ISBN 978-0-331-22604-1
PIBN 11033201

FB &c Ltd, Dalton House, 60 Windsor Avenue, London, SW19 2RR.
Company number 08720141. Registered in England and Wales.

For support please visit www.forgottenbooks.com

REPORT

OF THE

Superintendent of Public Schools

For the Fiscal Year 1904-1905. -1917

San Francisco, July 1, 1905.

To the Honorable Board of Education, in and for the City and County of San Francisco:

Gentlemen:—In accordance with the law, the Superintendent of Common Schools has the honor to submit herewith the Fifty-second Annual Report on the Public Schools of the City and County of San Francisco for the fiscal year terminating June 30, 1905.

W. H. LANGDON,
Supt. of Schools.

ANNUAL STATISTICAL REPORT OF THE SUPERINTENDENT OF SCHOOLS.

General Statistics.

Fiscal Year Terminating June 30.	1904	1905
Population of city (estimated)	435,000	450,000
Number of youth in city under 17 years of age	118,324	117,623
Number of school census children in the city upon which the appointment of state school funds is made	97,353	98,178
Assessment roll of taxable property of city	$545,866,446	$ 524,392,047.32
RECEIPTS OF SCHOOL DEPARTMENT.		
Balance on hand July 1	$ 62,409.02	$67,383.28
State apportionment	799,240.22	987,010.56
City taxes	507,521.69	323,364.32
Rents, etc.	59,148.75	58,476.75
Total	$1,428,319.68	$1,436,234.91
City and County tax per $100	.096	.064
Estimated value of school sites	$5,000,000.00	$5,005,000.00
Estimated value of school buildings	1,609,000.00	1,648,909.75
Estimated value of school furniture	160,000.00	165,000.00
Estimated value of school libraries	24,750.00	25,000.00
Estimated value of school apparatus	35,000.00	35,500.00
	$6,828.750.00	$6,879,409.75
Total receipts 1904–1905		$1,436,234.91
Total expenditures 1904–1905		1,405,215.80
Surplus on hand July 1, 1905		31,019.11

Note—Figures for Financial Report furnished by Board of Education.

SCHOOLS.	1904	1905
Number of High Schools	6	7
Number of Grammar Schools	23	27
Number of Primary Schools	47	46
Number of Evening Schools	6	6
Total number of schools	82	86
Number of Brick school buildings owned by the Department	7	7
Number of wooden school buildings owned by the Department	66	66
Number of buildings or rooms rented by the department	60	60
Total number of buildings owned by the Department	133	133

SCHOOL ATTENDANCE.

State Enrollment.	1905
High Schools (7)	4,105
Grammar Schools (27)	22,519
Primary Schools (46)	21,738
Evening Schools (6)	6,713
Total (86)	55,076

AVERAGE NUMBER BELONGING.

High Schools	3,076
Grammar Schools	18,970
Primary Schools	17,368
Evening Schools	2,526
	41,940

AVERAGE DAILY ATTENDANCE.

High Schools	2,870
Grammar Schools	18,180
Primary Schools	16,476
Evening Schools	2,194
	39,720

COMPARATIVE STATEMENT OF THE NUMBER ENROLLED AND THE AVERAGE DAILY ATTENDANCE IN THE PUBLIC SCHOOLS SINCE 1895.

	Number Enrolled	Average daily Attendance
During the Year ending June 30, 1895	44,822	32,974
During the ending June 30, 1896	45,435	33,508
During the year ending June 30, 1897	46,564	33,531
During the year ending June 30, 1898	50,101	35,116
During the year ending June 30, 1899	48,870	36,940
During the year ending June 30, 1900	48,058	35,004
During the year ending June 30, 1901	48,517	34,771
During the year ending June 30, 1902	49,090	35,943
During the year ending June 30, 1903	52,906	36,965
During the year ending June 30, 1904	52,969	37,797
During the year ending June 30, 1905	55,076	39,720

SCHOOL CENSUS REPORT SUBMITTED BY CHIEF CENSUS CLERK MR. T. E. ATKINSON, FOR THE YEAR ENDING JUNE 30, 1905, AS COMPARED WITH THE CORRESPONDING REPORT FOR THE YEAR ENDING JUNE 30, 1904.

Number of white children between 5 and 17 years of age—	
Boys	48,036
Girls	46,809
Total	94,845
School census, 1904	93,555
Increase	1,290
Number of negro children between 5 and 17 years of age:	
Boys	340
Girls	331
Total	671
School Census, 1904	462
Increase	209
Number of Indian children between 5 and 17 years of age:	
Girls	1
School Census, 1904	0
Increase	1
Native born Mongolians between 5 and 17 years of age:	
Boys	1,739
Girls	922
Total	2,661
School census, 1904	3,325
Decrease	664
Total number of census children between 5 and 17 years of age	98,178
School Census, 1904	97,353
Increase	825
Number of children under 5 years of age:	
White	19,267
Negro	102
Mongolian	76
Total	19,445
School Census, 1904	20,971
Decrease	1,526

Number of children between 5 and 17 years of age who have attended public schools at any time during the school year	58,962
School Census, 1904	58,856
Increase	106
Number of children between 5 and 17 years of age who have attended private schools, but no public schools at any time during the year	24,646
School Census, 1904	20,978
Increase	3,668
Number of children between 5 and 17 years of age who have not attended school at any time during the school year	14,570
School Census, 1904	17,519
Decrease	2,949
Nativity of children:	
Native born	115,847
Foreign born	1,776
Total	117,623
School Census, 1904	118,324
Decrease	701
Total decrease of children under 17 years of age	701

COMPARATIVE STATEMENT OF THE NUMBER OF CHILDREN IN THE CITY FROM 1895 to 1905, INCLUSIVE.

As reported by the Census Marshals.

Under seventeen years of age.	Number
May, 1895	93,558
May 1896	94,925
May 1897	98,506
May 1898	98,091
May 1899	98,368
May 1900	102,022
May 1901	105,512
May 1902	105,911
May 1903	111,190
May 1904	118,324
May 1905	117,623

NUMBER OF TEACHERS IN DEPARTMENT JUNE 30, 1905

	Men	Women	Total
Number of teachers in High Schools	61	54	115
Number of teachers in Grammar Grades	29	345	374
Number of teachers in Primary Grades	3	507	510
Number of High, Commercial, Grammar, Primary and Evening School Principals without classes	24	45	69
Supervisor of Music	0	1	1
Asst. Supervisor of Music	0	1	1
Supervisor of Drawing	0	1	1
Asst. Supervisor of Drawing	0	1	1
Supervisor of Manual Training	1	0	1
Asst. Supervisors of Manual Training	6	0	1
Supervisor of Cookery	0	1	6
Asst. Supervisors of Cookery	0	4	4
Supervisor of Physical Culture	1	0	1
Asst. Supervisors of Physical Culture	1	1	2
Day Substitutes	2	70	72
Evening Substitutes	9	13	22
Totals	137	1,044	1,181

STATEMENT OF GAINS AND LOSSES IN THE DEPARTMENT FOR SCHOOL YEAR ENDING JUNE 30, 1905.

Number of teachers in Department June 30, 1904		1,094
Losses:		
By resignation	23	
By retirement	1	
By death	2	26
		1,068
Gains:		
Teachers elected from July 1, 1904, to June 30, 1905		113
Total		1,181

NUMBER OF TEACHERS IN DEPARTMENT BY GRADES—JUNE 30, 1905.

	Special	Primary	Grammar	Principals without Class	Total	Men	Women
PRIMARY SCHOOLS							
1. Agassiz	..	13	3	1	17	..	17
2. Bergerot	..	2	2	..	4	..	4
3. Buena Vista	..	9	2	1	12	..	12
4. Chinese	..	7	1	1	9	..	9
5. Cleveland	..	9	1	1	11	..	11
6. Cooper	..	12	..	1	13	..	13
7. Deaf and Dumb	3	..	..	..	3	1	2
8. Douglas	..	9	1	1	11	..	11
9. Dudley Stone	..	12	3	1	16	..	16
10 Edison	..	8	2	1	11	..	11
11. Emerson	..	12	2	1	15	..	15
12. Garfield	..	13	1	1	15	..	15
13. Golden Gate	..	7	1	1	9	..	9
14. Grant	..	5	3	1	9	..	9
15. Haight	..	10	2	1	13	..	13
16. Harrison	..	6	1	..	7	..	7
17. Hawthorne	..	8	2	1	11	..	11
18. Henry Durant	..	11	1	1	13	..	13
19. Humboldt	..	10	2	1	13	..	13
20. Hunter's Point	..	1	..	..	1	1	..
21. Irving	..	7	1	1	9	..	9
22. Jackson	..	4	2	..	6	..	6
23. Jefferson	1	7	1	1	10	..	10
24. John W. Taylor	..	1	1	..	2	..	2
25. Lafayette	..	11	..	1	12	..	12
26. Laguna Honda	..	4	2	..	6	..	6
27. Madison	..	4	1	..	5	..	5
28. Marshall	..	13	..	1	14	..	14
29. Monroe	..	6	3	1	10	..	10
30. Moulder	..	10	2	1	13	..	13
31. Noe Valley	..	11	..	1	12	..	12
32. Ocean House	..	1	..	..	1	1	..
33. Oceanside	..	2	1	..	3	..	3
34. Park	..	5	..	..	5	..	5
35. Peabody	..	9	2	1	12	..	12
36. Redding	..	9	1	1	11	..	11
37. Sheridan	..	5	3	1	9	..	9
38. Sherman	..	10	2	1	13	..	13
39. South End	..	4	2	..	6	..	6
40. Starr King	..	11	1	1	13	..	13
41. Sunny Side	..	2	2	..	4	..	4
42. Sutro	..	5	4	1	10	..	10
43. West End	..	1	2	..	3	..	3
44. Whittier	..	16	2	1	19	..	19
45. Winfield Scott	..	3	2	..	5	..	5
Total	4	325	67	30	426	3	423

NUMBER OF TEACHERS IN DEPARTMENT BY GRADES, JUNE 30, 1905.

Continued.

	Special	Primary	Grammar	Principals without Classes	Total	Men	Women
GRAMMAR SCHOOLS.							
1. Adams Cosmopolitan	2	3	14	1	20	2	18
2. Bernal	..	9	5	1	15	..	15
3. Burnett	..	7	6	1	14	1	13
4. Clement	..	8	8	1	17	1	16
5. Columbia	..	12	8	1	21	..	21
6. Crocker	..	..	12	1	13	1	12
7. Denman	..	7	8	1	16	1	15
8. Everett	..	10	9	1	20	1	19
9. Fairmount	..	11	5	1	17	..	17
10. Franklin	..	9	10	1	20	2	18
11. Fremont	..	8	7	1	16	..	16
12. Hamilton No. 1	..	..	15	1	16	1	15
13. Hamilton No. 2	3	..	8	1	12	4	8
14. Hancock	2	1	10	1	14	2	12
15. Hearst	..	14	9	1	24	..	24
16. Horace Mann No. 1	..	..	18	1	19	1	18
17. Horace Mann No. 2	3	1	10	1	15	4	11
18. Humboldt No. 2	..	..	6	..	6	3	3
19. Irving M. Scott	..	10	6	1	17	..	17
20. James Lick	..	1	10	1	12	2	10
21. Jean Parker	..	8	7	1	16	..	16
22. John Swett	..	9	9	1	19	1	18
23. Lincoln No. 1	..	13	7	1	21	2	19
24. Lincoln No. 2	..	3	24	2	29	8	21
25. Mission	..	..	14	1	15	..	15
26. Pacific Heights	..	6	11	1	18	..	18
27. Parental	..	..	3	1	4	1	3
28. Richmond No. 1	..	8	4	1	13	..	13
29. Richmond No. 2	..	..	3	..	3	1	2
30. Rincon	..	7	5	1	13	..	13
31. Spring Valley	..	8	7	1	16	1	15
32. Washington No. 1	..	8	5	1	14	3	11
33. Washington No. 2	..	1	13	1	15	3	12
Total	10	182	296	32	520	46	474

NUMBER OF TEACHERS IN DEPARTMENT BY GRADES, JUNE 30, 1905.

Continued.

	Special	Primary	Grammar	Principals without Classes	Total	Men	Women
1. Commercial	15	..	..	1	16	4	12
2. Commercial Eve	13	..	..	1	14	5	9
3. Girls'	18	..	..	1	19	6	13
4. Humboldt Eve. High	21	..	..	1	22	20	2
5. Lowell	20	..	..	1	21	18	3
6. Mission	14	..	..	1	15	5	10
7. Polytechnic	14	..	..	1	15	10	5
Total	115	..	..	7	122	68	54
Primary, brought forward	4	325	67	30	426	3	423
Grammar, brought forward	10	182	296	32	520	46	474
High, brought forward	115	..	..	7	122	68	54
Physical Culture	3	..	..	..	3	2	1
Music	2	..	..	..	2	..	2
Drawing	2	..	..	..	2	..	2
Manual Training	7	..	..	..	7	7	..
Cookery	5	..	..	5	5	..	5
Day Substitutes	..	..	72	..	72	2	70
Evening substitutes	..	..	22	..	22	9	13
Total	148	507	457	69	1181	137	1044

REPORT

OF THE

Superintendent of Schools

AND

Board of Education

San Francisco, Cal.

FOR THE

FISCAL YEARS 1906-07 AND 1907-08

BOARD OF EDUCATION

THOMAS F. BOYLE, President

AARON ALTMANN DAVID OLIVER, JR.

JOSEPH O'CONNOR

ALFRED RONCOVIERI, Superintendent of Schools
(Ex-officio member of Board of Education)

E. C. LEFFINGWELL, Secretary

Neal Publishing Co.
PRINTERS AND BOOKBINDERS
66 FREMONT ST
SAN FRANCISCO

INDEX TO CONTENTS

55th

Report of Superintendent of Schools.

FISCAL YEAR 1906-1907

REPORT OF THE SUPERINTENDENT OF COMMON SCHOOLS OF THE CITY AND COUNTY OF SAN FRANCISCO, FOR THE YEAR ENDING JUNE 30, 1907.

San Francisco, August 20, 1907.

To the Honorable Board of Supervisors, in and for the City and County of San Francisco.

Gentlemen: I have the honor to submit herewith the Annual Report on the condition of the public schools of this City and County as required by the Charter, for the fifty-fifth year of the School Department, ending June 30, 1907.

ALFRED RONCOVIERI,

Superintendent of Common Schools, in and for the City and County of San Francisco.

ANNUAL STATISTICAL REPORT OF THE SUPERINTENDENT OF COMMON SCHOOLS FOR THE FISCAL YEAR ENDING JUNE 30, 1907.

GENERAL STATISTICS.

Population of the City, 1907 (estimated)	330,000
Number of youth in the City under 17 years of age	90,950
Number of youth in the City between 5 and 17 years of age who are entitled by law to draw public money	77,367
Assessment roll of the taxable property of the City	$375,932,477 00
City school tax on each hundred dollars	11.07 cts.
City and County taxes	434,488 38
Estimated value of school sites	$4,935,010
Estimated value of school buildings	1,229,000
Estimated value of school furniture	165,000
Estimated value of school libraries	46,000
Estimated value of school apparatus	32,000
Total value of school property	$6,407,010

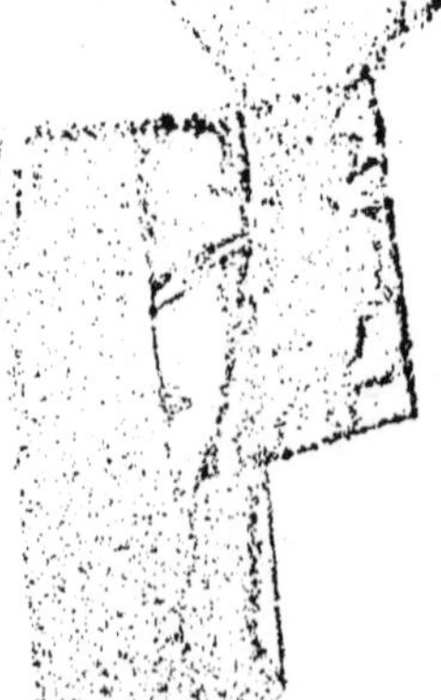

FINANCIAL REPORT.

RECEIPTS.

Balance on hand at the beginning of the year	$ 23,000 00
Receipts from State apportionments	689,530 82
Insurance	15,000 00
Rents	345 00
Sale of Girls' High School building	2,500 00
Sale of old material	2,971 84
From Red Cross Relief Fund for damage to the Crocker School building	400 00
City and County taxes	434,488 39
Total receipts	$1,168,236 05

Administration (Salaries of School Directors, Superintendent of Schools, Deputy Superintendents, Secretary, Board of Education, and Assistant Secretaries, Stenographers, Messengers, Storeroom and Shop Employees)	$46,065 14
Salaries of High School teachers	111,643 25
Salaries of primary and grammar teachers	807,075 05
Salaries of evening school teachers	49,428 00
Salaries of janitors	52,127 40
Repairs and temporary buildings	125,783 10
Supplies (labor)	15,218 00
Furniture	38,306 07
Blackboards	5,331 12
Stationery	8,050 10
Janitorial supplies	1,890 63
Printing	3,576 24
Light	2,514 14
Fuel	5,121 04
Water	13,871 00
Books (for indigents)	1,593 14
Apparatus	2,521 49
Rents	8,451 40
Census	7,240 25
Manual training supplies	2,171 74
Cookery supplies	512 65
Laboratory supplies	1,544 56
Cartage	3,529 00
Miscellaneous Incidentals	7,881 05
Miscellaneous supplies	3,869 78
Telegraph and telephone	118 34
Total	$1,325,433 68

RESUME.

Expenditures	$1,325,433 68	
Receipts	1,168,236 05	
Deficit		$157,197 63
Estimated July State appropriation for High Schools yet to be received		11,000 00
Estimated net deficit		$146,197 63

The Budget of appropriation adopted by the Board of Supervisors for the fiscal year ending June 30th, 1907, provided a public school fund of $1,200,000.

Including the July State apportionment for High Schools, the total receipts will be about $1,179,236 05, which leaves a deficit of $20,763 95. When the Board of Supervisors made the appropriation, they estimated that about $740,000 would be derived from State apportionments and $60,000 from rents. It will be observed that this estimate exceeded the income derived from the State by $40,000 and that, instead of receiving $60,000 from rents, only $345 were derived from that source.

In the deficit of $146,197 63 are included the so-called "Merchants' Claims," aggregating $109,035 54, leaving $37,162 09, which are required to satisfy outstanding salary demands of teachers and janitors for the month of June, 1907.

The Board of Supervisors in July, 1907, agreed to pay these "Merchants' Claims" by transferring the necessary funds from the surplus in the general fund.

COST OF MAINTAINING SCHOOLS PER PUPIL.

		Per Pupil on Enrollment.	Per Pupil on Av. Daily Attendance
High School	$142,380 02	$50 28	$80 82
Primary and grammar schools	1,117,257 00	30 05	42 21
Evening schools	65,796 66	13 48	47 00
Total	$1,325,433 68		

MEDAL FUNDS.

Name of Fund.	Deposited in.	In Fund June 30, 1907.
Bridge Silver Medal	Hibernia Savings and Loan Society	$1,952 63
Denman Grammar School	Hibernia Savings and Loan Society	1,051 98
Denman Silver Medal	German Savings and Loan Society	1,937 02
Hancock Grammar School	German Savings and Loan Society	581 44
Jean Parker Grammar School	German Savings and Loan Society	506 24
John Swett Grammar School	Hibernia Savings and Loan Society	259 50
Lincoln Grammar School	Hibernia Savings and Loan Society	3,175 94

SCHOOLS.

	1907.
Number of High Schools	5
Number of Grammar Schools	27
Number of Primary Schools	44
Number of Evening Schools	7
Total number of schools	83
Number of brick school buildings owned by the department	1
Number of wooden school buildings owned by the department	73
Number of buildings or rooms rented by the department	25
Total number of buildings used by the department	99

NUMBER OF TEACHERS IN DEPARTMENT, JUNE, 1907.

	Men	Women	Total
Number of teachers in High Schools	33	43	76
Number of teachers in grammar grades	19	285	304
Number of teachers in primary grades	3	458	461
Number of teachers in evening schools	24	57	81
Number of substitutes (day schools)	2	28	30
Number of substitutes (evening schools)			0
Number of teachers of manual training	7		7
Number of teachers (cooking)		5	5
Number of teachers (music)		3	3
Number of teachers (drawing)		2	2
Teachers of physical culture	2		2
Total number of teachers	90	881	971
Whole number of principals (included in total)	26	57	83
Number of principals not required to teach a class (included in total)	24	50	74
Number of vice-principals (included in total)	8	24	32

Decreased revenue and school attendance compelled the Board of Education to place on the unassigned, or waiting list, July, 1906, 232 teachers, 181 of whom still remain on said list.

BOARD OF EXAMINATION.

The Board of Examination is composed of:

Superintendent Alfred Roncovieri, Chairman.

Deputy Superintendent W. B. Howard, Secretary.

Deputy Superintendent T. L. Heaton.

Deputy Superintendent R. H. Webster.

Deputy Superintendent A. H. Suzzallo.

The Secretary of the Board of Examination, Deputy Superintendent W. B. Howard, furnishes the following facts respecting the work of the Board during the past year. The duties of the Secretary have been very extensive and onerous, due to the fact that all certificates of teachers and records of their certification were destroyed by the fire in April, 1906. This fact necessitated the restoration of certificates under the State law amended at the special session of the State Legislature, June, 1906, as well as that of the history of the department.

Nearly 1300 certificates have been restored and the history of their identity with the school department of more than 1200 teachers has been recorded.

Number of original certificates granted on examination during the year: to men, 0; to women, 5. Number of certificates granted on credentials: to men, 6; to women, 34; number of certificates renewed during the year, 36; number of applicants rejected during the year on examination, 12; on credentials, 0; amount of fees collected for examination and issuance of certificates, $220; number of teachers in the department who hold high school certificates, 133; number of teachers who hold certificates of the grammar grade, 771; number of teachers who hold certificates of primary grade, 33; number of teachers who hold special certificates, 34; number of teachers who are graduates of the University of California, 45; number of teachers who are graduates of other universities, 8; number of teachers who are graduates of the California State Normal Schools, 58; number of teachers who are graduates of other state normal schools, 2.

SCHOOL ENROLLMENT AND ATTENDANCE AND CENSUS STATISTICS FOR THE YEARS ENDING

	June 30,1906.	June 30, 1907.	
	ENROLLMENT.		DECREASE.
High School..........	5,188	2,823	2,365
Primary and Grammar	47,661	37,923	9,738
Evening.............	4,933	4,887	46
Total............	57,782	45,633	12,149

SCHOOL ENROLLMENT AND ATTENDANCE AND CENSUS STATISTICS FOR THE YEARS ENDING

	June 30,1906.	June 30,1907.	
	ENROLLMENT.		DECREASE.
Children 5 to 17 years	101,836	77,367	24,469
Children 0 to 17 years	125,191	90,955	34,236

Estimated population June 30, 1907..........................330,000

PRINCIPAL ITEMS OF SCHOOL CENSUS REPORT SUBMITTED BY CHIEF CENSUS CLERK, HON. SAMUEL H. BECKETT, FOR THE YEAR ENDING JUNE 30, 1907, AS COMPARED WITH THE CORRESPONDING REPORT FOR THE YEAR ENDING JUNE 30, 1906.

Number of white children between 5 and 17 years of age:

Boys	38,407	
Girls	38,182	
Total	76,589	
School census, 1906	98,319	
Decrease		21,730

Number of negro children between 5 and 17 years of age:

Boys	27	
Girls	24	
Total		51
School census, 1906		701
Decrease		650

Native born Mongolians between 5 and 17 years of age:

Boys	459	
Girls	267	
Total		726
School census, 1906		2,815
Decrease		2,089

Total number of census children between 5 and 17 years of age, including 1 Indian	77,367	
School census, 1906	101,836	
Decrease		24,469
Number of children under 5 years of age:		
White	13,531	
Negro	16	
Mongolian	40	
Indian	1	
Total	13,588	
School census, 1906	23,335	
Decrease		9,767
Number of children between 5 and 17 years of age who have attended public schools at any time during the school year	47,855	
School census, 1906	59,971	
Decrease		12,116
Number of children between 5 and 17 years of age who have attended private schools at any time during the year	14,103	
School census, 1906	24,902	
Decrease		10,799
Number of children between 5 and 17 years of age who have not attended school at any time during the school year	15,409	
School census, 1906	16,963	
Decrease		1,554
Nativity of children:		
Native born	90,782	
Foreign born	173	
Total	90,955	
School census, 1906	125,191	
Decrease		34,236
Total decrease of children under 17 years of age		34,236

MISCELLANEOUS.

Number of graduates from the grammar schools for the year:	
Boys	620
Girls	1,073
Total	1,693
Number of graduates from high schools for the year:	
Boys	84
Girls	164
Total	248
Average cost of instruction per pupil enrolled in the primary and grammar schools	$25.35
Average cost of instruction per pupil enrolled in high schools	$45.32

SALARY SCHEDULE, 1907-08.

Effect, July 1, 1907.

TO WHOM PAID.	Per Month.
Board of Education (4 members), each	$250.00
Secretary of Board of Education	150.00
Clerk of High School Board	50.00
Superintendent of Common Schools	333.33
Deputies (4), each	225.00

HIGH SCHOOLS.

Principals	$250.00
Vice-Principals	180.00
Heads of Departments	150.00
Heads of Departments in Science	160.00
Assistant Teachers (3 years on probation)	120.00
Assistants, after 1 year's experience	130.00
Assistants, after 2 year's experience	140.00
Assistants, after 3 year's experience	145.00
Teachers of Drawing	125.00
Head Teacher of Drawing, Wood Carving and Clay Modeling (Miss Van Vleck), Polytechnic High School	145.00
Assistant to Miss Van Vleck (Miss Murdock)	100.00
Teachers Modern Languages, Girls, Polytechnic High Schools	125.00
Teacher Spanish, Commercial High School	145.00
Teacher Iron Work, Manual Training Department, Polytechnic High School	145.00

PRIMARY AND GRAMMAR SCHOOLS.

Principals Grammar Schools	$180.00
Vice-Principals Grammar Schools	125.00
Principals Primary Schools, 14 or more classes	150.00
Principals Primary Schools, 10, 11, 12, or 13 classes	135.00
Principals Primary Schools, 4, 5, 6, 7, 8, 9 classes	120.00
Principals Primary Schools, 2 and 3 classes	105.00
Teachers in Charge of Primary Schools, 1 class	105.00

REGULAR TEACHERS OF GRAMMAR AND PRIMARY GRADE CLASSES.

Grades will be designated as 1st, 2d, 3d, 4th, 5th, 6th, 7th, and 8th.

		Dependent on special appropriation.
First year	$60.00	$65.00

1st, 7th, and 8th grades:

First year	$60.00	$65.00
Second year	63.50	68.50
Third year	66.75	71.50
Fourth year	70.00	75.00
Fifth year	73.50	79.00
Sixth year	76.75	82.50
Seventh year	80.00	86.00
Eighth year	83.00	89.00

2d, 3d, and 4th grades:

First year	$60.00	$65.00
Second year	62.75	67.50
Third year	65.50	70.00
Fourth year	68.00	73.00
Fifth year	70.75	76.00
Sixth year	73.50	79.00
Seventh year	76.00	82.00
Fifth and Sixth Grades	80.00	86.00

Assistants in Primary and Grammar Schools teaching German and English, or English and French, or Music and English, having special certificates to teach such special subjects, $5.00 per month in addition to their salaries according to the schedule. Any one special subject, $5.00 extra.

In fixing the salary of a teacher, after election as a regular teacher, credit shall be given such teacher for experience from the date of his or her appointment on the substitute list.

Teachers of the Day Substitute Class shall be paid $3.00 per day.

Substitutes teaching in High Schools shall receive $5.00 per day while actually engaged in work.

Teachers of the Evening Substitute Class shall receive $2.50 for each evening that they teach and $1.00 per evening for reporting.

EVENING SCHOOLS.

The salaries of Principals of Evening Schools shall be as follows:

Principal Humboldt Evening High School	$125.00
Schools having 300 or more average daily attendance	100.00
Less than 300 in average daily attendance	85.00
Assistants in Evening Schools	50.00
Head Bookkeeping Department, Lincoln Evening School	50.00
Teacher Typewriting, Lincoln Evening School	50.00
Teacher High School Class, Humboldt and Washington	60.00
All High School Branches	60.00

DEPARTMENT AT LARGE.

Vocal Music, Supervisor	$150.00
Assistant Teacher of Music	100.00
Supervisor of Drawing	150.00
Assistants in Drawing	90.00
Teacher of Physical Culture	100.00
Supervisor of Cooking	100.00
Assistant Teachers of Cooking	75.00
Supervisors of Manual Training	150.00
Six Assistants of Manual Training	100.00

OFFICE AND SHOP EMPLOYEES.

Financial Secretary	$160.00
Recording Secretary	150.00
Stenographers, Board of Education and Superintendent's Office (3)	80.00
Messenger, Board of Education	95.00
Messenger, Superintendent's Office	85.00
Telephone Operator	60.00
Storekeeper	150.00

Assistant Storekeeper	125.00
Foreman Storeroom	115.00
Inspector of Buildings and Head Carpenter	175.00
Storekeeper (Shop)	125.00
Scavenger	157.00
Teamster, Supply Department	115.00

FINES AND DEDUCTIONS.

Fine, 50 cents for tardiness day school (passed May 31, 1899).

Fine, 50 cents for tardiness evening school (passed May 10, 1899).

Fine, $2.50 for failure to acknowledge receipt of circulars or letters from Office (passed March 29, 1899).

Deduction of one-thirtieth for each day's absence.

No excuse to be absent from school, with pay, shall be granted to any principal or teacher of this Department except under suspension of rules, and by special action of the Board of Education (passed June 14, 1899), and adopted by the present Board, except for three days, on account of the death of a relative within the first degree of consanguinity, or of husband or wife (passed September 1, 1899).

Fine $5.00 for principals failing to make correct report of absentees on last school day of month.

JANITOR'S SALARIES.

$5.00 per class-room up to and including 10 class-rooms.

$4.50 per room, in excess of 10 rooms (except where this rate is impracticable).

AVERAGE MONTHLY WAGES.

	Male.	Female.
Superintendent of Schools (1)	$333.33⅓	
Deputy Superintendents of Schools (4)	225.00	
School Directors (4)	250.00	
Principals of High Schools (5)	250.00	
Principals of Primary, Evening and Grammar Schools	155.00	$138.00
Teachers in High Schools	140.00	126.00
Teachers in Grammar Schools	125.00	81.00
Teachers in Evening Schools	53.00	51.00
Teachers in Primary Schools	97.00	74.00

All Teachers, Principals and Superintendents................$86.00.

TEACHERS' INSTITUTE.

The Teachers' Institute for the teachers of the public schools of the City and County of San Francisco was convened by County Superintendent Alfred Roncovieri at the Alcazar Theater on June 26th, 27th and 28th, 1907.

All the sessions were attended by about 947 department teachers who declared that they were instructed, strengthened and entertained professionally by the following speakers and themes:

WEDNESDAY, JUNE 26, 1907.

Opening Address..Alfred Roncovieri
Superintendent of Schools.

Lecture—"Educational Value of the Playground"..........Dr. F. B. Dressler
Associate Professor of Education, University of California.

Lecture—"Moral Training and Education of the Young"........Dr. Felix Adler
Professor of Ethics, Columbia University.

THURSDAY, JUNE 27, 1907.

Lecture—"Education for Leisure"...................Professor T. L. Heaton
Deputy Superintendent of Schools, San Francisco.

Lecture—"The Place of the Emotions in Education".......Dr. Henry Suzzallo

Recess.

Lecture—"The Modern View of History Teaching".....Prof. H. Morse Stevens
Professor of History, University of California.

FRIDAY, JUNE 28, 1907.

Lecture—"The Function of Expression in Education"......Dr. Henry Suzzallo

Lecture—"Wide Education in America is Difficult"......Prof. E. P. Cubberley
Professor of Education, Stanford University.

Lecture—"Mechanism of Ideas"........................Prof. John Adams
Professor of Education, University of London.

REPORT OF THE EXPENDITURES OF THE SPECIAL APPROPRIATION MADE TO THE BOARD OF EDUCATION BY THE PEOPLE OF THE STATE OF CALIFORNIA, JUNE, 1906. (Approved June 14, 1906.)

The People of the State of California, represented in Senate and Assembly, do enact as follows:

Section 1. The sum of twenty-five thousand dollars is hereby appropriated out of any money in the State treasury not otherwise appropriated, to pay the claim of the Board of Education of the City and County of San Francisco, against the State of California.

Section 2. The Controller is hereby directed to draw his warrant in favor of said Board of Education of the City and County of San Francisco, for the sum of Twenty-five thousand dollars and the State Treasurer is directed to pay the same.

Section 3. This Act shall take effect immediately.

The Board of Education having obtained the sum of $25,000, resolved to expend the same in the purchase of school text books for the needy.

FINANCIAL STATEMENT.

Received		$25,000.00
Expended:		
Wells Fargo & Co., for the transportation of money and books	$ 286.50	
For School Text Books	22,775.55	$23,062.05
June 30, 1907: Balance in Fund		$1,937.95

24,562 school books have been sent to the schools to be used by children whose parents are in needy circumstances, and 14,301 books are in the storeroom of the department.

STATEMENT OF RECONSTRUCTION FUND CONTRIBUTED MAINLY BY SCHOOL CHILDREN AND SOCIETIES.

Alabama	$ 13.20
California	1,564.90
Colorado	194.90
Connecticut	42.43
Delaware	1.48
Florida	5.00
Iowa	154.04
Indiana	2,658.29
Indian Territory	15.78
Illinois	359.06
Idaho	55.30
Kansas	40.86
Kentucky	38.78
Massachusetts	6,321.64
Michigan	2,625.29
Minnesota	40.35
Mississippi	30.00
Maine	267.25
Missouri	45.07
Maryland	1,128.57
New York	238.18
New Jersey	499.85
New Mexico	99.22
New Hampshire	34.19
Nevada	288.82
Nebraska	180.82
North Carolina	44.45
North Dakota	15.00
Ohio	3,034.19
Oklahoma	1.70
Oregon	296.91
Pennsylvania	2,176.84
Rhode Island	607.85
South Carolina	2.00
South Dakota	40.27
Texas	557.97
Utah	2,108.40
Vermont	50.00
Washington	992.96
Wisconsin	1,788.02
Wyoming	92.95
West Virginia	51.91
Virginia	229.08
England	5.00
Native Daughters of Golden West	102.50
Order of the Eastern Star	176.10
Lady Maccabees of the World	25.00
Fraternal Order of Eagles	10.00
M. of R. L. C.	5.00
Rebekah Lodges	20.00
United Ancient Order of Druids	5.00
Women of Woodcraft	75.20
Total	$29,717.03

RECAPITULATION.

Contributions as specified, by individuals, cities and societies	$29,717.03
Coin Cards	155.55
Stamps	12.49
Chain letters	14.20
Contributions received directly by Anglo-California Bank	121.75
Interest	136.13
Grand total receipts	$30,157.15

RESUME.

Receipts	$30,157.15
Expenditures	1,365.74
Balance in Fund	$28,791.41
Deposited in Anglo-California Bank	239.30
Deposited in French American Bank	15,179.53
Deposited in Bank of California (Western Addition Branch)	13,372.58
Balance in Fund	$28,791.41

HISTORY OF THE DEPARTMENT SINCE THE CONFLAGRATION OF APRIL, 1906

The public schools have been operated during the fiscal year ending June 30th, 1907, under very adverse conditions caused by the earthquake and conflagration.

On Monday, April 23d, 1906, five days after the commencement of the fire and while it still smouldered upon the ruins it had wrought, the rehabilitation of the San Francisco School Department commenced. An inventory of the losses sustained revealed the fact that out of a total of seventy-four, twenty-nine school buildings had been burned. The handsome building occupied by the Girls' High School had been shattered and others slightly damaged by the earthquake, involving a loss computed on the original cost of nearly $1,250,000. It will require a sum of money greatly in excess of the loss to restore the buildings.

On the morning of Monday, April 23d, 1906, a meeting convoked by Superintendent Roncovieri at his home was attended by about 100 teachers. The following resolution was passed by unanimous vote:

"We, the teachers of San Francisco, instruct Superintendent Roncovieri to offer our services to the proper authorities to be used by them in any way they deem best for the interests of our city."

It was decided that, if safe, the Emerson Primary School, corner of Pine and Scott Streets, should be the official headquarters of the school department. All committees should meet there at 10 A. M. daily. Teachers and janitors should gather there April 24th, at 2 P. M., for the purpose of registering their addresses. Superintendent Roncovieri appointed Mrs. M. M. Fitzgerald, Vice-Principal of the Denman Grammar School, his secretary. The following committees were named:

1. Committee on headquarters for teachers and janitors, Chairman, C. W. Mark; James Ferguson, L. S. Melsted, Mark Felton.

2. Committee on registration, Chairman, Mrs. N. A. Wood; Mrs. M. Stewart, Miss Emma Madden, W. O. Smith, F. H. Clark, Miss S. A. Folsom.

3. Committee on general relief and sub-committee for relief of teachers, Chairman, A. E. Kellogg; F. A. Barthel, Mrs. C. Pechin, Miss P. Lewis, Miss Jennie Powers, Miss Emma Stincen, Miss Alice Stincen, Miss Mary Magner, William De Bell, Miss Julia Coffey, Miss E. M. Bartlett, Miss H. F. McFarland.

4. Committee on condition of school buildings, Chairman, R. H. Webster; Albert Armstrong, L. M. Shuck, J. M. Longley, Frank Morton, E. Knowlton, Robert Barth, J. H. Simmons.

5. Committee on ways and means to re-establish public instruction, President A. Altmann, and School Directors Thomas Boyle, D. Oliver, Lawrence Walsh, Superintendent Alfred Roncovieri, and his deputies and all principals and vice-principals.

6. Committee to confer with Dr. Ward of the Health Department as to the assistance teachers can give in restoring sanitary conditions, Chairman, Dr. A. W. Scott, Dr. P. Dolman, Dr. Sophie Kobicke, Dr. Margaret Mahoney, Dr. L. Deal, Dr. Pressley, Dr. Fisher.

7. Committee on janitorial service, Chairman, A. A. Macurda; Thomas Maginnis, W. H. Doyle, Frank Morton.

8. Committee on publicity, Chairman, Director Thos. Boyle; Secretary, Mrs. M. M. Fitzgerald, 405 Fillmore Street; James Ferguson, L. S. Melsted, C. W. Mark, Mark Felton, Miss M. A. Deane.

9. Committee on securing privileges from civil and military authorities, Chairman, Mrs. Mary Prag; Miss Agnes Regan, Miss R. B. Stolz, Miss M. Duraind, Mrs. S. W. McPherson, Miss F. Hodgkins, M. Cerf, A. Armstrong.

Miss Mary Callahan, formerly principal of Clement Grammar School, turned over to the Relief Committee her large residence at 2280 Pacific Avenue, for reception of distressed and homeless teachers.

The School Department repair headquarters were established at the residence of Mr. William Commary, Chief Inspector of School Buildings, 814 Hayes Street. It was reported that Assistant Secretary, Charles Berliner, at the risk of his personal safety, saved the financial records of the School Department from the flames in the City Hall.

LEGISLATION.

At a meeting held in the Emerson School building, May 2, 1906, Deputy Superintendent of Schools, R. H. Webster, made these suggestions as the basis of bills to be introduced at the proposed extra session of the State Legislature.

First. An Act enabling the school authorities of the City and County of San Francisco to comply with sub-divisions 5, 6, and 7, of Section 1696, sub-divisions 13, and 14, of Section 1543.

Suggestion, That affidavits of teachers regarding attendance of pupils may be substituted for destroyed records of year 1905-1906, and the same be accepted by Superintendent of Schools in and for the City and County of San Francisco, and by him be used in the compilation of all pertinent reports to the State Superintendent of Public Instruction.

Second. An Act enabling school authorities of the City and County of San Francisco to issue certificates to teachers. Section 1771, sub-division 3 (a), (b), and (c), Section 1775, sub-division 1 (a), (b), and (c); 4, 5, Section 1778.

Suggestion; Authorization to re-issue on affidavit of school authorities (Superintendent of Schools and his deputies), certificates destroyed.

Third. Special appropriation for State School Text Books.

Suggestion; That the People of the State of California do enact as follows, to wit:

That an appropriation of twenty-five thousand dollars be made for the purchase of State School Text Books, said books to be supplied on the requisitions of the Superintendent of Schools in and for the City and County of

San Francisco, and by him distributed to the pupils of the public schools of said City and County as may be required.

Fourth. An Act to amend Section 1551 of the Political Code of the State of California.

Suggestion; That it shall be competent for the Superintendent of Common Schools in and for the City and County of San Francisco to report the census returns of said City and County for the year 1904-1905, as the census returns for the year 1905-1906, and the same be accepted by State Superintendent of Public Instruction and the Board of Supervisors of said City and County, and constitute the school census for said City and County for the year terminating June 30, 1906, or that the average per cent of increase of school census children for next preceding ten years be added to the census returns of 1904-1905 and the same be accepted as the census of 1905-1906.

Bills incorporating these suggestions were adopted by the State Legislature convoked in special session in June, 1906.

OPERATION OF SCHOOLS.

The Board of Education met and suspended the operation of schools indefinitely, but in the month of June decided that they should reopen on Monday, July 23d.

On the 21st day of May, the Board of Education accepted the offer of A. M. Armstrong, Principal of the Parental School, and some teachers to conduct a Vacation School in tents at the Park. Between three and four hundred children availed themselves of the instruction offered.

A large number of teachers suffered by the disaster in the loss of their homes and personal effects. Many teachers volunteered their services to the Relief Committtee and were assigned to supply and relief stations and hospitals, and to the performance of clerical work.

The Board of Education about the first of May began the task of rehabilitating the department and worked strenuously for three months, during which time no less than thirty-six temporary buildings containing 256 rooms were built and equipped, affording accommodations for 8,000 school children. The Board of Education committed itself to the policy of recognizing seniority of service in the department. All teachers were attached to the schools whose buildings were burned. The greatly decreased school attendance preventd the employment of many, and therefore more than 200 were placed upon the waiting or unassigned list.

Day schools resumed sessions on July 23d, 1906, with an enrollment of 24,549 pupils as against 38,373 on the corresponding date of 1905. On August 3d, 1906, the enrollment in the primary and grammar schools had increased to 27,643 and in High Schools 1,985, with a total of 29,668.

JAPANESE PUPILS

On the 11th day of October, 1906, the Board of Education passed this Resolution:

''Resolved; That in accordance with Article 10, Section 1662, of the School Law of California, principals are hereby directed to send all Chinese, Japanese, and Korean children to the Oriental Public School, situated on the south side of Clay Street, between Powell and Mason Streets, on and after Monday, October 15th, 1906.''

The Board of Education had constructed a building on the site of that which had been the Chinese School and instead of limiting it to the admission of Chinese extended its operation to include, as per Resolution, Japanese and Korean children.

The result of the operation of the Resolution of the Board of Education just quoted was the exclusion of ninety-three Japanese who, prior to its passage, were attending the other public schools of this City and County, also twenty-three Chinese, three Koreans, and one Alaskan. Of these Japanese, fifty-four were under 15 years of age and thirty-nine from 15 to 20.

Many reasons can be cited which induced the Board of Education to pass this Resolution. Prominent among them was that frequently a matured Japanese would be seated in a room with little boys or girls from 9 to 12 years of age, thus presenting the spectacle of a little boy or girl having as a seat mate a grown Japanese in an overcrowded school. After the passage of this Resolution, the Board of Education and the Superintendent accepted an invitation from President Roosevelt at Washington. "Numerous interviews were had with the President from which we were satisfied that in the event that the amendment to the Immigration Bill introduced in both Houses of Congress of the United States on the 13th day of February, 1907, shall prove ineffectual, that every effort would be made by him not only to obtain a treaty with Japan, authorizing legislation by both Japan and the United States to exclude from each of their respective territories the immigration of all subjects of either of said nations, who are laborers, skilled and unskilled, but in any event would favor such form of legislation that will in the most speedy manner accomplish the result desired. That the national government has no purpose whatever to attempt to infringe upon the rights of California as a sovereign State and that the purpose of administration of the national government was merely to fulfill the bounden duty to a friendly nation with which it had a treaty, and to ascertain as a matter of international comity and courtesy whether or not by the true construction of their treaty such right or rights had been accorded to the subjects of Japan." The Board of Education and the Superintendent believing that the principle involved was one of comity and public policy, were fully in accord with the view of the administration to the effect that the attainment of the exclusion of all Japanese laborers, skilled and unskilled, should not be complicated with or endangered by the exercise of the right of segregation by the school board as authorized by Section 1662 of the Political Code of the State of California.

With the understanding that the Board did not concede or intend to concede that its action was in violation of any of the stipulations of the treaty between the United States and Japan, but on the contrary claiming and asserting that if any stipulation in said treaty contained anything that is inconsistent with or in conflict with the power and authority given by Section 1662 of the Political Code of the State of California, then so far as said treaty attempts to circumscribe the Board or prevent it from regulating its own school affairs, as the exercise of local police power, such provisions in said treaty are nugatory and void. The Board did modify the Resolution of October 11th, 1906, to read in words and figures as follows, to wit:

Section 1. Children of all alien races who speak the English language in order to determine the proper grade which they may be entitled to be enrolled, must first be examined as to their educational qualifications by the principal of the school where the application for enrollment shall have been made.

Section 2. That no child of alien birth over the ages of 9, 10, 11, 12, 13, 14, 15, and 16 years, shall be enrolled in any of the first, second, third, fourth, fifth, sixth, seventh or eighth grades respectively.

Section 3. If said alien children shall be found deficient in their ability to speak or deficient in the elements of the English language or unable to attend the course mentioned in Section 2, by reason of the restrictions mentioned therein, such children shall be enrolled in such schools or in such classes established exclusively for such children as and in the manner the Board of Education shall deem proper and most expedient.

Subsequently the Board of Education:

Resolved and Ordered; that children of alien races who are barred from other schools by age or educational qualifications, be received at the following schools, to wit: Hancock, Irving, Garfield, Washington (boy's), Jean Parker (girl's), Redding, and Oriental; and further that such children be enrolled in the ungraded classes of the following schools: Pacific Heights Grammar, Hamilton Grammar, Crocker Grammar, Hearst Primary and Grammar, and Emerson Primary.

COURSE OF STUDY.

The course of study for the common schools of this city and county has been revised by the Superintendent and his Board of Deputies, and will be issued during the third week of August, 1907.

The fiscal school year terminating June 30, 1907, was characterized by much inconvenience, the solution of new problems and much strenuous work produced by the disaster of April, 1906.

Notwithstanding these disadvantages, the teachers labored with an enthusiastic fidelity and the schools were in session 206 actual teaching days.

RECOMMENDATIONS

In conclusion, I desire to state forthwith these recommendations:

First. That in the interests of economy the Honorable Board of Supervisors include in its annual advertisement calling for bids on gas and water; the requirements of the Board of Education in these commodities.

Second. That a liberal appropriation not less than $8,000 be allowed for the purchase of supplementary and reference books.

Section 1714 of the Political Code refers to the expenditure of moneys for supplementary and reference books. Owing to the destruction of thirty school buildings during the conflagration of April, 1906, all the libraries contained therein were destroyed and therefore the appropriation asked for supplementary and reference books is considered moderate by the Board of Education and the Superintendent of Schools.

Third. That an appropriation be made of $12,000 for the purchase of charts, globes, typewriters, organs, pianos, and maps for use of the primary day and evening classes in accordance with Section 1617, Third Sub-division of the Political Code of the State of California.

Fourth. That ungraded classes in these schools: Adams, Fremont, Franklin, Hamilton, Hancock, Lincoln, Mission, Washington, Richmond, and Emerson, be maintained and that additional ungraded classes be established wherever there is sufficient demand.

In nearly every class of school, pupils will be found who, from various reasons, are deficient in one or two subjects. If special opportunity be not offered for overcoming these deficiencies, by individual or group instruction, such pupils become "misfits" in their classes, exercising a repressive influence upon their mates. If this special or group instruction be given by the regular teacher, it will result in the neglect of perhaps forty pupils for the teaching of five.

By segregating such pupils and placing them in an ungraded class, they can be taught individually or in groups. Certain pupils will thus do their work in an ungraded room for a month or a term, and then be prepared to join a regular grade. Others will be found who will remain permanently in the ungraded class, emphasizing the work they most need. Again, pupils may do grade work in all subjects save one. Such remain in the regular grade, but receive help in that one subject until it is mastered sufficiently to permit a resumption of regular grade work. Further, there are those, who, by being given special instructions in one subject for a limited time, may be so prepared as to be advanced a grade by being ahead of their class in all other subjects. The ungraded class keeps pupils in school, who, discouraged by failure in their regular classes would otherwise leave. It solves the problem of "leftovers." Permit me to inform you that Los Angeles has eighteen ungraded classes in operation. The Board of Education has satisfied a great need in establishing and maintaining the ungraded classes heretofore named, and it is to be hoped that sufficient means may be secured for the amplifying of this most important department of our public education.

Fifth. That an appropriation of not less than $2,500 be made for decoration and adornment of class rooms and school grounds; also, pictures, engravings, plaster reproductions, etc.

It is the desire of the Board of Education that more attention should be given to the proper decoration of class rooms and school buildings. Quite a number of teachers have shown great interest in this matter, and we have found many of them spending their own money to help make more agreeable and inviting the class rooms which are the scene of their labors.

The unconscious effect of proper esthetic surroundings upon children has hardly been given the attention it deserves. If we are to look for purity of speech, for gentleness of manner, for taste and cleanliness in dress, and for refinement and beauty of surroundings, we must have the means to enable us to carry out carefully prepared schemes for color and ornamentation of class rooms, and these schemes should be fully carried out in tinting the walls and in placing pictures and other works of art.

Sixth. Equipment of playgrounds provided for in the Bond Issue:

Few people, perhaps, realize how artificial child-life has become in our great cities. The change from village to city, and from city to metropolis has been so gradual that engrossed in cares of business life, the citizens of the great majority of large cities have failed to make any provision for the play of children, nor have they endeavored to retain for them an environment of nature. The country child lives with trees, flowers and animals. He is acted upon by all of those nature forces to which the brain most readily responds; he hunts, fishes, swims, and runs. In the transformation of village to metropolis, the "Commons" and the playground have become solid squares of masonry. The high price of land results in little or no yard space; this condition forces children upon sidewalks or streets often congested with traffic, endangering life and limb. Each gust of wind creates a cloud of dust that irritates lungs and inflames eyes.

Ball playing is prohibited and any form of play is either listless or impossible. The education of the street is generally demoralizing. Well has it been said that its moral code is, "They should take who have the power, and they should keep who can." This sentiment seems to be well inoculated, judging from the methods from which we often observe our great business interests operated. Our city has set aside some blocks of land for "breathing spaces" for parks; but their number is inadequate, and where they are most needed they are absent.

It is gratifying to note that the authorities of our large cities are commencing to supply a great need that avarice created. New York now sets aside $3,000,000 a year for the purchase of sites for playgrounds—a sum altogether too small, but a move in the right direction. Chicago has ninety-three acres of park playgrounds; Philadelphia has 146 acres; Boston much over 200 acres. But the play in the large majority of these playgrounds in UNDIRECTED, and therefore large boys and men monopolize them.

Municipal playgrounds are equipped with devices for facilitating play, and athletics of all varieties are under SUPERVISION. Cities are rapidly establishing such opportunities for well-directed wholesome play. New York has the best municipal playground in the world, containing more than three acres, accommodating about 3,000 children, and costing $2,500,000. The successful operation of the playgrounds established by the Board of Education of this city induces the hope that they may be extended. It would have been well had the authorities about fifty years ago set aside entire blocks for school sites which would have afforded ample room for activity. Where land is comparatively cheap, large yards should be secured for schools in existence. I cordially recommend that liberal appropriation be made for our playgrounds already in operation, for the establishment and maintenance of others when needed, and for the supervision of school yards after school hours, for play.

Seventh. The improvement of the Lincoln school site at the corner of Fifth and Market Streets so that it shall yield a large revenue to the city. This property was recently advertised for lease, for many weeks. Everything was done that could be done to invite proposals for leasing it, yet only one bid, that of $4050 per month, was received. This bid was rejected as too low. The rents of school property are always ostensibly (on paper) appropriated by the Board of Supervisors to the school department, but in reality, the more rent from school property increases, the lower goes the school tax levy, and just in proportion to our rent receipts. This fine jugglery of school rents has been going on for a long time, and the real effect of its has been to make our school rents a revenue for all municipal purposes. The people, believe in a sort of vague way, that rents of school properties are considered by the Supervisors, as a separate and additional school revenue. They are not. If a fire should destroy any income-bearing property of this department, there would be a deficit for that amount of rent at the end of the fiscal year.

My remedy, for amendment to the Charter, is that all rents received from school properties, shall be a distinct revenue and shall not be considered by the Board of Supervisors when making their annual appropriation for the maintenance of the department, and that all such rents shall go into an accumulating school building fund for the purpose of providing new buildings and repairing old ones. I believe that a bond election should be called for the purpose of issuing two million, or even three million dollars worth of bonds, if necessary, for the erection of a magnificent structure on the Lincoln School lot, 275 feet square, a magnificent temple of the people, a counterpart of the great James Flood building on the opposite corner, a monument of artistic architectural skill which will beautify our city and produce a rental of at least $30,000 per month. The Board of Education would have its offices in this building, and space would be set aside for an evening school of commerce. There would be no taxes on such a building, and in about ten years, the rents would have redeemed the bonds.

REPORT OF SUPERVISOR OF MUSIC.

San Francisco, June 30, 1907.

Mr. A. Roncovieri, Superintendent of Schools, City.

Dear Sir: In compliance with the rules of the Board of Education, and in reply to your request sent this week, I most respectfully submit a report of the Department of Music of the Public Schools of San Francisco.

My last report to you was at the close of the year 1905.

At the beginning of that year, I had given a series of eight meetings to the teachers of the different grades. I had instructed them in the work to be done, and I had illustrated my lectures with songs and exercises from the regular music books. I also gave out mimeographed copies of songs which I had selected, and vocal exercises and outlines which the teachers were to use for the work with the children.

The year, 1905, became notable in our School Department because of the great May Festival which was held in Mechanic's Pavilion for the benefit of the Teachers' Annuity Association.

The Innes Band of sixty pieces and three thousand children were lead by me on four afternoons, and I shall always hold the memory of these choruses as something rare and beautiful.

The children sang in four parts such selections as Gounod's "Praise Ye The Father," "Handel's Largo," and "The Blue Danube Waltzes," and other songs besides a number of "Patriotic and Folk Songs."

The sight of so many childish faces together, the perfect sweetness of the voices, the marvelous expression because of the perfect response to my slightest signal will never be forgotten by those who attended those concerts.

These performances were only possible because of the systematic training in the regular music work that had been given to the children for a number of years, through the regular teachers under my direction. These performances were also due to the hearty co-operation of the Board of Education and the Superintendent of Schools and the Principals and regular teachers and my assistant, Mrs. McGlade, and particularly to the special teachers in each school who took charge of the rehearsals. I shall ever be thankful for the magnificent work of these teachers.

During the year, 1905, my assistant and myself visited each class four times, and I noticed a remarkable improvement in the work from the time when I had become Supervisor of Music.

Wherever a teacher was capable of doing her own work, I insisted on the work being done by herself, but if I found a teacher not capable of doing the work, I would require her to exchange work with a capable teacher.

Now, in some schools, I found a number of teachers not capable of doing the song work, so a competent musical teacher was given the work to do, and paid five dollars a month extra. These teachers were recommended by me and in most cases they passed the regular music examinations for a music certificate. There were about twenty of these teachers, I wish here to commend their work. For the slight expenditure of money much good was accomplished.

During this year, I also held meetings after school for these teachers who needed help, and I and my assistant gave free private lessons to those who desired them.

The regular teachers as a whole do as much as they think themselves capable of doing. But many are more capable than they think.

One of the most important functions of a Supervisor of Music is to encourage each teacher to do her best. If each teacher strives each year to do the work well, then each year will give added power to the teacher.

Teachers' meetings are most desirable, because each teacher receives definite work to do, and instructions are given how to obtain the best results in the least time. Inspiration and enthusiasm are derived from personal contact with the Supervisor, and a sympathetic relation is established, because of a better understanding of the subject itself and because of a broader knowledge of methods of presenting the subject in the school room.

In January, 1906, I again gave my lectures and lessons to the grade teachers. My assistants and myself visited the schools and gave lessons to children and teachers.

By order of the Superintendent, I also made extensive preparations for the National Educational Association. A chorus of three thousand children were to sing, and definite directions were ready to be sent to the teachers, when the schools closed for the mid-term vacation.

It was during that time that the great disaster occurred, and of course all preparations were forgotten, and the National Educational Association had no meeting that year.

As soon as possible a school was started in Golden Gate Park, and I helped register the children for it, by going into the tents. With my assistants I started the music work, and every day I taught songs to the children who had lost their homes and were camped in the Park.

At the same time, with my assistant and some of the teachers I gathered together a chorus of five hundred children, and rehearesd them for the Park Graduation. These children formed the nucleus of a chorus of 2000 children, which I lead on June the second, in front of the Band Stand in Golden Gate Park. That day will always be an event in the history of the rebuilding of San Francisco. It will always furnish a text for a sermon on loyalty and energy.

Immediately after this, through the newspapers, I called rehearsals for a chorus to sing for the celebration on the Fourth of July. Fifteen children attended the first rehearsal, but special cars and free tickets were secured by the Fourth of July Committtee from the railroads and at the final performance at the Stadium in the Golden Gate Park, I lead 4000 children and the Park Band. San Francisco's Fourth of July celebration that year will be remembered, for Patriotism was not only talked of, it was lived.

At the opening of school in the Fall, I reorganized my work. My office, with its furniture, piano, equipment, and thousands of copies of songs were destroyed. Nearly half of the schools were destroyed. Where books and songs had not been burned with the school, they had been destroyed or taken by the people and soldiers who occupied the remaining schools. Fifty thousand sheets of music, and hundreds of books were taken. My whole department was disabled in almost every school by these conditions. Also, many teachers were transferred to new grade work, and sometimes the new work seemed difficult for them.

On account of the small number of children in the Shack School, I decided to give the same songs to all the children and have the singing lessons become school exercises.

I sent out a song called "San Francisco," and the patriotic songs with a circular suggesting that songs referring to our State and Nation should be taken first. I called attention to the fact that it was a most opportune time to instill in the hearts of the children love for "San Francisco, "California," and the "Union," and that the use of the right kind of songs would influence the characters of the children. I then decided that the whole year should be given to the study of "Patriotic and Folk Songs and all the Nations."

I had a fixed and definite idea what singing meant to the schools for that year. The songs should be a medium for the teaching of the grandest lessons in patriotism. They should furnish inspiration, for we needed it.

I walked and rode all over the city (not an easy thing to accomplish in those days) visiting the shack schools and getting acquainted with conditions and giving lessons for encouragement.

The memory of these first visits will never leave me. The brave characters of principals and teachers will never be forgotten. They worked under every inconvenience and patiently they did their part to build up the city.

Some of the schools were practically held together by the singing of the children. In some places there were no desks and no materials, but a wise teacher would gather the pupils together and keep them happy, singing songs.

It was out of the question to have Teachers' Meetings as formerly as distances were so great, and car service was so poor.

So I conceived the plan of printing my lectures and directions on the "Child Voice," "Sight Singing," and "Songs" with the regular outlines for the grade work. The pamphlet was called "Some Ideas on Children's Singing," and it was the means of starting my work, because the teachers could personally get my ideas on the subject even if there were no meetings.

In January, 1907, I sent these books out, and they proved a great assistance in the work. Regular work was encouraged wherever it was feasible.

I sent my assistants to the schools as usual and I visited many of them myself. Frequently I would call the whole number of pupils into the yard where we would all sing the Patriotic Songs.

We had during the Winter, many rainy days to reckon with, and later the car strike; still I managed to get to most of the schools to help them for the graduations, and I sent Mrs. McGlade to a number of schools for that purpose also.

I visited fifty-four schools during the year, and many of them I visited twice, and some of them I visited a number of times. I always try to strengthen the weak places.

I gave lessons to five hundred classes, and most of these classes I visited twice; I visited the Denman once a week for some months, and prepared the Eighth Grade Graduating Class for their closing exercises. I also helped the Adams School and many others for the graduation.

I sent Mrs. McGlade to thirty-five schools and about three hundred and fifty classes which she revisited a number of times, and she helped the Monroe, James Lick, Bernal, and Columbia Graduating Classes for their closing exercises.

I sent Miss Moran to twenty-seven schools and about two hundred and fifty classes which she revisited a number of times.

Besides their regular visits, my assistant stenciled and mimeographed eighty-three songs, making in all 20,000 sheets of music.

This was done, because I wished to emphasize the study of the songs of the various nations. I wished the children to become familiary with them for these songs came from the people and belong to the people. They never die. They are expressions of all that has touched the springs of action. Through them we can sympathize with the sorrows, joy with the happiness, and fight for the rights of those olden people.

This music which so easily affects the young minds, added to the stirring or tender words of the songs, will mold and influence the hearts of those who sing. In almost every one of these songs there is a particular story that reaches the interest and emotions of the children. Thus, new energy will be given and fresh courage will bring power to attain the best in character and citizenship.

These songs have soothed, comforted, and uplifted many great and noble men. These songs have stirred men to fight and die for their country. Think how the "Marseillaise" aroused one French army, and how many have been helped to better things by "Lead Kindly Light," and 'Abide With Me."

Though I have emphasized song singing during the past year, I have not forgotten that music in the school benefits the child in a threefold manner.

The correct study of music effects the child physically, mentally and spiritually.

Good health is essential to the student. It is the foundation of all effort and enjoyment. Deep breathing in conducive to good health and correct singing depends upon deep breathing. The chest expends, the physique is improved, the child is filled with vigor, and becomes more receptive.

After the child has been still in concentrated study there can be no better change than the relaxation that comes with the free flow of the breath, and for the little child the motion songs not only relieve the tense muscles, but also develop the brain centers, through muscle action.

The development of the human voice is no mean consideration. [illegible] who mumbles or whose voice is thin or throaty is hampered throughout his life; these faults are a constant annoyance and indeed sometimes causes the failure of a career. The singing voice itself, if used purely and with skill, is an unending joy to the owner and associates, and is a means whereby one may for a short while be lifted away from the struggles and difficulties of life.

The mentality of a child is greatly helped through the use of exercises for tone-perception and sight singing. Besides developing quickness of eye and voice, they exact the utmost concentration and make for memory and power. A knowledge of music is also gained, which will help the child unlock for himself the great store house of music. It will make him an interested and enthusiastic listener to the compositions of the masters.

The emotional life of the child is enriched by the singing of songs. His impulses will be more patriotic, more loving and reverent by the use of the right kind .of songs. Such songs will deepen and purify the emotions and will furnish the child with the world's songs, and thus he will understand better the joys and sorrows of other people. He will be able to better take his place as a social being.

The first two years of the school work in music is devoted to the singing of good songs, especially adapted to the little ones: to the formation of correct vocal habits so that the voice will not be harmed, and to the development of tone perception. This last is an important study in the younger years, because there is the time to make the impression upon the musical hearing. Some little children enter school without the power to imitate a given sound.

After a few years these children are able if trained carefully to sing simple lines by themselves. If children are neglected when they are younger, it is very hard to gain much development in later years.

Beginning with the third year the children study from the Staff Natation, and then the singing book is introduced in the fourth year. .Dictation work is given for eartraining and rhythm. Simple two part songs are introduced during the year and each year finds new difficulties presented in songs, sight singing and eartraining. Each subject is dealt systematically, and by the time the children leave the grammar school they should be able to think tones, sing at sight simple music, have a considerable knowledge of the theory of music, possess voices free and true, and enjoy keenly all things musical. If we can give them a sincere wish to become better acquainted with the beautiful songs and selections of the masters, then indeed we have accomplished a great deal.

Before the disaster, the music had taken rapid strides in progress. At the States Teacher's Association held here, twenty-seven songs in parts were sung by the children before the convention. At the Music Section I exemplified the work of my department in Songs and Sight Singing by the children singing.

Now after our City's misfortune, we are hampered, but nevertheless considering the hardships under which the whole department worked during last year I feel that the Music progressed.

I cannot but appreciate the faithfulness of the special teachers who still continued the extra work even though the extra compensation was discontinued.

There is yet much to be done, but I am hopeful that the coming year will bring splendid results.

I would like very much to have twenty minutes a day or one hour and a half a week given to the singing. We now only have one hour a week.

I should like to see the Principals interested in putting some choice song books in the library of their individual schools.

I would like a library myself as I had everything destroyed.

I would like a traveling library of sets of octavo music for the Eighth grades.

If possible, I should like to give a concert for the Eight grade children in the Mission High School where the children could have some of the works of the masters.

I wish sincerely to thank the Superintendent and the Board of Education for the cordial support that they have extended to me and my department during these strenuous days.

Yours respectfully,

ESTELLE CARPENTER,
Supervisor of Music.

REPORT OF SUPERVISOR OF DRAWING.

San Francisco, June 30, 1907.

Mr. Alfred Roncovieri,
Superintendent of Public Schools.

My Dear Sir: In reply to your request for a report of the work in Drawing, done during the past year, I take pleasure in submitting the following:

Before the great conflagration of this city, which occurred in April, 1906, the Drawing and Art of our schools were in a most promising condition.

For twelve years we had labored, diligently striving to evolve a system of instruction, which should not only meet the needs of our cosmopolitan population, but be one that could be successfully taught by the regular teachers of our Department.

We had passed through the same stages of experiment, common to most cities in this country—testing many methods, practicing many theories—and while we knew that we had not fully solved our problem, we did feel that we were working in the right direction.

We had come to the conclusion that the prevailing system of the times—though seemingly consistent, because so logical—was unsatisfactory since it failed to fulfill its claims.

We had followed the prescribed methods, and could get—from specially qualified teachers—immediate results having both technical and artistic qualities; but from the rank and file of the teaching force, we failed to get any final results, which would make for permanent power.

We were forced to abandon the logical system and substitute one that is psychological. The former is the system in vogue in special art schools; being vocational in purpose, it is not adapted to a general educational system which aims primarily at a faculty development and considers technique of secondary importance.

In shaping our system, we sought to create a course of instruction, which would not only permit of a free play of the independent activities of the perceptive and expressive faculties, but would also be untrammeled by cumbersome conventions of technique, and yet be one that would subtly guide the pupils into correct and orderly habits of working; a course that would recognize the limited aesthetic possibilities of immature mentalities, admitting of crude results as the true expression of childish ideas, and not demanding of young pupils, qualities of work that parallel the results of trained adult artists; a course that would give the pupil the opportunity to express himself in his own particular way and permit him to make mistakes and correct them; in short, a course by which the pupil may attain to power through natural stages of growth, instead of being dwarfed by forcing processes, merely to produce show work; a course that considers the child and not the subject; that makes for power and not for drawings.

Such a course should provide for the application of that great fundamental principle of achievement—practice—which principle is embodied in the old proverb, "Practice makes perfect," and should take into consideration the fact that it is not once doing that gives power, but the repetition upon repetition, before the idea is impressed and the vehicle of expression becomes spontaneous.

This is true of every form of expression. Reading and writing have constant practice, hence there is power. Drawing has but one hour a week, with long intervals of time between lessons. This very limited amount of time given to the subject, makes it necessary to question not only, how much can be done in one hour a week, but which of the various sub-subjects generally prescribed for a course in Drawing, are the most important fundamentally? Is it wise to try them all, and touch upon each slightly, or to select a few and by concentration upon these, teach them well? The problem is not only "to cut our garment to our cloth," but to select the proper garment.

The experiments we made in our search for a practical course of study, led us to drop one branch of the subject after another, until we found ourselves reduced to bare fundamentals, consisting of spontaneous story drawing in the Primary Grades, seeing lessons in the Intermediate and Grammar Grades and some elementary design and picture study in all grades.

As our system was distinctly local, there being no adopted text books, we found it necessary to prepare monographs of instruction for teachers.

During the years of 1904, 1905 and 1906 with the aid of Miss E. B. Murray, my only assistant, I distributed among the schools, twenty-five thousand pages of mimeographed matter, and had on hand—at the time of the fire—for future use, about half of this quantity most of which was destroyed. Our teachers found these outlines very helpful, as they gave definite instruction in the matter of the subject and the method of presenting it.

At the time of our historic disaster, we were preparing an exhibit of drawings for the National Teachers Association which was to convene in San Francisco the following summer. We had collected thousands of drawings, selected from the regular lessons, and representing every phase of the work. This collection, we felt to be the bloom of the plant we had so tenderly nurtured, and its exhibition, for the benefit of our visitors, was anticipated with much pleasure.

Our work shown at the St. Louis Exposition, had attracted universal commendation, bringing to us a first prize, but we felt that our later efforts had grown into something still better. The work was more of the child and less of the teacher, with much of that subtle quality of feeling that is the legitimate expression of the highest aesthetic understanding of a child, and not the particular artistic effect, which is the standard of the finished artist.

The work was principally in pencil, and colored crayon with some water-color in the design of the upper grades. We have in times passed, worked in every medium, changing from lead-pencil to charcoal and then to pen and ink. Then we adopted water-color. We were convinced of the value of using color, but found the technique of water-color, not only too difficult for pupils, but also for teachers. We had some good results, but most of them were happy accidents, which neither pupil nor teacher would repeat, and they failed to be progressive with the advancing grades.

We finally adopted colored crayons, which are now in use, and which are as satisfactory as is possible for so cheap a medium.

The colored crayon involves no special training. It has no particular technique related to it. It stays where it is put. It neither runs over the paper, nor is it responsible for unintentional and unwelcome pattering resulting from the use of too much or too little water, as in the case with water-colors. It is capable of fine effects, and being a coarsely pointed pencil, there is no danger of over-detail, or over-finish. Its results though crude, are at least bold and impressionistic, while it lends itself very happily to generalization.

In all our work, we have made color an important factor and our children have shown so much ability in this direction, that they are credited with having unusual color sense. This has been attributed to the favorable climate of California, which admits of so much outdoor life, and gives the opportunity for studying our beautiful country.

We know that environment exerts a tremendous influence upon people, but we also know that it takes educational training to fit them to appropriate all the environment affords. Before there was any teaching of color in our schools, there was no particular color sense manifest among the school children.

During the past year, terminating June 30, 1907, my being away on a leave of absence, Miss Murray did what she could to carry on the work. With twenty-seven schools housed in temporary structures, working under the most unfavorable conditions—not having any of the usual equipment or aids—and the remaining schools in the unsettled state following so great a catastrophe, and all alike suffering from an unusually severe winter and car strikes; it but follows that comparatively little was accomplished in the teaching of special subjects.

The adopted course of instruction was practically suspended, and the simplest possible line of work substituted. Miss Murray visited schools on an average of three times during the year, but was hampered in her work by the lack of outlines of instruction for the teachers, and of her inability to hold meetings. She did all that was possible under the unfavorable conditions.

In beginning the work this year, the outlook is much brighter, we mean to resume our work according to the old order of things, as rapidly as our present conditions will permit, and hope for great things for the future.

Respectfully yours,

KATHERINE M. BALL,
Supervisor of Drawing.

REPORT OF SUPERVISOR OF MANUAL TRAINING.

San Francisco, June 30, 1907.

Mr. Alfred Roncovieri,
Superintendent Schools, San Francisco, California.

Dear Sir: In accordance with your request for a general report, including other data, of the work in our Manual Training Department during school year ending June 30, 1907, I have the honor to submit the following, taken from reports of my assistants, now on file with me:

Total number days taught, 110 (except at Clement, 64).

Total enrollment at Clement Center	107
" " " Crocker "	274
" " " Everett "	218
" " " Hamilton "	237
" " " Horace Mann Center	253
" " " Irving Scott "	86
" " " Sherman "	284
Grand total enrollment at all laboratories	1,459

	Per cent.
Percentage of attendance at Clement Center	94
" " " " Crocker "	98.3
" " " " Everett "	96.6
" " " " Hamilton "	96.8
" " " " Horace Mann Center	95.1
" " " " Irving Scott "	92.4
" " " " Sherman "	97.5
General percentage of attendance at all laboratories	95.8

Immediately following the great fire, and largely since, there has been a marked falling off in the attendance of the larger boys, many having secured employment. With the opening this term, August, 1907, very many of these boys are returning to manual training.

A noticeable change has taken place in the Richmond District and also in the Mission and Sunnyside District. From one cause and another these sections are filling fast, with boys of manual training age, and, to meet requirements, I respectfully urge the building of two new Manual Training Centers, one at the Fairmont School site and one either at the Sutro or Richmond Schools, for one of which we have on hand an almost complete equipment. Even if temporary buildings can be had thy will relieve the situation.

It may be pardonable for me to add that schools which formerly sent us no boys (schools classed as Primary) are now sending them to manual training in ever increasing numbers. Among these are the Fremont, Laguna Honda, Oceanside, Winfield Scott, Grant, and McKinley schools.

Thus far we have managed to accommodate them, but I urgently beg that this matter of increase be considered and in some way provided for.

Your very kindly and helpful suggestion to me sometime since, that I introduce some simple additions to our mechanical drawing in the way of geometric forms and lines is proving very effective, and is not in the least beyond the capacity of the boys we get. This is particularly pleasing to me, and without going too far I am endeavoring to base objects made by the boys upon thep rinciples given, though this hampers design somewhat.

I should feel further obligated if you would interest sixth grade teachers in the beginnings of such drawing, since it would be the best preparatory work for our department conceivable in the high sixth grade.

I would be most willing, if no other means were found, to assist class teachers if time can be had for such.

Let me thank you also for the proffered desk room. It is something I shall be delighted to accept. It will facilitate matters and give me a "local habitation," so to speak.

Most sincerely yours,

M. DOYLE,
Supervisor Manual Training.

REPORT OF THE PUBLIC SCHOOL TEACHERS' ANNUITY AND RETIREMENT FUND COMMISSIONERS FOR THE FISCAL YEAR ENDING JUNE 30. 1907.

San Francisco, California, August 17, 1907.

To the Honorable, the Board of Supervisors in and for the City and County of San Francisco.

Gentlemen: I have the honor to submit herewith the report on the Public School Teachers' Annuity and Retirement Fund for the fiscal year terminating June 30, 1907.

ALFRED RONCOVIERI,
Superintendent of Schools and Secretary of Public School Teachers' Annuity and Retirement Fund Commission.

RECEIPTS.

Balance in fund June 30, 1906		$52,218.71
Contributions by teachers bound by provisions of the Annuity Law		9,742.00
Interest on funds deposited in Banks		1,774.27
Amounts received in accordance with Section 8 (a), from teachers retired during fiscal year—1906:		
August 1.	Miss E. R. Elder	250.00
August 1.	Mrs. C. Chalmers	230.00
October 1.	Miss H. E. Whirlow	277.00
Dec'r 1.	Mrs. V. Troyer	227.75
Jan'ary 1.	Miss Helen Thompson	213.80
April 1.	Adolph Herst	193.00
April 1.	Miss Q. O. McConnell	223.00
April 1.	Miss Annette Miley	207.05
April 1.	Miss Madge Sprott	111.50
Absence money allowed by Board of Education		1,793.70
Total Receipts		$67,461.78

DISBURSEMENTS.

Annuities to retired Teachers:	
October 1, 1906	$3,146.25
January 1, 1907	3,296.25
April 1, 1907	3,391.95
July 1, 1907	3,614.25
Clerical service	200.00
Stationery	68.15
Total	$13,716.85

RESUME.

Receipts	$67,461.78
Disbursements	13,716.85
Total	$53,744.93
In Banks	$50,866.56
Certified cheque on Western National Bank, favor of John H. Ryan accompanying bid for $50,000, School Bonds	2,500.00
On trays of Treasurer	378.37
	$53,744.93
Permanent Fund	$50,000.00
Annuity Fund	3,744.93
	$53,744.93

On March 11, 1907, the Board of Supervisors passed Bill No. 197, Ordinance No. 184 (New Series), approved March 12, 1907, providing for the sale of School Bonds for the City and County of San Francisco. Pursuant to this Resolution and the provisions of the Annuity Law, the Board of Public School Teachers' Retirement Fund Commissioners at a special meeting held March 30, 1907, did resolve unanimously to invest the $50,000 in the permanent fund, in School Bonds at par, and forthwith forwarded this bid with a certified check in favor of Mr. John H. Ryan, clerk of the Board of Supervisors, in the sum of $2,500.

The School Bonds appear to be unsalable and it is rumored that, the citizens so voting, they will be cancelled and 4 per cent bonds substituted. Therefore the Commissioners have petitioned the Board of Supervisors for permission to withdraw their bid and to have the certified check returned.

ANNUITANTS.

Date of Retirement	Name	Maximum or Fraction Thereof	Annuity Per Month	Annuity Per Quarter
1895.				
Nov. 27.	Mrs. L. T. Hopkins	Max.	$50.00	$150.00
1896.				
Jan. 22.	Miss L. B. Ryder	Max.	50.00	150.00
Jan. 22.	Mrs. M. H. Currier	"	50.00	150.00
April 24.	Miss V. M. Rachlet	9-10	45.00	135.00
1897.				
Sept. 11.	Miss M. Solomon	Max.	50.00	150.00
Dec. 8.	Miss F. S. Soule	"	50.00	150.00
1898.				
Sept. 14.	Miss Kate A. Kollmyer	8-15	26.66⅔	80.00
1899.				
April 18.	Miss M. J. Bragg	Max.	50.00	150.00
June 14.	Mrs. M. E. Caldwell	"	50.00	150.00
Aug. 1.	Mrs. E. M. Poole	11-15	36.66⅔	110.00
1900.				
Jan. 9.	Miss C. A. Templeton	Max.	50.00	150.00
July 18.	Mrs. A. Griffith	"	50.00	150.00
July 25.	Miss K. F. McColgan	"	50.00	150.00
Aug. 1.	Miss L. M. Barrows	13-15	43.33⅓	130.00
Aug. 1.	Miss Annie A. Hill	Max.	50.00	150.00
Oct. 15.	Miss M. J. Canham	14-15	46.66⅔	140.00
1901.				
July 20.	Miss J. B. Gorman	Max.	50.00	150.00
Oct. 4.	Miss E. Murphy	9-10	45.00	135.00
1902.				
Jan. 2.	Miss R. C. Campbell	Max.	50.00	150.00
Jan. 2.	Miss L. S. Templeton	"	50.00	150.00
Jan. 2.	Mr. A. T. Winn	"	50.00	150.00
Sept. 28.	Miss Emma J. Miller	11-15	36.66⅔	110.00
1903.				
Feb. 17.	Mrs. L. A. Chinn	Max.	50.00	150.00
Aug. 1.	Miss Lidis Hart	11-15	36.66⅔	110.00
	Miss Christine Hart	Max.	50.00	150.00
Aug. 1.	Mrs. S. A. Miles	"	50.00	150.00
Aug. 1.	Mr. T. B. White	"	50.00	150.00
Sept. 1.	Miss A. E. Slavan	"	50.00	150.00
Oct. 15.	Miss L. Burnham	¾	37.50	112.50

1904.				
Aug. 1.	Mr. Elishe Brooks	Max	50.00	150.00
Aug. 1.	Miss I. Patterson	"	50.00	150.00
Sept. 1.	Mrs. E. M. North Whitcomb.	"	50.00	150.00
1905.				
Jan. 16.	Miss E. O. Grant	Max	50.00	150.00
March 1.	Miss M. A. Smith	⅔	33.33⅓	100.00
"	Mrs. D. G. Webster	13-15	43.33⅓	130.00
"	Miss Jean Dean	Max	50.00	150.00
"	Mrs. T. C. Stohr Nicholl	"	50.00	150.00
"	Mr. Chas. Ham	"	50.00	150.00
"	Miss R. Jacobs	'	50.00	150.00
"	Mr. D. Lambert	" (Evening)	25.00	75.00
1906.				
Feb. 1.	Miss M. E. Carson	Max	50.00	150.00
Feb. 1.	Mrs. A. C. Taylor	"	50.00	150.00
Aug. 1.	Miss Elva R. Elder	"	50.00	150.00
Aug. 1.	Mrs. Christine Chalmers	"	50.00	150.00
Oct. 1.	Miss H. E. Whirlow	"	50.00	150.00
Dec. 1.	Mrs. V. Troyer	"	50.00	150.00
1907.				
Jan. 1.	Miss Helen Thompson	Max	50.00	150.00
April 1.	Miss Madge Sprott	½ (Evening)	25.00	75.00
April 1.	Miss Annette D. Miley	14-15	46.66⅔	140.00
April 1.	Miss Q. O. McConnell	Max	50.00	150.00
"	Prof. A. Herbst	"	50.00	150.00

Respectfully submitted,

ALFRED RONCOVIERI,
Superintendent of Common Schools, and Secretary of Public School Teachers' Annuity and Retirement Fund Commissioners.

Report of Superintendent of Schools

FISCAL YEAR 1907-1908

REPORT OF THE SUPERINTENDENT OF SCHOOLS OF THE CITY AND COUNTY OF SAN FRANCISCO FOR THE YEAR ENDING JUNE 30, 1908.

San Francisco, August 1st, 1908.

To the Honorable Edward R. Taylor, Mayor,
in and for the City and County of San Francisco.

Dear Sir: I have the honor to submit herewith the Annual Report on the condition of the public schools of this City and County, as required by the Charter, for the Fifty-sixth fiscal year of the School Department, ending June 30, 1908.

ALFRED RONCOVIERI,

Superintendent of Common Schools, in and for the City and County of San Francisco.

ANNUAL STATISTICAL REPORT OF THE SUPERINTENDENT OF COMMON SCHOOL.

FISCAL YEAR ENDING JUNE 30, 1908.

GENERAL STATISTICS.

Population of the City, 1908 (estimated)	365,000
Number of youth in the City under 17 years of age	96,792
Number of youth in the City between 5 and 17 years of age who are entitled by law to draw public money	87,696
Assessment roll of the taxable property of the City	$429,632,843.00
City school tax on each $100, 18.1c (plus 2.4c emergency)	20.5c
City and county taxes	$864,324.33
Estimated value of school sites	$4,840,000.00
Estimated value of school buildings	1,229,000.00
Estimated value of school furniture	265,000.00
Estimated value of school libraries	19,000.00
Estimated value of school apparatus	26,000.00
Total value of school property	$6,379,000.00

FINANCIAL REPORT.

DISBURSEMENTS.

	Amount	Total.
SALARIES—		
Teachers—		
High School	$ 159,590.90	
Primary and Grammar, (including Evening, $65,340 and Special $19,-033.75)	1,042,474.95	
Janitors—		
High School	6,440.00	
Primary and Grammar	51,546.85	
Board of Education	12,000.00	
Superintendent and Deputies	14,747.46	
Secretary and Attachees	12,072.65	
Storekeeper and Assistants	3,680.00	
Scavenger	2,281.00	
Teamster	1,450.00	
Superintendent of Repairs	2,505.00	
Bookkeeper: Repair Department	1,500.00	
Total Salaries		$1,310,288.81
Advertising		1,476.71
Cartage		2,458.00
Census		7,521.25
Conveyances		2,532.10
EQUIPMENT—		
Fifty classrooms	17,759.64	
Cooking centers	332.53	
Manual Training Centers	233.05	
Polytechnic High School	3,291.18	
Technical Department, Humboldt Evening	266.45	
Total equipment		23,872.85
Fences and benches		257.77
Fuel		9,547.17
Incidentals and Janitorial supplies		11,109.23
LABOR—		
Supply Department	12,967.00	
Repair Department	26,164.50	
Total labor		39,131.50
Light		3,257.52
Maps, charts, globes and books		3,244.98
Material for regular repairs		14,788.50
Printing		4,213.77
Rents		7,805.10
Roof for Burnett School building		312.06
School sites (Visitacion Valley)		5,950.00
Stationery		6,872.94
SUPPLIES—		
High School	6,817.37	
Cooking	846.22	
Manual Training	1,487.87	
Total supplies		9,151.46
Teachers' Annuity Fund		3,000.00
Teachers' Institute		300.00
Temporary Buildings		23,102.18
Water		12,589.65
Total ordinary expenses		1,500,793.55

(Payable from regular school revenues for year ending June 30, 1908.)

EXTRAORDINARY EXPENDITURES PAID BY BOARD OF SUPERVISORS

	Amount	Total.
Deficit for year 1906-07 (contracted by Board of Education in constructing and equipping necessary temporary buildings)	$151,009.06	
Rehabilitation Fund	38,938.01	
"Back Salary Claims"	23,142.50	
Total extraordinary expenditures		213,089.57
Expended from Bond Fund		220,472.14
Grand total of money expended on Public Schools		$1,934,355.26

RECEIPTS.

		Amount	Total.
City and County taxes, year ending June 30, 1908 (Auditor's figures)		$764,324.33	
Emergency tax (2.4c)		100,000.00	
State apportionment (High School)		21,762.40	
State apportionment (Primary and Grammar)		558,585.45	
Insurance		2,000.00	
Old material and miscellaneous		1,718.15	
Rents		431.40	
Total ordinary revenue		1,448,841.73	
GRANTS BY SUPERVISORS—			
Deficit, 1906-07	151,009.06		
Rehabilitation Fund	40,100.00		
"Back Salary Claims"	23,142.50		
Total		214,251.56	
Bond money		220,472.14	
Grand total receipts			1,883,565.43
Apparent deficit			50,789.83
Add unexpended balance, "Rehabilitation Fund"			1,161.99
Real deficit			51,951.82

This deficit was caused in the following manner: The Board of Supervisors appropriated $1,500,000.00, assuming that the revenue from rents, etc., and State apportionments would exceed $660,000.00. This revenue was but $584,-517.40, or over $75,000 below estimate. The Board of Education, however, knowing that, by law, it was entitled to the appropriation intact, audited 1-12 of $1,500,000.00 per month, thus expending $1,500,000.00, when less than $1,449,000.00 were received.

COST PER PUPIL.

(a) For instruction only.

	Per Pupil enrolled.	Per Pupil in Average Attendance. Daily
High Schools	$53.41	$78.88
Primary and Grammar Schools	25.54	32.76
Evening Schools	9.09	31.18

(b) For all expenditures, including maintenance, buildings, sites and furniture.

	Per Pupil enrolled.	Per Pupil in Average Daily Attendance.
High Schools	$78.28	$115.66
Primary and Grammar Schools	42.23	53.62
Evening Schools	14.17	48.61

SALARY SCHEDULE, 1907-1908.

All salaries are paid twelve months to the year.

To Whom Paid.	Per Month.
Board of Education (4 members), each	$250.00
Secretary of Board of Education	150.00
Clerk of High School Board	50.00
Superintendent of Common Schools	333.33
Deputies (4), each	225.00

HIGH SCHOOLS.

Principals	250.00
Vice-Principals	180.00
Heads of Departments	150.00
Heads of Departments in Science	160.00
Assistant Teachers (3 years on probation)	120.00
Assistants after 1 year's experience	130.00
Assistants after 2 years' experience	140.00
Assistants after 3 years' experience	145.00
Teachers of Drawing	125.00
Head Teacher, Drawing, Wood-carving and Clay Modeling (Miss Van Vleck), Polytechnic High School	145.00
Assistant to Miss Van Vleck (Miss Murdock)	100.00
Teachers of Modern Languages, Girls' High and Polytechnic High Schools	125.00
Teacher, Spanish, Commercial High School	145.00
Teacher, Iron Work, Manual Training Department, Polytechnic High School	150.00

PRIMARY AND GRAMMAR SCHOOLS.

To Whom Paid.	Per Month.
Principal Grammar Schools	180.00
Vice-Principals, Grammar Schools	125.00
Principals Primary Schools, 14 or more classes	150.00
Principals Primary Schools, 10, 11, 12 or 13 classes	130.00
Principals Primary Schools, 4, 5, 6, 7, 8, or 9 classes	120.00
Principals Primary Schools, 2 and 3 classes	105.00
Teachers in charge of Primary Schools, 1 class	105.00

REGULAR TEACHERS OF GRAMMAR AND PRIMARY GRADE CLASSES.

Grades will be designated as 1st, 2nd, 3rd, 4th, 5th, 6th, 7th, and 8th.

1st, 7th, and 8th Grades—	Per Month.
First year	$69.00
Second year	72.50
Third year	75.25
Fourth year	79.00
Fifth year	83.50
Sixth year	77.25
Seventh year	91.00
Eighth year	94.00
2nd, 3rd and 4th Grades—	
First year	69.00
Second year	71.25
Third year	73.50
Fourth year	77.00
Fifth year	80.25
Sixth year	83.50
Seventh year	87.00
5th and 6th Grades	97.00

Assistants in Primary and Grammar Schools teaching German and English, or English and French, or Music and English, having special certificates to teach such special subjects, $5.00 per month, in addition to their salaries according to the schedule. Any one special subject, $5.00 extra.

In fixing the salary of a teacher, after election as a regular teacher, credit shall be given such teacher for experience from the date of his or her appointment on the Substitute List.

Teachers of the Day Substitute Class shall be paid $3.00 per day.

Substitutes teaching in High Schools shall receive $5.00 per day while actually engaged in work.

Teachers of the Evening Substitute Class shall receive $2.50 for each evening that they teach and $1.00 per evening for reporting.

EVENING SCHOOLS.

The salaries of Principals of Evening Schools shall be as follows:

	Per Month.
Of Humboldt Evening School	$125.00
Of Schools having 300 or more average daily attendance	100.00
Less than 300 in average daily attendance	85.00
Assistants in Evening Schools	50.00
Teacher High School Class, Humboldt and Washington Evening	60.00
Head Teacher of Mechanical Drawing, Humboldt School	100.00
All High School branches	60.00

DEPARTMENT AT LARGE.

Vocal Music, Supervisor	150.00
Assistant Teachers of Music	90.00
Supervisor of Drawing	150.00
Assistant in Drawing	90.00
Teachers of Physical Culture	100.00
Supervisor of Cooking	100.00
Assistant Teachers of Cooking (4)	75.00
Supervisor of Manual Training	150.00
Assistants of Manual Training (6)	100.00

OFFICE AND SHOP EMPLOYEES.

Financial Secretary	160.00
Recording Secretary	150.00
Stenographers, Board of Education and Superintendent's Office (3)	80.00
Messenger, Board of Education	95.00
Messenger, Superintendent's Office	85.00
Telephone Operator	60.00
Storekeeper	150.00
Assistant Storekeeper	125.00
Foreman Storeroom	115.00
Inspector of Buildings and Head Carpenter	175.00
Storekeeper (Shop)	125.00
Scavenger	157.00
Teamster, Supply Department	115.00

FINES AND DEDUCTIONS.

Fine 50 cents for tardiness day school (passed May 31, 1899).

Fine 50 cents for tardiness evening school (passed May 10, 1899).

Fine $2.50 for failure to acknowledge receipt of circulars or letters from office (passed March 29, 1899).

Deduction of one-thirtieth for each day's absence.

No excuse to be absent from school, with pay, shall be granted to any principal or teacher of this Department, except under suspension of rules, and by special action of the Board of Education (passed June 14, 1899, and adopted by the present Board), except for three days, on account of the death of a relative within the first degree of consanguinity, or of husband or wife (passed September 1, 1899).

Fine $5.00 for principals failing to make correct report of absentees on last school day of month.

JANITOR'S SALARIES.

$5.00 per classroom up to and including 10 classrooms.

$4.50 per room, in excess of 10 rooms (except where this rate is impracticable).

AVERAGE ANNUAL SALARIES.

	Male.	Female.
Superintendent of Schools (1)	$4,000.00	
Deputy Superintendents of Schools (4)	2,700.00	
School Directors (4)	3,000.00	
Principals of High Schools (5)	3,000.00	
Principals of Primary, and Grammar Schools	2,035.40	$1,695.24
Teachers in High Schools	1,774.71	1,587.24
Teachers in Grammar Schools	1,240.00	1,106.70
Teachers in Primary Schools		1,053.11
Teachers in Evening Schools	746.84	626.00

All Teachers, Principals and Superintendents $1,149.44

MEDAL FUNDS.

Name of Fund.	Deposited in	In Fund June 30, 1908
Bridge Silver Medal	Hibernia Savings & Loan Society	$2,029.01
Denman Grammar School	Hibernia Savings & Loan Society	1,063.90
Denman Silver Medal	German Savings & Loan Society	2,013.23
Hancock Grammar School	German Savings & Loan Society	543.56
Jean Parker Gram. School	German Savings & Loan Society	444.87
John Swett Gram. School	Hibernia Savings & Loan Society	248.42
Lincoln Grammar School	Hibernia Savings & Loan Society	2,676.29

SCHOOLS.

Number of High Schools	5
Number of Grammar Schools	27
Number of Primary Schools	49
Number of Evening Schools	8
Total number of Schools	89
Number of brick school buildings owned by the Department	1
Number of wooden school buildings owned by the Department	80
Number of buildings or rooms rented by the Department	21
Total number of buildings used by the Department	102

NUMBER OF TEACHERS IN DEPARTMENT, JUNE, 1908.

	Men.	Women.	Total.
Number of teachers in High School	40	46	86
Number of teachers in Grammar Schools	18	318	336
Number of teachers in Primary Grades	1	510	511
Number of teachers in Evening School	38	60	98
Number of Substitutes and unassigned teachers, Day Schools	1	27	28
Number of unassigned teachers, Evening Schools	1	11	12
Number of teachers of Manual Training	8		8
Number of teachers, Cooking		7	7
Number of teachers, Music		4	4
Number teachers, Drawing		2	2
Teachers of Physical Culture	2		2
Special teacher of Reading		1	1
Total number of teachers in Department	109	986	1095
Whole number of Principals (included in total)	24	65	89
Number of Principals not required to teach a class (included in total)	22	50	72
Number of Vice-Principals (included in total)	7	26	33

LENGTH OF SERVICE OF TEACHERS, COUNTING ONLY THEIR SERVICE IN SAN FRANCISCO PUBLIC SCHOOLS.

Years of Service.	Men.	Women.	Total.
Less than 1 year	2	9	11
1 year	7	55	62
2 years	4	15	19
3 years	10	98	108
4 years	5	43	48
5 years	8	42	50
6 years	7	31	38
7 years	8	33	41
8 years		3	3
9 years	3	1	4
10 years	6	52	58
11 years	3	55	58
12 years	2	33	35
13 years		16	16
14 years	4	18	22
15 years	3	37	40
16 years	3	25	28
17 years	2	23	25
18 years	4	19	23
19 years	2	28	30
20 years	2	16	18
21 years	5	26	31
22 years		24	24
23 years	1	30	31
24 years	1	14	15
25 years	1	18	19
26 years		15	15
27 years	1	13	14
28 years	1	19	20
29 years		18	18
30 years		29	29
31 years	1	21	22
32 years	1	17	18
33 years		8	8
34 years	1	20	21
35 years		14	14
36 years	2	9	11
37 years		5	5
38 years		9	9
39 years	2	6	8
40 years		5	5
41 years		6	6
42 years	2	1	3
43 years		3	3
44 years		2	2
45 years			
46 years			
47 years			
48 years		1	1
49 years			
50 years		2	2

SCHOOL ENROLLMENT AND ATTENDANCE FOR THE YEAR ENDING JUNE 30, 1908.

Enrollment.		Increase over 1907.	For year ending April 17, '06
High Schools	2,990	167	5,188
Primary and Grammar Schools	37,866	decr'se 57	47,661
Evening Schools	7,189	2,256	4,993
Totals	48,045	2,067	57,782

Average Daily Attendance.		Increase over 1907.	For year ending April 17, '06
High Schools	2,023	261	3,211
Primary and Grammar Schools	29,812	3,047	35,753
Evening Schools	2,096	694	2,967
Totals	33,931	4,002	41,931

ENROLLMENT BY GRADES.

	Boys.	Girls.	Totals.
First Grade	5,515	4,680	10,195
Second Grade	2,858	2,432	5,290
Third Grade	2,546	2,316	4,862
Fourth Grade	2,481	2,392	4,873
Fifth Grade	2,190	2,140	4,330
Sixth Grade	1,637	1,951	3,588
Seventh Grade	1,249	1,506	2,755
Eighth Grade	800	1,173	1,973
Totals	19,276	18,590	37,866
First Year High School	450	791	1,241
Second Year High School	289	746	1,035
Third Year High School	183	270	453
Fourth Year High School	95	166	261
Totals	1,017	1,973	2,990

CENSUS.

I have estimated the population of this City to be 365,000, ascertained in the following manner:

The entire population of the City and County is determined by multiplying the number of school census children between the ages of 5 and 17 (87,696) by 4.1, this being the ratio which existed in 1900, between the number of such children and the population as determined by the federal census. To be exact, the figure for this year would be 359,554, but I have allowed 6,500 for a possible excess. I desire to explain the manner in which the factor 4.1 was obtained. The ratio which existed between the entire population of the State of California, as shown by the federal census of 1900, and the number of school census children between the ages of 5 and 17 years at that date, was 3.9. The ratio in San Francisco as has already been stated was 4.1 being, as will be observed, above the average. It must be remembered that the figure setting forth the number of census children in the various counties between 5 and 17 years of age is as liberal as it possibly can be, inasmuch as school authorities in each county give special instructions to census marshals to find every child between those ages, because, upon that number, State school money is apportioned to the various counties of the State. This ratio in Alameda county is 3.8; in Contra Costa county, 4.1; in Fresno county, 3.9; in Humboldt county, 3.7; in Inyo county, 4.4; in Lake county, 3.6; in Los Angeles county, 3.4; in Monterey county, 3.7, and in Sonoma county, 3.9. In the City of Alameda, 4; in the City of Berkeley, 3.9; in the City of Fresno, 3.8; in the City of Los Angeles, 3.2; in the City of Oakland, 3.9; in the City of Stockton, 5; in the City of Sacramento, 5, and in the City of San Jose, 3.65.

The ratio used by the State Superintendent of Public Instruction for the entire State for this year was 4, showing that the factor 4.1, used by my office to determine the population of San Francisco is liberal.

CENSUS.

	1906.	1907.	1908.
Children 0 to 17 years	125,191	90,955	96,640
Children 5 to 17 years	101,836	77,367	87,696
Population of City and County estimated on above	420,000	325,000	365,000

PRINCIPAL ITEMS OF THE SCHOOL CENSUS REPORT SUBMITTED BY CHIEF CENSUS CLERK, HON. SAMUEL H. BECKETT, FOR THE YEAR ENDING JUNE 30, 1908, AS COMPARED WITH THE CORRESPONDING REPORT FOR THE YEAR ENDING JUNE 30, 1907.

Number of white children between 5 and 17 years of age—

Boys	43,650	
Girls	43,301	
Total	86,951	
School Census, 1907	76,589	
Increase		10,362

Number of Negro children between 5 and 17 years of age—		
Boys	44	
Girls	29	
Total	73	
School Census, 1907	51	
Increase		52
Number of Native born Mongolians between 5 and 17 years of age—		
Boys	392	
Girls	279	
Total	671	
School Census, 1907	726	
Decrease		55
Total number of census children between 5 and 17 years of age, including 1 Indian	87,691	
School Census, 1907	77,367	
Increase		10,324
Number of children under 5 years of age—		
White	8,848	
Negro	6	
Mongolian	242	
Total	9,096	
School Census, 1907	13,588	
Decrease		4,492
Nativity of children—		
Native born	96,640	
Foreign born	152	
Total	96,792	
School Census, 1907	90,955	
Increase		5,837

MISCELLANEOUS.

Number of graduates from the grammar school for the year—	
Boys	579
Girls	881
Total	1,460
Number of graduates from High Schools for the year—	
Boys	57
Girls	164
Total	221

SCHOOL ENROLLMENT AND ATTENDANCE AND CENSUS STATISTICS FOR YEARS ENDING

	June 30, 1906	June 30, 1907		June 30, 1908	
	Enrollment	Enrollment	Decrease	Enrollment	
High School	5,188	2,823	2,365	2,990	167 inc. over 1907
Primary and Grammar	47,661	37,923	9,738	37,866	57 dec. from 1907
Evening	4,933	4,887	46	7,189	2,256 inc. over 1907
Total	57,782	45,633	12,149	48,045	2,366 inc. over 1907
	Average Daily Attendance	Average Daily Attendance	Decrease	Average Daily Attendance	
High School	3,211	1,762	1,449	2,023	261 inc. over 1907
Primary and Grammar	35,753	26,765	8,988	29,812	3,047 inc. over 1907
Evening	2,967	1,402	1,565	2,096	694 inc. over 1907
Total	41,931	29,929	12,002	33,931	4,002
			Decrease		
Children 5 to 17 years	101,836	77,367	24,469	87,696	10,329 inc. over 1907
Children 0 to 17 years	125,191	90,955	34,236	96,640	5,685 inc. over 1907

(Estimated population of the City and County of San Francisco, April, 1908, 365,000.)

SCHOOL ATTENDANCE AND POPULATION.

The figures set forth in the school census taken during April, 1908, and in the reports of Principals on school attendance, demonstrate the fact that San Francisco is quickly regaining its population. The city has gained about 35,000 people during the past year and the prospects are excellent that by 1910 the population will surpass what it was at the time of the earthquake and fire.

The table on the following page indicates the decrease and increase since April, 1906.

SALARIES OF TEACHERS.

It is gratifying to record the fact that the salaries of the teachers have been increased during the year about twenty per cent. This increase should be safe-guarded by an amendment to the Charter providing that the salary fund be increased from $28 to $50 per pupil in average daily attendance.

SCHOOL RECONSTRUCTION FUND.

Immediately after the conflagration of 1906, teachers and pupils of many cities, towns and school districts made contributions to aid in the reconstruction of school buildings.

My last report showed a balance in the fund of.................................. $28,791.41

Received since that time:

1907.			
Aug. 29. / Sept. 5. / Sept. 11.	"Citizen" San Francisco		30.00
Oct. 1.	School Children, Manitowoc, Wis.		12.10
Dec. 10.	Interest		192.74
Jan. 20.	From County Superintendent of Schools, Audubon, Ia.		22.85

DRAFTS.

Oct. 16.	Voucher No. 21, Lester Herrick & Herrick	$ 25.00	
Nov. 8.	Voucher No. 22, Phillips & Van Orden Co., Printing	228.00	
Jan. 3.	Cheque to order of A. Lacy Worswick, Architect, for preparation of Plans and Specifications for Yerba Buena School	700.00	
Jan. 3.	Crocker & Co., for printing 5,000 copies of financial statement of Reconstruction Committee	120.00	1,073.00

Balance in Fund on Special Deposit, City Treasury.............................. $27,976.10

It was decided to construct a school building commemorating these donations, to cost $60,000, and to be known as the Yerba Buena School, Yerba Buena being the original Spanish name of the peninsula of San Francisco. The Board of Supervisors has guaranteed $32,000, and the building is being constructed.

SWIMMING.

One who has acquired the art of swimming is possessed of an accomplishment, —the means of indulging in a most healthful exercise and in safe-guarding life in time of danger.

There are numerous and urgent requests that swimming instruction be provided for certain grades of public school children and for such persons as might wish to pay for instruction.

Franklin believed that swimming should be a part of national education and it is to be hoped that Boards of Education may make instruction in swimming a part of the practical physical education of school children.

Therefore, I earnestly recommend that the Board of Education lease the premises formerly occupied by the Lurline Bath Company, making necessary improvements thereon and furnish instruction to public school children in the art of swimming. The expenses for the operation of the swimming tank and for instruction to be paid from the revenue derived from rents of school property.

REPORTS.

No printed report on the condition of schools of this City and County has been issued since 1902. The office of Superintendent has been unable to satisfy either the local demand for such reports nor to exchange with the Superintendents of other cities. This has been commented upon unfavorably, and it illy becomes the largest city of the State and Pacific Coast not to furnish these reports when every other city of this State and of the other states having a population of 8000 or more issues them annually. I therefore recommend that the Superintendent's reports for 1906, 1907, and 1908 be printed for distribution.

STATE AID FOR OUR EVENING SCHOOLS.

The electors will have an opportunity at the general election to be held in November, 1908, of adopting or rejecting what is designated as Assembly Constitutional Amendment No. 8, proposing to amend Section 6 of Article IX of the Constitution of the State of California, defining the public school system.

This section now provides that the public school system shall include primary and grammar schools * * * and that the entire revenue derived from the State School Fund and from the general state school tax shall be applied exclusively to the support of the primary and grammar schools. The purpose of the proposed amendment is to include in the school system the elementary evening schools. It reads as follows: "The public school system shall include day and evening elementary schools, and such day and evening secondary schools, normal schools and technical schools as may be established by the legislature or by municipal or district authority. The entire revenue derived from the state school fund and from the general state school tax shall be applied exclusively to the support of day and evening elementary schools * * * ."

The City and County maintains eight evening schools at an annual expense of about $70,000. During the year ending June 30, 1908, there were enrolled in these schools 7,189 (5,962 boys and 1,227 girls) pupils, all over fourteen years, 85% of whom were employed during the day.

San Francisco and other cities of our State maintain evening schools entirely at their own expense. Is it just? Is not a boy or girl toiling during the day for a living yet possessed of such ambition and desire for self-improvement as to forego pleasure or rest during the evening, as valuable to the State and as worthy to receive State aid as the boy or girl attending school during the day? The adoption of this amendment would not increase state taxes but would increase the school revenue for this City, because the pupils, in average daily attendance in the evening schools, would participate in the apportionment of state school money. The average daily attendance of last year in the schools would have added $21,900 to the school fund of this City without increasing state taxes one cent.

Well taught evening schools are a most valuable feature of a school department. They furnish an opportunity for self-improvement to persons who are ambitious but whose circumstances will not allow them to take advantage of day school instruction. They have a good effect on the citizenship of the municipality, especially when the percentage of foreign-born people is large as here.

SCHOOL VISITATION.

During the past year the Superintendent and his deputies have made 4,049 visits to schools and classes. Material conditions and educational work have been inspected and examined. On the information gained by these visits reports have been made to the Board of Education. The good has been commended, deficiencies indicated and recommendations made for better equipment and operation where the same appeared necessary.

The teachers have labored against disadvantages, two of which are prominent. First the abbreviation of the school year to 188 actual teaching days, and second the presence in some schools of half-day classes. Dividing the day in the occupancy of the same building crippled the work of the Lowell and Girls' High Schools, also that of the Mission High and Commercial Schools. In order to meet the first disadvantage—the abbreviation of the year,—my office issued certain directions to teachers abbreviating the work as scheduled in the Course of Study.

The work of the great majority of teachers has been satisfactory; that of eight only has been reported poor and twenty-one not wholly satisfactory.

CONFERENCES.

The Superintendent and his deputies have met in weekly conferences for the purpose of discussing matters that have appeared from time to time in the course of official work. Plans of action have been formulated, policies adopted and recommendations made to the Board of Education designed to improve educational and material conditions and to adjust differences arising between principals and teachers, and teachers and pupils, and their parents. Much has been accomplished in this manner and official work has been defined and strengthened.

TEACHERS' INSTITUTE.

The Teachers' Institute for the teachers of the public schools of the City and County of San Francisco was convened by County Superintendent, Alfred Roncovieri, at the Auditorium of the Mission High School building on March 25, 26 and 27, 1908.

All the sessions were attended by 1,067 department teachers who were instructed and entertained professionally by the following speakers and themes:

Wednesday, March 25, 1908.

9:30. Opening Address..Alfred Roncovieri
Superintendent of Schools, San Francisco.

9:45. Lecture ,"A Visit to Burbank"..........................Hon. Edward Hyatt
State Superintendent of Public Instruction.

10:30. Recess.

10:45. Lecture, "The Common School"....................Dr. Benj. Ide Wheeler
President, University of California.

11:30. Lecture, "Characteristics of Spanish America"..Dr. Bernard Moses
Prof. of History and Political Science, University of California.

12:30. Adjournment.

Thursday, March 26, 1908.

9:30. Lecture, "The Juvenile Court"....................Hon. Frank J. Murasky
Judge of the Superior Court.

10:00. Soprano Solo, "Parla"..Arditi
Miss Julie Cotte.

10:15. Lecture, "Public Spirit and Education"........Dr. Alexis F. Lange
Professor of Education, University of California.

11:00. Recess.

11:15. Lecture, "Social and Industrial Education...............................
....Dr. James E. Russell
Dean of Teachers College, Columbia University.

12:30. Adjournment.

Friday, March 27, 1908.

9:30. Lecture, "The Ethical Aspect of Teaching"............................
....Dr. James E. Russell
Dean of Teachers College, Columbia University.

10:20. Baritone Solo from "Mille. Modiste," "I Want What I Want When I Want It." (Victor Herbert)........Mr. Arthur Cunningham
(By kind permission, Management Princess Theatre.)

10:35. Lecture, "The Forward Look"................................Mr. T. L. Heaton
Deputy Superintendent of Schools, San Francisco.

11:15. Recess.

11:30. Lecture, "The Latest Phase of Government Making in the Philippines"..Dr. Bernard Moses

12:30. Adjournment.

THE CIVIL SERVICE PLAN FOR THE APPOINTMENT OF TEACHERS FOR THE CITY AND COUNTY OF SAN FRANCISCO.

A sound plan for the selection and appointment of teachers is a much needed reform in the administration of public schools. Established custom and many private and personal interests at first bitterly opposed the competitive civil service system for the appointment of teachers as at present in vogue in the San Francisco School Department; but, after a trial of several years the system has come to stay, for it rests upon correct principles. Practical measures have been adopted for carrying these principles into effect. I believe that public sentiment will formulate our present plan into a law, making it compulsory on all City Boards of Education to select their teachers impersonally and on merit alone. In devising the present competitive system I was guided by the following principles found in a report addressed to the Board of Education in 1901 by a select committee composed of President Jordan, President Wheeler, State Superintendent Kirk, Professor Cubberley, Dr. Burk and Professor Brown.

PRINCIPLES UNDERLYING THE SELECTION OF TEACHERS.

1. The sole purpose of the public schools is education. No consideration whatever, other than educational interests of pupils can honestly enter into any plan for the appointment of teachers. In no sense do the schools exist to provide employment for teachers.

II. No one should be employed as a teacher who does not possess high personal character, liberal education and bodily health and vigor.

III. Successful experience is manifestly the best evidence of fitness for appointment.

IV. Pofessional training in the principles and practice of teaching is desirable, and is increasingly demanded in systems of public education.

V. The duty of the Board of Education requires that these officers should frequently take the initiative in securing the best possible teachers for the schools under their management. It is not sufficient that they should merely select from the candidates who apply for appointment.

VI. The employment of any sort of personal or political influence to secure appointment to the teaching force, or the urging of any consideration other than fitness for the work of teaching as a ground for such appointment, is held to be an act of unprofessional conduct.

Judging from the splendid corps of teachers which has been selected by our system I can only say that the results obtained have justified the system. I believe that we in San Francisco, approximate an ideal system in the selection and appointment of teachers, but if there are any who think differently we invite their criticism and we will be glad to receive any suggestions that may improve our plan.

As evidence of how impersonally our system works I would cite the fact that the President of one of our Normal Schools told me on an occasion, after an examination, that our system had selected the major part of the most capable graduates of his school. This is to me one of the greatest and most satisfactory proofs of the fact that our system leads to practical results in giving us the best teachers obtainable.

Many of our foremost educators are most emphatic in their advocacy of its adoption for cities, inasmuch as it so closely approximates an ideal system, the adoption of which insures a thoroughly equipped and competent teaching force.

As the real objective end of education is the rearing of a perfect citizen, so should it be the purpose of governing educational bodies to adopt and enforce a system through the exercise of which the services of the most competent pedagogues may be secured. It is not the educational qualifications alone which denote the successful teacher any more than the adoption of an excellent course of study could be said to insure the successful education of a pupil. A teacher must be, aside from the standpoint of academic qualifications, of agreeable disposition, strong personality, good bearing and address, as well as being perfectly sound in health and possessed of sufficient bodily vigor to do effective teaching. The importance of a teacher's life work can not be under estimated. To her is entrusted a solemn, sacred duty, as the child comes directly under her control during its formative period. None can gainsay the fact that the force of the teacher's example and the general environment of the classroom exercise an important part in this impressionable stage of a child's career.

The present competitive civil service method of appointing teachers of the San Francisco School Department has been in force for the past six years, but it was not formally adopted and made a permanent feature of the school administration of this City until May, 1904. In preparing the present competitive plan and in proposing its permanent adoption my object was to eliminate and prevent all political or social "pulls" from exercising their pernicious influences in the conduct of school affairs. The system is simple and has given us splendid results. The competitive examinations are based on questions relating to the theory and practice of teaching, and are both oral and written. They are held annually, generally in June or July. This time of the year is selected because it gives the teachers from every part of the State an opportunity to come to San Francisco to take the examinations. In the written examination which is the first held, ten questions are propounded, five in the forenoon session and the remainder in the afternoon. The papers are submitted to a committee of principals who mark the percentages. This Committee of Examiners' consists of ten persons, one and the same question being submitted to each of the Examiners for the determination of the percentage. To insure absolute impartiality a system has been adopted by which the identity of a candidate is completely hidden, and in fact is not devulged or known to any one until the percentages attained by the competitor in both the written and oral examinations have been decided.

The only conditions imposed upon candidates are that they must be the holders of at least a grammar grade certificate, of good moral character, bodily health and vigor.

The oral examination is conducted by the Board of Education, consisting of four members and the Superintendent of Schools. The main object of this examination is to ascertain the candidate's visible qualifications such as age, address, personality, education, experience, conscientiousness, enthusiasm, devotion and force of character. Two hundred is the maximum credits which a candidate may attain, one hundred credits being allowed for each examination.

The favor in which these examinations are held is evident by the increasing number of participants each year.

It is not difficult to account for the eagerness displayed by teachers to secure positions in this City. San Francisco offers the most attractive field of labor on the coast, higher salary, permanent tenure, social and educational advantages, and finally, the enjoyment of a pension at the time of retirement.

While the successful candidate in the examination secures a position in the Department as a member of the Substitute Class, the fact of such membership insures no guarantee of permanency to her position. Her future success or failure and the permanency of position depends upon the results of her own labor, for upon being assigned to a class from the Substitute list she enters upon what is known as a probationary period of two years duration. If upon the expiration of this probationary period, the reports of the principals under whom the teacher has taught are favorable as to her teaching qualifications and ability to enforce discipline, she is elected a regular member of the teaching force by the Board of Education, upon recommendation of the Superintendent. She now becomes what is known as a regular teacher, and the tenure of her occupation is for life, subject, however, to good behavior and efficiency and to her compliance with the rules governing teachers' positions. If, on the other hand, three unfavorable reports are made against a probationary teacher by three principals who have given the probationer a fair trial in classroom work, the probationer is dropped from the roll.

The probationary period under the eyes of competent judges of teachers' work is most important, for upon its successful termination depends the permanent employment of the teacher in the Department.

Even after election to a permanent regular position, under the San Francisco system, the teacher may be dismissed from the Department. But to do this, charges of insubordination, immoral or unprofessional conduct, or evident unfitness for teaching must be made and proved against her in regular form, her accuser must confront her with the charges, and she must be given a fair and impartial trial.

That the competitive civil service examination system is the only method by which teachers should be secured, the most skeptical must admit. Through its practical observation by an honest and loyal Board of Education, ready and willing to enforce the provisions governing the examination tests, the efficiency of our teachers can be elevated to the highest possible standard. It is my firm belief, after an experience of six years with this system that political pressure, social influence, personal intercession, and the exercise of improper and unworthy considerations must be relegated to the past in the selection of teachers.

Any suggestions, that might tend to benefit or perfect the system will be most gladly entertained. The system is a free-for-all competition for a permanent position in the San Francisco School Department. It gives the teachers selected under it dignity, independence and freedom from solicitude by delivering them from the necessity of securing an annual re-election.

The Civil Service plan eliminates completely the appointment of teachers from the activities of politics.

Applicants for positions are not obliged to expend their time, energy and money in "seeing" and "influencing" the members of the City Board of Education or the City Superintendent, nor of importuning their friends to do this for them. Those who are successful in the examination and receive appointments in the order of their rank, are relieved from anxiety and worry and are free to devote all their time to their work. They are not obliged to keep in touch with politicians nor to dance attendance on a too frequently complacent City Superintendent who is himself created by a Board of Education, many members of which are ordinarily controlled by political considerations.

Annually in the months of May and June most of the cities drop all their teachers from the roll. Great injustice is often done at this time. Frequently teachers of excellent character and ability are not re-elected because they are reported as not "satisfactory," which as a matter of fact too often means nothing more than that they are "not politically right."

The San Francisco Civil Service System of selecting teachers removes them from the often baneful influence of an official who holds his position by the grace of politicians and who, to retain it, is compelled to do politics perennially.

I am induced to elaborate thus in explanation of the San Francisco system because at times reflections have been cast upon the teachers and the administration of the San Francisco School Department, by self appointed educational critics holding official positions.

I believe that the school teachers of San Francisco comprise a corps of enthusiastic, able, faithful workers in the great educational system of our State and that this Civil Service plan of electing teachers has resulted, during the past six years, in the acquisition by this Department of the best available teaching talent in California.

I am pleased to note that the San Francisco Civil Service System is attracting favorable attention. The school authorities of the City of Los Angeles have recently adopted it.

PLAN FOR THE APPOINTMENT OF TEACHERS FOR THE CITY AND COUNTY OF SAN FRANCISCO.

The following system of appointing teachers to this Department is solely on merit (and without any reference to personal, social or political influence) —as determined by competitive "Civil Service" examination among applicants who already hold regular teachers' certificates. This system was inaugurated and carried out under the suggestions of Superintendent Alfred Roncovieri. From the standpoint of experience, and having in view the best interests of the children of the School Department which, after all, is the primary consideration, the Board of Education promulgates the following plan for the appointment of teachers:

No one shall be employed as a teacher who does not possess high personal character, liberal education and perfectly sound bodily health and vigor.

The Board of Education shall conduct annually a competitive examination for appointments to the substitute list. All teachers desiring to enter such examinations shall be required to take both a written and an oral examination on the Practice and Theory of Education and such other topics as may from time to time be announced.

The object of these examinations is not to test applicants in primary and grammar studies, but to select the best of those already certificated as teachers. Composition, penmanship and spelling, however, will be considered in the written examination. Applicants must furnish the Board of Education, before the time of the examination, full information relative to their academic preparation, their professional training (if any), and their experience in teaching (if any). Each applicant shall give not less than three nor more than seven references to persons who are competent to speak of his or her fitness for the work of teaching. Such references shall include the persons whose official position enables them to give the most exact and pertinent information with reference to the applicant's scholarship, training, experience and general character and efficiency. The Board of Education will not consider general letters of recommendation; but they will request from the persons referred to by the applicant a confidential statement as to the applicant's qualifications; such statement to be given in answer to a uniform list of questions to be furnished by the Board. The Board will also, in case of doubt, call for and make use of supplementary information, relating to the same set of questions, from other persons who may be deemed competent to speak intelligently of the candidate's qualifications.

At least five days prior to the time of examination, the Board of Education will canvass all of these evidences of qualifications of the several applicants, and will prepare the list of applicants who are to participate in the competitive examination. No applicant shall be included in this list, who does not hold a valid teacher's certificate of a grade not lower than the grammar grade, authorizing him or her to teach in the schools of San Francisco. Nor shall any applicant be included in this list, if the information obtained in the manner described in this section shall indicate, in the judgment of a majority of the Board, that such applicant would not be a suitable person to be appointed as a teacher in the schools of San Francisco.

No applicant shall be privileged to call on the members of the Board individually to press his or her claims for appointment, nor shall the friend of any applicant endeavor to use any personal, political or social influence with any member of the Board.

The employment of any sort of personal, political or social influence to secure appointment to the teaching force, or the urging of any consideration other than fitness, for the work of teaching, as a ground for such appointment, is held to be an act of unprofessional conduct, and shall debar the applicant from taking the examination.

During the oral examination, applicants will have ample opportunity to present in full their fitness and general ability.

If any applicant shall importune any member of the Board of Education, or be a party to importunities by any other person for the purpose of influencing any member of the Board of Education, with any argument or plea for his or her appointment to the Substitute List, assignment to a probationary teaching position, or election to a permanent teaching position (other than evidence of professional qualification for such appointment, assignment, or election), such applicant shall be deemed guilty of unprofessional conduct, and consequently disqualified.

It is the duty of every member of the Board of Education, whenever any such attempt is made to employ personal, political, or any improper influence, in connection with such appointment, assignment, or election to a teaching position, to immediately report the facts to the Board; and the applicant concerned in such attempt shall not thereafter be considered for appointment, assignment, or election to a teaching position by the Board, unless he or she shall satisfy the Board that he or she was not responsible, either directly or indirectly, for the actions so reported.

All assignments to teaching positions in the schools of San Francisco shall be from a Substitute List, and no person shall be appointed to this list, except by a unanimous vote of the Board, after having taken the regular Competitive Examination.

The Substitute List for assignment to positions in Primary and Grammar Schools shall at no time contain more than fifty names, and they shall be appointed to said list as vacancies occur in the order of their credit standing in the annual Competitive Examinations. A new list from which to select substitutes shall be formed annually after the Competitive Examination.

No married woman shall be appointed to any teaching position; and the position of any female teacher appointed after this date shall be declared vacant in case of her marriage.

Vacancies in the corps of regular teachers in Primary and Grammar Schools shall be filled by Probationary Teachers, taken from the Substitute List, in the order of their standing in the Competitive Examinations, the term of probation to date from the time of appointment to regular Substitute List.

Probationary teachers so appointed shall serve a probationary term of two years, from the date of their appointment as a regular substitute, before becoming eligible to be elected Regular Teachers.

After such final election they shall hold their positions for life, provided they shall at all times comply with and be subject to the rules of the Board of Education and the laws of the State, and the Charter of the City and County of San Francisco, so far as the same relate to the School Department.

No one suffering from tuberculosis or offensive catarrh shall be appointed to the Substitute List, and all teachers before being appointed to this list must obtain from one of the consulting physicians of the Board of Education, a certificate showing that the holder is perfectly sound in health, and possessed of sufficient bodily vigor to do effective teaching.

GENERAL PROVISIONS GOVERNING THE COMPETITIVE EXAMINATIONS FOR APPOINTMENT OF TEACHERS.

The Competitive Examinations will be held annually during the summer vacation. Announcement of dates will be made in the official daily newspaper. Examination for 1907 will begin at 9 o'clock on the morning of Wednesday, August 7th.

The Written Examination, at which ten questions are to be propounded for answer by the applicants, will be held in the Mission High School and will occupy the first day, and consist of two sessions, the first in the forenoon, beginning at 9, at which five questions will be given; the second at 2 o'clock, at which the five remaining questions will be given. A number system has been devised by which the identity of the examination papers of the candidates is completely lost, neither the candidates nor any one connected with the examination being able to identify them. In order to secure uniformity in marking and to prevent the personal equation of the examiners working for or against any candidate the answers will be marked, and the percentages determined by ten examiners, and instead of marking entire papers, each examiner will mark only one answer (the answer given to the same question by all the candidates).

The five examination questions for each session are complied in the following manner:

At 7:30 o'clock on the morning and at 12:30 on the afternoon of the day of the Written Examination, the four School Directors and the Superintendent meet in the Mission High School, and each submits a set of five questions. From these twenty-five questions five are selected after a careful consideration of the value of each one.

After the five questions have been selected, they are at once mimeographed in the presence and under the supervision of the Board and Superintendent, and at 9 A. M. and 2 P. M. sharp, the Examination sessions begin.

Candidates must be in their seats at 8:45 A. M. for the morning session and at 1:45 o'clock for the afternoon session. Candidates may leave the Examination rooms for rest and refreshment as soon as they shall complete their answers to the first five questions of the morning session, but they must return and be in their seats by 1:45 P. M. for the afternoon session.

The examination will be practical rather than academic in its nature and will be such as any well trained teacher of experience should answer. The questions will cover the field of general pedagogy that a teacher must understand to perform her work in the classroom, and will include such special fields as the general aims and principles of education, the general method of instruction, the special aims and methods of teaching the different elementary school subjects indicated in our course of study, classroom management and discipline, school hygiene, and educational psychology. Any standard pedagogical works may be consulted by applicants preparatory to examination. Successful experience, however, is the best preparation.

The Oral Examination will be held in the offices of the Board of Education, Pine and Larkin Streets. That for 1907 will begin on Thursday, August 8th, at 9 o'clock, and continue in morning and afternoon sessions until all applicants shall have been examined. Each candidate will appear before the Board of Education and the Superintendent, and be questioned for some fifteen minutes. His or her apparent fitness for teaching, experience and personality will be considered. Each of the examiners will cast a secret ballot with the percentage to which, in his opinion, the applicant is entitled. The average of these percentages will be taken as the marking for the oral examination.

The relative standing of the applicants will be determined by the combined markings of both the written and oral examinations, 100 credits being the maximum in each, and 200 for the two combined.

The examinations of 1905 were taken by 287 candidates. Of these the first 120 were appointed on the Substitute List, during the school year 1905-06.

The following instructions should be preserved for reference on the morning of the examination, as they must be carefully observed by all the candidates.

Directions to be followed at each session of the Teachers' Annual Competitive Written Examination.

You will find ten sheets of paper, one envelope, a small sheet of paper and a metal ''clasp'' on your desk.

First—Write your name and address in full on the small sheet of paper, fold it carefully, and place it in the envelope which YOU must seal immediately. Do not write your name or any name or address on anything but the small sheet which you must enclose and seal in the envelope. Any identification mark will exclude your examination paper. Write nothing on the outside of the envelope.

Second—Proceed to reply to the questions, using separate sheets of paper for each answer, supplied you for that purpose. Composition, penmanship and spelling will be considered in the marking. At both morning and afternoon sessions, when finished, clamp your five answers together consecutively, with the ''metal clasp'' which you will find on your desk, placing the sealed envelope containing your name on top; then deliver the finished set to the ''examiner'' in charge.

EXPLANATION.

At both the morning and afternoon sessions the envelope, together with the five sheets containing the answers of each candidate, are stamped with the same number. This stamping does not begin, however, until all the examination papers of each session have been turned in by the candidates. The envelope and the set of five answers of each candidate have a different number from those of every other candidate. There being two sessions, the two envelopes and two sets of five answers of each candidate must necessarily be stamped with two different numbers, but in order to avoid confusion the same number is never used twice. The two sets of envelopes (of the morning and afternoon sessions) after having been numbered, are all placed in a box which is locked and sealed and deposited in the safe of the Board of Education. The ten answers, each on a separate sheet of paper, are then given to ten San Francisco school principals, who, acting as examiners, will mark the answers to but one (and the same) question answered by all of the candidates.

After all the answers have been examined and marked, the ten answers of each candidate are re-assembled in two sets of five each and the markings thereon credited to the two numbers which appear on the sheets of the respective candidates. After this work is completed the seal is broken from the box containing the numbered envelopes. This is done in the presence of the Board of Education, Superintendent of Schools, and other public officials. The envelopes are opened, and the identity of the candidate is then disclosed for the first time. The markings of the oral and written examinations are then combined, and the standing of the candidates determined.

The following lists for 1902, 1903, 1904, 1905, 1907, and 1908 will give some idea of the general character of the questions:

QUESTIONS GIVEN IN 1902.

1. Interest. How would you rouse it? Is it all sufficient for accomplishing results?
2. State and describe three essential features of the class recitation.
3. State some IMPORTANT defects of a strictly graded system of classes and give one GOOD remedy for each defect mentioned.
4. Since about 70 per cent of the pupils attending the public schools, on an average, are in the primary grades, which three subjects of instruction do you regard as the most important in training the great mass of our pupils who never enter the grammar school? Give your reasons.
5. Do you think the State School Law which forbids teachers to assign any home-work to pupils under fifteen years of age is a wise provision, and give your reasons for or against this law?
6. What would you do to advance a very diffident or backward child?
7. Discuss the Use and Abuse of Text Books.
8. Discuss discipline, its necessity, aim or aims.
9. Discuss helps to memory.
10. Point out specifically some of the uses and common abuses of the memory in geography teaching, making your explanation show your knowledge of the psychology involved.
11. Explain what is meant by visual, auditory and motor types of thinking, and illustrate by reference to corresponding types of spellers.
12. Why is it that pupils who write neatly in their copy books frequently do much inferior work in original composition? Explain the psychological causes.

QUESTIONS GIVEN IN 1903.

1. What is the ultimate end of education? State specifically some of the things education should do for the individual. For society?
2. Considering the limited time at your disposal for the instruction of a large class, what methods would enable you to give maximum attention to

the special needs of individuals or groups of individuals that are particularly backward or brilliant?

3. How far can you teach parts of one school subject when you are definitely teaching another subject; for example, how far can you correlate geography with history? Should the attention of the child upon the history material be intesified or lessoned by such introduction of geography? Point out some dangers in attempting to correlate subjects.

4. What constitutes an ideal teacher?

5. Discuss the intellectual features particularly active in children and educational significance.

6. Give a description of a model lesson in arithmetic in a primary grade.

7. Discuss the development of the imagination in primary grades—its importance—means to secure it.

8. Discuss maintenance of strict discipline. How it may be tempered and how far relaxation from it may be allowed for the sake of promoting interest, emulation, and fellowship between teacher and pupils?

9. How can you make history teaching contribute directly to training for good citizenship? How far would you require children to learn facts of history, such as dates and names? What importance in history teaching would you give to the ideas and sentiments which have been the causes and results of historical events? What feelings should good history teaching awaken in the pupil?

10. Briefly outline the most approved general methods in use for teaching first grade pupils to read, and show by your explanation your comprehension of the mental process involved.

11. State three advantages and three disadvantages of department teaching in grammar grades.

12. Describe briefly any approved general method of teaching:

(a) Rapid and accurate addition.

(b) Geography.

Justify your methods by psychological reasons.

QUESTIONS FOR 1904.

1. Write a model lesson in geography and tell how you would make use of the following in teaching the same: 1, attention; 2, interest; 3, association; 4, memory; 5, imagination.

2. What standards or principles should guide a teacher in advancing or detaining a child at promotion time? Should all subjects have equal weight? If not, suggest some subjects that should have more weight than others. Give reasons in full for your answers.

3. Describe a remedy for each of the following cases: (a) Poor spellers; (b) faulty grammarians; (c) careless calculators; (d) thoughtless memorizing; (e) poor readers.

4. Why is it important to give special attention to ventilation of the schoolroom? Discuss fully the physiological processes involved.

5. What are your standards of good work in composition? Suggest the most effective way or methods of correcting composition in class. In your suggestion explain the defects as well as the merits of your method.

6. Discuss the method best calculated to secure the friendship and cooperation of a class.

7. How would you make use of the school or public library to the best advantage?

8. In teaching literature what would be your chief aims? What are the defects in the present methods? Would you use the sentences in literature as drills in grammar? Give reasons for answers.

9. How would you make the recitation of each pupil an intellectual activity for every member of the class?

10. Outline an inductive lesson in English grammar.

QUESTIONS FOR 1905.

1. By the history lesson, how may patriotism be best inculcated?

2. (a) What studies taught in school are especially adapted to the cultivation of the perceptive faculties?

(b) Give some illustrations.

3. Tell how you would teach a class to add columns of figures with accuracy and rapidity and justify your method by psychological reasons.

4. How would you direct and encourage home reading? Name ten books suitable for Sixth and Seventh grades.

5. Discuss the Art of Questioning with definite suggestions.

6. How would you teach the ready and correct use of the English language to the First, Second, and Third grades of the primary school.

7. How do you teach "pointing off" in division of decimals? Illustrate with examples showing various difficulties that perplex children.

8. Explain the method to be pursued in teaching writing during the first two years' of a the child's school life.

9. If you had a pupil with a remarkable gift of memory who succeeds but poorly in original work, such as composition and arithmetic, how would you work to correct the deficiency?

10. What devices would you employ to keep up a good standard attendance in your class?

QUESTIONS FOR 1907.

1. What are the purposes of school discipline?

What different ways of disciplining children has the teacher at command?

Suggest how you would vary in the use of these means: With incorrigible children as opposed to sensitive children. With boys as opposed to girls.

2. Suggest the various ways by which the teacher may rest a child from mental fatigue resulting from classroom instruction. Discuss the special merits of each way suggested.

3. When you find a pupil of normal mind who does not know how to study, how would you proceed to remedy the condition. Suggest as many detailed ways as you can of giving him desire and power to study by himself.

4. What are the different ways by which you can convey the meaning of an unfamiliar word, phrase, or sentence to a child? Discuss the relative value of each way.

5. What are the different elements which must be associated in the child's mind in order to make him a good speller? Suggest several ways of presenting and associating these elements.

6. What are the main advantages to be derived from nature study? How would you use the school garden and the school excursion in connection with this subject?

7. What are the objects to be kept in view in the teaching of history in the elementary schools? What are the most interesting and valuable kinds of historical facts to be learned in the primary grades? In the grammar grades?

8. In leading a child from home geography to world geography, how would you proceed?

9. State briefly in detail what means you would use in the primary grades to make your pupils speak and write good English.

10. In teaching arithmetic when would you let the child do the work mentally? When have him write it out in full? When mix both methods?

QUESTIONS FOR 1908.

1. There is a growing tendency to abolish corporal punishment as a means of correcting the faults of pupils:

(a) If you had charge of a school in which corporal punishment was not permitted state briefly how you would maintain order in the case of pupils disposed to be unruly.

(b) If you were allowed to inflict corporal punishment at your discretion, in exceptional cases, state some circumstances under which it might, in your opinion, be resorted to as a just and effective mode of correction.

(c) When a teacher decides that a pupil should be punished for wrong doing, what objects should he (the teacher) have in view; that is, what worthy ends would he expect to reach through the infliction of the punishment?

2. What would you do with a pupil who, from absence or other cause, has fallen behind the class?

3. What rules of order would you insist upon to be observed by pupils in passing from the building during fire drill?

4. (a) Tell how you would teach reading to beginners.

(b) Name the important qualities of good reading.

(c) What are the commonest faults which you have found in the reading of children? How would you correct these faults?

5. Our new Course of Study requires an exercise in rapid addition:

Make out a column of figures suited for this exercise, and say how you would best secure speed and accuracy in performing it.

6. (a) What is the main benefit to be derived from the study of general History? Of Geography?

(b) How would you use Geography in connection with History?

7. (a) Describe a good method of teaching the geographical idea of day and night.

(b) What conditions give a country large foreign commerce? Domestic commerce?

8. (a) In what school year would you introduce the regular study of fractions?

(b) With what other rules of Arithmetic would you correlate percentage?

9. Suppose you had charge of an elementary class consisting of pupils of two consecutive grades; make out a program of daily exercises therefor in regular form, showing the grades and divisions taught, the simultaneous work in each, the hour and duration of each subject, and the time for reviews, oral or written.

10. A great many pupils find it extremely difficult to concentrate their attention on the instruction and explanations of the teacher, or to record mentally the most important points set forth in their reading matter. In the case of normal children, what, in your opinion, is the chief cause of this defect, and how would you remedy it?

SCHOOL ACCOMMODATIONS.

Our school buildings are inadequate in number and size. The Board of Education and the Board of Supervisors have been generous in providing temporary and permanent buildings during the last two years. Within a few weeks handsome and permanent buildings will be ready for the accommodation of these schools:

Bay View Grammar,	Bergerot,
Glen Park Grammar,	Yerba Buena (Lafayette),
Laguna Honda,	Monroe Grammar,
Ocean House,	Winfield Scott.

BOND ISSUE.

At the last bond election, May 11, 1908, the Board of Supervisors was authorized by the voters of the City and County of San Francisco to issue bonds to the amount of $5,000,000 for school houses and lands. In the circular of information issued by the Board of Supervisors previous to the election, the following explanation was given:

SCHOOL BUILDINGS.

''This project is mainly a repetition of a similar one submitted in 1903, for which bonds to the amount of $3,595,000, were authorized. About $1,000,000 of the former issue has been sold and the money expended. To carry out the original designs for new school houses and to provide for the replacement of the buildings destroyed by fire (29 in number) the Board of Education estimated an expenditure of $8,000,000. The Board of Supervisors concluded that at least $5,000,000 of this sum was an immediate and pressing necessity, and consent of the voters is asked to bond to this amount.

''This sum will, according to the report of the City Architect, provide for the construction of twelve 'Class A' fireproof buildings to be constructed in the fire limits; nineteen 'Special Construction,' i. e. frame buildings covered both on exterior and interior with sheet metal, metal lath, and cement or hard finish. Also three 'Class A' High School buildings and a 'Class C' addition to the Mission High School. Also lands will be acquired for new sites, and additions to present sites to cost $595,000.

''The schools provided for are named in the architect's report as follows:

''CLASS A'' BUILDINGS.

''Adams Grammar School, 12 class rooms. North side of Eddy Street between Van Ness Avenue and Polk Street. Estimated cost, $120,000.

''Denman Grammar School, 16 class rooms. North side of Page Street, between Steiner and Pierce Streets. Estimated cost, $160.000.

''Franklin Grammar School, 12 class rooms. Eighth Street, near Harrison Street. Estimated cost, $120,000.

''Hancock Grammar School, 16 class rooms. Filbert Street, near Jones Street. Estimated cost, $160.000.

''Jean Parker Grammar School, 16 class rooms. Broadway between Powell and Mason Streets. Estimated cost, $160,000.

''John Swett Grammar School, 12 class rooms. McAllister Street between Franklin and Gough Streets. Estimated cost, $120,000.

''Jefferson Primary School, 8 class rooms. Bryant Street between Sixth and Seventh Streets. Estimated cost, $80,000.

''Lincoln Grammar School, 12 class rooms. Harrison Street near Fourth Street. Estimated cost, $120,000.

''Oriental Public School, 8 class rooms. Clay Street and Powell. Estimated cost, $80,000.

''Mission Grammar School, 16 class rooms. Mission Street between Fifteenth and Sixteenth Streets. Estimated cost, $160,000.

''Irving Primary School, 8 class rooms. Broadway, between Montgomery and Sansome Streets. Estimated cost, $80,000.

Spring Valley Grammar School, 12 class rooms. Washington Street, between Hyde and Larkin Streets. Estimated cost, $120,000.

SPECIAL CONSTRUCTION BUILDINGS.

''Bryant Cosmopolitan Primary School, 16 class rooms. York Street, between Twenty-second and Twenty-third Streets. Estimated cost, $100,000.

''Clement Primary School, 12 class rooms. Day and Noe Streets. Estimated cost, $80,000.

''Cooper Primary School, 16 class rooms. Greenwich Street, between Jones and Leavenworth Streets. Estimated cost, $100,000.

"Peabody Primary School, 16 class rooms. Sixth Avenue, near California Street. Estimated cost, $100,000.

"Holly Park Primary School, 16 class rooms. Holly Park Avenue, between Highland Avenue and West Park. Estimated cost, $100,000.

"Madison Primary School, 12 class rooms. Clay Street, between Walnut and Laurel Streets. Estimated cost, $80,000.

"Marshall Primary School, 16 class rooms. Nineteenth Street, between Valencia and Guerrero Streets. Estimated cost, $100,000.

"McKinley Primary School, 16 class rooms. Fourteenth and Castro Streets. Estimated cost, $100,000.

"Sheridan Primary School, 16 class rooms. Minerva Street, near Plymouth Avenue. Estimated cost, $100,000.

"South End Primary School, 16 class rooms. Burrow Street, between Berlin and Girard Streets. Estimated cost, $100,000.

"Grattan Primary School, 16 class rooms. Alma Street, near Grattan Street. Estimated cost, $100,000.

"Sutro Grammar School, 16 class rooms. Twelfth Avenue, between Clement and California Streets. Estimated cost, $100,000.

"West End Primary School, 12 class rooms. Mission Street, between Naglee and Worden Streets. Estimated cost, $75,000.

"Lakeview Primary School, 16 class rooms. On block bounded by Plymouth and Grafton Streets, Golden State and Holoway Avenues. Estimated cost, $100,000.

"Jackson Primary School, 16 class rooms. North of Panhandle, between Stanyan and Baker Streets. Estimated cost, $100,000.

"Cleveland Primary School, 12 class rooms. Block bounded by Persia, Brazil, Athen and Moscow Streets. Estimated cost, $75,000.

"Starr King Primary School, 16 class rooms. San Bruno Avenue, near Twenty-fifth Street. Estimated cost, $75,000.

"F. J. McCoppin Primary School, 16 class rooms. Sixth Avenue, between B and C Streets. Estimated cost, $100,000.

"CLASS A" HIGH SCHOOL BUILDINGS.

"Girls' High School, 20 class rooms. Scott Street, between O'Farrell and Geary Streets. Estimated cost, $450,000.

"Lowell High School, 20 class rooms. Octavia Street, between Bush and Sutter Streets. Estimated cost, $450,000.

"Commercial High School, 20 class rooms. Grove Street, between Larkin and Polk Streets. Estimated cost, $190,000.

"Addition to Mission High School, Church Street between Dorland and Eighteenth Streets. Estimated cost, $150,000.

"But the voters should be informed that the foregoing list is not to be considered as an absolute determination of the particular buildings to be constructed. Changing conditions may demand corresponding changes in the plan above stated."

The Board of Supervisors took great pains in consulting with the most expert lawyers on bond issues in this country. It is confidently believed that the bonds will be declared valid, and they are now being offered for sale.

On May 20th, the Board of Education passed a resolution selecting the following fifteen schools as the first to be constructed under the terms of the new bond issue and have requested the City Architect to prepare plans for the same: Commercial High, Hancock Grammar, Jackson Primary, Sheridan Primary, Mission Grammar, Sutro Grammar, Frank J. McCoppin Primary, Denman Grammar, Jean Parker Grammar, Bryant Cosmopolitan Primary, Madison Primary, Holly Park Primary, South End Primary, Marshall Primary, and Adams Cosmopolitan Grammar.

Within a few years the school accommodations of San Francisco will be second to none in the State.

ASSEMBLY HALLS IN PUBLIC SCHOOL BUILDINGS AND FREE PUBLIC LECTURES.

I regret that so few of our school houses have assembly rooms. The building of auditoriums, as a feature of school equipment, will be appreciated by the general public and particularly by the school patrons. They will afford a common place of meeting with small expense for all the people where there can be no bickerings, political or sectarian. The home life and the school life can be brought together in harmonious unity and much permanent good will result.

I would, therefore, recommend that every school building planned under the new Bond Issue be provided with an assembly hall to be built on the ground floor or first floor, where in addition to its use for general exercises, music and gymnastics, for the pupils of the school, it can be used for social center development. In such a room the principal can address a large number of pupils in a more impressive way than in separate class rooms. Such a room can be used for stereoptican exhibitions, for graduating exercises or as already indicated as a social center for citizens and parents of the district. The school houses belong to the people and under proper restrictions should be used for the diffusion of information and the promotion of a civic spirit among the adult population.

I respectfully recommend that free public lectures on American History, Physics, Mechanics, Economics, etc., for the student and adult population be given in the auditorium of the Mission High School, the Crocker, Girls' High, Polytechnic, Lowell, Hearst and the Horace Mann, and wherever possible in smaller buildings.

These lectures, combined with musical numbers, will be educational and elevating and will be appreciated by the general public and by the school patrons.

COMMERCIAL HIGH SCHOOL.

I am pleased to report excellent progress in the Commercial High School during the past term. Until the beginning of last year there had never been a fixed standard for graduation from this school. After consultation with the principal it was decided that the minimum requirement in Shorthand should be the ability to write new matter from dictation at the rate of 80 words per minute for five consecutive minutes, and to transcribe the same accurately upon the typewriter. In the tests which were given by my office in January, none of the candidates came up to the required standard of proficiency.

In response to the active work of this office during the second term the pupils, especially of the senior class, took unprecedented interest in their work. They were given permission to use the typewriters, under the supervision of an instructor, before and after regular school hours, for the transcription of their shorthand notes taken in class.

The result of the interest thus shown was seen in the test at the close of the term. Of thirty-seven pupils recommended by the Principal, three passed in the test at the rate of 110 words per minute, thirteen passed at 100 per minute, ten passed at 90 per minute, seven passed at 80 per minute, and only four failed to pass. All of the tests were given on new matter, and for five consecutive minutes.

These results are extremely gratifying to me, because, first of all, they prove the competency of those who took the examinations; also, because they show the correctness of our position in maintaining that the pupils of the Commercial High School were capable of doing better work than they had been doing, and also in requiring that better work be done.

The Board of Education provides generously for the Commercial High School, and many of the parents who send their sons and daughters there make sacrifices to do so. These parents expect that, at the end of the course of instruction, their children will be prepared to fill a position in the business world. And this can be done with the faithful application on the part of the pupil under the proper instruction of the teacher.

Hereafter, the transcription of notes upon the typewriter will be insisted upon as a regular class exercise, as it has been during the past term. These transcriptions will be examined by the teachers in charge and returned to the pupils for correction, to be afterwards placed on file for inspection.

Next term we hope to introduce touch typewriting in all of our beginning classes. Heretofore this has not been practicable, owing to the large numbers in the classes and the varied assortment of machines. It is of the utmost importance that pupils be taught correct fingering, for only in this way can the highest perfection in speed, neatness and accuracy be reached. For this reason I would recommend that only typewriters of standard keyboards, with blank keys be furnished the entering class. I would also recommend that for these classes only one standard make of machine be used, for it adds to the difficulties of the teacher in instruction, and particularly adds to the difficulties of the pupil in learning touch operating to be changed from one make of machine to another, especially during the first term.

The following plan, prepared by my office, was duly adopted by the Board of Education:

The rules and requirements are based upon those of the United States Civil Service Commission, and apply in all examinations given to candidates for graduation in stenography and typewriting.

All of the dictations in any examination in stenography are for five consecutive minutes. The minimum requirement for graduation is the ability to write new matter dictated at the rate of eighty words per minute for five consecutive minutes, and the ability to transcribe the same accurately upon the typewriter. Dictations will be given at higher rates of speed to those who express a desire for the same. Both speed and accuracy are considered in the rating, speed having a weight of 1 and accuracy a weight of 2. The ratings for speed for the different rates of dictation are as follows:

100 words per minute, 100 per cent.
90 words per minute, 95 per cent.
80 words per minute, 85 per cent.

The rating for accuracy shall be determined by the correctness of the transcript according to the following rules:

Mark each correct answer	100	The difference between the sum of the error marks of each answer and 100 will be the mark of the answer.
Mark every faulty answer according to its value on a scale of 100, as herein specifically directed, and deduct the sum of the erorr marks of each answer from 100.		

STENOGRAPHY.

	From 100 deduct
For each word omitted, added, substituted or misspelled, or for the use of the singular instead of the plural, or of the plural instead of the singular, when the grammatical correctness is affected	3
For each transposition	2
For each gross error in capitalization or punctuation; for each error in division of words; for each word repeated; for each failure to use the hyphen when required; for each abbreviation; or for the use of the plural for the singular, or of the singular for the plural, when the grammatical correctness is not affected	1

When the marks for accuracy is 10 or less no credit will be given for speed.

85 per cent shall be required for graduation.

To illustrate: When a pupil writes at the rate of eighty words per minute he receives 85 per cent on speed. Suppose he should make four errors in the transcription of his notes, amounting to 12 demerits, his credit on accuracy would be 88. According to this rule, giving accuracy a weight of 2 and speed a weight of 1, you multiply 88 by 2, giving a result of 176. Add to this the 85 per cent received in speed, and divide by three to get the percentage received in shorthand as a whole, as follows: 176 plus 85 equals 261, divided by 3 equals 87. Eighty-seven per cent would be the final mark on the examination in stenography, giving the pupil two credits more than required for passing.

In typewriting, the exercise consists of copying 400 to 500 words from plain copy, transcripts to be marked according to the following rules:

	From 100 deduct
For writing one line over another	10
For each error in orthography; for each word or figure omitted, provided that a deduction of 10 shall be made for the omission of two or more consecutive words if the words omitted do not constitute more than one printed line of the copy, and that a deduction of 20 shall be made for the omission of two printed lines, or more than one line, etc.; for each word added, substituted, or repeated; for each transposition; for each abbreviation not in copy; for each failure to capitalize or to punctuate as in copy; for each deviation from copy in paragraphing (maximum for the exercise, 10); for failure to indent as in copy (only one charge to be made in the exercise); for each error in compounding words or vice versa	5
For each case of inconsistent spacing between lines	3
For each space between letters of a word; for crowding letters in a word; for lack of space between words; for striking a letter instead of space-bar; for unfinished word due to coming to end of line when word is rewritten on next line; for striking letters in a line above band holding paper, thus making no impression on sheet, or for piling letters over each other at the end of a line when all the letters are decipherable, or for running off paper on right or left margin (maximum for the exercise, 10)	2
For each case of irregularity in left-hand margin or gross irregularity in right-hand margin (maximum for the exercise in each case, 5); for each strike over; for the misdivision of a word at end of line; for each omission of a hyphen, when needed, at end of line; for extra space between words (maximum for the exercise, 5); for each case of inconsistent spacing after punctuation marks; for each word interlined (maximum for a single interlineation of five or more words, 5); for each erasure (maximum for the exercise, 5)	1
For lack of neatness	1–5
For each error not specified above	1–5

Time consumed will be rated according to the following scale: For a speed of 35 words or more per minute, a credit of 100 will be given; for 30 words per minute, a credit of 95; for 25 words per minute, a credit of 85; and for 20 words per minute, 75. If the exercise is written at a rate of less than twenty words per minute no credit will be given for speed.

Both accuracy and speed are considered in rating, accuracy having a weight of 3 and speed a weight of 2. Eighty per cent shall be required for passing.

To illustrate how these rules would work out in practice, take a paper written at the rate of twenty words per minute. This would be marked 75 per cent on speed. If the paper had mistakes amounting to 10 demerits the credit for accuracy would be reduced to 90. To find the credit on the paper as a whole, multiply the credit for accuracy by three (90 multiplied by 3 equals 270), multiply the credit for speed by two (75 multiplied by 2 equals 150), and add both together (270 plus 150 equals 420). Divide the sum by five and the credit in typewriting is found (420 divided by 5 equals 84).

I have now in preparation a circular of instruction, to be sent to each teacher in this school, and to all other teachers of commercial branches in the evening as well as in the day schools, requiring that all of the work done by the pupils be kept in folders for inspection by the proper authorities, as is done in the case of other studies in our High Schools.

The commercial branches in our schools have been placed upon the list of college entrance subjects by both of our universities, and I desire to have this work in such form that it may be available for inspection at a moment's notice by anyone who may desire to see it.

Work in the other subjects taught in the school, such as Spanish, Business Law, Civics, Industrial History, Economics, English, etc., will also be kept up to a high point of excellence.

Too often boys or girls who desire to enter the commercial world think that they require only a little shorthand and typewriting or bookkeeping to be successful. With such a limited preparation they can not hope to become more than clerks. But our Commercial High School must stand for more. It must not only give the student the training that is necessary to make him successful as a clerk, but also offer to him the educational foundation that will enable him to become a successful man of business and an intelligent citizen.

A diploma from the Commercial High School should always be a guarantee to the business public that the holder has received such training and educational foundation.

EVENING SCHOOLS.

Throughout the year the following Evening Schools have held regular sessions: Humboldt Evening High, Commercial Evening, Horace Mann Evening, Lincoln Evening, Hamilton Evening, Richmond Evening, and the Washington Evening. During the second term it was found necessary to open additional rooms in the Washington School building to accommodate the pupils of that section of the city. Two classes were also established in the Irving M. Scott School, on Tennessee Street, near Twenty-second, principally for the accommodation of foreign born boys and girls and adults residing in that part of the city.

The following table gives the State enrollment, average number belonging and average daily attendance for each of the Evening Schools during the past year:

Name of School	Aver. No. Belonging	Aver. Daily Attendance	State Enrollment						Grand Total
			Primary		Grammar		Total		
			Boys	Girls	Boys	Girls	Boys	Girls	
Commercial	239	211	0	0	259	356	259	356	615
Hamilton	423	361	20	0	892	310	912	310	1222
Horace Mann	506	426	97	13	1191	167	1288	180	1468
Irving M. Scott	123	38	121	0	0	0	121	0	121
Lincoln	887	339	0	0	1161	100	1161	100	1261
Richmond	101	86	0	0	168	46	168	46	214
Washington	357	306	1016	131	281	71	1297	202	1499
Humboldt High	377	329	0	0	* 756	* 33	* 756	* 33	* 789
Total	2513	2096	1254	144	4708	1083	5962	1227	7189

* High School.

The above table shows the interesting facts that the young men and boys in attendance outnumber the young women and girls almost five to one, whereas in the day schools the number of girls is greater than the number of boys from the sixth grade upward. In the day high schools the girls outnumber the boys almost 2 to 1.

The total expense of the Evening Schools for the year was as follows:

Salaries of teachers, including back salaries	$ 71,936.25
Current expenses, books, supplies, etc	29,944.45
Total	$101,880.70

There is no more important part of our educational system than these schools. They are filling in a practical way the expressed wants of a large number of young men and women who are making a living during the day time. The courses of study are planned to supplement the practical work that these students are doing during the day, and to fit them for promotion in their chosen vocations. For instance, many young men who are employed in some manual pursuit in the Union Iron Works or other place of industry attend the Humboldt Evening High School and acquire the theoretical knowledge in Science, Mathematics, Language, Mechanical Drawing, etc., which under lies the practical work in their several lines of industry. In addition, those who work as stenographers or bookkeepers or clerks during the day, find in the Commercial Evening School and the Hamilton Evening School elementary and advanced courses in their vocational work. Courses in English, Arithmetic, History, etc., are given for those who recognize their need of a knowledge of such subjects as part of their vocational training. In this way we are able to adapt the work of our schools to the needs of the pupils in a practical and efficient manner.

In a recent visit of State Superintendent Hyatt to our evening schools, he commented most favorably upon this practical feature of the work, and commended the spirit of earnest application which pervaded the classes.

The Humboldt Evening High School consists of two departments, the Academic and the Technical, and is intended to supply secondary instruction to boys and girls who are employed during the day and who have finished the grade work of either the day or the evening school.

The course of the Academic Department embraces the chief studies of the Day High School and leads to admission into College.

With this school as part of our educational system, the ambitious young wage earner is afforded the opportunity of entering the walks of higher education, and the son of the most humble toiler is assured that the door to the learned professions is not closed against him. The idea is American and Democratic. Without evening secondary schools the boys and girls who are, by circumstances, forced early to become breadwinners, are deprived of all the opportunities attendant on advanced education.

The aim of the Technical Department of the Humboldt Evening High School is to assist young men who are engaged in any industrial pursuits or mechanical trades to become first-class workmen and master mechanics. The students gain their experience in manual training at their daily work in the shops of the city, and in their evening studies receive the explanation of the various processes they see in their work in the factory or shop. Thus is the instruction in Mathematics and Science directly applied to the practical work of the respective specialties of the students.

The instructors in this department have had practical experience in their respective lines of work.

The school manages to keep in touch with the foremen of the larger shops of the city, so that the students may receive from their employers prompt recognition for the efforts they are making to increase their efficiency by evening study.

The Commercial Evening School specializes upon those subjects of greatest importance to the young man or woman in the business world. Such technical subjects as Shorthand, Typewriting and Bookkeeping are supplemented by English, Arithmetic, History, Civics, Business Law and Modern and Foreign Languages. The work done is thorough.

The various Grammar Schools offer instructions in all of the subjects common to the day schools of like grade, and in addition have courses in the English language, especially adapted to foreign born adults who desire to acquire a knowledge of our language.

Under the present rules of the Board of Education, teachers holding the necessary State or County certificates may be appointed to positions in the Evening Schools without taking a competitive examination, as is required for appointment to the Day Schools. I recommend the adoption of a rule by the Board of Education applying the competitive examination system to all teachers who may hereafter be appointed to any teaching position in the department. To the average young man and woman the Evening Schools represent the last chance to get an education. For this reason the greatest care should be exercised in the appointment of Evening School teachers, and the work done by them should be given the most careful supervision.

ORAL SCHOOL FOR DEAF.

The Oral School for Deaf Children has had an enrollment of twenty-three for the year. Two instructors have been regularly in charge. The advance which has been made in the instruction of this class of children is remarkable. Instead of depending upon the old method of making the alphabet by signs with the hands and thus spelling out words, the children are taught to watch the lips of the person speaking and thus recognize the words spoken. They are also taught to produce the regular sounds of the language with such perfection that they can speak distinctly, and can carry on a conversation in the ordinary manner either with children similarly afflicted, or with others possessed of all the natural faculties.

Some of the children who have graduated from this school have continued their studies in the grammar schools and have graduated with honor. They have been able to understand all the instructions given by watching the lips of the speakers in the class, both teachers and pupils, and have been able to reply orally to the questions asked, although they were unable to hear the words spoken.

This shows the great advance that has been made in the last few years in the treatment and education of the deaf. That we have attained such excellent results in our school is due to the exceptional ability of the instructors, Mr. and Mrs. Holden.

UNGRADED CLASSES.

There are ungraded classes in each of the following schools: Adams, Fremont, Franklin, Hamilton, Hancock, Mission, Washington, Richmond, and in the Emerson and Whittier Primary Schools.

The Board of Education has satisfied a great need in establishing and maintaining these ungraded classes. In nearly every class of a school pupils will be found who, from sickness or other causes, are deficient in one or two subjects. If special opportunity be not offered for overcoming these deficiencies by individual or group instruction, such pupils become "misfits" in their classes, exercising a repressive influence upon their mates. If this special or group instruction be given by the regular teacher, it will result in the neglect of perhaps forty pupils for the teaching of five.

By segregating such pupils and placing them in an ungraded class, they can be taught individually or in groups. Certain pupils will thus do their work in an ungraded room for a month or a term, and then be prepared to join a regular grade. Others will be found who will remain permanently in the ungraded class, emphasizing the work they most need. Again, pupils may do grade work in all subjects save one. Such remain in the regular grade, but receive help in that one subject until it is mastered sufficiently to permit a resumption of regular grade work. Further, there are those, who, by being given special instructions in one subject for a limited time, may be so prepared as to be advanced a grade by being ahead of their class in all other subjects. The ungraded class keeps pupils in school who, discouraged by failure in their regular classes, would otherwise leave. It solves the problem of ''left-overs.''

READING IN THE PRIMARY GRADES.

During the past year the primary grades have been given special supervision. Since the appointment of Miss Lew Ball as Deputy Superintendent, in September, 1907, her entire time has been spent in directing the work in these grades, through teachers' meetings and through class teaching and supervision. The teachers have heartily co-operated with the Supervisor, and the close of the year showed worthy results, indicative of efficiency and effort.

CLASSES TOO LARGE.

Able work in the First Grades is much hindered because of the large classes. Greatly as this is to be deplored, it is unavoidable owing to the insufficient number of rooms in our small buildings. It has not always been possible to make suitable provision for the large numbers of children that enter our first grades through the year. Only with the opening of new schoolrooms and with the re-establishment of the burned-out public Kindergartens in various parts of the city can we hope to avoid the over-crowding of the first grades.

READING.

The most important branch in the primary grades is reading. Necessarily, the greater part of the time in these grades is given to it. To insure uniformity in the teaching of any branch in the schools, a systematically planned, clearly defined emthod is of great value. Such a method has been adopted and is being followed in the teaching of reading in all the first grades in the city. The results are surpassing our expectations. It is particularly satisfactory to note the results in schools where there are large numbers of foreign children. With the method in use, these children have made marvelous progress in learning to read the English language. During the coming year, this work in reading will be continued in the second and third grades.

SUPPLEMENTARY READERS.

Probably the greatest of our present needs in the proper equipment of our schools, is that of supplementary reading material. Particularly in the primary grades is our lack of material felt. During the first two years, while a child is mastering the mechanics of reading, he should have a sufficient supply of new books to read. It is only through reading new matter, not through re-reading that which has been memorized, that fluency and efficiency come. Within the past two years, but one set of supplementary readers has been provided for each first grade, two sets for each second grade. So proficient have our children proven themselves, that this has been far from sufficient, and the teachers of these grades have been unable to meet the demand.

Oakland averages about eight sets of supplementary readers to a grade. Los Angeles, realizing the futility of re-reading in primary grades, furnishes about fifteen different kinds of readers to a grade, with only a small number of each kind.

SEAT WORK.

Under another heading, attention was called to the large first grade classes in some of our schools. In some instances there have been from sixty or more children in charge of one teacher. With young children it is impossible to conduct class work except in small groups. Therefore, while the teacher is engaged with one group, the remaining children in the class must be provided with some occupation. Being too young to study, this necessitates provision being made for hand work in some of its great varieties—basket weaving with raffia, paper folding and cutting, block or stick building. Where this hand work is suitably chosen, the child's time is by no means wasted, as it developes in him qualities of accuracy, concentration, neatness, application and industry. It aids in training his sense of form and of number. Whatever occupation is used, material must be purchased. In many cases, the teachers themselves, through their great need, have purchased the materials for their classes. This expenditure on the teacher's part should not be necessary. Adequate provision should be made for the purchase of materials, as needed and selected for use in the schools.

CHILD LABOR LAW.

The Child Labor Law, as amended March 23, 1907, by our Legislature, and entitled "An act regulating the employment and hours of labor of children, etc.," throws around minors the safeguards which every community should seek to encourage. It fixes the maximum of hours per day which a child under eighteen may work. It also prohibits the employment in a mercantile institution, etc., of a child under sixteen between the hours of 10 o'clock in the evening and 6 o'clock in the morning. It also provides that minors under the age of fourteen must not work except on certificate as follows:

"Provided, that the judge of the juvenile court of the county, or city and county, or in any county or city and county in which there is no juvenile court, then any judge of the Superior Court of the county or city and county in which such child resides, shall have authority to issue a permit to work to any child over the age of twelve years, upon a sworn statement being made to him by the parent of such child that such child is past the age of twelve years, that the parent or parents of such child are incapacitated for labor, through illness, and after investigation by probation officer or truant officer of the city, or city and county, in which such child resides, or in cities and counties where there are no probation or truant officers, then by such other competent persons as the judge may designate for this purpose.

"And provided, that any such child, over the age of twelve years, may be employed at any of the occupations mentioned in this Act during the regular vacation of the public schools of the city, county, or city and county in which the place of employment is situated, upon the production of a permit signed by the principal of the school which such child has attended during the term next preceding any such vacation."

The law stops short of making a provision which I have found in my experience is needed. Many times parents or guardians apply for working certificates for children, claiming that their services are required to support the family, when, in fact, the children are not in physical condition to work, especially in any line requiring close confinement. This law should certainly be amended, providing for the proper medical examination of all children by a reputable physician, and the issuance of a certificate by him stating that the applicants are physically able to do the work which they will be required to do before working certificates can be issued to them. In the meantime, I believe it to be within the discretion of those authorized to issue these certificates to refuse to issue them to children who, in their judgment, are not physically able to do the work which their parents or guardians want them to do. I recommend that such discretion be exercised, and that provision be made for the medical examination of such children in cases of doubt.

COMPULSORY EDUCATION.

In accordance with the provisions of a special act of the Legislature entitled "An act to enforce the educational rights of children and providing penalties for the violation of the act," (amended March 4, 1907), two police officers are detailed by the Chief of Police, at the request of the Board of Education, to act as attendance officers. Their duties are stated in Section 5 of said Act to be as follows:

"It shall be the duty of the attendance officer to arrest during school hours, without warrant, any child between eight and fourteen years of age, found away from his home and who has been reported to him by the teacher, the Superintendent of Schools, or other person connected with the school department or schools, as a truant from instruction upon which he is lawfully required to attend within the county, city, or city and county, or school district. Such arresting officer shall forthwith deliver the child so arrested either to the parent, guardian, or other person having control or charge of such child, or to the teacher from whom said child is then a truant, or if such child shall have been declared a habitual truant, he shall bring such child before a magistrate for commitment by him to a parental school as provided in this act. The attendance officer or other arresting officer shall report promptly such arrest, and the disposition made by him of such child to the school authorities of such city, or city and county, or school district."

The following, a statement of the work done by these officers throughout the year is tabulated from the daily reports filed by them in my office:

Number of complaints from schools	1106
Number of complaints investigated	1106
Number of pupils found on street and sent or brought to school	142
Number of pupils brought to Parental School	16
Number of pupils arrested and brought to Detention Home	28
Number of pupils cited to appear before Judge Murasky, Juvenile Court	14
Parents arrested for violating compulsory education law and found guilty	2

THE PARENTAL SCHOOL.

The work of the Parental School has been along the same lines as that of the regular grammar schools, but has been done largely by individual instruction in ungraded classes. The average daily attendance for the past year has been 34, and the number of teachers towards the end of the year was two.

During the past term the California Woman's Club furnished manual training equipment for the school, and this has been installed. The boys have taken an unusual interest in this work. I hope it will be possible for us to develop this line of instruction until the school can give a thorough industrial training to every boy who enters it.

If to these boys the ordinary school studies are not attractive in our grammar schools, the same studies cannot be expected to attract them when given in another school merely of different name. It is the exception to find in this school a boy who is not industrious and possessed of unusual energy. It is only necessary for us to find out what his interests are, and see that his energy is used in acquiring the proper training and education. But we must fit the subject to the boy and not attempt to fit the boy to the subject.

The work which these pupils have done in manual training and in gardening, as well as in the regular studies, speaks well for their industry.

The present location of the school is not suitable. Boys who have had undesirable experiences should be removed as far as possible from an enviroment that recalls such experiences. Many of these boys have been arrested and brought before the Juvenile Court for trivial or other offenses. The Juvenile Court room immediately adjoins the school, and the sight of the patrol wagon recalls incidents that it would be better for them to forget.

When a policeman arrives with a young prisoner the word is passed around among the boys in the school, and for a time they are in spirit back in the old enviroment from which we desire to win them.

I hope it will be possible for the Board of Education to find a desirable location for this school, and to furnish the necessary plant with sufficient grounds for gardening, etc., where these boys can be trained in hand and in heart, as well as in mind, so that they may develop into useful citizens.

REPORT OF SUPERVISOR OF DRAWING.

San Francisco, July 30, 1908.

Mr. Alfred Roncovieri,
Superintendent of Schools.

My Dear Sir:—

I am pleased to submit to you a brief account of what the Department of Drawing has accomplished during the past year.

Owing to my absence immediately following the great fire, the year just closed has of necessity been one of rehabilitation. As our needs have been very great and more than could be supplied, we found ourselves at times seriously handicapped, not only in carrying out the course of study we had prepared. but in maintaining our former standards of excellence.

Inadequate office accommodation, limited equipment of furniture, reference books, and drawing models have obliged us to substitute increased energy, ingenuity and time unlimited, after school hours, in order to bring the work to any kind of successful conclusion.

To restore to our teachers the necessary aids, by way of a workable course of study and outlines of direction for teaching the subject—outlines consisting of supplementary monographs on every phase of the work, which were the accumulated product of many years of serious thought and effort—has been a tremendous task which still remains unfinished.

During the autumn term the work was principally drawing from objects, and to meet this need the Board of Education published my monograph entitled "Seeing Appearances." Subsequently, I prepared and presented to teachers a progressive series of mimeographed illustrated monographs on design, adapted to six different grades, and also mimeographed outlines on "Drawing Winter Berries" and "Flower Drawing from Nature."

Then, in order to illustrate to the pupils the character and quality of the work they were expected to do, and having no text-book on the subject for such work, I distributed among the schools over a thousand colored drawings and as many examples of good wall-paper designs as I was able to procure in the city. This supply stimulated a serious interest that led pupils to collect patterns of great variety—from useful objects and published matter—that were found to be most helpful.

Twice during the year I conducted teachers' meetings for instruction on the subject, while all through the year there were regular classes for the benefit of teachers who felt the need for further help.

In addition to the office work—which is of the greatest importance, because the success of the department depends upon the careful and definite planning of the work by the supervisor—every school in the city was visited a number of times, either by myself or my assistant, Miss Murray, upon which occasion the work of every class was examined, and, if necessary, the teacher interviewed. At these visits such lessons were given to pupils, in the presence of teachers, as were needed to demonstrate methods of teaching the subject.

The spring term was given almost exclusively to design, and in order to awaken an interest in the subject, I—in the schools under my supervision—and my assistant, in the schools under her supervision—gave talks on the meaning and uses of design to all grammar pupils, using a carefully selected collection of textiles and wall-papers to illustrate the subject. Subsequently many teachers took their classes to the Park Museum for similar study.

The pupils became exceedingly interested in the subject, and were not only able to do some good designs, but they have come to see beauty in the handiwork of man as well as in nature. They are now beginning to realize that they may derive as much pleasure from a fine building, a beautiful rug and a shapely vase, as from a stately tree and graceful flower.

At the close of the year every class in the city held an exhibition of the last term's drawings. The visiting parents and friends of the pupils expressed great surprise at the excellence of the work. The drawings were in pencil, brush and ink, water color, pastello and colored crayons, and included plant-drawing from nature and designs for applied purposes.

Considering all the difficulties we have been laboring under, the work reflected great credit not only on the pupils, but also on the teachers, whose conscientious and able efforts made our measure of success possible.

The coming year offers much of promise. With the new course of study in drawing, which has just been completed, and two additional assistant supervisors, whom the Board of Education has so generously added to the department, I feel that we may be able to do a quality of work that will be comparable with that done in any other city.

Thanking you and the Board of Education for your kindly assistance, and the principals and teachers for their hearty co-operation, I remain,

Yours sincerely,

KATHERINE M. BALL.

REPORT OF SUPERVISOR OF MUSIC.

San Francisco, July 28, 1908.

Mr. Alfred Roncovieri,

Superintendent of Schools.

Dear Sir:—

In compliance with the rules of the Board of Education, and in reply to a request from you, I respectfully submit a report of the Department of Music for year 1907-1908.

The year has found the Music Department accomplishing results. At the beginning of the year the work was organized by means of my course of study, "Some Ideas on Children's Singing." Each teacher was given a copy and so received an exact idea of the work to be done. Stress was laid on Voice-

Production, Song Singing, Sight Singing, and Music Writing, so that the teachers would understand the value of sweet tone, good expression, concentration derived from ear training sight work and theory.

The disorganization of the work on account of the fire was still noticeable, for teachers had been re-assigned and rooms were crowded. Some of the schools were not so advanced as others, therefore my aim was to lift the standard of these schools; consequently I visited some schools oftener than others, and instructed my assistants to do the same.

I called a meeting of all the new teachers, so that they would understand what was to be done.

During the year each child in this city has learned a number of patriotic and folk songs. By means of these songs the child is taught to love country, parents and right doing. These songs are a precious musical heritage, which each child should possess. In October I had to train a new assistant, so that she could be of some help.

I and my assistants visited each class at least twice during the term, and some of the schools were visited oftener.

In November, at the Mission Grammar School, I listened to some of the finest school singing I have ever heard. The chorus was out of doors, under the direction of Miss Jeanette Hillman. The songs were in four parts, and consisted of "Handel's Largo," "Neven's Boat Song," etc. The tone was beautiful and expression exquisite. The children followed their leader, and sang with their hearts as well as their voices.

In December I selected music for graduation, and drilled and conducted classes for closing exercises, including the Girls' High School.

The conditions of the shack schools necessarily impeded the formal side of my work, but I emphasized the sight singing and music writing. Before the fire there had been excellent work done, but there had been no writing book adopted. Through the efforts of the Hon Superintendent Roncovieri, a music writing book by H. J. Storer was adopted by the Board of Education, and I was instructed to map out definite work for the teachers.

I made an outline, consisting of Scale Writing, Musical Symbols, Dictation, and Copying Music. My aim in this direction is to develop the child musically, so that he will wish to express himself in simple melodies, and by giving him practice in music writing he will express these tunes on the staff.

Unfortunately, we have only one hour a week for music. There should be two hours a week given to the study. Singing is needed for the development of the child, and singing takes time; therefore there should be more time given for the formal side of music.

In January, 1908, I conducted eight grade meetings and so instructed about one thousand teachers for the term's work. I gave out many songs which my assistants mimeographed, and outlined the term's work.

Not long after, in all the grades except the three lowest, the regular music was given up for special preparation for the Fleet Chorus.

Feeling that the occasion was worthy of great effort, I exerted myself, and, through the teachers, I prepared a tremendous chorus. On May 13th, at the Stadium, I directed ten thousand children in twenty songs, a number of them being in three parts. That was a great day as all who were there know. The children and sailors will never forget it. Musically, the event will stand out always. As it was a living demonstration of Patriotism, it was worth all the trouble.

After this, I trained and conducted graduation choruses for the various schools and for the Girls' High School farce. I visited about 750 classes this year; my first assistant, 500 classes; and the other two assistants visited 300 classes each.

Two weeks after school closed, on the Fourth of July, I conducted children's choruses at the Park. This was a hardship, as the children were out of town and I was not given notice before the close of school in time to gather the children together.

I have attended to a large correspondence on school business during the year.

I recommend that new teachers entering the Department will be able to teach music, that when a musical teacher is needed in a school that she will be sent.

I recommend that I be given power to buy sets of octavo music for graduating classes, and that fifty copies of Mathews "Songs of All Lands" and 100 copies of McCaskey's "Favorite Songs and Hymns" be bought for the schools.

I recommend for supplementary reading for the grammar classes a little book called "Stories of Great Musicians," by Hurne and Scobey.

I wish some extra books for my personal musical library, and a small piano and two book cases for my office.

I wish to thank the Superintendent, the Board of Education, the teachers and my assistants for their generous support in my work. I am,

Respectfully,

ESTELLE CARPENTER,
Supervisor of Music.

REPORT OF SUPERVISOR OF DOMESTIC SCIENCE.

San Francisco, July 31, 1908.

Mr. Alfred Roncovieri,
Superintendent of Schools.

My Dear Mr. Roncovieri:—

In reply to your communication of the 28th inst., I take pleasure in submitting the following report on the Domestic Science Department in the San Francisco schools:

The School Department maintains six cookery centers, one at each of the following schools:

Central Manual Training School, Geary street, near Jones street;
Crocker Grammar School, Page street, near Broderick street;
Hamilton Grammar School, Geary street, near Scott street;
Hearst Grammar School, corner Fillmore and Hermann streets;
Horace Mann Grammar School, Valencia, near Twenty-second street;
Irving M. Scott Grammar School, Tennessee, near Twenty-second street.

Domestic science is not taught in any of our high schools. During the past year the following teachers have been in charge: Miss Bartlett, Supervisor, Miss Ballenger, Miss Congdon, Miss Gray, Miss Paulsell, and Miss Woodward, assistants.

The official course of study issued by your office states that domestic science is taught to the girls of the Seventh and Eighth grades. Owing to lack of cooking centers, this is possible only in certain schools. Last year we gave one lesson weekly to seventy-nine classes, or 1,698 girls. Our pupils came from thirty-two different schools. Fifty-eight classes, or 764 girls, who were supposed to have cooking lessons were disappointed because we lack accommodations for them.

During the first week of school, each term, I spend a good deal of time expressing my regrets to principals who ring up to know why their classes were left out. I hope that we will soon have centers enough to remedy this.

The San Francisco schools are not as well supplied with cooking centers as those of our neighboring cities.

We aim to teach our pupils good plain cooking, and the intelligent selection and care of foods. It is but a common place to affirm that virtue and vice are, to some extent, the result of good or bad digestion, and that digestion depends largely on the way in which one's food has been cooked.

Good courses in domestic science create an intelligent interest in public sanitation, such as water suppies, milk inspection, pure food laws, and clean streets.

In the grades, domestic science should include sewing as well as cooking. In the high schools, it should include the several things that English educators call "house-craft."

President Roosevelt tells us that it is as important to train a girl in the ways of household as it is to train a boy to make a living.

I am happy to report that the most cordial relations exist between the teachers of my department and the grade teachers. Several principals have gone out of their way to express their satisfaction and appreciation of the work done. The children themselves ask permission to attend cooking classes when the rest of the pupils are enjoying rainy day sessions.

I have also heard words of praise from many parents and I think that if we had conveniently situated centers, you would have no requests from parents who want their daughters excused from cooking class.

The professional standing of my assistants is high. My department has been visited by domestic science teachers from other places and they have been favorably impressed by the work done. Miss Paulsell, one of my assistants last year, has been made supervisor of domestic science in San Jose, and another of my teachers has been offered an excellent position elsewhere, which, fortunately for our school, she has declined.

Respectfully,

ELLEN M. BARTLETT.

REPORT OF THE SUPERVISOR OF MANUAL TRAINING IN THE GRAMMAR SCHOOLS.

Mr. Alfred Roncovieri,
Superintendent of Schools, San Francisco.

Dear Sir:

In answer to your request of July 1st, I take pleasure in submitting the following brief outline of what has been accomplished in our manual training department during the year just closed.

Practically all the "A-Seventh" grade boys in the city, those of the Sheridan School excepted, because of remoteness, have been instructed in such of the simplest geometric forms in mechanical drawing as were applicable to their first year's bench work. They have made an excellent showing in their wood work and are looking forward to next year's projects with an eagerness that is gratifying.

The boys of the "B-Seventh" grade have been advanced toward the more complex work promised them in the coming term, having of course, been given a more general view of constructive principles and design than was possible in the beginning. These also are full of anticipation.

Pupils in the "A-Eighth" grade made unusual progress in joinery during the year, particularly those going to the Hamilton Center, and some very remarkable mechanical drawings were made at the Crocker Center by boys of this grade. It is regrettable that many of these where not exhihibited outside the homes to which they were taken.

Another matter for congratulation is the spirit manifested and work done by the older boys, those of the "B-Eighth" grade, in the way of class gifts made individually and by groups. More than one principal and teacher was made glad and proud over the thoughtful presentation of some needed class room convenience. While some of these models were exhibited at the closing exercises of school, an effort should be made next year for a more general display of this kind.

A few boys of the Parental School should be mentioned in this connection. They were prompted by their principal, Miss Alexander, to make some grateful return to Judge Murasky and to a benevolent woman who had done much for the school. The boys actually undertook to make two large oak chairs, and, under proper guidance, succeeded beyond any one's expectation.

I am pleased to report also, that a new manual training center, that at the Moulder School, was put in successful operation during the year.

As you were good enough to welcome suggestions I would respectfully ask if a more liberal policy in the matter of suppiles could not be urged upon the Honorable Board of Education.

With highest esteem,

Yours sincerecly,

M. DOYLE, Supervisor Manual Training.''

BOARD OF EXAMINATION.

The Board of Examination is composed of

SUPERINTENDENT ALFRED RONCOVIERI, Chairman.
DEPUTY SUPERINTENDENT W. B. HOWARD, Secretary.
DEPUTY SUPERINTENDENT T. L. HEATON.
DEPUTY SUPERINTENDENT JAMES FERGUSON.
DEPUTY SUPERINTENDENT R. H. WEBSTER.

The Board of Examination has conducted two examinations (October, 1907, and April, 1908) according to law, of persons desirous of securing grammar grade or special certificates. It has met monthly and forwarded its recommendations to the Board of Education.

Herewith is a resume of its work:

Number of original certificates granted on examination during the year, to men	3
Number of original certificates granted on examination during the year, to women	16
Number of certificates granted on credentials, to men	13
Number of certificates granted on credentials, to women	139
Number of certificates renewed during the year	22
Number of applicants rejected during the year on examination	4
Number of applicants rejected during the year on credentials	1
Amount of fees collected for examination and issuance of certificates	232

CERTIFICATION AND SCHOLASTIC TRAINING OF TEACHERS.

Number of teachers in the department who hold High School certificates	173
Number of teachers who hold certificates of the grammar grade	848
Number of teachers who hold certificates of primary grade	28
Number of teachers who hold special certificates	46
Number of teachers who are graduates of the University of California	92
Number of teachers who are graduates of other universities	27
Number of teachers who are graduates of the California State Normal Schools	168
Number of teachers who are graduates of other State Normal Schools	28

RULES OF THE BOARD OF EXAMINATION OF THE CITY AND COUNTY OF SAN FRANCISCO.

Adopted at an adjourned meeting of the City and County Board of Examination, September 4, 1906, to go into effect January 1, 1907.

Section 1. The City and County Board of Examination shall consist of the County Superintendent of Schools, ex-officio chairman, and his deputies.

Sec. 2. The Board, at its first regular meeting in January of each year, shall select one of its number as Secretary, who shall hold office for one year or until his successor is elected.

Sec. 3. The Secretary of this Board shall keep his office open on Thursdays and Fridays of each week from two to five o'clock p. m.

MEETINGS.

Sec. 4. (a) The regular semi-annual meetings shall be during the spring and fall mid-term vacation of the Public Schools of the City and County of San Francisco.

(b) Regular monthly meetings shall be held on the first Monday of each calendar month at 1:30 p. m.

(c) Special meetings may be called at any time by the chairman, or upon the request of three members, the object of each special meeting to be stated in the call.

Sec. 5. (a) At the semi-annual meetings only, examinations for certificates shall be given, but special examinations for special certificates may be given at any time upon the order of this Board, when, in its judgment, the needs of the San Francisco School Department demand a specially certificated teacher and there be none available in the Department.

(b) The following shall be the order of business at the regular monthly meetings of the Board.

I. Roll Call.
II. Reading minutes of previous meeting.
III. Applications for granting and renewal of—
  (1) High School Certificates.
  (2) Grammar School Certificates.
  (3) Kindergarten-Primary Certificates.
  (4) Special Certificates.
IV. Applications for renewal of Primary Grade Certificates.
V. Applications for granting permanent Certificates on—
  (1) City and County Certificates and experience.
  (2) State Life or Educational Diplomas and experience.
VI. Applications for Recommendations for—
  (1) State Life Diplomas.
  (2) State University Documents.
  (3) State Normal Documents.
VII. Reports of Committees.
VIII. Unfinished business.
IX. New business.
X. Adjournment.

(c) Only such business shall come before special meetings as may be specified in the call therefor.

Sec. 6. Monthly and special meetings shall be held in the office of the Secretary, southwest corner of Pine and Larkin streets, San Francisco, California.

CERTIFICATES WITHOUT EXAMINATION.

Sec. 7. Recommendations for Certificates, without examination, may be made as follows:

(a) High School Certificates—on (1) Credentials issued by the State Board of Education in accordance with subdivision two of section fifteen hundred and twenty-one of the Political Code of California; (2) High School Certificates of other counties of California; (3) Normal School Diplomas, accompanied by documents from the faculty of the State University, provided for in subdivision five of section fifteen hundred and three of the Political Code of California.

(b) Grammar School Certificates—on (1) Life Diplomas or Certificates of any State, when properly accredited by the State Board of Education; (2) California State Normal School Diplomas; (3) San Francisco City Normal School Diplomas issued prior to July 1, 1899; (4) Diplomas from other legally accredited Normal Schools; (5) Diplomas from legally accredited Universities; (6) Grammar School or Grammar Grade Certificates of other counties of California.

(c) Kindergarten-Primary Certificates—on (1) Kindergarten-Primary Certificates of other counties; (2) Diplomas from Kindergarten Department of California State Normal Schools; (3) other credentials legally approved by the State Board of Education.

(d) Special Certificates—on any credential recognized by the State Board of Education, provided said credential be accompanied by a special recommendation in the subject desired from the faculty of the institution or head of the department in which work in said special subject was done.

CERTIFICATES ON EXAMINATION.

Sec. 9. Recommendations for Certificates on examination may be made as follows:

(a) Grammar School Certificates—to those who obtain on examination an average of 85 per cent in the following subjects:

Subject	
Algebra	50
Arithmetic, written	100
Arithmetic, oral	50
Bookkeeping	50
Composition	50
English Grammar, written	100
English Grammar, Oral	25
Elementary Physics	50
English and American Literature	50
Drawing	25
Geography—	
Industrial	25
Physical	25
Political	25
History of the United States and Civil Government	100
History—	
Ancient	25
Medieval	25
Modern	25
Methods of Teaching	50
Orthography and Defining	100
Penmanship	25
Physiology and Hygiene	50

Plane Geometry	50
Reading	50
School Law of California	50
Vocal Music	25
Totals	1,200

(Required to pass—1020 credits).

(2) To holders of San Francisco City and County Primary Grade Certificates, who obtain on examination an average of 85 per cent in the following subjects:

English and American Literature (Scope—English, one of requirements for entrance to University of California.)	50
Algebra (to Quadratics)	50
Plane Geometry	50
Elementary Physics	50
History (Ancient, Medieval and Modern)	75
Total	275

(Required to pass—233¾ credits.)

(b) Special Certificates—(1) To those who obtain 85 per cent on examination in the subject for which a Special Certificate is desired, and who, in addition thereto, attain in examination at least 60 per cent in each of the subjects of English Grammar, Orthography and Defining, and Methods of Teaching: (2) to those who are holders of regular City and County Certificates and who obtain 85 per cent on examination in the subject for which a Special Certificate is desired.

(c) Special Certificates may be issued in the following subjects:

1. Bookkeeping.*
2. Cookery.
3. Domestic Science (Cookery and Sewing combined).
4. Mechanical Drawing.
5. Architectural Drawing.
6. Naval Architectural Drawing.
7. Free-hand Drawing.
8. Free-hand Drawing and Clay Modeling (correlative and combined).
9. Free-hand Drawing and Wood Carving (correlative and combined).
10. Sloyd.
11. Iron Work.
12. Wood Work.
13. Physical Culture.
14. Penmanship.
15. Stenography and Typewriting (combined).
16. Music.
17. Manual Training—including as many of subjects 4 to 12 (both inclusive) as may be endorsed on the Certificate of the applicant upon legal proof of competency to teach the same.
18. Such other subjects as may be authorized by the City and County Board of Education.

Sec. 10. An applicant for any Certificate who fails to obtain at least 60 per cent in Arithmetic (if required), or in Grammar, or in Orthography and Defining, will be barred from further examination.

---

*An applicant for a Special Certificate in Bookkeeping shall, in addition to the other conditions imposed, also pass an examination in Commercial Arithmetic and Commercial Law. (Scope—Packard's Commercial Arithmetic, Lyon's Commercial Law.)

Sec. 11. The texts to be used as standard in the examinations shall be as follows:

Composition—Quackenbos, with Bancroft recommended.

Method of Teaching—Swett, Page or White.

Algebra—Tanner.

Physics—Carhart & Chutes.

Geometry—Wentworth, Chauvenet, or Edwards.

History (Ancient, Medieval and Modern)—A. B. Harts' Essentials.

Literature—English, one of entrance requirements to University of California.

Other Subjects—California State Series (if issued.)

Sec. 12. The papers containing the written answers of candidates must be preserved by the Secretary of the City and County Board of Examination, or his successors, for at least one year after the close of the examination.

Sec. 13. Papers of candidates for Certificates shall be examined by no person or persons other than the members of the City and County Board of Examination; provided, that, in special subjects, a member of the Board of Examination shall have authority to procure the assistance of competent persons, whose work shall be subject to the supervision of a member or members of the Board of Examination.

RENEWAL OF CERTIFICATES.

Sec. 14. (a) Evidence of good moral character shall be required from applicants for renewal of Certificates, unless such applicants are teaching in the Public Schools of San Francisco, or are personally known to members of this Board.

(b) Members of the San Francisco School Department must present, upon application for renewal of Certificates, a recommendation from their principals or from the Superintendent or one of his Deputies.

PERMANENT CERTIFICATES.

Sec. 15. Applicants for permanent Certificates of any kind or grade must make affidavit before the Secretary of this Board setting forth in detail (1) the amount and grade of their experience in the Public Schools of the City and County of San Francisco, and (2) the kind and grade of the Certificate or State Diploma held by the applicant.

Sec. 16. In computing the five years' experience required for a permanent Certificate, evidence of the receipt of sixty full months of compensation for services as teacher in the School Department of this city and county shall be sufficient.

REVOCATION OF CERTIFICATES.

Sec. 17. No recommendation to the City and County Board of Education for the revocation of any Certificate shall be made except on the following conditions:

(a) Complaints under subdivision four of section seventeen hundred and ninety-one of the Political Code of California must be in writing, signed by the complainant, and filed with the Secretary of this Board.

(b) Such complaints shall specifically state, in detail, the facts upon which the Certificate should be revoked.

(c) Such complaints must be accompanied by a list of the witnesses personally cognizant of the separate facts stated in the complaint, together with their addresses and also by a reference to all such documentary evidence pertinent to said charges as may be within the knowledge of the complainant.

LIFE DIPLOMAS AND STATE EDUCATIONAL DOCUMENTS.

Sec. 18. Applicants for State Life Diplomas or Educational Documents must make affidavit before the Secretary of this Board setting forth such facts as may be required by the State Board of Education.

FEES.

Sec. 19. (a) Applicants for Certificates (except temporary or permanent Certificates to be granted on State Life on Educational Diplomas) or for State Diplomas must deposit with the Secretary, at the time of application, a fee of two dollars.

(b) Applicants for State University or State Normal Documents must deposit with the Secretary, at the time of application, a fee of one dollar and twenty-five cents.

Sec. 20. These rules may be amended upon one week's written notice, given to each member of the Board, by a four-fifths' vote in favor thereof at any regular or called meeting.

EXTRACT FROM STATE CONSTITUTION, ARTICLE IX, SECTION SEVEN.

* * * * The county superintendents and the county Boards of Education shall have control of the examination of teachers and the granting of teachers' certificates within their respective jurisdiction. (The exercise of this power has been defined by legislative enactment as found in the Political Code of the State of California.)

EXTRACTS FROM THE POLITICAL CODE OF THE STATE OF CALIFORNIA.

Section 1503. (1) The board of trustees of each State Normal School upon the recommendation of the faculty, may issue to those pupils who worthily complete the full course of study and training prescribed, diplomas of graduation, either from the normal department or the kindergarten department, or both.

(2) Such diploma from the normal department shall entitle the holder thereof to a certificate (corresponding in grade to the grade of the diploma) from any county, or city and county, board of education in the State. One from the kindergarten department shall entitle the holder to a certificate to teach in any kindergarten class or any primary school in the State.

(3) Whenever any county, or city and county, board of education shall present to the state board of education a recommendation showing that the holder of a normal school diploma from the normal department of any State Normal School of the State of California, or of a diploma from any other normal school, that the state board of education shall declare to be equivalent to a diploma from the normal department of a state normal school of this State, has had a successful experience of two years in the public schools of this State, subsequent to the granting of such diploma, the state board of education shall grant to the holder thereof a document signed by the president and secretary of the state board, showing such fact. The said diploma, accompanied by said document of the state board attached thereto, shall become a permanent certificate of qualification to teach in any primary or grammar school in the State, valid until such time as the said diploma may be revoked, as provided in section fourteen hundred and eighty-nine of this code, or until such time as the document issued by the state board, as aforesaid, may be revoked or

suspended as provided in subdivision five of section fifteen hundred and twenty-one of this code.

(4) Upon presentation of the diploma and document referred to in subdivision three of this section to any county, or city and county, superintendent of schools, said superintendent shall record the name of the holder thereof in a book provided for that purpose in his office, and the holder thereof shall henceforth be absolved from the requirement of subdivision one of section sixteen hundred and ninety-six of this code.

(5) Said diploma of graduation from any state normal school in this State, when accompanied by a document granted by the faculty of the state university on or before the thirtieth day of June, nineteen hundred and three, showing that the holder of such diploma has successfully completed the course of instruction in said university prescribed for students who are graduates of a normal school of this state shall entitle such holder to a high school certificate authorizing the holder to teach in any grammar and primary school and in any high school in this State.

Section 1521. The powers and duties of the state board of education are as follows:

(2) (a) To prescribe by general rule the credentials upon which persons may be granted certificates to teach in the high schools of this State. No credentials shall be prescribed or allowed, unless the same, in the judgment of said board, are the equivalent of a diploma of graduation from the University of California, and are satisfactory evidence that the holder thereof has taken an amount of pedagogy equivalent to the minimum amount of pedagogy prescribed by the state board of education of this State, and include a recommendation for a high school certificate from the faculty of the institution in which the pedagogical work shall have been taken.

Sec. 1565. Except for a temporary certificate, and except as provided in subdivision second of section 1503 of the Political Code every applicant for a teacher's certificate, or for a renewal of a certificate, upon presenting his applition, shall pay to the county superintendent a fee of two dollars, to be by him immediately deposited with the county treasurer, to the credit of a fund to be known as the teachers' institute and library fund. All funds so credited shall be drawn out only upon the requisition of the county superintendent of schools upon the county auditor, who shall draw his warrant in payment of the services of instructors in the county teachers' institute; provided they be not teachers in the public schools of the county in which such institute is held; and for the purchase of books for a library for the use of the teachers of the county. At least 50 per cent of the teachers' institute and library fund shall be expended for books. The county superintendent shall take charge of the teachers' library, prepare a catalogue of its contents, and keep a correct record of books taken therefrom and returned thereto.

NORMAL SCHOOLS.

Note—The following named universities and colleges have been recognized (to November 1, 1906), by the state board of education under the provisions of this section:

Arizona Normal Schools:
- Flagstaff.
- Tempe.

Canadian Normal Schools:
- London,
- McGill Normal School, Quebec,
- New Brunswick,
- Ottawa,

Ontario Normal College, Hamilton,
Toronto,
Truro, Nova Scotia.
Colorado State Normal School, Greeley.
Connecticut State Normal Schools:
New Britain,
New Haven,
Willimantic.
Edge Hill Training College, Normal Department:
Liverpool, England.
Hawaiian Territorial Normal School, Honolulu.
Illinois State Normal Schools:
Chicago Normal School, Chicago.
Eastern Illinois State Normal School, Charleston.
Illinois State Normal University, Normal.
Northern Illinois State Normal School, De Kalb.
Southern Illinois State Normal School, Carbondale.
Indiana State Normal School, Terra Haute.
Iowa State Normal School, Cedar Falls.
Kansas State Normal School, Emporia.
Maine State Normal Schools:
Castine,
Farmington,
Gorham.
Massachusetts State Normal Schools:
Boston,
Bridgewater,
Framingham,
Fitchburg,
Hyannis,
Lowell,
North Adams,
Salem,
Westfield,
Worcester.
Michigan State Normal Schools:
Marquette,
Mt. Pleasant,
Ypsilanti.
Minnesota State Normal Schools:
Duluth,
Mankato,
Moorehead,
St. Cloud,
Winona.
Missouri State Normal Schools:
Cape Girardeau,
Kirksville,
Warrensburg.
Nebraska State Normal School, Peru.
Nevada State University, Reno; Normal Department.
New Hampshire State Normal School, Plymouth.
New Jersey State Normal School, Trenton.
New York State Normal Schools:
Albany,
Brockport,
Buffalo,

Cortland,
Fredonia,
Geneseo,
Jamacia,
Newplatz,
New York City Normal,
Oneonta,
Oswego,
Plattsburgh,
Potsdam.
North Carolina State Normal and Industrial College, Greensboro.
Oklahoma, Central Normal School, Edmond.
Pennsylvania State Normal Schools:
Bloomsburg,
California Clarion,
East Stroudsburg,
Edinboro,
Indiana,
Kutztown,
Lock Haven,
Mansfield,
Millersville,
Shippensburg,
Slippery Rock,
West Chester.
Rhode Island State Normal School, Providence.
South Dakota State Normal School, Spearfish.
Utah State Normal School (Normal Department Utah University), Salt Lake City.
Washington City Normal School No. 1, Washington, D. C.
Washington State Normal Schools:
Bellingham (Whatcom),
Cheney, from and after 1904;
Ellensburg.
Wisconsin State Normal Schools:
Milwaukee,
Oshkosh,
Platteville,
River Falls,
Stevens Point,
West Superior,
Whitewater.

STATE DOCUMENTS.

Arizona—Life Diploma.
Colorado—Complimentary Life Diploma only.
Idaho—Life Diploma.
Indiana—Life and Professional Certificates.
Iowa—Life Diploma.
Minnesota—Life Certificate.
Montana—Life Diploma.
Nevada—Life Diploma.
Ohio—Life Certificate, when obtained on forty-eight months' experience.
Oregon—Life Diploma, when obtained on sixty months' experience.
Rhode Island—Life Diploma, highest grade.
South Dakota—Life Diploma.
Virginia—Life Diploma.
Washington—Life Diploma.

KINDERGARTEN PRIMARY CERTIFICATES.

May be granted to holders of diplomas of graduation from any of the following named Kindergarten Training Schools:

Blackheath Kindergarten Froebelian School and Training College for Teachers, London, England.
Chicago Froebel Association, Chicago, Illinois.
Chicago Kindergarten College, Chicago, Illinois.
Chicago Kindergarten Institute, Chicago, Illinois.
Chicago Free Kindergarten Association, Chicago, Illinois.
Cincinnati Kindergarten Association, Cincinnati, Ohio.
Drake University Kindergarten Training School, Des Moines, Iowa.
Froebelian School, Longwood, Chicago, Illinois.
Golden Gate Kindergarten Association, San Francisco, California.
Indiana Kindergarten and Primary Normal Training School, Indianapolis, Indiana.
Kindergarten College, Pittsburg, Pennsylvania.
Kindergarten Department, Boston Normal School, Boston, Massachusetts.
Kindergarten Department, Edge Hill Training College, Liverpool, England.
Kindergarten Department of Teachers' College, Columbia University, New York.
Kindergarten Department, State Normal School, Greeley, Colorado.
Kindergarten Department, State Normal School, Oswego, N. Y.
Kindergarten Department, Wisconsin State Normal School, Milwaukee, Wisconsin.
Kindergarten Normal Department of the Ethical Culture School, New York, N. Y.
Kindergarten Training Department of Nebraska State Normal School, Peru, Nebraska.
Kindergarten Training Department, Omaha Public Schools, Omaha, Nebraska.
Kindergarten Training Department, Pratt Institute, Brooklyn, N. Y.
Kindergarten Training Department, State Normal School, Fredonia, N. Y.
Kindergarten Training School, Columbus, Ohio.
Kindergarten Training School of the Grand Rapids Kindergarten Association, Grand Rapids, Michigan.
Louisville Free Kindergarten Association's Training School, Louisville, Kentucky.
Minneapolis Kindergarten Training School, Minneapolis, Minnesota.
Miss Wheelock's Kindergarten Training School, Boston, Massachusetts.
Oakland Kindergarten Training School, Oakland, California.
Oberlin Kindergarten Training Association, Oberlin, Ohio.
The Froebel School, Providence, Rhode Island.
The Stout Training School for Kindergarten Teachers, Menominee, Wisconsin.
Utica Kindergarten Training School, Utica, N. Y.

HIGH SCHOOL CERTIFICATES.

University of California, Berkeley, California.
Catholic University of America, Washington, D. C.
University of Chicago, Chicago, Ill.
Clark University, Worcester, Mass.
Columbia University, New York City, N. Y.
Cornell University, Ithaca, N. Y.
Harvard University, Cambridge, Massachusetts.
John Hopkins University, Baltimore, Maryland.
Leland Stanford Junior University, Palo Alto, California.
University of Michigan, Ann Arbor, Michigan.
University of Pennsylvania, Philadelphia, Pennsylvania.
Princeton University, Princeton, New Jersey.
University of Wisconsin, Madison, Wisconsin.
University of Virginia, Charlottesville, Virginia.
Yale University, New Haven, Conn.

(b) The said board shall also consider the cases of individual applicants, who have taught successfully for a period of not less than twenty school months, and who are not possessed of the credentials prescribed by the board under the provisions of this section. The said board, in its discretion, may issue to such applicants special credentials upon which they may be granted certificates to teach in the high schools of the State. In such special cases, the board may take cognizance of any adequate evidence of preparation which the applicant may present. The standard of qualification in such special cases shall not be lower than that represented by the other credentials named by the board under the provisions of this section.

(3) To grant life diplomas of four grades, valid throughout the State, as follows:

(a) High School: Authorizing the holder to teach in any primary and grammar or high school.

(b) Grammar school: Authorizing the holder to teach in any primary or grammar school.

(c) Kindergarten-primary: Authorizing the holder to teach in the kindergarten class of any primary school.

(d) Special: Authorizing the holder to teach in any school such special branches and in such grades as are named in such diploma.

(4) Except as provided in sections fifteen hundred and three and seventeen hundred and seventy-five of this code, life diplomas may be issued only to such persons as have held for one year, and still hold a valid county, or city and county, certificate, corresponding in grade to the grade of diploma applied for, and who shall furnish satisfactory evidence of having had a successful experience in teaching of at least forty-eight months. Not less than twenty-one months of said experience shall have been in the public schools of California. Every application must be accompanied to the state board of education by a certified copy of a resolution adopted by at least a three-fourths vote of all the members composing a county, or city and county, board of education, recommending that the diploma be granted, and also by an affidavit of the applicant, specifically setting forth the places in which, and the dates between which said applicant has taught. The application must also be accompanied by a fee of two dollars for the purpose of defraying the expense of issuing the diploma.

(5) To revoke or suspend for immoral or unprofessional conduct or for evident unfitness for teaching, life diplomas, educational diplomas, documents issued under the provisions of section fifteen hundred and three and seventeen hundred and seventy-five of this code, or credentials issued in accordance with subdivision two of this section; and to adopt such rules for said revocation as they may deem expedient or necessary.

* * * * * * * * * *

Section 1663. (1) The public schools of California, other than those supported exclusively by the state, shall be classed as high schools, technical schools, and grammar and primary schools (including kindergarten classes), and no teacher shall be employed to teach in any school if the certificate held by the teachers is of a grade below that of the school or class to be taught; provided, that the holder of existing primary certificates or of the same when hereafter renewed shall be eligible to teach in any of the classes of the schools of the county, or city and county, which the county, or city and county superintendent shall have designated as of the primary grade, or in any school which said superintendent shall have designated as a primary school; and provided further, that nothing herein contained shall be construed as prohibiting the employment of any person holding a valid special certificate for kindergarten work heretofore granted by any county, or city and county, board of education in this State, as a teacher in any kindergarten class of a primary school in the county, or city and county, in which such valid special certificate for kindergarten work shall have been granted. The county, or city and county, board of education must, except in incorporated cities having boards of education, on or before the first day of July of each year, prescribe the course of study in each grade of the grammar and primary schools for the ensuing school year.

* * * * * * * * * *

Section 1696. Every teacher in the public schools must—

(1) Before assuming charge of a school, file his or her certificate with the superintendent of schools; provided, that when any teacher so employed is the holder of a California State normal school diploma, accompanied by the certificate of the state board of education, as provided in subdivision third of of section one thousand five hundred and three of the Political Code, an educational or a life diploma of California, upon presentation thereof to the superintendent he shall record the name of said holder in a book provided for that purpose in his office, and the holder of said diploma shall thereupon be absolved from the provisions of this subdivision.

1696a. Whenever the school register or registers of any teacher or teachers or other records of any public school district in any school year may have been or shall hereafter be destroyed by conflagration or other public calamity, thereby preventing the teacher or teachers and said school officers from making their monthly or annual reports in the usual manner and with accuracy the affidavits of the teacher or teachers, the school principals or other school officers of such school district certifying as to the contents of such destroyed registers or other records shall be accepted by all authorities for all school matters appertaining to such school district except that of average daily attendance. The average daily school attendance of any public school district or high school whereof the register or registers of the teacher or teachers, or any number of them or other records may have been or shall hereafter be destroyed by conflagration or other public calamity, or whereof, by reason of such conflagration or calamity the regular session or attendance of such district or high school has been interrupted and its average attendance materially affected thereby, shall be its average daily attendance of the next preceding school year increased or diminished by the average yearly percentage of increase or decrease calculated for the next preceding ten years; provided, that the average daily attendance of such school district or high school for the school year ending June 30, 1906, shall be its average daily attendance for the school year ending June 30, 1905, with five per cent (5%) thereof as increase added thereto.

* * * * * * * * * *

Section 1772. County boards of education may, on examination, grant certificates as follows:

(1) Grammar school certificates: To those who have passed a satisfactory examination in the following studies: Reading English grammar and advanced composition, English and American literature, orthography and defining,. penmanship, drawing, vocal music, bookkeeping, arithmetic, algebra to quadratics, plane geometry, geography (physical, political and industrial), elementary physics, physiology and hygiene, history of the United States and civil government, history (ancient, medevial and modern), school law, methods of teaching.

Section 1775. (1) County Boards of Education may, without examination, grant certificates as follows:

HIGH SCHOOL CERTIFICATES.

(a) High school certificates: (1) To the holders of credentials approved by the state board of education in accordance with subdivision two of section fifteen hundred and twenty-one of this code; (2) To the holders of special credentials issued by said state board, in accordance with said subdivision;

(3) To holders of high school certificates issued by any county, or city and county, board of education in this State; (4) To holders of normal school diplomas accompanied by documents from the faculty of the state university, provided for in subdivision five of section fifteen hundred and three of this code.

GRAMMAR SCHOOL CERTIFICATES.

(b) Grammar school certificates: To the holders of the following credentials: (1) Life diplomas or certificates of any state; provided, the state board of education in this state shall have decided that said diplomas or certificates represent experience and scholarship equivalent to the requirements for the elementary life diploma in California; (2) California state normal school diplomas, San Francisco city normal school diplomas heretofore granted, and other normal school diplomas; provided, that the state board of education of this state shall have recommended the normal school issuing said diploma as being of equal rank with the state normal schools of California; (3) Diplomas from the University of California, or from any other university that shall be declared by the state board of education to be of equal rank with the University of California, when the holders have completed the prescribed course in the pedagogical department of the state university, or a pedagogical course that said state board shall declare to be equivalent to such prescribed course, and have been recommended by the faculty of the university issuing such diploma; (4) Grammar school or grammar grade certificates of any county, or city and county, of California.

KINDERGARTEN PRIMARY CERTIFICATES.

(c) Kindergarten-primary certificates: (1) To the holders of kindergarten-primary certificates of any county, or city and county, of California; (2) To the holders of diplomas of graduation from the kindergarten department of any state normal school of this state; (3) To the holders of credentials, showing that the applicant has had professional kindergarten training in an institution approved by the state board of education, and also education equivalent to the requirements for graduation from the kindergarten department of a California state normal school; (4) To the holders of special kindergarten certificates of any county, or city and county, of California granted prior to July 1, 1901; provided, that the holders of such special kindergarten certificates have had at least two years' training in a kindergarten training school and have taught for a period of at least two years in a public kindergarten school in the county, or city and county, wherein such special kindergarten certificates were granted.

GRAMMAR SCHOOL CERTIFICATES ON PRIMARY AND EXAMINATION IN EXTRA STUDIES.

(2) Grammar school certificates may be granted to the holders of primary grade certificates who shall pass satisfactory examinations in such branches as do not appear on their certificates, or in the record of the examination upon which the original certificate was granted.

CERTIFICATES AND DIPLOMAS VALID.—RENEWAL OF CERTIFICATES.

(3) All certificates and diplomas now valid in California shall continue in force and effect for the full term for which they are granted. County boards of education may renew any certificate issued by them prior to the adoption of this law, and now in force, and may renew certificates granted by authority of this law. Renewed certificates shall be valid for a period equal to that for which they were originally granted.

PERMANENT CERTIFICATES.

(4) When the holder of any certificate or state diploma shall have taught successfully in the same county, or city and county, for five years, the board of education of such county, or city and county, may grant a permanent certificate of the kind and grade of the class in which said applicant has been teaching, valid in the county, or city and county, in which issued, during the life of the holder, or until revoked for any of the causes designated in subdivision four of section seventeen hundred and ninety-one of this code; provided, that such permanent certificate shall in no case be of a higher grade than the grade of the certificate or state diploma on which the teaching has been done; and for a permanent high school certificate twenty months of said teaching shall have consisted of regular high school work; and provided further, that a certificate when renewed the second time, or at any time thereafter, shall become, by such renewal, a permanent certificate, if the holder of said certificate shall have complied with all of the conditions of this subdivision.

DOCUMENT GRANTED ON STATE UNIVERSITY DIPLOMA OR DIPLOMAS OF ACCREDITED UNIVERSITIES.

(5) Whenever any holder of a diploma from the state university, or from any other university that shall be declared by the state board of education to be of equal rank with the state university, shall present to said state board satisfactory evidence of having had two years' successful experience as a teacher, subsequent to graduation, accompanied by satisfactory evidence that such holder has completed the prescribed course in the pedagogical department of the University of California, or a pedagogical course equivalent thereto, the state board of education shall grant to the holder of said university diploma a document signed by the president and secretary of the state board, showing such fact, and said diploma, accompanied by said document of the state board attached thereto, shall become a permanent certificate of qualification to teach in any grammar or primary or high school in the State, valid until such time as the said document shall be revoked by said state board of education, for any of the causes shown in subdivision four of section seventeen hundred and ninety-one of this code.

Section 1776. Any member of a county board of education, or of a city board of examination who shall, except in the regular course of study in the public schools, teach any classes where pupils are given special instruction to prepare them for passing examination to obtain teachers' certificates, or who shall give special instruction to any person preparing for examination to obtain a teacher's certificate, shall be deemed guilty of a misdemeanor, and, upon conviction thereof, his office shall be declared vacant. No certificates shall be issued to any applicant who has received special instructions, when preparing for examination, from any member of a county board of education, or of a city board of examination.

Section 1778. County or city and county boards of education shall have the power to issue permanent certificates valid, within the county, or city and county, in which issued, during the life of the holder, or until revoked for any of the causes shown in subdivision four of section seventeen hundred and ninety-one of this code. Said permanent certificates shall be issued on the following credentials and conditions:

Whenever the holder of any certificate shall have taught successfully in the same county or city and county for five years the board of education of said county or city and county may in addition to or in place of the renewal of such certificate, grant a permanent certificate of the kind and grade of the class in which said applicant has been teaching; provided, that in the issuance of a permanent high school certificates at least twenty months' successful high school experience, taught upon a high school certificate, shall be included in the five years' experience required.

(2.) Whenever the holder of any certificate shall have successfully completed five years of successful experience in any county or city and county, the board of education of said county, or city and county may, upon application and under the other conditions named in this section grant to said applicant a permanent certificate.

(3). Whenever the holder of any life or educational diploma shall have complied with the conditions as enumerated in subdivision one of this section, the said board of education shall, without fee, issue upon application, a permanent certificate of the grade of said life or educational diploma.

(4) No permanent certificate shall be of a higher grade, or, if special, of a different kind from the certificate upon which granted.

(5) (a) Upon the presentation of any certificate, except the primary grade, for renewal for the second time, or for any time thereafter, the board of education, in renewing said certificate shall by such renewal, cause such certificate to become permanent; provided, the applicant for said renewal shall have complied with the other conditions of this section.

(b) And it shall be the duty of the county superintendent to attach to said certificate a document giving it the full force and effect of a permanent certificate within said county or city and county.

(6 Each applicant for a permanent certificate must present to the county or city and county board of education satisfactory evidence of the experience upon which said permanent certificate may be issued.

(7) All permanent certificates shall be upon blank forms prepared by the state superintendent of public instruction.

Section 1790. The city, or city and county, board of examination must meet and hold examinations for the granting of teachers' certificates semi-annually, at such times as they may determine. They may also hold monthly meetings for the transaction of such other business as may come before them. Special meetings may be called by the city, or city and county superintendent, when, in his judgment the same are necessary; and on the recommendation, in writing, of any three members of the board, the city, or city and county superintendent shall call a special meeting. No business shall be transacted at any special meeting except such as is indicated in the call therefor; and of all such meetings, due notice shall be given to each member of the board. The place of meeting shall be designated by the chairman. The meetings of the city, or city and county board of examiners, shall be public and a record of their proceedings shall be kept in the office of the city, or city and county superintendent of schools.

Section 1791. Each city, or city and county board of examination has power:

First—To adopt rules and regulations, not inconsistent with the laws of this state, for its own government and for the examination of teachers.

Second—To examine applicants, and to prescribe a standard of proficiency which may entitle the person examined to receive: (a) A city, or city and county, grammar school certificate, valid for six years, authorizing the holder to teach any primary or grammar school or class in such city, or city and county; (b) A city, or city and county, special certificate, valid for six years, authorizing the holder to teach such special subjects in any school of the city, or city and county, and in such grades as are designated in such certificate. Applicants for special certificates by examination or any credentials, or by both, shall satisfy the board of their special fitness to teach one or more of the particular studies for which special certificates may be granted, and shall satisfy the board of their proficiency in English grammar, orthography, defining and methods of teaching. No special certificate shall be granted to teach in any school, studies other than drawing, music, physical culture, and commercial, technical or industrial work.

The board of examination shall report the result of the examination to the city, or city and county board of education; and said board of education shall thereupon issue to the successful applicants the certificates to which they shall be entitled.

Third—For immoral or unprofessional conduct, profanity, intemperance, or evident unfitness for teaching, to recommend to the city, or city and county board of education, the revocation of any certificates previously granted by said board of education in said city, or city and county.

Section 1792. The city, or city and county boards of examination may also recommend the granting of city, or city and county certificates and the renewal thereof, in the manner provided for the granting and renewal of county certificates by county boards of education in section seventeen hundred and seventy-five of this code.

Section 1793. (1) The holders of city, or city and county certificates are eligible to teach in the cities, or cities and counties, in which such certificates were granted, in schools or classes of grades corresponding to the grades of such certificates, and when elected shall be dismissed only for insubordination or other causes as mentioned in section seventeen hundred and ninety-one of this code, duly ascertained and approved by the boards of education of such cities, or cities and counties.

(3) The holders of special, city, or city and county certificates are eligible to teach the special branches mentioned in their certificates, in the grades of all the schools in the city, or city and county, in which such certificates were granted corresponding to the grade of said special certificates.

REPORT OF THE PUBLIC SCHOOL TEACHERS' ANNUITY AND RETIREMENT FUND COMMISSIONERS FOR THE FISCAL YEAR ENDING JUNE 30, 1908.

San Francisco, Cal., July 20, 1908.

Hon. Edward R. Taylor, Mayor,
In and for the City and County of San Francisco.

Dear Sir:—

I have the honor to submit herewith the report on the Public School Teachers' Annuity and Retirement Fund for the fiscal year terminating June 30, 1908.

ALFRED, RONCOVIERI,
Superintendent of Schools and Secretary
Public School Teachers' Retirement Fund
Commissioners.

RECEIPTS.

Balance in Fund June 30, 1907, including $50,000 in Permanent Fund	$52,322.13
Contributions by teachers under provisions of Annuity Law	11,605.00
Absence money granted by the Board of Education	3,000.00
Interest on Permanent Fund	1,983.19

Amounts received in accordance with Section 8 (A) from teachers retired during fiscal year:—

1907.				
July	1.	C. W. Moores	$209.00	
Sept.	1.	Miss V. E. Bradbury	231.30	
Sept.	1.	Miss Martha Stone	218.75	
Sept.	1.	Miss N. C. Stallman	235.75	
Sept.	1.	W. H. Edwards	210.00	
1908.				
Jan.	1.	Miss R. V. Claiborne	115.05	
Jan.	1.	Mrs. M. E. Steele	217.05	
Feb.	1.	Mrs. M. E. Michener	212.10	
Feb.	15.	Mrs. F. A. Banning	202.00	
Mar.	1.	Mrs. H. A. Hogan	193.70	
Mar.	1.	Miss Rose Fay	166.75	
May	1.	Miss Julia A. Danks	210.75	2,422.20

Total Receipts $71,332.52

DISBURSEMENTS.

Annuities to Retired Teachers—			
Oct. 1, 1907		$3,741.25	
Jan. 1, 1908		3,815.25	
April 1, 1908		4,057.95	
July 1, 1908		4,241.25	
Total		$15,855.70	
Clerical Services		50.00	
Lester, Herrick & Herrick (expert)		70.00	
Total Disbursements			15,975.70
Balance			$55,356.82
In Treasury		$ 255.57	
In Banks		55,101.25	$55,356.82
In Permanent Fund	$50,000.00		
In Annuity Fund	5,356.82		
	$55,356.82		

LIST OF ANNUITANTS.

Date of Retirement.	Name	Maximum or Fraction Thereof.	Annuity Per Month.	Annuity Per Quarter.
1895.				
Nov. 27,	Mrs. L. T. Hopkins,	Max.	$50.00	$150.00
1896.				
Jan. 22,	Miss L. F. Ryder,	Max.	50.00	150.00
Jan. 22,	Mrs. M. H. Currier,	Max.	50.00	150.00
April 24,	Miss V. M. Raclet,	9/10	45.00	135.00
1897.				
Sept. 11,	Miss M. Solomon,	Max.	50.00	150.00
Dec. 8,	Miss F. L. Soule,	Max.	50.00	150.00

Date of Retirement.	Name	Maximum or Fraction Thereof.	Annuity Per Month.	Annuity Per Quarter.
1898.				
Sept. 14,	Miss Kate Kollmyer,	8/15	26.66⅔	80.00
1899.				
April 18,	Miss M. J. Bragg,	Max.	50.00	150.00
June 14,	Mrs. M. E. Caldwall,	29/30	48.33⅓	145.00
Aug. 1,	Mrs. E. M. Poole,	11/15	36.66⅔	110.00
1900.				
Jan. 9,	Miss C. A. Templeton,	Max.	50.00	150.00
July 18,	Mrs. A. Griffith,	Max.	50.00	150.00
July 25,	Miss K. F. McColgan,	Max.	50.00	150.00
Aug. 1,	Miss L. M. Barrows,	13/15	43.33⅓	130.00
Aug. 1,	Miss Annie A. Hill,	Max.	50.00	150.00
Oct. 15,	Miss M. J. Canham,	14/15	46.66⅔	140.00
1901.				
July 20,	Miss J. B. Gorman.	Max.	50.00	150.00
Oct. 4,	Miss E. Murphy,	9/10	45.00	135.00
1902.				
Jan. 2,	Miss R. B. Campbell,	Max.	50.00	150.00
Jan. 2,	Miss L. S. Templeton,	Max.	50.00	150.00
Jan. 2,	Mr. A. T. Winn,	Max.	50.00	150.00
Sept. 28,	Miss Emma. J. Miller,	11/15	36.66⅔	110.00
1903.				
Feb. 17,	Mrs. B. A. Chinn,	Max.	50.00	150.00
Feb. 17,	Miss Lydia Hart,	11/15	36.66⅔	110.00
Feb. 17,	Miss Christine Hart,	Max.	50.00	150.00
Aug. 1,	Mrs. S. A. Miles,	Max.	50.00	150.00
Aug. 1,	Mr. T. B. White,	Max.	50.00	150.00
Sept. 1,	Miss A. E. Slavan,	Max.	50.00	150.00
Oct. 15,	Miss L. Burnham,	¾	37.50	112.50
1904.				
Aug. 1,	Mr. Elisha Brooks,	Max.	50.00	150.00
Aug. 1,	Miss I. Patterson,	Max.	50.00	150.00
Sept. 1,	Mrs. E. M. Whitcomb,	Max.	50.00	150.00
1905.				
Jan. 16,	Miss E. G. Grant,	Max.	50.00	150.00
Mar. 1,	Miss M. A. Smith,	⅔	33.33⅓	100.00
Mar. 1,	Miss Jean Parker,	Max.	50.00	150.00
Mar. 1,	Mrs. T. C. Nicholl,	Max.	50.00	150.00
Mar. 1,	Mr. Charles Ham,	Max.	50.00	150.00
Mar. 1,	Miss R. Jacobs,	Max.	50.00	150.00
Mar. 1,	Mr. D. Lambert,	Max. (Evening)	25.00	75.00
1906.				
Feb. 1,	Miss M. E. Carson,	Max.	50.00	150.00
Feb. 1,	Mrs. A. C. Taylor,	Max.	50.00	150.00
Aug. 1,	Miss E. R. Elder,	Max.	50.00	150.00
Aug. 1,	Mrs. C. Chalmers,	Max.	50.00	150.00
Oct. 1,	Miss H. E. Whirlow,	Max.	50.00	150.00
Dec. 1,	Mrs. V. Troyer,	Max.	50.00	150.00

Date of Retirement.	Name	Maximum or Fraction Thereof.	Annuity Per Month.	Annuity Per Quarter.
1907.				
April 1,	Miss Madge Sprott,	½ (Evening)	25.00	75.00
April 1,	Miss A. D. Miley,	14/15	46.66⅔	140.00
April 1,	Miss Q. O. McConnell,	Max.	50.00	150.00
April 1,	Prof. A. Herbst,	Max.	50.00	150.00
July 1,	Mr. C. W. Moores,	Max.	50.00	150.00
Sept. 1,	Miss V. E. Bradbury,	Max.	50.00	150.00
Sept. 1,	Miss Martha Stone,	Max.	50.00	150.00
Sept. 1,	Miss N. C. Stallman,	Max.	50.00	150.00
Sept. 1,	Mr. W. H. Edwards,	Max.	50.00	150.00
1908.				
Jan. 1,	Miss R. V. Claiborne,	⅔	33.33⅓	100.00
Feb. 1,	Mrs. M. E. Michener,	Max.	50.00	150.00
Feb. 15,	Mrs. F. A. Banning,	Max.	50.00	150.00
Mar. 1,	Miss Rose Fay,	11/15	36.66⅔	110.00
Mar. 1,	Mrs. Mary A. Hogan,	14/15	46.66⅔	140.00

The books and accounts of the Annuity and Retirement Fund were examined by Lester, Herrick & Herrick, Certified Public Accountants, and in a report on file in the office of the superintendent of schools made by this firm to the Public School Teachers' Retirement Fund Commissioners, the books and accounts were found to be correct and in good order.

I regret to state that no action was taken by the the Board of Supervisors in the matter of an appropriation of $16,000 asked for by Public School Teachers' Retirement Fund Commissioners, for the purpose of enabling the Commission to pay the full amount of the annuities due.

The request made to the Supervisors was as follows:

San Francisco, Cal., May 2d, 1908.

To the Honorable, the Board of Supervisors in and for the
City and County of San Francisco.

Gentlemen;

The Public School Teachers' Annuity and Retirement Fund Commissioners respectfully call your attention to a serious condition affecting those teachers who have served our City faithfully for long periods of time, and who, on account of becoming incapicitated, have been forced to retire.

The tenure of teachers elected to the San Francisco School Department is for life. After service of 25 to 40 years, teachers may become decrepit, and thereby be incapable of doing strong, systematic work in the school room. It is in the nature of things that the old should yield to the young, but we must treat the aged humanely and with the utmost consideration. Classes of forty to fifty pupils are benefited by receiving impressions through the personality of young and vigorous teachers who must take the place of the old.

The Board of Education, on account of the past records for efficiency of such teachers and on account of the influence and the pleas of their former pupils and friends, finds it practically impossible to dismiss them. In such cases the members of the Board of Education are human, and are not inclined to deprive a teacher of the means of earning a livlihood and thus rendering her an object of charity in her old age. Furthermore, a teacher who has spent her best years in the school room cannot change her occupation, because she lacks vigor, and, by the duties of her profession, has been deprived of training or experience in the affairs of the world.

Gradually the policy of granting pensions to old employees or those who have been injured in service is being recognized by the great corporations of the United States, and reports universally agree that this policy has resulted in greatly improving efficiency of service by increasing the enthusiasm and fidelity of employees. Old age pension movements are gaining strength annually in France, Germany, England, and Switzerland, and, from all indications, will ultimately become rules of conduct.

A pension fund is a convenient side-door by which aged or infirm teachers may be retired from the class room. By the law, commonly known as the Teachers' Annuity Fund Act, it is possible for the Board of Education to retire such teachers with a maximum pension of $50 per month. The fund from which the pensions are paid is made up entirely of assessments upon or deductions from the salaries of those actively engaged in teaching in the San Francisco School Department. So far this fund has been sufficient to pay only $25 a month to the retired teachers, or one-half of the sum allowed by law. At present the total number of retired teachers receiving pensions is sixty, making the sum of $31,000 necessary annually to pay each the maximum annuity allowed by law. The present income from the Teachers' Annuity Fund is only about $15,300, leaving a deficit of $15,700.

When it is remembered that this deficit bears directly upon the retired teachers, reducing the maximum annuity to which they are by law entitled from $50 a month down, it will be seen that they are suffering unjustly a very great hardship. Twenty-five dollars a month is not sufficient to provide even the necessities of life under our increased cost of living.

For these reasons, at a meeting of the Retirement Fund Commissioners held April 18th, 1908, the following was unanimously adopted:

Whereas, The present income of the San Francisco School Teachers' Annuity Fund is derived solely from assessments upon and deductions from the salaries of those actively engaged in teaching in the department; and

Whereas, The maximum annuity now paid to the retired teachers is only $25 per month instead of $50 as contemplated by law, owing to insufficient income; and

Whereas, Said $25 is insufficient to meet the advanced cost of living, and consequently works a great hardship on many of the pensioners; and

Whereas, The sum of $16,000, in addition to that above provided, is required in order to pay the maximum of $50 per month to said pensioners for next year; and

Whereas, the City of San Francisco has never contributed to the support of the Teachers' Annuity Fund as it very properly does to that of the Fire and Police Departments; therefore, be it

Resolved, That the Public School Teachers' Annuity and Retirement Fund Commissioners hereby respectfully ask the Honorable Board of Supervisors to appropriate to the School Teachers' Annuity Fund the sum of $16,000 in the budget for the next fiscal year to enable said commissioners to pay to the retired teachers of the San Francisco School Department the maximum pension of $50 per month contemplated by law.

We, therefore, respectfully ask your Honorable Board to appropriate to the School Teachers' Annuity and Retirement Fund the sum of $16,000 in the budget for the fiscal year, 1908-09, to enable the Public School Teachers' Retirement Fund Commissioners to pay the retired teachers of the San Francisco School Department the maximum pension of $50 per month contemplated by law.

Respectfully yours,

ALFRED RONCOVIERI,
Superintendent of Common Schools.

We concur in the above: Edward R. Taylor, Mayor; John E. McDougald, City and County Treasurer.

LIST OF BOOKS AND PRICES OF SAME USED IN THE SAN FRANCISCO SCHOOLS.

First Grade	California State Primer	$0.25
	California State First Reader	.30
	*Powers' Poems for Memorizing—Part I	.10
Second Grade	California State Second Reader	.35
	California State Speller—Book I	.25
	*Powers' Poems for Memorizing—Part I	.10
Third Grade	California State Third Reader	.50
	California State English Lessons—Book I	.35
	California State Speller—Book I	.25
	*Powers' Poems for Memorizing—Part I	.10
Fourth Grade	California State Third Reader	.50
	California State English Lessons—Book I	.35
	California State Introductory Geography	.65
	California State Speller—Book I	.25
	California State First Book in Arithmetic	.35
	*Powers' Poems for Memorizing—Part I	.10
	Natural Music Primer	.30
Fifth Grade	California State Fourth Reader	.60
	California State English Lessons—Book I	.35
	California State Introductory Geography	.65
	California State Introductory History	.55
	California State Speller—Book I	.25
	California State First Book in Arithmetic	.35
	*Powers' Poems for Memorizing—Part I	.10
	Natural Music Primer	.30
	Webster's Common School Dictionary	.75
Sixth Grade	California State Fourth Reader	.60
	California State English Lessons—Book II	.55
	California State Grammar School History	.95
	California State Grammar School Geography	1.20
	California State Grammar School Arithmetic	.60
	California State Speller—Book II	.25
	Powers' Poems for Memorizing—Part II	.10
	Natural Music Second Reader	.35
	Webster's Common School Dictionary	.75

Teachers select reading material from the following classics. The children are not asked to buy them all:

Lays of Ancient Rome—Macaulay	.25
King of The Golden River—Ruskin	.30
Water Babies—Kingsley	.40
Lamb's Tales from Shakespeare	.30
A Hunting of the Deer—Warner	.30
Courtship of Miles Standish—Longfellow	.10

Seventh Grade	California State English Lessons—Book II	.55
	California State Grammar School Geography	1.20
	California State Grammar School History	.95

* Teacher may recommend children to purchase.

	California State Grammar School Arithmetic	.60
	California State Speller—Book II	.25
	Powers' Poems for Memorizing—Part II	.10
	Natural Music Second Reader	.35
	Webster's Academic Dictionary	1.50
	Williams' & Fisher's Theory and Practice of Cookery	1.10

Teachers select reading material from the following classics. The children are not asked to buy them all:

	Hawthorne's Wonder Book	.15
	Longfellow's Leaflets	.30
	Coming of Arthur and Passing of Arthur	.30
	Benjamin Franklin's Autobiography	.15
	Rip Van Winkle and Sleepy Hollow	.15
	Goldsmith's Deserted Village	.30
	A Dog of Flanders	.30
Eighth Grade	California State English Lessons—Book II	.55
	California State Grammar School Geography	1.20
	California State Grammar School Arithmetic	.60
	California State Grammar School History	.95
	California State Speller—Book II	.25
	Powers' Poems for Memorizing—Part II	.10
	Natural Music Fourth Reader	.35
	Webster's Academic Dictionary	1.50
	Dunn's Community and the Citizen	.85
	Williams' & Fisher's Theory and Practice of Cookery	1.10

Teachers select reading material from the following classics. The children are not asked to buy them all:

	Evangeline	.15
	Dickens' Christmas Carol	.10
	Merchant of Venice	.10
	Snow Bound	.15
	Julius Caesar	.10
	Irvings Alhambra	.10
	Scott's Lady of The Lake	.10

HIGH SCHOOLS—COMMERCIAL

English	Scott's Ivanhoe, M. P. C.	.30
	Scott's Lady of the Lake—Riverside No. 53	.30
	Lowell's Vision of Sir Launfal—Riverside No. 31	.15
	Shakespeare's Merchant of Venice, M. P. C.	.30
	Shakespeare's Julius Caesar, M. P. C.	.30
	Williams' & Rogers' Commercial Correspondence	.35
	Kimball's Business Speller	.30
	California State English Lessons—Book II	.55
Spanish	Worman's First Spanish Book	.45
	Pinney's Spanish and English Conversation—First Book	.70
	Pinney's Spanish and English Conversation—Second Book	.70
	Monsanto & Languellier's Practical Spanish Course	1.40
History & Civics	Corman's Industrial History of the United States	1.40
	Ashley's American Government	1.10
Mathematics	Moore & Miner—Practical Business Arithmetic	1.10
Stenography	Gallagher & Marsh—Practical Shorthand Textbook	1.00
	Gallagher & Marsh—Shorthand Practice Book	1.00

Commercial Law	Huffcut's Elements of Business Law	1.10
Bookkeeping	Williams' & Roger's Modern Illustrative Bookkeeping Text Book—Complete Course	1.50
	Introductory Vouchers	.45
	Introductory Forms	.50
	Introductory Blanks	.40
	Commission Outfit	.70
	Dry Goods Outfit	.80
	Grocery Outfit	.40
	Manufacturing Outfit	.95
	Banking Textbook	.55
	Banking Outfit	.80

OFFICIAL LIST OF HIGH SCHOOL TEXT BOOKS.

1908-1909.

MATHEMATICS.

Beman & Smith's New Plane and Solid Geometry	1.40
Wells' Algebra	1.35
Crockett's Trigonometry	1.40

CLASSICS.

First Year	Pearson's Essentials of Latin for Beginners	1.00
	Tuell & Fowler's first book in Latin	1.10
	Arrowsmith & Whicher's First Latin Readings	1.40
Second Year	Caesar, Allen & Greenough	1.10
	Second Year Latin, Greenough, D'Ooge & Daniell	1.40
	Latin Composition, D'Ooge—Part I	.55
Third Year	Cicero, Allen & Greenough	1.55
	Latin Composition, D'Ooge—Parts II and III	.70
Fourth Year	Virgil, Greenough & Kittredge	1.65
	Latin Composition, D'Ooge—Parts II and III	.70
	Allen & Greenough's New Lattin Grammar	1.35

SCIENCE.

First Year	Physical Geography, Davis'	1.40
Second Year	Elements of Biology, Hunter	1.40
Third Year	Elementary Chemistry, Bradburg, with Laboratory Experiments	1.40
Fourth Year	First Course in Physics, Millikan & Gale, or Coleman's Elements of Physics	1.40

HISTORY.

First Year	West's Ancient History	1.65
Second Year	Meyer's Medieval and Modern	1.65
Third Year	Walker's Essentials in English History	1.65
Fourth Year	Hart's Essentials in American History	1.65
	Ashley's American Government	1.10

GERMAN.

First Year	Spannhoofd's Lehrbuch der Deutschen Sprache	1.10
	Immensee	.30
	Gluck Auf	.70
Second Year	Joyne's Meissner Grammar	1.25
	Fritz auf Ferien	.30
	Die Journalisten	*
	Aus Danischer Zeit	.40
	Bernhardt's Composition	1.00
	Heyse's Arrabiata	
	William Tell	
	Leander's Traumereien	

*Where there are several editions from which to select, price is not given.

ENGLISH.

First Year	Gayley's Classic Myths	1.65
	State Language Lessons	.55
	Poetry of the People, Gayley and Flaherty	.55
	Principals and Progress of Poetry, Gayley and Young	1.25
	Composition, Rhetoric, Brooks & Hubbard	1.10
	Scott's Ivanhoe	.30
	Scott's, "The Lady of the Lake"	.30
Second Year	Introduction to American Literature, Pancoast	1.50
	Snowbound, Whittier	.15
	The Merchant of Venice, Shakespeare	.30
	Julius Caesar, Shakespeare	.30
	The American Scholar, Emerson	.15
	Democracy, Lowell	.15
	Lincoln, Lowell	.15
Third Year	Orations (small editions instead of Bradley's), The Commemoration Ode, Lowell	.15
	Warren Hastings, Macaulay	.15
	Silas Marner, Eliot	.30
	The Vicar of Wakefield, Goldsmith	.30
	De Coverly Papers, Addison	.35
	Burns, Carlyle	.25
Fourth Year	Macbeth, Shakespeare	.30

FRENCH.

Fraser & Squair	Abridged French Grammar, first and second year	1.25
J. Lazare	Lectures Faciles, first year	.35
Francois	Introductory French Composition	
Comfort	Exercises in French Composition, second year	.35
Sanderson	Through France and the French Syntax, third year	.75

TEXTS FOR FIRST, SECOND OR THIRD YEAR.

About	La Mere de la Marquise	.55
	La Fille du Chanoine	
Angier	Le Gendrede M. Poirier	.45
Cameron	Tales of France	1.10

Corneille	Le Cid	
Daudet	Trois Contes Choisis	.25
Daudet	Tartarin de Tarascon	
Daudet	Choix de Contes	
Daudet	La Belle Nivernaise	.35
Dike	Scientific Reader	1.1υ
Dumas	La Tulipe Noir	
Dumas	Le Chevalier de Maison Rouge	.45

FRENCH REALISTS.

Halevy	L'Abbe Constantin	.45
Healy	La Comedie Classique en France	
Hugo	Hernani	
Labiche	Le Voyage de M. Perrichon	.35
Labiche	La Cigale chez les Fourmis	.25
Labiche	La Poudre aux Yeux	
Laurie	Memories d'un Collegien	.55
Loti	Pecheur d' Islande	.35
Maupassant	Huit Contes Choisis	.35
Merimee	Colomba	.40
Moliere	L'Avare	.40
Moliere	Le Bourgeios Gentilhomme	.35
Moliere	Les Precieuses Ridicules et les Femmes Savantes	
La Brete	Mon Oncle et mon Cure	.55
Pailbron	Le Monde ou l'on s'ennuie	.35
Pailbron	L'Etincelle	.45
Luquiens	Popular Science	.70
George Sand	La Mare Au Diablo	
Sandeân	Mlle. de la Seigliere	
Mme. de Sevigne	Lettres Choisies	.55
Saintine	Picciola	.50
St. Pierre	Paul et Virginie	.55
Schultz	La Neuvaine de Colette	.50
Racine	Athalie	
de Vigny	La Canne de Jonc	.45
	"How to Learn the Sense of 3,000 French words in an Hour."	

LIBRARY AND SUPPLEMENTARY BOOKS AND SCHOOL TEXTS FOR USE OF INDIGENTS.

High Schools	4,654	
Primary and Grammar Schools	61,530	
Evening Schools	1,601	
Total in Schools		67,785
In storerooms		13,372
Total number of volumes		81,157

Valued at $29,000.

LIST OF SCHOOLS AND TEACHERS.

Name.	Grade of Class.	When Elected.	Grade of Certificate	Salary per Year.
Adams Cosmopolitan Grammar School—				
McFarland, Miss H. F.	Principal	Nov. 30, 1877	Grammar	$2,160.00
Phillips, Miss H.	V. P., 8th	May 13, 1873	Grammar	1,500.00
Fairchild, Miss M. E.	Eighth	July 1, 1874	High	1,128.00
Doughty, Mary A.	Seventh	[illegible] 31, 1891	Grammar	1,128.00
Coons, Sarah S.	Seventh	Sept. 1, 1888	Grammar	1,128.00
Dolan, Mrs. C. M.	Sixth	Aug. 16, 1898	Grammar	1,092.00
Hesselmeyer, Miss C. A.	Sixth	Feb 11, 1892	Grammar	1,092.00
[illegible], Miss A. M.	Fifth	Sept. 29, 1892	Grammar	1,152.00
Littlefield, Eleanor A.	Fourth	June 15, 1866	Grammar	1,092.00
Hurley, [illegible] E.	Third	Sept. 10, 1884	Grammar	1,128.00
[illegible], Miss M. J.	Second	April 2, 1881	Grammar	1,128.00
Hawkins, Miss G. G.	French & Ungraded	Oct. 10, 1901	High	1,188.00
Hertz, Miss R.	German	Feb. 7, 1886	Grammar	1,104.00
Agassiz Primary—				
Jones, Miss S. J.	Principal	April 1, 1878	Grammar	1,800.00
Harney, Miss A.	First	July 31, 1889	Grammar	1,128.00
Phillips, Miss M. E.	Fifth	Nov. 18, 1884	Grammar	1,092.00
Brown, Miss R. F.	Fifth	July 18, 1902	Grammar	1,092.00
Glidden, Miss C. A.	Fifth	July 9, 1877	Grammar	1,092.00
[illegible], Ada M.	Fifth	Oct. 9, 1883	Grammar	1,152.00
Clausen, Miss E. A.	Fourth	Jan. 31, 1894	Grammar	1,044.00
Bartlett, Miss O. S.	Fourth	Jan. 31, 1894	Grammar	1,044.00
[illegible], Miss O. C.	Fourth	Oct. 1, 1905	Grammar	882.00
Rixon, Eliza A.	Fourth	Feb. 28, 1898	Grammar	1,044.00
[illegible]ricks, Miss E. L.	Third	Feb. 16, 1891	Grammar	1,044.00
[illegible], Miss R. F.	Third	[illegible] 23, 1901	Grammar	963.00
Hanson, Miss L.	Third	July 20, 1903	Grammar	963.00
Wright, Miss H.	Second	Dec. 1, 1890	Primary	1,044.00
Onyon, Miss A. M.	Second	Jan. 6, 1902	Grammar	963.00
Liner, Miss M. G.	Second	July 27, 1898	Grammar	1 044.00
Maloney, Miss K. A.	First	Jan. 10, 1881	Grammar	1,128.00
Bley, Miss M. R.	First	Nov. 11, 1890	Grammar	1,128.00
Sankey, Miss M. F.	First	Sept. 15, 1888	Grammar	1,128.00
Bay View—				
McElroy, Miss L.	Principal	Dec. 6, 1891	Grammar	1,440.00
Flynn, Miss M. E.	Fourth	Nov. 20, 1877	Primary	1,044.00
Schroeder, Miss S.	Second	Aug. 26, 1907	High	828.00
Curtis, Miss C. M.	First	July 6, 1882	Grammar	1,128.00

Name	Grade	Date of Appointment	Certificate	Salary
Hopkins, [illegible]s. J. M.	Second	[illegible]y 15, 1905	[illegible]ar	1,044.00
[illegible]n, Mrs. M. F.	First	July 6, 1877	[illegible]ar	1,128.00
Bernal Grammar—				
Regan, Miss A. G.	Principal	Oct. 5, 1887	Grammar	2,[illegible]60.00
McGivern, Miss K. A.	V. P., 8th	Oct. 13, 1892	Grammar	1,500.00
Scott, Mrs. E.	Ungraded	July 15, 1897	[illegible]ar	1,128.00
Schendel, Miss A.	Seventh	Sept. 27, 1880	[illegible]ar	1,128.00
Douglass, M. Louise	Sixth	Aug. 30, 1905	Grammar	1,092.00
Neppert, Miss L. C.	Sixth	Dec. 29, 1892	Grammar	1,092.00
[illegible]de, Miss M.	Fifth	Feb. 9, 1892	Grammar	1,092.00
Maxwell, Miss E.	Fifth	April 26, 1907	High	903.00
Benjamin, Miss M. O.	Fourth	[illegible]g. 26, 1903	Grammar	963.00
[illegible]t, Miss M. A.	Fourth	[illegible] 11, 1904	Grammar	963.00
[illegible]n, Sarah S.	Fourth	July 2, 1889	Grammar	1 044.00
[illegible], [illegible] F.	Third	Sept. 23, 1878	Grammar	[illegible]44.00
McCarthy, [illegible]iss M. C.	Third	[illegible]t. 23, 1901	Grammar	924.00
Folsom, Miss M. L.	Third	Nov. 18, 1896	Grammar	1,044.00
Gilchrist, Miss C. H.	Seventh	Sept. 15, 1901	Grammar	1,002.00
Madden, Miss E. L.	Third	July 27, 1898	Grammar	1,002.00
Bergerot Primary—				
Gavigan, [illegible]iss A. E.	Principal	July 20, 1875	Grammar	1,560.00
Simms, Miss E.	[illegible]ifth	April 5, 1883	Grammar	1,128.00
Oliver, [illegible]iss M. D.	Seventh	June 26, 1905	Grammar	903.00
Fairweather, Helen B.	Fifth	May 16, 1882	Grammar	1,092.00
Evans, Isabel	Sixth	June 21, 1904	High	963.00
Bonnell, Mrs. G. D.	[illegible]ird	Oct. 29, 1894	[illegible]	1,044.00
[illegible]n, [illegible]s. J. D.	Fifth	Jan. 27, 1886	Grammar	1,092.00
Davis, Miss F.	Fourth	Sept. 8, 1897	Grammar	1,044.00
Cassidy, [illegible]iss V.	Fourth	[illegible]g. 10, 1897	[illegible]r	1,044.00
Bowers, [illegible]iss E. B.	Second	Sept. 2, 1904	Grammar	1,044.00
Hanlon, Miss L. R.	First	Oct. 1, 1884	Grammar	1,128.00
[illegible]wi, Miss M.	F[illegible]st	Jan. 26, 1898	[illegible]	1,128.00
McDonnell, Miss A. F.	F[illegible]st	Sept. 1, 1897	[illegible]ar	1,128.00
Bryant [illegible]n School—				
Kelly, Miss E. E.	Principal	Oct. 5, 1887	Grammar	1,560.00
Giffard, Mrs. E. C.	French	Feb. 25, 1876	Special French	1,500.00
[illegible]rd, Miss B. M.	Seventh	Jan. 11, 1877	Grammar	1,188.00
Rutherford, Miss H. M.	Fifth	Nov. 7, 1888	Grammar	1,092.00
Kulmuk, Miss L.	[illegible]h, Third	July 22, 1886	[illegible]	972.00
[illegible]r, Miss L. C.	Third	July 8, 1872	Grammar	1,044.00
Curry, Miss M. E.	Second	Feb. 5, 1878	Grammar	[illegible]44.00
Mooney, [illegible]iss F. C.	First	Aug. 28, 1883	Grammar	1,188.00
[illegible]g, Miss L.	First, German	Aug. 15, 1873	Grammar	1,188.00
Roberts, Miss M. E.	First	July 14, 1871	Grammar	1,128.00

LIST OF SCHOOLS AND TEACHERS—Continued.

Name.	Grade of Class.	When Elected.	Grade of Certificate	Salary per Year.
Bryant ([illegible]politan School—Continued				
Koch, Miss L. H.	Fourth, German	Oct. 31, 1894	Grammar	1,104.00
Unger, Miss A. N.	First, German	Aug. 20, 1878	[illegible]mar	1,188.00
Duffy, Miss H. M.	Fifth	July 1, 1903	[illegible]r	1,002.00
Buena [illegible]ta Primary—				
Catlin, Miss A. G.	Principal	[illegible]. 5, 1878	Grammar	1,800.00
[illegible]t, Miss Emily	Sixth	Mar. 30, 1905	Grammar	1,002.00
Hunt, Charlotte F.	Fifth	[illegible]. 28, 1892	Grammar	1,092.00
[illegible]de, Miss M.	Fifth	July 22, 1896	[illegible]mar	1,152.00
[illegible]is, [illegible] R. P.	Fourth	Mar. 14, 1886	Grammar	1,044.00
[illegible]r, Nellie T.	Third	Dec. 23, 1903	[illegible]r	963.00
Paxton, Miss K. R.	Fourth	July 22, 1896	Grammar	1,092.00
Hilderth, Mrs. O.	Second	Nov. 11, 1896	Grammar	1,044.00
McFadden, Emma	Second	Jan. 1, 1887	[illegible]mar	1,044.00
Frank, Miss J. E.	Third	Dec. 13, 1896	Grammar	1,044.00
[illegible]g, Miss M. R.	F[illegible]st	[illegible]v. 14, 1896	Grammar	1,128.00
Rollins, [illegible]iss M. A.	First	Oct. 8, 1879	[illegible]mar	1,128.00
S[illegible]k, Rose M.	First	Feb. 23, 1898	[illegible]r	1,128.00
Crocker, [illegible]iss B. H.	First	Aug. 5, 1888	[illegible]mar	1,128.00
Burnett [illegible]—				
Prior, Philip	Principal	June 14, 1865	High	2,160.00
McGuire, Miss B. A.	V. P., [illegible]hth	Oct. 16, 1883	Grammar	1,500.00
Stolz, Miss R. C.	Seventh	Dec. 28, 1892	Grammar	1,128.00
Hanford, [illegible] E. V.	S[illegible]th	Sept. 1, 1886	[illegible]mar	1,128.00
[illegible]y, Miss M.	Sixth	Sept. 30, 1884	[illegible]mar	1,092.00
Perkins, [illegible]iss A. F.	Fifth	[illegible]v. 1, 1890	[illegible]r	1,092.00
[illegible]d, M[illegible]s. M. T.	Fifth	Aug. 19, 1907	Grammar	1,092.00
Kortick, [illegible] A. M.	First	Sept. 24, 1877	Grammar	1,128.00
[illegible]n, Miss J. I.	F[illegible]t	Aug. 7, 1888	G[illegible]mar	1,128.00
[illegible]r, [illegible]n	First	[illegible]. 2, 1905	Grammar	1,128.00
McGorey, [illegible] S.	Second	Feb. 12, 1890	Grammar	[illegible]044.00
Sleeper, Miss [illegible]y	[illegible]d	Nov. 18, 1873	Grammar	1,044.00
Piper, Miss L. K.	Third	[illegible]ly 19, 1885	[illegible]mar	1,044.00
Bailie, Miss M.	Fourth	June 9, 1897	Grammar	1,044.00
Cl[illegible]mont Primary—				
Quinlan, Mrs. F. L.	Principal	Aug. 10, 1898	[illegible]r	1,440.00
Bronson, Mrs. F. P.	First	Sept. 1, 1884	[illegible]gh	1,128.00
Meaney, Miss M. E.	Second	Aug. 7, 1893	[illegible]ar	1,044.00
[illegible]n, Miss Rose	Fourth	Jan. 3, 1889	[illegible]mar	1,044.00
Mayers, Miss Eliz.	Third	Jan. 20, 1886	[illegible]r	1,044.00
Cooke, Edith A.	First	Mar. 1, 1903	[illegible]mar	1,128.00

Name	Grade	Date of Appointment	Certificate	Salary
Columbia Grammar—				
Burke, Mrs. L. K.	Principal	Jan. 23, 1857	High	2,160.00
[illegible]h, Miss K.	V. P., Eighth	[illegible] 12, 1898	Grammar	1,500.00
Dunn, Miss M. L.	Fifth	Aug. 13, 1892	Grammar	1,128.00
Krauss, Miss L. H.	Seventh	Sept. 4, 1890	Grammar	1,128.00
Derrick, Miss A. L.	Seventh	June 24, 1884	Grammar	1,128.00
[illegible], M. M.	Sixth	[illegible] 29, 1877	Grammar	1,092.00
[illegible], M. E. R.	Sixth	Nov. 5, 1897	Grammar	1,092.00
Radford, Miss L. A.	Sixth	Jan. 12, 1898	Grammar	1,092.00
Doherty, Miss M. E.	Fifth	Oct. 29, 1891	Grammar	1,092.00
[illegible]s, Miss Maud L.	Fifth	Nov. 1, 1904	Grammar	1,092.00
Love, [illegible] S.	[illegible]h	O[illegible] 19, 1875	Grammar	1, [illegible]44.00
[illegible]y, Miss M.	Third	July 14, 1895	Grammar	1, [illegible]44.00
[illegible]t, Miss V.	Third	Mar. 15, 1884	Grammar	1,044.00
[illegible]n, Miss A. M.	Fourth	Dec. 14, 1892	Grammar	1, [illegible]44.00
Dolan, Miss Mary J.	Second	Feb. 3, 1888	Grammar	1,044.00
[illegible]s, Miss K. G.	Second	Dec. 20, 1896	Grammar	1,044.00
McKee, Eva M.	First	Sept. 14, 1892	Grammar	1,128.00
Bol[illegible], J[illegible] M.	First	Sept. 18, 1875	Grammar	1,128.00
[illegible]l, Mary I.	First	[illegible] 11, 1873	Grammar	1,128.00
[illegible]n, M[illegible] [illegible]ie M.	First	[illegible] 13, 1871	Grammar	1,128.00
Blumenthal, Miss A. A.	Fifth	Jan. 13, 1892	Grammar	1,092.00
[illegible]er Primary—				
[illegible]ll, Miss A. M.	[illegible]pal	Sept. 16, 1884	Grammar	[illegible]0.00
[illegible]r, Emma H.	[illegible]d	Jan. 6, 19[illegible]8	Grammar	828.00
Parker, Miss M. G.	First	Nov. 26, 1907	Grammar	1 044.00
Murray, Miss M. G.	Second	Nov. 11, 1907	Grammar	828.00
Hackett, Mrs. E. S.	First	Oct. 1873	Grammar	1,128.00
Paterson, Miss M.	First	Aug. 14, 1905	Grammar	1,128.00
[illegible]n, Miss L.	First	Aug. 1905	Grammar	1,128.00
[illegible]n, Miss C. Z.	First	Sept. 1, 1905	Grammar	1,128.00
[illegible]re, Eliz. B.	First	Sept. 30, 1901	Grammar	1,128.00
Vogelsang, Dorothy	First	Oct. 14, 1902	Grammar	1,128.00
[illegible]er [illegible]—				
[illegible]k, Mr. C. W.	Principal	July 10, 1893	High	2,160.00
Murphy, [illegible]te	Seventh	Dec. 20, 1890	Grammar	1,128.00
[illegible]a, Miss M. T.	V. P., Eighth	July 10, 1876	Grammar	1,500.00
[illegible], Miss S. A.	Fifth	Aug. 23, 1880	Grammar	1,128.00
[illegible]man, Miss [illegible]lra	Fifth	April 3, 1883	Grammar	1,128.00
Smith, Miss E. E.	Fifth	Jan. 7, 1895	Grammar	1,188.00
Harby, Miss R.	Fifth	May 5, 1879	Grammar	1,128.00
Durkin, Miss J. L. F.	Fifth	Aug. 1, 1882	Grammar	1,128.00
Barrett, Miss Mary A.	Seventh	Sept. 2, 1896	Grammar	1,128.00
[illegible]v, Miss M. M.	Sixth	Nov. 29, 1896	Grammar	1,128.00
[illegible]st[illegible]ng, Miss N.	[illegible]h	Dec. 26, 1877	Grammar	1,128.00

LIST OF SCHOOLS AND TEACHERS—Continued.

Name.	Grade of Class.	When Elected.	Grade of Certificate	Salary per Year.
Crocker [illegible]—Continued.				
[illegible]ke, Miss [illegible] T.	Seventh	April 3, 1892	[illegible]	1,128.00
[illegible], Jennie L.	Seventh	Nov. 4, 1886	Grammar	1,128.00
Saalburg, [illegible] J. E.	Sixth	[illegible] 5, 1889	Grammar	1,092.00
Carpenter, Miss E.	Sixth	July 6, 1905	Grammar	1,047.00
Coleman, Frances E.	Sixth	Dec. 14, 1877	[illegible]	1,092.00
Roberts, Miss B. E.	Sixth	Jan. 2, 1902	Grammar	1,002.00
[illegible], Miss Helen	Sixth	April 2, 1886	[illegible]	1,092.00
Maccuaig, Miss B.	Sixth	June 23, 1904	[illegible]	1,092.00
[illegible], [illegible] Mary T.	[illegible]	Dec. 10, 1890	Grammar	1,092.00
English, Virginia L.	Ungraded	Aug. 11, 1897	Grammar	1,128.00
Denman Grammar—				
Mann, Azro L.	Principal	Dec. 29, 1865	High	2,160.00
Smith, [illegible]	Eighth	Mar. 10, 1863	High	1,128.00
Gallagher, Margaret J.	Seventh	Aug. 30, 1870	Grammar	1,128.00
Childs, Miss K. B.	Seventh	July 5, 1866	[illegible]	1,128.00
[illegible], [illegible] R. A.	Sixth	Jan. 2, 1876	Grammar	1,092.00
D'Arcy, Miss A. M.	Fifth	July [illegible], 1870	[illegible]	1,092.00
Hazleton, Miss R. H.	Ungraded	April 6, 1873	[illegible]	1,128.00
Douglass Primary—				
[illegible], Miss W. L.	Principal	Aug. 19, 1884	[illegible]	1,560.00
Hetzer, Miss M.	Fourth	Sept. 12, 1894	[illegible]	1,044.00
Bishop, Louise M.	Fourth	Sept. 8, 1897	[illegible]	1,044.00
Curley, Miss A. G.	Third	April 1, 1903	Grammar	1,014.00
Houghton, Miss E.	First	Nov. 11, 1896	Grammar	1,104.00
Doherty, Miss M. A.	Second	June 9, 1897	Grammar	1,044.00
Reichling, Miss W. L.	Second	Jan. 8, 1902	[illegible]	1,044.00
[illegible], Miss E.	[illegible]	Aug. 20, 1907	Grammar	828.00
Bush, Miss E. S.	First	Oct. 1, 1905	Grammar	1,092.00
Parks, Miss M. R.	First	Sept. 15, 1891	Grammar	1,128.00
Grafe, Miss L.	First	July 15, 1902	Grammar	1,128.00
[illegible], Miss J.	First	Aug. 26, 1905	Grammar	1,128.00
Dudley [illegible] Primary—				
[illegible], Miss S. H.	Principal	July 20, 1869	High	1,800.00
Newman, Bertha K.	Third	Feb. 1, 1904	Grammar	1,044.00
Sexton, Miss J. L.	Fifth	Sept. 12, 1894	[illegible]	1,092.00
Carew, Miss M. R.	Fifth	Sept. 20, [illegible]	Grammar	1,092.00
Hare, [illegible] F.	Fifth	Oct. 21, 1873	[illegible]	1,092.00
Simpson, Miss M. L.	Fourth	Sept. 15, 1885	Grammar	1,104.00
Koch, Miss L.	Fourth	Feb. 11, 1903	Grammar	963.00

McBoyle, Miss A. B.	Fourth	Sept. 30, 1892	Grammar	1,044.00
Gambitz, Miss L.	Third	Nov. 11, 1896	Grammar	1,044.00
Cassinelli, Miss C. M.	Third	July 23, 1902	Grammar	1,044.00
Dwyer, Miss M. C.	Second	Sept. 1, 1897	Grammar	1,044.00
Gambitz, Miss N. R.	Second	Jan. 12, 1898	Primary	1,044.00
Fritz, Miss L. M.	Second	July 1, 1903	Grammar	924.0
[illegible]n, Miss J. A.	First	Nov. 1, 1883	Grammar	1,128.00
McGeough, Miss R.	First	Jan. 31, 1884	Grammar	1,128.00
Haslam, Mrs. J. P.	Ungraded	June 14, 1903	Grammar	1,128.00
[illegible]on Primary—				
Saunders, Miss J.	Principal	April 23, 1887	Grammar	1,560.0
Hucks, Miss A. E.	Third	Nov. 3, 1864	Grammar	1,044.00
Kelly, Miss M. C.	Fifth	Dec. 8, 1891	Grammar	1,092.00
Barry, Miss M. E.	Fifth	April 1, 1884	Grammar	1,092.00
Power, Miss A. R.	Fourth	Feb. 24, 1898	Grammar	1,044.00
Booth, Miss L.	Fourth	Feb. 1, 1889	Grammar	1,044.00
Wilson, Miss E. N.	Third	July 18, 1902	Grammar	924.00
Harrigan, Miss A. M.	Second	Sept. 19, 1891	Grammar	1,044.00
Robinett, Miss M. M.	First	Feb. 5, 1875	Grammar	1,128.00
McDermott, Miss C. M.	Second	Nov. 30, 1892	Grammar	1,044.00
Steele, Miss M. A.	First	Sept. 14, 1872	Grammar	1,128.00
Emerson Primary—				
Ephriam, Miss J.	Fifth	July 23, 1876	Grammar	1,092.00
Dennis, Miss E.	First	Dec. 5, 1888	Grammar	1,128.00
McLaughlin, Miss A. M.	Second	July 6, 1877	Grammar	1,128.00
Tiling, Miss A.	Second	Sept. 8, 1897	Grammar	1,044.00
Doran, Marie E.	Second	Sept. 4, 1871	Grammar	1,128.00
Kurlandzik, Miss R.	Second	Jan. 14, 1903	High	963.00
Pettigrew, Miss E. R.	Third	Nov. 26, 1888	Primary	989.00
Wolf, Miss E. R.	Third	Feb. 8, 1903	Grammar	960.00
Casamayou, Miss A. G.	Third	Sept. 10, 1897	Grammar	1,044.00
Bailey, Miss C. B.	Fourth	Sept. 13, 1894	Grammar	1,044.00
[illegible]n, Miss M. F.	Fourth	May 13, 1896	Grammar	1,044.00
Gambitz, Miss L. B.	Fourth	May 27, 1897	Grammar	1,044.00
[illegible]n, Miss M. A.	Fifth	Mar. 12, 1890	Grammar	1,092.00
Galloway, Miss M. S.	First	Nov. 28, 1881	Grammar	1,128.00
O'Brien, Miss L.	First	Mar. 12, 1890	Grammar	1,128.00
[illegible]r, Miss R.	First	Nov. 22, 1884	Grammar	1,128.00
Langdon, Miss M. M.	Ungraded	May 28, 1904	Grammar	1,128.00
Spafford, Miss D. B.	Third	Jan. 8, 1906	Grammar	1,002.00
Spencer, Mrs. T. F.	Principal	July 17, 1901	Grammar	1,800.00
Everett [illegible]—				
Sturges, Selden	Principal	July 6, 1875	Grammar	2,160.00
Leggett, Mr. W. A.	V. P., Eighth	Oct. 22, 1888	High	1,500.00
Lindberg, Emily U.	Eighth	Sept. 6, 1874	Grammar	1,236.00

LIST OF SCHOOLS AND TEACHERS—Continued.

Name.	Grade of Class.	When Elected.	Grade of Certificate	Salary per Year.
Everett Grammar—Continued.				
Theisen, Miss A. J.	Seventh	Dec. 20, 1892	Grammar	1,128.00
Devine, Miss M. E.	Sixth	July 14, 1895	Grammar	1,092.00
Hogan, Helen M.	Sixth	Sept. 30, 1900	Grammar	1,002.00
Johnson, Marie J.	Fifth	Feb. 1, 1876	Grammar	1,092.00
Grimm, Miss A. L.	Fifth	Feb. 14, 1881	Grammar	1,092.00
Casassa, Miss R. I.	Fifth	July 27, 1898	Grammar	1,044.00
Sullivan, Julia F.	Fifth	Aug. 1, 1897	Grammar	1,092.00
Perl, Ida May	Fourth	Nov. 11, 1896	Grammar	1,044.00
[illegible], Miss T. L.	Fourth	Jan. 8, 1906	Grammar	882.00
McKinnie, Eliza	Third	July 28, 1902	Grammar	963.00
Fenton, Miss E. R.	Third	July 27, 1898	Grammar	1,044.00
Spafford, Helen E.	Second	Jan. 6, 1902	Grammar	1,044.00
Gallagher, Miss R. C.	Second	July 29, 1889	Grammar	1,044.00
[illegible], Miss N. A.	Second	July 30, 1890	Grammar	1,044.00
Huntley, Miss A. M.	First	Oct. 21, 1873	Grammar	1,128.00
Gracier, Miss A. J.	First	July 6, 1877	Grammar	1,128.00
[illegible], Miss A. W.	Sixth	Jan. 3, 1893	Grammar	1,092.00
[illegible], Miss K. J.	First	April 3, 1887	Grammar	1,128.00
Fairmount Grammar—				
Johnston, Miss C. M.	Principal	Oct. 28, 1873	Grammar	2,160.00
Huskey, Mr. F. G.	V. P., Eighth	July 27, 1897	Grammar	1,500.00
[illegible], Miss E. E.	Seventh	Dec. 1, 1882	Grammar	1,128.00
Berard, Miss E. L.	Sixth	Sept. 30, 1901	Grammar	1,024.00
[illegible], Miss M. A.	Sixth	Aug. 11, 1897	Grammar	1,092.00
Fallon, Miss D. A.	Sixth	April 21, 1891	Grammar	1,092.00
Hortop, Miss C. E.	Fifth	Aug. 26, 1903	Grammar	1,002.00
Millhone, Belle	Fourth	July 27, 1898	Grammar	1,092.00
Harte, Mrs. S.	Fifth	Mar. 4, 1903	Grammar	963.00
[illegible], Miss K. L.	Third	Feb. 23, 1898	Grammar	1,044.00
Chandler, Miss M. G.	Third	Mar. 1, 1904	Grammar	1,044.00
Provost, Miss T. E.	Second	April 14, 1875	Grammar	1,044.00
O'Brien, Miss M. F.	Second	Nov. 19, 1905	Grammar	882.00
Foley, Miss Mary W.	First	Jan. 27, 1905	Grammar	1,128.00
Barry, Miss A. P.	First	Sept. 21, 1886	Grammar	1,128.00
Carey, Miss A. A.	First	Sept. 15, 1882	Grammar	1,128.00
Boyle, Edith M.	Fourth	[illegible] 15, 1896	Grammar	963.00
Frank J. McCoppin—				
Jenkins, Miss S. B.	Principal	Oct. 21, 1877	Grammar	1,560.00
Barber, Miss E. J.	Fifth	Mar. 1, 1884	Grammar	1,092.00

Dower, Miss J. E.	Fifth	Feb. 12, 1906	Grammar	1,092.00
[illegible]y, Miss S. L.	Fourth	Mar. 6, 1905	[illegible]	963.00
Jacobs, Miss H. H.	Fourth	Sept. 1, 1905	High	963.00
O'Neil, Miss M. E.	[illegible]	Sept. 14, 1898	Grammar	924.00
Hart, Miss E. I.	Second	July 18, 1902	High	963.00
Coggin, Miss E. M.	[illegible]	Nov. 28, 1881	Primary	1,044.00
Wright, [illegible] M. S.	First	July 1, 1871	[illegible]	1,128.00
Wade, Miss L. M.	First	July 30, 1886	[illegible]	1,128.00
Fay, Miss M. A.	First	Mar. 11, 1873	[illegible]	1,128.00
Franklin Grammar—				
Wood, Mrs. N. A.	Principal	Nov. 13, 1866	High	2,160.00
[illegible], [illegible] J. C.	V. P.	Sept. 11, 1895	[illegible]	1,500.00
Harris, Miss R. S.	Seventh	Mar. 30, 1905	[illegible]	1,128.00
[illegible]d, Miss E. B.	Fifth	July 21, 1902	High	948.00
McCullough, Miss M. J.	Fourth	Aug. 22, 1907	Grammar	828.00
Quinn, [illegible] [illegible]y	Sixth	Nov. 16, 1905	[illegible]	1,092.00
[illegible]as, Etta O.	[illegible]	Jan. 26, 1906	Grammar	1,092.00
Carroll, [illegible] A. T.	Third	June 25, 1905	[illegible]	963.00
Cadwalder, [illegible] E.	Second	June 21, 1895	[illegible]	[illegible]44.00
Roper, Miss B.	First	Nov. 23, 1869	[illegible]	1,128.00
Dunn, Miss C. E.	First	Oct. 22, 1884	Grammar	1,128.00
Fremont Grammar—				
Goldsmith, Miss R.	Principal	Mar. 1, 1873	Grammar	2,160.00
Ostrom, Mrs. I. D.	V. P., Eighth	[illegible]g. 10, 1898	Grammar	1,500.00
McKown, Mrs. M. E.	Seventh	April 14, 1869	High	1,128.00
Hanley, [illegible] B.	Ungraded	Sept. 30, 1890	Grammar	1,128.00
Rosenfeld, Miss F.	First	Aug. 1, 1888	Grammar	1,128.00
[illegible]t, Miss S. F.	First	Jan. 31, 1889	Grammar	1,128.00
[illegible]is, Mrs. R.	[illegible]	Sept. 27, 1880	Primary	1,044.00
Moran, Miss D. F.	Second	Dec. 1, 1898	Grammar	1,002.00
MacNichol, Mrs. J. E.	Second	Oct. 27, 1897	[illegible]	1,128.00
Lewis, Rose F.	Third	July 28, 1898	Grammar	1,002.00
Goldsmith, Miss B.	Fourth	Feb. 15, 1876	Grammar	1,092.00
Shorb, Mrs. M. E.	Fourth	Oct. 21, 1901	Grammar	1,023.00
Langstadter, Pauline	Fifth	[illegible]g. 13, 1872	Grammar	1,092.00
O'Connell, Miss M. C.	Fifth	July 18, 1902	Grammar	948.00
Classen, [illegible] L. M.	Sixth	April 9, 1875	[illegible]	1,128.00
Grant, Mrs. K. D.	Seventh	June 3, 1897	[illegible]	1,128.00
[illegible]ld Primary—				
Scherer, Miss M. A.	Principal	[illegible]g. 7, 1879	[illegible]	1,800.00
Bradley, [illegible] B.	Second	Oct. 22, 1882	Grammar	1,128.00
Woodland, Mrs. I. C.	First	Dec. 1, 1882	Grammar	1,128.00
McAllister, Mrs. F. R.	First	July 27, 1898	Grammar	1,128.00
Powers, Mrs. M. B.	First	Sept. 2, 1885	[illegible]	1,128.00

LIST OF SCHOOLS AND TEACHERS—Continued.

Name.	Grade of Class.	When Elected.	Grade of Certificate	Salary per Year.
Garfield Primary—Continued.				
Wehrli, Miss E.	First	Jan. 29, 1905	Grammar	1,128.00
[illegible], Miss H. E.	First	Dec. 14, 1892	Grammar	1,128.00
Cashman, Miss M. E.	Third	Nov. 19, 1905	Grammar	882.00
Moser, Mary E.	Third	Feb. 1, 1905	[illegible]	1,044.00
[illegible], Miss M. G.	Third	Jan. 6, 1902	Grammar	963.00
Irwin, Miss M. A.	Fourth	Nov. 4, 1891	Primary	1,044.00
Hess, [illegible]sa	Fifth	Oct. 17, 1904	High	948.00
Rea, Miss B.	Second	Jan. 6, 1908	Grammar	828.00
McWilliams, Miss B.	Second	Jan. 16, 1908	Grammar	882.00
[illegible], Miss N. V.	Second	Mar. 20, 1907	Grammar	[illegible]4.00
[illegible], Miss E. E.	Second	Aug. 27, 1907	High	848.00
Glen Park School—				
Pechin, Mrs. C. R.	Principal	Sept. 12, 1871	Grammar	2,160.00
Donnelly, Miss M. L.	V. P., Eighth	July 12, 1875	Grammar	1,500.00
Doran, Julia A.	Sixth	Jan. 7, 1869	Grammar	1,128.00
[illegible], Miss A.	First	July 22, 1882	Grammar	1,128.00
Dworzazek, Miss B. E.	Fourth	Jan. 3, 1882	[illegible]	1,044.00
[illegible], Miss I. T.	Fifth	[illegible] 21, 1873	Grammar	1,128.00
Crowley, Miss Mary E.	Third	Mar. 5, 1878	Grammar	1,092.00
McGuire, Miss Mary	Second	April 7, 1882	Grammar	1,044.00
Barron, Miss C. M.	Second	[illegible] 24, 1888	[illegible]	1,044.00
[illegible], M. J. H.	First	Mar. 20, 1877	Grammar	1,128.00
Golden Gate Primary—				
[illegible], Miss P.	Principal	July 6, 1870	High & [illegible]	1,440.00
[illegible], Mary L.	Fifth	Jan. 20, 1876	Grammar	1,092.00
[illegible], Mary A.	Fourth	Aug. 15, 1877	Grammar	1,044.00
Bonnelli, Mrs. E. M.	Fourth	Feb. 5, 1877	Grammar	1,044.00
Ryan, Miss E. T.	Third	Jan. 4, 1875	Primary	1,044.00
Kaplan, Miss M. E.	Second	[illegible] 8, 1884	Grammar	1,044.00
[illegible], [illegible]et G.	Second	April 4, 1886	Grammar	1,044.00
Hare, Mrs. K. M.	First	Oct. 2, 1873	Grammar	1,128.00
[illegible], Miss A. M.	First	Mar. 1, 1879	Grammar	1,128.00
[illegible]nt Primary—				
Shaw, Miss I. E.	Principal	May 30, 1882	Grammar	1,440.00
Kincaid, Miss B. C.	Seventh	Nov. 11, 1896	Grammar	1,128.00
Ryder, Miss V.	Sixth	Aug. 9, 1905	Grammar	903.00
Hart, Miss E. D.	Fifth	July 20, 1903	[illegible]	948.00
Cookson, Miss A. B.	Fifth	Jan. 12, 1898	Grammar	1,092.00
Sullivan, Emma G.	Fourth	Jan. 12, 1893	Grammar	1,044.00

Name	Grade	Date	Certificate	Salary
Berg, Miss F. C.	Second	April 14, 19[illegible]	Grammar	[illegible]
Deal, Miss V. V.	Second	Dec. 30, 1892	[illegible]	1,128.00
Campbell, [illegible]ne B.	First	Nov. 12, [illegible]87[illegible]	[illegible]	1,128.00
[illegible]n Primary—				
Butler, Mrs. E.	Principal	Aug. 4, 1882	[illegible]	1,440.00
Frontin, Miss E. A.	Fifth	Oct. 1, 1877	[illegible]	1,152.00
Sprague, Miss A. F.	Fourth	Sept. 14, 1867	[illegible]	1,128.00
[illegible]n, Miss M.	Second	Feb. 16, 1875	[illegible]	1,128.00
[illegible]rd, Miss K.	First	July 12, 1873	[illegible]	1,128.00
Maccord, Miss L.	Second and Third	Feb. 5, [illegible]87[illegible]	Primary	1,044.00
Drake, M[illegible]. A. K.	Second	Aug. 16, 1903	[illegible]	963.00
Haight Primary—				
Haswell, Miss M. A.	Principal	June 25, 1867	High	1,800.00
[illegible]d, Stella M.	Fourth	Feb. 16, 1906	High	828.00
Keegan, Miss A. R.	[illegible]	Feb. 21, 1905	[illegible]	924.00
Sweeney, Miss C. L.	[illegible]fth	Jan. 6, 1876	[illegible]mar	1,092.00
Rodgers, Miss C. E.	Fifth	Oct. 1, 1901	[illegible]	1,092.00
Gilmore, Miss E. M.	Fourth	Nov. 24, [illegible]89[illegible]	[illegible]	1,044.00
Donovan, Miss E.	[illegible]th	July 14, [illegible]86[illegible]	Primary	1,044.00
Hartrick, Miss L. A.	Second	Aug. 22, [illegible]90[illegible]	Grammar	828.00
[illegible]n, Mrs. A. H.	Third	July 3, 1873	[illegible]	[illegible]44.00
Neppert, Miss F. E.	Third	July 25, 1904	[illegible]	963.00
[illegible]n, M[illegible]. T.	[illegible]	[illegible] 26, [illegible]88[illegible]	Primary	[illegible]44.00
[illegible]t, Miss J.	Second	July 20, 9[illegible]	[illegible]	1,002.00
Haussler, Miss M. F.	First	Dec. 23, 1885	Grammar	1,128.00
Miller, Miss S. E.	First	Nov. 5, [illegible]86[illegible]	High	1,128.00
[illegible]h, Miss L. M.	First	Jan. 6, 1902	[illegible]	1,188.00
[illegible]n Grammar—				
Kellogg, Mr. A. E.	Principal	Sept. 1, 1886	High	2,160.00
Menley, Miss I. M.	Sixth	Aug. 12, 1903	[illegible]	1,092.00
[illegible]t, Miss E. E.	Seventh	July 18, 9[illegible]	[illegible]	1,128.00
Brown, Isabelle R.	[illegible]th	Aug. 5, 1885	[illegible]	1,128.00
Page, Catherine H.	[illegible]th	Sept. 1, 1886	[illegible]	1,128.00
Morton, Miss E. J.	[illegible]th, Vice Prin.	July 23, 1875	[illegible]	1,500.00
[illegible]s, Miss I. R.	[illegible]th	July 6, 1873	[illegible]	1,128.00
[illegible]h, Miss I. B.	Seventh	Jan. 31, [illegible]88[illegible]	[illegible]	1,128.00
Shaw, Mrs. L. A.	Seventh	Aug. 14, [illegible]89[illegible]	[illegible]	1,128.00
McDonnell, Miss L. A.	Seventh	Aug. 1, 1884	High	1,128.00
[illegible]d, M[illegible]y T.	Sixth	Dec. 7, 1905	[illegible]	1,092.00
[illegible]n, Miss A. C.	Seventh	Sept. 30, 9[illegible]	[illegible]	1,128.00
[illegible]n, Miss M[illegible]ry	Sixth	Sept. 16, 1901	[illegible]	1,092.00
Martin, Miss I. C.	Sixth	July 25, 9[illegible]	High	948.00
Boniface, Sara M.	Fifth	Sept. 14, [illegible]89[illegible]	High	1,092.00
Silverberg, Miss A.	Ungraded	[illegible] 2, 1903	High	[illegible],12[illegible].00

LIST OF SCHOOLS AND TEACHERS—Continued.

Name.	Grade of Class.	When [illegible]d.	Grade of [illegible]cate	Salary per Year.
[illegible] [illegible]ar—				
Carrol, Irene G. (nw Schwartz)	Third	Feb. 17, 1905	Grammar	960.00
[illegible]h, Miss F. C.	Second	Sept. 22, 1905	Grammar	882.00
O'Neil, Miss Agnes	Second	Oct. 14, 1905	Grammar	1,002.00
Gallagher, Miss N. G.	Principal	May 14, 1896	Grammar	2,160.00
Stuart, Mrs. M.	[illegible]th	April 10, 1885	[illegible]ar	1,500.00
Martini, [illegible]ry G.	Seventh	Nov. 24, 1889	Grammar	1,188.00
[illegible], Miss L. A.	Sixth	Sept. 30, 1901	Grammar	1,092.00
Scanlan, Miss Renee	Sixth	Aug. 14, 1905	Grammar	903.00
Burke, Miss M. C.	Fifth	Jan. 4, 1905	[illegible]ar	1,092.00
Pfeiffer, Miss L. M.	Fifth	Mar. 30, 1905	High	948.00
[illegible]o, Miss N. C.	[illegible]rd	Aug. 14, 1905	High	882.00
Furbush, Miss M. W.	Fourth	April 5, 1907	[illegible]ar	843.00
Harrison Primary—				
Derham, Miss T. E.	Principal	Jan. 3, 1888	[illegible]ar	[illegible]00
McCrosson, [illegible]ss A. F.	First	Mar. 28, 1907	[illegible]ar	828.00
Sullivan, Miss G. A.	First	June 25, 1904	High	1,128.00
Hawthorne Primary—				
Mann, Mrs. S. J.	Principal	Sept. 1, 1874	High	1,560.00
Lobenstein, Miss E.	[illegible]th	Jan. 28, 1905	Grammar	1,092.00
Barrington, Miss F. E.	Fifth	July 27, 1898	[illegible]ar	1,092.00
[illegible]h, Miss N. G.	Fourth	Aug. 1, 1888	[illegible]ar	1,044.00
[illegible]n, Miss M. A.	[illegible]th	Feb. 5, 1892	[illegible]ar	[illegible]44.00
Barrett, Alice L.	Third	Aug. 14, 1905	Grammar	882.00
Plagemann, Miss D. E.	Second	Sept. 1, 1905	High	[illegible]82.00
Simon, Miss L. F.	Se onde	Sept. 1, 1897	Grammar	1,044.00
Barrett, Miss N.	First	Jan. 12, 1898	[illegible]ar	1,128.00
[illegible]e, Miss M. L.	First	Sept. 8, 1897	[illegible]ar	1,128.00
Keith, Miss E. D.	Third	Jan. 29, 1891	Grammar	1,092.00
Hearst [illegible]—				
Sullivan, Miss N. F.	Principal	Aug. 13, 1876	[illegible]	2,160.00
Franklin, Miss F. M.	V. P., Eighth	[illegible]. 28, 1880	Grammar	1,500.00
[illegible]s, Miss R. H.	Third	July 23, 1905	Grammar	882.00
[illegible]tz, [illegible]se B.	[illegible]th	Oct. 15, 1885	[illegible]r	1,188.00
B[illegible]y, Miss L. F.	Seventh	Jan. 5, 1885	Grammar	1,128.00
Levison, Miss E.	Seventh	Aug. 17, 1891	[illegible]ar	1,128.00
Torpey, [illegible]s M. C.	[illegible]th	Sept. 8, 1897	[illegible]ar	1,092.00
[illegible]n, [illegible]ss A. W.	Sixth	Jan. 2, 1897	[illegible]r	1,092.00
[illegible]n, Miss M.	Sixth	[illegible]. 2, 1897	[illegible]r	1,092.00
Levey, Mrs. J. B.	Sixth	[illegible] 8, 1896	[illegible]r	1,092.00

Name	Grade	Date		Certificate	Salary
Humphrey, Miss K. A.	Fifth	May 1,	1896	Grammar	1,092.00
Van Den Bergh, Miss F.	Fifth	Aug. 9,	1880	Grammar	1,092.00
[illegible]n, Miss R.	Fifth	Jan. 12,	1898	[illegible]ar	1,092.00
Fairweather, Miss E.	Fifth	May 15,	189 0	Grammar	1,092.00
[illegible]t, Miss M. R.	Fourth	Jan. 2,	1901	Grammar	963.00
[illegible]y, Miss M. T.	Fourth	Aug. 21,	1905	Gr[illegible]mar	1,002.00
Peake, Mrs. B. M.	Third	July 1,	1883	Grammar	1,044.00
Martin, Miss A.	Fourth	Sept. 1,	1878	Grammar	1,044. 0
Levy, Miss A. M.	Second	Jan. 5,	1891	Grammar	1,044.00
Downing, Miss I. L.	First	Oct. 14,	1901	Grammar	1,128.00
Haas, Miss S.	Second	May 14,	1890	Grammar	1,044.00
Bigley, Jane A.	First	Nov. 6,	1877	Primary	1,128.00
[illegible]y, Miss E. A.	First	Oct. 29,	1877	Grammar	1,128.00
Grace, Miss H. M.	Ungraded	Dec. 29,	1896	High	1,128.00
[illegible]le, Miss L. C.	First	Aug. 1,	1882	[illegible]ar	1,128.00
Hynes, Miss F. S.	First	May 1,	1896	[illegible]ar	1,128.00
Henry Durant Primary—					
Washburn, Mrs. G.	Principal	Oct. 16,	1864	Grammar	1,560.00
Camblein, Mrs. M. F.	Fifth	Jan. 3,	1877	Grammar	1,092.00
Thompson, Miss R. A.	Fourth	Jan. 3,	1877	[illegible]ar	1,092.00
[illegible]enhood, Miss F.	Third	April 29,	1886	Grammar	1,044.00
[illegible]as, Miss L. F.	Fourth	Nov. 1,	1877	[illegible]ar	1,044.00
[illegible]e, Miss J. R.	Third	July 15,	1895	Gr[illegible]mar	1,044.00
Gillen, Miss E. J.	Third	Jan. 12,	1898	Grammar	1,044.00
Loud, Miss E. S.	Second	Nov. 2,	1879	Grammar	1,044.00
[illegible]as, Miss C.	Second	July 29,	1891	Grammar	1,044.00
Hill, Miss M. E.	First	April 15,	1885	Grammar	1,128.00
Heney, Miss F. S.	First	Jan. 2,	1877	[illegible]ar	1,128.00
Boukofsky, Miss R.	First	Sept. 1,	1886	[illegible]ar	1,128.00
[illegible]n, Miss S. R.	First	Nov. 5,	1875	[illegible]ar	1,128.00
Holly Park Primary—					
Sullivan, Miss N. M.	Principal	Dec. 15,	1877	[illegible]ar	1,560.00
Wool, Miss H. L.	Second	Aug. 15,	1867	Grammar	1,044. 0
Wilson, Miss May	[illegible]d	Feb. 2,	1904	[illegible]ar	1,044. 0
Foley, Eliz. M.	Second	Nov. 12,	1896	Grammar	1,044.00
[illegible]n, Miss G. J.	First	Jan. 1,	1893	[illegible]ar	1,128.00
[illegible]n, Mrs. S. F.	First	April 1,	1879	[illegible]ar	1,128.00
DeWitt, Miss Zora	Second	Jan. 6,	1908	[illegible]ar	1,044. 0
Nagle, Miss M. M.	Second	Jan. 17,	1905	High	882.00
O'Reilly, Miss J. F.	First	June 9,	1897	Grammar	1,128.00
Dworzazek, Miss P. A.	First	Jan. 2,	1897	Grammar	1,128.00
[illegible]as, Clara A.	First	Jan. 2,	1871	Grammar	1,128.00
Horace Mann Grammar—					
Faulkner, Mr. R. D.	Principal	[illegible] 22,	1888	High	2,160.00
O'Loughlen, Miss N.	V. P., Eighth	June 12,	1869	[illegible] & High	1,500.00

LIST OF SCHOOLS AND TEACHERS—Continued.

Name.	Grade of Class.	When Elected.	Grade of Certificate	Salary per Year.
Horace Mann Grammar—Continued.				
Elliott, Mary	Seventh	Mar. 18, 1879	Grammar	1,128.00
Hatch, Mrs. L. R.	Seventh	Jan. 2, 1881	Grammar	1,128.00
Carson, Miss E.	Seventh	Jan. 29, 1884	Grammar	1,128.00
McNicoll, Miss B.	Seventh	Aug. 6, 1872	Grammar	1,128.00
Thompson, Mrs. M. A.	Seventh	July 5, 1882	Grammar	1,128.00
Clary, Agnese E.	Sixth	Mar. 11, 1906	Grammar	1,092.00
Diggs, Miss A. B.	Sixth	July 21, 1903	Grammar	1,092.00
[illegible], Miss J. M.	Sixth	Jan. 2, 1895	Grammar	1,152.00
Dowd, Mary E.	Sixth	July 29, 1888	Grammar	1,092.00
Moore, Margaret M.	Sixth	April 5, 1883	Grammar	1,092.00
O'Brien, Miss Kate	Sixth	Sept. 14, 1878	Grammar	1,092.00
Stockton, Miss F.	Sixth	July 18, 1902	Grammar	1,092.00
[illegible], Mrs. M. C.	Sixth	Nov. 19, 1871	Grammar	1,092.00
Toland, Miss M.	Seventh	Feb. 19, 1906	Grammar	1,128.00
Iredale, Mrs. E. B.	Eighth	Dec. 1, 1876	Grammar	1,128.00
[illegible], Eliza J.	Eighth	Mar. 19, 1884	Grammar	1,128.00
Traynor, Miss M. E.	Eighth	Jan 3, 1876	Grammar	1,128.00
Casey, Miss M. E.	Eighth	April 6, 1875	Grammar	1,128.00
Hunters Point School—				
Itsell, Mr. A. J.	Principal	July 10, 1871	High	1,440.00
Irving Primary—				
Barlow, Miss C. B.	Principal	Aug. 1, 1868	Grammar	1,440.00
[illegible], Miss J. G.	Sixth	Mar. 13, 1895	Grammar	1,092.00
Erb, Miss N. V.	Third	July 28, 1898	High	1,044.00
McVerry, Miss M.	First	Sept. 2, 1884	Grammar	1,128.00
Fleming, Miss H.	Second	Feb. 1, 1907	Grammar	1,044.00
Laurent, Miss S. E.	First		Grammar	828.00
Irving M. Scott Grammar—				
Hamilton, Jas. T.	Principal	July 8, 1876	High	2,160.00
Croughwell, Miss A. T.	V. P., Eighth	Jan. 28, 1891	Grammar	1,500.00
Downey, Miss M. L.	Seventh	Sept. 1, 1886	Grammar	1,128.00
Gaffney, May T.	Sixth	Oct. 14, 1901	Grammar	1,002.00
McKinnon, Minnie	Sixth	Jan. 4, 1904	Grammar	1,002.00
[illegible], Miss M. F.	Fifth	Jan. 26, 1898	Grammar	1,092.00
Williamson, Mrs. E. G.	Fifth	Aug. 12, 1896	Grammar	1,092.00
Wright, Mary A.	Fourth	Feb. 23, 1898	Grammar	1,044.00
Marsh, Alice L.	Fourth	Aug. 26, 1903	Grammar	963.00
Bryan, Miss E. M.	Fourth	Feb. 5, 1906	Grammar	963.00
White, Miss J.	Third	Aug. 25, 1904	Grammar	963.00

Name	Grade	Date	Certificate	Salary
[illegible]y, Miss A. M.	Third	Oct. 6, 1904	[illegible]ar	924.00
[illegible]is, Miss K. M.	Third	Aug. 21, 1907	Grammar	1,044.00
Kincaid, Miss May	Second	Mar. 30, 1905	Grammar	924.00
Richards, Miss L. S.	First	Mar. 13, 1895	Grammar	1,128.00
Richards, Miss M. M.	First	Nov. 30, 1892	Primary	1,188.00
Edwards, [illegible]es M.	First	Nov. 30, 1892	Grammar	1,128.00
Herrick, Miss C. R.	First	S pt. e11, 1895	[illegible]ar	1,128.00
[illegible]k, Miss C. M.	First	Sept. 12, 1887	[illegible]ar	1,128.00
Finigan, Miss M. G.	Fourth	Aug. 20, 1907	[illegible]ar	828.00
[illegible]bs, Mrs. M. E.	Second	[illegible] 17, 1907	Grammar	1,044.00
Jackson Primary—				
Chalmers, Miss A.	Principal	Jan. 2, 1902	[illegible]ar	1,440.00
Hinds, Miss A.	First	[illegible] 23, 1880	Grammar	1,128.00
Ragan, Miss M. L.	Fifth	Mar. 10, 1897	High	1,[illegible]92.00
Conroy, Miss M. A.	First	July 1898	Grammar	1,128.00
Me l, Mrs. S. M.	Fourth	Mar. 1, 1900	Primary	1,044.00
[illegible]y, Miss R. V.	Third	Mar. 10, 1897	Grammar	1,044.00
James Lick Grammar—				
Lyser, Albert	Principal	June 10, 1868	High	2,160.00
[illegible]is, Frances R.	Eighth	June 10, 1879	Grammar	1,500.00
Boyle, [illegible]y	Eighth	July 23, 1875	High	1,128.00
Torpey, Miss M. M.	Seventh	Jan. 19, 1892	Grammar	1,128.00
Kedon, [illegible] A. E.	Seventh	Dec. 9, 1896	Grammar	1,128.00
[illegible]y, Miss M. A.	Seventh	Aug. 1894	Grammar	1,128.00
Henderson, Mary J.	Seventh	Jan. 29, 1872	Grammar	1,[illegible]92.00
Kinney, Miss L. M.	Sixth	Sept. 1, 1886	Grammar	1,092.00
Kilpatrick, [illegible]ce S.	Sixth	June 21, 1904	[illegible]ar	1,062.00
[illegible]on, Miss E. M.	Fifth	Mar. 30, 1905	Grammar	1,092.00
Kennedy, Josephine	First	Mar. 1, 1895	Grammar	1,128.00
[illegible]g, [illegible]ne B.	[illegible]th	Jan. 19, 1905	Grammar	1,047.00
Jean Parker Grammar—				
Campbell, Miss A. T.	Principal	July 10, 1866	High	2,160.00
Wade, Miss J.	V. P., Eighth	Jan. 2, 1878	Grammar	1,500.00
[illegible]all, Miss M. C.	Seventh	April 10, 1874	G[illegible]ar	1,128.00
[illegible]ll, Miss L.	[illegible]th	Aug. 23, 1880	Grammar	1,128.00
[illegible]t, Miss A.	Sixth	July 18, 1902	High	1,002.00
[illegible]n, Miss J.	Fourth	July 23, 1892	[illegible]ar	1,044.00
d'Erlach, Miss M. E.	Third	Aug. 26, 1903	[illegible]ar	963.00
Brooks, Lina M.	Second	Oct. 28, 1891	Grammar	1,044.00
Hopkins, Miss J. M.	First	[illegible] 1, 1903	Grammar	1,128.00
Heath, Miss R. E. L.	First	Aug. 29, 1885	[illegible]ar	1,128.00
Beardsley, Miss E. F.	Ungraded	Mar. 3, 1879	Grammar	1,128.00
[illegible]ty, Miss A.	Fourth	[illegible] 14, 1907	[illegible]ar	1,044.00
McEwen, Miss F. G.	Second	Oct. 12, 1895	Grammar	1,044.00

LIST OF SCHOOLS AND TEACHERS—Continued.

Name.	Grade of Class.	When Elected.	Grade of Certificate.	Salary per Year.
Jefferson Primary—				
Cohen, Miss J.	Principal	July 31, 1889	Grammar	1,440.00
Horgan, Miss K.	First	Oct. 26, 1905	Grammar	882.00
Duffy, Elizabeth A.	Third	July 23, 1902	Grammar	924.00
Moore, Miss K. T.	First	June 15, 1903	Grammar	1,128.00
John Swett Grammar—				
Fitzgerald, Mrs. M. M.	Principal	Mar. 4, 1879	High	2,160.00
Bow, Mrs. C. J.	V. P., Eighth	July 1, 1865	Grammar	1,500.00
Mitchell, Mrs. G. D.	Eighth	Feb. 11, 1879	Grammar	1,128.00
Boukofsky, Miss R. M.	Seventh	Aug. 1, 1884	Grammar	1,128.00
Brooks, Miss E. B.	Sixth	Dec. 27, 1896	Grammar	1,092.00
Carroll, Genevieve	Sixth	June 9, 1897	Grammar	1,092.00
Bean, Miss L.	Fifth	July 10, 1886	Grammar	1,092.00
Barry, Miss M. C.	Fourth	Feb. 29, 1872	Primary	1,044.00
Erkson, Mrs. J. H.	Third	Sept. 1, 1897	Grammar	1,044.00
Doud, Mrs. F. M.	Second	Dec. 1887	Grammar	1,044.00
Alderson, Mrs. A. E.	First	Mar. 3, 1888	Grammar	1,128.00
Laffayette Primary—				
Casey, Miss K. F.	Principal	Jan. 24, 1876	Grammar	1,800.00
L'Hommedieu, Miss M. G.	First	Aug. 26, 1891	Grammar	1,128.00
Carroll, Lyda A.	First	Dec. 27, 1896	High	1,128.00
[illegible], Miss M.	First	Nov. 1, 1881	Grammar	1,128.00
Bloch, Miss B. B.	First	July 5, 1873	Grammar	1,128.00
Morgan, Lulu V.	First	May 15, 1896	Grammar	1,128.00
Stewart, Miss J. M.	Fifth	Oct. 27, 1880	Grammar	1,092.00
Kennedy, Miss E.	Fourth	Jan. 9, 1906	Grammar	882.00
Mordecai, Miss C.	Second	Jan. 25, 1905	Grammar	1,002.00
Laguna Honda School—				
O'Neal, Mrs. M. L.	Principal	Jan. 20, 1874	Grammar	1,560.00
Carson, Mrs. N. E.	Seventh	July 14, 1898	High	1,128.00
Croughwell, Miss M. V.	Third	Aug. 1, 1904	Grammar	924.00
Lynch, Miss E.	Sixth	Feb. 25, 1905	Grammar	1,092.00
Sechrist, Mrs. A. M.	Eighth	Dec. 5, 1886	Grammar	1,128.00
Holmes, Miss E. T.	Fifth	July 27, 1898	Grammar	1,002.00
Coonan, Miss M.	Fifth	July 6, 1905	Grammar	996.00
Stack, Miss K.	Fourth	Jan. 28, 1905	High	924.00
Hofinghoff, Miss H. L.	Second	Feb. 1, 1905	Grammar	924.00
Child, Miss A. M.	First	Sept. 30, 1901	Grammar	1,128.00
Lewis, Miss J.	First	Jan. 1877	Grammar	1,128.00

Lake View School—				
Moran, Miss M. R.	Principal	Aug. 9, 1890	Grammar	1,440.00
Marks, Mary E.	Second	Oct. 2, 1907	Grammar	828.00
[illegible], Miss H. M.	First	Aug. 2, 1905	Grammar	1,128.00
Estes, Miss C.	Fourth	Oct. 14, 1907	Grammar	828.00
O'Flaherty, Miss M. E.	Third	Oct. 28, 1907	Grammar	1,044.00
Lincoln Grammar—				
Stone, Mr. W. W.	Principal	Feb. 11, 1873	High	2,160.00
[illegible], Mrs. F. L.	Seventh and Eighth	Sept. 3, 1883	Grammar	1,188.00
[illegible], Miss J. M.	Third	Sept. 1, 1904	High	948.00
Brown, Percy A.	Fifth	Aug. 21, 1907	High	1,092.00
Redmond, Miss J.	Fourth	Jan. 21, 1907	Grammar	1,044.00
Perry, Laura C.	Fourth	June 26, 1905	High	882.00
[illegible], Mrs. B. L.	Fifth	Jan. 29, 1884	Grammar	1,128.00
Lynch, Miss A. E.	First	Jan. 1, 1876	Grammar	1,128.00
Madison Primary—				
[illegible]tt, Miss E. F.	Principal	Aug. 5, 1885	Grammar	1,440.00
Lipman, Miss N. E.	Sixth	Sept. 7, 1897	Grammar	1,092.00
Howard, Miss F. G.	Fifth	Dec. 30, 1892	Grammar	1,092.00
Emmons, Miss I. C.	Fourth	July 30, 1876	Grammar	1,044.00
Rowland, Mrs. A. E.	Third	July 27, 1898	Grammar	1,002.00
[illegible], Miss Turid	Second	Aug. 14, 1905	Grammar	882.00
Breese, Miss A. A.	First	Oct. 29, 1897	Grammar	1,128.00
Bannon, Margaret F.	First	Jan. 3, 1873	Grammar	1,128.00
[illegible]all Primary—				
Walker, Mrs. M. J.	Principal	Aug. 13, 1869	High	1,800.00
Poppe, Miss M. H.	Third	April 30, 1886	Grammar	1,104.00
Harrigan, Miss J.	Fourth	July 1884	Grammar	1,044.00
Lundt, Miss J. C.	Fourth	Oct. 19, 1875	Grammar	1,044.00
Parker, Miss K. E.	Third	Jan. 3, 1904	Grammar	963.00
Belding, Mrs. M. L.	Second	Nov. 21, 1876	Primary	1,044.00
Herndon, Miss A. C.	First	Dec. 18, 1878	Grammar	1,128.00
Elliot, Miss E. F.	First	Nov. 18, 1885	Grammar	1,128.00
O'Connor, Miss C. J.	First	Sept. 12, 1904	Grammar	1,128.00
Gray, Mrs. H. W.	Fourth	July 28, 1892	Primary	1,044.00
O'Hara, Miss N. G.	Second	Mar. 30, 1905	Grammar	1,044.00
McKinley School—				
Cashman, Miss R. S.	Sixth	July 18, 1902	Grammar	1,128.00
[illegible], Miss A. E.	Sixth	Aug. 22, 1907	Grammar	828.00
Gallagher, Miss C.	Principal	Aug. 8, 1878	Grammar	[illegible]0.00
Kresteller, Miss S.	Fourth	Jan. 3, 1906	Grammar	828.00
O'Connell, Mary F.	Seventh	Jan. 29, 1906	Grammar	963.00
Moynihan, Nora	Fifth	July 7, 1877	Grammar	1,092.00
Davi[illegible]son, Miss E. R.	Fourth	Feb. 1, 1904	Grammar	[illegible]44.00

LIST OF SCHOOLS AND TEACHERS—Continued.

Name.	Grade of Class.	When Elected.	Grade of Certificate.	Salary per Year.
[illegible] **School**—Continued.				
[illegible]y, Mary E.	Third	April 2, 1888	Gr[illegible]mar	1,044.00
McKinney, Mary G.	Third	Nov. 7, 1888	Grammar	1,044.00
Kean, Miss K. E.	First	Jan. 1, 1885	Grammar	[illegible]
Sarles, [illegible]s. Julia	First	July 7, 1881	Grammar	1,128.00
Casey, Mary	First	June 6, 1888	Gr[illegible]mar	1,128.00
Mission Grammar—				
[illegible]y, Miss K. H.	Principal	Aug. 1, 1880	Grammar	2,160.00
Hillman, Miss J. C.	Eighth	Feb. 13, 1879	[illegible]r	1,500.00
[illegible]le, Miss M. E.	Eighth	Oct. 30, 1889	[illegible]ar	1,128.00
[illegible]s, [illegible]iss R. A.	Seventh	[illegible]g. 15, 1888	Grammar	1,128.00
Sykes, Mrs. M. A.	Fifth	[illegible]g. 11, 1897	[illegible]ar	1,128.00
[illegible]n, Miss M. A.	Seventh	Sept. 30, 1901	Grammar	1,188.00
[illegible]n, Miss M. G.	Seventh	May 15, 1883	[illegible]ar	1,128.00
Horn, [illegible]iss L. J.	Sixth	July 14, 1872	[illegible]r	1,092.00
O'Brien, Miss M. A.	Sixth	Aug. 11, 1897	[illegible]r	1,092.00
Hemmenway, Miss I. H.	Sixth	July 27, 1898	Grammar	1,092.00
Harvey, [illegible]ss E. F.	Fifth	Oct. 30, 1890	[illegible]r	1,092.00
Monroe [illegible]—				
Hagarty, Miss A. M.	Principal	Feb. 20, 1883	[illegible]ar	2,160.00
Gorham, Miss A. M.	[illegible]th	Aug. 22, 1907	[illegible]ar	828.00
Harrower, Miss A. W.	V. P., Eighth	Sept. 30, 1901	Grammar	1,500.00
[illegible]y, Miss M. R.	Seventh	Oct. 28, 1891	Grammar	1,128.00
Curtin, Ella J.	Seventh	Sept. 14, 1905	[illegible]r	1,128.00
[illegible]y, [illegible]L. J.	Sixth	Sept. 12, 1904	High	948.00
McIntyre, Miss J. L.	[illegible]th	[illegible] 2, 1905	Grammar	1,092.00
Maher, Miss J. G.	Fifth	Sept. 2, 1884	[illegible]r	1,092.00
Macauley, Miss H. I.	[illegible]th	Aug. 6, 1907	Grammar	828.00
Ward, [illegible]iss S. A.	Fifth	Oct. 30, 1894	G[illegible]ar	1,[illegible]88.00
Turney, Katherine	Third	Dec. 14, 1890	Primary	1,044.00
Lytton, Mrs. I. M.	Second	July 28, 1898	[illegible]ar	1,044.00
Ellis, Miss L.	Fourth	Jan. 3, 1889	Primary	1,044.00
d'Orr, M. F.	[illegible]t	Sept. 30, 1901	G[illegible]ar	1,128.00
Fleming, Miss J.	[illegible]st	Feb. 13, 1890	Grammar	1,128.00
Orr, Elizabeth A.	First	Jan. 5, 1881	Grammar	1,128.00
O'Brien, [illegible]iss A. T.	First	[illegible]v. 30, 1881	[illegible]ar	1,128.00
Rahilly, Ella T.	Second	[illegible] 7, 1907	[illegible]ar	882.00
[illegible]n, [illegible]iss A. J.	Third	Sept. 11, 1907	Grammar	828.00
Hussey, Miss N. E.	[illegible]d	Aug. 22, 1907	High	[illegible]9.00
[illegible]er Primary—				
Brogan, [illegible]s. K. E.	Principal	Jan. 7, 1873	[illegible]ar	1,560.00

Name	Class	Date	Certificate	Salary
Duncan, Miss C. L.	Sixth	Aug. 4, 1882	Grammar	1,092.00
Ecles, Mrs. L. B.	Fifth	Sept. 3, 1883	[illegible]mar	1,092.00
[illegible], Mrs. E. B.	Fourth	June 3, 1905	Grammar	1,044.00
Boukofsky, [illegible]ss S.	Fourth	Feb. 11, 1891	Grammar	1,[illegible]00
Franks, Miss A. E.	Third	Aug. 16, 1888	Primary	1,044.00
Fogarty, Miss N. T.	[illegible]rd	Dec. 19, 1896	Grammar	1,044.00
Tompkins, Mrs. C.	Second	April 16, 1872	Grammar	1,044.00
[illegible]n, Mrs. I.	First	Jan. 18, 1888	Grammar	1,128.00
Bristol, Miss M. K.	First	Aug. 10, 1882	Grammar	1,128.00
Noe Valle y Primary—				
Lyons, Mrs. E. H.	Principal	July 1, 1882	Grammar	1,800.00
Hall, Mrs. M. V.	First	Aug. 17, 1887	Grammar	1,128.00
Egan, Mrs. K. F.	Second	Mar. 11, 1897	Grammar	1,128.00
Brown, Miss M. L.	First	July 30, 1886	[illegible]mar	1,128.00
Gercke, Mrs. L.	Thi rd	April 1, 1903	[illegible]mar	1,128.00
Harrison, [illegible]ss E. D.	Second	Aug. 12, 1903	Grammar	984.00
MacDonald, Miss L. M.	Second		Grammar	828.00
[illegible]ll, Miss G. S.	Second	Aug. 23, 1907	Grammar	828.00
Hansell, Mrs. M. E.	S ond[illegible]	Aug. 9, 1897	[illegible]mar	1,044.00
Martin, Elizabeth R.	Third	May. 1, 1905	Grammar	924.00
[illegible]n, Miss M. L.	Thi rd	June 21, 1904	[illegible]mar	963.00
Gray, Mrs. J. E.	Third	Dec. 15, 1890	Grammar	1,044.00
Gray, Miss F. H.	[illegible]	Sept. 2, 1907	Grammar	882.00
Schnedel, Miss M. A.	Fourth	Sept. 30, 1901	[illegible]mar	963.00
Gaffney Miss S. A.	Fourth	July. 21, 1903	Grammar	924.00
Judson, Miss A. A.	Fifth	Jan. 16, 1903	[illegible]mar	1,092.00
Armstrong, Annie E.	Fifth	Aug. 19, 1897	Grammar	1,092.00
[illegible]e Primary—				
Heath, Miss V. D.	Principal	Jan. 4, 1894	Grammar	1,440.00
Allen, Miss S. H.	Fifth	Oct. 24, 1901	[illegible]mar	1,092.00
Hawkins, Miss B. C.	First	July 25, 1902	[illegible]	1,062.00
Vincent, Miss S. C.	Third	Feb. 25, 1904	[illegible]mar	963.00
Raas, Mrs. A.	Fourth	April 8, 1907	High	828.00
Kergan, Mrs. A. R.	Eighth	Jan. 26, 1905	Grammar	948.00
Ocean House School—				
Delay, Mr. D. J.	Principal	July 8, 1882	High	1,260.00
Oriental Public—				
Newhall, Mrs. C. C.	Principal	Feb. 13, 1870	Grammar	[illegible]0.00
Greer, Jane E.	Third	June 10, 1868	High	[illegible]4.00
Griffith, Miss A. C.	First	July 27, 1898	Grammar	1,092.00
Nixon, Miss V. E.	Seventh	June 30, 1902	Grammar	948.00
Branch, Miss C. A.	First	Feb. 27, 1905	Grammar	948.00
McInerney, Miss F. R.	First	Sept. 12, 1904	High	948.00
Austin, Miss E. D.	Fourth	Oct. 28, 1907	Grammar	828.00

LIST OF SCHOOLS AND TEACHERS—Continued.

Name.	Grade of Class.	When Elected.	Grade of Certificate	Salary per Year.
Pacific Heights [illegible]—				
[illegible]n, Miss A. M.	Principal	June 20, 1868	[illegible]. & High	2,160.00
Stincen, [illegible]ss Ella E.	Fourth	[illegible]ril 16, 1907	Grammar	861.00
Bl[illegible]n, Miss F. M.	Eighth	Sept. 3, 1880	Grammar	1,128.00
Earle, Miss C. B.	Eighth	Feb. 21, 1872	Grammar	1,128.00
Cook, Miss F. G.	Seventh	Dec. 4, 1904	Grammar	1,128.00
[illegible]th, [illegible]	Seventh	May 20, 1905	Grammar	948.00
Dreyfus, [illegible]ss R. E.	Seventh	Aug. 5, 1905	[illegible]ar	1,128.00
[illegible]h, Emma F.	Sixth	Jan. 21, 1883	Grammar	1,092.00
[illegible]is, Miss A. C.	Sixth	April 18, 1888	Grammar	[illegible]092.00
Boggs, Miss S.	[illegible]h	Feb. 18, 1903	Grammar	1 092.00
Spadoni, [illegible]ss F. C.	Fifth	Jan. 3, 1905	Grammar	948.00
[illegible]h, Mrs. L. L.	Fifth	Sept. 1886	[illegible]ar	1 002.00
Wollner, Miss M.	Fourth	Jan. 4, 1902	High	963.00
Donohue, Miss M. F.	[illegible]d	June 21, 1904	Grammar	963.00
[illegible]h, Miss G. M.	[illegible]d	Nov. 2, 1878	Grammar	1,044.00
Robertson, [illegible]ss A. C.	V. P., Eighth	July 16, 1867	High	1,500.00
Burnham, Miss C.	First	Aug. 1, 1885	Grammar	1,128.00
Dowling, Miss A. C.	First	[illegible]pt. 5, 1897	[illegible]r	1,128.00
Zweybruck, Miss E.	Ungraded	Feb. 20, 1885	Grammar	1,128.00
Morrison, Miss F. P.	Seventh	Aug. 20, 1888	Grammar	1,128.00
Peabody Primary—				
Dwyer, Miss A. M.	Principal	Mar. 17, 1879	High	1,440.00
Maguire, Mrs. M. E.	Fourth	Mar. 1, 1880	Grammar	1,044.00
Fitzgerald, [illegible]ss M. F.	[illegible]th	Nov. 13, 1889	[illegible]ar	1,[illegible]04.00
Watson, [illegible]s. M. G.	First	Jan. 12, 1898	Grammar	1,128.00
Reynolds, Mrs. I. M.	Third	April 1, 1903	Grammar	1,044.00
Duffy, Miss A. A.	Third	Aug. 18, 1884	[illegible]ar	1,044.00
[illegible]b, Mrs. E. S.	Second	Nov. 18, 1901	Grammar	1,044.00
Sullivan, Miss N. C.	First	Mar. 22, 1907	[illegible]ar	828.00
Ephriam, Miss A.	F[illegible]t	Dec. 2, 1882	Grammar	1,128.00
Ingram, Mrs. V. C.	First	Jan. 3, 1876	[illegible]ar	1,128.00
[illegible]g Primary—				
Deane, Miss M. A.	Principal	Aug. 2, 1872	[illegible]r	1,560.00
Sullivan, Miss T.	Fifth	Sept. 15, [illegible]8	Grammar	1,002.00
Geary, Miss M. E.	Fifth	Aug. 12, 1903	[illegible]ar	963.00
[illegible]r, Miss S. A.	Third	Feb. 14, 1881	[illegible]ar	1,044.00
[illegible]y, Miss A. C.	Second	July 10, 1869	Primary	1,044.00
Martin, Miss F.	First	Aug. 26, 1881	Grammar	1,128.00
Donahue, Mrs. L. E.	First	Dec. 23, 1885	Grammar	1,128.00

Name	Grade	Date	Certificate	Salary
Richmond Grammar—				
Keathing, Miss M. E.	Principal	July 12, 1880	Grammar	2,160.00
Sleator, Miss E. A.	V. P., Eighth	July 31, 1889	[illegible]mar	1,500.00
[illegible]e, Miss A. H.	Seventh	July 5, 1878	[illegible]mar	1,128.00
Cotrel, Miss E.	Sixth	Sept. 5, 1891	[illegible]mar	1,128.00
Browning, Miss E. F.	Sixth	Oct. 24, 1901	High	1,002.00
Ryan, [illegible]ss B.	Seventh	Sept. 16, 1886	Grammar	1,128.00
Hitchens, Florence J.	Sixth	Jan. 31, 1889	Grammar	1,092.00
[illegible]d, Miss A.	Fifth	Dec. 28, 1891	Grammar	1,092.00
McDonnell, [illegible]ss M. T.	Sixth	[illegible]r. 11, 1892	Grammar	1,092.00
H[illegible]s, Miss J. B.	Fifth	Dec. 9, 1896	Grammar	1,092.00
Gray, Miss M. E. A.	Fourth	Sept. 20, 1901	High	963.00
McDonald, Miss J.	Fourth	Jan. 21, 1898	Grammar	1,044.00
Grover, Mrs. E. J.	Seventh	Aug. 22, 1907	[illegible]mar	828.00
Harrigan, Miss M. A.	S[illegible]ond	Aug. 2, 1871	[illegible]mar	1,044.00
[illegible]n, Miss J. E.	S[illegible]ond	Sept. 16, 1879	[illegible]mar	1,044.00
[illegible]n, Miss K. E.	First	Nov. 7, 1884	[illegible]mar	1,188.00
Stark, Miss L. M.	First	Sept. 7, 1887	[illegible]mar	1,128.00
[illegible]ey, Miss A. F.	Third	April 27, 1888	Primary	1,044.00
Horton, Miss M.	First	Feb. 14, 1881	Grammar	1,155.00
Starr, Miss D. E.	Ungraded	Sept. 10, 1904	Grammar	1,128.00
Hawthorne, Miss M. E.	Third	Jan. 6, 1908	Grammar	828.00
Sheridan—				
Riordan, Miss C. F.	Principal	Dec. 10, 1890	[illegible]mar	1,560.00
Downey, Miss J.	Eighth	Aug. 26, 1891	[illegible]mar	1,128.00
[illegible]y, Miss H.	Seventh	Oct. 26, 1905	Grammar	1,002.00
Everett, Miss E. B.	Sixth	Jan. 13, 1892	[illegible]mar	1,092.00
Hussey, [illegible]ss E. G.	Fifth	Feb. 11, 1907	High	903.00
Tiern[illegible], Miss E. A.	Fifth	Oct. 13, 1904	[illegible]mar	948.00
[illegible]an, Miss M.	Fourth	Sept. 14, 1905	Grammar	882.00
[illegible]t, Mrs. M. I.	Third	July 7, 1905	Grammar	882.00
[illegible]o, Miss H.	Third	Sept. 8, 1897	Grammar	1,044.00
O'Connor, [illegible]ss A. J.	S[illegible]ond	Sept. 3, 1905	Grammar	924.00
Busteed, Miss M. W.	First	April 29, 1896	Grammar	1,128.00
Hawley, Miss M. E.	First	Jan. 6, 1879	Grammar	1,128.00
Sherman Primary—				
Hurley, Miss J. M. A.	Principal	Jan. 2, 1863	High	1,560.00
Featherly, Miss H.	Fourth	July 16, 1867	Gram. & High	1,044.00
Johnson, Miss M. C.	Fourth	June 21, 1904	Grammar	1,092.00
Nesfield, Miss E. M.	Fourth	Jan. 3, 1902	[illegible]mar	983.00
Crookham, Miss E. E.	[illegible]rd	Aug. 10, 1898	Grammar	[illegible]44.00
O'Brien, Miss M.	Third	Sept. 20, 1879	Primary	1,044.00
McLerie, Miss J. T.	S[illegible]d	May 17, 1896	Grammar	[illegible]44.00
[illegible]s, [illegible]ss E.	Fourth	Aug. 20, 1907	High	828.00
Unger, Miss R.	First	Aug. 20, 1885	[illegible]mar	1,128.00

LIST OF SCHOOLS AND TEACHERS—Continued.

Name.	Grade of Class.	When Elected.	Grade of Certificate	Salary per Year.
Sherman Primary—Continued.				
Sulli[illegible]n, Miss Nellie	Second	Aug. 15, 1890	Grammar	1,044.00
Roberts, Miss Maria	First	Dec. 23, 1884	[illegible]ar	1,128.00
Lyons, Miss E. H.	First	Sept. 30, 1885	Grammar	1,128.00
[illegible]ns, Elizabeth	First	Nov. 25, 1885	[illegible]ar	1,128.00
Gull, Mrs. M. S.	First	July 5, 1877	[illegible]ar	8[illegible]0
South End—				
Mills, Mrs. I. E.	Principal	Nov. 20, 1877	Grammar	1,560.00
Lapham, Miss E. M.	Eighth	Jan. 11, 1904	Grammar	1,002.00
Gillespie, Miss J. H.	Sixth	Aug. 1, 1888	Grammar	1,092.00
McDermott, Miss L.	F[illegible]th	Oct. 1, 1904	High	1,092.00
[illegible]y, Miss A.	Fifth	Aug. 22, 1907	Grammar	1,002.00
Tessmer, Miss E. H.	Fourth	July 20, 1903	Grammar	924.00
Laverene, Miss C. J.	Fourth	Oct. 28, 1907	[illegible]ar	828.00
Porter, Miss H. F.	Third	Jan. 28, 1907	Grammar	828.00
Wiley, Miss B.	Third	Aug. 22, 1907	Grammar	882.00
Prince, Miss R.	Second	Jan 18, 1903	Grammar	963.00
Grace, Miss J. G.	Second	Aug. 19, 1907	Grammar	828.00
Browne, Miss E.	First	Aug. 15, 1888	[illegible]ar	1,128.00
Johnson, Miss A. E.	First	April 29, 1891	[illegible]ar	1,128.00
[illegible]n, Miss M.	First	Sept. 25, 1905	Grammar	1,128.00
Spring Valley [illegible]ar—				
DeBell, W. H.	Principal	July 19, 1901	High	2160.00
Cregg, Miss A. C.	Eighth	Aug. 15, 1868	High	1,500.00
Holden, Mrs. A. F.	Eighth	Sept. 16, 1879	Grammar	1,188.00
[illegible]y, Miss A. J.	Seventh	Mar. 2, 1903	Grammar	1,128.00
[illegible]a, Miss A. B.	Seventh	Jan. 29, 1884	Grammar	1,128.00
H[illegible]gs, Mrs. M. A.	Sixth	Jan. 10, 1877	Grammar	1,092.00
Davis, Mrs. F. V.	Sixth	Feb. 20, 1872	Primary	1,092.00
Grozelier, Miss C. B. S.	Fifth	Sept. 14, 1905	[illegible]ar	903.00
Mandeville, Miss K.	S[illegible]v[illegible]nth	Aug. 10, 1885	[illegible]ar	1,128.00
Gallagher, Miss E. R.	F[illegible]th	Oct. 28, 1891	[illegible]ar	1,092.00
Starr King Primary—				
Finnegan, Miss C. L.	Sixth	Sept. 2, 1887	Grammar	1,092.00
Williams, Miss K. F.	Fourth	Oct. 17, 1884	Grammar	1,092.00
Thomas, Mildred A.	Third	July 29, 1903	Grammar	1,044.00
[illegible]n, Mrs. K. C.	Principal	Jan. 12, 1878	[illegible]ar	1,560.00
O'Sullivan, Elizabeth	First	April 18, 1897	Grammar	1,188.00
Foley, Kate J.	First	July 20, 1903	Grammar	1,128.00
Jordi, Mrs. S. J.	Second	June 14, 1885	[illegible]ar	1,044.00

Name	Grade	Date	Certificate	Salary
[illegible]n, Mrs. M. B.	[illegible]d	Aug. 6, 1904	Grammar	924.00
Louderback, Miss E. S.	F[illegible]t	Nov. 21, 1884	Grammar	1,128.00
[illegible]e Primary—				
Code, Mrs. E. S.	Principal	Jan. 22, 1857	High	1,440.00
Leeds, Miss B. E.	Eighth	Nov. 15, 1905	Grammar	1,128.00
[illegible]s, Miss G. A.	Fifth		Grammar	9 3. 0
King, Miss J. I.	F[illegible]t	Feb. 2, 1887	Grammar	1,128.00
Sunset School—				
Tiernan, Mrs. A. E.	Principal	July 6, 1869	High	1,560.00
Perlett, Mattie F.	Seventh	Dec. 28, 1896	Grammar	1,128.00
Rowe, Miss M. M.	Second	Aug. 3, 1871	High	1,128.00
Sutro [illegible]—				
Magner, Miss M.	Principal	July 25, 1876	Grammar	2,160.00
Duraind, Miss M. R.	[illegible]th, V. P.	Dec. 5, 1875	Grammar	1,500.00
Smullen, Miss A. M.	Seventh	Feb. 18, 1903	Grammar	1,188.00
[illegible]r, Miss M.	Seventh	July 28, 1902	High	1,128.00
Savage, Miss D. A.	Sixth	June 21, 1904	Grammar	1,002.00
Corbett, Miss A. M.	Sixth	Oct. 12, 1905	Grammar	903.00
Karatar, Miss A. C.	Fifth	Oct. 14, 1883	Grammar	1,092.00
Read, Miss M. F.	Fifth	July 18, 1902	Grammar	948.00
Curran, Miss M. M.	Fourth	Mar. 14, 1906	Grammar	1,044.00
Cullen, Miss R.	Third	Jan. 4, 1902	High	963.00
Faucompre, Miss M. E.	Third	Nov. 18, 1886	Grammar	1,044.00
O'Connell, Miss L.	Second	June 9, 1897	Grammar	1,044.00
[illegible]e, Miss H. E.	Second	Oct. 27, 1892	Grammar	1,044.00
O'Brien, Miss M. J.	First	Aug. 3, 1892	Grammar	1,128.00
Horton, Miss A. B.	First	May 13, 1896	Grammar	1,128.00
Bigelow, Mrs. S. H.	First	Sept. 1876	Grammar	1,128.00
[illegible]a, Miss K. L.	Ungraded	Sept. 10, 1904	Grammar	1,128.00
Visitacion Valley—				
Perolini, Mrs. M. J.	Principal	Mar. 1, 1866	High	1,440.00
[illegible]n, Miss M. A.	Eighth	Oct. 21, 1901	Grammar	1,002.00
Dailey, Miss A.	Fifth	Mar. 14, 1907	Grammar	1,092.00
Hart, Miss A. P.	Third	Aug. 19, 1907	Grammar	828.00
Kenny, Miss M.	First	April 8, 1907	Grammar	828.00
Healy, Miss C. L.	First	May 23, 1907	Grammar	828.00
Washington [illegible]—				
[illegible]y, Mr. T. H.	Principal	Mar. 20, 1891	High	2,160.00
Shuck, Mr. L. M.	V. P., Eighth	July 10, 1889	High	1,500.00
Kervan, Miss I. M.	Fifth	Sept. 9, 1872	Grammar	1,092.00
Bowman, Mr. L.	Sixth	Oct. 1, 1879	Grammar	1,092.00
Silvey, Paul A.	Ungraded	Aug. 22, 1907	High	1,128.00
[illegible]d, Miss A.	Second	Sept. 15, 1875	Grammar	1,044.00
[illegible]c, Miss Ella	First	Jan. 3, 1874	Grammar	1,128.00

LIST OF SCHOOLS AND TEACHERS—Continued.

Name.	Grade of Class.	When Elected.	Grade of Certificate	Salary per [illegible]ar.
[illegible]on Grammar—Continued.				
[illegible]ier, Miss J.	Eighth	May 1, 1878	[illegible]	1,128.00
Scott, [illegible]iss J.	First	Sept. 5, 1881	[illegible]ar	1,128.00
Kirkwood, Mr. W. H.	Fourth	Aug. 19, 1907	[illegible]	1,044.00
West End Primary—				
[illegible]y, Miss E. L.	Principal	Jan. 16, 1884	[illegible]ar	1,440.00
Dwyer, Miss A. C.	Fourth	Mar. 22, 1905	High	924.00
[illegible]er, Miss Nora	Third	Nov. 11, 1891	Primary	1,044.00
[illegible]r, Miss A. M.	First	Jan. 12, 1898	Grammar	1,128.00
[illegible]ld Scott Primary—				
Thomas, Miss M. E.	Principal	July 12, 1887	[illegible]	1,440.00
[illegible]s, [illegible]ss M. A.	Fifth	July 27, 1898	Grammar	1,092.00
Ryder, Miss P.	Eighth	June 23, 1904	[illegible]ar	1,002.00
[illegible], [illegible]s K.	Seventh	July 14, 1897	[illegible]	1,128.00
Horgan, Miss E. E.	Fifth	Sept. 1, 1905	[illegible]ar	903.00
Gavigan, Miss M. K.	Third	Feb. 1, 1889	Primary	1,044.00
Wright, Miss A. B.	Fourth	Jan. 6, 1902	High	963.00
Thomas, Miss A. G.	First	July 27, 1898	Grammar	1,128.00
Demmick, Mrs. M. F.	First	Dec. 10, 1890	Grammar	1,128.00
Oral School For Deaf—				
Holden, [illegible]s. J. B.	Principal	Aug. 15, 1901	Special	1,212.00
[illegible], Mr. A. N.	Fourth	Aug. 1, 1902	Special	1,032.00
Parental School—				
[illegible]r, Miss R.	Principal	Oct. 5, 1888	[illegible]ar	1,440.00
[illegible]s, Ang[illegible]ine	Seventh	Sept. 17, 1897	High	1,128.00
[illegible]al Hig[illegible]h—				
[illegible]y, Chas. H.	Principal	Nov. 27, 1890	High	3,000.00
Sykes, Jas. B.	V. P., [illegible] Law	Dec. 16, 1896	High	2,160.00
Durkee, Miss E. T.	Bookkeeping	[illegible]c. 30, 1891	Special	1,740.00
Armer, Miss E. D.	English	Aug. 15, 1898	High	1,740.00
McPherson, [illegible]s. S. W.	Arith. & Al[illegible]gebra	July 20, 1889	High	1,740.00
Salcido, [illegible]ss M. G.	[illegible]ish	July 30, 1890	Special	1,740.00
[illegible]n, Miss S. A.	Typewriting	July 20, 1904	Special	1,740.00
[illegible]s, Miss M. L.	Sten. & Typewriting	Aug. 15, 1889	Special	1,740.00
Espine, Mr. P. A.	Penmanship	S[illegible]pt. 13, 1887	[illegible]ial	1,740.00
Furlong, Miss I. M.	[illegible]ry & Civics	Jan. 14, 1905	[illegible]	1,740.00
[illegible]s, [illegible]s. I. D.	His., [illegible]t. & Eng.	Jan. 10, 1897	High	1,740.00
[illegible]y, [illegible]ss M. B.	Stenography	[illegible] 26, 1892	Special	1,740.00
Garbarino, Miss I.	Sten. & Typewriting	Nov. 13, 1889	Special	1,740.00

Name	Subject	Date	Grade	Salary
[illegible]s, Miss M. L.	Sten. & Typewriting	Sept. 1, 1904	Special	1,740.00
[illegible]r, Miss H. E.	Bookkeeping	May 15, 1887	Special	1,740.00
[illegible]n, Miss F. H.	Substitute	June 15, 1908	High	1,740.00
[illegible]n, Miss E.	Latin	June 17, 1903	High	1,740.00
[illegible], Miss E. L.	Bookkeeping	Sept. 30, 1901	High	1,440.00
Girls' High—				
Scott, Dr. A. W.	Principal	Jan. 5, 1883	High	3,000.00
[illegible]g, [illegible] M.	Vice-Principal	June 1864	High	2,160.00
Mitchell, Mr. G. O.	Science	Aug. 23, 1889	High	1,920.00
Dupuy, Mr. E. J.	[illegible]	May 15, 1899	Special	1,800.00
Goldstein, Mr. F. M.	Drawing	Mar. 1, [illegible]87	Special	1,800.00
[illegible]h, Miss N. E.	English	[illegible] 10, 1902	High	1,740.00
[illegible]s, Miss N. W.	English	Aug. 7, 1869	High	1,740.00
[illegible]le, Miss B.	[illegible]h, History	Mar. 13, 1905	High	1,740.00
[illegible]l, Miss L.	Science	Dec. 17, 1890	High	1,740.00
[illegible], Miss S. A.	[illegible]s	July 21, 1901	High	1,740.00
[illegible]t, Miss C. L.	[illegible]y, Zoology	Jan. 10, 1859	High	1,740.00
Croyland, Miss A. B.	[illegible]h	July 20, 1901	High	1,800.00
Stark, Miss C. M.	[illegible]n, [illegible]k	[illegible] 21, 1902	High	1,740.00
Zimmerman, Mr. Wm.	German	Jan. 4, 1871	High	1,740.00
S[illegible]n, Miss F. R.	[illegible]y, [illegible]ra	Jan. 3, 1903	High	1,740.00
[illegible]r, [illegible]n A.	[illegible]n	Aug. 19, 1907	High	1,800.00
Jewett, Miss F.	[illegible]s	Aug. 23, 1870	High	1,800.00
Lowell High—				
Morton, Frank	Principal	Aug. 1, 1886	High	3,000.00
[illegible]r, Dr. J. J.	Vice-Principal	July 27, 1898	High	2,160.00
[illegible]k, F. H.	History	July 8, 1889	High	1,800.00
[illegible]s, Francis E.	[illegible]s	Nov. 28, 1891	High	1,800.00
[illegible], Mr. J. L.	[illegible] [illegible]s	Aug. 5, 1888	High	1,740.00
Schmit, Mr. J. J.	Languages	Dec. 26, 1894	High	1,740.00
[illegible]e, Mr. J. P.	[illegible]n	Jan. 14, 1901	High	1,740.00
Longley, Mr. J. A.	History	July 20, 1901	High	1,740.00
Perham, Mr. F. E.	English	Sept. 4, 1901	High	1,740.00
Van Gorder, Mr. A. L.	Science	Sept. 1, 1904	High	1,920.00
[illegible]y, Mr. R. W.	Biology	Dec. 28, 1905	High	1,740.00
[illegible]r, Mr. C. L.	Drawing	April 20, 1896	High	1,740.00
[illegible]s, Mr. T. H.	Science	Nov. 15, 1906	High	1,740.00
Cronise, Miss C. B.	English	April 4, 1907	High	1,740.00
Cloud, Mr. A. J.	English	Jan. 15, 1905	High	1,800.00
[illegible], Mary M.	Language	Aug. 20, 1885	High	1,800.00
Rowell, [illegible]r I.	[illegible]tics & Latin	July 31, 1902	High	1,740.00
Dickerson, Mr. R. E.	Science	Jan. 2, 1907	High	1,740.00
Weigle, Miss E. A.	[illegible]y, [illegible]n	Oct. 1, 1907	High	1,740.00
Kelley, Mr. T. R.	English, Latin	Sept. 12, 1899	High	1,740.00

LIST OF SCHOOLS AND TEACHERS—Continued.

Name.	Grade of Class.	When Elected.	Grade of Certificate	Salary per Year.
Mission High—				
Smith, Mr. W. O.	Acting Principal	Aug. 1, 1901	High	3,000.00
Donnelly, Miss M. E.	English	July 9, 1872	High	2160.00
Goldsmith, Miss A.	History	Feb. 19, 1879	High	1,800.00
Ryan, Miss R.	Mathematics	July 15, 1898	High	1,800.00
Blanchard, Dr. M. E.	Classics	Jan. 5, 1890	High	1,800.00
Kelly, Miss A. G.	Mathematics	Oct. 10, 1895	High	1,740.00
[illegible]e, Miss E. R.	History	July 20, 1901	High	1,740.00
Graham, Elizabeth M.	English	Oct. 8, 1879	High	1,740.00
Cerf, Miss A.	Latin, French	July 21, 1904	High	1,740.00
Wing, Miss M. G.	German	Mar. 8, 1906	High	1,740.00
Downey, Mr. A. D.	Science	Jan. 21, 1907	High	1,920.00
Carin, Mr. P. A.	Drawing	Aug. 31, 1898	High	1,800.00
[illegible]y, Mr. E.	Science	Feb. 3, 1908	High	1,740.00
Michner, Miss M.	Drawing	Jan. 12, 1905	High	1,740.00
Harrison, Miss E. C.	French, German	Aug. 3, 1908	Special	
Polytechnic High—				
Bush, Mr. W. N.	Principal	July 20, 1886	High	3,000.00
Jordan, Mr. A. L.	V. P., Science	Jan. 26, 1899	High	2,160.00
Duffy, Miss A. G.	English & History	June 24, 1897	High	1,800.00
Van Vleck, Miss M.	Drawing	July 22, 1889	Special	1,800.00
Carniglia, Mr. E. S.	Iron-wk&Mech.Drg.	Mar. 25, 1905	High	1,800.00
Barthel, Mr. F. K.	Manual Training	Sept. 10, 1903	Special	1,800.00
Mohr, Mr. P. J.	Mathematics	Jan. 21, 1903	High	1,800.00
Hatch, Mr. I. C.	Language	Aug. 12, 1905	High	1,800.00
Brown, Mr. F. J.	English	Sept. 13, 1904	High	1,740.00
C[illegible]e, Miss E.	Algebra	Dec. 1, 1897	High	1,440.00
Castlehun, Miss E.	English, German	April 4, 1887	High	1,740.00
Murdoch, Miss R.	Drawing	Nov. 18, 1893	Special	1,200.00
Campbell, Miss N. L.	Sewing	Sept. 21, 1907	Special	1,200.00
Drew, Mr. W. J.	Drawing	Mar. 28, 1898	High	1,800.00
Walker, Mr. C. C.	Drawing	Sept. 30, 1907	Special	1,800.00
Cerf, Miss C.	French	Feb. 3, 1908	High	1,740.00
Kelly, Miss M. E.	English	July 20, 1904	High	1,740.00
[illegible]al Evening—				
R[illegible]y, Mr. Peter	Principal	July 17, 1901	High	1,200.00
Davidson, Mr. W. W.	Bookkeeping	July 5, 1884	Grammar	600.00
Dowling, Miss M. C.	Spanish, English	Dec. 20, 1899	High	600.00
Hitchcock, Miss H. M.	French	July 29, 1876	Grammar	600.00
Kozminsky, Miss D.	Stenography	Sept. 29, 1892	Special	600.00
O'Malley, Miss M. W.	Stenography	Aug. 18, 1897	Special	600.00

Rock, Miss A. J.	Bookkeeping	Jan. 12, 1898	Grammar	600.00
Trefts, Mr. W. E.	Sten. & Typewriting	April 1, 1903	Special	600.00
Freese, Miss L. E.	Penmanship	Mar. 8, 1894	Grammar	600.00
Kendrick, Miss N. K.	Stenography	Dec. 29, 1896	Grammar	600.00
Delaney, Mrs. K. F.	Bookkeeping	Mar. 25, 1886	Grammar	600.00
Hamilton Evening—				
Foulkes, Geo. W.	Principal	June 1, 1893	High	1,200.00
[illegible]h, Miss M. U.	Ninth	Aug. 11, 1897	Grammar	600.00
Lanahan, Mr. J. A.	Eighth	June 15, 1898	Grammar	600.00
Johns, Miss M. E.	Eighth	Aug. 4, 1906	Grammar	600.00
Bertz, Miss B. M.	Seventh	Sept. 16, 1886	Grammar	600.00
Hussey, Miss N. C.	Sixth	Feb. 26, 1896	Grammar	600.00
Israel, Miss D. T.	Sixth	Feb. 23, 1898	Grammar	600.00
Burnett, Miss S. C.	Foreign	Oct. 26, 1904	Grammar	600.00
Stimmel, Mrs. A.	Fifth	Sept. 1, 1897	Grammar	600.00
Enkle, Mrs. M. E.	Foreign	Sept. 1, 1872	Grammar	600.00
[illegible]s, Mr. F. A.	Foreign		Grammar	600.00
Daniels, John R.	Bookkeeping	Sept. 1, 1891	Special	600.00
Cohen, Miss R. B.	Stenography	Sept. 1, 1897	Grammar	600.00
Cronin, Miss K. F.	Typewriting	Jan. 2, 1903	Grammar	600.00
Kiely, Miss E. C.	Foreign	Sept. 14, 1905	Grammar	600.00
Spadoni, Miss A.	Foreign	Jan. 29, 1906	High	600.00
Painton, Mr. H. R.	Seventh	Oct. 2, 1905	Grammar	600.00
Melsted, Mr. L. D.	Stenography	Oct. 23, 1903	Special	600.00
Horace Mann Evening—				
Kratzer, Mr. D. W.	Principal	Aug. 14, 1897	Grammar	1,200.00
Bodkin, Miss A. J.	Foreign	Dec. 28, 1898	Special	600.00
Gorham, Miss K. L.	Bookkeeping	Aug. 30, 1897	Grammar	600.00
[illegible]r, Dr. G. J.	Fifth	July 20, 1903	Grammar	600.00
Kelly, Eliz. F.	Eighth	Aug. 18, 1904	Grammar	600.00
[illegible]e, Miss H. F.	Eighth	Sept. 1, 1905	Grammar	600.00
[illegible]g, Miss E. C.	Seventh	Dec. 15, 1896	Grammar	600.00
Martin, Miss A. G.	Seventh	July 28, 1898	Grammar	600.00
Marshall, Mrs. M. L.	Sixth	Sept. 1, 1897	Grammar	600.00
Kozminsky, Miss B.	Fifth	Aug. 31, 1892	Grammar	600.00
Dwyer, Mrs. M.	Fourth	Feb. 12, 1868	Primary	600.00
MacDonald, Miss F. M.	Foreign	Dec. 5, 1892	Grammar	600.00
Blum, Miss J. L.	Foreign	July 27, 1897	Grammar	600.00
Doyle, Miss J.	Ninth	July 28, 1898	Grammar	600.00
[illegible]s, Miss I. J.	Foreign	Aug. 19, 1907	Grammar	600.00
Irving M. Scott Evening—				
Ross, Mr. Louis	Principal	Feb. 17, 1908	High	600.00
Hall, Mr. H. C.	Foreign	July 1, 1903	High	600.00

LIST OF SCHOOLS AND TEACHERS—Continued.

Name.	Grade of Class.	When Elected.	Grade of Certificate	Salary pr Year.
[illegible]—				
MacDonald, Mr. A. H.	Principal	Sept. 2, 1880	High	1,200.00
[illegible], Miss E. J.	[illegible]	Jan. 31, 1889	[illegible]mar	600.00
Smith, Miss N. A.	Eighth	Jan. 3, 1887	[illegible]mar	600.00
Jordan, Mr. L. A.	Eighth	Aug. 1, 18[illegible]	High	600.00
MacDonald, Miss L. M.	Seventh	Aug. 23, 1907	[illegible]	600.00
Harvey, Miss M. A.	Fifth	Aug. 29, 1892	Grammar	600.00
Parlin, Mrs. A. E.	Ungraded	Aug. 31, 1892	Grammar	600.00
Rich, Mrs. L. A.	Vice Principal	Dec. 23, 1885	[illegible]mar	900.00
Greenan, Mrs. R. F.	Sixth	Mar. 26, 1877	[illegible]mar	600.00
Wigand, Mrs. S. S.	Foreign	Dec. 27, 1890	Primary	600.00
[illegible], Miss E.	Foreign	Oct. 23, 1901	Grammar	600.00
Rengla, Mrs. E.	Foreign	Sept. 15, 1887	Grammar	600.00
West, Miss E. L.	Foreign	Aug. 30, 1896	Primary	600.00
O'Neill, Miss L. C.	Foreign	Sept. 8, 1888	Grammar	600.00
Kinne, Mr. H. C.	Foreign	July 14, 1868	High	600.00
[illegible], Miss R. E.	Foreign	Nov. 4, 1878	High	600.00
Ri[illegible] Evening—				
Strauss, Miss M.	Principal	July 11, 1895	Grammar	1,020.00
Roesman, Mr. T. J.	Ninth	July 11, 1902	High	600.00
[illegible], Mr. N. B.	[illegible]	June 24, 1904	[illegible]mar	600.00
[illegible]y, Wm. J.	Sixth	Aug. 19, 1907	[illegible]	600.00
[illegible] Evening—				
[illegible], Mrs. P. M.	Principal	Dec. 14, 1886	Grammar	1,200.00
Williams, Mr. W. J.	Foreign	July 13, 1868	High	600.00
Fischer, Frank	High	July 6, 1886	[illegible]mar	720.00
[illegible], Miss A. M.	[illegible]	May 9, 1886	[illegible]mar	600.00
[illegible], Miss J. A.	[illegible]	June 9, 1897	Grammar	600.00
[illegible], Miss M. C.	Seventh	Dec. 10, 1896	[illegible]	600.00
Grosjean, Mrs. E. S.	Ungraded	May 17, 1883	[illegible]	600.00
[illegible], Ella B.	Foreign	Sept. 1, 1897	Grammar	600.00
Mahoney, Miss M. J.	Foreign	Sept. 30, 1879	[illegible]	600.00
[illegible], Mr. G. P.	Eighth	July 28, 1904	[illegible]	600.00
Bacigalupi, Miss B.	Italian		High	600.00
Nesfield, Miss M. C.	[illegible]	June 29, 1903	Grammar	600.00
Hollub, Miss M. C.	Fifth	April 5, 1892	Grammar	600.00
Humboldt Evening High—				
Taaffe, Mr. L. A.	[illegible]ipal	Dec. 2, 1886	High	1,500.00
Roberts, Mr. A. E.	Hd. of Drawing Dpt.	Dec. 31, 1892	Grammar	1,200.00
Riley, Mr. G. E.	Eng., Hist., C. Gov.	Sept. 1, 1902	High	720.00
[illegible], Mr. F. L.	High School	Feb. 11, 1904	High	720.00

Name	Position	Date	Grade	Salary
Leonard, Mr. E. M.	High School	Aug. 10, 1905	High	720.00
[illegible]y, Miss M. J.	Lie	Ag. 14, 1905	High	720.00
McHenry, Mr. John	Drawing	April 27, 1898	Special	720.00
Christie, Mr. L. C.	[illegible]g	Jan. 3, 1892	Special	720.00
Morgan, Mr. L.	Drawing	Aug. 21, 1902	Special	720.00
Harris, Mr. H. E.	Drawing	Sept. 4, 1902	Special	720.00
Hendry, Mr. C. S.	Drawing	April 27, 1898	Special	720.00
Carroll, Mr. W. E.	Drawing	April 15, 1905	Special	720.00
Blue, Mr. F. K.	Drawing	Aug. 5, 1901	Special	720.00
Roylance, Mr. L. S.	Drawing	April 1, 1905	Special	720.00
Barnett, Mr. A. T.	High School	Sept. 8, 1903	High	720.00
Blake, Mr. W. S.	Science	Jan. 5, 1901	High	720.00
Farmer, Mr. M. S.	[illegible]th	Jan. 8, 1906	[illegible]mmar	600.00
Department at Large—				
Doyle, Mr. M. J.	Mal Taining	Nv. 5, 1897	Special	1,800.00
Williams, Mr. J. B.	Mal Training	Jan. 4, 1906	Special	1,200.00
Davidson, Mr. L. E.	Mal Training	Aug. 1, 1901	Special	1,200.00
Bagot, Mr. H. C.	Manual Training	[illegible]b. 15, 1903	Special	1,200.00
Felton, Mr. M. A.	Mal Taining	July 30, 1902	Grammar	1,200.00
Dailey, Mr. P. F.	Mal Taining	Ag. 10, 1905	Special	1,200.00
Dowling, Mr. D. E.	Mal Taining	Mr. 4, 1906	Special	1,200.00
Silvia, Mr. A. M.	Mal Training	Mr. 11, 1905	High	1,200.00
Carpenter, Miss E.	Mc	Dec. 28, 1898	Special	1,800.00
[illegible]e, Mrs. M. G.	Music	Sept. 3, 1903	Special	1,080.00
Moran, Miss A. J.	Music	Nov. 16, 1905	Special	1,080.00
Crane, Ms. M. H.	Music	Oct. 1, 1907	Special	1,080.00
Ball, Miss K. M.	Drawing	July 1, 1894	Special	1,800.00
Murray, Miss E. B.	Drawing	Dec. 29, 1896	Special	1,080.00
Berth, Mr. R. H.	Physical Culture	[illegible] 31, 1892	Special	1,200.00
Miehling, Mr. O. S.	Physical Culture	Aug. 1, 1897	Special	1,200.00
Bartlett, Miss E. M.	Cookery	July 1, 1901	Special	1,200.00
Ballinger, Miss C. A.	Cookery	July 20, 1905	Special	900.00
[illegible]d, Miss F. M.	[illegible]y	Sept. 1, 1904	Special	900.00
Congdon, Miss M.	Cookery	Aug. 19, 1905	Special	900.00
[illegible]y, Miss E.	[illegible]	Aug. 19, 1907	Special	900.00
Ball, Miss L.	Sup. Prim. [illegible]ding	April 1, 1908	[illegible]	1,800.00
Paulsell, Miss J. N.	Cookery	Nov. 14, 1907	Special	900.00

TEACHERS ON LEAVE OF ABSENCE.

NAME.	SCHOOL.	When Elected.	Grade of Certificate.
Altmann, Mr. Aaron	Lowell High	July 15, 1903	Special
Altmann, Mrs. A	Humboldt	Nov. 1888	Grammar
Agnew, Miss E. O	Substitute	Jan. 29, 1906	Grammar
Adams, Miss E	Substitute	Sept. 1903	Grammar
Armstrong, Mr. A. M	Unassigned	May 28, 1903	High
Arnold, Miss M. V	Oriental	Nov. 1891	Grammar
Beanston, Mrs. E. W	Hawthorne	Aug. 31, 1902	Grammar
Baker, Mr. M. S	Lowell	Sept. 1901	High
Brampton, L. R	Substitute	Feb. 8, 1906	Grammar
Bloch, Mrs. F. V	Buena Vista	Feb. 25, 1905	Grammar
Baird, Mr. F. G	Lincoln Evening	Aug. 8, 1894	High
Boylan, Miss M. L	Burnett	Jan. 12, 1898	Grammar
Barrett, Mr. F. I	Hamilton Evening	Sept. 18, 1905	Special
Blackman, Miss R. E	Substitute	June 1, 1908	Grammar
Blue, Mr. F. K	Humboldt Evening	Aug. 1901	Special
Bartlett, A. G	Oceanside	Oct. 27, 1904	High
Brown, Miss H. A	Substitute	Feb. 12, 1906	Grammar
Connolly, Mr. G	Humboldt Evening	July 20, 1903	High
Crowley, M. I	Hearst	Sept. 21, 1891	Grammar
Crowley, A. T	Douglass	July, 1897	Grammar
Crook, Mrs. W. C. (nee A. J. Connelly)	Clement	No data	
Carson, A. M	Substitute	No data	
Cilker, J. A	Pacific Heights	No data	Grammar
Cozad, M	Substitute	No data	
Cove, E. A	Grattan	Dec. 28, 1880	Grammar
Carey, Mr. M. R	Horace Mann Evening	Oct. 13, 1904	Grammar
Cilker, M	Substitute	No data	
Casey, Miss A. E	Substitute	June 18, 1908	
Cullen, Miss L. R	Harrison	Feb. 14, 1882	Grammar
Coyle, M. G	Garfield	Dec. 5, 1892	Grammar
Cohen, D	Substitute	Jan. 7, 1908	Grammar
Daniel, Ella R	Grant	July 25, 1897	Grammar
Deal, Miss L. B	Hamilton Evening	Jan. 1, 1887	Grammar
Dispaux, K. G	Washington Evening	Sept. 5, 1888	Grammar
Drew, W. J	Humboldt Evening	Feb. 25, 1897	High
Doolan, C. L	Substitute	Oct. 1903	Grammar
Downey, M. V	Substitute	No data	
Deasy, Mr. D. C	Substitute	July 27, 1898	Grammar
Falk, Miss L	Substitute	Aug. 11, 1897	Grammar
Friedlander, C	Hamilton Evening	Oct. 9, 1905	Grammar
Geary, M. I	Pacific Heights	Sept. 1897	Grammar
Goodfriend, Mrs. B	Hamilton Evening	Sept. 12, 1904	Special
Hayes, Miss C. S	Substitute	Feb. 1, 1904	Grammar
Haggerty, Miss K	No date		
Hinds, M. W	Moulder	Dec. 1893	Grammar
Hodgkinson, Miss F	Lowell	May 27, 1885	High
Howell, E	Evening Substitute	Dec. 4, 1907	Grammar
Harrington, K	Substitute	May, 1890	Grammar

NAME.	SCHOOL.	When Elected.	Grade of Certificate.
Jacobs, N. A.	Lafayette	Sept. 5, 1888	Grammar
Kerns, Miss M.	Lafayette	July 25, 1904	Grammar
Koch, F. W.	Lowell	No data	
Lattimore, K.	Columbia	Sept. 19, 1888	Primary
Livingston, B.	Commercial Evening	Aug. 6, 1890	Special
Leszynsky, H. L.	Girls High	No data	High
Lyons, Grace	Substitute	Aug. 14, 1905	Grammar
Livingston, M.	Sutro	No data	
Ludlow, M. B.	Marshall	Nov. 4, 1904	No data
Monaco, N. I.	Jean Parker	Jan. 2, 1902	Grammar
Martin, A. M.	Clement	Dec. 30, 1880	Grammar
Michelson, J. A.	Pacific Heights	Mar. 1888	High
Miles, J. C.	Emerson	Jan. 12, 1908	Grammar
Morgan, W. R.	Humboldt Evening	Sept. 1896	Special
Miller, F. F.	Substitute	Sept. 1907	Grammar
MacLean, D. G.	Horace Mann Evening	April 6, 1908	High
McLellan, E. D.	Hamilton	No data	
McCabe, J.	Substitute	Aug. 14, 1905	Grammar
McDonnell, M.	Denman	Aug. 1880	Grammar
McCarty, Miss M. G.	Fairmount	Aug. 10, 1898	Grammar
McGraw, Miss M.	Substitute	June 8, 1908	Grammar
McMillan, K.	Substitute	Oct. 7, 1907	Grammar
Nunan, Miss K. T.	Irving M. Scott	May 14, 1890	Grammar
Nicholson, G.	Substitute	Aug. 14, 1905	No data
O'Connor, Joseph	Mission High	Oct. 1888	High
O'Connor, K. L.	Cooper	April 1, 1905	
O'Connell, A. E.	McKinley	July 6, 1905	Grammar
O'Neil, Mrs. N. T.	Hearst	Dec. 30, 1892	Grammar
O'Neil, M. F.	Substitute	Mar. 30, 1905	Grammar
Powers, J. L.	Humboldt Evening		
Parks, Miss C. E.	Douglass	Sept. 2, 1897	Grammar
Reed, F. S.	Jefferson	July 6, 1905	High
Ruff, M. C.	Substitute	Feb. 6, 1906	Grammar
Sutherland, A. E.	Spring Valley	Dec. 16, 1884	Grammar
Skahaen, L. C.	James Lick	Aug. 1, 1904	Grammar
Snyder, C. D.	Lowell High	No data	
Stokes, G.	Lowell High	No data	
Smith, M. J.	Marshall	July 9, 1885	Grammar
Senter, K. G.	Substitute	No data	
Tompkins, P. T.	Lowell High	Dec. 27, 1904	High
Vincent, Miss E. M.	Winfield Scott	June 23, 1904	Grammar
Wheeler, Miss. B.	Burnett	Feb. 1, 1905	Grammar
Wilson, L. S.	Winfield Scott	Jan. 5, 1903	High
Young, M. H.	Substitute	July 6, 1905	Grammar

NAMES AND LOCATION OF SCHOOLS AND DESCRIPTION OF SCHOOL PROPERTY.

Adams Cosmopolitan Grammar School. Temporary frame building, 12 rooms; Eddy Street, between Van Ness Avenue and Polk Street; lot in block 62 W. A., 137½x120 feet.

Agassiz Primary School. Eighteen rooms; Bartlett Street, between Twenty-second and Twenty-third Streets; lot in Mission Block 136, 150x250 feet, occupied also by Horace Mann Grammar School. On May 9, 1902, additional lot, Southwest corner Twenty-second and Bartlett Streets, S. 55 feet by W. 85 feet, was purchased from S. J. Hendy.

Bay View Primary School. Temporary building, 6 rooms. On July 10, 1905, additional lot in Silver Terrace Tract, block C, was purchased from Allen Riddell for $10,250. Commencing at the corner formed by the intersection of the Southerly line of Bay View Avenue and the Easterly line of Flora Street, and running thence Easterly along said Southerly line of Bay View Avenue, 200 feet, to the Westerly line of Pomona Street: thence at a right angle Southerly 350 feet; thence at a right angle Westerly 200 feet, to the Easterly line of Flora Street; thence Northerly along said line of Flora Street 350 feet, to the Southerly line of Bay View Avenue, and point of commencement. Recorded in Book 2,124 of Deeds, page 60. School located on Bay View Avenue and Flora Street.

Bergerot Primary School. New building, 12 rooms. Twenty-fifth Avenue and California Street. Block 95, 150x240 feet.

Bernal Grammar School. Frame building, 16 rooms. Courtland Avenue, between Andover Avenue and Moultrie Street. Lot in Gift Map No. 2, 140x148 feet 8½ inches.

Bryant Cosmopolitan Primary School. Temporary building, 12 rooms. York and Twenty-third Streets. Lot in Mission Block 147, between Twenty-second and Twenty-third Streets, Bryant and York Streets. 150 feet by 200 feet.

Buena Vista Primary School. Frame building, 13 rooms. Bryant Street, between Eighteenth and Nineteenth Streets. Lot on Potrero Block 39, 100x200 feet.

Burnett Grammar School. Frame building of 12 rooms and two adjacent rented rooms. L Street and Fourteenth Avenue South. Lot in South San Francisco Homestead Block 289. Lot 1, 75x100 feet; lot 2, 75x100 feet, and additional lot purchased from Cecilia Wright, August 26, 1903 for $500, South San Francisco Homestead. Commencing at a point on the Southwest line of Fourteenth Avenue South; distant 150 feet Northwesterly from the Northwesterly line of L Street South; thence Northwesterly along Fourteenth Avenue South, 32½ feet, by uniform depth of 100 feet.

Clement Primary School. Temporary frame building, 6 rooms. Day and Noe Streets.

Clement Cooking and Manual Training Center. Temporary frame building, 6 rooms. Geary, near Jones Street. Lot in Block 253, 77½x137½ feet. Additional lot commencing at a point on the Southerly line of Geary Street, distant 137 feet 6 inches Westerly from the Southwest corner of Geary and Jones Street; thence Northerly along said line of Geary Street, 25 feet by South 137 feet 6 inches in depth, being a portion of 50 vara lot 253. Purchased from S. L. and Mabel V. Starr, August 14, 1905 for $27,000. Recorded in Book 2,134 of Deeds, page 98.

Columbia Grammar School. Frame building, 18 rooms and three portable rooms. Florida Street, between Twenty-fifth and Twenty-sixth Streets. Lot in Mission Block 178. Lot No. 1, 100x200 feet; lot No. 2, 50x100 feet.

Cooper Primary School. Temporary frame building, 6 rooms. Greenwich Street, between Jones and Leavenworth Streets, lot in Block 237, 137½x137½ feet.

Commercial School. Afternoon session at Mission High School, Eighteenth and Dolores.

Crocker Grammar School. Frame building, 20 rooms. Page Street, between Broderick and Baker Streets. Lot in Block 523 W. A., 137½x137½ feet. Additional lot purchased from W. J. Hawkins, May 16, 1905, for $2,750. Commencing at a point on the Southerly line of Page Street, distant 96 feet, 10½ inches, Easterly from the Easterly line of Baker Street; thence Easterly 25 feet by uniform depth of 110 feet.

Denman Grammar School. Temporary frame building, 6 rooms. Bush Street, between Larkin and Hyde Streets. Lot in Block 307, 97½x137½ feet.

Douglass Primary School. Frame building, 10 rooms. Corner Nineteenth and Collingwood Streets. Lot in Horner's Addition, 135x135 feet.

Dudley Stone Primary School. Frame building, 16 rooms. Haight Street, between Lott and Masonic Avenues, lot in Block 657 W. A., 137½x137½ feet.

Edison Primary School. Frame building, 10 rooms. Church and Hill Streets. Lot in Mission Block 90, 101 feet 9 inches by 114 feet.

Emerson Primary School. Frame building, 20 rooms. Pine Street, between Scott and Devisadero Streets. Lot in Block 460 W. A., 137½x137½ feet.

Everett Grammar School. Frame building, 16 rooms; five additional rooms are rented. Sanchez Street, between Sixteenth and Seventeenth Streets. Lot in Mission Block 95, 125x160 feet.

Fairmount Grammar School. Frame building, 12 rooms. Chenery Street, near Randall Street, five portable rooms on premises. Lot in Fairmount Tract, Block 29. Lot 1, 112x125 feet; lot 2, 62x175 feet.

Franklin Grammar School. Temporary frame building, 12 rooms, Eighth Street, near Bryant Street. Lot in Block 410, 140x275 feet.

Frank J. McCoppin School. Temporary frame building, 9 rooms. Sixth Avenue, between B and C Streets. Lot in Block 375, West of First Avenue, 150x240 feet.

Fremont Grammar School. Frame building, 16 rooms. McAllister Street, between Broderick and Baker Streets. Lot in Block 530 W. A., 137½x137½ feet. Additional lot (No. 1) purchased from Herman Murphy, January 3, 1902, for $3,250. Commencing at a point on the Northerly line of McAllister Street, distant 112½ feet Westerly from the Westerly line of Broderick Street; thence Westerly 25 feet, by uniform depth of 137 feet, 6 inches. Recorded in Book 1,947 of Deeds, page 102. Additional lot (No. 2) purchased from Owen McHugh, July 1, 1902. Commencing at a point on the Northerly line of McAllister Street, distant 96 feet, 10½ inches Easterly from the Easterly line of Baker Street, running thence Easterly 25 feet, by uniform depth of 137 feet, 6 inches. Recorded in Book 1,962 of Deeds, page 138.

Garfield Primary School. Temporary frame building, 10 rooms (four additional rented rooms). Union Street, near Kearny Street. Lot in Block 62, 137½x137½ feet.

Girls' High School. Temporary frame building just completed at a cost of $16,000. Scott Street, near Geary Street. This school is not built on school property, but on property belonging to the City and which originally formed a part of Hamilton Square. In 1870 the Board of Education obtained permission to use a portion for the erection of school buildings. Lot 275 feet front on Scott Street, 341 feet 3 inches on Geary and O'Farrell Streets.

Glen Park Grammar School. New frame building, 12 rooms, costing $45,000. San Jose and Joost Avenues. Additional lot purchased from the Estate of John Pforr, May 20, 1905, for $5,600. Mission and Thirtieth Extension Homestead Union. Beginning at the corner formed by the intersection of the Southwesterly line of Berkshire Street with the Southeasterly line of Lippard Avenue; thence Southwesterly along Lippard Avenue, 400 feet; thence at right angles Southeasterly 200 feet, to the Northwesterly line of Fulton

Avenue; thence at right angles Northeasterly 400 feet along Fulton Avenue, to the Southwesterly line of Berkshire Street thence at a right angle Northwesterly along Berkshire Street to the point of beginning, being all of Block 3, Mission and Thirtieth Street Extension Homestead Union. Recorded in Book 2,125 of Deeds, page 76.

Golden Gate Primary. New building being built. Golden Gate Avenue, between Pierce and Scott Streets. Lot in Block 433 W. A., 100x137½ feet. Additional lot purchased from Fred L. Hansen, July 20, 1905, for $4,375. Commencing at a point on the Northerly line of Golden Gate Avenue, distant thereon 68 feet 9 inches, Westerly from the Westerly line of Pierce Street; thence Westerly 25 feet, by uniform depth of 137 feet 6 inches. Additional lot (No. 2) purchased from Margaret Poyelson, June 28, 1905, for $8,856. Commencing at a point on the Northerly line of Golden Gate Avenue, distant thereon 93 feet 9 inches, Westerly from the Westerly line of Pierce Street: thence Westerly 43 feet 9 inches, by uniform depth of 137 feet 8 inches. Additional lot (No. 3) purchased from Gustave A. DeManiel, June 14, 1905, for $12,462. Commencing at a point on the Northerly line of Golden Gate Avenue, distant 137 feet 6 inches, westerly from the Westerly line of Pierce Street; thence Westerly 37 feet six inches, by uniform depth of 137 feet 6 inches.

Grant Primary School. Frame building, 8 rooms. Pacific Avenue, between Broadway and Baker Streets. Lot in Block No. 546 W. A., 137½x137½ feet.

Grattan Primary. Temporary frame building, 6 rooms. Alma Street, near Grattan. Additional lot purchased from the Pope Estate Co., for $28,500. Recorded in Book 2,130 of Deeds, page 204. Western Addition Block 874. Commencing at the point of intersection of the Southerly line of Grattan Street with the Easterly line of Shrader Street; thence Easterly along Grattan Street, 203 feet 7¾ inches; thence at a right angle Southerly 249 feet, to the Northerly line of Alma Avenue; thence at a right angle Westerly and along said line of Alma Avenue, 203 feet 7¾ inches, to the Easterly line of Shrader Street; thence at a right angle Northerly 249 feet 11 inches, to the Southerly line of Grattan Street, and point of commencement.

Haight Primary. Frame building, 13 rooms. Mission Street, between Twenty-fifth and Twenty-sixth Streets. Lot in Mission Block 183. 150x117½ feet.

Hamilton Grammar. Frame building, 17 rooms. Geary Street, between Scott & Pierce Streets. (See Girls' High School).

Hancock Grammar. Temporary frame building, 10 rooms. Filbert Street, near Jones. Lot in Block 208, 100x120 feet.

Harrison Primary. Temporary frame building, 3 rooms. Railroad Avenue and Thirty-fourth Streets.

Hawthorne Primary. Frame building, 11 rooms. Shotwell Street, between Twenty-second and Twenty-third Streets, lot in Mission Block 138, 122½x122½ feet.

Hearst Grammar. Frame building, 25 rooms. Corner Fillmore and Hermann Streets, lot in Block 374 W. A., 137½ x 137½ feet.

Henry Durant Primary. Frame building, 12 rooms. Turk Street, between Buchanan and Webster Street, lot in Block 281 W. A., 137½x120 feet.

Holly Park Primary. Temporary frame building of 8 rooms. Andover Avenue and Jefferson Street. (Lot is leased).

Horace Mann Grammar. Frame building, 20 rooms. Valencia Street, between Twenty-second and Twenty-third Streets. (See Agassiz Primary).

Hunter's Point Primary. Temporary frame building of two rooms. Eighth Avenue, between C and D Streets. (Lot is leased).

Irving Primary. Temporary frame building, 6 rooms. Broadway, between Montgomery and Sansome Streets. Lot in Block No. 47, 68¾x137½ feet.

Irving M. Scott Grammar. Frame building, 20 rooms. Tennessee Street, near Twenty-second. Lot in Potrero Block No. 373, 150x200 feet.

Jackson Primary. Temporary portable frame building, 6 rooms. Oak and Stanyan Streets. (Lot is leased).

James Lick Grammar. Frame building, 14 rooms. Noe and Twenty-fifth Streets. Lot in Horner's Addition, Block No. 163, 114x116 feet.

Jean Parker Grammar. Temporary building, 10 rooms. Broadway, between Powell and Mason Streets. Lot in Block No. 157. Lot 1, 65 feet 2 inches by 137½ feet; lot 2, 30x91 feet 8 inches; lot 3, 39 feet 9 inches by 91 feet 8 inches.

Jefferson Primary. Temporary frame building, 6 rooms. Bryant and Seventh Streets. Lot in Block No. 397, 92½x275 feet.

John Swett Grammar. Temporary frame building, 12 rooms. McAllister Street, between Franklin and Gough Streets. Lot in Block No. 136 W. A., 137½x137½ feet.

Laguna Honda Primary. Building being built. Seventh Avenue, between I and J Streets. Lot in Block No. 678, 150x240 feet.

Lake View Primary. Temporary frame building, 4 rooms. Plymouth and Grafton Streets.

Lincoln Grammar School. Temporary frame building, 8 rooms. Harrison Street, near Fourth. Lot in Block No. 374, 195x160 feet. Additional lot (1) purchased from Bertha Gunnison, February 9, 1906, for $4,250. Commencing at a point on the Northwesterly line of Harrison Street, distant thereon 275 feet. Southwesterly on the Southwest line of Fourth Street, running thence Southerly along said line of Harrison Street; thence at a right angle Northwesterly 85 feet; thence at a right angle Northwesterly 85 feet, to the North line of Harrison Street, from the point of commencement. Additional lot (2) purchased from Herman Scholten, December 18, 1905, for $2,800. Commencing at a point on the Southeasterly line of Clara Street, distant 275 feet Southwesterly from the point of intersection of said Southeasterly line of Clara Street with the Southwesterly line of Fourth Street, running thence Southwesterly along said Southeasterly line of Clara Street, 25 feet; thence at a right angle Southeasterly, 75 feet; thence at a right angle Northeasterly, 25 feet; thence at a right angle Northwesterly, 75 feet, to the Southeasterly line of Clara Street and point of commencement.

Lowell High School. Frame building, 21 rooms. Sutter Street, between Octavia and Gough Streets. Lot in Block No. 158, W. A., 137½x120½ feet.

Madison Primary. Frame building, 8 rooms. Clay Street, near Walnut Street. Lot in Block No. 815, W. A., 137½x137½ feet.

Marshall Primary. Temporary frame building, 10 rooms. Julian Avenue, between Fifteenth and Sixteenth Streets. Lot in Mission Block No. 35, 200x182 feet. (Also occupied by Mission Grammar School).

McKinley Primary. Temporary frame building, 12 rooms. Fourteenth and Castro Streets. Additional lot purchased from Jas. Irvine, August 14, 1905. Cost $35,000. Mission Block No. 121. Commencing at the Southwesterly corner of Fourteenth and Castro Streets; thence Westerly along the Southerly line of Fourteenth Street, 320 feet; thence at right angle Southerly, 230 feet, to the Northerly line of Henry Street; thence Easterly along said last named line, 320 feet to the Westerly line of Castro Street; thence Northerly along said last named line, 230 feet, to the point of commencement.

Mission Grammar. Temporary frame building, 12 rooms. Mission, between Fifteenth and Sixteenth Streets. (See Marshall Primary.)

Mission High School. Brick building, 25 rooms. Eighteenth and Dolores Streets. Mission Block No. 85, 398x194 feet. Purchased in 1896 for $52,500.

Monroe Grammar. Building being built. China Avenue and London Streets. Lot in Block No. 14, Excelsior Homestead, 150x100 feet. Additional lot purchased from Thomas Shewbridge, August 30, 1902, Excelsior Homstead Block No. 14. New lot, corner China Avenue and Paris Street, Northwest 100 feet, by Northeast 150 feet, lot 4, Block 14, Excelsior Homestead.

Moulder Primary. Frame building, 10 rooms. Page and Gough Streets, lot in Block No. 145, W. A., 137½x120 feet.

Noe Valley Primary. Frame building, 15 rooms. Twenty-fourth and Douglas. Additional lot (No. 1) purchased from George and Christina Gies. Deed dated October 5, 1901. Horner's Estate, Block 244. Commencing at a point on the West line of Douglass Street, 139 feet North to Twenty-fourth Street; thence North on the West line of Douglass Street, 25 feet, by West, 125 feet in depth. Additional lot (No. 2) purchased from Mary E. Gies. Deed dated, October 7, 1901. Commencing at a point on the West line of Douglass Street, 114 feet North of Twenty-fourth Street; thence North on the West line of Douglass Street, 25 feet, by West 125 feet in depth. Additional lot (No. 3) commencing at a point on the West line of Douglass Street, 64 feet North of Twenty-fourth Street; thence North on Douglass Street, 50 feet, by West 125 feet in depth. Additional lot (No. 4) purchased from Jas. M. Curtin, deed dated September 6, 1901. Commencing at a point on the Northwest corner of Twenty-fourth and Douglass Streets; thence North 64 feet, West 125 feet, North 50 feet, West 51 feet 8 inches, South 114 feet, East 176 feet 8 inches. Additional lot (No. 5) purchased from Eliz. Overend, for $2,050. Commencing at a point on the South line of Elizabeth Street, 125 feet West of Douglass Street; thence West on Elizabeth Street, 51 feet 8 inches, by South 114 feet in depth.

Ocean House Primary. Frame building, 2 rooms. Corner Corbett Road and Ocean Avenue. Cost $1,401.58. Lot in San Miguel. 100 feet by 240 feet.

Oceanside Primary. New frame building, 8 rooms. Forty-second avenue and I Street. Lot in Block No. 714. 150 feet by 240 feet.

Oral School for Deaf. Temporary frame building, one room. McAllister Street, between Octavia and Gough Streets. (See John Sweet Grammar.)

Oriental Public School. Temporary frame building, 5 rooms. Clay Street, near Powell Street.

Parental School. Temporary frame building, 3 rooms. Harrison Street, near Tenth. Lot in Mission Block No. 8. 137½ feet by 137½ feet.

Pacific Heights Grammar. Frame building, 19 rooms. Jackson, between Fillmore and Webster Streets. Lot in Block 318 W. A. 137½ feet by 137½ feet.

Peabody Primary. Sixth Avenue, near California. Lot in Block No. 176; 150x240 feet.

Polytechnic High. Temporary frame building, 16 rooms. Frederick Street, near First Avenue. Additional lot purchased from the City Realty Company July 31, 1905, for $65,000. Western Addition Block No. 740. Commencing at a point on the South line of Frederick Street 121½ feet East from First Avenue; thence in a Southerly direction 175 feet; thence at a right angle Easterly 1 foot 6 inches; thence at a right angle Southerly 100 feet to a point in the North line of Carl Street 151½ feet East of First Avenue; thence easterly along Carl Street 464 and 8-12 feet to a point 269 4-12 feet West of Willard Street; thence Northerly 278 5-12 feet to a point on the South line of Frederick Street 226 11-12 feet West of Willard Street; thence West along South line of Frederick Street 505 10-12 feet to point of commencement.

Redding Primary. Temporary frame building, 6 rooms. Pine Street, between Polk and Larkin Streets. Lot in Block 114 W. A.; 200x120 feet.

Richmond Grammar. Frame building, 17 rooms. First Avenue, near Point Lobos Avenue. Lot in Academy of Science Block, W. A. O. L. R. 157 feet 7 inches by 240 feet. The Board of Education has permission to use this lot for school purposes.

Sheridan Primary. One-story frame building, comprising 12 rooms. Minerva Street, near Plymouth Avenue. Lot in Block S, Railroad Homestead Association. 100 feet by 125 feet.

Sherman Primary. Frame building, 14 rooms. Union Street, near Franklin Street. Lot in Block No. 117 W. A. 137½ feet by 137½ feet.

South End Primary. Frame building, comprising 13 rooms. Somerset Street, between Felton and Burrows Streets. Lot in University Mound Survey, 50 feet by 120 feet. Additional block purchased from P. J. Kennedy August 22, 1905, for $5,000.00. University Mound Survey Block 12. Commencing at a point formed by the intersection of the Northwesterly line of Bacon Street, in the Southwesterly line of Girard Street, running thence Northwesterly along Girard Street 200 feet and thence at a right angle 240 feet to Berlin Street, thence at a right angle Southeasterly and along Berlin Street 200 feet to the Northwesterly line of Bacon Street; thence at a right angle 240 feet to the Southwesterly line of Girard Street and point of commencement, being the Southerly half of Block No. 12, University Mound Survey.

Spring Valley Grammar. Temporary frame building, 9 rooms. Broadway near Polk Street. Lot in Block 21 W. A. 137½ feet by 137½ feet.

Starr King Primary. Temporary frame building, 9 rooms. San Bruno Avenue, near Twenty-fifth Street.

Sunnyside Primary. Building being built. 115 Flood Avenue. Additional Lots 10 to 24 inclusive. Sunnyside Tract. Purchased from the Sunnyside Land Company, July 19, 1902.

Sunset Primary. Temporary frame building, 6 rooms. Thirteenth Avenue and K Street. Block No. 780. West of First Avenue. 150 feet by 240 feet.

Sutro Grammar School. Frame building, comprising 13 rooms. Twelfth Avenue, between Clement and California Streets. Lot in Block No. 179; west of First Avenue; 150x240 feet.

Visitacion Valley Primary. Temporary frame building, 7 rooms. Sunnydale avenue and Cora Street.

Washington Grammar. Temporary frame building, 9 rooms. (New steel-concrete building being built). Washington and Mason Streets. Lot in Block No. 188: 137½x137½ feet. Additional new Lot No. 1; purchased from the estate of Louise C. Kauffman, March 10, 1905, for $7,500. Commencing at a point on the Southerly line of Washington Street 137 feet 6 inches Northerly from the Southwest corner of Mason and Washington Streets, thence Southerly 137 feet 6 inches by West 34 feet 4½ inches, being a portion of 50 Vara lot 188. Additional new lot No. 2, purchased from Julie Dunnier and others, July 12, 1905, for $9,500. Commencing at a point on the Southerly line of Washington Street, distant 170 feet 10½ inches from the Southwest corner of Mason and Washington Streets; thence Northerly 34 feet 4½ inches by South 137 feet 6 inches in depth, being a portion of 50 Vara lot 188.

West End Primary. One-story frame building, 3 rooms. 5630 Mission Street. Lot in West End Map. Block 23. 80x165 feet.

Winfield Scott Primary. Building being built. Lombard Street, between Broderick and Baker Streets. Lot in Block No. 553 W. A. 137½x137½ feet.

Yerba Buena Primary. Building being built. Greenwich street, between Webster and Fillmore Streets. Lot in Block No. 325 W. A. 137½x120 feet.

LIST OF UNOCCUPIED PROPERTIES BELONGING TO SCHOOL DEPARTMENT.

Lot in Block No. 220; northwest corner Bush and Taylor Streets; 137½x 137½ feet.

Lot in Block No. 3, W. A., Grove Street, near Larkin Street; 137½x137½ feet.

Lot in Block No. 286; Golden Gate Avenue, near Hyde Street; 110x137½ feet

Lot in Block 348; Tehama Street, between First and Second Streets; irregular in size; about 118x155 feet.

Lot in Block No. 82. Corner Filbert and Kearny Streets; 137½x137½ feet. Additional lot adjacent in litigation.

Lot in Block No. 160; Powell Street, between Washington and Jackson Streets; 68¾x137½ feet.

Lot in Block No. 371; Fifth Street, near Market Street; 275x275 feet. Leased to Wise Realty Company (later merged into the Lincoln Realty Company) for thirty-five years, at a total rental of $2,835,000, as follows: for the first five years a rental of $3,780 per month, and for the remaining thirty years a rental of $7,245 per month.

Lot in Block No. 137; Powell Street, between Clay and Sacramento Streets; 68¾x137½ feet.

Lot in Mission Block No. 21; West Mission Street, between Hermann and Ridley Streets; 133¾x137½ feet.

Lot in Block No. 118; corner Bush and Stockton Streets; 137½x137½ feet.

Lots in Block 358; Silver Street, between Second and Third Streets. Lot No. 1, 88x70 feet; Lot No. 2, 100x185 feet.

Lot in Mission Block No. 72. Commencing at a point formed by the intersection of the Southerly line of Nineteenth Street with the Easterly line of Angelica Street, running thence Southerly along said Easterly line of Cumberland Place; thence Easterly along said Northerly line of Cumberland Place and Cumberland Place Extension 183 feet; thence at a right angle Northerly 91 feet; thence at a right angle Northerly 50 feet; thence in a Northwesterly direction 118 feet 2½ inches to a point in the Southerly line of Nineteenth Street, which point is distant Easterly 102 feet from the Southeasterly corner of Nineteenth and Angelica Streets; thence Westerly along said Southerly line of Nineteenth Street 102 feet to the point of commencement. Purchased from P. W. Riordan, Roman Catholic Archbishop of San Francisco, for $33,625, as an alternate site for the Marshall Primary School. Recorded in Book 128 of Deeds, page 251, New Series.

Lot in Block 119, on Post Street, between Grant Avenue and Stockton Street; 70x122½ feet. Leased July 1, 1892, for ten years at $755 per month; later reduced to $600 per month.

Lot in Block 137, on Clay Street, between Stockton and Powell Streets; 26½x75 feet. Rented at $10 per month.

Lot in Block 183, on Northeast corner Taylor and Vallejo Streets; 137½x 137½ feet.

Lot in Block 302, on Washington Street, between Hyde and Leavenworth Streets; 137½x137½ feet.

Lot in Block 371, known as Lincoln School Lots, fronting 275 feet on Market Street by 100 feet in depth. Rented to various parties at $3,310 per month.

Lot in Block 374, corner Fourth and Clara Streets; 80x150 feet. Rented at $175 per month.

Lot in Mission Block 61, on Nineteenth Street, between Mission and Howard Streets; 137½x137½ feet, less 60 feet included in Capp Street. Title in litigation.

Lot in Mission Block 104, on south side of Sixteenth Street, between Sanchez and Noe Streets; 137½x137½ feet. In litigation.

Lot in Block 29 W. A., on south side of Francisco Street, between Larkin and Polk Streets; 137½x137½ feet.

Lot in Block 111 W. A., on south line of Bay Street, between Franklin and Gough Streets; 137½x137½ feet. In litigation.

Lot in Block 123 W. A., on south line of Washington Street, between Franklin and Gough Streets; 137¼x137½ feet.

Lot in Block 465 W. A., on north line of Jackson Street, between Scott and Devisadero Streets; 137½x137½ feet.

Lot in Block 848 W. A., on south line of Clay Street, between Cherry and First Avenue; 137½x137½ feet.

WEST OF FIRST AVENUE AND NORTH OF THE PARK, THE SCHOOL DEPARTMENT OWNS PROPERTY AS FOLLOWS:

(All 150x240 feet.)

Block 152; Thirty-first Avenue, between California and Clement Streets.
Block 164; Nineteenth Avenue, between California and Clement Streets.
Block 176; Seventh Avenue, between California and Clement Streets.
Block 242; Forty-third Avenue, between Point Lobos Avenue and A Street.
Block 248; Thirty-seventh Avenue, between Point Lobos Avenue and A Street.
Block 254; Thirty-first Avenue, between Point Lobos Avenue and A Street.
Block 260; Twenty-fourth Avenue, between Point Lobos Avenue and A Street.
Block 266; Nineteenth Avenue, between Point Lobos Avenue and A Street.
Block 272; Thirteenth Avenue, between Point Lobos Avenue and A Street.
Block 278; Seventh Avenue, between Point Lobos Avenue and A Street.
Block 339; Forty-third Avenue, between B and C Streets.
Block 345; Thirty-seventh Avenue, between B and C Streets.
Block 351; Thirty-first avenue, between B and C Streets.
Block 357; Twenty-fifth Avenue, between B and C Streets.
Block 363; Nineteenth Avenue, between B and C Streets.
Block 369; Thirteenth Avenue, between B and C Streets.
Block 395; Sixteenth Avenue, between C and D Streets.
Block 407; Twenty-eighth Avenue, between C and D Streets.
Block 418; Twenty-ninth Avenue, between C and D Streets.

ALSO WEST OF FIRST AVENUE AND NORTH OF THE PARK, AS FOLLOWS:

(All not otherwise stated are 150x240 feet.)

Block 673; First Avenue, between I and J Streets; 107x178 feet.
Block 690; Nineteenth Avenue, between I and J Streets.
Block 696; Twenty-fifth Avenue, between I and J Streets.
Block 702; Thirty-first Avenue, between I and J Streets.
Block 708; Thirty-seventh Avenue, between I and J Streets.
Block 775; Eighth Avenue, between K and L Streets.
Block 786; Nineteenth Avenue, between K and L Streets.
Block 792; Twenty-fifth Avenue, between K and L Streets.
Block 798; Thirty-first Avenue, between K and L Streets.
Block 804; Thirty-seventh Avenue, between K and L Streets.
Block 810; Forty-third Avenue, between K and L Streets.
Block 872; Thirteenth Avenue; between M and N Streets.
Block 878; Nineteenth Avenue, between M and N Streets.
Block 884; Twenty-fifth Avenue, between M and N Streets.
Block 890; Twenty-first Avenue, between M and N Streets.
Block 896; Thirty-seventh Avenue, between M and N Streets.
Block 902; Forty-third Avenue, between M and N Streets.
Block 952; Ninth Avenue, between O and P Streets; irregular; 147½x 182 feet.
Block 957; Thirteenth Avenue, between O and P Streets.
Block 963; Nineteenth Avenue, between O and P Streets.
Block 969; Twenty-fifth Avenue, between O and P Streets.
Block 975; Twenty-first Avenue, between O and P Streets.
Block 981; Thirty-seventh Avenue, between O and P Streets.
Block 987; Forty-third Avenue, between O and P Streets.
Block 1,035; Thirteenth Avenue, between Q and R Streets.
Block 1,044; Nineteenth Avenue, between Q and R Streets.
Block 1,050; Twenty-fifth Avenue, between Q and R Streets.

Block 1,056; Thirty-first Avenue, between Q and R Streets.
Block 1,062; Thirty-seventh Avenue, between Q and R Streets.
Block 1,068; Forty-third Avenue, between Q and R Streets.
Block 1,114; Thirteenth Avenue, between S and T Streets.
Block 1,120; Nineteenth Avenue, between S and T Streets.
Block 1,126; Twenty-fifth Avenue, between S and T Streets.
Block 1,132; Thirty-first Avenue, between S and T Streets.
Block 1,138; Thirty-seventh Avenue, between S and T Streets.
Block 1,144; Forty-third Avenue, between S and T Streets.
Block 1,186; Fourteenth Avenue, between U and V Streets; irregular; 161 x92½ feet.
Block 1,191; Nineteenth Avenue, between U and V Streets.
Block 1,197; Twenty-fifth Avenue, between U and V Streets.
Block 1,203; Twenty-first Avenue, between U and V Streets.
Block 1,209; Thirty-seventh Avenue, between U and V Streets.
Block 1,215; Forty-third avenue, between U and V Streets.
Block 1,258; Nineteenth Avenue, between W and X Streets.
Block 1,264; Twenty-fifth Avenue, between W and X Streets.
Block 1,276; Thirty-seventh Avenue, between W and X Streets; irregular; 125 feet 10 inches by 240 feet.
Block 1,282; Forty-third Avenue, between W and X Streets; irregular; 11 feet 2 inches by 240 feet.

LOTS IN POTRERO.

Block 46; York Street, between El Dorado and Alameda Streets; 100x200; Rented at $2 per month.
Block 85; Utah Street, between Yolo and Colusa Streets; 100x200 feet.
Block 127; Vermont Street, between Solano and Butte Streets; 120x200 feet.
Block 149; Kansas Street; between Yolo and Colusa Streets; 150x200 feet.
Block 163; Rhode Island Street, between Mariposa and Solano Streets; 100x200 feet. Rented $2 per month.
Block 226; Arkansas Street, between Nevada and Yolo Streets; 150x200 feet.
Block 254; Connecticut Street, between Yolo and Colusa Streets, 150 x 200 feet.
Block 265; Missouri Street, between Napa and Sierra Streets; 150x200 feet.
Block 287; Texas Street, between Nevada and Yolo Streets; 150x200 feet.
Block 391; Southeast corner Kentucky and Napa Streets; 150x200 feet.

OTHER OUTSIDE LOTS.

Precita Valley Lands; California Avenue, from Eve to Adam Streets; 150x 32 feet.

Paul Tract Homestead; Berlin Street, between Irving and Ward Streets; 85 feet and 2 inches by 120 feet.

RENTS.

	Per Mo.
Stapleton, William; Burnett School, room, Fourteenth Avenue South	$20.00
Anderson, H. B.; Hunter's Point School, lot, Ninth Avenue and G Street	2.50
Wallace, F. B. and Isabelle Sprague, Trustees; Burnett School, lot, Fifth-teenth Avenue and L Street	15.00
Cull, L. C.; Columbia School, lot, Florida and Twenty-fifth Streets	17.50
Hornung, C. F.; Everett School, lot, Sixteenth and Dehon Streets	8.35
Guinaw, E.; Everett School, one room, 375 Sanchez Street	25.00
Truman, A.; Everett School, three rooms, Seventeenth and Sanchez Sts.	60.00

Thomas, H. J.; Marshall School, Fifteenth and Julian Avenue.................... 41.75
Meisel, H. A.; Garfield School, one room, Northwest corner Union and Montgomery Streets 20.00
O'Neill, A. C.; Garfield School, one room, 1315 Montgomery Street............ 20.00
Hefferman, Mrs.; Garfield School, Montgomery and Filbert Streets............ 25.00
Iberg, Mrs. William; Hearst School, four rooms, Steiner and Hermann.... 60.00
Somers, W. J., Jackson School, lot, Oak Street..100.00
Bradrick, C.; James Lick School, lot, Twenty-sixth and Sanchez Streets.... 8.35
Oliva, J.; Monroe School, four rooms, London and China Avenues............ 30.00
Fair, J. O; Sunnyside School, house, 115 Flood Avenue................................ 25.00
Broderick, P.; Sheridan School, lot, Crafton and Plymouth............................ 5.00
Giannini, E.; South End School lot, corner Burrows and Somerset Streets 4.15
O'Callaghan, D.; Fairmount School, lot, corner Day and Noe Streets........ 40.00
O'Callaghan, D.; lot, Moscow and Brail Streets.. 20.00
O'Callaghan, D.; Winfield Scott School, lot, Lombard and Broderick Sts... 60.00
Deasy, D. C.; Lafayette School, lot, Greenwich and Webster Streets............ 30.00
Odland, S. P.; Holly Park School, rooms, 416 Andover Street..................... 25.00

REPORT

OF THE

Superintendent of Schools

San Francisco, Cal.

FOR THE

FISCAL YEAR 1908-09

ALFRED RONCOVIERI, Superintendent of Schools

(Ex-officio member of Board of Education)

INDEX

INDEX

Report of Superintendent of Schools

REPORT OF THE SUPERINTENDENT OF SCHOOLS OF THE CITY AND COUNTY OF SAN FRANCISCO FOR THE YEAR ENDING JUNE 30, 1909.

San Francisco, August 1, 1909.

To the Honorable Board of Supervisors, in and
for the City and County of San Francisco.

Gentlemen:—I have the honor to submit herewith the annual report on the condition of the public schools of this City and County, as required by the Charter, for the fifty-seventh fiscal year of the School Department, ending June 30, 1909.

ALFRED RONCOVIERI,

Superintendent of Common Schools, in and for the City and County of San Francisco.

GENERAL STATISTICS.

Population of the city, 1909, (estimated)	410,000
Number of youth in the city under 17 years of age	111,867
Number of youth in the city between 5 and 17 years of age who are entitled by law to draw public money	88,058
Assessment roll of the taxable property of the city	$454,334,160.00
City school tax on each $100	20.9c
City and County taxes for school purposes	952,257.17

Estimated value of school sites	$5,193,000
Estimated value of school buildings	1,700,000
Estimated value of school furniture	260,000
Estimated value of school libraries	28,513
Estimated value of school apparatus	25,000
Total value of school property	$7,206,513

FINANCIAL REPORT.

DISBURSEMENTS.

Salaries—		
Teachers'—		
High school (including Commercial $30,394.85 and Humboldt Evening High $13,629)..$	187,528.05	
Primary and Grammar	1,067,664.00	
Evening (excepting Humboldt Eve. High)	55,920.00	
Special (Manual Training, Domestic Science, Music, $4,140; Drawing, $5,124)	31,094.95	
Janitors—		
High school	6,420.00	
Primary and Grammar	55,380.50	
Board of Education	11,959.60	
Superintendent and Deputies	14,799.96	
Secretary and Attachees	12,950.00	
Storekeeper and assistants	2,287.85	
Scavenger (contract)	3,000.00	
Teamster	1,800.00	
Superintendent of repairs	2,100.00	
Foreman supply department	1,490.00	
Total salaries		$1,454,394.91
Advertising		186.40
Cartage		67.00
Census		8,126.97
Conveyances		1,495.50
Furniture		20,238.52
Fire escapes and repairs		5,000.00
Fuel		10,578.60
Labor (supply department)		11,352.00
Light		4,992.40
Maps, Charts, Globes and Books		3,166.71
Printing		2,023.61
Rents		7,473.70
Repairs (materials, $4,730.48; labor, $1,485)		6,215.48
School sites (Dudley Stone school)		6,000.00
Stationery		7,731.43
Supplies—		
Laboratory (High schools)..$	937.76	
High school	10,717.91	
Cooking	1,232.26	
Incidental	6,369.19	
Manual training	1,978.73	
Janitorial	3,533.12	
		24,768.97
Teachers' Annuity fund		3,000.00
Teachers' Institute		299.00
Telephone and Telegraph		124.32
Water		14,000.00
Total ordinary expenses		$1,588,235.52

In addition to the foregoing expenditures the Board of Supervisors made special appropriations:

(a) For the equipment of the Monroe, Glen Park, Laguna Honda, Golden Gate and Sunnyside schools (balance unexpended $928.97)	$ 13,000
(b) For repair of school buildings (totally expended by Board of Public Works and demands for labor and material outstanding)	100,000
Total	$113,000

FINANCIAL REPORT.

RECEIPTS.

City and County taxes (exclusive of $100,000 appropriated by the Board of Supervisors for the repair of school buildings to be expended by Board of Public Works)	$952,257.17	
Rents derived from school property	49,324.00	
Sale of old material	844.61	
State apportionment—High schools	25,727.72	
State apportionment—Primary and Grammar	633,807.35	
Total receipts		$1,661,960.85
Total ordinary expenditures		1,588,235.52
Balance (surplus)		$ 73,725.33

The deficit in the school fund for the year ending June 30, 1908, was $50,789.83. It still exists....................$50,789.83

Should a portion of the surplus this year be applied to the extinction of this deficit there would remain a surplus of....................$22,935.50

The Board of Supervisors appropriated $1,600,800 for the maintenance of schools for fiscal year ending June 30, 1909. The revenue was $1,661,960.85. The difference is due mainly to the State apportionments being $49,895.07 in excess of estimates.

GENERAL DEPARTMENT EXPENSES PROBATED AMONG HIGH, PRIMARY AND GRAMMAR AND EVENING SCHOOLS ON THE BASIS OF AVERAGE DAILY ATTENDANCE.

All salaries, except teachers' and janitors'		$ 50,387.41
All other expenses, except light, school sites, rents, supplies (High school, cooking, manual training) and repairs		93,813.88
Total prorated		$144,101.29
High schools	$ 9,353.16	
Primary and Grammar	125,496.00	
Evening schools	9,252.13	
		$144,101.29

DISTRIBUTION OF EXPENDITURES.

High Schools—		
Cost of instruction	$ 173,899.05	
Cost of janitors	6,420.00	
Cost of supplies (special)	11,849.82	
Cost of share (prorated on average daily attendance) of general department expenses	9,353.16	
Total cost of maintaining High schools		$ 201,522.03
Primary and Grammar Schools—		
Cost of instruction	$1,098,758.95	
Cost of janitors	55,380.50	
Rents	6,673.70	
School sites (Dudley Stone school)	6,000.00	
Supplies (cooking and manual training)	7,225.90	
Share of general department expenses	125,496.00	
Total cost Primary and Grammar schools		$1,299,535.05
Evening Schools—		
Cost of instruction	$ 69,549.00	
Light	4,625.29	
Share of general department expenses	9,252.13	
Total cost Evening schools		83,426.42
Unapportioned		3,752.02
Grand total		$1,588,235.52

The following is a report of the amounts expended by the Board of Public Works for improvements and repairs to school buildings during fiscal year 1908-1909 and paid out of a special appropriation of $100,000. This appropriation of $100,000 is in addition to the $1,600,800, appropriated for other school purposes:

Disbursed on permanent improvements	$ 58,095.00
Disbursed for incidental repairs	35,366.86
Salary of storekeeper for the year	1,500.00
Disbursed by Board of Public Works for the Lafayette school for temporary building—Henning and Burke	3,677.85
Disbursed by Board of Public Works for Horace Mann school (concrete bulkhead, curbing, etc.)—I. P. Leonard	222.97
Stock on hand, including lumber, hardware, plumbing material, etc.	1,132.23
	$100,000.00

IMPROVEMENTS AND REPAIRS TO SCHOOLS UNDER DIRECTION OF BOARD OF PUBLIC WORKS.

AGASSIZ:

July—	
Tinted all class rooms and halls	$ 572.65
March—	
Placing basement in sanitary condition, and general repairs to building	161.73

BERNAL:

September—	
Overhauling entire tin roof	247.54
October—	
Painting entire tin roof	112.25
December—	
Built two new toilets for boys and girls, installing individual toilet and urinal sinks, etc.; painting, carpenter work and plumbing complete; 16 toilets for boys, 20 toilets for girls..	3,414.19
February—	
Cutting extra doors in new toilet, and general overhauling of building	169.71

COLUMBIA:

October—	
Overhauling entire tin roof and new leaders	
November—	
New lunch room for teacher, new steps, treads and overhauling entire building	1,598.25
Tinting all class rooms and hallway; painting all new woodwork..	1,008.80

CLEVELAND:

August—	
One new 1,000-gallon water tank and fittings	126.98

CLEMENT:

September—	
Two new class rooms complete	892.32
Moving building from Sanchez street to Twenty-ninth and Day Streets	140.00

DUDLEY STONE:

March—	
Cleaning and painting exterior and interior of fire escapes	145.00

DOUGLASS:

August—	
Fitting up new class in basement	241.69

EVERETT:

August—
Tinted all class rooms and hallways; painted interior woodwork and new fire escapes 963.70
Alteration of building as per plans and specifications of City Architect; new stairs, new fire escapes, new floors where necessary 2,535.48

April—
Building new room for teacher; lunch room in yard 169.56

EMERSON:

July—
Tinted all class rooms and hallways 578.20

September—
New steps to two entrances 121.27

October—
New hand rail for entrance steps 142.66

FREMONT:

December—
Tinting entire interior of building and painting all woodwork 641.01

FAIRMOUNT:

December—
Building two new class rooms in lower yard, complete 864.09

GARFIELD:

August—
Two new class rooms, new toilet, and lunch room 1,182.11

HAWTHORNE:

July—
Tinted all class rooms and hallways, painted interior woodwork 394.85

March—
Reshingling two sides of roof and repairs to yard 201.41

HOLLY PARK:

January—
Building one new class room 438.69

HANCOCK:

December—
Building one new class room, installing new sink in Principal's office 421.54

HORACE MANN:

July—
Tinted all class rooms and hallway 583.80

September—
Painting entire roof 105.50

October—
New concrete steps, carpenter work 318.14

HEARST:

October—
Overhauling foundation of building, new mudsills, new stairs and fence, new exit, overhauling all plumbing, new leaders, fire escapes, etc. 3,971.63

HAMILTON:

July—
Tinted all class rooms and hallways, painted interior woodwork and fire escapes, stripped brickwork and foundation 829.70

August—
Alteration to hall and stairs, new fire escapes, etc., as per plans of City Architect 2,601.05

October—
Overhauling entire tin roof 162.55

HENRY DURANT:

August—
Tinted all class rooms and hallway ... 744.75

JAMES LICK:

July—
Tinted all class rooms and hallways ... 482.39
Overhauling entire tin roof ... 309.13

LINCOLN:

August—
One new class room complete ... 422.52

LOWELL HIGH:

July—
Tinted all class rooms and hallway, painted interior woodwork.... 1,107.25
August—
New fire escapes and alteration to stairway as per plans of City Architect ... 1,816.16

LAKE VIEW:

July—
Building one new class room 24x28 feet and moving toilet.......... 435.09

MOULDER:

December—
Tinting entire interior of building ... 673.62
Fitting and hanging 22 pairs sash ... 242.97
January—
Painting and varnishing all woodwork of interior of building; finishing painting exterior of building ... 326.04
February—
Building two new toilets, new steps to main entrance; general overhauling of building ... 1,757.97
New leader pipes ... 58.30
Installation of plumbing work in boys' and girls' toilets............ 696.38
April—
Buring and painting entire exterior of building and new toilets.. 1,057.04

MISSION HIGH.

January—
Painting all exterior sash and casing and refinishing fixtures...... 348.25

FRANK McCOPPIN:

September—
Painting and tinting two rooms and office; painting toilets, etc.... 157.25

MADISON:

July—
Overhauling entire tin roof ... 161.18

POLYTECHNIC:

August—
Installing 8 individual toilet and teachers' toilet, also 8 new sinks; alteration to building ... 1,022.00
May—
Moving and setting up 4 portable school buildings from Laguna Honda school to present site ... 300.00

PARENTAL:

December—
Building one new class room ... 418.35

ORIENTAL:

December—
Building new lunch room, office and teachers' toilet, complete.... 304.40

PACIFIC HEIGHTS:

August—	
Alteration to building, new fire escapes, new steps, two new wings and general overhauling of entire building	11,066.66
October—	
Roof painted, new addition, fire escapes pinned; office and hall tinted	786.43

RINCON:

June—	
Underway and partially finish of one new 3-room class room; entire room ceiled with T. & G.	2,343.19

RICHMOND:

January—	
Painting iron fire escapes, exterior and interior	188.19

SUTRO:

December—	
Moving shack from Board of Works to school site	202.40

SHERIDAN:

December—	
Moving shacks from Board of Works to school site	145.00

SPRING VALLEY:

August—	
Two new class rooms, new teachers' toilet and sinks complete	1,036.03

SHERMAN:

July—	
Tinted all class rooms and hallways	457.50

VISITACION VALLEY:

September—	
Two new class rooms, Principal's office complete, sink and toilets complete	1,058.21

WASHINGTON IRVING:

August—	
One new class room, teachers' toilet, etc.	498.43
December—	
One new class room complete adjoining previous class room	372.50

SCHOOL DIRECTORS' ROOM:

September—	
Fitting up room for Directors O'Connor and Altman; new toilet and wash basin	618.45
January—	
Fitting up new office for Director Hayden	156.49
	$58,095.09

PERMANENT BUILDINGS ERECTED SINCE APRIL 18, 1906.

Schools.	Location.	Cost.
Bergerot—	Twenty-fifth avenue and Lake street	$48,313.69
Winfield Scott—	Lombard street, between Baker and Broderick	40,440.93
Sunnyside—	Forester street, between Flood and Hearst avenues	37,888.57

Glen Park—	
San Jose and Joost avenues	49,455.10
Laguna Honda—	
Seventh avenue, between I and J streets	81,186.48
Monroe—	
China avenue and London street	78,583.30
Golden Gate—	
Golden Gate avenue, between Scott and Pierce streets	61,417.20
Washington—	
Broadway, between Montgomery and Sansome	74,909.96
Oceanside—	
Forty-second avenue and I street	48,845.24
Bay View—	
Bay View avenue and Flora street	118,673.17
Yerba Buena—	
Greenwich street, near Webster	54,043.00

COST PER PUPIL, 1908-1909.

(a) For Instruction Only—

	Per Pupil Enrolled.	Per Pupil in Average Attendance Daily.	Year '07-'08.
High schools	$53.94	$75.41	$78.88
Primary and Grammar schools	27.51	35.49	32.76
Evening schools	10.94	30.48	31.18

(b) For All Expenditures, Not Including Buildings and Sites—

	Per Pupil Enrolled.	Per Pupil in Average Attendance Daily.	Year '07-'08. Including Temporary Buildings.
High schools	$62.42	$87.25	$115.66
Primary and Grammar schools	32.54	41.98	53.62
Evening schools	13.12	36.58	48.61

SALARY SCHEDULE 1908-1909.

OFFICE AND STOREROOM.

	Per Month.
Deputies of Superintendent	$225.00
Secretary Board of Education	150.00
Clerk High School Board	50.00
Financial Secretary	165.00
Recording Secretary	150.00
Stenographers—Board of Education and Superintendent's office	100.00
Messenger Board of Education	100.00
Messenger Superintendent's Office	90.00
Storekeeper School Department	150.00
Teamster School Department (including use of two-horse team)	150.00
Telephone Exchange Operator	70.00
Superintendent of Building and Repairs	175.00
Foreman—Supply and Equipment Department	115.00

DEPARTMENT AT LARGE.

Supervisors of music, drawing manual training and primary reading and penmanship	$150.00
Assistants in manual training	100.00
Assistants in music and drawing	90.00
Supervisor of cooking	100.00
Assistants in cooking	75.00
Instructors in physical culture	100.00
Special teachers of Modern Languages in 3rd, 4th, 5th, 6th, 7th and 8th grades	100.00

HIGH SCHOOL.

YEAR OF SERVICE.		PRINCIPALS. Attendance (Daily Avg.) Over 800 Class 1		PRINCIPALS. Attendance (Daily Avg.) Up to 800 Class 2		V. Principals.		Heads of Department.		Assistants.	
		per Annum	per Month	per Annum	per Month	per Annum	per Month	per Annum	per Month	per Annum	per Month
Probationary Term	1	$3,000	$250	$3,000	$250	$2,160	$180	$1,920	$160	$1,440	$120
	2	3,000	250	3,000	250	2,160	180	1,920	160	1,440	120
	3	3,180	265	3,120	260	2220	185	2,040	170	1,560	130
	4	3,180	265	3,120	260	2,220	185	2,040	170	1,620	135
	5	3,360	280	3,240	270	2,280	190	2,100	175	1,620	135
	6	3,360	280	3,240	270	2,280	190	2,110	175	1,680	140
	7	3,540	295	3,360	280	2,340	195	2,160	180	1,680	140
	8	3,540	295	3,360	280	2,340	195	2,160	180	1,740	145
	9	3,720	310	3,480	290	2,460	205	2,220	185	1,800	150
	10	3,720	310	3,480	290	2,460	205	2,220	185	1,860	155
	11	4,000	333 ⅓	3,600	300	2,580	215	2,280	190	1,920	160

COMMERCIAL SCHOOL.

YEAR OF SERVICE.		Principal.		Vice-Principal.		Assistants.	
		Per Annum.	Per Month.	Per Annum.	Per Month.	Per Annum.	Per Month.
Probationary Term	1	$2,400	$200	$1,560	$130	$1,200	$100
	2	2,400	200	1,560	130	1,200	100
	3	2,520	210	1,680	140	1,320	110
	4	2,520	210	1,680	140	1,320	110
	5	2,640	220	1,800	150	1,380	115
	6	2,640	220	1,800	150	1,380	115
	7	2,760	230	1,920	160	1,440	120
	8	2,760	230	1,920	160	1,440	120
	9	2,880	240	2,040	170	1,560	130
	10	2,880	240	2,040	170	1,560	130
	11	3,000	250	2,160	180	1,740	145

Salaries of present teachers to continue unchanged.

ELEMENTARY SCHOOLS GRAMMAR.

YEAR OF SERVICE.		PRINCIPALS. Class 1.		PRINCIPALS. Class 2.		Vice-Principals.	
		Per Annum.	Per Month.	Per Annum.	Per Month.	Per Annum.	Per Month.
Probationary Term	1.	$2,100	$175	$2,100	$175	$1,500	$125
Probationary Term	2	2,100	175	2,100	175	1,500	125
	3.	2,220	185	2,160	180	1,560	130
	4.	2,220	185	2,160	180	1,560	130
	5.	2,340	195	2,220	185	1,620	185
	6	2,340	195	2,220	185	1,620	185
	7	2,460	205	2,280	190	1,680	140
	8.	2,460	205	2,280	190	1,180	140
	9.	2,580	215	2,340	195	1,740	145
	10.	2,580	215	2,340	195	1,740	145
	11.	2,700	225	2,400	200	1,800	150

ELEMENTARY SCHOOLS—PRIMARY PRINCIPALS.

	YEAR OF SERVICE.	CLASSES. 1 to 3.*		4 to 7.*		8 to 14.*		Over 14.	
		Per Annum.	Per Mth.	Per Annum.	Per Month.	Per Annum.	Per Mth.	Per Annum.	Per Month.
Probationary Term	1	$1,260	$105	$1,440	$120	$1,560	$130	$1,800	$150
	2	1,260	105	1,440	120	1,560	130	1,800	150
	3	1,320	110	1,512	126	1,620	135	1,872	156
	4	1,320	10	1,512	126	1,620	135	1,872	156
	5	1,380	115	1,584	132	1,680	140	1,944	162
	6	1,380	115	1,584	132	1,680	140	1,944	162
	7	1,440	120	1,656	138	1,740	145	2,016	168
	8	1,440	120	1,656	138	1,740	145	2,016	168
	9	1,500	125	1,728	144	1,800	150	2,088	174
	10	1,500	125	1,728	144	1,800	150	2,088	174
*Inclusive	11	1,560	130	1,800	150	1,860	155	2,160	180

ELEMENTARY SCHOOLS—CLASS TEACHERS.

YEAR OF SERVICE.		GRADES. 2d, 3d and 4th. Per Annum.	Per Mnth.	5th and 6th. Per Annum.	Per Mth.	1st, 7th and 8th. Per Annum.	Per Month.
Probationary Term	1	$840	$70.00	$840	$70.00	$840	$70.00
	2	840	70.00	840	70.00	840	70.00
	3	900	75.00	912	76.00	924	77.00
	4	930	77.50	948	79.00	966	80.50
	5	960	80.00	984	82.00	1,008	84.00
	6	984	82.00	1,014	84.50	1,044	87.00
	7	1,008	84.00	1,044	87.00	1,080	90.00
	8	1,032	86.00	1,074	89.50	1,116	93.00
	9	1,056	88.00	1,104	92.00	1,152	96.00
	10	1,080	90.00	1,134	94.50	1,[illegible]8	99.00
	11	1[illegible]4	92.00	1,164	97.00	1,224	102.00

PARENTAL SCHOOL.

The salary of the principal of the Parental school will remain as at present fixed by the Board ($1,440) until the experience or increase in the number of classes shall require an increase in salary under the schedule for primary principals.

Assistants in the Parental school will be paid under the schedule for teachers of ungraded classes.

EVENING SCHOOLS.

Principals of evening schools which have an average daily attendance of 300 or more pupils shall be paid $100 per month.

In the case of evening schools in which the average daily attendance is less than 300 the principal's salary will be fixed annually by the Board.

Principals.	Salary per Month.
Humboldt Evening	$125.00
Commercial	100.00
Vice-Principal, Lincoln Evening	75.00
Assistants in evening schools	50.00
Head teacher of drawing department, Humboldt Evening High school	100.00
Assistants teaching High school classes and assistant teachers of drawing in Humboldt Evening High school	60.00
Substitutes, when reporting, per evening	1.00
Substitutes, when teaching, per evening	2.50

JANITORS.

Janitors shall be paid five ($5.00) dollars per room up to and including ten rooms, and $4.50 per room thereafter.

This shall not apply to the schools mentioned below, nor to the janitorial service in buildings where more than one janitor is employed.

Hunter's Point school, per month	$15.00
Ocean House school, per month	20.00
Harrison Primary, per month	20.00

SUBSTITUTES.

Day substitutes and teachers on the day unassigned list in Primary and Grammar schools, when actually engaged in teaching, per day	$3.00
Substitutes in evening schools, per evening	2.50
Substitutes in evening schools, for reporting	1.00
High school substitutes, per day	5.00

FINES AND DEDUCTIONS.

See rules of the Board of Education.

GENERAL DIRECTIONS.

Teachers' annual salaries shall be paid in twelve equal installments, one installment for each month in the calendar year.

This schedule of salaries shall not, during the fiscal year 1908-1909, adversely affect the teaching force of those schools that were destroyed by the fire of 1906 and are now in process of rehabilitation.

Except for change of position, no salary shall be reduced by reason of the operation of this schedule.

Salaries of newly appointed teachers shall commence on the date of the beginning of actual and personal service; and all increase in the pay of teachers shall begin on the anniversary of such date.

In classes consisting of two grades, the salary of the higher grade will be paid when the average attendance in the higher grade equals or exceeds two-fifths of the average attendance for the class; provided, that when the average attendance of the entire class is less than forty, the salary of the lower grade shall be paid.

When there are more than two grades in a class, the Board will determine the salary of the teacher.

GRAMMAR SCHOOLS.

Class 1. Schools in which the total average daily attendance is 650 or over, and in which the average daily attendance in the 5th, 6th, 7th and 8th grades (grammar department) has been 400 or over for at least one school year immediately previous to their rating, shall be known as Class 1. Grammar schools.

Schools consisting entirely of grammar grade classes and having had an average daily attendance of 500 or more pupils for at least one school year immediately preceding their ranking, shall be rated as Class 1. Grammar schools, provided that all the grammar grades are represented therein.

Class 2. Schools in which the average daily attendance is 450 or over, and which have had an average daily attendance of 225 or more pupils in the 5th, 6th, 7th, and 8th grades for at least one school year immediately preceding their ranking, shall be rated as Class 2, Grammar schools.

Each principal of a high school or Class 1 grammar school may send to the Board for approval the name of an assistant who shall act as clerk of the school. Such appointees shall be paid fifteen dollars per month in high schools and ten dollars per month in Class 1, grammar schools, in addition to their regular salaries. School clerks shall assist in the preparation of reports, programs, etc.

Vice-principals of high schools acting as heads of departments will be paid the experience salary of the latter position where the experience salary of their positions as vice-principal would be lower.

Commercial and high school assistants holding only special certificates shall be paid a salary of $1,500 per annum.

No person shall be appointed head of a high school department nor, after the fiscal year 1907-1908, continued in that position, unless such person shall have at least one assistant under his or her supervision.

Current expenses of high school laboratories (including salary of student assistants) per school, shall not exceed $40 per month.

In all schools consisting of more than four classes, the minimum average daily attendance per primary class, exclusive of 1st grades and classes of more than two grades, shall be 40; and the minimum average daily attendance per grammar class shall be 45.

Experience shall be reckoned from date of assignment to the different positions in the San Francisco school department, but the salary of a promoted teacher shall in no case be less than that attaching to the position from which he or she may have been promoted. Experience acquired elsewhere shall not, so far as salaries are concerned, be considered.

A vice-principal, when acting in the capacity of principal, shall receive the minimum salary scheduled for the principal whose place he or she is temporarily filling.

Since Sec. 1687 of the school law provides that "Beginners shall be taught by teachers who have had at least two years' experience or by normal school graduates," normal school graduates who have successfully completed their probationary term as teachers of first grade classes will be allowed two years' experience as the equivalent of their normal school training.

Five ($5.00) dollars additional per month shall be paid to regular teachers in primary and grammar schools holding special certificates in music and teaching singing, provided, however, that such teachers shall be required to teach, as far as practicable, every class in the school, in this subject.

The minimum salary for teachers of ungraded classes shall be $1,008 per annum. This salary shall continue during their probationary period and until their experience in ungraded classes plus their previous experience in grammar classes of this department shall entitle them to an increase under the salary schedule for 1st, 7th and 8th grades.

Yard Assistant. In primary schools having an average daily attendance of 500 or over, the principal may name, for the approval of the Board, an assistant to perform yard duty, who shall be paid therefor ten dollars per month, in addition to her regular salary.

HIGH SCHOOLS.

All High school instructors who reached the maximum salary under the schedule of 1907-1908 are allowed the experience of four years under which the maximum was reached.

AVERAGE ANNUAL SALARIES.

	Male.	Female.
Superintendent of Schools (1)	$4,000.00	
Deputy Superintendents of Schools (4)	2,700.00	
School Directors (4)	3,000.00	
Principals of High Schools (5)	3,360.00	
Principals of Primary and Grammar Schools	2,194.28	$1,910.62
Teachers in High Schools	1,800.00	1,745.87
Teachers in Grammar Schools	1,437.35	1,190.80
Teachers in Primary Schools		1,014.48
Teachers in Evening Schools	768.30	633.35
All Teachers, Principals and Superintendents (except substitutes)		$1,155.75

MEDAL FUNDS.

NAME OF FUND.	Deposited in.	In fund June 30, 1909.
Bridge Silver Medal	Hibernia Savings & Loan Society	$2,045.49
Denman Grammar School	Hibernia Savings & Loan Society	1,076.55
Denman Silver Medal	German Savings & Loan Society	2,029.62
Hancock Grammar School	German Savings & Loan Society	419.42
Jean Parker Gram. School	German Savings & Loan Society	326.62
John Swett Gram. School	Hibernia Savings & Loan Society	227.39
Lincoln Grammar School	Hibernia Savings & Loan Society	2,641.53

SCHOOLS.

Number of High Schools	5
Number of Grammar Schools	27
Number of Primary Schools	51
Number of Evening Schools	9
Total number of Schools	92
Number of brick school buildings owned by the department	8
Number of wooden school buildings owned by the department	83
Number of buildings or rooms rented by the department	15
Total number of buildings used by the department	108

SCHOOL ENROLLMENT AND ATTENDANCE FOR THE YEAR ENDING JUNE 30, 1909.

Enrollment.		Increase over 1908.	For year ending April 17, '06.
High Schools (Day)	3,224	234	5,188
Primary and Grammar Schools	39,940	2,074	47,661
Evening Schools	5,345	decr'se1,846	4,993
Totals	48,509	462	57,782

Average Daily Attendance.		Increase over 1908.	For year ending April 17, '06.
High Schools	2,306	283	3,211
Primary and Grammar Schools	30,954	1,142	35,753
Evening Schools	3,281	185	2,967
Totals	35,541	1,610	41,931

ENROLLMENT BY GRADES.

	Boys.	Girls.	Totals.
First Grade	6,114	5,050	11,164
Second Grade	3,117	2,715	5,832
Third Grade	2,661	2,390	5,051
Fourth Grade	2,374	2,262	4,836
Fifth Grade	2,139	2,175	4,314
Sixth Grade	1,820	1,921	3,741
Seventh Grade	1,337	1,614	2,951
Eighth Grade	908	1,343	2,251
Totals	20,470	19,470	39,940

First Year High School	556	1,088	1,644
Second Year High School	306	568	874
Third Year High School	140	231	371
Fourth Year High School	137	198	335
Totals	1,139	2,085	3,224

PUPILS ENROLLED IN THE PUBLIC (DAY) SCHOOLS DURING THE YEAR ENDING JUNE 30, 1908.
ENUMERATED BY GRADES AND AGES.

Grades. BOYS—	6 yrs.	7 yrs.	8 yrs.	9 yrs.	10 yrs.	11 yrs.	12 yrs.	13 yrs.	14 yrs.	15 yrs.	16 yrs.	17 yrs.	18 yrs.	19 yrs.	20 yrs. and over	Total
First Grade	2,043	1,794	969	382	141	74	41	27	19	11	10	3	1			5,515
Second Grade	30	435	972	740	351	179	80	34	23	6	6	2				2,858
Third Grade	1	11	279	748	681	431	242	100	87	9	5		2			2,546
Fourth Grade			18	263	611	638	524	258	144	12	7	3		2	1	2,481
Fifth Grade				18	246	503	596	492	239	79	12	3	1		1	2190
Sixth Grade					15	187	432	522	342	109	17	10		2	1	1,637
Seventh Grade				1		23	183	413	394	185	37	7	2	2	2	1,249
Eighth Grade					1	1	25	167	274	230	89	12	1			800
Total Elementary	2,074	2,240	2,238	2,152	2,046	2,036	2,123	2,013	1,472	641	183	40	7	6	5	[illegible]
1st year high school							2	20	97	147	129	35	6	6	8	450
2d year high school								3	21	67	83	71	26	8	10	289
3d year high school									2	16	40	70	28	20	7	183
4th year high school											19	24	33	10	9	95
Total high school							2	23	120	230	271	200	93	44	34	1,017
Grand total (boys)	2,074	2,240	2,238	2,152	2,046	2,036	2,125	2,036	1,592	871	454	240	100	50	39	20,293

PUPILS ENROLLED IN THE PUBLIC (DAY) SCHOOLS DURING THE YEAR ENDING JUNE 30, 1908.

ENUMERATED BY GRADES AND AGES.

Grades.	GIRLS— 6 yrs.	7 yrs.	8 yrs.	9 yrs.	10 yrs.	11 yrs.	12 yrs.	13 yrs.	Ages. 14 yrs.	15 yrs.	16 yrs.	17 yrs.	18 yrs.	19 yrs.	20 yrs. and over	Total
First Grade	1,726	1,839	780	189	106	20	13	4	3							4,680
Second Grade	33	460	964	606	202	110	32	18	8	1						2,432
Third Grade	2	18	348	775	613	318	165	52	18	5	2					2316
Fourth Grade			10	307	635	765	398	201	60	13	2		1			2,392
Fifth Grade				30	280	619	580	399	167	56	6	2			1	2,140
Sixth Grade				2	28	271	631	585	326	86	17	3	1	1		1,951
Seventh Grade					1	30	261	501	500	178	33	1	1			1,506
Eighth Grade						6	30	201	464	347	110	15				1,173
Total elementary	1,761	2,317	2,102	1,909	1,865	2,139	2,110	1,961	1,544	686	170	21	3	1	1	18,590
1st year high school								40	202	275	206	41	20	6	1	791
2d year high school							1	2	30	219	289	145	44	12	4	746
3d year high school										13	90	109	49	7	2	270
4th year high school											9	48	63	37	9	166
Total high school							1	42	232	507	594	343	176	62	16	1,973
Grand total (girls)	1,761	2,317	2,102	1,909	1,865	2,139	2,111	2,003	1,776	1,193	764	364	179	63	17	([illegible]63

STATE ENROLLMENT OF THE PUBLIC DAY SCHOOLS OF SAN FRANCISCO DURING THE YEAR ENDING JUNE 30, 1908.

ENUMERATED BY SEX, AGE AND GRADE.

Grades. BOYS—	6 yrs.	7 yrs.	8 yrs.	9 yrs.	10 yrs.	11 yrs.	12 yrs.	13 yrs.	14 yrs.	15 yrs.	16 yrs.	17 yrs.	18 yrs.	19 yrs.	20 yrs.	Total
First Grade	2,253	1,995	1,070	428	165	83	46	29	21	11	10	3				6,114
Second Grade	33	476	1,069	815	382	180	85	39	26	5	6	1				3,117
Third Grade	2	13	294	786	716	442	245	103	39	11	6	3	1			2661
Fourth Grade			17	241	588	632	501	232	135	14	6	4	2	1	1	2374
Fifth Grade				16	241	501	575	481	234	75	11	3	2			2139
Sixth Grade					17	213	471	583	382	114	19	12	5	3	1	1,820
Seventh Grade				2	1	29	196	433	422	204	88	6	4	1	1	1,337
Eighth Grade					1		32	189	309	259	99	13	6			908
Total elementary	2,288	2,484	2,450	2,288	2,111	2,080	2,151	2,089	1,568	693	195	45	20	5	3	20,470
1st year high school							1	28	124	189	158	37	5	7	7	556
2d year high school								2	23	70	86	83	32	5	5	306
3d year high school									2	17	35	39	20	21	6	140
4th year high school										1	15	36	50	23	12	137
Total high school							1	30	149	277	294	195	107	56	30	1,139
Grand total (boys)	2,288	2,484	2,450	2,288	2,111	2,080	2,152	2,119	1,717	970	489	240	127	61	33	21,609

STATE ENROLLMENT OF THE PUBLIC DAY SCHOOLS OF SAN FRANCISCO DURING THE YEAR ENDING JUNE 30, 1908.

ENUMERATED BY SEX, AGE AND GRADE.

GIRLS—

Grades.	6 yrs.	7 yrs.	8 yrs.	9 yrs.	10 yrs.	11 yrs.	12 yrs.	13 yrs.	14 yrs.	15 yrs.	16 yrs.	17 yrs.	18 yrs.	19 yrs.	20 yrs.	Total
First Grade	1,874	1,989	823	188	125	26	15	6	3	1						5,050
Second Grade	37	504	1,096	684	229	104	33	18	8	2						2715
Third Grade	2	15	326	798	623	373	171	54	19	7	2					2390
Fourth Grade			12	298	627	670	391	187	58	14	4	1				2262
Fifth Grade				23	261	587	594	434	189	76	8	2	1			2175
Sixth Grade				1	31	280	592	589	322	81	19	4	1	1		1,921
Seventh Grade					1	34	272	520	529	212	39	4	2	1		1,[illegible]
Eighth Grade						1	31	248	521	393	129	19	1			1,343
Total elementary	1,913	2,508	2,257	1,992	1,897	2,075	2,099	2,056	1,649	786	201	30	5	2		19,470
1st year high school								49	269	381	299	52	29	8	1	1,088
2d year high school								2	31	161	199	124	39	10	2	568
3d year high school										12	84	91	37	6	1	231
4th year high school											8	55	87	42	6	198
Total high school								51	300	554	590	322	192	66	10	2,085
Grand total (girls)	1,913	2,508	2,257	1,992	1,897	2,075	2,099	2,107	1,949	1,340	791	352	197	68	10	21,555

CENSUS.

	April, 1906.	April, 1907.	April, 1909.
Children 0 to 17 years	125,191	90,955	111,867
Children 5 to 17 years	101,836	77,367	88,058
Population of City and County estimated on above	430,000	325,000	390,000

PRINCIPAL ITEMS OF THE SCHOOL CENSUS REPORT SUBMITTED BY CHIEF CENSUS CLERK, MR. J. N. ELBERT, FOR THE YEAR ENDING JUNE 30, 1909, AS COMPARED WITH THE CORRESPONDING REPORT FOR THE YEAR ENDING JUNE 30, 1908.

Number of families		50,654
Number of white children between 5 and 17 years of age—		
Boys	44,197	
Girls	42,646	
Total	86,843	
School Census, 1908	86,951	
Decrease		108
Number of negro children between 5 and 17 years of age—		
Boys	37	
Girls	30	
Total	67	
School census, 1908	73	
Decrease		6
Number of native born Mongolians between 5 and 17 years of age—		
Boys	731	
Girls	417	
Total	1,148	
School census, 1908	671	
Increase		477
Total number of census children between 5 and 17 years of age, including 1 Indian	88,058	
School census, 1908	87,691	
Increase		367
Number of children under 5 years of age—		
White	23,541	
Negro	11	
Mongolian	257	
Total	23,809	
School Census, 1908	9,096	
Increase		14,713
Nativity of children—		
Native born	108,173	
Foreign born	3,694	
Total	111,867	
School census, 1908	96,792	
Increase		15,075

GRADUATES.

Number of graduates from the grammar school for the year—

Boys	602
Girls	959
Total	1,561

Number of graduates from High schools for the year—

Boys	120
Girls	217
Total	337

SCHOOL ENROLLMENT AND ATTENDANCE AND CENSUS STATISTICS FOR YEARS ENDING

	June 30, 1906. Enrollment.	June 30, 1907. Enrollment.	Decrease.	June 30, 1909. Enrollment.	Increase. Over '07
High school	5,188	2,823	2,365	3,224	401
Primary and grammar	47,661	37,923	9,738	39,940	2,017
Evening	4,933	4,887	46	6,356	1,469
Total	57,782	45,633	12,149	49,520	3,887

	Average Daily Attendance.	Average Daily Attendance.	Decrease.	Average Daily Attendance.	Increase Over 1907.
High school	3,211	1,762	1,449	2,306	544
Primary and grammar	35,753	26,765	8,988	30,954	4,189
Evening	2,967	1,402	1,565	2,281	879
Total	41,931	29,929	12,002	35,541	5,612
Children 5 to 17 years	101,836	77,367	24,469	88,058	10,691
Children 0 to 17 years	125,191	90,955	34,236	111,867	20,912

(Estimated population of the City and County of San Francisco, April, 1909, 390,000).

NUMBER OF TEACHERS IN DEPARTMENT, JUNE, 1909.

	Men.	Women.	Total.
High school principals	5		5
High school vice-principals	4	1	5
High school teachers	34	51	85
Grammar principals	11	16	27
Grammar vice-principals	3	22	25
Grammar teachers	3	274	277
Primary principals	2	49	51
Primary teachers		552	552
Domestic science		6	6
Drawing		4	4
Manual training	9		9
Music		2	2
Physical culture	2		2
Reading (primary)		1	1
Total day schools	73	978	1,051
Evening school principals	7	2	9
Evening school teachers	34	58	92
Substitutes	2	41	43
Total number of teachers in department	116	1,079	1,195

LENGTH OF SERVICE OF TEACHERS, COUNTING ONLY THEIR SERVICE IN SAN FRANCISCO PUBLIC SCHOOLS.

Years of Service.	Men.	Women.	Total.
Less than 1 year	3	33	36
1 year	5	54	59
2 years	6	48	54
3 years	9	37	46
4 years	8	77	85
5 years	7	34	41
6 years	11	55	66
7 years	1	55	56
8 years	8	19	27
9 years	2	9	11
10 years	11	15	26
11 years	5	51	56
12 years	2	57	59
13 years	1	19	20
14 years	2	16	18
15 years	2	13	15
16 years	3	23	26
17 years	5	30	35
18 years	1	29	30
19 years	2	13	15
20 years	3	27	30
21 years	2	30	32
22 years	3	26	29
23 years	2	27	29
24 years	1	20	21
25 years	1	17	18
26 years	2	18	20
27 years	0	16	16
28 years	1	19	20
29 years	0	15	15
30 years	0	19	19
31 years	0	19	19
32 years	0	20	20
33 years	1	21	22
34 years	1	10	11
35 years	0	7	7
36 years	1	14	15
37 years	0	12	12
38 years	0	8	8
39 years	0	7	7
40 years	0	11	11
41 years	2	9	11
42 years	0	4	4
43 years	0	4	4
44 years	2	2	4
45 years	0	4	4
46 years	0	2	2
47 years	0	0	0
48 years	0	0	0
49 years	0	0	0
50 years	0	2	2
51 years	0	0	0
52 years	0	2	2
	116	1,079	1,195

VOLUMES IN SCHOOL LIBRARIES AND STORE-ROOM (INCLUDING BOOKS FOR USE OF INDIGENTS).

	Volumes.	Estimated Value.
High schools	5,225	$ 3,675
Primary and Grammar schools	63,926	21,309
Evening schools	2,346	709
In store-room	8,114	2,820
	79,611	$28,513

Books becoming useless or lost during year 2,718

SCHOOL VISITATION.

Official visits of superintendent and deputies	3,830
Official visits by members of the Board of Education	1,570
Visits by other persons	45,690

WORK OF TRUANT OFFICERS.

The following statement concerning the work performed by the five truant officers for the year ending June 30, 1909, was presented by Mr. T. J. Dugan, officer in charge:

Number of complaints of truancy investigated and reported back to principals	4,249
Number of children found on the street, cases investigated and reported to principals	2,133
Number of children taken to the Parental school	19
Number of children found upon the street possessed of working certificates	172
Number of complaints that children could not be located	51
Number of children placed in the public schools never having been enrolled therein before	287
Number of children brought before the Juvenile Court	141
Number of parents arrested, fined or reprimanded	6
Number of parents brought before the Juvenile Court	51
Total number of cases disposed of	7,109
Visits to schools on official business	1,410

Commenting on the foregoing statement, I desire to say that the enforcement of the Compulsory Education Law and the repression of truancy have been promoted very much during the past year. This is due to the efficient work of the attendance or truant officers. In the discharge of their duties they have exercised diligence, courtesy and firmness, and their work merits commendation.

REPORT OF THE BOARD OF EXAMINATION FOR THE YEAR ENDING JUNE 30, 1909.

The Board of Examination is composed of:
Superintendent Alfred Roncovieri, chairman;
Deputy Superintendent W. B. Howard, secretary;
Deputy Superintendent T. L. Heaton,
Deputy Superintendent James Ferguson,
Deputy Superintendent R. H. Webster.

The Board of Examination has conducted two examinations (October, 1908, and April, 1909,) according to law, of persons desirous of securing grammar grade or special certificates. It has met monthly and forwarded its recommendations to the Board of Education.

Herewith is a resume of its work:

Number of certificates granted on examination to men	5
Number of certificates granted on examination to women	14
Number of certificates granted on credentials to men	13
Number of certificates granted on credentials to women	16
Number of certificates renewed	102
Number of applicants rejected on examination	6
Number of applicants rejected on credentials	2
Amount of fees collected for examination and issuance of certificates	316

CERTIFICATION AND SCHOLASTIC TRAINING OF TEACHERS.

Number of teachers in the department who hold high school certificates	167
Number of teachers who hold certificates of the grammar grade	940
Number of teachers who hold certificates of primary grade	27
Number of teachers who hold special certificates	61
Number of teachers who are graduates of the University of California	130
Number of teachers who are graduates of Stanford University	10
Number of teachers who are graduates of other universities	27
Number of teachers who are graduates of the California State Normal schools	580
Number of teachers who are graduates of other Normal schools	33

TEACHERS' INSTITUTE.

The Teachers' Institute for the teachers of the public schools of the City and County of San Francisco was convened by County Superintendent Alfred Roncovieri at the auditorium of the Mission High School building on March 31, and April 1 and 2, 1909

All the sessions were attended by 1,156 department teachers who were instructed and entertained professionally by the following speakers and themes:

WEDNESDAY, MARCH 31, 1909.

9:30—Address, "Technical Education in Great Britain, Ireland, and France."
Alfred Roncovieri, Superintendent of Common Schools.

10:10—Lecture, "The Song" (illustrated)....Mrs. M. E. Blanchard

11:10—Recess.

11:25—Address....Mayor Edward R. Taylor

Violin Solo ....Selected
Miss Edna Cadwalader, of the Franklin Grammar School.
Accompanist, Mr. Wallace Sabin.

Lecture, "Art As Related to the Industries."
Professor James Edwin Addicott, B. S., A. M., President Manual Training Department, National Education Association.

12:30—Adjournment.

2. P. M.—SPECIAL SESSION.

Consideration of Proposed Amendment to the Annuity and Retirement Fund Law.

Principal T. H. McCarthy, President.

THURSDAY, APRIL 1, 1909.

9:30—Address, "Commercial Education in the United States and Abroad,"
Mr. James Ferguson, Deputy Superintendent of Schools, San Francisco.

10:00—Recess.

10:15—Duet, "The Gypsies," Viardot-Brahms.
Mrs. Cecil W. Mark and Mrs. F. Van Ness Cox.
Accompanist, Miss Mabel Gordon.

10:30—Lecture, "The Backward Child." Dr. Percival Dolman, Assistant Surgeon Eye, Ear, Nose and Throat Clinic, Cooper Medical College.

11:00—Soprano solo, "Love's Rapture" (Korthewer). Mrs. Cecil W. Mark.

11:15—Lecture, "Fundamentals in Education," Dr. Richard Gause Boone, University of California.

12:30—Adjournment.

FRIDAY, APRIL 2, 1909.

9:30—Lecture, "The Modern School" (illustrated with stereopticon views). Professor James Edwin Addicott, B. S., A. M., President Manual Training Department, National Educational Association.

10:30—Recess.

10:45—Address, "Observations on the Elementary Schools of Great Britain." Madame Celina R. Pechin, Principal of Jean Parker Grammar School.

11:15—Tenor solo, "Mother o'Mine" (Kipling-Tours). Mr. Mackenzie Gordon; Accompanist, Mr. Frederick Maurer.

11:30—Lecture, "Thinking and Doing." Dr. Richard Gause Boone, University of California.

12:30—Adjournment.

EDITORIAL.

THE UNGRADED CLASS.

The individual pupil is still an unsolved problem in all graded schools. Teaching fitted to a majority of a class will not meet the needs of each individual. Some pupils, able to do most of the work, are deficient or slow in a particular subject. Others, more mature than their classmates, are able to work at a more rapid pace than the grade to which their scholarship assigns them. Other pupils, immature or naturally slower of comprehension, will make sure and certain progress if they may take the work at a less rapid pace. Some of the soundest minds work slowly. Pupils from other school systems often do not fit into our course of study and grading. They need a little extra help in some subjects. A teacher with forty-five or fifty pupils cannot give sufficient attention to these individual needs.

Our ungraded class is the best method for combining individual with class instruction. We have several of these classes in operation. They are differently organized according to the needs of the school. In some, pupils go in groups of from six to a dozen for additional teaching in their weak subject. Each grade teacher sends pupils needing this special instruction to the ungraded room during a study period of her own class. The pupils who thus loses a study period must make up the time by home study. If a pupil is weak in arithmetic he gets the regular lesson from his own class teacher and another in the ungraded room. He may be able to understand the operation of percentage in his own grade work but is deficient in decimal or common fractions. Or a fifth grade pupil may be able to understand fractions but needs drill in the number combinations. Such pupils go to the ungraded room for drill in back work upon which present grade work depends.

In other schools the teacher has a number of permanent pupils who are either slow in all their work and need time for each grade, or who, because of maturity or ability, are able to do two terms in one or three terms in two, and thus gain time in completing their grammar school course. In addition to these permanent pupils the teacher has a limited number of groups who come from the classrooms for special drill. In the ungraded class the pupils are given either group instruction or individual instruction according to their needs. The principal assigns pupils to this class in conference with the teachers and carefully directs the work. This is never a deportment class and bad conduct or lack of application may at any time forfeit the privilege.

The ungraded class is found most effective in grammar schools, and in primary schools which have a large number of foreign pupils. Several of our large grammar schools are still unprovided with ungraded classes.

As soon as financial conditions permit every school of eight or more classes should have an ungraded class, and the larger schools should have two such. In schools of six or seven classes the principal should be teacher of the ungraded room for a half day and should have the other half of the day for supervising the building. First and second grades are divided into so many groups and the work is so largely individual that the ungraded class is not needed.

Failure of promotion is one of the chief causes for pupils dropping out of school. They are chagrined and discouraged at not going on with their classmates, the repeated work has little interest for them. A sufficient number of ungraded rooms will go far toward solving the problem of the "left-over." Pupils may be promoted in the subjects in which they are strong, and work in the ungraded room in the weak subjects. If weak in all subjects they are transferred to the ungraded room. Under a well organized system these defects should be remedied as soon as discovered, and discovered as soon as they exist. A pupil who shows marked weakness in any study should enter the proper group in the ungraded class; the pupil who needs more than a term to complete the work of a grade should join the permanent section of the ungraded class.

A larger amount of work for individual pupils should be done by all our grade teachers. It would be wise if a half hour after school were used for helping backward pupils.

SUBSTITUTE TEACHERS.

Teachers coming into our department are first assigned to the substitute list. They are generally young teachers with little experience. They may be sent to any grade for a single day, a week or a month. It takes the best teacher considerable time to know a class, and get them under good control, yet these substitutes are expected to take any grade in any part of the city on a minute's notice. The result is that a good teacher sometimes returns after a few days' absence to find her class thoroughly demoralized. They have learned nothing, and it takes time to reduce them again to law and order. The pupils had better have been dismissed. Only the strongest teachers can do successful substitute work.

I recommend that about twenty of our best teachers be selected for the substitute list, and be employed at full pay; that each substitute be assigned to a school where she shall report at 8:30 for clerical or ungraded work; that the secretary call such teachers and assign them by phone when needed for substituting. Thus each substitute is employed all of her time in clerical work, ungraded work, or substituting. She is near a group of schools, any one of which she may reach quickly on a call from the secretary. Teachers who show marked ability in substitute work, teaching any and every grade, often under unfavorable conditions, should be selected for primary principals, vice-principals, or for ungraded classes at a salary higher than that paid to the grade teacher. New teachers coming into the department should be assigned to regular classes, taking into consideration training, experience, and natural endowments for particular kinds of work.

CIVIL SERVICE COMPETITIVE EXAMINATIONS FOR TEACHERS' POSITIONS.

I believe that some change should be made in the civil service system of competitive examinations for positions in our elementary schools. It is fully as important to know a subject as to know how to teach it, in fact, knowledge of the subject matter must be at the very foundation of all pedagogy. The passing of a teachers' examination is not necessarily a test of scholarship. There are all kinds of examinations given in the various counties of this state. and the certificates so granted are good in every county. Girls complete the grammar school subjects in their early teens, go to a high school where grammar subjects are not reviewed, thence to a Normal school where they get methods on subject matter imperfectly learned and long since forgotten. These people come into our schools to teach. In the preparation of teachers there should be a thorough review and enlargement of elementary subjects. A knowledge of geography, history, grammar, arithmetic and literature possessed by a girl graduating from the eighth grade is not sufficient for a teacher of the eighth grade. How inadequate is it then, after six years of fading away. We give the best pay in the state and a life tenure and. should have the best teachers. I believe, therefore, that the examinations should include both professional and academic subjects. It is the function of good supervision and administration to improve the teaching power of those already in the department and to raise the standard for those entering it.

I therefore recommend that the system of civil service competitive examination be modified so as to include questions in grammar and arithmetic and that the system hereafter apply to candidates for positions in both the day and evening elementary service of this department.

I further recommend that candidates falling below 70% in either grammar or arithmetic, or an average of 80% in the two subjects be debarred from appointment to the San Francisco school department.

In the rules governing these examinations I recommend that the following be included:

(1) The answer to each question must be written on a separate sheet of paper and will be identified by a mark and not by the name of the candidate.

(2) The papers will be submitted to principals of the schools to be read and marked.

(3) Each paper will be marked by two readers, and the average of the marks which the different readers report will be the candidate's mark in grammar and arithmetic.

I further recommend that the following values be given to the examinations:

The examinations in grammar and arithmetic together, will be valued at one-third.

The written examination in Methods of Teaching will be valued at one-third.

The oral examination will be valued at one-third.

IMPROVING THE TEACHING FORCE.

We improve our schools by improving the teaching force. Educational thought is advancing and teachers should keep abreast of it. New subjects are coming into our course of study, old ones are being taught with different aims and different methods. There is a large amount of educational literature dealing in a practical, helpful way with educational material, aims and methods. Each school should be supplied with a small, well selected, pedagogical library to which teachers themselves should make additions. Each principal should hold two meetings a month with his teachers to discuss educational subjects. Superintendent's office will supply topics and references. The superintendent will conduct monthly meetings with the principals to discuss ways and means to improve the work of the department. To make work a success is to make it lighter, for success removes friction. Successful work holds the interest of pupils and eliminates questions of discipline. Successful work holds pupils in school. Our teaching must be less difficult, more interesting, and more profitable. Time spent in preparation is time saved in performance.

RAISING THE STANDARD.

During the year just passed the Superintendent's office has endeavored to raise the standard of work in our schools. Visits have been made to the schools by the Superintendent and his deputies. Circulars of instruction have been issued and principals' and teachers' meetings have been held. In visiting schools the aim has been to discover the weak points and to aid principals and teachers in correcting them. With the amount of office work which devolves upon us, it has been impossible to give all the help needed. The supervisor of primary reading, confining herself to the first and second grades, has accomplished wonderful results. We should have two more supervisors of special subjects, one for primary number work, and one for advanced arithmetic. It is considered necessary for one man to spend his entire time supervising only eight manual training teachers. Drawing, which occupies one hour a week, has three supervisors. Music, which has one hour a week, has two supervisors. The other twenty-three hours of school work are left to the supervision of five people. The force is inadequate.

We have found very different standards prevailing in the schools of our system. Pupils transferred from one school to another would not always fit into the grade to which they were transferred. Schools do the work in different ways, or are satisfied with different degrees of proficiency.

In order to unify standards the Superintendent has sent out to the schools examination questions in language and arithmetic. While the results were disappointing in many schools, the spirit in which these tests were received is very gratifying. Teachers are pleased to learn where their work is weak and to get help in improving it. Our office will send out tests in other subjects during the coming year. The object of these is not the comparison of teacher with teacher or school with school, but to furnish measuring rods by which a uniform standard of excellence may be attained. Each school should be as good as every other school. Children of one locality should have equal advantages with children of every other locality.

SUPPLEMENTARY BOOKS.

Before the earthquake our schools were very poorly furnished with supplementary books. One third of our schools with their equipment were destroyed by the fire. Since the fire the entire expenditure from our school fund for supplementary books would not adequately supply one large school.

With our new method of primary reading children require twice as much reading matter as four years ago, yet they have not half the quantity. We aim now by the end of the fourth year to make the child master of the printed page. He is no longer to be hampered in the grammar grades by difficulties of printed language. He must get the thought as readily from the book as from the teacher's voice. His geography, history, arithmetic, and literature will no longer be cumbered with his inability to read. To accomplish these results, however, we must have a liberal supply of supplementary readers. We need reference books for the grammar grades and supplementary books in history and geography. It will be difficult with a smaller appropriation this year to give our schools all of the books needed, but I would strongly urge that every dollar available be turned into supplementary books.

DEPARTMENTAL TEACHING.

Under the usual school management, pupils spend a year in each grade under a single teacher from whom they get all their instruction, moral training, and character building. This teacher stands to them in loco parentis, and if the teacher is of the right kind, the relation is warm and sympathetic. Conpleting the eighth grade they go to the high school, where they are daily brought in contact with four to six department teachers who are apt to be more interested in subjects taught than in pupils receiving instruction. The warm and sympathetic relation is gone. The pupil is now but one of several hundred. To this sudden change of control may be attributed much of the dropping out during the first year of high school. Last year we enrolled in the first year of our high schools 1,644, and but 874 in the second year.

The chasm between the grammar and the high school must be bridged from both sides. High school teachers must know better what pupils have done in the grammar school, and build upon it. They must show more clearly to their pupils the relation of subjects taught to the pupils' life, physical, industrial, intellectual and moral. They must simplify their teaching. They must bring into the high school more of the home spirit and personal interest in the individual pupil. They must remember that the entering class do not come to them ready-made high school students, but grammar grade pupils to be transformed into high school students.

The grammar school must prepare for the change. Pupils must be made more self-reliant, more capable of self-control, given greater power of independent study. Departmental work in the seventh and eighth grades will accustom them to instruction from more than one teacher.

Departmental teaching has been tried in many cities and has met with serious objections. Too many teachers have worked together, and so high school conditions and atmosphere have been thrust down upon elementary pupils, personal control of the teacher has been lost, and so discipline has weakened. Subjects, it is true, have been better taught by special teachers, but the moral influence has been weakened. In two of our schools during the past year we have tried a modified form of departmental teaching, and the results are to be highly recommended. Four classes, low seventh and high seventh, low eighth and high eighth, form a group for departmental work. Each class has its "class teacher," who has charge of attendance, deportment, home relations, and general welfare. With this teacher the class spends from one-third to one-half of the day. She remains their class teacher through the two years, getting and retaining a moral hold upon the individual pupil. Each of the four teachers of this group teaches one subject to each of the four classes. In this subject she is, or soon becomes an expert. She teaches the same subject to these pupils through the entire two years, giving continuity to the work. Thus the grammar in the seventh and eighth grades is taught by a single teacher, and if the work is found weak the responsibility cannot be shifted. Besides the main subjects which are taught departmentally, each teacher instructs her own class in a group of minor subjects. The class remaining with her for two years, the instruction in the minor subjects is continuous, and blame for poor work or credit for good work is easily placed. The principal holds frequent conference with these teachers and so correlates the work. Under the single teacher system, each teacher is inclined to over-emphasize the subjects which she likes best to the neglect of others. Under the departmental plan each study gets its proper quota of time, and each class gets the teachers in the best work. Pupils who have studied under our modified departmental system are ready for the transition to high school.

Success of departmental work rests very largely with the principal. I advise that the plan be extended to several more of our large grammar schools. We have principals in the department who are able to direct this work, and carry it through to success.

DIFFERENTIATED GRAMMAR SCHOOLS.

Modern life, intellectual, social and industrial, is so complex and makes so many demands upon the elementary school that it is impossible for any one school fully to satisfy them all. Some parents want modern languages taught in the elementary school, others prefer the ancient languages, a third class demand a more thorough knowledge of the mother tongue; some wish more stress laid upon music and art, others would give more manual training and domestic science, or more attention to commercial subjects. All these claims are supported by good arguments, yet no one school can meet all the demands made upon it.

I believe it is possible to make a minimum course of study including the materials in all the common branches, and preparing for the high school. With this minimum course as a basis, differentiation may be made, one group of schools adding modern languages (as is now done in our cosmopolitan schools) another beginning ancient languages, another giving more music, drawing and painting, another giving commercial ranches, and another manual training and domestic science. These schools should be so located that they are easy of access from different parts of the city and parents may choose the school which most nearly conforms to their ideas of education.

As a beginning in this differentiation, I would recommend that the Horace Mann school be designated as the technical grammar school, that sewing, cooking, mechanical drawing and manual training be given greater prominence in this school. To make place for these subjects the present course of study should be somewhat modified in history, arithmetic, geography, spelling and drawing. This school now has departmental work in the seventh and eighth grades, working in three groups of four teachers each. The modified work may be introduced into one or more of these groups, depending upon the demands made for it. A lot containing a large building has been purchased to enlarge the grounds of the Horace Mann school. This building may be sold for enough money to erect the workshops on this piece of ground, or the building may be modified as it now stands so as to supply workshops.

If this experiment is tried with the Horace Mann School during the coming year it will indicate in a measure the nature of the public demand made upon the schools, and show us in what direction improvements should be made.

MEDICAL INSPECTION.

Excellent work has been done by the Board of Health in giving our schools through its physicians and trained nurses an improved medical inspection. Vaccination has been inforced and the spread of contagious disease among pupils has been greatly checked. The nurses have visited the schools, sending home for treatment the most obvious cases of disease, and reserving for the attention of the physician all doubtful cases. Cases of sores and skin eruptions have been treated by the nurses at the schools. The force has been too small to accomplish the work in the most effective manner. Medical inspection ought to be under the Board of Education, but it has been undertaken by the Board of Health, who are anxious to co-operate with the school authorities. We should do everything possible to further their good work. There has been one specialist in eye, ear, nose and throat, who has given half his time to the schools, and has accomplished excellent results. It has been impossible, however, for him to accomplish one-tenth part of the work needed. The record of eyes fitted to glasses and of adenoids removed at the Parental School shows the great work to be done in removing physical hindrance to education. The work of medical inspection in Los Angeles shows what may be accomplished in schools in the way of improving general health, and removing those difficulties which deaden the senses, dull the brain, and dwarf the mind.

Following is the report of the Medical Inspector of Schools:

San Francisco, Cal., August 2, 1909.

Mr. Alfred Roncovieri, Superintendent of Schools.

Sir: I have the honor to enclose herewith the annual report of the Department of Medical Inspection of the public schools of San Francisco and we appreciate your co-operation in this work.

There is one thing that demands attention and I see that you have likewise considered it; namely, that a child should be of a certain age in order to enter the public schools. The only way to eliminate underaged children from school is to demand a birth certificate. This can be had in the majority of cases.

Hoping that this will meet with your consideration, I am,

Respectfully,

C. R. BRICCA,
Medical Inspector of Schools.

PHYSICAL EXAMINATIONS.

Condition—	
Enlarged glands	113
Poorly nourished	118
Total	231
Ear—	
Cerumen	5
Defective hearing	17
Discharging ears	25
Total	47
Eye—	
Chronic inflammation of lids	165
Chronic inflammation of conjunctive	62
Defective vision	295
Strabismus	88
Total	610
Lungs—	
Tuberculosis	2
Nervous System—	
Chorea	9
Defective mentality	35
Epilepsy	5
Total	49

Mouth, Nose and Throat—	
Adenoids and hypertrophied tonsils	463
Defective teeth—over 50%.	
Defective palate	2
Hypertrophied tonsils	237
Mouth breathers	48
Ozena	1
Total	741
Osseous Structure—	
Deformity of spine	8
Deformity of extremities	4
Hip disease	9
Total	21
Skin—	
Eczema	12
Furnunculosis	2
Impetigo	1,720
Pediculosis	1,643
Ringworm	770
Scabies	51
Total	4,208

Respectfully,

C. R. BRICCA,

Medical Inspector of Schools.

San Francisco, Cal., July 22, 1909.

To the Honorable, the Board of Health,

Through R. G. Broderick, Health Officer.

Gentlemen: I have the honor to submit herewith the annual report of the Department of Medical Inspection of Schools. This Department is concerned with nineteen of our primary and grammar public schools situated in the congested districts and enrolling 10,300 pupils.

The amount of work performed and the results obtained have been excellent, taking in consideration that these schools are by no means close together and that unfortunately we have had several nurse reappointments which naturally handicapped our work and results.

The Board of Education has at all times co-operated with this Department, and by so doing has been a great help. Without this co-operation, school medical inspection would be useless. The efficient and praiseworthy work of the nurses could not be passed over in silence, especially the work of those nurses who have worked since the beginning of school medical inspection.

Medical inspection of schools without the school nurse would be a farce. The combination of medical school inspection, examination and treatment, and school nurse co-operation is undoubtedly one of the greatest advancements that modern times has invented for the physical improvement of school children. We need good permanent nurses, as the frequent changing is detrimental, as we lose the co-operation of the willing principals and teachers.

The number of children excluded from school on account of infectious diseases is 859 or 8.34% of the enrollment. These cases were found either in the schools or in the homes, for the most in the latter. Every unaccounted for absentee of two or more days is visited at the home by the nurse and in this way a great number of infectious cases were found. This number does not include the number of contracts, as unfortunately this record was not kept until here of late. These cases and their contracts were not and most probably would not have been reported to the Board of Health. This certainly is a positive menace to community health. It is evident that the exclusion of these cases and contracts meant an increased school attendance. Trachoma has practically disappeared, as not one case has been found in months, while the original twenty cases have been found.

Of the 2,660 unvaccinated children, only 85 have not been re-vaccinated. Of the 2,575 re-vaccinations, 15 immune certificates were issued and the remaining 2,560 have been successful, with but few exceptions. The reason why vaccination is unsuccessful lies in the fact that the virus is not active, having been kept at an unsuitable temperature either in the drug store or in the practitioner's office. Mulford's vaccine virus has given most satisfactory results. Number of children vaccinated in the school with the consent of the parents by the School Medical Inspector, over 900.

The nurses have treated 2,441 cases in the schools. The number of times each case was treated has not been reported, but is at present, consequently does not appear in this report. These cases were simple contagious skin conditions, abrasions, and do not include the vaccinations, which vaccinations were performed by the Medical Inspector.

One hundred and eighty-two or 26.3% of the cases of hypertrophied tonsils and adenoids found have been operated upon by the family surgeon, while 162 others were medically treated. Of 383 cases of defective vision, 80 or 20.9% have received ocular attention. In all 2,843 or 27.04% of the total enrollment have been treated.

Twenty-seven cases have been reported to the Society for the Prevention of Cruelty to Children and to the Associated Charities.

One thousand six hundred and fifty school visits or 165 monthly visits have been made.

Two thousand four hundred and seventy-eight home visits or 225 monthly visits have been made.

Total 390 monthly visits have been made.

The record of the physical examinations is by no means complete, but most superficial, as our time was for the most part taken up with infectious diseases, vaccinations, vermin, contagious skin diseases and only the most evident cases of physical defects came under our observation. Two months before the close of the school term, the Medical Inspector began a systematic physical examination of the school children, taking a class at a time. Ninety-nine pupils were thus examined and 38.39% had defective vision, 50% enlarged tonsils and adenoids, 30% enlarged cervical glands, over 50% defective teeth. This proves conclusively the absolute necessity of physical examination.

Respectfully,

C. R. BRICCA,
Medical Inspector of Schools.

ASSEMBLY HALLS IN PUBLIC SCHOOL BUILDINGS AND FREE PUBLIC LECTURES.

Upon the subject of Assembly Halls and free public lectures, I desire to repeat what I said in my report for last year (page 62) in order to emphasize the very great importance of this matter. I also repeat the recommendation that I made at that time and respectfully ask the Board of Education to take action upon the matter at once.

> "I regret that so few of our school houses have assembly rooms. The building of auditoriums, as a feature of school equipment, will be appreciated by the general public and particularly by the school patrons. They will afford a common place of meeting with small expense for all the people where there can be no bickerings, political or sectarian. The home life and the school life can be brought together in harmonious unity and much permanent good will result.
>
> "I would, therefore, recommend that every school building planned under the new Bond Issue be provided with an assembly hall to be built on the ground floor or first floor, where in addition to its use for general exercises, music and gymnastics for the pupils of the school, it can be used for social center development. In such a room the principal can address a large number of pupils in a more impressive way than in separate class rooms. Such a room can be used for stereopticon exhibitions, for graduating exercises or as already indicated as a social center for citizens and parents of the district. The school houses belong to the people and under proper restrictions should be used for the diffusion of information and the promotion of a civic spirit among the adult population.
>
> "I respectfully recommend that free public lectures on American history, physics, mechanics, economics, etc., for the student and adult population be given in the auditorium of the Mission High School, the Crocker, Girls' High, Polytechnic, Lowell, Hearst and the Horace Mann, and wherever possible in smaller buildings.
>
> "These lectures, combined with musical numbers, will be educational and elevating and will be appreciated by the general public and by the school patrons."

Our evening schools are in session five evenings a week. The same buildings should be used for public lectures on educational subjects. There are many public spirited citizens who would give such lectures without charge. We should have lectures on all subjects pertaining to civic welfare. We should not wait till bubonic plague comes again before teaching people to be clean. Cleanliness in kitchens, back yards, alleys, streets, public and private morals, public and private decency, should be taught to both young and old. Such civic pride should be created that ugly billboards will disappear from our streets and that all entertainments of doubtful character will be prohibited.

Lectures should be given on public and private health, such as the prevention of tuberculosis. Physicians should give lectures on the physical care and training of children, and upon the dangers besetting adolescence.

COOKING AND MANUAL TRAINING.

Our cooking and manual training centers are open five days in the week for pupils attending the day schools. But no such opportunities are given the pupils of the evening schools. These centers should be open five evenings of the week and a large part of the work should be in advance of that done in the day school. Part of it should be done by lectures and part by laboratory work. A large number of young women are earning a living in domestic work who know nothing of the science underlying this work and very little of the best methods for doing it. The cooking centers should be crowded with young women eager to increase their earning capacity by increasing their knowledge and skill.

In the drawing department of the Humboldt Evening, hundreds of young men are making the work of their hands more profitable by training their heads. When a young man can read a drawing his work is more profitable to his employer. When he can make a drawing he is ready for promotion, and when he possesses the science of mathematics, he is ready for further advancement. The manual training centers should be open to a younger class of studentts than those attending the Humboldt Evening. They should be taught mechanical and architectural drawing, strength and quality of materials and should be given skill in the handling of wood-working tools.

Finances will not permit the opening of all of these centers the coming year, but we should open one or two centers this year and make plans for further development work the year following.

PARENTAL SCHOOL.

Our parental school is in reality only a day truant school. Most of its pupils are sent to it by the juvenile court and under the surveillance of probation officers from this court. It is situated next to the court and detention home, and boys detained at the detention home awaiting the decision of the court are sent to this school.

As soon as the boys show sufficient promise of reform they are sent back to a public school, but kept still in charge of a probation officer. The court and the school are doing excellent work for wayward boys, but owing to limitations are unable to do all that is necessary.

We should have a real parental school—a boarding parental situated on a ten acre tract of land. Here pupils may be kept day and night from bad home and street influences. Our present school has charge of them five hours of the day, but many boys and some girls need guidance and protection during twenty-four hours of the day. The school should have shops for teaching trades and plenty of ground for teaching practical agriculture. Many a boy, now a menace to public welfare, would leave such a school with an education and a trade, a self-supporting and self-respecting citizen.

The need of such a school should be kept in mind the coming year and every effort made to secure an appropriation for the ground and buildings.

In a previous report I pointed out serious objections to the present location of the parental school. Being alongside of the detention home and juvenile court the boys in this school are kept more or less in an environment which is to them suggestive of evil rather than of good. They should be in a place where they would be reminded of the right instead of the wrong.

The practical work in manual training introduced into the school during the past year has had a beneficent effect upon the pupils, and I recommend a still further extension of it.

I hope that as soon as possible proper facilities for washing and bathing will be provided for the schools; also that the present toilets will be replaced by modern ones. The present accommodations do not suggest either cleanliness or refinement. If anything is to be done for the social and physical welfare of the school these things must be given immediate attention.

HYGIENIC CLEANING.

In the future construction of our schools, I respectfully recommend that some suction system of cleaning be provided for in each school. We have adopted modern methods of heating and ventilating our schoolhouses at very great expense, and we find that these pay, but in the matter of cleaning, which is at least equally important, we employ the most antiquated and inefficient method known. The dust which is carried into the rooms by the children is laden with germs of the most dangerous diseases. The janitors are expected to sweep out and thoroughly clean each room every day. But only the coarser particles of dust or sand can be removed by the broom and duster; the finer particles which work themselves into the cracks in the floor, or into the woodwork on the walls, cannot be removed in this way. And this is what contains the greatest proportion of the deadly germs. Even when this fine dust is reached by the broom it is but stirred up and floats in the air, settling again in the room. Any movement by the children stirs this up in a greater or less degree, and the children inhale the germs of disease. Consumption is only one of the many diseases known to be transmitted in this way.

Where the janitors are forced to begin the sweeping of halls or stairways before the children have departed for their homes, the danger is very great, for millions of these germs are sent floating in the air which is breathed by the children as they pass out of the building.

With the use of dampened sawdust a very great amount of this disease-laden dust escapes the janitors and in scrubbing, a great deal of it will remain in the cracks and on the floor, to dry up and be stirred into the air by the children upon their first return to school.

Already the owners of large public office buildings are beginning to give up the antiquated method of broom and duster cleaning. Business men of mature years realize the danger they are subjected to through having dust stirred up in their offices. How much more important is it to safe-guard our school children, whose lungs are tender and most susceptible to the attacks of disease germs.

The number of obstacles fastened to the school room floor make it the most difficult of all floors to sweep. It is practically impossible to remove by our present method of cleaning the dust that accumulates in and around the feet and legs of the desks. But this can be removed with perfect ease by a vacuum system of cleaning. I therefore recommend that provision be made for the installation of such a system in all of the buildings to be constructed hereafter, and also that it be installed in the permanent buildings already constructed.

SANITARY DRINKING FOUNTAINS.

The danger of disease spreading through the indiscriminate use of ordinary drinking cups is well known. Examinations made of cups used in this manner at public fountains and in railroad trains show that they harbor millions of disease germs which have come from the lips of those who have used the cups. A clean, healthy child drinking from these cups is exposed to some of the most contagious diseases, and he may contract it in this way. The same conditions prevail in our schools where the children use a common drinking cup. Much of the sickness in our schools is undoubtedly due to this, and now that a thoroughly sanitary drinking device is available the old method should no longer be considered excusable. There are on the market sanitary drinking fountains by which the pupils can drink freely by simply placing the mouth over a jet of water, while at the same time it is impossible for the lips, tongue or face to come in contact with any substance other than the running water. It is certain that disease will not be transmitted from one child to another by this method of drinking. We cannot afford to risk the health of our school children and expose them to epidemics any longer by the use of a common drinking cup. I, therefore, recommend that sanitary drinking fountains be installed at once in every school in the department and that they be provided in all of the buildings now under construction.

FIRE ESCAPES AND PROVISIONS FOR INSURING SAFETY OF CHILDREN AGAINST THE DANGER OF FIRE.

In a communication to the Board of Education, on April 3, 1908, I called attention to the necessity of providing efficient protection against fire for the school children of our city, as follows:

> "The recent holocaust at Collingwood, Ohio, wherein one hundred and sixty-seven school children perished, demonstrated emphatically the necessity of providing all possible means to insure the safety of our children against the dangers of fire in school buildings.
>
> "I respectfully recommend that the Board of Supervisors be requested to provide in the next budget the necessary funds.
>
> "First—For an auxiliary fire alarm system connecting every school with the central station.
>
> "Second—For a large fire gong to be placed in each school.
>
> "Third—For at least two fire extinguishers to be placed on each floor of every school.
>
> "Fourth—For the purpose of widening all stair-cases sufficiently to permit four children to walk abreast of one another.
>
> "Section 1890 of the Political Code of the State of California reads, 'Each school building in the State shall, if two or more stories in height, be provided with suitable and sufficient fire escapes. The trustees of each school district and the Board of Education of each municipal corporation must provide sufficient and suitable fire escapes for each school building two or more stories in height under their jurisdiction.'
>
> "For years this office and the Board of Education have reminded the Board of Supervisors of this law and have applied earnestly to them to make it necessary to carry it into effect, but up to the present time only two schools have been equipped with fire escapes as the law requires. I recommend that this Board again request most emphatically the Board of Supervisors to appropriate specifically for the purchase and placement of necessary fire escapes on all buildings two or more stories in height to conform with Section 1890 of the Political Code of the State of California."

Notwithstanding my recommendations, eight of our new school buildings are without fire escapes. Neither is there any adequate protection against fire for the children in these buildings. This is in violation of the State law, above referred to, and also in violation of the city ordinance which provides for proper protection to school children, as follows:

> "For the proper and necessary protection of life and property, buildings that are already erected and built in this city or county shall be provided and equipped with fire escapes or facilities for escape in case of fire, and every school building of two stories in height, shall be provided and equipped with metallic fire escapes, combined with suitable metallic balconies, platforms and railings firmly secured to the outer walls, and erected and arranged in such a way and in such proximity to one or more windows, or to as many windows of each story above the first as may be necessary to make and render said fire escapes readily accessible, safe and adequate for the escape of inmates in case of fire."

In the presence of such a disaster as that at Collingwood, we become much exercised about the safety of human life, especially of our children. But such a lesson is often too soon forgotten. In order that San Francisco may never be in danger of giving to the world such an awful lesson, by the sacrifice of human life, the proper steps should now be taken to prevent it. Not only that, but it is a clear violation of the law, both state and city, for San Francisco to use for school purposes, any building of two or more stories in height, before such building is equipped with "sufficient and suitable fire escapes."

I respectfully, but most urgently request the Board of Education to call the attention of the Board of Supervisors to the above conditions in our Department, and urge that the necessary steps be taken to provide for all of our schools the necessary protection against fire, as required by law.

ELEMENTARY SCHOOLS.

Our Course of Study has not been changed during the past year. It was revised two years ago. Our best schools find the Course of Study well adapted to their needs. It is not too difficult; it is not too long. Schools which have most nearly followed its directions and suggestions have done the best work. Complaints against the Course of Study usually come from those who have paid too little attention to the work as outlined in it. Our schools should be unified by enforcing this Course of Study thoroughly. We have in our city as good primary and grammar schools as can be found in any portion of the state. Some of them, however, are falling below our high standard. It will be our effort next year to improve the work in the weaker schools and bring it, if possible, to a par with the best.

READING.

Primary reading is probably among the best work being done in the San Francisco schools. This is due to our system of supervision of the reading of the first and second grades. This shows what can be accomplished by expert supervision confined to a limited portion of work. We need more supervisors, so that more of this work may be done. The Superintendent and his deputies should take a broad view of the school system, co-ordinating part with part, directing the work of special supervisors, testing the work by examination questions, and seeing as much of the detail of schoolroom work as time will permit. Most of our grammar schools are doing superior work in oral reading.

This is due to the fact that my office has spent a great deal of time during the past three years working directly with the teachers and classes in this subject. As a result of this work, pupils are better able to interpret their literature and to read and understand arithmetic, history, geography, etc.

Literature is being read in all our grades above the fourth, and pupils are acquiring a taste for the best reading.

LANGUAGE.

The suggestions on Composition contained in our Course of Study are being followed by a large number of our schools with excellent results. The success of this work demonstrates beyond doubt the value of these suggestions, and we shall recommend that all schools follow hereafter the plan of work outlined in our Course of Study. In some schools Composition is taught too largely from the state text book. In such cases the results are poor. We shall recommend that next year composition books be kept in all grades above the fourth, and that a regular amount of work be placed in these books each month. The books shall be kept where they can be readily examined by the Board of Education or members of the Superintendent's staff. The results in formal language have been disappointing. Some schools have given excellent results in consequence of following closely the Course of Study. We shall endeavor to improve the work in this subject next year by means of teachers' meetings, circulars of information and test questions.

ARITHMETIC.

A few schools are disposed to complain of the difficulty of the work in arithmetic. Many good principals, however, have demonstrated in their schools that the work can be accomplished by the children; that it is satisfactorily and logically laid out and that it follows step by step. Difficulties have arisen where the work has not been thoroughly done and where the steps have not been followed in sequence. Here we ought to have the help of a special supervisor. The schools generally have done excellent problem work.

HISTORY.

History as taught from biographies and stories in the lower grades has been very successful. The Introductory History in the fifth grade has proved a very interesting study. The Grammar School History is a difficult book for the children, being better suited to high school pupils.

We need a large supply of supplementary books in history.

NATURE STUDY.

The home and school garden have been the form of nature study most used in our schools. We have distributed to schools flower and vegetable seeds received from the State University and from our representatives in Congress. This work has received special direction and encouragement from the Superintendent's office. In some schools 75% of the children have home gardens cultivated by themselves. Products of their labors have been brought to the schools. Gardening has been made the subject for composition work. Most of our schools have very little ground for school gardening, but in such cases boxes and pots of earth have been utilized. Properly used the school garden is but a demonstration where pupils learn how to plant and care for their home gardens.

Parents have greatly appreciated the interest taken in gardening and the work should receive strong support from the Board of Education. Other forms of nature study have been employed and made the basis of drawing and composition.

GEOGRAPHY.

One of the best forms of nature study has been the out-of-door geography which most schools have taught in excellent shape. Children study out of doors various land forms and observe the forces of nature actually at work shaping the surface of the earth. What they see after a rain is stream formation, transportation, deposit of soil, formation of ponds, deltas, river systems, gives them a means of interpreting the larger georgraphical features which they get only from the map or the printed page. This offers the very best of nature study and gives a firm foundation for geographic conceptions. The common vegetables and grains raised in the school or home garden give actual content to what would otherwise be empty words.

We have distributed during the year a large number of outline maps in the schools. Product maps have been of very great service. They have in fact been so useful that many schools have gone far beyond the requirement in making them. We regret to say, however, that the Superintendent's office looks in vain for product maps in some schools. It is for principals to see that the course of study is understood and carried out.

Another very important feature of geography is the excursion to factories, wholesale houses, shipping centers, etc. Before the fire this work was very satisfactorily carried on in the schools. It has been neglected during the past three years and should be revised. Principals and teachers should take classes during school hours to places where geography can be obtained at first hand. One bit of concreteness will be a center about which will crystalize a large amount of reading matter. Our parks contain a great deal of geography which is not being used. A few schools have done very valuable work at the Golden Gate Park.

We congratulate the schools on the progress of the present year and look forward to greater gains during the coming year.

HIGH SCHOOLS.

We have five high schools all in good standing and the four doing university preparatory work well accredited. These schools have received careful attention from the Superintendent's office this year.

Foreign languages are well taught. We would suggest, however, that the modern languages receive more attention as to conversation; that after the first term in any modern language all conversation should be in that language.

In Latin we suggest that much more attention be given to the use of Latin as the source of a large part of our English; that in the first year particularly English words be derived from the Latin words thus adding interest to the work and making pupils see that it has a real value.

We would further suggest that more attention be given to choice English in translation from Latin and other languages. Good Latin should be translated into equally good English. Where slovenly translation is permitted, not only is the value of Latin lost, but much of the work in English composition undone.

HISTORY.

History in our schools is rather better taught than in most high schools. The element of evolution should enter more largely into its teaching. Teaching of history should be the history of civilization, showing how each new institution is evolved from the old and in turn prepares for the next. Stress should be laid on great movements in history. The work should certainly be in the teacher and not in the text-book. The teacher should constantly give birds-eye views over long periods of history showing the relation of great events to each other. Events should be taught in relation to our own life and times. Events near at hand should be used to illustrate events and motives far remote. The development of great ideals should receive special attention. Moral standards have changed as much as material conditions. Children should be placed back into times long past, showing what ideals men then possessed, how new ideals were born, struggled for the mastery, conquered and became universal. Young people are so accustomed to the moral standards of today that they fail to realize the changes wrought by history.

SCIENCE.

We have good courses of science in all our high schools. Physics and chemistry should be less theoretical and more interpretive of nature and the mechanical arts as seen in the daily walks of life. Chemistry should be more organic and should bear upon physiology, hygiene and sanitation. Biology should be brought into relation with human life and health. Physical geography properly taught should be a laboratory subject. Each school should have a well equipped laboratory for this subject, and each teacher an abundance of time for field work with the classes; for the field is after all the best laboratory. Our laboratories are very poorly equipped and large classes make but a limited amount of field work possible. The girls' high school gives geology and astronomy in place of physical geography.

MATHEMATICS.

The university recognizes our high schools as strong in mathematics. The pupils entering from the grammar schools, however, find the work dry and uninteresting. It is recommended that the first work in Algebra be on the simple algebraic equations transposing, clearing fractions and solving such problems as have already been encountered in arithmetic. This gives the pupil an idea of the actual value of Algebra. He finds a new tool for solving knotty problems. Geometry should be made more concrete, more practical every-day problems given and models used wherever possible. A peck of large potatoes and a sharp knife will supply the best material for solid geometry. When the outside has dried over night, lines may be drawn on these potato models. Many a pupil is thus helped to see geometry.

POLYTECHNIC HIGH SCHOOL.

The bond election held on June 22d of this year resulted in a victory for the Polytechnic High school. By a vote of 17,893 for and 5,215 against, the issuance of bonds of the value of $600,000 was authorized by the electors of San Francisco for the purpose of building and equipping this school. Industrial education has thus received the approval of our people and it is earnestly hoped that the necessary steps will be taken at once to have the work of construction upon the new building begun at the earliest possible time.

The pupils now in the Polytechnic High school are suffering on account of the poor equipment in the school, and I can see no reason why a part of the permanent equipment for the new building should not be purchased so that these pupils may have the use of it during the next school year. Many of them will have finished their work in the school before the new building is completed. These young men and women made strong personal pleas to the electors in behalf of the bond issue for the Polytechnic High school and the people responded generously to them. For these reasons I respectfully recommend that the Board of Supervisors be requested to sell bonds to the amount of $15,000 as soon as possible so that funds may be immediately available for the purpose of providing permanent equipment in machinery and other apparatus urgently needed at the present time by the pupils now attending the Polytechnical High school.

This apparatus and equipment that I recommend can be transferred to the new building. It would be wrong to our present student body to delay the purchase of this apparatus until the new building is completed, for, as I have said, most of them will have completed their school work before that time.

In the canvass in behalf of the Polytechnic High school bonds the voters of San Francisco expressed themselves unmistakably in favor of scientific and technical education in evening continuation classes for apprentices and mechanics who are employed during the day time. And inasmuch as a costly plant, such as the Polytechnic High school will be, should be made use of for the benefit of the largest possible number of all classes of our people, and during as many hours of the day as it can be profitably used, I recommend that the City Architect be instructed to make provision for the necessary class rooms in the plans for the Polytechnic High school building so that evening continuation classes may be established wherein the apprentices and journeymen of our city may learn the theories and sciences underlying their various arts and crafts.

In 1904 additional bonds to the amount of $350,000 were issued for the Polytechnic High school, but as these are to bear interest at the rate of only 3½% per annum, and as there has been a great local demand for money at a higher rate of interest, these bonds have not yet been sold. A suggestion has been made that these be cancelled. I respectfully recommend that this be not done for the following reasons:

First—The Polytechnic High school will eventually require this money to provide additional equipment, etc., for the needs of the large number of pupils in day and evening classes. In European cities smaller than San Francisco such schools have an attendance of 5,000, and the San Francisco Polytechnic High school will undoubtedly have such an attendance if the needs of all classes in our community are met.

Second—It is not an easy or simple matter to have bonds voted at any time, and those which have been already voted should not be cancelled without good reasons.

Third—The money market will not always be so tight as at present, and undoubtedly in the future investors will be found who are willing to purchase these bonds bearing only 3½%.

Fourth—It costs the city nothing to save these bonds awaiting the development of the need of their sale to meet the requirements of the school.

COMMERCIAL INSTRUCTION.

During the past year instruction in commercial subjects has been given in two day schools (the Mission High and the Commercial) and in four evening schools (Commercial evening, Hamilton evening, Richmond evening, and Washington evening).

In the Mission High school the work is correlated with the regular high school subjects, and is accredited towards graduation upon the same basis as the other high school subjects.

The Commercial school gives a two-year course and does the work as thoroughly as it can be done in that time. This year the results were most gratifying. At the graduating exercises Colonel Murphy, the principal, subjected the graduating class to a severe test in stenography and typewriting in which the graduates wrote new matter dictated at the rate of 127 words per minute for five consecutive minutes, and immediately afterwards transcribed the same accurately upon the typewriter. There were at least 1,200 people present when the test was given.

This degree of efficiency, coupled with the general education these pupils received in the course required for graduation, fits them to fill responsible positions in the best offices and business houses. The importance of this for those young people cannot be over-estimated. When a graduate of a commercial school enters upon his business career, the first week is the trying time. Everything is strange to him. He works under the highest nervous tension and the strain is very great. It is therefore most important that the pupils should have the greatest facility possible in the taking of dictation and in the reading and transcribing of their stenographic notes.

With this end in view, the work in stenography and typewriting is thoroughly correlated. First of all, the pupils are required to read all of the shorthand notes made in class. They are also required to transcribe regularly upon the typewriter the different kinds of subject matter dictated to them. These transcriptions are carefully corrected by the teachers in typewriting and shorthand. The pupils are thus given systematic drill in practical amanuensis work, and every detail of it is criticised as thoroughly as it would be in any business establishment.

To thoroughly systematize this work the following instructions were issued by my office to the principals of all the schools in which these subjects are taught, and to the teachers:

San Francisco, February 4, 1909.

To Principals and Teachers of Shorthand and Typewriting.

Ladies and Gentlemen:—In addition to the instructions already given, the following shall apply in the teaching of your subjects:

SHORTHAND.

1. In elementary classes all shorthand exercises shall be corrected with red ink by the teacher, and pupils shall be required to copy all corrected words at least five times before writing the next lesson.

2. In speed classes teachers shall examine pupils' notes frequently and shall insist upon neat and correct outlines.

3. All pupils in speed classes shall be required to transcribe on the typewriter as much as possible of the exercise dictated each day. These papers shall be handed immediately to the instructor in typewriting for correction as to form and general neatness. (See rules and requirements for graduation referred to in 15 below). They shall be returned to the pupils not later than the following school day. The pupils shall then hand the papers to the teacher of shorthand for correction as to accuracy of transcript. (See 11 below).

4. Insofar as possible pupils shall be required to read every word they write in shorthand. Where dictation is given to be transcribed, the exercise shall not be read in class before the transcription is made.

5. When the teacher in typewriting desires certain "form" work done in typewriting by the speed pupils in shorthand, the teacher of shorthand shall secure the copy of such exercise or exercises in "form" work from the teacher in typewriting, and shall use same for the exercise in dictation in shorthand. (See 14 below).

6. Pupils shall be kept busy every minute of the recitation period, in both shorthand and typewriting, so that they may do the maximum amount of writing, and thus make the greatest possible progress.

7. In elementary and advanced shorthand classes all class and home exercises shall be kept in permanent form (either in book or folder).

8. Pupils shall not be promoted to advanced classes in shorthand until they have completed the work of the text-book and received a percentage of not less than 90 in an examination upon the general principles, and 95 per cent in examination upon word signs.

TYPEWRITING.

9. Pupils shall be taught to use all fingers in operating the typewriter.

10. Pupils shall strive to produce equal impressions in striking the keys, from capital M to the comma. Special care must be exercised in striking punctuation marks.

11. All papers written by the pupils shall be corrected by the teacher and returned not later than the following school day. Transcriptions of shorthand notes shall be corrected as to form and general neatness by the teacher of typewriting; as to accuracy of transcript they shall be corrected by the teacher of shorthand.. (See rules and requirements for graduation referred to in 15 below).

12. Pupils shall keep all typewriting exercises in permanent form.

13. Teachers shall insist upon accuracy, neatness and correct form in advanced as well as in elementary classes in typewriting.

14. All speed pupils in shorthand, who are equally well advanced in typewriting, shall spend one typewriting period each day in transcribing their shorthand notes. (See 5 above).

15. Teachers shall have every pupil in shorthand and typewirting make a copy for himself of the rules and requirements for graduation in these subjects sent out by this office last term and also at the beginning of this term.

16. See Rule 6 above.

Respectfully,

ALFRED RONCOVIERI,
Supt. of Schools."

The unusual success of this year I believe to be due in a large measure to the systematic work of the principals and teachers in following the instructions of my office, and I wish to heartily commend them for their hearty cooperation in the interests of the boys and girls studying these subjects. So that there might be a uniform requirement for graduation and a uniform standard of marking I issued the following instructions at the beginning of the school year:

"The following rules and requirements based upon those of the United States Civil Service Commission shall apply in all examinations given to candidates for graduation in stenography and typewriting:

"All of the dictations in any examination in stenography are for five consecutive minutes. The minimum requirement for graduation is the ability to write new matter dictated at the rate of 80 words per minute for 5 consecutive minutes, and the ability to transcribe the same accurately upon the typewriter. Dictations will be given at higher rates of speed to those who express a desire for the same. Both speed and accuracy are considered in the rating, speed having a weight of 1 and accuracy a weight of 2. The ratings for speed for the different rates of dictation are as follows:

100 words per minute	100 per cent
90 words per minute	95 per cent
80 words per minute	85 per cent

"The rating for accuracy shall be determined by the correctness of the transcript according to the following rules:

Mark every correct answer, 100.

Mark every faulty answer according to its value on a scale of 100, as herein specifically directed, and deduct the sum of the error marks of each answer from 100.

The difference between the sum of the error marks of each answer and 100 will be the mark of the answer.

STENOGRAPHY.

	From 100 deduct.
For each word omitted, added, substituted, or misspelled, or for the use of the singular instead of the plural, or of the plural instead of the singular, when the grammatical correctness is affected	3
For each transposition	2
For each gross error in capitalization or punctuation; for each error in division of words; for each word repeated; for each failure to use the hyphen when required; for each abbreviation, or for the use of the plural for the singular, or for the singular for the plural, when the grammatical correctness is not affected	1
For interlineations, erasures and lack of neatness	1-5

When the mark for accuracy is 10 or less, no credit will be given for speed.

85% shall be required for graduation.

To illustrate—When a pupil writes at the rate of 80 words per minute he receives 85% on speed. Suppose he should make four errors in the transcription of his notes amounting to 12 demerits, his credit on accuracy would be 88. According to this rule, giving accuracy a weight of 2 and speed a weight of 1, you multiply 88 by 2, giving a result of 176. Add to this the 85% received in speed, and divide by three to get the percentage received in shorthand as a whole, as follows: 176 plus 85 equals 261, divided by 3 equals 87. 87% would be the final mark on the examination in stenography, giving the pupil two credits more than required for passing.

TYPEWRITING.

In typewriting the exercise consists of copying 400 to 500 words from plain copy, transcripts to be marked according to the following rules:

	From 100 deduct.
For writing one line over another	10

For each error in orthography; for each word or figure omitted, provided, that a deduction of 10 shall be made for the omission of two or more consecutive words if the words omitted do not constitute more than one printed line of the copy, and that a deduction of 20 shall be made for the omission of two printed lines, or more than one line, etc.; for each word added, substituted, or repeated; for each transposition; for each abbreviation not in copy; for each failure to capitalize or to punctuate as in copy; for each deviation from copy in paragraphing (maximum for the exercise, 10); for failure to indent as in copy (only one charge to be made in the exercise); for each error in compounding words, or vice versa........ 5

For each case of inconsistent spacing between lines........ 3

For each space between the letters of a word; for crowding letters in a word; for lack of space between words; for striking a letter instead of space bar; for unfinished word due to coming to end of line when word is re-written on next line; for striking letters in a line over band holding paper, thus making no impression on sheet, or for piling letters over each other at the end of a line when all the letters are decipherable, or for running off paper on right or left margin (maximum for the exercise, 10)........ 2

For each case of irregularity in left-hand margin, or of gross irregularity in right-hand margin (maximum for the exercise in each case, 5); for each strike over; for the misdivision of a word at the end of line; for each omission of a hyphen, when needed, at end of line; for extra space between words (maximum for the exercise, 5); for each case of inconsistent spacing after punctuation marks; for each word interlined (maximum for a single interlineation of five or more words, 5; for each erasure (maximum for the exercise, 5)........ 1

For lack of neatness........ 1-5

For each error not specified above........ 1-5

Time consumed will be rated according to the following scale: For a speed of 35 words or more per minute, a credit of 100 will be given; for 30 words per minute a credit of 95; for 25 words per minute a credit of 85, and for 20 words per minute 75. If the exercise is written at a rate of less than 20 words per minute no credit will be given for speed.

Both accuracy and speed are considered in rating, accuracy having a weight of 3 and speed a weight of 2. 80 per cent shall be required for passing.

To illustrate how these rules would work out in practice, take a paper written at the rate of 20 words per minute. This would be marked 75% on speed. If the paper had mistakes amounting to 10 demerits the credit for accuracy would be reduced to 90. To find the credit on the paper as a whole, multiply the credit for accuracy by three (90 times 3 equals 270), multiply the credit for speed by two (75 times 2 equals 150), and add both together (270 plus 150 equals 420). Divide the sum by five and the credit in typewriting is found (420 divided by 5 equals 84).

Respectfully,

ALFRED RONCOVIERI,
Supt. of Schools."

August 14, 1908.

During the past year the touch method of operating the typewriting machines was put into effect in the entering classes of two of our schools. The machines were fitted with blank keys. By this method the pupil is taught the use of all of his fingers in typewriting, and receives such systematic drill in familiarizing himself with the keyboard that he can operate the machine without looking at the keys. He is thus able to look at his notes and at the same time continue operating the machine. The very great advantage of this is obvious.

In the last announcements issued by the University of California and Stanford University, shorthand, typewriting and bookkeeping are included among the subjects which will be accepted for entrance to these institutions. This is a decided step in advance, and the effect of it upon those subjects in our schools will be beneficial. For too long a time it has been thought that commercial subjects were suited to the needs of pupils of small mental caliber. But it has been demonstrated beyond a doubt that no subjects in the secondary school curriculum require greater mental alertness and power than these. Many college preparatory pupils who desired to learn shorthand and typewriting, but whose time was entirely taken up with accredited subjects, will now be able to do so. And many pupils who took the commercial courses will now be encouraged to go on with their school work and enter the university.

NEW REQUIREMENTS FOR TEACHERS' SPECIAL CERTIFICATES.

At the last regular meeting of the Board of Examination for the City and County of San Francisco, the requirements for teachers' special certificates in stenography and typewriting were fixed as follows:

"The speed test in stenography for a special teachers' certificate in stenography and typewriting shall consist of the writing of new matter dictated by the examiner at the rate of 110 words per minute for five consecutive minutes, and of the transcription of the same accurately upon the typewriter.

For passing, there shall be required a rating of 85% in the correctness of the transcripts under the following rules of marking:

STENOGRAPHY.

	From 100 deduct.
For each word omitted, added, substituted, or misspelled, or for the use of the singular instead of the plural, or for the plural instead of the singular when the grammatical correctness is affected	3
For each transposition	2
For each gross error in capitalization or punctuation; for each error in division of words; for each word repeated; for each failure to use the hyphen when required; for each abbreviation, or for the use of the plural for the singular, or of the singular for the plural, when the grammatical correctness is not affected	1
For interlineations, erasures and lack of neatness	1-5

TYPEWRITING.

The speed test in typewriting shall consist of the copying of 400 to 500 words from plain copy, at an average speed of not less than 40 words per minute. The transcript shall be corrected in accordance with the following rules, and 85% shall be required for passing in this test:

	From 100 deduct.
For writing one line over another	10

For each error in orthography; for each word or figure omitted, provided, that a deduction of 10 shall be made for the omission of two or more consecutive words if the words omitted do not constitute more than one printed line of the copy, and that a deduction of 20 shall be made for the omission of two printed lines, or more than one line, etc.; for each word added, substituted, or repeated; for each transposition; for each abbreviation not in copy; for each failure to capitalize or to punctuate as in copy; for each deviation from copy in paragraphing (maximum for the exercise, 10;) for failure to indent as in copy (only one charge to be made in the exercise); for each error in compounding words, or vice versa.................. 5

For each case of inconsistent spacing between lines.................. 3

For each space between the letters of a word; for crowding letters in a word; for lack of space between words; for striking a letter instead of space bar; for unfinished word due to coming to end of line when word is re-written on next line; for striking letters in a line over band holding paper, thus making no impression on sheet, or for piling letters over each other at the end of a line when all the letters are decipherable, or for running off paper on right or left margin (maximum for the exercise, 10).................. 2

For each case of irregularity in left-hand margin, or of gross irregularity in right-hand margin (maximum for the exercise in each case,5); for each strikeover; for the misdivision of a word at end of line; for each omission of a hyphen, when needed, at end of line; for extra space between words (maximum for exercise, 5); for each case of inconsistent spacing after punctuation marks; for each word interlined (maximum for a single interlineation of five or more words, 5); for each erasure (maximum for the exercise, 5).................. 1

For lack of neatness.................. 1-5

For each error not specified above.................. 1-5

The half-day sessions in the Mission High school and the Commercial school, due to the necessity of both schools being in the same building, have made the work harder upon both teachers and pupils. This has been particularly so for the Commercial school. The number of rooms available in the building for this school has not been equal to its needs. For this and other reasons it has been necessary for Commercial school classes to meet in the morning during the session of the Mission High school as well as in the afternoon, thus making it impossible for the principal to arrange the schedule of recitations in the best interests of the pupils. In many cases pupils and teachers are kept in school more than the required number of hours.

Some time ago I recommended to the Board of Education the fitting up of additional rooms on the lower floor of the building. With these rooms and the necessary equipment for them it will be possible to overcome the difficulties to which I have just referred. It will also enable the school to accommodate a greater number of pupils. The Commercial Evening school and the Humboldt Evening High, both of which occupy the Mission High school building in the evening, are also suffering because of a lack of room. Neither one of these schools has been able to receive all the applicants for admission. Besides in some cases two classes have had to hold recitations in the same room at the same time. This condition will also be remedied by the addition of the rooms above referred to.

The matter of typewriter equipment for our Commercial classes is an important one. The life of typewriting machines in a school is shorter than it would be in a business house, due to the fact that beginners are continually using the machines in school, whereas in business houses they are used by operators more or less expert. In addition the operator in an office who has the exclusive use of a machine and who is held responsible for it. and whose position depends upon the kind of work done by the machine, will take greater care of it than the pupil who is but one of eight or ten who operate the same typewriter.

New machines are guaranteed by the typewriter companies for from one to two years. During this period a repairman is sent weekly by the best companies to inspect and adjust the machines, and practically the only expense is for ribbons and new platens or rolls, which should be put on the machines at the end of each year.

After two years' service the expense of repairs may be very high. In most cases it is cheaper to trade out the old machines for new ones and pay the cash difference. To illustrate: The price of new machines in lots of fifty for school purposes is $50 each. To repair some of our old machines would cost as high as $18 each. Some of the standard companies would allow us as high as $35 each and perhaps more for these old machines in trade for new ones, thus making the cash difference not more than $15. Thus by giving out $15 and the old machine we would have a new one of the latest model in return guaranteed for one or two years, while on the other hand by giving out $18 (or $3 more) for repairs, we would still have the old machine, without any guarantee and with the possibility of having to pay out more money for repairs within a year. So from every point of view it would be wise to trade out these machines for new ones.

If we traded out our machines, say every two years, they would always be up to date, and the pupils would always be able to turn out the best work. Thus their eyes would be trained to neatness, and they would be more critical of their own work. Old machines not only give trouble in operation, but on account of the battered type and other defects, never produce good results, and the effect upon the pupils is bad.

The new course of study now being put into effect in our commercial classes requires the teaching of the use of the mimeograph, multigraph and adding machine. While it is impossible to give sufficient time to make the pupils as expert in the use of these as in the use of the typewriter, sufficient time can be given to have the pupils thoroughly familiar with their operation. It is highly important that this be done. I, therefore, recommend that one of the latest models of each of these machines be provided for use in the Commercial day and evening schools.

The required amount of instruction in penmanship was not given in the Commercial school owing to the fact that Mr. Espina, the regular instructor, was required to supervise the penmanship of the whole school department. As this subject is of great importance in the Commercial school, I recommend that a regular teacher be appointed to the position of teacher of penmanship in the Commercial school for the coming year.

Miss Freese, the regular instructor in penmanship in the Commercial Evening school, is doing excellent work, and I believe would fill the position acceptably in the day school. I therefore recommend her for the position.

TYPEWRITING IN GRAMMAR GRADES.

In this same connection I recommend an extension of typewriting to a number of the eighth grades in the grammar schools. This can be done at very little cost, by establishing at the Hamilton school a center for typewriting, where the necessary number of machines is already on hand, being used by the pupils of the evening school only. The center could be conducted in the same way that the cooking and manual training centers are conducted, by having the pupils of surrounding schools come to the Hamilton school for typewriting at regular hours of certain days of the week.

I do not wish to dwell upon the indirect advantages of this work in the eighth grades in connection with Engilsh, etc., although they are very great. The work in the eighth grade would be justified by this fact: Many of our grammar school pupils leave school upon graduation. By introducing typewriting into the eighth grade these pupils would be given an opportunity to acquire an art which could be used by them to very great advantage in the practical affairs of life. And this can be done without sacrificing any other essential work in the grammar schools.

Besides, it would be of very great advantage to every pupil who desires to enter the high school, and practically so to those who desire to enter the commercial classes. In the first place, it would help to bridge over most successfully the chasm now existing between the grammar schools and the high schools. Second, it would enable the pupils to enter the high schools with a high degree of efficiency in the operation of the typewriter and would enable them to devote more time to other work in the first year of the high school course.

I therefore recommend that a typewriter center be established in the Hamilton school for the coming school year.

EVENING SCHOOLS.

The total enrollment in the evening schools during the past year was 6,356, while that of the previous year was 7,189.

With one or two exceptions the discipline in the classes is to be commended in the highest terms. These pupils attend school with a definite end in view, and their actions show seriousness of purpose. Their ages range all the way from 14 to 45 years. Foreigners just landed in our country who cannot speak a word of English come to learn our language, and boys and girls of from 14 years of age upwards, who were forced to leave school early, come to continue their lessons in reading, writing and arithmetic. Young mechanics and draftsmen, employed during the day, come to study the particular branch of mechanical or architectural drawing and mathematics applicable to their chosen lines of work. In one department (the technical department of the Humboldt Evening High school) there were 706 of these this past year, and many more on the waiting list, for whom there was no room. Others who are working in business offices come to make themselves more expert in stenography and typewriting, or to learn bookkeeping or some other subject allied to their daily work, and those with literary or professional tastes and having a desire to prepare for entrance to the university, spend their time in studying the more formal academic subjects. But the mental environment in all the rooms is the same—the spirit of serious study permeates the whole atmosphere. This at once practically eliminates for the teacher the problem of discipline, and enables him to devote his whole energy to the teaching of the subject under consideration.

The course of study for the evening elementary schools is very similar to that for the day elementary schools. The same standard of proficiency is required for graduation in the evening and the day commercial schools. In the Humboldt Evening High school the subjects necessary for entrance to the university are completed so that the graduates are prepared to take the regular entrance examinations for full standing in a university.

The need of special evening classes to help those who are preparing for the Civil Service examinations given by the general Government has long been felt. In San Francisco examinations are given regularly for clerkships and other positions in the Federal service, not only in our city, but throughout the

United States and in our insular possessions. Civil Service examinations are also given for admission to and promotion in our city service, for instance, in the police and fire departments, and for clerkships and other positions in the various municipal departments. Those not in the service and who desire to prepare for these examinations must either work alone with such suggestions as they may be able to get from those already in the service or pay a substantial fee to some private tutor to coach them in the required branches. Many are not able to pay the fee, nor have they friends from whom they can get suggestions regarding how to prepare themselves. All of these young people are worthy of help, and I believe it to be one of our functions to provide help, especially to those who have a definite purpose in view and who require educational facilities to enable them to realize that purpose. Classes held two or three evenings a week in the special subjects required in these examinations would be well attended, and I recommend that the Board of Education organize Civil Service classes in connection with our evening schools.

Heretofore no state money has been received to help support evening schools in California. At the last state election a constitutional amendment was adopted by the people of California making evening schools a part of the state system of education. As a result of this money will henceforth be appropriated by the state local authorities upon the average daily attendance in these schools. This will give to San Francisco about $24,700 for the past year.

The passage of this constitutional amendment marks a step of progress in educational thought. It gives recognition to the fact that the boy who is compelled to quit school at an early age to enter the economic struggle for existence is entitled to an education at the expense of the state as well as is the boy who is not forced to earn his own living and who can spend his entire time in school and college up to the age of twenty-two or more. It gives recognition to the additional fact that the education which is directly related to a boy's daily vocation is worthy of support by the state. This is one of the most hopeful signs in the educational world.

While San Francisco has done much in evening schools for our working boys and girls. I feel that there is much more to be done. We have not one-quarter the attendance in these schools that we should have. There are thousands of boys and girls in San Francisco who ought to attend. Many of them possibly have no inclination to study, but I feel certain that if the advantages offered by our evening schools were properly advertised, the attendance would soon be doubled. In European cities as well as in the Eastern cities of our own country, an extensive campaign of advertising is carried on with remarkable results. I suggest, therefore, that announcements of the opening of our evening schools for next year be printed on large bills and posted in prominent places throughout the city. I also recommend that these announcements contain a brief statement of the several courses of instruction offered. There is no reason why young people in San Francisco should pay large tuition fees to correspondence schools or to private evening schools while the city offers superior advantages in its schools free.

MUSIC AND ART.

The University of California, in the Undergraduate Bulletin of 1909-10, has included music among the preparatory subjects for admission to the university. The Bulletin announces that "For the present, and until the schools of the state are prepared to give systematic instruction in music, credit will be given only by examination at the university."

The university, by this announcement, recognizes the educational value of serious study of music, and practically suggests that departments for systematic instruction in music be inaugurated, and opportunities presented by the schools of the state for courses in these subjects.

Pupils are taught music throughout the eight years of the grades. Music stops in the high school. It is not less important after the 8th year than before. Many a student who has carried music lessons up to the high school is compelled to drop the subject through high school and college, from pressure of other work, and yet, as a means of culture, refinement, power of enjoyment, and even of influence in the world and society, it ranks with the best of academic subjects. Opportunity should be given for chorus work. There should also be courses offered in musical notation, theory and history of music, which should count toward graduation. It is impossible to give instrumental and vocal music requiring individual teaching, and yet many a parent feels the loss when these have to be given up in the high school in order to carry four studies. I believe that we can recognize music taken outside of school and give credit for it towards graduation.

I therefore recommend, first, that a Board of Examiners, composed of experienced musicians of recognized ability, be appointed, whose duty shall be to pass upon the lessons and practice out of school hours, of students who desire credit therefor; secondly, that the music lessons and time of practice to the equivalent of three high school recitations per week be recognized as school work; thirdly, that class work in musical theory be given in the high schools. This would give five hours per week of elective work in music.

I further recommend that the lectures which have been given at the Summer school of the University of California by Mrs. M. E. Blanchard be repeated to our high school pupils.

The Oakland High school is giving two courses in the history of art, including sculpture, architecture and painting. This work has five recitations per week, counts five hours for graduation in the high school and for university entrance, or may be counted as three hours for advance university work. It was believed at first that the course would be taken by girls only, but nearly as many boys as girls are enrolled in the course, and six, as the result of the work, are preparing to study architecture.

Work similar should be offered in our high schools. One teacher can at present take charge of the work in two or more high schools. It should not displace anything now in the courses of study, but be given as an elective. If such work in Music and Art were offered, many students would take the present high school course, together with these subjects, and extend their work over four and a half or five years.

REPORT OF ESTELLE CARPENTER, SUPERVISOR OF MUSIC. JULY 6, 1909.

Hon. Alfred Roncovieri, Supt. of Schools, San Francisco, Cal.

Dear Sir:—In compliance with your request for a report from the Music Department, I submit the following:

From the inspection made during the past year, it is evident that a decided step in advance has been made in the music work.

The results have been observed in the daily work, and in the various dedications and graduations which have taken place.

There has been a many sided progression according to the respective grade. This progression has advanced along educational and musical lines, and embraces in the lower grades the intense interest of the child, the culture of the correct child-voice, the development of the lower preception and the delight in the interesting and musical song.

In the upper grades there is added the extended knowledge of the theory of music, the power to sing at sight from the printed page, the power to write simple exercises in the staff notation from dictation, and the delight given from singing the best songs in two and three parts.

During the past year, systematic work has been emphasized in oral and written dictation, and great encouragement has been given to individual effort in singing as well as in writing.

There has been a systematic study of the Patriotic and Folk songs. The very best songs from masters and from the modern composers have been given.

There has been an effort to increase the power for intelligent listening in music, and there has been an effort to stimulate and broaden the knowledge of the subject of music in every way.

All children are encouraged to cultivate their voices, to go to concerts, to study the piano and other musical instruments, and to take their places in the general musical life of the city.

Especial mention is made of the different graduation exercises where the very best selections were sung in three parts—such songs as "Pilgrims' Chorus" by Wagner, "Sextet from Lucia," "Lift Thine Eyes" from Elijah, "The Blue Danube" by Strauss, and "Serenade" by Gounod.

The effort is always made to give to the child the benefit of this knowledge of great songs, and to interpret these songs so that the right impulse may be quickened. This power of song is so needful in education, and so forceful because it reaches the "inmost center of us all where truth abides in fullness," and thence arouses the essence of the man and child and quickens the main-spring of action. It has the power to formulate the motive of life.

Thus through great songs and the inspirational teaching of them, we have endeavored to enrich the hearts and lives of the girls and boys and to give music its rightful place in education.

To the principals, teachers, special teachers, and my assistant, I wish to express my appreciation of the work done during the past year.

I cannot close without thanking the superintendent, deputy superintendents, and the Board of Education for their co-operation and kindness.

I am, respectfully

ESTELLE CARPENTER, Supervisor of Music.

REPORT OF MISS KATHERINE M. BALL, SUPERVISOR OF DRAWING.

San Francisco, June 11, 1909.

Mr. Alfred Roncovieri, Supt. of Schools.

My Dear Sir:—In reply to your request for a report from the Drawing Department of the city schools, I submit the following:

I am happy to inform you that our results this year are more satisfactory than those of any preceding year.

The best testimony of the success of the work was the exhibition of drawings and craft work, prepared for the Alaska-Yukon-Pacific Exposition, and shown at the San Francisco Institute of Art, the past month.

The exhibition included a remarkable collection of spontaneous story drawings—from pupils of six, seven and eight years of age—ranging from the very beginnings of children's efforts to express themselves by means of outline drawings, through various stages of growth, and culminating in compositions in color, which would be creditable to advanced workers.

There was also object drawing in color, from plant forms, fruits and vegetables and still life, showing not only a knowledge of the sciences of perspective, light and shade and color harmony, but also expressing a feeling for the beauty of the models represented.

In the design, geometric and floral motives were multiplied in all-over patterns, borders and single ornaments, decorating book covers, portfolios, boxes, candle shades, vases and printed cottons: all of which were made under the usual school-room conditions, within the very limited time of but one hour a week.

The exhibition attracted a great deal of favorable attention. The teachers and students of the Art Institute, as well as prominent art critics of the city, were profuse in their commendation of the work, all alike remarking upon its originality and unusual quality. A visiting art teacher from the East, surprised at what he saw and not understanding our system of art instruction, attributed the excellence of the work to local conditions, specifying the climate, the outdoor life, the beauty of scenery, our cosmopolitan population and the influence of the Oriental wares to be found in our shops; forgetting that all these may exist, and there still be no art in the community, unless there are teachers of art to cultivate it.

If we have achieved anything of consequence, it is due to our fifteen years of study, experiment, unceasing endeavor and attention to every detail. Interest, effort, energy and money have not been spared by the supervisor, who has never let an opportunity go by, to keep in touch with the world's work in art and education.

Through the addition to the Department of Drawing of two competent assistants, it has been possible to give more supervision to all the schools than was the case heretofore, and in so doing increase the efficiency of the work.

While we are gratified with our results, we feel that with more favorable conditions regarding time, equipment and additional assistants, there are still great possibilities for growth in many directions; possibilities which in time will come to be recognized as of the greatest value to the industrial development of this country.

Thanking you and the Board of Education for your kindly assistance and the principals and teachers for their hearty co-operation, I remain

Yours sincerely,

KATHERINE M. BALL, Supervisor of Drawing.

REPORT OF MISS LEW BALL, SUPERVISOR OF PRIMARY READING.

San Francisco, June 15, 1909.

Mr. A. Roncovieri, Superintendent of Schools.

Dear Sir:—I submit herewith my report for the school year 1908-09:

READING.

In our primary grades, the year just closed shows most encouraging results. Such deep interest has been evident, and such earnest work has been done by principals and teachers, that not only has the amount laid down in the course of study been completed, but in many schools even more has been accomplished.

With the full appreciation that teaching reading successfully means training the child in the right reading habit, that is the habit of reading for the purpose of getting thought from the printed page, we know that before the child can get the thought in any coherent manner, he must have power to read the printed symbols in which the thoughts are expressed—and this we call the mechanics of reading; that while it is necessary to give to the child as early as possible in his reading course full ability to read these printed symbols, yet to do this for the sake of perfection in mechanics only at the expense of thought in reading is disastrous, leading to the formation of a wrong reading habit. Therefore, from the beginning, we aim to make the teaching of reading successful in two-fold, (1) by providing the child with reading material that is suitable and interesting, through which (2) he begins to acquire the mechanics of reading.

While of necessity, the drill in mechanics must continue, the sentences and stories in which mechanics are applied need not be spoiled in interest for the child; so, while he is gaining in ability to read the printed page, he is also gaining in power to appreciate and interpret thought content.

It is not difficult to find subjects that are interesting to every child—games, toys, pets, doings of his playmates, his own activities and interests—and it is not difficult for the sympathetic teacher to know how to make best use of these in child-like sentences.

READING AND DRAMATIZATION.

There is always abundant opportunity to take advantage of the dramatic or "play" side of the child's nature. In those schools where the reading has been most successful, a great deal of dramatized reading has been carried on. In one first grade which I visited not long ago, the interest of an entire class of fifty-two children was held for a long period through the simple dramatization of a commonplace reading lesson, the children reading, interpreting, and acting, while encouraged by the sympathetic, skillful teacher. That the lesson was a success, no one who had watched the faces of the children could doubt. In another school, my visit fell upon a day when the children were reading and "playing" Mother Goose, and, with great satisfaction, Little Boy Blue went to sleep under the imaginary hay stack, while nimble Jack jumped over the candle-stick and Little Miss Muffet ate her curds and whey.

BLACKBOARD READING.

Throughout the first year, all teachers have given a great deal of reading from blackboard, reading slips, and mimeographed copies. This work is always indispensable in a first grade. The interested teacher will always resort to it, because (1) no book in print can make complete provision for the needs of all classes of children, nor for any children at all stages of the work; (2) it enables the teacher to supplement at just the right points and in just the right way to keep the work alive, and to give proper emphasis and repetition. While it will always be used, during the past year too much of it has been necessary because of the insufficient supply of supplementary readers.

CHILDREN'S VOICES.

In all oral reading, effort is made to keep the children's voices natural—soft and sweet. This leads to better enunciation, for when not permitted to raise his voice to an artificial pitch, the child makes greater effort to speak distinctly.

SUPERVISION.

Owing to the large number of schools having primary grades, I have been able to give direct supervision to the first and second grades only. With but few exceptions, at least one visit each term has been made to every first and second grade in the city, the length of time spent in each room varying from one-half hour to two hours in length. During the coming year it is planned to carry on the work now begun through the third and fourth grades.

Directions and instructions have been given to teachers at general teachers' meetings, at special meetings held in individual schools, and during weekly office hours for the reception of teachers.

SUPPLEMENTARY READERS.

In our primary grades the greatest drawback has been the great lack of supplementary readers. The children in these grades are asked to buy but one book for the entire term's work. In the process of learning to read, this is far from being sufficient. The child memorizes easily, and when a page is once memorized, its mission as part of the material used in teaching the child to read is gone. To hold the interest of the child, and to enable him to read a sufficient amount, an ample supply of reading matter must be furnished. In not one school has there been a sufficient supply, while in many schools almost no books have been furnished.

I most strongly recommend that ample provision be made for supplementary reading in all grades.

HAND WORK.

One of the ever present problems of the primary school room is that of keeping the children profitably employed between recitation periods. Every teacher of a large first grade must give much of her time daily to the teaching of one group of children at a time. This plan makes it necessary to provide occupation for all children not under her immediate charge. That the children may come to their recitation refreshed, rested, and receptive, these unsupervised periods should offer an entire change of work.

From kindergarten and manual training departments, suggestions have come which have led to the adaptation of certain forms of hand work that serve our purpose beyond a doubt. Particularly popular has been the raffis and yarn weaving on frames, discs and looms. This work is making a place for itself in the primary school room, and its value is recognized by teachers because (1) it offers change and rest to the child, enabling him to move about and freeing him from mental and physical strain; (2) having been taught the preliminary steps, he can work without direct supervision, making a large variety of articles that continue to hold his interest; (3) he works towards a definite end, and has a completed article to carry away with him at the end of his labor.

This work has been used in many of our first grades, and pronounced a success by those who have given it a trial. In some schools exhibits of the finished work of the children were held at the close of the term in December. Special attention was called to one exhibit which showed such excellence, and proved so interesting, that it attracted visiting parents and teachers in large numbers.

In closing this report, I wish to express appreciation of the earnest interest and co-operation of the principals and teachers with whom I have worked, and to convey thanks for the support given by the Board of Education, by the superintendent and his assistants.

Very respectfully,

LEW BALL, Supervisor of Primary Grades.

REPORT OF MISS ELLEN M. BARTLETT, SUPERVISOR OF DOMESTIC SCIENCE.

Central Manual Training School.

San Francisco, June 11, 1909.

Hon. Alfred Roncovieri, Superintendent of Schools.
San Francisco, Cal.

Dear Sir: I have the honor of submitting to you the following report of the Domestic Science Department for the school year 1908-1909.

There are nine cooking centers in the San Francisco public schools. They are found in the following schools:

Central Manual Training School, Crocker Grammar School, Glen Park Grammar School, Hamilton Grammar School, Hearst Grammar School, Horace Mann Grammar School, Irving M. Scott Grammar School, Laguna Honda Grammar School and Monroe Grammar School.

There are eight teachers employed:

One supervisor, salary $1,200 per annum.

Six assistants, salary $900 per annum.

One substitute, salary $3 per day.

The enrollment for the fall term, 1,616; spring term, after establishment of Glen Park center, 1,799.

Daily average attendance, 99.5 per cent.

Cost of supplies, $863.92.

Cost of supplies per pupil for one year, $0.515.

I am happy to report that there is a growing appreciation of the value of domestic science.

It was at the instigation of the Glen Park Improvement Club that gas was introduced into that neighborhood so that a cooking center might be opened in that school. The Improvement Clubs near the Monroe School are working to get a temporary gas main put in so that the Monroe center may be used.

The parents of the Bay View school children have presented a largely signed petition to the Board of Education asking to have a cooking center put in that school.

The most cordial relations exist between the domestic science teachers and the principals and teachers of our pupils. My assistants are all hard workers and are gaining in efficiency all the time. During the past term three new centers have been equipped. These are the Glen Park, Laguna Honda and Monroe centers.

More centers are still needed as there are yet several hundred girls without accommodation. A new teacher is also needed. I would suggest one who holds a diploma from a school of domestic science.

The enclosed table shows the course of lessons taught.

With many thanks for the courtesies received from your office, I am,

Very respectfully yours,

ELLEN M. BARTLETT,
Supervisor of Domestic Science.

SYNOPSIS OF FIRST YEAR OF COOKING COURSE.

A syllabus substantially the same as that employed in the first year is repeated in more extended form in the second.

Particulars of Course.

Length of course, 2 years.
Number of lessons per week, one.
Grades, VII and VIII.
Number in class, average, 20.
Time of lesson—
  Morning classes, 1½ hours.
  Afternoon classes, 2 hours.

Introductory.

1. Definition.
2. Purpose.
3. Process.
4. Incidental and general information respecting materials, sources, [illegible]es of preparation and [illegible]n, care and selection of materials. Table setting and serving of meals.

Boiling and Steaming.

(Materials.)

Definition.
Meats.
Soup-stock.
Fish.
Vegetables—
  Green.
  Underground.
Cereals.
Doughs—
  Dumplings.
  Puddings.
  Boston Brown Bread.
Liquids—
  [illegible]rds.
  Sauces.
  Beverages.

Stewing.

Definition.
Materials—
  Meat.
  Vegetables.
  Fruits.

Broiling.

Definition.
Materials—
  Meat.
  Fish.

Baking.

Definition.

(Materials.)

Quick breads., i. e, bread raised by the union of soda and an acid; bread raised by the expansion of air.

Bread raised by yeast.
Meat.
Fish.
Cake; pastry, puddings.
Vegetables.

Frying and Sauteing.

Definition.
Fish.
Batters—
  Doughnuts.
  Fritters.
Cakes—
  Griddle cakes.
  Vegetables—
  Potatoes.
  Parsnips.

Invalid Cookery.

(Diet.)

Liquid.
Sight.
Convalescent.

MANUAL TRAINING.

The following excerpts are taken from the report of Mr. F. K. Barthel, Supervisor of Manual Training.

"During the past year, instruction in Manual Training has been given to the boys of the seventh and eighth grades at the following laboratories: Sherman, Central, Hamilton, Crocker, Moulder, Everett, Horace Mann and Irving M. Scott. In addition, work was inaugurated in May in the newly equipped Monroe and Laguna Honda laboratories, and classes were held four times a week at the Parental School.

"The teachers under my supervision have been the following: Messrs. H. C. Bagot, D. E. Dowling, P. F. Dailey, L. E. Davidson, A. J. Hamilton (resigned), R. B. Thompson, A. M. Sylvia, I. H. Williams and M. A. Felton (on leave).

"In the preparation of a new course, I examined into the work of the Manual Training Departments of San Jose, Berkeley, Oakland and Sacramento, and also, as far as my facilities permitted, the work of a number of Eastern cities.

"In January the A seventh classes began the new course, both in woodwork and in drawing, and the results in the main have been highly satisfactory. In the preparation of this new course, I have endeavored to embody the following features:

1. A systematic introduction of tools.
2. A systematic introduction of processes.
3. A knowledge of materials.
4. A systematic development of certain principals of construction and elements of design.
5. The development of originality and initiative.
6. A linking with home and school interests, and with social and industrial life.
7. The development of skill and technique.
8. The undertaking of ambitious projects.
9. "Individual" and "community" work.
10. "Optional" and "prescribed" work.
11. An appreciation of good ornamentation and proper finish.
12. All-around development of the pupil.

"Submitted with the report are the outlines of the wood-work for the A and B seventh grades. The eighth grades will continue the old work, with some modifications for the present. By another year all grades will be working under the new course and we shall then be in a position to fully estimate results.

"Drawing is a very necessary and valuable part of manual training instruction. Every boy should know how to read and how to make the working plans necessary in the construction of his project. My first care was to eliminate all copy work. After consultation with Mr. Drew, head of the Mechanical Drawing Department of the Polytechnic High School, I adopted the same set of "conventions" as are used by him. This will obviate any "unlearning" by the boys who attend that school after leaving the grammar school. The work as outlined, a copy of which is submitted, was given this term to the A seventh classes and results indicate that, with some slight changes and with a better understanding by the instructors of what is wanted, the drawing of the future will be as satisfactory as the limited time at our disposal for this feature of our work will permit.

"The equipment of the new laboratories at the Monroe and Laguna Honda Schools provides accommodations for a large number of pupils heretofore crowded out for lack of room.

"The completion of the several new schools provided for in the Bond issue will soon afford opportunity for the extension of the work into lower grades, and it should be the policy of the school authorities to provide for such extension whenever and wherever laboratory accommodations will permit.

"The greatest drawback to good work in this Department today is the lack of room in our workshops. Our manual training rooms average less than 900 square feet of floor space. Such cramped quarters necessitates the use of the smallest manual training benches made; the placing of them so close together, often less than two feet, that there is not sufficient space to use the various tools properly, all of which interferes greatly with the quality of the work undertaken. No provision is made for the care or storing of large projects, nor for their proper finishing. In some laboratories the pupils literally walk over and on the work of each other, while the passage of the teacher from one pupil to another is possible only at the sacrifice of time and energy.

In the new Monroe, Laguna Honda and Washington Schools it is very evident that those who planned those structures had no very comprehensive idea of what are the requirements of a modern manual training room, and so in those buildings are small rooms unprovided with the accessories actually necessary in order that the work may be conducted economically and efficiently.

"In regard to supplies of lumber and hardware, the experience of myself and my predecessor might be properly expressed by saying that there have been "lean years and fat years," and I would suggest that a certain definite sum of money, based upon the enrollment of the grades taking the work, be set aside each year for supplies. I have endeavored to lessen the amount of the lumber bill by using almost exclusively the cheaper kinds; at the same time it should be kept in mind that too much economy in this regard will simply curtail the benefits that should be obtained from the work.

"During the year I have held one or more teachers' meetings per month. In addition I arranged for three talks, as follows: Miss Ball, "The Elements of Design" and the San Francisco "Drawing Course"; Mr. Altman, "Color Harmony"; Miss Van Vleck, "Ornament." These talks were of the utmost benefit and the speakers are entitled to our cordial thanks.

"My assistants attended in a body the meeting of the California Manual Training Association, and also visited the exhibit of manual training work held by the schools of Berkeley.

"From May 31 to June 6 inclusive, was held a joint exhibition of the work of the seventh and eighth grades of the San Francisco schools and the Polytechnic High School.

"This exhibition has had a most stimulating effect upon both pupils and teachers. I am sure that it was sufficiently beneficial to warrant the holding of such affairs at regular intervals."

Following is an outline of the work in manual training:

WORKING DRAWINGS.—FOR GRADE A7.

General Directions—

1. Names and use of instruments.
2. Placing of sheet.
3. Sharpening of and kinds of pencils.
4. "Light" and heavy lines. Use and value.
5. Drawing of margins.

First Sheet—Lettering and Conventions:

1. Draw guide lines.
2. Copy sample sheet.

Second Sheet—Working Drawings:

1. Explain their nature and use.
2. Explain and illustrate "plans" and "views."
3. Explain use of "extension" and "center" lines.
4. Have pupils construct from paper square and triangular prisms and cylinders.
5. Draw working plans, two views of each of above forms.

N. B.—Pay no attention to dimensions. Use center line in drawing cylinder. Discuss terms, square, rectangle. parallel, triangle, center, axis, radius, arc, circumference.

Third Sheet—Working Drawings:

1. Make working drawings of discs of various shapes; viz., circular, square, triangular, oblong, elliptical, etc.

N. B.—Pupils to make discs from paper or cardboard and draw in various positions. Use extension lines, axis lines. Omit dimension lines. Use terms, plan, elevation.

Fourth Sheet—Dimension Lines.

1. Distribute strips of paper, say, 1 inch by 6 inch.
2. Have pupils crease once and draw top and front views.
3. Apply dimensions.

N. B.—Have each pupil draw plans and views of at least three strips, varying size of strip and location of the crease.

Fifth Sheet—Invisible Edges:

1. Provide each pupil with two pieces of wood, one thicker than the other. Place in various positions, pieces touching. Draw top and side views. Teach and apply "Invisible Edges."

Sixth Sheet—Scale Drawing:

1. Teach why used.
2. Impress that real dimensions only appear on the drawing.
3. Draw working plans of bench hook one-twelfth scale.

Instruction to Teachers—

1. Use sample sheet as a type for all drawings.
2. Save first six sheets for inspection by supervisors.
3. Provide sandpaper blocks for sharpening pencils.
4. The first sheet need not be completed before starting the others.
5. Collect sheets at close of lesson, keeping each class separate.
6. Accept no careless nor dirty work.
7. These six sheets must be done well by each pupil before he will be permitted to begin wood-work.
8. Each class will be "examined" in the above work some time during the term.
9. Good work on these sheets will insure good drawing throughout the course.

WOOD WORK A SEVENTH GRADE.

No.	Model.	Drawing.	Wood.	New Tools.	New Operations.	Ornament.	Finish.	Instructions.
1.	Octagonal mat. 5½"x5½".	Blackboard.	Pine. Poplar.	Rule. Try-square. Blk. Plane. Bch. Hook.	Laying out. Working to line. N. B.—Plane working edge. Square ends to length. Gouge and plane to width.	Optional. Matt pattern.	None.	Plane working edge. "Square up" to size. Lay out octagon. Saw off corners. Block plane edges. All planing with Bch. Hook.
2.	Sun dial. 7"x7".	Pupils make.	Redwood base. Poplar dial.	Knife. Hammer. Bevel. Gouge. Screw driver.	Nailing. Screwing.	Optional. Figures. Motto. Cymbols.	Oil.	Square base and dial to size. Bevel base. Lay out and ornament dial. Make shadowstick, fasten to dial. Fasten dial to base, cross-ing grain oil.
3.	Box. 4"x6"x10".	Pupils make.	Redwood. Pine. Poplar. Cedar.	Mk. Gauge. Chisel.	Cutting groove.	Optional. Burnt pattern. Color. Carve.	Sand paper. Stain. Wax.	Give out two pieces, each 4½"x17". Plane working edge. Gauge width and plane to gauge line. Gauge lines for groove; cut groove. Cut off end pieces. Square four pieces to length. [illegible] groove off front end. Nail sides to ends. BOTTOM — Square two adjacent sides. Lay out other two sides from frame. Insert and nail. TOP—As with bottom, except fit to groove. Make thumb notch. N. B.—Pupils may make partitions.

WOOD WORK B SEVENTH GRADE.

No.	Model.	Drawing.	Wood.	New Tools.	New Operations.	Ornament.	Finish.	Instructions.
6.	Ironing board.	Blackboard.	Pine.	Jack plane. Spoke shave.	Edge planing. Surface planing. Spoke shaving.	None.	Sand paper.	Surface one side. Draw center line. Locate centers for arcs. Draw perpendiculars through centers. Draw arcs. Connect points of intersection of arcs and perpendiculars. Plane each side to line. Gauge and plane to thickness. Saw off corners—back saw. Spoke-shave to line.
	Hat rack.	Blackboard.	Redwood.	Brace and bit. Chisel.	Beveling. Boreing. Cutting pegs.	None.	Stain.	Square up stock. Surface both sides. Bevel edges. Locate and bore peg holes. Make and insert pegs. Stain. Screw eyes.
8.	Shelf.	Pupils make.	Optional.	As required.	As required.	Pupils design. Color. Relief.	Optional.	Give class instruction as to form, use, variety and ornamentation. Encourage "homework." Give individual criticism and instruction as to best method of construction.
9.	Box form.	Pupils make.	Optional.	As required.	As required.	Pupils design.	Optional.	Same as above. Suggestive models—Mail, glove, bird, handkerchief, necktie, collar, jewel and stationery boxes. In models 8 and 9 pupils are to be limited to 2 feet of stock unless they provide for themselves.

REPORT FOR ORAL SCHOOL FOR DEAF, 1908-1909.

MRS. J. B. HOLDEN IN CHARGE.

I desire at this time to submit to the Hon. Supt. of Schools a short report of our school work for the past year.

The school opened last August with 19 pupils in attendance. Since that time four more have been added to the roll.

The average daily attendance has been very good.

There has been little illness excepting colds.

It was our sad duty to record the death of one of our little pupils, who had suffered for almost a year with heart trouble.

The pupils in our school are required to take a special course in sense training, articulation voice training, lip reading and language. In cases where we find evidence of some hearing auricular training is given.

When far enough advanced, we begin the work outlined by your course of study for city schools.

Nine of Mr. Holden's class have accomplished the work thus mapped out as far as "A" 6th grade and are ready to begin "B" 6th grade work in August.

Five of the younger pupils are very well graded for "B" 3d grade work next year. Five more for "A" 2d grade. Four pupils are ungraded, one of them being a kindergarten tot of three years of age.

Three other children will enter in August or rather their parents have been here and desire to have them enter at that time.

One of our boys has been doing very good work in the "A" 7th grade in the John Swett school since January 1st.

Our pupils have made very good progress this year. They have worked faithfully and appreciatively.

We have every reason to feel that there is general satisfaction among the parents as to the condition of the school.

I would suggest that an additional teacher be hired in the fall if our enrollment is twenty-three or twenty-four.

Nine pupils in 6th grade is all one teacher ought to have and fourteen for the other teacher with a prospect of two or three more are more than she can do justice to.

Mr. Holden and I will spend the first two weeks of our vacation in visiting day schools for the deaf in Illinois and Wisconsin. We hope to bring back many new and useful ideas which may be of benefit to our pupils here.

We desire to express our appreciation of your interest in our work and the kindly consideration of the Board of Education.

Respectfully,

MRS. J. B. HOLDEN.

NAMES AND LOCATION OF SCHOOLS AND DESCRIPTION OF SCHOOL PROPERTY.

Adams Cosmopolitan Grammar School—Temporary frame building, 12 rooms; Eddy street, between Van Ness avenue and Polk street; lot in block 62 W. A., 137½x120 feet.

Agassiz Primary School—Eighteen rooms; Bartlett street, between Twenty-second and Twenty-third streets; lot in Mission block 136, 150x250 feet, occupied also by Horace Mann Grammar school. On May 9, 1902, additional lot, southwest corner Twenty-second and Bartlett streets, S. 55 feet by W. 85 feet. was purchased from S. J. Hendy, December 28, 1908, from H. J. Koepke a lot in Mission black 136, $5,000; March 19, 1909, from Johanna Sheehan, W. line of Bartlett street 255 feet S. to Twenty-second street., S. 25 feet by W. 125 feet Mission, block 136, $4,500; December 6, 1909, from G. W. Wepfer, lot W. line of Bartlett street, 205 feet S of Twenty-second street, S. 25 by W. 125 in Mission block 136, $7,000.

Bay View Grammar School—New building, twelve rooms. On July 10, 1905, additional lot in Silver Terrace tract, block C, was purchased from Allen Riddell for $10,250. Commencing at the corner formed by the intersection of the southerly line of Bay View avenue and the easterly line of Flora street, and running thence easterly along said southerly line of Bay View avenue 200 feet to the westerly line of Pomona street: thence at a right angle southerly 350 feet; thence at a right angle westerly 200 feet to the easterly line of Flora street; thence northerly along said line of Flora street 350 feet to the southerly line of Bay View avenue and point of commencement. Recorder in Book 2, 124 of Deeds, page 60. School located on Bay View Avenue and Flora street.

Bergerot Primary School—New building, 12 rooms; cost $37,000; Twenty-fifth avenue and California street, block 95, 150x240 feet.

Bernal Grammar School—Frame building, 16 rooms; Courtland avenue, between Andover avenue and Moultrie street. Lot in Gift Map No. 2, 140x148 feet 8½ inches. October 17, 1908, from Elizabeth S. Ford, lots Nos. 17, 19, 21 and 23, Gift Map No. 2, $2,600. January 15, 1909, lot on corner of Andover and Jefferson avenues, $2,600.

Bryant Cosmopolitan Primary School—Temporary building, 12 rooms. York and Twenty-third streets. Lot in Mission, block 147, between Twenty-second and Twenty-third streets, Bryant and York streets, 150x200 feet.

Buena Vista Primary School—Frame building, 13 rooms. Bryant street, between Eighteenth and Nineteenth streets. Lot on Potrero, block 39, 100x200 feet.

Burnett Primary School—Frame building of 12 rooms and two adjacent rented rooms. L street and Fourteenth Avenue South. Lot in South San Francisco Homestead, block 289. Lot 1, 75x100 feet, and additional lot purchased from Cecilia Wright, August 26, 1903, for $500. South San Francisco Homestead. Commencing at a point on the southwest line of Fourteenth Avenue South; distant 150 feet northwesterly from the northwesterly line of L Street South; thence northwesterly along Fourteenth Avenue South 32½ feet by uniform depth of 100 feet. September 27, 1909, from Martha A. Stapleton; commencing S.W. line Fourteenth avenue S. 182 feet 6 inches, N.W. on L. S. N.W. 42 feet 6 inches by S.W. 100 feet, Block 289, S. S. F. Homestead and R. R. Association, $1,750.

Clement Primary School—Temporary frame building, 6 rooms. Day and Noe streets. May 3, 1909, from Ellen S. McGowan and E. Connors, lot west line of Noe street 26½ feet north of 30th street, north 25 feet by west 105 feet in Horner Addition, block 172, $1,500. April 5, 1909, from Ellen S. McGowan and Delia Williams, lot southwestern corner Noe and Day streets, 105 feet by south on Noe street 26½ feet in Horner Addition, block 172, $6,000. April 12, 1909, from Ellen S. McGowan, west line Noe street, 25½ feet south of Day street, south 150 feet by west 105 feet, south 51½ feet by west 50 feet by north 228 feet by east 50 feet by south 26½ feet: thence east 105 feet, Horner Addition, block 172, $16,600. May 24, 1909, from W. E. Smith and Ellen McGowan, lot northwest corner Noe and 30th streets. North 26½ feet by west 105 feet, Horner Addition, block 172, $2,150. June 1, 1909, from Ellen S. McGowan and Joe Gottwald, lot south line of Day street 155 feet west of Noe street, west 25 feet by south 228 feet to the north line of 30th street in Horner Addition, block 172, $5,400.

Clement Cooking and Manual Training Center—Temporary frame building, six rooms. Geary near Jones street. Lot in block 253, 77½x137½ feet: additional lot commencing at a point on the southerly line of Geary street, distant 137 feet 6 inches westerly from the southwest corner of Geary and Jones streets: thence northerly along said line of Geary street, 25 feet by south 137 feet 6 inches in depth, being a portion of 50 vara lot 253. Purchased from S. L. and Mabel V. Starr, August 14, 1905, for $27,000. Recorded in Book 2, 134 of Deeds, page 98.

Cleveland Primary School—January 11, 1909, from Annie M. Creighton, lot northwest corner of Moscow street and Persia avenue, 100 feet by 300 feet, $6,500. February 15, 1909, from William McCall, lot in Excelsior Homestead Association, block 73, northeast corner Persia avenue and Athens street, 100 feet on Persia avenue by 300 feet on Athens street, $6,750.

Columbia Grammar School—Frame building, 18 rooms and three portable rooms. Florida street, between Twenty-fifth and Twenty-sixth streets. Lot in Mission, block 178. Lot No. 1, 100x200 feet; lot No. 2, 50x100 feet.

Cooper Primary School—Temporary frame building, 6 rooms. Greenwich street, between Jones and Leavenworth streets, lot in block 237, 137½x137½ feet.

Commercial School—Afternoon session at Mission High school, Eighteenth and Dolores streets. January 18, 1909, from F. Siefke, north line Grove street 100 feet west of Larkin street, 37½ feet by 120 feet, Western Addition, block No. 3, $15,000. February 8, 1909, from Dorothea Passman, west line of Grove street 112½ feet east from east line of Polk street, east 25 feet by 137½ feet Western Addition, block No. 3, $9,800. June 21, 1909, from Chas. Worth, lot north line Grove street, 82½ feet east of Polk street, east 30 feet by north 120 feet, Western Addition, block No. 3, $12,000; lot in block No. 3, Western Addition, Grove street near Larkin street, 137½ by 137½.

Crocker Grammar School—Frame building, 20 rooms. Page street, between Broderick and Baker streets. Lot in block 523, W. A., 137½x137½ feet. Additional lot purchased from W. J. Hawkins May 16, 1905, for $2,750. Commencing at a point on the southerly line of Page street, distant 96 feet 10½ inches, easterly from the easterly line of Baker street; thence easterly 25 feet by uniform depth of 110 feet.

Denman Grammar School—Temporary frame building, 6 rooms. Bush street, between Larkin and Hyde streets. Lot in block 307, 97½x137½ feet. A new building for this school will be constructed on the following property: May 17, 1909, from the Edwin Barron estate, lot northeast corner Fell and Pierce streets, 137 feet 6 inches on Fell street by 137 feet 6 inches on Pierce street, Western Addition, block 379, $29,118. October 18, 1909, from P. J. Stuparich and H. Adams, lot southeast corner Pierce and Hayes streets, 137½ by 137½, $37,125.

Douglass Primary School—Frame building, 10 rooms. Corner Nineteenth and Collingwood streets. Lot in Horner's Addition, 135x135 feet.

Dudley Stone Primary School—Frame building, 16 rooms, Haight street, between Lott and Masonic avenues, lot in block 657, W. A., 137½x137½ feet. August 12, 1908, from E. L. Pritchard: consideration $6,000. Lot on south line of Haight street 112 feet 6 inches west of Central avenue, west 25 feet by 137 feet 6 inches being a part of Western Addition, block 657. August 12, 1908, from J. L. Pritchard, out of School Fund, lot south line Haight street 112 feet 6 inches west of Central avenue, west 25 feet by 137 feet 6 inches, Western Addition block 657, $6,000.

Edison Primary School—Frame building, 10 rooms. Church and Hill streets. Lot in Mission, block 90, 101 feet 9 inches by 114 feet.

Emerson Primary School—Frame building, 20 rooms, Pine street, between Scott and Devisadero streets. Lot in block 460, W. A., 137½x137½ feet.

Everett Grammar School—Frame building, 16 rooms; five additional rooms are rented. Sanchez street, between Sixteenth and Seventeenth streets. Lot in Mission, block 95, 125x160 feet. A lot of land 28x160 feet on Sanchez street north of and contiguous to the present site of the Everett Grammar school, $10,000. November 29, 1909, from Frank L. Roseneau, lot east line of Sanchez street 202 feet south of Sixteenth street south 28 feet by east 80 feet, in Mission block 95, $6,900.

Fairmount Grammar School—Frame building, 12 rooms. Chenery street, near Randall street, five portable rooms on premises. Lot in Fairmount tract, block 29, lot 1, 112x125 feet; lot 2, 62x175 feet.

Franklin Grammar School—Temporary frame building, 12 rooms, Eighth street, near Bryant street. Lot in block 410, 140x275 feet.

Frank McCoppin School—Temporary frame building, 9 rooms. Sixth avenue, between B and C streets. Lot in block 375, west of First avenue, 150x240 feet. April 5, 1909, from Elizabeth M. Strand, lot west line Sixth avenue 200 feet south of B street, south 25 feet by west 120 feet O. L. block 375, $2,000. April 16, 1909, from Robert Bennett, lot east side Seventh avenue 200 feet south of B street, south 25 feet by east 100 feet O. L. block 375, $7,500.

Fremont Grammar School—Frame building, 16 rooms. McAllister street, between Broderick and Baker streets. Lot in block 530, W. A., 137½x137½ feet. Additional lot (No. 1) purchased from Herman Murphy, January 3, 1902, for $3,250. Commencing at a point on the northerly line of McAllister street, distant 112½ feet westerly from the westerly line of Broderick street; thence westerly 25 feet by uniform depth of 137 feet 6 inches. Recorded in book 1, 947 of Deeds, page 102; additional lot (No 2) purchased from Owen McHugh, July 1, 1902. Commencing at a point on the northerly line of McAllister street, distant 96 feet 10½ inches easterly from the easterly line of Baker street, running thence easterly 25 feet, by uniform depth of 137 feet 6 inches. Recorded in Book 1, 962 of Deeds, page 138.

Garfield Primary School—Temporary frame building, 10 rooms (four additional rented rooms). Union street, near Kearny street. Lot in block 62, 137½x137½ feet. A new building for this school is being built. Lot in block No. 82. Corner Filbert and Kearny streets; 137½x137½ feet. Additional lot adjacent in litigation. July 28, 1908, from Annie M. Gallagher and Mary B. Waller, lot on north line of Filbert street, distant 137 feet 6 inches west from Kearny street; thence west on Filbert street 68 feet 9 inches by 137 feet 6 inches, being a part of 50 vara lot No. 461 and 50 vara lot No. 82, $8,000. From Charles Huth, November 2, 1908, south line of Greenwich street, between Kearny and Dupont streets, 25 feet square, block 82, $750. November 2, 1908, from Charles Kosta, rear portion of lot adjoining above 25 feet square, $550. West line of Kearny street 112 feet 6 inches south from Greenwich; thence south along west line of Kearny street 25 feet; thence at right angles west 87 feet 6 inches; thence at right angles north 25 feet; thence east 87 feet 6 inches, purchased from the Hibernia Saving and Loan Society July 10, 1903, $850.

Girls' High School—Temporary frame building just completed at a cost of $16,000. Scott street, near Geary street. This school is not built on school property, but on property belonging to the city, and which originally formed a part of Hamilton Square. In 1870 the Board of Education obtained permission to use a portion for the erection of school buildings. Lot 275 feet front on Scott street, 341 feet 3 inches on Geary and O'Farrell streets.

Glen Park Grammar School—New frame building, 12 rooms, costing $42,500. San Jose and Joost avenues. Additional lot purchased from the estate of John Pforr, May 20, 1905, for $5,600. Mission and Thirtieth Extension Homestead Union. Beginning at the corner formed by the intersection of the southwesterly line of Berkshire street with the southeasterly line of Lippard avenue; thence southwesterly along Lippard avenue 400 feet; thence at right angles southeasterly 200 feet to the northwesterly line of Fulton avenue; thence at right angles northeasterly 400 feet along Fulton avenue to the southwesterly line of Berkshire street; thence at a right angle northwesterly along Berkshire street to the point of beginning, being all of block 3, Mission and Thirteenth Street Extension Homestead Union. Recorded in Book 2, 125 of Deeds, page 76.

Golden Gate Primary School—New building. Golden Gate avenue, between Pierce and Scott streets. Lot in block 433 W. A., 100x137½ feet. Additional lot purchased from Fred L. Hansen, July 20, 1905, for $4,375. Commencing at a point on the northerly line of Golden Gate avenue, distant thereon 68 feet 9 inches, westerly from the westerly line of Pierce street; thence westerly 25 feet, by uniform depth of 137 feet 6 inches. Additional lot (No. 2) purchased from Margaret Poyelson, June 28, 1905, for $8,856. Commencing at a point on the northerly line of Golden Gate avenue, distant thereon 93 feet 9 inches, westerly from the westerly line of Pierce street; thence westerly 43 feet 9 inches, by uniform depth of 137 feet 8 inches. Additional lot (No. 3) purchased from Gustave A. DeManiel, June 14, 1905, for $12,462. Commencing at a point on the northerly line of Golden Gate avenue, distant 137 feet 6 inches, westerly from the westerly line of Pierce street; thence westerly 37 feet 6 inches, by uniform depth of 137 feet 6 inches.

Grant Primary School—Frame building, 8 rooms. Pacific avenue, between Broadway and Baker streets. Lot in block No. 546 W. A., 137½x137½ feet.

Grattan Primary School—Temporary frame building, 6 rooms. Alma street, near Grattan. Additional lot purchased from the Pope Estate Co., for $28,500. Recorded in Book 2, 130 of Deeds, page 204. Western Addition, block 874. Commencing at the point of intersection of the southerly line of Grattan street with the easterly line of Shrader street; thence easterly along Grattan street 203 feet 7¾ inches; thence at a right angle southerly 249 feet to the northerly line of Alma avenue; thence at a right angle westerly and along said line of Alma avenue 203 feet 7¾ inches to the easterly line of Shrader street; thence at a right angle northerly 249 feet 11 inches to the southerly line of Grattan street, and point of commencement.

Haight Primary School—Frame building, 13 rooms. Mission street, between Twenty-fifth and Twenty-sixth streets. Lot in Mission block 183; 150x117½ feet.

Hamilton Grammar School—Frame building, 17 rooms. Geary street, between Scott and Pierce streets. (See Girls' High School).

Hancock Grammar School—Temporary frame building, 10 rooms. Filbert street, near Jones. Lot in block 208, 100x120 feet. December 21, 1908, from R. H. McColgan and Mary E. Russell, north line Filbert street 110 feet west from Taylor, west 60x120 feet, 50 vara lot No. 208, $10,800.

Harrison Primary School—Temporary frame building, 3 rooms. Railroad avenue and Thirty-fourth street.

Hawthorne Primary School—Frame building, 11 rooms. Shotwell street, between Twenty-second and Twenty-third streets, lot in Mission block 138, 122½x122½ feet.

Hearst Grammar School—Frame building, 25 rooms. Corner Fillmore and Hermann streets, lot in block 374 W. A., 137½x137½ feet.

Henry Durant Primary School—Frame building, 12 rooms. Turk street, between Buchanan and Webster streets, lot in block 281 W. A., 137½x120 feet.

Holly Park Primary School—Temporary frame building of 8 rooms. Andover avenue and Jefferson street. (Lot is leased). July 12, 1909, from A. B. Ruggles, lots 31, 32, 33, 34, 35, 36, 37, 38, 39, 40. Block 3, Holly Park tract, $13,700. July 6, 1909, from A. B. Ruggles, lots 31, 32, 33, 34, 35, 36, 37, 38, 39, 40, in block 3, Holly Park Tract, $13,700.

Horace Mann Grammar School—Frame building, 20 rooms. Valencia street, between Twenty-second and Twenty-third streets. (See Agassiz Primary). December 28, 1908, from Moore Investment Company, commencing 205 feet south from Twenty-second street, thence south on Valencia street 37½ feet by 125 feet, Mission block No. 136, $15,000.

Hunter's Point Primary School—Temporary frame building of 2 rooms. Eighth avenue, between C and D streets. (Lot is leased).

Irving Primary School—Temporary frame building, 6 rooms. Broadway, between Montgomery and Sansome streets. Lot in block No. 47, 68¾x137½ feet.

Irving M. Scott Grammar School—Frame building, 20 rooms. Tennessee street, near Twenty-second. Lot in Potrero, block No. 373, 150x200 feet.

Jackson Primary School—Temporary portable frame building, 6 rooms. Oak and Stanyan streets. (Lot is leased).

James Lick Grammar School—Frame building, 14 rooms. Noe and Twenty-fifth streets. Lot in Horner's Addition, block No. 163, 114x116 feet.

Jean Parker Grammar School—Temporary building, 10 rooms. Broadway, between Powell and Mason streets. Lot in block No. 157. Lot 1, 65 feet 2 inches by 137½ feet; lot 2, 30x91 feet 8 inches; lot 3, 39 feet 9 inches by 91 feet 8 inches. December 28, 1908, from Fannie Galloway, 228 feet 11 inches by 69 feet 7 inches of lot in 50 vara, block 157, 91 feet 8 inches perpendicularly distant from north line of Broadway, $2,000. January 4, 1909, from the estate of Jose M. Jininez, north line of Broadway, 137 feet east from east line of Mason street; thence east on Broadway 34 feet 4 inches by 137 feet 6 inches deep, 50 varas, lot No. 167, $8,925. November 15, 1909, from Bernardo Fernandez, lot north line of Broadway 171 feet 10 inches east of Mason, east 38 by north 137 feet 6 inches, 50 vara, block 167, $9,750.

Jefferson Primary School—Temporary frame building, 6 rooms. Bryant and Seventh streets. Lot in block No. 397, 92½x275 feet.

John Swett Grammar School—Temporary frame building, 12 rooms. McAllister street, between Franklin and Gough streets. Lot in block No. 136, W. A., 137½x137½ feet.

Lafayette School—(See Garfield School).

Laguna Honda Primary School—New building, cost $57,612; 14 rooms; brick, class B. Seventh avenue, between I and J streets. Lot in block No. 678, 150x240 feet.

Lake View Primary School—Temporary frame building, 4 rooms. Plymouth and Grafton streets. April 26, 1909, from John and Belle McCaffery, lot east line of Faxon avenue, 100 feet south from Halloway avenue, south 37½ feet by east 112½ feet lot 25, lot 19, Lake View, $1,025. April 26, 1909, from Spaulding & Neff, lots 19, 20, 21, 22, 23, half of lot 24, and lots from 26 to 41, inclusive, block 19, Lake View, $11,512.50.

Lincoln Grammar School—Temporary frame building, 8 rooms. Harrison street, near Fourth. Lot in block No. 374, 195x160 feet. Additional lot (1) purchased from Bertha Gunnison, February 9, 1906, for $4,250. Commencing at a point on the northwesterly line of Harrison street, distant thereon 275 feet, southwesterly on the southwest line of Fourth street, running thence southerly along said line of Harrison street; thence at a right angle northwesterly 85 feet; thence at a right angle northwesterly 85 feet to the north line of Harrison street from the point of commencement. Additional lot (2) purchased from Herman Scholten, December 18, 1905, for $2,800. Commencing at a point on the southeasterly line of Clara street, distant 275 feet southwesterly from the point of intersection of said southeasterly line of Clara street with the southwesterly line of Fourth street, running thence southwesterly along said southeasterly line of Clara street 25 feet; thence at a right angle southeasterly 75 feet; thence at a right angle northeasterly 25 feet; thence at a right angle northwesterly 75 feet to the southeasterly line of Clara street and point of commencement.

Lowell High School—Frame building, 21 rooms. Sutter street, between Octavia and Gough streets. Lot in block No. 158, W. A., 137½x120½ feet. November 29, 1909, from Ivan Treadwell, et al., the whole of Western Addition Block 667 bounded by Masonic avenue, Hayes, Ashbury and Grove streets, $116,500.

Madison Primary School—Frame building, 8 rooms. Clay street, near Walnut street. Lot in block No. 815, W. A., 137½x137½ feet.

Marshall Primary School—Temporary frame building, 10 rooms. Julian avenue, between Fifteenth and Sixteenth streets. Lot in Mission, block No. 35, 200x182 feet. (Also occupied by Mission Grammar school). July 13, 1908, from R. E. Archbishop of San Francisco, lot corner 19th and Angelica streets (resolution 1426 and 1757, Board of Supervisors). Commencing intersection south line 19th street with east line Angelica street, south 205 feet to Cumberland Place; thence east 183 feet by north 114 feet west 50 feet N. W., 118 feet 2½ inches to 19th street, west 102 feet to point of commencement. Mission, block 72, $33,625.

Commencing at point of intersection of the south line of 19th street with the east line of Angelica street, thence south along Angelica street 205 feet to the north line of Cumberland Place, thence east 183 feet, thence north 91 feet, thence at right angles west 50 feet, thence northwest 118 feet 2½ inches to a point in the south line of 19th street, which is distant east 102 feet from the southeast corner of 19th and Angelica streets; thence west on south line of 19th street 102 feet to point of commencement, being a portion of Mission block 72 purchased from Rev. P. W. Riordan, Roman Catholic Archbishop of San Francisco, a corporation sale for $33,625, as alternative site for the Marshall Primary authorized by the bond issue September 29, 1903.

McKinley Primary **School**—Temporary frame building, 12 rooms. Fourteenth and Castro streets. Additional lot purchased from Jas. Irvine August 14, 1905. Cost $35,000. Mission block No. 121. Commencing at the southwesterly corner of Fourteenth and Castro streets; thence westerly along the southerly line of Fourteenth street 320 feet; thence at right angle southerly

230 feet to the northerly line of Henry street; thence easterly along said last named line 320 feet to the westerly line of Castro street; thence northerly along said last named line 230 feet to the point of commencement.

Mission Grammar School—Temporary frame building, 12 rooms. Mission, between Fifteenth and Sixteenth streets. (See Marshall Primary).

Mission High School—Brick building, 25 rooms. Eighteenth and Dolores streets. Mission block No. 85, 398x194 feet. Purchased in 1896 for $52,500. April 19, 1909, from Owen M. V. Roberts, lot in Mission block 85, south line of Dorland street 88 feet east of Church street, east 25 feet by south 100 feet, $3,500. April 19, 1909, from J. and Winifred O'Donnell, lot south line Dorland street 138 feet southeast of Church street, southeast 25 feet by south 100 feet in Mission block 85, $5,225. April 19, 1909, from the Catholic Apostolic church, lot north line of 18th street 112 feet east of Church street, east 25 feet by north 114 feet, $7,800. June 1, 1909, from Amelia Dorland and Leonora Son, lot in Mission block No. 85, southeast corner Dorland and Church streets, south 35 feet 8 inches by east 88 feet, $6,300. June 1, 1909, from Herman D. Junck, lot in Mission block 85 south line Dorland street, 138 feet east from Church street; thence 100 feet east; east 25⅝ feet by north 100 feet; thence west 25⅝ feet, $17,000. June 1, 1909, from Jessie Hauser, lot east line of Church street 168 feet north of 18th street, north 27 feet by east 88 feet, $10,000; also northeast corner Church and 18th streets, 62 feet on 18th street by 114 feet on Church street, Mission block No. 85, $17,000. June 28, 1909, from Eva Topper, lot east line Church street 141 feet north 18th street, north 27 feet by east 88 feet Mission block 85, $11,085. October 4, 1909, lot north line Eighteenth street, 137 feet east of Church, east 25 by north 114 feet $9,000. From James A. Symon, lot north line Eighteenth street, 62 feet east from east line of Church, east 25 by north 114 feet, in Mission block 85, $8,500. November 1, 1909, from David Dorward, lot south line of Church street, 114 feet north of Eighteenth street north 27 by east 88 in Mission block 85, $9,100. November 15, 1909, from James A. Symon, exec., north line of Eighteenth street, 87 feet east of Church street, east 25 feet by north 114 feet, $8,500.

Monroe Grammar School—New building. China avenue and London streets. Lot in block No. 14, Excelsior Homestead, 150x100 feet. Additional lot purchased from Thomas Shewbridge, August 30, 1902, Excelsior Homestead, block No. 14. New lot, corner China avenue and Paris street, northwest 100 feet by northeast 150 feet, lot 4, block 14, Excelsior Homestead.

Moulder Primary School—Frame building, 10 rooms. Page and Gough streets, lot in block No. 145, W. A., 137½x120 feet.

Noe Valley Primary School—Frame building, 15 rooms. Twenty-fourth and Douglas. Additional lot (No. 1) purchased from George and Christina Gies. Deed dated October 5, 1901. Horner's Estate, block 244. Commencing at a point out the west line of Douglas street, 139 feet north to Twenty-fourth street; thence north on the west line of Douglas street 25 feet by west 125 feet in depth. Additional lot (No. 2) purchased from Mary E. Gies. Deed dated October 7, 1901. Commencing at a point on the west line of Douglass street 114 feet north of 24th street; thence north on the west line of Douglass street 25 feet by west 125 feet in depth. Additional lot (No. 3) commencing at a point on the west line of Douglass street, 64 feet north of Twenty-fourth street; thence north on Douglass street, 50 feet, by west 125 feet in depth from Mary Tobener, September 6, 1901. Additional lot (No. 4) purchased from James M. Curtin, deed dated September 6, 1901. Commencing at a point on the northwest corner of Twenty-fourth and Douglass streets; thence north 64 feet, west 125 feet, north 50 feet, west 51 feet 8 inches, south 114 feet, east 176 feet 8 inches. Additional lot (No. 5) purchased from Eliz. Overend for $2,050. Commencing at a point on the south line of Elizabeth street, 125 feet west of Douglass street; thence west on Elizabeth street, 51 feet 8 inches, by south 114 feet, in depth.

Ocean House Primary School—Frame building, 2 rooms. Corner Corbett road and Ocean avenue. Cost $1,401.58. Lot in San Miguel, 100 feet by 240 feet.

Oceanside Primary School—New frame building, 8 rooms, $38,000. Forty-second avenue and I street. Lot in block No. 714. 150 feet by 240 feet.

Oral School for Deaf—Temporary frame building, one room. McAllister street, between Octavia and Gough streets. (See John Swett Grammar).

Oriental Public School—Temporary frame building, 5 rooms. Clay street, near Powell street.

Parental School—Temporary frame building, 3 rooms. Harrison street, near Tenth. Lot in Mission block No. 8. 137½ feet by 137½ feet.

Pacific Heights Grammar School—Frame building, 19 rooms. Jackson, between Fillmore and Webster streets. Lot in block 318, W. A., 137½ feet by 137½ feet. May 17, 1909, from Mary W. Shannon, lot west line of Jackson street, 113 feet west from Webster street, west 24½ feet by north 90 feet, Western Addition, block 318, $11,500. June 1, 1909, from Lillie E. Lincoln, north side of Jackson street 112 feet east of Fillmore street, east 25½ feet by north 127 feet 8¼ inches, Western Addition, block 318, $12,000.

Peabody Primary School—Sixth avenue, near California. Lot in block No. 176; 150x240 feet.

Polytechnic High School—Temporary frame building, 16 rooms. Frederick street, near First avenue. Additional lot purchased from the City Realty Company, July 31, 1905, for $65,000. Western Addition, block No. 740. Commencing at a point on the south line of Frederick street 121½ feet east from First avenue; thence in a southerly direction 175 feet; thence at a right angle easterly 1 foot 6 inches; thence at a right angle southerly 100 feet to a point in the north line of Carl street 151½ feet east of First avenue; thence easterly along Carl street 464 and 8-12 feet to a point 269 4-12 feet west of Willard street; thence northerly 278 5-12 feet to a point on the south line of Frederick street 226 11-12 feet west of Willard street; thence west along south line of Frederick street 505 10-12 feet to point of commencement.

Redding Primary School—Temporary frame building, 6 rooms. Pine street, between Polk and Larkin streets. Lot in block 114, W. A., 200x120 feet.

Richmond Grammar School—Frame building, 17 rooms. First avenue, near Point Lobos avenue. Lot in Academy of Science block, W. A., O. L. R. 157 feet 7 inches by 240 feet. The Board of Education has permission to use this lot for school purposes.

Sheridan Primary School—One-story frame building, comprising 12 rooms. Minerva street, near Plymouth avenue. Lot in block S, Railroad Homestead Association. 100 feet by 125 feet. Lot No. 7. May 10, 1909, from W. S. Benthame, lot northwest corner of Farallones and Capital avenue in block L, Railroad Homestead Association, $3,450. September 23, 1908, from Welthy and Wm. S. Stafford, north side of Minerva street 150 feet west of Plymouth street; thence west on Minerva street 50 feet by north 125 feet. November 29, 1909, from Adolph Mueller, Caroline Bauer, admx. Wm. T. and Edward Bauer, interest and improvement in lot southwest corner of Capitol avenue and Lobos street, 50 feet by 125 feet, in R. R. Homestead Association, block L, $6,300.

Sherman Primary School—Frame building, 14 rooms. Union street, near Franklin. Lot in block No. 117, W. A., 137½ feet by 137½ feet.

South End Primary School—Frame building, comprising 13 rooms. Somerset street, between Felton and Burrows streets. Lot in University Mound survey, 50 feet by 120 feet. Additional block purchased from P. J. Kennedy, August 22, 1905, for $5,000. University Mound survey, block 12. Commencing at a point formed by the intersection of the northwesterly line of Bacon street, in the southwesterly line of Girard street, running thence northwesterly along Girard street 200 feet and thence at a right angle 240 feet to Berlin street; thence at a right angle southeasterly and along Berlin street 200 feet to the northwesterly line of Bacon street; thence at a right angle 240 feet to the southwesterly line of Girard street and point of commencement, being the southerly half of block No. 12, University Mound Survey.

Spring Valley Grammar School—Temporary frame building, 9 rooms. Broadway, near Polk street. Lot in block 21, W. A., 137½ feet by 137½ feet. May 24, 1909, from Margaret and Catherine Matthews, lot south line of Jackson street 137 feet 6 inches east from Larkin street, east 68 feet 9 inches by 137½ feet, $15,250. From Samuel Polack, lot south line of Jackson street 137 feet 6 inches west of Hyde street, west 34 feet 4½ inches by 137 feet 6 inches, 50 vara block 302, $6,975. July 19, 1909, from Edward P. McGeeney, et al., lot south line Jackson, 171 feet 10½ inches, west of Hyde west 34 feet 4½ inches, by south 137 feet 6 inches, $9,100.

Starr King Primary School—Temporary frame building, 9 rooms. San Bruno avenue, near Twenty-fifth street. Commencing on the east line of Utah street 100 feet south from 25th street, thence south on Utah street 100x200 feet in depth to San Bruno avenue, being lots 13, 14, 15, 16, 25, 26, 27, 28, of block. 85.

Sunnyside Primary School—New class C building. Cost $30,000. Block 85, 115 Flood avenue. Additional lots 10 to 24, inclusive, Sunnyside tract. Purchased from the Sunnyside Land Company, July 19, 1902. June 22, 1908, bought from Monarch Mutual Building and Loan Association sewer right of way for Sunnyside School portion of lot 23, Sunnyside, block 47, $400.

Sunset Primary School—Temporary frame building, 6 rooms. Thirteenth avenue and K street. Block No. 876. West of first avenue; 150 feet by 240 feet.

Sutro Grammar School—Frame building, comprising 13 rooms. Twelfth avenue, between Clement and California streets. Lot in block 179; west of First avenue; 150x240 feet. January 18, 1909, from F. C. Fish and J. J. Higgin, lot on west line Twelfth avenue 200 feet south from California street, 25 feet by 140 feet, in block 170, $7,100.

Visitacion Valley Primary School—Temporary frame building, 7 rooms. Sunnyside avenue and Cora street.

Washington Grammar School—New steel-brick building. Washington and Mason streets. Lot in block No. 188; 137½x137½ feet. Additional new lot No. 1; purchased from the estate of Louise C. Kauffman, March 10, 1905; for $7,500. Commencing at a point on the southerly line of Washington street 137 feet 6 inches northerly from the southwest corner of Mason and Washington streets; thence southerly 137 feet 6 inches by west 34 feet 4½ inches, being a portion of 50 vara, lot 188. Additional new lot No. 2, purchased from Julie Dunnier and others, July 12, 1905, for $9,500. Commencing at a point on the southerly line of Washington street, distant 170 feet 10½ inches from the southwest corner of Mason and Washington streets; thence northerly 34 feet 4½ inches by south 137 feet 6 inches in depth, being a portion of 50 vara, lot 188.

West End Primary School—One-story frame building, 3 rooms. 5630 Mission street. Lot in West End Map. Block 23; 80x165 feet. March 1, 1909, from D. A. Helbing et al., lot southwest corner Lowell, Mission and Morse, 267 by 213, being lots 49, 50 and 51, West End Homestead, $9,250.

Winfield Scott Primary School—Building being built. Lombard street, between Broderick and Baker streets. Lot in block No. 553, W. A.; 137½x137½ feet.

Yerba **Buena Primary** School—Building being built. Greenwich street, between Webster and Fillmore streets. Lot in block No. 325, W. A.; 137½x 120 feet. February 23, 1909, from McEwen Bros., lot Webster and Greenwich streets west 137½ feet by 120 feet in Western Addition, block No. 235, $17,000.

LIST OF UNOCCUPIED PROPERTIES BELONGING TO SCHOOL DEPARTMENT.

Lot in block No. 220; northwest corner Bush and Taylor streets; 137½x 137½ feet.

Lot in block No. 286; Golden Gate avenue, near Hyde street; 110x137½ feet.

Lot in block No. 348; Tehama street, between First and Second streets, irregular in size; about 118x155 feet.

Lot in block No. 160; Powell street, between Washington and Jackson streets; 68¾x137½ feet.

Lot in block 371; Fifth street, near Market street; 275x275 feet. Leased to Wise Realty Company (later merged into the Lincoln Realty Company) for thirty-five years, at a total rental of $2,835,000, as follows: for the first five years, a rental of $3,780 per month, and for the remaining thirty years, a rental of $7,245 per month.

Lot in block No. 137; Powell street, between Clay and Sacramento streets; 68¾x137½ feet.

Lot in Mission block No. 21; West Mission street, between Herman and Ridley streets; 133¾x137½ feet.

Lot in block No. 118; corner Bush and Stockton streets; 137½x137½ feet; 50 vara, lot 301.

Lots in block 358; Silver street, between Second and Third streets; lot No. 1, 88x70 feet; lot No. 2, 100x185 feet.

Lot in Mission Block No. 72. Commencing at a point formed by the intersection of the southerly line of Nineteenth street with the easterly line of Angelica street, running thence southerly along said easterly line of Cumberland Place; thence easterly along said northerly line of Cumberland Place and Cumberland Place Extension 183 feet; thence at a right angle northerly 91 feet; thence at a right angle northerly 50 feet; thence in a northwesterly direction 118 feet 2½ inches to a point in the southerly line of Nineteenth street, which point is distant easterly 102 feet from the southeasterly corner of Nineteenth and Angelica streets; thence westerly along said southerly line of Nineteenth street 102 feet to the point of commencement. Purchased from P. W. Riordan, Roman Catholic Archbishop of San Francisco, for $33,625, as an alternate site for the Marshall Primary school. Recorded in Book 128 of Deeds, page 251, new series.

Lot in block No. 119; on Post street, between Grant avenue and Stockton streets; 70x122½ feet. Leased at an average of $911.42 per month.

Total rental, 35 years	$382,800.00
Average rental, per month	911.42

Graduated Rentals—

First 4 months of lease, per month	$ 250.00
Second 4 month, per month	300.00
Third 4 month, per month	350.00
Second year, per month	400.00
Third year, per month	450.00
Fourth year, per month	500.00
Fifth year, per month	550.00
Sixth year, per month	650.00
Seventh year, per month	700.00
Eighth year, per month	750.00
Ninth year, per month	800.00
Tenth year, per conth	850.00
Eleventh year, per month	900.00
Twelfth year, per month	900.00
13th and 14th years, per month	950.00
15th year, per month	1,000.00
16th to 25th years, inc., per month	1,000.00
26th to 35th years, inc., per month	1,125.00

Lot in block No. 137; on Clay street, between Stockton and Powell streets; 26½x75 feet. Rented at $10 per month.

Lot in block No. 183, on northeast corner Taylor and Vallejo streets; 137½x137½ feet.

Lot in block No. 302, on Washington street, between Hyde and Leavenworth streets; 137½x137½ feet.

Lot in block No. 371, known as Lincoln school lots, fronting 275 feet on Market street by 100 feet in depth. Rented to various parties at $3,780 per month.

Lot in block No. 374, corner Fourth and Clara streets; 80x150 feet. Rented at $175 per month.

Lot in Mission Block No. 61, on Nineteenth street, between Mission and Howard streets; 137½x137½ feet, less 60 feet included in Capp street. Title in litigation.

Lot in Mission Block 104, on south side of Sixteenth street, between Sanchez and Noe streets; 137½x137½ feet. In litigation.

Lot in block No. 29, W. A., on south side of Francisco street, between Larkin and Polk streets; 137½x137½ feet.

Lot in block No. 111, W. A., on south line of Bay street, between Franklin and Gough streets; 137½x137½ feet. In litigation.

Lot in block No. 123, W. A., on south line of Washington street, between Franklin and Gough streets; 137¼x137½ feet.

Lot in block No. 465, W. A., on north line of Jackson street, between Scott and Devisadero streets; 137½x137½ feet.

Lot in block No. 848, W. A., on south line of Clay street, between Cherry and First avenue; 137½x137½ feet.

West of First avenue and north of the Park, the School Department owns property as follows. (Appraised by experts appointed by Board of Supervisors):

(All not otherwise stated are 150x240 feet.)

Block 152; Thirty-first avenue, between California and Clement streets.

Block 164; Nineteenth avenue, between California and Clement streets.

Block 176; Seventh avenue, between California and Clement streets.

Block 242; Forty-third avenue, between Point Lobos avenue and A street, $812.

Block 248; Thirty-seventh avenue, between Point Lobos avenue and A street, $1,250.

Block 254; Thirty-first avenue, between Point Lobos avenue and A street. $1,496.

Block 260; Twenty-fourth avenue, between Point Lobos avenue and A street, $837.

Block 266; Nineteenth avenue, between Point Lobos avenue and A street, $1,735.

Block 272; Thirteenth avenue, between Point Lobos avenue and A street, $1,916.

Block 278; Seventh avenue, between Point Lobos avenue and A street, $2,176.

Block 339; Forty-third avenue, between B and C streets, $259.

Block 345; Thirty-seventh avenue, between B and C streets, $750.

Block 351; Thirty-first avenue, between B and C streets, $587.

Block 357; Twenty-fifth avenue, between B and C streets, $300.

Block 363; Nineteenth avenue, between B and C streets, $4,032.

Block 369; Thirteenth avenue, between B and C streets, $525.

Block 395; Sixteenth avenue, between C and D streets, $463.

Block 407; Twenty-eighth avenue, between C and D streets, $293.

Block 418; Twenty-ninth avenue, between C and D streets, $268.

Also west of First avenue and south of the Park, as follows:

(All not otherwise stated are 150x240 feet.)

Block 673; First avenue, between I and J streets; 107x178 feet, $1,738.

Block 690; Nineteenth avenue, between I and J streets, $826.

Block 696; Twenty-fifth avenue, between I and J streets, $300.

Block 702; Thirty-first avenue, between I and J streets, $286.

Block 708; Thirty-seventh avenue, between I and J streets, $273.

Block 775; Eighth avenue, between K and L streets, $1,000.

Block 786; Nineteenth avenue, between K and L streets, $700.

Block 792; Twenty-fifth avenue, between K and L streets, $300.

Block 798; Thirty-first avenue, between K and L streets, $286.

Block 804; Thirty-seventh avenue, between K and L streets, $273.

Block 810; Forty-third avenue, between K and L streets, $259.

Block 872; Thirteenth avenue, between M and N streets, $776.

Block 878; Nineteenth avenue, between M and N streets, $750.

Block 884; Twenty-fifth avenue, between M and N streets, $300.

Block 890; Twenty-first avenue, between M and N streets, $286.

Block 896; Thirty-seventh avenue, between M and N streets, $273.

Block 902; Forty-third avenue, between M and N streets, $258.

Block 952; Ninth avenue, between O and P streets; irregular, 147½x182 feet, $656.

Block 957; Thirteenth avenue, between O and P streets, $250.

Block 963; Nineteenth avenue, between O and P streets, $700.

Block 969; Twenty-fifth avenue, between O and P streets, $300.

Block 975; Twenty-first avenue, between O and P streets, $286.

Block 981; Thirty-seventh avenue, between O and P streets, $272.

Block 987; Forty-third avenue, between O and P streets, $258.
Block 1,035; Thirteenth avenue, between Q and R streets, $250.
Block 1,044; Nineteenth avenue, between Q and R streets, $665.
Block 1,050; Twenty-fifth avenue, between Q and R streets, $300.
Block 1,056; Thirty-first avenue, between Q and R streets, $286.
Block 1,062; Thirty-seventh avenue, between Q and R streets, $273.
Block 1,068; Forty-third avenue, between Q and R streets, $258.
Block 1,114; Thirteenth avenue, between S and T streets, $500.
Block 1,120; Nineteenth avenue, between S and T streets, $685.
Block 1,126; Twenty-fifth avenue, between S and T streets, $300.
Block 1,132; Thirty-first avenue, between S and T streets, $286.
Block 1,138; Thirty-seventh avenue, between S and T streets, $273.
Block 1,144; Forty-third avenue, between S and T streets, $258.
Block 1,186; Fourteenth avenue, between U and V streets; irregular: 161x92½ feet, $310.
Block 1,191; Nineteenth avenue, between U and V streets, $606.
Block 1,197; Twenty-fifth avenue, between U and V streets, $606.
Block 1,203; Twenty-first avenue, between U and V streets, $606.
Block 1,209; Thirty-seventh avenue, between U and V streets, $605.
Block 1,215; Forty-third avenue, between U and V streets, $258.
Block 1,258; Nineteenth avenue, between W and X streets, $606.
Block 1,264; Twenty-fourth avenue, between W and X streets, $606.
Block 1,276; Thirty-seventh avenue, between W and X streets; irregular; 125 feet 10 inches by 240 feet, $221.
Block 1,282; Forty-third avenue, between W and X streets; irregular; 11 feet 2 inches by 240 feet, $31.

LOTS IN POTRERO.

Block 46; York street, between El Dorado and Alameda streets: 100x200. Rented at $2 per month.

Block 85; Utah street, between Yolo and Colusa streets; 100x200 feet.

Block 127; Vermont street, between Solano and Butte streets; 120x200 feet.

Block 149; Kansas street, between Yolo and Colusa streets; 150x200 feet, $1,663.

Block 163; Rhode Island street, between Mariposa and Solano streets; 100x200 feet. Rented $2 per month.

Block 226; Arkansas street, between Nevada and Yolo streets; 150x200 feet, $832.

Block 254; Connecticut street, between Yolo and Colusa streets; 150x200 feet.

Block 265; Missouri street, between Napa and Sierra streets; 150x200 feet.

Block 287; Texas street, between Nevada and Yolo streets; 150x200 feet.

Block 391; Southeast corner Kentucky and Napa streets; 150x200 feet.

Potrero block 254, O. L. R., also Potrero block 265, O. L. R., condemned and acquired by Western Pacific Railroad Company for $14,000.

Potrero Nuevo block 231, commencing on the west line of Connecticut street 125 feet north from 20th street, thence 150 feet by 200 feet from the Western Pacific Railroad Company, January 25, 1909, according to agreement in recondemnation suit, Potrero 254-265.

OTHER OUTSIDE LOTS.

Precita Valley lands; California avenue, from Eve to Adam streets; 150x32 feet.

Paul Tract Homestead; Berlin street, between Irving and Ward streets; 85 feet and 2 inches by 120 feet.

December 21, 1908, from Joseph B. and Carlotta L. Keenan, all of block No. 132 of University Extension Homestead, excepting one lot 25 feet by 100 feet on Pioche street, and one on Cambridge street, 25x120 feet, $8,250.

University Mound Survey, block 12. Commencing at the intersection of northwest line of Bacon street with southwest line Girard street; thence north along Girard street 200 feet; thence at a right angle 240 feet to the northeast line of Berlin street; thence southeast 200 feet to northwest line of Bacon street; thence at a right angle 240 feet to southwest line of Girard street and point of commencement, being south ½ of block No. 12, University Mound Survey, from P. J. and Jennie M. Kennedy, August 22, 1905; $5,000.

RENTS.

Cull, L. C.—Columbia school, lot, Florida and Twenty-fifth streets: $17.50.

Hornung, C. F.—Everett school, lot, Sixteenth and Dehon streets; $8.35.

Guinaw, E.—Everett school, one room, 375 Sanchez street; $25.

Truman, A.—Everett school, three rooms, Seventeenth and Sanchez streets; $60.

Thomas, H. J.—Marshall school, Fifteenth and Julian avenue; $41.75.

Meisel, H. A.—Garfield school, one room, northwest corner Union and Montgomery streets; $20.

O'Neill, A. C.—Garfield school, one room, 1315 Montgomery street; $20.

Hefferman, Mrs.—Garfield school, Montgomery and Filbert streets; $25.

Iberg, Mrs. William—Hearst school, four rooms, Steiner and Herman; $60.

Somers, W. J.—Jackson school, lot, Oak street; $100.

Bradrick, C.—James Lick school, lot, Twenty-sixth and Sanchez street; $8.35.

Fair, J. O.—Sunnyside school, house, 115 Flood avenue; $25.

Broderick, P.—Sheridan school, lot, Crafton and Plymouth; $5.

Giannini, E.—South End School, lot, corner Burrows and Somerset streets; $4.15.

O'Callaghan, D.—Fairmount school, lot, corner Day and Noe streets; $40.

O'Callaghan, D.—Lot, Moscow and Brazil streets; $20.

Odland, S. P.—Holly Park school, rooms, 416 Andover street; $25.

LIST OF SCHOOL BUILDINGS DESTROYED BY FIRE AND EARTHQUAKE, APRIL, 1906.

The contents of the offices of the Board of Education, their Secretary, and of the Superintendent of Schools and his deputies were destroyed by fire, involving the loss of all school records and of the elaborate Teachers' Library.

SCHOOL BUILDINGS DESTROYED BY FIRE.

Adams Cosmopolitan Grammar—Eddy, between Polk street and Van Ness avenue; three-story frame building, 18 rooms; constructed 1875; cost with improvements.............................$ 38,400.00

Chinese Primary School—916 Clay street; occupied a rented building.

Clement Grammar School—Geary, between Jones and Leavenworth streets; three-story frame building; 16 rooms; erected 1876 at a cost of $33,000. A two-story frame building was added in 1897 at an expense of $5,500. Total loss.......... 39,000.00

Cleveland Primary School—Harrison, between Tenth and Eleventh streets; a three-story frame building erected in 1875; cost $23,033.36 .... 23,033.36

Cooper Primary School—Greenwich, between Jones and Leavenworth; three-story frame building, 12 rooms; constructed in 1875 at a cost of $29,825.......... 29,825.00

Denman Grammar School—Northwest corner Bush and Taylor streets; three-story brick building with mansard roof and cupola, 16 rooms; constructed in 1864 at a cost of $53,800.... 53,800.00

Franklin Grammar School—Eighth, near Bryant street; a three-story frame building of 18 rooms; erected in 1871 at a cost of $25,860; and in the rear portion of the yard a two-story frame building of eight rooms erected in 1867 at a cost of $8,000. Total loss 33,860.00

Garfield Primary School—Union street, between Kearny and Montgomery streets; a two-story, twelve-room brick and frame building erected in 1854 at a cost of $33,321. Alterations and repairs in 1864 cost $1,734; in 1886, $1,900; in 1901, $4,200. Total loss 41,155.00

Hancock Grammar School—Filbert, between Taylor and Jones streets; three-story frame building erected in 1866; cost $16,500; building altered to twelve class rooms in 1895, cost $16,000. Total loss 32,500.00

Harrison Primary School—Grove, near Larkin street; erected in 1862 at a cost of $6,808; additions in 1865, $2,590; in 1872, $6,545; in 1896, $5,330. Total loss.......... 21,273.00

Humboldt Primary School—Golden Gate avenue, near Hyde street; three-story, twelve-room frame building erected in 1879 at a cost of $27,426. Alterations in 1898, $3,200. Total loss...... 30,626.00

Irving Primary School—Broadway, between Montgomery and Sansome streets; two-story, eight-room frame building; erected in 1871; cost $14,617; alterations and repairs, $3,000. Total loss 17,617.00

Jean Parker Grammar School—Broadway, between Powell and Mason streets; three-story brick building, 15 rooms, and 4 rooms in a cheap frame structure; altered originally from an old Jewish Synagogue at a cost of $12,910. Total loss........ 16,000.00

Jefferson Primary School—Tehama street, between First and Second streets; three-story, sixteen-room brick building; erected in 1866; cost, $27,910; repairs and alterations, $3,500. Total loss 31,410.00

John **Swett** Grammar School—McAllister, between Franklin and Gough streets; three-story frame building with wings, 18 rooms; erected in 1870 at a cost of $25,860. Total loss........ 25,860.00

Lafayette Primary School—Corner Filbert and Kearny streets; two-story, eight-room frame building; erected in 1867; cost $8,000; alterations, $5,000. Total loss.......... 13,000.00

Le Conte School—Powell, between Washington and Jackson streets; two-story frame building erected in 1851 at a cost of $4,000; additions in 1862, $1,700; additions in 1880, $1,970. Total loss	7,670.00
Lincoln Grammar School—Fifth street, near Market street; a three-story and basement brick building erected in 1865 at a cost of $93,940; partially destroyed by fire February 22, 1871, and rebuilt at a cost of $26,762.09. In the rear of the lot was the old Webster Primary Building, occupied by the Commercial High School, consisting of a one-story frame building of six rooms; cost $12,499. A one-story frame building of four rooms, erected in 1867, cost $2,700; building razed in 1873 and four rooms added at a cost of $2,690. Total loss	138,591.09
Marshall Primary School—Mission street, between Fifteenth and Sixteenth streets; two-story, ten-room frame building; erected in 1860; cost $11,383	11,383.00
Mission Grammar School—Mission street, between Fifteenth and Sixteenth streets; a three-story, twelve-room frame building; erected in 1875; cost $28,225; additions in 1884, $1,390. Total loss	29,615.00
Normal School Building—Powell street, between Clay and Sacramento; formerly the Boys' Latin High School; two-story brick and frame building with ells; erected in 1860; cost $17,962; alterations in 1887 cost $6,915; additional room in 1889, $598.15. Total loss	25,475.15
Peabody Primary School—West Mission, between Hermann and Ridley streets; three-story, fourteen-room frame building; erected in 1880; cost $18,305.75; additions in 1886 cost $694; building partially destroyed by fire in 1895 and repaired at a cost of $3,000. Total loss	21,999.75
Polytechnic High School—Corner Bush and Stockton streets; three-story frame building erected in 1867 at a cost of $26,390; a two-story brick building erected in 1854 at a cost of $11,300; this was razed and a new brick building erected in its place in 1894; cost $16,955.31. Total loss	43,345.31
Redding Primary School—Pine street, between Larkin and Polk streets. One-story frame building; erected in 1857, $3,700; two-story frame building erected in 1867, $8,000. Total loss	11,700.00
Rincon Grammar School—Silver street, between Second and Third streets; a two-story frame building with ells; erected in 1861; cost $10,566; alterations in 1875, cost $4,545. Total loss	15,111.00
Spring Valley Grammar School—Broadway, near Polk street; two-story frame building; erected in 1866; cost $13,423; enlarged to 12 rooms in 1875 at a cost of $7,650; alterations in 1888, $2,812.50. Total loss	22,885.50
Starr King Primary School—Bryant street, between Sixth and Seventh streets; three-story frame building of 12 rooms; erected in 1875 at a cost of $28,794	28,794.00
Whittier Primary School—A two-story frame building of 20 rooms erected in 1880 at a cost of $35,543.15; heating plant added in 1894 at a cost of $1,996. Total loss	37,539.15

SCHOOL BUILDINGS DAMAGED BY EARTHQUAKE.

Girls' High School—Scott street, near Geary street. This building is not on school property but on property belonging to the City and which originally formed a part of Hamilton Square. Permission was granted to the Board of Education, in 1870, to use a portion for a site for a school building. Three-story and basement brick building begun in 1890 and accepted in 1892, at a cost of $119,369.27. Experts differ in their opinion as to the amount of damage inflicted by the earthquake on this building, some declaring that the basement and first floor with their containing walls are in such a condition as to permit the reconstruction of the remainder of the building; others assert that it must be razed and a new building erected. This has been done	119,369.27
Mission High School—Eighteenth and Dolores streets. The tops of the two interior maintaining walls were shaken down, the bricks penetrating ceilings of the upper hall and laboratories. Damage inflicted estimated at about	2,500.00
Nearly all buildings were injured by having plastering loosened, chimneys broken and by being shifted more or less upon their foundations. Total damage wrought by earthquake, including Girls' High School, is estimated at $135,000	135,000.00
The aggregate loss by the destruction of school furniture, books and apparatus is estimated at $140,000	140,000.00
Total Loss	$1,227,154.58

In Memoriam

Miss Effie Douglas, Hamilton school; died April 23, 1906.

Miss Barbara Bannon, Emerson school; died June 5, 1906.

Mr. J. W. Gorman, Lincoln Evening school; died July 31, 1906.

Miss A. L. Hornsby, Laguna Honda school; died October 24, 1906.

Miss M. M. Murphy, principal Irving M. Scott school; died Dec. 24, 1906.

Mr. Madison Babcock, vice-principal Hancock school, ex-superintendent public schools, died December, 1906.

Miss Emma Stincen, principal Grattan school: died January 29, 1907.

Miss Leah C. Peckham, Laguna Honda school; died February 11, 1907.

Mr. J. B. Clarke, Polytechnic High school; died March, 1907.

Miss Helen Thompson, Girls' High school; died December 17, 1907.

Miss Josephine C. Evans, McKinley School; died February 5, 1908.

Mrs. M. E. Steele, Hearst school; died June, 1908.

Miss Margaret O'Brien, Sherman school; died August 13, 1908.

Miss L. R. Cullen, Burnett school; died September 3, 1908.

Miss Katherine Gaines, Winfield Scott school; died October 2, 1908.

Miss Adelaide C. Cherry, Redding school; died October 26, 1908.

Miss Rose Prince, Portola school; died October 31, 1908.

Mrs. Anne Armstrong, Noe Valley school; died November 20, 1908.

Miss S. M. Boniface, Hamilton school; died March 25, 1909.

Miss Mary Phillips, Agassiz school; died April 11, 1909.

Mrs. Georgia Washburn, principal Henry Durant school; died April 17, 1909.

Mrs. Anna M. Kortick, Burnett school; died May 3, 1909.

Miss Nell O'Hara, Marshall school; died May 27, 1909.

Mrs. M. B. Thompson, Starr King school; died June 25, 1909.

Mme. Ernestine Giffard, Bryant school; died July 24, 1909.

Mr. Leslie A. Jordan, ex-Deputy Superintendent of Schools, Lincoln Evening school; died July 30, 1909.

Mrs. Ellen R. Kenzla, Washington Evening school; died August 4, 1909.

REPORT OF THE PUBLIC SCHOOL TEACHERS' ANNUITY AND RETIREMENT FUND COMMISSIONERS FOR THE FISCAL YEAR ENDING JUNE 30, 1909.

San Francisco, July 20, 1909.

To the Honorable Board of Supervisors,
in and for the City and County of San Francisco.

Gentlemen:—I have the honor to submit herewith the report on the Public School Teachers' Annuity and Retirement fund for the fiscal year terminating June 30, 1909.

ALFRED RONCOVIERI,

Superintendent of Schools and Secretary Public School Teachers' Retirement Fund Commissioners.

RECEIPTS.

Balance in fund June 30, 1908, including $50,000 in permanent fund		$55,356.82
Contributions by teachers under provisions of Annuity law		11,243.18
Absence money granted by the Board of Education		3,000.00
Interest on permanent fund		2,122.74
Amounts received in accordance with Sections 8 (A) from teachers retired during fiscal year—		
1908—		
Aug. 21, Miss Laura T. Fowler	$219.00	
Sept. 1, Ruby A. Jewell	206.05	
Sept. 11, Margaret Gallagher	206.10	
Oct. 7, Regina Hertz	134.75	
1909—		
Jan. 5, Mrs. Mary Mayborn	199.40	
Jan. 30, Miss Lucy McNear	210.75	
Feb. 4, Miss Amy T. Campbell	197.00	
Feb. 17, Miss C. M. Johnston	191.00	
		1,564.05
Total receipts (including balance)		$73,286.79

DISBURSEMENTS.

Annuities to Retired Teachers—		
Oct. 1, 1908	$ 4,348.75	
Jan. 1, 1908	4,436.15	
April 1, 1909	4,561.80	
July 1, 1909	4,506.25	
	$17,852.95	
Clerical services	50.00	
Total disbursements		17,902.95
Balance		$55,383.84
In treasury	$ 4,033.42	
In banks	5,601.47	
	$9,634.89	
Subject to cheques outstanding and to be issued July 17, 1909	4,556.25	
Cash balance	$ 5,078.64	
In permanent fund, 44 S. F. Fire Protection System 5% bonds, (cost)	50,305.20	
		$55,383.84

LIST OF ANNUITIES.

Date of Retirement.		Name.	Maximum or Fraction Thereof.	Annuity Per Month.	Annuity Per Quarter.
1895.					
Nov.	27,	Mrs. L. T. Hopkins	Max.	$50.00	$150.00
1896.					
Jan.	22,	Miss L. F. Ryder	Max	50.00	150.00
Jan.	22,	Mrs. M. H. Currier	Max	50.00	150.00
April	24,	Miss V. M. Raclet	9/10	45.00	135.00
1897.					
Sept.	11,	Miss M. Solomon	Max.	50.00	150.00
Dec.	8,	Miss F. L. Soule	Max.	50.00	150.00
1898.					
Sept.	14,	Miss Kate Kollmyer	8/15	26.66⅔	80.00
1899.					
April	18,	Miss M. J. Bragg	Max.	50.00	150.00
1900.					
July	18,	Mrs. A. Griffith	Max.	50.00	150.00
July	25,	Miss K. F. McColgan	Max.	50.00	150.00
Aug.	1,	Miss L. M. Barrows	13/15	43.33⅓	130.00
Aug.	1,	Miss Annie A. Hill	Max.	50.00	150.00
Oct.	15,	Miss M. J. Canham	14/15	46.66⅔	140.00
1901.					
July	20,	Miss J. B. Gorman	Max.	50.00	150.00
Oct.	4,	Miss E. Murphy	9/10	45.00	135.00
1902.					
Jan.	2,	Miss R. B. Campbell	Max.	50.00	150.00
Jan.	2,	Miss L. S. Templeton	Max.	50.00	150.00
Jan.	2,	Mr. A. T. Winn	Max.	50.00	150.00
Sept.	28,	Miss Emma J. Miller	11/15	36.66⅔	110.00
1903.					
Feb.	17,	Mrs. B. A. Chinn	Max	50.00	150.00
Feb.	17,	Miss Lydia Hart	11/15	36.66⅔	110.00
Feb.	17,	Miss Christine Hart	Max.	50.00	150.00
Aug.	1,	Mrs. S. A. Miles	Max.	50.00	150.00
Aug.	1,	Mr. T. B. White	Max.	50.00	150.00
Sept.	1,	Miss A. E. Slaven	Max.	50.00	150.00
Oct.	15,	Miss L. Burnham	¾	37.50	112.50
1904.					
Aug.	1,	Mr. Elisha Brooks	Max.	50.00	150.00
Aug.	1,	Miss I. Patterson	Max.	50.00	150.00
Sept.	1,	Mrs. E. M. Whitcomb	Max.	50.00	150.00
1905.					
Jan.	16,	Miss E. G. Grant	Max.	50.00	150.00
March	1,	Miss M. A. Smith	⅔	33.33⅓	100.00
March	1,	Miss Jean Parker	Max.	50.00	150.00
March	1,	Mrs. T. C. Nicholl	Max.	50.00	150.00
March	1,	Mr. Charles Ham	Max.	50.00	150.00
March	1,	Miss R. Jacobs	Max.	50.00	150.00
March	1,	Mr. D. Lambert	Max. (Even)	25.00	75.00
1906.					
Feb.	1,	Miss M. E. Carson	Max.	50.00	150.00
Feb.	1,	Mrs. A. C. Taylor	Max.	50.00	150.00
Aug.	1,	Miss E. R. Elder	Max.	50.00	150.00
Aug.	1,	Mrs. C. Chalmers	Max.	50.00	150.00
Oct.	1,	Miss H. E. Whirlow	Max.	50.00	150.00
Dec.	1,	Mrs. V. Troyer	Max.	50.00	150.00
1907.					
April	1,	Miss Madge Sprott	½ (Even)	25.00	75.00
April	1,	Miss A. D. Miley	14/15	46.66⅔	140.00
April	1,	Miss Q. O. McConnell	Max.	50.00	150.00
April	1,	Prof. A. Herbst	Max.	50.00	150.00
July	1,	Mr. C. W. Moores	Max.	50.00	150.00
Sept.	1,	Miss V. E. Bradbury	Max.	50.00	150.00
Sept.	1,	Miss Martha Stone	Max.	50.00	150.00
Sept.	1,	Miss N. C. Stallman	Max.	50.00	150.00
Sept.	1,	Mr. W. H. Edwards	Max.	50.00	150.00

1908.				
Jan. 1,	Miss R. V. Claiborne	2/3	33.33 1/3	100.00
Feb. 1,	Mrs. M. E. Michener	Max.	50.00	150.00
Feb. 15,	Mrs. F. A. Banning	Max.	50.00	150.00
March 1,	Miss Rose Fat	11/15	36.66 2/3	110.00
March 1,	Mrs. Mary A. Hogan	14/15	46.66 2/3	140.00
May 1,	Miss Julia A. Danks	Max.	50.00	150.00
July 1,	Miss Laura T. Fowler	Max.	50.00	150.00
Aug. 1,	Miss M. J. Gallagher	Max.	50.00	150.00
Sept. 1,	Miss Ruby A. Jewell	Max.	50.00	150.00
Sept. 1,	Miss Regina Hertz	4/5	40.00	120.00
Jan. 1,	Miss A. T. Campbell	Max.	50.00	150.00
Jan. 1,	Mrs. Mary J. Mayborn	Max.	50.00	150.00
Jan. 1,	Miss C. M. Johnston	Max.	50.00	150.00
Jan. 1,	Miss L. C. McNear	Max.	50.00	150.00

RULES OF THE SAN FRANCISCO CITY AND COUNTY BOARD OF EXAMINATION, IN EFFECT JULY 1, 1909.

BOARD OF EXAMINATION.

JULY 1, 1909.

Superintendent, A. Roncovieri, Chairman.
Deputy Superintendent, T. L. Heaton.
Deputy Superintendent, James Ferguson.
Deputy Superintendent, R. H. Webster.
Deputy Superintendent, W. B. Howard, Secretary.

Office Hours of Secretary.

Thursdays and Fridays, 8:30 A. M. to 12 M., and 1 to 5 P. M.

Address all communications concerning examinations or certificates to the Secretary, southwest corner of Pine and Larkin streets, San Francisco, California.

RULES OF THE SAN FRANCISCO CITY AND COUNTY BOARD OF EXAMINATION: ALSO OF THE STATE BOARD OF EDUCATION; AND LAWS RELATING TO CERTIFICATION OF TEACHERS, IN EFFECT JULY 1, 1909.

RULES OF THE BOARD OF EXAMINATION OF THE CITY AND COUNTY OF SAN FRANCISCO.

Section 1. The City and County Board of Examination shall consist of the County Superintendent of Schools, ex-officio chairman, and his deputies.

Sec. 2. The Board, at its first regular meeting in January of each year, shall select one of its number as Secretary, who shall hold office for one year or until his successor is elected.

Sec. 3. The Secretary of this Board shall keep his office open on Thursdays and Fridays of each week from two to five o'clock p. m.

MEETINGS.

Sec. 4. (a) The regular semi-annual meetings shall be held in April and October.

(b) Regular monthly meetings shall be held on the first Monday of each calendar month at 1:30 p. m.

(c) Special meetings may be called at any time by the chairman, or upon the request of three members, the object of each special meeting to be stated in the call.

Sec. 5. (a) At the semi-annual meetings only, examinations for certificates shall be given, but special examinations for special certificates may be given at any time upon the order of this Board, when, in its judgment, the needs of the San Francisco School Department demand a specially certificated teacher and there be none available in the department.

(b) The following shall be the order of business at the regular monthly meetings of the Board:

I. Roll call.

II. Reading minutes of previous meeting.

III. Applications for granting and renewal of—
  (1) High School Certificates.
  (2) Grammar School Certificates.
  (3) Kindergarten-Primary Certificates.
  (4) Special Certificates.

IV. Applications for renewal of Primary Grade Certificates.

V. Applications for granting permanent Certificates on—
  (1) City and County Certificates and experience.
  (2) State Life or Educational Diplomas and experience.

VI. Applications for Recommendations for—
  (1) State Life Diplomas.
  (2) State University Documents.
  (3) State Normal Documents.

VII. Reports of Committees.

VIII. Unfinished business.

IX. New business.

X. Adjournment.

(c) Only such business shall come before special meetings as may be specified in the call therefor.

Sec. 6. Monthly and special meetings shall be held in the office of the Secretary, southwest corner of Pine and Larkin streets, San Francisco, California.

CERTIFICATES WITHOUT EXAMINATION.

Sec. 7. The following are the rules of the California State Board of Education relating to certificates granted on credentials; also a list of State Normal Schools and Universities accredited by the State Board of Education, etc. In effect July 1, 1909:

APPLICATION TO THE STATE BOARD OF EDUCATION FOR SPECIAL HIGH SCHOOL TEACHER'S CREDENTIAL, PROVIDED FOR IN (2) (b) SECTION 1521 OF THE POLITICAL CODE.

1. Name of Applicant: M..
(Give full name, avoiding initials and other abbreviations.)
2. Postoffice Address: ....
3. Birthplace: ....; Date of Birth:..

4. Academic Training:

(State in detail any courses you may have taken in institutions of secondary and higher education, giving dates, places, and names of institutions, and any degrees or diplomas you have received. Catalogues, carefully marked and annotated, and diplomas and certificates of record from the institutions concerned, should accompany this statement. Omit from this statement reference to courses in Normal Schools or other distinctively pedagogical institutions.)

....
....
....
....

5. Professional Training:

(State in detail any courses you may have taken in Normal Schools or other distinctively pedagogical institutions; and any distinctively pedagogical courses you may have taken in institutions of general education. In the latter case, show whether the courses referred to are included in those mentioned under heading number 4, above. If your professional training included practice-teaching, state amount, and grade of classes taught. Catalogues, carefully marked and annotated, and diplomas and certificates of record from the institutions concerned, should accompany this statement. Pedagogical courses taken in a college or university should be designated by subject, and by length of time pursued and hours per week for that time.)

....
....
....
....

6. Experience in Teaching:

State.	City, Town or District.	Name School.	Grade of School.	From (Date.)	To (Date.)	Months.
....	....	....	....	....	....	....
....	....	....	....	....	....	....
....	....	....	....	....	....	....
....	....	....	....	....	....	....
....	....	....	....	....	....	....
....	....	....	....	....	....	....
....	....	....	....	....	....	....
....	....	....	....	....	....	....

Total..............................

(Catalogues, printed announcements, and courses of study of schools in which teaching was done should, if possible, accompany this statement. Additional information concerning positions held, subjects taught, evidence of the grade of the schools referred to, etc., may be given below.)

7. Additional evidence of attainments:

(Statement of private studies, of special educational services, of publications; anything, in short, supported by adequate evidence of the excellence and worth of the performance which may help to a just estimate of your attainments.)

....

....

....

....

....

8. References:

(From two to five. Include the names of the persons best able, because of their personal knowledge of your work and their own educational competence, to give all needed information.)

....

....

....

....

....

9. List of documents submitted:

Health certificates from..................................., M. D.,.......................................

(The health certificate should accompany this application on a separate sheet.)

Other documents: ....

....

....

....

....

Signature of applicant:

....

(Applicants should forward 25c in stamps for return of documents.)

STATE OF..} ss.
County of..}

...., the applicant in the above and foregoing application, being duly sworn, says that the statements therein contained are true, and that the documents submitted with such application are in every case either the original or an exact copy of the original.

....

Applicant.

Subscribed and sworn to before me, this..............day

of................................., 190....

....

CIRCULAR 4—HYATT.

CONCERNING HIGH SCHOOL CERTIFICATION IN CALIFORNIA.

1. Regular certification by County Board of Education.

The law provides that the State Board of Education shall prescribe the general rules upon which County Boards and County and City Board of Education may grant regular high school certificates.

Those general rules have been thus formulated:

1. High School Certificates may be issued under the provisions of Section 1521, subdivision 2 (a), and Section 1775, subdivision 1 (a), of the Political Code of California, as follows:

(a) To candidates who have received the Bachelor's Degree from a college requiring not less than eight years of high school and college training, and who submit evidence that in addition to the course required for the Bachelor's Degree they have successfully completed at least one year of graduate study in a university belonging to the Association of American Universities; which year of graduate study shall include one half-year of advanced academic study (part of the time, at least, being devoted to one or more of the subjects taught in the high school), and such other time in a well-equipped training school of secondary grade directed by the Department of Education of any one of the universities of the association, as may be necessary to fulfill the pedagogical requirements prescribed by this Board.

(b) To candidates who have received the Bachelor's Degree from a college requiring not less than eight years of high school and college training, and who submit evidence that in addition to the courses required for the Bachelor's Degree they have successfully completed at least on half-year of graduate study in a university belonging to the Association of American Universities; which half-year of graduate study shall consist of advanced academic study (part of the time, at least, being devoted to one or more of the subjects taught in the high school); and six months as student teachers in a well-equipped school of secondary grade directed by a California State Normal, or its recognized equivalent, under conditions conforming to the requirements prescribed by this Board as the minimum amount of pedagogy.

(c) The minimum amount of pedagogy which Section 1521, subdivision 2 (a), of the Political Code, directs the State Board of Education to prescribe, is hereby declared to be as follows:

Satisfactory completion of courses, suitable and essential to acquiring efficient skill in teaching and an intelligent comprehension of the scope, and the attainable goals in high school instruction; said courses to be equivalent to not less than twelve hours per week for one half-year, provided, that at least one-third of this work shall consist of practical teaching under the direction of supervising instructors of academic competency and breadth of pedagogic comprehension who for a period of not less than two years have taught the subjects in which they supervise.

2. In lieu of the pedagogical training above prescribed, candidates may submit evidence showing that they are graduates of a California State Normal school, or other Normal school officially recognized by this Board as of equivalent rank, or have taught with decided success as regular teachers or as principals at least twenty months in any reputable school, elementary or secondary; and provided, that until further notice, the practical teaching prescribed may have been pursued in schools of grammar or secondary grade in connection with a California State Normal school, or under the direction of the Department of Education of the University of California or of Leland Stanford Junior University, as evidenced by a certificate of proficiency.

3. The institutions embraced in the Association of American Universities, mentioned in Rule 1 hereof, are the following:

University of California, Berkeley, Cal.
Catholic University of America, Washington, D. C.
University of Chicago, Chicago, Ill.
Clark University, Worcester, Mass.
Columbia University, New York City, N. Y.
Cornell University, Ithaca, N. Y.
Harvard University, Cambridge, Mass.
Johns Hopkins University, Baltimore, Md.
Leland Stanford Junior University, Palo Alto, Cal.
University of Michigan, Ann Arbor, Mich.
University of Pennsylvania, Philadelphia, Pa.
Princeton University, Princeton, N. J.
University of Wisconsin, Madison, Wis.
University of Virginia, Charlottesville, Va.
Yale University, New Haven, Conn.
University of Illinois, Champaign, Ill.
University of Missouri, Columbia, Mo.
University of Minnesota, Minneapolis, Minn.

For convenience, the above rules may be briefly summarized, as follows:

To apply to a County Board of Education for a High School Certificate you must present satisfactory evidence of three things, viz:

First, that you have had eight years of high school and college work, with Bachelor's Degree.

Second, that you have had a half-year of postgraduate work in one of the Association of American Universities.

Third, that you have had six months of practice-teaching in the training school of one of the above universities, or an accredited Normal school. [Twenty months of elementary or secondary teaching experience may be accepted in lieu of this six months' practice-teaching.]

Observe that if you can meet these conditions you have nothing to do with any State authorities, but that you go directly to the Board of Education of the county where you propose to teach. By "satisfactory evidence" is meant diplomas and recommendations of faculties certifying to the high character of the work performed and the personal fitness of the candidate.

2. The Special High School Credential.

The law provides that the State Board of Education may also consider the cases of individual candidates who have twenty months of successful elementary or secondary experience as teachers and who have not the exact credentials required above for regular certification. The State Board of Education in considering such cases will have in mind as the standard the same REQUIREMENTS AS FOR REGULAR CERTIFICATION ABOVE—that is, four years of high school work, four years of college work, and a half-year of postgraduate university work. As equivalent the Board may consider any evidences of scholarship, education, experience, training, travel, or culture, that may be offered. To candidates who in the judgment of the Board fully meet the ACADEMIC AND PROFESSIONAL STANDARDS OF REGULAR CERTIFICATION will be granted the Special High School Credential, upon which County and City Boards of Education may grant regular High School Certificates.

Candidates for the Special High School Credential will be guided by the following instructions in getting their cases before the State Board of Education:

A. Get a blank application for Special High School Credential from the office of the Superintendent of Public Instruction at Sacramento. Fill it out with a complete history of your case, and swear to it before some officer competent to administer an oath. Get together the diploma, recommendations, documents and catalogues that officially demonstrate your case. Get a certificate of sound bodily health from a reputable physician. Get a money order for two dollars, payable to the State Board of Education. Send all of these to the Superintendent of Public Instruction at Sacramento, California.

B. Do not expect early action upon your application, to meet some sudden emergency. The correspondence, investigation and consideration relating to it may be the work of months. The State Board of Education is an ex-officio body, meets at irregular intervals, and only three or four times per year.

C. Before a Special High School Credential can be issued, you must have a personal interview with some member of the State Board of Education. The credentials can not be issued to non-residents of California; but the Board will examine and report upon the application of non-residents when such applications are made as above described.

D. If you have had twenty months' elementary or secondary teaching experience and can not meet the standards described above, you may yet show your fitness for the Special High School Credential by taking an examination. Examinations will be given twice per year at Chico, Berkeley, and Los Angeles, simultaneously, under direction of the president of the Chico Normal school, the professor of pedagogy of the State University at Berkeley, and the president of the Los Angeles Normal school, respectively. Application blanks and further particulars may be obtained at the office of the Superintendent of Public Instruction at Sacramento.

EDWARD HYATT, Superintendent of Public Instruction.

CIRCULAR 3—HYATT.

EXAMINATION FOR SPECIAL HIGH SCHOOL CREDENTIALS.

The law for the granting of the Special High School Credential is found in Section 1521, Sub. 2, of the Political Code. It authorizes the State Board of Education to consider the cases of individual applicants who have taught successfully for a period of not less than twenty school months and who are not possessed of the credentials prescribed for regular certification by a County Board of Education. The State Board of Education may, in its discretion, grant to such persons the Special High School Credential, upon which County Boards of Education may grant regular High School Certificates. In granting these Special Credentials the State Board expects the equivalent of the following standard of qualification: First, four years of high school education; second, four years of college training; and, third, a half-year of postgraduate work in an accredited university. Usually these credentials are issued upon credentials, affidavits and recommendations; but, when necessary, the State Board will also examine applicants who wish to show their fitness in that way; and the examinations will be conducted by a standing committee of the State Board of Education, and according to the rules given below. The exact letter of the law upon which all this is based, is as follows:

> 2. (a) To prescribe by general rule the credentials upon which persons may be granted certificates to teach in the high schools of this State. No credentials shall be prescribed or allowed, unless the same, in the judgment of said Board, are the equivalent of a diploma of

graduation from the University of California, and are satisfactory evidence that the holder thereof has taken an amount of pedagogy equivalent to the minimum amount of pedagogy prescribed by the State Board of Education of this State, and include a recommendation for a high school certificate from the faculty of the institution in which the pedagogical work shall have been taken.

(b) The said board shall also consider the cases of individual applicants who have taught successfully for a period of not less than twenty school months, and who are not possessed of the credentials prescribed by the board under the provisions of this section. The said board, in its discretion, may issue to such applicants special credentials upon which they may be granted certificates to teach in the high schools of the State. In such special cases, the board may take cognizance of any adequate evidence of preparation which the applicants may present. The standard of qualification in such special cases shall not be lower than that represented by the other credentials named by the board under the provisions of this section.

RULES.

Observe that no one can be granted this credential unless he has had at least twenty months' successful experience in teaching.

The date of examination for 1908 has been fixed for May 13, 14, 15. Examinations will be conducted simultaneously, if there be candidates, at Chico, Berkeley, and Los Angeles, under the direct supervision of the following committee of the State Board of Education: C. C. Van Liew, State Normal School, Chico; A. F. Lange, University of California, Berkeley; J. F. Millspaugh, State Normal School, Los Angeles. For more detailed information as to the hour at which and the building wherein the examination will be held, the applicant should communicate with the committeeman at whose place he expects to take the examination.

All applicants for examination must register with the Superintendent of Public Instruction, Sacramento, California, not later than 5 days previous to the examination (May 8, 1909), stating at which of the three places they propose to take the examination. With such notice, each applicant should send a fee of five dollars, which will be used to defray the expenses of the examination. Upon request to the office of the Superintendent of Public Instruction, a blank will be sent prospective applicants, which they should fill out and return with the fee required.

The plan of examination, given herewith, is complete, and should be self-explanatory. If further information is desired concerning the examination of 1908, or those of subsequent years, address inquiries to any of the above-named committeemen.

PLAN OF EXAMINATION.

Candidates for the special credential for the High School certificate under Rule 3a will be required to pass an examination in Group I and one other of the following eight groups of subjects, as majors, and in any other two of the eight groups as minors:

I. Education: History of Education and particularly the values. aims, and methods of instruction of the several subjects of the High School curriculum.

II. Mathematics: Plain, Solid, and Spherical Geometry, Algebra, Plane Trigonometry.

III. History: Ancient, Mediaeval, and Modern European History, and English History.

IV. Literature: An intelligent familiarity with English literature and its masterpieces.

V. Language: First, a thorough acquaintance with the grammatical construction of the English language; and second, a reading ability in any two of the following languages: Latin, French, Greek, German.

VI. Physical Sciences: Physics, Chemistry, Physical Geography, and Geology.

VII. Biological Science: Physiology, Zoology and Botany.

VIII. First, American History; and, second, Economics and Civics, to include an intelligent comprehension of existing problems of general public interest and discussion.

THE EXAMINING COMMITTEE AND EXAMINERS.

The State Board shall annually appoint three members of its number as an Examining Committee, one of whom shall be designated as chairman.

At least one month previous to the examinations the State Board shall select expert examiners, at least two for each of the several groups of subjects above named, not necessarily members of the State Board.

PREPARATION OF QUESTIONS.

The work of preparing questions for the examination shall be distributed among the expert examiners so that one of each pair of examiners shall prepare the major questions and the other the minor. Not more than three days before the time appointed for the opening of an examination, these examiners shall have delivered to each member of the Examining Committee of the State Board of Education, a copy of the questions, assigned to him to prepare, in sealed envelopes; a separate envelope for each subdivision of the above eight groups. Questions for major examinations including group one should represent the average grade of college graduation, and require from five to six hours' work of the applicant. Questions for minor examination should represent average college entrance requirements and require from two and a half to three hours' work of applicant. All questions should be quite clear and definite.

HOLDING EXAMINATIONS.

Examinations shall be given simultaneously, under the personal supervision of a member of the Examining Committee, in the following places: Chico, Berkeley, and Los Angeles. The seal of the envelope containing the questions of a given subject shall be broken at the time designated by the member of the Examining Committee, and in the presence of the applicants.

Each applicant shall write his name and address upon a card and shall seal the same in a blank envelope. Upon completing the examination in each subject, the applicant shall fasten his papers and the envelope securely together. He shall not write his name nor any distinguishing mark upon his papers nor upon the outside of the envelope which contains his name and address. Each question, and only one question, shall be answered completely upon one sheet or half-sheet of paper.

When all the applicants shall have completed the examination in a given subject, the supervising member of the board shall seal the papers in double envelopes, writing upon the inner envelope the subject and place of examination. This package shall be immediately sent to the chairman of the Examining Committee.

NUMBERING PAPERS.

As soon as possible after the completion of the examination, a majority of the Examining Committee shall meet and open the sealed envelopes. Upon the back of each separate paper and upon the attached envelope (containing the name and address of the applicant) shall be stamped a number. When each paper shall have been thus carefully numbered, the envelope containing the names shall be detached, and these being collected shall be sealed in an envelope. This envelope shall not again be opened until all the papers have been duly examined, and under conditions hereinafter stated.

The Examining Committee shall arrange in separate packages the papers according to the groups of examiners and shall deliver or send the same to one of the two examiners with the instruction to forward, when markings are complete, to the other examiner, who shall be instructed to return the papers, when his markings are complete, to the Chairman of the Examining Committee.

EXAMINERS' MARKINGS.

The examiners shall mark the papers, upon the basis of 100 credits, and shall make a record of the papers, distinguishing them by number. This record for each of the numbers signed by the examiner shall be sealed in an envelope and sent to the Chairman of the Examining Committee. No examiner shall affix any mark upon the papers which might in any manner prejudice the mind of other examiners, nor shall there be any communication between them until after the board announces the results.

The Chairman of the Examining Committee shall retain the reports of the examiners, sealed, until all examiners have made their reports.

The sealed reports of the examiners shall be opened by the committee and the result of the examination for each subject by the duplicate examiners averaged In case of discrepancies indicating a misapprehension or inadvertency on the part of the examiners the committee may ask for a re-examination of the papers in question.

IDENTIFYING APPLICANTS.

The numbered envelopes containing the names of the applicants shall not be opened except in meeting of the Examining Committee, and not until the markings, according to the distinguishing numbers, are finally completed by the Examining Committee, and no markings shall be changed after the envelopes containing the names have been opened. The names shall then be substituted for the numbers.

THE STANDARD OF SUCCESS.

Applicants who fail to receive an average of 70 per cent upon all groups, or less than 50 per cent in any two groups, shall be marked as failed.

ORAL EXAMINATIONS.

The Chairman of the Examining Committee shall send the list of applicants who have passed the written test satisfactorily to the State Superintendent, who in turn shall notify such applicants to meet the Examining Committee of the board at a stated place and date for an oral examination as to experience, means of acquiring scholarship, health, age, general culture, habits, and such other matters affecting their qualification as teachers. At least two members of the committee must attest the result.

STATE BOARD ACTION.

At the following meeting of the State Board applicants who have passed the written examination satisfactorily and who are reported upon favorably by the Examining Committee conducting the oral examinations may be granted special high school credentials.

FEES AND EXPENSES.

All applicants before beginning the examination must pay a fee of five dollars. All successful applicants must pay an additional fee of ten dollars for credentials. The fund thus collected may be used by the board in payment of the services of the appointed examiners and for such incidental expenses as may be necessary. No member of the State Board shall receive any recompense for services.

Any candidate for the Special High School Credential whose application is pending or has been denied may be admitted to the annual examination conducted by the State Board of Education; and the State Board of Education may require any candidate concerning whose qualifications they are in doubt to take the whole or any part of such examination. The examination is regarded as a means of gaining information relative to the candidate's qualifications additional to the information regarding training and experience which may be presented in his formal application and accompanying documents.

All applicants must, before receiving credentials, submit a physician's certificate showing sound health.

By order of the State Board of Education

EDWARD HYATT, Secretary.

CIRCULAR 1—HYATT.

CALIFORNIA ACCREDITED LISTS OF NORMAL SCHOOLS, STATE LIFE DIPLOMAS AND KINDERGARTEN TRAINING SCHOOLS, UPON WHICH COUNTY BOARDS OF EDUCATION MAY GRANT CERTIFICATES WITHOUT EXAMINATION.

1. ACCREDITED LIST OF NORMAL SCHOOLS.

As authorized by law (Sec. 1775, Political Code) the State Board of Education has recommended the following list of Normal Schools as being of equal rank with the State Normal Schools of California. County Boards of Education may grant the Elementary (Grammar) School Certificate without examination to the holder of the highest grade diploma issued by any one of these Normal schools. In case the school issues more than one kind or grade of diploma the applicant must present evidence that his diploma is the highest issued, provided, that diplomas based on a two-year Normal school course, in addition to graduation from a four-year high school course, may be recognized. Duly certified statements from the faculty of any such school may be presented as evidence of any of the above facts:

Arizona Normal Schools—Flagstaff, Tempe.

Canadian Normal Schools—London, McGill Normal School, Quebec; New Brunswick, Ottawa, Ontario Normal College, Hamilton; Toronto, Truro, Nova Scotia.

Colorado State Normal School, Greeley.

Connecticut State Normal Schools—New Britain, New Haven, Willimantic.

Edge Hill Training College, Normal Department, Liverpool, England.

Hawaiian Territorial Normal School, Honolulu.

Illinois State Normal Schools—Chicago Normal School, Chicago; Eastern Illinois State Normal School, Charleston; Illinois State Normal University, Normal; Northern Illinois State Normal School, De Kalb; Southern Illinois State Normal School, Carbondale; Western Illinois State Normal School, Macomb.

Indiana State Normal School, Terre Haute.

Iowa State Teachers' College, formerly Iowa State Normal School, Cedar Falls.

Kansas State Normal School, Emporia.

Maine State Normal Schools—Castine, Farmington, Gorham.

Baltimore Training School for Teachers, Baltimore, Maryland.

Massachusetts State Normal Schools—Boston, Bridgewater, Farmingham, Fitchburg, Hyannis, Lowell, North Adams, Salem, Westfield, Worcester.

Michigan State Normal Schools—Marquette, Mt. Pleasant, Ypsilanti, Kalamazoo.

Minnesota State Normal Schools—Duluth, Mankato, Moorhead, St. Cloud, Winona.

Missouri State Normal Schools—Cape Girardeau, Kirkville, Warrensburg, Springfield.

Teachers' College, University of Missouri.

Montana State Normal School, Dillon, Montana.

Nebraska State Normal Schools—Peru, Kearney.

New Hampshire State Normal School, Plymouth.

Nevada State University, Normal Department, Reno.

New Jersey State Normal School, Trenton.

New Mexico Normal University, Las Vegas.

New Mexico Normal School, Silver City.

Normal Department, University of New Mexico, Albuquerque.

Provincial Normal School, Winnipeg, Manitoba.

St. Paul Teachers' Training School, St. Paul, Minnesota.

Normal Department, Baldwin University, Berea, Ohio.

New York State Normal Schools—Albany, Brockport, Buffalo, Cortland, Fredonia, Geneseo, Jamaica, Newpaltz, New York City Normal, Oneonta, Oswego, Plattsburgh, Potsdam.

North Carolina State Normal and Industrial College, Greensboro.

Oklahoma—Central Normal School, Edmond; Northwestern State Normal School, Alva.

Pennsylvania State Normal Schools—Bloomsburg, California, Clarion, East Stroudsburg, Edinboro, Indiana, Kutztown, Lock Haven, Mansfield, Millersville, Shippensburg, Slippery Rock, West Chester.

Philadelphia Normal School for Girls.

Rhode Island State Normal School, Providence.

South Carolina Winthrop Normal and Industrial College, Rock Hill.

South Dakota State Normal School, Spearfish.

Tennessee Peabody College for Teachers, Nashville.

Utah State Normal School (Normal Department, Utah University), Salt Lake City.

Washington City Normal School No. 1, Washington, D. C.

Washington State Normal Schools—Bellingham (Whatcom), Cheney, from and after 1904; Ellensburg.

Wisconsin State Normal Schools—Milwaukee, Oshkosh, Platteville, River Falls, Stevens Point, West Superior, Whitewater.

2. ACCREDITED LIST OF STATE LIFE DIPLOMAS.

The State Board of Education has decided that the State Life Diplomas and Certificates named below represent experience and scholarship equivalent to the Elementary (Grammar) School Life Diploma in California. County Boards of Education may grant an Elementary (Grammar) School Certificate without examination to the holder of one of these:

Arizona—Life Diploma.

Colorado—Complimentary Life Diploma only.

Idaho—Life Diploma.

Indiana—Life and Professional Certificates.

Iowa—Life Diploma.

Minnesota—Life Certificate.

Montana—Life Diploma.

Nevada—Life Diploma.

Ohio—Life Certificate, when obtained on forty-eight months' experience.

Oregon—Life Diploma, when obtained on sixty months' experience.

Rhode Island—Life Diploma, highest grade.

South Dakota—Life Diploma.

Washington—Life Diploma.

3. ACCREDITED LIST OF KINDERGARTEN TRAINING SCHOOLS.

The State Board of Education has approved the following institutions for professional kindergarten training. County Boards of Education may grant the Kindergarten-Primary Certificate without examination to the holders of diplomas of graduation from these institutions, who present recommendations for fitness and skill from the principals thereof dated within six months of the application:

Blackheath Kindergarten Froebelian School and Training College for Teachers, London, England.

Chicago Froebel Association, Chicago, Illinois.

Chicago Kindergarten College, Chicago, Illinois.

Chicago Kindergarten Institute, Chicago, Illinois.

Chicago Free Kindergarten Association, Chicago, Illinois.

Cincinnati Kindergarten Association, Cincinnati, Ohio.

Drake University Kindergarten Training School, Des Moines, Iowa.

Froebelian School, Longwood, Chicago, Illinois.

Golden Gate Kindergarten Association, San Francisco, California.

The Teachers' College of Indianapolis for the Training of Kindergarteners and Primary Teachers, formerly the Indiana Kindergarten and Primary Normal Training School, Indianapolis, Indiana.

Kindergarten College, Pittsburg, Pennsylvania.

Kindergarten Department, Boston Normal School, Boston, Massachusetts.

Kindergarten Department, Edge Hill Training College, Liverpool, England.

Kindergarten Department of Teachers' College, Columbia University, New York, N. Y.

Kindergarten Department, State Normal School Greeley, Colorado.

Kindergarten Department, State Normal School, Mankato, Minnesota.

Kindergarten Department, State Normal School, Oswego, N. Y.

Kindergarten Department, Teachers' Training School, St. Paul, Minnesota.

Kindergarten Department, Wisconsin State Normal School, Milwaukee, Wisconsin.

Kindergarten Normal Department of the Ethical Culture School, New York, N. Y.

Kindergarten Training Department of Nebraska State Normal School, Peru, Nebraska.

Kindergarten Training Department, Omaha Public Schools, Omaha, Nebraska.

Kindergarten Training Department, Pratt Institute, Brooklyn, N. Y.

Kindergarten Training Department, State Normal School, Fredonia, N. Y.

Kindergarten Training School, Columbus, Ohio.

Kindergarten Training School of the Grand Rapids Kindergarten Association, Grand Rapids, Michigan.

Louisville Free Kindergarten Association's Training School, Louisville, Kentucky.

The Law-Froebel Kindergarten Training School, Toledo, Ohio.

Kindergarten Department of the State Normal School, Westfield, Mass.

Kindergarten Training School, 82 St. Stephen Street, Boston, Mass.

Kindergarten Department State Normal School, New Britain, Conn.

Minneapolis Kindergarten Training School, Minneapolis, Minnesota.

Miss Wheelock's Kindergarten Training School, Boston, Massachusetts.

Oakland Kindergarten Training School, Oakland, California.

Oberlin Kindergarten Training Association, Oberlin, Ohio.

Philadelphia Training School for Kindergarteners, Senior Course, Philadelphia, Pennsylvania.

The Froebel School, Providence, Rhode Island.

The Stout Training School for Kindergarten Teachers, Menomonie, Wis.

Toronto Normal Kindergarten Training School, Toronto, Canada.

Utica Kindergarten Training School, Utica, N. Y.

Kindergarten Department of Normal School, Dayton, Ohio.

Pestalozzi-Froebel Kindergarten Training School, Chicago, Illinois.

Garland Kindergarten Training School, Boston, Massachusetts.

Perry Kindergarten Normal School, Boston, Massachusetts.

Miss Page's Normal Kindergarten School, Danvers, Massachusetts.

Kindergarten Training School of State Normal, Winona, Minnesota.

4. OBSERVATIONS.

These lists as printed above in 1909 supersede all previous ones. They are amended, brought up to date and printed only once per year. Institutions desiring place on the list may make formal application at any time, giving full information as to course of study, requirements for admission, conditions of graduation, faculty and equipment, accompanied by catalogue and other available printed matter. A blank for Kindergarten Training School application is furnished on request:

By order of the State Board of Education,

EDWARD HYATT, Secretary.

CIRCULAR 5—HYATT.

INFORMATION ABOUT CALIFORNIA SCHOOL SYSTEM.

SCHOOL OFFICERS.

For the State there is a Superintendent of Public Instruction and a State Board of Education composed of nine members. For each county there is a County Superintendent of Schools and a Board of Education composed of five members. For each school district there is a Board of Trustees composed of three members. In cities having charters there is a City Board of Education of five or more members.

FUNCTIONS OF OFFICERS.

The Superintendent of Public Instruction superintends the schools of the State, sells the State text-books, acts as the secretary of the State Board of Education, and prepares and distributes blanks, laws and registers for the use of school officers.

The State Board of Education issues Life Diplomas, adopts and publishes State text-books, prescribes the conditions of high school certification, and makes accredited lists of normal schools, kindergarten training schools, and universities.

The County Superintendent of Schools superintends the schools of the county, issues temporary certificates, conducts county institutes, and acts as the secretary of the County Board of Education.

The County Board of Education grants and revokes teachers' certificates, makes the course of study, conducts teachers' examinations, and graduates pupils from the grammar schools.

The Board of Trustees employs teachers and janitors, builds school houses, and manages the schools. One of their number is elected as clerk, and acts as an executive officer. In cities, the City Board of Education performs the same duties as the Board of Trustees does in the district.

PUBLIC SCHOOLS.

The public schools consist of primary schools, giving the first five or six years of instruction; grammar schools, giving the next three or four years of work, and high schools, usually giving four years of work additional to the grammar schools. There are also evening schools, kindergartens, manual training schools, and schools for the deaf in some of the cities.

OTHER STATE SCHOOLS.

There is a State university, located at Berkeley; five State Normal schools, at San Jose, Los Angeles, Chico, San Diego, and San Francisco respectively; a Polytechnic school at San Luis Obispo, and schools of a reformatory nature at Whittier and Ione. The presidents of any of these institutions will furnish information at request.

NUMBER OF TEACHERS.

There are about 8,000 primary and grammar school teachers, about 1,100 high school teachers, and about 300 kindergarten and night school teachers. Of these, about one-eighth are men.

PUPILS ENROLLED.

There are about 300,000 primary and grammar school pupils enrolled, and about 30,000 high school pupils. Their schooling costs about ten million dollars per year, for all purposes. Six millions of this is for teachers' salaries.

TEACHERS' SALARIES.

The lowest salaries are about $400 per year, for the teachers of small rural schools. Salaries for primary and grammar schools range from $400 to $800 per year, with an average of about $600. Principals get an average of about $800. High school teachers receive from $700 to $1,500 per year, with an average of about $1,000. High school principals average about $1,350. The cost of board ranges from $16 to $30 per month, averaging about $24.

TERMS AND TIMES.

The term of school varies from 8 to 10 months per year, averaging 9 in primary and grammar schools, 9½ in high schools. No school can fall below six months. The terms usually begin in September and close in May or June, although there are many exceptions in the high mountains and along the coast.

TEACHERS' CERTIFICATES.

There are four kinds of certificates issued by County Boards of Education: High school, Grammar school, Special and Kindergarten-Primary. All certificates require a fee of $2 before being issued.

HIGH SCHOOL CERTIFICATES.

High school certificates are issued only upon credentials, not upon examination. A circular (No. 4) giving the details of high school certificates will be furnished upon request, by the Superintendent of Public Instruction at Sacramento; or a copy may be seen at the office of the nearest County Superintendent of Schools. A high school certificate entitles the holder to teach in any high school, grammar school or primary school in the county.

GRAMMAR SCHOOL CERTIFICATES OR CREDENTIALS.

Grammar school certificates may be issued by the County Board of Education upon credentials, such as other California certificates, diplomas from California State normal schools, State diplomas and normal diplomas found on the accredited list prepared by the State Board of Education. A circular (No. 1) giving this accredited list and other details of grammar school and kindergarten certification upon credentials may be obtained upon request of the Superintendent of Public Instruction at Sacramento, or a copy may be seen at the office of the nearest County Superintendent of Schools.

GRAMMAR SCHOOL CERTIFICATES ON EXAMINATION.

Grammar school certificates may also be issued by the County Board of Education upon examination. Examinations are held twice a year and upon the following subjects: Reading, English grammar and advanced composition, English and American literature, orthography and defining, penmanship, drawing, vocal music, bookkeeping, arithmetic, algebra to quadratics, plane geometry, geography (physical, political and industrial), elementary physics, physiology and hygiene, history of the United States and Civil Government, history (ancient, mediaeval and modern), school law, methods of teaching. These examinations vary somewhat in the different counties, as each county is a law unto itself in details. Usually the examinations occur in December and June and occupy from three to five days of time; but there are many exceptions. All applicants pay a fee of $2. Detailed information of time, place, rules, and samples of questions may usually be obtained upon request of the County Superintendent of Schools. Any Grammar school certificate entitles the holder to teach in any grammar or primary school in the county.

SPECIAL CERTIFICATES.

The County Board of Education may issue Special certificates to those who, by examination or any credentials, or by both, shall satisfy the board of their special fitness to teach one or more of the particular studies for which special certificates may be granted, and who shall satisfy the board of their proficiency in English grammar, orthography, defining, and methods of teaching. No special certificate shall be granted to teach, in any school, studies other than drawing, music, physical culture, and commercial, technical, or industrial work. These special certificates do not entitle the holder to take charge of regular schools or to teach other branches than the technical ones specifically named in the certificate.

KINDERGARTEN PRIMARY CERTIFICATES.

The County Board of Education may grant kindergarten-primary certificates upon credentials only, not examination. Such certificates do not entitle the holder to teach primary or grammar school classes, but only kindergartens. Credentials that may be recognized are other California kindergarten-primary certificates, diplomas from the kindergarten department of a California State Normal school, and diplomas from kindergarten training schools on the accredited list. See remark concerning Circular No. 1 under Grammar School certificates, above.

TEMPORARY CERTIFICATES.

The County Superintendent has power to isuue, if he deem it proper to do so, temporary certificates, valid for six months, to persons holding certificates which in his judgment correspond in grade to certificates which may be issued under the provision of law, or to graduates of those schools of the State of California which in his judgment are the equivalent in scholarship required for graduation from the normal schools of California; provided, that no person shall be entitled to receive such temporary certificate more than once in the same county. The temporary certificate requires no fee.

TEACHERS' INSTITUTES.

Each County Superintendent of Schools conducts a County Teachers' Institute each year, at such time, in such manner, and with such instructors as he chooses. All teachers employed in the county are required to be present and take part in the proceedings. Teachers' salaries are not reduced by such attendance.

STATE TEXT-BOOKS.

California is the only State making its own text-books for the public schools. It has done so for about twenty-five years. Copyrights and plates of text-books adopted by the State Board of Education are leased of the publishers at royalties ranging from 15 to 25% of the price. The books are manufactured at the State printing office and furnished at cost to the children. The value of the books sold is more than $200,000 per year.

WHAT TO SEND FOR.

Address the Superintendent of Public Instruction, at Sacramento, for the following publications:

Superintendent's Biennial Report. (Postage, 9 cents.)

Circular 1—California Accredited Lists, concerning Grammar school and kindergarten certification on credentials.

Circular 3—On Examination for Special High School Credential.

Circular 4—On High School certification. (Also covers Special High School credential.)

Circular 5—Information on California school system.

Application for Special High School credential.

DO NOT APPLY FOR THESE.

Do not apply to the Superintendent of Public Instruction for a list of the teachers of the State; or for a State course of study; or for sample examination questions; or for lists of vacancies, chances for employment, or anything whatever that relates to applying for positions or securing places for teachers; or for the issue of teachers' certificates. These are things pertaining to the county, not to the State; wherefore, address the County Superintendent of Schools of the county where you are most interested. See accompanying list of superintendents for names and addresses.

EDWARD HYATT,
Superintendent of Public Instruction.

STATE, COUNTY, AND CITY SCHOOL OFFICERS.

STATE BOARD OF EDUCATION.

James N. Gillett, Governor, president of the board, Sacramento.

Edward Hyatt, Superintendent of Public Instruction, secretary of the board, Sacramento.

Morris E. Dailey, president of State Normal school, San Jose.

J. F. Millspaugh, president of State Normal school, Los Angeles.

C. C. Van Liew, president of State Normal school, Chico.

Samuel T. Black, president of State Normal school, San Diego.

Frederick L. Burk, president of State Normal school, San Francisco.

Benjamin Ide Wheeler, president of State University, Berkeley.

A. F. Lange, Professor of Pedagogy at State University, Berkeley.

COUNTY SUPERINTENDENTS OF SCHOOLS.

County.	Name.	Address.
Alameda	Geo. W. Frick	Oakland
Alpine	Mrs. E. A. Grover	Markleeville
Amador	W. H. Greenhalgh	Jackson
Butte	Mrs. Minnie Abrams	Oroville
Calaveras	Frank Wells	San Andreas
Colusa	Lillie L. Laugenour	Colusa
Contra Costa	W. H. Hanlon	Martinez
Del Norte	Mrs. A. M. Laduron	Crescent City
El Dorado	S. B. Wilson	Placerville
Fresno	E. W. Lindsay	Fresno
Glenn	S. M. Chaney	Willows
Humboldt	George Underwood	Eureka
Imperial	J. E. Carr	El Centro
Inyo	Mrs. M. A. Clarke	Bishop
Kern	Robert L. Stockton	Bakersfield
Kings	Mrs. N. E. Davidson	Hanford
Lake	Hettie Irwin	Lakeport
Lassen	W. B. Philliber	Susanville
Los Angeles	Mark Keppel	Los Angeles
Madera	Estelle Bagnelle	Madera
Marin	James Davidson	San Rafael
Mariposa	Julia L. Jones	Mariposa
Mendocino	L. W. Babcock	Ukiah
Merced	Mrs. Belle S. Gribi	Merced
Modoc	Eva W. Spargur	Alturas
Mono	Cordelia E. Hays	Bridgeport
Monterey	Duncan Stirling	Salinas
Napa	Lena K. Jackson	Napa
Nevada	J. G. O'Neill	Nevada City
Orange	R. P. Mitchell	Santa Ana
Placer	C. N. Shane	Auburn
Plumas	Miranda Ray Arms	Quincy
Riverside	Raymond Cree	Riverside
Sacramento	Mrs. Minnie O'Neill	Sacramento
San Benito	John H. Garner	Hollister
San Bernardino	A. S. McPherron	San Bernardino
San Diego	Hugh J. Baldwin	San Diego
San Francisco	Alfred Roncovieri	San Francisco
San Joaquin	E. B. Wright	Stockton
San Luis Obispo	F. E. Darke	San Luis Obispo
San Mateo	Roy W. Cloud	Redwood City
Santa Barbara	Mamie V. Lehner	Santa Barbara
Santa Clara	D. T. Bateman	San Jose
Santa Cruz	Champ S. Price	Santa Cruz
Shasta	Lulu E. White	Redding
Sierra	Belle Alexander	Downieville
Siskiyou	Mrs. E. Persons Wood	Yreka
Solano	D. H. White	Fairfield
Sonoma	DeWitt Montgomery	Santa Rosa
Stanislaus	Florence Boggs	Modesto
Sutter	L. L. Freeman	Yuba City
Tehama	Delia D. Fish	Red Bluff
Trinity	Nellie M. Jordan	Weaverville

Tulare	C. J. Walker	Visalia
Tuolumne	G. P. Morgan	Columbia
Ventura	James E. Reynolds	Ventura
Yolo	May E. Dexter	Woodland
Yuba	E. T. Manwell	Marysville

County Superintendents are Secretaries of their respective County Boards of Education.

CITY SUPERINTENDENTS OF SCHOOLS.

City.	County.	Name of Superintendent.
Alameda	Alameda	Fred T. Moore
Berkeley	Alameda	S. D. Waterman
Bakersfield	Kern	D. W. Nelson
Chico	Butte	Chas. H. Camper
Eureka	Humboldt	D. L. Thornbury
Fresno	Fresno	C. L. McLane
Long Beach	Los Angeles	J. D. Graham
Los Angeles	Los Angeles	E. C. Moore
Marysville	Yuba	E. T. Manwell
Oakland	Alameda	J. W. McClymonds
Pasadena	Los Angeles	A. L. Hamilton
Pomona	Los Angeles	P. W. Kauffman
Riverside	Riverside	A. N. Wheelock
Santa Ana	Orange	J. A. Cranston
Sacramento	Sacramento	O. W. Erlewine
Salinas	Monterey	L. F. Kilkenny
San Bernardino	San Bernardino	F. W. Conrad
San Buenaventura	Ventura	R. B. Haydock
San Diego	San Diego	Duncan MacKinnon
San Jose	Santa Clara	Alex. Sherriffs
San Pedro	Los Angeles	H. F. Pinnell
Santa Barbara	Santa Barbara	H. A. Adrian
Santa Cruz	Santa Cruz	J. W. Linscott
Santa Monica	Los Angeles	Horace M. Rebok
Santa Rosa	Sonoma	E. M. Cox
Stockton	San Joaquin	James A. Barr

CERTIFICATES ON EXAMINATION.

Sec. 9. Recommendations for Certificates on examination may be made as follows:

(a) Grammar School Certificates—to those who obtain on examination an average of 85 per cent in the following subjects:

Algebra	50
Arithmetic, written	100
Arithmetic, oral	50
Bookkeeping	50
Composition	50
English Grammar, written	100
English Grammar, oral	25
Elementary Physics	50
English and American Literature	50
Drawing	25

Geography—	
Industrial	25
Physical	25
Political	25
History of the United States and Civil Government	100
History—	
Ancient	25
Medieval	25
Modern	25
Methods of Teaching	50
Orthography and Defining	100
Penmanship	25
Physiology and Hygiene	50
Plane Geometry	50
Reading	50
School Law of California	50
Vocal Music	25
Totals	1,200

(Required to pass—1,020 credits.)

(2) To holders of San Francisco City and County Primary Grade Certificates, who obtain on examination an average of 85 per cent in the following subjects:

English and American Literature	50
Scope—English, one of requirements for entrance to University of California.	
Algebra (to Quadratics)	50
Plane Geometry	50
Elementary Physics	50
History (Ancient, Medieval and Modern)	75
Total	275

(Required to pass—233¾ credits.)

(b) Special Certificates—(1) To those who obtain 85 per cent on examination in the subject for which a special certificate is desired and shall satisfy the Board of Examination of their proficiency in English Grammar, Orthography and Defining, and Methods of Teaching; provided, that the test of proficiency in the subjects of English Grammar, Orthography and Defining and Methods of Teaching shall be one in which the applicant will be required to write as he would present the matter to a class the directions which he believes should be followed by pupils in accomplishing tasks pertaining to the subject in which he desires to be certificated; and provided further, that all tests of proficiency as herein referred to be heard or read and voted upon by the full Board of Examination; and that the sufficiency of the results secured by the applicant be satisfactory to the majority of the Board of Examination in order to pass such applicant; (2) to those who are holders of regular city and county certificates and who obtain 85 per cent on examination in the subject for which a special certificate is desired.

(b) 2. "The speed test in stenography for a special teachers' certificate in stenography and typewriting shall consist of the writing of new matter dictated by the examiner at the rate of 110 words per minute for five consecutive minutes, and of the transcription of the same accurately upon the typewriter."

For passing, there shall be required a rating of 85% in the correctness of the transcripts under the following rules of marking:

STENOGRAPHY.

	From 100 Deduct
For each word omitted, added, substituted, or misspelled, or for the use of the singular instead of the plural, or of the plural instead of the singular when the grammatical correctness is affected	3
For each transposition	2
For each gross error in capitalization or punctuation; for each error in division of words; for each word repeated; for each failure to use the hyphen when required; for each abbreviation; or for the use of the plural for the singular, or of the singular for the plural, when the grammatical correctness is not affected	1
For interlineations, erasures and lack of neatness	1-5

TYPEWRITING.

The speed test in typewriting shall consist of the copying of 400 to 500 words from plain copy at an average speed of not less than 40 words per minute. The transcript shall be corrected in accordance with the following rules, and 85% shall be required for passing in this test:

	From 100 Deduct
For writing one line over another	10
For each error in orthography; for each word or figure omitted, provided, that a deduction of 10 shall be made for the omission of two or more consecutive words if the words omitted do not constitute more than one printed line of the copy, and that a deduction of 20 shall be made for the omission of two printed lines, or more than one line, etc.; for each word added, substituted, or repeated; for each transposition; for each abbreviation not in copy; for each failure to capitalize or to punctuate as in copy; for each deviation from copy in paragraphing (maximum for the exercise 10); for failure to indent as in copy (only one charge to be made in the exercise); for each error in compounding words, or vice versa	5
For each case of inconsistent spacing between lines	3
For each space between the letters of a word; for crowding letters in a word; for lack of space between words; for striking a letter instead of space bar; for unfinished word due to coming to end of line when word is rewritten on next line; for striking letters in a line over band holding paper, thus making no impression on sheet, or for piling letters on sheet, or for piling letters over each other at the end of a line when all the letters are decipherable, or for running off paper on right or left margin (maximum for the exercise 10)	2
For each case of irregulariay in left-hand margin, or of gross irregularity in right-hand margin (maximum for the exercise in each case, 5); for each strike-over; for the misdivision of a word at end of line; for each omission of a hyphen, when needed, at end of line; for extra space between words (maximum for exercise, 5); for each case of inconsistent spacing after punctuation marks; for each word interlined (maximum for a single interlineation of five or more words, 5); for each erasure (maximum for the exercise, 5)	1
For lack of neatness	1-5
For each error not specified above	1-5

(c) Special certificates may be issued in the following subjects:

1. Bookkeeping.*
2. Cookery.
3. Domestic Science (Cookery and Sewing combined).
4. Mechanical Drawing.
5. Architectural Drawing.
6. Naval Architectural Drawing.
7. Free-hand Drawing.
8. Free-hand Drawing and Clay Modeling (correlative and combined).
9. Free-hand Drawing and Wood Carving (correlative and combined).
10. Sloyd.
11. Iron Work.
12. Wood Work.
13. Physical Culture.
14. Penmanship.
15. Stenography and Typewriting (combined).
16. Music.
17. Manual Training—including as many of subjects 4 to 12 (both inclusive) as may be indorsed on the certificate of the applicant upon legal proof of competency to teach the same.
18. Navigation.
19. Such other subjects as may be authorized by the City and County Board of Education.

*An applicant for a special certificate in bookkeeping shall, in addition to the other conditions imposed, also pass an examination in Commercial Arithmetic and Commercial Law. (Scope—Bookkeeping, Williams & Rogers complete course; Elements of Business Law, Huffcut; Practical Business Arithmetic, Moore & Miner.

Sec. 10. An applicant for a grammar school certificate who fails to obtain at least 60 per cent in Arithmetic (if required), or in Grammar, or in Orthography and Defining, will be barred from further examination.

Sec. 11. The texts to be used as standard in the examinations shall be as follows:

Composition—Brooks & Hubbard.
Methods of Teaching—Sweet or White, McMurry.
Algebra—Wells Secondary.
Physics—Coleman, Millikan & Gale.
Geometry—Beman & Smith; New, Plane, and Solid.
History and Civics—Meyers—Medieval and Modern.
West—Ancient World.
Ashley—American Government.
Literature—English, one of entrance requirements to University of California.
Other Subjects—California State Series (if issued).

Sec. 12. The papers containing the written answers of candidates must be preserved by the Secretary of the City and County Board of Examination, or his successors, for at least one year after the close of the examination.

Sec. 13. Papers of candidates for certificates shall be examined by no person or persons other than the members of the City and County Board of Examination; provided, that in special subjects a member of the Board of Examination shall have authority to procure the assistance of competent persons, whose work shall be subject to the supervision of a member or members of the Board of Examination.

RENEWAL OF CERTIFICATES.

Sec. 14. (a) Evidence of good moral character shall be required from applicants for renewal of certificates, unless such applicants are teaching in the public schools of San Francisco, or are personally known to members of this board.

(b) Members of the San Francisco School Department must present, upon application for renewal of certificates, a recommendation from their principals or from the Superintendent or one of his deputies.

PERMANENT CERTIFICATES.

Sec. 15. Applicants for permanent certificates of any kind or grade must make affidavit before the Secretary of this board setting forth in detail (1) the amount and grade of their experience in the public schools of the City and County of San Francisco, and (2) the kind and grade of the certificate or State diploma held by the applicant.

Sec. 16. In computing the five years' experience required for a permanent certificate, evidence of the receipt of sixty full months of compensation for services as teacher in the school department of this city and county shall be sufficient.

REVOCATION OF CERTIFICATES.

Sec. 17. No recommendation to the City and County Board of Education for the revocation of any certificate shall be made except on the following conditions:

(a) Complaints under subdivision four of section seventeen hundred and ninety-one of the Political Code of California must be in writing, signed by the complainant, and filed with the Secretary of this board.

(b) Such complaints shall specifically state, in detail, the facts upon which the certificate should be revoked.

(c) Such complaints must be accompanied by a list of the witnesses personally cognizant of the separate facts stated in the complaint, together with their addresses and also by a reference to all such documentary evidence pertinent to said charges as may be within the knowledge of the complainant.

LIFE DIPLOMAS AND STATE EDUCATIONAL DOCUMENTS.

Sec. 18. Applicants for State Life Diplomas or Educational Documents must make affidavit before the Secretary of this board setting forth such facts as may be required by the State Board of Education.

FEES.

Sec. 19. (a) Applicants for certificates (except temporary or permanent certificates to be granted on State Life or Educational Diplomas) or for State Diplomas must deposit with the Secretary, at the time of application, a fee of two dollars.

(b) Applicants for State University or State Normal Documents must deposit with the Secretary, at the time of application, a fee of one dollar and twenty-five cents.

Sec. 20. These rules may be amended upon one week's written notice, given to each member of the board, by a four-fifths' vote in favor thereof at any regular or called meeting.

EXTRACT FROM STATE CONSTITUTION, ARTICLE IX, SECTION SEVEN.

* * * The county superintendents and the county Boards of Education shall have control of the examination of teachers and the granting of teachers' certificates within their respective jurisdiction. (The exercise of this power has been defined by legislative enactment as found in the Political Code of the State of California.)

EXTRACTS FROM THE POLITICAL CODE OF THE STATE OF CALIFORNIA.

Sec. 1503. (1) The Board of Trustees of each State Normal school, upon the recommendation of the faculty, may issue to those pupils who worthily complete the full course of study and training prescribed, diplomas of graduation, either from the normal department or the kindergarten department, or both.

(2) Such diploma from the Normal department shall entitle the holder thereof to a certificate (corresponding in grade to the grade of the diploma) from any county, or city and county, Board of Education in the State. One from the kindergarten department shall entitle the holder to a certificate to teach in any kindergarten class of any primary school in the State.

(3) Whenever any county, or city and county, Board of Education shall present to the State Board of Education a recommendation showing that the holder of a Normal school diploma from the Normal department of any State Normal school of the State of California, or of a diploma from any other Normal school, that the State Board of Education shall declare to be equivalent to a diploma from the Normal department of a State Normal school of this State, has had a successful experience of two years in the public schools of this State, subsequent to the granting of such diploma, the State Board of Education shall grant to the holder thereof a document signed by the president and secretary of the State Board, showing such fact. The said diploma, accompanied by said document of the State Board attached thereto, shall become a permanent certificate of qualification to teach in any primary or grammar school in the State, valid until such time as the said diploma may be revoked, as provided in section fourteen hundred and eighty-nine of this code, or until such time as the document issued by the State Board, as aforesaid, may be revoked or suspended as provided in subdivision five of section fifteen hundred and twenty-one of this code.

(4) Upon presentation of the diploma and document referred to in subdivision three of this section to any county, or city and county, Superintendent of Schools, said Superintendent shall record the name of the holder thereof in a book provided for that purpose in his office, and the holder thereof shall henceforth be absolved from the requirement of subdivision one of section sixteen hundred and ninety-six of this code.

(5) Said diploma of graduation from any State Normal school in this State, when accompanied by a document granted by the faculty of the State University on or before the thirtieth day of June, nineteen hundred and three, showing that the holder of such diploma has successfully completed the course of instruction in said university prescribed for students who are graduates of a Normal school of this State, shall entitle such holder to a high school certificate authorizing the holder to teach in any grammar and primary school and in any high school in this State.

1521. The powers and duties of the State Board of Education are as follows:

1. To adopt rules and regulations not inconsistent with the laws of this State for its own government, and for the government of the public schools and district school libraries.

2. (a) To prescribe by general rule the credentials upon which persons may be granted certificates to teach in the high schools of this State. No credentials shall be prescribed or allowed, unless the same, in the judgment of said board, are the equivalent of a diploma of graduation from the University of California, and are satisfactory evidence that the holder thereof has taken an amount of pedagogy equivalent to the minimum amount of pedagogy prescribed by the State Board of Education of this State, and include a recommendation for a high school certificate from the faculty of the institution in which the pedagogical work shall have been taken.

(b) The said board shall also consider the cases of individual applicants who have taught successfully for a period of not less than twenty school months, and who are not possessed of the credentials prescribed by the board under the provisions of this section. The said board, in its discretion, may issue to such applicants special credentials upon which they may be granted certificates to teach in the high schools of the State. In such special cases the board may take cognizance of any adequate evidence of preparation which the applicants may present. The standard of qualification in such special cases shall not be lower than that represented by the other credentials named by the board under the provisions of this section.

3. To grant life diplomas for four grades, valid throughout the State, as follows:

(a) High School—Authorizing the holder to teach in any primary and grammar or high school.

(b) Grammar School—Authorizing the holder to teach in any primary or grammar school.

(c) Kindergarten-Primary—Authorizing the holder to teach in the kindergarten class of any primary school.

(d) Special—Authorizing the holder to teach in any school such special branches and in such grades as are named in such diploma.

4. Except as provided in sections fifteen hundred and three and seventeen hundred and seventy-five of this code, life diplomas may be issued only to such persons as have held for one year, and still hold a valid county, or city and county, certificate, corresponding in grade to the grade of diploma applied for, and who shall furnish satisfactory evidence of having had a successful experience in teaching of at least forty-eight months. Not less than twenty-one months of said experience shall have been in the public schools of California. Every application must be accompanied to the State Board of Education by a certified copy of a resolution adopted by at least a three-fourths vote of all the members composing a county, or city and county, Board of Education, recommending that the diploma be granted, and also by an affidavit of the applicant, specifically setting forth the places in which and the dates between which said applicant has taught. The application for any credential or diploma or document mentioned in this chapter must also be accompanied by a fee of two dollars, for the purpose of defraying the expense of issuing the credential, document or diploma.

5. To revoke or suspend for immoral or unprofessional conduct, or for evident unfitness for teaching, life diplomas, educational diplomas, documents issued under the provisions of sections fifteen hundred and three and seventeen hundred and seventy-five of this code, or credentials issued in accordance with subdivision two of this section; and to adopt such rules for said revocation as they may deem expedient or necessary.

6. To have done by the State printer, or other officer having the management of the State printing, any printing required by it; provided, that all orders for printing shall first be approved by the State Board of Examiners.

7. To adopt and use, in authentication of its acts, an official seal.

8. To keep a record of its proceedings.

9. To designate some educational monthly journal as the official organ of the department of public instruction. The publishers of such journal shall before the tenth day of each month, mail one copy of such journal to the clerk of every school district in the State and to the secretary of every Board of Education, and shall, on or before the tenth day of each month, file an affidavit with the superintendent of public instruction, showing that such copies have been so mailed for that month. Each clerk of a school district and each clerk of a board of education, receiving a copy of such journal so mailed to him, shall place such copy in the school library of his district, before the end of the month in which such copy shall be so received. The county superintendent of schools of each county, or city and county, shall draw warrant semi-annually in favor of the publishers of such school journal for an amount equal to one-half of the regular subscription price of such journal, not exceeding one dollar and fifty cents in any school year for each and every school district in his county, or city and county, and charge the same to the library fund of the district; provided, that such warrant shall not be drawn until such county superintendent of schools shall have received from the superintendent of public instruction a certificate to the effect that the affidavits aforesaid have been duly filed in his office, showing the mailing of copies of such journal as above required, for the half-year to be covered by such warrant.

Section 1543, subdivision Seventh—Power of Superintendent of Schools.—He shall have power to issue temporary certificates of equivalent grades to persons holding valid secondary or high school, elementary or grammar school, kindergarten-primary and special certificates granted by county boards of education of California; or to persons who are graduates of colleges, Normal schools, or universities and who hold valid certificates issued outside of California when, in the judgment of the superintendent, such certificates correspond in grade to any certificate which may be issued under the provisions of section 1775 of the Political Code of California; which temporary certificate when issued between July 1st and December 30th shall expire on January 1st following; and when issued between January 1st and June 29th shall expire on July 1st following; provided further, that he shall have power to issue temporary elementary certificates valid for two years to graduates of the University of California and to graduates of the Leland Stanford Junior University; and, provided further, that no person shall be entitled to receive a temporary certificate more than once in the same county.

1663. 1. The public schools of California, other than those supported exclusively by the State, shall be classed as day and evening elementary, and day and evening secondary schools.

The day and evening elementary schools of California shall be designated as primary and grammar schools.

The day and evening secondary schools of California shall be designated as high schools and technical schools, and either class may include a portion of the other class.

No teacher shall be employed to teach in any way, in any school, if the certificate held by the teacher is of a grade below that of the school or class to be taught; provided, that the holders of existing primary certificates or of the same when hereafter renewed or made permanent shall be eligible to teach in any of the grades of a day or evening elementary school below the sixth year and not including the kindergarten grades; and in any day or evening elementary school of the county, or city and county, which the county, or city and county, superintendent shall designate as a primary day or evening elementary school; and provided further, that the holder of any valid special certificate for work, or of any kindergarten -primary certificate, shall be eligible to teach in the kindergarten grades of day elementary schools.

2. The county, or city and county, Board of Education must, except in incorporated cities having Boards of Education, on or before the first day of July of each year, prescribe the course of study in and for each grade of the day and evening elementary schools for the ensuing school year

3. Except in city school districts having Boards of Education the county, or city and county, Board of Education shall provide for the conferring of diplomas of graduation by examination or otherwise upon those pupils who have satisfactorily completed the course of study provided for the day or evening elementary schools of the county, or city and county.

4. Whenever necessary the county, or city and county, Board of Education may amend and change, subject to section 1665 of this code, the course of study prescribed by them for the day and evening elementary schools.

1565. Except for a temporary certificate, every applicant for a teachers' certificate, or for the renewal of a certificate, upon presenting his application, shall pay to the county superintendent a fee of two dollars. All money so received by the county superintendent shall immediately be deposited by him in the county treasury. The county treasurer shall credit one-half of all moneys so received to a separate fund to be known as the Teachers' Institute fund, and the other half to a fund to be known as the Teachers' Library fund. The Teachers' Institute fund may be expended in payment of the services of such instructors in the County Teachers' Institute as are not teachers in the public schools of the county in which such institute is held. For this purpose warrants may be drawn by the auditor upon the request of the county superintendent. The Teachers' Library fund may be expended in a similar manner for the establishment of a teachers' library and for the transportation of library books, and other reading matter of the teachers' library, to and from the various schools of the county. The county superintendent may act as librarian thereof, but whenever in any county there is a county library, the county superintendent may require the county treasurer to credit all moneys payable to the Teachers' Library fund to the County Library fund, and may transfer to the county library all books and other property belonging to the teachers' library, and thereupon the county library shall administer the teachers' library as part of itself; but all funds received from the county superintendent in accordance with this section shall be expended exclusively for the purchase and maintenance of books of professional interest to teachers.

Sec. 1696. Every teacher in the public schools must—

(1) Before assuming charge of a school, file his or her certificate with the superintendent of schools; provided, that when any teacher so employed is the holder of a California State Normal school diploma, accompanied by the certificate of the State Board of Education, as provided in subdivision third of section one thousand five hundred and three of the Political Code, an educational or a life diploma of California, upon presentation thereof to the superintendent he shall record the name of said holder in a book provided for that purpose in his office, and the holder of said diploma shall thereupon be absolved from the provisions of this subdivision.

1696a. Whenever the school register or registers of any teacher or teachers, or other records of any public school district in any school year, may have been or shall hereafter be destroyed by conflagration or other public calamity, thereby preventing the teacher or teachers and said school officers from making their monthly or annual reports in the usual manner and with accuracy the affidavits of the teacher or teachers, the school principals or other school officers of such school district certifying as to the contents of such destroyed registers or other records shall be accepted by all authorities for all school matters appertaining to such school district except that of average daily attendance. The average daily school attendance of any public school district or high school whereof the register or registers of the teacher or teachers, or any number of them or other records may have been or shall hereafter be destroyed by conflagration or other public calamity, or whereof, by reason of such conflagration or calamity the regular session or attendance of such district or high school has been interrupted and its average attendance materially affected thereby, shall be its average daily attendance of the next preceding school year increased or diminished by the average yearly percentage of increase or decrease calculated for the next preceding ten years; provided, that the average daily attendance of such school district or high school for the school year ending June 30, 1906, shall be its average daily attendance for the school year ending June 30, 1905, with five per cent (5%) thereof as increase added thereto.

* * * * * *

Sec. 1772. County Boards of Education may, on examination, grant certificates as follows:

(1) Grammar School Certificates—To those who have passed a satisfactory examination in the following studies: Reading, English Grammar and Advanced Composition, English and American Literature, Orthography and Defining, Penmanship, Drawing, Vocal Music, Bookkeeping, Arithmetic, Algebra to Quadratics, Plane Geometry, Geography (physical, political and industrial), Elementary Physics, Physiology and Hygiéne, History of the United States and Civil Government, History (ancient, medevial and modern), School Law, Methods of Teaching.

1775. (1) County Boards of Education may, without examination, grant certificates as follows:

(a) High School Certificates—(1) To the holders of credentials approved by the State Board of Education in accordance with subdivision two of section fifteen hundred and twenty-one of this code; (2) to the holders of special credentials issued by said State board in accordance with said subdivision; (3) to holders of high school certificates issued by any county, or city and county, Board of Education in this State; (4) to holders of Normal school diplomas accompanied by documents from the faculty of the State University, provided for in subdivision five of section fifteen hundred and three of this code.

(b) Grammar School Certificates—To the holders of the following credentials: (1) Life diplomas or certificates of any State; provided, the State Board of Education in this State shall have decided that said diplomas or certificates represent experience and scholarship equivalent to the requirements for the elementary life diploma in California; (2) California State Normal school diplomas, San Francisco City Normal school diplomas heretofore granted, and other Normal school diplomas; provided, that the State Board of Education of this State shall have recommended the Normal school issuing said diploma as being of equal rank with the State Normal school of California; (3) to holders of diplomas of graduation of the four-year course of the University of California or Leland Stanford Junior University when said holder of such diploma shall have had six months' training in one of the State Normal schools of this State or has had eight months' successful experience in teaching in the public schools of California after graduation; (4) grammar school or grammar grade certificates of any county, or city and county, of California.

(c) Kindergarten-Primary Certificates—(1) To the holders of kindergarten-primary certificates of any county, or city and county, of California: (2) to the holders of diplomas of graduation from the kindergarten department of any State Normal school of this State; (3) to the holders of credentials, showing that the applicant has had professional kindergarten training in an institution approved by the State Board of Education, and also general education equivalent to the requirements for graduation from the kindergarten department of a California State Normal school; (4) to the holders of special kindergarten certificates of any county, or city and county, of California granted prior to July 1, 1901; provided, that the holders of such special kindergarten certificates have had at least two years' training in a kindergarten training school and have taught for a period of at least two years in a public kindergarten school in the county, or city and county, wherein such special kindergarten certificates were granted.

(2) Grammar school certificates may be granted to the holders of primary grade certificates who shall pass satisfactory examinations in such branches as do not appear on their certificates, or in the record of the examination upon which the original certificate was granted.

(3) All certificates and diplomas now valid in California shall continue in force and effect for the full term for which they were granted. County Boards of Education may renew any certificate issued by them prior to the adoption of this law, and now in force, and may renew certificates granted by authority of this law. Renewed certificates shall be valid for a period equal to that for which they were originally granted.

(4) When the holder of any certificate or State diploma shall have taught successfully in the same county, or city and county, for five years, the Board of Education of such county, or city and county, may grant a permanent certificate of the kind and grade of the class in which said applicant has been teaching, valid in the county, or city and county, in which issued, during the life of the holder, or until revoked for any of the causes designated in subdivision four of section seventeen hundred and ninety-one of this code; provided, that such permanent certificate shall in no case be of a higher grade than the grade of the certificate or State diploma on which the teaching has been done; and for a permanent high school certificate twenty months of said teaching shall have consisted of regular high school work; and provided further, that a certificate when renewed the second time, or any time thereafter, shall become, by such renewal, a permanent certificate, if the holder of said certificate shall have complied with all of the conditions of this subdivision.

Sec. 1776. Any member of a county Board of Education or of a city Board of examination who shall, except in the regular course of study in the public schools, teach any classes where pupils are given special instruction to prepare them for passing examination to obtain teachers' certificates, or who shall give special instruction to any person preparing for examination to obtain a teacher's certificate, shall be deemed guilty of a misdemeanor, and, upon conviction thereof, his office shall be declared vacant. No certificates shall be issued to any applicant who has received special instructions, when preparing for examination, from any member of a county Board of Education, or of a city Board of Examination.

Sec. 1778. County, or city and county, Boards of Education shall have the power to issue permanent certificates valid, within the county or city and county in which issued, during the life of the holder, or until revoked for any of the causes shown in subdivision four of section seventeen hundred and ninety-one of this code. Said permanent certificates shall be issued on the following credentials and conditions:

Whenever the holder of any certificate shall have taught successfully in the same county or city and county for five years the Board of Education of said county or city and county may, in addition to or in place of the renewal of such certificate, grant a permanent certificate of the kind and grade of the class in which said applicant has been teaching; provided, that in the issuance of a permanent high school certificate at least twenty months' successful high school experience, taught upon a high school certificate, shall be included in the six years' experience required.

2. Whenever the holder of any certificate shall have successfully completed five years of successful experience in any county, or city and county, the Board of Education of said county, or city and county, may, upon application and under the other conditions named in this section, grant to said applicant a permanent certificate.

3. Whenever the holder of any life or educational diploma shall have complied with the conditions as enumerated in subdivision one of this section, the said Board of Education shall, without fee, issue upon application a permanent certificate of the grade of said life or educational diploma.

4. No permanent certificate shall be of a higher grade, or, if special, of a different kind from the certificate upon which granted.

5. (a) Upon the presentation of any certificate except the primary grade for renewal for the second time, or for any time thereafter, the Board of Education, in renewing said certificate shall, by such renewal, cause such certificate to become permanent; provided, the applicant for said renewal shall have complied with the other conditions of this section.

(b) And it shall be the duty of the county superintendent to attach to said certificate a document giving it the full force and effect of a permanent certificate within said county, or city and county.

6. Each applicant for a permanent certificate must present to the county, or city and county, Board of Education satisfactory evidence of the experience upon which said permanent certificate may be issued.

7. All permanent certificates shall be upon blank forms prepared by the State Superintendent of Public Instruction.

Sec. 1790. The city, or city and county, Board of Examination must meet and hold examinations for the granting of teachers' certificates semi-annually, at such times as they may determine. They may also hold monthly meetings for the transaction of such other business as may come before them. Special meetings may be called by the city, or city and county, superintendent, when in his judgment the same are necessary; and on the recommendation, in writing, of any three members of the board, the city, or city and county, superintendent shall call a special meeting. No business shall be transacted at any special meeting except such as is indicated in the call therefor; and of all such meetings, due notice shall be given to each member of the board. The place of meeting shall be designated by the chairman. The meetings of the city, or city and county, Board of Examiners shall be public and a record of their proceedings shall be kept in the office of the city, or city and county, superintendent of schools.

Sec. 1791. Each city, or city and county, Board of Examination has power:

First—To adopt rules and regulations, not inconsistent with the laws of this State, for its own government and for the examination of teachers.

Second—To examine applicants, and to prescribe a standard of proficiency which may entitle the person examined to receive: (a) A city, or city and county, grammar school certificate, valid for six years, authorizing the holder to teach any primary or grammar school or class in such city, or city and county; (b) A city, or city and county, special certificate, valid for six years, authorizing the holder to teach such special subjects in any school of the city, or city and county, and in such grades as are designated in such certificates. Applicants for special certificates by examination or any credentials, or by both, shall satisfy the board of their special fitness to teach one or more of the particular studies for which special certificates may be granted, and shall satisfy the board of their proficiency in English grammar, Orthography, Defining and Methods of Teaching. No special certificate shall be granted to teach, in any school, studies other than drawing, music, physical culture, and commercial, technical or industrial work.

The Board of Examination shall report the result of the examination of the city, or city and county, Board of Education; and said Board of Education shall thereupon issue to the successful applicants the certificates to which they shall be entitled.

Third—For immoral or unprofessional conduct, profanity, intemperance, or evident unfitness for teaching, to recommend to the city, or city and county, Board of Education, the revocation of any certificates previously granted by said Board of Education in said city, or city and county.

Sec. 1792. The city, or city and county, Boards of Examination may also recommend the granting of city, or city and county, certificates and the renewal thereof, in the manner provided for the granting and renewal of county certificates by County Boards of Education in section seventeen hundred and seventy-five of this code.

Sec. 1793. (1) The holders of city, or city and county, certificates are eligible to teach in the cities, or cities and counties, in which such certificates were granted, in schools or classes of grades corresponding to the grades of such certificates, and when elected shall be dismissed only for insubordination or other causes as mentioned in section seventeen hundred and ninety-one of this code, duly ascertained and approved by the Boards of Education of such cities, or cities and counties.

(3) The holders of special, city, or city and county, certificates are eligible to teach the special branches mentioned in their certificates, in the grades of all the schools in the city, or city and county, in which such certificates were granted corresponding to the grade of said special certificates.

CHAPTER 186—STATUTES, PAGE 290.

An Act to amend an Act entitled, "An Act to continue in force school teachers' certificates, State educational diplomas, and life diplomas," approved February 5, 1880.

(Approved March 11, 1909.)

The people of the State of California, represented in Senate and Assembly, do enact as follows:

Section 1. All teachers' life diplomas, university documents, normal documents, city, city and county, and county certificates of all grades granted previons to the first day of February, A. D. 1909, shall be continued in full force and effect for the full time for which they were granted, and shall be deemed valid for all purposes and to the full extent of time that the same were and were intended respectively to be, under the laws in force at the time they were issued.

Sec. 2. This Act shall take effect and be in force on and after the date of its approval.

REPORT OF SUPERINTENDENT RONCOVIERI ON VISITS TO EUROPEAN SCHOOLS.

San Francisco, January, 1909.

To His Excellency, James N. Gillett, Governor of California; to His Honor, Mayor Edward R. Taylor; to the Honorable Board of Supervisors, and to the Honorable Board of Education, in and for the City and County of San Francisco.

Gentlemen:—In this report of my visit to European schools, my first duty, which is only a pleasure, shall be an expression of thanks to His Excellency, Governor James N. Gillett; to His Honor, Mayor Edward R. Taylor; to the Board of Supervisors, and to the Board of Education of this city and county, in acknowledgment of the very kind and courteous permission given to me to visit the schools of Great Britain and Ireland and France in answer to the invitation so generously tendered by the National Civic Federation, Mr. Alfred Mosely of the Mosely Educational Commission of England, and Mr. J. Bruce Ismay, Esq., president of the International Marine Company of England. I wish also to express my sincere appreciation of the generous hospitality and help so freely given me by Mr. Alfred Mosely and the many school officials whom I interviewed.

Technical education has always been a subject in which I have taken a deep interest, and believing that students, apprentices and journeymen who aim at success in the industrial arts and in vocational pursuits need more than ever, in these keenly competitive times, to possess a technical knowledge of their calling, my investigations abroad were directed mainly along the lines of technical and industrial education.

While taking a deep interest in all things educational, I paid special attention to this line of work and visited some of the most important technical and industrial schools of Great Britain, Ireland and France. Without in the least undervaluing the traditional classical studies for those who desire to enter professional careers, these countries are awake to the fact that their schools have for centuries been too much absorbed in the study of the dead languages and the philosophic studies which train memory and reasoning only, but which in our modern, complex industrial life fail altogether to give adequate discipline to the eye and the hand, and to fit the student for skilled labor and for practical life.

The modern trend of events seem to indicate that the prophecy of Crown Prince Frederick after the Franco-Prussian war of 1870 will soon be realized. He said: "We have conquered on the field of battle in war, and we will conquer on the field of battle in commerce and the industries." Englishmen and Frenchmen whom I met, everywhere admitted to me that the immense developmnt and progress of technical education in Germany is, in large measure, responsible for the great power and prosperity of her commerce.

There is a serious conviction in both of these countries, but in England especially, that the Crown Prince's prophecy is becoming a realized fact, and that Germany will soon be the conquerer in the fields of commerce and industry. With the example of Germany as a stimulus, and recognizing that her wonderful advance in the industries is to be traced to a very large extent to her technicai training schools, Great Britain especially, is exerting every effort to create and support an elaborate system of technical schools which shall be the means of retaining her immense trade.

In France the development of art as applied to the industries has been successfully taught in technical schools long before the establishment of the present technical education system in England and Germany. In the higher arts and crafts the products of French industrial taste and intelligence are the direct result of special training along the industrial art lines, and continue to maintain their supremacy in the markets of the world. It must be admitted by all thinking persons that the nation having the greatest industrial average efficiency of her workmen, along the lines of the common trades and industries, is more certain to take its place in the front rank in its invasion of the world of trade, and the governments of Germany, England and France realizing this are putting forth every effort in support of their technical schools. This battle for the conquest of the world's markets, though peaceful, is none the less severe, and is attracting the attention of the manufacturers, importers and exporters of the United States. That England and France look upon the growing commercial and industrial world-influence of Germany with much concern is admittedly due to her splendid system of industrial training. English royal commissions on technical education have been appointed to make careful investigations. International Congresses on technical education have been held in Paris, and all have agreed that besides energy, brains and physique, the young of these countries must be trained in the technical and industrial arts, if they would remain in the forefront of the commercial and industrial world.

The battle, in the field of commerce and industries, as predicted by Crown Prince Frederick in 1870 is actually on. The field of battle is the manufactury and the counting-house. The battle is bloodless, but none the less intense, and the captains of industry will win, whose industrial army is best equipped with technical knowledge. Confronted as is the United States, by the great advances being made in technical and industrial education in the leading countries of Europe, the question naturally arises, where will the United States stand when our immense natural resources shall begin to wane, and the fertility of the soil will be less, as in the very nature of things our limit will in the near future be attained, unless we teach the science of agriculture and industrialism? I shall quote an extract from a comparatively recent article in the ''Monde Economique'' to illustrate the generally accepted French view of German progress: ''The Germans have shown themselves during the last few years to be on the way to become pastmasters in commercial matters. Their energy, patience, activity, and spirit of enterprise are remarkable, and at the pace they are going they will soon succeed in obtaining the commercial supremacy of the chief markets of the world.'' The English Technical Education Board is also alive to the necessity for immediate action. In one of its late reports the Board says: ''One of the subjects constantly kept in view by the Board has been the importance of technical and commercial education. There is no direction than which instruction is likely to be more effective in promoting the industry and well-being of England. Indeed, there are indications that in the immediate future our countrymen will have to encounter a competition far more acute than anything they have yet had to grapple with.'' Besides the battle for supremacy in the world's markets, it is coming to be realized the world over, that apprentices are no longer formed in workshops, hence the disturbing prospect of a scarcity of skilled workmen in the future. This state of things, if not shortly remedied, will lead insensibly to the decadence of the natural industries where expert skill is required.

The English and French technical and industrial schools do not pretend to teach the trade of the carpenter, the mason, the plumber or any other particular business. It must be conceded by all that there is no trade which does not depend more or less upon scientific principles, and to teach what these are, and to point out their practical application, is the essence of technical and industrial education in the schools of these countries. For he who unites a thorough knowledge of the scientific principles underlying his art, with that dexterity which only actual practice in the workshop can give, will, of necessity, be the most completely skilled, and probably the most successful artisan. I was agreeably surprised both in England and France to find that the objects and purposes of a technical education are not in conflict with labor union principles, and that the relation of each to the other is one of helpfulness and unity of purpose. Many labor unions in the United States are opposed to developing apprentices in their trades, because of the increase in the number of workers in that particular trade, and the consequent competition to hold up the scale of wage. A technical education, however, in all the European schools that I visited, does not mean the making of apprentices who shall enter the competitive ranks of labor. It means the teaching of the various branches of science, which underlie the majority of trades, and which are of practical application to mechanics in the several trades, so that they may the better comprehend the reason for each individual operation that passes through their hands, and have more certain rules to follow, than the mere imitation of what they may have seen done by another.

The labor unions of Great Britain and France recognize the beneficent influence of the technical schools and are giving them hearty support by naming representative labor leaders as advisory members of the Boards of Control of these schools, and by giving cash prizes to be competed for by the students in the various trades. In Scotland I found that the advisory members from the labor unions gives to these schools their hearty support and spend much time in consultation with the governing boards. They assist in examining candidates for instructorships. They visit the schools and render to the students much valuable assistance on graduation. A true spirit of fellowship and good feeling is thus developed which has brought about the most cordial relations between the technical schools and the labor unions.

In England and France it is clearly understood by the unions and the school authorities that the expensive equipment of tools and appliances of technical schools shall not be used for anything approaching the apprenticeship system, nor to give the young students who want to learn a trade the chance of acquiring the practice of the trade, which is best acquired in the factory and shop, where work is done on commercial lines. The instruction given in the technical schools is intended to be supplementary to the dexterity and proficiency which only shop experience can give. In England and France the expensive equipment of the technical school is used only to show the students how certain processes are performed, and to enable him to perform those processes himself, with the especial object in view of giving him the why and wherefore of the sciences underlying his trade, rather than the shop experience. The students are taught how the tool is used; the principles and theories underlying its construction; the errors to avoid, and the means of rectifying them when they occur; the nature of the materials to be wrought and the means of distinguishing different qualities of such material; and having learned all this, and having acquired a certain degree of manipulative skill, the school does not require him to constantly repeat the same process, in order to obtain the rapidity of execution that is expected of a professional workman; but instead, proceeds to the explanation of the use of some other machine, and to the learning of some other process, and the sciences and theories underlying it. The skilled labor unionists know full well that the individual who is content to do things by "rule of thumb" can never lift himself above the common level. "There is always room on top" is an old saying, but its truth is never better exemplified than in the crafts. The worker who increases his technical knowledge is on the road to promotion, and the higher pay which promotion brings. The experts in crafts owe their success to technical instruction. The advance of the foreign worker in the industries is to be traced to technical training. He has recognized its need and taken full advantage of it. For these reasons the trades unions of England and France are friendly to the development of technical schools. No conflict can possibly exist, when it is clearly understood that although a technical school may be equipped almost as completely as a trade shop, the equipment serves a very different purpose. It is used, as I have pointed out. to enable the student to understand the why and wherefore of his trade, and to use the appliances with care and scientific judgment. The trades unions of these countries thoroughly understand the technical school to be one whose object is the production of highest type of scientific workers, capable of holding the highest positions in the industrial world, and not simply to produce competitive cheap labor, that will later enter into a fierce rivalry with the unions. The unions understand that the machinery and tools employed in an English and French technical school are used with different objects, and with a different intention from those of the factory or commercial workshop. The good will of the trades unions and their support means much to the technical schools of Great Britain and France, and accounts in a large measure for the impetus given to industrial education, and its present efficient standards.

Nor is it only the trades unions that approve of this great work, and collaborate with the school authorities in favor of technical instruction; but also the manufacturers, Chambers of Commerce, philanthropic and economic associations. Each of these give to the cause the fullest measure of its strength and influence, and assists in the creation of the new education that is to develop and solve the great economic and social problems of these nations.

The time has come for the youth of the United States to rebel at the modern tendency to make him a small, insignificant cog in the wheel of industry, and to be thus converted into human machinery. The great captains of industry, through the complex machinery which American genius has for the most part invented, use our boys as mere tools to feed this machinery. They are not expected to develop skill, and their lives are consecrated to dull routine and the endless spinning, grinding and hammering of the modern workshop. Their days and years are regulated by the factory whistles and the time clock; slaves of the wheel, they have no opportunity of mastering a trade or handicraft. The machinery does the work, and the man seldom understands the why and wherefore of its movements. It is only too true that the apprentice who learns his trade under our modern system, learns only a single part of it and usually knows little or nothing of the several processes involved in the trade as a whole. He has become an automatic working part of the "machine" on which he is working. He knows nothing of its complicated construction. A workman who is only capable of doing one thing and cannot readily turn to other branches of the same trade, is practically unskilled and a prey to those who would lower his wages. The man who does not understand the science of his trade, and who feeds the machine without the fundamental knowledge of its functions, is the modern "Man at the Hoe" hopelessly bound to it, and the weak object of attack in the constant war to lower his wages, and most apt to be thrown out of employment in times of depression. Few men there are today engaged, for example, in the shoemakers' trade, who could make a pair of shoes complete in all its parts, for the reason that this trade, and many others likewise, is divided into many different parts, and men work a lifetime at one part, not knowing or understanding anything about the trade as a whole. I have been informed that the shoe trade is divided into thirty different parts, and that few men working at these separate parts are able to make a complete shoe. Such men are hopelessly handicapped in the struggle for better wages and conditions, because the captains of industry hold them as slaveworkers to one part of the trade. The spirit and independence of such workmen are crushed, and they are doomed never to rise above their present level, a condition repugnant to every liberty-loving American who has a hope in his future uplift, and in the rise and individual initiative of his sons and daughters. The technical and scientific training received by the student in a particular trade, tends to discourage others from being content with a simple knowledge of only one or perhaps two branches of a trade. They are all stimulated to become all-around, efficient workers able to cope with the every varying conditions of the industry in which they are engaged, demanding and receiving the maximum rate of wages and certain of steady employment. Such an education gives broad views of life and develops men of natural power, capable of initiative, with the highest ideals of work and citizenship, just as certainly as does a clerical and professioual education. Education can have no higher objects.

My itinerary abroad included a visit to the schools of Dublin and Belfast in Ireland, to the schools of Glasgow and Edinburgh in Scotland, to the schools of Manchester, Birmingham and London, England, and to schools in Paris, France. The history of public education in England is of comparatively recent date. It was not until 1870 that a national system of education was established in England. Not until that late date did the Government recognize the civil obligation to enable every boy and girl to attain higher development. England was the last of the great nations to establish a national system of free education, and to understand Macauley's motto, "The first business of the State is the education of its citizens." In order to give a short historical retrospect of the state of public education in England at the beginning of the 19th century, I quote from "A Short History of National Education in Great Britain and Ireland," published in 1908 by Thos. Lloyd. Humberstone, B. Sc., (Lond.), of the University of London Administrative Staff, the following most interesting historical account:

"In 1807 the question of national education was fully discussed in connection with Mr. Whitbread's Bill for providing parish schools. The bill passed successfully through the House of Commons, but was rejected in the House of Lords.

"The difficulties in the way of legislative action at that time were indeed insuperable. Some of the most enlightened members of both Houses of Parliament thought that the project of giving education to the laboring classes would be prejudicial to their morals and happiness, teaching them to despise their lot in life. It may here be remarked that, in the minds of many Englishmen at this time. the idea that popular education would cause discontent among the poor was closely associated with a 'genuine, hearty, craven fear' of all political change. induced by the appalling events of the French Revolution. Wise men saw that the events of the French Revolution formed perhaps the strongest justification for an attempt to raise the moral and intellectual standard of the people: that a contented and intelligent people were more easily governed than a brutal and ignorant populace. The view that popular education was one of the most effective means of improving social conditions was indorsed by many of the leading philosophers and social reformers of the time—by Adam Smith in the 'Wealth of Nations,' by Malthus in his 'Essay on Population,' by Robert Owen. the founder of Socialism, and many others. The same message came across the English Channel from the French philosophers, across the Atlantic from the founders of the American Constitution, and across the Tweed from the parish schools of Scotland. But abstract reasoning and lessons drawn from other countries had less effect than the object lessons of social conditions in England. The prevalence of crime called for some drastic remedy. As many as forty people were sometimes hanged in one day; forgery and blackmailing were rife: the highways outside London were infested with footpads, and the police, we are told, were unable to give protection even to shopkeepers and householders. The industrial revolution induced in the large towns a state of social disorder, due to overcrowding, unsanitary conditions, drunkenness, and vice in all its forms, which could not fail to suggest to public-minded men the imperative need for education. The plight of the children in mining and industrial centers was indeed pitiable. Employed for long hours in exhausting labor in mines and factories, they grew up to a stunted manhood, without education or any other civilizing influence. The apprenticeship system, established originally for very different conditions, was exploited for the supply of child labor, and a regular traffic in pauper children grew up, between the parish authorities and the factory owners. Elizabeth Barrett Browning has given expression in some poignant lines to the cry of these unhappy children:

"'For oh' say the children, "'We are weary
And we cannot run or leap:
If we cared for any meadows, it were merely
To drop down in them and sleep.

"'For all day we drag our burden tiring
Through the cold, dark underground;
Or, all day, we drive the wheels of iron
In the factories, round and round.

"Happily for England, the children's cry has not gone unheeded, but it was not until the Education Act of 1870, introduced by Mr. Gladstone's Ministry, that an efficient system of public elementary education was introduced."

In many English schools in addition to public moneys received from the State, endowments have been given by philanthropic men, and in many cases fees are charged to the pupils in order to aid in the support of the schools. This is especially the case of the secondary schools, many of which besides receiving State aid are richly endowed, but still charge fees, giving away only a few scholarships, on competition, to the children whose parents cannot afford to pay for their education. I am of the opinion that no country can boast of a national system of free education, which denies absolutely free secondary education to all who may desire it. Education in Great Britain and England is free only in the elementary grades. It is true that certain bursaries or special scholarships are used to defray the expenses of the unusually bright children of the poor who seek secondary education, but the great majority of those attending secondary schools are required to pay for their tuition.

While visiting a school in London I heard of the son of a poor man, who paid the required fees rather than accept the free scholarship and endure among his fellows the social caste difference. This boy was sent to a pay elementary school, rather than to the free school, because of the social differences that exist among those who attend free schools and pay schools. The father of this boy made sacrifices in order to pay these fees, with a view that his son should move in a higher social plane. In the "pay school" the boy would meet and form friendships with the sons of a more exclusive set. The baneful old English "charity" school system was upon this father. The old charity schools provided a sort of free education for the children of the poor, but compelled these children to wear a special uniform which had the effect to degrade and produce in them a subservient spirit. It also had a pauperizing effect on the parents. The endowed schools, including the large schools at Eton, Harrow, Winchester and Rugby, which have been given the incomprehensible misnomer of "public" schools, form the core of England's secondary education. They do not seem to have been intended for the children of the poor. They are "public" schools only to those who can afford the price. There is, however, a strong tendency developing among intelligent Englishmen to establish free public secondary schools, where the children of rich and poor may attend without any class distinctions. If progress continues as it has since 1870, England may hope to have a free, complete and efficient system of secondary education in the reasonably near future, where the children of rich and poor shall meet on the same common ground, and all caste and social differences may be obliterated.

The educational system of England seems to me to lack unification, and that co-ordination between the elementary schools, the high schools and the universities which is so manifest in the United States. In England there is no uniform course of study for the elementary schools. It is a mere outline. Each headmaster makes out the course for his own school according to the general outline which has been prepared by the Board of Education of England. It is subject, however, to approval of the school inspector, who presides over the district in which this school may be. The consequence is that there is no uniformity of work in the elementary schools of England and they form isolated units instead of an integral part of the general school system. As an example of this go-as-you-please arrangement, I found one headmaster who was teaching vertical writing under approval of the inspector, and another headmaster who was an advocate of the slant system. In different schools I found different text-books in the same subject.

EDUCATION IN SCOTLAND AND IRELAND.

Quoting again from "A Short History of National Education" by Humberstone:

"The educational systems of Scotland and Ireland are entirely different in origin and character from the English system. Scotland has always set an example to England in her zeal for education. Even before the Reformation there was a system of parish schools in Scotland, and so early as 1696 an Act was passed in the Scottish Parliament for the establishment of a system of national education, under which the duty of providing schools was imposed on the landowners. It is interesting to know that as early as 1807 the success achieved by education in Scotland in raising the standard of civilization in that century was put forward as one of the chief reasons for the establishment of parish schools in England. In her secondary and technical schools and her four universities (St. Andrews, founded in 1411; Glasgow, in 1450; Aberdeen, in 1498; Edinburgh, in 1582), Scotland has educational resources which are certainly relatively superior to those possessed by England.

"Education in Ireland has a sadder history. Ireland had the use of letters long before England, and to Ireland, a trustworthy authority has said, England chiefly owed her knowledge. But for reasons for which England, it is to be feared, was to blame, Ireland was never able to profit by its start in the educational race. For centuries the work of education in Ireland was closely associated with proselytising. Since 1831, when the Board of Commissioners of National Education in Ireland was established, the educational system has been more in consonance with the desires of the Irish people; but it is generally admitted that the present system of elementary education in Ireland is in need of reform. In recent years considerable progress has been made in the encouragement of scientific education in Irish schools by means of grants administered by the Board of Agriculture and Technical Instruction. Belfast has built a large and finely-equipped technical school of the best character. Dublin University, founded in 1591, and the Royal University of Ireland, founded in 1880, are at present the only universities in Ireland; but a Bill for the establishment of two new universities (in Dublin and Belfast), and involving the abolition of the Royal University of Ireland, has been submitted to Parliament, and there is a good prospect of its becoming law in the near future."

In Scotland there is a carefully planned uniform course of study, adopted by the Board of Education of the Scotch Educational Department, a body whose functions are entirely distinct from those of the Board of Education of England and Wales.

In Ireland the system of national education is controlled by a Board of Commissioners. They are representative men who adhere to the policy of strict impartiality in religious matters. The schools under this board are supported by state and local funds, and may be Roman Catholic, Protestant or mixed in respect to religion. But in Ireland, as well as in Great Britain, the rights of parents in religious matters are guarded by a "Conscience Clause" in the school regulations making the attendance at religious exercises optional with the parents. The school programs are so arranged that no child is allowed to attend a religious exercise of a denomination other than his own, except upon the written request of the parent.

The schools of the Christian Brothers form a large and important part of Ireland's elementary education. These schools are both numerous and justly flourishing. Their system of education where the development of character goes strongly hand in hand with the training of the minds has taken a deep hold upon the people and they number among their former pupils some of the most influential men in every city and large town in Ireland. At the competitive examinations given by the commissioners of national education in Ireland last September, the largest number of distinctions and prizes were won by the Christian Brothers' schools. Fully one thousand prizes of varying degrees of value were awarded to the successful students of the eighty-five schools and colleges which took part in the competition. Twenty-eight of those schools are under the control of the Christian Brothers, and the highest places on the list and the larger share of the prizes were taken by the Christian Brothers' schools. The "Christian" schools throughout Ireland literally swept the boards in experimental science, which gives proof that the work in these schools is far in advance of that done in the other schools. The North Richmond Street school in Dublin, under the direction of the Christian Brothers, beat the record of every other school in the country this year, securing first place in all Ireland with eighty-three distinctions.

In Ireland, technical instruction is controlled by "The Department of Agriculture and Technical Instruction," which has an advisory board of technical instruction. The department aims at the co-ordination of its work with that of other educational authorities. Throughout Ireland technical instruction is being organized in the various counties, and thousands of students attend the technical schools. The teaching of Irish textile industries is a natural instance of the attempt that is being made to make Ireland the exclusive home of this industry. The problem of educational administration in Ireland, as I saw it, shows that there is not a comprehensive system of public education as in this country. Reform of the system is needed so that efficient direction and co-ordination between the schools may bring about a unified purpose. The Board of National Education and the Board of Technical Education with close co-operation will undoubtedly reach this result in the near future.

Our perfectly articulated California system of free education from kindergarten to university, entirely supported from public funds, adapted as it is to produce equality in citizenship and equality in opportunity, when given with due regard to the development of character, obliterates all snobbish social relations and walls of caste all too frequently evident in Great Britain and Ireland. The American democratic ideal in absolutely free higher education for all, without any class distinctions based on "fees" or other snobbish forms or previous conditions of servitude in the English social scale, is not yet accomplished in Great Britain and Ireland. Progressive men in these countries are stimulating the popular demand to develop and foster this ideal in secondary education, for without it, education can never reach the high plain of usefulness to all the people, which it has attained in the United States.

The entire social school structure of England is so hidebound, stratified and even fossilized into classes that the children of the poor are hopelessly down deep in the lowest strata of English society without the slightest hope and apparently without even ambition to break into the upper crust.

In America there is a total absence of formalities required in the manner of visiting schools. Everywhere the visitor is welcome whether he be a citizen or a stranger, but in Europe bundles of official red-tape have to be cut before one is permitted to visit the schools. Special letters of identification and recommendation are required. The visitor is not permitted to enter the school without first having obtained special permission from some high official in the office of the administration. This is another refreshing evidence that our splendid free school system in America is founded on the broadest principles of democracy, for freedom to visit and criticise the work of our free public schools is the acknowledged prerogative of every American citizen and visitor from any land.

Our American system of encouraging inquiry, training to think and bringing out self-expression on the part of our pupils in elementary schools, producing as it does mental alertness and quickness of mind, is vastly superior to the English method, which does not countenance the idea of a pupil asking questions. Such freedom is considered familiarity. The English pupil is made to feel his subordinate position, and not treated as an intellectual equal, as in our system. The consequence is that the children in England seem to take less interest in their studies than in our country.

A well-organized, graded and co-ordinated system of public education absolutely free and open to all from infancy to manhood, from kindergarten to university, is woefully inadequate, incomplete and expensive, and England must remedy this greatest of all defects in her educational system if the traditional differences in social positions are ever to be obliterated and the now practically submerged lower classes are ever to rise by means of their educational strength and feel themselves the intellectual equals of the upper classes.

If I have shown some of the faults and weaknesses of the elementary schools, I desire with equal fairness and frankness to sound the praise of the magnificent English technical schools, their equipment, and their effect upon the various trades of the United Kingdom. There is also virtue in English conservatism as against our tendency to carry experimentation too far in subjects which in a short while are declared to be useless fads. Such, for example, the sudden and irresistible tidal wave which brought the now almost entirely discarded system of vertical penmanship. Leading public men and educators everywhere in England realize the close connection between the welfare of the country and education, and that to secure the prosperity of the State, the system of education must be made as good, as complete and far-reaching and up-to-date as possible. They know that the expenditure of money on education is the wisest investment the nation can make, provided the expenditure is carefully directed and applied, as is the rule in the United States. It is acknowledged everywhere in England and France, that in the United States there is a justified belief in the value of education, and a universal zeal in promoting it. They admit that there is a deeper rooted sympathy in the hearts and minds of the American people, that national prosperity, and national safety and freedom, depend upon an educated people.

In the countries visited by me, I found that the most important principle of our democratic institutions, viz: equal opportunities for all, through education from kindergarten to university and through equal rights before the law, giving to the young of our country the opportunity to make the most of himself (by raising himself to any social level to which he may aspire), through his character, capacity, and industry, does not exist, and is not even understood by the masses of Europe. The stratified conditions in which the classes in the social scale are so clearly defined and hopelessly fixed for the terms of their natural lives, and the apparent lack of ambition of the so-called "lower classes" to look above them, gave me the impression that class distinctions, based on wealth or lineage, govern the people and control their destinies.

In England I was impressed with the general feeling of unrest that I found in some of the large manufacturing centers, such as Manchester and Birmingham. While I was in Manchester there were bread riots, due to the great "problem of the unemployed," which for some years back has been growing more acute. In my opinion the problem of the unemployed is, to a very large extent, the problem of the unskilled. The men who marched in the streets whom I saw charged upon by the mounted police, were not skilled artisans, they were the unskilled men who fed machines in the mills, and who had become a part of those machines, so that when the large manufacturers declared a lockout in order to reduce their wages, these men were confronted with the alternative of either accepting the wages offered, or of finding employment in some other industry. My observations convinced me that the problem of the unemployed is undoubtedly the result of two main causes: the failure and almost complete disappearance of the apprenticeship system, and the consequent impossibility of finding work for such a large army of unskilled workers in the trades. The problem is clearly understood by the educational authorities of England, and day and evening technical and industrial trade schools are being fostered to meet it. There is no question but that the superior and most successful nation yet to be in the world's history, will be the one whose workmen are the most energetic, intelligent and industrious, highly skilled in their vocations and whose spirit of initiative is most developed. We in the United States, and especially in California, should therefore direct all our energy along these lines if we would maintain ourselves in the front rank. In the leading countries of Europe a wonderful advance is being made in the development of skilled and scientific workmen through technical schools, and we must not forget that to remain stationary in such a race is really to go backwards. The mission of our future technical and industrial schools should be to give a solid preparation for the battle of life; to form draftsmen, designers, foremen in the shops, architects, engineers, skilled artisans; in a word, men well armed for the rough combat of life, ready to defend any of our threatened industries in the industrial and commercial war that is going on around us all the time in our modern complex life. We must develop men highly skilled in all the arts and crafts, who will give to the United States the industrial rank which it should hold among the great nations.

Among the schools which I visited, and from which I formed my impressions, was the Belfast Municipal Technical Institute. This is an immense institution presided over by Mr. Francis C. Forth, a gentleman of unusual executive ability. There are 5,000 students attending this school; about 500 of these attend in the day and 4,500 in the evening. The trade subjects are taught only to those who work at the trade. A boy must be not less than 12 years of age and have passed the sixth standard of the National schools before being admitted. The principal object of the trade classes of this school is to provide a specialized training for boys who are intended for industrial occupations. While due regard is paid to the subjects of a general education, special attention is devoted to imparting a sound training in the elements of science, and in science as applied to local arts and manufactures such as mechanical engineering, naval architecture, the building trades and the textile industries. The complete course covers three years, and includes, besides theoretical instruction, practical work in the laboratories, the workshops and the drawing school.

Boys who take the complete course are in a position to enter on their life work in the mill, factory, or workshop and soon outstrip the lads who have not had these advantages. These classes are intended chiefly for apprentices who wish to obtain a thorough grasp of all the fundamentals of their own and allied trades. It is not an object of these classes to teach a trade, but the aim is to make the progress of the apprentice more rapid, and to give him a broader view of the trade with which he is associated and to enable him to acquire a familiarity with trades closely allied to his own.

I visited classes in patternmakers' work, moulders' work, boilermakers' work, machine shop practice, marine engineering for sea-going engineers, motor-car construction, naval architecture, electrical engineering, telephone, telegraphy, electric wiring and fitting, building trades classes, such as sanitary engineering and practical plumbers' classes, cabinet making, building construction, practical painting and decoration classes, the practical classes in linen weaving and the textile industries, cotton and linen bleaching and dyeing, etc., etc.

Fees are charged in this school varying from one pound to twelve pounds per annum, but a number of scholarships covering tuition and the necessary books and instruments are awarded to those pupils who are poor but deserving and who have passed a competitive examination.

The daily sessions in this school are of six hours duration.

There is, besides a trade school, a technical course for older students. It provides a sound training in the science and technology of mechanical engineering, electrical engineering, the textile industries and pure and applied chemistry. The students in this course aim at filling positions of responsibility, such as mechanical engineers, electrical engineers, naval architects, spinners, manufacturers, manufacturing chemists, or other industrial occupations. All classes of Irish society attend this school. Young men and young women who come in automobiles are seated along side of poor girls who come with shawls on their heads. This great school has a distinct social leveling tendency. The magnet that draws all these people together is the knowledge that a practical education that will train the hand and eye as well as the brain can be obtained at reasonable cost.

In the evening school I visited the classes in housewifery. There were present in the class I visited about 30 young women ranging from 18 to 30 years of age. It was a most interesting sight. Some were cooking on coal and gas ranges making soups, roasts, bread, etc. Others were washing and ironing; others were learning to sew and darn and mend. Some were doing dressmaking; others were learning the chemistry of the kitchen, the use of caustics, the making of soap, dyeing fabrics, etc. The students are permitted to purchase excellent roasts that are cooked in the class. I was informed that many of these students were young married women whose education in the homely house duties had been neglected as single girls, and who attended these classes so as to make their homes more pleasant and to learn housewifery economy.

The demand for a bread and butter education would be just as great in San Francisco if we would only establish a school like the Belfast school. The proof is shown by the way the correspondence schools of the East are thriving, and all students have to pay for this education. In San Francisco many students are paying for such a correspondence education simply because San Francisco has not established anything of the kind. If San Francisco can only awake to the necessity for action, and compare her supineness in this matter to the progressiveness of Belfast, Ireland, we will be doing something that will forever benefit our children and our children's children. The splendid Belfast school which I have just described cost 150,000 pounds and the equipment cost 50,000 pounds in addition, a total of a million dollars for Belfast, a city of 350,000 people.

The equipment was very complete and machines and lathes of every description were in the shops. I noted with pleasure that there were in the shops machines of American manufacture, such as the excellent Brown & Sharp milling machine No. 12, made in Providence, R. I., and a No. 7 lathe of the Hendey Machine Co. of Torrington, Conn.

In Glasgow, Scotland, I visited several interesting schools, notably the Glasgow Athenaeum Commercial College, Mr. John Lauder, Supt.; the Allan Glen's Technical school, of which Dr. John G. Kerr is the headmaster; also the Glasgow and West of Scotland Technical College, Mr. Herbert F. Stockdale, director.

The Glasgow Athenaeum Commercial College, besides giving a thorough course in bookkeeping, commercial arithmetic, English, French, German, shorthand and typewriting, also has special classes to teach bank clerks, railroad clerks, insurance clerks and shipping clerks. There is also a specially strong department of music in this school. In the evening school I heard a large and splendid orchestra and talented vocalists, all pupils of this school, rehearsing with marked ability Hayden's Oratorio of the Creation. It is the aim of Allan Glenn's Technical school to combine the essential elements of a liberal education with a thorough training in science. It contains a primary and secondary department and emphasizes mechanics, physics, chemistry, freehand, geometrical, mechanical, and architectural drawing, mechanical and electric engineering and a large amount of workshop practice. In this school stress is laid on scientific studies.

In the Glasgow and West of Scotland Technical College, I found a school of even greater importance than the Belfast school. The students number over 5,000 in the evening and more than 600 in the day classes. The building is a large modern and imposing one of brown stone. Large elevators are provided for the pupils. The heating and ventilating system is a modern plenum system on the same plan as those placed in our new schools. This great school was built and equipped at a cost of 300,000 pounds. Private subscriptions furnished 50,000 pounds, the National Government furnished 50,000 pounds, and the city of Glasgow furnished 200,000 pounds. The equipment of the school cost over 60,000 pounds. The school was completed in 1905. In one large room I saw scientific apparatus and machines for hydraulic testing which the director told me cost 8,000 pounds. Every department of this great school has been as generously equipped as the hydraulic testing room. I saw everywhere at work earnest, busy students who were learning the why and wherefore, and delving into the science underlying their trades. Most of the students were either apprentices or full-fledged workers in the various trades. I visited the bootmakers, the tailors, the plumbers, the machinists, the sheet metal classes, the bakers and confectioners, the weaving, dyeing and bleaching classes, motor car engineering, naval architecture, the electric engineering classes. To illustrate the spirit of the people of Glasgow and their interest in technical education, I was informed that the master bakers and the Bakers' Union had recently, in co-operation, presented to the school a complete outfit of tools, ovens and equipment which cost 4,000 pounds. One of the donors to the fund was a large manufacturer of bakery machinery. Instruction was being given in all branches of the trade from the kneading of dough to the most complex cake ornamentation. This co-operation between employers and employees extends to all the trades. The unions of the various crafts assist the school and recognize it as a friend. On my way to the school I saw in the windows of a union paint shop, signs advertising and illustrating the work done by the classes for painters and decorators and inviting all apprentices to join them. The impression which one receives after visiting this school is, that through unity of action and a sensible understanding of the purposes of the school on the part of manufacturers and workmen, captains of industry and leaders in the labor union movement, perfect harmony prevails in the management of the school. The school is managed through a board of governors composed of leading men of the city, and the general public and the municipality give to this school all the support, both moral and financial, that its excellent work entitles it to. In Edinborough I visited the Heriot-Watt Technical College and the

George Heriot Technical School. This latter is in a very old building, and while the architecture is pleasing from the exterior its interior is poorly arranged. No thought was given to scientific lighting, heating and ventilating. The hallways were all too narrow and the main doors opened inwardly. A panic in such a school would result disastrously. The Heriot-Watt College has the advantage of a magnificent and very complete collection of working models of steam engines and other complicated machinery in the Edinburgh Museum. Boys enter the George Heriot school at 8 and the average age of graduation is 17. It covers the field of technical and industrial education. There is in this school a fine white tiled swimming tank which holds 25,000 gallons of water heated by steam. It is complete and has diving spring boards, rings, trapese slides, etc. The water is heated by steam. There are two regular instructors of swimming and every boy in the school is compelled to learn. The evening technical schools of Edinburgh require the payment of a fee for tuition, but the fee is returned at the end of the year to students who make 80% of attendance for the year. The Board of Education sends out printed circulars to employers in the various trades and professions and invite them to inform their employees that classes are to be in session at which instruction in the trade will be given. Large posters are pasted in various parts of the city advertising the school and the courses of instruction. This advertising of the technical schools is done in all the cities of Ireland, Scotland, England and France. Every possible method of advertising the work of the school is used. There are four schools that have large swimming tanks. These schools are used as centers to teach swimming, which is obligatory except where a child is excused for good reason. These four swimming tanks not being sufficient, the municipal corporation baths are used and the Board of Education pays one cent per pupil admission.

From Edinburgh I proceeded to Manchester to attend the Education Conference of the teachers of the United Kingdom. The subject under discussion was "The Feeding of the Children of the Poor." Relating their personal experiences some of the teachers told sad tales of hungry children forced to school under the compulsory education law. One teacher said he had gazed on the pitiable spectacle of nearly 60 children, with sunken eyes and quivering lips and few would apply for a free meal. Another teacher told of knowing mothers who remained at home without food that their children might have it and attend school. The result of the conference was that inasmuch as it was impossible to educate a starving child an appeal should be made to the government to extend the system of providing meals for hungry children in premises other than the school. The discussion developed that the teachers had always stood between the children of the unemployed and starvation, and it was resolved to demand the immediate approval of the "Provision of Meals Act," under which the feeding of poor children would be regarded as an Act of right and due without humiliation, rather than as a charity.

I visited the municipal school of technology and municipal school of art in Manchester. Here again I was struck with the importance of technical education. Another great technical school of five thousand students in the evening and five hundred in the day. The value of the structure and equipment amounts to upwards of three hundred thousand pounds. The school accommodates the mechanical, electrical and sanitary engineering industries; the chemical and textile industries; architecture and all of the building trades, printing and allied trades. The building is modern and the equipment has been generously provided. On each floor (there are six stories covering sixty-five hundred square yards of ground) and in the machine shops, I noticed cabinets containing a book on First Aid to the Injured, and bottles of medicines, such as Friar's Balsam Antiseptic Wash for cuts, bruises, dressing for burns and scalds, spirits of sal volatile, picric acid, boric ointment, carbolic wool, bandages, lint, strapping, a little glass and a bottle of brandy. The cabinet is of glass, and the key is in a small case next to it to be used only when needed, by breaking the glass. A red cross is painted over the glass case. In this school I saw the largest plumbing and sanitary workshop that I have seen in my travels. The students were all young plumbers' apprentices and being given instruction in the theory and construction of gas and water meters. In the evening classes, the architectural drawing rooms have an excellant arrangement that reflects the electric light on the white ceiling. This softens and diffuses the light more evenly through the rooms. I visited classes in electric wiring, electric testing instrument laboratory and electro chemical engineering. I saw the students at work at the electro furnaces making calcium carbide. I visited classes in domestic science, dressmaking, millinery and plain needle work. The fee charged in each of these subjects was five guineas for the term. It would take a volume to describe in detail the work done in these schools. Besides a large library, there is also a restaurant and kitchen for the benefit of the students and especially for the students of the evening classes who cannot go to their homes for their dinner and return to school in time. The school is another instance of an immense workshop in all its varied industries.

The school is so large and important and covers instruction in such a large field in the mechanical industries that to avoid accidents notices like the following are posted on each floor and in the shops and laboratories:

THE MUNICIPAL SCHOOL OF TECHNOLOGY,
MANCHESTER.

SPECIAL NOTICE TO STUDENTS.

Students in laboratories and workshops are warned to exercise the utmost care in the use of machines and appliances and materials, and in the use of the electric current or other motive power. All reasonable precautions are taken by the school committee, but it will not hold itself responsible for damages or injury to students caused by their own carelessness and disregard of the directions issued to them.

(Signed) J. H. REYNOLDS, Principal.

From Manchester I went to Birmingham, where I visited the Municipal Technical School on Suffolk street. Mr. W. E. Sumpner, the principal, showed me around and explained the work of his school. This is also another such school as I have just described, and it would be tiresome repetition to go into details. Suffice it that in Birmingham, Liverpool and London I found that they were as far in advance of us here in California in the matter of scientific and industrial education as it is possible to conceive. In London I visited the Central School of Arts and Crafts, the Borough Polytechnic school, the South Lambeth Road school, the Ponton Road Day Industrial school, the East London Industrial school, Brookbank Road, Lewisham, the William Street school, and the educational exhibit at the Franco-British Exposition. I also attended the conference of the International Moral Education Congress at the University of London.

EDUCATION IN FRANCE.

Public education in France is divided into three parts. First, primary instruction patronized by the great majority of French children. To the department of primary instruction belongs the kindergarten, the elementary primary schools, and the superior primary. Second, the department of secondary education to which belong the lycees or state classical colleges and the "College

Communal'' equivalent to our classical high schools, and third, the department of superior instruction to which belong the university and those special schools of high order, which are under the Minister of Education of France. These latter include the College of France, the Museum of Natural History, the practical school of high studies ''Ecole Pratique des Hautes Etudes,'' the Conservatoire des Arts et Metiers, and the Ecole Nationale Superieure des Mines. Paris is the seat of these special schools and also of the principal university.

There are separate schools for boys and for girls; co-education is unknown in France or England, except in the case of kindergartens. There is a strong antagonism toward co-education in Europe. The general opinion is that bad in itself it is infinitely worse when the teachers are mostly women, as in the United States. In both England and France commiseration was expressed on many occasions that women should predominate over the men in education and the fear was freely expressed that combined with co-education it would result in developing effeminate men, lacking in virility with a sexless tone of thought.

No one in France is permitted to teach in any capacity in a public school unless provided with a state certificate. The state pays a fixed annual salary ranging for full teachers in the elementary primaries from $200 to $400 for men and for women from $200 to $300. In addition to the salary, however, every teacher is provided with a residence or with a money equivalent for the same.

Primary teachers may be retired upon a pension after reaching sixty years of age if they have been in the service thirty years. The minimum pension is, for men $120 a year, and for women $100. The total state appropriation amounts to more than $50,000,000, of which over $40,000,000 are expended for primary education. To this sum is added the amounts received from local taxes in the cities and communes of France. In addition to the schools for general education under the control of the Minister of Public Instruction there are many special schools, technical, agricultural, commercial and art, which, with the numerous municipal technical schools, complete the public provision for education in France. The state, however, assumes no monopoly of education and private institutions of all conditions exist side by side with the public institutions. Primary education is absolutely free in France. Secondary education is patronized chiefly by the children of the wealthy classes, but it is accessible to those children who, however poor are meritorious. The poor children obtain admission to these institutions of secondary education on competitive examination and their expenses are paid by endowments.

There is a compulsory education law compelling all the children of France to attend school until they shall have attained the age of 13 years, or they may leave school earlier if they have received a certificate of graduation from the primary schools, and provision is made to furnish food and even clothing to the children of worthy poor. I was informed by the Minister of Public Instruction that in 1854 statistics showed that 31.6% of the men and 47.4% of the women were illiterate; in 1870 the figures were 25% of illiterates for the men and 37.7% for the women, but in 1898, due to the free public education in the primary schools and to the great compulsory laws and interest taken in education generally in France, these figures fall to 4.7% of illiterates for men and 7.2% for the women.

Secondary education is of a high order both for boys and for girls, especially in technical education in the arts. As in England so in France, since 1870 a great forward movement has taken place in free public education. In Paris I was informed that in many cities of France new buildings have been constructed richly endowed and equipped with all modern appliances.

Each primary school is placed under the patronage of an appointed school commission. This commission watches over the welfare of the children of the poor, gives shoes to those who have none, warm clothes in winter and a good lunch at mid-day. The children of the poor who graduate from the "Ecole Primaire Superieure" schools equivalent to our high school are given an opportunity through a competitive examination to enter higher institutions of learning, however distant these higher schools may be situated from the city which they graduated. All expenses of maintenance and of transportation are paid out of bursaries or endowments established for that purpose. The meritorious child of the peasant is thereby given the advantages of a higher education at public expense. To be admitted into an "Ecole Primaire Superieure" a pupil must have reached the age of 12 years and must have obtained his certificate of primary studies or pass an examination showing equivalent attainments, which examination is not open to candidates below 13 years of age. Promotions from class to class are made upon the basis of a right examination and pupils who fail in the same must either leave the school or stay another year in the division in which they have been studying.

Very liberal provisions have been made to provide normal schools in which teachers are trained. Two normal schools exist in every department of France, one for men and one for women.

The compulsory period of primary education extends from the sixth to the thirteenth year, but a child who passes the examination for the certificate of primary studies is exempt from the obligation to attend school. Candidates may be admitted to this examination at eleven years of age, and a large proportion of the children seek their certificates at that early age. The majority of children leave school at an earlier age than thirteen. The schools begin at 8 in the morning and close at 6 p. m.

Manual training and technical education in all the primary schools holds a strong place in the curriculum. The French system of industrial schools is highly developed. Machinery models, laboratories and general equipment are of the highest order and have been lavishly supplied to these schools in large quantities. The equipment and school plant of the "Central School of Art and Manufactures" in Paris cost over $2,000,000. Special trade schools exist in which shoemaking, carriage-making, furniture-making, and metal working are taught, together with practical schools of commerce and industry in all of which tuition is free. The instruction is both theoretical and practical.

In the "Boulle Municipal School" of Paris, which I visited, I saw students at work in cabinet-making and making real furniture of most beautiful designs instead of the small sloyd models made in our schools. They were learning upholstering, woodcarving, sculpture, application of art to bronzes, goldsmith's work, jewelry, and iron work. In this school the application of arts and sciences to the furniture industry predominates. It was founded in 1886 by the City of Paris with the object of creating skilled workmen and educate artisans capable of maintaining the traditions of taste, and the superiority of the genuinely partisian industries in the production of artistic designs in furniture. It is essentially a trades school. The students pass through a real apprenticeship and at the same time receive a scientific high school education appropriate to the profession they have chosen. The boys all wear jumpers and overalls, and the school looks like a busy factory. The pupils must be not less than thirteen years nor more than sixteen years of age to enter. In the course, instruction is given in industrial economy, industrial drawing and geometry, lectures on the history of art, art designing, clay modeling and water color painting. In manual training, instruction is given in moulding in sand, inlaying, blacksmithing, wood turning, joinery, upholstery and jewelry work. The pupils are required to visit manufacturing establishments and work under the guidance of the teachers. At the noon hour a lunch is prepared for the pupils. It was an interesting sight to see these two hundred and ninety-two boys seated at tables enjoying a fine meal table d'hote style. On the day of my visit to the "Ecole Boulle;" I was invited by the director to partake of the lunch that was prepared for the pupils. It was an excellent, warm lunch and consisted of maccaroni and cheese, a veal roast and sardines in oil. The pupils pay for this excellent meal the sum of ten cents. Women cooks and waiters attend the boys. To develop a spirit of camaraderie all the students must partake of the same food. They are not permitted to bring their own lunches or any extras. At the end of the year the balance which accumulates is used by the pupils for the purchase of a gift of some kind for the school. The annual expense of this school is two hundred and fifty thousand francs. Everything is furnished free to the two hundred and ninety-two students.

I also visited the "Bernard Palissy" school, whose chief purpose is the application of art to the industries. The object of the school is to develop workmen of artistic taste, skilled in the application of art to the industries such as ceramics, decorative and practical sculpture, drawing and designs on cloths, or wall paper, and decorative painting. Instruction is absolutely free in this school. In addition to the practical application of the arts, instruction is given in free-hand drawing, linear and perspective drawing, modeling, comparative anatomy, lectures on the history of art, and decorative compositions.

The "Germain-Pillon" School of Design and Modeling, as applied to the industries is under the direction of Mons. John Labusquiere, who is also the director of the Bernard-Palissey school. The City of Paris has voted 1,000,000 francs for a new building which will house both of these schools. They are supported entirely by municipal funds. Pupils are admitted to this school only on a competitive examination which is held in June of each year. The school aims to develop original and capable art workers with the ability to create original designs as well as to reproduce the designs of others. Drawing is here taught not alone from the viewpoint of the trades, but also from the viewpoint of the decorative arts. Strong efforts are made in this school to develop the artistic sense in drawing, which shall give originality to industrial products. Its graduates are skilled artisans in such art industries as ceramics, wood-carving, marble and other stone carving, textiles and wall-paper designing and decorative painting. Designing and modeling are given from plaster casts and living models; water-colors, from plants, living models and the many objects employed in the industries. Modeling is given through practical exercises. Practical and applied geometry, industrial drawing, architectural drawing and the theory of shadows and perspective are taught. Lectures on the practical setting up of furniture in its relation to the colors involved and the taste of arrangement. As the director, Mons Labusquiere, said to me, "Il ne faut pas force' les eleves de voir comme nous voyons ni de pense' comme nous pensons." "We must not force our students to see as we see nor to think as we think." To the class he said, "Do not imitate; find your own way; be yourselves. This struck me as the keynote of the splendid work under the direction of this able principal. Copies or imitations of the works of others are never tolerated in this school. Originality in the conception of work was his thought. The ideal of this school is the development of the creative faculties. "We give them general outlines," he said, "and let them finish in their own way and according to their own conception. We want our boys to develop initiative, no artificial method of obtaining results is permitted, such as the use of mirrors, as is often seen in other schools. The drawings must be conceived and originate in the brains of the boys and composed in that way only." The "Germain-Pillon" school emphasizes education in the decorative arts. All of the materials used in the school, such as wood, stone, paints, plaster, etc., etc., are supplied gratuitously by the city.

The manual training department of "L'Ecole Arago," an ecole primaire superiere which I visited, consisted of the screw propeller made from pieces of wood, models of an engine head and cylinder and other practical applications of manual training. The designs of artistic iron work were also very meritorious. In this school, as in those previously alluded to, drawing in all its branches and particularly original work in architectural drawing is emphasized. The "Ecole Arago," which is a regular ecole primaire superieure, is really equivalent to a four years' American high school with scientific studies and where only modern languages are taught. It is a free public school, having also a preparatory department of four years equivalent to the four years' of grammar grades. The daily sessions are from 8 a. m. to 6 p. m., with four recesses of ten minutes each. It is a combination grammar and high school, four years being devoted to each department. Professor G. Hugnot, the surveillant general, told me that the famous architect, Bernard, who prepared the plans for the University of California, is a graduate of this school, although he finished his studies at the Beaus Arts.

The "Conservatoire National des Arts et Metiers" is both an industrial museum and a school of industrial arts and science. It contains mechanical, physical and chemical laboratories. The museum contains precious and rare collections of scientific instruments, models of machines and objects of art. All the arts and sciences applied to the industries are largely represented. Physical and mechanical, weights and measures, geometry, geodesy, topography, astronomy, architecture and constructions, hygiene, agriculture, transportation and railroads, mining, metallurgy, light and heat, chemistry, glass, porcelains, textiles, printing, photography, etc. The library contains a rich collection of works relating to the sciences, arts, agriculture and the industries. It contains more than 40,000 volumes and over 2,000 prints.

There are 22 chairs occupied by men of the greatest renown in France. Fifteen chairs are devoted to the teaching of the applied sciences to the arts, and the applied arts to the trades. The remainder of the chairs are devoted to political and industrial economy, social economy, commerce, industrial hygiene and the prevention of accidents in the industries. The rapid transformations that are taking place in the industries is actively watched and the most recent inventions are discussed. All this work is made practical.

This magnificent institution is attended by nearly 2,000 students.

The technical and industrial trade schools of France are under governmental control, well developed and comprehensive in character. There are of course many private and semi-private organizations. The government controlled schools furnish a broad, fundamental training in scientific and technical work which prepares the pupil for the battle of life far more practically than the classical academic education can do. There are over 5,000 technical schools in France. They represent the entire gamut of the industries and the arts, sciences and agriculture.

What particularly distinguishes French technical industrial education is not only the splendid organization of the courses of study in the technical schools, but the variety of types of educational institutions adapted as far as possible to the requirements and necessities of local needs.

The evening industrial schools also act as ties between the apprentices and the employers which unite the interests of both and conduce toward the harmony of the whole labor problem.

Such institutions as I have just described from personal visits are the glory of the country that possesses them. These splendid technical institutions, the great museums, and schools of applied arts are the inspiration from which French artisans, both men and women, derive their keen sense of the beautiful, and develop that delicacy of touch which they apply with their natural artistic instinct in the pure realms of decorative design and which compel the admiration of the world of modern fashion. This kind of education brings to France a never ceasing stream of the world's gold in return for what? A touch of art more skillfully executed, on account of their training, than by the artisans of any other country in the world. Does industrial and technical education pay? I say it does. For when our country shall become, as in the course of time it must, as poor in natural resources as the countries of Europe, when our forests shall have been cut away, our coal mines exhausted; when our land shall become exhausted through our present wasteful methods of agriculture, and refuse to yield, then will we become as China and India, a starving unproductive race, and our entire social structure degenerate to their level, unless we heed the advice of our scientists and the cry of our great thinkers to protect our great natural resources and conserve them for our posterity by establishing technical and industrial education throughout the land that will give to our people the skill and intelligence to protect these resources and create markets for the work of our artisans because of their superior excellence. Our complex and ever changing industrial conditions demand of our youth that they perfect themselves in technical education. The rapid discoveries and inventions are daily throwing men out of one employment into another. These rapid changes require men of skill, men who understand the fundamental sciences that underlie all physical inventions.

Only through technical education can the problems of the future generations be solved, developing as it does skillful and capable workmen and able foremen and managers who form the elite of the working population.

The sooner we realize the personal advantages for our children and posterity and the incalculable advantages that technical education will give to our country as a whole in the international contest for supremacy in industry, in commerce, and in agriculture, the sooner will we begin a forward movement which will place our nation at the head of the column.

I wish this report to be taken merely as a summary of the most important things observed by me in connection with technical education abroad. I have endeavored to plainly state the facts and relate the impressions I have formed, making use of my notes and observations and such information as I have been able to gather in my travels.

The general provisions for technical instruction in California, and especially in San Francisco, are as yet incomparably inferior to that of the countries I visited. We have neither buildings nor equipment, nor have we ever received the financial aid which should be ours. To illustrate this apathy I would state that in the recent bond issue not a single dollar was provided for our public Polytechnic High school. In the manual training and domestic science department of our elementary schools a miserable pittance of a few hundred dollars is appropriated for a term's work. We must make the humiliating confession that practically nothing has been done in the public schools of San Francisco that compares with the splendid schools and liberal provisions made for technical instruction abroad.

In San Francisco we have been drifting helplessly along old lines and traveling in old ruts, falling behind in the great technical education race. Every city of importance in the United States is ahead of us. European countries are awake to the situation and the incalculable prize is the control of the markets of the world.

I hope San Francisco will soon awake from her Rip Van Winkle sleep in this most vital educational need by making provision for a great technical and industrial school on the lines of the Belfast, Glasgow, Manchester or Birmingham schools and of the Paris Schools of Arts and Crafts. To do this successfully we must awaken the interest of all our citizens and as far as the teaching of trades is concerned we must secure the intelligent co-operation of capital and labor in these schools or they cannot succeed.

The subdivision of labor more and more prevalent in this country requires that there shall be either a preliminary or supplementary education along scientific and technical lines to supply the deficiency of the old apprentice system as is now done in England and France.

The usual objections made to technical and trade schools by labor unions in this country have been entirely overcome in Great Britain, Ireland and France. The unions in these countries have the same industrial problems to contend with that have the unions in this country, but they have learned to encourage and protect these schools as their best friends. Labor leaders of known ability and probity are elected by the unions as advisory committees to the Boards of Education in all matters that concern these schools. This brings the labor unions into close and friendly relation to the industrial school, and nothing is done without first seeking the advice and opinion of the labor union committee. On the other hand, many of the largest employers of labor are invited by the Board of Education to sit at the conferences between the Board of Education and the labor advisors, and a genuine feeling of fraternity is developed which tends to co-operation and is of the greatest advantage in tightening the friendly relations between labor and capital.

As an illustration of the friendly co-operation of unions in the matter of technical education, permit me to quote what the general secretary of the Machinists' Union of France says:

"There was a time when trade unions were opposed to the schools. That opposition, however, came from a misunderstanding of their intended scope. It has been totally effaced, and now we look upon the schools and instructors as our best friends, and the graduates as the greatest assets of our trade unions, since they enable us to select from our ranks the best artisans obtainable. One is able to get an idea of how much sought after these graduates are, when he learns that there are more than 20,000 machinists employed in the construction of high-class automobiles alone in the Department of the Seine, and many thousands in the construction of locomotives, not to speak of the great numbers engaged in the various other branches of the machine industry of the very highest class.

"For the various schools we appoint members of our organization to act as advisory and visiting members of boards of control; thus we are kept in touch with the school and its work, and are bound to keep the standard the very highest."

As a further illustration let me quote what the general secretary of the Printing Trades of France says:

"I believe we may be justly proud of our schools of printing, and we have perfect confidence in the ability of the director. Personally, I have given much time to the students, and am ever ready to assist in the maintenance of the highest standard of excellence of equipment and instruction. You are aware, no doubt, that the seventeen trades comprising the printing industry have in France the foundation for the attainment of the highest intelligence. Thus our schools are called upon to supply the several trades with most efficient artisans; and that they do this we are bound to believe, for we are receiving the best wage and the shortest day of any craft in France.

"As you probably know, we have the best school of printing in existence today, with all the modern types of machines and every facility for instruction. There is no doubt that as artisans we compare favorably with those of any other country. We take great pride in assisting the apprentices from these schools, both educationally and industrially."

On the subject of technical education, President Roosevelt says:

"No industrial school can turn out a finished journeyman; but it can furnish the material out of which a finished journeyman can be made, just as an engineering school furnishes the training which enables its graduates speedily to become engineers.

"We hear a great deal of the need of protecting our workmen from competition with pauper labor. I have very little fear of the competition of pauper labor. The nations with pauper labor are not the formidable industrial competitors of this country. What the American workingman has to fear is the competition of the highly skilled workingman of the countries of greatest industrial efficiency. By the tariff and by our immigration laws we can always protect ourselves against the competition of pauper labor here at home; but when we contend for the markets of the world we can get no protection, and we shall then find that our most formidable competitors are the nations in which there is the most highly developed business ability, the most highly developed industrial skill; and these are the qualities which we must ourselves develop."

* * * * * *

"The calling of the skilled tiller of the soil, the calling of the skilled mechanic, should alike be recognized as professions, just as emphatically as the callings of lawyer, of doctor, of banker, merchant, or clerk. The printer, the electrical worker, the house painter, the foundry man, should be trained just as carefully as the stenographer or drug clerk. They should be trained alike in head and in hand. They should get over the idea that to earn twelve dollars a week and call it 'salary' is better than to earn twenty-five dollars a week and call it 'wages.'

* * * * * *

"I am glad that societies have already been formed to promote industrial education, and that their membership includes manufacturers and leaders of labor unions, educators and publicists, men of all conditions, who are interested in education and in industry. It is such co-operation that offers most hope for a satisfactory solution of the question as to what is the best form of industrial school, as to the means by which it may be articulated with the public school system, and as to the way to secure for the boys trained therein the opportunity to acquire in the industries the practical skill which alone can make them finished journeymen."

I plead for more technical schools for the good of my State, believing that we need them to develop the men who do things, the men who move forward and revolutionize things and work the wonders of modern civilization. Men skilled in the trades and possessing a knowledge of the sciences underlying their particular art or craft, possess independence of thought, and an initiative which directs them toward the development of new creations and new inventions, thereby preventing and controlling over-production in the existing fields.

This report is based on personal observation and inquiry, and is the result of my deep interest in the cause of industrial and vocational training. I trust the study of this report will result in bearing good fruit and in improving our educational work in San Francisco. We cannot close our eyes to the fact that our Spanish-American trade is slowly but surely slipping away from us. That German, English and French commerce and manufactures are acquiring a foothold in neighboring Spanish America, and supplanting American trade to such an extent that unless we do something, and do it now, we will lose the rich trade of our neighbors. We must act. We must employ all the means at our disposal while it is yet time. We must educate our rising generation in the commercial and technical arts and crafts.

Power and superiority must incontestably belong to the most energetic, intelligent and highly skilled people, whose spirit of initiative is the best developed. It is only through technical and vocational schools that we can develop the skill to defend our threatened industries in the markets of the world, and keep our country in the first rank of the great nations. The successful German invasion of the world's markets, which bids fair to completely displace the influence of other nations, is the logical outcome of the greater average efficiency of her workmen. Their energy, patience, activity, and spirit of enterprise are remarkable, and at the pace they are going they will soon succeed in obtaining the commercial supremacy of the chief markets of the world.

We in the United States are facing the grandest future of any country on the globe. With no traditions to hinder us or wed us to conservatism, we should take advantage of our patrimony by enlarging the scope of our education and make it include the utilitarian "bread and butter" subjects of education, in order that we may forever lead all the nations of the earth. I appeal to the patriotism and intelligence of the members of the Board of Supervisors, the labor unions, the mercantile and manufacturing interests, and all the civic bodies of San Francisco. I appeal to all to give heed to the call for funds to build and properly equip our Polytechnical High school and such other technical schools as may be established. Owing to the complex nature of modern life and its industries, I am firmly convinced that to develop the whole man education must have an industrial basis as well as a moral one.

I respectfully submit this report to the kind attention of all who are interested in the development of technical education, the prosperity of our industries, and the consequent greatness of our City, State and Nation.

Respectfully yours,

ALFRED RONCOVIERI,

Superintendent of Schools.

LIST OF SCHOOLS AND TEACHERS.

Name.	Grade of Class.	When Elected.	Grade of Certificate	Salary per Year.
[illegible] [illegible]olitan [illegible] School—				
McFarland, [illegible]iss H. F.	Principal	Nov. 30, 1877	Grammar	2, [illegible]60.00
[illegible]is, [illegible]s H.	V. P., 8th	May 13, 1873	[illegible]	1,620.00
Fairchild, [illegible]iss M. E.	[illegible]th	July 1, 1874	High	1,224.00
Doughty, [illegible]ry A.	Seventh	Oct. 31, 1891	Grammar	1,164.00
Coons, Sarah S.	[illegible]th	Sept. 1, 1888	[illegible]ar	1,224.00
Dolan, Mrs. C. M.	Sixth	Aug. 16, 1898	[illegible]ar	1,164.00
Hesselmeyer, Miss C. A.	Sixth	Feb 11, 1892	[illegible]mar	1,104.00
Grozelier, [illegible]iss A. M.	Fifth	Sept. 29, 1892	[illegible]ar	1,200.00
Littlefield, Eleanor A.	Fourth	June 15, 1866	Grammar	1,104.00
Hurley, Mamie E.	Third	Sept. 10, 1884	Grammar	1,164.00
Houston, Miss M. J.	Second	April 2, 1881	[illegible]	1,224.00
Jacobs, E.	Fourth	Aug. 20, 1907	High	1,200.00
Agassiz Primary—				
Jones, Miss S. J.	Principal	April 1, 1878	Grammar	2, [illegible]60.00
Harney, Miss A.	First	July 31, 1889	[illegible]	1,224.00
Brown, Miss R. F.	F[illegible]h	July 18, 1902	[illegible]ar	1,164.00
Glidden, Miss C. A.	Fifth	July 9, 1877	[illegible]ar	1,164.00
[illegible]n, Ada M.	Fifth	Oct. 9, 1883	[illegible]ar	1,224.00
Clausen, Miss E. A.	[illegible]h	Jan. 31, 1894	Grammar	1,104.00
Bartlett, Miss O. S.	Fourth	Jan. 31, 1894	[illegible]ar	1,104.00
[illegible]le, Miss O. C.	Fourth	[illegible] 1, 1905	[illegible]ar	[illegible]84.00
Rixon, Eliza A.	Fourth	Feb. 28, 1898	[illegible]ar	1,104.00
Fredericks, Miss E. L.	Third	Feb. 16, 1891	[illegible]	1,104.00
[illegible]y, [illegible]iss R. F.	Third	Oct. 23, 1901	[illegible]ar	1,032.00
Hanson, Miss L.	Third	July 20, 1903	Grammar	1, [illegible]
[illegible]t, Miss H.	Second	Dec. 1, 1890	Primary	1,224.00
[illegible]n, Miss A. M.	Second	Jan. 6, 1902	Grammar	1,032.00
Liner, [illegible]iss M. G.	Second	July 27, 1898	Grammar	1,224.00
Maloney, Miss K. A.	First	Jan. 10, 1881	Grammar	1,224.00
B[illegible]y, Miss M. R.	First	Nov. 11, 1890	Grammar	1,224.00
Sankey, Miss M. F.	First	Sept. 15, 1888	[illegible]ar	1,224.00
Burnett Primary—				
McElroy, Miss L.	Principal	Dec. 6, 1891	Grammar	1,860.00
Flynn, Miss M. E.	Fourth	Nov. 20, 1877	Primary	1,104.00
Schroeder, Miss S.	Second	Aug. 26, 1907	High	900.00
Curtis, Miss C. M.	First	July 6, 1882	Grammar	1,224.00
Hopkins, Mrs. J. M.	Second	May 15, 1905	[illegible]ar	1,104.00

Name	Grade	Date of appointment	Certificate	Salary
Gannon, Mrs. M. F.	[illegible]rst	July 6, 1877	[illegible]ar	1,224.00
McGorey, Miss S.	Second	Feb. 12, 1890	Grammar	1,104.00
Woelffel, Miss E.	Second	Aug. 3, 1908	Grammar	1,008.00
Kean, Miss J. I.	First	Aug. 7, 1888	Grammar	1,224.00
Bernal [illegible]—				
Regan, Miss A. G.	Principal	Oct. 5, 1887	Grammar	2,400.00
McGivern, Miss K. A.	V. P., Eighth	Oct. 13, 1892	[illegible]ar	1,620.00
Scott, Mrs. E.	[illegible]ed	July 15, 1897	Grammar	1,188.00
Schendel, Miss A.	Seventh	Sept. 27, 1880	[illegible]ar	1,244.00
Douglass, M. Louise	Sixth	[illegible]g. 30, 1905	[illegible]ar	1,158.00
Neppert, Miss L. C.	Sixth	Dec. 29, 1892	Grammar	1,164.00
[illegible]e, Miss M.	Fifth	Feb. 9, 1892	[illegible]ar	1,164.00
Maxwell, Miss E.	Fifth	April 26, 1907	High	984.00
Benjamin, Miss M. C.	Fourth	Aug. 26, 1903	Grammar	1,044.00
[illegible]n, Sarah S.	Fourth	July 2, 1889	[illegible]ar	1,104.00
[illegible]bby, Georgie F.	Third	Sept. 23, 1878	[illegible]ar	1,[illegible]04.00
McCarthy, Miss M. C.	Thi[illegible]d	[illegible]t. 23, 1901	[illegible]ar	1,032.00
Folsom, Miss M. L.	Thi[illegible]d	Nov. 18, 1896	Grammar	1,104.00
Gilchrist, [illegible]iss C. H.	Seventh	Sept. 15, 1901	[illegible]ar	1,224.00
Madden, Miss E. L.	Third	July 27, 1898	[illegible]ar	1,104.00
McGraw, Miss M.	[illegible]th	Aug. 3, 1908	[illegible]ar	1,104.00
Bergerot Primary—				
Gavigan, Miss A. E.	Principal	July 20, 1875	Grammar	1,860.00
[illegible]s, [illegible]iss E.	Eighth	April 5, 1883	[illegible]	1,284.00
Oliver, Miss M. D.	Seventh	June 26, 1905	Grammar	1,164.00
Fairweather, Helen B.	Fifth	May 16, 1882	Grammar	1,104.00
[illegible]s, Isabel	Sixth	J[illegible]ne 21, 1904	High	1,032.00
[illegible]n, Mrs. J. D.	Fifth	Jan. 27, 1886	[illegible]ar	1,104.00
Cassidy, Miss V.	Fourth	Aug. 10, 1897	Grammar	1,104.00
Hanlon, Miss L. R.	F[illegible]st	Oct. 1, 1884	[illegible]ar	1,224.00
Loewi, Miss M.	First	Jan. 26, 1898	Grammar	1,224.00
[illegible]ll, [illegible]iss A. F.	First	Sept. 1, 1897	[illegible]ar	1,224.00
Savage, Miss D. A.	Sixth	June 21, 1904	[illegible]ar	1,044.00
Hawthorne, Miss M. E.	Sixth	Jan. 8, 1908	[illegible]ar	912.00
Waters, Mrs. K.	[illegible]th	[illegible]v. 1, 1875	L. D. High	1,164.00
[illegible]n, M. A.	Third	Aug. 2, 1871	[illegible]ar	1,104.00
Lynch, Miss Florence	First	Sept. 22, 1905	[illegible]ar	1,044.00
Bryant Cosmopolitan School—				
Kelly, Miss E. E.	Principal	Oct. 5, 1887	Grammar	1,680.00
Giffard, Mrs. E. C.	French	Feb. 25, 1876	Special [illegible]h	1,200.00
Stanford, Miss B. M.	[illegible]h	Jan. 11, 1877	[illegible]ar	1,164.00
Rutherford, Miss H. M.	Fifth	Nov. 7, 1888	[illegible]ar	1,104.00
Kulmuk, Miss L.	French, Third	July 22, 1886	G[illegible]ar	1,[illegible]04.00
Curry, Miss M. E.	Second	Feb. 5, 1878	[illegible]ar	1,104.00

LIST OF SCHOOLS AND TEACHERS—Continued.

Name.	Grade of Class.	When Elected.	Grade of Certificate	Salary per Year
Bryant Cosmopolitan School—Continued				
M[illegible]y, Miss F. C.	First	Aug. 28, 1883	Grammar	1,224.00
Heineberg, Miss L.	First	Aug. 15, 1873	Grammar	1,224.00
Roberts, Miss M. E.	First	July 14, 1871	Grammar	1,224.00
Koch, Miss L. H.	Third	Oct. 31, 1894	Grammar	1,104.00
Unger, Miss A. N.	First	Aug. 20, 1878	Grammar	1,224.00
Duffy, Miss H. M.	Fifth	July 1, 1903	Grammar	1,104.00
Cassamayou, Miss A.	Second	Aug. 3, 1908	Grammar	840.00
Wing, Miss M. G.	German	Mar. 8, 1906	High	1,200.00
Buena Vista Primary—				
Catlin, Miss A. G.	Principal	Mar. 5, 1878	Grammar	1,860.00
Hunt, Charlotte F.	Third	Oct. 28, 1892	Grammar	1,104.00
Lewis, Miss R. P.	Fourth	Mar. 14, 1886	Grammar	1,104.00
Paxton, Miss K. R.	Fourth	July 22, 1896	Grammar	1,104.00
Hilderth, Mrs. O.	Second	Nov. 11, 1896	Grammar	1,104.00
[illegible], Emma	Second	Jan. 1, 1887	Grammar	1,104.00
Frank, Miss J. E.	Third	Dec. 13, 1896	Grammar	1,104.00
Fleming, Miss M. R.	First	Nov. 14, 1896	Grammar	1,224.00
Rollins, Miss M. A.	First	Oct. 8, 1879	Grammar	1,224.00
S[illegible]k, Rose M.	First	Feb. 23, 1898	Grammar	1,224.00
[illegible]er, Miss B. H.	First	Aug. 5, 1888	Grammar	1,224.00
Bay View Grammar—				
Prior, Philip	Principal	June 14, 1865	High	2,400.00
McGuire, Miss B. A.	V. P., Eighth	Oct. 16, 1883	Grammar	1,680.00
Stolz, Miss R. C.	Seventh	Dec. 28, 1892	Grammar	1,224.00
Hanford, Miss E. V.	Seventh	Sept. 1, 1886	Grammar	1,224.00
[illegible]y, Miss M.	Sixth	Sept. 30, 1884	Grammar	1,164.00
Perkins, Miss A. F.	Fifth	Nov. 1, 1890	Grammar	1,164.00
Fitzgerald, Mrs. M. T.	Fifth	Aug. 19, 1907	Grammar	1,164.00
[illegible]r, [illegible]n	First	[illegible] 2, 1905	Grammar	1,224.00
Sleeper, Miss Mary	Third	Nov. 18, 1873	Grammar	1,104.00
Piper, Miss L. K.	Fourth	July 19, 1885	Grammar	1,104.00
Bailie, Miss M.	Fourth	June 9, 1897	Grammar	1,104.00
[illegible]n, Miss A. A.	Fifth	Jan. 16, 1903	Grammar	1,164.00
Boylan, M. L.	Fourth	Jan. 12, 1898	Grammar	1,104.00
Clement Primary—				
Quinlan, Mrs. F. L.	Principal	Aug. 10, 1898	Grammar	1,620.00
Bronson, Mrs. F. P.	First	Sept. 1, 1884	High	1,224.00
[illegible]y, Miss M. E.	Second	Aug. 7, 1893	Grammar	1,104.00
Cohen, Miss Rose	Fourth	Jan. 3, 1889	Grammar	1,104.00

Mayers, Mss Eliz.	Third	Jan. [illegible], 1886	Grammar	1,104.00
Cooke, Edith A.	First	Mar. 1, 1903	[illegible]mar	1,224.00
[illegible]ll, Miss A.	Fourth	July 6, 1905	Grammar	1,032.00
[illegible]n, Miss E.	Third	Aug. 23, 1880	[illegible]mar	1,104.00
Hansell, [illegible] M.	Second	Aug. 9, 1897	[illegible]mar	1,104.00
O'Connor, Miss E.	Second	Jan. 6, 1908	Grammar	900.00
D'Or, Miss M.	First	Sept. 30, 1901	Grammar	1,224.00
Cl [illegible]d Primary—				
Parolini, Mrs. M. J.	Principal	Mar. 1, 1866	L. D. High	1,866.00
Davis, [illegible] F. V.	Third	Jan. 15, 1884	Primary	1,[illegible]04.00
Green, Mrs. A. H.	Fourth	July 3, 1873	[illegible]mar	1,104.00
Cove, Miss E. A.	Second	Dec. 28, 1880	[illegible]mar	1,104.00
Turney, Mrs. K.	Second	Dec. 14, 1890	Primary	1,104.00
Lytton, Mrs. I. M.	First	July 28, 1898	[illegible]r	1,224.00
Ward, Miss S. A.	First	Oct. 30, 1894	Grammar	1,224.00
[illegible]ley, Miss A.	First	Oct. 21, 1873	[illegible]mar	1,224.00
Col [illegible]ia Grammar—				
Burke, Mrs. L. K.	Principal	Jan. 23, 1857	High	2,700.00
McGeough, Miss K.	V. P., Eighth	Jan. 12, 1898	[illegible]mar	1,560.00
[illegible]n, Miss M. L.	Eighth	[illegible]g. 13, 1892	[illegible]mar	1,224.00
Krauss, Miss L. H.	Seventh	Sept. 4, 1890	[illegible]mar	1,224.00
Derrick, Miss A. L.	Seventh	June 24, 1884	[illegible]mar	1,224.00
Simon, Mrs. M.	Sixth	Jan. 29, 1877	[illegible]mar	1,164.00
Canar, Mrs. E. R.	Sixth	Nov. 5, 1897	[illegible]mar	1,224.00
Doherty, Miss M. E.	Sixth	Oct. 29, 1891	Grammar	1,164.00
[illegible]es, Miss [illegible]d L.	Fifth	Nov. 1, 1904	[illegible]mar	1,164.00
Love, [illegible]ne S.	Fourth	Oct. 19, 1875	[illegible]mar	1,104.00
[illegible]ay, Miss M.	Fifth	July 14, 1895	Grammar	1,164.00
Stewart, Miss V.	Third	Mar. 15, 1884	Grammar	1,044.00
Lyons, Miss K. G.	[illegible]th	Dec. 20, 1896	[illegible]mar	1,164.00
McKee, Eva M.	First	Sept. 14, 1892	[illegible]mar	1,224.00
Boland, Joanna M.	First	Sept. 18, 1875	[illegible]mar	1,224.00
Connell, Mary I.	First	Mar. 1, 1873	[illegible]mar	1,224.00
Brown, Mrs. [illegible]ie M.	First	[illegible]. 13, 1871	Grammar	1,224.00
Blumenthal, Miss A. A.	Sixth	Jan. 13, 1892	[illegible]mar	1,164.00
Malarin, M.	Spanish	June 3, 1908	[illegible]mar	1,200.00
Cooper Primary—				
O'Connell, Miss A. M.	Principal	Sept. 16, 1884	Grammar	1,620.00
Murray, Miss M. G.	Second	Nov. 11, 1907	[illegible]r	840.00
Hackett, Mrs. E. S.	First	Oct. 1873	[illegible]mar	1,224.00
Paterson, Miss M.	First	Aug. 14, 1905	[illegible]mar	1,224.00
Roden, Miss L.	F[illegible]st	[illegible]g. 1905	[illegible]mar	1,224.00
Gleason, Miss C. Z.	Second	Sept. 1, 1905	[illegible]mar	1,224.00
Moore, Eliz. B.	First	Sept. 30, 1901	[illegible]mar	1,224.00

LIST OF SCHOOLS AND TEACHERS—Continued.

Name.	Grade of Class.	When Elected.	Grade of Certificate	Salary per Year.
Cooper Primary—Continued.				
[illegible]g, Dorothy	Second	Oct. 14, [illegible]2	[illegible]ar	1,224.00
Miel, Mrs. M. E.	Second	Mar. 1, 1900	Primary	1,104.00
Deal, Miss V. V.	Second	Dec. 30, 1892	Grammar	1,224.00
[illegible]d, Mrs. I. C.	First	Dec. 1, 1882	Grammar	1,224.00
[illegible]r Grammar—				
Mark, Mr. C. W.	Principal	[illegible]ly 10, 1893	High	2,340.00
[illegible]y, [illegible]te	Seventh	Dec. 20, 1890	[illegible]mar	1,224.00
[illegible]a, [illegible]iss M. T.	V. P., Eighth	July [illegible], 1876	Grammar	1,620.00
Folsom, Miss S. A.	Eighth	[illegible]g. 23, 1880	Grammar	1,224.00
[illegible]n, Miss Elvira	[illegible]th	April 3, 1883	Grammar	1,224.00
Smith, Miss E. E.	Eighth	[illegible]. 7, 1895	Grammar	1,224.00
Harby, Miss R.	[illegible]th	May 5, 1879	Grammar	1,224.00
Durkin, Miss J. L. F.	[illegible]h	[illegible]g. 1, 1882	Grammar	1,224.00
Barrett, Miss [illegible]y A.	Seventh	Sept. 2, 1896	[illegible]r	1,224.00
[illegible]w, [illegible]s M. M.	[illegible]h	Nov. 29, 1896	[illegible]r	1,224.00
Armstrong, [illegible]iss N.	Seventh	Dec. 26, 1877	Grammar	1,224.00
Burke, Miss [illegible]h T.	Seventh	April 3, 1892	[illegible]r	1,224.00
Murphy, [illegible]ie L.	Seventh	Nov. 4, 1886	Grammar	1,224.00
Saalburg, [illegible]iss J. E.	Sixth	Dec. 5, 1889	Grammar	1,164.00
Carpenter, [illegible]iss E.	[illegible]th	July 6, 1905	Grammar	1,164.00
[illegible]n, Frances E.	Sixth	Dec. 14, 1877	Grammar	1,164.00
Roberts, Miss B. E.	Sixth	Jan. 2, 1902	Grammar	1,074.00
Hefron, Miss Helen	Sixth	April 2, 1886	[illegible]r	1,164.00
[illegible]g, [illegible]iss B.	Sixth	June 23, 1904	[illegible]r	1,164.00
[illegible]n, [illegible]ss Mary T.	F[illegible]th	Dec. 10, 1890	[illegible]ar	1,164.00
English, Virginia L.	[illegible]d	Aug. 11, 1897	Grammar	1,136.00
Denman Grammar—				
[illegible]n, Azro L.	Principal	Dec. 29, 1865	High	2,160.00
Smith, Jessie	Eighth	Mar. 10, 1863	High	1,224.00
[illegible]lds, Miss K. B.	Seventh	July 5, 1866	[illegible]r	1,224.00
D'Arcy, Miss A. M.	Fifth	July , 1870	[illegible]r	1,[illegible]64.00
Hazleton, Miss R. H.	Ungraded	April 6, 1873	[illegible]r	1,224.00
Mandeville, Miss K.	Sixth	Aug. 10, 1885	[illegible]r	1,164.00
Douglass Primary—				
Tarpy, [illegible]iss W. L.	Principal	Aug. 19, 1884	Grammar	1,860.00
Hetzer, Miss M.	Fourth	Sept. 12, 1894	Grammar	1,104.00
Bishop, Louise M.	Fourth	Sept. 8, 1897	Grammar	1,104.00
[illegible]y, [illegible]iss A. G.	Second	April 1, 1903	[illegible]ar	1,008.00

Name	Grade	Date	Certificate	Salary
[illegible]n, Miss E.	Third	Nov. 11, 1896	[illegible]ar	1,164.00
Doherty, Miss M. A.	Second	June 9, 1897	Grammar	1,104.00
Reichling, Miss W. L.	[illegible]d	[illegible] 6, 1902	[illegible]ar	1,104.00
[illegible]h, Miss E. S.	First	Oct. 1, 1905	Grammar	1,224.00
Parks, Miss M. R.	First	Sept. 15, 1891	Grammar	1,224.00
[illegible], Miss L.	First	July 15, 1902	[illegible]ar	1,224.00
Sullivan, Miss E. G.	Third	Jan. 12, 1898	[illegible]ar	1,104.00
[illegible]on, Miss A. J.	Second	Sept. 11, 1907	Grammar	900.00
Brown, Miss M. L.	First	July 30, 1886	Grammar	1,224.00
Dudley Stone Primary—				
[illegible]e, Miss S. H.	Principal	July 20, 1869	High	2,160.00
[illegible]an, Bertha K.	Third	Feb. 1, 1904	[illegible]ar	1,1[illegible]4.00
Sexton, Miss J. L.	Fifth	Sept. 12, 1894	[illegible]ar	1,284.00
Carew, Miss M. R.	First	Sept. 20, 1894	[illegible]ar	1,224.00
Hare, Miss F.	Fifth	[illegible] 21, 1873	Grammar	1,[illegible]64.00
[illegible]n, Miss M. L.	[illegible]th	Sept. 15, 1885	[illegible]ar	1,[illegible]64.00
[illegible]h, Miss L.	[illegible]th	[illegible]b. 11, 1903	[illegible]ar	1,008.00
McBoyle, Miss A. B.	[illegible]th	Sept. 30, 1892	[illegible]ar	1,104.00
[illegible], Miss L.	Third	Nov. 11, 1896	[illegible]ar	1,104.00
Dwyer, Miss M. C.	[illegible]d	Sept. 1, 1897	Grammar	1,104.00
[illegible]tz, Miss N. R.	Second	[illegible] 12, 1898	Primary	1,104.00
[illegible]tz, Miss L. M.	Second	[illegible]ly 1, 1903	[illegible]ar	[illegible]84.00
Cullen, Miss J. A.	First	Nov. 1, 1883	Grammar	1,224.00
[illegible]h, Miss R.	First	Jan. 31, 1884	[illegible]ar	1,224.00
[illegible]m, [illegible] W. D.	Ungraded	June 14, 1903	[illegible]ar	1,224.00
[illegible]s, Miss M. A.	Third	July 27, 1908	Grammar	1,224.00
Edison Primary—				
[illegible]s, Miss J.	[illegible]pal	[illegible]ril 23, 1887	[illegible]ar	1,800.00
Hucks, Miss A. E.	Third	Nov. 3, 1864	Grammar	1,104.00
K[illegible]ly, [illegible]ss M. C.	[illegible]th	Dec 8, 1891	Grammar	1,164.00
Barry, Miss M. E.	[illegible]th	April 1, 1884	[illegible]ar	1,[illegible]64.00
Power, Miss A. R.	Fourth	Feb. 24, 1898	Grammar	1,104.00
Booth, Miss L.	Fourth	Feb. 1, 1889	[illegible]ar	1,104.00
Wilson, Miss E. N.	[illegible]rd	July 18, 1902	[illegible]ar	1,008.00
Harrigan, Miss A. M.	Second	Sept. 19, 1891	[illegible]ar	1,104.00
Robinett, [illegible]ss M. M.	First	Feb. 5, 1875	[illegible]ar	1,224.00
McDermott, [illegible]s C. M.	Second	Nov. 30, 1892	Grammar	1,164.00
Steele, [illegible]ss M. A.	First	Sept. 14, 1872	[illegible]ar	1,224.00
Emerson Primary—				
Spencer, Mrs. T. F.	[illegible]pal	July 17, 1901	[illegible]ar	1,944.00
Ephriam, Miss J.	o[illegible]th	July 23, [illegible]76	[illegible]ar	1,104.00
Dennis, Miss E.	First	Dec. 5, 1888	[illegible]ar	1,224.00
L[illegible]in, Miss A. M.	First	J[illegible]y 6, 1877	[illegible]ar	1,224.00
Tiling, Miss A.	Second	Sept. 8, 1897	Grammar	1,104.00

LIST OF SCHOOLS AND TEACHERS—Continued.

Name.	Grade of Class.	When Elected.	Grade of Certificate.	Salary per Year.
Emerson Primary—Continued.				
Kurlandzik, Miss R.	Second	Jan. 14, 1903	High	1,032.00
[illegible], Miss A. G.	Third	Sept. 10, 1897	Grammar	1,[illegible]04.00
Bailey, Miss C. B.	Third	Sept. 13, [illegible]94	Grammar	1,104.00
Nelson, Miss M. F.	[illegible]th	May 13, [illegible]96	[illegible]ar	1,104.00
Gambitz, Miss L. B.	Fourth	May 27, 1897	[illegible]	1,104.00
[illegible], Miss M. A.	Fifth	Mar. 12, 1890	Grammar	1,164.00
O'Brien, Miss L.	First	Mar. 12, 1890	Grammar	1,224.00
[illegible], Miss R.	First	Nov. 22, 1884	Grammar	1,224.00
Spafford, Miss D. B.	Third	Jan. 8, 1906	Grammar	1,[illegible]04.00
Mordecai, Miss C.	Third	Jan. 25, 1905	[illegible]ar	1,[illegible]04.00
Estes, Miss C.	Second	Oct. 14, 1907	[illegible]ar	840.00
[illegible]tt Grammar—				
Sturges, Selden	Principal	July 6, 1875	Grammar	2,220.00
Lindberg, Emily U.	Eighth	Sept. 6, 1874	Grammar	1,224.00
Theisen, Miss A. J.	Seventh	Dec. 20, 1892	Grammar	1,224.00
[illegible], Miss M. E.	Sixth	July 14, 1895	Grammar	1,164.00
Johnson, Marie J.	Sixth	Feb. 1, 1876	Grammar	1,1[illegible]4.00
Grimm, Miss A. L.	Fifth	Feb. 14, 1881	Grammar	1,164.00
Casassa, Miss R. I.	Fifth	July 27, 1898	Grammar	1,164.00
Sullivan, Julia F.	Fifth	Aug. 1, 1897	Grammar	1,164.00
Perl, [illegible] May	Fifth	Nov. 11, 1896	Grammar	1,1[illegible]4.00
Fenton, Miss E. R.	Third	July 27, 1898	Grammar	1,[illegible]04.00
Spafford, [illegible] E.	Second	Jan. 8, 1902	Grammar	1,[illegible]04.00
Morse, Miss N. A.	Second	July 30, 1890	Grammar	1,[illegible]04.00
Gracier, Miss A. J.	First	July 8, 1877	Grammar	1,224.00
Quinn, Miss A. W.	Seventh	Jan. 3, 1893	Grammar	1,224.00
[illegible], Mrs. K. J.	First	April 3, 1887	Grammar	1,224.00
[illegible], Mrs. M.	Eighth	April 10, 1885	Grammar	1,560.00
Wheeler, Miss C.	Sixth	Nov. 1, [illegible]05	Grammar	1,164.00
Moore, Miss M.	Ungraded	April 5, 1883	Grammar	1,224.00
Fairmount Grammar—				
De Bell, Mr. W. H.	Principal	July 19, 1901	[illegible]	2,400.00
[illegible]ond, Miss E. E.	Seventh	Dec. 1, 1882	Grammar	1,224.00
Berard, Miss E. L.	Eighth	Sept. 30, [illegible]01	Grammar	1,116.00
McCauley, Miss M. A.	Seventh	Aug. 11, 1897	Grammar	1,224.00
[illegible], Miss D. A.	Sixth	April 21, 1891	Grammar	1,164.00
Hortop, Miss C. E.	Fifth	Aug. 26, 1903	[illegible]ar	1,014.00
Millhone, Belle	Fifth	July 27, [illegible]	[illegible]ar	1,[illegible]64.00
[illegible], Miss K. L.	Fourth	Feb. 23, 1898	[illegible]ar	1,[illegible]04.00

Name	Grade	Date of birth	Certificate	Salary
Chandler, Miss M. G.	Third	Mar. 1, 1904	Grammar	1,104.00
Provost, Miss T. E.	Second	April 14, 1875	Grammar	1,104.00
O'Brien, Miss M. F.	Fourth	Nov. 19, 1905	Grammar	930.00
Foley, Miss Mary W.	First	Jan. 27, 1905	Grammar	1,224.00
Barry, Miss A. P.	First	Sept. 21, 1886	Grammar	1,224.00
Carey, Miss A. A.	First	Sept. 15, 1882	Grammar	1,224.00
Shuck, Mr. L. M.	Sixth	July 10, 1889	High	1,800.00
[illegible], Miss K. R.	Sixth	July 18, 1902	Grammar	1,164.00
Grant, Miss E. W.	Fifth	Mar. 30, 1905	Grammar	1,164.00
[illegible], Miss N. T.	Third	Dec. 23, 1903	Grammar	984.00
Crowley, Miss N. T.	Second	July 26, 1897	Grammar	1,104.00
McCarthy, Miss M. G.	First	Oct. 23, 1901	Grammar	1,224.00
Frank J. [illegible] Primary—				
[illegible], Miss S. B.	Principal	Oct. 21, 1877	Grammar	1,860.00
Barber, Miss E. J.	Fifth	Mar. 1, 1884	Grammar	1,164.00
Higby, Miss S. L.	Fourth	Mar. 6, 1905	Grammar	1,030.00
Jacobs, Miss H. H.	Third	Sept. 1, 1905	High	1,080.00
O'Neil, Miss M. E.	Third	Sept. 14, 1898	Grammar	1,032.00
Hart, Miss E. I.	Second	July 18, 1902	High	1,008.00
Coggin, Miss E. M.	Second	Nov. 28, 1881	Primary	1,1 4000
Wright, Mrs. M. S.	First	July 1, 1871	Grammar	1,224.00
Wade, Miss L. M.	First	July 30, 1886	Grammar	1,224.00
Fay, Miss M. A.	First	Mar. 11, 1873	Grammar	1,224.00
Franklin Grammar—				
[illegible], Mrs. N. A.	Principal	Nov. 13, 1866	High	2,160.[illegible]
[illegible], Miss J. C.	V. P., Eighth	Sept. 11, 1895	Grammar	1,560.00
Harris, Miss R. S.	[illegible]	Mar. 30, 19[illegible]	Grammar	1,224.00
McCullough, Miss M. J.	Fifth	Aug. 22, 1907	Grammar	984.00
[illegible], Etta O.	Fifth	Jan. 26, 1906	Grammar	1,164.00
Carroll, Miss A. T.	Fourth	June 25, 1905	Grammar	960.00
Cadwalder, Miss E.	Second	June 21, 1895	Grammar	1,164.00
Roper, Miss B.	First	Nov. 23, 1869	Grammar	1,224.00
Dunn, Miss C. E.	First	Oct. 22, 1884	Grammar	1,224.[illegible]
McIntyre, Miss J. L.	Sixth	Oct. 2, 1905	Grammar	1,164.00
Browne, Frank J.	Sixth	Sept. 13, 1904	High	1,164.00
Coyle, Miss M. G.	Third	Dec. 5, 1892	Grammar	1,104.00
[illegible], Miss Etta F.	Third	June 15, 1908	Grammar	930.00
Fremont Grammar—				
Goldsmith, Miss R.	Principal	Mar. 1, 1875	Grammar	2400.00
Ostrom, Mrs. I. D.	V. P., Eighth	Aug. 10, 1898	Grammar	1,560.00
McKown, Mrs. M. E.	Seventh	April 14, 1869	High	1,224.00
Hanley, [illegible] B.	Ungraded	Sept. 30, 1890	Grammar	1,224.00
Rosenfeld, Miss F.	First	Aug. 1, 1888	Grammar	1,224.00
M[illegible]unt, Miss S. F.	First	Jan. 31, 1889	Grammar	1,224.[illegible]

LIST OF SCHOOLS AND TEACHERS—Continued.

Name.	Grade of Class.	When Elected.	Grade of Certificate	Salary per Year.
Fremont Grammar—Continued.				
Luis, Mrs. R.	Second	Sept. 27, 1880	Primary	1,104.00
MacNichol, Mrs. J. E.	Second	Oct. 27, 1897	Grammar	1,224.00
Lewis, Rose F.	Fourth	July 28, 1898	Grammar	1,104.00
[illegible], Miss B.	Third	Feb. 15, 1876	Grammar	1,104.00
Shorb, Mrs. M. E.	Fourth	Oct. 21, 1901	Grammar	992.00
Langstadter, Pauline	Fifth	Aug. 13, 1872	Grammar	1,064.00
[illegible], Miss M. C.	Sixth	July 18, 1902	Grammar	1,074.00
[illegible], Miss L. M.	Sixth	April 9, 1875	Grammar	1,164.00
Grant, Mrs. K. D.	Eighth	June 3, 1897	Grammar	1,224.00
[illegible], E. T.	Fifth	Oct. 17, 1904	Grammar	1,044.00
McGough, R. M.	Third	Jan. 31, 1884	Grammar	1,080.00
Garfield Primary—				
Scherer, Miss M. A.	Principal	Aug. 7, 1879	Grammar	2,160.00
Bradley, Mrs. A.	First	Oct. 27, 1882	Grammar	1,224.00
[illegible], Mrs. F. R.	First	July 27, 1898	Grammar	1,224.00
Powers, Mrs. M. B.	First	Sept. 2, 1885	Grammar	1,224.00
[illegible], Miss E.	First	Jan. 29, 1905	Grammar	1,284.00
[illegible], [illegible] E.	Fourth	Feb. 1, 1905	Grammar	1,104.00
Klein, Miss M. G.	Third	Jan. 6, 1902	Grammar	1,080.00
[illegible], Miss M. A.	Fourth	Nov. 4, 1891	Primary	1,104.00
[illegible], [illegible]	First	Oct. 17, 1904	High	1,272.00
Rea, Miss B.	Second	Jan. 6, 1908	Grammar	930.00
[illegible], Miss N. V.	Third	Mar. 20, 1907	Grammar	1,104.00
Busch, Miss E. E.	Second	Aug. 27, 1907	High	984.00
[illegible], Miss E.	Third	Jan. 29, 1906	Grammar	1,104.00
Hanlon, Miss M.	Second	April 1908	Adv. Doc.	840.00
Young, Miss M.	Second	July 6, 1905	Grammar	1,104.00
Carroll, Miss L.	First	Dec. 27, 1896	Grammar	1,224.00
Haussler, Miss M.	First	Dec. 28, 1885	Grammar	1,224.00
Soule, Miss M.	[illegible]	July 22, 1896	Grammar	1,224.00
Glen Park Grammar—				
[illegible], Miss [illegible]	Principal	Jan. 2, 1878	Grammar	2,100.00
Donnelly, Miss M. L.	V. P., Eighth	July 12, 1875	Grammar	1,680.00
Doran, Julia A.	Seventh	Jan. 7, 1869	Grammar	1,164.00
[illegible], Miss A.	First	July 22, 1882	Grammar	1,224.00
Dworzazek, Miss B. E.	Fourth	Jan. 3, 1882	Grammar	1,104.00
[illegible], Miss I. T.	Sixth	Oct. 21, 1873	Grammar	1,164.00
[illegible], Miss Mary E.	Third	Mar. 5, 1878	Grammar	1,104.00
McGuire, Miss Mary	Second	April 7, 1882	Grammar	1,104.00

Barron, Miss C. M.	Second	Oct. 24, 1888	Grammar	1,104.00
Phelps, Mrs. J. H.	First	Jan. 20, 1877	Grammar	1,224.00
Smith, Mrs. V. E.	Fifth	April 16, 1877	Grammar	1,164.00
Walters, Miss T. L.	Fourth	Jan. 8, 1906	Grammar	930.00
Golden Gate Primary—				
Hart, Miss P.	Principal	July 6, 1870	High	1,860.00
Wiseman, Mary L.	Fifth	Jan. 20, 1876	Grammar	1,164.00
Houston, Mary A.	Fourth	Aug. 15, 1877	Grammar	1,104.00
Bonnelli, Mrs. E. M.	Fourth	Feb. 5, 1877	Grammar	1,104.00
Ryan, Miss E. T.	Third	Jan. 4, 1875	Primary	1,104.00
Kaplan, Miss M. E.	Second	Nov. 8, 1884	Grammar	1,104.00
[illegible], Margaret G.	Second	April 4, 1886	Grammar	1,104.00
Hare, Mrs. K. M.	First	Oct. 2, 1873	Grammar	1,224.00
Johnson, Miss A. M.	First	Mar. 1, 1879	Grammar	1,224.00
Grant Primary—				
Shaw, Miss I. E.	Principal	May 30, 1882	Grammar	1,860.00
Kincaid, Miss B. C.	Seventh	Nov. 11, 1896	Grammar	1,224.00
Ryder, Miss V.	Sixth	Aug. 9, 1905	Grammar	984.00
Hart, Miss E. D.	Eighth	July 20, 1903	Grammar	984.00
Cookson, Miss A. B.	Fifth	Jan. 12, 1898	Grammar	1,164.00
Berg, Miss F. C.	Fourth	April 14, 1905	Grammar	1,032.00
Campbell, Anne B.	First	Nov. 12, 1878	Grammar	1,224.00
Austin, Miss E.	Third	Oct. 28, 1907	Grammar	930.00
Aune, Miss T.	Second	Aug. 14, 1905	Grammar	930.00
Gratton Primary—				
Butler, Mrs. E.	Principal	Aug. 4, 1882	Grammar	1,800.00
Frontin, Miss E. A.	Third	Oct. 1, 1877	Grammar	1,164.00
Sprague, Miss A. F.	Fourth	Sept. 14, 1867	Grammar	1,104.00
[illegible], Miss M.	First	Feb. 16, 1875	Grammar	1,224.00
Shepheard, Miss K.	First	July 12, 1873	Grammar	1,224.00
Maccord, Miss L.	Second	Feb. 5, 1878	Primary	1,104.00
Drake, Mrs. A. K.	Second	Aug. 16, 19[illegible]3	Grammar	1,032.00
Haight Primary—				
Hall, Miss M. A.	Principal	June 25, 1867	High	1,860.00
Wieland, Stella M.	Third	Feb. 16, 1906	High	900.00
Keegan, Miss A. R.	Fourth	Feb. 21, 1905	Grammar	1,032.00
Sweeney, Miss C. L.	Fifth	Jan. 6, 1876	Grammar	1,164.00
Rodgers, Miss C. E.	Fifth	Oct. 1, 1901	Grammar	1,164.00
Gilmore, Miss E. M.	Fourth	Nov. 24, 1897	Grammar	1,104.00
Donovan, Miss E.	Fourth	July 14, 1868	Primary	1,104.00
Neppert, Miss F. E.	Third	July 25, 1904	Grammar	960.00
Davidson, Mrs. T.	Second	Oct. 26, 1880	Primary	1,224.00
McDevitt, Miss J.	Second	July 20, 1903	Grammar	1,104.00

LIST OF SCHOOLS AND TEACHERS—Continued.

Name.	Grade of Class.	When Elected.	Grade of Certificate	Salary per Year.
Haight Primary—Continued.				
Miller, Miss S. E.	First	Nov. 5, 1866	High	1,22[illegible]
Fersyth, Miss L. M.	First	Jan. 6, 1902	Grammar	1,248.00
Knowlton, [illegible]ss G. W.	Third	Mar. 9, 1903	[illegible] mar	1,032.00
Gallagher, Miss R. G.	Second	July 29, 1889	Grammar	1,104.00
O'Connor, Miss J.	First	Aug. 3, 1905	Grammar	1,044.00
Hamilton Grammar—				
Kellogg, Mr. A. E.	Principal	Sept. 1, 1886	High	2,700.00
Menley, Miss I. M.	Sixth	Aug. 12, 1903	[illegible]ar	1,164.00
[illegible]lt, Miss E. E.	Seventh	July 18, 1902	Grammar	1,224.00
Brown, Isabelle R.	Eighth	Aug. 5, 1885	Grammar	1,224.00
Page, [illegible]ne H.	Eighth	Sept. 1, 1886	Grammar	1,224.00
Morton, Miss E. J.	Eighth, Vice Prin.	July 23, 1875	Grammar	1,800.00
[illegible]s, Miss I. R.	Eighth	July 6, 1873	Grammar	1,224.00
[illegible]h, Miss I. B.	Seventh	Jan. 31, [illegible]89	[illegible]ar	1,224.00
Shaw, [illegible] L. A.	Seventh	Aug. 14, 1895	Grammar	1,224.00
McDonnell, Miss L. A.	Seventh	Aug. 1, 8[illegible]	High	1,224.00
Redmond, Mary T.	Fifth	Dec. 7, 1905	[illegible]ar	1,164.00
[illegible]n, Miss A. C.	Sixth	Sept. 30, 1901	[illegible]ar	1,164.00
Martin, Miss I. C.	Sixth	July 25, 1901	High	1,174.00
Whitley, Miss A.	Seventh	Sept. 29, 1901	High	1,116.00
[illegible]e, Mrs. M. E.	Fifth	Sept. 1, 1872	Grammar	1,164.00
[illegible]g, Miss A.	Ungraded	[illegible] 2, 1903	High	1,044.00
Hancock Grammar—				
Gallagher, Miss N. G.	Principal	May 14, 1896	Grammar	2,160.00
Leggett, Mr. [illegible]	V. P., Eighth	[illegible] 22, 1888	High	1,800.00
O'Neil, Miss Agn se	Third	[illegible] 14, 1905	Grammar	[illegible]80.00
Martini, Mrs. M. G.	Seventh	[illegible]v. 24, 1889	[illegible]ar	1,284.00
Scanlan, Miss Renee	Sixth	Aug. 14, 1905	[illegible]ar	948.00
B[illegible]ke, Miss M. C.	Fifth	Jan. 4, 1905	[illegible]ar	1,164.00
Pfeiffer, Miss L. M.	Fifth	Mar. 30, 1905	High	[illegible]84.00
[illegible]o, Miss N. C.	Third	[illegible]g. 14, 1905	High	930.00
Furbush, Miss M. W.	[illegible]th	April 5, 1907	[illegible]ar	1,008.00
[illegible], Miss L.	Sixth	Aug. 1, 1904	[illegible]ar	1,164.00
Hartrick, Miss L.	Fourth	Aug. 22, 1907	Grammar	984.00
[illegible]s, Miss B.	Third	Jan. 16, 1908	Grammar	1,032.00
O'Connor, Miss V.	Second	Jan. 6, 1908	Grammar	984.00
Harrison Primary—				
[illegible]m, Miss T. E.	Principal	Jan. 3, 1888	Grammar	1,260.00
Sullivan, Miss G. A.	First	June 25, 1904	High	[illegible]00
Dolan, Miss Mary J.	First	Feb. 3, 1888	[illegible]ar	1,224.00

Name	Grade	Date	Certificate	Salary
Hawthorne Primary—				
Mann, Mrs. S. J.	Principal	Sept. 1, 1874	High	1,860.00
Lobenstein, Miss E.	First	Jan. 28, 1905	Grammar	1,224.00
Barrington, Miss F. C.	Fifth	July 27, 1898	Grammar	1,124.00
Walsh, Miss N. G.	Fourth	Aug. 1, 1888	Grammar	1,104.00
McLean, Miss M. A.	Fourth	Feb. 5, 1892	Grammar	1,104.00
Barrett, Alice L.	Third	Aug. 14, 1905	Grammar	930.00
Plagemann, Miss D. E.	Fourth	Sept. 1, 1905	High	930.00
Simon, Miss L. F.	Second	Sept. 1, 1897	Grammar	1,104.00
Barrett, Miss N.	First	Jan. 12, 1898	Grammar	1,224.00
[illegible], Miss M. L.	First	Sept. 8, 1897	Grammar	1,224.00
McKinne, Miss E.	Second	July 28, 1902	Grammar	1,008.00
Hearst Grammar—				
Sullivan, Miss N. F.	Principal	Aug. 13, 1876	Grammar	2,460.00
[illegible], Miss F. M.	V. P., Eighth	Dec. 28, 1880	Grammar	1,620.00
Haynes, Miss R. H.	Third	July 23, 1905	Grammar	960.00
[illegible], Rose B.	Eighth	[illegible] 15, 1885	Grammar	1,284.00
Bray, Mss L. F.	Seventh	Jan. 5, 1885	Grammar	1,224.00
[illegible], Mss E.	Eighth	Aug. 17, 1891	Grammar	1,224.00
Torpey, Miss M. C.	Sixth	Sept. 8, 1897	Grammar	1,164.00
Thompson, Miss A. W.	Seventh	Jan. 2, 1897	Grammar	1,224.00
Brierton, Miss M.	Sixth	Jan. 2, 1897	Grammar	1,164.00
Levey, Mrs. J. B.	Seventh	May 8, 1896	Grammar	1,224.00
Humphrey, Miss K. A.	Fifth	May 1, 1896	Grammar	1,164.00
Van Den Bergh, Miss F.	Fifth	Aug. 9, 1880	Grammar	1,164.00
McKeon, Miss R.	Fifth	Jan. 12, 1898	Grammar	1,164.00
Fairweather, Miss E.	Sixth	May 15, 1896	Grammar	1,164.00
Pencovic, Mrs. M.	Fourth	Jan. 2, 1901	Grammar	1,032.00
[illegible], Miss M. T.	Sixth	Aug. 21, 1905	Grammar	1,164.00
Peake, Mrs. B. M.	Third	July 1, 1883	Grammar	1,104.00
Martin, Miss A.	Fourth	Sept. 1, 1878	Grammar	1,164.00
Downing, Miss I. L.	Second	Oct. 14, 1901	Grammar	1,104.00
[illegible], Miss E. A.	First	[illegible] 29, 1877	Grammar	1,224.00
[illegible], Miss H. M.	Ungraded	Dec. 29, 1896	High	1,224.00
[illegible], Miss L. C.	First	Aug. 1, 1882	Grammar	1,224.00
Hyn se Miss F. S.	First	May 1, 1896	Grammar	1,224.00
Davidson, Miss E.	[illegible]	Feb. 1, 1904	Grammar	1,104.00
Connor, Miss E.	Third	1908	Grammar	840.00
O'Neil, Mrs. N.	Second	Dec. 30, 1892	Grammar	1,104.00
Henry Durant Primary—				
Camblein, Mrs. M. F.	Principal	Jan. 3, 1877	Grammar	1,560.00
Thompson, Miss R. A.	Fifth	Jan. 3, 1877	Grammar	1,164.00
Greenhood, Miss F.	Fourth	April 29, 1886	Grammar	1,104.00
Adams, Miss L. F.	Fourth	Nov. 1, 1877	Grammar	1,104.00

LIST OF SCHOOLS AND TEACHERS—Continued.

Name.	Grade of Class.	When Elected.	Grade of Certificate	Salary per Year.
Henry Durant Primary—Continued.				
Ambrose, Miss J. R.	Third	July 15, 1895	Grammar	1,104.00
Gillen, Miss E. J.	Third	Jan. 12, 1898	Grammar	1,104.00
Loud, Mrs. E. S.	Second	Nov. 2, 1879	Grammar	1,104.00
[illegible]s, Miss C.	Second	July 29, 1891	Grammar	1,104.00
Hill, Mrs. M. E.	First	April 15, 1885	Grammar	1,224.00
[illegible]y, Miss F. S.	First	Jan. 2, 1877	Grammar	1,224.00
Boukofsky, Miss R.	First	Sept. 1, 1886	Grammar	1,224.00
[illegible]n, Miss S. R.	First	Nov. 5, 1875	Grammar	1,224.00
Holly Park Primary—				
Sullivan, Miss N. M.	Principal	Dec. 15, 1877	Grammar	1,560.00
[illegible]l, Miss H. L.	Second	Aug. 15, 1867	Grammar	1,104.00
[illegible]n, Miss May	Second	Feb. 2, 1904	Grammar	1,224.00
Foley, Eliz. M.	Second	Nov. 12, 1896	Grammar	1,104.00
[illegible]n, Miss G. J.	First	Jan. 1, 1893	Grammar	1,224.00
[illegible]n, Mrs. S. F.	First	April 1, 1879	Grammar	1,224.00
Nagle, Miss M. M.	Third	Jan. 17, 1905	High	1,008.00
[illegible]illy, Miss J. F.	First	June 9, 1897	Grammar	1,224.00
Dworzazek, Miss P. A.	First	Jan. 2, 1897	Grammar	1,224.00
[illegible]s, [illegible]ra A.	First	Jan. 2, 1871	Grammar	1,224.00
Parker, Miss M.	Third	Nov. 26, 1907	Grammar	1,104.00
Kendrick, Miss M. E.	Second	Mar. 25, 1908	Grammar	1,104.00
O'Connell, Miss M.	Second	Jan. 29, 1906	Grammar	1,008.00
[illegible] Mann Grammar—				
Faulkner, Mr. R. D.	Principal	Oct. 22, 1888	High	2700.00
O'Loughlen, Miss N.	V. P., Eighth	June 12, 1869	Gram. & High	1,800.00
Elliott, Mary	Seventh	[illegible] 18, 1879	Grammar	1,224.00
Hatch, Mrs. L. R.	Sixth	Jan. 2, 1881	Grammar	1,224.00
Carson, Miss E.	Ungraded	Jan. 29, 1884	Grammar	1,224.00
[illegible]ll, Miss B.	Sixth	Aug. 6, 1872	Grammar	1,164.00
Clary, Agnes E.	Seventh	Mar. 11, 1906	Grammar	1,164.00
Diggs, Miss A. B.	Sixth	July 21, 1903	Grammar	1,164.00
[illegible]t, Miss J. M.	Seventh	Jan. 2, 1895	Grammar	1,284.00
Dowd, Mary E.	Seventh	July 29, 1888	Grammar	1,224.00
[illegible]n, Miss Kate	Sixth	Sept. 14, 1878	Grammar	1,[illegible].00
Stockton, Miss F.	Sixth	July 18, 1902	Grammar	1,164.00
[illegible]d, Miss M.	Seventh	Feb. 19, 1906	Grammar	1,224.00
Iredale, Mrs. E. B.	Eighth	Dec. 1, 1876	Grammar	1,224.00
Moynihan, Eliza J.	Eighth	Mar. 19, 1884	Grammar	1,224.00
Traynor, Miss M. E.	Eighth	Jan 3, 1876	Grammar	1,224.00

Casey, Miss M. E.	Eighth	April 6, 1875	Grammar	1,224.00
Peckham, Miss L.	Seventh	Sept. 30, 1901	Grammar	1,224.00
Keith, Miss E. D.	Seventh	Jan. 29, 1891	Grammar	1,224.00
Finnegan, Miss C. L.	Sixth	Sept. 2, 1887	Grammar	1,164.00
Hunters Point School—				
Itsell, Mr. A. J.	Principal	July 10, 1871	High	1,560.00
Irving M. Scott Grammar—				
Hamilton, Jas. T.	Principal	July 8, 1876	High	2,400.00
Croughwell, Miss A. T.	V. P., Eighth	Jan. 28, 1891	Grammar	1,800.00
Downey, Miss M. L.	Seventh	Sept. 1, 1886	Grammar	1,224.00
Gaffney, May T.	Sixth	Oct. 14, 1901	Grammar	1,074.00
Duggin, M. M.	Sixth	Jan. 4, 1904	Grammar	1,074.00
Mooney, Miss M. F.	Fifth	Jan. 26, 1898	Grammar	1,164.00
[illegible]n, M. E. G.	Fifth	Aug. 12, 1896	Grammar	1,164.00
Wright, [illegible]y A.	[illegible]th	Feb. 23, 1898	Grammar	1,104.00
M[illegible]h, Alice L.	Second	[illegible] 26, 1903	Grammar	1,008.00
Bryan, Miss E. M.	Fourth	Feb. 5, 1906	Grammar	1,080.00
White, Miss J.	Third	Aug. 25, 1904	Grammar	1,080.00
Gaffney, Miss A. M.	Third	Oct. 6, 1904	Grammar	960.00
[illegible]is, Miss K. M.	Sixth	Aug. 21, 1907	Grammar	1,164.00
[illegible]d, Miss May	Second	Mar. 30, 1905	Grammar	960.00
[illegible]s, Miss M. M.	First	Nov. 30, 1892	Primary	1,284.00
[illegible]s, Frances M.	First	Nov. 30, 1892	Grammar	1,224.00
Herrick, Miss C. R.	First	Sept. 11, 1895	Grammar	1,224.00
[illegible]k, Miss C. M.	First	Sept. 12, 1887	Grammar	1,224.00
[illegible]n, Miss M. G.	Fourth	Aug. 20, 1907	Grammar	900.00
Erb, Miss N. V.	Second	July 28, 1898	Grammar	1,104.00
Doran, Miss M. E.	First	Sept. 4, 1871	Grammar	1,224.00
[illegible]n Primary—				
Chalmers, Miss A.	Principal	Jan. 2, 1902	Grammar	1,440.00
Hinds, Miss A.	First	Aug. 23, 1880	Grammar	1,224.00
Ragan, Miss M. L.	Fifth	Mar. 10, 1897	High	1,164.00
[illegible]y, Miss R. V.	Third	Mar. 10, 1897	Grammar	1,104.00
Cashman, Miss May	Fourth	Nov. 19, 1905	Grammar	924.00
[illegible]y, Miss F. H.	First	Sept. 2, 1907	Grammar	1,188.00
James Lick Grammar—				
Graham, Miss E. W.	Principal	[illegible] 8, 1879	High	2,100.00
Lewis, Frances R.	Fifth	June 10, 1879	Grammar	1,569.00
Boyle, Mary	Eighth	July 23, 1875	High	1,224.00
Torpey, Miss M. M.	Seventh	Jan. 19, 1892	Grammar	1,224.00
Henderson, Mary J.	Seventh	Jan. 29, 1872	Grammar	1,224.00
Kinney, Miss L. M.	Seventh	Sept. 1, 1886	Grammar	1,164.00
Kilpatrick, Grace S.	Sixth	June 21, 1904	Grammar	1,044.00

LIST OF SCHOOLS AND TEACHERS—Continued.

Name.	Grade of Class.	When Elected.	Grade of Certificate	Salary per Year.
James Lick Grammar—Continued.				
Johnson, Miss E. M	Fifth	Mar. 30, 1905	Grammar	1,164.00
Kennedy, Josephine	First	Mar. 1, 1895	Grammar	1,224.00
Manning, Catherine B.	Fifth	Jan. 19, 1905	Grammar	1,104.00
Hogan, Miss H. M	Sixth	Sept. 30, 1900	Grammar	1,074.00
Harte, Mrs. H. S	Fifth	Mar. 4, 1903	[illegible]	1,044.00
Gray, Miss M. E. A	Fifth	Sept. 20, 1901	High	990.00
Jean Parker [illegible]—				
Pechin, Mrs. C. R	Principal	Sept. 12, 1872	Grammar	2,160.00
Haswell, Miss M. C	V. P., Eighth	April 10, 1874	Grammar	1,500.00
McCorkell, Miss L	Seventh	Aug. 23, 1880	Grammar	1,164.00
Tabrett, Miss A	Fifth	July 18, 1902	High	1,074.00
Anderson, Miss J	Fourth	July 23, 1892	Grammar	1,104.00
d'Erlach, Miss M. E	Third	Aug. 26, 1903	Grammar	984.00
Hopkins, Miss J. M	First	Oct. 1, 1903	Grammar	1,116.00
Heath, Miss R. E. L	First	Aug. 29, 1885	Grammar	1,224.00
Beardsley, Miss E. F	Ungraded	Mar. 3, 1879	Grammar	1,224.00
McCarty, Miss A	Fifth	[illegible] 14, 1907	Grammar	1,[illegible]64.00
McEwen, Miss F. G	Second	Oct. 12, 1895	Grammar	1,[illegible]04.00
Monaco, Miss N	Sixth	Jan. 2, 1902	Grammar	1,074.00
W[illegible]dland, Miss E	Third	July 21, 1902	High	1,008.00
Jefferson Primary—				
Cohen, Miss J	Principal	July 31, 1889	Grammar	1,440.00
Horgan, Miss K	Fourth	Oct. 26, 1905	Grammar	930.00
Carson, Miss A. M	Third	Feb. 12, 1906	Grammar	930.00
Orr, Miss Eliz A	First	Jan. 5, 1881	Grammar	1,224.00
John Swett Grammar—				
Fitzgerald, Mrs. M. M	Principal	Mar. 4, 1879	High	2,160.00
Bigelow, M[illegible] C. J	V. P., Eighth	July 1, 1865	Grammar	1,800.00
[illegible]ll, Mrs. G. D	Seventh	Feb. 11, 1879	Grammar	1,224.00
Boukofsky, Miss R. M	Seventh	Aug. 1, 1884	Grammar	1,224.00
Brooks, Miss E. B	Sixth	Dec. 27, 1896	Grammar	1,164.00
[illegible]ll, Genevieve	Sixth	June 9, 1897	Grammar	1,164.00
Bean, Miss L	Fifth	July 10, 1886	Grammar	1,[illegible]64.00
Erkson, Mrs. J. H	Third	Sept. 1, 1897	Grammar	1,104.00
Doud, Mrs. F. M	Second	Dec. 1887	Grammar	1,[illegible]04.00
Alderson, Mrs. A. E	First	Mar. 3, 1888	Grammar	1,224.00
[illegible]s, Mrs. M. C	Fifth	Nov. 19, 1871	Grammar	1,[illegible]64.00
Brown, Miss H	Fourth	Feb. 12, 1906	Grammar	840.00

Name	Grade	Date	Certificate	Salary
Laffayette Primary—				
McLeran, Miss M.	Principal	Sept. 16, 1901	Grammar	1,260.00
Bigelow, Mrs. S. H.	Third	Sept. 1876	Grammar	[illegible]
Sullivan, Miss H.	First	Aug. 2, 1905	Grammar	1,224.00
Laguna Honda School—				
O'Neal, Miss M. L.	Principal	Jan. 20, 1874	Grammar	1,860.00
Carson, Miss N. E.	Seventh	July 14, 1898	High	1,224.00
Croughwell, Miss M. V.	Third	Aug. 1, 1904	Grammar	1,008.00
Lynch, Miss E.	Seventh	Feb. 25, 1905	Grammar	[illegible]
Sechrist, Mrs. A. M.	Eighth	Dec. 5, 1886	Grammar	1,224.00
Holmes, Miss E. T.	Fifth	July 27, 1898	Grammar	1,164.00
[illegible], Miss M.	Fourth	July 6, 1905	Grammar	1,104.00
[illegible], Miss K.	Fourth	Jan. 28, 1905	High	960.00
[illegible], Miss H. L.	Second	Feb. 1, 1905	Grammar	960.00
[illegible], Miss A. M.	First	Sept. 30, 1901	Grammar	1,188.00
[illegible], Miss J.	First	Jan. 1877	Grammar	1,224.00
[illegible], Miss B. E.	Third	Nov. 15, 1905	Grammar	1,104.00
Lake View Primary—				
Moran, Miss M. R.	Principal	Aug. 9, 1890	Grammar	1,140.00
Moran, Miss D. F.	First	[illegible] 1, 1898	Grammar	1,104.00
McDonald, Miss J.	First	Jan. 21, 1898	Grammar	1,224.00
Anderson, Miss L.	Second	Aug. 3, 1908	Grammar	840.00
Seavy, Miss J.	Third	Aug. 3, 1908	High	840.00
Wagner, Miss H.	Fourth	Aug. 3, 1908	Grammar	840.00
Lincoln Grammar—				
Stone, Mr. W. W.	Principal	[illegible] 11, 1873	High	2160.00
Backman, Mrs. F. L.	Eighth	Sept. 3, 1883	Grammar	1,284.00
[illegible], Miss J.	Fourth	Jan. 21, 1907	Grammar	1,104.00
Perry, Laura C.	Second	June 26, 1905	High	930.00
Macdonald, Mrs. B. L.	First	Jan. 29, 1884	Grammar	1,224.00
[illegible], Miss A. E.	First	Jan. 1, 1876	Grammar	1,224.00
[illegible], Miss J. E.	Sixth	[illegible] 12, 1906	Grammar	1,164.00
Perlet, Miss M.	Fifth	Dec. 28, 1896	Grammar	1,164.00
Barry, Miss Mary C.	Third	Feb. 12, 1872	Primary	1,104.00
Madison Primary—				
Bartlett, Miss E. F.	Principal	Aug. 5, 1885	Grammar	1,800.00
Lipman, Miss N. E.	Second	Sept. 7, 1897	Grammar	1,104.00
Howard, Miss F. G.	Fifth	Dec. 30, 1892	Grammar	1,164.00
Emmons, Miss I. C.	Fourth	July 30, 1876	Grammar	1,104.00
Rowland, Mrs. A. E.	Third	July 27, 1898	Grammar	1,104.00
Breese, Miss A. A.	First	Oct. 29, 1897	Grammar	1,104.00
Bannon, Margaret F.	First	Jan. 3, 1873	Grammar	1,224.00

LIST OF SCHOOLS AND TEACHERS—Continued.

Name.	Grade of Class.	When El[illegible]d.	[illegible]de of Certificate	Salary per Year.
Marshall Primary—				
[illegible]r, Mrs. M. J.	Principal	Aug. 13, 1869	High	1,860.00
Poppe, Miss M. H.	Third	April 30, 1886	[illegible]ar	1,164.00
Harrigan, [illegible]ss J.	Fourth	July 1884	[illegible]ar	1,104.00
Lundt, Miss J. C.	Fourth	Oct. 19, 1875	Grammar	1,1[illegible]4.00
Belding, Mrs. M. L.	Second	Nov. 21, 1876	Primary	1,104.00
[illegible]n, [illegible]ss A. C.	First	[illegible] 18, 1878	[illegible]ar	1,224.00
Elliot, Miss E. F.	First	Nov. 18, 1885	[illegible]ar	1,224.00
O'Co[illegible]nr, [illegible]ss C. J.	First	Sept. 12, 1[illegible]04	[illegible]ar	1,080.00
[illegible]y, Mrs. H. W.	Fourth	July 28, 1892	Primary	1,104.00
[illegible]—				
Gallagher, Miss Cora	Principal	Aug. 6, 1878	Grammar	1,680.00
Dearin, M[illegible]ss A. E.	Third	Aug. 22, 1907	[illegible]ar	930.00
[illegible]r, Miss S.	Fourth	Jan. 3, 1906	[illegible]ar	930.00
[illegible]n, Nora	Fourth	July 7, 1877	Grammar	1,[illegible]04.00
Curry, Mary E.	Third	April 2, 1888	Grammar	1,104.00
[illegible]y, [illegible]ry G.	Second	Nov. 7, 1888	[illegible]ar	1,104.00
Kean, Miss K. E.	First	Jan. 1, 1885	[illegible]ar	1,224.00
Sarles, Mrs. Julia	First	July 7, 1881	Grammar	1,224.00
Casey, Mary	Fourth	June 6, 1888	[illegible]mar	1,[illegible]04.00
[illegible]n Grammar—				
[illegible]y, [illegible]ss K. H.	Principal	Aug. 1, 1880	[illegible]ar	2400.00
Hillman, [illegible]ss J. C.	[illegible]th	Feb. 13, 1879	[illegible]ar	1,680.00
[illegible]ss M. E.	Eighth	Oct. 30, 1889	[illegible]r	1,224.00
Fitzsimmons, Miss R. A.	Seventh	Aug. 15, 1888	Grammar	1,224.00
Sykes, Mrs. M. A.	Fifth	Aug. 11, 1897	Grammar	1,164.00
[illegible]n, [illegible]ss M. A.	Seventh	Sept. 30, 1901	Grammar	1,176.00
Noon, Miss M. G.	Seventh	May 15, 1883	[illegible]mar	1,164.00
Horn, Miss L. J.	Sixth	July 14, 1872	[illegible]mar	1,164.00
O'Brien, Miss M. A.	Sixth	Aug. 11, 1897	[illegible]mar	1,164.00
Hemmenway, Miss I. H.	Sixth	July 27, 1898	G[illegible]mmar	1,164.00
Harvey, Miss E. F.	Fifth	[illegible] 30, 1890	[illegible]mar	1,164.00
Monroe [illegible]—				
Hagarty, Miss A. M.	Principal	Feb. 20, 1883	[illegible]ar	2,400.00
Gorham, Miss A. M.	Fifth	Aug. 22, 1907	[illegible]ar	840.00
Harrower, Miss A. W.	Eighth	Sept. 30, 1901	[illegible]ar	1,560.00
[illegible]y, Miss M. R.	Eighth	Oct. 28, 1891	[illegible]ar	1,224.00
Curtin, Ella J.	Seventh	Sept. 14, 1905	[illegible]ar	1,224.00
Beardsley, [illegible]ss L. J.	Seventh	Sept. 12, 1904	High	1,008.00
Maher, Miss J. G.	Sixth	Sept. 2, 1884	[illegible]r	1,164.00

[illegible], Miss H. I.	Sixth	Aug. 6, 1907	Grammar	840.00
Ellis, Miss L.	Fourth	Jan. 3, 1889	Primary	1,104.00
[illegible], Miss J.	First	Feb. 13, 1890	[illegible]	1,224.00
O'Brien, Miss A. T.	First	Nov. 30, 1881	[illegible]	1,224.00
[illegible], Ella T.	Third	Oct. 7, 1907	Grammar	1,132.00
Hussey, Miss N. E.	Fifth	Aug. 22, 1907	High	1,164.00
Flaherty, Miss E.	Fourth	Oct. 28, 1907	Grammar	1,104.00
Purvine, Miss E. M.	Third	Aug. 1907	Grammar	900.00
Cilker, Miss J. A.	Second	Aug. 1904	Grammar	1,104.00
Ryan, Miss M. T.	Second	Aug. 3, 1908	Grammar	840.00
Morgan, Miss L. V.	First	May 15, 1896	Grammar	1,224.00
Langdon, Miss M.	[illegible]	May 28, 1904	Grammar	1,188.00
[illegible] Primary—				
[illegible], Miss K. E.	Principal	Jan. 7, 1873	Grammar	1,860.00
Duncan, Miss C. L.	First	Aug. 4, 1882	Grammar	1,224.00
Eccles, Miss L. B.	Third	Sept. 3, 1883	Grammar	1,104.00
[illegible], Miss E. B.	[illegible]	[illegible] 3, 1905	Grammar	1,104.00
Boukofsky, Miss S.	[illegible]	[illegible] 11, 1891	Grammar	1,104.00
[illegible], Miss A. E.	Second	Aug. 16, 1888	Primary	1,104.00
Fogarty, Miss N. T.	Third	Dec. 19, 1896	Grammar	1,104.00
[illegible]kins, Mrs. C.	Second	April 16, 1872	Grammar	1,104.00
Tobin, Mrs. I.	First	Jan. 18, 1888	Grammar	1,224.00
Bristol, Miss M. K.	First	Aug. 10, 1882	Grammar	1,224.00
[illegible]ey Primary—				
[illegible], Miss E. H.	Principal	July 1, 1882	[illegible]	2,160.00
Hall, Mrs. M. V.	First	Aug. 17, 1887	Grammar	[illegible]44.00
Egan, Miss K. F.	First	Mar. 11, 1897	[illegible]	1,224.00
[illegible], Mrs. L.	First	April 1, 1903	Grammar	1,152.00
Harrison, Miss E. D.	Second	Aug. 12, 1903	Grammar	[illegible]44.00
MacDonald, Miss L. M.	Second	Aug. 1907		840.00
[illegible]ll, Miss G. S.	Second	Aug. 23, 1907	Grammar	840.00
Martin, Elizabeth R.	Third	May 1, 1905	Grammar	960.00
Nolan, Miss M. L.	Third	June 21, 1904	Grammar	1,008.00
[illegible], Miss J. E.	Second	Dec. 15, 1890	Grammar	1,104.00
Schnedel, Miss M. A.	Fourth	Sept. 30, 1901	Grammar	[illegible]32.00
Gaffney, Miss S. A.	Fourth	July 21, 1903	Grammar	1,032.00
McLane, Miss H. E.	First	Dec. 14, 1892	Grammar	1,224.00
Marx, Miss M. E.	Third	Oct. 7, 1907	Grammar	840.00
Conroy, Miss M. A.	Third	July 1898	Grammar	1,104.00
Kerns, Miss [illegible]	Fourth	July 25, 1904	Grammar	1,104.00
[illegible] Primary—				
[illegible]th, Miss V. D.	Principal	Jan. 4, 1894	Grammar	1,680.00
Allen, Miss S. H.	Sixth	Oct. 24, 1901	Grammar	1,164.00
[illegible]kins, Miss B. C.	Second	July 25, 1902	Grammar	1,284.00

LIST OF SCHOOLS AND TEACHERS—Continued.

Name.	Grade of Class.	When Elected.	Grade of Certificate	Salary per Year.
[illegible]e Primary—Continued.				
Vincent, Miss S. C.	Fourth	Feb. 25, 1904	Grammar	960.00
Raas, Mrs. A.	Fifth	April 8, 1907	High	840.00
Bartlett, Miss A. G.	Eighth	Oct. 27, 1904	High	966.00
[illegible]an House School—				
Day, Mr. D. J.	Principal	July 8, 1882	High	1,560.00
Oriental Public—				
Newhall, Mrs. C. C.	Principal	[illegible]. 13, 1870	Grammar	1,680.00
Greer, [illegible]ne E.	Third	June 10, 1868	High	1,104.00
[illegible]th, Miss A. C.	First	July 27, 1898	Grammar	1,224.00
Nixon, Miss V. E.	Fourth	June 30, 1902	Grammar	1,008.00
Branch, Miss C. A.	First	Feb. 27, 1905	Grammar	1,080.00
McInerney, Miss F. R.	Second	Sept. 12, 1904	High	1,008.00
Jacobs, Mrs. M. E.	Eighth	Oct. 17, 1907	Grammar	1,164.00
[illegible]tt, Miss K. C.	Fifth	Aug. 5, 1907	High	840.00
Arnold, Miss M. V.	First	Nov. 9, 1891	Grammar	1,224.00
Pacific Heights Grammar—				
Stincen, Miss A. M.	Principal	June 20, 1863	High	2,700.00
[illegible]n, Miss Ella E.	Third	April 16, 1907	Grammar	960.00
Bliven, Miss F. M.	Eighth	Sept. 3, 1880	Grammar	1,224.00
Earle, Miss C. B.	Second	Feb. 21, 1972	Grammar	1,224.00
[illegible]k, Miss F. G.	Seventh	Dec. 4, 1904	Grammar	1,224.00
[illegible]th, [illegible]ne	Sixth	May 20, 1905	Grammar	1,014.00
Dreyfus, Miss R. E.	Fifth	Aug. 5, 1905	Grammar	1, [illegible]64.00
[illegible]h, Emma F.	Sixth	Jan. 21, 1883	Grammar	1,164.00
[illegible]s, Miss A. C.	Sixth	April 18, 1883	Grammar	1,164.00
Boggs, Miss S.	Seventh	Feb. 18, 1903	Grammar	1,224.00
Spadoni, Miss F. C.	Fifth	Jan. 3, 1905	Grammar	984.00
[illegible]r, Miss M.	Fourth	Jan. 4, 1902	High	1,032.00
Donohue, Miss M. F.	Fourth	June 21, 1904	Grammar	960.00
Wentworth, Miss G. M.	Second	Nov. 2, 1878	Grammar	1,224.00
Robertson, Miss A. C.	V. P., Eighth	July 16, 1867	High	1,800.00
Burnham, Miss C.	Fifth	Aug. 1, 1885	Grammar	1, [illegible]64.00
Dowling, Miss A. C.	First	Sept. 5, 1897	Grammar	1,224.00
Zweybruck, Miss E.	Ungraded	Feb. 20, 1885	Grammar	1,224.00
Morrison, Miss E. P.	Eighth	Aug. 20, 1888	Grammar	1,224.00
Cotrel, Miss E.	Seventh	July 7, 1889	Grammar	1,224.00
Peabody Primary—				
Dwyer, Miss A. M.	Principal	Mar. 17, 1879	High	1,860.00
Maguire, Mrs. M. E.	Fourth	Mar. 1, 1880	Grammar	1,104.00

Fit[illegible]ld, Miss M. F.	Fourth	Nov. 13, 1889	Grammar	1,164.00
[illegible]on, [illegible] M. G.	Second	Jan. 12, 1898	Grammar	1,104.00
Duffy, Miss A. A.	Third	Aug. 18, 1884	[illegible]mar	1[illegible]4.00
[illegible]b, Mrs. E. S.	Third	Nov. 18, 1901	Grammar	1,104.00
Sullivan, Miss N. C.	Second	Mar. 22, 1907	Grammar	840.00
Ephriam, Miss A.	First	Dec. 2, 1882	[illegible]mar	1,224.00
Ingram, [illegible] V. C.	First	Jan. 3, 1876	[illegible]mar	1,224.00
Redding Primary—				
Deane, Miss M. A.	Principal	Aug. 2, 1872	Grammar	1,800.00
Sullivan, Miss T.	Fifth	Sept. 15, [illegible]98	Grammar	1[illegible]44.00
[illegible]y, Miss M. E.	Fourth	Aug. 12, 1903	[illegible]mar	[illegible]84.00
[illegible]r, Miss S. A.	Second	Feb. 14, 1881	[illegible]mar	1,104.00
Martin, Miss F.	First	Aug. 26, 1881	[illegible]mar	1,224.00
[illegible]e, Mrs. L. E.	First	Dec. 23, 1885	[illegible]mar	1,224.00
Duffey, Miss Alma	Third	July 23, 1902	Grammar	1,008.00
Richmond Grammar—				
[illegible]r, Mr. Albert	Principal	June 10, 1868	High	2,400.00
Lalande, Miss A. H.	Eighth	July 5, 1878	[illegible]mar	1,224.00
Sleator, [illegible]ss E. A.	V. P., Eighth	July 31, 1889	Grammar	1,620.00
Browning, Miss E. F.	Sixth	[illegible] 24, 1901	High	1,074.00
Ryan, Miss B.	Seventh	Sept. 16, 1886	Grammar	1,224.00
Hitchens, Florence J.	Fifth	Jan. 31, 1889	[illegible]mar	1,164.00
Theobald, Miss A.	Fourth	Dec. 28, 1891	[illegible]mar	1, [illegible]04.00
McDonnell, [illegible]ss M. T.	Fourth	[illegible]r. 11, 1892	[illegible]mar	1, 1[illegible]4.00
Hinds, Miss J. B.	Sixth	Dec. 9, 1896	[illegible]mar	1,164.00
Grover, Mrs. E. J.	Fifth	[illegible]g. 22, 1907	[illegible]mar	840.00
[illegible]an, Miss J. E.	Third	Sept. 16, 1879	Grammar	1,104.00
Meighan, Miss K. E.	First	[illegible]v. 7, 1884	Grammar	1,224.00
Stark, [illegible]ss L. M.	First	Sept. 7, 1887	Grammar	1,224.00
Hurley, Miss A. F.	Third	April 27, 1888	Primary	1, [illegible]04.00
Horton, Miss M.	Second	Feb. 14, 1881	Grammar	1,104.00
Starr, Miss D. E.	Ungraded	Sept. 10, 1904	Grammar	1,224.00
Levy, Miss M. A.	Seventh	Aug. 1894	Grammar	1,224.00
Kedon, [illegible]s. A. E.	Seventh	Dec. 9, 1896	Grammar	1,224.00
[illegible]e, Mrs. N. E.	Sixth	Jan. 21, 1907	Grammar	1,164.00
[illegible]—				
[illegible]in, Miss C. F.	Principal	Dec. 10, 1890	Grammar	1,860.00
Downey, Miss J.	Eighth	Aug. 26, 1891	[illegible]	1,224.00
Murphy, Miss H.	Seventh	Oct. 26, 1905	Grammar	1,152.00
Everett, Miss E. B.	Sixth	Jan. 13, 1892	Grammar	1,164.00
Hussey, Miss E. G.	Sixth	Feb. 11, 1907	High	984.00
Tierney, Miss E. A.	Fifth	Oct. 13, 1904	[illegible]mar	984.00
Miklan, Miss M.	Fifth	Sept. 14, 1905	Grammar	948.00
Ehat, Mrs. M. I.	Fourth	July 7, 1905	Grammar	930.00

LIST OF SCHOOLS AND TEACHERS—Continued.

Name.	Grade of Class.	When Elected.	Grade of [illegible]cate	Salary per [illegible]r.
Sheridan S ho le—Continued.				
Brignardello, Miss H.	Third	Sept. 8, 1897	[illegible]	1,104.00
[illegible]hor, Miss A. J.	Second	Sept. 3, 1905	[illegible]	[illegible]
[illegible], Miss M. W.	[illegible]	April 29, 1896	[illegible]	[illegible]
a[illegible]y, Miss M. E.	First	Jan. 6, 1879	[illegible]	1,224.00
Crowley, [illegible]iss M. I.	[illegible]rd	Sept. 21, 1901	[illegible]	1,104.00
Kyne, Miss E. M.	Second	Aug. 3, 1908	Grammar	840.0
[illegible] Primary—				
Hurley, Miss J. M. A.	Principal	Jan. 2, 1863	[illegible]	1,860.00
Featherly, [illegible]iss H.	[illegible]th	July 16, 1867	High	1,104.00
[illegible]on, Miss M. C.	Fourth	June 21, 1904	Grammar	1,104.00
Nesfield, Miss E. M.	Third	Jan. 3, 1902	[illegible]	1,032.00
Crookham, Miss E. E.	Third	Aug. 10, 1898	Grammar	1,104.00
[illegible], Miss J. T.	Second	May 17, 1896	[illegible]	1,104.00
Unger, Miss R.	First	Aug. 20, 1885	Grammar	1,224.00
Sullivan, Miss Nellie	[illegible]	Aug. 15, 1890	[illegible]	1,104.00
Roberts, Miss Maria	Third	Dec. 23, 1884	[illegible]	1,104.00
Lyons, [illegible]iss E. H.	[illegible]	Sept. 30, 1885	[illegible]	1,224.00
Hitchens, Elizabeth	First	[illegible]v. 25, 1885	[illegible]	1,224.00
Gull, [illegible] M. S.	[illegible]	July 5, 1877	[illegible]	1,224.00
Sutherland, Miss M. C.	Second	July 1888	Primary	1,104.00
McDermott, [illegible]ss L.	Second	Oct. 1, 1904	High	1,104.00
Portola Primary (South End)—				
[illegible]s, Mrs. I. E.	Principal	Nov. 20, 1877	[illegible]	1,860.00
Lapham, Miss E. M.	Eighth	Jan. 1, 1904	[illegible]	1,080.00
[illegible], [illegible]iss J. H.	Sixth	Aug. 1, 1888	[illegible]	[illegible]64.00
[illegible]y, [illegible]ss B.	Sixth	Aug. 22, 1907	[illegible]	[illegible]4.00
Tessmer, Miss E. H.	Fourth	July 20, 1903	[illegible]	1,032.00
Laverene, Miss C. J.	[illegible]rd	Oct. 28, 1907	[illegible]	930.00
Porter, Miss H. F.	Thi rd	Jan. 28, 1907	Grammar	840.00
Wiley, Miss A.	Sixth	Aug. 22, 1907	Grammar	1,032.00
Grace, Miss J. G.	Second	Aug. 19, 1907	[illegible]	930.00
Browne, Miss E.	First	Aug. 15, 1888	Grammar	1,224.00
Johnson, Miss A. E.	First	April 29, 1891	[illegible]	1,224.00
Sullivan, Miss M.	First	Sept. 25, 1905	Grammar	1,224.00
Flanagan, [illegible]ss G.	First	Aug. 3, 1908	Grammar	840.00
Ruff, Miss M.	Second	Feb. 2, 1906	Grammar	[illegible]4.00
Spring [illegible]—				
Keating, Miss M. E.	Principal	July 12, 1880	[illegible]mar	2,400.00
Cregg, Miss A. C.	[illegible]th	Aug. 15, 1868	High	1,560.00

Name	Grade	Date	Rank	Salary
Holden, Mrs. A. F.	Eighth	Sept. 16, 1879	[illegible]mar	1,284.00
Murphy, Miss A. J.	[illegible]th	Mar. 2, 1903	[illegible]mar	1,224.00
Shea, Miss A. B.	Seventh	Jan. 29, 1884	Grammar	1,224.00
Hoggs, Mrs. M. A.	Sixth	Jan. 10, 1877	Grammar	1,[illegible]64.00
Davis, Mrs. F. V.	Sixth	[illegible]b. 20, 1872	Primary	1,164.00
Grozelier, Miss C. B. S.	Fifth	Sept. 14, 1905	[illegible]mar	948.00
Gallagher, Miss E. R.	Fifth	Oct. 28, 1891	Grammar	1,1[illegible]4.00
McCrossen, Miss A.	Fifth	Mar. 28, 1907	Grammar	840.00
Starr King Primary—				
McGrath, M[illegible] K. C.	Principal	Jan. 12, 1878	[illegible]mar	1,860.00
[illegible]s, Miss K. F.	Fourth	Oct. 17, 1884	[illegible]ar	1,104.00
[illegible]n, [illegible]beth	First	April 18, 1897	[illegible]mar	1,284.00
[illegible]y, [illegible]e J.	Second	July 20, 1903	[illegible]mar	1,104.00
Jordi, M[illegible] S. J.	Third	June 14, 1885	[illegible]mar	1,104.00
[illegible]n, Mrs. M. B.	Third	Aug. 6, 1904	[illegible]mar	960.00
Louderback, Miss E. S.	First	Nov. 21, 1884	[illegible]mar	1,224.00
Rhine, Miss E.	[illegible]th	July 5, 1903	Grammar	1,104.00
Ellis, Miss M.	Second	Feb. 3, 1908	[illegible]mar	930.00
Sunnyside Primary—				
Code, Mrs. E. S.	Principal	Jan. 22, 1857	High	1,560.00
McGinnis, Miss G. A.	Fourth	[illegible] 1907	[illegible]mar	1,032.00
Moore, Miss K.	First	June 15, 1903	[illegible]mar	1,224.00
Sunset School—				
Tiernan, Mrs. A. E.	Principal	July 6, 1869	High	1,560.00
Rowe, Miss M. M.	Second	[illegible]g. 3, 1871	High	1,224.00
Quinn, Miss May	Eighth	Nov. 12, 1905	Grammar	1,164.00
Sutro Grammar—				
[illegible]r, Miss M.	Principal	July 25, 1876	[illegible]mar	2400.00
[illegible]d, Miss M. R.	Eighth	Dec. 5, 1875	[illegible]mar	1,560.00
Smullen, Miss A. M.	Eighth	Feb. 18, 1903	[illegible]ar	1,284.00
Karatar, Miss A. C.	Fifth	Oct. 14, 1883	[illegible]mar	1,164.00
Read, Miss M. F.	Sixth	July 18, 1902	[illegible]ar	1,104.00
Curran, [illegible]ss M. M.	Seventh	Mar. 14, 1906	[illegible]mar	1,224.00
Cullen, [illegible]ss R.	Fourth	Jan. 4, 1902	Grammar	1,032.00
Faucompre, Miss M. E.	Fifth	Nov. 18, 1886	High	1,[illegible]64.00
O'Connell, Miss L.	Second	June 9, 1897	Grammar	1,1[illegible]4.00
Maguire, Miss H. E.	Second	[illegible]t. 27, 1892	Grammar	1,104.00
O'Brien, Miss M. J.	First	Aug. 3, 1892	Grammar	1,224.00
[illegible]n, Miss A. B.	First	May 13, 1896	Grammar	1,224.00
McNamara, Miss K. L.	Ungraded	Septe. 10, 1904	[illegible]mar	1,224.00
Grace, Miss K.	[illegible]rd	Aug. 1907	[illegible]mar	1,104.00
Hart, Miss A. P.	Fourth	Aug. 19, 1907	[illegible]mar	840.00

LIST OF SCHOOLS AND TEACHERS—Continued.

Name.	Grade of Class.	When Elected.	Grade of Certificate	Salary per Year.
Visitacion Valley—				
Galloway, Miss M.	Principal	Nov. 28, 1881	Grammar	1,560.00
Nolan, Miss M. A.	Eighth	Oct. 21, 1901	Grammar	1,092.00
Dailey, Miss A.	Fifth	Mar. 14, 1907	Grammar	1,164.00
Kenny, Miss M.	First	April 8, 1907	Grammar	924.00
[illegible], Miss C. L.	First	May 23, 1907	[illegible]	924.00
McArthur, Miss M. A.	Fourth	Feb. 3, 1908	Grammar	1,104.00
Mack, Miss A.	Third	Aug. 5, 1908	Grammar	840.00
Blackman, Miss R. E.	Second	June 1, 1908	Grammar	960.00
Corbett, Miss A. M.	First	Oct. 12, 1905	Grammar	1,188.00
[illegible]—				
[illegible]hy, Mr. T. H.	Principal	Mar. 20, 1891	High	2,160.00
Kervan, Miss I. M.	[illegible]	Septe 9, 1872	Grammar	1,164.00
Bowman, Mr. L.	Sixth	Oct. 1, 1879	Grammar	1,164.00
[illegible], Paul A.	Sixth	Aug. 22, 1907	High	1,152.00
Weed, Miss A.	Second	Sept. 15, 1875	Grammar	1,104.00
Chase, Miss [illegible]	First	Jan. 3, 1874	Grammar	1,224.00
[illegible], Miss J.	Seventh	May 1, 1878	Grammar	1,224.00
Scott, Miss J.	First	Sept. 5, 1881	Grammar	1,224.00
Kirkwood, Mr. W. H.	Fifth	Aug. 19, 1907	Grammar	1,164.00
[illegible], M[illegible] M. A.	Third	July 20, 1903	Grammar	1,104.00
[illegible], Miss A. E.	[illegible]	June 18, 1908	Grammar	1,104.00
Huskey, M[illegible] F. G.	[illegible]ighth	July 27, 1897	Grammar	1,800.00
[illegible] Irving Pr.—				
Barlow, Miss C. B.	Principal	Aug. 1, 1868	Grammar	1,800.00
Miller, Miss J. G.	Fifth	Mar. 13, 1895	Grammar	1,104.00
McVerry, Miss M.	First	Sept. 2, 1884	Grammar	1,224.00
[illegible]g, Miss H.	Second	Feb. 1, 1907	Grammar	1,104.00
[illegible], Miss S. T.	First	Feb. 1, 1907	Grammar	1,008.00
Ennewold, Miss A. T.	Third	Aug. 3, 1908	Grammar	840.00
West End Primary—				
[illegible]y, Miss E. L.	Principal	Jan. 16, 1884	Grammar	1,800.00
Dwyer, Miss A. C.	Second	Mar. 22, 1905	High	930.00
Dwyer, Miss Nora	Third	Nov. 11, 1891	Primary	1,104.00
[illegible]r, Miss A. M.	First	[illegible] 12, 1898	Grammar	1,224.00
[illegible]ld S[illegible]tt Primary—				
Thomas, Miss M. E.	Principal	July 12, 1887	Grammar	1,680.00
[illegible]r, Miss P.	Eighth	June 23, 1904	Grammar	1,116.00
Horgan, Miss E. E.	Sixth	Sept. 1, 1905	Grammar	948.00

Name	Grade / Subject	Date		Certificate	Salary
Gavigan, Miss M. K.	Third	Feb. 1, 1889		Primary	1,104.00
Wright, Miss A. B.	Second	Jan. 6, 1902		High	1,032.00
Thomas, Miss A. G.	First	July 27, 1898		[illegible]	1,224.00
Demmick, Mrs. M. F.	First	Dec. 10, 1890		[illegible]mar	1,224.00
Birch, Mrs. Lily	[illegible]	[illegible] 18, 1907		Grammar	[illegible]64.00
Hortenstein, Miss M. L.	Fourth	Jan. 22, 1908		[illegible]mar	960.00
Yerba Buena Primary—					
Casey, Miss K. F.	Principal	Jan. 24, 1876		[illegible]mar	1,860.00
Klaus, Miss B. J.	Fourth	Oct. 9, 1903		[illegible]mar	1,032.00
Stewart, Miss J. M.	Third	[illegible] 27, 1880		[illegible]mar	[illegible]04.00
Kennedy, Miss E.	[illegible]ird	Jan. 9, 1906		[illegible]mar	984.00
Bloch, Miss B.	Second	July 5, 1873		Grammar	1,104.00
Waltenspiel, Miss M.	Second	Aug. 3, 1908		[illegible]mar	930.00
Jacobs, Miss N. A.	First	Sept. 5, 1888		Grammar	1,224.00
McHugh, [illegible]iss M.	First	Nov. 1, 1881		Grammar	1,224.00
Hochheimer, Miss J.	First	Jan. [illegible]		Grammar	1,224.00
L'Hommedieu, Miss G.	First	Aug. 26, 1891		[illegible]mar	1,224.00
Oral School For Deaf—					
Holden, Mrs. J. B.	[illegible]ipal	Aug. 15, 1901		Special	1,248.00
Holden, Mr. A. N.	Sixth	Aug. 1, 1902		[illegible]ial	996.00
Parental School—					
Alexander, Miss R.	Principal	Oct. 5, 1888		[illegible]mar	1,512.00
[illegible], Angeline	Ungraded	Sept. 17, 1897		High	1,224.00
Schwartz, Mrs. I. C.	Ungraded	Feb. 17, 1905		[illegible]mar	1,008.00
[illegible]y, Miss A.	Ungraded	Jan. 5, 1891		[illegible]mar	1,224.00
[illegible]al High—					
[illegible], Chas. H.	[illegible]pal	[illegible] 27, 1890		High	3,000.00
Sykes, Jas. B.	Law, Gov.	Dec. 16, 1896		High	2,[illegible]60.00
[illegible], Miss E. D.	English	Aug. 15, 1898		High	1,740.00
McPherson, Mrs. S. W.	[illegible]th.	July 20, 1889		High	1,740.00
Sal i[illegible]o, Miss M. G.	Spanish	July 30, 1890		Special	1,740.00
[illegible], Miss S. A.	[illegible]ing	July 20, 1904		Special	1,740.00
Richards, Miss M. L.	Stenography	Aug. 15, 1889		Special	1,740.00
[illegible], Miss I. M.	English	Jan. 14, 1905		High	1,740.00
Reeves, [illegible] I. D.	Arithmetic	Jan. 10, 1897		High	1,740.00
Conway, Miss M. B.	Stenography	Oct. 26, 1892		[illegible]ial	1,740.00
Garbarino, Miss 1.	Typewriting	Nov. 13, [illegible]		Special	1,740.00
[illegible]s, Miss M. L.	Sten. & Typewriting	Sept. 1, 1904		Special	1,740.00
Rademaker, Miss H. E.	Bookkeeping	May 15, 1887		[illegible]ial	1,740.00
Sallman, Miss F. H.	English	June 15, 1908		High	1,740.00
Bowman, Miss E.	Arithmetic	June 17, 1903		High	1,740.00
Noonan, Miss E. L.	Bookkeeping	Sept. 30, 1901		High	1,440.00
Willard, Mr. O. C.	Bookkeeping	July 1, 1908		Special	1,320.00

LIST OF SCHOOLS AND TEACHERS—Continued.

Name.	Grade of Class.	When Elected.	Grade of Certificate	Salary per Year.
Girls' High—				
Scott, Dr. A. W.	Principal	Jan. 5, 1883	High	3,600.00
Prag, Mrs. M.	Fourth A	June 27, 1864	High	2280.00
[illegible]ll, Mr. G. O.	Science	Aug. 23, 1889	High	2280.00
Dupuy, Mr. E. J.	Fourth B	May 15, 1899	Special	1,500.00
Goldstein, Mr. F. M.	Drawing	Mar. 1, 1887	Special	1,500.00
Roth, Miss N. E.	First B	Jan. 10, 1902	High	1,740.00
[illegible]s, Miss N. M.	Second B	Aug. 7, 1869	High	1,920.00
Levicle, Miss B.	French	Mar. 13, 1905	High	1,920.00
[illegible]iel, Miss L.	Second B	Dec. 17, 1890	High	1,920.00
Hobe, Miss S. A.	First A	July 21, 1901	High	1,740.00
Hunt, Miss C. L.	First B	Jan. 10, 1859	High	1,920.00
Croyland, Miss A. B.	Third A	July 20, 1901	High	2040.00
[illegible]k, Miss C. M.	Second A	July 21, 1902	High	1,740.00
Zimmerman, Mr. Wm.	First B	Jan. 4, 1871	High	1,920.00
Stevenson, Miss E. R.	First A	Jan. 3, 1903	High	1,800.00
[illegible]r, Martin A.	Third B	Aug. 19, 1907	High	1,920.00
[illegible]t, Miss F.	Fourth B	Aug. 23, 1870	High	2,280.00
Maher, Miss M.	Second A	July 28, 1902	High	1,440.00
Jones, Miss M.	First A	July 23, 1908	Special	1,500.00
Lowell High—				
Morton, Frank	Principal	Aug. 1, 1886	High	3, 60.00
Gallagher, Dr. J. J.	Second	July 27, 1898	High	2220.00
Clark, F. H.	First	July 8, 1889	High	2280.00
Crofts, Francis E.	Fourth	Nov. 28, 1891	High	2220.00
Schmit, Mr. J. J.	First	Dec. 26, 1894	High	1,920.00
Nourse, Mr. J. P.	Second	Jan. 14, 1901	High	1,920.00
[illegible]y, Mr. J. A.	Third	July 20, 1901	High	1,860.00
Perham, Mr. F. E.	Third	Sept. 4, 1901	High	1,920.00
Van [illegible]der, Mr. A. G.	First	Sept. 1, 1904	High	1,920.00
Harvey, Mr. R. W.	Biology	Dec. 28, 1905	High	1,680.00
Rhodes, Mr. T. H.	First	Nov. 15, 1906	High	1,920.00
Cronise, Miss C. B.	Second	April 4, 1907	High	1,920.00
Cloud, Mr. A. J.	Fourth	Jan. 15, 1905	High	2040.00
Cox, Mary M.	Third	Aug. 20, 1885	High	2040.00
[illegible]le, Miss E. A.	First	Oct. 1, 1907	High	1,800.00
Kelley, Mr. T. R.	First	Sept. 12, 1899	High	1,800.00
Hodgkinson, Miss F.	Second	May 27, 1885	High	1,920.00
[illegible]gh, Miss E.	First	Dec. 1, 1897	High	1,440.00
Sheldon, Mr. H.		Aug. 3, 1908	High	1,920.00

Altmann, Mr. A.	Drawing	July 15, 1903	Special	1,500.00
Koch, Mr. F. W.	Science	July 29, 1901	High	1,920.00
Mon High—				
Smith, Mr. W. O.	Acting Principal	Aug. 1, 1901	High	3,000.00
Donnelly, Miss M. E.	First A 2	July 9, 1872	High	2,280.00
Goldsmith, Miss A.	Fourth B & B 2	Feb. 19, 1879	High	2,200.00
Ryan, Miss R.	Second A	July 15, 1898	High	2,200.00
Blanchard, Dr. M. E.	Third B	Jan. 5, 1890	High	2,100.00
Kelly, Miss A. G.	Fourth A & Third A	Oct. 10, 1895	High	1,920.00
[illegible], Miss E.	Second B 1	July 20, 1901	High	1,740.00
Cerf, Miss A.	First B 1	July 21, 1904	High	1,740.00
Downey, Mr. A. D.	Science	Jan. 21, 1907	High	2,100.00
[illegible], Mr. P. A.	Drawing	Aug. 31, 1898	High	1,920.00
Carey, Mr. E. P.	Science	Feb. 3, 1908	High	1,920.00
Dal Piaz, M. M.	Drawing	Jan. 12, 1905	High	1,740.00
Harrison, Mrs. E. C.	First B 2	Aug. 3, 1908	Special	1,500.00
Townsend, Mr. I.	First A 1	Jan. 2, 1909	High	1,680.00
[illegible], Miss M. C.	Spanish	Dec. 20, 1899	High	1,440.00
[illegible], Mr. F. M.	Commercial	Aug. 17, 1908	Special	1,500.00
Polytechnic High—				
Bush, Mr. W. N.	Principal	July 20, 1886	High	3,000.00
Jordan, Mr. A. L.	Science	Jan. 26, 1899	High	2,280.00
Duffy, Miss A. G.	English & History	June 24, 1897	High	1,920.00
Van Vdk, Miss M.	Drawing	July 22, 1889	Special	1,500.00
Carniglia, Mr. E. S.	Head Mach. Shop	Mar. 25, 1905	High	1,920.00
[illegible], Mr. P. J.	Mathematics	Jan. 21, 1903	High	1,920.00
Hatch, Mr. I. C.	Language	Aug. 12, 1905	High	2,280.00
Castlehun, Miss E.	English, German	April 4, 1887	High	1,740.00
[illegible], Miss R.	Drawing	Nov. 18, 1893	Special	1,500.00
[illegible], Miss N. L.	Sewing	Sept. 21, 1907	Special	1,500.00
Drew, Mr. Wm. J.	Drawing	Mar. 28, 1898	High	2,160.00
Walker, Mr. C. C.	Drawing	Sept. 30, 1907	Special	1,500.00
Cerf, Miss C.	French	Feb. 3, 1908	High	1,800.00
Kelly, Miss M. E.	English	July 20, 1904	High	1,740.00
Crittenden, Mr. J. L.	Maths.	Aug. 5, 1888	High	1,920.00
Dickerson, Mr. R. R.	Science	Jan. 2, 1907	High	1,800.00
Doyle, Mr. M. J.	Woodwork	Nov. 5, 1897	Special	1,500.00
Ferrea, Miss E.	Ind.-Art	Oct. 3, 1904	Special	1,500.00
McTiernan, J. J.	Asst. Forge	Sept. 14, 1908	Special	1,500.00
Commercial Evening—				
Riley, Mr. Peter	Principal	July 17, 1901	High	1,200.00
Davidson, Mr. W. W.	Bookkeeping	July 5, 1884	[illegible]	600.00
Hitchcock, Miss H. M.	French	July 29, 1876	[illegible]	600.00

LIST OF SCHOOLS AND TEACHERS—[illegible]d.

Name.	Grade of Class.	[illegible] Elected.	Grade of Certificate	Salary per Year.
Commercial Evening—Continued.				
Kozminsky, Miss D.	Stenography	Sept. 29, 1892	Special	0.00
[illegible]y, Miss M. W.	Typewriting	Aug. 18, 1897	Special	600.00
Rock, Miss A. J.	Bookkeeping	Jan. 12, 1898	Grammar	600.00
[illegible]s, Mr. W. E.	Sten. & Typewriting	April 1, 1903	Special	600.00
Freese, Miss L. E.	Penmanship	Mar. 8, 1894	Grammar	600.00
Kendrick, Miss N. K.	Stenography	Dec. 29, 1896	Grammar	600.00
Delaney, Mrs. K. F.	Bookkeeping	Mar. 25, 1886	Grammar	600.00
[illegible]n, Mr. J. R.	Spanish	April 30, 1908	High	[illegible]00.00
Kellerher, Mr. J. B.	Sten. & Com. Arith.			600.00
Hamilton Evening—				
Foulkes, Geo. W.	Principal	June 1, 1893	High	1,200.00
[illegible]h, Miss M. U.	Ninth	Aug. 11, 1897	Grammar	600.00
Lanahan, Mr. J. A.	Eighth	June 15, 1898	Grammar	600.00
Johns, Miss M. E.	Eighth	Aug. 4, 19[illegible]	Grammar	600.00
Hussey, Miss N. C.	Sixth	Feb. 26, 1896	Grammar	600.00
Israel, Miss D. T.	Seventh	Feb. 23, 1898	Grammar	600.00
Burnett, Miss S. C.	Foreign	Oct. 26, 1904	Grammar	600.00
[illegible]l, Mrs. A.	Fifth	Sept. 1, 1897	Grammar	600.00
[illegible]s, Mr. F. A.	Foreign	[illegible] 14, 1907	Grammar	600.00
Regan, Miss V.	Seventh	Aug. 3, 190[illegible]	Grammar	600.00
Livingston, Miss B.	Sten.	Aug. 1907	Special	600.00
Daniels, John R.	Bookkeeping	Sept. 1, 1891	Special	600.00
Cohen, Miss R. B.	Stenography	Sept. 1, 1897	Grammar	600.00
[illegible]n, Miss K. F.	Typewriting	Jan. 2, 1903	Grammar	600.0
Kiely, Miss E. C.	Foreign	Sept. 14, 1905	Grammar	600.00
Spadoni, Miss A.	Foreign	Jan. 29, 1906	High	600.00
Horace Mann Evening—				
Kratzer, Mr. D. W.	Principal	Aug. 14, 1897	Grammar	1,2[illegible]0.00
Bodkin, Miss A. J.	Sixth	Dec. 28, 1898	Special	600.00
Gorham, Miss K. L. (now Mrs. C. L. Murphy)	Seventh	Aug. 30, 1897	Grammar	600.00
[illegible]r, Dr. G. J.	Sixth	July 20, 1903	[illegible]	600.00
Kelly, Eliz. F.	Eighth	Aug. 18, 1904	Grammar	600.00
[illegible]e, Miss H. F.	[illegible]th	Sept. 1, 1905	Grammar	600.00
Martin, Miss A. G.	Seventh	July 28, 1898	Grammar	600.00
[illegible]ll, M. M. L.	Sixth	Sept. 1, 1897	Grammar	600.[illegible]
Kozminsky, Miss B.	Fifth	Aug. 31, 1892	Grammar	600.00
[illegible]r, M. M.	Fourth	Feb. 12, 1868	Primary	600.00
MacDonald, Dr. F.	Foreign	Dec. 5, 1892	Grammar	0.00

Name	Class	Date of appointment	Certificate	Salary
Blum, Miss J. L.	Foreign	July 27, 1897	Grammar	600.00
Doyle, Miss J.	Ninth	July 28, 1898	Grammar	600.00
Lahaney, Miss K.	Eighth	April 2, 1906	Grammar	600.00
Cleary, Miss A. C.	Seventh	Jan. 29, 1906	High	600.00
Irving M. Scott Evening—				
Hall, Mr. H. C.	Foreign	July 1, 1903	High	600.00
Lincoln Evening—				
MacDonald, Mr. A. H.	Principal	Sept. 2, 1880	High	1,200.00
Onyon, Miss E. J.	Ninth	Jan. 31, 1889	Grammar	600.00
Smith, Miss N. A.	Eighth	Jan. 3, 1887	Grammar	600.00
Jordan, Mr. L. A.	Eighth	Aug. 1, 1894	High	600.00
MacDonald, Miss L. M.	Seventh	Aug. 23, 1907	Grammar	600.00
Harvey, Miss M. A.	Fifth	Aug. 29, 1892	Grammar	600.00
Parlin, Mrs. A. E.	Ungraded	Aug. 31, 1892	Grammar	600.00
Rich, Mr. L. A.	Vice Principal	Dec. 23, 1885	Grammar	900.00
Greenan, Mrs. R. F.	Sixth	Mar. 26, 1877	Grammar	600.00
Wigand, Mrs. S. S.	Foreign	Dec. 27, 1890	Primary	600.00
[illegible], Miss E.	Foreign	Oct. 23, 1901	Grammar	600.00
West, Miss E. L.	Foreign	Aug. 30, 1896	Primary	600.00
O'Neill, Miss L. C.	Seventh	Sept. 8, 1888	Grammar	600.00
Kinne, Mr. H. C.	Foreign	July 14, 1868	High	600.00
Morgan, Miss R. E.	Foreign	Nov. 4, 1878	High	600.00
Richmond Evening—				
Strauss, Miss M.	Principal	July 11, 1895	Grammar	1,020.00
Gould, Mr. N. B.	Eighth	June 24, 1904	Grammar	600.00
Dougherty, Wm. J.	Sixth	Aug. 19, 1907	Grammar	600.00
Walsh, Mr. C. F.	Ninth	Sept. 10, 1908	High	600.00
Finn, Mrs. E. C.	Seventh	Dec. 15, 1896	Grammar	600.00
Faure, Mrs. E.	Bookkeeping	April 23, 1908	Grammar	600.00
Sherman Evening—				
Fenton, Mr. F. L.	Principal	Feb. 11, 1904	High	1,020.00
Williams, Mr. W. J.	Foreign	July 15, 1868	High	600.00
Fischer, Dr. Frank	High School	July 5, 1886	High	720.00
Roden, Miss J.	Ninth	June 9, 1897	Grammar	600.00
Reed, Miss C.	Eighth	Aug. 3, 1908	Grammar	600.00
Ventura, Mr. L. D.	Italian	July 29, 1908	High	600.00
Fiala, Miss A. M.	Foreign	May 9, 1886	Grammar	600.00
Washington Evening—				
Goodman, Mrs. P. M.	Principal	Dec. 14, 1886	Grammar	1,020.00
Roden, Miss J. A.	Foreign	June 9, 1897	Grammar	600.00

LIST OF SCHOOLS AND TEACHERS—Continued.

Name.	Grade of Class.	When Elected.	Grade of Certificate.	Salary per Year.
Washington Evening—Continued.				
Robinson, Miss M. C.	Seventh	Dec. 10, 1896	[illegible]	600.00
Grosjean, [illegible] E. S.	Foreign	May 17, 1883	[illegible]	600.00
[illegible], Ella B.	Foreign	Sept. 1, 1897	[illegible]	600.00
[illegible], [illegible] M. J.	Foreign	Sept. 30, 1879	[illegible]	600.00
[illegible], Mr. G. P.	Ninth	July 28, 1904	Grammar	600.00
Bretz, Miss B.	Foreign	Sept. 16, 1886	Grammar	[illegible]
Kengla, [illegible] E. R.	Foreign	Sept. 15, 1887	[illegible]	600.00
[illegible], Miss M. C.	Foreign	June 29, 1903	[illegible]	600.00
Hollub, Miss M. C.	Fourth	April 5, 1892	[illegible]	600.00
Humboldt [illegible] High—				
Taaffe, Mr. L. A.	Principal	Dec. 2, 1886	High	1,500.00
Roberts, Mr. A. E.	Hd. of Drawing Dpt.	Dec. 31, 1892	Grammar	[illegible]
[illegible], Mr. G. E.	High [illegible]	Sept. 1, 1902	High	720.00
Leonard, Mr. E. M.	[illegible] School	[illegible] 10, 1905	High	720.00
[illegible], Miss M. J.	High School	Aug. 14, 1905	[illegible]	720.00
[illegible], Mr. John	Drawing	[illegible] 27, 1898	Special	720.00
Christie, Mr. L. C.	Drawing	Jan. 3, 1892	Special	720.00
Harris, Mr. H. E.	Drawing	Sept. 4, 1902	Special	720.00
Hendry, Mr. C. S.	Drawing	April 27, 1898	Special	720.00
Carroll, Mr. W. E.	Drawing	April 15, 1905	Special	720.00
Blue, Mr. F. K.	Drawing	[illegible] 5, 1901	Special	720.00
Roylance, Mr. L. S.	Drawing	April 1, 1905	Special	720.00
Barnett, Mr. A. T.	High School	Sept. 8, [illegible]	High	720.00
Blake, Mr. W. S.	Science	Jan. 5, 1901	High	720.00
[illegible], Mr. [illegible] L.	High School	April 20, 1896	High	720.00
McMillan, Mr. J. T.	Navigation	Aug. 1908	Special	720.00
[illegible], Mr. E.			Special	720.00
Power, Miss J. L.				720.00
Department at Large—				
Barthel, Mr. F. K.	Supt. Manual Trng.	Jan. 15, 1904	Gram. & Special	1,800.00
Williams, Mr. J. B.	Manual Training	Jan. 4, 1906	Special	1,200.00
Davidson, Mr. L. E.	Manual Training	[illegible] 1, 1901	Special	1,200.00
[illegible], Mr. H. C.	Manual Training	Feb. 15, 1903	Special	1,200.00
Dailey, Mr. P. F.	Manual Training	[illegible] 10, 1905	Special	1,200.00
Dowling, Mr. D. E.	Manual Training	Mar. 4, 1906	Special	1,200.00
Silvia, Mr. A. M.	Manual Training	Mar. 11, 1905	High	1,200.00
Thompson, Mr. R. D.	Manual Training	Jan. 2, 1909	Special	1,200.00
Carpenter, Miss E.	Music	[illegible] 28, 1898	Special	1,800.00

McGlade, Mrs. M. G.	Music	Sept. 3, 1903	[illegible]	1,080.00
Ball, Miss K. M.	Drawing	July 1, 1894	Special	1,800.00
McKillop, Mrs. E. M.	Drawing	Dec. 29, 1896	Special	1,164.00
Martin, [illegible] E. H.	Drawing	Aug. 3, 1908	Special	1,080.00
Dewing, Miss A. B.	Drawing	Aug. 3, 1908	[illegible]	1,080.00
Barth, Mr. R. H.	[illegible] Culture	Aug. 31, 1892	Special	1,200.00
[illegible], Mr. O. S.	Physical Culture	[illegible] 1, 1897	Special	1,200.00
Bartlett, Miss E. M.	Cookery	July 1, 1901	Special	1,200.00
Ballinger, Miss C. A.	[illegible]	July [illegible], 1905	Special	900.00
[illegible], Miss F. M.	Cookery	Sept. 1, 1904	Special	900.00
Congdon, [illegible] M.	[illegible]	Aug. 19, 1905	Special	900.00
Gray, Miss E.	[illegible]	Aug. 19, 1907	Special	900.00
Wright, Miss P. E.	Cookery	Mar. 11, 1908	Special	900.00
[illegible], Miss I.	Cookery	Aug. 20, 1908	Special	900.00
Ball, Miss L.	Supt. Pr. Read	[illegible] 1, 1908	[illegible]	1,800.00
Espina, Mr. P. A.	Penmanship	Sept. 13, 1887	Special	1,800.00

Report of Board of Education

San Francisco, August 4, 1909.

Honorable Edward H. Taylor, Mayor.

Dear Sir:—In compliance with Charter provision, I have the honor to transmit to you herewith a report of the appropriation and disbursements of the Board of Education for the fiscal year 1908-1909, just closed.

Very respectfully,

E. C. LEFFINGWELL,

Secretary Board of Education.

DISBURSEMENTS, FISCAL YEAR 1908-1909.

Board of Education	$ 11,959.60
Superintendent and Deputies	14,799.96
Secretary and Attaches	12,950.00
Storekeeper and Assistant	2,287.85
Scavenger	3,000.00
Superintendent of Building and Repair	2,100.00
Foreman, Supply Department	1,490.00
Teamster	1,800.00
Teachers, Primary and Grammar	1,132,848.00
Teachers, High	157,133.20
Teachers, Commercial	30,394.85
Teachers' Special	21,830.95
Janitors	61,800.50
Rents	7,473.70
Wages in Supply Department	11,352.00
Stationery	7,731.43
Conveyances	1,495.50
Incidentals, Supplies	6,369.19
Laboratory Supplies	937.76
Furniture	20,238.52
Manual Training Supplies	1,978.73
Janitorial Supplies	3,533.12
Printing	2,023.61
Indigent Books, Maps, Globes and Charts	3,166.71
Fuel	10,578.60
Telephone and Telegraph	124.32
School Sites	6,000.00
Census	8,126.97
Water	14,000.00
Light	4,992.40
Teachers' Institute	299.00
Fire Escapes and Repairs	5,000.00
Cartage	67.00
Cooking Supplies	1,232.26
High School Supplies	10,717.91
Advertising	186.40
Wages for building temporary Schools	1,485.00
Material for building temporary Schools	4,730.48
Total Disbursements, fiscal year 1908-1909	$1,588,235.52

SUMMARY.

Appropriation, fiscal year 1908-1909	$1,600,800.00
Disbursed as above	1,588,235.52
Surplus	$ 12,564.48

Annual Report *of the* Board of Education and the Superintendent *of* Schools

San Francisco, California

For the Fiscal Year Ending June 30, 1910—

Printed by A. Carlisle & Company, *San Francisco*

90

CONTENTS.

BOARD OF EDUCATION

City and County of San Francisco, California

OFFICERS, 1909-10

President: July-November, Joseph O'Connor; December, Thomas E. Hayden; January-June, Thomas R. Bannerman.

Secretary: July-August, Elmore Leffingwell; September-June, Melvin G. Dodge.

Members, 1909-10

David Oliver, July-September.
Joseph O'Connor, July-November.
Thomas E. Hayden, July-December.
Mary W. Kincaid, July-June.
Thomas R. Bannerman, October-June.
Henry Payot, December-June.
Richard I. Whelan, January-June.
Alfred Roncovieri, Superintendent of Schools, ex-officio Member.

Report of the Board of Education

San Francisco, California,
August 1, 1910.

To the Honorable Board of Supervisors,
City and County of San Francisco.

Gentlemen:—

In accordance with provision of the Charter, I have the honor to submit herewith the annual report of the Board of Education, embracing reports of the Secretary and of the Superintendent of Schools, for the fifty-eighth fiscal year of the School Department, ending June 30, 1910.

Respectfully,

THOMAS R. BANNERMAN,
President Board of Education City and County of San Francisco.

SECRETARY'S REPORT.

San Francisco, California.
August 1, 1910.

To the Honorable Board of Education
City and County of San Francisco.

Madam and Gentlemen:—

I have the honor to submit herewith my report of the financial transactions of the Board of Education for the fiscal year ending June 30, 1910; to which is appended a list of the teachers in the Department, the amount of salary paid each, the dates of their appointments, and the character of the certificates held by them.

Respectfully yours,

MELVIN G. DODGE,
Secretary Board of Education.

RECEIPTS, 1909–10.

City Taxes	$ 909,678 85
City Taxes (collected in July)	4,548 68
First Installment from State (including High School)	460,748 11
Second Installment from State (including High School)	217,433 35
Rents	50,322 00
Sales of Junk	300 00
Miscellaneous	40 05
Total Receipts from all sources	$1,643,071 04

DISBURSEMENTS, 1909–10.

Board of Education	$ 12,000 00
Superintendent and Deputies	14,799 96
Secretary and Attaches	13,180 00
Clerk, Repair Shop	1,500 00
Teachers, Primary and Grammar	1,173,974 55
Teachers, High School	171,791 30
Janitors	67,726 53
Rents	9,577 45
Wages in Supply Department	10,337 50
Storekeeper and Assistant	2,550 00
Scavenger	2,370 00
Superintendent Building and Repair	2,100 00
Foreman Supply Department	1,500 00
Stationery	8,770 59
Cooking Supplies	1,170 49
Forward	$1,493,348 37

Disbursements, forward	$1,493,348 37
Janitorial Supplies	3,832 81
Incidental Supplies	7,145 14
High School Supplies	1,941 45
Books	5,208 34
Fuel	10,309 54
Printing	2,718 97
Cartage	932 50
Advertising	138 52
Telegrams and Telephones	32 32
Water	11,865 18
Manual Training Supplies	3,285 26
Light	6,124 04
Teamster	300 00
Census	10,901 25
Furniture	10,301 40
Equipment, Polytechnic High	8,552 42
Teachers' Institute	200 00
Total Disbursements	$1,577,137 51
Appropriation, fiscal year 1909–10	$1,584,300 00
Disbursed during the year	1,577,137 51
Balance to Credit of Appropriation	$ 7,162 49

RECAPITULATION

Total Receipts	$1,643,071 04
Total Disbursements	1,577,137 51
Surplus	$ 65,933 53
Add Surplus of Fiscal Year, 1908–09	23,000 00
Total Surplus, July 1, 1910	$ 89,933 53

Report of the Superintendent of Schools

San Francisco, August 1, 1910.

To the Honorable Board of Education,
in and for the City and County of San Francisco.

Gentlemen:—I have the honor to submit herewith the annual report on the condition of the public schools of this City and County, as required by the Charter, for the fifty-eighth fiscal year of the School Department, ending June 30, 1910.

ALFRED RONCOVIERI,
Superintendent of Common Schools, in and for the City and County of San Francisco.

GENERAL STATISTICS.

FISCAL YEAR ENDING JUNE 30, 1910.

Population of the City and County (estimate)	420,000
Number of children in the City and County, under 17 years of age.	100,183
Number of school census children in the City and County, between 5 and 17 years of age (a basis of apportionment of State School funds)	74,729
Assessment roll of the taxable property of the City and County (Assessor's valuation)	$492,867,374 00
The same assessed by State Board of Equalization	539,097,371 00
City and County School Tax on each $100	1838
City and County Taxes for school purposes	909,678 85
Apportionments of State School Funds	678,181 46

ESTIMATED VALUE OF SCHOOL PROPERTY—

Sites occupied by Elementary Schools		$ 2,346,000 00
Sites occupied by Secondary Schools		600,000 00
Sites not occupied by schools		2,376,000 00
Total Value of Land		$ 5,322,000 00
BUILDINGS—		
Elementary Schools	$ 2,698,894 00	
Secondary Schools	412,000 00	
Administration	12,000 00	
Total Value of Buildings		$ 3,122,894 00
FURNITURE—		
Elementary Schools	$ 170,300 00	
High Schools	20,500 00	
Administration	3,500 00	
Total Value of Furniture		$ 194,300 00
APPARATUS AND LABORATORIES—		
Elementary Schools including Manual Training and Cooking	25,700.00	
High Schools	31,450 00	
Total Value of Apparatus and Laboratories.		57,150 00
LIBRARY—		
Elementary Schools	$ 31,286 00	
High Schools	5,055 00	
Teachers	600 00	
Total Value Libraries		36,941 00
Total Value (estimated) of all School Property		$ 8,733,285 00

FINANCIAL REPORT.

DISBURSEMENTS.

SALARIES—		
Teachers—		
High School (including Newton J. Tharp Commercial, $24,623.35, and Humboldt Evening High $13,546.85)	$ 171,791 30	
Primary and Grammar	1,065,335 75	
Evening (except Humboldt Evening High $13,546.85)	51,360 00	
Primary and Grammar Substitutes	24,458 80	
Special (Domestic Science, $8,400: Drawing $4,060: Manual Training, $11,400: Music, $3,120: Penmanship, $1,500: Physical Culture, $2,400: Primary Reading, $1,920)	32,820 00	
Janitors—		
High School	6,840 00	
Primary and Grammar	60,886 53	
Board of Education	12,000 00	
Superintendent and Deputies	14,800 00	
Secretary and Attaches	13,180 00	
Clerk of Repair Shop	1,500 00	
Storekeeper and Assistant	2,550 00	
Superintendent Buildings and Repairs	2,100 00	
Foreman Supply Department	1,500 00	
Scavenger	2,370 00	
Teamster	300 00	
Total Salaries		$1,463,792 38
Advertising		138 52
Cartage		930 00
Census		10,896 25
Furniture		10,292 40
Fuel		10,309 54
Labor (Supply Department)		10,337 50
Light		6,124 04
Maps, Books and Charts		5,208 34
Printing		2,818 57
Rents		9,577 45
		$1,530,424 99
Stationery		8,633 69
SUPPLIES—		
Cooking	$ 1,169 64	
High School	1,941 45	
Incidental	7,241 42	
Janitorial	3,827 25	
Manual Training	3,285 26	
Polytechnic High (Supplies, Laboratory and Machinery)	8,552 42	
Total Supplies		26,017 44
Teachers' Institute		200 00
Forward		$1,565,276 12

Disbursements, forward	$1,565,276 12
Telephone and Telegraph	32 32
Water	11,865 18
Total Expenses (excluding Sites, Building and Repairs)	$1,577,173 62

RECEIPTS.

City and County Taxes (exclusive of $120,000 appropriated by the Board of Supervisors to be expended by Board of Public Works for repairing school buildings)	$ 909,678 85
State Apportionment High Schools	29,344 18
State Apportionment Primary and Grammar Schools	648,837 28
Rents derived from School Property	50,322 00
Sale of Old Material	340 05
Total Receipts	$1,638,522 36
Surplus for year 1909—$73,725.33. The deficit of the year 1908 was paid from this surplus, leaving	22,935 50
Total Revenue Year 1909–1910	$1,661,457 86
Total ordinary expenses for year ending June 30, 1910	1,577,173 62
Surplus	$ 84,284 24

REPAIRS—

The Board of Supervisors appropriated for the repairing of School Buildings to be expended by the Board of Public Works	$ 120,000 00

GENERAL DEPARTMENT EXPENSES PRORATED AMONG HIGH, PRIMARY AND GRAMMAR AND EVENING SCHOOLS, ON THE BASIS OF AVERAGE DAILY ATTENDANCE.

All Salaries, except teachers' and janitors'	$ 50,300 00	
All other expenses except light, rents, supplies (high school, cooking, manual training)	82,730 98	
Total Prorated		$ 133,030 98
High Schools	$ 8,747 74	
Primary and Grammar Schools	115,627 94	
Evening (including Humboldt Evening High)	8,655 30	
		$ 133,030 98

DISTRIBUTION OF EXPENDITURES.

(Not Including Sites, Buildings and Repairs.)

High Schools—

Cost of Instruction	$ 158,244 45	
Cost of Janitors	6,360 00	
Cost of Supplies	10,493 87	
Cost of share of department expenses prorated	8,747 74	
		$ 183,846 06

Primary and Grammar Schools—

Cost of Instruction	$1,122,614 55	
Cost of Janitors	60,886 53	
Rents	9,577 45	
Supplies (Cooking and Manual Training)	4,454 90	
Share of department expenses prorated	115,627 94	
		$1,313,161 37

Evening Schools (including Humboldt)—

Cost of Instruction	$ 64,906 85	
Cost of Janitor	480 00	
Light	6,124 04	
Share of department expenses prorated	8,655 30	
		80,166 19
Grand Total		$1,577,173 62

COST PER PUPIL, 1909–1910.

	Per Pupil Enrolled	Per Pupil in Average Daily Attendance	Year 1908—1909
(a) For Instruction only—			
High Schools	$40 38	$65 50	$75 41
Primary and Grammar Schools	28 34	35 12	35 49
Evening Schools (including Humboldt)	9 20	27 15	30 48
(b) For all expenditures (including repairs but not including buildings and sites)—			
High Schools	48 20	78 16	87 25
Primary and Grammar Schools	35 96	44 55	41 98
Evening Schools	11 92	35 20	36 58

SCHOOL BONDS.

Bonds authorized by the election of 1908: sold during the year ending June 30, 1910	$ 900,000 00
Premium on same	61,470 00
Total realized from sale of Bonds	$ 961,470 00
Total realized from sale of Bonds—1908-1909	2,100,000 00

STATEMENT OF THE EXPENDITURE OF MONEY REALIZED FROM SALE OF BONDS, DURING THE YEAR ENDING JUNE 30, 1910.

SCHOOL	Sites	Buildings	Equipment
Agassiz Primary	$ 7,000 00	....	....
Bryant Cos. Primary	....	$ 99,578 70	$ 2,671 95
Burnett Primary	1,750 00	....	....
Clement Primary	....	34,329 99	....
Cleveland Primary	....	150 00	....
Denman Grammar	46,625 00	36,748 90	....
Douglass Primary	4,500 00	....	....
Everett Grammar	6,900 00	....	....
Frank McCoppin	....	51,450 14	....
Franklin	....	218 30	....
Garfield	....	89,191 24	....
Hancock	....	85,296 97	....
Harrison	10,000 00	....	....
Holly Park	13,700 00	28,387 14	....
Jean Parker Grammar	9,750 00	31,728 51	389 76
John Swett Grammar	46,750 00	68 35	....
Farragut	....	35,023 44	....
Madison	....	85,177 91	2,445 70
McKinley	....	55,753 66	....
Mission Grammar	....	169,365 74	3,213 35
Sheridan Grammar	6,300 00	65,175 24	....
Portola	....	93,892 76	3,609 75
Spring Valley Grammar	9,100 00	1,754 00	....
Sutro Grammar	....	97,580 48	3,604 98
Washington Grammar	....	8,944 00	....
Longfellow (West End)	....	36,978 77	....
Girls' High	....	5,380 00	....
Lowell High	116,500 00	....	....
Mission High	35,100 00	....	....
Newton J. Tharp Commercial	....	168,689 44	....
Totals	$313,975 00	$1,280,863 68	$ 15,935 49

Total Bond Money Expended during Year	$1,610,774 17

RECAPITULATION.

Operating Expenses of Department	$1,577,173 62
Repairs (Special Appropriation)	120,000 00
Bond Money for Sites, Buildings and Equipment	1,610,774 17
Grand Total of Money Expended on Schools	$3,307,947 79

Salary Schedule 1909-1910

OFFICE AND STOREROOM.

	Per Month
Deputy Superintendents	$225 00
Secretary, Board of Education	150 00
Clerk, High School Board	50 00
Financial Secretary	165 00
Recording Secretary	155 00
Stenographers—Board of Education and Superintendent's office	100 00
Messenger, Board of Education	100 00
Messenger, Superintendent's office	90 00
Storekeeper, School Department	150 00
Teamster, School Department (including use of two-horse team)	150 00
Telephone Exchange Operator	80 00
Superintendent of Building and Repairs	175 00
Foreman—Supply and Equipment Department	125 00
Storekeeper of Repair Shop	125 00

DEPARTMENT AT LARGE.

Supervisors of Music, Drawing and Primary Reading	$160 00
Supervisor of Manual Training	150 00
Supervisor of Penmanship	125 00
Assistants in Manual Training	100 00
Assistants in Music and Drawing	90 00
Supervisor of Cooking	100 00
Assistants in Cooking	75 00
Instructors in Physical Culture	100 00
Special Teachers of Modern Languages in 3d, 4th, 5th, 6th, 7th and 8th grades	100 00

HIGH SCHOOL SALARIES.

	Per Annum	Per Month
Principals—		
Principals of schools having fewer than 400 pupils enrolled, will be paid a salary of	$2,700 00	$225 00
Principals having over 400, but under 700 pupils enrolled, will be paid a salary of	3,000 00	250 00
Principals having more than 700 pupils enrolled, will be paid a salary of	3,300 00	275 00
Heads of Departments—		
Heads of Departments will be paid	$1,980 00	$165 00
Assistants—		
Assistants will be paid, during their probationary term, at the rate of	1,440 00	120 00
Afterwards, at the rate of	1,620 00	135 00
High School Assistants holding only special certificates, shall be paid a salary of	1,500 00	125 00

DAY COMMERCIAL SCHOOL.

	Per Annum	Per Month
Principal—		
Principal will be paid a salary of	$2,400 00	$200 00
Assistants—		
Assistants will be paid, during their probationary term, at the rate of	1,200 00	100 00
After probationary term, at the rate of	1,440 00	120 00

ELEMENTARY SCHOOLS.

Grammar.

	Per Annum	Per Month
Schools in which the enrollment is 800 or over, and in which the number of grammar grade pupils is 325 or over, will be ranked as Class 1, Grammar Schools, and the principals will be paid a salary of	$2,460 00	$205 00
Schools in which the total enrollment is 400 or more, but less than 800, and in which the number of grammar grade pupils is 225 or more, will be ranked as Class 2, Grammar Schools, and the principals will be paid a salary of	2,160 00	180 00
Vice-Principals—		
Vice-Principals, during their probationary term, will be paid at the rate of	1,500 00	125 00
Afterwards the salary will be	1,620 00	135 00

ELEMENTARY SCHOOLS.

Primary.

	Per Annum	Per Month
In primary schools, having an enrollment of 700 or more pupils, the principal's salary will be	$2,160 00	$180 00
In primary schools, having an enrollment of 400, and less than 700 pupils, the principal's salary will be	1,800 00	150 00
In primary schools, having an enrollment of 150 pupils, but less than 400, the principal's salary will be	1,560 00	130 00
In primary schools having an enrollment of less than 150 pupils, the principal's salary will be	1,320 00	110 00

ELEMENTARY SCHOOLS.

CLASS TEACHERS.

Class Teachers of Elementary Schools shall be paid the same salaries during the fiscal year 1909–1910, as were paid for the month of May, 1909, as per pay roll.

EVENING SCHOOLS.

	Salary Per Month
Principals—	
Humboldt Evening High	$100 00
Commercial	85 00
Hamilton	80 00
Horace Mann	80 00
Lincoln	80 00
Richmond	65 00
Sherman	75 00
Washington	80 00
Assistants in Evening Schools	50 00
Head Teacher of Drawing Department, Humboldt Evening High School	100 00
Assistants teaching High School Classes and Assistant Teachers of Drawing in Humboldt Evening High School	60 00
Substitutes, when teaching, per evening	2 50

ELEMENTARY SCHOOLS.
CLASS TEACHERS.

Year of Service		GRADES 2d, 3d and 4th Per Annum	2d, 3d and 4th Per Month	5th and 6th Per Annum	5th and 6th Per Month	1st, 7th and 8th Per Annum	1st, 7th and 8th Per Month
Probationary Term	1	$ 840	$70 00	$ 840	$70 00	$ 840	$70 00
	2	840	70 00	840	70 00	840	70 00
	3	900	75 00	912	76 00	924	77 00
	4	930	77 50	948	79 00	966	80 50
	5	960	80 00	984	82 00	1,008	84 00
	6	984	82 00	1,014	84 50	1,044	87 00
	7	1,008	84 00	1,044	87 00	1,080	90 00
	8	1,032	86 00	1,074	89 50	1,116	93 00
	9	1,056	88 00	1,104	92 00	1,152	96 00
	10	1,080	90 00	1,134	94 50	1,188	99 00
	11	1,104	92 00	1,164	97 00	1,224	102 00

SUBSTITUTES.

Day Substitutes and Teachers on the Day Unassigned List in Primary and Grammar Schools, when actually engaged in teaching, per day	$ 3 00
Substitutes in Evening Schools, per evening	2 50
High School Substitutes, per day	5 00

FINES AND DEDUCTIONS.

See Rules of the Board of Education.

GENERAL DIRECTIONS.

Teachers' Annual Salaries shall be paid in twelve equal installments, one installment for each month in the calendar year.

Salaries of newly appointed teachers shall commence on the date of the beginning of actual and personal service.

In classes consisting of two grades, the salary of the higher grade will be paid when the average attendance in the higher grade equals or exceeds two-fifths of the average attendance for the class: provided, that when the average attendance of the entire class is less than forty, the salary of the lower grade shall be paid.

When there are more than two grades in a class, the Board will determine the salary of the teacher.

HIGH SCHOOLS.

No person shall be appointed Head of a High School Department, nor after the fiscal year 1908–1909, continued in that position, unless such person shall have at least one assistant under his or her supervision.

GRAMMAR SCHOOLS.

In all schools consisting of more than four classes, the minimum average daily attendance per primary class, exclusive of first grades and classes of more than two grades, shall be forty: and the minimum average daily attendance per grammar class shall be forty-five.

A vice-principal, when acting in the capacity of principal, shall receive the minimum salary scheduled for the principal whose place he or she is temporarily filling.

Since Sec. 1687 of the school law provides that "Beginners shall be taught by teachers who have had at least two years' experience or by normal school graduates," normal school graduates who have successfully completed their probationary term as teachers of first grade classes will be allowed two years' experience as the equivalent of their normal school training.

The salary for teachers of ungraded classes in the Grammar Schools of this department shall be the same as paid to such teachers during the month of May, 1909, as per Pay Roll.

PARENTAL SCHOOL

The salary of the principal of the Parental School is hereby fixed at $1,440 per year.

Assistants in the Parental School shall be paid the same salaries during the fiscal year 1909-1910 as were paid for the month of May, 1909, as per Pay Roll.

YARD ASSISTANTS.

In Primary Schools having an average daily attendance of 500 or over, the principal may name for the approval of the Board, an assistant to perform yard duty, who shall be paid therefor ten dollars per month in addition to her regular salary.

Five ($5.00) dollars additional, per month, shall be paid to regular teachers in Primary and Grammar Schools holding special certificates in

Music, and teaching Singing; provided, however, that such teachers shall be required to teach, as far as practicable, every class in the school, in this subject.

No teacher shall be paid any salary for the Christmas or Spring vacation, unless such teacher shall have been present for at least twenty school days of the period preceding the vacation.

Teachers shall be paid one-tenth of the salary of the Summer vacation, for each school month of the preceding fiscal year during which they shall have been present.

AVERAGE ANNUAL SALARIES.

	Male	Female
Superintendent of Schools (1)	$4,000 00	....
Deputy Superintendents of Schools (4)	2 700 00	....
School Directors (4)	3,000 00	$3,000 00
Principals of High Schools (5)	2,820 00	....
Principals of Primary and Grammar Schools	2,130 00	1,905 60
Teachers in High Schools	1,866 67	1,513 46
Teachers in Grammar Schools	1,352 22	1,154 68
Teachers in Primary Schools	....	1,024 32
Teachers in Evening Schools	729 48	616 45
All Teachers, Principals and Superintendents (except substitutes)	....	1,145 88

MEDAL FUNDS.

Name of Fund	Deposited in	In Fund June 30, 1910
Bridge Silver Medal	Hibernia Savings & Loan Society	$2,045 14
Denman Grammar School	Hibernia Savings & Loan Society	1,080 50
Denman Silver Medal	German Savings & Loan Society	2,024 13
Hancock Grammar School	German Savings & Loan Society	401 41
Jean Parker Grammar School	German Savings & Loan Society	326 59
John Swett Grammar School	Hibernia Savings & Loan Society	212 02
Lincoln Grammar School	Hibernia Savings & Loan Society	2,733 77

SCHOOLS.

Number of High Schools, including N. J. Tharp Commercial	5
Number of Grammar Schools	25
Number of Primary Schools	55
Number of Evening Schools	9
Total Number of Schools	94

Number of concrete school buildings owned by the department	2
Number of brick school buildings owned by the department	12
Number of wooden school buildings owned by the department	68
Number of buildings or rooms rented by the department	9
Total number of buildings used by the department	

ENROLLMENT BY GRADES.

First Grade—A	6,530
First Grade—B	5,604
Second Grade	8,316
Third Grade	8,019
Fourth Grade	6,727
Fifth Grade	6,153
Sixth Grade	5,317
Seventh Grade	3,954
Eighth Grade	3,215
Totals	53,835

First Year High School—A	1,045
First Year High School—B	978
Second Year High School	1,051
Third Year High School	391
Fourth Year High School	448
Totals	3,913

These figures are the numbers of pupils enrolled in each and admits duplication: e.g., twenty pupils in a B-6th grade during the first term are promoted to an A-7th in January. They are counted in both B-6th and A-7th grades. This is different from the State enrollment which admits of no duplication. In the above example the twenty pupils would be enumerated in the State enrollment as 6th grade pupils only.

STATE SCHOOL ENROLLMENT AND ATTENDANCE AND CENSUS STATISTICS FOR YEARS ENDING

	June 30, 1910		June 30, 1909
	Enrollment	Increase over 1909	Enrollment
High School	3,545	321	3,224
Primary and Grammar	39,610	330 (Decrease)	39,940
Evening	7,057 ✓	1,712	5,345
Total	50,212	1,703	48,509
	Average Daily Attendance		Avg. Daily Atten.
High School	2,416	110	2,306
Primary and Grammar	31,967	1,013	30,954
Evening	2,391 ✓	110	2,281
Total	36,774	1,233	35,541

✓ 876 in Humboldt.
✓ 399 in Humboldt.

STATE ENROLLMENT.

State Enrollment of the Public Day Schools of San Francisco during the year ending June 30, 1910, enumerated by sex, age and grade. (State enrollment admits no duplication. Pupils promoted during the year are enumerated in the grades from which they were promoted.

BOYS.

GRADES	6 Yrs.	7 Yrs.	8 Yrs.	9 Yrs.	10 Yrs.	11 Yrs.	12 Yrs.	13 Yrs.	14 Yrs.	15 Yrs.	16 Yrs.	17 Yrs.	18 Yrs.	19 Yrs.	20 Yrs. or over	Grade Total
First Grade	2,726	1,486	548	226	114	59	46	35	35	16	13	9	3	2	3	5,321
Second Grade	34	598	1,153	769	302	51	37	19	5	4	4	1	1	....	......	2,978
Third Grade	......	64	493	820	697	437	259	106	50	12	9	1	....	3	......	2,951
Fourth Grade	......	......	71	543	856	672	386	132	52	11	6	4	....	....	......	2,733
Fifth Grade	......	......	......	27	299	689	637	421	107	8	2	3	....	....	......	2,193
Sixth Grade	......	......	......	......	15	353	601	442	380	15	4	....	1	....	......	1,811
Seventh Grade	......	......	......	......	1	44	217	388	364	181	43	12	3	2	1	1,256
Eighth Grade	......	......	......	......	1	2	49	246	337	299	98	19	3	2	......	1,056
Age Total Elementary	2,760	2,148	2,265	2,385	2,285	2,307	2,232	1,789	1,330	546	179	49	11	9	4	20,299
1st Year High School	......	......	......	......	......	......	23	83	176	183	121	43	16	16	15	676
2d Year High School	......	......	......	......	......	......	1	15	65	108	71	32	6	10	9	317
3d Year High School	......	......	......	......	......	......	......	1	4	29	55	28	27	7	3	154
4th Year High School	......	......	......	......	......	......	......	......	......	2	20	48	30	19	11	130
Total High School	......	......	......	......	......	......	24	99	245	322	267	151	79	52	38	1,277
Grand Total (Boys)	2,760	2,148	2,265	2,385	2,285	2,307	2,256	1,888	1,575	868	446	200	90	61	42	21,576

STATE ENROLLMENT.

State Enrollment of the Public Day Schools of San Francisco during the year ending June 30, 1910, enumerated by sex, age and grade. (State enrollment admits no duplication. Pupils promoted during the year are enumerated in the grades from which they were promoted.

GIRLS.

GRADES	6 Yrs.	7 Yrs.	8 Yrs.	9 Yrs.	10 Yrs.	11 Yrs.	12 Yrs.	13 Yrs.	14 Yrs.	15 Yrs.	16 Yrs.	17 Yrs.	18 Yrs.	19 Yrs.	20 Yrs. or over	Grade Total
First Grade	2,812	1,274	445	116	64	19	15	3	......	1	....	....	1	....	......	4,750
Second Grade	31	580	1,025	693	305	52	29	2	1	2	....	....	....	....	......	2,720
Third Grade	......	51	411	635	508	313	208	83	44	7	....	....	....	....	......	2,260
Fourth Grade	......	......	67	380	644	563	370	153	55	10	6	....	....	....	......	2,248
Fifth Grade	......	......	......	31	328	757	645	457	105	4	1	....	....	....	......	2,328
Sixth Grade	......	......	......	......	15	383	711	452	405	52	16	1	1	....	......	2,036
Seventh Grade	......	......	......	......	......	65	298	531	473	191	55	1	2	....	......	1,616
Eighth Grade	......	......	......	......	......	5	57	347	442	364	116	19	1	1	1	1,353
Age Total Elementary	2,843	1,905	1,948	1,855	1,864	2,157	2,333	2,028	1,525	631	194	21	5	1	1	19,311
1st Year High School	......	......	......	......	......	......	12	113	412	411	199	48	15	9	6	1,225
2d Year High School	......	......	......	......	......	......	2	8	52	193	191	92	29	1	......	568
3d Year High School	......	......	......	......	......	......	......	......	14	55	82	77	28	2	......	258
4th Year High School	......	......	......	......	......	......	......	......	......	4	35	104	50	19	5	217
Total High School	......	......	......	......	......	......	14	121	478	663	507	321	122	31	11	2,268
Grand Total (Girls)	2,843	1,905	1,948	1,855	1,864	2,157	2,347	2,149	2,003	1,294	701	342	127	32	12	21,579

EVENING SCHOOLS.

	14 Years	15 Years	16 Years	17 Years	18 Years	19 Years	20 Years	Total Pupils
Boys	484	671	614	571	489	363	2,491	5,683
Girls	111	142	175	196	179	126	445	1,374
Totals by Age	595	813	789	767	668	489	2,936	7,057

CENSUS.

	April 1906	April 1907	April 1910
Children 0 to 17 years	125,191	90,955	100,183
Children 5 to 17 years	101,836	77,367	74,729
Population of City and County, estimated on above	430,000	325,000	360,000

PRINCIPAL ITEMS OF THE SCHOOL CENSUS REPORT SUBMITTED BY CHIEF CENSUS MARSHAL AND CLERK, MR. W. D. SCURLOCK, FOR THE YEAR ENDING JUNE 30, 1910, AS COMPARED WITH THE CORRESPONDING REPORT FOR THE YEAR ENDING JUNE 30, 1909.

Number of families		46,766
Decrease		3,888
Number of white children between 5 and 17 years of age—		
Boys	36,937	
Girls	36,556	
Total	73,493	
School Census, 1909	86,843	
Decrease		13,350
Number of negro children between 5 and 17 years of age—		
Boys	35	
Girls	23	
Total	58	
School Census, 1909	67	
Decrease		9
Number of native born Mongolians between 5 and 17 years of age—		
Boys	754	
Girls	424	
Total	1,178	
School Census, 1909	1,148	
Increase		30

Total number of census children between 5 and 17 years of age	74,729	
School Census, 1909	88,058	
Decrease		13,329
Number of children under 5 years of age	25,454	
School Census, 1909	23,809	
Increase		1,645
Nativity of children—		
Native born	96,926	
Foreign born	3,257	
Total	100,183	
School census, 1909	111,867	
Decrease		11,684

TABLE SHOWING NUMBER OF CHILDREN OF COMPULSORY SCHOOL AGE (8 TO 14 YEARS) ATTENDING SCHOOL AND NOT ATTENDING SCHOOL. ASSEMBLY DISTRICTS 28 TO 45, INCLUSIVE.

School Children (Boys)— Age	Public	Private	No School
8	2,532	319	66
9	2,388	314	41
10	2,287	309	34
11	2,246	337	19
12	2,482	407	35
13	2,255	398	53
14	2,387	435	139
	16,577	2,559	387
School Children (Girls)— Age			
8	2,347	406	64
9	2,293	345	26
10	2,450	396	27
11	2,130	401	30
12	2,326	464	49
13	2,108	446	42
14	2,131	512	155
	15,785	2,970	393
Boys—8 to 14	16,577	2,559	387
Girls—8 to 14	15,785	2,970	393
	32,362	5,529	780

GRADUATES.

Number of graduates from the grammar schools for the year—	
Boys	789
Girls	1,016
Total	1,805
Number of graduates from the high schools for the year—	
Boys	169
Girls	225
Total	394

NUMBER OF TEACHERS IN DEPARTMENT, JUNE, 1910.

	Men	Women	Total
High School Principals	5	.....	5
High School Teachers	37	55	92
Grammar Principals	9	16	25
Grammar Vice-principals	2	23	25
Grammar Teachers	4	292	296
Primary Principals	4	51	55
Primary Teachers	...	523	523
Domestic Science	...	8	8
Drawing	...	3	3
Manual Training	9	.....	9
Music	...	2	2
Physical Culture	1	1	2
Reading (Primary)	...	1	1
Total Day Schools	71	975	1,046
Evening School Principals	7	2	9
Evening School Teachers	29	60	89
Substitutes	5	49	54
Total number of teachers in department	112	1,086	1,198

LENGTH OF SERVICE OF TEACHERS, COUNTING ONLY THEIR SERVICE IN SAN FRANCISCO PUBLIC SCHOOLS.

Years of Service	Men	Women	Total
1 year	...	17	17
2 years	6	18	24
3 years	8	65	73
4 years	6	55	61
5 years	2	40	42
6 years	10	73	83
7 years	7	42	49
8 years	8	79	87
9 years	8	30	38
10 years	9	12	21
11 years	3	1	4
12 years	4	50	54
13 years	5	55	60
14 years	1	31	32
15 years	...	17	17
16 years	1	10	11
17 years	1	3	4
18 years	2	37	39
19 years	3	24	27
20 years	2	22	24
21 years	3	20	23
22 years	2	26	28
23 years	2	16	18
24 years	4	33	37
25 years	...	27	27
26 years	1	31	32
27 years	1	17	18

LENGTH OF SERVICE OF TEACHERS—Continued.

28 years	1	27	28
29 years	...	13	13
30 years	1	16	17
31 years	...	18	18
32 years	...	18	18
33 years	...	27	27
34 years	1	16	17
35 years	2	22	24
36 years	...	6	6
37 years	...	14	14
38 years	2	9	11
39 years	2	8	10
40 years	...	5	5
41 years	...	7	7
42 years	4	5	9
43 years	...	4	4
44 years	...	4	4
45 years	2	2	4
46 years	...	2	2
47 years	...	3	3
48 years	...	.....	.....
49 years	...	.....	.....
50 years	...	2	2
51 years	...	1	1
52 years	...	2	2
53 years	...	2	2
	112	1,086	1,198

VOLUMES IN SCHOOL LIBRARIES AND STOREROOM (INCLUDING BOOKS FOR USE OF INDIGENTS).

	Volumes	Estimated Value
High Schools	5,353	$ 5,055
Primary and Grammar Schools	70,844	30,422
Evening Schools	2,163	864
In Storeroom	12,881	6,500
	91,241	$42,841

Books becoming useless or lost during year 2,369

SCHOOL VISITATION.

Official visits of Superintendent and deputies	4,231
Official visits by members of the Board of Education	2,017
Visits by other persons	44,486

WORK OF TRUANT OFFICERS.

The following statement concerning the work performed by the five truant officers for the year ending June 30, 1910, was presented by Mr. T. J. Dugan, officer in charge;

Number of complaints of truancy investigated and reported back to principals.	5,280
Number of children found on the street, cases investigated and reported to principals	4,039
Number of children taken to the Parental School	10
Number of children found upon the street possessed of working certificates	321
Number of complaints that children could not be located	59
Number of children placed in the public schools never having been enrolled therein before	258
Number of children brought before the Juvenile Court	98
Number of parents arrested, fined or reprimanded	2
Number of parents brought before the Juvenile Court	86
Number of boys brought before the Board of Education for acts of vandalism committed on school property and fined or reprimanded	31
Total number of cases disposed of	10,184
Visits to schools on official business	2,494

Commenting on the foregoing statement, I desire to say that the enforcement of the Compulsory Education Law and the repression of truancy have been promoted very much during the past year. This is due to the efficient work of the attendance or truant officers. In the discharge of their duties they have exercised diligence, courtesy and firmness, and their work merits commendation.

REPORT OF THE BOARD OF EXAMINATION.

The Board of Examination is composed of;

Superintendent Alfred Roncovieri, Chairman

Deputy Superintendent W. B. Howard, Secretary

Deputy Superintendent T. L. Heaton

Deputy Superintendent James Ferguson.

Deputy Superintendent R. H. Webster.

The Board of Examination has conducted two examinations (October, 1909, and April, 1910), according to law, of persons desirous of securing grammar grade or special certificates. It has met monthly and forwarded its recommendations to the Board of Education.

Herewith is a resume of its work;

Number of certificates granted on examination to men	2
Number of certificates granted on examination to women	10
Number of certificates granted on credentials to men	13
Number of certificates granted on credentials to women	135
Number of certificates renewed	60
Number of applicants rejected on examination	14
Number of applicants rejected on credentials	1
Amount of fees collected for examination and issuance of certificates	$412

CERTIFICATION AND SCHOLASTIC TRAINING OF TEACHERS.

Number of teachers in the department who hold high school certificates........	154
Number of teachers who hold certificates of the grammar grade................	944
Number of teachers who hold certificates of primary grade....................	24
Number of teachers who hold special certificates.............................	76
Number of teachers who hold Kindergarten certificates........................	1
Number of teachers who are graduates of the University of California..........	117
Number of teachers who are graduates of Stanford University..................	14
Number of teachers who are graduates of other universities...................	29
Number of teachers who are graduates of S. F. City or High School Normal prior to 1901..	401
Number of teachers who are graduates of S. F. State Normal after 1901........	104
Number of teachers who are graduates of Chico State Normal.................	11
Number of teachers who are graduates of Los Angeles State Normal............	2
Number of teachers who are graduates of San Diego State Normal.............	0
Number of teachers who are graduates of San Jose State Normal..............	79

TEACHERS' INSTITUTE.

The Teachers' Institute for the teachers of the public schools of the City and County of San Francisco was held in conjunction with the Teachers' Institutes of the counties of Alameda, Contra Costa, Marin and San Mateo, under the auspices of the annual convention of the California Teachers' Association which was convened in this City and County December 27, 28, 29 and 30, 1909. All the sessions were attended by 1,068 department teachers.

REPORT OF THE PUBLIC SCHOOL TEACHERS' ANNUITY AND RETIREMENT FUND COMMISSIONERS.

San Francisco, July 20, 1910.

To the Honorable Board of Education,

in and for the City and County of San Francisco.

Gentlemen:—I have the honor to submit herewith the report on the Public School Teachers' Annuity and Retirement Fund for the fiscal year terminating June 30, 1910.

ALFRED RONCOVIERI,

Superintendent of Schools, and Secretary Public School Teachers' Retirement Fund Commissioners.

RECEIPTS.

Balance in fund June 30, 1909, including $50,000—permanent fund—invested in 44 $1,000 San Francisco Fire Protection System 5% bonds................................	$55,383 44
Contributions by teachers under provisions of Annuity Law.	12,315 50
Absence money granted by Board of Education............	3,000 00
Interest on Permanent Fund........	2,200 00
Forward..	$72,898 94

Receipts, forward		$72,898 94
Interest on Annuity Fund in Savings Banks		246 50
Amounts received in accordance with Section 8 (A) from teachers retired during fiscal year;		
1909		
Sept. 3—Mrs. N. Seabrook	$149 75	
July 30—Miss Rose E. Morgan	217 75	
Aug. 30—Miss Jessie I. King	195 10	
1910		
Jan. 3—Paul A. Garin	248 00	
March 4—Miss Emma R. Pettigrew	73 70	
March 15—Miss Emma R. Pettigrew	12 00	
April 2—Miss Anne B. Campbell	195 10	1,091 40
Total		$74,236 84

DISBURSEMENTS.

Annuities to Retired Teachers.

1909		
October 1	$4,641 25	
1910		
January 1	4,708 75	
April 1	4,841 45	
July 1	4,811 25	
	$19,002 70	
Clerical Service	50 00	
Printing	29 50	19,082 20
Balance in fund		$55,154 64

LIST OF ANNUITIES.

Date of Retirement	Name	Maximum or Fraction Thereof	Annuity Per Month	Annuity Per Quarter
1895				
Nov. 27,	Mrs. L. T. Hopkins	Max.	$50 00	$150 00
1896				
Jan. 22,	Miss L. F. Ryder	Max.	50 00	150 00
Jan. 22,	Mrs. M. H. Currier	Max.	50 00	150 00
April 24,	Miss V. M. Raclet	9/10	45 00	135 00
1897				
Sept. 11,	Miss M. Solomon	Max.	50 00	150 00
Dec. 8,	Miss F. L. Soule	Max.	50 00	150 00
1898				
Sept. 14,	Miss Kate Kollmyer	8/15	26 66⅔	80 00

Date of Retirement	Name	Maximum or Fraction Thereof	Annuity Per Month	Annuity Per Quarter
1900				
July 18,	Mrs. A. Griffith	Max.	50 00	150 00
July 25,	Miss K. F. McColgan	Max.	50 00	150 00
Aug. 1,	Miss L. M. Barrows	13/15	43 33⅓	130 00
Aug. 1,	Miss Annie A. Hill	Max.	50 00	150 00
Oct. 15,	Miss M. J. Canham	14/15	46 66⅔	140 00
1901				
July 20,	Miss J. B. Gorman	Max.	50 00	150 00
Oct. 4,	Miss E. Murphy	9/10	45 00	135 00
1902				
Jan. 2,	Miss R. B. Campbell	Max.	50 00	150 00
Jan. 2,	Miss L. S. Templeton	Max.	50 00	150 00
Jan. 2,	Mr. A. T. Winn	Max.	50 00	150 00
Sept. 28,	Miss Emma J. Miller	11/15	36 66⅔	110 00
1903				
Feb. 17,	Mrs. B. A. Chinn	Max.	50 00	150 00
Feb. 17,	Miss Lydia Hart	11/15	36 66⅔	110 00
Feb. 17,	Miss Christine Hart	Max.	50 00	150 00
Aug. 1,	Mrs. S. A. Miles	Max.	50 00	150 00
Aug. 1,	Mr. T. B. White	Max.	50 00	150 00
Sept. 1,	Miss A. E. Slaven	Max.	50 00	150 00
Oct. 15,	Miss L. Burnham	3/4	37 50	112 50
1904				
Aug. 1,	Mr. Elisha Brooks	Max.	50 00	150 00
Aug. 1,	Miss I. Patterson	Max.	50 00	150 00
Sept. 1,	Mrs. E. M. Whitcomb	Max.	50 00	150 00
1905				
Jan. 16,	Miss E. G. Grant	Max.	50 00	150 00
March 1,	Miss M. A. Smith	2/3	33 33⅓	100 00
March 1,	Miss Jean Parker	Max.	50 00	150 00
March 1,	Mrs. T. C. Nicholl	Max.	50 00	150 00
March 1,	Mr. Charles Ham	Max.	50 00	150 00
March 1,	Miss R. Jacobs	Max.	50 00	150 00
March 1,	Mr. D. Lambert	Max. (Even)	25 00	75 00
1906				
Feb. 1,	Miss M. E. Carson	Max.	50 00	150 00
Feb. 1,	Mrs. A. C. Taylor	Max.	50 00	150 00
Aug. 1,	Miss E. R. Elder	Max.	50 00	150 00
Aug. 1,	Mrs. C. Chalmers	Max.	50 00	150 00
Oct. 1,	Miss H. E. Whirlow	Max.	50 00	150 00
Dec. 1,	Mrs. V. Troyer	Max.	50 00	150 00
1907				
April 1,	Miss Madge Sprott	1/2 (Even)	25 00	75 00
April 1,	Miss A. D. Miley	14/15	46 66⅔	140 00
April 1,	Miss Q. O. McConnell	Max.	50 00	150 00
April 1,	Prof. A. Herbst	Max.	50 00	150 00
July 1,	Mr. C. W. Moores	Max.	50 00	150 00

Date of Retirement	Name	Maximum or Fraction Thereof	Annuity Per Month	Annuity Per Quarter
1907—Continued				
Sept. 1,	Miss V. E. Bradbury	Max.	50 00	150 00
Sept. 1,	Miss Martha Stone	Max.	50 00	150 00
Sept. 1,	Miss N. C. Stallman	Max.	50 00	150 00
Sept. 1,	Mr. W. H. Edwards	Max.	50 00	150 00
1908				
Jan. 1,	Miss R. V. Claiborne	2/3	$33 33⅓	$100 00
Feb. 1,	Mrs. M. E. Michener	Max.	50 00	150 00
Feb. 15,	Mrs. F. A. Banning	Max.	50 00	150 00
March 1,	Miss Rose Fay	11/15	36 66⅔	110 00
March 1,	Mrs. Mary A. Hogan	14/15	46 66⅔	140 00
May 1,	Miss Julia A. Danks	Max.	50 00	150 00
July 1,	Miss Laura T. Fowler	Max.	50 00	150 00
Sept. 1,	Miss Ruby A. Jewell	Max.	50 00	150 00
Sept. 1,	Miss Regina Hertz	4/5	40 00	120 00
1909				
Jan. 1,	Miss A. T. Campbell	Max.	50 00	150 00
Jan. 1,	Mrs. Mary J. Mayborn	Max.	50 00	150 00
Jan. 1,	Miss C. M. Johnston	Max.	50 00	150 00
Aug. 1,	Mrs. N. Seabrook	7/10	35 00	105 00
Aug. 1,	Miss Rose E. Morgan	Max.	50 00	150 00
Aug. 1,	Miss Jessie I. King	Max.	50 00	150 00
1910				
Jan. 1,	Paul A. Garin	Max.	50 00	150 00
Jan. 1,	Miss E. R. Pettigrew	3/5	30 00	90 00
Jan. 10,	Miss Anne B. Campbell	Max.	50 00	150 00

COMPETITIVE EXAMINATION FOR APPOINTMENT OF TEACHERS.

Questions, December 20th, 1909.

ARITHMETIC.

1. (a) A pupil writes 425 words in 5 minutes, 3 seconds. At next lesson she writes 521 words in 4 minutes, 5 seconds. At next lesson she writes 593 words in 4 minutes, 17 seconds. At what average rate of speed per minute does she write?

(b) Hale & Co., Stockton, bought of Lamont & Co., San Francisco, 3 doz. plain gold rings at $20.00 per dozen; 4 gold rings, diamond settings, at $50.00 each; 6 gold watches at $15.00 each; 4 sets teaspoons at $6.00 each. Make out the bill allowing a discount of 25%.

2 (a) A commission merchant received $50.00 from a country customer with orders to send him ribbon, worth 6¼c per yard, and to pay himself for his trouble. The merchant charged 2¼%. How many yards of ribbon did the merchant send to his customer?

(b) A ship worth $75,000.00 was insured for three-fifths of its value at 1⅞%. The cargo, valued at $7,500.00, was insured for 4-5 of its value at 2½%. Find amount of premiums.

3 (a) If it cost $312 to fence a piece of land 216 rods long and 24 rods wide, what will it cost to fence a square piece of equal area with the same kind of fence?

(b) Find the interest on $125.50 from January 1st, 1898, to July 7th, 1899, at 7% per annum.

4 (a) What will it cost to dig a cellar 60'x30'x9' at 33 1-3 cents per cubic yard?

(b) A room is 15 feet square and the walls are 9 feet high. What will it cost to paint the four walls at 25 cents per square yard, making no allowance for doors or windows?

5 (a) If four men build 12¼ rods of fence in 3¼ days, how long will it take 18 men to build 237 6-13 rods?

(b) Four persons engage in manufacturing, and invest together $22,500.00. At the end of a certain time A's share of the gain is $2,000.00, B's share $2,800.75, C's share $1,685.25, and D's share $1,014.00. How much capital did each put in?

GRAMMAR.

1. "In the bosom of one of those spacious coves which indent the eastern shore of the Hudson, at that broad expansion of the river denominated by the ancient Dutch navigators the Tappan Zee, and where they always prudently shortened sail and implored the protection of St. Nicholas when they crossed, there lies a small market town or rural port, which by some is called Greensburgh, but which is more generally and properly known by the name of Tarry Town."

(a) Draw one line under the entire subject, and two lines under the entire predicate.

(b) Parse the underlined phrases and clauses in above.

2. "The sun that brief December day
Rose cheerless over hills of gray,
And, darkly circled, gave at noon
A sadder light than waning moon."
Diagram or analyze the above.

3. What is a synopsis?
What is meant by voice?
What is declension?
Give the principal parts of lay, set, go, give and lie (to recline).
Singing birds are silent at this season.
The bird's singing under the window awakened us.
What is the use of "singing" in each of the above sentences?

.4 "In the Old Colony days, in Plymouth, the land of the Pilgrim,
To and fro in a room of his simple and primitive dwelling,
Clad in doublet and hose, and boots of Cordovan leather,
Strode with a martial air, Miles Standish, the Puritan Captain,
Buried in thought he seemed, with his hands behind him, and pausing
Ever and anon to behold his glittering weapons of warfare,
Hanging in shining array along the walls of the chamber."

In the above selection, tell the part of speech of each underlined word.

5. (a) Give sentences illustrating the following uses of clauses. (Underline each clause.)
   1. Adverbial,
   2. Adjective,
   3. As object,
   4. As subject.

   Give an example of an infinitive used as subject.

(b) Give an example of a compound and a complex sentence, and explain the difference between them.

METHODS OF TEACHING.

1. (a) Which study do you consider the most valuable in the ordinary school curriculum, and give several reasons for your choice.

(b) 1. Upon what is the science of teaching based?
   2. What should be the great object of teaching?
   3. What are the characteristics of any good method of teaching?

2. (a) What method would you adopt to prevent tardiness; and to secure regular attendance in school?

(b) What is to be accomplished in teaching English Grammar?

3 (a) What special training is given by Literature, by History?

(b) By Mathematics, by Science?

4. (a) For what definite purpose and to what extent would you use analysis or the diagram?

(b) In teaching composition, in any grade above the fourth, state your method as to choosing subject, writing the composition, or correcting it. Name the grade or class you have in mind.

5. (a) Distinguish between principle, method, device. Which may change?

(b) 1. When is a schoolroom in good order?
   2. What incentive will you put before children for study?

QUESTIONS, MARCH 21, 1910.

ARITHMETIC.

1. (a) The longitude of Portland, Maine, is 70 degrees 15 minutes, and that of Chicago is 87 degrees, 38 minutes. What is the difference in time between the two places?

(b) How many square inches of tin are there in a dozen tin pails of cylindrical shape, the diameter of each being 8 inches and the height 10 inches? (No top.)

2. (a) A rectangular field having an area of 135 1/5 acres is 3 1/5 times as long as it is wide. Find the length of its diagonal.

(b) If 9 bricklayers can lay a wall 80 ft. long, 20 ft. high, 1½ ft. thick, in 15 days and 9 hours each, in how many days of 10 hours each can 12 bricklayers lay a wall 100 ft. long, 25 ft. high and 2 ft. thick?

3. (a) On $860.56, $149.63 interest was paid for 2 years, 8 months, 3 days. What was the rate?

(b) An agent received $10,200 with which to purchase wheat at $1.25 per cental at a commission of 2%. How many centals did he buy?

4. (a) The distance from San Francisco to San Jose is 50.6 miles. An automobile party leaves San Francisco at 10:35 A. M. and arrives at San Jose at 1:20 P. M. What was the average speed on the trip?

(b) A man owns 3/5 of a ship that is worth $85,000. If the ship is insured for 57½% of its value, how much money would this man receive if the ship were a total loss, and how much would he lose?

5. (a) Subtract 5⅜ from 9.65 and divide the difference by (3⅞—2.65). What number is that from which if we deduct 3/7 of itself and 2/9 of the remainder, 28 will be left?

(b) A shed is 15 ft. long and 10 ft. wide. It is 12 ft. high in front and 7 ft. high in the back. How much lumber (one inch boards) should be ordered to cover the four sides, adding 10% for waste?

How many full bundles of shingles should be ordered for the roof, if there are 250 shingles in a bundle, and they are laid so that one thousand cover an area 80 square feet?

GRAMMAR.

1 Part of speech of the underlined words, and why?

(a) (b) He is as honest as he looks.

(c) He came as he had promised.

(d) There is little hope, but I shall try.

(e) There is no lad but honors his mother.

(f) The game is not worth the candle.

(g) This is the book that I prefer.

(h) Not that I love Caesar less.

(i) The longer we live, the more we learn.

2. Name the principal and subordinate clauses, and tell how subordinate clauses are used:

> The drawbridge dropped with a surly clang,
> And through the dark arch a charger sprang,
> Bearing Sir Launfal, the maiden knight,
> In his gilded mail, that flamed so bright
> It seemed the dark castle had gathered all
> Those shafts the fierce sun had shot over its wall
> In his siege of three hundred summers long,
> And, binding them all in one blazing sheaf,
> Had cast them forth.

3. In the above selection tell what each participial and prepositional phrase modifies.

4. Give the case of nouns and pronouns and why, and parse all finite verbs in the following selection:

The investigations and prosecutions initiated by Secretary Hitchcock and carried on by his successor, Secretary Garfield, demonstrated conclusively that land thieves have been for some time getting possession of the public domain, and that they have had sometimes the direct, sometimes the indirect, aid of public officials in and out of Congress.

5. Are the following correct? Give your reasons:
(a) I saw him many times this year.
(b) One of his best friends were accused of the crime.
(c) It looks like it would rain to-day.

METHODS OF TEACHING—SCHOOL MANAGEMENT—HYGIENE.

(Write not more than one page on each lettered division of a question.)

11. (a) Discuss the importance of the personal life and character of the teacher in relation to her profession. Illustrate.

(b) How much time should a teacher spend daily out of school hours in preparation of her work, and how should that time be spent?

12 (a) How would you handle the "topical method" in History, in study and recitation, and what are its advantages over the "question and answer method"?

(b) How may the judgment be trained in History study?

13. (a) What are the causes of impure air in a schoolroom, and what are its effects on the children? How can a room be ventilated by doors and windows without subjecting some to cold air?

(b) Name two books on "Methods," or History of Education, you have read. Give a brief summary of the contents of one of these.

14. (a) Name the most important factors in moral training. Illustrate by suggesting how the different school subjects might contribute.

(b) How do you teach division and pointing off of decimals? How would you secure accuracy in number combinations?

15. (a) How would you give individual aid to backward pupils in a class of 40 to 50 pupils?

(b) How do you estimate a pupil's fitness for promotion?

APPENDIX

NAMES AND LOCATION OF SCHOOLS AND DESCRIPTION OF SCHOOL PROPERTY.

Adams Cosmopolitan Grammar School—Temporary frame building, 12 rooms; Eddy street, between Van Ness avenue and Polk street; lot in block 62 W. A., 137½x120 feet.

Agassiz Primary School—Frame building. Cost, $31,500; 18 rooms; Bartlett street, between Twenty-second and Twenty-third streets; lot in Mission block 136, 150x250 feet, occupied also by Horace Mann Grammar school. On May 9, 1902, additional lot, southwest corner Twenty-second and Bartlett streets, S. 55 feet by W. 85 feet, was purchased from S. J. Hendy, December 28, 1908, from H. J. Koepke a lot in Mission block 136, $5,000; March 19, 1909, from Johanna Sheehan, W. line of Bartlett street 255 feet S. to Twenty-second street, S. 25 feet by W. 125 feet Mission, block 136, $4,500; December 6, 1909, from G. W. Wepfer, lot W. line of Bartlett street, 205 feet S. of Twenty-second street, S. 25 by W. 125 in Mission block 136, $7,000.

Bay View Grammar School—New building, 12 rooms. On July 10, 1905, additional lot in Silver Terrace tract, block C, was purchased from Allen Riddell for $10,250. Commencing at the corner formed by the intersection of the southerly line of Bay View avenue and the easterly line of Flora street, and running thence easterly along said southerly line of Bay View avenue 200 feet to the westerly line of Pomona street; thence at a right angle southerly 350 feet; thence at a right angle westerly 200 feet to the easterly line of Flora street; thence northerly along said line of Flora street 350 feet to the southerly line of Bay View avenue and point of commencement. Recorded in Book 2, 124 of Deeds, page 60. School located on Bay View avenue and Flora street.

Bergerot Primary School—New building, 12 rooms; cost $37,000; Twenty-fifth avenue and California street, block 95, 150x240 feet.

Bernal Grammar School—Frame building, 16 rooms; cost $30,560; Courtland avenue, between Andover avenue and Moultrie street. Lot in Gift Map No. 2, 140x148 feet 8½ inches. October 17, 1908, from Elizabeth S. Ford, lots Nos. 17, 19, 21 and 23, Gift Map No. 2, $2,600. January 15, 1909, lot on corner of Andover and Jefferson avenues, $2,600.

Bryant Cosmopolitan Primary School—Temporary building, 12 rooms. York and Twenty-third streets. Lot in Mission, block 147, between Twenty-second and Twenty-third streets, Bryant and York streets, 150x 200 feet.

Buena Vista Primary School—Frame building, 13 rooms. Bryant street, between Eighteenth and Nineteenth streets. Lot on Potrero, block 39, 100x200 feet.

Burnett Primary School—Frame building of 12 rooms and two adjacent rented rooms. L street and Fourteenth Avenue South. Lot in South San Francisco Homestead, block 289. Lot 1, 75x100 feet, and additional lot purchased from Cecilia Wright, August 26, 1903, for $500,

South San Francisco Homestead. Commencing at a point on the southwest line of Fourteenth Avenue South; distant 150 feet northwesterly from the northwesterly line of L Street South; thence northwesterly along Fourteenth Avenue South 32½ feet by uniform depth of 100 feet. September 27, 1909, from Martha A. Stapleton; commencing S.W. line Fourteenth avenue S. 182 feet 6 inches, N.W. on L. S. N.W. 42 feet 6 inches by S.W. 100 feet, Block 289, S. S. F. Homestead and R. R. Association, $1,750.

Clement Primary School—Temporary frame building, 6 rooms. Day and Noe streets. May 3, 1909, from Ellen S. McGowan and E. Connors, lot west line of Noe street 26½ feet north of 30th street, north 25 feet by west 105 feet in Horner Addition, block 172, $1,500. April 5, 1909, from Ellen S. McGowan and Delia Williams, lot southwestern corner Noe and Day streets, 105 feet by south on Noe street 26½ feet in Horner Addition, block 172, $6,000. April 12, 1909, from Ellen S. McGowan, west line Noe street, 25½ feet south of Day street, south 150 feet by west 105 feet, south 51½ feet by west 50 feet by north 228 feet by east 50 feet by south 26½ feet; thence east 105 feet, Horner Addition, block 172, $16,600. May 24, 1909, from W. E. Smith and Ellen McGowan, lot northwest corner Noe and 30th streets. North 26½ feet by west 105 feet, Horner Addition, block 172, $2,150. June 1, 1909, from Ellen S. McGowan and Joe Gottwald, lot south line of Day street 155 feet west of Noe street, west 25 feet by south 228 feet to the north line of 30th street in Horner Addition, block 172, $5,400.

Clement Cooking and Manual Training Center—Temporary frame building, 6 rooms. Geary near Jones street. Lot in block 253, 77½x137½ feet; additional lot commencing at a point on the southerly line of Geary street, distant 137 feet 6 inches westerly from the southwest corner of Geary and Jones streets; thence northerly along said line of Geary street, 25 feet by south 137 feet 6 inches in depth, being a portion of 50 vara lot 253. Purchased from S. L. and Mabel V. Starr, August 14, 1905, for $27,000. Recorded in Book 2, 134 of Deeds, page 98.

Cleveland Primary School—January 11, 1909, from Annie M. Creighton, lot northwest corner of Moscow street and Persia avenue, 100 feet by 300 feet, $6,500. February 15, 1909, from William McCall, lot in Excelsior Homestead Association, block 73, northeast corner Persia avenue and Athens street, 100 feet on Persia avenue by 300 feet on Athens street, $6,750.

Columbia Grammar School—Cost $30,300; frame building, 18 rooms and three portable rooms. Florida street, between Twenty-fifth and Twenty-sixth streets. Lot in Mission, block 178. Lot No. 1, 100x200 feet; lot No. 2, 50x100 feet.

Cooper Primary School—Temporary frame building, 6 rooms, Greenwich street, between Jones and Leavenworth streets, lot in block 237, 137½x137½ feet.

Commercial School—Afternoon session at Mission High school, Eighteenth and Dolores streets. January 18, 1909, from F. Siefke, north line Grove street 100 feet west of Larkin street, 37½ feet by 120 feet, Western Addition, block No. 3, $15,000. February 8, 1909, from Dorothea Fassman, west line of Grove street 112½ feet east from east line of Polk street, east 25 feet by 137½ feet, Western Addition, block No. 3, $9,800. June

21, 1909, from Chas. Worth, lot north line Grove street, 82½ feet east of Polk street, east 30 feet by north 120 feet, Western Addition, block No. 3, $12,000; lot in block No. 3, Western Addition, Grove street near Larkin street, 137½ by 137½.

Crocker Grammar School—Frame building, 20 rooms; cost, $26,547. Page street, between Broderick and Baker streets. Lot in block 523, W. A., 137½x137½ feet. Additional lot purchased from W. J. Hawkins May 16, 1905, for $2,750. Commencing at a point on the southerly line of Page street, distant 96 feet 10½ inches, easterly from the easterly line of Baker street; thence easterly 25 feet by uniform depth of 110 feet.

Denman Grammar School—Temporary frame building, 6 rooms. Bush street, between Larkin and Hyde streets. Lot in block 307, 97½x137½ feet. A new building for this school will be constructed on the following property: May 17, 1909, from the Edwin Barron estate, lot northeast corner Fell and Pierce streets, 137 feet 6 inches on Fell street by 137 feet 6 inches on Pierce street, Western Addition, block 379, $29,118. October 18, 1909, from P. J. Stuparich and H. Adams, lot southeast corner Pierce and Hayes streets, 137½ by 137½, $37,125. June 13, 1910, from Emery B. Hopkins, lot north side of Fell street 137 feet 6 inches east from easterly line of Pierce street, 55 feet by 137½ feet, W. A. block 379, $9,500.00.

Douglass Primary School—Cost, $28,787; frame building, 10 rooms. Corner Nineteenth and Collingwood streets. Lot in Horner's Addition, 135x135 feet. June 27, 1910, from Alfred H. Grant, lot E. line of Nineteenth street, 113 feet west of Collingwood street, W. 30 feet by S. 135 feet, Horner's Addition block 194, $4,500.00.

Dudley Stone Primary School—Frame building, 16 rooms, cost, $28,755. Haight street, between Lott and Masonic avenues, lot in block 657, W. A., 137½x137½ feet. August 12, 1908, from E. L. Pritchard; consideration, $6,000. Lot on south line of Haight street, 112 feet 6 inches west of Central avenue, west 25 feet by 137 feet 6 inches, being a part of Western Addition, block 657. August 12, 1908, from J. L. Pritchard, out of School Fund, lot south line Haight street, 112 feet 6 inches west of Central avenue, west 25 feet by 137 feet 6 inches, Western Addition block 657, $6,000.

Edison Primary School—Frame building, 10 rooms, cost, $27,936. Church and Hill streets. Lot in Mission, block 90, 101 feet 9 inches by 114 feet.

Emerson Primary School—Frame building, 20 rooms, cost, $28,155. Pine street, between Scott and Devisadero streets. Lot in block 460, W. A., 137½x137½ feet.

Everett Grammar School—Frame building, 16 rooms, cost, $24,132; five additional rooms are rented. Sanchez street, between Sixteenth and Seventeenth streets. Lot in Mission, block 95, 125x160 feet. A lot of land 28x160 feet on Sanchez street north of and contiguous to the present site of the Everett Grammar school, $10,000. November 29, 1909, from Frank L. Roseneau, lot east line of Sanchez street 202 feet south of Sixteenth street, south 28 feet by east 80 feet, in Mission block 95, $6,900.

Fairmount Grammar School—Frame building, 12 rooms. Chenery street, near Randall street, five portable rooms on premises. Lot in Fairmount tract, block 29, lot 1, 112x125 feet; lot 2, 62x175 feet.

Franklin Grammar School—Temporary frame building, 12 rooms. Eighth street, near Bryant street. Lot in block 410, 140x275 feet.

Frank McCoppin School—Temporary frame building, 9 rooms. Sixth avenue, between B and C streets. Lot in block 375, west of First avenue, 150x240 feet. April 5, 1909, from Elizabeth M. Strand, lot west line Sixth avenue 200 feet south of B street, south 25 feet by west 120 feet, O. L. block 375, $2,000. April 16, 1909, from Robert Bennett, lot east side Seventh avenue, 200 feet south of B street, south 25 feet by east 100 feet, O. L. block 375, $7,500.

Fremont Grammar School—Frame building 16 rooms, cost, $35,873. McAllister street, between Broderick and Baker streets. Lot in block 530, W. A., 137½x137½ feet. Additional lot (No. 1) purchased from Herman Murphy, January 3, 1902, for $3,250. Commencing at a point on the northerly line of McAllister street, distant 112½ feet westerly from the westerly line of Broderick street; thence westerly 25 feet by uniform depth of 137 feet 6 inches. Recorded in book 1, 947 of Deeds, page 102; additional lot (No. 2) purchased from Owen McHugh, July 1, 1902. Commencing at a point on the northerly line of McAllister street, distant 96 feet 10½ inches easterly from the easterly line of Baker street, running thence easterly 25 feet, by uniform depth of 137 feet 6 inches. Recorded in Book 1, 962 of Deeds, page 138.

Garfield Primary School—Temporary frame building, 10 rooms (four additional rented rooms). Union street, near Kearny street. Lot in block 62, 137½x137½ feet. A new building for this school is being built. Lot in block No. 82. Corner Filbert and Kearny streets; 137½x137½ feet. Additional lot adjacent in litigation. July 28, 1908, from Annie M. Gallagher and Mary B. Waller, lot on north line of Filbert street, distant 137 feet 6 inches west from Kearny street; thence west on Filbert street 68 feet 9 inches by 137 feet 6 inches, being a part of 50 vara lot No. 461 and 50 vara lot No. 82, $8,000. From Charles Huth, November 2, 1908, south line of Greenwich street, between Kearny and Dupont streets, 25 feet square, block 82, $750. November 2, 1908, from Charles Kosta, rear portion of lot adjoining above 25 feet square, $550. West line of Kearny street 112 feet 6 inches south from Greenwich; thence south along west line of Kearny street 25 feet; thence at right angles west 87 feet 6 inches; thence at right angles north 25 feet; thence east 87 feet 6 inches, purchased from the Hibernia Saving and Loan Society July 10, 1903, $850.

Girls' High School—Temporary frame building just completed at a cost of $16,000. Scott street, near Geary street. This school is not built on school property, but on property belonging to the city, and which originally formed a part of Hamilton Square. In 1870 the Board of Education obtained permission to use a portion for the erection of school buildings. Lot 275 feet front on Scott street, 341 feet 3 inches on Geary and O'Farrell streets:

Glen Park Grammar School—New frame building, 12 rooms, costing $42,500. San Jose and Joost avenues. Additional lot purchased from the estate of John Pforr, May 20, 1905, for $5,600. Mission and Thirtieth Extension Homestead Union. Beginning at the corner formed by the intersection of the southwesterly line of Berkshire street with the southeasterly line of Lippard avenue; thence southwesterly along Lippard avenue 400 feet; thence at right angles southeasterly 200 feet in the northwesterly line of Fulton avenue; thence at right angles northeasterly

400 feet along Fulton avenue to the southwesterly line of Berkshire street; thence at a right angle northwesterly along Berkshire street to the point of beginning, being all of block 3, Mission and Thirtieth Streets Extension Homestead Union. Recorded in Book 2, 125 of Deeds, page 76.

Golden Gate Primary School—New building. Golden Gate avenue, between Pierce and Scott streets. Lot in block 433 W. A., 100x137½ feet. Additional lot purchased from Fred L. Hansen, July 20, 1905, for $4,375. Commencing at a point on the northerly line of Golden Gate avenue, distant thereon 68 feet 9 inches, westerly from the westerly line of Pierce street; thence westerly 25 feet, by uniform depth of 137 feet 6 inches. Additional lot (No. 2) purchased from Margaret Poyelson, June 28, 1905, for $8,856. Commencing at a point on the northerly line of Golden Gate avenue, distant thereon 93 feet 9 inches, westerly from the westerly line of Pierce street; thence westerly 43 feet 9 inches, by uniform depth of 137 feet 8 inches. Additional lot (No. 3) purchased from Gustave A. DeManiel, June 14, 1905, for $12,462. Commencing at a point on the northerly line of Golden Gate avenue, distant 137 feet 6 inches, westerly from the westerly line of Pierce street; thence westerly 37 feet 6 inches, by uniform depth of 137 feet 6 inches.

Grant Primary School—Frame building, 8 rooms, cost, $18,499. Pacific avenue, between Broderick and Baker streets. Lot in block No. 546, W. A., 137½x137½ feet.

Grattan Primary School—Temporary frame building, 6 rooms. Alma street, near Grattan. Additional lot purchased from the Pope Estate Co.; for $28,500. Recorded in Book 2, 130 of Deeds, page 204. Western Addition, block 874. Commencing at the point of intersection of the southerly line of Grattan street with the easterly line of Shrader street; thence easterly along Grattan street 203 feet 7¾ inches; thence at a right angle southerly 249 feet to the northerly line of Alma street thence at a right angle westerly and along said line of Alma street 203 feet 7¾ inches to the easterly line of Shrader street; thence at a right angle northerly 249 feet 11 inches to the southerly line of Grattan street, and point of commencement.

Haight Primary School—Frame building, 13 rooms, cost, $23,488. Mission street, between Twenty-fifth and Twenty-sixth streets. Lot in Mission block 183; 150x117½ feet.

Hamilton Grammar School—Frame building, 17 rooms, cost, $27,650. Geary street, between Scott and Pierce streets. (See Girls' High School.)

Hancock Grammar School—Temporary frame building, 10 rooms. Filbert street, near Jones. Lot in block 208, 100x120 feet. December 21, 1908, from R. H. McColgan and Mary E. Russell, north line Filbert street 110 feet west from Taylor, west 60x120 feet, 50 vara lot No. 208, $10,800.

Harrison Primary School—Temporary frame building, 3 rooms. Railroad avenue and Thirty-fourth street. All of block 584, Bay View Tract, Sub. 2, bounded by Railroad avenue, J street S., Thirty-fourth avenue S. and Thirty-fifth avenue S., except lot S line of Thirty-fourth avenue S., 100 feet west of J street, S. W. 50xS. 100 feet, $10,000.

Hawthorne Primary School—Frame building, 11 rooms, cost, $11,500. Shotwell street, between Twenty-second and Twenty-third streets, lot in Mission block 138, 122½x122½ feet.

Hearst Grammar School—Frame building, 25 rooms, cost, $25,007. Corner Fillmore and Hermann streets, lot in block 374, W. A., 137½x137½ feet.

Henry Durant Primary School—Frame building, 12 rooms, cost, $18,294. Turk street, between Buchanan and Webster streets, lot in block 281, W. A., 137½x120 feet.

Holly Park Primary School—Temporary frame building of 8 rooms. Andover avenue and Jefferson street. (Lot is leased.) July 12, 1909, from A. B. Ruggles, lots 31, 32, 33, 34, 35, 36, 37, 38, 39, 40. Block 3, Holly Park tract, $13,700.

Horace Mann Grammar School—Frame building, 20 rooms, cost, $33,149. Valencia street, between Twenty-second and Twenty-third streets (See Agassiz Primary.) December 28, 1908, from Moore Investment Company, commencing 205 feet south from Twenty-second street, thence south on Valencia street 37½ feet by 125 feet, Mission block No. 136, $15,000.

Hunter's Point Primary School—Temporary frame building of 2 rooms. Eighth avenue, between C and D streets. (Lot is leased.)

Irving Primary School—Temporary frame building, 6 rooms. Broadway, between Montgomery and Sansome streets. Lot in block No. 47, 68¾x137½ feet.

Irving M. Scott Grammar School—Frame building, 20 rooms, cost, $35,360. Tennessee street, near Twenty-second. Lot in Potrero, block No. 373, 150x200 feet.

Jackson Primary School—Temporary portable frame building, 6 rooms. Oak and Stanyan streets. (Lot is leased.)

James Lick Grammar School—Frame building, 14 rooms, cost, $21,877. Noe and Twenty-fifth streets. Lot in Horner's Addition, block No. 163, 114x116 feet.

Jean Parker Grammar School—Temporary building, 10 rooms. Broadway, between Powell and Mason streets. Lot in block No. 157. Lot 1, 65 feet 2 inches by 137½ feet; lot 2, 30x91 feet 8 inches; lot 3, 39 feet 9 inches by 91 feet 8 inches. December 28, 1908, from Fannie Galloway, 228 feet 11 inches by 69 feet 7 inches of lot in 50 vara, block 157, 91 feet 8 inches perpendicularly distant from north line of Broadway, $2,000. January 4, 1909, from the estate of Jose M. Jininez, north line of Broadway, 137 feet east from east line of Mason street; thence east on Broadway 34 feet 4 inches by 137 feet 6 inches deep, 50 varas, lot No. 167, $8,925. November 15, 1909, from Bernardo Fernandez, lot north line of Broadway 171 feet 10 inches east of Mason, east 38 by north 137 feet 6 inches, 50 vara, block 167, $9,750.

Jefferson Primary School—Temporary frame building, 6 rooms. Bryant and Seventh streets. Lot in block No. 397, 92½x275 feet.

John Swett Grammar School—Temporary frame building, 12 rooms. McAllister street, between Franklin and Gough streets. Lot in block No. 136, W. A., 137½x137½ feet. June 27, 1910, from Elizabeth M. Kreuz, lot on south line of Golden Gate avenue, 169½ feet west of Franklin street, west 27½ by south 120 feet, W. A., block 136, $11,000. From Sara Patek, lot on south line of Golden Gate avenue, 197 feet west from Franklin street, West 25 feet by South 120 feet, W. A., block 136, $9,750. From Mary Mocker, lot on south side of Golden Gate avenue, 222 feet west from Franklin street, 28x120 feet, W. A., block 136, $12,000. July 5, 1910, from Veronica J. Porcher, lot on the south line of Golden Gate avenue, 137½ feet west from Franklin street, west 32 feet by south 137½ feet, W. A., block 136, $14,000.

Lafayette School—(See Garfield School).

Laguna Honda Primary School—New building; cost, $57,612; 14 rooms; brick, class B. Seventh avenue, between I and J streets. Lot in block No. 678, 150x240 feet.

Lake View Primary School—Temporary frame building, 4 rooms. Plymouth and Grafton streets. April 26, 1909, from John and Belle McCaffery, lot east line of Faxon avenue, 100 feet south from Halloway avenue, south 37½ feet by east 112½ feet, lot 25, lot 19, Lake View, $1,025. April 26, 1909, from Spaulding & Neff, lots 19, 20, 21, 22, 23, half of lot 24, and lots from 26 to 41, inclusive, block 19, Lake View, $11,512.50.

Lincoln Grammar School—Temporary frame building, 8 rooms. Harrison street, near Fourth. Lot in block No. 374, 195x160 feet. Additional lot (1) purchased from Bertha Bunnison, February 9, 1906, for $4,250. Commencing at a point on the northwesterly line of Harrison street, distant thereon 275 feet, southwesterly on the southwest line of Fourth street, running thence southerly along said line of Harrison street; thence at a right angle northwesterly 85 feet; thence at a right angle northwesterly 85 feet to the north line of Harrison street from the point of commencement. Additional lot (2) purchased from Herman Scholten, December 18, 1905, for $2,800. Commencing at a point on the southeasterly line of Clara street, distant 275 feet southwesterly from the point of intersection of said southeasterly line of Clara street with the southwesterly line of Fourth street, running thence southwesterly along said southeasterly line of Clara street 25 feet; thence at a right angle southeasterly 75 feet; thence at a right angle northeasterly 25 feet; thence at a right angle northwesterly 75 feet to the southeasterly line of Clara street and point of commencement.

Lowell High School—Frame building, 21 rooms. Sutter street, between Octavia and Gough streets. Lot in block No. 158, W. A., 137½x120½ feet. November 29, 1909, from Ivan Treadwell, et al., the whole of Western Addition Block 667, bounded by Masonic avenue, Hayes, Ashbury and Grove streets, $116,500.

Madison Primary School—Frame building, 8 rooms. Clay street, near Walnut street. Lot in block No. 815, W. A., 137½x137½ feet.

Marshall Primary School—Temporary frame building, 10 rooms. Julian avenue, between Fifteenth and Sixteenth streets. Lot in Mission, block No. 35, 200x182 feet. (Also occupied by Mission Grammar school.) July 13, 1908, from R. E. Archbishop of San Francisco, lot corner Nineteenth and Angelica streets (resolution 1426 and 1757, Board of Supervisors). Commencing intersection south line Nineteenth street with east line Angelica street, south 205 feet to Cumberland Place; thence east 183 feet by north 114 feet west 50 feet N. W., 118 feet 2½ inches to Nineteenth street, west 102 feet to point of commencement. Mission, block 72, $33,625.

Commencing at point of intersection of the south line of Nineteenth street with the east line of Angelica street, thence south along Angelica street 205 feet to the north line of Cumberland Place, thence east 183 feet, thence north 91 feet, thence at right angles west 50 feet, thence northwest 118 feet 2½ inches to a point in the south line of Nineteenth street, which is distant east 102 feet from the southeast corner of Nineteenth and Angelica streets; thence west on south line of Nineteenth street 102 feet to point of commencement, being a portion of Mission block 72, purchased from Rev. P. W. Riordan, Roman Catholic Archbishop of San Francisco, a corporation sale, for $33,625, as alternative site for the Marshall Primary authorized by the bond issue September 29, 1903.

McKinley Primary School—Temporary frame building, 12 rooms. Fourteenth and Castro streets. Additional lot purchased from Jas. Irvine, August 14, 1905. Cost, $35,000. Mission block No. 121. Commencing at the southwesterly corner of Fourteenth and Castro streets; thence westerly along the southerly line of Fourteenth street 320 feet; thence at right angle southerly 230 feet to the northerly line of Henry street; thence easterly along said last named line 320 feet to the westerly line of Castro street; thence northerly along said last named line 230 feet to the point of commencement.

Mission Grammar School—Temporary frame building, 12 rooms. Mission, between Fifteenth and Sixteenth streets. (See Marshall Primary.)

Mission High School—Brick building, 25 rooms. Eighteenth and Dolores streets. Mission block No. 85, 398x194 feet. Purchased in 1896 for $52,500. April 19, 1909, from Owen M. V. Roberts, lot in Mission block 85, south line of Dorland street 88 feet east of Church street, east 25 feet by south 100 feet, $3,500. April 19, 1909, from J. and Winifred O'Donnell, lot south line Dorland street 138 feet southeast of Church street, southeast 25 feet by south 100 feet in Mission block 85, $5225. April 19, 1909, from the Catholic Apostolic church, lot north line of Eighteenth street 112 feet east of Church street, east 25 feet by north 114 feet, $7,800. June 1, 1909, from Amelia Dorland and Leonora Son, lot in Mission block No. 85, southeast corner Dorland and Church streets, south 35 feet 8 inches by east 88 feet, $6,300. June 1, 1909, from Herman D. Junck, lot in Mission block 85 south line Dorland street, 138 feet east from Church street; thence 100 feet east, 25⅝ feet by north 100 feet; thence west 25⅝ feet, $17,000. June 1, 1909, from Jessie Hauser, lot east line of Church street 168 feet north of Eighteenth street, north 27 feet by east 88 feet, $10,000; also northeast corner Church and Eighteenth streets, 62 feet on Eighteenth street by 114 feet on Church street, Mission block No. 85, $17,000. June 28, 1909, from Eva Topper, lot east line Church street 141 feet north Eighteenth street, north 27 feet by east 88 feet Mission block 85, $11,085. October 4, 1909, from Ida G. Shade, lot north line Eighteenth street, 137 feet east of Church, east 25 by north 114 feet, $9,000. From James A. Symon, lot north line Eighteenth street, 62 feet east from east line of Church east 25 by north 114 feet, in Mission block 85, $8,500. November 1, 1909, from David Dorward, lot south line of Church street, 114 feet north of Eighteenth street north 27 by east 88 in Mission block 85, $9,100. November 15, 1909, from James A. Symon, exec., north line of Eighteenth street, 87 feet east of Church street, east 25 feet by north 114 feet, $8,500.

Monroe Grammar School—New building. China avenue and London streets. Lot in block 14, Excelsior Homestead, 150x100 feet. Additional lot purchased from Thomas Shewbridge, August 30, 1902, Excelsior Homestead, block No. 14. New lot, corner China avenue and Paris street, northwest 100 feet by northeast 150 feet, lot 4, block 14, Excelsior Homestead.

Moulder Primary School—Frame building, 10 rooms. Cost, $21,100. Page and Gough streets, lot in block 145, W. A., 137½x120 feet.

Noe Valley Primary School—Frame building, 15 rooms. Twenty-fourth and Douglass. Additional lot (No. 1) purchased from George and Christina Gies. Deed dated October 5, 1901. Horner's Estate, block 244. Commencing at a point out the west line of Douglass street, 139 feet north to Twenty-fourth street; thence north on the west line of Douglass street 25 feet by west 125 feet in depth. Additional lot (No. 2) purchased from Mary E. Gies. Deed dated October 7, 1901. Commencing at a point on the west line of Douglass street 114 feet north of Twenty-fourth street; thence north on the west line of Douglass street 25 feet by west 125 feet in depth. Additional lot (No. 3) commencing at a point on the west line of Douglass street, 64 feet north of Twenty-fourth street; thence north on Douglass street, 50 feet, by west 125 feet in depth from Mary Tobener, September 6, 1901. Additional lot (No. 4) purchased from James M. Curtin, deed dated September 6, 1901. Commencing at a point on the northwest corner of Twenty-fourth and Douglass streets; thence north 64 feet, west 125 feet, north 50 feet, west 51 feet 8 inches, south 114 feet, east 176 feet 8 inches. Additional lot (No. 5) purchased from Eliz. Overend for $2,050. Commencing at a point on the south line of Elizabeth street, 125 feet west of Douglass street; thence west on Elizabeth street, 51 feet 8 inches, by south 114 feet, in depth.

Ocean House Primary School—Frame building, 2 rooms. Cost $1401.58. Corner Corbett road and Ocean avenue. Lot in San Miguel, 100 feet by 240 feet.

Oceanside Primary School—New frame building, 8 rooms, $38,000. Forty-second avenue and I street. Lot in block No. 714. 150 feet by 240 feet.

Oral School for Deaf—Temporary frame building, one room. McAllister street, between Octavia and Gough streets. (See John Swett Grammar).

Oriental Public School—Temporary frame building, 5 rooms. Clay street, near Powell street.

Parental School—Temporary frame building, 3 rooms. Harrison street, near Tenth. Lot in Mission block No. 8. 137½ feet by 137½ feet.

Pacific Heights Grammar School—Frame building, 19 rooms. Cost $31,270. Jackson, between Fillmore and Webster street. Lot in block 318, W. A., 137½ feet by 137½ feet. May 17, 1909, from Mary W. Shannon, lot west line of Jackson street, 113 feet west from Webster street, west 24½ feet by north 90 feet. Western Addition, block 318, $11,500. June 1, 1909, from Lillie E. Lincoln, north side of Jackson street 112 feet east of Fillmore street, east 25½ feet by north 127 feet 8¼ inches, Western Addition, block 318, $12,000.

Parkside—On T street near Thirteenth avenue. Lot in block 1114. 150x240 feet. One room frame building.

Peabody Primary School—Sixth avenue, near California. Lot in block No. 176; 150x240 feet.

Polytechnic High School—Temporary frame building, 16 rooms. Frederick street, near First avenue. Additional lot purchased from the City Realty Company, July 31, 1905, for $65,000. Western Addition, block No. 740. Commencing at a point on the south line of Frederick street 121½ feet east from First avenue; thence in a southerly direction 175 feet; thence at a right angle easterly 1 foot 6 inches; thence at a right angle southerly 100 feet to a point in the north line of Carl street 151½ feet east of First avenue; thence easterly along Carl street 464 and 8-12 feet to a point 269 4-12 feet west of Willard street; thence northerly 278 5-12 feet to a point on the south line of Frederick street 226 11-12 feet west of Willard street; thence west along south line of Frederick street 505 10-12 feet to point of commencement.

Redding Primary School—Temporary frame building, 12 rooms. Pine street, between Polk and Larkin streets. Lot in block 114, W. A., 200x120 feet.

Richmond Grammar School—Frame building, 17 rooms. First avenue, near Point Lobos avenue. Lot in Academy of Science block, W. A., O. L. R. 157 feet 7 inches by 240 feet. The Board of Education has permission to use this lot for school purposes.

Sheridan Primary School—One-story frame building, comprising 12 rooms. Minerva street, near Plymouth avenue. Lot in block S, Railroad Homestead Association. 100 feet by 125 feet. Lot No. 7. May 10, 1909, from W. S. Benthame, lot northwest corner of Farallones and Capital avenue in block L, Railroad Homestead Association, $3,450. September 23, 1908, from Welthy and Wm. S. Stafford, north side of Minerva street 150 feet west of Plymouth street; thence west on Minerva street 50 feet by north 125 feet. November 29, 1909, from Adolph Mueller, Caroline Bauer, admx. Wm. T. and Edward Bauer, interest and improvement in lot southwest corner of Capital avenue and Lobos street, 50 feet by 125 feet, in R. R Homestead Association, block L, $6,300.

Sherman Primary School—Frame building, 14 rooms. Union street, near Franklin. Lot in block 117, W. A., 137½ feet by 137½ feet.

South End Primary School—Frame building, comprising 13 rooms. Somerset street, between Felton and Burrows streets. Lot in University Mound survey, 50 feet by 120 feet. Additional block purchased from P. J. Kennedy, August 22, 1905, for $5,000. University Mound survey, block 12. Commencing at a point formed by the intersection of the northwesterly line of Bacon street, in the southwesterly line of Girard street, running thence northwesterly along Girard street 200 feet and thence at a right angle 240 feet to Berlin street; thence at a right angle southeasterly and along Berlin street 200 feet to the northwesterly line of Bacon street; thence at a right angle 240 feet to the southwesterly line of Girard street and point of commencement, being the southerly half of block No. 12, University Mound Survey.

Spring Valley Grammar School—Temporary frame building, 9 rooms. Broadway, near Polk street. Lot in block 21, W. A., 137½ feet by 137½ feet. May 24, 1909, from Margaret and Catherine Matthews, lot south line of Jackson street 137 feet 6 inches east from Larkin street, east 68 feet 9 inches by 137½ feet, $15,250. From Samuel Polack, lot south line of Jackson street 137 feet 6 inches west of Hyde street, west 34 feet 4½ inches by 137 feet 6 inches, 50 vara block 302, $6,975. July 19, 1909, from

Edward P. McGeeney, et al., lot south line Jackson, 171 feet 10½ inches, west of Hyde west 34 feet 4½ inches, by south 137 feet 6 inches, $9,100.

Starr King Primary School—Temporary frame building, 9 rooms, San Bruno avenue, near Twenty-fifth street. Commencing on the east line of Utah street 100 feet south from Twenty-fifth street; thence south on Utah street 100x200 feet in depth to San Bruno avenue, being lots 13, 14, 15, 16, 25, 26, 27, 28, of block 85.

Sunnyside Primary School—New class C building. Cost $30,000. Block 85, 115 Flood avenue. Additional lots 10 to 24 inclusive, Sunnyside tract. Purchased from the Sunnyside Land Company, July 19, 1902. June 22, 1908, bought from Monarch Mutual Building and Loan Association sewer right of way for Sunnyside School portion of lot 23, Sunnyside, block 47, $400.

Sunset Primary School—Temporary frame building, 6 rooms. Thirteenth avenue and K street. Block No. 876. West of First avenue; 150 feet by 240 feet.

Sutro Grammar School—Frame building, comprising 13 rooms. Twelfth avenue, between Clement and California streets. Lot in block 179; west of First avenue; 150x240 feet. January 18, 1909, from F. C. Fish and J. J. Higgin, lot on west line Twelfth avenue 200 feet south from California street, 25 feet by 140 feet, in block 170, $7,100.

Visitacion Valley Primary School—Temporary frame building, 7 rooms. Sunnyside avenue and Cora street.

Washington Grammar School—New steel-brick building. Washington and Mason streets. Lot in block No. 188; 137½x137½ feet. Additional new lot No. 1; purchased from the estate of Louise C. Kauffman, March 10, 1905, for $7,500. Commencing at a point on the southerly line of Washington street 137 feet 6 inches northerly from the southwest corner of Mason and Washington streets; thence southerly 137 feet 6 inches by west 34 feet 4½ inches, being a portion of 50 vara, lot 188. Additional new lot No. 2, purchased from Julie Dunnier and others, July 12, 1905, for $9,500. Commencing at a point on the southerly line of Washington street, distant 170 feet 10½ inches from the southwest corner of Mason and Washington streets; thence northerly 34 feet 4½ inches by south 137 feet 6 inches in depth, being a portion of 50 vara, lot 188.

West End Primary School—One-story frame building, 3 rooms. 5630 Mission street. Lot in West End Map. Block 23; 80x165 feet. March 1, 1909, from D. A. Helbing et al., lot southwest corner Lowell, Mission and Morse, 267 by 213, being lots 49, 50 and 51, West End Homestead, $9,250.

Winfield Scott Primary School—Building being built. Lombard street, between Broderick and Baker streets. Lot in block No. 553, W. A.; 137½x137½ feet.

Yerba Buena Primary School—Building being built. Greenwich street, between Webster and Fillmore streets. Lot in block No. 325, W. A.; 137½x120 feet. February 23, 1909, from McEwen Bros., lot Webster and Greenwich streets west 137½ feet by 120 feet in Western Addition, block No. 235, $17,000.

LIST OF UNOCCUPIED PROPERTIES BELONGING TO SCHOOL DEPARTMENT.

Lot in block No. 220; northwest corner Bush and Taylor streets; 137½x137½ feet.

Lot in block No. 286; Golden Gate avenue, near Hyde street; 110x 137½ feet.

Lot in block No. 348; Tehama street, between First and Second streets, irregular in size; about 118x155 feet.

Lot in block No. 160; Powell street, between Washington and Jackson streets; 68¾x137½ feet.

Lot in block 371; Fifth street, near Market street; 275x275 feet. Leased to Wise Realty Company (later merged into the Lincoln Realty Company) for thirty-five years, at a total rental of $2,835,000, as follows: For the first five years, a rental of $3,780 per month, and for the remaining thirty years, a rental of $7,245 per month.

Lot in block No. 137; Powell street, between Clay and Sacramento streets; 68¾x137½ feet.

Lot in Mission block No. 21; West Mission street, between Herman and Ridley streets; 133¾x137½ feet.

Lot in block No. 118; corner Bush and Stockton streets; 137½x137½ feet; 50 vara, lot 301.

Lots in block 358; Silver street, between Second and Third streets; lot No. 1, 88x70 feet; lot No. 2, 100x185 feet.

Lot in Mission block No. 72. Commencing at a point formed by the intersection of the southerly line of Nineteenth street with the easterly line of Angelica street, running thence southerly along said easterly line of Cumberland Place; thence easterly along said northerly line of Cumberland Place and Cumberland Place Extension 183 feet; thence at a right angle northerly 91 feet; thence at a right angle northerly 50 feet; thence in a northwesterly direction 118 feet 2½ inches to a point in the southerly line of Nineteenth street, which point is distant easterly 102 feet from the southeasterly corner of Nineteenth and Angelica streets; thence westerly along said southerly line of Nineteenth street 102 feet to the point of commencement. Purchased from P. W. Riordan, Roman Catholic Archbishop of San Francisco, for $33,625, as an alternate site for the Marshall Primary school. Recorded in Book 128 of Deeds, page 251, new series.

Lot in block No. 119; on Post street, between Grant avenue and Stockton streets; 70x122½ feet. Leased at an average of $911.42 per month.

Total rental, 35 years	$382,800.00
Average rental, per month	911.42

Graduated Rentals—

First 4 months of lease, per month	$ 250.00
Second 4 months, per month	300.00
Third 4 months, per month	350.00
Second year, per month	400.00
Third year, per month	450.00

Fourth year, per month........................	$500.00
Fifth year, per month........................	550.00
Sixth year, per month........................	650.00
Seventh year, per month........................	700.00
Eighth year, per month........................	750.00
Ninth year, per month........................	800.00
Tenth year, per month........................	850.00
Eleventh year, per month........................	900.00
Twelfth year, per month........................	900.00
13th and 14th years, per month................	950.00
15th year, per month........................	1,000.00
16th to 25th years, inc., per month............	1,000.00
26th to 35th years, inc., per month............	1,125.00

Lot in block No. 137; on Clay street, between Stockton and Powell streets; 26½x75 feet. Rented at $10 per month.

Lot in block No. 183, on northeast corner Taylor and Vallejo streets; 137½x137½ feet.

Lot in block No. 302, on Washington street, between Hyde and Leavenworth streets; 137½x137½ feet.

Lot in block No. 374, corner Fourth and Clara streets; 80x150 feet. Rented at $175 per month.

Lot in Mission block No. 61, on Nineteenth street, between Mission and Howard streets; 137½x137½ feet, less 60 feet included in Capp street. Title in litigation.

Lot in Mission block No. 104, on south side of Sixteenth street, between Sanchez and Noe streets; 137½x137½ feet. In litigation.

Lot in block No. 29, W. A., on south side of Francisco street, between Larkin and Polk streets; 137½x137½ feet.

Lot in block No. 111, W. A., on south line of Bay street, between Franklin and Gough streets; 137½x137½ feet. In litigation.

Lot in block No. 123, W. A., on south line of Washington street, between Franklin and Gough street; 137¼x137½ feet.

Lot in block No. 465, W. A., on north line of Jackson street, between Scott and Devisadero streets; 137½x137½ feet.

Lot in block No. 848, W. A., on south line of Clay street, between Cherry and First avenue; 137½x137½ feet.

West of First avenue and north of the Park, the School Department owns property as follows. (Appraised by experts appointed by the Board of Supervisors):

(All not otherwise stated are 150x240 feet.)

Block 152; Thirty-first avenue, between California and Clement streets, $5,000.

Block 164; Nineteenth avenue, between California and Clement streets, $6,000.

Block 176; Seventh avenue, between California and Clement streets,

Block 242; Forty-third avenue, between Point Lobos avenue and A street, $3,000.

Block 248; Thirty-seventh avenue, between Point Lobos avenue and A street, $4,000.

Block 254; Thirty-first avenue, between Point Lobos avenue and A street, $4,000.

Block 260; Twenty-fourth avenue, between Point Lobos avenue and A street, $3,000.

Block 266; Nineteenth avenue, between Point Lobos avenue and A street, $6,000.

Block 272; Thirteenth avenue, between Point Lobos avenue and A street, $6,000.

Block 278; Seventh avenue, between Point Lobos avenue and A street, $7,000.

Block 339; Forty-third avenue, between B and C streets, $1,000.

Block 345; Thirty-seventh avenue, between B and C streets, $2,000.

Block 351; Thirty-first avenue, between B and C streets, $1,500.

Block 357; Twenty-fifth avenue, between B and C streets, $1,000.

Block 363; Nineteenth avenue, betweent B and C streets, $12,000.

Block 369; Thirteenth avenue, between B and C streets, $1,500.

Block 395; Sixteenth avenue, between C and D streets, $1,500.

Block 407; Twenty-eighth avenue, between C and D streets, $1,200.

Block 418; Twenty-ninth avenue, between C and D streets, $1,200.

Also west of First avenue and south of the Park, as follows:

(All not otherwise stated are 150x240 feet.)

Block 673; First avenue, between I and J streets; 107x178 feet, $5,000.

Block 690; Nineteenth avenue, between I and J streets, $3,000.

Block 696; Twenty-fifth avenue, between I and J streets, $800.

Block 702; Thirty-first avenue, between I and J streets, $1,000.

Block 708; Thirty-seventh avenue, between I and J streets, $700.

Block 775; Eighth avenue, betweent K and L streets, $3,500.

Block 786; Nineteenth avenue, between K and L streets, $2,000.

Block 792; Twenty-fifth avenue, between K and L streets, $700.

Block 798; Thirty-first avenue, between K and L streets, $700.

Block 804; Thirty-seventh avenue, between K and L streets, $700.

Block 810; Forty-third avenue, between K and L streets, $800.

Block 872; Thirteenth avenue, between M and N streets, $1,500.

Block 878; Nineteenth avenue, between M and N streets, $3,100.

Block 884; Twenty-fifth avenue, between M and N streets, $800.

Block 890; Twenty-first avenue, between M and N streets, $700.

Block 896; Thirty-seventh avenue, between M and N streets, $700.

Block 902; Forty-third avenue, between M and N streets, $700.

Block 952; Ninth avenue, between O and P streets; irregular, 147½x 182 feet, $1,000.

Block 957; Thirteenth avenue, between O and P streets, $700.

Block 963; Nineteenth avenue, between O and P streets, $1,500.

Block 969; Twenty-fifth avenue, between O and P streets, $1,000.

Block 975; Twenty-first avenue, between O and P streets, $900.

Block 981; Thirty-seventh avenue, between O and P streets, $900.

Block 987; Forty-third avenue, between O and P streets, $1,000.

Block 1,035; Thirteenth avenue, between Q and R streets, $500.

Block 1,044; Nineteenth avenue, between Q and R streets, $1,500.

Block 1,050; Twenty-fifth avenue, between Q and R streets, $800,

Block 1,056; Thirty-first avenue, between Q and R streets, $800.

Block 1,062; Thirty-seventh avenue, between Q and R streets, $600.

Block 1,068; Forty-third aveune, between Q and R streets, $1,000.

Block 1,120; Nineteenth avenue, between S and T streets, $1,800.

Block 1,126; Twenty-fifth avenue, between S and T streets, $1,500.

Block 1,132; Thirty-first avenue, between S and T streets, $1,500.

Block 1,138; Thirty-seventh avenue, between S and T streets, $1,500.

Block 1,144; Forty-third avenue, between S and T streets, $1,500.

Block 1,186; Fourteenth avenue, between U and V streets; irregular; 161x92½ feet, $1,000.

Block 1,191; Nineteenth avenue, between U and V streets, $1,500.

Block 1,197; Twenty-fifth avenue, betweent U and V streets, $1,500.

Block 1,203; Twenty-first avenue, between U and V streets, $1,500.

Block 1,209; Thirty-seventh avenue, between U and V streets, $1,000.

Block 1,215; Forty-third avenue, between U and V streets, $1,000.

Block 1,258; Nineteenth avenue, between W and X streets, $1,000.

Block 1,264; Twenty-fourth avenue, between W and X streets, $1,000.

Block 1,276; Thirty-seventh avenue, between W and X streets; irregular; 125 feet 10 inches by 240 feet, $700.

Block 1,282; Forty-third avenue, between W and X streets; irregular; 11 feet 2 inches by 240 feet, $100.

LOTS IN POTRERO.

Block 46; York street, between El Dorado and Alameda streets; 100x 200 feet. Rented at $2 per month.

Block 85; Utah street, between Yolo and Colusa streets; 100x200 feet.

Block 127; Vermont street, between Solano and Butte streets; 120x200 feet.

Block 149; Kansas street, between Yolo and Colusa streets; 150x200 feet, $1,663.

Block 163; Rhode Island street, between Mariposa and Solano streets; 100x200 feet. Rented $2 per month.

Block 226; Arkansas street, between Nevada and Yolo streets; 150x200 feet, $832.

Block 254; Connecticut street, between Yolo and Colusa streets; 150x 200 feet.

Block 265; Missouri street, between Napa and Sierra streets; 150x200 feet.

Block 287; Texas street, between Nevada and Yolo streets; 150x200 feet.

Block 391; Southeast corner of Kentucky and Napa streets; 150x200 feet.

Potrero block 254, O. L. R., also Potrero block 265, O. L. R., condemned and acquired by Western Pacific Railroad Company for $14,000.

Potrero Nuevo block 231, commencing on the west line of Connecticut street 125 feet north from Twentieth street; thence 150 feet by 200 feet from the Western Pacific Railroad Company, January 25, 1909, according to agreement in recondemnation suit, Potrero 254-265.

OTHER OUTSIDE LOTS.

Precita Valley lands; California avenue, from Eve to Adam streets; 150x32 feet.

Paul Tract Homestead; Berlin street, between Irving and Ward streets; 85 feet and 2 inches by 120 feet.

December 21, 1908, from Joseph B. and Carlotta L. Keenan, all of block No. 132 of University Extension Homestead, excepting one lot 25 feet by 100 feet on Pioche street, and one on Cambridge street, 25x120 feet, $8,250.

University Mound Survey, block 12. Commencing at the intersection of northwest line of Bacon street with southwest line Girard street; thence north along Girard street 200 feet; thence at a right angle 240 feet to the northeast line of Berlin street; thence southeast 200 feet to northwest line of Bacon street; thence at a right angle 240 feet to southwest line of Girard street and point of commencement, being south ½ of block No. 12, University Mound Survey, from P. J. and Jennie M. Kennedy, August 22, 1905, $5,000.

WITHIN THE PRESIDIO WALL.

Block 553, W. A. Commencing on the north line of Lombard street, 137½ feet west from Broderick street; thence west on Lombard street, 137½ feet by 137½ feet in depth. Lot. 2. Outside Land Reservation.

Block 810, W. A. Commencing on the north line of Broadway, 137½ feet west from Walnut street; thence west on Broadway, 137½ feet by 137½ feet in depth. Lot 2. Outside Land Reservation.

Block 841, W. A. Commencing on the north line of Pacific Avenue, 137½ feet west from Maple street; thence west on Pacific Avenue, 137½ feet by 137½ feet in depth. Lot 2. Outside Land Reservation.

LIST OF SCHOOLS AND TEACHERS.

Name	Grade of Class	When Elected	Grade of Certificate	Salary per Year
Adams Cosmopolitan Grammar—				
McFarland, Miss H. F.	Principal	Nov. 30, 1877	Grammar	$2,160
Phillips, Miss H	V. P., Eighth	May 13, 1873	Grammar	1,620
Fairchilds, Miss M. E.	Third	July 1, 1874	High	1,104
Doughty, Mary A.	Seventh	Oct. 31, 1891	Grammar	1,224
Dolan, Mrs. C. M.	Sixth	Aug. 16, 1878	Grammar	1,164
Hesselmeyer, Miss C. A.	Second	Feb. 11, 1892	Grammar	1,104
Grozelier, Miss A. M.	Frencl.	Sept. 29, 1892	Grammar ard Special	1,200
Littlefield, Eleanor A.	Fifth	June 15, 1866	Grammar	1,164
Hurley, [illegible] E.	Seventh	Sept. 16, 1884	Grammar	1,274
Houston, Miss M. J.	First	April 2, 1881	Grammar	1,224
Jacobs, Edith	German	Aug. 20, 1907	High	1,200
Jacobs, Margaret E.	Fourth	[illegible] 17, 1907	Grammar	1,104
Agassiz Primary—				
Jones, Miss S. J.	Principal	April 1, 1878	Grammar	2,160
Harney, Miss A.	First	July 31, 1889	Grammar	1,224
Brown, Miss R. F.	Fifth	July 18, 1902	Grammar	1,164
[illegible], Miss C. A.	Fifth	July 9, 1877	Grammar	1,164
Josselyn, Ada M.	Fifth	Oct. 9, 1883	Grammar and Special	1,224
[illegible], Miss E. A.	Fourth	Jan. 31, 1894	Grammar	1,104
[illegible], Miss O. S.	Fourth	Jan. 31, 1894	Grammar	1,104
Boyle, Miss O. C.	Fourth	Oct. 1, 1905	Grammar	984
Rixon, Ella A.	Second	Feb. 28, 1898	Grammar	1,104
Fredericks, Miss E. L.	Third	Feb. 16, 1891	Grammar and Special	1,104
Cleary, Miss R. F.	Third	Oct. 23, 1901	Grammar	1,032
Hanson, Miss L.	Third	July 20, 1903	Grammar	1,008
Wright, Miss H.	Second	[illegible] 1, 1890	Primary	1,224
[illegible], Miss A. M.	Second	Jan. 6, 1902	Grammar	1,104

LIST OF SCHOOLS AND TEACHERS.—Continued.

Name	Grade of Class	When Elected	Grade of Certificate	Salary per Year
Agassiz Primary—Continued				
Liner, Miss M. G.	Second	July 27, 1898	Grammar	1,224
Maloney, Miss K. A.	First	Jan. 10, 1881	Grammar	1,224
Sankey, Miss M. K.	First	Sept. 15, 1888	Grammar	1,224
Knowlton, Grace W.	Second	Mar. 9, 1903	Grammar	1,032
Burnett Primary—				
McElroy, Miss L.	Principal	Dec. 6 1891	Grammar	1,560
Flynn, Miss M. E.	Third	Nov. 20, 1877	Primary	1,104
Schroeder, Miss S.	Third	Aug. 26, 1907	High	990
Curtis, Miss C. M.	First	July 6, 1882	Grammar	1,224
Hopkins, Mrs. J. M.	Second	May 15, 1905	Grammar	1,224
Gannon, Mrs. M. F.	First	July 6, 1877	Grammar	1,224
McGorey, Miss S.	Second	Feb. 12, 1890	Grammar	1,104
Woelffel, Miss E.	Second	Aug. 3, 1908	Grammar	1,008
Kean, Miss J. I.	First	Aug. 7, 1888	Grammar	1,224
Reichling, Miss Wanda L.	Second	Jan. 6, 1902	Grammar	1,104
Bernal Grammar—				
Regan, Miss A. G.	Principal	Oct. 5, 1887	Grammar	2,160
McGiveren, Miss K. A.	V. P., Eighth	Oct. 13, 1892	Grammar	1,620
Quinn, May	Fifth	Nov. 16, 1905	Grammar	1,164
Scott, Mrs. E.	Ungraded	July 15, 1897	Grammar	1,188
Schendel, Miss A.	Seventh	Sept. 27, 1880	Grammar	1,244
Douglass, Louise M.	Sixth	Aug. 30, 1905	Grammar	1,152
Meaney, Miss M. E.	Sixth	Aug. 7, 1893	Grammar	1,104
Neppert, Miss L. C.	Sixth	Dec. 29, 1892	Grammar	1,164
McQuaid, Miss M.	Fifth	Feb. 9, 1892	Grammar	1,164

LIST OF SCHOOLS AND TEACHERS.—Continued.

Name	Grade of Class	When Elected	Grade of Certificate	Salary per Year
Bernal Grammar—Continued				
[illegible]all, Miss E.	Fifth	April 26, 1907	High	964
Benjamin, Miss M. O.	Fourth	Aug. 26, 1903	Grammar	1,044
[illegible]n, Sarah S.	Fourth	July 2, 1889	Grammar	1,104
Libby, [illegible]ie F.	Third	Sept. 23, 1878	Grammar	1,104
[illegible]st, Miss C. H.	Seventh	Sept. 15, 1901	Grammar	1,224
Senter, [illegible] K. G.	Fifth	Aug. 5, 1907	Grammar	1,020
[illegible]s, Miss M. F.	Fourth	Aug. 3, 1910	Grammar	840
Schoof, Miss L[illegible]lu	Fourth	Aug. 3, 1910	Grammar	840
Bergerot Primary—				
[illegible]n, Miss A. E.	Principal	July 20, 1875	Grammar	1,800
Simms, Miss E.	Fifth	April 5, 1883	Grammar	1,284
[illegible]r, Miss M. D.	Seventh	June 26, 1905	Grammar	1,044
Fairweather, Helen B.	Second	May 16, 1882	Grammar	1,104
Evans, Isabel	Fourth	June 21, 1904	High	1,104
[illegible]n, Mrs. J. D.	Fourth	Jan. 27, 1886	Grammar	1,104
Cassidy, Miss V.	Second	Aug. 10, 1897	Grammar	1,104
Hanlon, Miss L. R.	First	Oct. 1, 1884	Grammar	1,224
McDonnell, Miss A. F.	First	Sept. 1, 1897	Grammar	1,224
Savage, Miss D. A.	Seventh	June 21, 1904	Grammar	1,044
Hawthorne, Miss M. E.	Sixth	Jan. 6, 1908	Grammar	912
Powers, Miss M. V.	First	Sept. 2, 1885	Grammar	1,224
Waters, Mrs. K.	Ungraded	Nov. 1, 1875	L. D. High	1,224
Harrigan, M. A.	Third	Aug. 2, 1871	Grammar	1,104
Bryant Cosmopolitan—				
Kelly, Miss E. E.	Principal	Oct. 5, 1887	Grammar	1,800

LIST OF SCHOOLS AND TEACHERS.—Continued.

Name	Grade of Class	When Elected	Grade of Certificate	Salary per Year
Bryant Cosmopolitan—Continued				
Stanford, Miss B. M.	Seventh	Jan. 11, 1877	[illegible]ar ard Special	1,164
Rutherford, Miss H. M	Fifth	Nov. 6, 1888	[illegible]ar	1,104
Kalmuk, Miss L.	French—Third	July 22, 1886	[illegible]ar	1,104
Curry, Miss M. E	Second	Feb. 5, 1878	[illegible]ar	1,104
Mooney, Miss F. C.	First	Aug. 28, 1883	[illegible]ar ard Special	1,224
Heineberg, Miss L	First—German	Aug. 15, 1873	[illegible]ar ard Special	1,224
Roberts, Miss M. E	First	July 14, 1871	[illegible]ar	1,224
Koch, Miss L. H	Fourth—German	Oct. 31, 1894	Grammar	1,104
[illegible]r, Miss A	First	Aug. 20, 1878	Grammar and Special	1,224
Duffy, Miss H. M	Fifth	July 1, 1903	Grammar	1,104
Casamayou, Miss A	Third	Aug. 3, 1908	Grammar	840
Wing, M. G	German-Latin	Mar. 8, 1906	High	1,200
[illegible]ck, H. M	French	July 29, 1876	Grammar and Special	1,200
Buena Vista Primary—				
Catlin, Miss A. G	Principal	Mar. 5, 1878	Grammar	1,800
Hunt, Charlotte F	Fifth	Oct. 28, 1892	Grammar	1,164
Hildreth, Mrs. O. P	Second	Nov. 11, 1896	Grammar	1,104
Mooney, Miss M. F	Second—Third	Nov. 24, 1909	Grammar	840
McFadden, Emma	Second	Jan. 1, 1887	Grammar	1,104
Fleming, Miss M. R	First	Nov. 14, 1896	Grammar	1,224
Rollins, Miss M. A	First	Oct. 8, 1879	Grammar	1,224
Stack, Rose M	First	Feb. 23, 1898	Grammar	1,224
Crocker, Miss B. H	First	Aug. 5, 1888	Grammar	1,224
O'Connor, Miss L. B	Fourth	Aug. 3, 1909	Grammar	840
Anderson, Miss L. E	Fourth	Aug. [illegible] 1908	Grammar	840

LIST OF SCHOOLS AND TEACHERS.—Continued.

Name	Grade of Class	When Elected	Grade of [illegible]	Salary per Year
Bay View Grammar—				
Prior, Philip	Principal	June 14, 1865	High	2,160
[illegible]e, Miss B. A	V. P., Eighth	[illegible] 16, 1883	Grammar	1,620
Stolz, Miss A. C	Seventh	Dec. 28, 1892	Grammar	1,224
Hanford, Miss E. V	Seventh	Sept. 1, 1886	Grammar	1,224
Casey, Miss M	Sixth	Sept. 30, 1884	Grammar	1,164
Perkins, Miss A. F	Fifth	Nov. 1, 1890	Grammar	1,164
Fitzgerald, [illegible] M. T	Fifth	Aug. 19, 1907	Grammar	1,164
[illegible]y, Miss A. A	Fifth	Sept. 15, 1882	Grammar	1,224
Sleeper, Miss [illegible]	Third	Nov. 18, 1873	Grammar	1,[illegible]04
Piper, Miss L. K	Fourth	July 19, 1885	Grammar	1,104
Bailie, Miss M	Fourth	June 9, 1897	Grammar	1,104
Judson, Miss A. A	Sixth	Jan. 16, 1903	Grammar	1,164
Boylan, Miss M. L	Fourth	Jan. 12, 1898	Grammar	1,104
Clement Primary—				
Quilan, Mrs. F. L	[illegible]	Aug. 1, 1884	Grammar	1,800
Bronson, Mrs. F. P	First	Sept. 1, 1884	High	1,224
[illegible]n, Miss Rose	Fourth	Jan. 3, 1889	Grammar	1,104
Mayers, Miss Eliz	Third	Jan. 20, 1886	Grammar	1,[illegible]04
[illegible]ke, Edithe A	First	Mar. 1, 1903	Grammar	1,224
O'Connell, Miss A	[illegible]th	July 6, 1905	Grammar	1,032
[illegible]n, Miss E	Third	Aug. 23, 1880	Grammar	1,104
Hansell, [illegible] M. E	First	Aug. 9, 1897	Grammar	1,224
[illegible]r, Miss E. M	Second	Jan. 6, 1908	Grammar	900
d'Or, Miss M	First	Sept. 30, 1901	Grammar	1,224
Young, Miss M. M	Third	July 6, 1905	Grammar	1,[illegible]04

LIST OF SCHOOLS AND TEACHERS.—Continued.

Name	Grade of Class	When Elected	Grade of Certificate	Salary per Year
Cleveland Primary—				
Parolini, Mrs. M. J.	Principal	Mar. 1, 1866	L. D. High	1,560
Davis, Mrs. F. V.	Third	Jan. 15, 1884	Primary	1,104
Green, Mrs. A. H.	Fourth	July 3, 1873	Grammar	1,104
Cove, Miss E. A.	Second	Dec. 28, 1880	Grammar	1,104
Ward, Miss S. A.	First	Oct. 30, 1894	Grammar	1,224
Brown, Miss H. A.	Fourth	Feb. 12, 1906	Grammar	840
[illegible]a Grammar—				
[illegible]ke, Mrs. L. K.	Principal	Jan. 23, 1857	High	2,460
Shu[illegible]ke, Mr. L. M.	Sixth—Seventh	July 10, 1889	High	1,620
Quinn, Miss A. M.	Fifth	Dec. 14, 1892	Grammar	1,164
Dunn, Miss M. L.	Eighth	Aug. 13, 1892	Grammar	1,224
Krauss, Miss L. H.	Seventh	Sept. 4, 1890	Grammar	1,224
[illegible]rethead, Mrs. A. L.	Seventh	June 24, 1884	Grammar	1,224
Simon, Mrs. M.	Sixth	Jan. 29, 1877	Grammar	1,164
Veuve, Miss M.	Sixth	Aug. 2, 1909	Grammar	840
Canar, Mrs. E. R.	Seventh	Nov. 5, 1897	Grammar	1,224
Doherty, Miss M. E.	Sixth	Oct. 29, 1891	Grammar	1,164
Jones, Miss [illegible]d L.	Fifth	Nov. 1, 1904	Grammar	1,[illegible]64
[illegible]de, Miss J. S.	Fourth	Oct. 19, 1875	Grammar	1,104
Lahanney, Miss M.	Fifth	July 14, 1895	Grammar	1,164
Stewart, Miss V.	Second	Mar. 15, 1884	Grammar	1,104
Lyons, Miss K. G.	Fifth	Dec. 20, 1896	Grammar	1,164
McKee, Eva M.	First	Sept. 14, 1892	Grammar	1,224
Boland, [illegible]na M.	First	Sept. 18, 1875	Grammar	1,224
Connell, Mary I.	First	Mar. 11, 1873	Grammar	1,224
Brown, Mrs. Annie M.	First	Feb. 13, 1871	Grammar	1,224
Bl[illegible]al, Miss A. A.	Fifth	Jan. 13, 1892	Grammar	1,164

LIST OF SCHOOLS AND TEACHERS.—Continued.

Name	Grade of Class	When Elected	Grade of Certificate	Salary per Year
Columbia Grammar—Continued				
Malarin, Mrs. Margaret	Spanish	June 3, 1908	Grammar	1,800
Haslam, J. Pearl	Ungraded	June 14, 1903	Grammar	1,224
Bailey, Miss V	Second	Aug. 22, 1907	High	840
Cooper Primary—				
Brogan, [illegible] K. E	[illegible]	Nov. 15, 1882	[illegible]	1,800
Traynor, Miss M. E	Third	Jan. 3, 1876	Grammar	1,224
[illegible]y, Miss M. C	Second	[illegible] 11, 1907	Grammar	840
[illegible]tt, Mrs. E. S	First	[illegible] 1873	[illegible]	1,224
Eager, Miss N. V	Second	Mar. 21, 1909	[illegible]	840
Boukofsky, Miss S	Fourth	Feb. 11, 1891	[illegible]	1,104
Paterson, Miss M	First	Aug. 14, 1905	[illegible]	1,224
[illegible]n, Miss I	First	Jan. 18, 1888	Grammar	1,224
Roden, Miss L	First	Aug. 1905	[illegible]	1,224
Franks, Miss A. E	Second	Aug. 16, 1888	[illegible]	1,104
Moore, Eliz. B	First	Sept. 30, 1901	[illegible]	1,224
[illegible]l, Miss M. K	First	Aug. 10, 1882	[illegible]	1,224
Vogelsang, Miss D	First	Oct. 14, 1902	[illegible]	1,224
Duncan, Miss C. L	Sixth	Aug. 4, 1882	[illegible]	1,224
Woodland, [illegible] I. C	First	Dec. 1, 1882	[illegible]	1,224
Rea, Miss J. M	Second	Sept. 1, 1904	High	1,008
Crocker Grammar—				
Mark, Mr. C. W	Principal	July 10, 1893	High	2,460
Murphy, Annette	Seventh	Dec. 20, 1890	[illegible]	1,224
Shea, Miss M. T	V. P., Eighth	July 10, 1876	Grammar	1,620
Folsom, Miss S. A	Eighth	Aug. 23, 1880	[illegible]	1,224

LIST OF SCHOOLS AND TEACHERS.—Continued.

Name	Grade of Class	When Elected	Grade of Certificate	Salary per Year
Crocker Grammar—Continued				
Coleman, Miss Elvira	Fifth	April 3, 1883	Grammar	1,224
Smith, Miss E. E	Eighth	Jan. 7, 1895	Grammar and Special	1,284
Harby, Miss Rosalie	Fifth	May 5, 1879	Grammar	1,224
Durkin, Miss J. L. F	Sixth	Aug. 1, 1882	Grammar	1,164
Barrett, Miss Mary A	Seventh	Sept. 2, 1896	Grammar	1,224
Carew, Miss M. M	Seventh	Nov. 29, 1896	Grammar	1,224
Armstrong, Miss N	Seventh	Dec. 26, 1877	Grammar	1,224
Burke, Miss Eliz. T	Seventh	April 3, 1892	Grammar	1,224
[illegible]y, Jennie L	Seventh	Nov. 4, 1886	Grammar	1,224
Brampton, Miss L. R	Fifth	Feb. 12, 1908	Grammar	960
Carpenter, Miss E	Fifth	July 6, 1905	Grammar	1,164
Coleman, Frances E	Sixth	Dec. 14, 1877	Grammar	1,164
Ryder, Miss P. E	Sixth	June 23, 1904	Grammar	1,074
Hefron, Miss Helen	Sixth	April 2, 1886	Grammar	1,164
Maccuaig, Miss B	Sixth	June 23, 1904	Grammar	1,164
Gleason, Miss Mary T.	Fifth	Dec. 10, 1890	Grammar	1,164
English, Virginia L	Ungraded	Aug. 11, 1897	Grammar	1,116
Denman Grammar—				
Mann, Mr. A. L.	Principal	Dec. 29, 1865	High	2,160
Smith, Miss Jessie	Eighth	Mar. 10, 1863	High	1,224
Childs, Miss K. B.	Seventh	July 5, 1866	Grammar	1,224
D'Arcy, Miss A. H.	Fifth	July 1870	Grammar	1,164
Hazelton, Miss R. H.	Ungraded	April 6, 1873	Grammar	1,224
Douglass Primary—				
Tarpy, Miss W. L.	Principal	Aug. 19, 1884	Grammar	1,800

LIST OF SCHOOLS AND TEACHERS.—Continued.

Name	Grade of Class	When Elected	Grade of Certificate	Salary per Year
Douglass Primary—Continued				
Hetzer, Miss M.	[illegible]	Sept. 12, 1894	[illegible]	1,104
[illegible], [illegible] M.	Fourth	Sept. 8, 1897	[illegible]	1,104
[illegible], Miss A. G.	Third	April 1, 1903	Grammar	1,152
Houghton, [illegible] E.	[illegible]	Nov. 11, 1896	Grammar and Special	1,164
Doherty, [illegible] A.	Second	June 9, 1897	[illegible]	1,104
Elmes, Kate C.	Third	Mar. 5, 1909	[illegible]	840
[illegible], Miss E. S.	First	[illegible] 1, 1905	[illegible]	1,224
Parks, Miss M. R.	First	Sept. 15, 1891	[illegible] and Special	1,224
Grafe, Miss L.	First	July 15, 1902	Grammar	1,224
Schou, Elsie M.	Third	Aug. 3, 1908	Grammar	840
[illegible], Miss A. J.	Second	Sept. 11, 1907	[illegible]	900
Brown, Miss M. L.	First	July 30, 1886	Grammar	1,224
Stewart, Miss A. R.	Third	Aug. 6, 1909	[illegible]	840
Dudley Stone Primary—				
Earle, Miss S. H.	Principal	July 20, 1869	Hgh	1,800
Newman, Bertha K.	Fourth	Feb. 1, 1904	Grammar	1,104
[illegible], N lliee.	Fourth	Aug. 15, 1890	Grammar	840
[illegible], Miss M. R.	First	Sept. 20, 1894	[illegible]	1,224
Hare, Miss F.	Fifth	Oct. 21, 1873	[illegible]	1,164
Simpson, Miss M. L.	Fourth	Sept. 16, 1885	[illegible] and Special	1,164
Koch, Miss L.	Fourth	Feb. 11, 1903	[illegible]	1,164
McBoyle, Miss A. B.	Fourth	Sept. 30, 1892	[illegible]	1,104
Gambitz, Miss L.	[illegible]	Nov. 11, 1896	[illegible]	1,104
Dwyer, Miss M. C.	Second	Sept. 1, 1897	[illegible]	1,104
[illegible]abitz, Miss L. M.	Second	Jan. 12, 1898	Primary	1,104
Fritz, Miss L. M.	Second	July 1, 1903	[illegible]	984
Cullen, [illegible] J. A.	First	Nov. 1, 1883	[illegible]	1,224

LIST OF SCHOOLS AND TEACHERS.—Continued.

Name	Grade of Class	When Elected	Grade of Certificate	Salary per Year
Dudley Stone Primary—Continued				
McGeough, Miss R.	First	Jan. 31, 1884	Grammar	1,224
Owens, Miss M. A.	Third	July 27, 1908	Grammar	1,104
Edison Primary—				
Saunders, Miss J.	Principal	April 23, 1887	Grammar	1,800
Kelly, Miss M. C.	Fifth	Dec. 8, 1891	Grammar	1,164
Barry, Miss M. E.	Fifth	April 1, 1884	Grammar	1,164
Power, Miss A. R.	Fourth	Feb. 24, 1898	Grammar	1,224
Booth, Miss L.	Fourth	Feb. 1, 1889	Grammar	1,104
Wilson, Miss E. N.	Third	July 18, 1902	Grammar	1,008
Harrigan, Miss A. M.	Second	Sept. 19, 1891	Grammar	1,104
Robinett, Miss M. M.	First	Feb. 5, 1875	Grammar	1,224
McDermott Miss C. M.	Second	Nov. 30, 1892	Grammar	1,104
Serex, Mrs. M. E. H.	Third	Aug. 7, 1883	Grammar	1,104
Emerson Primary—				
Spencer, Mrs. T. F.	Principal	July 17, 1901	Grammar and Special	1,800
Davidson, Miss E. R.	Fourth	Feb. 1, 1904	Grammar	1,104
Dennis, Miss E.	First	Dec. 5, 1888	Grammar	1,344
McLaughlin, Miss A. M.	First	July 0, 1877	Grammar	1,224
Tiling, Miss A.	Second	Sept. 8, 1897	Grammar	1,104
Folsom, Miss M. L.	Third	Nov. 18, 1896	Grammar	1,104
Casamayou, Miss A. G.	Third	Sept. 10, 1897	Grammar	1,104
Bailey, Miss C. B.	Third	Sept. 13, 1894	Grammar	1,104
Nelson, Miss M. F.	Fourth	May 13, 1896	Grammar	1,104
Gambitz, Miss L. B.	Fourth	May 27, 1897	Grammar	1,104
Watson, Miss M. A.	Ungraded	Mar. 12, 1890	Grammar	1,224

LIST OF SCHOOLS AND TEACHERS.—Continued.

Name	Grade of Class	When Elected	Grade of [illegible]	Salary per Year
Emerson Primary—Continued				
O'Brien, Miss L.	First	Mar. 12, 1890	[illegible]ar	1,224
Meyer, Miss R.	First	Nov. 22, 1884	[illegible]ar	1,224
Spafford, Miss D. B.	Second	Jan. 8, 1906	[illegible]ar	1,104
Mordecai, Miss G.	Second	Jan. 25, 1905	[illegible]ar	1,104
Estes, Miss C.	Third	Oct. 14, 1907	Grammar	840
Everett Grammar—				
Sturges, Selden	Principal	July 6, 1875	Grammar	2,1[illegible]0
Lindberg, Emily U.	Eighth	Sept. [illegible]	Grammar and Special	1,224
Theisen, Miss A. J.	Seventh	Dec. 20, 1892	Grammar	1,224
Devine, Miss M. E.	Sixth	July 14, 1895	Grammar	1,164
Johnson, Marie J.	Sixth	Feb. 1, 1876	[illegible]ar	1,164
Grimm, Miss A. L.	Sixth	Feb. 14, 1881	[illegible]ar	1,164
Casassa, Miss R. I.	Fifth	July 27, 1898	[illegible]ar	1,164
Sullivan, Julia F.	Fifth	[illegible]g. 1, 1897	Grammar	1,164
Perl, [illegible] May	Fifth	Nov. 11, 1896	[illegible]ar	1,164
Fenton, Miss E. R.	Third	July 27, 1898	Grammar	1,[illegible]04
Spafford, Helen E.	Second and Third	Jan. 6, 1902	[illegible]ar	1,104
Morse, Miss N. A.	[illegible]rd	July 30, 1890	[illegible]ar	1,104
Gracier, Miss A. J.	First	July 6, 1877	[illegible]ar	1,224
Quinn, Miss A. W.	First	Jan. 3, 1893	Grammar	1,224
[illegible]y, Mrs. K. J.	First	April 3, 1887	[illegible]ar	1,224
Stuart, Mrs. M.	Eighth	April 10, 1885	Grammar	1,620
[illegible]e, Miss M.	Ungraded	April 5, 1883	Grammar	1,224
Grant, Emily W.	Fifth	Mar. 30, 1905	Life Diploma Grammar	1,164

LIST OF SCHOOLS AND TEACHERS.—Continued.

Name	Grade of Class	When Elected	Grade of Certificate	Salary per Year
Fairmount Grammar—				
De Bell, Mr. W. H.	Principal	July 19, 1901	High	2,460
McGough, Miss Kathryn	Eighth	Jan. 12, 1898	Grammar	1,620
Hammond, Miss E. E.	Seventh	Dec. 1, 1882	Grammar	1,224
Berard, Miss E. L.	Eighth	Sept. 30, 1901	Grammar	1,116
McCauley, Miss M. A.	Fifth	Aug. 11, 1897	Grammar	1,164
Fallon, Miss D. A.	Sixth	April 21, 1891	Grammar	1,164
Hortop, Miss C. E.	Sixth	Aug. 26, 1903	Grammar	1,014
Millhone, Belle	Fifth	July 27, 1898	Grammar	1,164
Torpey, Miss K. L.	Fourth	Feb. 23, 1898	Grammar	1,104
Chandler, Miss M. G.	Second	Mar. 1, 1904	Grammar	1,104
Provost, Miss C. E.	Second	April 14, 1875	Grammar	1,104
O'Brien, Miss M. F.	Fourth	Nov. 19, 1905	Grammar	930
Foley, Miss Mary W.	First	Jan. 27, 1905	Grammar	1,224
Woeffel, Anna M.	Fourth	Jan. 10, 1910	Grammar	720
Holden, Mrs. A. F.	Ungraded	Jan. 13, 1902	Grammar	1,284
Meighan, Katherine E.	First	Nov. 7, 1884	Grammar and Special	1,224
Smith, Mrs. A. H.	Second	Sept. 2, 1908	Primary	840
Burke, Miss M. A.	Seventh	Jan. 10, 1910	Grammar	720
O'Connor, Miss N. T.	Third	Dec. 23, 1903	Grammar	984
Austin, Miss E. D.	Sixth	Oct. 28, 1907	Grammar	940
McCarthy, Miss M. G.	First	Oct. 23, 1901	Grammar	1,224
Bain, Miss A. J.	Sixth	June 10, 1910	Grammar	720
Farragut Primary—				
Derham, Miss T. E.	Principal	Jan. 3, 1888	Grammar	1,560
McDonald, Miss J.	First	Jan. 21, 1898	Grammar	1,164
Sullivan, Miss G. A.	First	June 25, 1904	Grammar	1,224
Anderson, Miss L.	Second	Aug. 3, 1908	Grammar	840

LIST OF SCHOOLS AND TEACHERS.—Continued.

Name	Grade of Class	When Elected	Grade of Certificate	Salary per Year
Farragut—Continued				
Seavey, Miss J	Third	Aug. 3, 1908	High	840
Wagner, Miss H. R	Fourth	Aug. 3, 1908	Grammar	840
Frank McCoppin Primary—				
Jenkins, Miss S. B	Principal	[illegible] 21, 1877	Grammar	1,560
Barber, Miss E. J	First	Mar. 1, 1884	Grammar	1,224
Higby, Miss S. L	Fourth	Mar. 6, 1905	Grammar	1,030
[illegible], Miss H. H	Fifth	Sept. 1, 1905	High	1,134
O'Neill, Miss M. E	Third	Sept. 14, 1898	Grammar	1,032
Hart, Miss E. I	Fourth	July 18, 1902	High and Special	1,044
Goggin, Miss E. M	Second	Nov. 28, 1881	Primary	1,[illegible]04
[illegible], Miss L. M	First	July 30, 1886	Grammar	1,224
Irwin, Miss M. A	Fourth	Nov. 4, 1891	Grammar and Special	1,104
Fay, Miss M. A	First	Mar. 11, 1873	Grammar	1,224
Brierton, Mary	Sixth	Jan. 2, 1897	Grammar	1,164
Franklin Grammar—				
Wood, Miss N. A	Principal	Nov. 13, 1866	High	1,800
Harris, Miss R. S	Seventh	[illegible] 30, 1905	Grammar	1,344
Nesfield, Miss E. M	Second	Jan. 3, 1902	Grammar	1,032
McCullough, Miss M. J	Fifth	Aug. 22, 1907	Grammar	984
Thomas, Miss E. O	Fourth	Jan. 26, 1906	Grammar	1,104
Carroll, Miss A. T	Third	June 25, 1905	Grammar	960
Roper, Miss B	First	Nov. 23, 1869	Grammar	1,224
Dunn, Miss C	First	Oct. 22, 1884	Grammar	1,224
[illegible], Miss J. L	Sixth	Oct. 2, 1905	Grammar	1,164
Browne, Frank J	Sixth	Sept. 13, 1904	High	1,224

LIST OF SCHOOLS AND TEACHERS.—Continued.

Name	Grade of Class	When Elected	Grade of Certificate	Salary per Year
Franklin Grammar—Continued				
Parker, Miss A. A	Second	Sept. 27, 1909	Grammar	840
Miller, Miss Etta F	Fifth	June 15, 1908	Grammar	940
Cowan, Miss M. A	Third	Jan. 12, 1910	Grammar	720
Fremont Grammar—				
Goldsmith, Miss R	Principal	Mar. 1, 1875	[illegible]ar	2,160
Ostrom, Mrs. I. D	V. P., Eighth	Aug. 10, 1898	[illegible]ar	1,620
[illegible]n, Miss D. F	S[illegible]ond	Dec. 1, 1898	[illegible]ar and Special	1,104
Hanley, [illegible]ra B	Ungraded	Sept. 30, 1890	[illegible]ar	1,224
Rosenfeld, Miss F	F[illegible]st	Aug. 1, 1888	Grammar	1,224
[illegible]t, Miss S. F	First	Jan. 31, 1889	[illegible]ar	1,224
L[illegible]s, Mrs. R	S[illegible]ond	Sept. 27, 1880	Primary	1,104
[illegible]l, Mrs. J. E	S[illegible]ond	Oct. 27, 1897	[illegible]ar	1,224
Lewis, Rose F	Fourth	July 28, 1898	Grammar	1,104
Shorb, Mrs. M. E	Fourth	[illegible] 21, 1901	Grammar	1,032
Langstadter, Miss P	Fifth	Aug. 13, 1872	[illegible]ar	1,064
[illegible]ll, Miss M. C	Sixth	July 18, 1902	[illegible]ar	1,074
Classen, Miss L. M	Seventh	April 9, 1875	[illegible]ar	1,224
Grant, Mrs. K. D	Eighth	June 3, 1897	[illegible]ar	1,224
Ramage, E. T	Fifth	Oct. 17, 1904	[illegible]ar	1,044
[illegible]h, Rose	Third	Jan. 31, 1884	G[illegible]mar	1,080
M[illegible], Miss J. A	Third	Jan. 31, 1910	[illegible]ar	720
Garfield Primary—				
Scherer, Miss M. A	Principal	Aug. 7, 1879	Grammar	1,800
Bradley, Mrs. A	First	Oct. 27, 1882	Grammar	1,224
McAllister, Mrs. F	First	July 27, 1898	Grammar	1,224

LIST OF SCHOOLS AND TEACHERS.—Continued.

Name	Grade of Class	When Elected	Grade of Certificate	Salary per Year
Garfield Primary—Continued				
Lynch, Miss F. C.	First	Sept. 22, 1905	Grammar	1,044
Powers, Mrs. M	First	Sept. 2, 1885	Grammar	1,224
[illegible]li, Miss E	First	Jan. 29, 1905	Grammar	1,284
[illegible]e, Miss K. L	First	Aug. 3, 1908	Grammar Life Diploma	720
[illegible]r, Miss M	Fourth	Feb. 1, 1905	Grammar Life Diploma	1,[illegible]04
Klein, Miss M. G.	Third	Jan. 6, 1902	Grammar	1,080
Hess, Miss T	First	Oct. 17, 1904	High	1,284
[illegible]a, Miss B	Second	Jan. [illegible]0, 1908	Grammar	930
Casey, Miss N	Third	Mar. 20, 1907	Grammar	1,104
Busch, Miss E. E	Second	Aug. 27, 1907	High	984
Agnew, Miss E	Fourth	Jan. 29, 1906	Grammar Life Diploma	1,104
Hanlon, Miss M	Second	April 1908	High	840
Hucks, Miss A. E	Third	Nov. 3, 1864	High	1,104
Carroll, Miss L	First	do. 27, 1896	Grammar	1,224
Haussler, Miss M	First	do. 23, 1885	Grammar	1,224
Soule, Miss M	Ungraded	July 22, 1896	Grammar and Special	1,224
Glen Park Grammar—				
Wade, Miss Janet	Principal	Jan. 2, 1878	Grammar	1,800
Ganter, Miss C	Fourth	Nov. 30, 1909	Grammar	840
Doran, Julia A	Eighth and Sixth	Jan. 7, 1869	Grammar	1,224
[illegible]ty, Miss A	Sixth	Oct. 14, 1907	Grammar	1,224
[illegible]y, Miss A. T	Second	July 26, 1897	Grammar	1,104
[illegible]n, Miss I. T	Sixth	Oct. 21, 1873	Grammar	1,164
[illegible]y, Miss M. E	Third	Mar. 5, 1878	Grammar	1,104
McGuire, Miss [illegible]y	Second	April 7, 1882	Grammar	1,104
Barron, Miss C. M	First	Oct. 24, 1888	Grammar	1,224
Phelps, Mrs. J. H	First	Mar. 20, 1877	Grammar	1,224

LIST OF SCHOOLS AND TEACHERS—**Continued.**

Name	Grade of Class	When Elected	Grade of Certificate	Salary per Year
Glen Park Grammar—Continued				
Smith, Mrs. V. E.	Fifth	Apr. 16, 1877	Grammar	1,164
McNeil, Miss F.	Fifth	Feb. 26, 1909	Grammar	840
Walters, Miss T. L.	Fourth	Jan. 8, 1906	Grammar	930
Golden Gate Primary—				
[illegible]rt, Miss P.	Principal	July 6, 1870	High	1,560
[illegible]n, Miss M. L.	Fifth	Jan. 20, 1876	Grammar	1,164
Houston, Mary A.	Fourth	Aug. 15, 1877	[illegible]	1,104
Bonelli, [illegible] E. M.	Third	Feb. 5, 1877	G[illegible]mr	1,104
Ryan, Miss E. T.	Third	Jan. 4, 1875	Primary	1,104
[illegible]n, Miss M. E.	Second	Nov. 8, 1884	G[illegible]mar	1,104
Cashin, Miss M. G.	Second	April 4, 1886	G[illegible]mr	1,104
Hare, [illegible] K. M.	First	Oct. 2, 1873	Grammar	1,224
Johnson, Miss A. M.	First	Mar. 1, 1879	Grammar	1,224
Grant Primary—				
Shaw, Miss I. E.	Principal	May 30, 1882	Grammar	1,560
Kincaid, Mss B. C.	Seventh and Eighth	Nov. 11, 1896	Grammar	1,224
Ryder, Miss V.	Seventh	Aug. 9, 1905	G[illegible]mar	984
Downing, Ida L.	First	Oct. 14, 1901	Grammar	1,224
Cookson, Miss A.	Fifth	Jan. 12, 1898	G[illegible]mar	1,164
Berg, Miss F. C.	Third	April 14, 1905	Grammar	1,032
[illegible]er, Miss J. A.	Sixth	Jan. 27, 1908	Grammar	840
Body, Miss [illegible]a	Fourth and Fifth	Mar. 8, 1909	Grammar	840
Aune, Miss T.	Second	Aug. 14, 1905	Grammar	930

LIST OF SCHOOLS AND TEACHERS.—Continued.

Name	Grade of Class	When Elected	[illegible]de of [illegible]te	Salary per Year
Grattan Primary—				
Butler, [illegible] E.	Principal	Aug. 4, 1882	[illegible]ar	1,560
Frontin, Miss E. A.	Third	Oct. 1, 1877	[illegible]ar	1,164
Sprague, Miss A. F.	Fourth	Sept. 14, 1867	[illegible]ar	1,104
[illegible]in, Miss M.	Second	Feb. 16, 1875	[illegible]ar	1,224
Shepheard, Miss K.	First	July 12, 1873	[illegible]ar	1,224
[illegible]l, Miss L.	Second	Feb. 5, 1878	Primary	1,104
Drake, [illegible] A. K.	Second	Aug. 16, 1903	[illegible]ar	1,032
Haight Primary—				
Haswell, Miss M. A.	Principal	June 25, 1867	High	1,800
[illegible]d, Stella M.	Third	Feb. 16, 1906	High	900
Enewold, [illegible]y T.	Second	[illegible]g. 3, 1908	[illegible]r	840
Sweeney, Miss C. L.	Fifth	Jan. 6, 1876	[illegible]ar	1,164
Rodgers, Miss C. E.	F[illegible]h	Oct. 1, 1901	[illegible]ar	1,164
Gilmore, Miss E. M.	Fourth	[illegible]v. 24, 1897	[illegible]ar	1,104
Donovan, [illegible] E.	[illegible]th	July 14, 1868	Primary	1,104
Neppert, Miss F. E.	Third	July 25, 1904	Grammar	960
Davidson, [illegible] T.	Second	Oct. 26, 1880	Primary	1,224
McDevitt, Miss J.	First	July 20, 1903	[illegible]ar	1,104
[illegible]er, Miss S. E.	First	[illegible]v. 5, 1866	High	1,224
Forsyth, Miss L. M.	First	Jan. 6, 1902	[illegible]r and Special	1,248
[illegible]er, Miss R. C.	S[illegible]ond	July 29, 1889	Primary	1,104
[illegible]r, Miss J.	First	Aug. 3, 1905	[illegible]ar	1,0[illegible]4
Hamilton Grammar—				
Kellogg, Mr. A. E.	Principal	Sept. 1[illegible], 1886	High	1,800
Manley, Miss I. M.	Sixth	Aug. 12, 1903	Grammar	1,164

LIST OF SCHOOLS AND TEACHERS.—Continued.

Name	Grade of Class	When Elected	Grade of Certificate	Salary per Year
Hamilton Grammar—Continued				
Hauselt, Miss E. E.	Eighth	July 18, 1902	Grammar	1,224
Brown, Miss I. R.	Seventh	Aug. 5, 1885	Grammar	1,224
Page, Mrs. K. H.	Seventh	Sept. 1, 1886	Grammar	1,224
Morton, Miss E. J.	V. P., Eighth	July 23, 1875	Grammar	1,620
Strauss, Miss I. R.	Eighth	July 6, 1873	Grammar	1,224
French, Miss I. V.	Seventh	Jan. 31, 1889	Grammar	1,224
Shaw, Miss L. A.	Seventh	Aug. 14, 1895	Grammar	1,224
McDonnell, Miss L. A.	Sixth	Aug. 1, 1884	High	1,164
Redmond, Miss M. T.	Fifth	do. 7, 1905	High	1,164
Brittan, Miss A. C.	Fifth	Sept. 30, 1901	Grammar	1,164
Martin, Miss I. C.	Sixth	July 25, 1901	High	1,174
Whitley, Miss A.	Sixth	Sept. 29, 1901	High	1,116
Kurlandzik, Miss R.	Second	Jan. 4, 1903	High	1,074
Silverberg, Miss A.	Ungraded	Oct. 2, 1903	High	1,044
Hancock Grammar—				
Gallagher, Miss N. G.	Principal	May 14, 1896	Grammar	2,160
Cereghino, Miss J.	Italian	Feb. 14, 1910	Grammar	1,200
Leggett, Wm.	V. P., Eighth	Oct. 22, 1888	High	1,620
O'Neil, Miss A.	Fourth	Oct. 14, 1905	Grammar	1,104
Martini, Mrs. M.	Seventh	Nov. 24, 1889	Grammar	1,284
Scanlan, Miss R.	Seventh	Aug. 14, 1905	Grammar	966
Burke, Miss M.	Fifth	Jan. 4, 1905	Grammar	1,[illegible]64
Pfeiffer, Miss L. M.	Sixth	Mar. 30, 1905	High	984
[illegible], Miss N. C.	Third	Aug. 14, 1905	High	930
Furbush, Miss M. W.	Fifth	April 5, 1907	Grammar	1,044
[illegible], Miss N. E.	Ungraded	Jan. 21, 1907	Grammar	1,224
Skaba ne Miss L.	Sixth	Aug. 1, 1904	Grammar	1,164

LIST OF SCHOOLS AND TEACHERS.—Continued.

Name	Grade of Class	When Elected	Grade of Certificate	Salary per Year
Hancock Grammar—Continued				
Hartrick, Miss L. A.	Fourth	Aug. 22, 1907	Grammar	984
McWilliams, Miss B.	Third	Jan. 16, 1908	Grammar	1,032
O'Connor, Miss E. H.	Third	Jan. 6, 1908	Grammar	984
Harrison Primary—				
Moran, Miss M. R.	Second (Principal)	Aug. 9, 1890	Grammar	1,320
Dolan, Miss Mary J.	First	Feb. 3, 1888	Grammar	1,224
North, Mrs. E. H.	Third and Fourth	Jan. 14, 1910	Grammar	720
Hawthorne Primary—				
[illegible]n, [illegible] S. J.	Principal	Sept. 1, 1874	High	1,800
Dacre, Mrs. E. L.	First	Jan. 28, 1905	Grammar	1,224
Barrington, Miss F. C.	Fifth	July 27, 1898	G[illegible]mar	1,164
Walsh, Miss N. G.	Third	Aug. 1, 1888	Grammar	1,104
[illegible]n, Miss M. A.	Fourth	Feb. 5, 1892	Grammar	1,104
[illegible]tt, Miss A. L.	Third	Aug. 14, 1905	Grammar	930
Drewry, Miss [illegible]	Second	Aug. 3, 1908	[illegible]	840
[illegible]n, Miss L. F.	Second	Sept. 1, 1897	[illegible]	1,104
Barrett, Miss N. L.	First	Jan. 12, 1898	[illegible]	1,224
Love, Miss M. L.	First	Sept. 8, 1897	[illegible]	1,224
Norton, [illegible] B.	Fourth	Sept. 22, 1909	G[illegible]mar	840
Hearst Grammar				
Sullivan, Miss N. F.	Principal	Aug. 13, 1876	Grammar	2,460
Franklin, Miss F. M.	V. P., Eighth	Dec. 28, 1880	Grammar	1,620
Haynes, Miss R. H.	Second	July 23, 1905	Grammar	960

LIST OF SCHOOLS AND TEACHERS.—Continued.

Name	Grade of Class	When Elected	Grade of Certificate	Salary per Year
Hearst Grammar—Continued				
Stoltz, Rose B.	Eighth	Oct. 15, 1885	Grammar and Special	1,284
Bray, Miss L. F.	Seventh	Jan. 5, 1885	Grammar	1,224
Levison, Miss E.	Fifth	Aug. 17, 1891	Grammar	1,224
Torpey, Miss M. C.	Sixth	Sept. 6, 1897	Grammar	1,164
Thompson, Miss A. W.	Seventh	Jan. 2, 1897	Grammar	1,224
Brierton, Miss M.	Sixth	Jan. 2, 1897	Grammar	1,164
Finnegan, Miss C. L.	Fifth and Sixth	Sept. 2, 1884	Grammar	1,164
Humphrey, Miss K. A.	Fifth	May 1, 1896	Grammar	1,164
Van Den [illegible], Miss F.	Fifth	Aug. 9, 1880	Grammar	1,164
McKeon, Miss R.	Fifth	Jan. 12, 1898	Grammar	1,164
Fairweather, Miss E.	Sixth	May 15, 1896	Grammar	1,164
Lahey, Miss M. T.	Fourth	Aug. 21, 1905	Grammar	1,104
Pake, Mrs. B. M.	Third	July 1, 1883	Primary	1,104
Martin, Miss A.	Fourth	Sept. 1, 1878	Grammar	1,104
[illegible]y, Miss E. A.	Second	Oct. 29, 1877	Grammar	1,224
[illegible], Miss H. M.	Ungraded	Dec. 29, 1896	High	1,224
Cole, Miss L. C.	First	Aug. 1, 1882	Grammar	1,224
Haynes, Mrs. F. S.	First	May 1, 1896	Grammar	1,224
O'Neil, Mrs. N.	Third	Dec. 30, 1892	Grammar	1,104
Mary Durant Primary—				
[illegible]n, Mrs. M. T.	Principal	Jan. 3, 1877	Grammar	1,800
[illegible]n, Miss R. A.	Fifth	Jan. 3, 1877	Grammar	1,164
[illegible]d, Miss F.	Fourth	April 29, 1886	Grammar	1,104
Adams, Miss L. F.	Fourth	Nov. 1, 1877	Grammar	1,104
Ambrose, Miss J. R.	Third	July 15, 1895	Grammar	1,104
Gillen, Miss E. J.	Third	Jan. 12, 1898	Grammar	1,104
[illegible]ud, Mrs. E. S.	First	Nov. 2, 1879	Grammar	1,224

LIST OF SCHOOLS AND TEACHERS.—Continued.

Name	Grade of Class	When Elected	Grade of Certificate	Salary per Year
Henry Durant Primary—Continued				
Haas, Miss Carrie	Second	July 29, 1891	Grammar	1,104
Haas, Miss Susie	Second	May 14, 1890	Grammar	1,104
Hill, Mrs. M. E.	First	April 15, 1885	Grammar	1,224
Boukofsky, Miss R.	First	Sept. 1, 1886	Grammar	1,224
Thompson, Miss S. R.	First	Nov. 5, 1875	Grammar	1,224
Powers, Mrs. E.	Second	Nov. 25, 1908	Grammar	840
Holly Park Primary—				
Sullivan, Miss N. M.	Principal	Dec. 15, 1877	Grammar	1,800
Wooll, Miss H. L.	Second	Aug. 15, 1867	Grammar	1,104
Wilson, Miss May	First	Feb. 2, 1904	Grammar	1,224
Ely, Miss E. M.	Second	Nov. 12, 1896	Grammar	1,224
Cohen, Miss G. J.	First	Jan. 1, 1895	Grammar	1,224
Laven, Mrs. S. F.	First	April 1, 1879	Grammar	1,224
O'Reilly, Miss J. F.	First	June 9, 1897	Grammar	1,224
Dworsazek, Miss P. A.	First	Jan. 2, 1897	Grammar	1,224
Adams, Miss Clara A.	First	Jan. 2, 1871	Grammar	1,224
Parker, Miss M. C.	Third	Nov. 26, 1907	Grammar	1,104
Kendrick, Miss M. E.	Second	Mar. 25, 1908	Grammar	1,104
O'Connell, Miss M. F.	Second	Jan. 29, 1906	Grammar	1,008
Horace Mann Grammar—				
Faulkner, Mr. R. D.	Principal	Oct. 22, 1888	High	2,460
O'Loughlin, Miss N.	V. P., Eighth	June 12, 1869	Grammar	1,620
Elliot, Miss Mary	Seventh	Mar. 18, 1879	Grammar	1,224
Hatch, Mrs. L. R.	Sixth	Jan. 2, 1881	Grammar	1,224
Carson, Miss E.	Ungraded	Jan. 29, 1884	Grammar	1,224

LIST OF SCHOOLS AND TEACHERS.—Continued.

Name	Grade of Class	When Elected	Grade of Certificate	Salary per Year
[illegible]ce Mann Grammar—Continued				
McNicoll, Miss B	Sixth	Aug. 6, 1872	Grammar	1,164
Clary, Miss A. E	Seventh	Mar. 11, 1906	Grammar	1,224
Diggs, Miss A. B	Sixth	July 21, 1903	Grammar	1,164
[illegible]pert, Miss J. M	Seventh	Jan. 2, 1895	Grammar and Special	1,284
Dowd, Miss M. E	Seventh	July 29, 1888	Grammar	1,224
O'Brien, Miss Kate	Sixth	Sept. 14, 1878	Grammar	1,164
[illegible]n, Miss F	Sixth	July 18, 1902	Grammar	1,164
Toland, Miss M	Seventh	Feb. 19, 1906	Grammar	1,224
Iredale, Mrs. E. B	Eighth	Dec. 1, 1876	Grammar and Special	1,224
Moynihan, Miss E. J	Eighth	Mar. 19, 1884	Grammar	1,224
Casey, Miss M. E	Eighth	April 0, 1875	Grammar	1,224
Peckham, Miss L	Seventh	Sept. 30, 1901	Grammar	1,224
Keith, Miss E. D	Seventh	Jan. 29, 1891	Grammar	1,224
McCrosson, Miss A. F	Fifth	[illegible] 28, 1907	Grammar	840
Hunter's Point—				
Itsell, Mr. A. J	Principal	July 10, 1871	High	1,440
Irving M. Scott Grammar—				
Hamilton, [illegible]es T	Principal	July 8, 1876	High	2,160
Croughwell, Miss A. T	V. P.; Eighth	Jan. 28, 1891	Grammar	1,620
Downey, Miss M. L	Seventh	Sept. 1, 1886	Grammar	1,224
Colgan, Mrs. J. J	Fifth	Mar. 10, 1884	Grammar	720
Duggin, Mrs. M	Sixth	Jan. 4, 1904	Grammar	1,116
[illegible]y, Miss M. F	Fifth	Jan. 26, 1898	Grammar	1,164
Wright, Miss Mary A	Fourth	Feb. 23, 1898	Grammar	1,104
Marsh, Miss Alice L	Second	Aug. 26, 1903	Grammar	1,008

LIST OF SCHOOLS AND TEACHERS.—Continued.

Name	Grade of Class	When Elected	Grade of Certificate	Salary per Year
Irving M. Scott Grammar—Continued				
Bryan, Miss E. M	Fourth	Feb. 5, 1906	Grammar	1,080
[illegible], Miss J	Third	Aug. 25, 1904	Grammar	1,080
Gaffney, Miss A. M	Third	Oct. 0, 1904	Grammar	960
Davis, Miss K. M	Sixth, Fifth and Eighth	Aug. 21, 1907	Grammar	1,164
Kincaid, Miss May	Second	Mar. 30, 1905	Grammar	840
McManus, [illegible] A. F	Ungraded	Sept. 17, 1897	High and Special	1,284
Edwards, Miss F. M	First	Nov. 30, 1892	Grammar	1,224
[illegible] C. M.	First	Sept. 12, 1887	Grammar	1,224
Erb, Miss N. V	Second	July 28, 1898	Grammar and High	1,104
[illegible], Miss A. M	First	Oct. 21, 1873	Grammar	1,224
Jackson Primary—				
Chalmers, Miss A	Principal	Jan. 2, 1902	Grammar	1,560
Hinds, Miss A	First	Aug. 23, 1880	Grammar	1,224
Ragan, Miss M. L	Fifth	Mar. 10, 1897	High and Special	1,164
McFeely, Miss R. V	Third	Mar. 10, 1897	Grammar	1,104
Cashman, Miss May	Fourth	Nov. 19, 1905	Grammar	930
Gray, Miss F. H	First	Sept. 2, 1907	Grammar	1,188
James Lick Grammar—				
Graham, Miss E. M	Principal	Oct. 8, 1879	High	2,160
Lewis, Miss F. R	Eighth	June 10, 1879	Grammar	1,620
Boyle, Miss Mary	Eighth	July 23, 1875	High	1,224
Torpey, Miss M. M	Seventh	Jan. 19, 1892	Grammar	1,224
Henderson, Miss M. J	Seventh	Jan. 29, 1872	Grammar	1,224
Kinney, Miss L. M	Seventh and Sixth	Sept. 1, 1886	Grammar	1,224
Kilpatrick, Miss Grace	Sixth	June 21, 1904	Grammar and Special	984

LIST OF SCHOOLS AND TEACHERS.—Continued.

Name	Grade of Class	When Elected	Grade of Certificate	Salary per Year
James Lick Grammar—Continued				
Johnson, Miss E. M.	Sixth	[illegible]. 30, 1905	[illegible]	1,164
Kennedy, Mrs. J.	First	[illegible]. 1, 1895	[illegible] and Special	1,224
Manning, Miss O. V.	Fifth	Jan. 19, 1905	Grammar	1,104
Hogan, Miss H. M.	Seventh	Sept. 30, 1900	Grammar	1,116
Harte, Mrs. Susie	Fifth	Mar. 4, 1903	Grammar	1,044
Gray, Miss M. E. A.	Sixth	S pte20, 1901	High	1,074
Jean Parker Grammar—				
[illegible]in, Mrs. C. R.	Principal	Sept. 12, 1871	[illegible]	2,160
[illegible]en, Miss E. L.	Fifth	July 27, 1898	Grammar	1,164
[illegible]ll, [illegible] N. C.	V. P., Sixth	April 10, 1874	Grammar	1,500
[illegible]ll, Miss L.	Fifth and Sixth	Aug. 23, 1880	Grammar	1,224
Tabrett, Miss A.	Sixth	July 18, 1902	High	1,074
[illegible]in, Miss J.	Fifth	July 23, 1892	G[illegible]mar	1,164
d'Erlach, Miss M.	Third	Aug. 26, 1903	Grammar	984
[illegible]s, Miss J.	First	Oct. 1, 1903	Grammar	1,116
[illegible]g, [illegible]	First	July 22, 1882	Grammar	1,224
[illegible]h, Miss R. E. L.	First	Aug. 29, 1885	G[illegible]mar	1,224
Beardsley, Miss E. F.	Ungraded	Mar. 3, 1879	Grammar	1,224
Dworzarek, Miss B. E.	Second	Jan. 3, 1882	[illegible]	1,104
McEwen, Miss E. G.	Third	Oct. 12, 1895	Grammar	1,104
Woodland, Miss E. B.	Fourth	July 21, 1902	High	1,008
Coons, Sarah E.	Sixth	Sept. 1, 1888	Grammar	1,164
Thompson, Miss R. V.	Second	Dec. 7, 1908	[illegible]	840
Jefferson Primary—				
Roberts, Miss B. E.	Fourth	Jan. 2, 1902	Grammar and Special	1,320
Spozio, Mrs. E.	F[illegible]st	Jan. 4, 1904	Grammar	1,020

LIST OF SCHOOLS AND TEACHERS.—Continued.

Name	Grade of Class	When Elected	Grade of Certificate	Salary per Year
John Swett Grammar—				
Fitzgerald, Mrs. M. M.	Principal	Mar. 4, 1879	High and Special	2,160
Schirerin, Mrs. L.	Third	July 10, 186[illegible]	Grammar	1,104
Bigelow, Mrs. C. J.	V. P., Eighth	July 1, [illegible]85	Grammar	1,620
[illegible]e, Miss K.	Ungraded	Aug. 10, 185	Grammar	1,224
[illegible]l, Mrs. G. D.	Seventh	Feb. 11, 1879	Grammar	1,224
[illegible]ky, Miss L. M.	Seventh	Aug. 1, [illegible]84	Grammar	1,224
[illegible]n, Mrs. E. G.	Fifth and Sixth	Aug. 12, 1[illegible]6	Grammar	1,104
Brooks, Miss E. B.	Sixth	[illegible] 27, 1[illegible]96	Grammar	1,164
Carroll, Miss G.	Sixth	June 9, 1897	Grammar	1,164
Horgan, Miss K.	Fourth and Fifth	Oct. 26, 1[illegible]05	Grammar	940
Erkson, Mrs. J. H.	Third	Sept. 1, 1897	Grammar	1,104
Doud, Mrs. E. [illegible]	Second	Dec. 1887	Grammar	1,104
Alderson, Mrs. A. E.	First	Mar. 3, 1[illegible]88	Grammar	1,224
Williams, Mrs. M. C.	Sixth	Nov. 19, 1877	Grammar	1,164
Lafayette Primary—				
McLeran, Miss Mary	Principal	Sept. 16, 1901	Grammar	1,320
Lissak, Miss M.	Kindergarten	Oct. 1, 1909	Kindergarten	840
Bigelow, Mrs. S. H.	Third and Second	Sept. 1876	Grammar	1,224
Sullivan, Miss H. M.	First	Aug. 2, 1905	Grammar	1,224
Hewitt, M. A.	Fifth and Sixth	June 10, 1910	Grammar	720
Longfellow Primary—				
McCarthy, Miss E. L.	Third and Fourth	Jan. 16, 1884	Grammar	1,560
Dwyer, Miss A. C.	Second	Mar. 22, 1905	High	930
Dwyer, Miss Nora	Third	Nov. 11, 1891	Primary	1,224

LIST OF SCHOOLS AND TEACHERS.—Continued.

Name	Grade of Class	When Elected	Grade of Certificate	Salary per Year
Longfellow Primary—Continued				
O'Connor, Miss A. M.	First	Jan. 12, 1898	Grammar	1,224
Wilcox, Miss M. A.	Fifth	Mar. 1, 1909	Grammar	840
Laguna Honda—				
O'Neal, Mrs. M. L.	Principal	[illegible] 20, 1 84	[illegible]ar	2,160
Donnelly, [illegible] M. L.	V. P.	July 23, 1 85	[illegible]ar	1,620
Carson, [illegible] N. E.	Seventh	July 14, 1 98	High	1,224
[illegible]ll, Miss M. V.	Third	Aug. 1, 1 04	[illegible]ar	1,008
[illegible], Miss E.	Sixth	Feb. 25, 1 05	[illegible]ar	1,164
Sechrist, Mrs. A. M.	Seventh	Dec. 5, 186	[illegible]ar	1,224
[illegible]es, Miss E. T.	Fifth	July 27, 198	[illegible]ar	1,164
[illegible]n, [illegible] M.	Fourth	July 6, 1 05	[illegible]ar	1,104
Stack, Miss K.	Fourth	[illegible]n. 28, 1 05	High	960
H[illegible]ff, Miss H. L.	Second	Feb. 1, 1 05	[illegible]ar	960
McDonald, [illegible] A. M.	First	[illegible]t. 30, 1901	[illegible]ar	1,188
Lewis, Miss J.	First	Jan. 1 87	[illegible]ar	1,224
Leeds, Miss B. E.	Third	[illegible]v. 15, 1 05	[illegible]ar	1,104
McKown, Mrs. M. E.	Sixth	April 14, 1 89	High	1,164
Lincoln Grammar—				
Stone, Mr. W. W.	Principal	Feb. 11, 1 83	High	1,560
Backman, Mrs. F. L.	Eighth	Sept. 3, 1 83	Grammar and Special	1,284
Redmond, Miss J.	Fourth	Jan. 21, 1 07	Grammar	1,104
Perry, Miss L. C.	Second	June 26, 1 05	High	930
Macdonald, Mrs. B. L.	First	Jan. 29, 1 84	Grammar	1,224
Lynch, Miss A. E.	First	Jan. 1, 1 86	Grammar	1,224
Dower, Miss J. E.	Sixth	Feb. 12, 1 06	Grammar	1,164

LIST OF SCHOOLS AND TEACHERS.—Continued.

Name	Grade of Class	When Elected	Grade of Certificate	Salary per Year
Lincoln Grammar—Continued				
Perlet, Mrs. M. F.	Fifth	Dec. 28, 1896	Grammar	1,164
Barry, Miss Mary C.	Fourth	Feb. 12, 1872	Primary	1,104
Rincon (In charge of principal of Lincoln)—				
Coyle, Mrs. Mary G.	Fourth	Dec. 5, 1892	Grammar	1,164
Barry, Miss A. P.	First	Sept. 21, 1886	Grammar	1,224
Madison Primary—				
Bartlett, Miss E. F.	Principal	Aug. 5, 1885	Grammar	1,560
Cobb, Miss E. S.	Second	Nov. 18, 1901	Grammar	1,104
Howard, Miss E. G.	Fifth	Dec. 30, 1892	Grammar	1,164
Emmons, Miss I. C.	Fourth	July 30, 1876	Grammar	1,104
Rowland, Mrs. A. E.	Third	July 27, 1898	Grammar	1,104
Breése, Miss A. A.	First	Oct. 29, 1897	Grammar	1,104
Bannan, Miss M. F.	First	Jan. 3, 1873	Grammar	1,224
Plageman, Miss D. E.	Fifth	Sept. 1, 1905	High	940
Marshall Primary—				
[illegible], Mrs. M. H.	Principal	Aug. 13, 1869	High	1,800
Flanagan, Miss M. C.	Third	Aug. 1908	Grammar	840
Poppe, Miss M. H.	Third	April 30, 1886	Grammar and Special	1,164
Harrigan, Miss J.	Fourth	July 1884	Grammar	1,104
Anderson, Miss L. A.	Third	Aug. 3, 1908	Grammar	840
[illegible], Miss J. C.	Fourth	Oct. 19, 1875	Grammar	1,104
Belding, Mrs. M. L.	Second	Nov. 21, 1876	Primary	1,104
Herndon, Miss A. C.	First	Dec. 18, 1878	Grammar	1,224

LIST OF SCHOOLS AND TEACHERS.—Continued.

Name	Grade of Class	When Elected	Grade of Certificate	Salary per Year
Marshall Primary—Continued				
Elliot, Miss E. F.	First	Nov. 18, 1885	Grammar	1,224
O'Connor, Miss C. J.	First	Sept. 12, 1904	Grammar	1,080
Gray, Mrs. H. W.	Fourth	July 28, 1892	Primary	1,104
Smith, Mary J.	First	July 9, 1895	Grammar	1,224
McKinley School—				
Gallagher, Miss [illegible]	Principal	Aug. 6, 1878	Grammar	1,560
Dearin, Miss A. E.	Third and Fourth	Aug. 22, 1907	[illegible]	930
Kresteller, Miss S.	Fourth	Jan. 3, 1906	Grammar	930
[illegible], Miss Nora	Fifth	July 7, 1877	[illegible]	1,164
Curry, Mary E.	[illegible]	April 2, 1888	[illegible]	1,104
McKinney, [illegible] C.	Third	[illegible] 7, 1888	[illegible]	1,104
[illegible], Miss K. E.	First	Jan. 1, 1885	[illegible]	1,224
Sarles, Mrs. J.	First	July 7, 1881	[illegible]	1,224
[illegible], Miss [illegible]	[illegible]	June 6, 1888	Grammar	1,104
Mission Grammar—				
[illegible], Miss K. H.	Principal	Aug. 1, 1880	Grammar	2,160
[illegible], Miss J. C.	[illegible]	Feb. 13, 1879	[illegible]	1,620
Doyle, Miss M. E.	[illegible]	Oct. 30, 1889	[illegible]	1,224
[illegible], Miss R. A.	Seventh	Aug. 15, 1888	[illegible]	1,224
Sykes, Mrs. M. A.	Fifth	Aug. 11, 1897	[illegible]	1,164
Noon, Miss M. A.	Seventh	Sept. 30, 1901	[illegible]	1,176
[illegible], Miss M. G.	Sixth	May 15, 1883	[illegible]	1,164
Horn, Miss L. J.	Sixth	July 14, 1872	[illegible]	1,164
O'Brien, Miss M. A.	Sixth	Aug. 11, 1897	[illegible]	1,164

LIST OF SCHOOLS AND TEACHERS.—Continued.

Name	Grade of Class	When Elected	Grade of Certificate	Salary per Year
Mission Grammar—Continued				
Harvey, Miss E. F	Fifth	Oct. 30, 1890	Grammar	1,164
Cashman, Miss R. S	Sixth	July 18, 1902	Grammar	1,164
Monroe Grammar—				
Hagarty, Miss A. M	Principal	Feb. 20, 1883	Grammar	2,160
Read, Mrs. A. G	Fifth	Aug. 22, 1907	Grammar	840
Harrower, Miss A. W	V. P., Eighth	Sept. 30, 1901	Grammar	1,620
McLay, Miss M. R	Eighth	Oct. 28, 1891	Grammar	1,224
Enkle, Mrs. M. E	Fourth	Sept. 1, 1872	Grammar	1,104
Curtin, Miss E. J	Seventh	Sept. 14, 1905	Grammar	1,224
Beardsley, Miss L. J	Seventh	Sept. 12, 1904	High	1,008
Maher, Miss J. G	Fifth	Sept. 2, 1884	Grammar	1,164
Macauley, Miss H. I	Sixth	Aug. 6, 1907	Grammar	840
Ellis, Miss L	Fourth	Jan. 3, 1889	Primary	1,104
Fleming, Miss J	First	Feb. 13, 1890	Grammar	1,224
O'Brien, Miss A. T	First	Nov. 30, 1881	Grammar	1,224
Rahilly, Miss E. T	Fifth	Oct. 7, 1907	Grammar	1,074
Hussey, Miss N. E	Sixth	Aug. 22, 1907	High	1,164
O'Flaherty, Miss M. E	Fourth	Oct. 28, 1907	Grammar	1,104
Purvine, Miss E. M	First	Aug. 21 1907	Grammar	900
Jones, Miss M. M	Third	Jan. 10, 1910	Grammar	720
Ryan, Miss M. T	Second	Aug. 3, 1908	Grammar	840
Morgan, Miss L. V	First	May 15, 1896	Grammar	1,224
Langdon, Miss M. M	Ungraded	May 28, 1904	Grammar	1,188
Devine, Miss C. N	Third	Jan. 12, 1910	Grammar	720
Moulder Primary—				
O'Connell, Miss A. M	Principal	Sept. 7, 1884	Grammar	1,560

LIST OF SCHOOLS AND TEACHERS.—Continued.

Name	Grade of Class	When Elected	Grade of Certificate	Salary per Year
Moulder Primary—Continued				
Miel, Mrs. S. M.	Second	Mar. 1, 1900	Primary	1,104
c[illegible], Mrs. L. B.	Fifth	Sept. 3, 1883	Grammar	1,104
[illegible]der, Edna	Second	June 21, 1895	Grammar	1,104
Deal, Miss V. V.	First	Dec. 30, 1892	Grammar	1,224
Fogarty, Miss N. T.	Third	[illegible] 19, 1896	Grammar	1,104
Tompkins, Mrs. C.	Se onde	April 16, 1872	Grammar	1,104
Kellogg, [illegible]ele E.	Fourth	Aug. 3, 1908	Grammar	840
Hackett, Mrs. E. S.	First	[illegible] 1873	Grammar	1,224
Noe Valley Primary—				
[illegible]on, Mrs. E. H.	Principal	July 1, 1882	Grammar	2,160
Hall, [illegible] M. V.	First	Aug. 17, 1887	Grammar	1,344
Egan, Mrs. K. T.	First	Mar. 11, 1897	Grammar	1,224
[illegible]ke, Mrs. L.	First	April [illegible] 1903	Grammar	1,152
Harrison, Miss E. D.	Second	Aug. 12, 1903	Grammar and Special	1,044
[illegible], Miss L. M.	Second	Aug. 23, 1907	Grammar	840
Merell, Miss G. S.	Se onde	Aug. 23, 1907	Grammar	840
Martin, Miss Eliz. R.	Third	May 1, 1905	Grammar	960
Nolan, Miss M. L.	Third	June 21, 1904	Grammar	1,008
Gray, Mrs. J. E.	Second	Dec. 15, 1890	Grammar	1 104
Schendel, Mss M. A.	Fourth	Sept. 30, 1901	Grammar	1,032
Gaffney, Miss S. A.	Fourth	July 21, 1903	Grammar	1,032
D[illegible]ne, Miss H. E.	First	Dec. 14, 1892	Grammar	1,224
Schulteis, Miss D. B.	Fourth	Aug. [illegible] 1908	Grammar	840
[illegible]y, Miss M. A.	Third	July 1898	[illegible]	1,104
Kerns, Miss May	Third	July 25, 1904	Grammar	1,104

LIST OF SCHOOLS AND TEACHERS.—Continued.

Name	Grade of Class	When Elected	Grade of Certificate	Salary per Year
Oceanside Primary—				
Heath, Miss V. D.	Principal	Jan. 4, 1894	Grammar	1,560
Allen, Miss S. H.	Sixth	Oct. 24, 1901	Grammar	1,164
Hawkins, Miss B. C.	Second	July 25, 1902	Grammar	1,284
Vincent, Miss S. C.	Fourth	Feb. 25, 1904	Grammar	960
Raas, Mrs. C.	Fifth	April 8, 1907	High	840
Bartlett, Miss A. G.	Eighth	Oct. 27, 1904	High	960
Ocean House School—				
Delay, Mr. D. J.	Principal	July 8, 1882	High	1,308
Oriental Public—				
Newhall, Mrs. C. C.	Principal	Feb. 13, 1870	Grammar	1,560
[illegible]r, Miss J. E.	Second	June 10, 1868	High	1,104
[illegible]h, Miss A. C.	First	[illegible]ly 27, 1898	[illegible]ar	1,224
Nixon, Miss V. E.	Fourth	June 30, 1902	[illegible]ar	1,008
Branch, Miss C. A.	F[illegible]t	Feb. 27, 1905	[illegible]ar	1,[illegible]80
[illegible]y, Miss F. R.	First	Sept. 12, 1904	High	1,008
Barrett, Miss K. C.	Sixth	Aug. 5, 1907	High	840
Arnold, Miss M. V.	First	Nov. 9, 1891	Grammar	1,224
Cilker, Miss J. A.	Seventh and Eighth	Aug. 1904	Grammar	1,224
Pacific Heights Grammar—				
Stincen, Miss A. M.	Principal	June 20, 1863	High	2,160
Stincen, Miss E. E.	Fourth	April 16, 1907	Grammar	900
Bliven, Miss F. M.	Eighth	Sept. 3, 1880	Grammar	1,224
Earle, Miss C. B.	Eighth	Feb. 21, 1872	Grammar	1,224

LIST OF SCHOOLS AND TEACHERS.—Continued.

Name	Grade of Class	When Elected	Grade of Certificate	Salary per Year
Pacific Heights Grammar—Continued				
Cook, Miss F. G.	Seventh	Dec. 4, 1904	Grammar	1,224
Griffith, Miss K.	Fifth	May 20, 1905	Grammar	1,014
Dreyfus, Miss R. E.	Seventh	Aug. 5, 1905	Grammar	1,164
[illegible]th, Miss E. F.	Sixth	Jan. 21, 1883	Grammar	1,164
Timmins, Miss A. C.	Sixth	April 18, 1883	Grammar	1,164
Boggs, Miss S.	Seventh	Feb. 18, 1903	Grammar	1,224
Spadoni, Miss F. C.	Fifth	Jan. 3, 1905	Grammar	984
Wellner, Miss M.	Fourth	Jan. 4, 1902	High	1,032
Donahue, Miss M. F.	Third	June 21, 1904	Grammar	960
Wentworth, Miss G. M.	Second	Nov. 2, 1878	Grammar	1,224
Robertson, Miss A. C.	V. P., Eighth	July 16, 1867	High	1,620
Burnham, Miss C.	Third	Aug. 1, 1885	Grammar	1,104
Dowling, Miss A. C.	First	Sept. 5, 1897	Grammar	1,224
Zweybruck, Miss E.	Ungraded	Feb. 20, 1885	Grammar	1,224
Morrison, Miss F. P.	Eighth	Aug. 20, 1888	Grammar	1,224
[illegible]rel, Miss Lucy	Seventh	July 7, 1889	Grammar	1,224
Peabody—				
Dwyer, Miss A. M.	Principal	Mar. 17, 1879	High	1,560
[illegible]re, Mrs. M. E.	Fourth	Mar. 1, 1880	Grammar	1,164
Harris, Miss E. L.	Second	Aug. 3, 1908	Grammar	840
Fitzgerald, Miss M. F.	Fourth	Nov. 13, 1889	Grammar and Special	1,164
[illegible]n, Mrs. M. G.	First	Jan. 12, 1898	Grammar	1,224
Duffy, Miss A. A.	Third	Aug. 18, 1884	Grammar	1,104
[illegible]n, Miss N. E.	Second	Sept. 7, 1897	Grammar	1,104
[illegible]nagh, Mary E.	Third	Aug. 3, 1908	Grammar	840
Ephraim, Miss A.	First	Dec. 2, 1882	Grammar	1,224

LIST OF SCHOOLS AND TEACHERS.—Continued.

Name	Grade of Class	When Elected	[illegible] of Certificate	Salary per Year
Portola—				
[illegible], [illegible] I. E.	Principal	Nov. 20, 1877	G [illegible]mar	1,800
Lapham, Miss E. M.	Eighth	Jan. 11, 1904	G [illegible]mar	1,080
[illegible], Miss J. H.	Sixth	[illegible]g. 1, 1888	[illegible]	1,164
Tessmer, Miss E. H.	Fourth	July 20, 1903	[illegible]	1,032
Laverene, Miss C. J.	Third	Oct. 28, 1907	[illegible]	930
Porter, Miss H. F.	Fourth	Jan. 28, 1907	[illegible]	840
Grace, Miss J. G.	Second	Aug. 19, 1907	[illegible]	930
Browne, Miss H.	First	[illegible]g. 15, 1888	[illegible]	1,224
Johnson, Miss A. E.	First	[illegible] 29, 1891	[illegible]	1,224
[illegible], Miss M.	First	Sept. 25, 1905	[illegible]	1,224
Flannigan, Miss G. M.	Third.	Aug. 3, 19[illegible]	[illegible]	840
Ruff, Miss M.	Second	Feb. 2, 1905	[illegible]	984
Dougherty, Miss J. C.	[illegible]	[illegible]v. 23, 1908	[illegible]	840
[illegible], Miss Mary	Fifth	June 8, 1908	[illegible]	840
McDonald, Miss A. A.	Second	Aug. 3, 1908	Grammar	840
Potrero—				
Coffey, Miss J. C.	Principal—Third	Sept. 11, 1895	Grammar	1,560
Loewi, Miss M.	First	Jan. 26, 1898	Grammar	1,224
Herrick, Miss C. R.	First	Sept. 11, 1895	Grammar	1,224
Doran, Miss Marie E.	First	Sept. 4, 1871	Grammar	1,224
Carson, Alice M.	Second	Feb. 12, 1906	Grammar	930
Finnigan, Miss M. G.	Third and Second	Aug. 20, 1907	Grammar	900
Redding—				
Deane, Miss M. A.	Principal	Aug. 2, 1872	Grammar	1,560
Sullivan, Miss T.	Sixth	Sept. 15, 1898	Grammar	1,152

LIST OF SCHOOLS AND TEACHERS.—Continued.

Name	Grade of Class	When Elected	Grade of Certificate	Salary per Year
Redding—Continued				
[illegible]ry, Miss M. E.	Ungraded	Aug. 12, 1903	Grammar	1,044
May, Miss H. M.	Fourth	Sept. 23, 1909	Grammar	840
Webster, Miss S. A.	First	Feb. 14, 1881	Grammar	1,224
White, Mrs. E. B.	Fifth	June 3, 1905	Grammar	1,164
Martin, Miss F.	First	Aug. 26, 1881	Grammar	1,224
[illegible], Mrs. Elizabeth	First	Dec. 23, 1885	Grammar	1,224
Duffy, Miss E. A.	Second	July 23, 1902	Grammar	1,008
Sullivan, Miss E. G.	Second	Jan. 12, 1898	Grammar	1,104
Roosevelt Grammar—				
Lyser, Mr. Albert	Principal	June 10, 1868	High	2,160
Lalande, Miss A. H.	Seventh	July 5, 1878	Grammar and Special	1,224
[illegible]r, Miss E. A.	V. P., Eighth	July 31, 1889	Grammar	1,620
Browning, Miss E. F.	Sixth	Oct. 24, 1901	High	1,074
Ryan, Miss B ll e.	First	Sept. 16, 1886	Grammar	1,224
[illegible]s, Miss F. J.	Sixth	Jan. 31, 1889	Grammar	1,164
Theobald, Miss A.	Second	Dec. 28, 1891	Grammar	1,104
McDonnell, Miss M. T.	Fourth	[illegible]r. 11, 1892	Grammar	1,224
[illegible]ls, Miss J. B.	Fifth	Dec. 9, 1896	Grammar	1,164
Grover, Mrs. E. J.	Sixth	Aug. 22, 1907	Grammar	940
Stark, Miss L. M.	First	Sept. 7, 1887	Grammar	1,224
Cotrel, Edna	Fifth	Sept. 5, 1892	Grammar	1,164
[illegible]ss A. F.	Third	April 27, 1890	Primary	1,104
Hon, Miss M.	First	Feb. 14, 1881	Grammar	1,224
[illegible], Miss M. A.	Seventh	Mar. 1896	Grammar	1,224
Kedon, Mrs. A. E.	Eighth	Dec. 9, 1896	Grammar	1,224
Sutherland, Margaret	Third	July 16, 1888	Primary	1,104
Kelly, Marg[illegible] F.	Fourth	[illegible]pt. 2[illegible], 1909	Grammar	840

LIST OF SCHOOLS AND TEACHERS.—Continued.

Name	Grade of Class	When Elected	Grade of Certificate	Salary per Year
Sheridan School—				
Riordan, Miss C. F.	Principal	Dec. 10, 1890	Grammar	2,160
[illegible]ey, Miss J.	Eighth	Aug. 26, 1891	Grammar	1,500
Murphy, Miss H.	Seventh	Oct. 26, 1905	Grammar	1,152
Everett, Miss E. B.	Sixth	Jan. 13, 1892	Grammar	1,164
Hussey, Miss E.	Sixth	Feb. 11, 1907	High	984
[illegible]y, Miss E. A.	Fifth	Oct. 13, 1904	Grammar	984
Miklau, Miss M.	Fifth	Sept. 14, 1905	Grammar	940
[illegible]t, Mrs. M. I.	Fourth	July 7, 1905	Grammar	930
[illegible]o, Miss H.	Third	Sept. 8, 1897	Grammar	1,104
[illegible]r, Miss A. J.	Second	Sept. 3, 1905	Grammar	1,104
Busteed, Miss M. W.	First	April 29, 1896	Grammar	224
Hawley, Miss M. E.	First	Jan. 6, 1879	Grammar	1,224
Crowley, Miss M. I.	Third	Sept. 21, 1891	Grammar	1,104
Kyne, Miss E. M.	Second	Aug. 3, 1908	Grammar	840
Sherman—				
Hurley, Miss J. M. A.	Principal	Jan. 2, 1863	High	1,800
Johnson, Miss M. C.	Fourth	June 21, 1904	Grammar	1,104
Millar, Mrs. S. H.	Third	July 6, 1880	Grammar	104
[illegible]rie, Miss J. T.	Second	May 17, 1896	Grammar	1,104
Unger, Miss R.	First	Aug. 20, 1885	Grammar	1,224
Sullivan, Miss [illegible]e	Second	Aug. 13, 1890	Grammar	1,164
[illegible]briner, Miss Elsie	Third	Aug. 3, 1908	High	840
Lyons, Miss E. H.	First	Sept. 30, 1885	Grammar	1,224
Hitchens, Miss E.	First	Nov. 25, 1885	Grammar	1,224
[illegible]t, Miss M. C.	Third	Jan. 16, 1910	Grammar	720
Erb, Miss F. M.	Second	Aug. 3, 1908	Grammar	840

LIST OF SCHOOLS AND TEACHERS.—Continued.

Name	Grade of Class	When Elected	Grade of Certificate	Salary per Year
Sherman—Continued				
McDermott, Miss L.	Second	Oct. 1, 1904	High	1,104
Fleming, Miss L. M.	Fourth	Sept. 27, 1909	Grammar	840
Spring Valley—				
Keating, Miss M. E.	Principal	July 12, 1880	Grammar	2,160
G[illegible]gg, Miss A. C.	Eighth	Aug. 15, 1868	High	1,620
[illegible], Miss A. J.	Seventh	Mar. [illegible] 1903	Grammar	1,224
Hause, Miss E. N.	Fifth	Mar. [illegible] 1909	High	840
Shea, Miss A. B.	Seventh	Jan. 29, 1884	High	1,224
Hoogs, Miss M. A.	Eighth	Jan. 10, 1877	Grammar	1,224
Davis, Miss Florence	Sixth	Sept. [illegible] 1897	Grammar	1,164
Grozelier, Miss B. S. C.	Fifth	Sept. 14, 1905	Grammar	940
Gallagher, Miss E. R.	Sixth	Oct. 22, 1891	Grammar	1,164
Dittenhoefer, Miss M. B.	Fifth	Sept. 10, 1908	High	720
Starr King—				
McGrath, Mrs. K. C.	Principal	Jan. 12, 1878	Grammar	1,560
Williams, Miss K. F.	[illegible]th	Oct. 17, 1884	Grammar	1,104
O'Sullivan, Miss E.	First	April 18, 1897	Grammar and Special	1,164
[illegible]y, Miss L. E.	Fourth	April 12, 1909	Grammar	840
Foley, Miss K. J.	Second	July 20, 1903	Grammar	1,104
Jordi, Miss S. J.	Third	June 14, 1885	Grammar	1,[illegible]04
Louderback, Miss E.	First	Nov. 21, 1884	Grammar	1,224
Ellis, Miss M.	Second	Feb. 5, 1908	Grammar	930
[illegible], Miss J. E.	Third	Sept. 16, 1879	Grammar	1,104

LIST OF SCHOOLS AND TEACHERS.—Continued.

Name	Grade of Class	When Elected	Grade of Certificate	Salary per Year
Sunnyside Primary—				
Code, Mrs. E. S.	Principal	Jan. 22, 1857	High	1,320
McGinness, Miss G. A.	Fourth	Oct. 1907	Grammar	1,032
Moore, Miss K. T.	First	June 15, 1903	Grammar	1,224
Sunset Primary—				
Tiernan, Mrs. A. E.	Third and Fourth (Prin.)	July 6, 1869	High	1,320
Rowe, Miss M. M.	Second	Aug. 3, 1871	High	1,224
Barkley, Miss A. G.	4-5-6-7-8	Sept. 27, 1909	High	840
Sutro Grammar—				
Magner, Miss M.	Principal	July 25, 1876	Grammar	2,160
Duraind, Miss M. R.	[illegible]	Dec. 5, 1875	Grammar	1,620
Smullen, Miss A. M.	Eighth	Feb. 18, 1903	Grammar	1,284
Karatar, Miss A. C.	Fifth	Oct. 14, 1883	Grammar	1,164
[illegible]d, Miss M. H.	Second	July 18, 1902	Grammar	1,104
Curr[illegible], Miss M. M.	Seventh	Mar. 14, 1906	Grammar	1,224
[illegible]r, E. L.	Third	Aug. 3, 1908	Grammar	840
Faucompre, Miss M. E.	Sixth	Nov. 18, 1886	Grammar	1,164
[illegible]ll, Miss L.	Second	June 9, 1897	Grammar	1,104
Maguire, Miss H. E.	Second	Oct. 27, 1892	Grammar	1,104
O'Brien, Miss M. J.	First	Aug. 3, 1892	Grammar	1,224
Norton, Miss A. B.	First	May 13, 1896	Grammar	1,224
McNamara, Miss K. L.	Ungraded	Sept. 10, 1904	Grammar	1,224
Hart, Miss A. P.	Fourth	Aug. 19, 1907	Grammar	840
Connolly, Miss M. J.	Third	Aug. 3, 1908	Grammar	840
Lewis, Miss R. P.	Sixth	Mar. 14, 1886	Grammar and Special	1,164

LIST OF SCHOOLS AND TEACHERS.—Continued.

Name	Grade of Class	When Elected	Grade of Certificate	Salary per Year
Visitacion Valley—				
[illegible], Miss M.	Principal	Nov. 28, 1881	Grammar	1,560
Nolan, Miss M. A.	Fifth	Oct. 24, 1901	Grammar	1,052
Dailey, Miss A. A.	Sixth	Mar. 14, 1907	Grammar	1,164
Kenny, Miss M. A.	First	April 8, 1907	Grammar	960
[illegible]lly, Miss C. A.	Second	May 23, 1907	Grammar	960
McArthur, Miss M. A.	Fourth	Feb. 3, 1908	Grammar	1,104
[illegible]k, Miss [illegible]	Third	Aug. 5, 1908	Grammar	840
Blackman, Miss R. E.	Second	June 1, 1908	Grammar	960
[illegible]tt, Miss A. M.	First	Oct. 12, 1905	Grammar	1,188
Washington Grammar—				
McCarthy, Mr. T. H.	Principal	[illegible] 20, 1891	High	2,160
Kervan, Miss I. M.	Fifth	Sept. 9, 1872	Grammar	1,164
Silvey, Paul A.	Ungraded	Aug. 22, 1907	High	1,116
Weed, Miss A.	Second	Sept. 15, 1875	Grammar	1,[illegible]04
Cl[illegible]se, Miss Ella	First	Jan. 3, 1874	Grammar	1,224
Fischer, Miss Jennie	Seventh	May 1, 1878	Grammar	1,224
Scott, Miss J.	First	Sept. 5, 1881	Grammar	1,224
Kirkwood, Mr. W. A.	Fourth	Aug. 19, 1907	Grammar	1,164
Thomas, Mrs. M. A.	Third	July 20, 1903	Grammar	1,104
[illegible]y, Miss A. E.	Fourth	June 18, 1908	Grammar	1,164
Huskey, Mr. F. G.	Eighth	July 27, 1897	Grammar	1,620
Washington Irving—				
Barlow, Miss C. B.	Principal	Aug. 1, 1868	Grammar	1,560
Miller, Miss J. G.	Fifth	Mar. 13, 1895	Grammar	1,164
McVerry, Miss M.	First	Sept. 2, 1884	Grammar	1,224

LIST OF SCHOOLS AND TEACHERS.—Continued.

Name	Grade of Class	When Elected	[illegible]de of [illegible]te	Salary per Year
Washington Irving—Continued				
Fleming, Miss Hilda	Second	Feb. 1, 1907	[illegible]ar	1,104
Laurent, Miss S. E.	First	Jan. 7, 1908	[illegible]r	1,008
Lloyd, Miss E. L.	Third	Aug. 3, 1909	High	840
Winfield Scott—				
Thomas, Miss M. E.	[illegible]	July 12, 1887	[illegible]r	1,560
Ryder, Miss Pauline	[illegible]	June 23, 1904	[illegible]r	1,116
Horgan, Mss Eliz.	Seventh	Sept. 1, 1905	[illegible]r	940
Gavigan, Miss M. K.	Third	Feb. 1, 1889	Primary	1,104
[illegible]ht, [illegible]ss A. B.	Second	[illegible]n. 6, 1902	High	1,032
[illegible]s, Mss A. G.	[illegible]	[illegible] 27, 1898	[illegible]r	1,224
Demmick, Mrs. M. F.	[illegible]	Dec. 10, 1890	Grammar	1,224
[illegible]h, [illegible]rs. [illegible]e	[illegible]	Mar. 18, 1907	Grammar	1,164
Hortenstine, Miss M. L.	[illegible]	Jan. 22, 1908	Grammar	960
Yerba Buena—				
Cas y, Miss K. F.	Principal	Jan. 24, 1876	Grammar	1,560
K[illegible]s, [illegible]s B. J.	Fourth	Oct. 9, 1903	Grammar	1,032
Stewart, Mss J. M.	Third	Oct. 27, 1880	Grammar	1,104
Kennedy, [illegible]ss E.	S ond e	[illegible]n. 9, 1906	Grammar	984
B[illegible]h, Miss B.	First	[illegible] 5, 1873	Grammar	1,104
[illegible]l, Mss M.	Third	Aug. 3, 1903	Grammar	930
Jacobs, [illegible]s N. A.	[illegible]	Sept. 5, 1888	Grammar	1,224
McHugh, Miss M.	[illegible]	[illegible]v. 1, [illegible]	Grammar	1,224
Hochheimer, Miss J.	[illegible]	[illegible]n. 1877	Grammar	1,224
I [illegible]u, Miss G.	[illegible]	Aug. 26, 1891	Grammar	1,224
Purvine, Alice	Fourth	[illegible] 1908	Grammar	840
Keegan, Mss A. R.	Fifth	Feb. 21, 1905	Grammar	1,074

LIST OF SCHOOLS AND TEACHERS.—Continued.

Name	Grade of Class	When Elected	Grade of Certificate	Salary per Year
Oral School for Deaf—				
Holden, Mrs. J. B.	Principal	Aug. 15, 1901	Special	1,248
Holden, Mr. A. N.	Sixth	Aug. 1, 1902	Special	1,008
Parental School—				
Alexander, Miss R.	Principal	Oct. 5, 1888	Grammar	1,440
Schwartz, Mrs. I. C.	Ungraded	Feb. 17, 1905	Grammar	1,008
Levy, Miss A.	Second	Jan. 5, 1891	Grammar	1,224
Newton J. Tharp Commercial—				
Murphy, [illegible] H.	Principal	[illegible]. 27, 1890	High	2,400
Deacon, [illegible] Eldora	Bookkeeping	Sept. 1, 1887	Special	1,200
Sykes, Jas. B.	Law and [illegible]	Dec. 16, 1896	High	1,440
[illegible]n, Mrs. S. W.	Arithmetic	July 20, 1889	High	1,440
[illegible]do, Miss M. G.	Spanish	July 30, 1890	Special	1,440
Langdon, Miss S. A.	Typewriting	July 20, 1904	[illegible]ar and Special	1,440
Richards, Miss L.	Stenography	Aug. 15, 1889	Special	1,800
Furlong, Miss Irene	English	Jan. 14, 1905	High	1,440
Freese, Louise E.	Penmanship	Mar. 8, 1894	Special	1,200
Reeves, Mrs. I. D.	[illegible]tic	Jan. 10, 1897	High	1,440
[illegible], Miss I.	Typewriting	[illegible]v. 13, 1889	Special	1,440
Hayes, Miss M. L.	Sten. and Typewriting	Sept. 1, 1904	Special	1,440
Rademaker, Miss H. E.	Bookkeeping	May 15, 1887	Special	1,440
[illegible]e, Miss H. I.	Stenography	Jan. 24, 1910	High	1,200
Hawkins, Miss G. G.	[illegible]tic	[illegible]. 10, 1901	High	1,200
Sollman, Miss F. H.	English	June 15, 1908	High	1,200
Willard, Mr. O. C.	Bookkeeping	July 1, 1908	Special	1,200
Cullen, Rene	English	Jan. 4, 1902	High	1,200

LIST OF SCHOOLS AND TEACHERS.—Continued.

Name	Grade of Class	When Elected	Grade of Certificate	Salary per Year
Girls' High—				
Scott, Dr. A. W	Principal	Jan. 5, 1883	High	3,000
Prag, Mrs. Mary	History	June 27, 1864	High	1,980
Mitchell, Mr. Geo. Ctis	Science	Aug. 23, 1889	High	1,980
Dupuy, Mr. E. J	French	May 15, 1899	Special	1,980
Kirwin, Clarice A	History	Aug. 3, 1909	High	1,440
[illegible]in, Mr. F. M	Drawing	[illegible] 1, 1887	High	1,980
Roth, Miss N. E	English	Jan. 10, 1902	High	1,620
Leviele, Miss B	French	Mar. 13, 1905	High	1,620
Daniel, Miss L	Assistant, Science	Dec. 17, 1890	High	1,620
Armer, Miss E. D	English	Aug. 15, 1898	High	1,620
Hunt, Miss C. L	Biology	Jan. 10, 1859	High	1,620
Croyland, Miss A. B	English	July 20, 1901	High	1,980
Stark, Miss C. M	Latin	July 21, 1902	High	1,620
Noonan, Miss E. L	Mathematics	Sept. 30, 1901	High	1,440
Zimmerman, Mr. Wm	German	Jan. 4, 1871	High	1,620
Stevenson, Miss E. R	English	Jan. 3, 1903	High	1,620
Centner, Martin A	Latin	Aug. 19, 1907	High	1,980
[illegible]t, Miss F	Mathematics	Aug. 23, 1870	High	1,980
[illegible]r, Miss M	History	July 28, 1902	High	1,440
Jones, Miss Marion	Drawing	July 23, 1908	Special	1,500
More, Miss Isabel	Domestic Science	Aug. 20, 1908	Special	1,200
Lowell High—				
Morton, Frank	Principal	Aug. 1, 1886	High	3,300
Clark, F. H	History	July 8, 1889	High	1,980
Crofts, Francis E	History	Nov. 28, 1891	High	1,980
Schmit, Mr. J. J	History	Dec. 26, 1894	High	1,980
Nourse, Mr. J. P	History	Jan. 14, 1901	High	1,980

LIST OF SCHOOLS AND TEACHERS.—Continued.

Name	Grade of Class	When Elected	Grade of Certificate	Salary per Year
Lowell High—Continued				
Bowman, Elsie	Latin	June 17, 1903	High	1,620
Longley, Mr. J. A.	History	July 20, 1901	High	1,620
Perham, Mr. F. E.	English	Sept. 4, 1901	High	1,620
Gray, Mr. E. P.	Science	Feb. 3, 1908	High	1,440
[illegible]les, Mr. T. H.	Latin and Spanish	Nov. 15, 1906	High	1,620
[illegible], Miss C. B.	English	April 4, 1907	High	1,620
Cloud, Mr. A. J.	English	Jan. 15, 1905	High	1,980
Cox, Miss M. M.	Modern Language	Aug. 20, 1885	High	1,980
[illegible]e, Miss E. A.	German	Oct. 1, 1907	High	1,440
Kelley, Mr. T. R.	Latin	Sept. 12, 1899	High	1,620
Hodgkinson, Miss F.	Latin	May 27, 1885	High	1,620
Smith, Thos. A.	Chemistry	Aug. 2, 1909	High	1,440
[illegible]n, Mr. H.	Head Science	Aug. 3, 1908	High	1,980
Altmann, Mr. A.	Drawing	July 15, 1903	Special	1,500
[illegible]ch, Mr. F. W.	Science	July 29, 1901	High	1,620
[illegible]n, Carl L.	History	Aug. 2, 1909	High	1,440
Stephens, L. H.	History	Aug. 13, 1909	High	1,440
Mission High				
O'Connor, Joseph	Principal	[illegible] 1, 1868	High	2,700
Smith, W. O.	Head Science	Aug. 1, 1901	High	1,980
Donnelly, Miss M. E.	English	July 9, 1872	High	1,980
Goldsmith, Miss A.	History	Feb. 19, 1879	High	1,980
Ryan, Miss R.	Mathematics	July 15, 1898	High	1,980
Blanchard, Dr. M. E.	Latin	Jan. 5, 1890	High	1,980
Kelly, Miss A. G.	Mathematics	Oct. 10, 1895	High	1,920
[illegible]e, Miss E.	History	July 20, 1901	High	1,620
Cerf, Miss A.	French and Latin	July 21, 1904	High	1,620

LIST OF SCHOOLS AND TEACHERS.—Continued.

Name	Grade of Class	When Elected	Grade of Certificate	Salary per Year
Mission High—Continued				
Downey, Mr. A. D	Science	Jan. 21, 1907	High	1,620
Garin, Mr. P. A	Drawing	Aug. 31, 1898	High	1,920
Dal Piaz, [illegible] Marion	Drawing	Jan. 12, 1905	High	1,620
Harrison, Mrs. E. C	German and French	Aug. 3, 1908	High and Special	1,980
Townsend, Irving	English	Jan. 2, 1909	High	1,440
Dowling, Miss M. C	Spanish	Dec. 20, 1899	High	1,500
[illegible]k, Mr. F. M	Commercial Studies	Aug. 17, 1908	Special	1,500
Castelhun, Miss Ella	English	April 4, 1887	High	1,620
Polytechnic High—				
Bush, Mr. W. N	Principal	July 20, 1886	High	2,700
[illegible]n, Mr. A. L	Science	Jan. 26, 1899	High	1,980
Duffy, Miss A. G	English and History	[illegible]ne 24, 1897	High	1,980
Van [illegible]k, Miss M	Drawing	July 22, 1889	Special	1,980
Carniglia, Mr. E. S	Head Machine Shop	Mar. 25, 1905	High	1,980
[illegible]n, Jas. R	Spanish	April 30, 1908	High	1,440
Mohr, Paul J	Mathematics	Jan. 21, 1903	High	1,980
Hatch, I. C	Language	Aug. 12, 1905	High	1,980
[illegible]e, Etta	Algebra	Dec. 1, 1897	High	1,620
Murdoch, Miss R	Drawing	Nov. 18, 1893	Special	1,500
Campbell, Miss N. L	Sewing	S pte21, 1907	Special	1,500
Drew, Wm. J	Drawing	[illegible] 28, 1898	High	1,980
Cerf, Miss C	French	Feb. 3, 1908	High	1,440
Kelly, Miss May E	English	July 20, 1904	High	1,620
Dickerson, Roy E	Science	Jan. 2, 1907	High	1,620
McTiernan, John J	Assistant Forge	Sept. 14, 1908	Special	1,500
[illegible]n, Carmel	Drawing	Jan. 10, 1901	Special	1,500
Carne, Harry L	Pattern Making	Aug. 2, 1909	Special	1,500

LIST OF SCHOOLS AND TEACHERS.—Continued.

Name	Grade of Class	When Elected	Grade of Certificate	Salary per Year
Commercial Evening—				
Riley, Mr. P. T.	Principal	July 17, 1901	High	1,014
Davidson, Mr. W. W.	Bookkeeping	July 5, 1884	Grammar and Special	600
Kozminsky, Miss Dora	Stenography	Sept. 29, 1892	Special	600
[illegible]y, Miss M. W.	Typewriting	Aug. 18, 1897	Special	600
Rock, Miss A. J.	Bookkeeping	Jan. 12, 1898	Grammar and Special	600
Trefts, Mr. W. E.	Stenography	April [illegible] 1903	Grammar and Special	600
Kendrick, Miss N. K.	Stenography	Dec. 29, 1896	Grammar and Special	600
Delaney, M[illegible] K. F.	Bookkeeping	[illegible], 2[illegible]96	Grammar	600
Kelleher, [illegible]es V.	Sten. and Com'l Arith.	Jan. [illegible]08	Grammar L. D.	600
Dickson, M[illegible] Mary	Penmanship	April 7, 1910	High	600
Hamilton Evening—				
Lenahan, Mr. J. A.	Principal	June 1[illegible], 1898	Grammar	600
Walsh, Miss M. U.	[illegible]th	Aug. 11, 1897	Grammar	600
[illegible]ms, Miss M. E.	Eighth	Aug. 4, 1906	Grammar	600
Hussey, Miss N. C.	Sixth	Feb. 26, 1896	Grammar	600
Israel, Miss D. T.	Sixth	Feb. 23, 1898	Grammar	600
[illegible]tt, Miss E. C.	Foreign	Oct. 26, 1904	Grammar	600
Stimmel, Mrs. Agnes	Fifth	Sept. [illegible] 1897	Grammar	600
Regan, Mrs. V. E.	Seventh	Aug. 3, 1908	Grammar	600
[illegible]n, Miss B.	Stenography	Aug. [illegible] 1897	Special	600
Daniels, John R.	Bookkeeping	Sept. 1, 1891	Special	600
Cronin, Miss K. F.	Typewriting	Jan. 2, 1903	Grammar and Special	600
H[illegible]y, Miss E. C.	Foreign	Sept. 14, 1905	Grammar	600
Spadoni, Miss A.	Foreign	Jan. 2[illegible] 1906	High	600
Boehm, Mrs. M.	Stenography	Aug. 3, 1909	Special	600

LIST OF SCHOOLS AND TEACHERS.—Continued.

Name	Grade of Class	When Elected	Grade of Certificate	Salary per Year
[illegible] Evening—				
Kratzer, Mr. D. W	Principal	Aug. 14, 1897	Grammar	960
Bodkin, Miss A. J	Seventh	Dec. 28, 1898	Special and Grammar	0
Gorham, Miss K. L. (Mrs. C. L. Murphy)	Seventh	Aug. 30, 1897	Grammar	0
Deal, Louise B	Eighth	Jan. 1, 1887	Grammar	0
Kelly, Mrs. E. F	Ninth	Aug. 18, 1904	Grammar	600
Lane, Miss H. F	[illegible]	Sept. 1, 1905	Grammar	0
[illegible], Miss A. G	Seventh	July 28, 1898	Grammar	0
Finn, Mrs. E. F	Eighth	Dec. 15, 1896	Grammar	600
Marshall, Mrs. M. L	Sixth	Sept. 1, 1897	Grammar	0
[illegible], Mr. F. A	Seventh	Oct. 7, [illegible]	Grammar	0
Kozminsky, Miss B	Fifth	Aug. 31, 1892	Grammar	0
Dwyer, Mrs. M	Fourth	Feb. 12, 1868	Primary	600
MacDonald, Dr. F	Foreign	Dec. 5, 1892	Grammar	600
[illegible], Miss J. L	Foreign	July 27, 1897	Grammar	0
Doyle, Miss J	Ninth	July 28, 1898	Grammar	600
[illegible], Miss K	Ninth	April [illegible]	Grammar	600
Irving M. Scott Evening—				
Hall, Mr. H. C	All	July 1, 1903	High	600
[illegible] Evening—				
Goodman, Mrs. P. M	Principal	Dec. 14, 1880	Grammar	960
Onyon, Miss E. J	Ninth	Jan. 31, 1889	Grammar	600
Smith, Miss M. A	Eighth	Jan. 3, 1887	Grammar	600
[illegible], Miss M. R	Seventh	Aug. 14, 1907	Grammar	0
[illegible], Miss K	Eighth	Aug. 12, 1908	Grammar	600
Harvey, Miss M. A	Fifth	Aug. 29, 1892	Grammar	0
Parlin, Mrs. A	Ungraded	Aug. 31, 1892	Grammar	0

LIST OF SCHOOLS AND TEACHERS.—Continued.

Name	Grade of Class	When Elected	Grade of Certificate	Salary per Year
Lincoln Evening—Continued				
Rich, M[illegible] L. A.	Vice-Principal	Dec. 23, 1885	Grammar	900
[illegible]n, M[illegible] R.	Sixth	Mar. 26, 1877	Grammar	600
Wigand, M[illegible] S.	Foreign	Dec. 28, 1890	Primary	600
Heineman, Mrs. E.	Foreign	Oct. 23, 1901	Grammar	600
[illegible]t, Miss E. L.	Foreign	Aug. 30, 1896	Primary	600
O'Neill, Miss L. C.	Seventh	Sept. 8, 1888	Grammar	600
Kinne, Mr. H. C.	Foreign	July 14, 1868	High	600
[illegible]n, Miss A.	Seventh	July 15, 1884	Grammar	600
Roosevelt Evening—				
Strauss, Miss M. E.	Eighth and Ninth—Prin.	July 11, 1895	Grammar	780
Kennedy, Mrs. A.	Eighth and Ninth	Sept. 21, 1908	Grammar	600
Gould, Mr. N. B.	Eighth and Ninth	June 24, 1904	Grammar	600
Dougherty, Wm. J	Seventh and Eighth	Aug. 19, 1907	Grammar	600
Madden, Janet C.	Fourth—Fifth—Sixth	July 29, 1908	Grammar	600
Sherman Evening—				
Fenton, Frank L.	Principal	Feb. 11, 1904	High	900
Williams, Walter J	Foreign	July 15, 1868	High	600
Roden, Miss Jessie	Eighth	June 9, 1897	Grammar	600
Reed, Miss C.	Seventh	Aug. 4, 1908	Grammar	600
Cella, Miss E. L.	Italian	Aug. 2, 1909	Grammar	600
Fiala, Miss A. M.	Foreign	May 9, 1886	Grammar	600
Faure, Mrs. E. S.	Bookkeeping	April 23, 1908	Grammar	600
Washington Evening—				
McDonald, A. H.	Principal	Dec. 2, 1880	High	960
Roden, Miss Jennie	Foreign	June 9, 1897	Grammar	600

Name	Grade of Class	When Elected	Grade of Certificate	Salary per Year
W[illegible] Evening—Continued				
Hatch, G. P.	[illegible]th and Ninth	July 28, 1[illegible]04	[illegible]ar	600
[illegible]n, [illegible]ss [illegible]. C.	Seventh	Dec. 10, 1896	[illegible]ar	600
Grosjean, [illegible] Lily	[illegible]	May 17, 1883	[illegible]ar	600
[illegible]r, Frank	High School	[illegible]y 6, 1886	[illegible]ar	720
T[illegible]r, Miss E. B.	[illegible]	Sept. 1, 1897	[illegible]ar	600
[illegible]y, Dr. M.	Foreign	Sept. 30, 1879	G[illegible]mar	600
[illegible]an, [illegible]rs. P. S.	Sixth	July 11, 1870	[illegible]ar	600
Bretz, [illegible]ss B. M.	Foreign	Sept. 16, 1886	G[illegible]mar	600
[illegible]y, [illegible] E. S.	[illegible]	[illegible]y 17, 1883	C[illegible]mar	60
[illegible]a, Mrs. E. [illegible]	Foreign	Sept. 15, 1887	[illegible]ar	[illegible]0
[illegible]d, Miss M. C.	Spanish	[illegible]e 29, 1903	G[illegible]mar	600
Hollub, Miss Minnie	[illegible]	April 5, 1892	G[illegible]mar	600
Humboldt Evening High—				
[illegible]e, Mr. Lawrence	Princi[illegible]al	Dec. 2, 1886	High	1,200
[illegible]s, A. E.	[illegible] Drawing	Dec. 31, 1892	Grammar	1,200
[illegible]y, [illegible]. E.	[illegible]gh S[illegible]hool	Sept. 1, 1902	High	720
[illegible]d, Mr. E. M.	High School	[illegible]ug. 10, 1905	[illegible]	720
[illegible]y, Miss M. J.	[illegible]gh S[illegible]hool	Aug. 14, 1905	[illegible]	720
McHenry, John	Drawing	April 27, 1898	Special	720
[illegible]h, Mr. C. F.	[illegible]	Sept. 10, 1908	High	720
Christie, Mr. L. C.	Drawing	Jan. 3, 1892	Special	720
Harris, Mr. H. E.	Drawing	Sept. 4, 1902	Special	720
Hendry, [illegible] C. S.	Drawing	April 27, 1898	Special	720
Harvey, [illegible] R. W.	B[illegible]ology	Dec. 28, 1905	Special	720
Carroll, W. E.	Drawing	April 15, 1905	Special	720
Blue, Mr. F. K.	Drawing	Aug. 5, 1901	Special	720
[illegible]e, L. [illegible] D.	Drawing	April 1, 1905	Special	720

LIST OF SCHOOLS AND TEACHERS.—Continued.

Name	Grade of Class	When Elected	Grade of Certificate	Salary per Year
Humboldt Evening High—Continued				
Barnett, Mr. A. T.	High School	Sept. 8, 1903	High	720
McMillan, Mr. J. T.	Navigation	Aug. 1908	Special	720
Cuthbertson, G. W.	Science	Dec. 1, 1905	High	720
Drew, John S.	Science	Feb. 25, 1897	High	720
Department at Large—				
Barthel, F. K.	Supervisor Manual Train.	Jan. 15, 1904	Special	1,800
[illegible], Mr. L. E.	[illegible] Training	Aug. 1, 1901	Special	1,200
Bagot, H. C.	Manual [illegible]	[illegible]. 15, 1903	Special	1,200
Dailey, P. F.	Manual Training	Aug. 10, [illegible]05	Special	1,200
Dowling, Mr. D. E.	Manual [illegible]	Mar. 4, 1906	Special	1,200
Silvia, A. M.	Manual Training	Mar. 11, 1905	[illegible]	1,200
Thompson, R. D.	Manual T[illegible]	[illegible]. 2, 1909	Special	1,200
Doyle, M. J.	Manual Training	[illegible]. 5, 1897	Special	1,200
Felton, M. A.	Manual [illegible]	July 30, 1902	Special	1,200
Telfer, G. J.	Manual Training	July 1, 1903	Special	1,200
Carpenter, Miss L.	Music	[illegible]. 28, 1898	Special	1,920
[illegible], Mrs. M. G.	Music	Sept. 1, [illegible]	Special	1,200
Ball, Miss K. M.	Drawing	July 1, 1894	Special	1,920
McKillop, Mrs. E. M.	Drawing	[illegible]. 29, 1896	Special	1,080
Dewing, Miss A. B.	Drawing	Aug. 3, 1908	Special	1,080
Martin, Miss E. H.	Drawing	Aug. 3, 1908	Special	1,080
Miehling, Mr. G. S.	Physical Culture	Aug. 1, 1897	Special	1,200
Bartlett, Miss E. M.	[illegible]	July 1, 1901	Special	1,200
Ballinger, Miss C. A.	Cookery	July 20, 1905	Special	900
[illegible], Miss L. G.	[illegible]	Aug. 2, 1909	Special	[illegible]
Woodward, Miss F. M.	[illegible]ery	Sept. 1, 1904	Special	900
Fenton, [illegible] M. N.	Cookery	Sept. 1, 1909	Special	900

LIST OF SCHOOLS AND TEACHERS.—Continued.

Name	Grade of Class	When Elected	Grade of Certificate	Salary per Year
Department at Large—Continued				
Congdon, Miss M.	Cookery	Aug. 19, 1905	Special	900
Gerhardt, Mrs. M.	Cookery	Oct. 25, 1909	Special	900
Gray, Miss E.	Cookery	Aug. 10, 1907	Special	900
Joralemon, Miss B. H	Cookery	Jan. 3, 1910	Special	900
Ball, Miss Lew	Supervisor Prim. Reading	April 1, 1908	Grammar	1,920
Espina, Mr. P. A.	Penmanship	Sept. 13, 1887	Special	1,500

c 59th

Annual Report of The Board of Education and The Superintendent of Schools

San Francisco, California

For the Fiscal Year Ending June 30, 1911

105

CONTENTS

BOARD OF EDUCATION

City and County of San Francisco

OFFICERS, 1910-11

President: July-December, Thomas R. Bannerman; January-June, Hiram G. Vaughan.
Secretary: Melvin G. Dodge.

MEMBERS, 1910-11

Mary W. Kincaid, July-June.
Thomas R. Bannerman, July-December.
Henry Payot, July-June.
Richard I. Whelan, July-December.
Hiram G. Vaughan, January-June.
James E. Power, January June.
Alfred Roncovieri, Superintendent of Schools, ex officio Member.

Report of Board of Education

San Francisco, California, August 1, 1911.

To the Honorable Board of Supervisors,
City and County of San Francisco.

Gentlemen:

In accordance with provision of the Charter, I have the honor to submit herewith the annual report of the Board of Education, embracing the report of the Superintendent of Schools, for the fifty-ninth fiscal year of the School Department, ending June 30, 1911.

Respectfully,

H. G. VAUGHAN,
President Board of Education, City and County of San Francisco.

Report of Superintendent of Schools

San Francisco, August 1, 1911.

To the Honorable the Board of Education, in and
for the City and County of San Francisco.

Mrs. Kincaid and Gentlemen:—I have the honor to submit herewith the annual report on the condition of the public schools of this City and County, as required by the Charter for the fifty-ninth fiscal year of the School Department, ending June 30, 1911.

ALFRED RONCOVIERI,

Superintendent of Common Schools, in and for the City and County of San Francisco,

GENERAL STATISTICS.

Fiscal Year ending June 30, 1911.

Population of the City and County (estimate)	420,000
Assessment roll of the taxable property of the City and County (Assessor's valuation)	$515,028,100.00
City and County School Tax on each $100	17.47
City and County Taxes for school purposes	900,778.38
Apportionments of State School Funds	638,791.89

ESTIMATED VALUE OF SCHOOL PROPERTY.

Sites occupied by Elementary Schools	$2,483,700.00	
Sites occupied by Secondary Schools	525,000.00	
Sites not occupied by schools	2,490,000.00	
Total value of land		$5,498,700.00
Buildings—		
Elementary Schools	$3,868,828.00	
Secondary Schools	541,252.00	
Administration	15,000.00	
Total Value of Buildings		$4,425,080.00
Furniture—		
Elementary Schools	$ 192,287.00	
High Schools	23,350.00	
Administration	3,500.00	
Total Value of Furniture		$ 219,137.00
Apparatus and Laboratories—		
Elementary Schools, including Manual Training and Cooking	27,000.00	
High Schools	49,000.00	
Total Value of all Apparatus and Laboratories		$ 76,000.00
Library—		
Elementary Schools	$ 35,728.00	
High Schools	4,635.00	
Teachers'	700.00	
Storeroom	1,512.00	
Total Value Libraries		$ 42,575.00
Total Value (Estimated) of all School Property		$10,161,492.00

FINANCIAL REPORT.

DISBURSEMENTS.

Salaries—		
Teachers—		
High School (including San Francisco Commercial, $27,979.95 and Humboldt Evening High, $15,900.00)	$ 181,742.10	
Substitutes	6,000.00	
Primary and Grammar	*1,122,590.25	
Evening (except Humboldt Evening High, $15,900.00)	50,220.00	
Primary and Grammar Substitutes	45,000.00	
Special (Domestic Science, $10,500; Drawing, $4,320; Manual Training, $12,228; Music, $4,740; Penmanship, $1,620; Physical Culture, $2,400; Primary Reading, $1,920)	37,728.00	
Janitors—		
High School	9,480.00	
Primary and Grammar	65,546.00	
Evening	3,600.00	
Board of Education	12,000.00	
Superintendent and Deputies	15,640.00	
Secretary and Attaches	13,530.00	
Attendance Officer	250.05	
Clerk of Repair Shop	1,500.00	
Storekeeper and Assistant	2,700.00	
Superintendent Buildings and Repairs	2,100.00	
Foreman Supply Department	1,500.00	
Inspector of Boilers	187.50	
Scavenger	2,070.00	
Total Salaries		$1,563,903.90
Advertising		450.39
Athletics		3,000.00
Cartage		1,303.50
Contribution to Reception expenses National Education Assn.		1,500.00
Census		348.00

* Includes $12,857.50 back salaries for 1908-1909.

Drinking Fountains	3,000.00
Furniture, $9,425.19. (This does not include money derived from sale of bonds and spent by Board of Supervisors for equipment $)	9,453.56
Fuel	14,818.07
Labor (Supply Department)	14,191.00
Light	7,835.23
Loam for School Gardens	700.00
Maps, Books and Charts	11,235.97
Pacific Heights Yard (Concrete work)	4,667.20
Printing	3,937.15
Rooms and Equipment for Cooking and Manual Training Centers at Roosevelt, James Lick and Pacific Heights Schools	15,000.00
Rents	9,044.35
Stationery	11,461.19

Supplies—		
Cooking	1,541.30	
High School	2,195.80	
Incidental	15,090.86	
Janitorial	4,184.27	
Manual Training	3,301.81	
Polytechnic High (Supplies, Laboratory and Machinery)	3,453.56	
Total Supplies		29,767.60
Teachers' Institute		1,432.00
Telephone and Telegraph		87.14
Water		10,225.15
Total Expenses (excluding sites, building and repairs)		1,726,813.03

RECEIPTS.

City and County Taxes (exclusive of $102,000.00 appropriated by the Board of Supervisors to be expended by Board of Public Works for repairing school buildings)	$ 900,778.38
State Apportionment High Schools	26,608.04
State Apportionment Primary and Grammar Schools	612.183.85
Rents derived from School Property	50,888.00
Sale of Old Material	682.72
Total Receipts	$1,591,140.99
Surplus for year ending June 30, 1910	89,311.52
Total Revenue Year 1910-1911	$1,680,452.51
Total ordinary expenses for year ending June 30, 1911	1,726,813.03
Deficit *	46,360.52

Repairs—

The Board of Supervisors appropriated for the repairing of School Buildings to be expended by the Board of Public Works, $102,000.00.

GENERAL DEPARTMENT EXPENSES PRORATED AMONG HIGH, PRIMARY AND GRAMMAR AND EVENING SCHOOLS, ON THE BASIS OF AVERAGE DAILY ATTENDANCE.

All Salaries, except Teachers' and Janitors'	$ 51,477.65	
All other expenses except light, rents, supplies (high school, cooking, manual training) Loam, Manual Training and Cooking Centers, Pacific Heights yard	105,689.88	
Total Prorated		$ 157,167.43
High Schools	11,267.69	
Primary and Grammar Schools	135,440.94	
Evening (including Humboldt Evening High)	10,458.90	
		157,167.43

* There are a few outstanding bills which will increase this deficit.

DISTRIBUTION OF EXPENDITURES.

(Not Including Sites, Buildings and Repairs.)

High Schools—		
Cost of Instruction	$ 171,842.10	
Cost of Janitors	8,880.00	
Cost of Supplies	5,649.36	
Cost of share of department expenses prorated..	11,267.69	
		$ 197,639.15
Primary and Grammar Schools—		
Cost of Instruction	$1,205,318.25	
Cost of Janitors	65,546.00	
Rents	9,044.35	
Supplies (cooking and manual training, etc.)....	25,210.31	
Share of department expenses prorated	135,440.94	
		1,440,559.85
Evening Schools (including Humboldt)—		
Cost of Instruction	66,120.00	
Cost of Janitor	4,200.00	
Light	7,835.23	
Share of department expenses prorated	10,458.80	
		88,614.03
Grand Total		$1,726,813.03

COST PER PUPIL, 1910-1911

	Per Pupil Enrolled	Per Pupil Avge. Daily Attendance	Year 1909-10
(a) For Instruction Only—			
High Schools	$35.88	$63.48	$65.50
Primary and Grammar Schools	29.98	37.04	35.12
Evening Schools including Humboldt	8.83	26.62	27.15
(b) For all Expenditures (not including repairs, buildings and sites—			
High Schools	41.27	73.01	78.16
Primary and Grammar Schools	35.84	44.26	44.55
Evening Schools	11.83	35.70	35.20

STATEMENT OF EXPENDITURE OF MONEY DERIVED FROM SALE OF SCHOOL BONDS.

(ISSUE OF 1908.)

School	Equipment	Extras	Sites	Paid on Contract.
Adams Cosmopolitan		$ 8,130.84		$ 27,645.00
Bryant Cosmopolitan	$ 3,580.31	9,886.86		96,419.29
Burnett		3,266.30	$ 5,500.00	22.095.00
Clement	1,178.88	10,065.81		88,360.70
Cleveland	6,725.27			29,841.75
Denman		9,267.74	18,750.00	100,596.50
Douglas			6,250.00	
Farragut	1,339.65	11,209.67		83,160.15
Franklin		7,256.10		25,458.75
Frank McCoppin	4,046.37	8,433.49		94,765.90
Garfield	4,844.49	12,709.58		87,752.75
Girls' High		10,288.00		5,380.00
Grattan		6,304.57		6,975.00
Hancock	4,059.68	20,575.99		143,737.00
Harrison		2,773.41		10,303.50
Holly Park	4,127.03	9,697.14		79,360.20
James Lick			5,600.00	
Jean Parker	389.76	10,550.78		102,183.73
John Swett		2,970.90	25,000.00	12,500.00
Lincoln		3,425.22		
Longfellow	2,618.33	11,704.64		63,054.00
Lowell	12,136.13			12,136.13
Madison	2,967.86	6,864.22		80,081.50
Marshall	2,628.10			
McKinley	3,293.08	11,473.23		88,225.15
Peabody		3,499.60		29,785.00
Portola	3,700.00	5,835.23		89,056.00
San Francisco Commercial	15,342.43	15,787.04		244,464.60
Sheridan	4,915.08	10,604.06	9,350.00	94,838.00
Spring Valley		9,458.03		33,217.50
Sutro	4,317.98	9,881.49		91,115.00
Visitacion Valley		2,644.92		2,595.00
Washington Grammar				8,944.00
Mission Grammar	4,006.85	10,840.94		160,607.62
Washington Irving	26.62			
Apparatus		953.36		
Total	$64,727.82	$274,073.62	$70,450.00	$2,001,838.59

SOME SCHOOL STATISTICS FROM THE OPENING OF THE FIRST FREE

Year Ending Oct. 31.	No. of Schools.	Teachers.	Pupils Enrolled.	Average Daily Attendance.
1850	1	2	150	......
1851	1	4	325	......
1852	7	15	700	445
1853	....	16	2,870	1,182
1854	....	19	4,199	1,727
1855	....	29	4,694	1,638
1856	9	61	3,347	2,516
Year Ending June 30.				
1857	....	60	2,821	2,155
1858	....	67	5,273	2,521
1859	11	75	6,201	2,829
1860	....	68	6,180	2,837
1861	13	73	6,617	3,377
1862	17	82	8,204	3,786
1863	....	94	8,177	4,389
1864	20	108	7,075	5,470
1865	....	138	8,000	6,718
1866	32	206	10,152	8,131
1867	37	253	13,385	10,177
1868	39	285	17,426	11,871
1869	42	326	19,885	13,113
1870	55	371	22,152	15,394
1871	56	416	26,406	16,978
1872	56	480	27,664	18,272
1873	58	506	27,722	18,550
1874	64	510	29,449	19,434
1875	64	552	31,128	21,014
1876	66	574	34,029	22,761
1877	66	632	37,268	24,899
1878	65	672	38,672	26,292
1879	64	696	38,129	27,075
1880	59	686	38,320	28,150
1881	62	719	40,187	29,092
1882	65	675	40,752	29,435
1883	63	687	40,722	30,827
1884	64	714	41,942	31,578
1885	65	734	43,265	32,183
1886	65	773	43,140	32,146
1887	68	799	43,311	31,316
1888	68	806	42,330	30,191
1889	71	838	42,626	31,609
1890	72	859	42,926	31,352
1891	73	879	43,626	31,809
1892	75	897	46,172	32,431
1893	76	929	45,775	32,799
1894	73	866	44,349	32,939
1895	75	904	44,822	32,974
1896	76	927	45,435	33,508
1897	77	974	46,564	33,531
1898	92	1,070	50,101	35,116
1899	90	1,074	48,972	36,830
1900	86	1,061	48,058	35,004
1901	82	1,017	48,517	34,771
1902	84	1,052	48,893	35,691
1903	84	1,086	48,345	37,077
1904	85	1,121	49,600	37,700
1905	85	1,181	55,067	40,920
1906	86	1,115	57,782	41,932
1907	83	971	45,633	29,929
1908	89	1,095	48,045	33,931
1909	92	1,195	48,509	35,541
1910	95	1,198	50,212	36,774
1911	100	1,227	51,462	37,736
		Total		

PUBLIC SCHOOL BY J. C. PELTON, DECEMBER, 1849, TO JUNE 30, 1911.

Expenses for All Purposes.	Cost per Capita on Average Daily Attendance.	School Census Children 4 to 18 Years.	Value of School Property.	Assessment of City and County Property.
....	....	500	....	....
....	....	1,510		
$23,125	51.96	2,132		
35,040	296.5	2,730		....
159,249	125.19	3,268	....	....
136,580	83.38	4,531	....	....
125,064	49.71	4,751	....	
92,955	43.14	4,755		
104,808	41.57	6,375		
134,731	47.62	7,767	....	....
156,407	55.13	9,025		....
158,855	47.04	13,316	....	....
134,576	35.58	13,358		
178,929	47.67	16,501		
228,411	41.76	18,748	....	
346,862	50.15	21,013		....
		5 to 15 Years.		
361,668	44.48	17,369	....	$70,202,000
507,822	49.89	20,253	$1,057,000	74,976,000
416,654	35.09	23,306	1,368,000	84,689,000
397,842	30.34	24,817	1,531,000	95,700,000
526,625	33.56	27,055	1,729,800	114,759,500
705,116	41.53	28,971	1,786,400	....
668,262	36.02	31,936	1,810,000	(?)97,000,000
611,818	35.45	34,676	....	....
		5 to 17 Years.		
689,022	35.40	38,084	2,227,620	212,407,505
707,445	33.71	41,029	2,367,000	264,000,000
867,755	38.12	46,238	2,505,500	269,105,141
732,324	29.41	53,210	2,585,000	260,576,978
989,259	37.62	55,899	2,711,000	254,702,960
876,489	32.37	62,105	3,047,303	244,477,360
809,133	28.74	58,492	3,073,000	217,487,074
827,324	28.44	55,115	3,137,000	253,545,476
735,435	24.98	55,880	3,137,000	222,336,400
791,175	25.66	58,061	3,137,000	201,992,152
797,452	25.25	63,029	3,137,000	201,763,762
840,367	25.80	69,000	3,137,000	223,509,560
815,778	25.37	74,079	3,189,000	230,386,325
843,297	26.93	78,246	3,184,575	230,151,009
926,662	30.69	59,517	3,230,598	251,746,111
916,644	28.99	60,642	4,772,180	273,389,616
983,014	31.35	61,144	4,757,724	306,041,440
1,053,610	33.12	62,456	4,798,427	301,444,140
1,098,839	33.88	63,933	4,932,754	311,566,079
1,134,757	34.59	65,317	5,019,317	346,224,706
989,009	30.05	68,390	5,063,364	342,644,179
1,043,067	26.09	70,006	5,140,258	325,108,898
1,086,571	32.42	71,822	5,284,000	327,805,147
1,222,941	36.52	74,840	5,354,859	330,401,154
1,319,829	37.58	76,336	5,474,739	351,784,094
1,507,163	40.92	75,292	5,514,200	405,111,615
1,274,696	36.41	78,554	5,514,200	410,155,304
1,152,631	30.27	82,173	5,207,600	413,417,241
1,316,170	36.88	82,391	5,334,000	413,338,420
1,322,585	35.67	91,386	5,649,651	420,555,541
1,398,296	37.09	97,353	5,702,001	564,070,301
1,403,349	34.29	98,127	5,800,000	583,056,457
1,498,275	35.73	101,836	6,984,000	524,392,047
1,325,433	44.28	77,367	6,207,010	375,932,477
1,934,355	57.01	87,696	6,379,000	429,632,843
1,701,236	47.86	88,058	7,206,573	454,334,160
3,307,948	89.98	74,729	8,733,285	492,867,374
3,137,825	83.18	abolished	10,161,492	515,028,100
$51,588,590				

STATE SCHOOL ENROLLMENT AND ATTENDANCE STATISTICS FOR YEARS ENDING

	June 30, 1911		June 30, 1910.
	Enrollment.	Increase over 1910.	Enrollment.
High School	3,789	244	3,545
Primary and Grammar	40,190	580	39,610
Evening	7,483	426	7,057
Total	51,462	1,250	50,212
	Av. Daily Attend.		Av. Daily Attend.
High School	2,707	291	2,416
Primary and Grammar	32,545	578	31,967
Evening	2,484	93	2,391
Total	37,736	962	36,774
	Tardiness.	Av. Daily Absence.	
High School	8,221	135	
Primary and Grammar	23,381	1,513	
Evening	7,145	258	

ENROLLMENT OF PUPILS FOR THE FIRST AND FIFTH DAYS OF SCHOOL YEAR.

FIRST DAY.

	1906.	1907.	1908.	1909.	1910.	1911.
High School	1,759	2,275	2,463	2,681	2,600	2,687
Elementary	22,790	29,012	31,014	32,115	32,673	33,403
Evening	Not open.	1,841	2,006	2,089	2,198	2,255
Totals	27,549	33,128	35,483	36,885	37,471	38,345

FIFTH DAY.

	1906.	1907.	1908.	1909.	1910.	1911.
High School	1,964	2,306	2,465	2,702	2,798	2,888
Elementary	25,585	30,210	32,144	33,168	34,390	35,056
Evening	Not open.	1,970	2,371	2,389	2,542	2,581
Totals	27,549	34,486	36,980	38,259	39,730	40,525

STATE ENROLLMENT OF THE DAY PUBLIC SCHOOLS OF SAN FRANCISCO DURING THE YEAR ENDING JUNE 30, 1911, ENUMERATED BY SEX, AGE AND GRADE. STATE ENROLLMENT ADMITS NO DUPLICATION. PUPILS PROMOTED DURING THE YEAR ARE ENUMERATED IN THE GRADES FROM WHICH THEY WERE PROMOTED. AGES AT DATE OF ENTRANCE TO GRADES.

BOYS—

Grades.	6 Yrs.	7 Yrs.	8 Yrs.	9 Yrs.	10 Yrs.	11 Yrs.	12 Yrs.	13 Yrs.	14 Yrs.	15 Yrs.	16 Yrs.	17 Yrs.	18 Yrs.	19 Yrs.	20 Yrs. or over.	Grade Total.
First Grade	2,967	1,497	582	170	86	36	30	17	19	8	2	4	2	2	2	5,424
Second Grade	79	701	1,037	730	347	120	74	38	30	9	7	2	3		1	3,178
Third Grade		61	499	836	702	443	257	110	51	13	10	1	2	2		2,987
Fourth Grade			65	550	870	671	394	131	50	13	5	4	1			2,754
Fifth Grade			2	40	310	535	553	398	208	37	11	6	3	2		2,105
Sixth Grade					57	268	527	499	309	120	25	14	3			1,822
Seventh Grade					1	46	245	451	398	212	49	10	1	1		1,414
Eighth Grade						2	51	229	380	269	120	18	4	3		1,076
Age Totals	3,046	2,259	2,185	2,326	2,373	2,121	2,131	1,873	1,445	681	229	59	19	10	3	20,760
High Schools—																
First Year						1	2	51	194	252	184	97	31	15	14	841
Second Year								5	30	72	98	64	31	10	8	318
Third Year									1	10	38	40	35	14	4	142
Fourth Year										3	13	41	25	15	7	104
Total High School						1	2	56	225	337	333	242	122	54	33	1,405
Grand Total Boys	3,046	2,259	2,185	2,326	2,373	2,122	2,133	1,929	1,670	1,018	562	301	141	64	36	22,165

GIRLS—

Grades.	6 Yrs.	7 Yrs.	8 Yrs.	9 Yrs.	10 Yrs.	11 Yrs.	12 Yrs.	13 Yrs.	14 Yrs.	15 Yrs.	16 Yrs.	17 Yrs.	18 Yrs.	19 Yrs.	20 Yrs. or over.	Grade Total.
First Grade	2,760	1,117	453	124	47	16	8	8	3	2	1		1			4,540
Second Grade	122	863	1,018	586	227	89	41	19	2		1					2,968
Third Grade		43	439	664	529	327	219	91	39	5						2,356
Fourth Grade			72	398	697	592	388	178	56	9	3	1	1			2,395
Fifth Grade			1	61	422	632	551	340	121	31	6	1	1			2,167
Sixth Grade				1	54	332	615	539	277	64	14	2				1,898
Seventh Grade						66	338	573	497	205	63	3	2			1,747
Eighth Grade					1	3	73	288	482	316	160	35	1			1,359
Age Totals	2,882	2,023	1,983	1,834	1,977	2,057	2,233	2,036	1,477	632	248	42	6	—	—	19,430
High Schools—																
First Year							2	43	393	406	232	114	28	10	7	1,235
Second Year							1	2	31	229	217	103	36	9	9	637
Third Year									2	22	128	102	31	4	2	291
Fourth Year										1	23	104	58	27	8	221
Total High School							3	45	426	658	600	423	153	50	26	2.384

EVENING SCHOOLS.

	14 yrs.	15 yrs.	16 yrs.	17 yrs.	18 yrs.	19 yrs.	20 yrs. or over	Total Pupils
Boys	514	703	637	641	540	393	2,589	6,017
Girls	113	163	177	217	210	129	465	1,474
Total by Age	627	866	814	858	750	522	3,054	7,491

GRADUATES.

Number of graduates from the grammar school for the year—

Boys	Day 810, Evening 302	1,112
Girls	Day 969, Evening 108	1,077
Total		2,189

Number of graduates from the High schools for the year—

Boys	Day 99, Evening 57	156
Girls	Day 299, Evening 16	315
Total		471

NUMBER OF TEACHERS IN DEPARTMENT, JUNE, 1911.

	Men	Women	Total
High School Principals	5		5
High School Teachers	45	61	106
Grammar Principals	9	18	27
Grammar Vice-principals	2	25	27
Grammar Teachers	4	270	274
Primary Principals	3	50	53
Primary Teachers		531	531
Special Schools, (Oral School for Deaf, Parental, Ungraded)	1	8	9
Domestic Science		11	11
Drawing		4	4
Manual Training	10		10
Music		3	3
Physical Culture	1	1	2
Reading (Primary Grades)		1	1
Penmanship	1		1
Total Day Schools	81	983	1,064
Evening School Principals	10	2	12
Evening School Teachers	34	60	94
Substitutes	4	53	57
Total number of teachers in department	129	1,098	1,227

LENGTH OF SERVICE OF TEACHERS, COUNTING ONLY THEIR SERVICE IN SAN FRANCISCO PUBLIC SCHOOLS.

Years of Service.	Men	Women	Total
1 year	11	42	53
2 years	6	44	50
3 years	8	65	73
4 years	8	47	55
5 years	3	21	24
6 years	12	72	84
7 years	4	40	44
8 years	6	38	44
9 years	4	32	36
10 years	9	29	38
11 years	1	4	5
12 years	2	1	3
13 years	4	43	47
14 years	7	50	57
15 years	2	31	33
16 years	1	15	16
17 years	1	10	11
18 years	1	4	5
19 years	3	37	40
20 years	4	26	30
21 years	2	21	23
22 years	2	20	22
23 years	1	27	28
24 years	2	15	17
25 years	3	22	25
26 years		25	25
27 years	1	31	32
28 years	1	16	17
29 years	1	18	19
30 years		12	12
31 years	1	16	17
32 years		19	19
33 years		16	16
34 years		28	28
35 years	1	16	17
36 years	1	18	19
37 years		6	6
38 years	1	15	16
39 years		10	10
40 years	2	6	8
41 years	1	5	6
42 years		6	6
43 years	3	6	9
44 years		5	5
45 years		5	5
46 years	1	0	1
47 years	0	2	2
48 years		3	3
49 years			
50 years			
51 years			
52 years			
53 years			

AVERAGE NUMBER BELONGING, AND AVERAGE DAILY ATTENDANCE OF EACH SCHOOL FOR YEAR ENDING JUNE 30, 1911.

DAY ELEMENTARY SCHOOLS.	Average Number Belonging.	Average Daily Attendance.	Per Cent. Av. Daily Att. to Av. No. Blg.
Adams Grammar	287	274	95.47
Agassiz Primary	727	703	95.87
Bay View Grammar	467	451	96.66
Bernal Grammar	605	578	95.63
Bergerot Primary	448	433	96.56
Bryant Cosmopolitan	483	464	96.06
Buena Vista Primary	332	316	95.45
Burnett Primary	370	351	94.96
Clement Primary	461	448	97.22
Columbia Grammar	892	870	97.80
Cleveland	345	333	96.55
Cooper Primary	482	454	94.24
Crocker Grammar	799	772	96.62
Denman Grammar	27	26	97.40
Douglass Primary	485	464	95.01
Dudley Stone Primary	463	444	95.44
Edison Primary	427	412	96.46
Emerson Primary	517	496	96.03
Everett Grammar	720	696	91.14
Fairmount Grammar	939	899	95.73
Frank McCoppin Primary	510	492	96.43
Franklin Grammar	415	390	94.04
Fremont Grammar	675	642	95.14
Garfield Primary	788	743	94.82
Glen Park Grammar	522	499	95.54
Golden Gate Primary	360	343	95.41
Grant Primary	373	359	96.17
Grattan Primary	249	238	95.77
Haight Primary	581	557	96.19
Hamilton Grammar	587	571	97.22
Hancock Grammar	493	476	96.63
Harrison Primary	114	108	94.98
Hawthorne Primary	388	375	96.39
Hearst Grammar	686	667	97.19
Henry Durant Primary	452	430	95.10
Junipero Serra Primary	601	576	95.82
Horace Mann Grammar	854	827	96.88
Hunter's Point	41	39	95.60
Irving Primary	246	231	93.90
Irving M. Scott Grammar	611	581	95.07
Jackson Primary	158	151	95.56
James Lick Grammar	522	501	96.01
Jean Parker Grammar	601	576	95.87
Jefferson Primary	93	91	98.50
John Swett Grammar	512	496	96.60
Lafayette Primary	27	26.5	98.15
Laguna Honda Primary	621	598	96.36
Lake View Primary	218	206	94.49
Lincoln Grammar	285	272	95.44
Madison Primary	341	329	96.48

Marshall Primary	489	470	96.12
McKinley Primary	349	338	96.84
Mission Grammar	407	400	98.18
Monroe Grammar	839	806	96.06
Moulder Primary	237	228	96.20
Noe Valley Primary	678	649.7	95.87
Ocean House	33	32	96.96
Ocean Side Primary	163	155	95.09
Oriental Public	318	306.5	96.38
Pacific Heights Grammar	716	690	96.64
Parkside	20	19	95.00
Peabody Primary	224	215	95.89
Potrero	323	306	94.73
Redding	358	345	96.34
Richmond Grammar	653	627	96.02
Rincon	83	78	93.97
Sheridan Primary	625	592	94.72
Sherman Primary	375	364	97.06
South End Primary	610	586	96.06
Spring Valley Grammar	433	424	97.92
Starr King Primary	274	264	96.13
Sunnyside Primary	120	114	95.00
Sunset Primary	52	51	98.07
Sutro Grammar	521	500	95.97
Visitacion Valley Primary	243	234	96.29
Washington Grammar	470	456	94.89
West End Primary	254	239	94.09
Winfield Scott Primary	259	248	95.75
Yerba Buena	448	431	96.29

SPECIAL SCHOOLS.

Oral for Deaf	......	......	....
Parental	46	45.6	98.27

HIGH SCHOOLS.

Commercial	594	581	97.81
Girls'	644	606	94.10
Lowell	781	742	95.00
Mission	496	478	96.37
Polytechnic	319	300	94.04

EVENING SCHOOLS.

Commercial	321	280	87.23
Hamilton	394	337	85.49
Horace Mann	438	363	82.59
Irving M. Scott	34	29	84.55
Lincoln	362	308	85.09
Roosevelt	96	84	87.50
Washington	304	258	84.87
Humboldt High	516	451	87.40
Bernal	......	......	....
Monroe	......	......	....
Portola	......	......	....
Sherman	176	159.4	90.57
Washington High	37	31	80.38
Laguna Honda	36	27	75.00
Monroe	69	59	85.51

SCHOLASTIC TRAINING AND CERTIFICATION OF TEACHERS.

Number of Teachers (including Principals and excluding Substitutes)

	Men	Women
Who are graduates of University of California	29	88
Who are graduates of Leland Stanford Jr. University	11	5
Who are graduates of Other Universities	18	7
Who are graduates of Other Colleges	22	10
Who are graduates of S. F. City Normal School or Class	1	393
Who are graduates of Chico State Normal School	1	11
Who are graduates of Los Angeles State Normal	2	2
Who are graduates of San Diego State Normal		3
Who are graduates of San Francisco State Normal		103
Who are graduates of San Jose Normal	4	87
Who are graduates of Normal Schools of other States	10	26

CERTIFICATES.

	Men	Women
No. holding certificates of High School Grade	71	118
No. holding certificates of Grammar School Grade	22	828
No. holding certificates of Primary School Grade		32
No. holding Special Certificate in Bookkeeping	5	13
No. holding Special Certificate in Domestic Science		5
No. holding Special Certificate in Drawing (all departments)	13	8
No. holding Special Certificate in Languages		27
No. holding Special Certificate in Manual Training (all depts.)	12	1
No. holding Special Certificate in Music	1	42
No. holding Special Certificate in Physical Culture	1	1
No. holding Special Certificate in Stenography and Typewriting	3	22

VOLUMES IN SCHOOL LIBRARIES AND STOREROOM (INCLUDING BOOKS FOR USE OF INDIGENTS).

	Volumes	Estimated Value.
High schools	5,677	$ 4,635
Primary and grammar schools	88,154	35,728
Evening schools	2,240	880
In Storeroom	3,183	1,512
	94,254	$42,755
Books becoming useless or lost during year		2,603

SCHOOL VISITATION.

Official visits of Superintendent and deputies	3,451
Official visits by members of the Board of Education	1,392
Visits by other persons	45,020

MEDAL FUNDS.

Name of Fund.	Deposited in.	In Fund June 30, 1911.
Bridge Silver Medal	Hibernia Savings & Loan Society	$2,002.97
Denman Grammar School	Hibernia Savings & Loan Society	1,131.43
Denman Silver Medal	German Savings & Loan Society	1,980.51
Hancock Grammar School	German Savings & Loan Society	394.31
Jean Parker Grammar School	German Savings & Loan Society	331.82
John Swett Grammar School	Hibernia Savings & Loan Society	187.19
Lincoln Grammar School	Hibernia Savings & Loan Society	2,635.67

SCHOOLS.

Number of High Schools, including San Francisco Commercial	5
Number of Grammar Schools	27
Number of Primary Schools	53
Number of Special Schools	3
Number of Evening Schools	12
Total Number of Schools	100

Number of concrete school buildings owned by the department, Class "A"	8
Number of brick school buildings owned by the department, "Special Construction"	17
Number of wooden school buildings owned by the department, "Class C"	59
Number of buildings or rooms rented by the department	4
Total number of buildings used by the department	88

WORK OF TRUANT OFFICERS.

The following statement concerning the work performed by the five truant officers for the year ending June 30, 1910, was presented by Mr. T. J. Dugan, officer in charge.

Complaints of truancy, etc., investigated	4,055
Found on street during school hours	3,058
Children brought before Juvenile Court	116
Parents brought before Juvenile Court	69
Boys brought before the Board of Education	13
Children found on street having working certificates	281
Children not located	23
	7,615

Commenting on the foregoing statement, I desire to say that the enforcement of the Compulsory Education Law and the repression of truancy have been promoted very much during the past year. This is due to the efficient work of the attendance or truant officers. In the discharge of their duties they have exercised diligence, courtesy and firmness, and their work merits commendation.

Since last October the number of officers has been reduced from five to three; therefore, the foregoing statement of activity is the more commendable.

SCHOOL LECTURES.

FREE PUBLIC LECTURE SYSTEM FOR ADULTS.

As far back as my report of 1907 (page 62), I respectfully recommended the holding of free public lectures in school buildings, believing that they would "be educational and elevating . . . . and appreciated by the general public and by the school patrons." Again in my report of 1908-09 I made the same recommendation, urging the Board of Education to take action upon the matter at once (page 37). The language of my recommendation at that time is herewith repeated:

"I regret that so few of our school houses have assembly rooms. The building of auditoriums, as a feature of school equipment, will be appreciated by the general public and particularly by the school patrons. They will afford a common place of meeting with small expense for all the people where there can be no bickerings, political or sectarian. The home life and the school life can be brought together in harmonious unity and much permanent good will result.

"I would, therefore, recommend that every school building planned under the new Bond Issue be provided with an assembly hall to be built on the ground floor or the first floor, where in addition to its use for general exercises, music and gymnastics for the pupils of the school, it can be used for social center development. In such a room the principal can address a large number of pupils in a more impressive way than in separate class rooms. Such a room can be used for stereopticon exhibitions, for graduating exercises or as already indicated as a social center for citizens and parents of the district. The school houses belong to the people and under proper restrictions should be used for the diffusion of information and the promotion of a civic spirit among the adult population.

"I respectfully recommend that free public lectures on American history, physics, mechanics, economics, etc., for the student and adult population be given in the auditoriums of the Mission High School, the Crocker, Girls' High, Polytechnic, Lowell, Hearst and the Horace Mann, and where-ever possible in smaller buildings.

"These lectures, combined with musical numbers, will be educational and elevating and will be appreciated by the general public and by the school patrons."

"Our evening schools are in session five evenings a week. The same buildings should be used for public lectures on educational subjects. There are many public spirited citizens who would give such lectures without charge. We should have lectures on all subjects pertaining to civic welfare. We should not wait till bubonic plague comes again before teaching the people to be clean. Cleanliness in kitchens, back yards, alleys, streets, public and private morals, public and private decency, should be taught to both young and old. Such civic pride should be created that ugly billboards will disappear from our streets and that all entertainments of doubtful character will be prohibited."

"Lectures should be given on public and private health, such as the prevention of tuberculosis. Physicians should give lectures on the physical care and training of children, and upon the dangers besetting adolescence."

Early in January, 1910, primarily through the active efforts of Mrs. Louis Hertz of the California Club, the Board of Education endorsed the plan to hold in school auditoriums lectures for adults, and co-operated with the following committee to take charge of the movement:

Mrs. Mary Kincaid, representing the Board of Education; Dr. Caroline Rosenberg, the Council of Jewish Women; Miss Amy Sussman and Miss Katherine Felton, the Collegiate Alumnae; Mrs.Louis Hertz, the California Club; Mrs. James Crawford, the Women's Auxiliary to the Juvenile Court; Dr. R. G. Brodrick, the Board of Health; Walter Macarthur, the Civic League; Dr. Langley Porter, the San Francisco Milk Improvement Association, and William P. McCabe, R. I. Wisler and Leo Michelson representing the community at large.

The ideas of the Committee were well set forth in the beginning in an interview by Mr. Walter Macarthur, who said:

''This innovation in educational work has proved extremely successful in other cities and has been indorsed by numerous labor organizations. The meetings will be short, beginning at 8 o'clock p. m. and ending about 9.30 o'clock. The lectures will, whenever possible, be accompanied by stereopticon views or moving pictures. The services of the lecturers and others will be gratuitous and admission will be free.''

The Board of Education designated the Mission High, Washington Grammar, Portola, Laguna Honda, Monroe, Lafayette and Girls' High School buildings as centers in which the lectures should be held. The first lecture, under the direction of Mrs. Hertz, was delivered at the Mission High School on January 19, 1910 by Mr. J. C. Astredo, his subject being ''The Panama Canal,'' and his address being illustrated by moving pictures of life in the canal zone. Introductory remarks were made by Mr. Thomas Bannerman, President of the Board of Education, and musical selections were rendered by Mrs. Joseph Artigues and Dr. M. W. Fredericks. The event was signalized by the attendance of 1,200 persons, the total capacity of the assembly room. During the year illustrated lectures on ''British Columbia'' by Mr. E. J. Le Breton, ''Russia'' by Mr. Harris Weinstock, and ''Syria'' by Mr. W. H. Jordan were delivered. To Mrs. Hertz and Dr. Caroline Rosenberg, secretary of the committee, we tender our thanks for their untiring zeal in establishing and carrying on this work in its preparatory period.

At this stage, a new friend of the idea appeared in the person of Mr. Henry Payot, who had been appointed to a seat upon the Board of Education. He, henceforth, fathered the movement, and at his request toward the opening of 1911, the Board firmly established the system by adopting a resolution, to wit:

''Whereas, the Board of Education believes that a system of free public lectures for school pupils and adults is desirable, said lectures giving the results of the latest developments in science, history, hygiene, art, music, travel, and political science, etc., thereby encouraging reading and study to definite ends, and developing a wider and deeper interest in the schools on the part of the people, by making said schools and their equipment more effective social and community centers; therefore be it

''Resolved. That such a system to be known as the Lecture Bureau be and is hereby ordered instituted under the control of the Board of Education, in the City of San Francisco, the lectures to be at once arranged for, and lecture centers established for the present, at the following school buildings:

Lincoln	Monroe
Girls' High	Adams
Sheridan	Spring Valley
Yerba Buena	Sutro
Frank McCoppin	Laguna Honda
Burnett	Junipero Serra
Hancock	Mission High
Mission Grammar	Glen Park

also

"Resolved, That the following named persons interested in all that makes for the betterment of conditions in this city, be invited to act as an Advisory Commission to this Board of Education in carrying out the purposes above mentioned, namely:

Mr. J. P. Young,	Dr. R. G. Brodrick,
Dr. Langley Porter,	Raphael Weill,
James Ferguson,	Dr. C. Rosenberg,
Walter Macarthur,	C. S. Stanton,
Willis Polk,	Harris Weinstock,
E. S. Simpson,	Paul Steindorff,
Thos. E. Hayden,	James Rolph, Jr.

and further

"Resolved, That Prof. M. E. Blanchard, Ph. D., of the Mission High School, and Prof. G. O. Mitchell, A. B., of the Girls' High School, be and they are hereby appointed Secretary of the Lecture Bureau and Director of Lectures, respectively, each in his own line, to arrange for and carry out all details necessary for the proper and successful outcome of the system hereby instituted, and each to serve for such time and at such compensation as this Board may determine."

These public-spirited citizens having accepted the invitation, the body in control became:

COMMITTEE ON LECTURES

H. G. Vaughan	President of the Board of Education
Mary W. Kincaid	Member Board of Education
Henry Payot	Member Board of Education
Jas. E. Power	Member Board of Education
Alfred Roncovieri	Superintendent of Schools
Milton E. Blanchard, Ph. D.	Supervisor of Lectures
G. O. Mitchell, A. B.	Director of Lectures

ADVISORY COMMISSION ON LECTURES

Raphael Weill	Willis Polk
Harris Weinstock	Dr. Caroline Rosenberg
John P. Young	Paul Steindorff
Ernest S. Simpson	Dr. Langley Porter
C. S. Stanton	Dr. R. G. Brodrick
James Rolph, Jr.	James Ferguson
Walter Macarthur	A. J. Cloud
Thos. E. Hayden	

The aims and ideals of the course, and their practical realization, are best seen in the appended list of topics and speakers for the year.

DATE	PLACE.	SUBJECT AND SPEAKER.
esday, Jan. 4.	Mission High School Eighteenth and Dolores	Aviation. LIEUT. PAUL W. BECK, U. S. A.
y, Jan. 27.	Girls' High School O'Farrell and Scott Streets	Castles and Legends of the Rhine. B. R. BAUMGARDT
ay, Jan. 30.	Laguna Honda School Seventh Ave., bet. I and J	Animal Traits. MATTHEW McCURRIE
esday, Feb. 1.	Mission High School Eighteenth and Dolores	Ascent of the Matterhorn. DAVID STARR JORDAN
day, Feb. 2.	Sutro School 13th Ave., bet. Clement and California	A Trip through Syria. WM. H. JORDAN
esday, Feb. 8.	Monroe School China Ave. and London Street	Continental Europe. J. EMMET HAYDEN
lay, Feb. 11.	Frank McCoppin School Seventh Ave., bet B and C	The Beauties of Hawaii. ROGER SPRAGUE
esday, Feb. 15.	Crocker School Page St., bet. Broderick and Baker	Wanderings along the Equator. FORD E. SAMUEL
day, Feb. 16.	Madison School Clay Street and First Avenue	Educational value of Museums. JOHN P. YOUNG
day, Feb. 23.	Laguna Honda School Seventh Ave., bet. I and J	Java, the Pearl of the Orient. ALEXANDER RUSSELL
, Feb. 24.	Mission High School Eighteenth and Dolores Streets	Land of the Rising Sun. HENRY PAYOT
esday, Mar. 1.	Mission High School Eighteenth and Dolores Streets	Abraham Lincoln. RILEY R. ROSS
day, Mar. 2.	Sutro School 13th Ave., bet. Clement and California	Homes Without Hands. HERBERT L. COGGINS
, Mar. 3.	Girls' High School O'Farrell and Scott	Playgrounds and the Wider Use of Schools. L. H. WEIR, Field Sec'y Playground Ass'n of America.
y, Mar. 6.	Mission Grammar School Mission, near Sixteenth	The Incas of Peru. A. L. KROEBER
esday, Mar. 8.	Monroe School Excelsior Ave. and London St.	Yosemite and Hetch-Hetchy. CHAS. WESLEY REED
, Mar. 10.	Frank McCoppin School Seventh Ave., bet. B and C	A Run Through Russia. HARRIS WEINSTOCK
y, Mar. 13.	Yerba Buena School Greenwich and Webster	The Tenement House Plague. R. G. BRODRICK, M. D.
esday, Mar. 15.	Mission High School Eighteenth and Dolores	The Ancient Cliff Dwellers. MR. & MRS. EDW. H. KEMP
day, Mar. 16.	Crocker School Page, near Baker	The Child and His Environment. ERNEST B. HOAG, M. D.

DATE	PLACE.	SUBJECT AND SPEAKER.
iday, Mar. 17.	Girls' High School O'Farrell and Scott	The Land of Poco Tiempo. MRS. MARY DICKSON
onday, Mar. 20.	Madison School Clay, near First Ave.	Scenes in the South Seas. ALMON E. ROTH
ednesday, Mar. 22.	Garfield School Filbert and Kearny	Roma, Torino, e Esposizione Internazionale. ARTURO SPOZIO
iday, Mar. 24.	Portola School Bacon and Girard	Scenic California. FRANCIS HOPE
esday, Mar. 28.	Mission Grammar School Mission, near Sixteenth	The Parcels Post. EDWARD BERWICK
ednesday, Mar. 29.	Mission High School Eighteenth and Dolores	Wonders of the Heavens. MAYNARD SHIPLEY
ursday, Mar. 30.	Laguna Honda School Seventh Ave., bet I and J	Romance of California History. FRANK H. POWERS
iday, Mar. 31.	Girls' High School O'Farrell and Scott	Rostand's Chantecler. EDW. J. DUPUY and MLLE. BLANCHE LEVEILLE
ednesday, April 5.	Monroe School Excelsior and London Ave.	Wanderings along the Equator. FORD E. SAMUEL
ednesday, April 5.	Sutro School 13th Ave., bet. Clement and California	The Holy Land. ROBT. P. TROY
ursday, April 6.	Mission High School Eighteenth and Dolores	Palestine and Syria. WM. H. JORDAN
iday, April 7.	Bryant School Twenty-third and York	A Trip to Mexico. J. EMMET HAYDEN
onday, April 17.	Hancock School Filbert, near Taylor	The Races of the World. A. L. KROEBER
esday, April 18.	Crocker School Page, near Broderick	Fur Seals of Bering Sea. G. A. CLARK
ednesday, April 19.	McCoppin School Seventh Ave., bet. B and C	The Queen of the Adriatic. HENRY PAYOT
ursday, April 20.	Madison School Clay, near First Ave.	In and About Jerusalem. MARTIN A. MEYER
iday, April 21.	Girls' High School O'Farrell, near Scott	The Development of Song. MRS. M. E. BLANCHARD
onday, April 24.	Junipero Serra School Holly Park, near Highland Ave.	Java, the Gem of the East Indies. ALEXANDER RUSSELL
onday, April 24.	Mission Grammar School Mission, near Sixteenth St.	The Open Air Life. WM. C. VOORSANGER, M. D.
esday, April 25.	Garfield School Filbert and Kearny	Tahiti and Its People. ROSWELL S. WHEELER
ursday, April 27.	Laguna Honda School Seventh Ave., bet. I and J	Wireless Telegraphy. A. L. JORDAN

DATE	PLACE.	SUBJECT AND SPEAKER.
iday, April 28.	Mission High School Eighteenth and Dolores	Orchestral Instruments: 1. The Violin. WM. J. McCOY
dnesday, May 3.	Mission High School Eighteenth and Dolores Sts.	A Wider Democracy. ALBERT H. ELLIOT
ursday, May 4.	Yerba Buena School Greenwich near Webster	A Trip to Mexico. MRS. MARY DICKSON
iday, May 5.	Mission Grammar School Mission, near Sixteenth St.	India. HARRIS WEINSTOCK
turday, May 6.	Portola School Bacon and Girard	Tuberculosis and its Remedy. R. G. BRODRICK, M. D.
nday, May 8.	Monroe School Excelsior Ave. and London	Newcomers to America. MARTIN A. MEYER
esday, May 9.	Hancock School Filbert, near Taylor	Mexico, the Egypt of America. W. C. EVANS
dnesday, May 10.	Girls' High School O'Farrell, near Scott	Conservation of Childhood. WILL C. WOOD
ursday, May 11.	Frank McCoppin School Seventh Ave., bet. B and C	The Health of the Child. ERNEST B. HOAG, M. D.
ursday, May 11.	Junipero Serra School Holly Park near Highland Ave.	Panorama of the Peoples. A. L. KROEBER
day, May 12.	Madison School Clay, near First Ave.	Fur Seals of Bering Sea. G. A. CLARK
day, May 12.	Mission High School Eighteenth and Dolores	Richard Wagner. WM. GREER HARRISON and FRED. MAURER, JR.
nday, May 15.	Garfield School Filbert and Kearny	The Open Air Life. WM. C. VOORSANGER, M. D.
sday, May 16.	Sutro School 13th Ave., bet. Clement and Cal.	Java, the Gem of the East Indies. ALEXANDER RUSSELL
dnesday, May 17.	Girls' High School O'Farrell, near Scott	What is Music? ALBERT ELKUS
dnesday, May 17.	Crocker School Page, near Broderick	My First Trip Abroad. MRS. FLORENCE RICHMOND
irsday, May 18.	Mission Grammar School Mission, near Sixteenth St.	Climbing Mt. Shasta. RULIFF S. HOLWAY
day, May 19.	Mission High School Eighteenth and Dolores	St. Francis of Assisi. H. MORSE STEPHENS
nday, May 22.	Madison School Clay, near First Ave.	Japan. HENRY PAYOT
sday, May 23.	Hancock School Filbert, near Taylor	Through the South Seas. ALMON E. ROTH
irsday, May 25.	Yerba Buena School Greenwich, near Webster	Our Animals. MATTHEW McCURRIE

DATE	PLACE.	SUBJECT AND SPEAKER.
hursday, May 25.	Laguna Honda School Seventh Ave., bet. I and J.	Electricity and Heat. A. L. JORDA
riday, May 26.	Mission High School Eighteenth and Dolores	Orchestral Instruments: 2. The Flute. WM. J. McCO
onday, May 29.	Bryant School York, near Twenty-second	Yosemite and Hetch-Hetchy. CHAS. WESLEY REE
ednesday, May 31.	Girls' High School O'Farrel, near Scott	Maeterlinck's Bluebird. EDWARD J. DUPU

It is to be readily observed from the above programs that the staff of lecturers has been drawn from all walks of life and that the subjects of the discourses have covered a very broad expanse of human thought and experience. The schedule for the month of May, 1911, gives the best index to the number and location of the lecture centers. A striking proof that the system has met with popular approval is to be found in the fact that the audiences have been very large in numbers, 25,000 people in all having attended the set of sixty lectures, or approximately 400 to an evening. The cost of installing and operating the bureau has been relatively very small. The equipment expense for moving picture machines, stereopticons, lanterns, screens, curtains, wiring, etc., has approximated $3,000. The schools that have been equipped with stereopticon apparatus are: Bryant Cosmopolitan, Crocker, Garfield, Glen Park, Hancock, Horace Mann, Junipero Serra, Laguna Honda, Madison, Mission Grammar, Frank McCoppin, Monroe, Portola, Sheridan, Sutro, Yerba Buena, Girls' High and Mission High. The salary of the operator of the lantern was $100 for the year. The speakers have without exception very kindly offered their services free of charge, and to them we gladly acqnowledge our obligation.

For the coming year great prosperity for this valuable work is predicted. The Board of Supervisors has provided, at the request of the Board of Education, the sum of $2,500 for the furtherance of this movement. Out of this amount payments for services will be made to the directors of the Bureau and to such speakers as should receive remuneration. Three new lecture centers are projected.

LECTURES FOR TEACHERS.

During the year, the Board of Education and the Superintendent were enabled to secure a number of speakers to address the Department. The principal ones of these and their subjects were:

November 28, 1910, Christian Science Hall, "Songs and Stories of Nature," by Mr. Kellogg, "The Nature Singer."

February and March, 1911, a series of four lectures by Professor B. R. Baumgardt, including "The Age of Pericles" and "Castles and Legends of the Rhine."

March 7, 1911, Mission High School Building, "Modern Boys and Girls—Assets or Liabilities," by Dr. A. E. Winship.

July 31, 1911, Mission High School Building, "The Problem of the Exceptional Child," by Dr. Maximilian P. E. Groszmann.

August 8, 1911, Mission High School, "New Thought in Education," by W. L. Tomlins, and "The Chicago Teachers' Victory," by Miss Margaret Haley.

LECTURES IN SCHOOLS FOR PUPILS.

Side by side with the Free Public Lectures for adults, there has been conducted during the year 1910-11 a system of lectures for pupils in the auditoriums of the different schools. These lectures have been of two kinds, one under the immediate direction of the lecture bureau of the Board of Education, the other arranged by the Board in conjunction with the San Francisco Association for the Study and Prevention of Tuberculosis, under the immediate supervision of Dr. R. G. Brodrick.

The lectures given by the Bureau, Dr. M. E. Blanchard, Director, were as follows:

December, 1910, Crocker School, "The True Sportsman."
DR. M. E. BLANCHARD.

December, 1910, Crocker School, "Personal and National Thrift."
DR. M. E. BLANCHARD.

March, 1911, Girls' High School, "Dickens: The Man and His Works."
MRS. C. W. PLATT.

March, 1911, Girls' High School, "The Yosemite and Hetch-Hetchy."
MR. CHAS. W. REED.

March, 1911, Girls' High School, "The Chateaux of Northern France."
MR. HENRY PAYOT.

April, 1911, Bryant Cosmopolitan School, "Our Animals."
MR. MATTHEW McCURRIE.

May, 1911, Mission High School, "Fur Seals of Bering Sea."
MR. G. A. CLARK.

These addresses were all illustrated by stereopticon views.

The lectures given under the direction of Dr. Brodrick were authorized by a Resolution passed by the Board of Education on January 4, 1911, as follows:

"RESOLVED: That this Board hereby authorizes the giving of stereopticon lectures on Tuberculosis, to pupils in the high schools and in the 7th and 8th grades of the grammar schools, by Dr. R. G. Brodrick, in accordance with the following schedule:

Girls' High	Friday,	Jan. 20,	2:00 P. M.
Mission High	"	Jan. 27,	"
Mission Grammar	"	Feb. 3,	"
Sutro Grammar		Feb. 17,	
Laguna Honda		Mar. 3,	
Sheridan		Mar. 24,	
Monroe		Mar. 31,	
Glen Park		April 14,	"
Crocker		April 28,	
Horace Mann		May 12,	

Each school auditorium was furnished with black curtains, fitted in such manner that day light could be excluded and stereopticon lamps already furnished these schools through the Lecture Bureau were employed. Mr. Richard C. M. Page, a pupil at the Mission High School, kindly offered to operate the lamp.

So far as we know, San Francisco is the only city in the United States, in which stereopticon lectures on Tuberculosis are given to the pupils during school hours.

Through these illustrated lectures several thousand children were shown the cause and nature of this scourge, statistical data, such as mortality compared with other diseases, and its relative prevalence in various states and cities; the evil effects of violating the tenement house law; insanitary factories and workshops; good results which have followed municipal and state control; benefit of outdoor treatment in homes or sanitaria, and illustrations of outdoor schools. Great emphasis was laid on the truth that consumption is a preventable disease, and that it is also curable, if wise treatment be begun early. It was vividly shown that impure air and unclean surroundings are conditions favorable to its spread while, on the contrary, fresh air and clean surroundings destroy its possibilities of existence. Great credit is due Dr. Brodrick for having contributed his time, energy, and thought to this cause.

In this connection I respectfully call to the special attention of the Board the necessity of providing our teachers with a card form, outlining briefly a practical program that will aid the teacher in understanding and dealing with simple cases as they arise. A copy of such a form issued in a Massachusetts city is herewith added:

Some general symptoms of disease in children which teachers should notice and on account of which the children should be referred to the School Physician:

Emaciation.
Pallor.
Puffiness of the Face.
Shortness of Breath.
Swellings in the Neck.
General Lassitude and other Evidences of Sickness.
Flushing of the Face.
Eruptions of Any Sort.
A Cold in the Head with Running Eyes.
Irritating Discharge from the Nose.
Evidences of a Sore Throat.
Coughs.
Vomiting.
Frequent Requests to Go Out.

MOVING-PICTURES.

I also respectfully recommend, most earnestly, that the lecture system for pupils in our schools be extended so as to include moving-picture films on educational themes. In other places such a plan has been tried with eminent success. While it is true that the moving-picture has its limits of usefulness, and can only supplement and reinforce the work of the class-room, it is also true that it has been proved to have great value in impressing geographical facts, historical events and natural phenomena on the minds of children. From these pictures the facts of geography gain a form, size, mass, movement and color impossible in verbal presentation only. The reality of historical events is strengthened by reason of the stimulus given to the imagination by this device. In no other way can the study of nature be so powerfully developed, for plant and bird life are thus brought before the child directly in their own environment. It is helpful in the teaching of literature, because it gives optical illustration of the idea presented by the author.

A writer on this subject, Mr. John Collier, says:

"The school will use the motion picture because it is graphic. The growth of a plant from seed to harvest is shown in a ten-minute space on the screen, not with gaps and halts, but in a continuous process amazing to behold. The almost infinitely swift motion of an insect's wing has been dissected by pictures at the rate of 2000 a second. Too much passive instruction weakens the will of a child. The motion picture, when it presents a dramatic theme, impels the child away from a merely receptive attitude and into an active mood. 'Education through doing the thing, not merely studying about it,' is a watchword of pedagogical reform, and the school which believes this will find a great use for motion pictures."

Believing that we should move ever in the van, I again respectfully urge that our schools be equipped with these machines, and that competent operators and lecturers be employed for this purpose.

THE COMPETITIVE EXAMINATION SYSTEM OF APPOINTMENT OF TEACHERS TO THE SAN FRANCISCO SCHOOL DEPARTMENT.

Upon the recommendation of Alfred Roncovieri the present system of civil service examinations was formally adopted by the Board of Education in May, 1904, as a part of the Rules and Regulations of this Department. It provides for the appointing of teachers to this Department solely on merit, (and without any reference to personal, social or political influence), as determined by competitive "Civil Service" examinations among applicants who already hold regular teachers' certificates.

The object of these examinations is to enable the Board of Education to select the best for its corps of teachers. No one who does not possess high personal character, liberal education and perfectly sound bodily health and vigor need apply as a candidate for examination. No married woman need apply, or any teacher who may not be in position to accept an appointment to the substitute list whenever such appointment may be made during the year.

The details of the plan and the method of operation are best found in the following excerpts from the pamphlets on the subject issued by the Board of Education:

The original rule ran:

"It shall be the duty of the Board........

9. To annually conduct a competitive Civil Service examination for the appointment of teachers to the substitute list of the elementary schools of the City and County of San Francisco, provided that such examination shall be both written and oral on the Theory and Practice of Teaching, and on such other topics as may from time to time be announced by the Board of Education; and, further provided, that no person shall be permitted to take said examination unless, after examination by physicians to be appointed by the Board, he or she shall be pronounced sound in health mentally and physically. Every applicant must be the holder of a teacher's certificate of a grade not lower than the grammar grade, valid under the laws of the State of California. Teachers successful in said examination shall be placed on the substitute list in the order of their standing, and shall be appointed to regular positions in the same order, subject however, to a satisfactory probationary service of two years before final election.''

To this first section, the following amendments have been joined:

March 2, 1910:

"1. The competitive examinations for the appointment of teachers shall include all teachers for both day and evening elementary schools.

2. The examination shall consist of three parts: a. Written examination in Arithmetic and Grammar. b. Written examination in Methods of Teaching, School Management, Hygiene, etc. c. Oral examination in Methods of Teaching, School Management, Hygiene, and the references submitted by the candidate.

3. Any candidate who falls below 70% in either Arithmetic or Grammar, or below an average of 75% in both subjects, or below 65% in Methods of Teaching, School Management, Hygiene, etc., shall be barred from the oral and hence from any appointment as a result of that examination, provided that failure in one examination shall not bar the candidate from any future competitive examination.

4. Each of the three parts of the examination designated in "2" shall be marked on the basis of 100, and the average of the three shall be the candidate's percent. in the examination, on which he or she shall be ranked.

5. The subjects and method of conducting this examination shall be given the widest publicity at the earliest date, to the end that the best possible teachers may be secured.

6. Each answer shall be credited by two readers, and the average of their credits shall be the credit assigned to the answer."

March 22, 1911:

"7. To complete each examination, applicants shall be allowed two hours and thirty minutes from the time, when having received the questions, they begin to write their answers."

These examinations are held annually, or more frequently, as occasion demands. Application blanks will be furnished all those asking for them. They should be filled out and forwarded to the Secretary of the Board of Education, if possible, not later than one week prior to the examination. Applicants must furnish full information relative to their academic preparation, their professional training (if any), and their experience in teaching (if any). Each applicant shall give not less than three references to persons who are competent to speak of his or her fitness for the work of teaching. Such references shall include the persons whose official position enables them to give the most exact and pertinent information with reference to the applicant's scholarship, training, experience and general efficiency. The Board of Education will not consider general letters of recommendation; but it will request from the persons referred to by the applicant a confidential statement as to the applicant's qualifications; such statement to be given in answer to a uniform list of questions to be furnished by the Board. The Board will also, in case of doubt, call for and make use of supplementary information, relating to the same set of questions, from other persons, who may be deemed competent to speak intelligently of the candidate's qualifications.

Before entering the examination each candidate must have secured from one of the physicians appointed by the Board a certificate stating that he or she is in sound health. The expense of the physical examination must be borne by the applicant, each physician having agreed upon a uniform charge of $2.50.

Those applicants will be considered as having successfully passed the examination who receive an average grade of 75% for both written and oral tests. All such will be notified at the close of the oral examination that they have been successful, and will be placed at once on what is known as the "Eligible List," to be called upon for substitute duty as soon as needed. A new list from which to select substitutes shall be formed annually after the competitive examination.

All assignments to teaching positions in the schools of San Francisco shall be from the Substitute List, and no person shall be so assigned except by a unanimous vote of the Board, and from the three highest on the list at the time.

Before becoming eligible to be elected Regular Teachers in the Department, those who have been thus elected to positions must serve two years as probationers. Before receiving final election the teachers must receive the recommendation of the Superintendent of Schools. After such final election they shall hold their positions for life, provided they shall at all times comply with and be subject to the rules of the Board of Education and the laws of the State, and the Charter of the City and County of San Francisco, so far as the same relate to the School Department.

The examinations of December, 1910 were taken by 125 candidates, of whom 46 were successful; those of June, 1911 by 115 candidates, of whom 67 passed.

The following sets of exxamination questions from 1902 through 1911 give an idea of the general character of the questions asked:

QUESTIONS GIVEN IN 1902.

1. Interest. How would you rouse it? Is it all sufficient for accomplishing results?

2. State and describe three essential features of the class recitation.

3. State some IMPORTANT defects of a strictly graded system of classes and give one GOOD remedy for each defect mentioned.

4. Since about 70 per cent of the pupils attending the public schools, on an average, are in the primary grades, which three subjects of instruction do you regard as the most important in training the great mass of our pupils who never enter the grammar school? Give your reasons.

5. Do you think the State School Law which forbids teachers to assign any home-work to pupils under fifteen years of age is a wise provision, and give your reasons for or against this law?

6. What would you do to advance a very diffident or backward child?

7. Discuss the Use and Abuse of Text Books.

8. Discuss discipline, its necessity, aim or aims.

9. Discuss helps to memory.

10. Point out specifically some of the uses and common abuses of the memory in geography teaching, making your explanation show your knowledge of the psychology involved.

11. Explain what is meant by visual, auditory and motor types of thinking, and illustrate by reference to corresponding types of spellers.

12. Why is it that pupils who write neatly in their copy books frequently do much inferior work in original composition? Explain the psychological causes.

QUESTIONS GIVEN IN 1903.

1. What is the ultimate end of education? State specifically some of the things education should do for the individual. For society?

2. Considering the limited time at your disposal for the instruction of a large class, what methods would enable you to give maximum attention to the special needs of individuals or groups of individuals that are particularly backward or brilliant?

3. How far can you teach parts of one school subject when you are definitely teaching another subject; for example, how far can you correlate geography with history? Should the attention of the child upon the history material be intensified or lessened by such introduction of geography? Point out some dangers in attempting to correlate subjects.

4. What constitutes an ideal teacher?

5. Discuss the intellectual features particularly active in children and their educational significance.

6. Give a description of a model lesson in arithmetic in a primary grade.

7. Discuss the development of the imagination in primary grades—its importance—means to secure it.

8. Discuss maintenance of strict discipline. How it may be tempered and how far relaxation from it may be allowed for the sake of promoting interest, emulation, and fellowship between teacher and pupils?

9. How can you make history teaching contribute directly to training for good citizenship? How far would you require children to learn facts of history, such as dates and names? What importance in history teaching would you give to the ideas and sentiments which have been the causes and results of historical events? What feelings should good history teaching awaken in the pupil?

10. Briefly outline the most approved general methods in use for teaching first grade pupils to read, and show by your explanation your comprehension of the mental process involved.

11. State three advantages and three disadvantages of department teaching in grammar grades.

12. Describe briefly any approved general method of teaching:

(a) Rapid and accurate addition.

(b) Geography.

Justify your methods by psychological reasons.

QUESTIONS FOR 1904.

1. Write a model lesson in geography and tell how you would make use of the following in teaching the same: 1, attention; 2, interest; 3, association; 4, memory; 5, imagination.

2. What standards or principles should guide a teacher in advancing or detaining a child at promotion time? Should all subjects have equal weight? If not, suggest some subjects that should have more weight than others. Give reasons in full for your answers.

3. Describe a remedy for each of the following cases: (a) Poor spellers; (b) faulty grammarians; (c) careless calculators; (d) thoughtless memorizing; (e) poor readers.

4. Why is it important to give special attention to ventilation of the schoolroom? Discuss fully the physiological processes involved.

5. What are your standards of good work in composition? Suggest the most effective way or method of correcting compositions in class. In your suggestion explain the defects as well as the merits of your method.

6. Discuss the method best calculated to secure the friendship and co-operation of a class.

7. How would you make use of the school or public library to the best advantage?

8. In teaching literature what would be your chief aims? What are the defects in the present methods? Would you use the sentences in literature as drills in grammar? Give reasons for answers.

9. How would you make the recitation of each pupil an intellectual activity for every member of the class?

10. Outline an inductive lesson in English grammar.

QUESTIONS FOR 1905.

1. By the history lesson, how may patriotism be best inculcated?

2. (a) What studies taught in school are especially adapted to the cultivation of the perceptive faculties?

(b) Give some illustrations.

3. Tell how you would teach a class to add columns of figures with accuracy and rapidity and justify your method by psychological reasons.

4. How would you direct and encourage home reading? Name ten books suitable for Sixth and Seventh grades.

5. Discuss the Art of Questioning with definite suggestions.

6. How would you teach the ready and correct use of the English language to the First, Second, and Third grades of the primary school.

7. How do you teach "pointing off" in division of decimals? Illustrate with examples showing various difficulties that perplex children.

8. Explain the method to be pursued in teaching writing during the first two years' of a child's school life.

9. If you had a pupil with a remarkable gift of memory who succeeds but poorly in original work, such as composition and arithmetic, how would you work to correct the deficiency?

10. What devices would you employ to keep up a good standard attendance in your class?

QUESTIONS FOR 1907.

1. What are the purposes of school discipline?

What different ways of disciplining children has the teacher at command?

Suggest how you would vary in the use of these means: With incorrigible children as opposed to sensitive children. With boys as opposed to girls.

2. Suggest the various ways by which the teacher may rest a child from mental fatigue resulting from classroom instruction. Discuss the special merits of each way suggested.

3. When you find a pupil of normal mind who does not know how to study, how would you proceed to remedy the condition. Suggest as many detailed ways as you can of giving him desire and power, to study by himself.

4. What are the different ways by which you can convey the meaning of an unfamiliar word, phrase, or sentence to a child? Discuss the relative value of each way.

5. What are the different elements which must be associated in the child's mind in order to make him a good speller? Suggest several ways of presenting and associating these elements.

6. What are the main advantages to be derived from nature study? How would you use the school garden and the school excursion in connection with this subject?

7. What are the objects to be kept in view in the teaching of history in the elementary schools? What are the most interesting and valuable kinds of historical facts to be learned in the primary grades? In the grammar grades?

8. In leading a child from home geography to world geography, how would you proceed?

9. State briefly in detail what means you would use in the primary grades to make your pupils speak and write good English.

10. In teaching arithmetic when would you let the child do the work mentally? When have him write it out in full? When mix both methods?

QUESTIONS FOR 1908.

1. There is a growing tendency to abolish corporal punishment as a means of correcting the faults of pupils:

(a) If you had charge of a school in which corporal punishment was not permitted, state briefly how you would maintain order in the case of pupils disposed to be unruly.

(b) If you were allowed to inflict corporal punishment at your discretion, in exceptional cases, state some circumstances under which it might, in your opinion, be resorted to as a just and effective mode of correction.

(c) When a teacher decides that a pupil should be punished for wrong doing, what objects should he (the teacher) have in view; that is, what worthy ends would he expect to reach through the infliction of the punishment?

2. What would you do with a pupil who, from absence or other cause, has fallen behind the class?

3. What rules of order would you insist upon to be observed by pupils in passing from the building during fire drill?

4. (a) Tell how you would teach reading to beginners.

(b) Name the important qualities of good reading.

(c) What are the commonest faults which you have found in the reading of children? How would you correct these faults?

5. Our new Course of Study requires an exercise in rapid addition:

Make out a column of figures for this exercise, and say how you would best secure speed and accuracy in performing it.

6. (a) What is the main benefit to be derived from the study of general History? Of Geography?

(b) How would you use Geography in connection with History?

7. (a) Describe a good method of teaching the geographical idea of day and night.

(b) What conditions give a country large foreign commerce? Domestic commerce?

8. (a) In what school year would you introduce the regular study of fractions?

(b) With what other rules of Arithmetic would you correlate percentage?

9. Suppose you had charge of an elementary class consisting of pupils of two consecutive grades; make out a program of daily exercise therefor in regular form, showing the grades and divisions taught, the simultaneous work in each, the hour and duration of each subject, and the time for reviews, oral or written.

10. A great many pupils find it extremely difficult to concentrate their attention on the instruction and explanations of the teacher, or to record mentally the most important points set forth in their reading matter. In the case of normal children, what, in your opinion, is the chief cause of this defect, and how would you remedy it?

QUESTIONS, DECEMBER 20TH, 1909.

ARITHMETIC.

1 (a) A pupil writes 425 words in 5 minutes 3 seconds. At next lesson she writes 521 words in 4 minutes 5 seconds. At next lesson she writes 593 words in 4 minutes 17 seconds. At what average rate of speed per minute does she write?

(b) Hale & Co., Stockton, bought of Lamont & Co., San Francisco, 3 doz. plain gold rings at $20.00 per dozen; 4 gold rings, diamond settings, at $50.00 each; 6 gold watches at $15.00 each; 4 sets teaspoons at $6.00 each. Make out the bill, allowing a discount of 25%.

2. (a) A commission merchant received $50.00 from a country customer with orders to send him ribbon, worth 6¼c per yard, and to pay himself for his trouble. The merchant charged 2¼%. How many yards of ribbon did the merchant send to his customer?

(b) A ship worth $75,000.00 was insured for three-fifths of its value at 1⅞%. The cargo, valued at $7,500.00, was insured for 4/5 of its value at 2½%. Find amount of premiums.

3. (a) If it cost $312 to fence a piece of land 216 rods long and 24 rods wide, what will it cost to fence a square piece of equal area with the same kind of fence?

(b) Find the interest on $125.50 from January 1st, 1898, to July 7th, 1899, at 7% per annum.

4. (a) What will it cost to dig a cellar 60x30x9 feet at 3½ cents per cubic yard?

(b) A room is 15 feet square and the walls are 9 feet high. What will it cost to paint the four walls at 25 cents per square yard, making no allowance for doors or windows?

5. (a) If four men build 12¼ rods of fence in 3¼ days, how long will it take 18 men to build 237 6/13 rods?

(b) Four persons engage in manufacturing, and invest together $22,500.00. At the end of a certain time A's share of the gain is $2,000.00: B's $2,800.75: C's share $1,685.25; and D's share $1,014.00. How much capital did each put in?

GRAMMAR.

6. "In the **bosom** of one of those spacious coves which indent the eastern shore of the Hudson, **at that broad expansion** of the river denominated by the ancient Dutch navigators the Tappan Zee, and **where they always prudently shortened sail** and implored the protection of St. Nicholas when they crossed, there lies a small market town or rural port, which by some is called Greensburgh, but **which is more generally and properly known** by the name of Tarry Town."

(a) Draw one line under the entire subject, and two lines under the entire predicate.

(b) Parse the phrases and clauses in black-face type in above.

7. The sun that brief December day
Rose cheerless over hills of gray,
And, darkly circled, gave at noon
A sadder light than waning moon."

Diagram or analyze the above.

8. What is a synopsis?
What is meant by voice?
What is declension?
Give the principal parts of lay, set, go, give and lie (to recline).
Singing birds are silent at this season.
The bird's singing under the window awakened us.

What is the use of "singing" in each of the above sentences?

9. "In the Old Colony days, in Plymouth, the land of the Pilgrim,
To and fro in a room of his simple and primitive dwelling,
Clad in doublet and hose, and boots of Cordovan leather,
Strode with a martial air, Miles Standish, the Puritan Captain.
Buried in thought he seemed, with his hands behind him, and pausing
Ever and anon to behold his glittering weapons of warfare,
Hanging in shining array along the walls of the chamber."

In the above selection, tell the part of speech of each word in black-faced type.

10. (a) Give sentences illustrating the following uses of clauses. (Underline each clause).

1. Adverbial.
2. Adjective.
3. As object.
4. As subject.

Give an example of an infinitive used as subject.

(b) Give an example of a compound and a complex sentence, and explain the difference between them.

METHODS OF TEACHING.

11. (a) Which study do you consider the most valuable in the ordinary school curriculum, and give several reasons for your choice.

(b) 1. Upon whta is the science of teaching based?
2. What should be the great object of teaching?
3. What are the characteristics of any good method of teaching?

12. (a) What method yould you adopt to prevent tardiness; and to secure regular attendance in school?

(b) What is to be accomplished in teaching English Grammar?

13. (a) What special training is given by Literature, by History?

(b) By Mathematics, by Science?

14. (a) For what definite purpose and to what extent would you use analysis or the diagram?

(b) In teaching composition, in any grade above the fourth, state your method as to choosing subject, writing the composition, or correcting it. Name the grade of class you have in mind.

15. (a) Distinguish between principle, method, device.
Which may change?

(b) 1. When is a schoolroom in good order?
2. What incentive will you put before children for study?

March 21, 1910.

ARITHMETIC.

1. (a) The longitude of Portland, Maine, is 70 degrees, 15 minutes, and that of Chicago is 87 degrees, 38 minutes.
What is the difference in time between the two places?

(b) How many square inches of tin are there in a dozen tin pails of cylindrical shape, the diameter of each being 8 inches and the height 10 inches? (No top).

2. (a) A rectangular field having an area of 135 1-5 acres is 3 1-5 times as long as it is wide. Find the length of its diagonal.

(b) If 9 bricklayers can lay a wall 80 ft. long, 20 ft. high, 1½ ft. thick, in 15 days and 9 hours each, in how many days of 10 hours each can 12 bricklayers lay a wall 100 ft. long, 25 ft. high and 2 ft. thick?

3. (a) On $860.56, $149.63 interest was paid for 2 years, 8 months, 3 days. What was the rate?

(b) An agent received $10,200, with which to purchase wheat at $1.25 per cental at a commission of 2%. How many centals did he buy?

4. (a) The distance from San Francisco to San Jose is 50.6 miles. An automobile party leaves San Francisco at 10:35 A. M., and arrives at San Jose at 1:20 P. M. What was the average speed on the trip?

(b) A man owns 3-5 of a ship that is worth $85,000. If the ship is insured for 57½% of its value, how much money would this man receive if the ship were a total loss, and how much would he lose?

5. (a) Subtract 5⅜ from 9.65 and divide the difference by (3⅞-2.65).

What number is that from which if we deduct 3-7 of itself and 2-9 of the remainder, 28 will be left?

(b) A shed is 15 ft. long and 10 ft. wide. It is 12 ft. high in front and 7 ft. high in the back.

How much lumber (one inch boards) should be ordered to cover the four sides, adding 10% for waste?

How many full bundles of shingles should be ordered for the roof, if there are 250 shingles in a bundle, and they are laid so that one thousand cover an area 80 square feet?

GRAMMAR.

6. Parts of speech of the heavy-faced type words, and why?

(a) He is **as** honest **as** he looks.
(b) He came **as** he had promised.
(c) There is little hope, **but** I shall try.
(d) There is no lad **but** honors his mother.
(e) The game is not **worth** the candle.
(f) This is the book that I prefer.
(g) Not that I love Caesar less.
(h) **The** longer we live, the more we learn.

7. Name the principal and subordinate clauses, and tell how subordinate clauses are used:

The drawbridge dropped with a surly clang,
And through the dark arch a charger sprang.
Bearing Sir Launfal, the maiden knight,
In his gilded mail, that flamed so bright
It seemed the dark castle had gathered all
Those shafts the fierce sun had shot over its wall.
In his siege of three hundred summers long,
And, binding them all in one blazing sheaf,
Had cast them forth.

8. In the above selection tell what each participal and prepositional phrase modifies.

9. Give the case of nouns and pronouns and why, and parse all finite verbs in the following selection:

The investigations and prosecutions initiated by Secretary Hitchcock and carried on by his successor, Secretary Garfield, demonstrated conclusively that land thieves have been for some time getting possession of the public domain, and that they have had sometimes the direct, sometimes the indirect, aid of public officials in and out of Congress.

10. Are the following correct? Give your reasons:

(a) I saw him many times this year.
(b) One of his best friends were accused of the crime.
(c) It looks like it would rain to-day.

METHODS OF TEACHING—SCHOOL MANAGEMENT—HYGIENE.

(Write not more than one page on each lettered division of a question).

11. (a) Discuss the importance of the personal life and character of the teacher in relation to her profession.
Illustrate.

(b) How much time should a teacher spend daily out of school hours in preparation of her work, and how should that time be spent?

12. (a) How would you handle the "topical method" in History, in study and recitation; and what are its advantages over the "question and answer method"?

(b) How may the judgment be trained in History study?

13. (a) What are the causes of impure air in a schoolroom, and what are its effects on the children? How can a room be ventilated by doors and windows without subjecting some to cold air?

(b) Name two books on "Methods", or History of Education, you have read. Give a brief summary of the contents of one of these.

14. (a) Name the most important factors in moral training. Illustrate by suggesting how the different school subjects might contribute.

(b) How do you teach division and pointing off of decimals? How would you secure accuracy in number combinations?

15. (a) How would you give individual aid to backward pupils in a class of 40 to 50 pupils?

(b) How do you estimate a pupil's fitness for promotion?

QUESTIONS DECEMBER 30, 1910.

ARITHMETIC.

1a. If a note, dated March 20, 1910, due in 90 days, for $760.00, bearing 6% interest, de discounted on April 9, 1910, what will be the proceeds, if the rate of discount be 4%?

1b. If a 5-cent loaf of bread weighs 8 oz. when flour is $5.00 a barrel, what should a 10-cent loaf weigh if flour is $8.00 per bbl.?

2a. If I buy shoes at $2.00 per pair, how much must I mark them so that I can abate 25% of the asking price and still make a profit of 12½%?

2b. If I sell ½ of an article for ⅔ of its cost, what per cent. do I gain?

3a. In how many days of 8 hours each will 10 men build a wall of 120 feet long, 15 feet high, 2½ feet thick, if 12 men build a wall 100 feet long, 12 feet high, and 3 feet thick, in 10 days of 10 hours each?

3b. If a field of 30 acres is three times as long as it is wide, what will it cost to fence it at $2.50 a rod?

4a. A ship valued at $90,000.00 is insured under the "average clause" for $75,000.00. It is damaged to the extent of $30,000.00. What is the owner's loss?

4b. The longitude of San Francisco is 122° 26′ 45″ W.; and of Manila,

120° 52′ E. When it is 10:30 A. M. solar time, Dec. 30, 1910, at San Francisco, what is the time at Manila?

5a. The floor of a room is 15′x18′, and height 12′. What is the distance from the S. E. corner (on floor) to the N. W. corner (on ceiling)?

5b. The circumference of the smaller wheel of a locomotive is 8 feet, and of the larger wheel 20 feet. A spoke of each is red. At the start both of these spokes are at a right angle to the rail. How many times will they occupy this relative position in traversing a mile?

GRAMMAR.

6 (a)

Combine the following into a complex sentence:
1. Napoleon was imprisoned on the island of St. Helena.
2. This happened after the battle of Waterloo.
3. This battle occurred in 1815.

6 (b)

Change the following to a complex and then to a compound sentence:

"Besides being kind, lazy, and good-natured, this boy went continually into debt with the tart man."

7.

Correct where necessary, and write reasons:
1. I saw some one who I took to be she.
2. He gave the books to Alice and myself.
3. I didn't know it was that late.
4. I used to always think that that was correct.
5. Be sure and get your lessons.

8.

Select and name all complements and indirect objects:
1. By perseverance Lincoln became a great man.
2. Honesty of purpose brought the boy his reward.
3. Jack made his brother a kite.
4. He pumped the well dry.
5. The teacher asked them five questions.

9.

1. Write sentences using a present participle as a noun.
2. Past participle as an adjective.
3. An infinitive as an adverb.

Parse all participles and infinitives in the following:

4. It is difficult to learn to paint.
5. He saw the enemy fall.
6. The crew attracted attention by waving the flag.

10.

Parse the black-faced type words in the following:

People talk of liberty **as** if it meant liberty **to** do just what **a** man likes. I call that man free **who** fears doing wrong, **but** fears nothing else. I call that man free who has learned the most blessed of all truths, **that** liberty consists **in** obedience to the power **and** to the will and to the law that his higher soul reverences and approves. He is not free **because** he does what he likes; but he is free because he does **what** he ought, and there is no protest in his soul against the **doing**.

METHODS OF TEACHING.

11. (a) What is the value of Psychology to the teacher?

11. (b) Of what educational value is discipline in the school?

12. (a) How would you introduce the subject of number in the lowest primary grade?

12. (b) How would you introduce the study of Geography in the lower primary grades?

13. What would you do to cultivate honesty, truthfulness, and moral courage among your pupils?

14. (a) Give some device to secure regular and prompt attendance.

14. (b) Do you favor giving medals for superior work in school? Give reasons for your answer.

15. (a) If interest on the part of the pupils is lacking, where would you look for the cause?

15. (b) How would you teach a class to study History?

QUESTIONS JUNE 12, 1911.

ARITHMETIC.

1. (a) The people of a school district wish to build a new school house which will cost $2,850. The taxable property of the district is valued at $190,000. What will be the rate of taxation?

1. (b) A man had three lots, each containing 6¼ acres, which he redivided into building lots of ⅝ of an acre each. How many building lots did he have?

2. (a) How many square inches are there in the surface of a cube whose solid contents are 2,744 cubic inches?

2. (b) If 120 bushels of oats last 14 horses 56 days, in how many days will 6 horses consume 90 bushels? (No analysis. To be answered by proportion.)

3. (b) A grocer bought 7 gallons of wine, and lost two gallons by leakage. He sold the remainder for $8.05 a gallon, making 25% on the whole. What was the cost per gallon?

4. (a) Mary bought a piece of silk for $63.50; she found, on measuring the silk, that she had only $61.25 in value. How many inches to a yard were given her?

4. (b) For what sum must a three months note be drawn so that, when discounted at a bank at 6%, the proceeds will pay for 75 barrels of flour at $8.50 per bbl.?

5. (a) Find the difference between the simple and compound interest, computed annually, of $1,200, for three years, three months, at 8%.

5. (b) Berlin is 13° 23′ 53″ east longitude, and San Francisco is 122° 26′ 12″ west longitude. When it is 12 M at San Francisco, what time is it at Berlin?

GRAMMAR.

6. Correct where necessary, giving reasons:
   - (a) "It is them."
   - (b) "Who will the book be read by?"
   - (c) "Than who none higher sat."
   - (d) "Every man, woman, and child lifted their voice in anger."
   - (e) "I do not like those kind of people."

7. Choose the better tense, with reasons:

(a) "It had happened before I saw him," or
"It had happened before I had seen him."

(b) "I should have liked to have done it," or
"I should like to have done it."

(c) "We have met on a great battlefield," or
"We are met on a great battlefield."

8. Give the principal parts of:

Awake, begin, blow, break, do, sing, swim, drink, steal, write, teach, catch, forget, take, fall.

9. Distinguish the adverbs and the adjectives in the following sentences:

He was sick nigh unto death.
The tumult shows the battle nigh.
How ill this taper burns.
All left the world much as they found it.
Much learning doth make thee mad.

10. Tell the part of speech each black-faced type word is, and give reason for your classification:

Heaven still guards the **right**.
Be sure you are **right** and then go ahead.
He will **right** the wrongs of the innocent.
And that my soul knoweth **right** well.
He is an **American** and glories in the right of an **American** citizen.

His years **but** young, **but** his experience old.
Quick! **man** the lifeboat.
Man wants but **little** here below.
Nor wants that little long.

METHODS OF TEACHING.

June 12, 1911.

Answer to each question to be limited to one page.)

11. (a) How best may the problem of retardation be met by the class teacher.

11. (b) When, if ever, is corporal punishment justifiable? What are the special dangers in its use?

12. (a) State three ways in which interest may be aroused and facility be developed in the writing of compositions.

12. (b) State the educational justification of the school garden?

13. (a) Discuss the relationship between the personal character of the teacher and its effect upon the moral development of the child.

13. (b) Name five essential qualities for a good teacher to possess.

14. (a) What qualities should characterize the work of a "good disciplinarian"?

14. (b) How would you deal with a restless class of fourth grade children placed indefinitely in your charge?

15. (b) Do you favor the holding of examinations at regular intervals in the grades? State your reasons for or against.

15. (b) What degree of self-government would you allow to children in the elementary school? On the playground? In the classroom? On the way to and from school?

MAINTAIN ITS INVIOLABILITY.

The system has now been on trial a sufficient time for its worth to be fully tested, and its results to be clearly exhibited. As a result of that test, I am positively of the belief that the present high standing of our teaching force, and the freedom from political scandals in appointments to the service are the outcome of the establishment and enforcement of the provisions of the existing Civil Service plan. I am also sure that my conviction is shared by our foremost educators and our interested citizenry in general.

The Civil Service System for the appointment of teachers to this department was on March 15, 1911, suspended for the first time since it had become a rule of the department. Three teachers now have the unenviable distinction of being the only ones ever appointed to the department under a suspension of the Civil Service System. I wish to register my most emphatic protest against the establishment of such a precedent. No exception should ever be made for any one. No political, religious or social influence should count. Let those who wish to join the San Francisco school department compete in the open. Let them enter this department honorably and through the only door that is open to all, whether strong or weak in "pull." Nothing should count but character, and ability to do the work.

I sincerely trust that no suspension of the Civil Service will ever again take place. Unfortunately, the Civil Service System is but a rule of the Board which can be suspended at any time. As long as it remains only a rule of the Board, it can be suspended in order that certain favored candidates for positions as teachers may be appointed, or it may be abolished altogether. Its beneficial effects, its absolute fairness and justice to candidates have been universally commended by prominent educators as well as by many of those who have taken the examinations. It is the only plan that has permitted absolute independence among candidates.

It is therefore, with the direct object of preserving this institution in all its solidity, and preventing attacks upon its integrity, that I respectfully recommend most strongly that every effort be made to have it incorporated expressly in our City Charter by amendment submitted to the qualified electors of our city. I pledge myself to work assidously for the adoption of an amendment such as proposed, to the end that neither open assault nor stratagem of any kind, resorted to by any party, should ever succeed in overthrowing or circumventing those on guard behind this bulwark of our educational progress and development.

REPORT OF OBSERVATIONS

made by Sup't. Alfred Roncovieri and Deputy Sup't. A. J. Cloud, on a visit to the Los Angeles Schools, April 3, 4, and 5, 1911.

We visited in Los Angeles four great High Schools, viz., in the order of our inspection, the Los Angeles Polytechnic High School, the Manual Arts High School, the Los Angeles High School, and the Hollywood High School,. We were accompanied in all but the latter instance by Sup't. J. H. Francis of Los Angeles, who extended to us every courtesy. Many of the facts which are herewith given were derived from the conversations we had with Mr. Francis and with the principals and teachers of the schools visited. I shall treat of this subject first with reference to such matters as appear to be common to all of the schools; secondly, some particular phases of the work in the individual schools; and, at the end, add certain recommendations which seem to me to be pertinent as the outgrowth of both these general and particular considerations.

GENERAL.

It is a striking fact that the number of students in attendance at the High Schools of Los Angeles, combined, is, at the present time, over 7,000. This student population has been built up from approximately 2,000 within a period of five or six years, having, therefore, more than kept pace with the increase of population, even when the annexation of surrounding territory by the City of Los Angeles is kept in mind.

The second broad fact that cannot escape notice is the very large number of courses of study, something over forty, that is presented to an entering pupil for his choice. It is true that each High School in the Los Angeles system emphasizes a certain specific line of work, as will appear more in detail later in this report; but, nevertheless, the boy or girl living in Los Angeles and wishing to attend a public High School, has the opportunity of choosing between about forty-two different and distinct courses of instruction, so he may practically obtain that which he believes to be best for his own case.

The next general subject worthy of consideration is that of organization. The Los Angeles school authorities have been ready to put into the schools a large corps of teachers, and particularly have not been slow in relieving the principals of these High Schools of routine detail duties, thus leaving the principals free to deal with bigger questions of educational policy, as also will be shown later in this report. The principal is assisted by two vice-principals, one a man, the other a woman, who take from his shoulders and dispose of all the minor matters incident to the conducting of a large institution. Thus the principal becomes in effect the manager of a great business corporation, with assistants upon whom he may depend for relief from petty exactions. In this connection it is important to state that all agree that difficulties of administration decrease rather than increase when the attendance rises above seven or eight hundred. The reason is that more sections in fixed courses of instruction may be formed, and hence a greater flexibility of program result, so that irregularities on study-cards of pupils take care of themselves.

PARTICULAR PHASES.

Los Angeles Polytechnic High School.

The aim of this school is to give its students thorough preparation in specialized branches of education that will prepare them for the actualities of life, both industrially and commercially. Perhaps some emphasis should be laid upon the fact that this school presents not only industrial, but also commercial branches; yet it by no means neglects the cultural elements so necessary in the educating of the boy or girl, if he or she is to be, not a machine, but a human being.

The present attendance at this school is about 2,200, of whom about 1,200 are boys. This student assemblage is contained in a large, fine building with a ground space of perhaps half a city block; yet this seems to be hardly enough room for the institution. This school has eighty-five teachers, a principal, and two vice-principals, averaging a little less than one teacher to twenty-six pupils. The students in this school have a possibility of choice from eighteen different courses of study.

Some of the special features of the work which we inspected were:

A. A domestic science department, in which 240 girls are enrolled. We saw these girls perfecting themselves in the arts of cooking, patterning and designing.

B. The shops in wood-working and iron-working, including blacksmithing. The best line on the results in this department is found in the fact that the school is equipping itself through the labor of these students with furniture and other school apparatus. Thus we saw in the principal's office, chairs, desks, and a couch, which we were told were the handiwork of students of the school. The boys in the shops have made the stoves that are being used by the girls in the cooking department. In the shops we noticed a sign issued by the Board of Education of Los Angeles reading: "The High School Board of Education of Los Angeles City High Schools will not be responsible for any accident resulting from the use of these machines." Precaution is taken, however, against accidents in the use of the machinery, as was evidenced by the boxes built around the belts connecting one part of a machine with another part. We were told that a single accident only had occurred in the school in this work in the past several years.

C. The physical laboratory is admirably fitted with the most modern apparatus, especially that which bears upon the science of electricity. It has taken about $10,000 to purchase and install this equipment. One piece alone cost $460.00.

D. There is an outdoor gymnasium upon the roof. The roof is flat, and it is also used as a lunch place.

E. The assembly hall is of dimensions sufficient to hold nearly the whole student body.

F. The library, containing a complete collection of books of reference, was just being re-fitted so as to give facilities for study at the time of our visit.

G. The most highly organized instruction in all branches of oral English, from the simple personal narrative through the well-prepared debate, including parliamentary law, is being given.

H. A cafeteria, having a holding capacity equal to one-half to two-thirds of the total attendance of the school, is run within the school by the students' organization, of which I shall speak immediately below. Here lunch service is provided for students with the utmost rapidity and at minimum prices. 1,200 students are served within an hour and thirty minutes, from noon on. A commedious kitchen adjoins the lunch-room.

I. A remarkably effective student organization is in full swing. This is chiefly due to the efforts of Sup't. Francis, who was principal of this school for a number of years before he was elevated to his present position. The system is somewhat elaborate, but the end and aim of it is to train the students in the science of self-government. Under this plan, discipline has been reduced to the smallest dimensions in this school. Especially valuable to the student is the training that he gets in the managing of financial affairs. The student body of this school handles the sum of about $25,000 a year. A rigid system of accounting is maintained under the broad direction of a Faculty member who acts as Treasurer of the Students' Association. This money comes from various sources, particularly from athletic events and from the receipts of the cafeteria mentioned above. The general effect is to give the students a sense of responsibility and a pride in their school which they otherwise would not have.

POLYTECHNIC HIGH NIGHT SCHOOL.

Our attention was drawn to the fact that a night school is conducted in the building of the Los Angeles Polytechnic High School. having an attendance of 700. These students are admitted to the same courses as if they came in the day-time.

MANUAL ARTS HIGH SCHOOL.

The main distinction between this School and the Polytechnic is that the former does not develop such a high degree of specialization as does the latter. This may be illustrated by saying that the Polytechnic offers a three years' course in chemistry, while the Manual Arts has but a one year's course of instruction in that subject. This is a new school, which was opened about six months ago only. It is located rather far out in the city, but with good car connections. There are at present three large buildings, with an immediate prospect of a fourth one, to serve as an Administration Building. The school stands on a large tract of land 600 feet square. The present enrollment is slightly over 500. The students are just about evenly divided between boys and girls. The Faculty consists of fifty-three teachers, a principal and two vice-principals, or an average of one teacher to ten or eleven pupils. The students in this school have the choice between six different courses of study, with the further proviso that parents and students may submit others for consideration under the agreement that such course shall include work for at least two years in advance and meet with the approval of the principal. This school is equipped with fine shops, a gymnasium for boys, and one for girls, outdoor playgrounds of every kind, and a cafeteria. The student organization conducts the cafeteria on the same principle as at the Polytechnic. A dry-kiln for the curing of lumber is one of the features of the shops.

THE LOS ANGELES HIGH SCHOOL.

This is the old-line school of the city, which still places the emphasis upon the academic branches of study, but is nevertheless adapting itself to the practical needs of life. It is housed in a fine old brick building which was evidently the original structure, a big brick annex, and a wooden shack across the street, into which it has overflowed. The attendance at this school is about 2,100, with a ratio of three girls to two boys. It was thought, when the Polytechnic High School was opened, that there might possibly come to be a falling-off in the registration at the Los Angeles High School, but quite the contrary has been the case. The number of teachers in this school is eighty-two, besides a principal, two vice-principals and a clerk. This makes an average of about twenty-five pupils to each teacher. Twelve distinct courses of study are presented to the students of this school. Some of the noteworthy points that we had brought to our attention here were:

A. A very fine Art Course of four years' duration is given. The students themselves pose as living models while their fellow-students draw from them. Thus we saw one boy holding a tennis racket in his hand as he stood upon a platform; the other students were drawing his picture from life. Some fine crayon and color work is included in the course of instruction. Architectural drawing is given in the fourth year. Classes for sketching out-of-doors are formed. A complete line of instruction in mechanical drawing, in which surveying is incorporated, is also conducted. All of this work, both in the freehand and mechanical, is a part of the regular course of the school.

B. Special emphasis is placed upon musical instruction in this institution. Two women devote their entire time to choral and class teaching of music. Besides this, there is a students' glee club. A special room is set aside for the music. This branch is also given full credit upon the school program.

C. There is a gymnasium for boys, and one for girls. The plan in this school is that each student must take some physical exercise every day of his school life throughout the whole time of his attendance there. The first year's work is prescribed in-door gymnastics under the direction of most competent men and women. The second year's work for boys is military drill. A cadet corps has been established in the school with an armory attached. The students of their own accord arrange summer camps in outlying regions. The commandant of this department is a trained military officer. In the third and fourth years the students are given a very considerable latitude of election of the kind of physical exercise or athletic sport that they will undertake. For example, we saw a group of young men playing a game of tennis on the courts located on the school grounds, and found upon inquiry that these players were performing a given part of the regular school work, and that their attendance at the same had been registered by a teacher in charge.

D.. A school garden, in which those interested in agriculture have full opportunity to learn the practical side of the subject, is located at one side of the athletic ground of the school.

E. A very considerable museum, in which has been gathered a collection of fossils and other geological and zoological specimens under the supervision of a competent scientist, who acts as curator, is located in a group of rooms in the main building, and the students who are interested in that department of study have most excellent opportunities to advance.

F. There are here both large and small study rooms. Some of the smallest study rooms are fitted up to bring vividly to the student's mind a realization of a special kind of work, as, for example, one of these smaller study rooms is decorated with many beautiful pictures of California scenes and people, and is known as the "California Room." There is a large assembly hall with a stage such as would be found in a thoroughly equipped theatre.

G. The library is one of the most valuable features of this school. Several hundred volumes for reference purposes are so placed as to be easy of access to the students of the school. A librarian, who is a regular member of the Faculty of the school, is in charge. Perhaps thirty or forty students were quietly and silently studying at tables in this large library room when we visited it. The students are permitted to take out selected lists of books for a period of not over twenty-four hours. The subject-teacher finds it a tremendous gain to be able to post in the library a list of books, especially in the literature and history courses, so that pupils may make further investigation than they would otherwise be able to do from the classroom text-books alone.

H. A cafeteria is conducted by the Students' Association of this school, somewhat on the plan of that at the other two High Schools above noted. We had an excellent lunch here, being waited upon by young ladies of the school, who, we were assured, at the beginning of each term volunteered their services and considered it a privilege to perform this duty for the Students' Association. The average cost of the lunch to each student is between ten and fifteen cents. The student body officers attend to all of the details of management. The chief cook is a woman of most excellent qualifications who is also employed by the student body. As an adjunct to the cafeteria, there stands outside a candy wagon from which the students buy such supplies as they desire. The Students' Association derives a very considerable revenue from this business, which sum it devotes to the establishment of three scholarships in the Universities.

I. The Students are organized here on the basis of self-government along the same lines as at the Polytechnic High School. The financial income of the organization is more than $40,000 a year. The discipline in this school seemed to us to be remarkably high and to be the direct reflex of the inculcation of ideas of self-government in the minds of the students. There was no monitoring by teachers in the hallways. The students passed from room to room at the end of periods, yet no disorder of any kind whatever was observed.

J. Many beautiful paintings, photographs and pieces of statuary adorned the rooms and hallways of the building. This is also true of the other two schools above named. The aesthetic nature of these students is being cultivated by their being brought daily into association with fine works of art.

HOLLYWOOD HIGH SCHOOL.

This school is located in a recently annexed portion of the City of Los Angeles and therefore has not been long under the control of the City Board of Education. It combines in itself more nearly all of the distinctive features of the other three High Schools just above mentioned than any other secondary school that we have seen. In other words, it is a composite of a highly technical and of a thoroughly organized academic school. It is almost ideally located on a tract of twelve and one-half acres of land. It has six fine buildings, arranged in a group plan at certain intervals apart. The ground was being broken for a new building which, we were told, was to be erected immediately. The total investment in buildings to date is $180,000 and in land $30,000. The student population of Hollywood totals 500. A principal, vice-principal and twenty-five teachers direct the lines of work. This gives an average of twenty pupils to a teacher. The pupil has a choice between twelve different courses of study. The school session lasts until 3:10 P. M., out of which time three assembly periods of twenty minutes each are taken to enable pupils and teachers to get together. The school day is divided into eight periods. The teachers hold no more than five recitations each day. The heads of departments are given one-half of their time off for supervision of the work in their respective branches. A few of the noteworthy facts that we found existing in this school were:

A. A most artistic and complete theatre is located in a building by itself with an adjoining music-room and reading-room under the same roof, which may be opened into the theatre by sliding doors if it is desired, to accommodate an overflow. The auditorium proper will seat about 700. The music-room is furnished with a raised platform of sufficient size to seat a class receiving instruction, so that the conductor may direct the recital from below. The acoustic properties are admirable. The reading-room is similarly fitted. In it we found a class holding a session. The individual members were standing upon the platform and reading aloud, with fine expression, to their associates. It was one of the best recitations in oral expression that I have ever had the good fortune to hear.

B. The school has an orchestra taught and led by a regular member of the Faculty. This is a part of the music course of the school, which embraces instruction over a period of four years. We listened to a rendition of good music by this orchestra.

C. In the main academic building the recitation and study rooms are particularly bright and airy and are artistically decorated. The study rooms are organized on the plan of classes; for example, there are study halls for pupils of the upper classes and others for those of the lower classes. It is very easy to locate a given teacher at any time of the day becauses a type-written schedule of his or her hours and subjects is affixed to the outside of the door of his own room.

Lockers built in the shops of the school are arranged along the sides of the walls in the hallways, and in them the students keep their books and personal property, each student having an individual key to his locker. There are rest rooms for the teachers in this and in several of the other buildings.

D. Two buildings are set aside for Domestic Science and industrial work. The girls in the Domestic Science Department have almost unlimited scope in the choice of subjects they wish to pursue. Sewing, cooking, basketry, leather work, metal work, designing, dress-making and freehand drawing are samples of what they have to choose from. They are given practical instruction in the art of housekeeping. In one part of this building a series of six or seven rooms is set aside for the practice of home-making. It is equipped with all such modern conveniences as would be found in a well regulated household. Here the girls prepare a meal and perform all of the ordinary duties that devolve upon the housekeeper.

The furniture of this particular set of rooms was made by the boys of the school in the shops, and all of the wall decorations, coverings, cushions, etc., by the girls of the schools. In fact, the same statement would hold for this building throughout, and for the academic building as well.

A thoroughly equipped laundry with tubs, drying apparatus, gas heaters, irons, etc., is established in conjunction with the teaching of Domestic Science here. A hospital is also found in this building.

E. The shops are not so extensive as those at the Polytechnic High School. The courses are chiefly in wood and iron working. The chemical and physical laboratories are as complete as can be made. The principal, who is an expert in this direction, devoted a great deal of time to their building and equipment.

F. Outside, to the rear, comes a ground space of some acres which has been turned into a farm. The land is cultivated by the students, who take two hours every morning to practical application of their knowledge in Agriculture. Athletic grounds also are laid out on the school plot.

G. A cafeteria is conducted, much the same as in the other places already referred to. Gymnasium facilities are also provided.

H. In the matter of administration the principal of this school has established a system to which great praise must be accorded. He has had notices printed with this heading: "Possible Failures." Notices are sent in regularly each week by the class teachers giving the names of pupils who may be lax, with comment by the teacher on the reasons why the given pupil is failing, and what he or she would suggest as a remedy. The entire faculty of the school meets each week to go over these records and to discuss ways and means of coping with the individual problems. Usually the method adopted is that of kind advice to the pupil, with the suggestion of extra work that he may undertake under the guidance of the teacher, who thus becomes, in effect, an "ungraded" teacher for the special case. The result of this plan has been that in the Hollywood High School of over five hundred pupils, there were at the end of last term not to exceed five pupils who were requested to repeat their courses. This method also gives the principal an idea of the work that is being done by each pupil in his school, and thus enables him to keep close watch upon individuals. The principal makes it a point to find out exactly why each pupil leaves his school. The mortality in his school is reduced to the lowest possible figure; thus he is meeting one of the gravest problems in the High Schools today, that of the great number of pupils who drop out before graduation.

GRAMMAR SCHOOLS.

We visited several grammar schools in Los Angeles, but chiefly with the express purpose of looking at the school gardens which we heard were being established. In Los Angeles this year the Board of Education has set aside $6,000 for the purpose of improving grounds and making school gardens. This development is still in its first stages, however, but will undoubtedly grow larger and larger in proportion.

We saw two school gardens upon grammar school lots and adjacent vacant property that made an excellent appearance. The Los Angeles plan is to give over to a certain class or section of a class, a certain prescribed part of ground for special care. The students plant both vegetables and flowers and, in some places, trees. The aim is not only that the pupils may gain practical knowledge of agriculture, but also that the school grounds may be beautified.

THE LOS ANGELES NORMAL SCHOOL.

We visited this school, but it is not necessary at this time to speak of its work except in one respect, that is the system by which those attending it are enabled to serve in the City Department of Los Angeles, as so-called "Cadet Teachers." This is accomplished by an arrangement between the Superintendent of Schools at Los Angeles and the Normal School authorities. Members of the final year in the Normal School spend a large part of their time in practical teaching in the public schools of Los Angeles, where they act as assistants to the regular teachers in the class rooms or as substitutes without pay. Both the President of the Normal School and the Superintendent of Schools at Los Angeles declare that the plan brings the very best results.

RECOMMENDATIONS.

From the foregoing statements of fact I desire to draw certain conclusions which I respectfully submit as recommendations:

1. The elective system of courses of study should be widely extended in the San Francisco High Schools. This should be done with proper safeguards and with a grouping around certain fundamental studies. This will help to get pupils into the High Schools.

2. We should improve the machinery in our High Schools for watching the progress of individual students and for maintaining a closer personal contact with them. This will keep the students in the schools when we get them there.

3. We should work toward the six year High School plan.

4. We should still continue to have High Schools of various kinds with different ideals and purposes; but in some ways there could well be a closer correlation between them.

5. We should try to make an arrangement with the San Francisco Normal School by which we could gain the services of cadet teachers.

PUBLIC SCHOOL ATHLETICS.

Athletics that make for strong character among our boys and girls have been fostered in our city by the Public Schools Athletic League, an organization of public-spirited citizens consisting of Mr. S. S. Peixotto, President; Mr. Ray Dougherty, Secretary; Mr. Eustace Peixotto, Athletic Director; and Directors T. F. Boyle, John Elliott, Judge F. J. Murasky, Judge T. F. Graham, Robert Roos, L. A. Wolff, A. C. Skaife, J. C. Astredo, Geo. A. Schlitter, Alfred Roncovieri, John Hammersmith, C. W. Conlisk, John McLaren, A. Katschinski, I. F. Moran, Jos. Hickey and A. J. Cloud. The best index of the work of the League during the past season is to be found in the report of Athletic Director Eustace Peixotto, which is here submitted:

"The Public Schools Athletic League has completed a most successful year in all lines of activity undertaken by the organization. In every branch of sport, great and widely distributed interest has been shown by the boys of the city's grammar schools. Competition has been keen, but at the same time there has been a lessening of the intensity of feeling that has characterized some of the school contests in the past. This result is due, I believe, partly to the plan of playing tournaments on a percentage basis, so that everything does not hinge on the winning or losing a single game, and also to the fact that the boys, and teachers as well, are growing to have more confidence in the League, its officials and their rulings. The fact that the same umpires are used all through a given series has greatly contributed to the success of the tournaments. Boys come to understand an umpire and his rulings, and he to understand the boys. There has been no trouble whatever experienced in the conduct of games or behaviour of boys on the basketball court or on the diamond.

The track meets have been uniformly well conducted. The boys are learning to report for their events promptly and heed the slightest request of the officials, making the work of conducting the meets easier all the time.

Nevertheless, successful as the competitive sports carried on by the League have been, I believe that the future of the League's work is going to lie in other directions. There is a great field of endeavor in public school athletics which we have only just scratched. Although we have had as many as 700 boys taking part in a single meet, and although nearly all the schools have entered one or more teams in baseball and basketball tournaments, still but a small proportion of the pupils in the schools have had an opportunity to take part in the League's activities, and, judging from present indications the proportion is likely to grow smaller rather than larger, especially in track and field events. More and more, as athletics become a settled institution in the schools, the boys of ability along this line become known, the time in which races can be won is known, and boys who feel they have but small chance or no chance at all of winning do not enter in the meets. Much can be done toward getting boys of lesser ability interested in athletics through holding of novice meets and district meets, but even then a great many of those who need the athletics most will not take part. It should therefore be the line of work in the future to develop interclass competition in the various schools, and carry on class athletics and athletic badge contests by which means all the boys can be given the stimulus of athletic competition.

It is a great pity that we have not a more adequate department of physical training in our public schools, for all this athletic work should be supplemented by careful gymnastic training. It is to be hoped that this will come in time. The present system appears to me entirely inadequate. There is but one instructor for 75 schools, and it stands to reason that no matter how competent he may be, he will not be able to accomplish much in the way of results. It may be found possible during the next year for the Public Schools Athletic League to assist in this matter of gymnastic training.

The League should also assist in the development of the school playgrounds, which I am happy to say the Board of Education is now giving its attention to in the construction of the new school houses, and should foster the idea that an adult (preferably one of the teachers) should supervise these playgrounds after school. This system is in vogue in Los Angeles, where the teachers get a small extra compensation for the work.

The League must keep before it the object of getting every school boy and girl, if possible, interested in his physical as well as his mental development, and giving them normal, healthy bodies, without which they cannot be said to be fully equipped for the battle of life. I hope that next year, as I have said, at least a beginning can be made along these lines, although I must confess it is an herculean task. The actual carrying on of the competitive tournaments of the League takes a great deal of time, more perhaps than one would realize at first sight, and with the schedules of the different sports crowding one after another there is but little time left the Athletic Director for such work as outlined above. It is time, however, that a beginning at least should be made, and this will be part of the programme for next year.

We have a splendid beginning here in San Francisco, because we have started in right. We have a control of the athletic situation and are able to manage things from the League headquarters much as athletics are generally carried on within a single school. The Board of Education has given its financial support to the League's work, and with an increase in this regard promised in the future, the outlook is a rosy one.''

In order to strengthen and emphasize one part of this report, I respectfully recommend to the Board of Education that play on school-grounds after school hours be supervised by a teacher in sympathy with this movement, and that he or she be given additional renumeration for this service.

UNGRADED CLASSES.

I desire at this time to repeat the subject matter of my discussion of this theme in the report of 1908-09, pages 28 and 29.

"The individual pupil is still an unsolved problem in all graded schools. Teaching fitted to a majority of a class will not meet the needs of each individual. Some pupils, able to do most of the work, are deficient or slow in a particular subject. Others, more mature than their classmates, are able to work at a more rapid pace than the grade to which their scholarship assigns them. Other pupils, immature or naturally slower of comprehension, will make sure and certain progress if they may take the work at a less rapid pace. Some of the soundest minds work slowly. Pupils from other school systems often do not fit into our course of study and grading. They need a little extra help in some subjects. A teacher with forty-five or fifty pupils cannot give sufficient attention to these individual needs.

Our ungraded class is the best method for combining individual with class instruction. We have several of these classes in operation. They are differently organized according to the needs of the school. In some, pupils go in groups of from six to a dozen for additional teaching in their weak subject. Each grade teacher sends pupils needing this special instruction to the ungraded room during a study period of her own class. The pupils who thus loses a study period must make up the time by home study. If a pupil is weak in arithmetic he gets the regular lesson from his own class teacher and another in the ungraded room. He may be able to understand the operation of percentage in his own grade but is deficient in decimals or common fractions. Or a fifth grade pupil may be able to understand fractions but needs drill in the number combinations. Such pupils go to the ungraded room for drill in back work upon which present grade work depends.

In other schools the teacher has a number of permanent pupils who are either slow in all their work and need time for each grade, or who, because of maturity or ability, are able to do two terms in one or three terms in two, and thus gain time in completing their grammar school course. In addition to these permanent pupils the teacher has a limited number of groups who come from the classrooms for special drill. In the ungraded class the pupils are given either group instruction or individual instruction according to their needs. The principal assigns pupils to this class in conference with the teachers and carefully directs the work. This is never a deportment class and bad conduct or lack of application may at any time forfeit the privilege.

The ungraded class is found most effective in grammar schools, and in primary schools which have a large number of foreign pupils. Several of our large grammar schools are still unprovided with ungraded classes.

As soon as financial conditions permit every school of eight or more classes should have an ungraded class, and the larger schools should have two such. In schools of six or seven classes the principal should be teacher of the ungraded room for a half day and should have the other half of the day for supervising the building. First and second grades are divided into so many groups and the work is so largely individual that the ungraded class is not needed.

Failure of promotion is one of the chief causes for pupils dropping out of school. They are chagrined and discouraged at not going on with their classmates; the repeated work has little interest for them. A sufficient number of ungraded rooms will go far toward solving the problem of the "left-over." Pupils may be promoted in the subjects in which they are strong, and work in the ungraded room in the weak subjects. If weak in all subjects they are transferred to the ungraded room. Under a well organized system these defects should be remedied as soon as discovered, and discovered as soon as they exist. A pupil who shows marked weakness in any study should enter the proper group in the ungraded class; the pupil who needs more than a term to complete the work of a grade should join the permanent section of the ungraded class.

A larger amount of work for individual pupils should be done by all our grade teachers. It would be wise if a half hour after school were used for helping backward pupils."

In line with the above policy Ungraded Classes have been established in the following schools:

Bergerot, Bernal, Columbia, Crocker, Denman, Emerson, Everett, Fairmount, Fremont, Garfield, Hamilton, Hancock, Hearst, Horace Mann, Irving M. Scott, James Lick, Jean Parker, John Swett, Monroe, Noe Valley, Pacific Heights, Parental (all classes), Redding, Roosevelt, Sutro and Washington.

The Board of Education has satisfied a great need in establishing and main taining these ungraded classes. The results are already seen in progress that is being made toward the solution of the problem of the "left-over."

NEW VACCINATION LAW.

In accordance with the provisions of an act passed by the last legislature, relaxing to some extent the stringent provisions of former years relative to the vaccination of children enrolled in public schools, the Board of Education has issued a blank form to comply with the statute, as follows:

San Francisco, California.

(Date)..

I hereby declare that I am conscientiously opposed to the practice of vaccination and will not consent to the vaccination of..

(Signed)..

Parent or Guardian.

AROUSING INTEREST IN HOME INDUSTRIES.

In April of 1911 the Board of Education and the Superintendent of Schools co-operated with the Home Industry League of California in interesting the pupils of the upper grammar grades and of the high schools in "Made in California" goods and products. A competition for prizes was conducted in the schools, it being in the nature of the writing of a composition that would bring out best the character of the work of the League. The following were some of the sub-topics which the pupils were asked to investigate and treat of in their writings:

First: The natural resources of the State of California; the best means to develop these resources.

Second: The different commodities that are manufactured in the State of California. Enumerate products that are finished and made ready for the market.

Third: How will the developing of home industries improve the general business conditions of the State?

Fourth: How can converting raw material into manufactured products ready for the market be encouraged?

Fifth: How may the consumption of California manufactured products be encouraged and increased? What benefits may be derived therefrom?

Sixth: If the home industry movement of California could greatly increase the number of factories in the State, resulting in the employment of thousands of additional factory hands, what effect would it have on the prosperity of your father's business?

Seventh: If it is impossible to increase the number of factories in the State of California, what employment would you suggest for the increased population that we expect during the next ten years?

Such great interest was taken in this contest that about 1,500 compositions were presented to the League. The effects will undoubtedly be beneficial in awakening in our boys and girls a desire to gain more accurate information concerning the opportunities that our State affords for creating the finished article from the raw material. The officials of the League expressed themselves as being more than satisfied with the outcome.

THE CONVENTION OF THE NATIONAL EDUCATION ASSOCIATION.

The Forty-ninth Convention of the National Education Association, popularly known as the "N. E. A.", in our city from July 8th to 14th inclusive, was the most significant educational event of the year in our community. This great meeting was looked upon as the deferred convention of 1906 for which every preparation had been completed by the city of San Francisco when the destruction of the city by fire made the meeting for that year impossible. Since the rebuilding of our metropolis, delegations of eminent educators from California had asked that San Francisco be granted the privilege of entertaining the Association, first at the meeting at Denver, and again at Boston, and at the latter place were successful in presenting their claim. As soon as the choice of a convention city had definitely been made, a group of enthusiastic workers issued an invitation which is so expressive of the cordiality of our people in bidding the teachers of America to come, that it is herewith quoted in full:

THE INVITATION.

San Francisco, California, Dec. 15, 1910.

TO THE TEACHERS OF AMERICA:

All California invites you to the **New San Francisco** in July, **1911**, to attend the National Education Association Convention. The hotel facilities in the rebuilt city will accommodate 60,000 people, and every hotel is pledged not to advance rates. After seeing the marvelous work of a great city rebuilt in four short years, you can make San Francisco the center for "Seeing California." Why not plan to attend the Convention—then visit the Yosemite, the various groves of the Big Trees, the Redwood country, the Tahoe or Shasta resorts, Southern California, the great Canyons of the Sierras or some of the many beach or mountain resorts scattered throughout our Wonderland? If you are interested in Industrial California, we shall be glad to show you our orange groves, our orchards, our vineyards, our great wheat ranches, our gold mines and our forests. Why not make definite plans now for a real vacation in California? It will never be more enjoyable; it will never cost so little. The latch string will be out when you cross the California line. We shall hope to see you in the New San Francisco next July. Remember, the latch string will be out.

YOURS FOR SAN FRANCISCO AND CALIFORNIA

Edward Hyatt, Superintendent of Public Instruction, Sacramento.
P. H. McCarthy, Mayor of the City and County of San Francisco.
Duncan MacKinnon, Director N. E. A. for California, San Diego.
Benjamin Ide Wheeler, President University of California, Berkeley.
Alfred Roncovieri, City Superintendent of Schools, San Francisco.
David Starr Jordan, President Stanford University.
Mark Keppel, County Superintendent of Schools, Los Angeles.
James A. Barr, City Superintendent of Schools, Stockton.
M. E. Dailey, President State Normal School, San Jose.
Alexis F. Lange, Dean of Faculties University of California, Berkeley.
John Swett, Martinez.
J. W. McClymonds, City Superintendent of Schools, Oakland.
J. H. Francis, City Superintendent of Schools, Los Angeles.
Kirk Harris, President San Francisco Convention League.
William L. Gerstle, President San Francisco Chamber of Commerce.

The California organization for the convention was effected by co-operation between school people and the officials of the San Francisco Convention League. The membership of the General Committee, to whose able management was due much of the success of the convention, was:

GENERAL COMMITTEE.

William B. Pringle, Chairman, 378 Russ Building, San Francisco.
Felton Taylor, Secretary, Merchants' Exchange Bldg., San Francisco.

MEMBERS AT LARGE.

Hon. Hiram W. Johnson, Governor of California, Sacramento.
Hon. P. H. McCarthy, Mayor of City and County of San Francisco.
Duncan MacKinnon, State Director N. E. A. for California, San Diego.
Benjamin Ide Wheeler, Pres., University of California, Berkeley.
David Starr Jordan, President, Leland Stanford Junior University.
Miss Agnes E. Howe, Pres. California Teachers' Association, San Jose.
Miss Jessica Peixotto, Assistant Prof., University of California.
Morris E. Dailey, Pres., State Normal School, San Jose.
Alexis F. Lange, Dean of Faculties, University of California.
J. W. Linscott, Sup't. of Schools, Santa Cruz.
Arthur H. Chamberlain, University of California, Berkeley.
Kirk Harris, Pres., San Francisco Convention League.

EXECUTIVE COMMITTEE.

William B. Pringle, Chairman, 378 Russ Building, San Francisco.
Felton Taylor, Secretary, Merchants' Exc. Bldg., San Francisco.
Alexis F. Lange, Dean of Faculties, University of California.
James A. Barr, Sup't. of Schools, Stockton.
Alfred Roncovieri, Sup't. of Schools, San Francisco.
L. E. Armstrong, Editor "Sierra Educational News," San Francisco
J. W. McClymonds, Sup't. of Schools, Oakland.
Kirk Harris, Pres., San Francisco Convention League.
Arthur H. Chamberlain, University of California, Berkeley.
Paul T. Carroll, San Francisco.

SUB-COMMITTEES.

James A. Barr, Sup't. of Schools, Stockton.
Chairman, Committee on Publicity and Attendance.
Paul T. Carroll, San Francisco.
Chairman, Finance and Auditing Committee.
Alfred Roncovieri, Sup't. of Schools, San Francisco.
Chairman, Committee on Music.
Mrs. E. L. Baldwin, San Francisco.
Chairman, Committee on Hospitality.
Mrs. M. W. Kincaid, Member of Board of Education, San Francisco.
Chairman, Committee on Reception.
Joseph A. Stulz, San Francisco.
Chairman, Committee on Printing.
F. H. Meyer. Director School of Arts and Crafts, Berkeley.
Chairman, Committee on Decorations and Badges.
A. J. Cloud, Deputy Sup't. of Schools, San Francisco.
Chairman, Committee on Hotels and Headquarters.
Mark Keppel, County Sup't. of Schools, Los Angeles.
Chairman, Advance Membership Com. (South of Tehachapi).
C. L. McLane, Sup't. of Schools, Fresno.
Chairman, Advance Membership Com. (San Joaquin Valley).
Miss Lulu E. White, County Sup't. of Schools, Redding.
Chairman, Advance Membership Com. (Sacramento Valley).
J. W. McClymonds, Sup't. of Schools, Oakland.
Chairman, Advance Membership Com. (Coast and Bay Counties).
Richard D. Faulkner, Prin., Horace Mann Grammar School, San Francisco
Chairman, Committee on Halls.
Edward Hyatt, Sup't. of Public Instruction, Sacramento.
Chairman, Committee on California Headquarters.
Robert Newton Lynch, California Development Board, San Francisco.
Chairman, Committee on Excursions.
L. E. Armstrong, Editor, "Sierra Educational News," San Francisco
Chairman, Committee on Press.
Will C. Wood, Sup't. of Schools, Alameda.
Chairman, Committee on Exhibits.

The Board of Education manifested its interest in the meeting by passing on March 22, 1911 a resolution appointing one of its members, Mrs. Mary W. Kincaid, Chairman of a Reception Committee of members of the department to arrange for the entertainment of delegates to the convention, and by appropriating funds to carry out that object. Principals and teachers loyally responded to the call for service on this committee, and to the invitation to subscribe for membership in the association, approximately 1,200 joining from the San Francisco Department, a very remarkable record. Three hundred principals and teachers gave their time and energy to work on committees, especially those on Reception and Hospitality, where they performed their duties in such a manner as to reflect the greatest credit on our city, as was repeatedly testified to by both the officials and lay-members of the Association.

We should be happy to reprint here a complete digest of the discussions of the Convention, but, as space forbids, we shall confine ourselves to the furnishing of the program of the general sessions only. Yet we shall preface that by saying that the dominant note of the proceedings may be stated as having been the spirit of public welfare as developed by education, carrying with it the conviction that education is the most potent force in civilization that works toward the improvement of the human race.

The program of the General Sessions:

MONDAY AFTERNOON, JULY 10, 3:30 O'CLOCK.

Session in Greek Theatre, State University, Berkeley.
Music—March, "Daughters of the American Revolution" .... Lampe
Selections from Offenbach, arranged by .... Godfrey
Potpourri "The Sunny South" .... Lampe
March, "Pro Patria" .... Roncovieri
Overture "William Tell" .... Rossini
Presiding—Wm. B. Pringle, Chairman of General Committee.
Invocation—Rev. Wm. K. Guthrie, First Presbyterian Church, San Francisco.
Addresses of Welcome:
Honorable Hiram W. Johnson, Governor of California.
Mr. R. B. Hale, Director of the Panama-Pacific Exposition Company.
Honorable P. H. McCarthy, Mayor of the City and County of San Francisco.
President Benjamin Ide Wheeler, of the University of California.
Introduction of Ella Flagg Young, President of the National Education Association, by Josiah Little Pickard, Cupertino, California, ex-President of the N. E. A., for the year 1871.
Response to Addresses of Welcome:
Robert J. Aley, President, University of Maine, Orono, Maine.
Music—Fantaisie on "American Songs," .... Herbert
Appointment of Committee on Resolutions.
"The Relation of Education to Temperance"—David Starr Jordan, President of Leland Stanford Junior University, Stanford University, California.
"The Cause of Education"—Helen Marsh Wixson, State Superintendent of Public Instruction, Denver, Colo.
Meetings of active members by states to elect members of the Committee on Nominations immediately after the close of the session, 5:30 p. m., at places designated by State Signs in the Greek Theatre.

MONDAY EVENING, JULY 10, 8:30 O'CLOCK.

A general reception to President Ella Flagg Young and the members of the N. E. A. was held in Pavilion Rink, corner of Sutter and Pierce Streets, on Monday evening, July 10th. The following musical program was rendered:

1. March "Golden State" .... Weldon
2. Overture, "Light Cavalry" .... Suppe
3. "Reminiscences of Verdi" .... Godfrey
4. Selections from the "Chocolate Soldier" .... Strauss
5. Paraphrase on "My Old Kentucky Home" .... Dalby
6. Intermezzo from "Contes de Hoffman" .... Offenbach
7. Pizzicati Polka .... Strauss
8. Introduction and Soldiers' Chorus from "Carmen" .... Bizet
9. Waltz, "Dolores" .... Waldteufel
10. March, "Under Freedom's Banner" .... von Blon

TUESDAY EVENING, JULY 11, 8 O'CLOCK.

All evening sessions were held in Pavilion Rink Auditorium, Sutter Street, between Steiner and Pierce Streets.

Music—March, "Our National Emblem," .... Bagley
Selection from "Faust" .... Gounod
March, "La Fiesta" .... Roncovieri

Overture, "Poet and Peasant" .... Suppe
Invocation—Rev. E. R. Dille, Central M. E. Church, San Francisco.
President's Address—Ella Flagg Young, Superintendent of Schools, Chicago, Ill., President of the National Education Association.
"An Appreciation"—Alfred Roncovieri, Superintendent of Schools, San Francisco, California.
Music—National Songs, "The American Patrol" .... Meacham
"Reorganization of American Education"—James H. Baker, President, University of Colorado, Boulder, Colo.

WEDNESDAY EVENING, JULY 12, 8 O'CLOCK.

Music—Selections from "Woodland" .... Lueders
Intermezzo, "Love in Idlesness" .... Macbeth
Selection from "The Serenade" .... Herbert
March from the "Ring of the Niebelungen" .... Wagner
Invocation—Rev. Charles M. Lathrop, Church of Advent, San Francisco.
"The Opportunity of the Teacher"—Mrs. Emmons Blaine, Chicago, Ill.
"The Development of Personality Through Education"—Margaret E. Schallenberger, Principal of Training Department, State Normal School, San Jose, Cal.
Music—"Victorious America" .... Tobani
"The Compensation of the Teacher"—Joseph Scott, President, Board of Education, Los Angeles, Calif.
"The Life of the Teacher"—Charles Zueblin, Lecturer, Boston, Mass.
Appointment of Committee on Nominations.

THURSDAY EVENING, JULY 13, 8 O'CLOCK.

Music—March, "Centennial Evacuation" .... Conterno
Selection, "Echoes of the Metropolitan Opera" .... Tobani
Medley of Songs, "Gems from Erin" .... Beyer
Waltz, "Blue Danube" .... Strauss
March from "Tannhauser" .... Wagner
Invocation—Rev. George E. Burlingame, First Baptist Church, San Francisco.
"Can We Shorten the Term of Years Without Decreasing the Efficiency of Education in American Schools"—Samuel Avery, Chancellor, University of Nebraska, Lincoln, Nebraska.
Music—Piano Solo by George Kruger.
(a) "Rhapsodie Hongroise" .... Liszt
(b) "Faust Fantaisie" .... Liszt
"Present Problems in English Education"—Kate Stevens, North Islington Central School, Tollington Park, London, England.

FRIDAY EVENING, JULY 14, 8 O'CLOCK.

Music—March, "Stars and Stripes Forever" .... Sousa
Selection, "Recollections of the War" .... Beyer
"Melody in F" .... Rubinstein
Medley of National Songs "America" .... Moses
Overture, "Orpheus" .... Offenbach
Invocation—Rev. Charles A. Ramm, Secretary to His Grace, the Archbishop Riordan.
"Peace in the School"—Katherine Devereux Blake, Principal, Public Schools, City of New York.
"Progress in Public Education"—Francis G. Blair, State Superintendent of Public Instruction, Springfield, Ill.
Music—March, "The American Republic" .... Thiele
Closing exercises.
Music—"America."

In accordance with an established custom of the Association, Sunday, July 9th, was observed as Educational Sunday by a large number of the churches of San Francisco. The themes of several of these sermons are here given:

"Honey and Enlightenment: A Study of Happiness as a Social Asset" (morning).—"The Earth and The Woman: In the First Century and the Twentieth" (evening).—Rev. Charles S. Aked, First Congregational Church.

"The Purpose of an Education" (morning).—"Religious Doubt, its Cause and Cure" (evening).—Rev. Hugh K. Hamilton, California Street M. E. Church.

"The Great Teacher" (morning).—"How Knoweth This Man Letters" (evening).—Rev. W. H. Bagley, West Side Christian Church.

"Real Education Leads Godward" (morning).—"The Incomparable Teacher" (evening).—Rev. Louis J. Sawyer, Hamilton Square Baptist Church.

"The Teacher and Society"—Rabbi Martin A. Meyer, Temple Emanuel. Services on Saturday, July 8.

"Ethical Ideals in Modern Educational Theories"—Rev. Bernard Kaplan, Congregation Beth Israel. Services on Saturday, July 8.

"Christian Training a Necessary Element of True Culture"—Rev. T. W. Clampett, Trinity Episcopal Church.

"Religion and Education"—Rev. Charles Lathrop, Church of Advent Episcopal.

"The Teacher's Calling" (morning).—"Education for Character" (evening).—Rev. George E. Burlingame, First Baptist Church.

"The Bible Supreme as an Educational Force" (evening).—Rev. George W. Rine, Seventh Day Adventist Church.

"Education a Factor in National Life"—Rev. J. Fuendeling, St. Markus Kirche.

"The Place and Scope of Education in Religious Life" (Swedish Language).—Rev. Alfred E. Lindberg, First Swedish Baptist Church.

"Our Master's Model Mind"—Rev. James McElhinnery, Holly Park Presbyterian Church.

"The Place of Knowledge in the Christian System"—Rev. Robert Irwin, University Mound Presbyterian Church.

"Public School: Its Influence on the Republic"—Rev. Dr. M. S. Levy, Geary Street Temple. Services on Saturday, July 8.

"The Religious Elements in Education"—Rev. William P. Sullivan, St. Mary's Cathedral, Catholic.

"The Ideal Woman"—Swami Trigunatita, Hindu Temple, 2963 Webster Street.

"Religion and Public Education"—Rev. E. R. Dille, Central Methodist Episcopal Church.

"Present Day Tendencies in Education"—Rev. R. Logan, Lebanon Presbyterian Church.

"Religious Education in the Public Schools"—Rev. C. S. Tanner, Richmond Presbyterian Church, 31st Avenue and Clement St.

"Religion Cannot Be Taught But Must Be Cherished" (morning).—"Education Without Religion Dangerous" (evening).—Rev. W. K. Guthrie, First Presbyterian Church.

"Personal Education"—Rev. F. M. Larkin, Ph. D., of Los Angeles, Grace M. E. Church, 21st and Capp Streets.

The words of Alfred Roncovieri on the subject "An Appreciation," delivered at the general session of July 11th, are thought to be worthy of repetition here, inasmuch as they preserve an interesting bit of San Francisco's educational history.

"AN APPRECIATION."

"Madam President and Teachers who have come from every section of our Republic:

"I deem it a flattering compliment to be called upon to speak on this occasion and to add my small tribute to the gracious words that have been spoken.

I assure you that we feel deeply the honor you have conferred on us by choosing San Francisco as the place of the forty-ninth Annual Convention of the National Education Association.

We rejoice in your coming, the effect of which must be to elevate the character and advance the interest of the profession of teaching and promote the cause of popular education. Your presence will inspire us with fresh enthusiasm for our work, and we will carry into our school rooms renewed energy. Our 50,000 school children will reap the benefit of our contact with you.

In 1906 it was to have been our pleasure and honor to welcome and entertain the National Education Association, but a conflagration unparalleled in ancient or modern times overwhelmed us and laid our beloved city in ruins. Our business was wiped out and our people were without food and shelter. Homeless, we could not entertain you. Fate had decreed that we should become instead the recipients of the bounty of the world.

We experienced the fact, however, that a calamity has its compensations. No sooner had the wires flashed the news of our catastrophe to the world than there followed the greatest outpouring of brotherly love and sympathy recorded in the annals of history. While the embers of the great fire were yet alive and still smouldering amid the ruins that had been wrought, and before our citizens had even partially recovered from the appalling devastation, by land and by sea there flowed to our city streams of relief. The sympathy of the Republic and of the nations beyond the seas was awakened, and magnificent was the generosity that was exhibited toward our people.

Teachers and school children of the United States were animated by this common spirit of brotherhood. Immediately there came substantial aid. Carloads of food and clothing were hurried to us from every village and hamlet of California and neighboring States. Cheered by the sympathy and the generous charity of the nation, aided and sustained by the millions of dollars which were so magnanimously given to us, we resolved that a new San Francisco should arise; that the beautiful one of yesterday should be restored, and that the future city should transcend the old in solidity, elegance, and in all things which make a community great and attractive. In a miraculously short time our people were fed, clothed, and housed, and the new San Francisco was begun.

Among the hundreds and thousands of benefactions bestowed upon us during the dark days of affliction, and in the midst of those distressing times, nothing was more touching than the thought of teacher for fellow teacher, of school child for school child, and none was more grateful than the contributions of the school children of our country for the construction of a school building, and the many gifts of food, clothing and money sent for the special relief of teachers made destitute by the great fire. These spontaneous offerings relieved much actual distress, and developed in its fullest significance the text, "It is more blessed to give than to receive," for many of our teachers had fled from burning buildings with no wordly goods but the scant clothing which they wore.

The funds for the relief of teachers were distributed by a special committee of teachers and citizens and members of the Board of Education, presided over by the then President of the Board, Hon. Aaron Altmann. With the contributions of the children, a beautiful school building was in large part erected. It is located in the northern portion of our city, graceful in its architecture, and characteristic of the early Mission fathers of California. It was given the Spanish name of "Yerba Buena," to commemorate the first name of the village of '49 that has since grown to be the metropolis of San Francisco. It stands as an eloquent memorial and a fitting monument to the generosity and loving thoughts of the school children of the Republic towards the school children of San Francisco.

The rehabilitation of the San Francisco School Department was commenced five days after the calamity of April 18, 1906. An inventory of the losses sustained revealed the fact that 32 schools, out of a total of 83, had been destroyed, involving a loss of nearly $2,000,000. Then came a splendid exhibition of hope, pluck and energy. Our teachers, many of whom were themselves refugees, volunteered their services to those more unfortunate than themselves. They served with the Red Cross society on committees of relief, health and order. They did yeoman service wherever duty called. For our refugee children schools were opened in tents in Golden Gate Park. Although school rehabilitation was carried on under most adverse conditions, yet, three months after the catastrophe, our schools reopened for regular work.

Ever alive to the educational needs of the children, our citizens have authorized school bond issues amounting to nearly $9,000,000. Many of our new school buildings are now finished. They far exceed in their beauty, strength and equipment those that were destroyed. Behold the Phoenix has risen from the ashes! We point with pardonable pride to our achievements, with the realization that the compensations of calamity are only made apparent after the lapse of time.

Let me say to you that the people of San Francisco glory in the good men and women engaged in the work of our public schools. Without flinching and without retreating, undaunted in the presence of the greatest conflagration of all time, our teachers bravely stood their ground, shoulder to shoulder, and notwithstanding the difficulties and adverse conditions that have confronted them ever since the dire calamity that befell our beloved city, our department has, through the zeal and patient efforts of our teachers, produced the most satisfactory results in education and thus has earned the approbation of our citizens. Our people recognize in the fullest, that teaching is an exalted calling, that the work and influence of the teacher abides in the boys and girls, and that when the men and women of a profession are brought together through sympathy and become associated on the plane of mutual aid and common labor, they become united by the gentle bond of fraternal love.

We acknowledge your gifts with deep gratitude. We appreciate the generous impulse which prompted you to help us in our hour of need. We abundantly value your kindly thoughts and your friendship, your cordial good-will and the closer expression of the great brotherhood of the teachers of the United States, far more than the material things you sent to us. To withdraw something from oneself and give to another is a point of common humanity. It exemplifies altruism and the brotherhood of man in the highest. To carry with us the consciousness of your generous deeds and the thankful remembrance of the love and benevolence of which we have been the object, brings joyful pleasure and everlasting gratitude to our hearts. Like brethren, whether you had little or much, you divided with us in time of need. For all this loving thought, the children and the teachers of the old and the new San Francisco extend to you, and to those whom you represent from every corner of our great country, their sincere thanks and deep appreciation.

You shared our sorrows of 1906, and now do we welcome you and bid you share and pass the cup overflowing with the joys of 1911. We "open our hearts to you wider than our gates," and welcome you to our homes and firesides. And now, with devout thanksgiving to the "Lord of Hosts," through whose love, power, and blessings we have been enabled to right ourselves, we pray that your deliberations may be crowned with success, and that you may enjoy your sojourn with us as your labors deserve; and when you have gone hence we shall remember with grateful hearts the welcome guests that gave much more than they received."

Several special features of the convention deserve recognition by reason of the active participation in them, or immediate direction of them, by our own pople; and to such events we now refer.

On Friday evening, July 8th, Mrs. Ella Flagg Young, President of the National Education Association, was the honored guest at a banquet tendered by the reception sub-committee of the Hospitality Committee of the California organization, under the immediate charge of Mrs. Henry Payot. Six hundred school people and their guests were seated at the tables, all of whom voted the entertainment to have been thoroughly enjoyable. Toasts were responded to by Mrs. Young, President Benjamin Ide Wheeler, President David Starr Jordan, Mrs. O. S. Barnum of Los Angeles, Professor E. C. Moore of Yale University, and Dean W. T. Sumner of Chicago, while Mr. Thomas E. Hayden officiated as toastmaster.

The San Francisco Board of Education maintained head-quarters, during the week, in the Girls' High School building. The hospitality there bestowed on our guests, and the beauty and restful atmosphere of the surroundings, were unsurpassed in the history of our city. Great credit for this achievement is the due of Mrs. M. W. Kincaid, Chairman of the Committee in charge, who devoted her exceptional executive talents unsparingly to this labor. Exhibits of the "busy-work," such as woven baskets and small blankets, of children of the primary grades, trained by Miss Lew Ball, Supervisor of primary reading; and of wood and metal-work by pupils of the upper grammar grades, under the direction of Mr. F. K. Barthel, Supervisor of manual training; gave rise to most commendatory criticism by hundreds of Eastern and Californian educators. A distinct novelty was a Chinese room, fashioned to represent a pagoda, furnished and decorated in gorgeous Oriental style. In this temple tea was served daily by pupils of the Chinese public school, arrayed in native costume. These head-quarters served as a resting-place for many hundreds during the Convention. Trained nurses and a physician were in constant attendance. Mrs. Kincaid as Chairman was assisted by Mrs. Henry Payot, Mrs. James E. Power, Mrs. H. G. Vaughan, and by leading principals and teachers of the Department.

An exhibition of drawing and design, the work of the children of the primary and grammar public schools of San Francisco, trained by Miss Katherine Ball, Supervisor of drawing, that attracted most favorable comment among the many visitors who attended it, was held at the S. F. Institute of Art.

Through the courtesy of Colonel John P. Wisser, Commander of the Troops, the Presidio and Fort Winfield Scott were opened to members of the N. E. A. during the sessions of the Convention. Mrs. Alfred Roncovieri originated the idea and laid the plans. On Wednesday afternoon fully ten thousand people were given free access to the reservation that they might inspect the fortifications, see the great disappearing guns and visit the quarters, being guided by officers of the post. Afterward a vast throng remained to witness the parade and drill under command of Colonel Wisser, and to enjoy the strains of martial music as furnished by the fine regimental band.

Among the most delightful affairs of Convention Week were the informal receptions given at Golden Gate Hall, on Wednesday and Thursday evenings, by the San Francisco Association of Teachers' Councils, with Mrs. M. L. O'Neal as Chairman of the Committee having direction of the entertainment.

That San Francisco is to hold a great exposition for the whole world in 1915 was given wide publicity during the meeting of the N. E. A. Especially, Thursday, July 13th, was set aside as "Exposition Day," and special receptions were held at the Palace and St. Francis Hotels, to which invitations were accepted by large numbers of delegates, and at which addresses were delivered by prominent citizens.

The Newman Club of San Francisco, Miss Agnes Regan, President, gave an elaborate reception on Wednesday afternoon, July 12th, which was well attended by delegates to the Convention.

Due to the indefatigable energy of Miss Estelle Carpenter, Superintendent of Music in the S. F. School Department, who arranged the program, a recital of California Composers presenting their own compositions was given on Friday afternoon, July 14th. This event proved to be such a rare musical feast that by almost unanimous request it was given again on the following day. The program follows:

FRIDAY AFTERNOON, JULY 14, 2:00 O'CLOCK.

Recital of California Composers in Scottish Rite Hall, corner of Van Ness Avenue and Sutter Street.

Arthur Fickenscher—
Songs: (a) "Where go the Boats." Words by Robert Louis Stevenson.
(b) "The First Kiss." Words by Goebel.
(c) "The Winds." Words by Robert Louis Stevenson.
(d) "The Brass Band." Words by Charles Keeler.
Sung by Mrs. Arthur Fickenscher.
Accompanied by Mr. Arthur Fickenscher.

H. B. Pasmore—
Songs: (a) "The Message."
Sung by Mrs. Joseph Mora.
Accompanied by the Misses Pasmore.
(b) "Love's Annals."
Sung by Miss Sophye Rottanzi.
Accompanied by the Misses Pasmore.

Albert Elkus—
Piano Solo: "Four Pieces in Folk Tone."
Rendered by Miss Stella Elkus.

William H. McCoy—
Songs: "Prayer and Duett," from Opera "Cleopatra."
Sung by Miss Catharine McCoy and Mr. Ernest McCandish
Accompanied by Mr. William H. McCoy.

Edward Schneider—
Violin Solo: "The Romanza."
Rendered by Miss Elsie Sherman.
Accompanied by Mr. Edward Schneider.

Edith Simonds—
Songs: (a) "In the Glow of the Morning."
(b) "Resurgam."
(c) "Anthem of the Sea."
Words by Charles Keeler.
Sung by Miss Fernando Pratt.
Accompanied by Mrs. Edith Simonds.

Theodore Vogt—
Songs: (a) "Ich Liebe Dich."
(b) "A Canadian Lullaby."
Sung by Mrs. Anna Covert.
Accompanied by Theodore Vogt.

H. B. Pasmore—
Cello Solo: "Barcarolle."
Rendered by Miss Dorothy Pasmore.
Accompanied by Miss Suzanne Pasmore.

Samuel Savannah—
Songs: (a) "The Four Seasons."
(b) "Ocean Lullaby."
(c) "The Crested Jay." Words by Kieler.
Sung by Mrs. Arthur Fickenscher.
Accompanied by Mr. Arthur Fickenscher.

H. B. Pasmore—
Arrangement of Violin Solo: "Baby Bunting."
Rendered by Miss Mary Pasmore.
Accompanied by Miss Suzanne Pasmore.

Kathleen De Young—
Songs: (a) "Castles in the Air."
(b) "Morning o' March."
(c) "Sylvia's Lips."
Sung by Mrs. B. M. Stitch.
Accompanied by Dr. H. J. Stewart.

Dr. H. J. Stewart—
Songs: "Legends of Yosemite." Words by Allan Dunn.
Sung by Mrs. Lillian Birmingham.
Accompanied by Dr. H. J. Stewart.

John Haradeen Pratt—
Trio in G Major, for Piano, Violin and Violoncello.
Moderato con Moto.
Ben Sustenuto.
Allegro Vivace.
Rendered by the Misses Suzanne, Mary, and Dorothy Pasmore.

John Metcalf—
Songs: (a) "O Sing, Ye Birds."
(b) "Hark as the Twilight Pale."
(c) "Little House o' Dreams."
(d) "Love and Springtime."
Sung by Miss Mabel Riegelman.
Accompanied by John Metcalf.

Wallace Sabin—
Selections from "St. Patrick of Tara," composed for Bohemian Club Jinks.
Words by Henry Morse Stephens.
Sung by Mr. Wilfred Glenn.
Accompanied by Mr. W. F. Husband.

Our teachers must indeed have been inspired for renewed work of still greater usefulness in our profession as they listened to the stirring messages brought from other parts of our land. It is with very deep gratification that we are able to record that the Convention was in every way a pronounced success, and that the leaders of educational thought, who attended, went away with a multitude of words on their lips of highest praise for the kindness and attention lavished upon them during their stay.

COMPULSORY EDUCATION.

One of the functions of the Superintendent of Schools has become that of issuing certificates under the provisions of the so-called Child Labor Law. We transcribe here a digest of that act as prepared by the State Labor Bureau:

DIGEST OF CHILD LABOR LAW.

(As amended Stats. 1911, Chap. 456.)

PLACES AFFECTED—

Any mercantile institution, office, laundry, manufacturing establishment, workshop, place of amusement, restaurant, hotel, apartment house, or in the distribution or transmission of merchandise or messages.

CHILDREN WHO SHALL NOT BE EMPLOYED—

No child under 15 years of age shall be employed except those between 12 and 15 years of age who are provided with a Juvenile Court Permit. This permit is issued by the Judge of the Juvenile Court only when the parents or parent of the child are incapacitated for labor, through illness, and is good only for the period of time and at the kind of work specified therein, provided, that during the Regular Vacations of the public schools, children over 12 years of age may be employed if provided with a Vacation Permit. This permit is issued by the principal or vice-principal of a school or by the secretary of school trustees or board of education, and is good only for the time of the vacation specified therein.

No child between 15 and 16 years of age shall be employed unless provided with an Age and Schooling Certificate. This certificate is issued by the city superintendent of schools or a person designated by him, or by a person authorized by the local school trustees or by a superintendent of a school of recognized standing; provided, that if the certificate states that the child cannot read and write simple English sentences there must also be obtained a Certificate of Attendance at Night School. This certificate is issued by the principal of the school attended.

Exceptions: Nothing in this Act shall be construed to prohibit the employment of minors at agricultural, horticultural or viticultural, or domestic labor during the time the public schools are not in session, or during other than school hours.

CHILDREN WHO MUST BE AT WORK OR IN SCHOOL—

No child under 16 years of age shall, while the public schools are in session, be and remain idle or unemployed for a period longer than two weeks, but must enroll and attend school.

Within one week after a child shall have ceased to be employed by any employer, such employer shall, in writing, giving the latest correct address of such child known to such employer, notify, in the case of a child having a Juvenile Court Permit, the judge of the juvenile court, in the county of said child's residence, or the probation officer of such juvenile court, or in case of a child having an Age and Schooling certificate, the county superintendent of schools of such county, that the child is no longer employed by such employer; and such judge of the juvenile court, or such probation officer or such county superintendent of schools, shall thereupon immediately notify the attendance officer in the place of such child's residence, giving the said latest correct address of such child, that such child is neither at work or in school; and provided, further, that no such child shall be permitted to cease school attendance without securing a Juvenile Court Permit, or an Age and Schooling certificate.

FILING OF CERTIFICATES AND POSTING OF NOTICES—

All the certificates mentioned above must be kept on file by the employer while the child is in his employ.

Every person, firm or corporation employing minors under 18 years of age, in any manufacturing establishment, shall post, and keep posted, in a conspicuous place in every room where such help is employed, a written or printed notice stating the number of hours per day for each day of the week required of such persons.

HOURS OF LABOR OF CHILDREN—

No minor under the age of 18 years shall be employed more than nine hours in one day, except when it is necessary to make repairs to prevent the interruption of the ordinary running of the machinery, or when a different apportionment of the hours of labor is made for the sole purpose of making a shorter day's work for one day of the week, and in no case shall the hours of labor exceed fifty-four hours in a week.

No minor under the age of 18 years shall be employed or permitted to work between the hours of ten o'clock in the evening and five o'clock in the morning.

PENALTIES FOR VIOLATIONS—

Any person, firm, corporation, agent, or officer of a firm or corporation that violates or omits to comply with any of the foregoing provisions of this act, or that employs or suffers or permits any minor to be employed in violation thereof is guilty of a misdemeanor, and shall, upon conviction thereof, be punished by a fine of not less than $50.00 or more than $200.00, or by imprisonment for not more than sixty days; or by both such fine and imprisonment for each and every offense.

ENFORCEMENT—

It shall be the duty of the Bureau of Labor Statistics to enforce the provisions of this act. The commissioner, his deputies, and agents, shall have all powers and authority of sheriffs to make arrests for violations of the provisions of this act.

NUMBER ISSUED IN SAN FRANCISCO—

The number of "Age and Schooling Certificates" issued by the City and County for the year ending June 30, 1911, was Boys 417, Girls 211, Total 628. It is to be observed that the age now required before such certificates can be issued by the Superintendent is 15 years, whereas heretofore the age fixed was 14.

TECHNICAL EDUCATION

Our city has made and is making liberal provision for various forms of handiwork in the elementary schools, the aim having been almost purely cultural.

We hope for a still farther extension of these studies with a greater bent toward the applied arts. In the Polytechnic High School the latter lines have been more closely followed, the aim there having been more technical through the introduction of trade processes and the recognition of industrial conditions. Our laboring people have consistently supported this institution.

The trend of modern educational thought indicates that there is necessity for further development of the trade and industrial idea if the public school system of our city is properly to prepare our young men and women for the stations that they will assume as they undertake their vocational duties in the world of affairs.

With the desire of indicating as fully and completely as possible this situation by reason of its vast significance to our community, I append here an address entitled "The Relations of Organized Labor and Technical Education," delivered originally at the University of California, and afterwards read before the Ninth Annual Convention of the State Building Trades Council:

THE RELATIONS OF ORGANIZED LABOR AND TECHNICAL EDUCATION.

By Alfred Roncovieri.

I have been honored by an invitation to address you on the subject of Technical and Industrial Education and its relation to the Labor Union movement. Technical education and labor unionism have been subjects in which I have always taken a deep and sympathetic interest. I propose to address you on my observations on technical education made during a recent trip to Europe.

It must be admitted by all thinking persons that the nation having the greatest average industrial efficiency is likely to take its place in the front rank in the world of trade; realizing this, the governments of Germany, England, and France are putting forth every effort in support of their technical schools. England and France look upon the growing commercial and industrial influence of Germany with much concern; and this influence is admittedly due to Germany's splendid system of industrial training.

The battle in the field of commerce and industries is actually on. The field of battle is the manufactory and the counting house. The battle is bloodless, but none the less intense, and those nations will win whose industrial army is best equipped with technical knowledge. Confronted, as we are, by the great advances being made in technical and industrial education in the leading countries of Europe, the question naturally arises, where will the United States stand when our immense natural resources shall begin to wane, unless we teach the sciences of agriculture and industrialism?

The English and French technical and industrial schools do not pretend to teach the trade of the carpenter, the mason, the plumber, or any other particular business. It must be conceded by all that there is no trade that does not depend more or less upon scientific principles: to teach what these principles are, and to point out their practical application, is the essence of technical and industrial education in the schools of these countries. For he who unites a thorough knowledge of the scientific principles underlying his art with that dexterity which only actual practice in the workshop can give, will, of necessity, be the most completely skilled and probably the most successful artisan.

I was agreeably surprised, both in England and France, by the fact that objects and purposes of a technical education are not in conflict there with labor union principles. A technical education in all the European schools that I visited does not mean the making of apprentices who shall enter the competitive ranks of labor. It means the teaching of the various branches of science which underlie the majority of trades, and which are of practical application, to mechanics in the several trades, so that they may the better comprehend the reason for each individual operation that passes through their hands, and have more certain rules to follow than the mere imitation of what they may have seen done by another.

The Labor Unions of Great Britain and France recognize the beneficent influence of the technical schools, and are giving them hearty support by naming representative labor leaders as advisory members of the Boards of Control of these schools and by giving cash prizes to be competed for by the students in the various trades. In Scotland especially I found that the advisory members from the Labor Unions give to these schools their hearty support, spending much time in consultation with the governing boards, in examining candidates for instructorships, in visiting schools, and in rendering the students much valuable assistance on graduation. A true spirit of fellowship and good feeling is thus developed, which brings about the most cordial relations between the schools and the Labor Unions.

It is clearly understood in England and France that the expensive equipment of tools and appliances of technical schools shall not be used for anything approaching the apprenticeship system, nor to give the young students who want to learn a trade the chance of acquiring the practice of the trade, which is best acquired in the factory and shop, where work is done on commercial lines. The instruction given in the technical schools is intended to be supplementary to the dexterity and proficiency which only shop experience can give. In England and France the expensive equipment of the technical school is used only to show the student how certain processes are performed and to enable him to perform those processes himself, with the special object in view of giving him the why and the wherefore of the sciences underlying his trade rather than the shop experience. The students are taught how the tool is used, the principles and theories underlying its construction, the errors to avoid and the means of rectifying them when they occur, the nature of the materials to be wrought, and the means of distinguishing different qualities of such material; and having learned all this, and having acquired a certain degree of manipulative skill, the school does not require the student constantly to repeat the same process in order to obtain the rapidity of execution that is expected of a professional workman, but instead proceeds to the explanation of the use of some other machine and to the learning of some other process and the sciences and theories underlying it.

The individual who is content to do things by rule of thumb can never lift himself above the common level. "There is always room on top" is an old saying, but its truth was never better exemplified than in the crafts. The worker who increases his technical knowledge is on the road to promotion and the higher pay which promotion brings. The experts in crafts owe their success to technical instruction. The advance of the foreign worker in the industries is to be traced to a great extent to technical training. He has recognized its need and taken full advantage of it. It will be seen, therefore, that for these reasons the trades unions of England and France are friendly to the development of technical schools and that no conflict can possibly exist when it is clearly understood that although a technical school may be equipped almost as completely as a trade shop, the equipment serves a very different purpose. The trades unions of these countries thoroughly understand the object of the technical school to be the production of intelligent working people capable of holding the highest positions in the industrial world,—not simply to produce competitive cheap labor that will later enter into a fierce rivalry with the Unions. The Unions understand that the machinery and tools employed in an English and French technical school are used with different objects, and with a different intention from those of the factory or commercial workshop. The good will of the trades unions and their support means much to the technical schools of Great Britain and France, and accounts in a large measure for the impetus given to industrial education and its present efficient standards.

Nor is it only the trades unions that approve of this great work, and collaborate with the school authorities in favor of technical instruction; but also the manufacturers, chambers of commerce, philanthropic and economic associations. Each of these gives to the cause the fullest measure of its strength and influence, and assists in the creation of the new education that is to develop and solve the great economic and social problems of these nations.

I want the youth of the United States to rebel at the modern tendency to make him a small, insignificant cog in the wheel of industry, a piece of human machinery. The great captains of industry, through the complex machinery which American genius has for the most part invented, use our boys as mere tools to feed this machinery. They are not expected to develop skill; their lives are consecrated to dull routine and the endless spinning, grinding, and hammering of the modern workshop. Their days and years are regulated by the factory whistle and the time clock; slaves of the wheel, they have no opportunity of mastering a trade or handicraft. The machinery does the work and the man seldom understands the wherefore of its movements. Few men there are today engaged, for example, in the shoe-maker's trade, who can make a pair of shoes complete in all its parts, for the reason that this trade, and many others, are divided into many different parts, and men work a life-time at one part, not knowing or understanding anything about the trade as a whole. I have been informed that the shoe trade is divided into forty or fifty different parts, and that few men working at these separate parts are able to make a complete shoe. Such men are hopelessly handicapped in the struggle for better wages and conditions, because the plutocrats hold them as slave-workers to one part of the trade. The spirit and independence of such workmen are crushed and they are doomed never to rise above their present level,—a condition repugnant to every liberty loving American who has a hope in his future uplift and in the rise and individual initiative of his sons and daughters. It is only too true that if the apprentice is only capable of doing one thing and cannot readily turn to other branches of the same trade, he is practically unskilled and a prey to those who would lower his wages. The man who does not understand the science of the trade and who feeds the machine without the fundamental knowledge of its functions, is the modern "Man with the Hoe," hopelessly bound to it,—the weak object of attack in the constant war to lower his wages, and the one most apt to be thrown out of employment in times of depression.

The technical and scientific training received by the student in a particular trade tends to discourage others from being content with a simple knowledge of only one or perhaps two branches of a trade. They are all stimulated to become all-round, efficient men, able to cope with the ever varying conditions of the industry in which they are engaged, demanding and receiving the maximum rate of wages, and certain of steady employment. Such an education gives broad views of life, and develops men of natural power with the highest ideals of work and citizenship, just as certainly as does a clerical and professional education. Education can have no higher objects.

In England I was impressed with the general feeling of unrest in some of the large manufacturing centers, such as Manchester and Birmingham. While I was in Manchester there were bread riots, due to the great problem of the unemployed which for some years back has been growing more acute. In my opinion the problem of the unemployed is to a very large extent the problem of the unskilled. The men who marched in the streets, and whom I saw charged upon by the mounted police, were not skilled artisans; they were the unskilled men who fed the machines in the cotton mills, and who had become so much a part of those machines that when the large manufacturers declared a lockout in order to reduce their wages these men were confrontd with the alternative of either accepting the wages offered or of finding employment in some other industry.

The problem is clearly understood by the educational authorities of England, and day and evening technical and industrial trade schools are being fostered to meet it. Among the schools which I visited was the Belfast Municipal Technical Institute. This school and its equipment cost $1,000,000. About 5000 students attend it, of whom about 500 attend in the day and 4500 in the evening. The trade subjects are taught only to those who work at the trade in the daytime. Organized labor has absolute control of this school. A boy must be not less than twelve years of age and must have passed the sixth standard of the national schools before being admitted to the school. The principal object of the trade classes of this school is to provide a specialized training for boys who are intended for industrial occupations. While due regard is paid to the subjects of a general education, special attention is devoted to imparting a sound training in the elements of science, and in science as applied to local arts and manufactures, such as mechanical engineering, naval architecture, the building trades, and the textile industries. The complete course covers three years, and includes, besides theoretical instruction, practical work in the laboratories and the drawing school.

The classes are intended chiefly for apprentices who wish to obtain a thorough grasp of all the fundamentals of their own and allied trades. It is not an object of these classes to teach a trade, but the aim is to make the progress of the apprentice more rapid, and to give him a broader view of the trade with which he is associated, and to enable him to acquire a familiarity with trades closely allied to his own. Boys who take the complete course are in a position to enter on their life work in the mill, factory, or workshop; they soon outstrip the lads who have not had these advantages.

I visited classes in pattern maker's work, moulder's work, boiler-maker's work, machine shop practice, marine engineering for sea-going engineers, motor-car construction, naval architecture, electric engineering, telephone, telegraphy, electric wiring and fitting, building trades classes—such as sanitary engineering and practical plumbers' classes, cabinet making, building construction, practical painting and decoration classes—the practical classes in linen weaving and the textile industries, cotton and linen bleaching and dyeing, and many others. There is also a technical course for older students. It provides a sound training in the science and technology of mechanical engineering, electrical engineering, the textile industries, and pure and applied chemistry. The students in this course aim at filling positions of responsibility, such as mechanical engineers, electrical engineers, naval architects, manufacturing chemists, or other industrial occupations.

All classes of Irish society attend this school. Young men and young women who come in automobiles are seated beside poor girls who come with shawls on their heads. This great school has a distinct social-leveling tendency. The magnet that draws all these people together is the knowledge that a practical education that will train the hand and eye as well as the brain can be obtained at reasonable cost.

In the evening school I visited the classes in housewifery. There were present in the class I visited about thirty young women ranging from eighteen to thirty years of age. It was a most interesting sight. Some were cooking on coal and gas ranges, making soups, bread, and roasting meat. Others were washing and ironing; others were learning to sew, darn, and mend. Some were engaged in dressmaking; others were learning the chemistry of the kitchen, the use of caustics, the making of soap, the dyeing of fabrics. The students are permitted to purchase the excellent roasts which are cooked in the class. I was informed that many of these students were young married women whose education in the homely house duties had been neglected.

The demand for a bread-and-butter education would be just as great in California if we would only establish a school like the Belfast school. The proof is shown by the way the correspondence schools of the East are thriving. In San Francisco many students are paying for such a correspondence education simply because San Francisco has not established anything of the kind. If California can only awake to the necessity for action, and compare her supineness in this matter to the progressiveness of Belfast, Ireland, we shall be doing something that will forever benefit our children, and our children's children. The splendid Belfast school which I have just described cost £150,000 and the equipment has cost £50,000 in addition: a total of a million dollars for Belfast, a city of 350,000 people.

In Glasgow, Scotland, I visited several interesting technical schools, notably the Glasgow and West of Scotland Technical College. I found a school of even great importance than the Belfast school. This great school was built and equipped at a cost of £300,000. The equipment of the school cost over £60,000. I saw everywhere at work earnest, busy students who were learning the why and wherefore, and delving into the science underlying their trades. Most of the students were either apprentices or full fledged union workers in the various trades. I visited the shoemakers, the tailors, the plumbers, the machinists, the bakers and confectioners, the sheet metal classes, the weaving, dyeing, and bleaching classes, and those in motor car engineering, naval architecture, and electric engineering.

As an illustration of the spirit of the people of Glasgow and their interest in technical education, I was informed that the Master Bakers and the Bakers' Union had recently, in cooperation, presented to the school a complete outfit of tools, ovens, and other equipment which cost four thousand pounds. One of the donors to the fund was a large manufacturer of bakery machinery. Instruction was being given in all branches of the trade from the kneading of dough to the most complex cake ornamentation. This cooperation between employers and employees extends to all the trades. The unions of the various crafts assist the school and recognize it as a friend. On my way to the school I saw in the windows of a union paint shop signs advertising and illustrating the work done by the classes for painters and decorators and inviting all apprentices to join them. The impression which one receives after visiting this school is that through unity of action and a sensible understanding of the purposes of the school on the part of manufacturers and workmen, captains of industry and leaders in the labor union movement, perfect harmony prevails in the management of the school. The school is managed by a board of governors composed of leading men of the city, labor leaders, and employers, and the general public and the municipality give to this school all the support both moral and financial to which its excellent work entitles it.

It would be mere repetition to describe similar institutions in Edinburgh, Manchester, Birmingham, London, and Paris. In all of these cities every effort is being put forth in support of technical and industrial education. The buildings and equipment far surpass anything of the kind in California. We must make the humiliating confession that practically nothing is being done in the public schools of California that compares with the splendid schools and liberal provisions made for technical instruction abroad. We have been drifting helplessly along old lines and traveling in old ruts, falling behind in the great technical education race. Every city of importance in the United States is ahead of us. European countries are awake to the situation and the incalculable prize is the control of the markets of the world.

I hope California will soon awake to this most vital educational need by making provision for great technical and industrial schools on the lines of the Belfast, Glasgow, Manchester, and Birmingham schools, and of the Paris school of arts and crafts. To do this successfully we must awaken the interest of all our citizens, and as far as the teaching of skill in the trades is concerned, we must secure the intelligent cooperation of capital and labor in these schools, or they cannot succeed.

The usual objection made to technical and trade schools by labor unions in this country have been entirely overcome in Great Britain, Ireland, and France. The unions in these countries have the same industrial problems to contend with as the unions in this country; but they have learned to encourage and protect these schools as their best friends. Labor leaders of known ability and probity are elected by the unions as advisory committees to the Boards of Education in all matters that concern these schools. This brings the labor unions into close and friendly relation to the industrial schools, and nothing is done without first seeking the advice and opinion of the labor union committee. On the other hand, many of the largest employers of labor are invited by the Board of Education to sit at the conferences between the Board of Education and the union labor advisors, and a genuine feeling of fraternity is developed which tends to cooperation and is of the greatest advantage in tightening the friendly relations between labor and capital.

I plead for the support of organized labor for more technical schools, believing that we need them to develop the men who do things, the men who move forward and revolutionize things, and work the wonders of modern civilization. Men skilled in the trades and possessing a knowledge of the sciences underlying their particular art or craft, possess independence of thought, and an initiative which directs them toward the development of new creations and new inventions, thereby preventing and controlling over-production in the existing fields.

The achievements of science during the last century have been marvelous. The possibilities of electricity no imagination can compass. Almost every daily paper tells of discoveries of the X-ray, liquid air, wireless telegraph, aerial navigation, and other valuable discoveries and inventions. Each new discovery opens the door for yet more wonderful disclosures, all demanding a new activity of mind, increasing the necessity for a thorough scientific education in connection with industrial enterprises. Nearly every advance in theoretic science has in late years been followed by the growth of some industry dependent on that science. The discoveries of Fulton, Howe, Whitney, Pasteur, Bell, Edison, Marconi, Goodyear, and others have found immediate echo of practical advantage to the industrial world; such too was the result in the last century of the triumphs of astronomical science in the perfection of the telescope, the spectroscope, and of sidereal photography. Consider microscopic science and its present perfection and utility; the advance in medicine and surgery, especially in the case of anaesthetics; consider the science of mining and the invention of giant explosives, such as nitroglycerine, dynamite, giant powder; consider the perfection of photography and kindred methods of producing pictures by the aid of sunlight; consider electricity as a motor, messenger, illuminator, and heater, unknown one hundred years ago; consider aniline colors, the telegraph, the telephone, the "wireless," the phonograph, the steam engine, the steam printing press, the sewing machine, the typewriter; consider the glorious achievements of science, and remember that it is in a modern technical and industrial school that such studies are emphasized as helping the student to comprehend the labor of the past and to obtain glimpses of the possibilities of the future.

We cannot close our eyes to the fact that our Spanish-American trade is slowly but surely slipping away from us; that German, English, and French commerce and manufactures are acquiring a foothold in neighboring Spanish

America, and supplanting American trade to such an extent that unless we do something, and do it now, we shall lose the rich trade of our neighbors. We must act. We must employ all the means at our disposal while there is yet time. We must educate our rising generation in the commercial and technical arts and crafts. Power and superiority will beyond doubt belong to the most energetic, intelligent, and highly skilled people; and it is only through technical and vocational schools that we can develop the skill to defend our threatened industries in the markets of the world, to keep our country in the first rank of the great nations. While we must train our youth in the power to know, we must, to meet the demands of modern life, also train them in the power to do. The successful German invasion of the world's markets, which bids fair to displace completely the influence of other nations, is the logical outcome of the greater average efficiency of her workmen. Their energy, patience, activity, and spirit of enterprise are remarkable. At the pace they are going they will soon succeed in obtaining the commercial supremacy of the chief markets of the world.

We in California are facing the grandest future of any state in the Union. With no traditions to hinder us or wed us to conservatism, we should take advantage of our patrimony by enlarging the scope of our education, and making it include the technical and utilitarian subjects.

TYPEWRITING IN THE UPPER GRAMMAR GRADES.

In order also to promote those features of vocational training that had been found suitable for boys and girls in the upper grades of the grammar school, in January, 1910, I respectfully recommended the introduction of typewriting into the Hamilton Grammar School to be taken up by the A and B Eighth Grades. I then stated to the Board that "In time I hope to see industrial subjects placed nearer than they now are to the boys and girls who require them. Too many of them drop out of school before they reach the subjects that could be of greatest economic value to them. This recommendation is a step in the direction of a policy of revision and expansion which I hope to see brought about in our schools."

The Hamilton School was selected for the purpose both because there was available there the typewriting equipment used by the evening school which occupies the same building, and because Mr. A. E. Kellogg, the Principal, was in hearty sympathy with the plan.

The Board of Education followed the recommendation as above made, and now that the system has been in practical operation for a year and a half, deductions may easily be drawn as to its effectiveness in reaching the object sought. That it has been a striking success is the united testimony of Principal and teachers, and all other educational observers who have watched it in working. One of the chief advantages of the course is that the typewriting proves to be of great assistance to the pupil in his other school studies, particularly English. Many of the mechanical difficulties met in the study of composition, such as arise in spelling, punctuation, etc., are much more quickly overcome by continued practice on the typewriting machine than in the regular classroom drill. The teachers of the English branches and the teacher of typewriting at the Hamilton, under direction of the Principal, have co-operated zealously in correlating the technical with the academic studies in the school. One of the best indications of the success of this school-subject is that, although it is optional, all of the members of the Eighth Grade, both boys and girls, have without exception chosen to enter the course in typewriting. That in itself proves conclusively not only that the pupil sees some immediate benefit from the work, but that he must find in it also such other elements of interest as attract the mind of the boy or girl.

Since this idea has now proceeded beyond the speculative and even beyond the experimental stage, and has established its own worth, I desire at this time respectfully to submit that courses in typewriting be established in others of our large grammar schools, with this object, that our school children may acquire to a greater degree an efficiency that will be of direct practical service to them, but from the acquiring of which the major part are now excluded.

DEPARTMENTAL TEACHING.

On this subject permit me to quote a few sentences, not originally grouped together, from my report of 1908-09: (Page 32.)

"The chasm between the grammar and the high school must be bridged from both sides. High school teachers must know better what pupils have done in the grammar school, and build upon it. The grammar school must prepare for the change. Departmental work in the Seventh and Eighth grades will accustom the pupils to instruction from more than one teacher. Pupils who have studied under our modified departmental system are ready for the transition to high schools. Success of departmental work rests very largely wtih the principal. I advise that the plan be extended to several more of our large grammar schools. We have principals in the department who are able to direct this work, and carry it through to success."

This system of departmental teaching has now been tried for several years in two of our largest grammar schools, the Hamilton and the Horace Mann, and a beginning has been made in the last year at the Bernal and Roosevelt. The principals of the two former schools have kindly submitted reports on this subject and I take pleasure in presenting here their views as to the results.

San Francisco, June 2, 1911.

Mr. Alfred Roncovieri,
Superintendent of Common Schools.

Dear Sir: In the Seventh and Eighth Grades a plan of organization which may be called a modified departmental system, has been in operation in several of our Grammar Schools. Four branches of instruction—arithmetic, history, geography, language, the last comprising grammar and literature with reading, have been included in the scheme. A teacher is assigned to each of these subjects, and the group of four teachers forms a working unit, or team.

All other subjects of instruction are outside the departmental program, and each teacher is responsible for their conduct in her own class. Between a third and a half of a teacher's time is thus spent with her own class, and the program is so arranged that the teacher is with her class at all entrance or dismissal movements.

The class teacher is, under this plan, with her assigned class a sufficient time and at such times as to make it truly her own and to establish nearness of personal relation. Her absence at the other periods gives a restful variety to her own experience and to that of the class as well.

To the teacher it means the enrichment of her equipment along the line of some special aptitude, and an escape from the narrowing tendencies of teaching a single grade, perhaps for years.

Altogether the departmental system arranged as described has proved, so far as tried, a distinct advance upon the single-teacher plan.

In practical administration of the school, it assists in making any grade in the scheme of equal dignity, since each teacher deals with several grades and carries her class finally to the highest grade in the team, it may be to graduation.

It means that a conference of two teachers and a principal carries instant application of some better method or finer continuity in the work to eight classes.

It altogether demands and brings about more conference and co-operation between the principal and the teachers engaged.

The child enjoys the advantage of having four persons instead of one to awaken his possibilities and to modify all judgments that touch his interests.

This larger contact makes for the pupil easier transition to High School experience, and, more essential still, it prepares better for the many-sided contacts of life outside the school room. Respectfully,

A. E. KELLOGG,
Principal Hamilton Grammar School.

San Francisco, June 2, 1911.

Mr. Alfred Roncovieri,
Superintendent of Common Schools.

Dear Sir: In June 1909 I submitted you a report of my work in connection with the introduction of departmental teaching in the Horace Mann Grammar School which, I understand, was omitted inadvertently from your report of 1908-09.

I have nothing to add to my report of 1909 other than to say that with your hearty approval and cooperation, the Board of Education in December of last year passed two resolutions which enabled me to put my two year plan into operation. The Board also passed a resolution relative to the salary of the class teacher of a sixth grade, when such a grade is included in a departmental group. These several resolutions have been incorporated in the Rules of the Board.

REPORT OF 1909.

In the fall term I organized three groups of departmental work. I put three teachers in each group. The subjects specialized were geography, history and arithmetic. The A Seventh, B Seventh and A Eighth grades were represented in each group. I omitted the B Eighths, as the term was not only short, but, owing to other causes, it was impossible to organize the departmental work at once. At the beginning of the spring term the grades that had been doing departmental work became, of course, B Sevenths, A Eighths and B Eighths. I then added an A Seventh to each group and English as the fourth special subject. It will be observed that a division of each grade is represented in each group. Under this plan continuity is given to the instruction. Further, it gives interest and breadth of view to the teacher.

In order to make a working programme I found it necessary to modify the "Suggested Time Schedule" contained in the course of study, but as the modifications were so slight, I will not particularize them. No changes have been made in the programme since the beginning of this term, when the fourth teacher was added to each group.

The only vital problem in connection with departmental teaching in the Seventh and Eighth grades is whether the children will suffer in the formation of their character by coming in contact with several personalities during a year rather than with a single one. It has therefore been my aim to minimize, if not overcome, this one alleged weakness. I have attempted to minimize it by not putting too many teachers in a group and by not specializing too many subjects. In other words, each teacher is not only a subject teacher, but a class teacher as well. As a subject teacher she teaches a single subject to four classes, to one of which she also teaches the subjects of the course of study other than the major ones. As a class teacher she begins and ends her day with her class, besides being with them a short period after recess. In a word, while giving to a class the superior instruction which come with the specialization of the teacher, I attempt to give each teacher an opportunity to impress her personality upon a class.

The school is stronger for the introduction of departmental teaching. It has given the teachers a new point of view. It has forced instruction in accordance with the "suggested time schedule," thus preventing special subjects in which special teachers are interested, as well as favorite subjects of regular teachers, being taught at the expense of other subjects. It prevents cramming for examinations either from the principal or the superintendent. It fixes responsibility. It gives the opportunity for closer supervision. Finally, it cannot fail to produce pupils who will be able, on their entrance to the high school, to adapt themselves to secondary methods without loss of time.

Of the twelve teachers who are doing departmental work, eleven are in favor of its continuance. One teacher was not in favor of it in the beginning, nor is she now, but she has not permitted her fixed opinion to interfere with the carrying out of the plan. In only one particular have the teachers failed to follow every suggestion I have made in connection with the plan.

I wish the teacher who becomes the class teacher of the A Seventh grade to continue with the class until its graduation. Or to put it another way, I wished the B Eighth grade teachers at the close of the fall term to take the newly promoted A Seventh grade at the beginning of the spring term, just as I now wish the B Eighth grade teachers to take the newly promoted A Seventh grade at the opening of the fall term. The teachers have not seen their way clear to follow me in this request. The Eighth grade teachers fear if they accept assignment by subject rather than by grade, that they may be stranded with a Seventh grade in case departmental teaching should be discontinued. But it is senseless to organize departmental teaching, not only in relation to subjects, but also in relation to the rank of teachers according to grade and to seniority within the grade. It is absurd deliberately to weaken the plan when it could be strengthened at the point of its single possible weakness.

The keeping of the register of Eighth grade children should not be permitted to stand in the way of the two year plan, since there is no difference of salary between the Seventh and Eighth grades, and since each teacher teaches her major subject equally to each grade. If departmental teaching succeeds in schools where Seventh and Eighth grades exist, the teachers must be assigned as subject teachers rather than as grade teachers. I am satisfied that nothing so much prevents the introduction of departmental teaching or makes its failure so frequent, as the inability of grade teachers to come to regard themselves as subject teachers. If departmental teaching fails for this reason, or if it be not introduced where it should be, it will force the organization and centralization of Seventh and Eighth grades into separate schools—"pre-academic schools"—or their absorption into the high school, for the belief is general that these grades must be made to afford not only a better preparation for entrance to high school, but for life. If such preparation cannot be given through departmental teaching in schools as now organized—it will be given in the "pre-academic school" or in the high school.

I trust that the Board of Education will make such regulations as will enable me to put the two year plan into operation without teachers feeling that in accepting assignment by subject they have given up their rank by grade, for I believe a teacher who instructs a class two years in a major subject as well as in the minor ones, will impress her personality upon it stronger than she would if teaching the same class a single year under the ordinary plan. In two years she would know not only the child, but its home, and during all that time she would have the consciousness of feeling that children were being taught in the major subjects other than her own with the same preparation and enthusiasm she was giving to hers. Further, it would give continuity and fix responsibility in the minor subjects as well as the major ones.

RESOLUTIONS OF THE BOARD OF EDUCATION.

December, 1910.

Resolved, That the rank of departmental teachers shall be in accordance with their seniority, regardless of the grade they instruct as class teachers.

Resolved, That whenever departmental teaching shall be discontinued in any school, the departmental teachers shall be assigned to grades within the school in accordance with the seniority of their appointment to said school.

Resolved, That whenever a sixth grade is included with seventh and eighth grades in a departmental group, the class teacher of the sixth grade shall receive the salary of the other teachers of the group.

Very Sincerely,

RICHARD D. FAULKNER,
Principal Horace Mann Grammar School.

REPORT ON MEDICAL INSPECTION IN THE S. F. SCHOOL DEPARTMENT.

San Francisco, Cal., August 25, 1911.

Mr. Alfred Roncovieri,
Sup't. Public Schools, San Francisco, Cal.

Dear Sir:

As per your request I beg leave to submit a tabulated list of work performed in this Department during the fiscal year July, 1910 to June, 1911 inclusive. I trust that the figures will give you an idea of the volume of work accomplished among the schools under inspection.

The figures on the extreme right show that the nurse has examined over 30,000 children in the schools and has made over 3,000 visits to homes. During the year the Inspector has physically examined over 3,000 children.

Under the heading, "exclusions from schools under inspection" the figures indicate the actual number of contagious diseases discovered by the nurse and the inspector, both in the school and in the home.

Under the heading, "vaccination" these figures mean that the nurse has actually made this number of vaccination examinations.

Under the heading, "disposition of special cases" it will be seen that a large amount of medical treatment has been accomplished. Each one of these cases has come under the direct supervision of the nurse and has been closely followed up until necessary treatment or operation has been furnished. Those cases referred to clinic are those children whose parents are unable to pay for medical treatment. In every case it is the aim of this Department to refer pupils to their family physician for treatment. They are not permitted to receive the benefit of a clinic unless they are actually deserving. Those cases referred to societies are ones of either neglect or cruelty on the part of the parent and ones needing the benefit of a charitable society.

A glance at the totals of the columns of figures will show the amount of work the nurse has had to do during the fiscal year.

During the present year we are pursuing the same course, and am pleased to say that we are establishing, through the principals of the schools, a much better system than heretofore.

On September 1st, 1911 we will add four nurses to our working staff, thereby enabling us to medically inspect all of the public schools in the City.

Yours respectfully,

E. L. WEMPLE,
Chief Medical Inspector of Schools.

Health Inspectresses

Mrs. Madge Dake — Josephine Graham — Anna Shepler — Edith Flynn — Katherine Winne
Mrs. A. Frisbie — Grace McIntyre — Elizabeth McKenzie — Evangeline Phelan — Mrs. M. B. Wynne

EXAMINATIONS, FINDINGS AND TREATMENTS.

SCHOOL.	Enrollment	No. of Visits	Pediculosis		Impetigo		Ringworm		Eczema	Eye Diseases	Infected Wounds	Scabies	Not Vaccinated			Dressings	Treatments	Exclusions
			New	Old	New	Old	New	Old										
Adams	375	21	20	4	8	10	1	4	....	10	....	7	62	....	....	11	3	13
Agassiz	703	110	28	6	34	46	12	7	....	30	5	7	9	....	....	18	156	24
Bay View	433	124	....	30	81	68	7	2	1	18	1	....	1	....	....	142	178	4
Bernal	660	62	36	3	18	11	1	1	....	13	2	1	....	....	....	17	78	5
Bryant	576	115	34	38	21	8	1	....	....	2	10	2	....	....	....	64	16	13
Buena Vista	399	65	32	38	6	1	....	....	1	....	2	....	....	....	....	3	6	1
Burnett	430	109	8	25	41	28	2	....	....	8	2	....	1	....	....	54	57	17
Clement	544	18	33	17	....	....	....	....	....	....	....	....	8	....	....	1	....	....
[illegible]nd	410	11	9	20	3	2	....	....	....	....	....	....	....	....	....	7	5	3
Columbia	1,009	118	118	30	13	7	....	....	....	....	7	4	....	....	....	45	10	6
Cooper	592	67	22	35	66	60	8	2	....	4	2	2	5	....	....	335	18	6
Denman	31	17	5	13	....	....	2	4	8	12	....	2	41	....	....	....	....	1
Douglas	582	18	18	25	....	....	....	....	....	....	....	....	....	....	....	....	....	1
Edison	559	15	14	9	2	2	....	....	1	....	....	....	1	....	....	3	7	3
Emerson	617	15	11	15	16	48	....	....	1	....	....	1	....	....	....	7	44	1
Everett	812	18	5	....	1	2	....	....	2	....	2	3	....	....	....	2	....	4
Fairmount	1,092	22	11	42	1	....	....	....	....	....	....	....	....	....	....	....	5	25
Franklin	519	24	118	76	1	4	....	....	....	....	....	2	44	....	....	....	....	...
Frank McCoppin	576	7	5	....	....	....	....	....	....	....	....	....	....	....	....	8	5	...
Fremont	776	29	23	22	5	7	5	3	2	....	....	2	....	....	....	3	5	...
Garfield	940	97	77	90	64	50	12	6	2	3	6	5	2	....	....	621	39	...

Golden Gate	428	81	48	77	5	6	4	10	....	....	....	....	1	....	....	10	17	1
Grant	462	15	5	5	....	....	....	....	....	....	....	....	5	....	....	....	....	1
Haight	667	97	91	....	38	29	....	2	1	8	1	4	2	....	....	16	237	3
Hancock	529	68	5	20	6	2	1	....	....	....	1	....	....	....	....	45	....	....
Hawthorne	515	29	5	5	11	....	1	....	1	1	....	1	....	....	....	10	1	....
Hearst	795	18	38	24	2	....	2	....	....	....	....	2	38	....	....	....	....	....
Henry Durant	629	16	87	93	19	51	11	35	3	....	....	....	3	....	....	26	61	1
Irving Scott	699	79	16	70	57	44	24	4	6	18	2	1	....	....	....	50	195	3
James Lick	567	11	8	7	....	....	1	....	....	....	....	1	....	....	....	....	....	2
Jean Parker	673	18	27	15	2	....	....	....	....	....	....	1	4	....	....	2	....	....
John Swett	652	21	26	13	7	2	17	7	2	35	4	2	10	....	....	1	....	9
Junipero Serra	680	83	81	9	52	43	....	3	4	13	9	5	10	....	....	26	312	12
Lincoln	374	33	81	78	4	11	4	4	....	....	....	4	34	....	....	....	....	....
Marshall	652	14	6	4	3	12	....	....	....	2	....	....	10	....	....	1	12	1
Marshall Annex		11	5	2	1	....	....	....	2	....	....	....	10	....	....	....	....	2
Monroe	942	21	13	33	1	8	1	1	....	....	....	1	....	....	....	4	44	19
Muir	307	18	35	34	1	....	....	....	....	....	....	....	33	....	....	....	....	....
Noe Valley	806	21	37	30	3	6	....	....	....	1	....	3	1	....	....	7	6	15
Oriental	462	8	8	8	....	1	....	....	....	1	....	....	....	....	....	7	....	....
Pacific Heights	834	16	14	10	....	....	....	....	....	....	....	1	7	....	....	....	3	2
Portola	698	79	14	100	157	154	8	....	3	20	3	2	....	....	....	93	336	8
Potrero	380	21	15	25	21	10	1	7	....	4	....	1	8	....	....	3	13	4
Redding	637	13	19	....	1	1	2	9	4	6	....	2	....	....	....	....	....	5
Rincon	142	25	40	34	3	4	....	....	....	4	....	....	19	....	....	....	....	....
Roosevelt	736	15	41	18	4	1	4	2	6	....	....	....	....	....	....	....	....	....
Sheridan	711	22	11	41	3	1	....	....	....	....	....	....	....	....	....	....	....	32
Sherman	503	17	9	16	1	1	4	4	....	....	....	....	18	....	....	....	....	2
Spring Valley	464	22	27	25	3	....	14	17	4	12	1	6	103	....	....	2	....	17
Starr King	328	76	59	32	13	....	5	5	3	6	3	15	....	....	....	27	9	12
Sutro	606	10	....	16	....	....	....	....	....	....	....	....	....	....	....	....	....	....
Visitacion	272	41	3	16	31	37	10	1	3	4	3	2	....	....	....	32	90	3
Washington Irving	320	79	9	32	36	45	1	3	....	2	....	3	5	....	....	249	9	1
Washington Grammar	564	23	8	5	2	....	....	....	....	....	....	3	4	....	....	3	....	....
Winfield Scott	316	14	72	75	6	....	2	1	1	....	....	....	21	....	....	1	2	2
Yerba Buena	519	88	65	47	38	52	9	11	3	2	4	....	5	....	....	323	14	....
Total	32219	2275	1666	1584	919	881	188	165	64	239	70	108	515	....	....	2271	2007	291

DIVISION OF SCHOOL MEDICAL INSPECTION—Continued

TOTALS.

No. Primary and Grammar Day schools in San Francisco	85
Schools under inspection	57
Pupils examined by Inspector	3,542
Pupils examined by Nurse	30,958
Visits to home by Nurse	3,036

Exclusions from Schools Under Inspection

Chickenpox	250
Contagious Skin Diseases	77
Choreá	7
Diptheria	29
Measles	456
Mumps	340
Scarlatina	117
Tonsilitis (cute)	81
Whooping Cough	140
Contacts	788
Tuberculosis (Pulm)	2

VACCINATIONS

Remaining from last month	1,657
Found to be unsuccessfully vaccinated	1,023
Never vaccinated	484
Total	2,680
Vaccinated during month	56
Remaining to be vaccinated	2,624
Examinations	9,716

Disposition of Special Cases

Treated by Family Physician	170
Treated by Family Physician (Operation)	154
Referred to Clinic	171
Referred to Societies	66

APPORTIONMENT OF STATE SCHOOL FUNDS.

As the law relating to the taking of the school census was repealed by the last Legislature, (see Chapter 333, page 529 of the Statutes for 1911), the State school money is now apportioned in accordance with Section 1858 of the Political Code, (as amended March 31, 1911), of which the salient features are here re-produced: (See pages 527, and 528 of the Statutes for 1911).

"The school superintendent of every county and city and county must apportion all State and county school moneys for the elementary grades of his county or city and county as follows:

"1. He must ascertain the number of teachers each school district is entitled to by calculating one teacher for every district having 35 or less number of units of average daily attendance and one additional teacher for each additional 35 units of average daily attendance, or fraction of 35 not less than ten units of average daily attendance as shown by the annual school report of the school district for the next preceding school year; and two additional teachers shall be allowed to each district for every 700 units of average daily attendance.

"3. $550 shall be apportioned to every school district for every teacher so allowed to it; provided, that to districts having over 35 or multiple of 35 units of average daily attendance and a fraction of less than ten units of average daily attendance, $40 shall be apportioned for each unit of average daily attendance in said fraction.

"5. Units of average daily attendance wherever used in this section shall be construed to be the quotient arising from dividing the total number of days of pupils' attendance in the schools of the district by the number of days school was actually taught in the district. A school day is hereby construed and declared to be that portion of the calendar day or night in which school is maintained and in which one-twentieth of the work of a school month may be performed. The attendance of pupils present less than one-fourth of any day shall not be counted for that school day and pupils present for one-fourth of a day or for more than one-fourth of a day shall be counted as present for one-fourth of a day, one-half of a day, three-fourths of a day, or for a whole day, as the case may be."

Under the terms of the bill as at first proposed, every district in the State having a remainder of fifteen or more pupils in average daily attendance after dividing the whole number by the unit 35, was to be entitled to a teacher and, consequently to $250 for that teacher. I found that several counties had many more than 100 districts and that if each district could, under the proposed system, receive an appropriation of $250 for the remainder of 15 or more, this would give an unfair advantage to all counties having many districts, and that a city and county like San Francisco having but one school district would be at a distinct disadvantage for the simple reason that it could have but one remainder. I at once planned to remedy this defect in the proposed law, and accomplished my purpose by prevailing upon Assemblyman Benedict to offer an amendment to section 1858 providing that two additional teachers should be allowed for every seven hundred pupils and receive the State appropriation therefor. This he did, the amendment carried, and became a part of the law as finally enacted. This gives San Francisco at present 98 more teachers at $250 per teacher, and thus $24,500 have been saved to us annually.

SCHOOL HOLIDAYS

The Legislature of 1911 amended Section 10 of the Political Code relating to legal holidays. The provisions of the present law that affect the schools are:

"The public schools of this State shall close on Saturday, Sunday, the first day of January, the 30th day of May, the Fourth Day of July, the 25th day of December and on every day appointed by the President of the United States or the Governor of this State for a public fast, thanksgiving or holiday. Said public schools shall continue in session on all other legal holidays and shall hold proper exercises commemorating the day. Boards of School Trustees and City Boards of Education shall have power to declare a holiday in the public schools under their jurisdiction when good reason exists therefor."

The other legal holidays to which reference is made in the second sentence of the part of the act just quoted are:

The 12th day of February, to be known as "Lincoln Day;" the 22nd day of February, or Washington's Birthday; the 9th day of September, or Admission Day; the first Monday in September, or Labor Day; the 12th day of October, to be known as "Columbus Day;" and every day on which an election is held throughout the State.

THE SCHOOL LIBRARY FUND

Ever since the disaster of 1906 the San Francisco schools have suffered from a paucity of supplementary books. Our schools have not been re-supplied with volumes sufficient adequately to meet their needs. This was in part due to the interpretation placed on section 1714 of the Political Code relating to the library fund in cities, which originally read:

"In cities not divided into school districts the library fund shall consist of a sum not to exceed fifty dollars, for every one thousand children or fraction thereof of five hundred or more, between the ages of 5 and 17 years, annually taken from the City or County school fund apportioned to the city. The Superintendent shall apportion the Library Fund in cities not divided into districts among the several schools in proportion to the average number of children belonging to each school."

In the past the words "not to exceed" in line 2 of the section above have been taken advantage of, with the result that comparatively insignificant amounts of money have been devoted to this laudable purpose.

With these ideas in mind, at the last session of the Legislature I prepared an amendment to the section just above quoted attaching to its final words the following proviso:

"Provided, that in each city and county the Library Fund shall consist of a sum equal to at least ten dollars for each teacher employed in such city and county." This amendment was introduced by Assemblyman James Ryan and was enacted into law. Under this act the Board of Education of San Francisco will be required to appropriate approximately $12,000 a year at the present time for the purpose of placing supplementary books in the schools, an increase of about $8,000 per year.

THE TEACHERS' PENSION BILL.

At the session of the Legislature in 1911 the teachers of this Department strove earnestly, in company with the educational forces of the entire State, to secure the enactment of effective pension legislation, believing that such a law would prove to be of the greatest value to school-workers and the children alike. a measure known as the "Williams' Bill" was passed by the Assembly on March 16th and by the Senate on March 24th, but failed to receive the signature of the Governor. We reprint here the terms of this act as finally presented to His Excellency, Governor Johnson.

An act to provide for retirement salaries for public school teachers of this State, and to provide for the revenue therefor.

The people of the State of California, represented in Senate and Assembly, do enact as follows:

Section 1. A fund is hereby created, to be known as the "public school teachers' retirement salary fund of California." So much of the taxes collected under the succession and inheritance tax laws of this state and not specifically appropriated to the uses of the state school fund and for other educational purposes as may be necessary to provide for the retirement salaries, specified in sections three and four of this act shall constitute this fund.

Sec. 2. The superintendent of public instruction shall each year determine, from reports made to him by city, county, and city and county superintendents, the amount that will be needed for the following fiscal year to pay the said retirement salaries, and shall report the same to the state controller, annually, between the tenth day of August and the first day of September. This amount the state controller shall certify to the state treasurer, who shall pay such retirement salaries upon warrants properly drawn by the state controller.

Sec. 3. Any public school teacher who shall have served on a teacher's legal certificate, as teacher or partly as teacher and partly as superintendent or supervising executive, or educational administrator, for at least thirty school years in the public schools of this state, including the last ten years preceding retirement, shall be entitled to receive upon retirement after such service an annual tirement salary payable quarterly, which salary shall be equal to one and one-half per cent of the average salary of the last ten years of service multiplied by the total number of years of service; provided that the term "ten years" as used in this act shall not be construed as meaning ten consecutive years, and that, on the other hand, the interruptions of service during this period, however caused, shall not exceed a total of three years; and provided further, that the term "public schools" shall be construed, for the purposes of this act, as meaning all schools supported by public funds and subject to city, county, or city and county, or state control; and provided further, that the above requirement of a teacher's legal certificate for the full thirty years shall not apply to those who entered the public school service of this state, prior to the passage of this act, except that no person shall be entitled to receive said retirement salary who is not the holder of such a teacher's legal certificate at the time of retirement.

Sec. 4. Any public school teacher, as described in section three, who shall have served, on a teacher's legal certificate, for at least twenty years, in the public schools of this state, and who shall, by reason of bodily or mental infirmity, have become totally incapacitated for further school service, shall be entitled to receive, during the period of such disability, an annual retirement salary, payable quarterly, equal to one and one-half per cent of the average annual salary of the last ten years immediately preceding retirement, multiplied by the total number of years of service, provided application for such retirement salary is made within two years after the last month of service; provided, however, that the above requirement of a teacher's legal certificate for the full twenty years shall not apply to those who entered the public school service of California before the passage of this act, except that no person shall be entitled to receive a retirement salary who is not the holder of such a teacher's legal certificate at the time of becoming so incapacitated.

Sec. 5. If any teacher retired under the provisions of section four of this act shall be re-employed in any public or private school of this, or any other state, his or her retirement salary shall cease, and in case such teacher qualifies for a retirement salary already received by such teacher under section four shall be deducted year by year in the amounts originally received.

If any teacher retired, under section three of this act, shall be re-employed in any public or private school of this or any other state, his or her retirement salary shall cease.

Sec. 6. No one shall be permitted to draw from the state, directly or indirectly, more than one retirement salary. This act shall not be so construed, however, as to prevent local communities or bodies of teachers from increasing the retirement salary received from the state.

Sec. 7. The state board of education shall determine and prescribe what shall constitute a "school year," under section three and the other provisions of this act, and shall define in detail the periods of service specified in this act, and shall make all needful regulations for the method or methods of applying for and drawing said retirement salaries, and for the method or methods of determining the eligibility of each applicant, and the amount of the retirement salary, under the provisions of this act.

Sec. 8. The minimum retirement salary for teachers retiring under section three of this act shall not be less than three hundred and sixty dollars per annum; nor shall the maximum for teachers retiring under section three or section four of this act be more than nine hundred dollars per annum.

Sec. 9. All teachers already retired, are eligible to be retired, under the act to amend an act approved March 26, 1895, entitled "An act to create and administer a public school teachers' annuity and retirement fund in the several counties, and cities and counties in the state" (approved March 29, 1897, amended March 20, 1903,) shall be entitled to receive annual retirement salaries under the provisions of this act.

Sec. 10. This act shall take effect July 1, 1911.

CONCLUSION

I take this means of commending the spirit shown by the people of this city toward their schools since the calamity of April 18, 1906. The people at large have manifested a deep interest in public education and have never hesitated to take up any project which has had for its object the improvement of the schools. Bond issues for school purposes whenever submitted to popular vote have invariably been carried by overwhelming majorities. The people are coming into closer contact with our work. Parents' Clubs have been organized in several schools. Improvement Clubs take an active interest in all that pertains to the welfare of the children. This spirit is reflected in our teaching force. The esprit de corps which exists among our teachers has resulted in honest, conscientious work and the establishment of the highest standards in education. I shall continue to exert every influence at my command to develop this community interest in our schools and thus make them more useful, not only to the children, but as real social centers in which our citizens may gather to discuss ways and means for the benefit of our city.

REPORT OF THE SUPERVISOR OF LECTURES FOR THE SCHOOL YEAR 1910-1911.

San Francisco, July 1, 1911.

To the Board of Education of the City of San Francisco.

Madam and Gentlemen:

Herewith I respectfully submit my first annual report on public lectures, for the school year ending June 30, 1911.

This, the first year of the existence of the Bureau of Lectures, has seen the equipment and opening of fifteen school auditoriums as lecture centers, in which sixty-four free evening lectures for adults have been given, besides several afternoon lectures to children, pupils of the schools. The subjects of the lectures have been varied, representing the fields of Geography and Travel, History and Biography, Science, Health, and Social Topics, Literature and Music. Most of the lectures have been illustrated with the stereopticon, several with moving pictures or concrete scientific experiments; while literary and musical topics have been enlivened with selections of a high order, in every instance (I believe) rendered with superior artistic taste and skill. Yet such has been the generosity and public spirit of the friends of the public lecture system (including men from the faculties of Stanford and California universities, as well as citizens of San Francisco), that all this service has cost the city of San Francisco not one dollar. The speakers and artists have understood that the Bureau of Lectures was without funds with which to repay their services, and in no instance has that fact made any difference: the service was rendered for love and the public welfare. Even expensive appliances, views and musical instruments have been loaned to the Bureau for its use, without charge. Of this, more specific acknowledgment is elsewhere made.

The response on the part of the people to this plan for their instruction and entertainment has been very gratifying, in point of attendance, attention, and after-comment. The total attendance at seventy lectures has been 25,236, an average of 360 to each lecture, or nearly double the average last year in New York City. The attention paid at the lectures has been generally all that could be desired, and the comments made at the close of many evenings have been most appreciative, while some of the auditors have taken pains to write their enthusiastic approval. Especially gratifying has it been to the workers in the Bureau to have men and women, entire strangers, speak to them at the close of lectures, or even accost them later, on the streets of the city, and declare our lectures quite equal to those of New York, which, with its elaborate system, may be regarded as a standard.

Principals of schools used as lecture centers have not only attended the lectures given in their schools, but have without exception expressed approval of the system as a wise use of public property, leading to a closer and better relation between school aud neighborhood. From others, not connected with our schools, kindly suggestions have come, and offers of help, even beyond our immediate power to use.

The lecture idea is simple. It rests on the fundamental fact that language is the keenest tool of intellect and speech the most facile medium of man's intercourse with man. Given a log with Mark Hopkins seated on one end and a student on the other, and you have a university, said Emerson. In such a university one may be sure the instruction would be oral and not printed—winged words flying from the lips of the wise teacher to the listening ear of the eager learner. Though the printed page has its uses, it can never replace the speaker in liveliness, in facility, in appeal to an assembly. It is agreed by all that the success of a lecture turns on the personality of the lecturer. Given a magnetic speaker, fortified in his knowledge of his subject, and facing a receptive audience, —then the conditions for instruction are ideal.

And all the people, even the most fortunate of us, need enlightenment on many subjects, our life long; a ready means for which is the public lecture, given in the halls of the public schoolhouse built with public money.

Prof. Edmund J. James, President of the University of Illinois, says:—

> "We must reach out and provide systematic means of educating and training the adult population of the country. The church, the theatre, the book, the library, the newspaper, valuable as they are, are still far from accomplishing the necessary result. We must adopt a more comprehensive, a more scientific, a more systematic method of work.
>
> "It is fortunate for us that the means for this work are so close at hand. The public school buildings in this country represent an enormous investment of capital, most of which, from an industrial point of view, is lying idle most of the time. A schoolroom is used for perhaps six hours a day, not to exceed ten months in the year. The plant is, in a word, very much underworked. We must make a new departure. Every schoolhouse should be the center of a system of adult education, as well as of infantile and youthful education. Every city schoolhouse ought to contain a large, well-equipped auditorium, able to take in of an evening, for purposes of further study and instruction, the parents of the children who attend it in the day time.

Prof. Charles Zueblin, of the University of Chicago, writes to Dr. Leipziger:—

> "New York is doing a great work for the world, as for itself, in indorsing and supporting the ideas that education is the process of a lifetime and that the millions we have invested in our public school buildings belong to the people and should be used for their benefit. I meet no more responsive audiences than those in the New York public schools, and I find no feature of our public school system which seems worthier of support or brings more immediate returns in good citizenship. I hope the authorities will continue to subsidize you as in the past, and enable you to respond to the growing demands of your intelligent citizens."

But will the people come, and will they continue receptive to lectures that aim to be something more than merely entertaining?

To quote an eminent Harvard professor:

> "With the multitude of other opportunities for education that American life affords, will any large body of men and women attend public lectures; will they attend when the novelty has worn off, say, during the third year; will they do nothing more than attend; will they follow courses of study, write essays and pass examinations; will the extension system (and the free public lecture is a form of educational extension) —no better than its decayed predecessor, the old Lyceum System—resist the demands of popular audiences and keep itself from slipping out of serious instruction into lively and eloquent entertainment?

We are informed by Dr. Henry M. Leipziger, Supervisor of Lectures in New York City, that the twenty years' experience of his city gives a satisfactory reply to every item in the above question. Will San Francisco,—like New York City in the cosmopolitan character of her people; its counterpart in geographic and economic position, but a century and a half younger, three thousand miles farther removed from their common parentage in the riper civilization of Europe; with fresher, cruder traditions of transcontinental travel, toiling miners, Mexican and Indian life, and with a milder sky encouraging improvidence, putting a premium on picnics, play and outdoor display—will dear, distressing, patient, human San Francisco keep step with the metropolis in the matter of public educational lectures? Time alone can tell, but the experience of the past six months makes us believe that she will.

HISTORICAL. The Bureau of Lectures, as it now exists, is a child of the enthusiasm of Director Henry Payot. San Francisco had seen scattering lectures, even systematic courses of lectures, given to limited audiences, in hired halls, for an admission fee; in isolated schools, notably the Laguna Honda, free lectures have been provided; but not before 1910 were free lectures offered to the public on a large and systematic plan, in our school buildings. In that year a volunteer committee of ladies and gentlemen, among whom Dr. Caroline Rosenberg was perhaps the most active, under permission from the Board of Education, arranged for a series of public lectures; eight such lectures were given in 1910. In December last, Director Henry Payot (who for many years had found pleasure in lecturing on topics suggested by his travels, before audiences in San Francisco and other cities, and had himself heard many of the public lectures in New York City), believing that the time was ripe, introduced the resolution creating a Bureau of Lectures, a copy of which is appended to this report.

This resolution being unanimously adopted by the Board of Education, and warmly supported by Superintendent of Schools Alfred Roncovieri, meetings of the Advisory Commission on Lectures were held early in January, a schedule of lectures approved, and lanterns and screens having already at the instance of Mr. Henry Payot been installed in a number of schools, lectures were commenced. Beginning thus in January, 1911, at first twice a week, they were continued as frequently as five or even seven lectures weekly until the end of May, with the excellent attendance stated above.

NEEDS OF THE BUREAU. A good beginning has been made, but only a beginning. Many auditoriums are still without equipment, and few of the halls fitted as centers are in use oftener than once a month. This raises the item of expense. New York City, where free lectures for adults have been systematically provided for over twenty years, and which may well be regarded as the standard for the country, spent in 1909-10 the sum of $125,000 for this purpose. With one-tenth the population, San Francisco might eventually, at a like rate, expect to expend some $12,000 for lectures. In May, last, the Board of Education named $6,000 as desirable for the fiscal year 1911-12, and was allowed $2,500—perhaps a reasonable grant, considering the youth of the experiment here. Half a loaf, indeed a quarter loaf, is far better than no bread; and with this small fund, carefully husbanded, the Bureau expects to continue the lectures about as frequently as heretofore, to open several more lecture centers, to equip a number of auditoriums for moving pictures, and—not least in importance—to allow a small fee to a few, a very few, of its lecturers and assistants. These men and women have thus far tendered their services to the city, gratis. But an adequate free lecture system cannot be indefinitely continued on a charity basis. Assuming a complete material equipment of school auditoriums, seats, lights, lanterns, slides, electrical fittings, screens, and the rest,—and ours is far from being complete,—there is a constant expense for lighting, printing, operation, and supervision; and above all, the lectures and music, which so far have cost nothing, will properly require an increasing appropriation if the service is to be extended to meet the present demand.

But more than this, the scope and the quality of the lectures should be improved. In order to do this, we must be able to call on the scholars and specialists of our universities. Several of these men, both from Stanford and the University of California, have already generously rendered volunteer service, but we need many more if we are to raise the standard of our lectures. A university is not merely a company of scholars; it is a nursery of knowledge, a place—it might almost be said the place—where truth is brooded over, and hatched into the world. It is difficult, almost impossible, for the man of affairs to look at scientific truth so steadily or to utter it so truly, as can the professional scholar who dwells amid academic shades in the traditional atmosphere of study. And truth is what the people desire; to offer them aught else were to insult their intelligence. The Bureau of Lectures should therfore be enabled to secure, preeminently, the assistance of a number of university lecturers for systematic courses as well as for single lectures. Nor does it seem right any longer to permit these men, some of them on lamentably small salaries, to give their evenings, and sometimes their afternoons, also, without compensation, in service and in travel to and from our city, meeting their own traveling expenses into the bargain. The city's departments of police, fire, libraries, and public health have each a fund whereby they serve the adult population. Why should education, the diffusion of knowledge that makes for better citizenship and in some degree tends increasingly to render other expenditures less necessary, why should education be confined to children? Goethe said: "The best is good enough for children." Let us say, The best is none too good for all.

ACKNOWLEDGMENT. It is with great pleasure that, on behalf of the Board of Education, I here record the names of the following ladies and gentlemen who have given lectures, addresses, or musical assistance without fee:—Mr. V. Arrillaga, Mr. B. R. Baumgardt, Lieut. P. W. Beck, U. S. A., Mr. Edward Berwick, Mrs. M. E. Blanchard, Dr. R. G. Brodrick, Mr. G. A. Clark, Mr. Herbert L. Coggins, Rev. D. O. Crowley, Mrs. Mary Dickson, Mr. Edw. J. Dupuy, Mr. Albert I. Elkus, Hon. Albert H. Elliot, Dr. W. C. Evans, Miss Lucy D. Hannibal, Mr. Wm. Greer Harrison, Hon. J. Emmet Hayden, Mr. Elias M. Hecht, Dr. Ernest B. Hoag, Prof. R. S. Holway, Mr. Francis Hope, Mr. M. Hrubanik, Mr. A. L. Jordan, Dr. David Starr Jordan, Hon. Wm. H. Jordan, Mrs. Edw. H. Kemp, Prof. A. L. Kroeber, Mlle. Blanche Leviele, Mr. Fred Maurer, Jr., Mr. Wm. J. McCoy, Mr. Matthew McCurrie, Rabbi Martin A. Meyer, Hon. Henry Payot, Mrs. C. W. Platt, Mr. Frank H. Powers, Hon. C. Wesley Reed, Mrs. Richard Rees, Mrs. Florenz Richmond, Mr. Riley R. Ross, Mr. Almon E. Roth, Mr. Alexander Russell, Mr. Ford E. Samuel, Mr. Maynard Shipley, Mr. Arturo Spozio, Mr. Roger Sprague, Prof. H. Morse Stephens, Mr. Robert P. Troy, Dr. Wm. C. Voorsanger, Mr. L. H. Weir, Col. Harris Weinstock, Mr. Roswell S. Wheeler, Mr. Hother Wismer, Supt. Will C. Wood, Mr. John P. Young.

In conclusion, I desire to thank the Board of Education, for support and assistance; the daily papers for numerous notices and articles; the members of the Advisory Commission on Lectures for their support and advice; the lecturers and musical artists for generous services; Messrs. Sherman, Clay & Co. for the loan of Steinway pianos on several occasions; Mr. George Kanzee for the use of his fine collection of lantern slides as well as for services; Mr. Edw. H. Kemp for services and the use of valuable appliances; Mr. G. O. Mitchell for constant support and skillful projection; and, in particular, Director Henry Payot, to whose devoted zeal, business acumen, and experience in lecturing the cause of Free Public Lectures in San Francisco owes a debt that can never be paid.

MILTON E. BLANCHARD,
Supervisor of Lectures.

APPENDIX A. Resolution creating a Lecture Bureau, introduced December 21, 1910, by Director Henry Payot:

> Whereas, The Board of Education believes that a system of free public lectures for adults is desirable, said lectures giving the results of the latest developments in science, history, hygiene, art, music, travel, and political science, etc., thereby encouraging reading and study to definite ends, and developing a wider and deeper interest in the schools on the part of the people, by making said schools and their equipment more effective social and community centers: Therefore, be it
>
> Resolved, That such a system, to be known as the Lecture Bureau, be and is hereby ordered instituted under the control of the Board of Education in the City of San Francisco, the lectures to be at once arranged for, and lecture centers established for the present at the following school buildings: Lincoln, Girls' High, Sheridan, Yerba Buena, Frank McCoppin, Burnett, Hancock, Mission Grammar, Monroe, Adams, Spring Valley, Sutro, Laguna Honda, Junipero Serra, Mission High, Glen Park.
>
> Also Resolved, That the following named persons interested in all that makes for the betterment of conditions in this City, be invited to act as Advisory Commission to this Board of Education in carrying out the purposes above mentioned, namely:

COMMITTEE ON LECTURES.

H. G. Vaughan....................President of the Board of Education
Mary W. Kincaid..........................Member Board of Education
Henry Payot ....Member Board of Education
Jas. E. Power.................................Member Board of Education
Alfred Roncovieri ....Superintendent of Schools
Milton E. Blanchard, Ph. D...................Supervisor of Lectures
G. O. Mitchell, A. B. ....Director of Lectures

ADVISORY COMMISSION ON LECTURES.

Raphael Weill
Harris Weinstock
John P. Young
Ernest S. Simpson
C. S. Stanton
James Rolph, Jr.
Walter Macarthur
Thos. E. Hayden
Willis Polk
Dr. Caroline Rosenberg
Paul Steindorff
Dr. Langley Porter
Dr. R. G. Brodrick
James Ferguson
A. J. Cloud

APPENDIX B. Classification of lectures given since the establishment of the bureau, in January to May, 1911:

> Geography and Travel, 35; History and Biography, 3; Science, 14; Health, 6; Social Topics, 5; Literature, 2; Music, 5: Total, 70 lectures. Total attendance, 25,236, being an average attendance per lecture of 360.

REPORT OF THE BOARD OF EXAMINATION.

The Board of Examination is composed of:

Superintendent Alfred Roncovieri, Chairman;
Deputy Superintendent W. B. Howard, Secretary;
Deputy Superintendent T. L. Heaton;
Deputy Superintendent A. J. Cloud;
Deputy Superintendent R. H. Webster.

The Board of Examination has conducted two examinations (October 1910 and April, 1911, according to law, of persons desirous of securing certificates. It has met monthly and forwarded its recommendation to the Board of Education.

Herewith is a resume of its work:

CERTIFICATES GRANTED ON CREDENTIALS.
HIGH SCHOOL.

Men	14
Women	16
	30

GRAMMAR.

Men	6
Women	80
	86

SPECIALS.

Men	16
Women	33
	49

RENEWALS.

Men	5
Women	38
	43

ON EXAMINATION.

GRAMMAR.

Men	0
Women	2
	2

REJECTED.

Men	6
Women	34
	40

SPECIALS.

Men	2
Women	17
	19

Number of Certificates issued	186
Number of Certificates renewed	43
Number of applicants rejected	40
Amount fees collected of applicants, including renewals	$538.00

REPORT OF THE PUBLIC SCHOOL TEACHERS' ANNUITY AND RETIREMENT FUND COMMISSIONERS.

San Francisco, July 30, 1911.

To the Honorable Board of Supervisors
in and for the City and County of San Francisco.

Gentlemen:

I have the honor to submit herewith the report on the Public School Teachers' Annuity and Retirement Fund for the fiscal year terminating June 30, 1911.

ALFRED RONCOVIERI,
Superintendent of Schools and Secretary Public School Teachers' Retirement Fund Commissioners.

RECEIPTS.

Balance in fund June 30, 1910, including $50,000—permanent fund—invested in 44 $1,000 San Francisco Fire Protection System 5% bonds	$55,154.64
Contributions by teachers under provisions of Annulty law	12,848.50
Absence money granted by Board of Education	3,000.00
Interest on Permanent Fund	2,200.00
Interest on Annuity Fund in Banks	279.34
Amount received from teachers retiring during the year	493.90
Total Receipts	$73,976.38

DISBURSEMENTS.

ANNUITIES TO RETIRED TEACHERS.

1910—		
October 1	$ 4,803.75	
1911—		
January 1	4,838.75	
April 1	4,828.75	
July 1	4,828.75	
	$19,300.00	
Clerical Service	271.25	
		$19,571.25
		$54,405.13

LIST OF ANNUITIES.

Limited revenue admits the payment of but fifty per cent (50%) of these annuities.

Date of Retirement.	Name.	Maximum or Fraction Thereof.	Annuity Per Month.	Annuity Per Quarter.
1895.				
Nov. 27,	Mrs. L. T. Hopkins	Max.	$50.00	$150.00
1896.				
Jan. 22,	Mrs. M. H. Currier	Max	50.00	150.00
April 24,	Miss V. M. Raclet	9/10	45.00	135.00
1897.				
Sept. 11,	Miss M. Solomon	Max.	50.00	150.00
Dec. 8,	Miss F. L. Soule	Max.	50.00	150.00
1898.				
Sept. 14,	Miss Kate Kollmyer	8/15	26.66⅔	80.00
1900.				
July 18,	Mrs. A. Griffith	Max.	50.00	150.00
July 25,	Miss K. F. McColgan	Max.	50.00	150.00
Aug. 1,	Miss L. M. Barrows	13/15	43.33⅓	130.00
Aug. 1,	Miss Annie A. Hill	Max.	50.00	150.00
Oct. 15,	Miss M. J. Canham	14/15	46.66⅔	140.00
1901.				
July 20,	Miss J. B. Gorman	Max.	50.00	150.00
Oct. 4,	Miss E. Murphy	9/10	45.00	135.00
1902.				
Jan. 2,	Miss R. B. Campbell	Max.	50.00	150.00
Jan. 2,	Miss L. S. Templeton	Max.	50.00	150.00
Jan. 2,	Mr. A. T. Winn	Max.	50.00	150.00
Sept. 28,	Miss Emma J. Miller	11/15	36.66⅔	110.00
1903.				
Feb. 17,	Mrs. B. A. Chinn	Max	50.00	150.00
Feb. 17,	Miss Lydia Hart	11/15	36.66⅔	110.00
Feb. 17,	Miss Christine Hart	Max.	50.00	150.00
Aug. 1,	Mrs. S. A. Miles	Max.	50.00	150.00
Aug. 1,	Mr. T. B. White	Max.	50.00	150.00
Sept. 1,	Miss A. E. Slaven	Max.	50.00	150.00
Oct. 15,	Miss L. Burnham	¾	37.50	112.50
1904.				
Aug. 1,	Mr. Elisha Brooks	Max.	50.00	150.00
Aug. 1,	Miss I. Patterson	Max.	50.00	150.00
Sept. 1,	Mrs. E. M. Whitcomb	Max.	50.00	150.00
1905.				
Jan. 16,	Miss E. G. Grant	Max.	50.00	150.00
March 1,	Miss M. A. Smith	⅔	33.33⅓	100.00
March 1,	Miss Jean Parker	Max.	50.00	150.00
March 1,	Mrs. T. C. Nicholl	Max.	50.00	150.00
March 1,	Mr. Charles Ham	Max.	50.00	150.00
March 1,	Miss R. Jacobs	Max.	50.00	150.00
March 1,	Mr. D. Lambert	Max. (Even)	25.00	75.00
1906.				
Feb. 1,	Miss M. E. Carson	Max.	50.00	150.00
Feb. 1,	Mrs. A. C. Taylor	Max.	50.00	150.00
Aug. 1,	Miss E. R. Elder	Max.	50.00	150.00
Aug. 1,	Mrs. C. Chalmers	Max.	50.00	150.00
Oct. 1,	Miss H. E. Whirlow	Max.	50.00	150.00
Dec. 1,	Mrs. V. Troyer	Max.	50.00	150.00
1907.				
April 1,	Miss Madge Sprott	½ (Even)	25.00	75.00
April 1,	Miss A. D. Miley	14/15	46.66⅔	140.00
April 1,	Miss O. O. McConnell	Max.	50.00	150.00
April 1,	Prof. A. Herbst	Max.	50.00	150.00
July 1,	Mr. C. W. Moores	Max.	50.00	150.00
Sept. 1,	Miss V. E. Bradbury	Max.	50.00	150.00
Sept. 1,	Miss Martha Stone	Max.	50.00	150.00
Sept. 1,	Miss N. C. Stallman	Max.	50.00	150.00
Sept. 1,	Mr. W. H. Edwards	Max.	50.00	150.00

1908.			
Jan. 1, Miss R. V. Claiborne	⅔	33.33⅓	100.00
Feb. 1, Mrs. M. E. Michener	Max.	50.00	150.00
Feb. 15, Mrs. F. A. Banning	Max.	50.00	150.00
March 1, Miss Rose Fay	11/15	36.66⅔	110.00
March 1, Mrs. Mary A. Hogan	14/15	46.66⅔	140.00
May 1, Miss Julia A. Danks	Max.	50.00	150.00
July 1, Miss Laura T. Fowler	Max.	50.00	150.00
Sept. 1, Miss Ruby A. Jewell	Max.	50.00	150.00
Sept. 1, Miss Regina Hertz	4/5	40.00	120.00
1909.			
Jan. 1, Miss A. T. Campbell	Max.	50.00	150.00
Jan. 1, Mrs. Mary J. Mayborn	Max.	50.00	150.00
Jan. 1, Miss C. M. Johnston	Max.	50.00	150.00
Aug. 1, Mrs. N. Seabrook	7/10	35.00	105.00
Aug. 1. Miss Rose E. Morgan	Max.	50.00	150.00
Aug. 1, Miss Jessie I. King	Max.	50.00	150.00
1910.			
Jan. 1, Paul A. Garin	Max.	50.00	150.00
Jan. 1, Miss E. R. Pettigrew	3/5	30.00	90.00
Jan. 10, Miss Anne B. Campbell	Max.	50.00	150.00
July 1, Miss E. S. Heney	Max.	50.00	150.00
Aug. 1, Mrs. R. H. Hazelton	Max.	50.00	150.00

SALARY SCHEDULE, 1911-1912.

OFFICE AND STOREROOM.

	Per Month.
Deputy Superintendents	$250.00
Secretary, Board of Education	150.00
Clerk, High School Board	50.00
Chief Clerk, Board of Education	200.00
Financial Secretary	180.00
Recording Secretary	170.00
Stenographers, Board of Education and Superintendent's Office	100.00
Messenger, Board of Education	100.00
Messenger, Superintendent's Office	95.00
Storekeeper	150.00
Assistant Storekeeper	90.00
Teamster (including use of two-horse team)	150.00
Telephone Exchange Operator	90.00
Superintendent of Building and Repair	175.00
Inspector of Boilers	125.00
Inspector of Water and Gas Supply	125.00
Chauffeur, Board of Education	125.00
Attendance Officer	83.35
Foreman, Supply Department	125.00
Supervisor of Lectures	50.00
Director of Lectures	40.00

DEPARTMENT AT LARGE.

Supervisor of Primary Grades	170.00
Supervisor of Drawing	160.00
Supervisor of Manual Training	160.00
Supervisor of Music in Elementary Schools	160.00
Supervisor of Penmanship	150.00
Supervisor of Cooking	135.00

Instructors in Physical Culture	100.00
First Assistant Supervisor in Music in Elementary Schools	135.00
Assistants in Manual Training	105.00
Assistant Supervisors in Drawing	100.00
Assistants in Cooking	85.00
Special Teachers of Modern Languages in 3rd, 4th, 5th, 6th, 7th and 8th Grades	100.00

HIGH SCHOOLS.

	Per Annum.	Per Month.
Principals of High Schools having less than 400 pupils enrolled, shall be paid a salary of	$2,700.00	$225.00
Principals having over 400, but under 700 pupils enrolled, shall be paid a salary of	3,000.00	250.00
Principals having more than 700 pupils enrolled, shall be paid a salary of	3,300.00	275.00
Vice-Principals in High Schools shall be paid	2,160.00	180.00
Heads of Departments shall be paid	2,040.00	170.00
Assistants in High Schools excepting Sewing, shall be paid, during their probationary term	1,500.00	125.00
Afterwards, at the rate of	1,680.00	140.00
The Salary of the Principal of the Polytechnic High School is hereby fixed at	3,000.00	250.00
Supervisor of Music, in High and Commercial Schools	1,620.00	135.00
Teachers of Sewing in High Schools	1,200.00	100.00
Assistants in Commercial Subjects in High Schools teaching Bookkeeping, Penmanship, Typewriting and Stenography, shall be paid during their probationary period, at the rate of	1,500.00	125.00
Afterwards, at the rate of	1,620.00	135.00
Teachers of Woodwork, and Ironwork in Polytechnic High School:		
1st Year	1,500.00	125.00
2nd Year	1,560.00	130.00
3rd Year	1,620.00	135.00
4th Year	1,680.00	140.00
5th Year	1,740.00	145.00
6th Year (maximum)	1,800.00	150.00

SAN FRANCISCO COMMERCIAL SCHOOL.

	Per Annum.	Per Month.
Principal	$3,000.00	$250.00
Vice-Principal	2,160.00	180.00
Assistants in Academic Subjects shall be paid during their probationary period at the rate of	1,500.00	125.00
Afterwards, at the rate of	1,680.00	140.00
Assistants in Special Subjects, shall be paid during their probationary period, at the rate of	$1,500.00	$125.00
Afterwards, at the rate of	1,620.00	135.00
Substitutes, when teaching, per day $4.00		

ELEMENTARY SCHOOLS.

The salaries of Grammar and Primary School Principals, in this department, for the Fiscal Year 1911-1912, shall be based on the enrollment, as per regular report, submitted on May 5th, 1911, but the salary of no principal shall be affected where the total enrollment is within twenty-five of the number required for a particular rating of a school.

GRAMMAR SCHOOL PRINCIPALS.

	Per Annum.	Per Month.
Schools in which the enrollment is 800 or over, and in which the number of grammar grade pupils is 325 or over, shall be ranked as Class I Grammar Schools, and the principals shall be paid a salary of	$2,460.00	$205.00
Schools in which the enrollment is 600, and less than 800, and in which the number of Grammar Grade pupils is 265, shall be ranked as Class II, Grammar Schools, and the principals shall be paid a salary of	2,340.00	195.00
Schools in which the enrollment is 400, but less than 600, and in which the number of Grammar Grade pupils is 225, shall be ranked as Class III, Grammar Schools, and the principals shall be paid a salary of	2,160.00	180.00
Owing to the exceptional classification of the Adams Cosmopolitan School, the same shall be, and is hereby ranked as a Class III Grammar School, during the fiscal year 1911-1912.		
Vice Principals, during their probationary term, shall be paid at the rate of	1,500.00	125.00
Afterwards, the salary shall be	1,620.00	135.00

PRIMARY SCHOOL PRINCIPALS.

	Per Annum.	Per Month.
In Primary Schools, having an enrollment of 700 or more pupils, the principal's salary shall be	$2,160.00	$180.00
In Primary Schools, having an enrollment of 400, and less than 700 pupils, the principal's salary shall be	1,800.00	150.00
In Primary Schools, having an enrollment of 150 pupils but less than 400, the principal's salary shall be	1,560.00	130.00
In Primary Schools, having an enrollment of less than 150 pupils, the principal's salary shall be	1,320.00	110.00
The following exceptions to the above schedule, are hereby ordered, as follows:		
Harrison School	1,560.00	130.00
Hunter's Point	1,440.00	120.00

CLASS TEACHERS.

	GRADES.			
	2nd, 3rd, 4th, 5th and 6th		1st, 7th and 8th	
Years of Service.	Per Annum.	Per Month.	Per Annum.	Per Month.
Probationary Term—1	$ 840	$70	$ 840	$ 70
Probationary Term—2	840	70	840	70
Beg. 1st year after probation	900	75	960	80
Beg. 2nd year after probation	960	80	1,008	84
Beg. 3rd year after probation	1,020	85	1,056	88
Beg. 4th year after probation	1,080	90	1,104	92
Beg. 5th year after probation	1,140	95	1,152	96
Beg. 6th year and thereafter	1,164	97	1,224	102

Maximum reached at the beginning of the 8th year of teaching.

EVENING SCHOOLS.

Principals—

	Per Annum.	Per Month.
Humboldt Evening High School	$1,320.00	$110.00
Commercial Evening School	1,320.00	110.00
Hamilton Evening School	1,020.00	85.00
Horace Mann Evening School	960.00	80.00
Lincoln Evening School	960.00	80.00
Roosevelt Evening School	780.00	65.00
Sherman Evening School	900.00	75.00
Washington Evening School	960.00	80.00
Head Teacher of Drawing Department in Humboldt Evening High School	1,260.00	105.00
Vice-Principal and Clerk in Lincoln Evening School	1,200.00	100.00
Teacher in Charge of Washington Evening High School	780.00	65.00
Teacher in Charge of Irving Scott Evening School	660.00	55.00
Teacher in Charge of Monroe Evening School	900.00	75.00
Teacher in Charge of Laguna Honda Evening School	660.00	55.00
Teacher in Charge of Bernal Evening School	900.00	75.00
Teacher in Charge of Portola Evening School	660.00	55.00
Assistants teaching High and Commercial classes, and assistants in Drawing Department in Humboldt Evening High and Commercial Evening Schools	780.00	65.00
Assistants in evening Schools	660.00	55.00

PARENTAL SCHOOL.

The salary of the Principal of the Parental School, is hereby fixed at	1,680.00	140.00
Assistants in the Parental School	1,320.00	110.00
The salary of the first assistant in Oral-Deaf is hereby fixed at	1,260.00	105.00
The salary of the second assistant in Oral-Deaf is hereby fixed at	1,164.00	97.00

SUBSTITUTES.

Day Substitutes and Teachers on the Day Unassigned List in Primary and Grammar Schools, when actually engaged in teaching, per day................$3.00
High School Substitutes, per day 5.00
Evening School Substitutes, per evening.............. 2.50
Substitutes in San Francisco Commercial School, per day 4.00

Principals not teaching classes shall not call for a substitute for the first day's absence of any teacher, but shall notify the Secretary of such absence at once.

NORMAL SCHOOL GRADUATES.

Since Section 1687 of the School Law provides that "Beginners shall be taught by teachers who have had at least two years' experience or by Normal School graduates,'' Normal School graduates who have successfully completed their probationary term as teachers of first grade classes, shall be allowed two years' experience as the equivalent of their Normal School training.

YARD ASSISTANTS.

In primary schools having an average daily attendance of 500 or over, the principal may recommend for the approval of the Board, an assistant to perform yard duty, who shall be paid therefor, ten ($10.00) Dollars per month in addition to the regular salary.

TEACHERS OF SINGING.

Five ($5.00) Dollars additional, per month, shall be paid to regular teachers in primary and grammar schools, holding special certificates in Music, and teaching singing; provided, however, that said teachers shall be required to teach, as far as practicable, every class in the school, in this subject.

TEACHERS OF LANGUAGES.

Five ($5.00) Dollars additional, per month, shall be paid to regular teachers in primary and grammar schools, holding special certificates and teaching English and French or English and German.

VACATION SALARY.

No teacher shall be paid any salary for the Christmas or Spring vacation, unless such teacher shall have been present for at least twenty (20) school days of the period immediately preceding the vacation.

Teachers shall be paid one-tenth of the salary of the Summer vacation, for each school month of the preceding fiscal year during which they shall have been present.

All rules in conflict with this schedule are hereby rescinded and annulled.

JANITORS.

Janitors shall be paid five ($5.00) dollars per room up to and including ten rooms, and $4.50 per room thereafter.

This shall not apply to the janitorial service in buildings where more than one janitor is employed, or in schools of less than 4 rooms.

FINES AND DEDUCTIONS.

See Rules of the Board of Education.

GENERAL INSTRUCTIONS.

A probationary term of two years must be served by every teacher elected into this department, and by every teacher elected or promoted to the position of principal, vice-principal, head of department, or high school assistant.

No increase in salary under this schedule shall be allowed until after a recommendation by the Superintendent and confirmation by the Board of Education in the case of each teacher serving a probationary term.

Experience outside of this department shall not be counted in fixing the salary of any teacher during the fiscal year 1911-1912 as this schedule permits the maximum salary to be reached after seven years of teaching.

No person shall be appointed Head of a High School Department, nor after the fiscal year 1910-1911, continued in that position, unless such person shall have at least one assistant under his or her supervision.

A Vice-Principal when acting in the capacity of Principal for more than one day in any calendar month, shall receive the salary of the Principal whose place he or she is temporarily filling.

Teachers' annual salaries shall be paid in twelve equal installments, one installment for each month in the calendar year.

Salary shall be computed from the time a teacher is appointed to a probationary class.

In classes consisting of two grades, the salary of the higher grade shall be paid when the average attendance in the higher grade equals or exceeds two-fifths of the average attendance for the class; provided, that when the average attendance of the entire class is less than forty, the salary of the lower grade shall be paid.

When there are more than two grades in a class, the Board will determine the salary of the teacher—A AND B DIVISIONS OF ANY GRADE SHALL CONSTITUTE ONE GRADE.

In all schools consisting of more than 4 classes, the minimum average daily attendance per primary class, exclusive of first grades and classes of more than 2 grades, shall be 40; and the minimum average daily attendance per grammar class, shall be forty-five.

AVERAGE ANNUAL SALARIES.

	Male.	Female.
Superintendent of Schools (1)	$4,000.00	
Deputy Superintendents of Schools (4)	2,820.00	
School Directors (4)	3,000.00	$3,000.00
Principals of High Schools (5)	3,000.00	
Principals of Primary and Grammar Schools	2,142.00	1,780.00
Teachers in High Schools	1,803.20	1,597.24
Teachers in Grammar Schools	1,336.00	1,197.15
Teachers in Primary Schools		1,118.24
Teachers in Evening Schools	730.50	620.40
All Teachers, Principals and Superintendents (except substitutes)		1,217.95

ANNUAL SALARIES AND NUMBER OF TEACHERS RECEIVING EACH.

Teachers		Salaries	Teachers		Salaries
1	at	$3,300	1	at	1,260
3	at	3,000	283	at	1,224
1	at	2,700	23	at	1,200
5	at	2,460	347	at	1,164
9	at	2,340	7	at	1,152
2	at	2,240	17	at	1,140
18	at	2,160	2	at	1,104
26	at	1,980	12	at	1,080
4	at	1,920	8	at	1,020
17	at	1,800	16	at	960
57	at	1,620	21	at	900
26	at	1,560	93	at	840
23	at	1,500	1	at	780
10	at	1,440	38	at	720
8	at	1,344	49	at	600
4	at	1,320			
19	at	1,284	1,151	average	$1,216

There were on an average, 57 substitutes who were paid about $51,000 for the year, or an average of nearly $895.00.

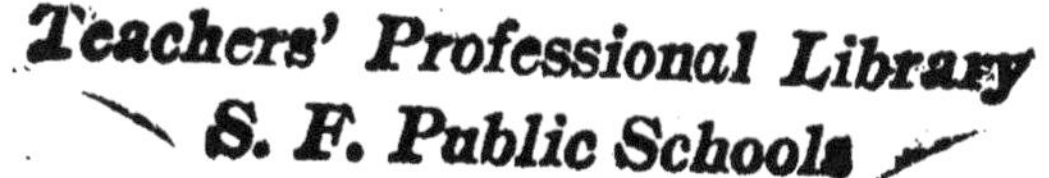

NAMES AND LOCATION OF SCHOOLS AND DESCRIPTION OF SCHOOL PROPERTY.

CLASS "A"

Designates a strictly fireproof building with steel frame concrete or tile floors or partitions, brick or stone or concrete walls.

"SPECIAL CONSTRUCTION"

Designates a building with fireproof stairways, concrete basement walls with concrete first floor, wood frame above with metal lath and plaster interior and exterior, metal frame and sash.

"CLASS C"

Designates a steel frame with exterior brick walls, fireproof stairways and wooden joists and partitions.

Adams Grammar School—Eddy street, between Van Ness avenue and Polk street, 2-story, 14-room and basement Class "C" building. Now in course of construction. Appropriation, $105,500.00. Lot in Western Addition, Blk. 62, 120 x 137½ feet.

Agassiz Primary School—Frame building; cost $31,500; eighteen rooms; Bartlett street, between Twenty-second and Twenty-third streets; lot in Mission block 136, 150x250 feet, occupied also by Horace Mann Grammar school. On May 9, 1902, additional lot, southwest corner Twenty-second and Bartlett streets, S. 55 feet by W. 85 feet, was purchased from S. J. Hendy, December 28, 1908, from H. J. Koepke a lot in Mission Block 136, $5,000; March 19, 1909, from Johanna Sheehan, W. line of Bartlett street 255 feet S. to Twenty-second street, S. 25 feet by W. 125 feet Mission, block 136, $4,500; December 6, 1909, from G. W. Wepfer, lot W. line of Bartlett street, 205 feet S. of Twenty-second street, S. 25 by W. 125 in Mission, block 136, $7,000.

Bay View Grammar School—New building of 18 rooms and assembly hall, Class "A". Costing nearly $117,000.00. On July 10, 1905, lot in Silver Terrace tract, block C, was purchased from Allen Riddell for $10,250. Commencing at the corner formed by the intersection of the southerly line of Bay View avenue and the easterly line of Flora street, and running thence easterly along said southerly line of Bay View avenue 200 feet to the westerly line of Pomona street; thence at a right angle southerly 350 feet; thence at a right angle westerly 200 feet to the easterly line of Flora street; thence northerly along said line of Flora street 350 feet to the southerly line of Bay View avenue and point of commencement. Recorded in Book 2, 124 of Deeds, page 60. School located on Bay View avenue and Flora street.

Bergerot Primary School—New building, 12 rooms; cost $37,000; Twenty-fifth avenue and California street, block 95, 150x240 feet.

Bernal Grammar School—Frame building, 16 rooms; cost $30,560; Courtland avenue, between Andover avenue and Moultrie street. Lot in Gift Map No. 2, 140x148 feet 8½ inches. October 17, 1908, from Elizabeth S. Ford, lots Nos. 17, 19, 21 and 23, Gift Map No. 2, $2,600. January 15, 1909, lot on corner of Andover and Jefferson avenues, $2,600.

Bryant Cosmopolitan Grammar School—Bryant street, between Twenty-second and Twenty-third; 2-story, 18-rooms and basement; "Special Construction'' building. Occupied by Board of Education June 9, 1910; cost approximately $105,000.00. Lot in Mission block 147, between Twenty-second and Twenty-third streets, Bryant and York streets, 150x200 feet.

Buena Vista Primary School—Frame building, 13 rooms; costing $21,867.00. Bryant street, between Eighteenth and Nineteenth streets. Lot on Potrero, block 39, 100x200 feet.

Burnett Primary School—Fourteenth Avenue South, near Railroad Avenue, 2-story, 12-room and basement ''Frame-Cement and Plaster'' building. Now in course of construction. Appropriation $52,500.00. Lot in South San Francisco Homestead, block 289. Lot 1, 75x100 feet, and additional lot purchased from Cecilia Wright, August 26, 1903, for $500, South San Francisco Homestead. Commencing at a point on the southwest line of Fourteenth Avenue South; distant 150 feet northwesterly from the northwesterly line of L Street South; thence northwesterly along Fourteenth Avenue South 32½ feet by uniform depth of 100 feet. September 27, 1909, from Martha A. Stapleton; commencing S. W. line Fourteenth avenue S. 182 feet 6 inches, N.W. on L. S. N.W. 42 feet 6 inches by S.W. 100 feet, Block 289, S. S. F. Homestead and R. R. Association, $1,750. August, 1910, lot in Homestead Association, block 189; $5,500.

Clement Primary School—Noe and Thirtieth streets; 2-story, 15-room and basement ''Special Construction'' building. Occupied by Board of Education, March 20, 1911. Cost approximately $99,000. May 3, 1909, from Ellen S. McGowan and E. Connors, lot west line of Noe street 26½ feet north of 30th street, north 25 feet by west 105 feet in Horner Addition, block 172, $1,500. April 5, 1909, from Ellen S. McGowan and Delia Williams, lot southwestern corner Noe and Day streets, 105 feet by south on Noe street 26½ feet in Horner Addition, block 172, $6,000. April 12, 1909, from Ellen S. McGowan, west line Noe street, 25½ feet south of Day street, south 150 feet by west 105 feet, south 51½ feet; by west 50 feet by north 228 feet by east 50 feet by south 26⅛ feet; thence east 105 feet, Horner Addition, block 172, $16,600. May 24, 1909, from W. E. Smith and Ellen McGowan, lot northwest corner Noe and 30th streets. North 26½ feet by west 105 feet, Horner Addition, block 172, $2,150. June 1, 1909, from Ellen S. McGowan and Joe Gottwald, lot south line of Day street 155 feet west of Noe street, west 25 feet by south 228 feet to the north line of 30th street in Horner Addition, block 172, $5,400.

Clement Cooking and Manual Training Center—Temporary frame building, 6 rooms. Geary near Jones street. Lot in block 253, 77½x137½ feet; additional lot commencing at a point on the southerly line of Geary street, distant 137 feet 6 inches westerly from the southwest corner of Geary and Jones streets; thence northerly along said line of Geary street, 25 feet by south 137 feet 6 inches in depth, being a portion of 50 vara block 253. Purchased from S. L. and Mabel V. Starr, August 14, 1905, for $27,000. Recorded in Book 2, 134 of Deeds, page 98.

Cleveland Primary School—Persia, between Moscow and Athens; 2-story, 14-room and basement ''Special Construction'' building. Now in course of construction. Appropriation $61,500. January 11, 1909, from Annie M. Creighton, lot northwest corner of Moscow street and Persia avenue, 100 feet by 300 feet, $6,500. February 15, 1909, from William McCall, lot in Excelsior Homestead Association. block 73, northeast corner Persia avenue and Athens street, 100 feet on Persia avenue by 300 feet on Athens street, $6,750.

Columbia Grammar School—Cost $30,300; frame building, 18 rooms and three portable rooms. Florida street, between Twenty-fifth and Twenty-sixth streets. Lot in Mission, block 178. Lot No. 1, 100x200 feet; lot No. 2, 50x100 feet.

Cooper Primary School—Temporary frame building, 15 rooms. Greenwich street, between Jones and Leavenworth streets, lot in block 237, 137½x137½ feet.

Crocker Grammar School—Frame building, 20 rooms; cost $26,547; Page street, between Broderick and Baker streets. Lot in block 523, W. A., 137½x 137½ feet. Additional lot purchased from W. J. Hawkins May 16, 1905, for $2,750. Commencing at a point on the southerly line of Page street, distant 96 feet 10½ inches, easterly from the easterly line of Baker street; thence easterly 25 feet by uniform depth of 110 feet.

Denman Grammar School—Pierce street, between Fell and Hayes; 2-story, 18-room and basement Class "A" building. Now in course of construction. Appropriation $153,000. May 17, 1909, from the Edwin Barron estate, lot northeast corner Fell and Pierce streets, 137 feet 6 inches on Fell street by 137 feet 6 inches on Pierce street, Western Addition, block 379, $29,118. October 18, 1909, from P. J. Stuparich and H. Adams, lot southeast corner Pierce and Hayes streets, 137½ by 137½, $37,125. June 13, 1910, from Emery B. Hopkins, lot N. side of Fell street, 137 feet 6 inches E. from E. line of Pierce street, 55 feet by 137½ feet, W. A. block 379, $9,500.00. September, 1910; 2 lots in W. A. block 379, $13,100.00.

Douglass Primary School—Cost $28,787; frame building, 11 rooms. Corner Nineteenth and Collingwood streets. Lot in Horner's Addition, 135x113 feet. June 27, 1910, from Alfred H. Grant, lot east line of Nineteenth street, 113 feet west of Collingwood street, west 30 feet by south 135 feet, Horner's Addition block 194, $4,500.00. On Nineteenth street, 143 feet west of Collinwood street. West 40 feet x South 135 feet, Horner's Addition block 194, $6,250.00.

Dudley Stone Primary School—Frame building, 16 rooms; cost $28,755; Haight street, between Lott and Masonic avenues, lot in block 657, W. A., 137½x137½ feet. August 12, 1908, from E. L. Pritchard; consideration $6,000. Lot on south line of Haight street 112 feet 6 inches west of Central avenue, west 25 feet by 137 feet 6 inches being a part of Western Addition, block 657. August 12, 1908, from J. L. Pritchard, out of School Fund, lot south line Haight street 112 feet 6 inches west of Central avenue, west 25 feet by 137 feet 6 inches, Western Addition block 657, $6,000.

Edison Primary School—Frame building, 10 rooms; cost $27,936; Church and Hill streets. Lot in Mission, block 90, 101 feet 9 inches by 114 feet.

Emerson Primary School—Frame building, 20 rooms; cost $28,155; Pine street, between Scott and Devisadero streets. Lot in block 460, W. A., 137½x 137½ feet.

Everett Grammar School—Frame building, 16 rooms; cost $24,132; five additional rooms are rented. Sanchez street, between Sixteenth and Seventeenth streets. Lot in Mission, block 95, 125x160 feet. A lot of land 28x160 feet on Sanchez street north of and contiguous to the present site of the Everett Grammar school, $10,000. November 29, 1909, from Frank L. Roseneau, lot east line of Sanchez street 202 feet south of Sixteenth street south 28 feet by east 80 feet, in Mission block 95, $6,900.

Fairmount Grammar School—Frame building, 12 rooms. Chenery street, near Randall street, five portable rooms on premises. Lot in Fairmount tract, block 29, lot 1, 112x125 feet; lot 2, 62x175 feet.

Franklin Grammar School—Eighth, between Bryant and Harrison; 2-story, 14-room and basement "Special Construction" building. Now in course of construction. Appropriation $85,500.00. Lot in 100 vara block 410, 140x275 feet.

Frank McCoppin Primary School—Seventh avenue, between B and C; 2-story, 18-room and basement "Special Construction" building. Occupied by Board of Education, October 24, 1910. Cost approximately $105,000.00 Lot in block 375, west of Sixth avenue, 150x240 feet. April 5, 1909, from Elizabeth M. Strand, lot west line Sixth avenue 200 feet south of B street, south 25 feet by west 120 feet O. L. block 375, $2,000. April 16, 1909, from Robert Bennett, lot east side Seventh avenue 200 feet south of B street, south 25 feet by east 100 feet O. L. block 375, $7,500.

Fremont Grammar School—Frame building, 16 rooms; cost $35,873; McAllister street, between Broderick and Baker streets. Lot in block 530, W. A., 137½x137½ feet. Additional lot (No. 1) purchased from Herman Murphy, January 3, 1902, for $3,250. Commencing at a point on the northerly line of McAllister street, distant 112½ feet westerly from the westerly line of Broderick street; thence westerly 25 feet by uniform depth of 137 feet 6 inches. Recorded in book 1, 947 of Deeds, page 102; additional lot (No. 2) purchased from Owen McHugh, July 1, 1902. Commencing at a point on the northerly line of McAllister street, distant 96 ft. 10½ inches easterly from the easterly line of Baker street, running thence easterly 25 feet, by uniform depth of 137 feet 6 inches. Recorded in Book 1, 962 of Deeds, page 138.

Garfield Primary School—Filbert and Kearny; 2-story, 19-room and basement "Special Construction" building. Occupied by Board of Education, November 21, 1910. Cost approximately $107,500.00. Lot in block No. 82. Corner Filbert and Kearny streets; 137½x137½ feet. Additional lot adjacent in litigation. July 28, 1908, from Annie M. Gallagher and Mary B. Waller, lot on north line of Filbert street, distant 137 feet 6 inches west from Kearny street; thence west on Filbert street 68 feet 9 inches by 137 feet 6 inches, being a part of 50 vara lot No. 461 and 50 vara lot No. 82, $8,000. From Charles Huth, November 2, 1908, south line of Greenwich street, between Kearny and Dupont streets, 25 feet square, block 82, $750. November 2, 1908, from Charles Kosta, rear portion of lot adjoining above 25 feet square, $550. West line of Kearny street 112 feet 6 inches south from Greenwich; thence south along west line of Kearny street 25 feet; thence at right angles west 87 feet 6 inches; thence at right angles north 25 feet; thence east 87 feet 6 inches, purchased from the Hibernia Saving and Loan Society July 10, 1903, $850.

Girls High School—Scott street, between Geary and O'Farrell; 2-story, 20 class-rooms and basement, Class "C" building. Appropriation $350,000.00. Plans being prepared. Temporary frame building completed at a cost of $16,000.00 Scott street, near Geary stret. This school is not built on school property, but on property belonging to the city, and which originally formed a part of Hamilton Square. In 1870 the Board of Education obtained permission to use a portion for the erection of school buildings. Lot 275 feet front on Scott street, 341 feet 3 inches on Geary and O'Farrell streets.

Glen Park Grammar School—New frame building, 12 rooms, costing $42,500, San Jose and Joost avenues. Additional lot purchased from the estate of John Pforr, May 20, 1905, for $5,600. Mission and Thirtieth Extension Homestead Union. Beginning at the corner formed by the intersection of the southwesterly line of Berkshire street with the southeasterly line of Lippard avenue; thence southwesterly along Lippard avenue 400 feet; thence at right angles southeasterly 200 feet to the northwesterly line of Fulton avenue; thence at right angles northeasterly 400 feet along Fulton avenue to the southwesterly line of Berkshire street; thence at a right angle northwesterly along Berkshire street to the point of beginning, being all of block 3, Mission and Thirteenth Street Extension Homestead Union. Recorded in Book 2, 125 of Deeds, page 76.

Golden Gate Primary—New building; 12 rooms, Class "C", costing $73,533. Golden Gate avenue, between Pierce and Scott streets. Lot in block 433 W. A., 100x137½ feet. Additional lot purchased from Fred L. Hansen, July 20, 1905, for $4,375. Commencing at a point on the northerly line of Golden Gate avenue, distant thereon 68 feet 9 inches, westerly from the westerly line of Pierce street; thence westerly 25 feet, by uniform depth of 137 feet 6 inches. Additional lot (No. 2) purchased from Margaret Poyelson, June 28, 1905, for $8,856. Commencing at a point on the northerly line of Golden Gate avenue, distant thereon 93 feet 9 inches, westerly from the westerly line of Pierce street; thence westerly 43 feet 9 inches, by uniform depth of 137 feet 8 inches. Additional lot (No. 3) purchased from Gustave A. DeManiel, June 14, 1905, for $12,462. Commencing at a point on the northerly line of Golden Gate avenue, distant 137 feet 6 inches, westerly from the westerly line of Pierce street; thence westerly 37 feet 6 inches, by uniform depth of 137 feet 6 inches.

Grant Primary School—Frame building, 8 rooms; cost $18,499; Pacific avenue, between Broderick and Baker streets. Lot in block No. 546, W. A., 137½x137½ feet.

Grattan Primary School—Shrader street, between Alma and Grattan; 2-story, 16-room "Frame" building. Now in course of construction. Appropriation $76,500. Additional lot purchased from the Pope Estate Co., for $28,500. Recorded in Book 2, 130 of Deeds, page 204. Western Addition, block 874. Commencing at the point of intersection of the southerly line of Grattan street with the easterly line of Shrader street; thence easterly along Grattan street 203 feet 7¾ inches; thence at a right angle southerly 249 feet to the northerly line of Alma street; thence at a right angle westerly and along said line of Alma street 203 feet 7¾ inches to the easterly line of Shrader street; thence at a right angle northerly 249 feet 11 inches to the southerly line of Grattan street, and point of commencement.

Haight Primary School—Frame building, 13 rooms; cost $23,488; Mission street, between Twenty-fifth and Twenty-sixth streets. Lot in Mission block 183; 150x117½ feet.

Hamilton Grammar School—Frame building, 17 rooms; cost $27,650; Geary street, between Scott and Pierce streets. (See Girls' High School).

Hancock Grammar School—Filbert street, between Jones and Taylor; 2-story, 18-room and basement Class "A" building. Now occupied by Board of Education. Cost approximately $164,000. Lot in block 208, 100x120 feet. December 21, 1908, from R. H. McColgan and Mary E. Russell, north line Filbert street, 110 feet west from Taylor, west 60x120 feet, 50 vara lot No. 208, $10,800.

Harrison Primary School—Jamestown avenue, between Railroad and Jennings; 1-story, 6-room and basement "Special Construction" building. Occupied by Board of Education, May 15, 1911. Cost approximately $19,000. All of block 584, Bay View Tract, Sub. 2, bounded by Railroad avenue, J street South, Thirty-fourth avenue South, and Thirty-fifth avenue South, except lot south line of Thirty-fourth avenue South, 100 feet west of J street, S. W. 50xS. 100 feet, $10,000.

Hawthorne Primary School—Frame building, 11 rooms; cost $11,500; Shotwell street, between Twenty-second and Twenty-third streets, lot in Mission block 138, 122½x122½ feet.

Hearst Grammar School—Frame building, 25 rooms; cost $25,007; corner Fillmore and Hermann streets, lot in block 374 W. A., 137½x137½ feet.

Henry Durant Primary School—Frame building, 12 rooms; cost $18,294; Turk street, between Buchanan and Webster streets, lot in block 281 W. A., 137½x120 feet.

Horace Mann Grammar School—Frame building, 20 rooms; cost $33,149; Valencia street, between Twenty-second and Twenty-third streets. (See Agassiz Primary). December 28, 1908, from Moore Investment Company, commencing 205 feet south from Twenty-second street, thence south on Valencia street 37½ feet by 125 feet, Mission block No. 136, $15,000.

Hunter's Point Primary School—Temporary frame building of 2 rooms. Eight avenue, between C and D streets. (Lot is leased).

Irving M. Scott Grammar School—Frame building, 20 rooms; cost $35,360; Tennessee street, near Twenty-second. Lot in Potrero, block No. 373, 150x200 feet.

Jackson Primary School—Temporary portable frame building, 6 rooms. Oak and Stanyan streets (Lot is leased).

James Lick Grammar School—Frame building, 14 rooms; cost $21,877; Noe and Twenty-fifth streets. Lot in Horner's Addition, block No. 163, 114x116 feet. November, 1910, additional lot, $5,600.

Jean Parker Grammar School—Broadway, between Powell and Mason streets; 2-story, 18-room and basement Class "A" building. Now in course of construction. Appropriation $171,900. Lot in block No. 157. Lot 1, 65 feet 2 inches by 137½ feet; lot 2, 30x91 feet 8 inches; lot 3, 39 feet 9 inches by 91 feet 8 inches. December 28, 1908, from Fannie Galloway, 227 feet 11 inches by 69 feet 7 inches of lot in 50 vara, block 157, 91 feet 8 inches perpendicularly distant from north line of Broadway, $2,000. January 4, 1909, from the estate of Jose M. Jininez, north line of Broadway, 137 feet east from east line of Mason street; thence east on Broadway 34 feet 4 inches by 137 feet 6 inches deep, 50 varas, lot No. 167, $8,925. November 15, 1909, from Bernardo Fernandez, lot north line of Broadway 171 feet 10 inches east of Mason, east 38 by north 137 feet 6 inches, 50 vara, block 167, $9,750.

Jefferson Primary School—Temporary frame building, 6 rooms. Bryant and Seventh streets. Lot in block No. 397, 92½x275 feet.

John Swett Grammar School—McAllister street, between Gough and Franklin streets; 2-story, 16-room and basement Class "C" building. Now in course of construction. Appropriation $101,800.00. Lot in block No. 136, W. A., 137½x137½ feet. June 27, 1910, from Elizabeth M. Kreuz, lot south line of Golden Gate avenue 169½ feet west of Franklin street, west 27½ by south 120 feet, W. A. block 136, $11,000.

From Sara Patek, lot south line of Golden Gate avenue, 197 feet west from Franklin street, west 25 feet by south 120 feet, W. A. block 136, $9,750.

From Mary Mocker, lot south side of Golden Gate avenue, 222 feet west from Franklin street, 28x120 feet, W. A. block 136, $12,000.

July 5, 1910, from Veronica J. Porcher, lot on the south line of Golden Gate avenue, 137½ feet west from Franklin street, west 32 feet by south 137½ feet, W. A. block 136, $14,000. July 25, 1910, west 32 feet x south 137½ feet, W. A. block 136, $14,000.

August 15, 1910, from Alexander and Elizabeth Lynch, lot on south line Golden Gate avenue, 137½ feet east from Gough street, east 25 feet x south 137½ feet, W. A. block No. 136.

Junipero Serra Primary School—Holly Park avenue, between Highland and West Park; 2-story, 18-room and basement "Special Construction" building. Occupied by Board of Education, January 5, 1911. Cost approximately $87,000. July 12, 1909, from A. B. Ruggles, lots 31, 32, 33, 34, 35, 36, 37, 38, 39, 40. Block, 3, Holly Park tract, $13,700.

Lafayette School—Thirty-seventh avenue, near Point Lobos.

Laguna Honda Primary School—New building; cost $91,418.99; 14 rooms; brick, class B. Seventh avenue, between I and J streets. Lot in block No. 678, 150x240 feet.

Farragut Primary School—Holloway avenue, between Capitol and Faxon; 2-story, 18-room and basement "Special Construction" building. Occupied by Board of Education, March 29, 1911. Cost approximately $96,000. April 26, 1909, from John and Belle McCaffefy, lot east line of Faxon avenue, 100 feet south from Halloway avenue, south 37½ feet by east 112½ feet, lot 25, lot 19, Lake View, $1,025. April 26, 1909, from Spaulding & Neff, lots 19, 20, 21, 22, 23, half of lot 24, and lots from 26 to 41. inclusive, block 19, Lake View, $11,-512.50.

Lincoln Grammar School—Harrison street, near Fourth street; 1-story, 12-room "Frame-Cement-Plaster" building. Now in course of construction. Appropriation $85,500. Lot in block No. 374, 195x160 feet. Additional lot (1) purchased from Bertha Gunnison, February 9, 1906, for $4,250. Commencing at a point on the northwesterly line of Harrison street, distant thereon 275 feet, southwesterly on the southwest line of Fourth street, running thence southerly along said line of Harrison street; thence at a right angle northwesterly 85 feet; thence at a right angle northwesterly 85 feet to the north line of Harrison street from the point of commencement. Additional lot (2) purchased from Herman Scholten, December 18, 1905, for $2,800. Commencing at a point on the southeasterly line of Clara street, distant 275 feet southwesterly from the point of intersection of said southeasterly line of Clara street with the southwesterly line of Fourth street, running thence southwesterly along said southeasterly line of Clara street 25 feet; thence at a right angle southeasterly 75 feet; thence at a right angle northeasterly 25 feet; thence at a right angle northwesterly 75 feet to the southeasterly line of Clara street and point of commencement.

Longfellow (see West End Primary).

Lowell High School—Frame building, 21 rooms. Sutter street, between Octavia and Gough streets. Lot in block No. 158, W. A., 137½x120½ feet. November 29, 1909, from Ivan Treadwell, et al., the whole of Western Addition Block 667 bounded by Masonic avenue, Hayes, Ashbury and Grove streets, $116.500, on which will be built a 3-story, 60-room and basement Class "C" building. Now in course of construction. Appropriation $350,000.

Madison Primary School—Clay street, between Cherry and First avenue; 2-story, 14-room and basement "Special Construction" building. Occupied by Board of Education, May 24, 1910. Cost approximately $87,000. Lot in block No. 848, Western Addition, 137½x137½ feet.

Marshall Primary School—Temporary frame building, 15 rooms. Julian avenue, between Fifteenth and Sixteenth streets. Lot in Mission, block No. 35, 200x182 feet. (Also occupied by Mission Grammar school). July 13, 1908, from R. A. Archbishop of San Francisco, lot corner Nineteenth and Angelica streets (resolution 1426 and 1757, Board of Supervisors). Commencing intersection south line Nineteenth street with east line Angelica street, south 205 feet to Cumberland Place; thence east 183 feet by north 114 feet west 50 feet N. W., 118 feet 2½ inches to Nineteenth street, west 102 feet to point of commencement. Mission, block 72, $33,625.

Commencing at point of intersection of the south line of Nineteenth street with the east line of Angelica street, thence south along Angelica street 205 feet to the north line of Cumberland Place, thence east 183 feet, thence north 91 feet, thence at right angles west 50 feet, thence northwest 118 feet 2½ inches to a point in the south line of Nineteenth street, which is distant east 102 feet from the southeast corner of Nineteenth and Angelica streets; thence west on south line of Nineteenth street 102 feet to point of commencement, being a portion of Mission block 72 purchased from Rev. P. W. Riordan, Roman Catholic Archbishop of San Francisco, a corporation sale for $33,625, as alternative site for the Marshall Primary authorized by the bond issue September 29, 1903.

McKinley Primary School—Fourteenth and Castro; 2-story, 18-room and basement "Special Construction" building. Occupied by Board of Education, November 21, 1910. Cost approximately $109,000. Lot purchased from Jas. Irvine, August 14, 1905. Cost 35,000. Mission block No. 121. Commencing at the southwesterly corner of Fourteenth and Castro streets; thence westerly along the southerly line of Fourteenth street 320 feet; thence at right angle southerly 230 feet to the northerly line of Henry street; thence easterly along said last named line 320 feet to the westerly line of Castro street; thence northerly along said last named line 230 feet to the point of commencement.

Mission Grammar School—Mission, between Fifteenth and Sixteenth; 2-story, 19-room and basement Class "A" building. Occupied by Board of Education, January 26, 1910. Cost approximately $170,500. Land (See Marshall School).

Mission High School—Brick building, 25 rooms; costing about $173,000. 18th and Dolores streets. Mission block No. 35, 398x194 feet. Purchased in 1896 for $52,500. April 19, 1909, from Owen M. V. Roberts, lot in Mission block 85, south line of Dorland street 88 feet east of Church street, east 25 feet by south 100 feet $3,500. April 19, 1909, from J. and Winifred O'Donnell, lot south line Dorland street 138 feet southeast of Church street, southeast 25 feet by south 100 feet in Mission block 85, $5,225. April 19, 1909, from the Catholic Apostolic church, lot north line of Eighteenth street 112 feet east of Church street, east 25 feet by north 114 feet, $7,800. June 1, 1909, from Amelia Dorland and Leonora Son, lot in Mission block No. 85, southeast corner Dorland and Church streets, south 35 feet 8 inches by east 88 feet, $6,300. June 1, 1909, from Herman D. Junck, lot in Mission block 85 south line Dorland street, 138 feet east from Church street; thence 100 feet east, 25⅝ feet by north 100 feet; thence west 25⅝ feet, $17,000. June 1, 1909, from Jessie Hauser, lot east line of Church street 168 feet north of Eighteenth street, north 27 feet by east 88 feet, $10,000; also northeast corner Church and Eighteenth streets, 62 feet on Eighteenth street by 114 feet on Church street, Mission block No. 85, $17,000. June 28, 1909, from Eva Topper, lot east line Church street 141 feet north Eighteenth street, north 27 feet by east 88 feet Mission block 85, $11,085. October 4, 1909, from Ida G. Shade, lot north line Eighteenth street, 137 feet east of Church, east 25 by north 114 feet, $9,000. From James A. Symon, lot north line Eighteenth street, 62 feet east from east line of Church, east 25 by north 114 feet, in Mission block 85, $8,500. November 1, 1909, from David Dorward, lot south line of Church street, 114 feet north of Eighteenth street north 27 by east 88 in Mission block 85, $9,100. November 15, 1909, from James A. Symon, exec., north line of Eighteenth street, 87 feet east of Church street, east 25 feet by north 114 feet, $8,500.

Monroe Grammar School—New building; Class "C", costing $83,500. China avenue and London streets. Lot in block 14, Excelsior Homestead, 150x 100 feet. Additional lot purchased from Thomas Shewbridge, August 30, 1902, Excelsior Homestead, block No. 14. New lot, corner China avenue and Paris street, northwest 100 feet by northeast 150 feet, lot 4, block 14, Excelsior Homestead.

Moulder Primary School—Frame building, 10 rooms; cost $21,100; Page and Gough streets, lot in block No. 145, W. A., 137½x120 feet.

Noe Valley Primary School—Frame building, 15 rooms, cost $29,474. 24th and Douglass. Additional lot (No. 1) purchased from George and Christina Gies. Deed dated October 5, 1901. Horner's Estate, block 244. Commencing at a point out the west line of Douglas street, 139 feet north to Twenty-fourth street; thence north on the west line of Douglas street 25 feet by west 125 feet in depth. Additional lot (No. 2) purchased from Mary E. Gies. Deed dated October 7, 1901. Commencing at a point on the west line of Douglass street 114 feet north of Twenty-fourth street; thence north on the west line of Douglass street 25 feet by west 125 feet in depth. Additional lot (No. 3) commencing at a point on the west line of Douglass street, 64 feet north of Twenty-fourth street; thence north on Douglass street, 50 feet, by west 125 feet in depth from Mary Tobener, September 6, 1901. Additional lot (No. 4) purchased from James M. Curtin, deed dated September 6, 1901. Commencing at a point on the northwest corner of Twenty-fourth and Douglass streets; thence north 64 feet, west 125 feet, north 50 feet, west 51 feet 8 inches, south 114 feet, east 176 feet 8 inches. Additional lot (No. 5) purchased from Eliz. Overend for $2,050. Commencing at a point on the south line of Elizabeth street, 125 feet west of Douglass street; thence west on Elizabeth street, 51 feet 8 inches, by south 114 feet, in depth.

Ocean House Primary School—Frame building, 2 rooms; cost $1,401.58; corner Corbett road and Ocean avenue. Cost $1,401.58. Lot in San Miguel, 100 feet by 240 feet.

Oceanside **Primary** School—New frame building, 8 rooms, $38,000. Forty-second avenue and I street. Lot in block No. 714. 150 feet by 240 feet.

Oral School for **Deaf**—Temporary frame building, one room. McAllister street, between Octavia and Gough streets. (See Golden Gate Primary.)

Oriental Public School—Temporary frame building, 5 rooms. Clay street, near Powell street, 50 vara block No. 137.

Parental School—Temporary frame building, 3 rooms. Harrison street, near Tenth. Lot in Mission block No. 8. 137½ feet by 137½ feet.

Pacific Heights Grammar School—Frame building, 19 rooms; cost $31,270; Jackson, between Fillmore and Webster streets. Lot in block 318, W. A., 137½ feet by 137½ feet. May 17, 1909, from Mary W. Shannon, lot west line of Jackson street, 113 feet west from Webster street, west 24½ feet by north 90 feet, Western Addition, block 318, $11,500. June 1, 1909, from Lillie E. Lincoln, north side of Jackson street 112 feet east of Fillmore street, east 25½ feet by north 127 feet 8¼ inches, Western Addition, block 318, $12,000.

Parkside—On Taraval street, near Thirteenth avenue. Lot in O. L. block 1114, 150x240 feet; 1 room, frame building; value $1,700.

Peabody Primary School—Sixth avenue, between California and Clement streets; 2-story, 14-room and basement "Special Construction" building. Now in course of construction. Appropriation $76,500. Lot in block No. 176; 150x 240 feet.

Potrero—Temporary frame building; Potrero Nuevo Block 231, west line of Connecticut street; 125 feet north from Twentieth street; thence 150 feet by 200 feet from the Western Pacific R. R. Co., January 25, 1909; agreement in condemnation suit.

Polytechnic High School—Temporary frame building, 16 rooms. Frederick street, near First avenue. Lot purchased from the City Realty Company, July 31, 1905, for $65,000. Western Addition, block No. 740. Commencing at a point on the south line of Frederick street 121½ feet east from First avenue; thence in a southerly direction 175 feet; thence at a right angle easterly 1 foot 6 inches; thence at a right angle southerly 100 feet to a point in the north line of Carl street 151½ feet east of First avenue; thence easterly along Carl street 464 and 8-12 feet to a point 269 4-12 feet west of Willard street; thence northerly 278 5-12 feet to a point on the south line of Frederick street 226 11-12 feet west of Willard street; thence west along south line of Frederick street 505 10-12 feet to point of commencement.

(Main Building.) 3-story, 61-room, attic and basement. Class "C" building;

(Shop Building.) 2-story, 13-room, shops and drafting rooms, Class "A" building.

Appropriation $600,000. Contracts for construction of shop buildings awarded.

Portola (see South End Primary).

Redding Primary School—Temporary frame building, 12 rooms. Pine street, between Polk and Larkin streets. Lot in block 14, W. A., 200x120 feet.

Rincon Primary School—Temporary frame building, two rooms. Lots in 100 vara block 358; Silver street, between Second and Third streets. Lot No. 1, 88x70 feet; lot No. 2, 100x185 feet.

Roosevelt **Grammar** School—Frame building, 17 rooms, costing $31,216. First avenue, near Point Lobos avenue. Lot in Academy of Science block, W. A., block No. 647, O. L. R. 157 feet 7 inches by 240 feet. The Board of Education has permission to use this lot for school purposes.

San Francisco Commercial School—Grove street, between Polk and Larkin streets; 3-story, 31-room and basement Class "A" building. Occupied by Board of Education, December 14, 1910. Cost approximately $261,000. Lot in block 3, W. A., 137½x120 feet. January 18, 1909, from F. Siefke, north line Grove street 100 feet west of Larkin street, 37½ feet by 120 feet, Western Addition, block No. 3, $15,000. February 8, 1909, from Dorothea Fassman, west line of Grove street 112½ feet east from east line of Polk street, east 25 feet by 137½ feet, Western Addition, block No. 3, $9,800. June 21, 1909, from Chas. Worth, lot north line Grove street, 82½ feet east of Polk street, east 30 feet by north 120 feet, Western Addition, block No. 3, $12,000.

Sheridan Primary **School**—Capitol Avenue, between Farallones and Lobos; 2-story, 18-room and basement "Special Construction" building. Occupied by Board of Education, December 12, 1910. Cost $105,443. Lot in block S, Railroad

Homestead Association. 100 feet by 125 feet. Lot No. 7, May 10, 1909, from W. S. Benthame, lot northwest corner of Farallones and Capital avenue in block L, Railroad Homestead Association, $3,450. September 23, 1908, from Welthy and Wm. S. Stafford, north side of Minerva street 150 feet west of Plymouth street; thence west on Minerva street 50 feet by north 125 feet. November 29, 1909, from Adolph Mueller, Caroline Bauer, admx. Wm. T. and Edward Bauer, interest and improvement in lot southwest corner of Capitol avenue and Lobos street, 50 feet by 125 feet, in R. R. Homestead Association, block L, $6,300.

Sherman Primary School—Frame building, 14 rooms. Union street, near Franklin. Lot in block No. 117, W. A., 137½ feet by 137½ feet.

South End (now Portola) Primary School—Bacon street, between Berlin and Girard streets; 2-story, 18 rooms, "Special Construction" building. Occupied April 22, 1910. Cost $97,315.00. Lot in University Mound survey, 50 feet by 120 feet. Additional block purchased from P. J. Kennedy, August 22, 1905, for $5,000. University Mound survey, block 12. Commencing at a point formed by the intersection of the northwesterly line of Bacon street, in the southwesterly line of Girard street, running thence nortwesterly along Girard street 200 feet and thence at a right angle 240 feet to Berlin street; thence at a right angle southeasterly and along Berlin street 200 feet to the northwesterly line of Bacon street; thence at a right angle 240 feet to the southwesterly line of Girard street and point of commencement, being the southerly half of block No. 12, University Mound Survey.

Spring Valley Grammar School—Washington street, between Hyde and Larkin streets; 2-story, 14-room and basement Class "A" building. Now in course of construction. Appropriation $111,500. Temporary frame building, 9 rooms, Broadway, near Polk street. Lot in block 21, W. A., 137½ feet by 137½ feet. May 24, 1909, from Margaret and Catherine Matthews, lot south line of Jackson street 137 feet 6 inches east from Larkin street, east 68 feet 9 inches by 137½ feet, $15,250. From Samuel Polack, lot south line of Jackson street 137 feet 6 inches west of Hyde street, west 34 feet 4½ inches by 137 feet 6 inches, 50 vara block 302, $6,975. July 19, 1909, from Edward P. McGeeney, et al., lot south line Jackson, 171 feet 10½ inches, west of Hyde west 34 feet 4½ inches, by south 137 feet 6 inches, $9,100.

Starr King Primary School—Temporary frame building, 9 rooms, San Bruno avenue, near Twenty-fifth street. Commencing on the east line of Utah street 100 feet south from Twenty-fifth street, thence south on Utah street 100x200 feet in depth to San Bruno avenue, being lots 13, 14, 15, 16, 25, 26, 27, 28, in Potrero block No. 85.

Sunnyside Primary School—New class C building. Cost $30,000. Sunnyside block No. 219. Additional lots 10 and 24, inclusive, Sunnyside tract. Purchased from the Sunnyside Land Company, July 9, 1902. June 22, 1908, bought from Monarch Mutual Building and Loan Association sewer right of way for Sunnyside School portion of lot 23, Sunnyside, block 47, $400.

Sunset Primary School—Temporary frame building, 6 rooms. Thirteenth avenue and Kirkham street. Block No. 780. West of First avenue; 150 feet by 240 feet.

Sutro Grammar School—Thirteenth avenue, between California and Clement streets; 2-story, 18-room and basement "Special Construction" building. Occupied by Board of Education, July 25, 1910. Cost approximately $101,000. Lot in block 179; west of First avenue; 150x240 feet. January 18, 1909, from

F. C. Fish and J. J. Higgin, lot on west line Twelfth avenue 200 feet south from California street, 25 feet by 140 feet, in block 170, $7,100.

Visitacion Valley Primary School—Visitacion Avenue, between Leland and Schwerin streets; 2-story, 12 rooms, "Frame'' building, in course of construction; appropriation $47,500.

Washington Grammar School—New steel-brick building; 20 rooms and auditorium; Washington and Mason streets. Lot in 50 vara block No. 188; 137½x 137½ feet. Additional new lot No. 1; purchased from the estate of Louise C. Kauffman, March 10, 1905, for $7,500. Commencing at a point on the southerly line of Washington street, 137 feet 6 inches northerly from the southwest corner of Mason and Washington streets; thence southerly 137 feet 6 inches by west 34 feet 4½ inches, being a portion of 50 vara, lot 188. Additional new lot No. 2, purchased from Julie Dunnier and others, July 12, 1905, for $9,500. Commencing at a point on the southerly line of Washington street, distant 170 feet 10½ inches from the southwest corner of Mason and Washington streets; thence northerly 34 feet 4½ inches by south 137 feet 6 inches in depth, being a portion of 50 vara, lot 188.

Washington Irving Primary School—Temporary frame building, 6 rooms. Broadway, between Montgomery and Sansome streets. Lot in 50 vara block No. 47, 68¾x137½ feet.

West End (now Longfellow) Primary School—Corner Morse and Lowell streets; 2-story, 14 rooms and basement, ''Special Construction.'' Occupied January 3, 1911. Cost $66,500. Lot in West End Map. Block 23; 80x165 feet. March 1, 1909, from D. A. Helbing et al., lot southwest corner Lowell, Mission and Morse, 267 by 213, being lots 49, 50 and 51, West End Homestead, $9,250.

Winfield Scott Primary School—Building cost $42,206.43. Lombard street, between Broderick and Baker streets. Lot in block No. 553, W. A.; 137½x 137½ feet.

Yerba Buena Primary School—Building cost $59,206.43. Greenwich street, between Webster and Fillmore streets. Lot in block No. 325, W. A.; 137½x120 feet. February 23, 1909, from McEwen Bros., lot Webster and Greenwich streets west 137½ feet by 120 feet in Western Addition, block No. 235, $17,000. $30,000 of the above cost were contributed by the school children of the United States immediately subsequent to the Great Fire of 1906.

Ungraded School—Temporary frame building, 10 rooms (four additional rented rooms). Union street, near Kearny street. Lot in 50 vara block 62, 137½x137½ feet.

LIST OF UNOCCUPIED PROPERTIES BELONGING TO SCHOOL DEPARTMENT.

Lot in 50 vara block No. 220; northwest corner Bush and Taylor streets; 137½x137½ feet.

Lot in 50 vara block No. 286; Golden Gate avenue, near Hyde street; 110x137½ feet.

Lot in 100 vara block No. 348; Tehama street, between First and Second streets, irregular in size; about 118x155 feet.

Lot in 50 vara block No. 160; Powell street, between Washington and Jackson streets; 68¾x137½ feet.

Lot in 100 vara block 371; Fifth street, near Market street; 275x275 feet. Leased to Wise Realty Company (later merged into the Lincoln Realty Company) for thirty-five years, at a total rental of $2,835,000, as follows: for the first five years, a rental of $3,780 per month, and for the remaining thirty years, a rental of $7,245 per month.

Lot in Mission block No. 21; West Mission street, between Herman and Ridley streets; 133¾x137½ feet.

Lot in 50 vara block No. 118; corner Bush and Stockton streets; 137½x 137½ feet; 50 vara, lot 301.

Lot in Mission Block No. 72. Commencing at a point formed by the intersection of the southerly line of Nineteenth street with the easterly line of Angelica street, running thence southerly along said easterly line of Cumberland Place; thence easterly along said northerly line of Cumberland Place and Cumberland Place Extension 183 feet; thence at a right angle northerly 91 feet; thence at a right angle northerly 50 feet; thence in a northwesterly direction 118 feet 2½ inches to a point in the southerly line of Nineteenth street, which point is distant easterly 102 feet from the southeasterly corner of Nineteenth and Angelica streets; thence westerly along said southerly line of Nineteenth street 102 feet to the point of commencement. Purchased from P. W. Riordan, Roman Catholic Archbishop of San Francisco, for $33,625, as an alternate site for the Marshall Primary school. Recorded in Book 128 of Deeds, page 251, new series.

Lot in 50 vara block No. 119; Post street, between Grant avenue and Stockton streets; 70x122½ feet. Leased at an average of $911.42 per month.

Total rental, 35 years	$382,800.00
Average rental, per month	911.42

Graduated Rentals—

First 4 months of lease, per month	$ 250.00
Second 4 months, per month	300.00
Third 4 months, per month	350.00
Second year, per month	400.00
Third year, per month	450.00
Fourth year, per month	500.00
Fifth year, per month	550.00
Sixth year, per month	650.00
Seventh year, per month	700.00
Eighth year, per month	750.00
Ninth year, per month	800.00
Tenth year, per month	850.00
Eleventh year, per month	900.00
Twelfth year, per month	900.00
13th and 14th years, per month	950.00
15th year, per month	1,000.00
16th to 25th years, inc., per month	1,000.00
26th to 35th years, inc., per month	1,125.00

Lot in 50 vara block No. 182, on northeast corner Taylor and Vallejo streets; 137½x137½ feet.

Lot in 50 vara block No. 302, on Washington street, between Hyde and Leavenworth streets; 137½x137½ feet. (Site of new Spring Valley School.)

Lot in Mission Block No. 61, on Nineteenth street, between Mission and Howard streets; 137½x137½ feet, less 60 feet included in Capp street. Title in litigation.

Lot in block No. 29, W. A., on south side of Francisco street, between Larkin and Polk streets; 137½x137½ feet.

Lot in block No. 111, W. A., on south line of Bay street, between Franklin and Gough streets; 137½x137½ feet. In litigation.

Lot in block No. 123, W. A., on south line of Washington street, between Franklin and Gough streets; 137¼x137½ feet.

Lot in block No. 253, W. A., on south line of Geary street, between Jones and Leavenworth streets; 102½x137½ feet. (Present location of school repair shop.)

Lot in block No. 465, W. A., on north line of Jackson street, between Scott and Divisadero streets; 137½x137½ feet.

Lot in block No. 848, W. A., on south line of Clay street, between Cherry and First avenue; 137½x137½ feet.

West of First avenue and north of the Park, the School Department owns property as follows. (Appraised by experts appointed by Board of Supervisors):

(All not otherwise stated are 150x240 feet.)

Block 152; Thirty-first avenue, between California and Clement streets, $5,000.

Block 164; Nineteenth avenue, between California and Clement streets, $6,000.

Block 242; Forty-third avenue, between Point Lobos avenue and A street, $3,000.

Block 248; Thirty-seventh avenue, between Point Lobos avenue and A street, $4,000.

Block 254; Thirty-first avenue, between Point Lobos avenue and A street, $4,000.

Block 260; Twenty-fourth avenue, between Point Lobos avenue and A street, $3,000.

Block 266; Nineteenth avenue, between Point Lobos avenue and A street, $6,000.

Block 272; Thirteenth avenue, between Point Lobos avenue and A street, $6,000.

Block 278; Seventh avenue, between Point Lobos avenue and A street $7,000.

Block 339; Forty-third avenue, between B and C streets, $1,000.

Block 345; Thirty-seventh avenue, between B and C streets, $2,000.

Block 351; Thirty-first avenue, between B and C streets, $1,500.

Block 357; Twenty-fifth avenue, between B and C streets, $1,000.

Block 363; Nineteenth avenue, between B and C streets, $12,000.

Block 369; Thirteenth avenue, between B and C streets, $1,500.

Block 395; Sixteenth avenue, between C and D streets, $1,500.

Block 407; Twenty-eighth avenue, betwen C and D streets, $1,200.

Block 418; Twenty-ninth avenue, between C and D streets, $1,200.

Also west of First avenue and south of the Park, as follows:

(All not otherwise stated are 150x240 feet.)

Block 673; First avenue, between I and J streets; 107x178 feet, $5,000.

Block 690; Nineteenth avenue, between I and J streets, $3,000.

Block 696; Twenty-fifth avenue, between I and J streets, $800.

Block 702; Thirty-first avenue, between I and J streets, $1,000.

Block 708; Thirty-seventh avenue, between I and J streets, $700.

Block 775; Eighth avenue, between K and L streets, $3,500.

Block 786; Nineteenth avenue, between K and L streets, $2,000.

Block 792; Twenty-fifth avenue, between K and L streets, $700.

Block 798; Thirty-first avenue, between K and L streets, $700.

Block 804; Thirty-seventh avenue, between K and L streets, $700.

Block 810; Forty-third avenue, between K and L streets, $800.

Block 872; Thirteenth avenue, between M and N streets, $1,500.

Block 878; Nineteenth avenue, between M and N streets, $3,100.

Block 884; Twenty-fifth avenue, between M and N streets, $800.

Block 890; Twenty-first avenue, between M and N streets, $700.

Block 896; Thirty-seventh avenue, between M and N streets, $700.

Block 902; Forty-third avenue, between M and N streets, $700.

Block 952; Ninth avenue, between O and P streets; irregular, 147½x182 feet, $1,000.

Block 957; Thirteenth avenue, between O and P streets, $700.

Block 963; Nineteenth avenue, between O and P streets, $1,500.

Block 969; Twenty-fifth avenue, between O and P streets, $1,000.

Block 975; Twenty-first avenue, between O and P streets, $900.

Block 981; Thirty-seventh avenue, between O and P streets, $900.

Block 987; Forty-third avenue, between O and P streets, $1,000.

Block 1,038; Thirteenth avenue, between Q and R streets, $500.

Block 1,044; Nineteenth avenue, between Q and R streets, $1,500.

Block 1,050; Twenty-fifth avenue, between Q and R streets, $800.

Block 1,056; Thirty-first avenue, between Q and R streets, $800.

Block 1,062; Thirty-seventh avenue, between Q and R streets, $600.

Block 1,068; Forty-third avenue, between Q and R streets, $1,000.

Block 1,120; Nineteenth avenue, between S and T streets, $1,800.

Block 1,126; Twenty-fifth avenue, between S and T streets, $1,500.

Block 1,132; Thirty-first avenue, between S and T streets, $1,500.

Block 1,138; Thirty-seventh avenue, between S and T streets, $1,500.

Block 1,144; Forty-third avenue, between S and T streets, $1,500.

Block 1,186; Fourteenth avenue, between U and V streets; irregular 161x92½ feet, $1,000.

Block 1,191; Nineteenth avenue, between U and V streets, $1,500.

Block 1,197; Twenty-fifth avenue, between U and V streets, $1,500.

Block 1,203; Twenty-first avenue, between U and V streets, $1,500.

Block 1,209; Thirty-seventh avenue, between U and V streets, $1,000.

Block 1,215; Forty-third avenue, between U and V streets, $1,000.

Block 1,258; Nineteenth avenue, between W and X streets, $1,000.

Block 1,264; Twenty-fourth avenue, between W and X streets, $1,000.

Block 1,276; Thirty-seventh avenue, between W and X streets; irregular; 125 feet 10 inches by 240 feet, $700.

Block 1,282; Forty-third avenue, between W and X streets; irregular; 11 feet 2 inches by 240 feet, $100.

LOTS IN POTRERO.

Block 46; York street, between Fifteenth and Alameda streets; 100x200. Rented at $2 per month.

Block 127; Vermont street, between Eighteenth and Nineteenth streets; 120x 200 feet.

Block 149; Kansas street, north of Army street; 150x200 feet, $1,663.

Block 163; Rhode Island street, between Mariposa and Eighteenth streets; 100x200 feet. Rented $2 per month.

Block 226; Arkansas street, south of Twenty-third street; 150x200 feet, $832.

Block 287; Texas street, betwewen Twenty-third and Twenty-fourth streets; 150x200 feet.

Block 391; southwest corner Kentucky and Twentieth street; 150x200 feet.

Potrero block 254, O. L. R., also Potrero block 265, O. L. R., condemned and acquired by Western Pacific Railroad Company for $14,000.

OTHER OUTSIDE LOTS.

Precita Valley lands; Eve street, between Army and Adam streets; 150x32 feet.

S.Paul Tract Homestead; Berlin street, between Ordway and Ward streets; 85 feet and 2 inches by 120 feet.

December 21, 1908, from Joseph B. and Carlotta L. Keenan, all of block No. 132 of University Mound Homestead Association, excepting one lot 25 feet by 100 feet on Pioche street, and one on Cambridge street, 25x120 feet, $8,250.

WITHIN THE PRESIDIO WALL.

Block 553, W. A. Commencing on the north line of Lombard street, 137½ feet west from Broderick street; thence west on Lombard street, 137½ feet by 137½ feet in depth. Lot 2. Outside Land Reservation.

Block 810, W. A. Commencing on the north line of Broadway, 137½ feet west from Walnut street; thence west on Broadway, 137½ feet by 137½ feet in depth. Lot 2. Outside Land Reservation.

Block 841, W. A. Commencing on the north line of Pacific avenue, 137½ feet west from Maple street; thence west on Pacific avenue, 137½ feet by 137½ feet in depth. Lot 2. Outside Land Reservation.

REPORT OF MISS KATHERINE M. BALL, SUPERVISOR OF DRAWING

San Francisco, June 3, 1911.

Mr. Alfred Roncovieri,
Superintendent of Schools.

My Dear Sir:

In reply to your request for a report concerning the Drawing and Art in our city schools, I submit the following:

I am happy to inform you, that we are progressing in our work. Not only is there a marked growth in power, on the part of our children, but the aesthetic quality of their work is much improved.

Considering that the subject of Drawing and Art is given the minimum quantity of time, our results seem quite remarkable. An hour a week is a very short time, when so much is expected, notwithstanding that the subject continues consecutively for eight years. No matter how well graded a course of study may be, the instruction lacks continuity on account of the prevailing custom of transferring teachers from grade to grade, and from school to school.

That the percentage of classes in the city doing creditable work is much larger this year than ever before, is a source of great encouragement, and if it were possible to demand of incoming teachers the same knowledge of subject matter in Drawing as is required in other subjects they are obliged to teach, a greater uniformity of results would be possible in all the schools.

Public School Drawing and Art is elementary in character. That all certificated teachers can learn its principles and teach them successfully is proven by the work done by a large number of our present corps. A supervisor can plan the work, but to the body of teachers belongs the credit of successfully carrying out the given directions.

The drawing of the elementary schools is sometimes criticised by the upper schools. If our pupils cannot draw with the same degree of skill that they read and write, we should remember that the technique of any subject requires more than an hour a week. The results of art schools are acquired only after years of hard work—not on a basis of one hour a week, but of all the working hours of every day, while the student is at work.

Public School Drawing and Art is intended to be educational, not technical. It does not aim to produce draftsmen or artists. It really does not intend to teach drawing for the purpose of learning to draw. The latter is merely the result, the effect or consequence of the effort of thought expression, through graphic channels.

The real aim of this subject is to teach the pupil to see size, proportion and shapes in relation to space; to acquire a knowledge of structure and the geometrical principles involved; to discern beauty of form and color in nature and in art—developing intelligent discrimination; to calculate and plan so that the product will be true and useful; to work methodically and accurately, acquiring habits of order, patience, perseverance and conscientious effort, and to stay by a piece of work until it is finished.

Every drawing a pupil makes,—whether it is a representation of a plant, model, or a design for an applied purpose—is a construction, which first has to be planned and then executed, according to method. This requires serious thought and not only gives as fine mental training as any other subject in the curriculum, but it creates habits of thinking and working, which become a most valuable asset in life, whatever the vocation exacts.

Under the present conditions, we are able to do much for the child, but with increased facilities it might be possible to do more in accomplishing greater skill in technique.

One of the most important functions of the teaching of drawing is the discovery of the talented child, but as yet popular appreciation of the value of talent is very limited. The time will come when the nation will see the wisdom of fostering its genius and conserving for its own special benefit all kinds of native ability.

Ample provision should be made for the careful training—in a specially equipped school and under carefully prepared teachers—of all talented children.

Manual training high schools and polytechnic schools for older children abound, but the technical school for the younger children is yet to be established.

The development of the creative faculty should begin in the kindergarten and continued all through the school life. If it is neglected until the time of the high school it may be too late.

The industrial supremacy of a nation is dependent upon its trained and skilled workmen, and in the preparation of these workmen the public school should take an important place by giving a proper fundamental training.

California is frequently spoken of as the "Nursery of Genius." Why should not the city of San Francisco become this in reality, by making more favorable conditions for teaching the industries and their allied arts?

At the exposition of St. Louis we received the first award, and at Seattle the gold medal. Increase our time and equipment and we will promise you still greater results.

Respectfully submitted,

KATHERINE M. BALL,
Supervisor of Drawing.

REPORT OF THE DOMESTIC SCIENCE DEPARTMENT.

San Francisco, California, June 2, 1911.

Mr. Alfred Roncovieri,
Superintendent of Schools,
San Francisco.

My Dear Mr. Roncovieri:

I beg to submit the folowing report of the Domestic Science Department for the fiscal year 1910-1911.

The following table shows the location of the Cookery Centers, the names of the teachers in charge, the number of pupils enrolled, the cost of supplies and laundry, and the cost of supplies per pupil; also the number of visitors.

Center.	Teacher.	Average Monthly Enrollment.	Cost of Food Supplies and Laundry.	Cost of Supplies per Pupil.	Visitors, School Officials.	Visitors, Others.
Bay View	Miss Taber	71.5	$35.45	$0.487	1	90
Crocker	Miss Ballinger	317.1	130.95	.411	2	162
Glen Park	Mrs. Fenton	255.5	107.54	.457	0	161
Hamilton	Miss Martin	300.7	142.85	.467	2	62
Hearst	Miss Gray	271.8	100.95	.374	6	117
Horace Mann	Miss Tobiner	347.6	123.63	.342	7	100
Irving M. Scott	Miss Tabor	47.6	31.76	.661	0	85
Laguna Honda	Miss Tomlin	104.3	50.05	.561	2	73
Mission	Miss Congdon	308.3	127.10	.41	8	86
Monroe	Miss Tabor	184.7	47.85	.537	1	60
Sheridan (1 term)	Mrs. Fenton	53.5	19.65	.369	0	35
Sutro	Miss Tomlin	199.5	54.60	.269	3	154
Washington	Miss Woodward	311.	136.50	.50	0	69

Average monthly enrollment 2,773.1
Cost of supplies $1,108.88
Average cost of supplies per pupil .... .431
Number visits from school officials 32
Number visits from others 1,254
—— 1,286

PARENTAL SCHOOL LUNCH ROOM

Mrs. Mathilde Gerhardt in Charge.

Average number of meals served daily 48
Average cost per meal (supplies) .... $ 0.024
Cost of supplies to School Department 129.017
Cost of supplies to Parental School 91.65

$220.67

Average daily attendance in cooking classes	17
Average number of baths supervised (daily)	17
Cost of supplies for Domestic Science Department	$1,108.88
Cost of supplies for Parental School	220.67
	$1,329.55

NEW COOKERY CENTERS.

Cooking Centers were equipped this year in the recently completed Mission, Sutro, and Sheridan Grammar Schools. The equipment is good and the rooms are attractive.

The Hancock Grammar School is now completed, and the cooking laboratory should be made ready for the Fall Term.

I would suggest that the use of the cooking laboratory at the Washington School be discontinued, and that the equipment be transferred to the Hancock School. The Washington School, being a boys' school, does not need a cooking laboratory.

The new Denman and Franklin Schools are nearing completion and will be equipped for domestic science.

Plans have also been drawn for special buildings to house the Domestic Science and Manual Training departments at the Roosevelt, James Lick, and Pacific Heights schools. When these six proposed centers are ready, as they should be, at the beginning of the fall term, most of the girls of the seventh and eighth grades will have their cooking lessons in their own schools, and few will have to travel far to cooking centers.

SEWING.

During the past year there has been a demand from some of the grammar school principals for the establishment of sewing classes for the girls of the fifth and sixth grades. With the permission of the School Board, several domestic science teachers have taught sewing during the past year. There were twelve sewing classes during part of the fall term and nine during the spring term, at practically no expense to the Board. The pupils and teachers have furnished almost all the materials, and the time taken was some that was not available for cooking lessons.

Mrs. Fenton, at the earnest request of the parents and pupils of the Fairmount School, taught after school hours, giving her time for several months. At the Horace Mann, the supervisor relieved Miss Tobriner of three cooking classes a week so that she might teach sewing. The experiment has demonstrated that sewing classes in the public schools would be useful, and that their usefulness would be appreciated.

Domestic Art is very generally taught in the public schools of this country, and I would suggest that it be included in our next course of study, and provided for in the budget.

GIFTS TO THE DOMESTIC SCIENCE DEPARTMENT.

The following is a report of the gifts made to the Domestic Science Department this year. The gifts have very materially lessened the cost of our cooking lessons.

Received from the—

Globe Mills, about 2,000 lbs. flour;
Golden Gate Yeast Co., 800 yeast tickets;
Johnson-Locke Mercantile Co., 6 cases Royal Baking Powder;

Johnson-Locke Mercantile Co., 1 case Kingsford Corn Starch;
Johnson-Locke Mercantile Co., 1 case Karo Corn Syrup;
N. K. Fairbanks Co., 8 cases Cottolene;
Sperry Mills, 50 lbs. flour.

During the past term, manufacturers belonging to the Home Industry League have presented several collections of specimens illustrating food productions and manufacture. They have also invited the Domestic Science teachers to visit their factories. Parties of teachers have visited the Carlson Currier Silk Mills and the Nolan Shoe factory in Petaluma, also the A. C. Boldemann chocolate factory in San Francisco. Our pupils take great interest in these collections of food products and textiles, and we hope to get more. At present the best display of collections is at the Mission Grammar School.

SUGGESTIONS.

CERTIFICATIONS OF DOMESTIC SCIENCE TEACHERS.—I would like to suggest that your office draw up a list of schools giving a normal school course in Domestic Science, and that only graduates from such schools be given certificates for teaching domestic science. This plan has been adopted, as you know, in most school departments. The field of Domestic Science has so broadened in the past few years that only regularly trained people can do the work required efficiently. A rule requiring applicants for certificates and positions in the Domestic Science department to have this special training would not only raise the standing of the department, but would also relieve your office, and the Board of Education, of the importunities of uninformed, though estimable people, who consider themselves fit to teach cookery because they can cook.

PURCHASING COOKING SUPPLIES.—I would also like to make a suggestion about the ordering of groceries, etc., for my department. Instead of getting the small amounts needed at one time on requisition, I would suggest that each teacher be given a triplicating order book, such as salesmen use, for her weekly grocery supply. One copy to be given to the grocer, another to remain in her book for reference, and the third to be O. K.'d at the end of the month by the supervisor and sent to the store-room of the School Board. The grocer attaches the order that he receives to the bill for comparison. The method of getting supplies, although a hundred per cent better than that in vogue before Mrs. Kincaid became School Director, is still cumbersome and expensive. I have calculated that the cost of buying supplies is sometimes five times that of the supplies themselves.

A cooking teacher's requisition, which may be for no more than for one-half pound of butter and one-half dozen eggs, passes through the hands of one supervisor, one storekeeper, two school directors, and one recording secretary. This course is expensive and offers no compensating advantage.

I have studied the question of getting supplies for cooking classes, and find that the best service is obtained when each teacher orders from a local grocer. It is noted that the tradesman who is apt to regard a school board as a remote abstraction, unacquainted with the price of eggs, will give excellent service to his little girl's cooking teacher.

In a school department where several centers are maintained, it is found best to deal with several grocers, conveniently located near the schools, rather than with one firm only. The remoteness of some of the centers, and the smallness of some orders, make delivery expensive for the firm, and the groceries cost more in consequence to the School Board. It also deprives the teacher of the opportunity of selecting what she needs, and of returning unused goods, should rainy-day sessions, unexpected class examinations or singing rehearsals interrupt the sequence of cooking lessons.

COOKING CENTER AT LONGFELLOW SCHOOL.—Last December the Board of Education passed a resolution to devote the old Longfellow School building and yard to the use of Domestic Science and school gardening. Nothing has been done as yet to prepare the building and grounds to such purposes.

I would suggest that part of the building be demolished, leaving only three rooms, and that these be fitted up very simply as a cottage home. A good deal of the furnishings might be made by the pupils in class, as sewing and manual training work, and would afford useful lessons in economical house fitting. Many of the people of that neighborhood live in shacks that date from earthquake times, and such a lesson would be useful.

CONCLUSION.

In conclusion I would like to state that the work of this department has progressed successfully this year. My assistants have enjoyed the co-operation and appreciation of the principals and teachers in whose schools they have been placed. At the end of each term the pupils of the B 8th grades have kept open house for their parents and friends, and these affairs have been very pleasant. The class-rooms have been open to inspection and garnished with flowers, and the pupils have taken pleasure in explaining the equipment and work of the department to their visitors. They also have served refreshments of their own making.

I have attended most of these ''teas,'' and have been very much gratified by the expressions of appreciation that I have heard from the mothers of our pupils. Both the value of the Domestic Science work and the efficiency of the Domestic Science teachers have been pleasantly commented upon.

NEW TEACHERS.

At the beginning of the fall term the supervisor was absent on leave for five weeks, attending the summer session of Teachers' College, Columbia University. During her absence, Miss Florence M. Woodward was acting supervisor, and superintended the installation of equipment at the new Mission Grammar and Sutro Centers.

The completion of new centers and the resignation of one of our Domestic Science teachers, who was married last fall, made necessary the appointment of three teachers. The School Board made very happy selections, and the department has profited by new blood.

With many thanks for the courtesies that I have received from you and your deputies, I am,

Respectfully,

ELLEN M. BARTLETT,
Supervisor of Domestic Science

REPORT OF MANUAL TRAINING DEPARTMENT.

San Francisco, Cal., June 30, 1911.

Superintendent Alfred Roncovieri.

Dear Sir:

I herewith submit annual report of the work under my supervision for the school year ending June 30, 1911.

The enrollment by grades for the term just concluded is as follows:

A Sixth, 72; B Sixth, 134; A Seventh, 710; B Seventh. 629; A Eighth, 601; B Eighth, 445: Ungraded—Parental School, 27. Total 2,616.

These pupils have been under the instruction of the following men: H. C. Bagot, R. J. Brower (three-fifths time); M. J. Doyle, D. E. Dowling, P. F. Dailey, L. E. Davidson, M. A. Felton, A M. Sylvia and G. J. Telfer.

During the year a laboratory at the Sheridan School was equipped and instruction begun; the Hancock laboratory was partially equipped and will be ready for use this fall; at the Horace Mann School a large laboratory was fully equipped for both wood and metal work, thus accommodating the Sixth grade and also affording an additional lesson per week for some of the Eighth grades.

Detached manual training laboratories are now in course of erection at the James Lick, Pacific Heights and Roosevelt Schools. The early completion of several of the new-bond school buildings will give us a total of more than twenty laboratories; three years ago we had but eight.

While this increase in laboratory facilities is very gratifying, there is immediate need for an increase in our teaching force, to permit of the extension of the work through the Sixth grades, at least.

With the teaching force now employed, our laboratories in the aggregate are idle more than two-fifths of the time. There is perhaps no one other thing which would do more to keep the Sixth-grade boy from leaving school than this kind of work.

It has been extremely gratifying to note the increasing numbers of large projects undertaken by the Eighth-grade pupils, the materials for which are furnished by the pupils themselves.

When a parent will readily supply his boy with several dollars' worth of lumber to be used in the manual training class, it is certainly good evidence of his high regard and faith in our system of manual training.

The introduction of metal work at the Horace Mann School has proven a great success. Work in metal supplements work in wood, and affords opportunity to present various tools and processes of great educational value and interest.

Since design and decoration enter so largely into this type of work, there is great need for either additional work in drawing or else greater correlation with the present drawing course.

The designing and preparation of plans and patterns should be done before coming to the laboratory, in order to leave the full lesson period for actual tool-practice.

At the close of the term the customary semi-annual exhibits of the term's work were held in the several laboratories, and were viewed by large numbers of parents and citizens. From these exhibits we have selected a limited but representative amount of work to show during the meeting of the National Education Association.

In conclusion, I wish to express my appreciation of the cordial co-operation of my assistants and of the many teachers and principals of the department. The good work done was only possible through this co-operation, together with the liberal support of the Board of Education and your own well-known favorable attitude toward this kind of school work.

Respectfully submitted,

F. K. BARTHEL,
Supervisor of Manual Training.

REPORT OF MISS ESTELLE CARPENTER, SUPERVISOR OF MUSIC.

June 2, 1911.

Hon. Alfred Roncovieri,
Superintendent Schools,
San Francisco, Cal.

My Dear Sir:

In reply to your request for report from the Music Department of the City Schools, I submit the following:

From the inspection of the work made during the past year, the results have been more satisfactory than those of preceding years since the fire. The regular class-room work was much disturbed by the great disaster of 1906. Since then the work has been gradually improving, and this year finds the music most systematically given.

The best evidence of the work is found in the results obtained by the in-individual child and the results obtained in the systematic class work.

Variety of songs, expression in singing, and development of sweet and fervent tones have all been admirably exemplified in the singing at dedications, graduations and concerts. There have been a grêat many dedications in the schools since the fire, and with each dedication, singing has been a prominent feature. This is as it should be, as such an occasion proves the value of the children's singing to the community. The school joined hands with the parents on these occasions and the music of the schools extended to the homes, carried there by the memories of the songs of the little ones. On the other hand, the children's singing was a part of the great life of the city, and thus singing by the children in the community became a factor in the building of the city.

As to graduations, in each and every graduation class, twice a year, there have been given in three parts, beautiful songs from the Masters, such as the "Intermezzo" from Cavelleria Rusticana, "Sextette" from Lucia, selections from "Stabat Mater," "Pilgrims' Chorus," "Miserere" from Il Trovatore, "Blue Danube," "Arditi's Waltz," Handel's "Largo," etc. Aside from these, we have had some songs from the Romance Composers of Germany and France, and well-known Folk Songs. In the Cosmopolitan Schools, songs are sung in French, German, Spanish and Italian.

Nature inspires true Folk Melody which is born in a moment, and contains truth and beauty. A Folk Melody reflects the spirit of the race which gave it birth. It is our duty to preserve these priceless values which have come down to us from the various nations.

Aside from the Graduations, the past year has been noted in our school music for a monster chorus which was conducted at Union Square for the benefit of the Native Sons in honor of the Admission Day Festival. This chorus comprised five thousand eight hundred voices, composed of children from all the schools of the city. It was given in the open air, and the greatest enthusiasm was manifested by the people at the singing. The songs rendered were "Sextette" from Lucia, "Carmen" in three parts, and the patriotic songs were sung amidst the flying of the Red, White and Blue colors. One cannot dream of the beauty and grandeur of the "Pilgrims' Chorus" from Tannhauser, sung by six thousand sweet, fresh children's voices, unless one has actually experienced the sensation of hearing such a thing. It took five weeks of work to prepare this chorus, while the Portola took twelve weeks to accomplish the same results.

Another notable event in the music world of children's singing was the chorus which had the honor of singing before Madam Tetrazzini in Dreamland Rink. The children from the Garfield, Hancock and Jean Parker Schools, with nine days' preparation, sang "Anvil Chorus," and "Intermezzo" from Cavelleria Rusticana, and the patriotic songs, besides some songs in Italian. The artistic interpretation given by these children and their beautiful tone production, were the wonder of all who heard this performance. The memory of that performance is a perpetual delight.

The Admission Day Chorus, and the Tetrazzini Chorus, were directed by myself, and also a chorus for the benefit of the Hayes Valley Carnival. This chorus was unique in that the children actually sang on the street. Though it was a day in February, still the weather was mild and balmy; a day peculiar to California climate. The children were most responsive, and carried off the honors of the day.

During the year a number of dedications have occurred on Sundays, and the supervisor and assistant have conducted the songs on these occasions. On a number of occasions the children have sung at the Mothers' Club meetings, which are held in the school buildings. In a series of eight meetings given for the one thousand teachers of San Francisco, the supervisor outlined the work of the year and sang seventy-five various songs to be given the children of different grades.

The child has, during the last term, been held responsible for his individual effort and interest along the line of development in tone quality, ear training, sight singing, formal work and song singing. The effort of the child to give and hear beautiful tones, and to read at sight, results in a quickened interest in tone appreciation, and ultimately brings the mind of the child into responsive attitude toward the music world. This tone appreciation is the foundation of musicianship, and gives results, so that the child deals in tonality as easily as he deals in words and figures and makes him a quickened, mental and spiritual being.

During the past year systematic work has been emphasized in oral and written dictation. The motive or impulse in artistic education, lies in the desire of the individual to express himself. Unfortunately our curriculum allows us only one hour per week in which to give music, and this has been too short a time to go deeply into the expression of one's self in written music. So far we have expressed ourselves through beautiful tone and beautiful compositions, through the grasping of new situations in the tone world; but there is still another side which we hope to initiate soon, which will be the actual expression of thought by means of creative work. We are told that melody started in language, inflection and rhythm, in the savage ages; so in instructing the child, we aim to develop the melody instinct with the rhythmical. Much stress in the lower grades is put upon the rhythmical steps so that the child's body is thoroughly in accord with accent and impulse. The expression of time is but a reflex action, and comes where the child is taught to move in rhythm and to enjoy each movement. As the child progresses, this movement is transferred to the printed page, and helps on toward rapid mental conception of the rhythm of the printed page.

In every way the knowledge of the subject of music is encouraged. All children are encouraged to listen to the best music, to go to concerts, study the piano and other instruments, to cultivate their voices and put their lives into the general musical life of the city. Talks are given on the care of the vocal organs and how much the voice depends on the simple healthy life which conserves energy for usefulness.

In a large department, some of the schools are more advanced than others, and consequently some schools have been visited frequently and others not so often, in order that the whole department would attain an even degree of efficiency in the work. On some of the occasions, some of the schools were visited twice and some were visited more, according to the need. Where each regular teacher does the work thoroughly and artistically, there the work becomes more proficient. The strength of the department lies in the ability of the individual teachcer, and it becomes necessary to strengthen the weak places. Consequently, where a teacher is not capable, endeavor is made to increase her knowledge and give her methods to make her a stronger teacher. In some cases it is impossible to get desired results from the teachers. In such cases the Supervisor or Assistant Supervisor arranges for the exchange of work. In classes where there are a number of incapable teachers, the work is put into the hands of one particular teacher who assumes the responsibility of the work of these classes. These teachers possess special certificates in music, and are given a slight extra compensation for their work. There are about thirty such teachers in the San Francisco School Department, and here I take occasion to thank them for the work they have so ably done during the past year. These teachers have particularly been helpful not only for the regular work, but for all extra work such as the tremendous choruses given for the "Fleet," for "Portola," and for "Admission Day Festival." I am glad to say that the Board of Education appointed about five such teachers during the past year.

As I was appointed Secretary of the Music Section of the N. E. A., I organized these special teachers and others into a reception committee, and everything will be done to welcome the N. E. A. visitors.

During the last year a number of new pianos have been installed in the various schools by the Board of Education, for which I am most grateful. Each new school dedicated has been given a new piano.

I wish to recommend to the Honorable Superintendent and to the Board of Education, that more time be given to music in the public schools of this city. One hour a week is very little. I recommend that in the transfer of teachers, the Board of Education make it a rule to see that musical teachers are put in classes where musical teachers are needed. I wish to make mention of the fact that a piano be bought for the office of the Supervisor of Music, as it is very hard to carry on the work without a piano.

The Board of Education has for the past year supplied the teachers with mimeographed songs and printed music sheets, which is most satisfactory. I recommend that when supplementary books are sent to the school libraries by the Superintendent or Board of Education, that some of the books be music books. I specially recommend that each school possess a copy of "Favorite Songs and Hymns" by McCasky, and "Songs of All Lands" by Matthews, "The Rote Song Book" and "No. 1 of the Shorter Chorus" by Ripley & Tapper. These books were in each school before the fire, and should be sent to the schools that lost them during that catastrophy.

I wish to make mention of the good work done by our faithful regular teachers; of the support given to me and my department by the principals; of the excellent work done by the first assistant, and the special teachers of the various schools.

Thanking you, the Deputy Superintendents, and the Board of Education for your co-operation and kindness, I am,

Sincerely yours,

ESTELLE CARPENTER,
Supervisor of Music, San Francisco School Department.

REPORT OF PARENTAL SCHOOL GARDEN.

In August, 1909, we moved from our old school building on Harrison street, near Tenth, to the present location on Bryant and Seventh streets.

Adjacent to the school building was an immense sand lot covered with debris left by the fire of 1906. The boys of the school, fifty in number, were organized into squads to clear this debris. The time for this was found in the early morning before the 9 o'clock session, and also at the first recess at 10:30. Little by little the work of this debris commission began to show, the bricks were removed, and after several months of good hard work the ground was comparatively clear.

At this juncture, through the kind interest of Mr. J. C. Astredo, of the Playground Commission, the ground was plowed, then through the additional assistance of several loads of street sweepings as a fertilizer, the former barren, unattractive sand lot was transformed into good material for a garden.

The ground was then staked off, each class was given a certain portion, with a superintendent. Seeds were distributed, viz.: lettuce, beets, peas, onions, etc. This was in the spring of 1910. Many boys became so interested that they would prefer to work at the noon hour instead of playing.

This first venture in gardening was an experiment, not only with the boys but also with the teachers and myself. None of us was over-burdened with exact knowledge about the cultivation and care of a vegetable garden. However, the results were of an encouraging nature, the boys' interest was awakened, good-natured rivalry existed among the young gardeners; then came the closer association between the teachers and pupils, especially valuable with this type of boy, and, lastly, the practical results, the use of the product at the noon-day meal.

As the result of this pioneering in gardening, we were encouraged by the kindly and timely advice of Professor T. Heaton.

In the fall the ground was cleared again, old stalks taken up, a more ambitious garden staked out. The school, numbering about fifty boys, worked daily through the fall and winter months, and in the spring of 1911 the ground was again ready. Carefully selected seeds were sent to us by the Board of Education, through Professor T. Heaton, and this time we went to work more intelligently, with the knowledge gained by former experience, backed up by the unremitting interest of Professor Heaton, who sent us two agricultural students from the University of California at Berkeley, who gave us valuable assistance.

We planted radishes, lettuce, potatoes, cabbages, Swiss chards, etc.

The first practical results have been as follows:

Enough radishes to supply fifty boys for several meals, Swiss chard, lettuce salad, new potatoes used daily. The strawberry plants have yielded only fairly. They are fine, healthy plants, and are of great interest. We think next year the yield will be greater.

With proper care through the summer months, there are enough vegetables to supply the table throughout the season.

The garden has been a great factor in helping to upbuild the character of the boys. It aids them to form habits of industry, developing thought and concentration, awakening a living interest in things about them, bringing them close to Nature, who restores and invigorates, displacing the bad habits engendered by years of living in the streets, at the best displacing the artificial with the real, teaching the boys to do things which will make them useful members of the community.

RAE ALEXANDER,
Principal Parental School.

REPORT OF MRS. AMY W. DEANE, DIRECTOR OF MUSIC IN HIGH SCHOOLS.

To Hon. Alfred Roncovieri,
Superintendent of Common Schools.

Music has long been embodied in the course of study of the grammar grades in our public schools, and also for some time in the curriculum of the University of California. During this time there has existed an illogical hiatus in the high schools. There were, of course, glee clubs and orchestras under the direction of music-loving teachers, but no regularly authorized course. This matter had for some time attracted the attention of the Board of Education, there being no more loyal supporter of the cause than the Superintendent, Mr. Alfred Roncovieri. After due consideration, at a meeting of the Board held October 26, 1910, the Chair of Music in the High Schools was established. To me fell the great honor of being the first incumbent.

As in the case with all new departures, more or less uncertainty attached to the undertaking. I visited the Oakland high schools, where music, under the most capable direction of Mrs. Wood, had for some two years formed part of the regular course. This visit was followed by a conference with Dr. Wolle, Professor of Music in the State University. I was further greatly aided by valuable suggestions from Mr. W. J. McCoy. Data were also obtained through correspondence with many schools in the United States where music had long been established. Thus equipped, I began instruction Tuesday, November 1, 1910, the experimental school, so to speak, being the Girls' High, presumably because girls are supposed to be more musically inclined than boys. By way of parenthesis, I will here say that I have since had reason to alter considerably this opinion, the boys of the Mission, Commercial and Polytechnic High Schools being quite as enthusiastic and studious as the girls.

Dr. Scott, principal of the Girls' High, being a most ardent advocate of music, rendered me all possible assistance in my new work. The class which was to graduate in December was the first body of pupils to receive instruction. The singing of this class at the graduating exercises reflected the utmost credit on the interest and intelligence of the pupils.

At the beginning of the new year in January, my work was greatly extended, covering the entire field of five high schools. Dr. Scott, Mr. Ferguson, Mr. O'Connor, and Colonel Murphy, principals, respectively, of Girls', Polytechnic, Mission and Commercial, entered with great interest and willingness upon the task of so arranging my classes that at some time during one of the study periods I might have all pupils desiring to take up the new study. Being purely elective and voluntary, it was most gratifying to see the very large classes that greeted me. I was particularly surprised at the Commercial, with which we usually associated a strictly business course. The enrollment of 231 pupils was highly encouraging. The classes manifesting great interest, and the equipment in the splendid new buildings affording splendid aid, it is not surprising that the chorals on Class Day made a remarkably fine showing.

The enrollment at Mission and Polytechnic taught me that the boys are not behind the girls in interest. In fact, at Polytechnic the boys were, if possible, more enthusiastic than the girls. At the closing exercises of this school, music was a prominent feature—proof that trades and art may go hand in hand and tend to mutual development.

At Mission High, the singing of the chorals on Class Day was one of the marked successes on a program of unusual interest. The Faculty, which had not before heard the united strength of the different chorals, expressed surprise and pleasure at the proficiency attained in so short a time. The total enrollment in music in this school is very large, rendering the chorals of fine volume and excellent effect.

The musical program for the graduating exercises at Girls' High was quite ambitious, but excellently rendered, phrasing and shading being most intelligently observed. The school orchestra played the march. One of the red-letter days (or evenings, to be exact) of this school in the term just ended, was May 29, when the Glee Club gave its concert. It will long be remembered for its really artistic merit, the girls entering into the spirit of the numbers given, not only musically, but dramatically. A charming addition to the program was the rendering by the school orchestra, under the leadership of Dr. Scott, of several difficult and classical numbers.

Mr. Morton, of Lowell High, regretted that the work could not, for the time, be taken up in his school, there being not an unoccupied nook or corner in the building. I was, however, not deprived of the pleasure of having at least a foothold in the school, for, at the beginning of the term, the Girls' Glee Club requested me to assume the position of Director. The work was, of course, accomplished after school hours. The girls proved musical, intelligent, and apt. The result of the term's work was a concert, because of the excellence of which the Club was requested to repeat it at Yerba Buena Island for the benefit of officers and men stationed there. There are also in this school a Boys' Glee Club and an orchestra. Certainly, so musical an aggregation should be given the possibility of the more serious musical study afforded by a regular course. Space is the only requirement.

I have written this lengthy report and have gone into these minute details for a reason. The work was, in a measure, experimental. We believed that there must exist in the high schools good voices and musical ability. I, for one, now know it, and I trust this report may lead your Honorable Body to the same conviction. That there should be found good voices is not surprising. It is the musical intelligence and the keen appreciation of the dramatic side of music, possessed by the California boy and girl, that impresses the musician. With comparatively few explanations, some of my chorals have grasped the dramatic as well as the vocal values of an operatic selection, and, considering their inexperience, have given an astonishingly good interpretation.

I would not have you glean from all this that I desire your aid in making this a town of professional musicians. The study of literature is given a prominent place in the high school curriculum. This does not argue that every graduate is to become an author or a writer, and there is no more reason why the artisan, the merchant, or the professional, should not have an equally correct knowledge of music. Simply as a relaxation after a day of toil, the pleasure of listening to music is increased tenfold if the listener has an analytical understanding of the music he hears. It is a pleasure when it appeals to the senses alone; it is a delight when added to this is the intellectual enjoyment that only knowledge and understanding can bring. There seems, therefore, to exist no more logical reason that the study of music should be barred from the high school course than that literature should be discontinued on similar grounds.

Respectfully submitted,

AMY WATERS DEANE.

June, 1911.

REPORT OF PEDRO A. ESPINA, SUPERVISOR OF PENMANSHIP.

San Francisco, June 5, 1911.

Hon. Alfred Roncovieri,
Superintendent of Schools.

Dear Sir:

I most respectfully submit my report for the year's work in penmanship.

The progress made in the entire department is most satisfactory. The blackboard work is excellent.

In the primary grades, where the greatest progress has been made, I find that by beginning the forms of letters in the last ten weeks of the first term of the A Division of First Grade, much better results can be obtained.

I herewith submit the few changes that I desire in my department.

Thanking you for your generous support, and the teachers for their faithful work, I remain,

Yours very respectfully,

P. A. ESPINA,
Supervisor of Writing.

NEW COURSE OF STUDY FOR PENMANSHIP.

A FIRST GRADE.—Blackboard work with movement exercise. Teachers may begin to teach letters the last ten weeks of the term.

B FIRST GRADE.—Movement on blackboard, teach form of letters. Teachers may begin to teach pupils how to write their names and may begin the use of pencil the last ten weeks of the term; pencil should be held the same as the pen.

A SECOND GRADE.—Continue to use pencil, and use much care in the position of the hand.

B SECOND GRADE.—Continue with pencils and with movement exercises, and promote pupils to a pen and ink division if the hand is held correctly.

Use No. 1 Copy Book.

A AND B THIRD GRADE.—Use No. 2 Copy Book, give movement exercises, and drill on position.

A AND B FOURTH AND A AND B FIFTH GRADES.—Use No. 3 Copy Book, follow movement exercises, and position of the pen.

A AND B SIXTH AND A AND B SEVENTH GRADES.—Use No. 4 Copy Book. Great care must be used in teaching position of hand and pen.

A AND B EIGHTH GRADES.—Use No. 5 Copy Book; take twenty minutes once a week for movement and forms of letters. Must insist on correct position of hand and pen.

P. A. ESPINA.

REPORT OF GEO. S. MIEHLING, SUPERVISOR OF PHYSICAL CULTURE.

The results of the Physical Culture and Drills given in the public schools during the year ending June, 1911, were demonstrated to the public during the Native Sons' Celebration, September 10, 1910, at the Golden Gate Park Stadium, where one thousand school children under the direction of Professor Geo. S. Miehling of P. S. of S. F., marched and engaged in their calisthenic exercises.

The scene was an inspiring one as they marched in review in military order and evolutions. The excellent drill shown was the result of the good behavior and attention insisted upon while learning in the past year. The class work of the graduating boys and girls of the Fremont School was given at the Girls' High School in the presence of the Superintendent of Schools, Alfred Roncovieri, and the Board of Education. Dumb-bell drill by the graduating boys and girls of the Monroe School was also shown.

Calisthetics, yard drill and saluting the flag were witnessed by the Chinese Educator, who had just finished his tour around the world, the Chinese Consul, and Superintendent Alfred Roncovieri, at the Madison School. All the school children of San Francisco are taught the same exercises.

SUMMARY OF WORK ACCOMPLISHED.

Schools visited	81
Classes	862
Children enrolled	37,047
Days at school	160½
Visits	218
Grand total of children taught	101,629
Cases of special duty and assistance (days)	27
Average daily (children taught)	633
Holidays	14
Absence	2

Yours respectfully,

GEO. S. MIEHLING,
Physical Culture Department.

PRINCIPALS' MONTHLY MEETINGS.

San Francisco, June 22, 1911.

Hon. Alfred Roncovieri,
Superintendent of Schools,
San Francisco, Cal.
Dear Sir:

As Secretary of the Monthly Meetings of Principals, and in compliance with the request from your office, I have the honor to submit the following report of those meetings, beginning with the one held October 20, 1910, at which I was appointed Secretary pro tem.

At a meeting of principals held at the Mission Grammar School in May, 1911, a motion prevailed that a monthly meeting of principals be held during the school year 1910-1911, to consider the problems that relate especially to the work of the principal, and it was in pursuance of this motion that the various meetings of the year were held. Other matters, however, of broader import than the problems of the principal were discussed. It is not proposd to embody in this report anything like a detailed report of the topics discussed, the reports submitted, and the papers read, but only a mere outline of these things from which may be derived something approaching an adequate conception of their scope and interest. It may be remarked here that the meetings were held at 2 p. m. on school days, the principals being allowed and expected to leave their schools at that time in order to attend the meetings. Hence they were well attended, and deep interest was evinced in all the discussions and proceedings. The discussions sometimes waxed warm and demonstrated the fact that school principals may differ as widely in their opinions and maintain their views as stubbornly and eloquently as other folks. The early part of each meeting was usually occupied by the chairman, Deputy Superintendent T. L. Heaton, in short talks on various topics of interest, which always elicited the closest attention of the principals, as they were terse, pointed, and derived from a close observation and wide experience.

Among the topics discussed by him may be mentioned the following:

"How to make the visiting days of teachers and principals more profitable," "Outside Geography," "Art of Questioning," "Teachers' Libraries," "Medical Inspection," "Changes in the Course of Study," "Cumulative Reviews," "Honorary Promotion," "School Gardens," "Composition," etc.

Among the topics discussed by the principals were such as "Outside Interruptions," "Health and Sanitation," "Course of Study," "Retardation," "Dropping out of Pupils from Grammar and High Schools," "Compulsory Education," "Graduation Exercises," "Manual Training," "Conservation of the Principal's Time," etc.

A part of the time of each of several meetings was also devoted to five-minute talks by principals previously appointed by Deputy Heaton, on McMurry's book, "How to Study."

Under "Good of the Order," which was a feature of the meetings, many of the principals made very suggestive and helpful talks varying in length from three to five minutes.

Committees were appointed to consider the subjects of "Retardation," "Graduation Exercises," "Medals," "Professional Library," and "Admission to the High Schools." These committees submitted carefully prepared reports, some of which evoked considerable discussion, but were generally adopted, either with or without modification. The recommendations embodied in these recommendations have in some instances received favorable consideration by the Board of Education, but not always.

Among the excellent prepared papers read at these meetings should be mentioned those on (1) "The Public School Athletic League," by Principal Frank Morton of the Lowell High School; (2) "Retardation," by Principal A. E. Kellogg, of the Hamilton Grammar School; (3) "Arithmetic," by Deputy Superintendent R. H. Webster; and (4) "Courtesy to One Another and Respect for Older Persons," by Principal Miss M. A. Deane, of the Redding School.

Finally it would be discourteous to omit to mention the fact that many of these meetings were attended by our Superintendent, who greatly encouraged us by his kindly sympathy and readiness to approve of any good action that was taken. He also assisted by participating in discussions, and, at the last meeting gave a talk on some of the more important educational enactments of the late Legislature.

Respectfully submitted,

S. STURGES,
Secretary

READ AT PRINCIPALS' MEETING.

FOR THE GOOD OF THE DEPARTMENT.

By Miss M. A. Deane, Principal Redding Grammar School.

When I was asked to say something, or suggest some idea for the good of the Department, I at once thought of a talk on Word Analysis—its value in helping our young people to grasp the meaning of ordinary words, and thereby gain facility of expression. Then suddenly I changed my mind, for I realized that I was not consigned to McMurry or any other Mc., but that I was asked simply for a thought on "The Good of the Department,"—my own thought, to be expounded in three minutes. So I concluded to drop for a time my offshoot of "The Three R's," and take up a subject that to me is of equal importance to the Department, since it is equally helpful to our pupils, i. e.: Courtesy to Each Other and Respect for the Elderly.

Is not the lack of courtesy at present truly deplorable? How many of the young give up their place in cars to old people, stand when spoken to, assist with a bundle, enter or leave a room properly, remember the prefatory "Please," acknowledge a favor with "I thank you"? Is it a wonder that some are tempted to speak of courtesy as a lost art? But being optimistic, I believe it is not dead but sleepeth, and that we of the Department might do much to wake it up.

Courtesy could be considered under different heads, as, Home, Street, School (and Professional etiquette too, which is very important though sometimes forgotten)—and could be part of our day's work. Ten minutes spent on rules of politeness is time well invested, the income of which our young people can enjoy all their lives.

Many of you will say, that belongs to the Home Training. But do we not have these little ones half of their waking time, and are not many of the thoughts that help and guide them given by us? And can we exclude the little conventionalities that make life so much sweeter, and sacrifice for home so much easier? Our training should not be apart from home training, but correlated with it.

You may not agree with me as to the vital importance of my subject; each may think his hobby a better mount: as our worthy Superintendent might favor music; one of his deputies, arithmetic; another, farming; another, reading; and still another, language and composition—all good and very good indeed in their proper places. But let us not fill our Course of Study so full that there is not a little space left for the small amenities of life. No matter what path our pupils take, let them find time to stop by the roadside and extend a common courtesy. How much better all feel when politely treated, and how aggressive when rudely treated?

I plead, then, for a few rules each month that would help ennoble the young of our Department.

CHRONOLOGY OF SUPERINTENDENTS OF SCHOOLS OF THE CITY AND COUNTY OF SAN FRANCISCO

APPOINTED BY BOARD OF EDUCATION.

Thomas J. Nevins .... Nov. 17, 1851, to Dec., 1853
William H. O'Grady .... 1854 and 1855
E. A. Theller 1856

COUNTY SUPERINTENDENT (ELECTED BY THE PEOPLE).

John C. Pelton 1856

CITY AND COUNTY SUPERINTENDENTS (ELECTED BY THE PEOPLE).

John C. Pelton 1857
Henry P. Janes 1857-59
James Denman 1859-60
George Tait 1861-62-63-64
John C. Pelton 1865-66-67
James Denman 1868-69-70
J. H. Widber 1871-72-73
James Denman 1874-75
H. N. Bolander 1876-77
Azro L. Mann .... Dec. 1, 1877, to Jan. 3, 1880

UNDER NEW CONSTITUTION

John W. Taylor .... Jan., 1880, to Jan., 1883
Andrew Moulder .... Jan., 1883, to Jan., 1887
Jas. W. Anderson .... Jan., 1887, to Jan., 1891
John Swett .... Jan., 1891, to Jan., 1895
Andrew Moulder .... Jan., 1895, to Nov., 1895 (died)
Madison Babcock (appointed by Bd. of Education) Nov., 1895, to Dec. 26, 1896
Reginald H. Webster .... Dec. 26, 1896, to Jan. 8, 1903
William H. Langdon .... Jan. 8, 1903, to Jan. 8, 1906
Alfred Roncovieri .... Jan. 8, 1906, to ~~date~~

THE SAN FRANCISCO TEACHERS' INSTITUTE OF 1910

The annual institute of the teachers of the San Francisco Department was called at the Alcazar Theatre for the mornings of Tuesday, Wednesday and Thursday, December 27, 28 and 29, 1910, with an evening concert in Dreamland Pavilion Wednesday, December 28. Superintendent Alfred Roncovieri presided.

The meetings of the Institute were so arranged that teachers could also attend the sessions of the California Teachers' Association at Berkeley.

Superintendent Roncovieri, in opening the Institute on Tuesday morning, declared himself strongly in favor of a readjustment of the school system in such wise that it should meet the needs of industrial advancement. "In a city like San Francisco," he said, "where the industrial development during the next generation will, I believe, astonish the world, technical education must lead the way. Our Course of Study must be adjusted to meet the situation."

Dean George F. James, of the University of Minnesota, in his address entitled "A Pedagogical Relic," maintained that our traditional grouping of school classes into four primary, four grammar, four high school, four college, and four professional years, should be replaced by groups of three. He advocated a combination six-year couse, of which three should be chiefly liberal and the other three distinctly technical, or professional. The speaker suggested separate instruction for the two sexes in many subjects, but not in all.

Professor Lee Emerson Bassett, of Stanford University, developed his conception of the true teaching of poetry. He opposed that method of studying poetry by which the appeal was made to the intellectual faculties rather than to the imaginative and emotional. He advised frequent reading of poetry aloud and repetition of memorized poems. Enjoyment, or aesthetic pleasure, should be the chief gain from the reading of poetry, he declared.

On the first morning the Institute adjourned out of respect to the memory of Mrs. Margaret Deane, who had been a pioneer teacher in the department. Resolutions presented by Mrs. Mary Prag, of the Girls' High School, in recognition of the distinguished services of Mrs. Deane, and as a tribute to her memory, were unanimously adopted by the Institute.

On Wednesday, the first lecture was delivered by Dr. M. L. Gardner, of the Los Angeles Polytechnic High School, on the subject "Agriculture in Our Schools." He advocated the establishment of agricultural courses in the public school and, wherever possible, the founding of school farms near the cities as practical adjuncts to the work.

In her address on "The Ideals of Amateur Singing," Mrs. Mary Roberts Coolidge favored the confining of class teaching of music to such simple melodies as would fall within the range of the voices of all. She sang a number of lullabies and old-time songs to exemplify her ideas.

Superintendent James M. Greenwood, of Kansas City, spoke on "The Automatic Element in Education." He divided children into four classes—the idea-nervous, the muscular-motor, the idea-motor, and the muscular-corpulent. He divided teachers into three classes—those of genuine skill who can develop all children, even the stupid; of little proficiency, who can scarcely educate the average pupil; and of no qualification, whose effect is to discourage the brightest pupil. The great teacher, he said, is the one who in each subject picks out universal truths and teaches them.

The musical features of the program of each day's session were very popular and enjoyable. On Wednesday evening over three thousand people attended the grand concert which marked the initial appearance in San Francisco of Madame Gerville-Reache, the great contralto singer from New York. The welcome given her was remarkable for the sincerity of its warmth. A leading musical critic said of the concert: "Mr. Roncovieri will do well for the future of the town's culture if he is able to repeat the program which was given last night at Dreamland Rink when Madame Gerville-Reache sang for the pedagogues."

On Thursday morning the session was opened by a lecture by Dr. James A. Blaisdell, President of Pomona College, whose subject was "The Vocational Problem in Education." He advised the study of the fit vocation for each child from the time that it is ten years of age. "It is by the training of every man for his proper sphere of work," said the lecturer, "that the peril of the land in the problem of the unemployed is to be solved."

An illustrated discourse by Dr. Charles U. Clark, of Yale University, on "The Romance and Grandeur of Spain," was then delivered. In his introduction to his lecture, Professor Clarke dwelt on the value of cultural studies before the life vocation is taken up. He declared that in America we lack the culture influence in the home, and that this must be supplied in the school.

At the end of the Thursday's session, Mr. Selden Sturges, Principal of the Everett Grammar School, paid a tribute to the work of Superintendent Roncovieri in conducting the Institute, and a set of resolutions, as follows, introduced by him, was unanimously adopted:

"Resolved, That we tender to Superintendent Roncovieri our very high appreciation of the thoughtful care evidenced in the preparation of the program of this most delightful session of our teachers' institute, and our hearty thanks for the great pleasure we have experienced in attendance upon its various exercises."

The program is herewith reproduced in full:

TUESDAY MORNING, DECEMBER 27th—

9:15 Opening Address

ALFRED RONCOVIERI
Superintendent of Schools

9:30 Lecture.."The Teaching of Poetry"

PROFESSOR LEE EMERSON BASSETT
Professor of English, Stanford University

10:30 Intermission

10:40 Address

HON. P. H. McCARTHY
Mayor of the City and County of San Francisco

10:55 Songs (a) Mignon's Lied—Liszt.
(b) Der Nussbaum—Schumann
(c) Sous les Branches—Massenet
(d) Le Chevalier Belle—Etoile, Augusta Holmes

MRS. LILLIAN BIRMINGHAM
(Miss Alma Birmingham, Accompanist)

11:15 Lecture.."A Pedagogical Relic"

Dr. GEORGE F. JAMES
Dean of the College of Education, University of Minnesota

12:15 Adjournment

WEDNESDAY MORNING, DECEMBER 28th—

9:15 Lecture..."Agriculture in Our City Schools"

DR. N. L. GARDNER
Head of the Department of Biology, Los Angeles Polytechnic High School

10:00 Lecture on the Ideals of Amateur Singing, "Classic Lullabies and Old-Time Songs," with illustrations in several languages.

MARY ROBERTS COOLIDGE, Ph. D.
Author, Lecturer and Ballad-Singer
Formerly Associate Professor of Sociology, Stanford University

11:00 Intermission

11:15 Lecture..."The Automatic Element in Education"

SUPERINTENDENT JAMES M. GREENWOOD
Of Kansas City, Mo.

12:15 Adjournment

WEDNESDAY EVENING, DECEMBER 28th—

Grand Concert at Dreamland Pavilion, Steiner Street, near Sutter Street. The following special musical program of unusual educational value and entertainment was rendered by Mme. Gerville-Reache, one of the world's greatest contraltos. Mme. Gerville-Reache was accompanied by Miss Ina Grange, pianist, and by a full symphony orchestra under the direction of Mr. Paul Steindorff.

1. Overture, "William Tell" .... Rossini

ORCHESTRA
Alfred Roncovieri, Director

2. Arioso, "Ah Mon Fils" (Le Prophete) .... Meyerbeer

MME. GERVILLE-REACHE AND ORCHESTRA

3. Songs in English—
   (a) Hindu Slumber Song .... Harriet Ware
   (b) Kathleen Mavourneen .... Crouch

MME. GERVILLE-REACHE

4. Grand Fantasia from "La Boheme" .... Puccini

ORCHESTRA

5. Songs in German—
   (a) Ich grolle nicht .... Schumann
   (b) Der Erlkonig .... Schubert

MME. GERVILLE-REACHE

6. Songs in French—
   (a) "Plaisir d'Amour" .... Martini
   (b) "L'Air du Tigre," from Paul et Virginie .... Victor Masse

MME. GERVILLE-REACHE

7. Ballet Music from "Coppelia" .... Delibes
   (a) Mazourka
   (b) Czardas

ORCHESTRA

8. Aria, "Mon coeur s'ouvre a ta voix" (Samson et Dalila) .... Saint-Saens

MME. GERVILLE-REACHE AND ORCHESTRA

9. Marche Triumphale "Coronation" (Le Prophette) .... Meyerbeer

ORCHESTRA

MISS INA GRANGE, Accompanist

MR. PAUL STEINDORFF, Director of Orchestra

THURSDAY MORNING, DECEMBER 29th—

9:30 Lecture..''The Vocational Problem in Education''

DR. JAMES A. BLAISDELL
President Ponoma College

10:15 Violin Solos—
(a) Nocturne .... Chopin-Wilhelmj
(b) Spanish Dance .... Rehfeld

MR. NATHAN LANDSBERGER
Mrs. Nathan Landsberger, Accompanist

10:40 Intermission

11:00 Illustrated Lecture.......................................''Romance and Grandeur of Spain''

DR. CHARLES UPSON CLARK
Assistant Professor of Latin in Yale University

12:00 Adjournment

DEPARTMENT OF EDUCATION, CITY AND COUNTY OF SAN FRANCISCO, CALIFORNIA.

BOARD OF EDUCATION.

Name	Term	Salary
VAUGHAN, H. G., President	Term expires Jan. 8, 1914	$3,000.00
POWER, JAMES E., Member	Term expires Jan. 8, 1915	3,000.00
KINCAID, Mrs. M. W., Member	Term expires Jan. 8, 1913	3,000.00
PAYOT, H., Member	Term expires Jan. 8, 1912	3,000.00

OFFICIALS.

Name	Term	Salary
RONCOVIERI, ALFRED, Superintendent of Schools	Term expires Jan. 8, 1915	$4,000.00

(Ex-officio member of the Board of Education without right to vote).

DEPUTY SUPERINTENDENTS OF SCHOOLS.

Name	Term	Salary
Webster, R. H.	Term expires May 1, 1912	$2,820.00
Cloud, A. J.	Term expires Dec. 1, 1912	2,820.00
Heaton, T. L.	Term expires Mar. 1, 1914	2,820.00
Howard, W. B.	Term expires Mar. 1, 1914	2,820.00

EMPLOYES.

Dodge, M. G.	Secretary, Board of Education	Term at pleasure of Board of Education	$2,400.00
Berliner, C. A.	Financial Secretary, Board of Education	Term at pleasure of Board of Education	2,100.00
[illegible]e, R. P.	Recording Secretary, Board of Education	Term at pleasure of Board of Education	2,040.00
Walsh, E. A., Miss	Stenographer, Board of Education	Term at pleasure of Board of Education	1,200.00
O'Rourke, J., Miss	Stenographer, Board of Education	Term at pleasure of Board of Education	1,200.00
O'Connor, T. S., Miss	Stenographer, [illegible]ice Supt. of Schools	Term at pleasure of Board of Education	1,200.00
[illegible]n, S. A., Miss	Phone Exchange Operator	Term at pleasure of Board of Education	960.00
[illegible]s, J.	Messenger, Board of Education	Term at pleasure of Board of Education	1,200.00
Larkin, R.	Messenger, Supt. of Schools	Term at pleasure of Board of Education	1,080.00
Sweeney, E.	Truant Officer	Assigned by Chief of Police.	
[illegible]n, T. J.	Truant Officer	Assigned by Chief of Police.	
Ewing, G. F.	Truant Officer	Assigned by Chief of Police.	
Foley, James	Store Keeper	Term at pleasure of Board of Education	$1,800.00
Hunt, John	[illegible]t Store Keeper	Term at pleasure of Board of Education	1,080.00
McGinnis, T. J.	Foreman	Term at pleasure of Board of Education	1,500.00
Regan, L.	Building and Repairs	Term at pleasure of Board of Education	2,100.00
Alford, T.	Clerk	Term at pleasure of Board of Education	1,500.00
Handy, W. L.	Chauffeur	Term at pleasure of Board of Education	1,500.00

SCHOOLS AND TEACHERS.

Name.	Grade of Class.	When Elected.	Grade of Certificate	Salary per Year.
Adams [illegible]politan Grammar School—				
McFarland, Miss H. F.	Principal	Nov. 30, 1877	High	2,160.00
Phillips, Miss H.	V. P., 8th	May 13, 1873	Grammar	1,620.00
[illegible]d, Miss M. E.	Third	July 1, 1874	High	1,164.00
[illegible]y, Mary A.	Seventh	April 2, 1881	Grammar	1,224.00
[illegible], M[illegible] C. M.	Fifth	Aug. 16, 1898	Grammar	1,164.00
Hesselmeyer, Miss C. A.	First	Feb. 11, 1892	Grammar	1,224.00
Grozelier, Miss A. M.	French	Sept. 29, 1892	Grammar and Special	1,200.00
[illegible]field, [illegible]or A.	Sixth	June 15, 1866	Grammar	1,164.00
Hurley, Mamie E.	Sixth	Sept. 10, 1884	Grammar	1,164.00
[illegible]obs, E.	[illegible]an	Aug. 20, 1907	High	1,200.00
[illegible]obs, [illegible]ret	[illegible]th	[illegible] 17, 1907	Grammar	1,164.00
Grace, Miss K. L.	Third	Aug. 3, 1908	High	1,164.00
Grozlier, Miss A. M.	French	Sept. 29, 1892	Grammar	1,200.00
[illegible]obs, Miss E.	German	Aug 20, 1907	High	1,200.00
Agassiz Primary—				
[illegible]s, M[illegible]s S. J.	Principal	April 1, 1878	Grammar	2,160.00
Harney, Miss A.	First	July 31, 1889	Grammar	1,224.00
Brown, Miss R. F.	Fifth	July 18, 1902	Grammar	1,164.00
[illegible]n, Miss C. A.	Fifth	July 9, 1877	Grammar	1,164.00
Josselyn, Ada M.	Fifth	Oct. 9, 1883	Grammar and Special	1,224.00
[illegible]n, Miss E. A.	Fourth	Jan. 31, 1894	Grammar	1,164.00
Bartlett, Miss O. S.	[illegible]th	Jan. 31, 1894	Grammar	1,164.00
Boyle, Miss O. C.	Third	Oct. 1, 1905	Grammar	1,164.00
Rixon, [illegible]iss A. E.	Second	Feb. 28, 1898	Grammar	1,164.00
Fredericks, Miss E. L.	Third	Feb. 16, 1891	Grammar and Special	1,164.00
Hanson, Miss L.	Second	July 20, 1903	Grammar	1,164.00
Wright, Miss H.	Second	Dec. 1, [illegible]	Primary	1,284.00
[illegible]n, Miss A. M.	Second	Jan. 6, 1902	Grammar	1,164.00

Schoof, Miss L.	Fourth	July 27, 1908	Grammar	840.00
Walters, Miss T.	Fourth	Jan. 8, 1906	Grammar	1,080.00
Liner, Miss M. G.	First	July 27, 1898	Grammar	1,224.00
Maloney, Miss K. A.	First	Jan. 10, 1881	Grammar	1,224.00
Sankey, Miss M. F.	First	Sept. 15, 1888	Grammar	1,224.00
Knowlton, Grace W.	Third	Mar. 9, 1903	Grammar	1,164.00
Bay View Grammar—				
Prior, Philip	Principal	June 14, 1865	High	2,160.00
McGuire, Miss B. A.	V. P., Eighth	Oct. 16, 1883	Grammar	1,620.00
Stolz, Miss R. C.	Seventh and Eighth	Dec. 28, 1892	Grammar	1,224.00
[illegible]rd, Miss E. V.	Seventh	Sept. 1, 1886	Grammar	1,224.00
Casey, Miss M.	Sixth	Sept. 30, 1884	Grammar	1,164.00
Perkins, Miss A. F.	Fifth	Nov. 1, 1890	Grammar	1,164.00
Fitzgerald, Mrs. M. T.	Fifth	Aug. 19, 1907	Grammar	1,164.00
Carey, Miss A. A.	First	Sept. 15, 1882	Grammar	1,224.00
Sleeper, Miss Mary	First	Nov. 18, 1873	Grammar	1,164.00
Piper, Miss L. K.	[illegible]	July 19, 1885	Grammar	1,164.00
[illegible], Miss A. A.	Sixth	Jan. 16, 1903	Grammar	1,164.00
Boylan, M. L.	Fourth	Jan. 12, 1898	Grammar	1,164.00
North, Mrs. E.	Fifth	Jan. 14, 1910	Grammar	840.00
Bernal Grammar—				
Regan, Miss A. G.	Principal	Oct. 5, 1887	Grammar	2,340.00
McGivern, Miss K. A.	V. P., 8th	Oct. 13, 1892	Grammar	1,620.00
Quinn, May	Sixth	Nov. 16, 1905	Grammar	1,164.00
Scott, Mrs. E.	Ungraded	July 15, 1897	Grammar	1,224.00
Schendel, Miss A.	Seventh	Sept. 27, 1880	Grammar	1,224.00
Neppert, Miss L. C.	Sixth	Dec. 29, 1892	Grammar	1,164.00
[illegible], Miss M.	Fifth	Feb. 9, 1892	Grammar	1,164.00
Powell, Mrs. O. T.	Fourth	Jan. 26, 1906	Grammar	1,164.00
Maxwell, Miss E.	Seventh	April 26, 1907	High	1,224.00
Benjamin, Miss M. O.	Sixth	Aug. 26, 1903	Grammar	1,164.00

SCHOOLS AND TEACHERS—Continued.

Name.	Grade of Class.	When Elected.	Grade of Certificate.	Salary per Year.
Bernal Grammar—Continued				
Simpson, Sarah S.	Fourth	July 2, 1889	Grammar	1,164.00
[illegible]bby, [illegible]gie F.	Third	Sept. 23, 1878	Grammar	1,164.00
H[illegible]st, Miss C. H.	Eighth	Sept. 15, 1901	Grammar	1,284.00
[illegible]r, Miss K. G.	Fifth	Aug. 5, 1907	Grammar	1,164.00
Bliss, Miss M. F.	Fifth	Aug. 3, 1910	Grammar	840.00
Millhone, Miss B.	Fifth	July 27, 1898	Grammar	1,164.00
Powell, M[illegible] O.	Fourth	Jan. 26, 1906	Grammar	1,164.00
Bergerot Primary—				
[illegible]e, Miss J. L.	Fifth	[illegible] 2, 1905	Grammar	1,164.00
Gavigan, Miss A. E.	Principal	July 20, 1875	Grammar	1,800.00
[illegible]is, Miss E.	Fifth	April 5, 1883	Grammar	1,284.00
[illegible]r, Miss M. D.	Seventh	June 26, 1905	Grammar	1,224.00
Fairweather, [illegible]en B.	Second	May 16, 1882	Grammar	1,164.00
Evans, Isabel	Fourth	June 21, 1904	High	1,164.00
[illegible]n, M[illegible] J. D.	Third	Jan. 27, 1886	Grammar	1,164.00
Hanlon, Miss L. R.	First	[illegible] 1, 1884	Grammar	1,224.00
McDonnell, Miss A. F.	Third	Sept. 1, 1897	Grammar	1,164.00
Savage, Miss D. A.	Seventh	June 21, 1904	Grammar	1,224.00
Powers, Miss M. V.	First	Sept. 2, 1885	Grammar	1,224.00
[illegible]s, Mrs. C. K.	Ungraded	Nov. 1, 1875	L. D. High	1,224.00
Bell, Miss L. V.	Fifth	Jan. 10, 1910	Grammar	840.00
Wilbur, Mrs. V.	Second	Aug. 10, 1897	Grammar	1,164.00
Bryant Cosmopolitan School—				
Kelly, Miss E. E.	Principal	Oct. 5, 1887	Grammar	1,800.00
Stanford, Miss B. M.	Seventh	Jan. 11, 1877	Grammar and Special	1,224.00
Rutherford, Miss H. M.	Fourth	Nov. 6, 1888	Grammar	1,164.00
Kulmuk, Miss L.	Second	July 22, 1886	Grammar	1,164.00

Name	Grade	Date	School	Salary
Curry, Miss M. E.	Second	Feb. 5, 1878	Grammar	1,164.00
[illegible]ney, Miss F. C.	First	Aug. 28, 1883	Grammar and Special	1,224.00
Heineberg, Miss L.	First	Aug. 15, 1873	Grammar and Special	1,224.00
Roberts, Miss M. E.	First	July 14, 1871	Grammar	1,224.00
Koch, Miss L. H.	4th German	Oct. 31, 1894	Grammar	1,164.00
Unger, Miss A. N.	Second	Aug. 20, 1878	Grammar and Special	1,224.00
[illegible], Miss H. M.	Fourth	July 1, 1903	Grammar	1,164.00
[illegible], Miss A.	Third	Aug. 3, 1908	Grammar	900.00
Wing, Miss M. G.	[illegible]	Mar. 8, 1906	High	1,200.00
Hitchcock, H. M.	French	July 29, 1876	Grammar and Special	1,200.00
Buena [illegible]ta Primary—				
Catlin, Miss A. G.	Principal	Mar. 5, 1878	[illegible]	1,560.00
Hunt, Charlotte F.	Fifth	Oct. 28, 1892	Grammar	1,164.00
Hilderth, M. O.	Fourth	Nov. 11, 1896	Grammar	1,164.00
[illegible], Miss M. T.	Third	Nov. 24, 1909	Grammar	840.00
McFadden, Emma	Second	Jan. 1, 1887	Grammar	1,164.00
Fleming, Miss M. R.	Second	Nov. 14, 1896	Grammar	1,164.00
Rollins, Miss M. A.	First	Oct. 8, 1879	Grammar	1,224.00
[illegible]k, [illegible]se M.	First	Feb. 23, 1898	Grammar	1,224.00
[illegible]r, Miss B. H.	First	Aug. 5, 1888	Grammar	[illegible]
O'Connor, Miss L. B.	Fourth	Aug. 3, 1909	Grammar	840.00
Lewis, Miss R. P.	Fifth	Mar. 14, 1886	Grammar	1,164.00
Burnett Primary—				
[illegible]y, Miss L.	Principal	Dec. 6, 1891	Grammar	1,560.00
Flynn, Miss M. E.	[illegible]	Nov. 20, 1877	Primary	1,164.00
Schroeder, Miss S.	Third	Aug. 26, 1907	High	1,020.00
Curtis, Miss C. M.	First	July 6, 1882	[illegible]	1,224.00
Hopkins, M. J. M.	Second	May 15, 1905	[illegible]	1,164.00
Gannon, M. M. F.	First	July 6, 1877	Grammar	1,224.00
[illegible]y, Miss S.	Second	Feb. 12, 1890	Grammar	1,164.00
Woelffel, Miss E.	Second	Aug. 3, 1908	Grammar	1,164.00

SCHOOLS AND TEACHERS—Continued.

Name.	Grade of Class.	When Elected.	Grade of Certificate.	Salary per Year.
Burnett Primary—Continued				
Kean, Miss J. I.	First	Aug. 7, 1888	Grammar	1,224.00
Reichling, Miss Wanda L.	Second	Jan. 6, 1902	Grammar	1,164.00
Cl[illegible]mont Primary—				
Quinlan, [illegible] F. L.	Principal	Aug. 1, 1884	Grammar	1,800.00
Bronson, [illegible] F. P.	First	Sept. 1, 1884	High	1,224.00
Cohen, Miss Rose	Fourth	Jan. 3, 1889	Grammar	1,164.00
[illegible], Miss Eliz.	Third	Jan. 20, 1886	Grammar	1,164.00
[illegible], Edith A.	First	Mar. 1, 1903	Grammar	1,224.00
O'Connell, Miss A.	Fourth	July 6, 1905	Grammar	1,164.00
[illegible], Miss E.	Second	Aug. 23, 1880	Grammar	1,164.00
Hansell, [illegible] M.	First	Aug. 9, 1897	Grammar	1,224.00
[illegible], Miss E.	Second	Jan. 6, 1908	Grammar	1,020.00
D'Or, Miss M.	First	Sept. 30, 1901	Grammar	1,224.00
Young, Miss M.	Fourth	July 6, 1905	Grammar	1,164.00
O'Connell, Miss Mary C.	Third	July 18, 1902	Grammar	1,164.00
[illegible]d Primary—				
Parolini, [illegible] M. J.	Principal	Mar. 1, 1866	High	[illegible]
Davis, Mrs. F. V.	Second	Jan. 15, 1884	Primary	1,164.00
[illegible], [illegible] A. H.	Third	July 3, 1873	Grammar	1,164.00
[illegible], Miss E. A.	Fourth	Dec. 28, 1880	Grammar	1,164.00
[illegible]rd, Miss S. A.	First	Oct. 30, 1894	Grammar	1,284.00
[illegible], Miss [illegible] A.	Fourth	Feb. 3, 1908	[illegible]	1,164.00
Curley, Miss Alice G.	First	April 1, 1903	Grammar	1,224.00
[illegible], Miss [illegible] A.	First	May 23, 1907	Grammar	1,104.00
Harrigan, Miss Mary A.	Second	Aug. 2, 1871	Grammar	1,164.00
Columbia Grammar—				
Burke, Mrs. L. K.	Principal	Jan. 23, 1857	High	2,460.00
Shuck, Mr. L. M.	V. P., 6th	July 10, 1889	High	1,620.00

Name	Grade	Date	School	Salary
[illegible]n, Miss A. M.	Fifth	Dec. 14, 1892	Grammar	1,164.00
Dunn, Miss M. L.	E[illegible]h	Aug. 13, 1892	[illegible]ar	1,224.00
Krauss, Miss L. H.	Eighth	Sept. 4, 1890	[illegible]ar	1,224.00
[illegible]d, Mrs. A. L.	[illegible]h	June 24, 1884	[illegible]ar	1,224.00
[illegible]n, Mrs. M.	Seventh	Jan. 29, 1871	[illegible]ar	1,224.00
Veuve, Miss M.	[illegible]th	Aug. 2, 1909	[illegible]ar	840.00
[illegible], Mrs. E. R.	Seventh	Nov. 5, 1897	[illegible]ar	1,224.00
[illegible]y, [illegible] M. E.	Sixth	Oct. 29, 1891	[illegible]ar	1,164.00
[illegible]s, Miss [illegible] L.	Fifth	Nov. 1, 1904	[illegible]ar	1,164.00
[illegible]y, Miss M.	Fifth	July 14, 1895	[illegible]ar	1,164.00
[illegible]t, [illegible] V.	Fourth	Mar. 15, 1884	[illegible]ar	1,164.00
[illegible]s, [illegible] K. G.	Fifth	Dec. 20, 1896	[illegible]ar	1,164.00
[illegible]e, Eva M.	First	Sept. 14, [illegible]2	[illegible]ar	1,224.00
Bol[illegible]d, [illegible] M.	First	Sept. 18, [illegible]5	[illegible]ar	1,224.00
Connell, [illegible] I.	Second	Mar. 11, [illegible]3	[illegible]ar	[illegible]
Brown, Mrs. [illegible]ie M.	First	Feb. 13, [illegible]1	[illegible]ar	1,224.00
[illegible]al, Miss A. A.	Sixth	Jan. 13, [illegible]2	[illegible]ar	1,164.00
Lahanney, Miss K.	Fourth	April 2, [illegible]6	[illegible]ar	960.00
[illegible]tt, Miss Mary A.	Third	Jan. 10, [illegible]0	[illegible]ar	840.00
[illegible]n, Mrs. M.	Spanish	June 3, [illegible]8	[illegible]ar	1,200.00
[illegible]h, Mrs. J. Pearl	[illegible]	June 4, 1[illegible]03	Grammar	1,224.00

[illegible]er Primary—

Name	Grade	Date	School	Salary
Brogan, Mrs. K. E.	Pri[illegible]ipal	Nov. 15, 1882	[illegible]ar	1,[illegible]60.00
Murray, Miss M. G.	Second	Nov. 11, [illegible]7	[illegible]r	960.00
Eager, [illegible] N. V.	Second	Mar. 21, [illegible]9	[illegible]ar	[illegible]00
[illegible], Miss S.	Fourth	Feb. 11, [illegible]1	[illegible]ar	1,164.00
Paterson, Miss M.	First	Aug. 14, [illegible]5	[illegible]ar	1,224.00
Tobin, Miss I.	F[illegible]t	Jan. 18, [illegible]8	Grammar	1,344.00
Roden, Miss L.	First	Aug. [illegible]5	[illegible]	1,224.00
Franks, Miss A. E.	Second	Aug. 16, 1888	[illegible]ar	1,164.00
Moore, Eliz. B.	F[illegible]t	Sept. 30, 1901	[illegible]ar	1,224.00
[illegible]l, Miss M. K.	First	Aug. [illegible], 1[illegible]82	[illegible]ar	1,224.00
[illegible]gel[illegible]g, Dorothy	Second	Oct. 14, 1902	[illegible]ar	1,164.00

SCHOOLS AND TEACHERS—Continued.

Name.	Class. Grade of	Elected. When	Grade of Certificate.	Salary per Year.
Cooper Primary—Continued				
Duncan, Miss C. L.	First	Aug. 4, 1882	Grammar	1,224.00
Woodland, Mrs. I. C.	First	Dec. 1, 1882	Grammar	1,224.00
Rea, Miss J. M.	Second	Sept. 1, 1904	High	1,164.00
Crocker [illegible]—				
[illegible]k, Mr. C. W.	Principal	July 10, 1893	High	2,460.00
Murphy, Annette	[illegible]	Dec. 20, 1890	[illegible]mar	1,164.00
[illegible], Miss M. T.	V. P., Eighth	July 10, 1876	[illegible]ar	1,620.00
Folsom, Miss S. A.	[illegible]fth	Aug. 23, 1880	Grammar	1,224.00
Smith, [illegible]ss E. E.	Seventh	Jan. 7, 1895	[illegible]ar and Special	1,284.00
Harby, Miss R.	[illegible]fth	May 5, 1879	Grammar	1,224.00
Durkin, Miss J. L. F.	Seventh	Aug. 1, 1882	[illegible]ar	1,224.00
Barrett, Miss [illegible]ry A.	Seventh	Sept. 2, 1896	[illegible]	1,224.00
Carew, Miss M. M.	Seventh	Nov. 29, 1896	[illegible]ar	1,224.00
Armstrong, Miss N.	Seventh	Dec. 26, 1877	Grammar	1,224.00
[illegible], Miss [illegible]th T.	[illegible]fth	April 3, 1892	Grammar	1,224.00
Murphy, J[illegible]nniee L.	Seventh	Nov. 4, 1886	Grammar	1,224.00
Carpenter, Miss E.	Fifth	July 6, 1905	[illegible]ar	1,164.00
Coleman, Fran[illegible] E.	Sixth	Dec. 14, 1877	[illegible]ar	1,164.00
Ryder, Miss P. E.	Sixth	June 23, 1904	Grammar	1,164.00
Hefron, Miss Helen	Sixth	April 2, 1886	[illegible]ar	1,164.00
Maccuaig, [illegible]ss B.	Sixth	June 23, 1904	[illegible]ar	1,164.00
[illegible]n, Miss [illegible]y T.	Fifth	Dec. 10, 1890	Grammar	1,164.00
E[illegible]h, Virginia L.	Ungraded	Aug. 11, 1897	Grammar	1,224.00
Burlingame, Mrs. J. E.	Fifth	Dec. 5, 1889	[illegible]ar	[illegible]00
Denman Grammar—				
Smith. Jessie	Eighth	Mar. 10, 1863	High	1,224.00
Childs, Miss K. B.	Seventh	July 5, 1866	High	1,224.00
D'Arcy, Miss A. H.	Fifth	July , 1870	Grammar	1,164.00

Name	Grade	Date	Certificate	Salary
Goldsmith, Miss B.	Eighth	Feb. 15, 1876	Grammar	1,164.00
Houstin, Miss J.	[illegible]	April 2, 1881	Grammar	1,224.00
[illegible] Primary—				
Tarpy, Miss W. L.	Principal	Aug. 19, 1884	Grammar	1,800.00
Cashman, Miss M. E.	Second	Nov. 14, 1905	Grammar	1,140.00
Dacre, Miss E. L.	First	[illegible] 28, 1905	Grammar	1,224.00
[illegible], Miss M.	Fourth	Sept. 12, 1894	Grammar	1,164.00
Bishop, Louise M.	Fourth	Sept. 8, 1897	Grammar	1,164.00
Houghton, Miss E.	Third	Nov. 1, 1896	Grammar & Special	1,224.00
[illegible], Miss M. A.	Second	June 9, 1897	Grammar	1,164.00
El[illegible], Kate C.	Third	Mar. 5, 1909	Grammar	[illegible]
[illegible], Miss E. S.	First	Oct. 1, 1905	Grammar	1,224.00
P[illegible], Miss [illegible] R.	First	Sept. 15, 1891	Grammar & Special	1,224.00
[illegible], Miss L.	First	July 15, 1902	Grammar	1,224.00
Stewart, Miss A. R.	Third	Aug. 6, 1909	Grammar	840.00
Dowling, Miss E. P.	Second	[illegible] 10, 1910	[illegible]	[illegible]
[illegible] Stone Primary—				
Earle, Miss S. H.	Principal	July 20, 1869	Grammar	[illegible]
[illegible], Bertha K.	Third	Feb. 1, 1904	Grammar	1,164.00
Carew, Miss M. R.	First	Sept. 20, 1894	Grammar	1,224.00
Hare, Miss F.	Fourth	Oct. 21, 1873	Grammar	1,164.00
[illegible], Miss M. L.	Fourth	Sept. [illegible], 1885	Primary & Special	1,224.00
Koch, Miss L.	[illegible]	Feb. 11, 1903	Grammar	1,164.00
[illegible], Miss Natalie	Second	Nov. 11, 1896	Primary	1,164.00
Dwyer, Miss M. C.	Second	Sept. 1, 1897	Grammar	1,164.00
Gambitz, Miss L. M.	Third	[illegible] 12, 1898	Grammar	1,164.00
Fritz, Miss L. M.	Second	July 1, 1903	Grammar	1,164.00
[illegible], Miss J. A.	First	Nov. 1, 1883	Grammar	1,224.00
McGeough, Miss R.	First	Jan. 31, 1884	Grammar	1,224.00
Edison Primary—				
Saunders, Miss J.	Principal	April 23, 1887	Grammar	1,800.00
Kelly, Miss M. C.	Fifth	Dec 8, 1891	Grammar	1,164.00

Name.	Grade of [illegible]	[illegible] Elected.	Grade of Certificate.	Salary per Year.
Edison Primary—Cont[illegible]d.				
Barry, [illegible] M. E.	Fifth	April 1, [illegible]	[illegible]	1,164.00
[illegible], Miss A. R.	[illegible]	Feb. 24, 1898	[illegible]	1,224.00
Wilson, [illegible] E. N.	[illegible]	July 18, 1902	[illegible]	1,164.00
Harrigan, Miss A. [illegible]	[illegible]	Sept. 19, [illegible]	[illegible]	1,224.00
Robinett, Miss M. M.	First	[illegible] 5, 1875	[illegible]	1,224.00
McDermott, [illegible] C. M.	[illegible]	Nov. 30, [illegible]	[illegible]	1,164.00
[illegible], [illegible] E. H.	[illegible]	[illegible] 7, 1883	[illegible]	1,164.00
F[illegible], Miss H. A.	Fourth	Jan. 13, [illegible]	[illegible]	840.00
Porter, [illegible] H.	Second	[illegible] 28, [illegible]	Grammar	[illegible]
Emerson Primary—				
Spencer, Mrs. T. F.	Principal	July 17, [illegible]	[illegible] & Special	[illegible]
Dennis, Miss E.	First	[illegible] 5, 1888	Grammar	1,344.00
McLaughlin, Miss A. M.	First	July 6, [illegible]	[illegible]	1,224.00
[illegible], [illegible] A.	Second	Sept. 8, 1897	[illegible]	[illegible]
Fol[illegible], Miss M. L.	[illegible]	Nov. 18, 1896	Grammar	[illegible]
[illegible], [illegible] A. G.	[illegible]	Sept. 10, [illegible]	[illegible]	[illegible]
[illegible], Miss C. B.	Third	[illegible] 13, [illegible]	Grammar	[illegible]
[illegible], Miss M. F.	Fourth	May 13, [illegible]	[illegible]	1,164.00
Gambitz, [illegible] L. B.	Fourth	[illegible] 27, [illegible]	[illegible]	1,164.00
Watson, Miss M. A.	Ungraded	Mar. 12, 1890	Grammar	1,224.00
O'Brien, [illegible] L.	First	[illegible] 12, 1890	[illegible]	1,224.00
Meyer, Miss R.	First	Nov. 22, [illegible]	Grammar	1,224.00
Spafford, [illegible] D. B.	Second	[illegible] 8, [illegible]	[illegible]	1,164.00
[illegible], Miss C.	Second	Jan. 25, 1905	[illegible]	1,164.00
Estes, Miss C.	[illegible]	Oct. 14, [illegible]	Grammar	[illegible]
Everett Grammar—				
Sturges, Selden	Principal	July 6, 1875	[illegible]	2,340.00

Name	Grade	Date	School	Salary
[illegible], Miss A. J.	[illegible]hth	Dec. 20, 1892	Gr[illegible]	1,224.00
Devi[illegible], M[illegible]s M. E.	Seventh	July 4, [illegible]5	Gr[illegible]	1,224.00
Johnson, Marie J.	Seventh	Feb. 1, [illegible]6	Gr[illegible]	1,284.00
Grimm, M[illegible]s A. L.	Sixth	Feb. 14, 1881	Gr[illegible]	1,164.00
[illegible], M[illegible]s R. I.	Fifth	[illegible] 2, [illegible]8	Gr[illegible]	1,164.00
Sullivan, Julia F.	Sixth	[illegible] 1, [illegible]7	Gr[illegible]	1,164.00
[illegible], Ida May	Fifth	Nov. 11, [illegible]6	Gr[illegible]	1,164.[illegible]
Fenton, M[illegible]s E. R.	Third	July 27, [illegible]8	Grammar	1,164.00
Spafford, Hel[illegible]n E.	S[illegible]ond	Jan. 6, [illegible]2	Gr[illegible]	1,164.00
Morse, Miss N. A.	Second	July 30, [illegible]0	Gr[illegible]	1,164.00
Gracier, M[illegible]s A. J.	[illegible]	[illegible] 6, [illegible]7	Gr[illegible]	1,224.00
McClain, Mrs. A. W.	First	[illegible] 3, 1893	Gr[illegible]	1,224.00
[illegible], Mrs. E. J.	First	April 3, [illegible]7	Gr[illegible]	1,224.00
Stuart, Mrs. M.	[illegible] P., 8th	April [illegible], [illegible]5	Gr[illegible]	1,620.00
Moore, M[illegible]s M.	[illegible]	April 5, [illegible]3	Gr[illegible]	1,224.00
Grant, Emily W.	Fourth	Mar. 30, 1905	L. D. [illegible]	1,164.00
[illegible], Miss E. M.	Fifth	Jan. [illegible], [illegible]0	[illegible]	840.00
Erb, Miss N. V.	Third	July 8, [illegible]8	High	[illegible],164.00

Fai[illegible] [illegible]—

Name	Grade	Date	School	Salary
[illegible] Bell, Mr. [illegible] H.	Pri[illegible]ipal	July 19, 1901	High	2,460.00
[illegible]gh, Miss Kathryn	V. P., 8th	Jan. 12, 1898	Grammar	1,620.00
Hammond, Miss E. E.	Seventh	Dec. 1, [illegible]2	Gr[illegible]	1,224.00
Berard, M[illegible]s E. L.	Eighth	Sept. 30, 1901	Gr[illegible]mar	1,224.00
[illegible], Miss M. A.	Fifth	Aug. 11, [illegible]7	Gr[illegible]	1,164.00
Fallon, M[illegible]s D. A.	Seventh	April 21, 1891	Gr[illegible]	1,224.00
Torpey, Miss K. L.	Fourth	Feb. [illegible], [illegible]8	Gr[illegible]	1,164.00
Chandler, M[illegible]s M. G.	Second	Mar. 1, [illegible]4	Grammar	1,164.00
Provost, M[illegible]s C. E.	Second	April 14, [illegible]5	Gr[illegible]ar	1,164.00
[illegible]n, Miss M. F.	Fourth	Nov. 19, [illegible]5	Gr[illegible]ar	1,140.00
Foley, Miss Mary [illegible].	First	Jan. 27, 1905	Gr[illegible]	1,224.00
Woeffel, [illegible]a M.	Fourth	[illegible] [illegible], 1[illegible]0	Grammar	840.00
[illegible]n, Mrs. A. F.	Ungraded	Sept. [illegible], [illegible]9	Grammar	1,284.00
Smit[illegible], Mrs. A. [illegible]	Second	Sept. 2, 1908	Primary	840.00

Name.	Grade of [illegible]	[illegible]	Grade of [illegible]	Salary [illegible]
Fairmount Grammar—Continued				
Burke, Miss M. A.	[illegible]	[illegible] [illegible], [illegible]	[illegible]	[illegible]
C'Connor, [illegible] N. T.	Third	[illegible] [illegible], [illegible]	[illegible]	1,164.00
[illegible], [illegible] E. D.	[illegible]	Oct. [illegible], [illegible]	[illegible]	1,080.00
[illegible], Miss M. G.	First	[illegible] [illegible], [illegible]	[illegible]	1,224.00
[illegible], [illegible] [illegible] J.	Seventh	June 10, 1910	[illegible]	840.00
Barrington, [illegible] F. E.	[illegible]	July [illegible], [illegible]	[illegible]	[illegible]
Traynor, Miss M. E.	First	[illegible] 3, [illegible]	[illegible]	[illegible]
Prichard, [illegible]. C. B.	Fifth	[illegible] 1, [illegible]	[illegible]	1,164.00
Flanagan, Miss I. R.	Fifth	[illegible] [illegible], 1910	[illegible]	840.00
Farragut Primary—				
Derham, Miss T. E.	Principal	[illegible] 3, 1888	[illegible]	1,560.00
McDonald, Miss J.	First	[illegible] [illegible], 1898	[illegible]	1,224.00
Sullivan, Miss G. A.	First	June [illegible], 1904	[illegible]	1,224.00
Seavy, Miss J.	Third	Aug. 3, 1908	Grammar	900.00
Wagner, Miss H. R.	Fourth	[illegible] 3, 1908	[illegible]	900.00
Caswell, Miss A. E.	Second	[illegible] [illegible], 1910	[illegible]	840.00
Frank [illegible]—				
[illegible], [illegible] S. B.	Principal	[illegible] [illegible], [illegible]	[illegible]	[illegible]
Barber, [illegible] E. J.	First	[illegible] 1, 1884	Grammar	[illegible]
Jacobs, [illegible] H. H.	Fifth	Sept. 1, [illegible]	[illegible]	[illegible]
[illegible]Neil, Miss M. E.	Second	[illegible] [illegible], [illegible]	[illegible]	[illegible]
Hart, [illegible] E. I.	Fourth	[illegible] [illegible], [illegible]	High [illegible] Special	[illegible]
Wade, [illegible] L. M.	[illegible]	July [illegible], [illegible]	[illegible]	1,224.00
Irwin, [illegible] M. A.	[illegible]	Nov. [illegible], [illegible]	Gram. [illegible] Spec.	1,164.00
Fay, Miss M. A.	First	Mar. 11, [illegible]	[illegible]	1,284.00
Brierton, Mary	[illegible]	[illegible] 2, 1897	[illegible]	1,224.00
[illegible], [illegible] E.	Second	Aug. 3, [illegible]	[illegible]	840.00
[illegible], [illegible] N.	Third	Aug. 15, [illegible]	[illegible]	840.00
[illegible], Mrs. J. S.	Fourth	[illegible] 19, [illegible]	Grammar	1,164.00

Name	Grade	Date	School	Salary
Sullivan, Miss N. C.	Third	Mar. 22, 1907	[illegible]	960.00
Hall, M. S.	Seventh	May 2, 1910	[illegible]	840.00
Meek, A.	Sixth	July 25, 1910	[illegible]	840.00
Bailie, M.	Fifth	June 9, 1897	[illegible]	840.00
Fr[illegible]—				
[illegible], Mrs. N. A.	Principal	Nov. 13, 1866	[illegible]	1,800.00
[illegible], Miss [illegible] S.	[illegible]	Mar. 30, 1905	[illegible]	1,344.00
[illegible], Miss E. M.	Second	Jan. 3, 1902	[illegible]	1,164.00
[illegible], Miss M. J.	Si[illegible]th	Aug. 22, 1907	[illegible]	1,140.00
Roper, Miss B.	First	Nov. 23, 1869	[illegible]	1,224.00
[illegible], Miss C. E.	First	Oct. 22, 1884	[illegible]	1,224.00
Browne, Mr. Frank J.	S[illegible]venth	Sept. 13, [illegible]4	[illegible]	1,344.00
[illegible], M[illegible]s A. A.	Second	Sept. 27, 1909	Grammar	840.00
[illegible], Miss Etta F.	[illegible]	June 15, 1908	Grammar	1,020.00
[illegible], Miss M. [illegible]	[illegible]	Jan. 12, 1910	Grammar	840.00
[illegible], Miss E. G.	Third	April 4, 1910	[illegible]	840.00
Fremont Grammar—				
Von [illegible] L[illegible]h, Miss O.	Sixth	April 18, [illegible]10	Gram. [illegible] S[illegible]al	840.00
Ostrom, Mrs. I. D.	V. P., [illegible]hth	Aug. 10, 1898	[illegible]	2,340.00
Moran, [illegible]s D. F.	S[illegible]ond[illegible]	Dec. 1, 1898	Gram. [illegible] Special	1,164.00
[illegible], Nora B.	[illegible]	Sept. 30, 1890	[illegible]	1,620.00
Rosenfeld, Miss F.	First	Aug. 1, 1888	[illegible]	1,224.00
[illegible], Miss S. F.	First	Jan. 31, 1889	[illegible]	1,224.00
[illegible], Mrs. R.	Second	Sept. 27, 1880	Primary	1,224.00
[illegible]Nichol, Mrs. J. E.	Second	Oct. 27, 1897	[illegible]	1,164.00
[illegible], Rose F.	Fourth	July 28, 1898	[illegible]	1,164.00
Shorb, Mrs. [illegible] E.	Fourth	Oct. 21, 1901	[illegible]	1,164.00
[illegible], Miss L. M.	Seventh	April 9, 1875	[illegible]	1,284.00
Grant, Mrs. K. D.	Ei[illegible]h	June 3, 1897	[illegible]	1,224.00
[illegible], E. T.	Fifth	Oct. 17, 1904	[illegible]	1,164.00
McGough, R. M.	Third	~~Jan. 31, 1884~~	[illegible]	1,164.00
[illegible], M[illegible]s J. A.	Seventh	Jan. 31, 1910	[illegible]	840.00
Barrett, Miss C.	Third	April 13, 1910	[illegible]	840.00

SCHOOLS AND TEACHERS—[illegible]

Name.	Grade of Class.	[illegible] El[illegible]ted.	Grade of Certificate	Salary [illegible] Year.
Garfield [illegible]—				
Scherer, Miss [illegible] A.	[illegible]	Aug. 7, [illegible]	[illegible]	2,160.00
[illegible], [illegible] E.	[illegible]	Jan. 17, [illegible]	[illegible]	840.00
[illegible], [illegible] L.	[illegible]	Oct. 28, [illegible]	[illegible]	1,164.00
Barkley, [illegible]	[illegible]	[illegible] 27, [illegible]	High	840.00
Lyton, Mrs. I.	First	[illegible] 28, [illegible]	Grammar	1,224.00
[illegible], [illegible] C.	First	[illegible] 22, [illegible]	[illegible]	1,224.00
Wehrli, [illegible] E.	First	[illegible] 29, [illegible]	[illegible]	1,284.00
[illegible], [illegible] E.	First	Feb. 1, [illegible]	Life Diploma	1,224.00
[illegible], Teresa	First	Oct. 17, [illegible]	[illegible]	1,344.00
[illegible], Miss N. V.	Fourth	[illegible] [illegible], [illegible]	[illegible]	1,164.00
Busch, [illegible] E.	Fourth	Aug. [illegible], [illegible]	[illegible]	1,164.00
[illegible], [illegible]	Fourth	Jan. [illegible], [illegible]	L. [illegible] Grammar	1,164.00
[illegible], [illegible] M.	Third	[illegible] , [illegible]	High	[illegible].00
[illegible], [illegible] A. [illegible]	Third	Nov. 3, 1864	[illegible]	1,164.00
Carroll, Miss L. A.	First	[illegible] [illegible], [illegible]	[illegible]	1,224.00
[illegible], [illegible] M.	First	[illegible] [illegible], [illegible]	[illegible]	1,224.00
[illegible], [illegible]	[illegible]	[illegible] 2, [illegible]	Grammar-Special	[illegible]
[illegible], Mrs. C.	Second	July 23, [illegible]	[illegible]	1,164.00
Glen Park [illegible]—				
[illegible], [illegible] Janet	Principal	[illegible] 2, [illegible]	Grammar	2,160.00
[illegible], [illegible] C.	Fourth	[illegible] [illegible], [illegible]	Grammar	840.00
Doran, Julia A.	Sixth-Eighth	Jan. 7, [illegible]	[illegible]	1,500.00
[illegible], [illegible] A.	Seventh	[illegible] 4, [illegible]	[illegible]	1,224.00
Crowley, [illegible] A. T.	[illegible]	July [illegible], [illegible]	[illegible]	1,164.00
[illegible], [illegible] I. T.	Sixth	Oct. [illegible], [illegible]	[illegible]	1,164.00
Crowley, [illegible] Mary E.	Third	[illegible] 5, [illegible]	Grammar	1,164.00
[illegible], [illegible] Mary	[illegible]	April 7, [illegible]	Grammar	1,164.00
Barron, Miss C. M.	First	Oct. [illegible], [illegible]	Grammar	1,224.00

Phelps, Mrs. J. H.	First	Mar. 20, 1877	Grammar	1,224.00
Gray, Mrs. O. P.	Fifth	July 25, 1910	Grammar	840.00
McDermott, Miss L.	Third	Oct. 1, 1904	High	1,164.00
Smith, Mrs. V. E.	Sixth	April 16, 1877	Grammar	1,164.00
McNeil, Miss F. A.	Fifth	Feb. 26, 1909	Grammar	840.00
Golden Gate Primary—				
[illegible]rt, Miss P.	Principal	July 6, 1870	High	1,560.00
[illegible]n, Mary L.	Fifth	Jan. 20, 1876	Gr[illegible]	1,164.00
[illegible]n, Mary A.	Fourth	[illegible]g. 15, 1877	Gr[illegible]	1,164.00
Bonnelli, Mrs. E. M.	Fourth	Feb. 5, 1877	[illegible]	1,164.00
Ryan, Miss E. T.	Third	Jan. 4, 1875	[illegible]	1, [illegible]4.00
Kaplan, M[illegible]s M. E.	Third	Nov. 8, 1884	Gr[illegible]	1,164.00
[illegible]n, [illegible]t G.	Second	[illegible]il 4, 1886	Gr[illegible]	1,164.00
Hare, Mrs. K. M.	First	O[illegible]. 2, 1873	Gr[illegible]	1,224.00
[illegible]n, M[illegible]s [illegible]. M.	First	Mar. 1, 1879	Gr[illegible]	1,224.00
Oral School for Deaf—				
Holden, Mrs. J. B.		Aug. 15, 1901	Special	1,260.00
Holden, Mr. A. N.		Aug. 1, 1902	Special	1,164.00
Grant Primary—				
Shaw, [illegible]ss I. [illegible]	[illegible]al	[illegible] 6, [illegible]2	Gr[illegible]	1,560.00
[illegible], M[illegible]s B. C.	Ei[illegible]th	Nov. 1, [illegible]6	Gr[illegible]	1,224.00
[illegible]r, Miss V.	[illegible]	[illegible]g. 9, [illegible]5	Gr[illegible]	1,152.00
[illegible]n, Miss A. B.	[illegible]th [illegible] Sixth	Jan. [illegible], [illegible]8	Gr[illegible]	1,164.00
Berg, M[illegible]s F. C.	First	April [illegible], [illegible]5	Gr[illegible]	1,224.00
Wagner, M[illegible]s J. A.	Sixth	Jan. [illegible], [illegible]8	Gr[illegible]	840.00
Body, M[illegible]s [illegible]	[illegible]-Fifth	Mar. 8, 1[illegible]99	Gr[illegible]	[illegible]0.00
[illegible]e, M[illegible]s T.	Second	[illegible]g. [illegible], [illegible]5	Gr[illegible]	1,080.00
Rhine, M[illegible]s E.	F[illegible]h	[illegible]y 5, 1903	Gr[illegible]	1,164.00
Davids[illegible] Miss E.	Third	[illegible]g. 10, 1898	Gr[illegible]	1,164.00

SCHOOLS AND TEACHERS—[illegible].

Name.	Grade of Class.	[illegible] Elected.	Grade of [illegible]ate.	Salary [illegible]r Year.
[illegible] Primary—				
[illegible]tler, Mrs. E.	Prin. and Second	Aug. 4, [illegible]82	[illegible]	1,560.00
Frontin, Miss E. A.	Third and Fourth	Oct. 1, [illegible]87	[illegible]	1,224.00
Sprague, Miss A. F.	Fourth	Sept. 4, [illegible]67	[illegible]	1,164.00
[illegible], [illegible] M.	Second	Feb. 16, 1875	[illegible]	1,224.00
[illegible], [illegible] K.	First	July 2, [illegible]83	[illegible]	1,224.00
Maccord, [illegible] L.	Second	Feb. 5, [illegible]878	Primary	1,164.00
[illegible], [illegible] A.	Third	July 2, [illegible]98	[illegible]	1,164.00
[illegible]—				
Haswell, [illegible] M. A.	Principal	[illegible] 25, [illegible]87	High	1,900.00
[illegible], Stella [illegible]	Fourth	[illegible] 16, [illegible]06	[illegible]	1,020.00
[illegible], [illegible] T.	Second	Aug. 3, [illegible]08	[illegible]	900.00
Sweeney, [illegible] C. L.	Fifth	[illegible] 6, [illegible]86	[illegible]	1,164.00
Gilmore, [illegible] E. M.	[illegible]	[illegible] 24, [illegible]87	[illegible]	1,164.00
Donovan, [illegible] E.	Fourth	[illegible] 14, [illegible]88	Primary	1,[illegible].00
[illegible], [illegible] F. E.	Third	[illegible] 25, [illegible]04	[illegible]	1,[illegible]64.00
Davidson, Mrs. T.	S[illegible]ond	[illegible] 26, [illegible]80	Primary	1,[illegible]84.[illegible]
McDevitt, [illegible] J.	First	[illegible] 20, [illegible]03	[illegible]	[illegible]24.00
Miller, [illegible] S. E.	First	[illegible] 5, [illegible]86	[illegible]	1,[illegible]24.00
Forsyth, [illegible] L. M.	[illegible]rst	[illegible] 6, [illegible]92	Gram. and Special	1,[illegible]84.00
[illegible], [illegible] C.	[illegible]	[illegible] 29, [illegible]89	Primary	1,[illegible]64.00
[illegible], [illegible] J.	First	Aug. 3, [illegible]95	[illegible]	1,[illegible]24.00
Grace, [illegible] J. G.	Third	Aug. [illegible], [illegible]97	[illegible]	1,080.00
[illegible], Miss G. M.	Third	Aug. 3, [illegible]98	[illegible]	1,080.00
Hamilton Grammar—				
Kellogg, Mr. A. E.	Principal	Sept. 1, 1886	[illegible]	2,340.00
Manley, Miss I. M.	Sixth	Aug. 12, 1903	[illegible]	1,164.00
Allen, Miss S. H.	Fifth	Oct. 24, 1901	[illegible]	1,164.00

Name	Grade	Date of Appointment	Certificate	Salary
Hauselt, [illegible] E. E.	[illegible]th	July [illegible], [illegible]2	[illegible]r	1,224.00
[illegible]n, [illegible]elle R.	Eighth	Aug. 5, [illegible]5	Gr	1,224.00
Morton, [illegible] E. J.	Seventh, V.-Prin.	July [illegible], [illegible]5	Gr	1,620 0
Strauss, Miss I. R.	Seventh	July 6, 1873	[illegible]r	1,224.00
[illegible]h, [illegible] I. B.	Seventh	Jan. 31, 1889	Gr	1,224.00
[illegible]w, Mrs. L. A.	Ei[illegible]h	Aug. 14, 1895	Grammar	1,224.00
[illegible]l, [illegible] L. A.	[illegible]th	Aug. 1, [illegible]4	[illegible]h	1,224.00
[illegible]d, Mary T.	Fifth	Dec. 7, [illegible]5	[illegible]h	1,164.00
Brittan, [illegible] A. C.	Fifth	Sept. 30, 1901	[illegible]r	1,164.00
Martin, [illegible] I. C.	[illegible]th	July 25, 1901	[illegible]h	1,164.00
Whitley, Miss A.	Seventh	Sept. 29, 1901	[illegible]h	1,224.00
Silverberg, Miss A.	Ungraded	Oct. 2, [illegible]3	[illegible]h	1,224.00
Moldrup, Miss E.	Fifth	July [illegible], [illegible]0	Gr	840.00
[illegible] Grammar—				
[illegible]er, Miss N. [illegible]	Principal	May 14, 1896	Gr	2,160.00
Cereghino, Miss J.	Italian	Feb. 14, [illegible]0	Gr	1,200.00
O'Neil, [illegible]ss [illegible]s	Fourth	Oct. 4, 1[illegible]95	Gr	1,164.00
[illegible]i, Mrs. [illegible] G.	[illegible]th	Nov. [illegible], [illegible]9	Gr	1,560.00
Scanlan, [illegible] Renee	Seventh	[illegible]g. [illegible], [illegible]5	[illegible]r	1,152.00
Burke, [illegible] M. C.	Third.	Jan. 4, 1905	[illegible]r	1,164.00
[illegible]r, [illegible]s L. M.	E[illegible]h	Mar. 30, 1905	[illegible]h	1,224.00
[illegible]o, [illegible] N. C.	[illegible]h	[illegible]g. 14, [illegible]5	[illegible]h	1,080.00
Furbush, Miss M. W.	Fifth	April 5, [illegible]	[illegible]r	1,164.00
Deane, Mrs. N. E.	Ungraded	Jan. 21, [illegible]	Gr	1,224.00
Barry, [illegible] May D.	Fifth	Mar. 3, [illegible]0	[illegible]h	840.00
[illegible]s, Miss A.	Third	Jan. 10, [illegible]0	Gr	840.00
Leibold, [illegible] E.	Sixth	[illegible]r. 23, [illegible]1	Gr	1,164.00
Hartrick, [illegible]s L.	Fifth	Aug. 22, [illegible]7	Gr	1,164.00
[illegible]s, [illegible]s [illegible]	Fourth	Jan. 16, [illegible]8	Gr	1,164.00
O'Connor, Miss V.	Third	Jan. 6, [illegible]8	Grammar	1,164.00
Harrison Primary—				
Moran, Miss M. R.	Third & Fourth, P'l	[illegible]g. 9, 1890	Grammar	1,560.00
Dolan, Miss Mary J.	First	Feb. 3, 1888	Grammar	1,224.00

SCHOOLS AND TEACHERS—[illegible]

Name.	Grade of Class.	When Elected.			Grade of Certificate.	Salary per Year.
Hawthorne Primary—						
[illegible], Mrs. S. J.	[illegible]	Spt.	1,	[illegible]	High	1,80C 00
Curran, Mrs. N. W.	[illegible]	Aug.	1,	[illegible]	[illegible]	1,164.00
[illegible], Mrs.	[illegible]	[illegible]	5,	[illegible]	[illegible]	1,164.00
Barrett, [illegible] L.	[illegible]	[illegible]	14,	[illegible]	[illegible]	1,140.00
Drewry, [illegible] Mable	Second	Aug.	3,	[illegible]	[illegible]	[illegible]0.00
Simon, [illegible] [illegible] F.	S onde	[illegible]	1,	[illegible]	[illegible]	1,164.00
Barrett, [illegible] N. [illegible]	First	[illegible]	12,	[illegible]	[illegible]	1,224.00
[illegible], [illegible] M. L.	First	Spt.	8,	[illegible]	[illegible]	1,224.00
[illegible], Mrs. [illegible] [illegible]	Fourth	Aug.	1,	[illegible]	[illegible]	840.00
Hill, Mrs. M. [illegible]	Second	[illegible]	9,	[illegible]	[illegible]	1,224.00
Hearst Grammar—						
Sullivan, [illegible] N. F.	[illegible]	[illegible]	13,	[illegible]	[illegible]	2,340.00
[illegible], [illegible] [illegible] M.	[illegible]	[illegible]	28,	[illegible]	[illegible]	1,620.00
[illegible], [illegible] R. H.	S onde	[illegible]	23,	[illegible]	Gram n ar	1,164.00
[illegible], Mrs. R.	[illegible]	[illegible]	15,	[illegible]	Grammar-Special	1, [illegible] 00
Bray, [illegible] [illegible] F.	Seventh	[illegible]	5,	[illegible]	[illegible]	1,224.00
Levison, [illegible] [illegible]	Seventh	Ag.	17,	[illegible]	[illegible]	1,224.00
Torpey, [illegible] M. C.	[illegible]	Sept.	6,	[illegible]	[illegible]	1,164.00
[illegible], [illegible] [illegible] [illegible]	Seventh	[illegible]	2,	[illegible]	[illegible]	1,224.00
[illegible], [illegible] C. L.	Sixth	Sept.	2,	[illegible]	[illegible]	1,164 00
[illegible], [illegible] K. A.	Fifth	[illegible]	1,	[illegible]	[illegible]	1,164.00
Van [illegible] Bergh, [illegible] F.	Fi [illegible]	[illegible]	9,	[illegible]	[illegible]	1,164.00
[illegible], [illegible] R.	F [illegible]	[illegible]	12,	[illegible]	Grammar	1,164.00
Fairweather, [illegible] E.	[illegible]	[illegible]	15,	[illegible]	[illegible]	1,164.00
[illegible], [illegible] [illegible] [illegible]	[illegible]	Aug.	21,	[illegible]	[illegible]	1,164.00
Peake, Mrs. B. M.	[illegible]	[illegible]	1,	[illegible]	[illegible]	1,164.00
Martin, [illegible] A.	[illegible]	Spt.	1,	[illegible]	[illegible]	1,164.00
Crowley, [illegible] E. A.	Second	[illegible]	29,	[illegible]	Grammar	1,224.00

Name	Grade	Date	School	Salary
Grace, Miss H. M.	Ungraded	Dec. 29, 1896	High	1,224.00
Cole, Miss L. C.	First	Aug. 1, 1882	Grammar	1,224.00
Hynes, Miss F. S.	First	May 1, 1896	Grammar	1,224.00
O'Neil, Mrs. N.	Fourth	Dec. 30, 1892	Grammar	1,164.00
Henry Durant Primary—				
[illegible]n, M[illegible] M. F.	[illegible]ci[illegible]al	Jan. 3, [illegible]7	[illegible]r	1,300.00
[illegible]n, M[illegible]s R. A.	Fifth	[illegible]n. 3, [illegible]7	[illegible]r	1,164.00
[illegible]d, M[illegible]s [illegible]	[illegible]h	[illegible]ril 29, 1886	[illegible]r	1,164.00
[illegible]s, M[illegible]s [illegible] F.	[illegible]h	Nov. 1, [illegible]7	[illegible]r	1,164.00
[illegible]e, [illegible]s [illegible] [illegible]	[illegible]	[illegible]y [illegible], [illegible]5	[illegible]r	1,164.00
[illegible], Miss E. J.	Third	[illegible]n. 12, 1898	[illegible]r	1,164.00
[illegible]d, Mrs. E. S.	First	[illegible]v. 2, [illegible]9	[illegible]r	1,224.00
[illegible], M[illegible]s C.	Se[illegible]ond	[illegible]y 29, 1891	[illegible]r	1,164.00
[illegible], M[illegible]s [illegible]	[illegible]	May [illegible], [illegible]0	[illegible]r	1,164.00
Hill, [illegible]s. [illegible] [illegible]	[illegible]st	April 15, 1885	[illegible]r	1,224.00
Boukofsky, M[illegible]s [illegible]	First	[illegible]t. 1, [illegible]6	[illegible]r	1,224.00
[illegible]n, M[illegible]s S. R.	First	Nov. 5, [illegible]5	[illegible]r	1,224.00
Powers, Mrs. E.	Second	Nov. 25, [illegible]8	Grammar	840.00
Horace Mann Grammar—				
Faulkner, [illegible] Richard D.	[illegible]ri[illegible]ci[illegible]al	Oct. 2, [illegible]8	[illegible]h	2,460.00
[illegible]t, Mary	Seventh	Mar. [illegible], [illegible]9	[illegible]r [illegible] S[illegible]al	1,224.00
Hatch, [illegible]s. L. [illegible]	S[illegible]h	[illegible]n. 2, [illegible]1	[illegible]r	1,224.00
[illegible], Miss [illegible]	[illegible]	Jan. [illegible], [illegible]4	Grammar	1,224.00
Grant, Miss [illegible] [illegible]	Seventh	Jan. [illegible], [illegible]0	[illegible]r	840.00
[illegible]oll, Miss B.	S[illegible]h	Aug. 6, [illegible]2	[illegible]r	1,164.00
[illegible], Agnes E.	Ei[illegible]th	Mar. 11, [illegible]6	[illegible]r	1,224.00
[illegible]s, M[illegible]s A. [illegible]	S[illegible]th	[illegible]y 21, [illegible]3	[illegible]r	1,164.00
[illegible]t, M[illegible]s [illegible] M.	Ei[illegible]h	[illegible]n. 2, [illegible]5	[illegible]r-Special	1,284.00
[illegible]d, Mary E.	Eighth	[illegible]y 26, [illegible]8	[illegible]r	1,224.00
O'Brien, M[illegible]s Kate	Si[illegible]h	Sept. 14, [illegible]8	[illegible]r	1,164.00
Stockt[illegible]n, Miss F.	Sixth	July 18, [illegible]2	[illegible]r	1,164.00

SCHOOLS AND TEACHERS—[illegible]

Name.	Grade of Class.	When Elected.	Grade of Certificate.	Salary per Year.
Horace Mann Grammar—Continued				
Toland, Miss M.	Seventh	Feb. [illegible], 1906	[illegible]	1,224.00
Moynihan, Eliza J.	Eighth	[illegible]. [illegible], 1884	[illegible]	1,224.00
Casey, Miss M. E.	Eighth	[illegible] 6, 1875	[illegible]	1,620.00
Peckham, Miss L.	Seventh	[illegible]. [illegible], 1901	[illegible]	1,224.00
Keith, Miss E. D.	Seventh	[illegible] [illegible], 1891	[illegible]	1,224.00
Cooney. Miss K.	Fifth	[illegible]. [illegible], 1910		840.00
Hunters Point School—				
Itsell, Mr. A. J.	Principal	July 10, 1871	High	1,440.00
[illegible] M. Scott [illegible]—				
Hamil[illegible], Jas. T.	[illegible]	[illegible] 8, 1876	High	2, [illegible]0.00
Croughwell, Miss A. T.	V. P., Eighth	[illegible]. 8, [illegible]	Gr[illegible]	1, [illegible] 00
Downey, Miss M. L.	S[illegible]	[illegible]. 1, 1886	Gr[illegible]	1, [illegible]4.00
Duggin, Mrs. M.	Sixth	[illegible]. 4, 1904	Grammar	1, [illegible]4.00
Mooney, Miss M. F.	Fifth	Jan. [illegible], [illegible]	[illegible] and Special	1, [illegible]4.00
[illegible], Mary A.	[illegible]	Feb. 23, 1898	[illegible]	1, [illegible]4.00
Marsh, Alice L.	S[illegible]	Aug. [illegible], [illegible]	[illegible]	1, [illegible]4.00
Bryan, [illegible] E. M.	Fifth	[illegible]. 5, 1906	[illegible]	1, [illegible]4.00
[illegible], Miss M. J.	[illegible]	[illegible]. [illegible], [illegible]	[illegible]	1, [illegible]4.00
Gaffney, Miss A. M.	Third	Oct. 6, 1904	[illegible]	1, [illegible]4.00
Davis, [illegible] K. M.	Fifth-Sixth	[illegible]. [illegible], [illegible]	Grammar	1, [illegible]4.00
Kincaid, [illegible]	Second	[illegible]. [illegible], [illegible]	[illegible]	1,164.00
[illegible], Mrs. A. F.	[illegible] & Music	Sept. [illegible], [illegible]	[illegible]pecial	1,284.00
Edwards, Frances M.	First	[illegible]. [illegible], [illegible]	Grammar	1,224.00
Stack, [illegible] C. M.	First	[illegible]. [illegible], [illegible]	Grammar	1,224.00
[illegible]	First	Oct. [illegible], [illegible]	[illegible]	1,224.00
Jackson Primary—				
Chalmers, Miss A.	Prin. & Second	[illegible]. 2, 1902	Grammar	1,560.00
Hinds, Miss A.	First	Aug. 23, 1880	Grammar	1,224.00

Name	Grade	Date	Certificate	Salary
Ragan, Miss M. L.	Fourth	Mar. 10, 1897	[illegible]cial	1,164 00
Gray, Miss F. H.	First	Sept. 2, 1907	G[illegible]r	1,224.00
Cooney, Mrs. M. C.	Third	June 21, 1904	G[illegible]r	1,164.00

James [illegible] Grammar—

Name	Grade	Date	Certificate	Salary
[illegible]n, Miss E. M.	Principal	Oct. 8, 1879	[illegible]h	2,160 00
Lewis, Miss F. R.	V. P., 8th	June 10, 1879	[illegible]r	1,620 00
Torpey, Miss [illegible]	Seventh	Jan. 19, 1892	[illegible]r	1,224.00
Henderson, Mary J.	[illegible]	Jan. 29, 1872	[illegible]r	1,224.00
Kinney, [illegible] L. M.	Eighth	Sept. 1, 1886	G[illegible]r	1,224 00
[illegible]k, G[illegible]ce S.	Seventh	June 21, 1904	G[illegible]r & Special	1,152.00
Wolff, Miss M.	Fifth	Nov. 18, 1893	[illegible]r	840.00
Langstader, [illegible] P.	Fifth	Aug. 13, 1872	Grammar	1,164.00
[illegible]n, Miss E. M.	Sixth	Mar. 30, 1905	[illegible]r	1,164.00
Kennedy, [illegible]e	First	Mar. 1, 1895	G[illegible]ar-Special	1,224 00
Manning, [illegible] C. V.	Sixth	Jan. 19, 1905	Grammar	1,164.00
Hogan, Miss H. M.	Ungraded	Sept. 30, [illegible]	[illegible]r	1,224.00
Gray, Miss M. E. A.	Sixth	Sept. 30, 1901	High	1,164.00

J[illegible] Parker Grammar—

Name	Grade	Date	Certificate	Salary
Pechin, Mrs. C. R.	Princi[illegible]al	Sept. 12, 1871	G[illegible]r	2,160.00
Haswell, [illegible] M. C.	V.-P., [illegible]h & 8th	April 10, 1874	G[illegible]r	1,620.0.0
McCorkell, Miss L.	[illegible]th	Aug. 23, 1880	Gramn ar	1,224.00
Anderson, Miss J.	Fifth	July 23, 1892	[illegible]r	1,164 00
d'Erlach, Miss [illegible] E.	Third	Aug. 26, 1903	G[illegible]r	1,164.00
[illegible]s, [illegible] M.	First	Oct. 1, 1903	[illegible]r	1,224.00
[illegible]g, Miss Anna	First	July 22, 1882	[illegible]r	1,224 00
Heath, Miss R. E. L.	First	Aug. 29, 1885	[illegible]r	1,224.00
a[illegible], [illegible] F.	[illegible]	Mar. 3, 1879	[illegible]r	1,224.00
Dworzarek, Miss B. E.	Second	Jan. 3, 1882	[illegible]r	1,164.00
[illegible]d, [illegible] E.	Sixth	July 21, 1902	H[illegible]h	1,164.00
[illegible], Sarah E.	Third	Sept. 1, 1888	[illegible]r	1,164.00
[illegible]n, [illegible] R. V.	Second	Dec. 7, 1908	G[illegible]r	840 00
Glazier, Miss M.	Fifth	Mar 10, 1910	[illegible]r	840.00

SCHOOLS AND TEACHERS—Continued.

Name.	Grade of Class.	When Elected.	Grade of [illegible]ate.	Salary per Year.
Jean Parker Grammar—Continued				
Carroll, Miss Agnes	Fourth	June 25, 1905	[illegible]	1,164.00
McBoyle, Miss A. B.	Fourth	Sept. 30, 1892	[illegible]	1,164.00
Jefferson Primary—				
Roberts, Miss B. E.	Fifth	Jan. 2, 1902	[illegible]cial	1,320.00
Carmichael, Miss B.	Third	July 25, 1910	Gramm[illegible]r	840.00
Brown, Miss M. L.	Seventh	[illegible]y 30, 1908	[illegible]	1,224.00
[illegible]				
[illegible]	Princi[illegible]al	Mar. 4, 1879	Hi[illegible]al	2,160.00
[illegible]in, Mrs. L. B.	[illegible]	July 10, 1886	Gramm[illegible]r	1,164.00
[illegible] K.	Ungraded	Aug. 10, 1885	[illegible]	1,224.00
[illegible]	Seventh	Feb. 11, 1879	[illegible]	1,224.00
[illegible]ky, Miss [illegible]	[illegible]th	Aug. 1, 1884	[illegible]	1,500.00
[illegible]ty, [illegible]s. E. [illegible]	Sixth	Dec. 27, 1896	[illegible]	1,164.00
Carroll, [illegible]	Sixth	June 9, 1897	[illegible]	1,164.00
Horgan, [illegible]s K.	Fourth	Oct. 26, 1905	[illegible]	1,140.00
[illegible]n, Mrs. J. H.	Second	Sept. 1, 1897	[illegible]	1,164.00
Doud, Mrs. E. M.	First	Dec. [illegible], 1887	[illegible]	1,224.00
[illegible]n, Mrs. A. E.	First	Mar. 3, 1888	[illegible]	1,224.00
[illegible]s, Mrs. [illegible] C.	Fifth	Nov. 19, 1877	[illegible]	1,164.00
[illegible]h, Miss [illegible]	[illegible]th	June 15, 1895	[illegible]	1,152.00
[illegible]n, Miss E. L.	Fourth	July 27, 1898	[illegible]	1,164.00
Junipero Serra—				
Sullivan, Miss N. M.	Principal	Dec. 15, 1877	Grammar	1,800.00
Wool, Miss H. L.	Second	Aug. 15, 1867	Grammar	1,164.00
Wilson, Miss May	First	Feb. 2, 1904	Grammar	1,224.00
Foley, Eliz. M.	Second	Nov. 12, 1896	Grammar	1,164.00

Name	Grade	Date	Certificate	Salary
[illegible], [illegible] [illegible] J.	First	Jan. 1, 1895	[illegible]	1,224.00
Laven, Mrs. S. F.	[illegible]	April 1, 1879	[illegible]	1,224.00
[illegible]lly, [illegible] J. F.	[illegible]rst	June 9, 1897	[illegible]	1,224.00
Dworsazek, [illegible] P. A.	First	Jan. 2, 1897	[illegible]	1,224.00
Adams, Clara [illegible]	[illegible]	Jan. 2, 1871	[illegible]	1,224.00
Parker, [illegible] [illegible]	[illegible]	Nov. 26, 1907	[illegible]	1,164.00
[illegible], Miss M. E.	Third	Mar. 25, 1908	[illegible]	1,164.00
[illegible], Miss M.	Second	Jan. 29, 1906	[illegible]	1,164.00
McInerney, Miss L. E.	[illegible]	April 24, 1909	[illegible]	840.00
Douglas, [illegible] M. L.	[illegible]	Aug. 30, 1905	[illegible]	1,164.00
[illegible], Miss A. C.	[illegible]	Jan. 11, 1910	High	840.00
Frank, [illegible] J.	S[illegible]ond[illegible]	Dec. 13, 1896	Grammar	1,164.00
McCarty, [illegible] May A.	Second	Jan. 11, 1911	[illegible]	840.00
Lafayette Primary—				
McLeran, Miss M.	Principal	Sept. 16, 1901	Grammar	1,560.00
Lissak, Miss M.	Kindergarten	Oct. 1, 1909	Kindergarten	840.00
Bigelow, Mrs. S. H.	Second and Third	Sept. 1876	[illegible]	1,224.00
Sullivan, Miss H.	First	Aug. 2, 1905	[illegible]	1,224.00
Livingston, Miss N.	6th, 7th & 8th	Nov. 29	[illegible]	840.00
Longfellow Primary—				
McCarty, [illegible] E. L.	Principal	Jan. [illegible], [illegible]	[illegible]	1,560.00
Dwyer, [illegible] A. C.	Second	Mar. 22, 1905	[illegible]	1,080.00
Dwyer, [illegible] Nora	First	Nov. 11, [illegible]	Primary	1,224.00
Young, Mrs. [illegible] A.	Fourth	Jan. 10, 1910	[illegible]	840.00
Meaney, [illegible] [illegible] E.	Fifth	Aug. 7, [illegible]	Grammar	1,164.00
O'Connor, Miss A. M.	[illegible]	Jan. [illegible], [illegible]	[illegible]	1,224.00
[illegible]x, Miss M. A.	Third	[illegible] 1, [illegible]	[illegible]	840.00
[illegible], Mrs. A. [illegible]	Third	[illegible] [illegible]	[illegible]	1,1[illegible].00
Laguna Honda School—				
O'Neal, Mrs. M. L.	Principal	Jan. 20, 1874	Grammar	2,160.00
Donnelly, Miss M. L.	Vice-Principal, 8th	July 2, 1875	Grammar	1,620.00

SCHOOLS AND TEACHERS—[illegible]

Name.	Grade of Class.	When Elected.	Grade of Certificate	Salary per Year.
Laguna Honda School—Continued				
Carson, [illegible]s. N. E.	Seventh	July 14, [illegible]	[illegible]	1,224.00
[illegible], Miss M. V.	Second	Aug. 1, [illegible]	[illegible]	1,164.00
[illegible], Miss E.	Sixth	Feb. 25, [illegible]	[illegible]	1,164.00
Sechrist, Mrs. A. M.	Seventh and Eighth	[illegible] 5, [illegible]	[illegible]	1,224.00
[illegible], Miss E. T.	[illegible]	July 27, [illegible]	[illegible]	1,164.00
[illegible], Miss M.	[illegible]	[illegible] 6, [illegible]	[illegible]	1,164.00
[illegible], Miss E.	[illegible]	[illegible] 8, [illegible]	High	1,164.00
[illegible], Miss H. L.	Second	Feb. 1, [illegible]	[illegible]	1,140.00
[illegible], Miss A. M.	[illegible]	Sept. 6, [illegible]	[illegible]	1,224.00
[illegible], Miss J.	First	[illegible]	[illegible]	1,224.00
[illegible], Miss B. E.	Third	[illegible] [illegible], [illegible]	[illegible]	1,164.00
McKown, Mrs. M. E.	[illegible]	April 14, 1869	[illegible]	1,164.00
Bertagna, Miss L.	Fourth	[illegible] 1, [illegible]	[illegible]	840.00
Lincoln Grammar—				
[illegible], Mr. [illegible] W.	Principal	Feb. 1, [illegible]	[illegible]	1,560.00
[illegible], Mrs. F. L.	Seventh and Eighth	Sept. 3, [illegible]	[illegible] & Special	1,284.00
[illegible], Miss J.	[illegible]	[illegible]	[illegible]	1,284.00
[illegible], Mrs. B. L.	First	[illegible]	[illegible]	1,224.00
[illegible], Miss A. E.	First	[illegible] 1, [illegible]	[illegible]	1,224.00
Dower, Miss J. E.	Si[illegible]	[illegible] 12, [illegible]	[illegible]	1,164.00
[illegible], Mr. M. P.	[illegible]	Mar. [illegible], [illegible]	[illegible]	840.00
Perlet, Mrs. M.	[illegible]	[illegible] 28, 1896	[illegible]	1,164.00
[illegible], Miss Mary C.	[illegible]	[illegible]	Primary	1,164.00
Rincon (In charge of Principal of Lincoln)—				
Coyle, Mrs. Mary G.	Fourth	Dec. 5, 1892	Grammar	1,164.00
Barry, Miss A. P.	First	Sept 21, 1886	Grammar	1,344.00

[illegible] Primary—

Name	Grade	Date	Certificate	Salary
Bartlett, [illegible] E. F.	Principal	Aug. 5, 1885	Grammar	1,560.00
[illegible], Miss E. S.	Second	Nov. 18, 1901	[illegible]	1,164.00
[illegible], [illegible] F. G.	[illegible]th	Dec. 30, 1892	[illegible]	1,224.00
Emmons, [illegible] I. C.	Fourth	July 30, 1876	[illegible]	1,164.00
[illegible], Mrs. A. E.	Third	July 27, 1898	Grammar	1,164.00
Breese, [illegible] A. A.	First	Oct. 29, 1897	[illegible]	1, 24.00
Bannon, Margaret F.	First	Jan. 3, 1873	[illegible]	1,224.00
Plageman, [illegible] D. E.	Seventh [illegible] Sixth	Sept. 1, 1905	[illegible]	1,140.00
[illegible], [illegible] E.	Fifth	Aug. 3, 1908	High	840.00
Fitzgerald, Miss [illegible] F.	Fourth	Nov. 13, 1899	Gram. & Spec.	1,164.00
[illegible], Mrs. L.	Si[illegible]h	Feb. 12, 1906	Grammar	1,164.00

[illegible] Primary—

Name	Grade	Date	Certificate	Salary
Walker, Mrs. M. J.	P[illegible]al	Aug. [illegible], [illegible]69	[illegible]	1,800.00
Flanagan, Miss M. C.	Third	Aug. 5, [illegible]98	[illegible]	840.00
Poppe, [illegible] M. H.	[illegible]	April 30, 1886	Gram. & Spec.	1,224.00
Harrigan, Miss J.	[illegible]h	July [illegible]84	G[illegible]	1,164.00
Robinson, Mrs. L.	Third	Aug. 3, [illegible]98	[illegible]	960.00
[illegible], [illegible] J. C.	Fourth	Oct. 19, [illegible]85	[illegible]	1,164.00
[illegible], [illegible] [illegible] L.	S[illegible]ond	Nov. 21, [illegible]86	Primary	1,164.00
[illegible], [illegible] A. C.	First	Dec. 18, [illegible]88	[illegible]	1,224.00
[illegible], [illegible] [illegible] F.	[illegible]	[illegible]. 10, 1910	[illegible]	840.00
Elliot, [illegible] E. F.	First	Nov. [illegible], [illegible]85	[illegible]	1,224.00
O'Connor, Miss C. J.	First	Sept. 12, 1904	[illegible]	1,224.00
Gray, Mrs. H. W.	Second	July 8, [illegible]92	Primary	1,164.00
Smith, Mary J.	First	July 9, [illegible]95	[illegible]	1,224.00

McKinley School—

Name	Grade	Date	Certificate	Salary
Gallagher, Miss Cora	Principal	Aug. 6, 1878	Grammar	1,560.00
Dearin, Miss A. E.	Third	Aug. 22, 1907	Grammar	1,080.00
Kresteller, Miss S.	Fourth and Fifth	Jan. 3, 1906	Grammar	1,140.00
Moynihan, Nora	Fifth	July 7, 1877	Grammar	1,164.00
Gurry, Miss Mary E.	Second	April 2, 1888	Grammar	1,164.00

SCHOOLS AND TEACHERS—Continued.

Name	Grade	Date	Certificate	Salary
McKinley School—Continued				
McKinney, Mary C.	Third	Nov. 7, 1888	Grammar	1,164.00
Kean, Miss K. E.	First	Jan. 1, 1885	Grammar	1,224.00
Sarles, Mrs. Julia	First	July 7, 1881	Grammar	1,224.00
Casey, Mary	Fourth	June 6, 1888	Grammar	1,164.00
Smith, Miss M. A.	Sixth	Jan. 3, 1887	Grammar	1,164.00
[illegible] Grammar—				
Crowley, [illegible] K. H.	[illegible]	Aug. 1, [illegible]	[illegible]	2,160.00
[illegible], [illegible] J. C.	V. P., 8th	Feb. 13, [illegible]	[illegible]	1,620.00
[illegible], Miss M. E.	E[illegible]th	Oct. 30, [illegible]	[illegible]	1,224.00
[illegible], Miss R. A.	Seventh	Aug. 15, [illegible]	[illegible]	1,224.00
Sykes, Mrs. M. A.	Fifth	Aug. 11, [illegible]	[illegible]	1,164.00
[illegible], [illegible] M. A.	Seventh	Sept. 30, [illegible]	[illegible]	1,284.00
[illegible], [illegible] M. G.	[illegible]th	May 15, [illegible]	[illegible]	1,224.00
Horn, [illegible] L. J.	[illegible]	July 14, [illegible]	[illegible]	1,164.00
O'Brien, [illegible] M. A.	[illegible]th	Aug. 11, [illegible]	[illegible]	1,164.00
Doyle, [illegible] J.	[illegible]th	July 28, [illegible]	[illegible]	1,140.00
Harv[illegible], Miss E. F.	[illegible]th	Oct. 30, [illegible]	[illegible]	1,164.00
[illegible], Miss R. S.	[illegible]th	July 18, [illegible]	[illegible]	1,164.00
Monroe Grammar—				
Hagarty, Miss A. M.	Principal	Feb. 20, 1883	[illegible]	2,460.00
[illegible], Mrs. A. M.	Third	Aug. 22, 1907	[illegible]	960.00
Harrower, [illegible] A. W.	V.-P., Eighth	Sept. 30, 1901	[illegible]	1,620.00
[illegible], [illegible] M. R.	E[illegible]	Oct. 28, 1891	Grammar	1,224.00
[illegible], [illegible] I. E.	Fifth	Sept. 1, 1872	[illegible]	1,164.00
Curtin, Ella J.	Seventh	Sept. [illegible], 1905	Grammar	1,224.[illegible]
Beardsley, [illegible] L. J.	Seventh	[illegible]t. [illegible], 1904	[illegible]	1,224.00
[illegible], [illegible] J. G.	Sixth	Sept. 2, 1884	[illegible]	1,164.00
El[illegible], [illegible] L.	Fourth	Jan. 3, 1889	Primary	1,164.00
Fleming, [illegible] J.	First	[illegible]b. 13, 1890	[illegible]	1,224.00

Name	Grade	Date of Appointment	Certificate	Salary
O'Brien, [illegible] A. T.	First	Nov. [illegible], [illegible]	[illegible]	1,224.00
[illegible]lly, Ella T.	Fifth	Oct. 7, [illegible]97	[illegible]	1,164.00
Hussey, [illegible] N. E.	Sixth	Aug. 2, [illegible]97	[illegible]	1,164.00
[illegible], [illegible] M. E.	Fourth	Oct. 28, 1907	[illegible]	1,164.00
[illegible]s, [illegible] M. M.	Fourth	Jan. [illegible], [illegible]90	[illegible]	840.00
[illegible]n, Miss M. T.	First	Aug. 3, [illegible]98	[illegible]	1,020.00
Morgan, Miss L. V.	First	May [illegible], [illegible]96	[illegible]	1,224.00
[illegible]n, [illegible] M.	Ungraded	May [illegible], [illegible]904	[illegible]	1,224.00
[illegible]e, [illegible] C. N.	Fifth	[illegible] [illegible], [illegible]90	[illegible]	840.00
[illegible]e, [illegible] G. E.	Third	[illegible] [illegible], [illegible]90	[illegible]	840.00
Colgan, Mrs. K.	Second	Mar. [illegible], [illegible]84	[illegible]	1,164.00
[illegible]y, [illegible] N. C.	Second	Feb. [illegible], 1896	[illegible]	1,164.00
[illegible] Primary—				
[illegible]ll, [illegible] A. M.	Principal	Sept. 7, 1884	Grammar	1,560.00
[illegible]s, Miss G.	Third	Feb. 4, 1907	[illegible]	1,164.00
[illegible]M, Mrs. S. M.	Second	[illegible] 1, 1900	Primary	1,164.00
Eccles, Mrs. L. B.	Fifth	Sept. 3, 1883	[illegible]	1,164.00
[illegible]r, Edna	[illegible]th	June 21, 1895	[illegible]	1,164.00
[illegible]ll, [illegible] V. V.	First	[illegible] 30, 1892	Grammar	1,224.00
Kellogg, [illegible] E.	Fourth	Aug. 3, 1908	[illegible]	840.00
[illegible]tt, Mrs. E. S.	First	Oct. 1873	[illegible]	1,224.00
[illegible] Valley Primary—				
[illegible]s, Mrs. E. H.	Principal	July 1, [illegible]82	[illegible]	2,160.00
Hall, Mrs. [illegible] V.	First	Aug. 17, 1887	[illegible]	1,344.00
Egan, Mrs. K. F.	First	Mar. 11, 1897	[illegible]	1,224.00
Gercke, Mrs. L.	First	April 1, 1903	[illegible]	1,224.00
[illegible]n, [illegible] E. D.	Second	Aug. 12, 1903	Gram. & Spec.	1,224.00
[illegible]d, [illegible] L. M.	Second	Aug. 23, 1907	Grammar	960.00
Merell, Miss G. S.	Second	Aug. 23, 1907	[illegible]	960.00
Martin, Eli[illegible]beth R.	Third	May 1, 1905	[illegible]	1,164.00
[illegible]lan, Miss M. L.	Third	June 21, 1904	[illegible]	1,164.00
Gray, Mrs. [illegible] E.	Second	Dec. 15, 1890	Grammar	1,164.00

SCHOOLS AND TEACHERS—[illegible]

Name.	Grade of Class.	When Elected.	Grade of Certificate.	Salary per Year.
Noe Valley Primary—Continued				
Schnedel, Miss M. A.	Fourth	Sept. 6, [illegible]91	[illegible]	1,164.00
Gaffney Miss S. A.	Fourth	July 2, [illegible]93	[illegible]	1,164.00
McLane, Miss H. E.	First	Dec. 4, [illegible]	[illegible]	1,224.00
Conroy, Miss M. A.	Third	July [illegible]98	[illegible]	1,164.00
Kerns, Miss May	Third	July 3, [illegible]94	[illegible]	1,164.00
King, Miss Ellen	Fourth	Sept. 6, [illegible]90	[illegible]	840.00
Oceanside Primary—				
Heath, Miss V. D.	Principal	Jan. 4, 1894	Grammar	1,560.00
Hawkins, Miss B. C.	First	[illegible] 3, 1902	[illegible]	1,284.00
DeForest, Mrs. J. J.	Third	F[illegible]b. 3, 1904	[illegible]	1,140.00
Bartlett, Miss A. G.	Eighth	Oct. 2, 1904	[illegible]	1,152.00
Ashley, Miss B.	Seventh and Eighth	[illegible] 1, 1910	[illegible]	840.00
Timmins, Miss K.	Sixth	[illegible] 4, 1910	[illegible]	840.00
Ocean House School—				
Delay, Mr. D. J.	Principal	July 8, 1882	[illegible]	1,320.00
[illegible] Public—				
[illegible], Mrs. C. C.	Principal	F[illegible]b. [illegible], [illegible]80	[illegible]	1,560.00
Greer, Jan[illegible]e E.	Second	[illegible], [illegible]88	[illegible]	1,164.00
Griffith, [illegible] A. C.	First	[illegible] 2, [illegible]98	[illegible]	1,224.00
[illegible], [illegible] V. E.	Fourth	[illegible] 6, [illegible]92	[illegible]	1,164.00
Branch, [illegible] C. A.	First	Feb. 2, [illegible]95	[illegible]	1,224.00
[illegible], Miss F. R.	First	[illegible] 2, [illegible]94	High	1,164.00
Barrett, Miss [illegible] C.	[illegible]	[illegible] 5, [illegible]97	[illegible]	960.00
Arnold, Miss M. V.	First	[illegible] 9, [illegible]	[illegible]	1,224.00
Cilker, [illegible] A.	Seventh and E[illegible]	Aug., [illegible], [illegible]94	[illegible]	1,224.00
Brown, [illegible] H. A.	Fifth	Feb. 2, [illegible]96	[illegible]	1,020.00

Pa[illegible]c [illegible]s Grammar—

Name	Position	Date	Grade	Salary
S[illegible]n, Miss A. M.	[illegible]al	June 20, 1868	High	2,340.00
S[illegible]n, M[illegible]s Ella E.	Second	April 16, 1907	G[illegible]r	1,020.00
[illegible]n, M[illegible]s I. M.	[illegible]h	[illegible]t. 3, 1880	G[illegible]r	1,224.00
[illegible]e, Miss C. B.	[illegible]h	Feb. 21, 1872	G[illegible]r	1,224.00
[illegible]k, M[illegible]s F. G.	Fifth	[illegible]. 4, 1904	Grammar	1,164.00
G[illegible]h, Katherine	[illegible]h	[illegible]y 20, 1905	G[illegible]r	1,164.00
Dreyfus, M[illegible]s R. E.	S[illegible]th	Aug. 5, 1905	G[illegible]r	1,164.00
[illegible]h, Emma F.	[illegible]th	[illegible]. 21, 1883	G[illegible]r	1,164.00
Timmins, M[illegible]s A. C.	[illegible]th	April 18, 1883	G[illegible]r	1,164.00
Boggs, M[illegible]s S.	Seventh	[illegible]b. 18, 1903	G[illegible]r	1,224.00
S[illegible]i, M[illegible]s I. C.	Fourth	[illegible]n. 3, 1905	G[illegible]r	1, [illegible]4.00
W[illegible]r, M[illegible]s M.	[illegible]	Jan. 4, 1902	[illegible]h	1, [illegible].[illegible]0
Donohue, M[illegible]s M. F.	Third	June 21, [illegible]4	G[illegible]r	1, [illegible]4.00
[illegible]rth, M[illegible]s G. M.	First	[illegible]v. 2, 1878	G[illegible]r	1, [illegible]24.00
Robertson, M[illegible]s A. C.	V. P., [illegible]hth	[illegible]y 16, 1867	[illegible]h	1, [illegible]0.00
Burnham, M[illegible]s C.	[illegible]h	[illegible]g. 1, 1885	G[illegible]r	1, [illegible]4.00
[illegible]g, [illegible]s A. C.	First	[illegible]t. 5, 1897	G[illegible]r	1, [illegible]24.00
Zweybruck, Miss E.	Ungraded	Feb. 20, 1885	G[illegible]r	1, [illegible]24.00
Morrison, Miss E. P.	Seventh	[illegible]g. 20, 1868	G[illegible]ar	1,224.00
Cotrel, M[illegible]s E.	Seventh	[illegible]y 7, 1889	G[illegible]r	1,224.00

Parental School—

Name	Position	Date	Grade	Salary
Alexander, Miss R.	Principal	Oct. 5, 1888	Grammar	1,560.00
Schwartz, Mrs. I. C.	Ungraded	Feb. 17, 1905	Grammar	1,140.00
Levy, Miss A.	Second	Jan. 5, 1891	Grammar	1,224.00

Peabody Primary—

Name	Position	Date	Grade	Salary
Dwyer, Miss A. M.	Principal	[illegible]r. [illegible], 1879	Grammar	1,560.00
Maguire, Mrs. M. E.	Fourth	M[illegible]r. 1, 1880	Grammar	1,164.00
Harris, Miss E. L.	Third	Aug. 3, 1908	Grammar	840.00
Watson, Mrs. M. G.	First	[illegible]. [illegible], 1898	Grammar	1,224.00
Duffy, Miss A. A.	Third	Aug. 18, 1884	Grammar	1,164.00

SCHOOLS AND TEACHERS—Continued.

Name.	Grade of Class.	When Elected.	Grade of Certificate.	Salary per Year.
Peabody Primary—Continued				
Lipman, Miss N. E.	Second	Sept. 7, 1897	Gr[illegible]	1,164.00
Cavanagh, Mary E.	Third	Aug. 3, 1908	Gr[illegible]	840.00
Ephriam, Miss A.	First	Dec. 2, 1882	Gr[illegible]	1,224.00
Parkside—				
Code, Mrs. E. S.	Primary	July 18, 1871	[illegible]	1,560.00
Portola—				
Mills, Mrs. I. E.	Principal	Nov. [illegible], [illegible]7	Grammar	1,[illegible]80.00
Lapham, Miss E. M.	[illegible]th	Jan. 11, [illegible]04	Gr[illegible]	1,[illegible]24.00
G[illegible]e, Miss J. H.	Sixth	[illegible]g. 1, [illegible]8	Gr[illegible]	1,[illegible]64.00
T[illegible]er, Miss E. H.	[illegible]th	July [illegible], [illegible]3	Gr[illegible]	1,[illegible]64.00
Laverene, Miss C. J.	Third	Oct. 8, [illegible]7	Gr[illegible]	1,[illegible]80.00
Brown, Mrs. E.	First	[illegible]g. [illegible], [illegible]8	Grammar	1,[illegible]24.00
Johnson, Miss A. E.	First	April 29, 1891	Gr[illegible]	1,224.00
[illegible]h, Miss M.	First	Sept. 25, 1905	Gr[illegible]	1,344.00
[illegible]iff, M[illegible]s M.	Second	Feb. 2, [illegible]5	Gr[illegible]	1,164.00
McGraw, Miss Mary	Third	June 8, [illegible]	Gr[illegible]	840.00
[illegible]al[illegible], Miss A. A.	Second	Aug. 3, 1908	Gr[illegible]	840.00
Potrero—				
Coffey, Miss J. C.	Principal Third	Sept. 11, [illegible]5	Gr[illegible]	1,560.00
Loewi, M[illegible]s M.	First	Jan. 26, [illegible]8	Gr[illegible]	1,224.00
Herrick, M[illegible]s C. R.	First	Sept. 11, [illegible]5	Gr[illegible]	1,224.00
Doran, Miss M[illegible]ie E.	[illegible]t	Sept. 4, [illegible]1	Gr[illegible]	1,224.00
Carson, Alice M.	S[illegible]ond	Feb. 12, [illegible]6	Gr[illegible]	1,080.00
Finnegan, M[illegible]s M. G.	Third	[illegible]g. 20, 1907	Gr[illegible]	960.00
McFeeley, Miss R.	Second	M[illegible]. 10, [illegible]7		1,164.00
Hollub, Miss M[illegible]C.	Fourth	April [illegible], [illegible]2	Gr[illegible]	1,164.00
Anderson, Miss Lena E.	Third	Aug. 3, [illegible]8	Gr[illegible]	840.00

Redding—

Name	Grade	Date	Certificate	Salary
Deane, Mrs. M. A.	Principal	Aug. 2, 1872	Gr	2,160.00
[illegible]s, Miss D.	F[illegible]th	Aug. 5, 1908	Gr	840.00
[illegible]n, Miss A. M.	[illegible]	Mar. 20, [illegible]09	Gr	840.00
Sullivan, Miss T.	[illegible]h	Jan. 15, 1903	Gr	1,224.00
[illegible]y, Miss M. E.	Ungraded	Aug. 12, 1903	Gr	1,224.00
[illegible]y, Miss [illegible] M.	Third	Sept. 23, 1909	[illegible]r	840.00
[illegible]r, Miss S. A.	First	Aug. 14, 1881	Gr	1,224.00
[illegible]e, Mrs. E. B.	[illegible]ixth	June 3, 1905	Gr	1,164.00
Martin, Miss F.	First	Aug. 26, 1881	Gr	1,224.00
Donahue, Mrs. L. E.	[illegible]st	Dec. 23, 1885	Gr	1,224.00
Duff[illegible]y[illegible], Miss [illegible]a	First	July 23, 1902	Gr	1,224.00
Sulli[illegible]n, Miss E. G.	Second	Jan. 12, 1898	Gr	1,164.00

Roosevelt Grammar—

Name	Grade	Date	Certificate	Salary
Lyser, Mr. [illegible]bert	Princi[illegible]al	June 10, [illegible]8	[illegible]h	2,340.00
Lalande, Miss A. H.	Seventh	July 5, [illegible]8	Gram. & Spec.	1,620.00
Browning, Miss E. F.	S[illegible]th	[illegible] 24, [illegible]1	[illegible]h	1,224.00
Ryan, Miss B.	Second	Sept. 16, [illegible]6	Grammar	1,[illegible]64.00
[illegible]s, F[illegible]e J.	Fourth	[illegible]n. 31, [illegible]9	Gr	1,164.00
[illegible]d, Miss A.	S[illegible]cond	Dec. 28, [illegible]1	Gr	1,164.00
[illegible]ll, Miss M. T.	[illegible]	M[illegible]r. 11, [illegible]2	Gr	1,224.00
Hinds, Miss J. B.	Sixth	Dec. 9, [illegible]6	Gr	1,164.00
Stark, Miss L. M.	First	Sept. 7, [illegible]7	Gr	1,224.00
Cotrel, Edna	Fifth	Sept. 5, [illegible]2	Gr	1,164.00
Hurl[illegible]y, Miss A. F.	Third	April 27, [illegible]8	Primary	1,164.00
Horton, Miss M.	First	Feb. 14, [illegible]1	Gr	1,224.00
Levy, Miss M. A.	[illegible]h	Mar. [illegible] [illegible]6	Gr	1,224.00
Kedon, Mrs. [illegible] E.	[illegible]h	Dec. 9, [illegible]6	Grammar	1,224.00
Kell[illegible]y, Margery F.	Fifth	Sept. 2, [illegible]9	Gr	840.00
Boyle, M[illegible]ry	Seventh	July 3, [illegible]5	Grammar	1,224.00
McEachern, Miss M. V.	Third	July 3, [illegible]0	Gramm[illegible]r	840.00

SCHOOLS AND TEACHERS—Continued.

Name.	Grade of Class.	When Elected.			Grade of Certificate.	Salary per Year.
Sheridan—						
Riordan, Miss C. F.	Principal	Dc.	10,	90	Gr	2,160.00
Downey, Miss J.	gh	Ag.	26,	91	Gr	1,500.00
Murphy, Miss H.	Seventh and Eighth	Ot.	26,	95	Gr	1,224.00
Everett, Ms E. B.	Seventh	Jan.	13,	92	Gr	1,164.00
Hussey, Ms E. G.	Sixth	Fb.	11,	97	High	1,140.00
Tierney, M ss B. A.	Fifth	Ot.	13,	94	Gr	1,164.00
Miklau, Miss M.	Fifth	Spt.	14,	95	Gr	1,140.00
Eat, Is. I. I.	Fourth and Fifth	Jly	7,	95	Gr	1,200.00
Frign allo, Miss H.	Third	Spt.	8,	97	Gr	1,164.00
Gor, Is A. J.	Second	Sept.	3,	95	Gr	1,224.00
Bdd, M ss I. W.	First	April	29,	96	Gr	1,224.00
Hley, Miss M. E.	First	Jn.	6,	89	Gr	1,224.00
Kyne, Miss E. M.	Second	Ag.	3,	98	Gr	900.00
Harte, Mrs. S.	Fourth	Mar.	4,	93	Gr	,164.00
Christman, Miss E. A.	Fourth	July	6,	90	Gr	840.00
Sherman Primary—						
Hurley, Miss J. M. A.	Principal	Jn.	2,	83	High	1,800.00
Millar, Mrs. S. H.	Fh	July	6,	80	Gr	1,164.00
McLerie, Miss J. T.	Second	My	1,	86	Gr	1,164.00
Unger, Miss R.	First	Ag.	2,	85	Gr	1,224.00
Sullivan, Miss Nellie	Second	Ag.	5,	80	Gnar	1,164.00
Is, Miss E. H.	Second	Sept.	6,	81	Grammar	1,224.00
els, Elizabeth	First	Nv.	3,	85	Gr	1,224.00
Erb, Miss I. M.	Third	Aug.	3,	88	Grammar	840.00
Kinsey, Miss L.	Third	Jn.	3,	90	Gr	840.00
Hull, Mrs. M.	Ft	Jly	7,	87	Gr	1,224.00
Fl eg, Miss L. M.	Frth	St.	27,	99	Gr	840.00

Spring Valley Grammar—

Name	Grade	Date	Certificate	Salary
Keating, Miss [illegible] E.	Principal	[illegible]y 12, 1880	Grammar	2,160.00
Gregg, M[illegible]s A. C.	[illegible] P., 8th	Aug., [illegible], [illegible]8	[illegible]h	1,620.00
Murphy, M[illegible]s A. J.	Seventh	[illegible]r. 2, [illegible]3	[illegible]r	1,224.00
Hause M[illegible]s E. N.	[illegible]h	[illegible]r. 9, [illegible]9	[illegible]h	840.00
S[illegible]a, Miss A. B.	[illegible]h	[illegible]n. 29, [illegible]4	[illegible]h	1,224.00
Hoggs, Mrs. M. A.	Ei[illegible]hth	[illegible]n. 10, [illegible]7	[illegible]r	1,224.00
Davis, Mrs. F.	Si[illegible]th	[illegible]t. 8, [illegible]7	[illegible]r	1,164.00
Grozelier, M[illegible]ss C. B. S.	[illegible]h	[illegible]t. 14, [illegible]5	[illegible]r	1,140.00
Gallagher, Miss [illegible] R.	S[illegible]h	[illegible]t. 28, [illegible]1	[illegible]r	1,164.00
Dittenhoefer, M[illegible]ss [illegible]. B.	[illegible]h	[illegible]pt. 10, [illegible]8	[illegible]h	840.00
Bradley, Mrs. A. B.	First	Oct. 7, [illegible]2	[illegible]r	1,224.00

Starr King Primary—

Name	Grade	Date	Certificate	Salary
[illegible]rath, [illegible]s. K. C.	Pri[illegible]ipal	[illegible]n. 12, [illegible]8	G[illegible]r	1,560.00
Willi[illegible]s, Miss K. F.	Fourth	Oct. 17, [illegible]84	G[illegible]r	1,164.00
O'Sullivan, Miss L.	First	April 18, [illegible]7	Gram.-Spec.	1,284.00
Fol[illegible]y, Kate J.	Third	[illegible]y 20, [illegible]3	G[illegible]r	1,164.00
Jordi, Mrs. S. J.	[illegible]	June 14, [illegible]5	G[illegible]r	[illegible]164.00
Louderback, Miss E. S.	First	[illegible]v. 21, [illegible]4	G[illegible]r	1,224.00
Ellis, Miss M. R.	Second	[illegible]b. 3, [illegible]8	G[illegible]r	1,080.00
[illegible]n, Miss J. E.	Thi[illegible]d	[illegible]pt. [illegible], [illegible]9	G[illegible]r	1,164.00
Keegan, Miss M. E.	Third	[illegible]n. [illegible], [illegible]0	G[illegible]r	840.00

Sunnyside Primary—

Name	Grade	Date	Certificate	Salary
Moore, Miss K.	First	June 15, 1903	Grammar	1,224.00
Eprhaim, Miss J.	1st, 4th and 3d	July 23, 1876	Grammar	1,560.00

Sunset School—

Name	Grade	Date	Certificate	Salary
Tiernan, Mrs. A. E.	Principal 3d & 4th	July 6, 1869	High	1,320.00
Rowe, Miss M, M.	Second	Aug. 3, 1871	High	1,224.00

SCHOOLS AND TEACHERS—[illegible]d.

Name.	Grade of Class.	When Elected.	Grade of Certificate	Salary per Year.
Sutro Grammar—				
[illegible]r, Miss M.	Principal	[illegible]y 3, [illegible]6	Gr[illegible]ar	2,160.00
[illegible]d, Miss M. R.	V. P., 8th	[illegible]c., 5, [illegible]5	[illegible]	1,620.00
[illegible]n, Miss A. M.	Ei[illegible]th	[illegible]b. [illegible], [illegible]3	[illegible]	1,284.00
Karatar, Miss [illegible] C.	Fifth	Oct. [illegible], [illegible]3	[illegible]	1,164.00
Read, [illegible] H.	Second	[illegible]y [illegible], [illegible]2	G[illegible]ar	1,164.00
Curran, [illegible] M. M.	Seventh	M[illegible]. 4, [illegible]6	[illegible]	1,224.00
[illegible]r, E. L.	Third	A[illegible]g. 3, [illegible]8	[illegible]	900.00
[illegible]e, Miss M. E.	[illegible]	N[illegible]v. 18, [illegible]6	[illegible]	1,164.00
[illegible]e, [illegible] H. E.	Second	Oc[illegible]. 27, [illegible]2	[illegible]	1,164.00
O'Brien, Miss M. J.	First	[illegible]g. 3, [illegible]2	[illegible]	1,224.00
Horton, [illegible] A. B.	First	[illegible]y 13, [illegible]6	[illegible]	1,224.00
[illegible], Miss K. L.	[illegible]	[illegible]t. 10, [illegible]4	[illegible]	1,224.00
Hart, [illegible] A. [illegible]	[illegible]	Aug. 19, [illegible]7	[illegible]	960.00
[illegible], [illegible] M. J.	Third	Aug. 3, [illegible]8	[illegible]	840.00
Gordon, [illegible] H.	[illegible]	April 18, [illegible]0	[illegible]	840.00
[illegible], [illegible] A. J.	Fif[illegible]h	[illegible]t. 11, [illegible]7	[illegible]	1,020.00
Ungraded School—				
Klien, Miss M. G.	[illegible]	Jan. 6, 1902	[illegible]	1,164.00
McAllister, Mrs. F. H.	Ungraded	July 27, 1898	[illegible]	1,224.00
[illegible]—				
Iredale, Mrs. E. B.	[illegible]	[illegible] 1, [illegible]6	[illegible] & Spec.	1,560.00
[illegible], [illegible] M. A.	[illegible]	[illegible]t. [illegible], [illegible]1	[illegible]	1,224.00
Dailey, [illegible] Alice	Fifth	[illegible]r. [illegible], [illegible]7	[illegible]	1,164.00
Kenny, [illegible] M.	First	[illegible] 8, [illegible]7	[illegible]	1,104.00
[illegible]k, [illegible] A.	Fourth	[illegible]g. 5, [illegible]8	[illegible]	960.00
Bl[illegible], Miss R. E.	Second	June 1, [illegible]8	[illegible]	1,140.00
Corbett, Miss A. M.	F[illegible]st	[illegible]. [illegible], [illegible]5	[illegible]	1,224.00

[illegible] [illegible]—

Name	Grade	Date of appointment	Certificate	Salary
McCarthy, Mr. T. H.	Principal	Mar. 20, 1891	[illegible]	2,160.00
[illegible], Miss I. M.	Sixth	Sept. 9, 1872	[illegible]	1,164.00
Silvey, [illegible]	[illegible]	Aug. 22, 1907	[illegible]	1,152.00
[illegible], Miss A.	Second	Sept. [illegible], [illegible]	[illegible]	1,164.00
[illegible], Miss Ella	First	Jan. 3, 1874	[illegible]	1,224.00
Fischer, Miss J. G.	[illegible]	May 1, [illegible]	[illegible]	1,224.00
Sc[illegible], Miss J.	First	Sept. 5, [illegible]	Grammar	1,224.00
Kirkwood, Mr. W. H.	Seventh	Aug. 19, [illegible]	[illegible]	1,224.00
[illegible], Mrs. M. A.	Third	July 20, [illegible]	[illegible]	1,164.00
[illegible], Miss A. E.	Sixth	June 18, [illegible]	Grammar	1,164.00
[illegible], Mr. [illegible] G.	V. P., 8th	July 27, [illegible]	[illegible]	1,620.00
[illegible], Miss [illegible] A.	Fourth	April 18, [illegible]	[illegible]	840.00
Zul[illegible], Mr. C.	Italian	July 24, [illegible]	[illegible]	1,200.00

[illegible] [illegible] Pr.—

Name	Grade	Date of appointment	Certificate	Salary
Barlow, Miss C. B.	Principal	Aug. 1, 1868	Grammar	1,560.00
Mi[illegible], Miss J. G.	Fifth	Mar. 13, 1895	Grammar	1,164.00
McVerry, Miss M.	First	Sept. 2, 1884	Grammar	1,224.00
Fleming, Miss I.	Second	Feb. 1, 1907	Grammar	1,164.00
Laurent, Miss S. E.	First	Jan. 7, 1908	Grammar	1,152.00
Lloyd, Miss E. L.	Third	Aug. 3, [illegible]	High	840.00
Miller, Miss Mary A.	Second	Jan. 16, 1910	Grammar	840.00

Winfield Scott Primary—

Name	Grade	Date of appointment	Certificate	Salary
Thomas, Miss M. E.	Principal	July 12, 1887	[illegible]	1,560.00
Horgan, Miss E. E.	[illegible] Eighth	Sept. [illegible], [illegible]	[illegible]	1,140.00
Wright, Miss [illegible] B.	Second	Jan. 6, 1902	High	1,164.00
[illegible], Miss A. G.	First	July 27, 1898	[illegible]	1,224.00
Demmick, Mrs. M. F.	First	Dec. 10, 1890	[illegible]	1,224.00
Birch, Mrs. Lily	Fifth	Mar. 18, 1907	Grammar	1,164.00
[illegible], Miss M. L.	Fourth	Jan. 22, 1908	Grammar	1,140.00
Lin[illegible], Miss Emily	Third	Sept. 6, 1874	Gram. & French	1,164.00

SCHOOLS AND TEACHERS—[illegible]

Name.	Grade of Class.	When Elected.			Grade of Certificate.	Salary per Year.
Yerba Buena Primary—						
[illegible]y, M[illegible]s K. F.	Principal	[illegible]	[illegible],	[illegible]6	[illegible]r	1,800.00
[illegible]s, [illegible]s 3. J.	Seventh	[illegible]t.	9,	[illegible]3	G[illegible] r	1,224.00
Stewart, [illegible]s J. [illegible]	Third	[illegible]t.	[illegible],	[illegible]0	G[illegible]r	1,164.00
[illegible]h, [illegible]s 3. 3.	Third	[illegible]y	1,	[illegible]3	G[illegible]r	1,164.00
[illegible]l, M[illegible]s M. C.	Third	Aug.	3,	[illegible]3	G[illegible]r	1,164.00
c[illegible]s, [illegible]ss N. A.	First	[illegible]t.	5, 1	88	G[illegible]r	1,224.00
[illegible]h, Mi[illegible]s M.	First	[illegible]v.	1,	[illegible]1	G[illegible]r	1,224.00
c[illegible]r, [illegible]s J.	First	[illegible]		[illegible]7	[illegible]r	1,224.00
[illegible]u, [illegible]s M. G.	First	Aug.	[illegible],	[illegible]1	G[illegible]r	1,224.00
Purvine, Al[illegible]oe	Fourth	[illegible]ril		[illegible]8	G[illegible]r	840.00
K[illegible]n, Miss [illegible] R.	Fifth	[illegible]b.	[illegible],	[illegible]5	G[illegible]r	1,164.00
[illegible]n, M[illegible]s J. [illegible].	Sixth	[illegible]g.	[illegible],	[illegible]6	G[illegible]r	840.00
San Francisco Commercial—						
[illegible]y, [illegible]s. H.	Prin[illegible]l	[illegible]v.	27,	[illegible]	i[illegible]h	3,000.00
Deacon, Mrs. Eldora	Bookkeeping	[illegible]t.	1,	[illegible]7	1 [illegible]l	1,500.00
Sykes, [illegible]s. B.	Law, Gov.	e[illegible].	16,	[illegible]6	[illegible]h	1,620.00
[illegible]n, Mrs. S. W.	Arith.	[illegible]y	20,	[illegible]9	[illegible]h	1,620.00
[illegible]o, [illegible]s [illegible]. G.	S[illegible]h	Jy	30,	[illegible]0	Special	1,500.00.
Langdon, M[illegible]s S. A.	[illegible]ng	[illegible]y	20,	[illegible]4	Gram. & Spec.	1, [illegible]60.00
[illegible]s, [illegible]s [illegible]y L.	S[illegible]y	Aug.	15,	[illegible]9	Special	1, [illegible]60.00
Furlong, Miss M. I.	[illegible]gh	[illegible]n.	14,	[illegible]5	[illegible]h	1, [illegible]80.00
[illegible]e, [illegible]e [illegible]	Penmanship	[illegible]r.	8,	[illegible]4	Gram. & Special	1,500.00
[illegible]s, Mrs. I. D.	[illegible]ic	[illegible]n.	[illegible],	[illegible]7	[illegible]h	1, [illegible]80.00
Garbarino, M[illegible]s I.	[illegible]g	[illegible]v.	[illegible],	[illegible]9	Special	1,500.00
Hayes, M[illegible]s M. L.	S[illegible]y	[illegible]t.	1,	[illegible]4	Special	1,500.00
[illegible]r, Miss H. E.	Bookkeeping	[illegible]y	[illegible],	[illegible]7	Special	1,500.00
Hawkins, Miss G. G.	[illegible]etic	Oct.	[illegible],	[illegible]1	[illegible]h	1,620.00
G[illegible]ll[illegible]e, [illegible]e	Engl[illegible]h	Jan.	4,	[illegible]2	High	1.440.00

Name	Position	Date	Grade	Salary
Barnes, Mr. J. E.	Stenography	Aug. 18, 1910	Special	1,500.00
Kirwin, Miss C. A.	English	Aug. 2, 1909	High	1,440.00

Girls' High—

Name	Position	Date	Grade	Salary
[illegible]t, [illegible] A. W.	Principal	Jan. 5, 1883	[illegible]h	3,000.00
Prag, Mrs. M.	History	June 27, 1864	[illegible]h	1,980.00
[illegible]l, Mr. [illegible] O.	Science	Aug. 23, 1889	[illegible]h	2240.00
[illegible]y, Mr. E. J.	Fren[illegible]h	May 15, 1899	Special	1,980.00
[illegible]h, Mr. F. M.	[illegible]g	Mar. 1, 1887	[illegible]h	1,980.00
[illegible]h, M[illegible]s N. E.	[illegible]h	Jan. 10, 1902	[illegible]h	1,620.00
Levicle, M[illegible]s B.	[illegible]h	Mar. 13, 1905	[illegible]h	1,620.00
[illegible]l, Miss L.	[illegible]t. Science	Dec. 17, 1890	[illegible]h	1,620.00
[illegible]r, M[illegible]s E. D.	[illegible]h	Aug. 15, 1898	[illegible]h	1,620.00
[illegible]d, M[illegible]s [illegible] B.	[illegible]h	July 20, 1901	[illegible]h	1,980.00
Stark, Miss C. [illegible]	[illegible]n	July 21, 1902	[illegible]h	1,620.00
[illegible], M[illegible]s E. L.	[illegible]atics	Sept. 30, 1901	[illegible]h	1,620.00
Zimmerman, Mr. [illegible]	[illegible]n	Jan. 4, 1871	[illegible]h	1,620.00
[illegible]n, M[illegible]s E. R.	[illegible]h	Jan. 3, 1903	[illegible]h	1,620.00
[illegible]r, Martin A.	[illegible]n	Aug. 19, 1907	[illegible]h	1,980.00
[illegible]t, M[illegible]s [illegible]	[illegible]at[illegible]s	Aug. 23, 1870	[illegible]h	1,980.00
[illegible], Miss M.	[illegible]g	July 23, 1908	Special	1,500.00
Moore, [illegible]s Isabel	Dom. Science	Aug. 20, 1908	S[illegible]l	1,200.00
[illegible]s, Miss N[illegible]lli e M.	History	Aug. 7, 1869	H[illegible]h	1,620.00
Hobe, M[illegible]s S. A.	Mat[illegible]s	July 21, 1901	High	1,620.00

Lowell High—

Name	Position	Date	Grade	Salary
Morton, Mr. Frank	Principal	Aug. 1, 1886	High	3,300.00
Clark, Mr. F. H.	Head History	July 8, 1889	High	1,980.00
Crofts, Francis E.	Head Mathematics	Nov. 28, 1891	High	1,980.00
Schmit, Mr. J. J.	Head Drawing	Dec. 26, 1894	High	1,980.00
Nourse, Mr. J. P.	Head Anc. Lang.	Jan. 14, 1901	High	1,980.00

SCHOOLS AND TEACHERS—[illegible]

Name.	Grade of Class.	When Elected.	Grade of [illegible].	Sal[illegible] [illegible]
Lowell High—Continued				
Duffy, [illegible] A. G.	Head Engl[illegible]	[illegible] [illegible], [illegible]	[illegible]	1, [illegible]0.00
[illegible] F. [illegible]	[illegible]	Jan. 3, [illegible]	[illegible]	1, 40.00
Bowman, Elsie	[illegible] Mat[illegible]atics	[illegible] [illegible], [illegible]	[illegible]	1, [illegible]0.00
Longley, Mr. J. A.	History	[illegible] [illegible], [illegible]	[illegible]	1, [illegible]0.00
Perham, Mr. F. E.	[illegible]	[illegible] 4, [illegible]	[illegible]	1,620.00
Carey, Mr. E. P.	S[illegible]	Feb. 3, [illegible]	[illegible]	1, [illegible].00
[illegible], Mr. T. H.	[illegible]	Nov. [illegible], [illegible]	[illegible]	1, [illegible]0.00
[illegible], Miss C. B.	English	April 4, [illegible]	[illegible]	1, [illegible]0.00
[illegible], Mary M.	Head Modern [illegible]	[illegible] [illegible], [illegible]	[illegible]	1, [illegible]0.00
[illegible], [illegible] A.	[illegible]	[illegible] 1, [illegible]	[illegible]	1, [illegible]0.00
[illegible], [illegible] F.	Latin-[illegible]	May [illegible], 1885	[illegible]	1, [illegible]0.00
[illegible], [illegible] A.	[illegible]istry	[illegible] 2, [illegible]	[illegible]	1, 40.00
[illegible], Mr. H.	Head Science	Aug. 3, [illegible]	[illegible]	1,980.00
[illegible], Mr. A.	Drawing	[illegible] [illegible], [illegible]	Special	1,500.00
Koch, Mr. F. W.	Science	July [illegible], [illegible]	[illegible]	1,620.00
[illegible], [illegible] Carl L.	[illegible] & [illegible]	[illegible] 2, [illegible]	[illegible]	1,440.00
[illegible], Mr. L. H.	Latin [illegible] Greek	[illegible] [illegible], [illegible]	[illegible]	1,440.00
[illegible], Mr. F. B.	Latin and Greek	July [illegible], [illegible]	[illegible]	1,440.00
[illegible]—				
[illegible], [illegible]	[illegible]	Oct. 1, [illegible]	[illegible]	3, 00.00
[illegible], [illegible] W. O.	Head Science	[illegible] 1, [illegible]	[illegible]	1, [illegible]0.00
[illegible], [illegible] E.	[illegible]	[illegible] 9, [illegible]	[illegible]	1, [illegible]0.00
[illegible], [illegible] A.	[illegible]	Feb. [illegible], [illegible]	[illegible]	1, [illegible]0.00
Blanchard, Dr. M. E.	Latin	[illegible] 5, [illegible]	[illegible]	2, [illegible]0.00
Kel[illegible], [illegible] A. [illegible]	[illegible]	[illegible] [illegible], [illegible]	[illegible]	1, [illegible]0.00
[illegible], Miss E.	History	[illegible] [illegible], [illegible]	H[illegible]	1, [illegible]0.00
[illegible], [illegible] A.	[illegible]atin	July [illegible], [illegible]	[illegible]	1,620.00
Maher, Miss M.	English	July [illegible], [illegible]	H[illegible]	1, [illegible]0,00

Name	Subject	Date of Appointment	Certificate	Salary
[illegible], Miss N. K.	[illegible]	Dec. 29, 1896	Gram. & [illegible]	1,500.00
Downey, Mr. A. D.	Science	Jan. 21, 1907	[illegible]	1,620.00
[illegible], Mrs. M.	[illegible]	Jan. 12, 1905	[illegible]	1,620.00
[illegible], Mrs. E. C.	[illegible] Languages	Aug. 3, 1908	[illegible] and Sp.	1,980.00
Dowling, [illegible] C.	[illegible]	Dec. 20, 1899	[illegible]	1,620.00
[illegible], [illegible] E.	[illegible] & [illegible]	April 4, 1887	[illegible]	[illegible]
[illegible], Mr. C. L.	Drawing	April 20, 1896	[illegible]	1,980.00
[illegible], Mr. R. L.	[illegible]	Nov. 2, [illegible]	Special	1,500.00

Polytechnic High—

Name	Subject	Date of Appointment	Certificate	Salary
Ferguson, James	Principal	Aug. 21, 1905	[illegible]	[illegible]
Jordan, Mr. A. L.	Head Science	Jan. 26, 1899	[illegible]	[illegible]
[illegible] Vleck, [illegible] M.	Head Ind. Arts	July 22, 1889	Special	[illegible]
[illegible], [illegible] E. S.	[illegible]	Mar. 25, 1905	[illegible]	[illegible]
[illegible], [illegible] R.	[illegible]	April 30, 1908	[illegible]	[illegible]
[illegible], Mr. P. J.	Head [illegible]	Jan. 21, 1903	[illegible]	[illegible]
Hatch, Mr. I. C.	Head [illegible]	Aug. 12, [illegible]	[illegible]	[illegible]
[illegible], Etta	[illegible]atics	Dec. 1, 1897	[illegible]	[illegible]
Murdoch, Miss R.	Drawing	Nov. 18, 1893	[illegible]	1,500.00
[illegible], Miss N. L.	Sewing	Sept. 21, 1907	Special	1,500.00
Drew, Mr. [illegible] J.	Head Mech. Draw.	Mar. 28, 1898	[illegible]	1,980.00
[illegible], Miss C.	French	Feb. 3, 1908	[illegible]	1,620.00
Kell[illegible], Miss M. E.	Head [illegible]	July 20, [illegible]	[illegible]	1,980.00
Dickerson, Mr. R. R.	Science	Jan. 2, 1907	[illegible]	1,620.00
[illegible], Mr. J. J.	Asst. Forge	Sept. 14, [illegible]	Special	1,500.00
Ostrom, Carmel	Drawing	Jan. 10, [illegible]	Special	1,500.00
Carne, Harry L.	Pattern [illegible]	Aug. 2, [illegible]	Special	1,500.00
[illegible]tt, Miss [illegible]	[illegible]	July 18, [illegible]	Special	[illegible]
[illegible], Mr. C. C.	[illegible] Drawing	Sept. 30, [illegible]	Special	1,500.00

Bernal Evening—

Name	Subject	Date of Appointment	Certificate	Salary
Van Gorder, Mr. A. G.	All	Sept. 1, 1904	High	900.00

SCHOOLS AND TEACHERS—[illegible].

Name.	Grade of Class.	When [illegible].	Grade of Certificate.	Salary [illegible] Yr.
Commercial Evening—				
Riley, [illegible] T.	Principal	[illegible]y 17, 1901	[illegible]	1,[illegible]00
[illegible]n, Mr. W. W.	Bookkeeping	[illegible]y 5, [illegible]	[illegible] & Spec.	720.00
Kozminsky, M[illegible]s D.	[illegible]	[illegible]t. 29, [illegible]	Special	720.00
O'Mall[illegible], [illegible] W.	Typewriting	Aug. 18, [illegible]	Special	720.00
[illegible]k, Miss A. J.	Bookkeeping	[illegible] 12, [illegible]	Gram. & S[illegible]c.	720.00
Treff[illegible]s, Mr. W. E.	[illegible]	[illegible]ril 1, [illegible]	[illegible] & S[illegible]c.	720.00
[illegible]ey, Mrs. K. F.	Bookkeeping	[illegible]r. 25, [illegible]	[illegible]r	720.00
[illegible]r, Mr. J. [illegible]	Eng. & [illegible] Arith.	[illegible] 8, [illegible]	[illegible]r, L. D.	720.00
Dickson, Mrs. Mary	[illegible]ip	April 7, [illegible]	[illegible]	720.00
[illegible], Miss [illegible]	Seventh	[illegible] 28, [illegible]	[illegible] & Spec.	720.00
[illegible]r, Mrs. M. E.	Stenography	[illegible]v. [illegible], [illegible]	Spe[illegible]ial	720.00
[illegible], Mr. D. A.	Bookkeeping	[illegible]v. [illegible], [illegible]	Grammar	720.00
[illegible]n, Miss Alma	[illegible]	Feb. 3, [illegible]	[illegible]	720.00
Hamilton Evening—				
Lenahan, Mr. J. A.	[illegible]al	[illegible]e 15, [illegible]	[illegible]r	960.00
Israel, [illegible] T.	[illegible]h and [illegible]th	[illegible] 23, [illegible]	[illegible]r	600.00
Burnett, M[illegible]s S. C.	[illegible]	[illegible]t. 26, [illegible]	[illegible]r	600.00
L[illegible]st[illegible], M[illegible]s B.	Sten.	Aug. [illegible]	Special	720.00
Daniels, John R.	Bookkeeping	[illegible]pt. 1, [illegible]	S[illegible]al	720.00
Cronin, Miss K. F.	Typewriting	[illegible] 2, [illegible]	Gram. & Spec.	720.00
Wirt, [illegible]	Ninth	[illegible] 9, [illegible]	[illegible]	600.00
Cohn, M[illegible]s D.	Seventh	[illegible] 7, [illegible]	[illegible]r	600.00
Ringnalda, Wm. F.	[illegible]	[illegible]v. 12, [illegible]	[illegible]	600.00
[illegible]k, Miss Mary	St[illegible]g[illegible]y	[illegible]y 27, [illegible]	Special	600.00
Horace Mann Evening—				
Kratzer, Mr. D. W.	Principal	Ag. 14, 1897	Grammar	960.00
Murphy, Mrs. C. L.	Ninth	Aug. 30, 1897	Gram. & Spec.	600.00

Name	Grade	Date of appointment	Certificate	Salary
Deal, Louise B.	Eighth	Jan. 1, [illegible]87	Gram[illegible]ar	600.00
Kelly, Eliz. F.	Eighth	Aug. 18, [illegible]04	[illegible]r	600.00
Lane, M[illegible]s H. F.	[illegible]h	Sept. 1, [illegible]05	[illegible]r	600.00
Martin, M[illegible]s A. G.	Seventh	July 28, [illegible]98	[illegible]r	600.00
Finn, Mrs. E. C.	[illegible]h	Dec. 15, [illegible]96	Gramm[illegible]ar	600.00
[illegible]ll, Mrs. M. L.	Sixth and S[illegible]v[illegible]nth	Sept. 1, [illegible]97	[illegible]r	600.00
McManus, Mr. [illegible]. A.	Seventh	Oct. 7, [illegible]97	G[illegible]r	600.00
K[illegible]ny, Miss B.	Fifth [illegible]d Sixth	Aug. 31, [illegible]92	G[illegible]r	600.00
Dwyer, Mrs. M.	First [illegible]d Fourth	Feb. 12, [illegible]88	Primary	600.00
M[illegible]ld, [illegible]. F.	Foreign	Dec. 5, [illegible]92	[illegible]r	600.00
Mann, Mr. R. L.	[illegible]h	Feb. 2, [illegible]95	High	600.00

Humboldt Evening High—

Name	Subject	Date of appointment	Certificate	Salary
Taaffe, Mr. L. A.	Principal	Dec. 2, [illegible]96	[illegible]h	1,200.00
[illegible]rts, Mr. A. E.	Hd. of Drawing Dpt.	Dec. [illegible], [illegible]92	Gram. & Spec.	1,200.00
Riley, [illegible]. G. E.	[illegible]h [illegible]l	Sept. 1, [illegible]02	High	[illegible]20.00
[illegible]d, [illegible]. E. M.	High [illegible]l	Aug. 10, 1905	High	[illegible]20.00
[illegible]y, Miss [illegible]. J.	[illegible]h [illegible]ol	Aug. [illegible], [illegible]05	[illegible]h	720.00
McHenry, Mr. John	Drawing	April 27, 1898	S[illegible]al	[illegible]20.00
Walsh, Mr. C. F.	[illegible]tin	Sept. 10, 1908	High	720.00
Christie, [illegible]. L. C.	Drawing	Jan. 3, [illegible]92	Special	720.00
Harris, Mr. H. E.	Drawing	Sept. 4, [illegible]02	Special	720.00
Hendry, Mr. C. S.	Drawing	April 27, 1898	Special	720.00
Harvey, Mr. R. W.	Biology	Dec. 28, [illegible]05	Special	720.00
Carroll, Mr. W. E.	Drawing	April 15, 1905	Special	720.00
Blue, Mr. [illegible]. K.	Drawing	Aug. 5, [illegible]01	Special	720.00
[illegible]e, Mr. L. 8.	Drawing	April 1, [illegible]05	Special	720.00
Bailey, Mr. S. E.	[illegible]atics	Jan. 3, [illegible]91	High	720.00
Hall, Mr. H. C.	[illegible]ting	July 1, [illegible]03	High	720.00
Antonovich, Mr. E. P.	Drawing	Aug. 8, [illegible]90	Special	720.00
Little, John W.	M[illegible]h. Drawing	Oct. 10, 1910	Special	720.00

Name.	Grade of Class.	When Elected.	Grade of Certificate.	Salary per Year.
Humboldt Evening High—Continued				
McMillan, Mr. J. T.	Navigation	Aug. [illegible]	Special	720.00
Cuthbertson, Mr. G. W.	Science	Dec. 1, [illegible]	High	720.00
Drew, John S.	Science	Feb. 25, [illegible]	High	720.00
Irving M. Scott Evening—				
Maries, Mr. L. B.	All	April 18, 1910	Grammar	600.00
Lagunda Honda—				
Dunkley, Mr. L. P.	All	Jan. 9, 1908	Grammar	600.00
[illegible] Evening—				
[illegible], [illegible] A. H.	Principal	[illegible] 2, [illegible]	[illegible]	960.00
[illegible], [illegible] E. J.	[illegible]nth	[illegible] 31, [illegible]	[illegible]	[illegible]60.00
[illegible], Miss L. M.	Ninth	[illegible] 14, [illegible]	[illegible]	[illegible]60.00
McDermott, Miss K.	[illegible]	Aug. 12, [illegible]	Grammar	600.00
Harvey, [illegible] M. A.	5th, [illegible], 3d	Aug. 4, [illegible]	[illegible]	600.00
Parlin, Mrs. A. E.	Ungraded	Aug. 31, [illegible]	[illegible]	600.00
[illegible], [illegible] P. S.	[illegible]	[illegible] 11, [illegible]	[illegible]	600.00
[illegible], [illegible] I. A.	[illegible]	[illegible] 23, [illegible]	[illegible]	1,200.00
[illegible], Mrs. S. S.	[illegible]	[illegible] 27, [illegible]	Primary	600.00
Heineman, Mrs. E.	[illegible]	Oct. 23, [illegible]	[illegible]	600.00
[illegible], [illegible] E. L.	[illegible]	Aug. 30, [illegible]	[illegible]	600.00
O'Neill, [illegible] L. C.	[illegible]nth	Sept. 8, [illegible]	[illegible]	600.00
Monroe Evening—				
Nolan, Mr. W. C.		Jan. 24, 1910	Grammar	720.00
Stokes, Mr. G. W.		Aug. 1, 1901	High	900.00

Name	Grade	Date	Certificate	Salary
Portola Evening—				
Prusch, Mr. N. H.		Feb. 1, 1906	Grammar	600.00
Roosevelt Evening—				
Strauss, Miss M.	Principal	July 11, 1895	Grammar	780.00
Kennedy, Mrs. A.	Eighth and Ninth	Sept. 21, 1908	Grammar	600.00
Dougherty, Wm. J.	Seventh and Eighth	Aug. 19, 1907	Grammar	600.00
Madden, Janet C.	Fourth, Fifth, Sixth	July 29,1908	Grammar	600.00
Sherman Evening—				
Fenton, Mr. F. L.	Principal	[illegible] 11, 1904	High	900.00
Williams, Mr. W. J.	Foreign	July 15, 1868	High	600.00
Reed, Miss C.	6th, 7th, 8th	[illegible]g. 4, 1908	Grammar	600.00
Cella, Miss E. L.	Italian	[illegible]g. 2, 1909	Grammar	600.00
Fiala, Miss A. M.	Ninth	May 9, 1886	Grammar	600.00
Jones, Mrs. Jennie	Commercial	July 29, 1910	Grammar	600.00
Washington Evening—				
Goodman, Mrs. P.	[illegible]	[illegible] 4, [illegible]	[illegible]	960.00
R[illegible]d[illegible]n, Miss J. A.	[illegible]	June 9, 1897	[illegible]	600.00
[illegible], [illegible] E. J.	Ninth	[illegible]g. 22, [illegible]	Grammar	600.00
Caglieri, Mrs. V.	Eighth	Nov. 19, [illegible]	Grammar	600.00
Robinson, Miss M. C.	Seventh	Dec. 10, [illegible]	[illegible]	600.00
[illegible]n, Mrs. E. S. M.	Foreign	[illegible] 17, [illegible]	[illegible]	600.00
Taylor, Ella B.	Foreign	Sept. 1, 1897	[illegible]	600.00
[illegible], Dr. M.	Foreign	[illegible]t. 30, 1879	[illegible]	600.00
Bretz, Miss B.	[illegible]	[illegible]t. 16, [illegible]	[illegible]	600.00
[illegible]ly, Mr. C.	Foreign	Nov. 22, [illegible]	[illegible]	600.00
M[illegible]Laughlin, Miss A.	Foreign	July 15, [illegible]	[illegible]	600.00
Washington Evening High—				
Fischer, Dr. F.	All	July 6, 1886	High	720.00

SCHOOLS AND TEACHERS—Continued.

Name.	Grade of Class.	When Elected.	Grade of Certificate.	Salary per Yr.
[illegible] at Large—				
[illegible]hel, Mr. F. K.	Supt. Manual Trng.	Jan. 15, 1904	Grammar and Special	1,920.00
[illegible]on, Mr. L. E.	Manual Training	Aug. 1, 1901	Special	1,200.00
[illegible]ot, Mr. I. C.	[illegible]ing	Feb. 15, 1903	Special	1,200.00
Dailey, Mr. P. F.	Manual Training	Aug. 10, 1905	Special	1,200.00
Dowling, Mr. D. E.	Manual Training	Mar. 4, 1906	Special	1,200.00
[illegible]ia, Mr. A. M.	Manual [illegible]ing	Mar. 11, 1905	High and Special	1,200.00
[illegible]le, Mr. M. J.	[illegible] [illegible]ing	Nov. 5, 1897	Special	[illegible],200.00
Felton, Mr. M. [illegible]	[illegible] Training	July 30, 1902	Grammar and Special	[illegible],200.00
Telfer, Mr. G. J.	[illegible] [illegible]	July 1, [illegible]03	[illegible] and Special	1,200.00
[illegible]er, Mr. R. J.	[illegible]ing	Mar. 23, 1905	Special	720.00
[illegible]r, Miss E.	Music	[illegible] 28, 1908	[illegible] Primary	1,920.00
[illegible]e, Mrs. M. G.	Music	[illegible] 3, 1903	Special	1,320.00
[illegible]ne, Mrs. A. W.	Music	Nov. 1, 1910	Special	1,500.00
Ball, Miss K. M.	Drawing	July 1, 18[illegible]4	Special	1,920.00
[illegible]ing, Miss A. B.	Drawing	Aug. 3, 1908	Special	1,080.00
[illegible]in, Miss E. H.	Drawing	Aug. 3, 1908	Special	[illegible],0[illegible]0.00
[illegible]ng, Mr. O. S.	[illegible]re	Aug. 1, 1897	Special	1,200.00
Tharp, Mrs. N. J.	[illegible] [illegible]ture	Jan. 1, 1910	Special	1,200.00
[illegible]t, Miss E. M.	Cookery	July 1, [illegible]01	Special	1,500.00
[illegible]er, Miss C. A.	Cookery	July 20, 1905	Special	900.00
[illegible]n, Miss L. G.	Cookery	Aug. 2, 1909	Grammar and Special	900.00
[illegible]rd, Miss F. M.	Cookery	Sept. 1, 1904	Special	[illegible]
[illegible]on, Mrs. M. N.	Cookery	Sept. 1, 1909	Special	900.00
Tobriner, Miss A.	Cookery	Aug. 18, 1910	Special	900.00
[illegible]in, Miss V. N.	Cookery	July 25, 1910	Special	900.00
[illegible]or, Miss H. S.	Cookery	Oct. 14, 1910	Special	900.00
[illegible]n, Miss M.	Cookery	Aug. 19, 1905	Special	900.00
[illegible]t, Mrs. M.	Cookery	Oct. 25, 1909	Special	900.00
Gray, Miss E.	Cookery	Aug. 19, 1907	Special	900.00
Ball, Miss L.	Supt. Pr. Grades	April 1, 1908	[illegible]mar	1,920.00
[illegible]na, Mr. P. A.	[illegible]	[illegible] 13, 1887	Special	1,620.00

NECROLOGY.

Name.	Position Occupied.	Died.
Miss Lucy McNear	Bryant Cosmopolitan Primary	Jan. 21, 1910
Mrs. V. C. Ingram	Peabody	Mar. 10, 1910
Miss Minnie R. Bley	Agassiz	Apr. —, 1910
Miss Mary L. Marks	Bernal	Apr. 20, 1910
Mrs. M. A. Steele	Edison	Apr. 25, 1910
Mr. George Foulks	Principal Hamilton Evening	June 7, 1910
Mrs. J. B. Levey	Hearst Grammar	July 25. 1910
Mrs. Cora B. Tompkins	Moulder	Oct. 8, 1910
Miss Laura C. Perry	Lincoln	Oct. 26, 1910
Mrs. Clara Bigelow	V.-Prin. John Swett Grammar	Dec. 6, 1910
Mr. Azro L. Mann	Principal Denman Grammar, Superintendent of Schools 1878-1879	Feb. 28, 1911
Mr. Ebenezer Knowlton	Formerly Principal of Rincon Grammar, Vice-Principal of Lincoln Grammar and Teacher in Boys' High, Commercial and Roosevelt Evening Schools	Feb. 9, 1911
Mr. John C. Pelton	Founder of the first free public school in San Francisco or California, December, 1849. Principal Grammar Schools, Superintendent of Schools 1856, 1857, 1865, 1866, 1867	Mar. 5, 1911
Mr. William A. Leggett	Vice-Principal Franklin	Mar. 31, 1911
Miss Martha Galloway	Principal Visitacion Valley	Apr. 5, 1911
Mrs. Rebecca Greenan	Lincoln Evening	Apr. 12, 1911
Mr. W. N. Bush	Formerly Teacher Lowell High and Principal Polytechnic High	May 21, 1911
Mrs. M. S. Wright	Frank McCoppin	Mar. 9, 1911
Miss Emily Wickman	Jackson	
Miss Katherine E. Meighan	Fairmount	1910
Mr. A. C. Kinne	Lincoln Evening	Oct. —, 1910

JANITORS.

SCHOOL.	NAME.	SALARY. per Month.		per Annum.
Adams	Sample, R.	$60.00	=	$720.00
Agassiz	Caveney, K.	55.00	=	660.00
Agassiz	Dempsey, P.	55.00	=	660.00
Bergerot	Stelljes, H.	72.50	=	870.00
Bernal	Murphy, J.	90.00	=	1,080.00
Bay View	Jacobs, J. *	75.00	=	900.00
Bay View	Gorman, A.	30.00	=	360.00
Bryant	O'Donnell, A.	60.00	=	720.00
Bryant	Foster, Wm. *	75.00	=	900.00
Buena Vista	McCullough, M.	55.00	=	660.00
Burnett	Davis, S.	50.00	=	600.00
Columbia	McCarthy, M.	50.00	=	600.00
Columbia	Adams, M.	55.00	=	660.00
Clement	McHugh, M.	55.00	=	660.00
Cleveland	Lee, K.	45.00	=	540.00
Cooper	Spinetti, M.	62.50	=	750.00
Crocker	Creegan, C.	55.00	=	660.00
Crocker	Brennan, T.	55.00	=	660.00
Denman	Fordyce, M.	40.00	=	480.00
Douglass	Carter, K.	72.50	=	870.00
Dudley Stone	Byrne, B.	70.00	=	840.00
Edison	Swanson, A.	55.00	=	660.00
Emerson	Dunn, G. *	85.00	=	1,020.00
Everett	Cormack, W. *	90.00	=	1,080.00
Farragut	Bassett, Mrs.	60.00	=	720.00
Fairmount	Cuddy, J.	60.00	=	720.00
Fairmount	Kellerher, N.	60.00	=	720.00
Franklin	Mullane, J.	60.00	=	720.00
Fremont	Gunn, S. *	80.00	=	960.00
McCoppin, Frank	Johnson, M.	40.00	=	480.00
McCoppin, Frank	Haigermoser, J. *	75.00	=	900.00
Garfield	Stoermer, M.	60.00	=	720.00
Garfield	Post, A. L. *	85.00	=	1,020.00
Glen Park	O'Connor, E.	72.50	=	870.00
Golden Gate	Dehoney, E.	75.00	=	900.00
Grant	McAdams, J. W.	55.00	=	660.00
Grattan	Dawson, M.	40.00	=	480.00
Haight	Lavelle, M.	70.00	=	840.00
Hamilton	Creighton, J.	47.50	=	570.00
Hamilton and Eve	Hanley, J.	85.00	=	1,020.00
Hancock	Heine, J.	50.00	=	600.00
Hancock	Costello, L. *	75.00	=	900.00
Harrison	Earl, A.	35.00	=	420.00
Hawthorne	Allen, R.	50.00	=	600.00
Hearst and Lincoln Eve	Ferbeek, H. *	140.00	=	1,680.00
Henry Durant	McQuaide, E.	65.00	=	780.00
Horace Mann and Eve	McGowan, J. *	72.50	=	870.00
Horace Mann and Eve	Herring, D. T. *	72.50	=	870.00
Hunter's Pt	Koch, A.	15.00	=	180.00
Washington Irving	McMahon, B.	40.00	=	480.00
Irving M. Scott	Rollins, E.	50.00	=	600.00

School	Janitor	Monthly		Annual
Irving M. Scott	Clark, M. E.	60.00	=	720.00
Jackson	Dolan, M.	35.00	=	420.00
James Lick	Foley, J.	60.00	=	720.00
Jean Parker	Kennedy, J.	72.50	=	870.00
Jefferson	Baker, A.	20.00	=	240.00
John Swett	Kaskell, A. *	65.00	=	780.00
Junipero Serra	Murphy, E.	50.00	=	600.00
Junipero Serra	Staff, G. F. *	75.00	=	900.00
Lafayette	Hemenez, D. F.	35.00	=	420.00
Laguna Honda	Cavanagh, M. R.	50.00	=	600.00
Laguna Honda	Nolan, D. A.	80.00	=	960.00
Lincoln	McShea, S.	40.00	=	480.00
Longfellow	Cook, J. F. *	75.00	=	900.00
Madison	Powers, P. F. *	75.00	=	900.00
Madison	Devine, M.	40.00	=	480.00
Marshall	Kelly, E.	55.00	=	660.00
McKinley	Langan, R.	75.00	=	900.00
Mission Grammar	Belden, A.	50.00	=	600.00
Mission Grammar	Whiting, C. E. *	75.00	=	900.00
Monroe	Buttle, Wm. *	85.00	=	1,020.00
Monroe	Savage, O.	52.50	=	630.00
Moulder	Jones, J.	60.00	=	720.00
Noe Valley	Kelly, J. *	77.50	=	920.00
Ocean House	Davis, M.	20.00	=	240.00
Oceanside	Benson, M.	50.00	=	600.00
Oriental	Naughton, J.	50.00	=	600.00
Pacific Heights	McDonald, J.	50.00	=	600.00
Pacific Heights	McMahon, K.	50.00	=	600.00
Parental	McQuaide, J.	35.00	=	420.00
Parkside	Jileck, M.	15.00	=	180.00
Peabody	Bole, N.	40.00	=	480.00
Potrero	Hayes, A.	45.00	=	540.00
Redding	Curran, D.	60.00	=	720.00
Roosevelt and Eve	Fevrier, I.	50.00	=	600.00
Roosevelt and Eve	Lillis, M. B.	50.00	=	600.00
Rincon	Hogan, J.	30.00	=	360.00
Sheridan	Moran, A.	50.00	=	600.00
Sheridan	Arnold, S. T. *	75.00	=	900.00
Sherman and Eve	Kelly, M.	85.00	=	920.00
Portola	Holmes, B.	65.00	=	780.00
Portola	Foley, M. A. *	75.00	=	900.00
Spring Valley	Branley, A.	55.00	=	660.00
Starr King	Neary, J.	40.00	=	480.00
Sunnyside	Morris, K.	50.00	=	600.00
Sunset	Aubertine, G.	25.00	=	300.00
Sutro	Ganzert, W.	50.00	=	600.00
Sutro	Rossiter, J. J. *	75.00	=	900.00
Ungraded and Cooper	Fitzpatrick, A.	32.50	=	390.00
Visitacion Valley	Freelond, R. I.	40.00	=	480.00
Washington Eve	Guinasso, N.	65.00	=	780.00
Washington	Kane, D. *	100.00	=	1,200.00
Winfield Scott	McEvoy, E. *	75.00	=	900.00
Yerba Buena	Hill, A.	70.00	=	840.00
Yerba Buena	Andrews, A.	40.00	=	480.00
Girls' High	Connors, M.	70.00	=	840.00
Girls' High	Nellman, E. *	90.00	=	1,080.00

Lowell High	Power, P. *	120.00	=1,440.00
Mission High & Humboldt Evening High	Boyd, E. *	125.00	=1,500.00
Mission High & Humboldt Evening High	Norton, K. *	80.00	= 960.00
Polytechnic High	Majnussen, G. *	110.00	=1,320.00
S. F. Commercial	Mahoney, J. F. *	100.00	=1,200.00
S. F. Commercial	Cohen, J. *	100.00	=1,200.00

*Names starred (*) are men.
All others are women.

Annual Report of The Board of Education and The Superintendent of Schools

San Francisco, California

For the Fiscal Year Ending June 30, 1912

105

CONTENTS

BOARD OF EDUCATION

City and County of San Francisco

OFFICERS 1911-12.

President: July-December, Hiram G. Vaughan; January-June, A. A. D'Ancona.
Secretary: Melvin G. Dodge.

MEMBERS 1911-12

Mary W. Kincaid.
Henry Payot, July-January.
Hiram G. Vaughan, July-January.
James E. Power.
Mary A. Deane, January '12; Died March 1912.
Sarah J. Jones, March-July 1912.
Alfred Roncovieri, Superintendent of Schools, ex-officio Member.

Report of Board of Education

San Francisco, California, July 1, 1912.

To the Honorable Board of Supervisors,
City and County of San Francisco.

Gentlemen:

In accordance with provision of the Charter, I have the honor to submit herewith the annual report of the Board of Education, embracing the report of the Superintendent of Schools, for the fifty-ninth fiscal year of the School Department, ending June 30, 1912.

Respectfully,

A. A. D'ANCONA,
President Board of Education, City and County of San Francisco.

Report of Superintendent of Schools

San Francisco, July 1, 1912.

To the Honorable, the Board of Education, in and
for the City and County of San Francisco.

Ladies and Gentlemen:—I have the honor to submit herewith the annual report on the condition of the public schools of this City and County, as required by the Charter, for the sixtieth fiscal year of the School Department, ending June 30, 1912.

ALFRED RONCOVIERI,

Superintendent of Common Schools, in and
for the City and County of San Francisco.

GENERAL STATISTICS.

Fiscal Year Ending, June 30, 1912.

Population of the City and County		450,000
Municipal Assessment—		
Real Estate	$405,516,520.00	
Personal Property	57,333,505.00	
Total	$461,850,025.00	
State Assessment	83,207,566.00	
Total Assessable		$545,057,591.00
Assessment just completed on which taxes will be collected for year 1912-1913—		
Municipal	$511,194,525.00	
State	94,293,628.00	
Total		$605,488,153.00
Gain for Year		60,330,562.00

City and County School Tax on each $100.00: 23½c.

Total rate (including Panama-Pacific In. Ex. Co. 5c): $2.05, 1911-1912.

City and County School Tax on each $100.00: 1912-1913 22 4/10 cts.

Total rate (including Panama-Pacific In. Ex. Co. 5c): $2.10, 1912-1913.

City and County Taxes for school purposes		$ 1,082,531.39
Apportionments of State School Funds—		
High Schools	$ 37,421.57	
Elementary Schools	601,182.56	
Total		$ 638,604.13

ESTIMATED VALUE OF SCHOOL PROPERTY.

Sites occupied by Elementary Schools	$2,616,700.00	
Sites occupied by Secondary Schools	547,000.00	
Sites not occupied by schools	2,600,000.00	
Total value of land		$ 5,763,700.00
Buildings—		
Elementary Schools	$5,140,470.00	
Secondary Schools	1,176,294.00	
Administration	15,000.00	
Total Value of Buildings		$ 6,331,764.00
Furniture—		
Elementary Schools	$ 292,396.00	
High Schools	23,350.00	
Administration	3,500.00	
Total Value of Furniture		$ 319,246.00
Apparatus and Laboratories—		
Elementary Schools, including Manual Training and Cooking	$ 30,000.00	
High Schools	50,000.00	
Total Value of all Apparatus and Laboratories		$ 80,000.00
Library—		
Elementary Schools	$ 35,819.00	
High Schools	4,710.00	
Teachers'	890.00	
Storeroom	800.00	
Total Value Libraries		$ 42,219.00
Total Value (Estimated) of all School Property		$12,536,929.00

FINANCIAL REPORT.

DISBURSEMENTS.

Salaries—		
Teachers—		
High School	$ 148,337.10	
Commercial	34,313.45	
Humboldt Evening High	19,083.20	
Primary and Grammar	1,200,404.35	
Evening (except Humboldt)	55,961.00	
Special (Athletics, Domestic Science, Industrial Work, Manual Training, Music, Penmanship, Physical Culture, Primary Reading)	44,918.35	
Total of Teachers' Salaries		$1,503,017.45
Janitors—		
High School	$ 9,300.00	
Humboldt Evening High	300.00	
Primary and Grammar	80,603.80	
Evening	2,910.00	
Total of Janitors' Salaries		$ 93,113.80
Board of Education, (4 members)	$ 11,947.50	
Chauffeur	1,562.50	
Inspector of Boilers (abolished Feb. 12)	875.00	
Inspector (Gas and Water Supply)	1,550.00	
Scavenger	3,900.00	
Secretary and Attaches (10 persons)	14,146.00	
Storeroom —Bookkeeper	608.35	
Storekeeper and Assistant	2,880.00	
Superintendent Buildings	2,094.15	
Superintendent of Schools and 4 Deputies	15,975.96	
Supply Department—Foreman, (abol. Feb. 12)	875.00	
Wages, Mechanics	9,522.75	
Total Miscellaneous Salaries		$ 65,937.21
Grand Total of Salaries		$1,662,068.46
Advertising	$ 138.00	
Athletics	1,213.79	
Books and Charts	7,873.61	
Buildings, Additions to	2,356.61	
Cartage	1,829.75	
Cooking Center Equipment	358.90	
Drinking Fountains	3,000.00	
Fuel	17,954.00	
Furniture	9,887.61	
Home Economics	239.95	
Lectures, Free Public	1,041.41	
Light	6,301.71	
National Education Association, Convention Expense—		
Polytechnic High School Equipment	2,222.56	
Printing	3,605.71	
Rents ($20 Polytechnic)	5,115.75	
Stationery	11,569.00	

Supplies—

Cooking	$ 2,143.48
High School	2,716.36
Incidental	14,139.31

SUPPLIES—Continued.

Industrial	874.22		
Janitorial	3,535.86		
Manual Training	2,208.87	25,618.12	
Teachers' Institute		1,365.00	
Telephone and Telegraph		76.41	
Toilets (New)		1,394.00	
Water		11,643.57	$ 115,553.16
Repairs to Buildings, (expended by Board of Public Works)		100,000.00	
Grand Total Expenditures			$1,877,621.62

RECEIPTS.

City and County Taxes		$1,082,531.39
State Apportionment High Schools	$ 37,421.57	
State Apportionment Elementary Schools	601,182.56	
Total		638,604.13
Rents derived from School Property		52,854.00
Money from sale of Old Material		100.00
Special Appropriation by Board of Supervisors expended by Board of Works for Repairs		100,000.00
Grand Total Receipts		$1,874,089.52

RESUME'.

Expenditures	$1,877,621.62
Receipts	1,874,089.52
Deficit year ending June 30, 1912	*3,532.10
Deficit year ending June 30, 1911	27,173.37
Total Deficit	$ *30,705.47

Including redemption of bonds ($89,600.00) and expenditure of bond money for land, buildings and equipment ($1,866,542.00) there was spent on the public schools of San Francisco for the year ending June 30, 1912, $3,833,763.62.

DEPARTMENT EXPENSES PRORATED AMONG HIGH, ELEMENTARY AND EVENING SCHOOLS, ON THE BASIS OF AVERAGE DAILY ATTENDANCE.

All Salaries, except Teachers' and Janitors'	$ 65,937.21	
All other expenses except additions to buildings, equipment Cooking Center, Drinking Fountains, Home Economics, Light, Polytechnic High School equipment, Rents, Supplies, Toilets	68,945.56	
Repairs, (Board of Public Works)	100,000.00	
Total Pro-rated		$234,882.77
High Schools (4)	$ 12,141.44	
Commercial	4,337.80	
Elementary	202,687.53	
Humboldt Evening	4,001.00	
Other Evening	11,715.00	
		$234,882.77

*Expected additional revenue will reduce this deficit by possibly $1000.00.

DISTRIBUTION OF EXPENSES AMONG SCHOOLS.

(Not including Sites and Buildings.)

High Schools—		
Equipment (Polytechnic)	$ 2,222.56	
Instruction	148,337.10	
Janitors	7,500.00	
Light and Electricity	600.00	
Rent (Polytechnic)	20.00	
Supplies	3,228.20	
Share of Department Expenses pro-rated	12,141.44	
		$ 174,049.30
Commercial School—		
Instruction	$ 34,313.45	
Janitors	1,800.00	
Supplies	727.74	
Share of Department Expenses pro-rated	4,444.65	
		41,285.84
Elementary Schools (Day)—		
Buildings (additions to)	$ 2,356.61	
Cooking Center Equipment	358.00	
Drinking Fountains	3,000.00	
Instruction	1,254,322.70	
Janitors	80,603.80	
Supplies	20,400.33	
Rents	5,095.75	
Toilets (New)	1,394.00	
Share of Department Expenses pro-rated	202,687.53	
		1,561,219.62
Humboldt Evening High School—		
Instruction	$ 19,083.20	
Janitors	300.00	
Light	1,505.21	
Supplies	267.00	
Share of Department expenses pro-rated	4,001.00	
		25,156.41
Other Evening Schools—		
Home Economics	239.95	
Instruction	55,961.00	
Janitors	2,910.00	
Light	4,196.50	
Supplies	888.00	
Share of Department expenses pro-rated	11,715.00	
		75,910.45
Total Expenditures		$1,877,621.62

Exclusive of Bond Money for Sites, Buildings and Equipment.

COST PER PUPIL, 1911-1912.

	Per Pupil Enrolled	Per Pupil Avge. Daily Attendance	Year 1910-11
(a) For Instruction Only—			
High Schools	$54.68	$64.35	$63.48
Primary and Grammar Schools	29.70	35.70	37.04
Evening Schools including Humboldt	9.65	27.73	26.62
(b) For all Expenditures (not including buildings and sites—			
High Schools	58.80	69.16	73.01
Primary and Grammar Schools	37.00	44.52	44.26
Evening Schools	13.02	37.15	35.70

MEDAL FUNDS.

Name of Fund.	Deposited in.	In Fund June 30, 1912.
Bridge Silver Medal	Hibernia Savings & Loan Society	$2,003.26
Denman Grammar School	Hibernia Savings & Loan Society	1,158.99
Denman Silver Medal	German Savings & Loan Society	1,962.50
Hancock Grammar School	German Savings & Loan Society	387.92
Jean Parker Grammar School	German Savings & Loan Society	336.04
John Swett Grammar School	Hibernia Savings & Loan Society	164.33
Lincoln Grammar School	Hibernia Savings & Loan Society	2,204.36

STATEMENT SETTING FORTH THE EXPENDITURE OF MONEY DERIVED FROM SALE OF BONDS (ISSUE OF 1904, 1908 AND 1909), TO JUNE 30, 1912.

School	Site	Buildings	Furniture or Equipment.
Girls' High		$ 225,502.60	
Lowell High	$ 138,500.00	207,805.20	
Mission High	103,910.00		
Polytechnic High	65,000.00	202,919.22	
S. F. Commercial	36,800.00	261,635.28	$ 15,462.43
Adams		94,739.36	4,159.98
Agassiz	16,500.00		
Bay View	10,250.00	116,892.00	5,296.00
Bernal	11,800.00		
Bryant		106,306.15	4,545.89
Burnett	10,000.00	54,372.92	3,800.08
Cleveland	13,250.00	64,782.24	3,566.44
Crocker	2,750.00		
Denman	88,843.00	158,494.85	3,502.02
Douglass	10,750.00		
Dudley Stone	12,000.00		
Edison	17,400.00		
Everett	20,400.00		
Farragut	12,537.50	101,914.91	2,474.30
Francis Scott Key		38,904.00	2,869.40
Frank McCoppin	9,500.00	106,294.69	4,085.56
Franklin		75,926.83	4,284.62
Fremont	6,750.00		
Garfield	10,150.00	111,188.18	4,884.99
George Peabody		80,545.02	2,951.80
Glen Park	5,600.00	45,750.00	3,672.00
Golden Gate	25,693.00	73,533.00	4,200.00
Grant	44,500.00		
Grattan	28,500.00	68,579.17	3,484.88
Hancock	10,800.00	166,321.20	5,233.72
Harrison	10,000.00	22,435.41	441.39
Horace Mann	15,000.00		
Jackson	37,500.00		
James Lick	5,600.00		
Jean Parker	20,675.00	173,355.57	5,720.17
John Swett	56,750.00	91,156.74	3,010.02
Junipero Serra	21,815.00	91,603.59	4,545.89
Kate Kennedy	31,650.00	102,370.57	3,697.44
Laguna Honda		91,418.99	4,283.28
Le Conte	14,000.00		
Lincoln	7,050.00	74,650.96	4,020.76
Longfellow	9,250.00	78,675.38	2,645.83
McKinley	35,000.00	111,018.18	3,523.33
Madison		87,945.72	3,500.00
Marshall	67,250.00	3,419.70	
Mission Grammar		171,836.66	4,053.10
Monroe	13,800.00	84,296.00	3,600.00
Noe Valley	13,250.00		
Pacific Heights	23,500.00		
Portola	5,000.00	97,042.23	3,700.00

Rochambeau	39,489.00	38,900.00	3,891.00
Sheridan	9,750.00	105,749.60	4,991.58
Spring Valley	31,325.00	118,595.67	5,233.72
Starr King	14,500.00		
Sunnyside	2,000.00	31,000.00	
Sutro	7,100.00	101,341.49	4,448.78
Visitacion Valley		46,623.88	2,918.53
Washington	17,000.00	118,944.00	4,988.00
Washington Irving		26.62	
Winfield Scott		42,206.43	3,590.58
Yerba Buena	17,000.00		
Miscellaneous Plans, Specification		57,656.08	
Lot on Geary St	27,000.00		
	$1,264,437.00	$4,305,018.65	$155,275.15

Grand Total Expended $5,724,730.80

STATEMENT CONCERNING THE ISSUANCE OF SCHOOL BONDS.

1. 3½% SCHOOL BONDS DATED JULY 1, 1904—

Authorized at a special election Sept. 29, 1903
Total vote, 27,308: ⅔ of the vote necessary to carry—18,206.
Votes in favor 23,327; excess of votes necessary, 5,121.

Amount authorized	$3,595,000.00
Issued	1,305,500.00
Redeemed to date	628,600.00
Face value of bonds outstanding	$ 676,900.00
Canceled	$1,975,600.00
Annual redemption	$ 89,800.00

Sinking Fund ends, 1922.

Condition of Fund, July 1, 1912—

Issued 1904-1905	$1,077,600.00
Issued 1910-1911	39,000.00
Issued 1911-1912	188,900.00
Total Issued	$1,305,500.00
Expended	1,303,515.82
Balance in Fund July 1, 1912	$ 1,984.18

2. 5 PER CENT SCHOOL BONDS DATED JULY 1, 1908—

Election May 11, 1908.
Total vote cast 23,560: ⅔ necessary to carry—15,707.
Votes in favor 21,397; excess of votes necessary, 5,694.

Amount authorized	$5,000,000.00
Issued and outstanding, July 1, 1912	$4,000,000.00

Redemption commences July 1, 1914, when $140,000 will be redeemed and $140,000, every year thereafter until July 1, 1938. Annual sinking fund required, if all bonds are issued, $200,000.

Condition of Fund—

Issued 1908-1909	$2,000,000.00
Issued 1909-1910	900,000.00

Issued 1910-1911	600,000.00
Issued 1911-1912	500,000.00
Premium	287,051.40
Total realized	$4,287,051.40
Expended	4,218,295.16
Balance in Fund, July 1, 1912	$ 68,755.64

3. POLYTECHNIC HIGH SCHOOL 4½% BONDS, DATED JAN. 1, 1910—

Authorized by election June 22, 1909.

Total vote, 24,058; ⅔ of vote necessary to carry, 16,039.

Votes in favor, 17,979; excess of votes necessary, 1,940.

Issue authorized	$600,000.00
Issued and outstanding, July 1, 1912	$456,000.00

Annual redemption of $19,000 commences July 1, 1914.

Annual sinking fund, if all bonds are issued, $25,000; commences 1914 and ends in 1937.

Condition of Fund, July 1, 1912—

Issued	$456,000.00
Premium	1,758.00
Realized	$457,758.00
Expended	202,919.22
Balance in Fund	$245,838.78

SCHOOLS.

Number of High Schools, including San Francisco Commercial and Humboldt Evening High School	6
Number of Grammar	25
Number of Primary Schools	55
Number of Special Schools	3
Number of Evening Schools	16
Total Number of Schools	105
Number of concrete school buildings owned by the department, Class "A"	9
Number of brick school buildings owned by the department, "Special Construction"	18
Number of concrete school buildings owned by the department	12
Number of wooden school buildings owned by the department, "Class C"	50
Number of rooms rented by the department	2
Total number of buildings used by the department	91

"STATE ENROLLMENT" BY GRADES AND SEX.

(State Enrollment ADMITS NO DUPLICATION. PUPILS PROMOTED DURING THE YEAR ARE ENUMERATED ONLY in the grades from which they were promoted.)

DAY SCHOOLS.

	Boys	Girls	Total
Kindergarten	33	37	70
First Grade	5,746	4,840	10,586
Second Grade	3,286	2,775	6,061

Third Grade	3,136	2,790	5,926
Fourth Grade	2,787	2,663	5,450
Fifth Grade	2,376	2,271	4,647
Sixth Grade	1,856	1,976	3,832
Seventh Grade	1,584	1,533	3,117
Eighth Grade	1,109	1,246	2,355
Totals Elementary and Kindergarten	21,913	20,131	42,044
High Schools—			
First Year	427*	488*	915*
Second Year	292	456	748
Third Year	145	329	474
Fourth Year	104	271	375
Total High	968	1,544	2,512
Commercial—			
First Year	156*	329*	485*
Second Year	84	257	341
Total Commercial	240	586	826
Grand Totals (Day Schools)	23,121	22,261	45,382

EVENING SCHOOLS.

	Boys	Girls	Total
Humboldt Evening High—			
First Year	887	215	1,102
Second Year	280	8	288
Third Year	101	13	114
Totals	1,268	236	1,504
North Beach High and Evening Technical School—			
First Year	609	497	1,106
Second Year	134	108	242
Third Year	12	3	15
Totals	755	608	1,363
Elementary Evening Schools—			
First Grade	846	308	1,154
Second Grade	445	61	506
Third Grade	409	64	473
Fourth Grade	405	60	465
Fifth Grade	359	26	385
Sixth Grade	418	126	544
Seventh Grade	563	174	737
Eighth Grade	572	75	647
Totals	4,017	894	4,911
Grand Totals Evening Schools	6,040	1,738	7,778
Grand Totals Day Schools	23,121	22,261	45,382
Grand Totals	29,161	23,999	53,160

*These figures EXCLUDE those enrolling in January and who during the year were enrolled in the Grammar (8th) grade.

STATE SCHOOL ENROLLMENT AND ATTENDANCE STATISTICS FOR THE YEAR ENDING

	June 30, 12. Enrollment	Increase (I) over or Decrease (D) from 1911.	June 30, '11. Enrollment
High Schools	2,512	D. 401*	2,913
S. F. Commercial	826	D. 50*	876
Elementary	41,974	I. 1,784	40,190
Kindergarten	70	I. 7	63
Humboldt Evening High	1,504	I. 480	1,024
Other Evening Schools	6,274	D. 122	6,396
	53,160	I. 1,698	51,462

AVERAGE DAILY ATTENDANCE.

	Av. Daily Attend.		Av. Daily Attend.
High Schools	2,091	D. 35	2,126
S. F. Commercial	747	I. 166	581
Elementary	34,879	I. 2,334	32,545
Kindergarten	25	D. 4	29
Humboldt Evening High	689	I. 238	451
Other Evening Schools	2,017	I. 13	2,004
	40,448	I. 2,712	37,736

Last year the San Francisco Commercial School was regarded as a high school.

GRADUATES.

Number of graduates from the grammar school for the year—

Boys	Day 752, Evening 140	892
Girls	Day 771, Evening 73	844
Total		1,736

Number of graduates from the high schools for the year—

Boys	Day 104, Evening 60	164
Girls	Day 335 Evening 40	375
Total		539

---

*This year all pupils entering high schools who were enrolled at any time during the year in a grammar school are omitted by order of State Superintendent; such pupils were included last year.

TEACHERS EMPLOYED DURING THE YEAR ENDING JUNE 30, 1912.

	Principals or Supervisors of Special Subjects		Teachers	
	Men	Women	Men	Women
(4) High Schools (Day)	4	0	A37	A43
Humboldt Evening High	1	0	22	4
North Beach Evening High	1	0		
San Francisco Commercial	1	0	B 3	17
(25) Elementary (Day) Grammar	8	17	C 7	D354
(55) Elementary (Day) Primary	3	52	1	543
Oral for Deaf		1	1	
Special Subjects	4	5	11	18
Elementary Evening	11	2	10	53
Commercial Evening	1		7	7
Jean Parker Evening School of Home Economics				4
Substitutes (Emergency, June 1912)				53
Teachers on leave who were employed some time during the year (four of these in evening service			5	29
Totals	34	78	105	1125

Grand Total (employed)	Men	139,	Women	1203=1342
Less Leaves	Men	5,	Women	29= 34
Net number on pay roll June 1912	Men	134,	Women	1174=1308

A= 2 Vice Principals.
B= 1 Vice Principals.
C= 2 Vice Principals.
D=21 Vice Principals.

SCHOLASTIC TRAINING AND CERTIFICATION OF TEACHERS.

Number of Teachers (including Principals.)

	Men	Women
Who are graduates of University of California	35	89
Who are graduate of Leland Stanford Jr. University	10	7
Who are graduates of Other Universities	18	7
Who are graduates of other Colleges	20	17
Who are graduates of S. F. City Normal School or Class	2	363
Who are graduates of Chico State Normal School	1	13
Who are graduates of Los Angeles State Normal	1	5
Who are graduates of San Diego State Normal		3
Who are graduates of San Francisco State Normal		129
Who are graduates of San Jose Normal	3	93
Who are graduates of Normal Schools of other States	9	27

CERTIFICATES.

No. holding certificates of High School Grade	70	129
No. holding certificates of Grammar School Grade	22	1,020
No. holding certificates of Primary School Grade		21
No. holding Special Certificate in Bookkeeping	6	14
No. holding Special Certificate in Domestic Science		11
No. holding Special Certificate in Drawing, (all departments)	12	8
No. holding Special Certificate in Languages		28
No. holding Special Certificate in Manual Training (all Depts.)	13	1
No. holding Special Certificate in Music	1	43
No. holding Special Certificate in Physical Culture	4	3
No. holding Special Certificate in Stenography and Typewriting	5	26

VOLUMES IN SCHOOL LIBRARIES AND STOREROOM (INCLUDING BOOKS FOR USE OF INDIGENTS).

	Volumes	Estimated Value
High Schools, including Humboldt Evening and S. F. Com'l	6,223	$ 4,710
Primary and Grammar Schools	84,113	35,819
Evening Schools	2,414	890
In Storeroom	1,610	800
	94,360	$42,219

SCHOOL VISITATION.

Official visits of Superintendent and deputies	4,295
Official visits by members of the Board of Education	4,289
Visits by other persons	67,057

SOME SCHOOL STATISTICS FROM THE OPENING OF THE FIRST

Year Ending Oct. 31.	No. of Schools.	Teachers.	Pupils Enrolled.	Average Daily Attendance.	Popul
1850	1	2	150	------	
1851	1	4	325	------	
1852	7	15	700	445	
1853	----	16	2,870	1,182	
1854	----	19	4,199	1,727	
1855	----	29	4,694	1,638	
1856	9	61	3,347	2,516	
Year Ending June 30.					
1857	----	60	2,821	2,155	
1858	----	67	5,273	2,521	
1859	11	75	6,201	2,829	
1860	----	68	6,180	2,837	
1861	13	73	6,617	3,377	
1862	17	82	8,204	3,786	
1863	----	94	8,177	4,389	
1864	20	108	7,075	5,470	
1865	----	138	8,000	6,718	
1866	32	206	10,152	8,131	
1867	37	253	13,385	10,177	
1868	39	285	17,426	11,871	
1869	42	326	19,885	13,113	
1870	55	371	22,152	15,394	1
1871	56	416	26,406	16,978	
1872	56	480	27,664	18,272	
1873	58	506	27,722	18,550	
1874	64	510	29,449	19,434	
1875	64	552	31,128	21,014	
1876	66	574	34,029	22,761	
1877	66	632	37,268	24,899	
1878	65	672	38,672	26,292	
1879	64	696	38,129	27,075	
1880	59	686	38,320	28,150	2
1881	62	719	40,187	29,092	
1882	65	675	40,752	29,435	
1883	63	687	40,722	30,827	
1884	64	714	41,942	31,578	
1885	65	734	43,265	32,183	
1886	65	773	43,140	32,146	
1887	68	799	43,311	31,316	
1888	68	806	42,330	30,191	
1889	71	838	42,626	31,609	
1890	72	859	42,926	31,352	2
1891	73	879	43,626	31,809	
1892	75	897	46,172	32,431	
1893	76	929	45,775	32,799	
1894	73	866	44,349	32,939	
1895	75	904	44,822	32,974	
1896	76	927	45,435	33,508	
1897	77	974	46,564	33,531	
1898	92	1,070	50,101	35,116	
1899	90	1,074	48,972	36,830	
1900	86	1,061	48,058	35,004	3
1901	82	1,017	48,517	34,771	
1902	84	1,052	48,893	35,691	
1903	84	1,086	48,345	37,077	
1904	85	1,121	49,600	37,700	
1905	85	1,181	55,067	40,920	
1906	86	1,115	57,782	41,932	
1907	83	971	45,633	29,929	
1908	89	1,095	48,045	33,931	
1909	92	1,195	48,509	35,541	
1910	95	1,198	50,212	36,774	4
1911	100	1,227	51,462	37,736	
1912	105	1,308	53,160	40,448	

Total...

PUBLIC SCHOOL BY J. C. PELTON, DECEMBER, 1849, TO JUNE 30, 1912.

Expenses for All Purposes.	Cost per Capita on Average Daily Attendance.	School Census Children 4 to 18 Years.	Value of School Property.	Assessment of City and County Property.
....	....	500	....	....
....	....	1,510		....
$23,125	51.96	2,132		
35,040	296.5	2,730	....	....
159,249	125.19	3,268	....	....
136,580	83.38	4,531	....	....
125,064	49.71	4,751	....	....
92,955	43.14	4,755	....	
104,808	41.57	6,375	....	....
134,731	47.62	7,767	....	....
156,407	55.13	9,025	....	....
158,855	47.04	13,316	....	....
134,576	35.58	13,358	....	
178,929	47.67	16,501	....	....
228,411	41.76	18,748	....	
346,862	50.15	21,013	....	....
		5 to 15 Years.		
361,668	44.48	17,369	....	$70,202,000
507,822	49.89	20,253	$1,057,000	74,976,000
416,654	35.09	23,306	1,368,000	84,689,000
397,842	30.34	24,817	1,531,000	95,700,000
526,625	33.56	27,055	1,729,800	114,759,500
705,116	41.53	28,971	1,786,400	....
668,262	36.02	31,936	1,810,000	(?)97,000,000
611,818	35.45	34,676	....	....
		5 to 17 Years.		
689,022	35.40	38,084	2,227,620	212,407,505
707,445	33.71	41,029	2,367,000	264,000,000
867,755	38.12	46,238	2,505,500	269,105,141
732,324	29.41	53,210	2,585,000	260,576,978
989,259	37.62	55,899	2,711,000	254,702,960
876,489	32.37	62,105	3,047,303	244,477,360
809,133	28.74	58,492	3,073,000	217,487,074
827,324	28.44	55,115	3,137,000	253,545,476
735,435	24.98	55,880	3,137,000	222,336,400
791,175	25.66	58,061	3,137,000	201,992,152
797,452	25.25	63,029	3,137,000	201,763,762
840,367	25.80	69,000	3,137,000	223,509,560
815,778	25.37	74,079	3,189,000	230,386,325
843,297	26.93	78,246	3,184,575	230,151,009
926,662	30.69	59,517	3,230,598	251,746,111
916,644	28.99	60,642	4,772,180	273,389,616
983,014	31.35	61,144	4,757,724	306,041,440
1,053,610	33.12	62,456	4,798,427	301,444,140
1,098,839	33.88	63,933	4,932,754	311,566,079
1,134,757	34.59	65,317	5,019,317	346,224,706
989,009	30.05	68,390	5,063,364	342,644,179
1,043,067	26.09	70,006	5,140,258	325,108,898
1,086,571	32.42	71,822	5,284,000	327,805,147
1,222,941	36.52	74,840	5,354,859	330,401,154
1,319,829	37.58	76,336	5,474,739	351,784,094
1,507,163	40.92	75,292	5,514,200	405,111,615
1,274,696	36.41	78,554	5,514,200	410,155,304
1,152,631	30.27	82,173	5,207,600	413,417,241
1,316,170	36.88	82,391	5,334,000	413,338,420
1,322,585	35.67	91,386	5,649,651	420,555,541
1,398,296	37.09	97,353	5,702,001	564,070,301
1,403,349	34.29	98,127	5,800,000	583,056,457
1,498,275	35.73	101,836	6,984,000	524,392,047
1,325,438	44.28	77,367	6,207,010	375,932,477
1,934,355	57.01	87,696	6,379,000	429,632,843
1,701,236	47.86	88,058	7,206,573	454,334,160
3,307,948	89.98	74,729	8,733,285	492,867,374
3,137,825	83.18	abolished	10,161,492	545,057,591
3,744,073	92.54		12,536,929	605,488,153
$55,302,663				

REPORT OF THE BOARD OF EXAMINATION.

The Board of Examination is composed of: Superintendent Alfred Roncovieri, Chairman; Deputy Superintendent W. B. Howard, Secretary; Deputy Superintendent T. L. Heaton, Deputy Superintendent A. J. Cloud, Deputy Superintendent R. H. Webster.

The Board of Examination has conducted two examinations (October 1911 and May 1912), according to law, of persons desirous of securing certificates. It has met monthly and forwarded its recommendation to the Board of Education.

Herewith is a resume of its work:

CERTIFICATES GRANTED ON CREDENTIALS.

HIGH SCHOOL.

Men	12
Women	20
	32

GRAMMAR.

Men	3
Women	104
	107

SPECIALS.

Men	5
Women	28
	33

RENEWALS.

Men	4
Women	32
	36

ON EXAMINATION.

GRAMMAR.

Men	0
Women	0
	0

REJECTED.

Men	12
Women	46
	58

SPECIALS.

Men	5
Women	24
	29

Number of Certificates issued	201
Number of Certificates renewed	36
Number of Applicants rejected	58
Amount fees collected of applicants, including renewals	590

RECOMMENDATIONS MADE BY THE SUPERINTENDENT OF SCHOOLS SINCE JULY, 1906.

July, 1906—

First. That in the interests of economy the Honorable Board of Supervisors include in its annual advertisement calling for bids on gas and water: the requirements of the Board of Education in these commodities.

Second. That a liberal appropriation not less than $8,000 be allowed for the purchase of supplementary and reference books.

Section 1714 of the Political Code refers to the expenditure of moneys for supplementary and reference books. Owing to the destruction of thirty school buildings during the conflagration of April, 1906, all the libraries contained therein were destroyed and therefore the appropriation asked for supplementary and reference books is considered moderate by the Board of Education and the Superintendent of Schools.

Third. That an appropriation be made of $12,000 for the purchase of charts, globes, typewriters, organs, pianos, and maps for use of the primary day and evening classes in accordance with Section 1617, Third Sub-division of the Political Code of the State of California.

Fourth. That ungraded classes in these schools: Adams, Fremont, Franklin, Hamilton, Hancock, Lincoln, Mission, Washington, Richmond, and Emerson, be maintained and that additional ungraded classes be established wherever there is sufficient demand.

Fifth. That an appropriation of not less than $2,500 be made for decoration and adornment of classrooms and school grounds: also, pictures, engravings, plaster reproductions, etc.

Sixth. Equipment of playgrounds to be provided for in a bond issue.

May, 1908—

To have Supervisors appropriate a sufficient sum of money to enable the Board of Education to pay entire (not 50% as now) pensions of retired teachers.

March, 1909—

That medical inspection of school children be extended and improved.

That streets in front of school houses be bituminized.

July, 1909—

That departmental teaching be extended.

That evening schools and their work be advertised.

That a Parental School equipped with dormitories, shops and other things necessary for a detention or reformatory home be established on twenty acres of land.

August, 1909—

Recommending that supplementary books be purchased by the Board of Education and giving a list of such books.

November, 17—

That experience gained outside of the city be allowed in fixing salaries of teachers.

November 29, 1909—

That the Board of Education enter into contract with prominent steam boiler inspection and insurance companies, for the regular inspection of these boilers and the insurance of the same.

May 24, 1910—

That the name of the Newton J. Tharp Commercial School be changed to the "Commercial High School" and that the Superintendent of Schools and the Principal of the Commercial High School be and are hereby requested to prepare and submit for the consideration of this Board, a one-year's Course of Study, a two years' Course of Study and a four years' Course of Study.

July, 1909—

To extend and improve the subject of Manual and Industrial Training based on observations while on an European tour of inspection.

1911—

That Sanitary Drinking Facilities be supplied in all schools.

That Typewriting be introduced into the Hamilton Grammar School.

That elective system of Courses of Study be extended in the San Francisco High Schools, with proper safeguards and with a grouping around certain fundamental studies.

That greater care should be used in our high schools to watch the progress of individual students and for maintaining a closer personal contact with them.

That we should work toward the six-year high school plan.

That arrangements be made with the San Francisco Normal School by which we could gain the services of cadet teachers.

That the civil service rules be amended and a filing of a protest against their violation.

That a Burbank Agricultural High School be established.

That the number of school gardens be increased and school premises be beautified with flowers, etc.

That the Board of Education set aside $12,270 for supplementary books.

At the suggestion of the Superintendent of Schools, a bill was introduced at the last session of the Legislature by Assemblyman James J. Ryan and enacted into law.

I regret to state that a majority of the Board of Education instead of observing this necessary and beneficent law in its full intent, requested the opinion of the City and County Attorney concerning the necessity on their part of obeying it. That official declared that in his opinion it is unconstitutional in so far as it relates to San Francisco.

1912—

That credit be given in high schools for work along the lines of school activities and music.

March 20, 1912—

That the Courses of Study used in the high schools be remodeled and brought to date and the same be printed, and that at least one course of four years' duration leading to a department in the University be introduced into the Commercial School so that that school be included under law in the apportionment of State High School money.

I regret that failure to so modify the course of study has resulted in a loss of State funds to the school revenue of this city and county of $8,000.00.

That public school swimming baths be constructed on the school property at Pine and Larkin Streets.

That Vacation Schools be established.

That only experienced teachers be employed as substitutes:

REPORT OF THE PUBLIC SCHOOL TEACHERS' ANNUITY AND RETIREMENT FUND COMMISSIONERS.

San Francisco, June 30, 1912.

To the Honorable Board of Supervisors,
in and for the City and County of San Francisco.

Gentlemen:—I have the honor to submit herewith the report on the Public School Teachers' Annuity and Retirement Fund for the fiscal year terminating June 30, 1912.

ALFRED RONCOVIERI,

Superintendent of Schools and Secretary Public School Teachers' Retirement Fund Commissioners.

RECEIPTS.

Balance in Fund July 1, 1911, not deducting sinking fund for Fire Protection Bonds to replace premium paid for them	$ 4,405.13	
Contributions by teachers under provisions of Annuity Law	13,404.00	
Absence money granted by Board of Education	3,000.00	
Interest on Permanent Fund, ($50,000 invested in 44 $1,000 Bonds, S. F. Fire Protection)	2,200.00	
Interest on funds in bank	296.33	
Amount received from teachers retiring during the year..	1,398.60	
Total Receipts		$24,704.06

DISBURSEMENTS.

Annuities to Retired Teachers.

1911—		
October 1	$ 5,088.25	
1912—		
January 1	5,176.25	
April 1	5,301.25	
July 1	5,284.35	
Total	$20,850.10	
Clerical services	120.00	
Postage	5.00	
Sinking Fund ($142.86 semi-annually commencing July, 1909) to pay premium paid on Fire Protection Bonds ($44,000 par)	990.02	
Total Disbursements		$21,965.12
Balance June 30, 1912, E. & O. E.		$ 2,738.94

LIST OF ANNUITIES.

Limited revenue admits the payment of but fifty per cent (50%) of these annuities.

Date of Retirement.	Name.	Maximum or Fraction Thereof.	Annuity Per Month.	Annuity Per Quarter.
1895.				
Nov. 27,	Mrs. L. T. Hopkins	Max.	$50.00	$150.00
1896.				
Jan. 22,	Mrs. M. H. Currier	Max	50.00	150.00
April 24,	Miss V. M. Raclet	9/10	45.00	135.00
1897.				
Sept. 11,	Miss M. Solomon	Max.	50.00	150.00
Dec. 8,	Miss F. L. Soule	Max.	50.00	150.00
1898.				
Sept. 14,	Miss Kate Kollmyer	8/15	26.66⅔	80.00
1900.				
July 18,	Mrs. A. Griffith	Max.	50.00	150.00
July 25,	Miss K. F. McColgan	Max.	50.00	150.00
Aug. 1,	Miss L. M. Barrows	13/15	43.33⅓	130.00
Aug. 1,	Miss Annie A. Hill	Max.	50.00	150.00
Oct. 15,	Miss M. J. Canham	14/15	46.66⅔	140.00
1901.				
July 20,	Miss J. B. Gorman	Max.	50.00	150.00
Oct. 4,	Miss E. Murphy	9/10	45.00	135.00
1902.				
Jan. 2,	Miss R. B. Campbell	Max.	50.00	150.00
Jan. 2,	Miss L. S. Templeton	Max.	50.00	150.00
Jan. 2,	Mr. A. T. Winn	Max.	50.00	150.00
Sept. 28,	Miss Emma J. Miller	11/15	36.66⅔	110.00
1903.				
Feb. 17,	Mrs. B. A. Chinn	Max	50.00	150.00
Feb. 17,	Miss Lydia Hart	11/15	36.66⅔	110.00
Feb. 17,	Miss Christine Hart	Max.	50.00	150.00
Aug. 1,	Mr. T. B. White	Max.	50.00	150.00
Sept. 1,	Miss A. E. Slaven	Max.	50.00	150.00
Oct. 15,	Miss L. Burnham	¾	37.50	112.50
1904.				
Aug. 1,	Mr. Elisha Brooks	Max.	50.00	150.00
Aug. 1,	Miss I. Patterson	Max.	50.00	150.00
Sept. 1,	Mrs. E. M. Whitcomb	Max.	50.00	150.00
1905.				
Jan. 16,	Miss E. G. Grant	Max.	50.00	150.00
March 1,	Miss M. A. Smith	⅔	33.33⅓	100.00
March 1,	Miss Jean Parker	Max.	50.00	150.00
March 1,	Mrs. T. C. Nicholl	Max.	50.00	150.00
March 1,	Mr. Charles Ham	Max.	50.00	150.00
March 1,	Miss R. Jacobs	Max.	50.00	150.00
March 1,	Mr. D. Lambert	Max. (Even)	25.00	75.00
1906.				
Feb. 1,	Miss M. E. Carson	Max.	50.00	150.00
Feb. 1,	Mrs. A. C. Taylor	Max.	50.00	150.00
Aug. 1,	Miss E. R. Elder	Max.	50.00	150.00
Oct. 1,	Miss H. E. Whirlow	Max.	50.00	150.00
Dec. 1,	Mrs. V. Troyer	Max.	50.00	150.00
1907.				
April 1,	Miss Madge Sprott	½ (Even)	25.00	75.00
April 1,	Miss A. D. Miley	14/15	46.66⅔	140.00
April 1,	Miss Q. O. McConnell	Max.	50.00	150.00
April 1,	Prof. A. Herbst	Max.	50.00	150.00
July 1,	Mr. C. W. Moores	Max.	50.00	150.00
Sept. 1,	Miss V. E. Bradbury	Max.	50.00	150.00
Sept. 1,	Miss Martha Stone	Max.	50.00	150.00
Sept. 1,	Miss N. C. Stallman	Max.	50.00	150.00
Sept. 1,	Mr. W. H. Edwards	Max.	50.00	150.00

1908.				
Jan. 1,	Miss R. V. Claiborne	⅔	33.33⅓	100.00
Feb. 1,	Mrs. M. E. Michener	Max.	50.00	150.00
Feb. 15,	Mrs. F. A. Banning	Max.	50.00	150.00
March 1,	Miss Rose Fay	11/15	36.66⅔	110.00
May 1,	Miss Julia A. Danks	Max.	50.00	150.00
July 1,	Miss Laura T. Fowler	Max.	50.00	150.00
Sept. 1,	Miss Ruby A. Jewell	Max.	50.00	150.00
Sept. 1,	Miss Regina Hertz	4/5	40.00	120.00
1909.				
Jan. 1,	Miss A. T. Campbell	Max.	50.00	150.00
Jan. 1,	Mrs. Mary J. Mayborn	Max.	50.00	150.00
Jan. 1,	Miss C. M. Johnston	Max.	50.00	150.00
Aug. 1,	Mrs. N. Seabrook	7/10	35.00	105.00
Aug. 1.	Miss Rose E. Morgan	Max.	50.00	150.00
Aug. 1,	Miss Jessie I. King	Max.	50.00	150.00
1910.				
Jan. 1,	Paul A. Garin	Max.	50.00	150.00
Jan. 1,	Miss E. R. Pettigrew	3/5	30.00	90.00
Jan. 10,	Miss Anne B. Campbell	Max.	50.00	150.00
July 1,	Miss E. S. Heney	Max.	50.00	150.00
Aug. 1,	Mrs. R. H. Hazelton	Max.	50.00	150.00
1911.				
July 1,	Miss Emily M. Goggin	29/30	48.33⅓	145.00
July 1,	Miss Caroline L. Hunt	Max.	50.00	150.00
July 1,	Miss E. A. Sutherland	18/30	30.00	90.00
Sept. 1,	Mrs. Kate Waters	Max.	50.00	150.00
Nov. 1,	Mr, Jas. T. Hamilton	Max.	50.00	150.00
1912.				
Jan. 2,	Miss K. B. Childs	Max.	50.00	150.00
March 1,	Miss Bertha Goldsmith	Max.	50.00	150.00
April 1,	Mrs. Katherine Turney	2/3	33.33⅓	100.00

THE SAN FRANCISCO TEACHERS' INSTITUTE OF 1912.

The regular annual institute of the teachers of the San Francisco Department, in accordance with State law, was called at the Alcazar Theatre on the days of Monday, Tuesday and Wednesday, of May 27, 28 and 29, of 1912. Superintendent Alfred Roncovieri presided.

A varied and interesting program of addresses and musical numbers was presented. Among those whose lectures were greatly appreciated for the educational messages delivered were: Hon. Samuel Shortridge, Professor Lee Emerson Bassett, Dr. Richard Gause Boone and Dr. Benjamin Ide Wheeler. The afternoons were devoted to wonderfully instructive and entertaining illustrated lectures by Mr. B. R. Baumgardt.

At the close of Wednesday's session, Mr. Selden Sturges, Principal of the Everett Grammar School, moved the adoption of the following set of resolutions, which motion, being put to a vote, was unanimously adopted:

"Resolved, That, the hearty thanks of the teaching body of San Francisco be tendered to Superintendent Roncovieri as a token of our deep appreciation of his earnest efforts in having prepared and carried out this splendid program to a most successful termination."

The program is herewith reproduced in full:

ANNUAL INSTITUTE OF THE TEACHERS OF THE CITY AND COUNTY OF SAN FRANCISCO, ALCAZAR THEATRE, O'FARRELL STREET, NEAR POWELL, MAY 27TH, 28TH AND 29TH, 1912.

Morning Session..........................9:20 to 12:15 o'clock
Afternoon Session......................2:15 to 4:15 o'clock

The afternoons will be devoted to artistic, educational lecture entertainments by Mr. B. M. Baumgardt

"As for truth, it endureth and is always strong; it liveth and conquereth for evermore."—Esdras, 450 B. C.

MONDAY, MAY 27—9:20 A. M.

Overture—"American Fantaisie" ....Victor Herbert

Alcazar Theatre Orchestra Under the Direction of Mr. Edward B. Lada.

Introductory Address—"A Review," Alfred Roncovieri, Sup't. of Schools.

Roll Call—"Departed Teachers," (Jan., 1911, to May 27, 1912), Mr. Selden Sturges.

Address—"The Life of the Teacher," Hon. Samuel M. Shortridge.

Address—Dr. A. A. D'Ancona, President of the Board of Education.

Recess (ten minutes), during which the Orchestra will render a selection from "The Girl of the Golden West" ....Puccini

Address—Hon. Charles A. Murdock, Member of Board of Supervisors.

Baritone Solo—

(a) Aria "Toreador" from Carmen ....Bizet
(b) Spanish Serenade "Lolita" ....Buzzi-Peccia

Signor F. Avedano.

Lecture—"The Educational Uses of Literature," Professor Lee Emerson Bassett, Department of English Literature, Leland Stanford Junior University.

Orchestra—March, "La Lorraine" ....Ganne

MONDAY, MAY 27—2:15 P. M.

Orchestra—Overture, "William Tell" ....Rossini

The following musical numbers will be rendered during the two intermissions:

First Intermission.

Orchestra—Grand March from "Tannhauser" ....Wagner

Second Intermission.

Piano Solo—

(a) Polonaise A flat Major ....Chopin
(b) Romance ....Leschetizky
(c) La Campanella ....Paganini-Liszt

Mr. Georg Kruger

Illustrated Lecture—"The Latest from the Heavens," Mr. B. R. Baumgardt.

"Two things fill me with awe; the starry heavens, and the sense of moral responsibility in man."—Immanuel Kant.

"Why did not someone, when I was a child, teach me the constellations and make me at home in the starry heavens, which I do not half know today."—Carlyle.

Finale—Orchestra, "Marche Triomphale" ....Elgar

TUESDAY, MAY 28—9:20 A. M.

Orchestra—Overture, "Jubel" ....Von Weber

Lecture—"A Trunk-Line in Education," Mr. Archibald J. Cloud, B. L., Deputy Superintendent of Schools, San Francisco.

Recess (ten minutes), during which the Orchestra will render a selection from "The Spring Maid" ....Reinhardt

Lecture—"The Music of Poetry," Professor Lee Emerson Bassett, Leland Stanford Junior University.

Trio—

(a) Minuet in G........Beethoven
(b) Humoreske ....Dvorak
(c) Hungarian Dance ....Brahms

Miss Edna Cadwalader, Violinist. (Moulder School),
Assisted by Miss Mabel Stierlen, 'Cellist,
Miss Grace Hendricks, Piano.

Lecture—"Learning by Means of Experience and Language," Dr. Richard Gause Boone, University of California.

Orchestra—Coronation March from "Le Prophete"........Myerbeer

TUESDAY, MAY 28—2:15 P. M.

Orchestra—Suite "Peer Gynt" ....Edvard Grieg

(a) Morning.
(b) Asa's Death.
(c) Anitra's Dance.
(d) In the Hall of the Mountain King.

The following numbers will be rendered during the two intermissions:

First Intermission.

Orchestra—"Saeterjenten's Sondag" ....Ole Bull
Group of Songs by Edvard Grieg—
(a) "With a Violet."
(b) "I Love Thee."
(c) "Morning Dew."
Mrs. M. E. Blanchard,
Accompanist, Miss Edna M. Willcox.

Second Intermission.

Aria—"Dost Thou Know That Sweet Land" (Mignon) ....Thomas
Mrs. M. E. Blanchard,
Accompanist, Miss Edna M. Willcox.

Illustrated Lecture—"The Fjelds and Fjords of Norway," Mr. B. R. Baumgardt.

A lecture of great educational value, on the land of the Midnight Sun. The beauty of the "Fjelds and Fjords" is graphically portrayed on the screen with more than one hundred and thirty beautiful views.

Finale—
"The Norwegian National Anthem" ....Nordraak
"The Star Spangled Banner" ....Francis Scott Key

WEDNESDAY, MAY 29—9:20 A. M.

Orchestra—Overture, "The Merry Wives of Windsor" ....Nicolai
Lecture—"Group Work in All Grades," Dr. Richard Gause Boone.
Recess (ten minutes), during which the Orchestra will render a selection from "Carmen" ....Bizet
Address—"The American Need," Dr. Benj. Ide Wheeler, President of the University of California.
Tenor Solo—"Che gelida Manina" from "La Boheme" ....Puccini
Senor Manuel Carpio,
Accompanist, Mr. E. M. Rosner.

Recital—From "Idylls of the King" ....Tennyson
(a) The Coming of Arthur.
(b) Guinevere.
(c) The Passing of Arthur.
Professor Lee Emerson Bassett.
Orchestra—March, "La Fiesta" ....Roncovieri

WEDNESDAY, MAY 29—2:15 P. M.

Orchestra—Overture, "Maximilian Robespierre" ....Litolff
A tone-poem depicting the arrest and execution of the Dictator amid the shouts and rejoicings of the maddened Parisian mob.
The following musical numbers will be rendered during the intermissions:

First Intermission.

Orchestra—"Marche Pontificale" ....Gounod
Soprano Solo—
(a) "Non so piu" (Figaro) ....Mozart
(b) Irish Folk Song ....Foote
(c) Open Secret ....Woodman
Mabel Riegelman, Member Chicago Grand Opera Co.

Second Intermission.

Soprano Solo—

(a) Aria Pagliacci .... Leoncavallo
(b) Rococo Standchen .... Meyer Helmund
(c) Ecstacy .... Rummel

Mabel Riegelman,

Bass Solo—"The Two Grenadiers" .... Schumann

Mr. Henry L. Perry.

Illustrated Lecture—"Napoleon, Conquerer and Captive of the Earth," Mr. B. R. Baumgardt.

A beautiful, historical review of the life of the Great Emperor. The major part of five years has been devoted to the preparation of this lecture, during which Mr. Baumgardt has repeatedly visited all the important Napoleonic battlefields, from Madrid to Moscow. The art galleries in Europe (the Louvre, Versailles, Chantilly, Fontainebleau, St. Petersburg and Moscow) have been drawn upon for the views.

Finale—Orchestra, "La Marseillaise" .... Rouget de Lisle
"The Star Spangled Banner .... Francis Scott Key

Adjournment.

PROGRAM FOR WEDNESDAY AFTERNOON, MAY 29TH, 1912 AT 2 O'CLOCK ANNUAL INSTITUTE OF THE TEACHERS OF THE CITY AND COUNTY OF SAN FRANCISCO, ALCAZAR THEATRE.

It is a pleasure to announce that an extra attraction has been secured in the person of the celebrated German Royal Court Singer, Alexander Heinemann, who has kindly consented to sing two groups of songs for the teachers of San Francisco on Wednesday afternoon, at the Alcazar Theatre, Mr. George Stewart McManus at the piano. Steinway Piano will be used, Sherman, Clay & Co.

PROGRAM.

Orchestra—Overture, "Maximilian Robespierre" .... Litolff

A tone-poem depicting the arrest and execution of the Dictator amid the shouts and rejoicings of the maddened Parisian mob.

The following musical numbers will be rendered during the two intermissions:

First Intermission.

Orchestra—"Marche Pontificale" .... Gounod

MABEL RIEGELMAN, Member Chicago Grand Opera Co.

Soprano Solo—

(a) "Non so piu" (Figaro) .... Mozart
(b) Irish Folk Song .... Foote
(c) Open Secret .... Woodman

ALEXANDER HEINEMANN

Group I

(a) Talismane .... R. Schumann
(b) Litanei .... Franz Schubert
(c) Wohin .... "
(d) Teufelslied .... Eugen Haile

MABEL RIEGELMAN

Second Intermission.

Soprano Solo—

(a) Aria Pagliacci ....Leoncavallo
(b) Rococò Standchen ....Meyer Helmund
(c) Ecstacy ....Rummel

ALEXANDER HEINEMANN

Group II.

(a) Die Naechtliche Heerschau ....Carl Loewe.
(b) Robespierre ....Hans Hermann
(c) Die beiden Grenadiere ....R. Schumann

Illustrated Lecture—"Napoleon, Conqueror and Captive of the Earth,"

MR. B. R. BAUMGARDT.

A beautiful, historical review of the life of the Great Emperor. The major part of five years has been devoted to the preparation of this lecture, during which Mr. Baumgardt has repeatedly visited all the important Napoleonic battlefields, from Madrid to Moscow. The art galleries in Europe (the Louvre, Versailles, Chantilly, Fontainebleau, St. Petersburg and Moscow) have been drawn upon for the views.

Finale—Orchestra, "La Marseillaise" ....Rouget de Lisle
"The Star Spangled Banner" ....Francis Scott Key

Adjournment.

TEACHERS' COMPETITIVE EXAMINATION, CITY AND COUNTY OF SAN FRANCISCO.

The competitive examination for 1912 was held at the San Francisco Commercial School building, on Grove Street, just west of Larkin Street, beginning Saturday, June 8, 1912, at 9 a. m.

QUALIFICATIONS OF CANDIDATES.

The applicant must be the holder of a teacher's certificate of a grade not lower than the grammar grade valid under the laws of the State of California.

The candidate must not be over thirty-five years of age.

Applicants must possess high personal character, liberal education and perfectly sound bodily health and vigor.

No married woman, unless her husband be totally incapacitated because of illness or infirmity, need apply, or any teacher who may not be in a position to accept an appointment to the substitute list whenever such appointment may be made during the year.

SCOPE OF THE EXAMINATION.

Examinations will be given to test the qualifications of the candidates as follows:

1. Ability to speak and write correct, forceful English.
2. United States history and current American institutions.
3. Arithmetic.
4. Methods of teaching and school management.

(Notice is hereby given that the examinations to be held after June, 1912, in addition to the subjects named above, will include elementary biology, hygiene and physics.)

In the determination of the qualifications of applicants due credit will be allowed for successful experience in teaching, graduation from State Normal Schools, and academic training in institutions of collegiate grade.

SAN FRANCISCO TEACHERS' EXAMINATION JUNE 10, 1912.

AMERICAN HISTORY AND INSTITUTIONS.

1. What parts of American History should be taught, and during what years, to children before the Seventh Grade?
2. What purposes would you have in mind in teaching the "Revolution Period" to a Seventh Grade class? and how would you use the material?
3. Name 10 characters in American history a study of whose lives and public services would give a fairly connected view of the Nation since 1750.
4. Give your reasons for and against teaching Grammar Grade pupils both sides of the Civil War struggle, fairly.
5. Among "current" happenings since June, 1911, in political, industrial, religious and cultural interests, what do you consider suitable for instruction in the Grammar Grades?
6. Had the Panama Canal been built by private enterprise, would it have been a fact of "history" as much as when built by the Government? Why?

Answer the first, third and fifth questions, and two of the other three.

SCHOOL METHODS AND MANAGEMENT.

(Write legibly and make your answers concise.)

(Answer two out of the first four, and five others.)

1. (a) It is often urged that we should teach reading, history, geography and civics in close relation, making each serve the purpose of all. Is this a good plan or should we keep the subjects of the curriculum separate? Explain.

(b) Is it better teach geography by topics or by countries? Give reasons for your answer.

2. Which is better; to keep the class upon a topic (e. g. alcohol, the Revoluntionary War, interest, etc.) until they have mastered it, or to return to the topic at different times and from different points of view? Explain.

3. In the teaching of U. S. history what would be the relative emphasis placed on (1) industrial development, and (2) political and military events? Why?

4. (a) Mention some general principles which ought to govern the selection of topics for nature study.

(b) With what subjects is nature study readily correlated?

5. (a) What should be done with the dull pupil who is over-age for his grade but has not done his year's work satisfactorily?

(b) State some important facts and list some important questions relating to the general problem of retardation.

6. Name as many recent books as you can bearing on the pedagogy of the following subjects: reading, writing, spelling, nature study, arithmetic.

7. (a) State as specifically as possible what you would do to improve the spelling of children who continually miss even the simplest words.

(b) In the teaching of spelling what objection or objections could be raised to the use of such words as the following taken from the State Series Speller? Fillet, timorous, frieze, fuchsia, epaulet, aconite, lapidary.

8. (a) What is the proper temperature for a classroom?

(b) What special considerations should govern the seating of pupils in the classroom?

(c) What are some specific effects of Open Air schools upon pupils?

(d) Will you require home study? If any, how much and in what studies?

9. (a) What is the best method of preventing disorder?

(b) To what extent, if at all, would you permit one pupil to help another with his lessons?

(c) Is it better to punish rarely and severely. or to punish less severely but to exercise great care in calling to account for every offense? Explain briefly.

10. Define or explain each of the following terms: experimental pedagogy, adolescence, school clinic, vocational guidance, Binet mental Tests, social center activities, ungraded class, Batavia teacher, inductive method.

ARITHETIC—FIRST 6 YEARS.

1. Write out in full all the possible combinations of change one can make for a quarter of a dollar. With what age of children could such problem be used?

2. What common fractional forms (specify) can be taught to children profitably, during the first 3 years? Why should these be taught? Why not others?

3. A newsboy buys nickle papers, three for a dime; how many papers must he sell to clear $1.00? What preparatory teaching would you want to do before giving this problem to a class of Fourth Graders?

4. How early can decimal fractions be taught profitably? Is the notion, one tenth, more difficult than one-fifth? Why?

5. In "reduction of fractions" you accustom the pupil to see the given fraction in two or more forms having the same value: as 1-2=2-4=5-10=7-14, etc. What use do you make of this principle in working with integers, as in addition or subtraction?

Answer all five questions.

ARITHMETIC, JUNE 10, 1912.

(Write legibly. Answer ten.)

1. A man bought a lot for $1,500 and built a house on it costing $3,000. He rented his property for $300 a year. Taxes, repairs and insurance cost him $74.00 a year. What per cent does make on his investment?

2. There are 48 pupils and a teacher in a room 36 ft. long, 30 ft. wide and 14 ft. high. If fresh air is introduced at the rate of 30 cu. ft. per person per minute how often is the air of the entire room renewed?

3. If a city raises $13,093.75 from a ¼% tax, what is the assessed valuation of the property in the city?

4. The diameter of a circular tank is 8 feet. How high must it be to contain 15,000 gallons?

5. (a) $48.225 \div 15 = ?$

(b) $\dfrac{.124}{132} = ?$

6. The sum of two numbers is 10, and the sum of their squares is 52. Find the numbers by algebra.

7. What arithmetical knowledge should children entering the seventh grade possess? Answer fully.

8. In seventh and eighth grade arithmetic which is better; to teach the short cuts and abbreviated forms of solution used by accountants and business men, or to require the pupil to make a detailed analysis of his solution by formally setting forth each step in the process? Give reason.

9. If a pupil in the seventh grade is excellent in all his studies save arithmetic, but fails in that branch, should he be promoted? Give reason for your answer.

10. What are some of the newer trends in the teaching of seventh and eighth grade arithmetic as regards:

(a) The subject matter covered,

(b) The nature of the problems used in the teaching of a given topic.

11. Does the reasoning ability which is gained through the study of arithmetic enable the pupil to reason better in matters pertaining to history, geography, etc? Defend your answer.

FREE PUBLIC LECTURES FOR ADULTS.

The system of free public lectures for school pupils and adults instituted 1910, has completed its second year.

Over two hundred lectures were delivered in the auditoria of our public schools during the year ending June 30, 1912. M. E. Blanchard, Ph. D. of the Mission High School, and G. O. Mitchell, A. B., of the Girls' High School, respectively Secretary and Director of the Lecture Bureau, arranged interesting and instructive programmes as the following schedules demonstrate.

DEPARTMENT OF EDUCATION, ANNOUNCEMENT OF FREE PUBLIC LECTURES FOR ADULTS (ILLUSTRATED—USUALLY WITH STEREOPTICON.)

SCHEDULE FOR AUGUST, 1911.

Wednesday, August 2.—Yerba Buena School, Greenwich, near Webster; Homes Without Hand, Herbert L. Coggins.

Friday, August 4.—Mission High School, Dolores and Eighteenth; Continental Europe, J. Emmet Hayden.

Tuesday, August 8.—Hancock School, Filbert, near Taylor, Tuberculosis (in Italian), Salvatori Schiro, M. D.

Thursday, August 10.—Monroe School, Excelsior Ave. and London, Java, the Gem of the East Indies, Alexander Russell.

Friday, August 11.—Girls' High School, O'Farrell and Scott, Robert Louis Stevenson in the South Seas, Mrs. Lloyd Osbourne.

Monday, August 14.—Mission Grammar School, Mission, bet. 15th and 16th; Athletics in Education, Eustace M. Peixotto.

Tuesday, August 15.—Portola School, Bacon and Girard; Our Animals, Matthew McCurrie.

Thursday, August 17.—Madison School, Clay, near Cherry; The Yosemite National Park, Chas. W. Reed.

Friday, August 18.—Crocker School, Page, near Broderick; Maeterlinck's Bluebird, Edw. J. Dupuy.

Monday, August 21.—Sutro School, 13th Ave., bet. Clement and Cal.; The Open Air Life, Wm. C. Voorsanger, M. D.

Tuesday, August 22.—Junipero Serra School, Holly Park, near Highland Ave.; Snapshots in the Orient, W. G. Hartranft.

Wednesday, August 23.—Garfield School, Filbert and Kearny; Newcomers to America, Martin A. Meyer.

Thursday, August 24.—Frank McCoppin School, Seventh Ave., bet. Balboa and Cabrillo; Electro-Magnetism, A. L. Jordan.

Friday, August 25.—Bryant School, York, near Twenty-second; Experiences in India, Harris Weinstock.

Monday, August 28.—Girls' High School, O'Farrell and Scott; The Cornet, Trumpet, and Trombone, Wm. J. McCoy, W. Mahood and A. Roncovieri.

Wednesday, August 30.—Mission High School, Dolores and Eighteenth; Sioux and the Yellowstone, Mr. and Mrs. Edw. H. Kemp.

Thursday, August 31.—Laguna Honda School, Seventh Ave., bet. Irving and Judah; The Land of the Rising Sun, Henry Payot.

SCHEDULE FOR SEPTEMBER, 1911.

Tuesday, September 5.—Madison School, Clay, near Cherry; The Relation of Pure Milk to Public Health, E. C. Fleischner, M. D.

Wednesday, September 6.—Adams Cosmopolitan School, Eddy, near Van Ness; Au Pays du Soleil Levant (in French), Henry Payot.

Wednesday, September 6.—Garfield School, Filbert and Kearny, L'Italia, il bel Paese (in Italian), Arturo Spozio.

Thursday, September 7.—Monroe School, Excelsior Ave. and London; Seven Vacation Walking Trips of the Columbia Park Boys' Club, Sidney S. Peixotto.

Friday, September 8.—Mission High School, Dolores and 18th Sts.;Fur Seals of Bering Sea, G. A. Clark.

Monday, September 11.—Mission Grammar School, Mission St., bet. 15th and 16th Sts.; Java, the Pearl of the East Indies, Alexander Russell.

Tuesday, September 12.—Junipero Serra School, Holly Park, near Highland Ave.; A Trip to Yosemite, Chas. Wesley Reed.

Tuesday, September 12.—Bryant School, York, near 22nd St.; Newcomers to America, Martin A. Meyer.

Wednesday, September 13.—Portola School, Bacon and Girard; Continental Europe, J. Emmet Hayden.

Thursday, September 14.—Frank McCoppin School, 7th, bet. Balboa and Cabrillo; Robert Louis Stevenson in the South Seas, Mrs. Lloyd Osbourne.

Friday, September 15.—Adams Cosmopolitan School, Eddy, near Van Ness; Die Wichtigkeit der Deutschen Sprache in Amerika (in German), Albin Putzker.

Monday, September 18.—Girls' High School, O'Farrell, near Scott; The Cradle of the Renaissance, Henry Payot.

Tuesday, September 19.—Crocker School, Page, near Broderick; Winters in Egypt, Clarence Reed.

Wednesday, September 20.—Yerba Buena School, Greenwich, near Webster; Snapshots in the Orient, W. G. Hartranft.

Wednesday, September 20.—Madison School, Clay, near Cherry; Outline of the Development of Music, Albert Elkus.

Thursday, September 21.—Hancock School, Filbert, near Taylor; Glimpses of China and Corea, Roswell S. Wheeler.

Friday, September 22.—Mission High School, Dolores and 18th Sts.; Young Australia and its Aims, J. J. Simons.

Monday, September 25.—Jean Parker School, Broadway, near Mason; A Summer in Mexico, Mrs. Mary Dickson.

Wednesday, September 27.—Sutro School, 13th Ave., bet. Clement and California; Electric Lights, A. L. Jordan.

Thursday, September 28.—Laguna Honda School, 7th Ave., bet. Irving and Judah; A Run Through Russia, Harris Weinstock.

Friday, September 29.—Mission High School, Dolores and 18th; Reminiscences of an Army Chaplain, Joseph M. Gleason.

SCHEDULE FOR OCTOBER, 1911.

Monday, October 9.—Yerba Buena School, Greenwich, near Webster; The Story of San Francisco, Mrs. Ella M. Sexton.

Wednesday, October 11.—Madison School, Clay, near Cherry; Recent Excavations in Palestine, Edward A. Wicher.

Thursday, October 12.—Jean Parker School, Broadway, near Powell; Shanghai and its Vicinity, John Fryer.

Friday, October 13.—James Lick School, Noe and Twenty-fifth; The Land of the Castanet, Henry Payot.

Monday, October 16.—Monroe School, Excelsior Ave. and London; The Pioneer Mother and Her Times, Mrs. Ella S. Mighels.

Tuesday, October 17.—Portola School, Bacon and Girard; Newcomers to America, Martin A. Meyer.

Wednesday, October 18.—Adams Cosmopolitan School, Eddy, near Van Ness; The Sonata: its Form and Meaning, Albert Elkus.

Wednesday, October 18.—Garfield School, Filbert and Kearny; Scenes in the South Seas, Almon E. Roth.

Friday, October 20.—Mission High School, Dolores and Eighteenth; San Francisco's Water Supply, Hermann Schussler.

Monday, October 23.—Crocker School, Page, near Broderick; The Greatest Discovery is Electricity, A. L. Jordan.

Tuesday, October 24.—Bryant School, Bryant, near Twenty-second; Our Southwest, the Land of Little Rain, Mrs. Mary Dickson.

Wednesday, October 25.—Frank McCoppin School, 7th Ave., bet. Balboa and Cabrillo; The Open-Air Life, W. C. Voorsanger, M. D.

Thursday, October 26.—Laguna Honda School, 7th Ave., bet. Irving and Judah; Shakespeare's Romeo and Juliet, John D. Barry.

Friday, October 27.—Adams Cosmopolitan School, Eddy, near Van Ness; Hugo's Hernani and the Literary Revolution, Edward J. Dupuy and Mlle. Blanche Levielle.

Friday, October 27.—Mission Grammar School, Mission, bet. 15th and 16th; The Fur Seals of Behring Sea, G. A. Clark.

Monday, October 30.—Sutro School, 13th Ave., bet. Clement and California; Folk-Lore, Folk-Dance and Ballad, Mrs. Fred W. Stowell.

Tuesday, October 31.—Hancock School, Filbert, near Taylor; Scenes in Three Continents, W. G. Hartranft.

SCHEDULE FOR NOVEMBER, 1911.

Wednesday, November 1.—Monroe School, Excelsior Ave. and London; The Pioneer Mother and Her Times, Mrs. Ella S. Mighels.

Thursday, November 2.—Garfield School, Filbert and Kearny; Continental Europe, J. Emmet Hayden.

Friday, November 3.—Mission Grammar School, Mission St., bet. 15th and 16th; Florence, the Cradle of the Renaissance, Henry Payot.

Monday, November 6.—Yerba Buena School, Greenwich, near Webster; The Lessons of the Southeast Wind, Marsden Manson.

Wednesday, November 8.—Adams Cosmopolitan School, Eddy, near Van Ness; Methods and Aims in Studying Languages, Albin Pützker.

Thursday, November 9.—Mission High School, Dolores and Eighteenth Sts.; Conquest of the Far North, Lincoln Wirt.

Friday, November 10.—Jean Parker School, Broadway, near Powell; Modern Subways and the Rapid Transit Problem, Sherman A. Jubb.

Monday, November 13.—Hancock School, Filbert, near Taylor; San Francisco in Early Days, Chas. B. Turrill.

Tuesday, November 14.—Bryant School, Bryant, near Twenty-second; The Child in the Home, Miss Lillian McCarthy, Dr. E. C. Fleischner.

Wednesday, November 15.—Frank McCoppin School, 7th Ave., bet. Balboa and Cabrillo; Ups and Downs of the Santa Cruz Coast, R. S. Holway.

Wednesday, November 15.—Madison School, Clay, near Cherry; A Run Through Russia, Harris Weinstock.

Thursday, November 16.—Mission High School, Eighteenth and Dolores; Ishi, the Last of the Deer Creeks, A. L. Kroeber.

Friday, November 17.—Denman School, Hayes and Pierce; Rostand's "Distant Princess," Edward J. Dupuy.

Monday, November 20.—Crocker School, Page, near Broderick; Recent Excavations in Palestine, Edward A. Wicher.

Wednesday, November 22.—Sutro School, 13th Ave., bet. Clement and California; Newcomers to America, Martin A. Meyer.

Wednesday, November 22.—Jean Parker School, Broadway, near Powell; Development of the Opera, Albert Elkus.

Thursday, November 23.—Laguna Honda School, 7th Ave., bet. Irving and Judah; Dress and Ornamentation of Primitive Peoples, T. T. Waterman.

Friday, November 24.—Burnett School, 14th Ave. So. and L St.; Fur Seals of Behring Sea, G. A. Clark.

Friday, November 24.—Adams School, Eddy, near Van Ness; From Waterfall to Street-car, A. L. Jordan.

Monday, November 27.—James Lick School, Noe and 25th Sts.; The Open-Air Life, Dr. W. C. Voorsanger.

Tuesday, November 28.—George Peabody School, 7th Ave., bet. Clement and California; Shakespeare's "Hamlet," John D. Barry.

SCHEDULE FOR DECEMBER, 1911.

Monday, December 4.—Crocker School, Page, near Broderick; Glimpses of Korea, Peking and the Yang-tse, Roswell S. Wheeler.

Tuesday, December 5.—George Peabody School, 7th Ave., bet. Clement and California; Paris, Queen of Beauty, Culture, and Pleasure, Henry Payot.

Wednesday, December 6.—Mission High School, Eighteenth and Dolores; Crossing the Plains Fifty Years Ago, C. W. Childs.

Thursday, December 7.—Adams Cosmopolitan School, Eddy, near Van Ness; A Trip to Palestine, Harris Weinstock.

Friday, December 8.—Yerba Buena School, Greenwich, near Webster; Napa County: Scenery, Resources, and Industries, Chas. B. Turrill.

Monday, December 11.—Girls' High School, Hamilton Square; Algeria, illustrating the Garden of Allah, I. H. Morse.

Tuesday, December 12.—Jas. Lick School, Noe and Twenty-fifth; Scientific Prevention of Accidents, Carl M. Hansen.

Tuesday, December 12.—Bryant School, Bryant, near Twenty-second; Three Trips to the Top of Mt. Shasta, R. S. Holway.

Wednesday, December 13.—Mission Grammar School, Mission, bet. 15th and 16th; In and About Jerusalem, Martin A. Meyer.

Thursday, December 14.—Frank McCoppin School, 7th Ave., bet. Balboa and Cabrillo; Houses and Homes in European and American Cities, Wm. S. Morgan.

Friday, December 15.—Denman School, Hayes and Pierce; History of Music: 1. Period of Foundations, Albert Elkus.

Friday, December 15.—Madison School, Clay, near Cherry; Social Life on the French Stage, 1850-1875, Edward J. Dupuy.

SCHEDULE FOR JANUARY, 1912.

Friday, January 5.—Girls' High School, Hamilton Square; French Wit in French Comedy, 1850-1890, Edward J. Dupuy.

Monday, January 8.—Portola School, Bacon and Girard; Scientific Prevention of Accidents, Carl M. Hansen.

Tuesday, January 9.—Garfield School, Kearny and Filbert; Napa County: Scenery, Resources, and Industries, Chas. B. Turrill.

Wednesday, January 10.—Madison School, Clay, near Cherry; Oriental Rugs, Genuine and "Faked," Thos. H. Kullujian.

Thursday, January 11.—Mission High School, Eighteenth and Dolores; Our Southwest, the Land of Little Rain, Mrs. Mary Dickson.

Friday, January 12.—Junipero Serra School, Holly Park and Highland Ave.; Tuberculosis vs. Open-Air Life. Dr. W. C. Voorsanger.

Monday, January 15.—Crocker School, Page, near Broderick; Washington, the Nation's Capital, Robert P. Troy.

Tuesday, January 16.—Monroe School, London and Excelsior Ave.; Scenes in Three Continents, W. G. Hartranft.

Wednesday, January 17.—Girls' High School, Hamilton Square; Turrets, Towers and Spires, Henry Payot.

Thursday, January 18.—Frank McCoppin School, 7th Ave., bet. Balboa and Cabrillo; Romance of Early California History, Frank H. Powers.

Friday, January 19.—Jean Parker School, Broadway, near Mason; Occupational and Social Diseases (in Italian), Dr. Salvatore Schiro.

Friday, January 19.—Adams School, Eddy, near Van Ness; The Spell of Italy, Frank S. Brush.

Monday, January 22.—Girls' High School, Hamilton Square; Travels in India, I. H. Morse.

Tuesday, January 23.—George Peabody School, 7th Ave., bet. Clement & California; Java, the Gem of the East Indies, Alexander Russell.

Wednesday, January 24.—Mission High School, Eighteenth and Dolores; Country Life in Modern Greece, Oliver M. Washburn.

Thursday, January 25.—Laguna Honda School, 7th Ave., bet. Irving and Judah; Three Trails up Mt. Shasta, R. S. Holway.

Friday, January 26.—Bryant School, Bryant, near Twenty-second; The Fur Seals of Behring Sea, George A. Clark.

Monday, January 29.—Adams School, Eddy, near Van Ness; Shakespeare's "Merchant of Venice," John D. Barry.

Tuesday, January 30.—Burnett School, 14th Ave. South and L St.; Glimpses of Korea, Peking and the Yang-tse, R. S. Wheeler.

Wednesday, January 31.—Mission Grammar School, Mission, near Sixteenth; History of Music: 2. Classical Period, Albert Elkus.

SCHEDULE FOR FEBRURARY, 1912.

Thursday, February 1.—Sutro School, 13th Ave., bet. Clement and California; The Physical Observation of Children, Dr. Ernest B. Hoag.

Friday, February 2.—Portola School, Bacon and Girard; Scientific Prevention of Accidents, Carl M. Hansen.

Monday, February 5.—Yerba Buena School, Greenwich and Webster; The Yosemite National Park; Arthur H. Chamberlain.

Tuesday, February 6.—Denman School, Hayes and Pierce; Oriental Rugs, Genuine and "Faked," Thos. H. Kullujian.

Wednesday, February 7.—Mission High School, Eighteenth and Dolores; Dickens as Novelist and Man, John D. Barry.

Thursday, February 8.—Girls' High School, Hamilton Square; Opportunities in California, Fred G. Athearn.

Friday, February 9.—Grattan School, Shrader and Alma; Turrets, Towers and Spires, Henry Payot.

Monday, February 12.—James Lick School, Twenty-fifth and Noe; Scenes in China and the Far East, W. G. Hartranft.

Tuesday, February 13.—Hancock School, Filbert, near Taylor; America in the Philippines, Gilbert M. Brink.

Wednesday, February 14.—Crocker School, Page, near Broderick; Citizenship in California; Albert H. Elliot.

Thursday, February 15.—Adams School, Eddy, near Van Ness; Across the Jordan, Martin A. Meyer.

Friday, February 16.—McKinley School, Fourteenth and Castro; Three Trails Up Mt. Shasta, Ruliff S. Holway.

Monday, February 19.—Madison School, Clay, near Cherry; What the Microscope Reveals in Our Bodies, Dr. A. A. D'Ancona.

Monday, February 19.—Monroe School, London and Excelsior Ave.; San Francisco's Place Among Cities, Percy V. Long.

Tuesday, February 20.—Jean Parker School, Broadway, near Mason; Around the World with My Kodak, Wallace Bradford.

Wednesday, February 21.—Mission Grammar School, Mission, near Sixteenth; George Washington, the Man and the Statesman, Robt. P. Troy.

Friday, February 23.—Girls' High School, Hamilton Square; The Cosmopolitan in the Modern French Theatre, Edw. J. Dupuy.

Friday, February 23.—Bryant School, Bryant, near Twenty-second; From Waterfall to Electric Car, A. L. Jordan.

Monday, February 26.—Junipero Serra School, Holly Park and Highland Ave.; San Francisco in Early Days, Chas. B. Turrill.

Tuesday, February 27.—Adams School, Eddy, near Van Ness; Open-air Life vs. Tuberculosis, Dr. Wm. C. Voorsanger.

Tuesday, February 27.—Mission High School, Eighteenth and Dolores; California, the Land of Alluring Contrasts, Francis Hope.

Wednesday, February 28.—Laguna Honda School, 7th Ave., bet. Irving and Judah; Bird Life in California, Gretchen L. Libby.

Thursday, February 29.—Geo. Peabody School, 7th Ave., bet. Clement and California; The X-Ray, Dr. G. R. Hubbell.

SCHEDULE FOR MARCH, 1912.

Friday, March 1.—Frank McCoppin School, 7th Ave., bet. Balboa and Cabrillo; Glimpses of Korea, Peking and the Yang-tse, R. S. Wheeler.

Monday, March 4.—Jean Parker School, Broadway, near Mason; Life and Works of Mario Rapisardi (in Italian), Gastone Bertini.

Tuesday, March 5.—Grattan School, Schrader and Alma; Robert Louis Stevenson in the South Seas, Mrs. Lloyd Osbourne.

Wednesday, March 6.—Hancock School, Filbert, near Taylor; America in the Philippines, Gilbert M. Brink.

Thursday, March 7.—Crocker School, Page, near Broderick; The Yosemite National Park, Arthur H. Chamberlain.

Friday, March 8.—Madison School, Clay, near Cherry; Scenes in Syria, Wallace Bradford.

Monday, March 11.—Girls' High School, Hamilton Square; Tennyson's "Enoch Arden," (Richard Strauss's Musical Setting), Mrs. Sidney Ashe and Miss Ada Clement.

Tuesday, March 12.—McKinley School, Castro and Fourteenth St.; San Francisco's Water Supply, Hermann Schussler.

Wednesday, March 13.—Yerba Buena School, Greenwich, near Webster; Shakespeare's "Merchant of Venice," John D. Barry.

Thursday, March 14.—Adams School, Eddy, near Van Ness; Rome, the Eternal City, Henry Payot.

Friday, March 15.—Burnett School, Lane St. and Newcomb Ave.; A Trip to Mexico, J. Emmet Hayden.

Monday, March 18.—Girls' High School, Hamilton Square; Maeterlinck, the Writer, Edward J. Dupuy.

Tuesday, March 19—Sutro School, 13th Ave., bet. Clement and California; At the Edge of the Artic, Mrs. J. Dennis Arnold.

Wednesday, March 20.—Bryant School, Bryant, near Twenty-second; Open-Air Life vs. Tuberculosis, Dr. G. R. Hubbell.

Thursday, March 21.—Mission High School, Eighteenth and Dolores; Ireland in Views, John P. Tobin.

Friday, March 22.—Adams School, Eddy, near Van Ness; Radium, the Realization of the Alchemist's Dream, E. P. Lewis.

Monday, March 25.—George Peabody School, Seventh Ave., near California; The Fur Seals of Behring Sea, George A. Clark.

Tuesday, March 26.—Monroe School, Excelsior Ave. and London; A Trip through the Holy Land, Robert P. Troy.

Wednesday, March 27.—Laguna Honda School, Seventh Ave., bet. Irving and Judah; What the Microscope Reveals in Our Bodies, Dr. A. A. D'Ancona.

Wednesday, March 27.—Girls' High School, Hamilton Square; History of Music, 3: Classical Period, Albert Elkus.

Thursday, March 28.—James Lick School, Noe and Twenty-fifth St.; Across the Jordan, Martin A. Meyer.

Friday, March 29.—Mission High School, Eighteenth and Dolores; The Passion Play of Ober-Ammergau, Frank S. Brush.

SCHEDULE FOR APRIL.

Monday, April 8.—Portola School, Bacon and Girard; The Fur Seals of Behring Sea, George A. Clark.

Tuesday, April 9.—Mission High School, Eighteenth and Dolores; San Francisco in Early Days, Charles B. Turrill.

Wednesday, April 10.—Garfield School, Kearny and Filbert; Our Southwest, the Land of Little Rain, Mrs. Mary Dickson.

Thursday, April 11.—Sheridan School, Capitol Av., bet. Lobos and Farallones; Newcomers to America, Martin A. Meyer.

Friday, April 12.—Madison School. Clay, near Cherry; Glimpses of Korea, Peking and the Yang-tse, R. S. Wheeler.

Friday, April 12.—Junipero Serra School, Holly Park and Highland Ave.; The Evolution of Sierra Scenery, R. S. Holway.

Monday, April 15.—McKinley School, Fourteenth and Castro Sts.; The Recreation Movement in Large Cities, Jas. E. Rogers.

Tuesday, April 16.—Grattan School, Schrader and Alma; What the Microscope Reveals in Our Bodies, Dr. A. A. D'Ancona.

Wednesday, April 17.—Adams School, Eddy, near Van Ness; Rome: the City Beautiful, H. R. Fairclough.

Thursday, April 18.—Frank McCoppin School, 7th Ave., bet. Balboa and Cabrillo; Java, the Gem of the East Indies, Alexander Russell.

Thursday, April 18.—James Lick School, Noe and Twenty-fifth; Yellowstone Park, H. H. Bell.

Friday, April 19.—Mission Grammar School, Mission, bet. Fiftetenth and Sixteenth; Alaska, Our Northern Empire, H. H. Hildreth.

Friday, April 19.—Crocker School, Page, near Broderick; Shakespeare's "Julius Cæsar," John D. Barry.

Monday, April 22.—Girls' High School, Hamilton Square; Edmond Rostand, the Writer, Edward J. Dupuy.

Tuesday, April 23.—Bryant School, Bryant, near Twenty-second; The Spell of Italy, Frank S. Brush.

Wednesday, April 24.—Laguna Honda School, Seventh Ave., bet. Irving and Judah; From the Alps to the Adriatic, Henry Payot.

Thursday, April 25.—Adams School, Eddy, near Van Ness; The Standard French Play—Racine's Athalie (in French), E. B. Lemare.

Thursday, April 25.—Mission High School, Dolores and Eighteenth; Our Western Wonderland, Arthur H. Chamberlain.

Friday, April 26.—Visitacion Valley School, Visitacion Ave. and Schwerin St.; A Trip to Continental Europe, J. Emmet Hayden.

Monday, April 29.—Burnett School, Newcomb Ave. and Lane St.; The Open-air Life vs. Tuberculosis, Dr. G. R. Hubbell.

Tuesday, April 30.—Sutro School, 13th Ave., bet. Clement and California; Scientific Prevention of Accidents, Carl M. Hansen.

SCHEDULE FOR MAY.

Thursday, May 2.—Visitacion Valley School, Visitacion Ave. and Schwerin St.; A Trip to Continental Europe, J. Emmet Hayden.

Friday, May 3.—Spring Valley School, Jackson, bet. Hyde and Larkin; Florence, the Cradle of the Renaissance, Dr. A. H. Giannini.

Monday, May 6.—Yerba Buena School, Greenwich, near Webster; Chemistry in Everyday Life, R. R. Rogers.

Tuesday, May 7.—Girls' High School, Hamilton Square; Robert and Elizabeth Barrett Browning, John D. Barry, Mrs. Lillian Quinn Stark, Miss Helen Heath, Mrs. W. J. Batchelder.

Wednesday, May 8.—Jean Parker School, Broadway, near Mason; Giovanni Pascoli, the Poet, (in Italian), Arturo Spozio.

Thursday, May 9.—Denman Grammar School, Hayes and Pierce; Physical Training Among the Greeks, Walter E. Magee.

Friday, May 10.—Geo. Peabody School, 7th Ave., bet. California and Clement; Scientific Prevention of Accidents, Carl M. Hansen.

Friday, May 10.—Mission High School, Eighteenth and Dolores; The Folk-dance in Physical Culture, (Illustrated by pupils of Laguna Honda School), Mrs. Fred W. Stowell.

Monday, May 13.—Adams School, Eddy, near Van Ness; Under the Eaves of the World, Henry Payot.

Tuesday, May 14.—Hancock School, Filbert, near Taylor; The Yosemite National Park, Arthur H. Chamberlain.

Wednesday, May 15.—Monroe School, Excelsior Ave. and London; Open-air Life vs. Tuberculosis, Dr. G. R. Hubbell.

Thursday, May 16.—Bryant School, Bryant, near Twenty-second; Early San Francisco, Chas. B. Turrill.

Friday, May 17.—McKinley School, Castro and Fourteenth; Glimpses of Korea, Peking and the Yang-tse, R. S. Wheeler.

Friday, May 17.—Burnett School, Newcomb Ave. and Lane St.; Our Animals, Matthew McCurrie.

Monday, May 20.—Sheridan School, Capitol Ave., bet. Lobos and Farallones; Java, the Gem of the East Iidies, Alexander Russell.

Monday, May 20.—Mission Grammar School, Mission, bet. Fifteenth and Sixteenth; Relation of the Consumer to the Pure Food Law, M. E. Jaffa.

Tuesday, May 21.—Girls' High School, Hamilton Square; Paris, la Reine des Capitales (in French), Edward J. Dupuy.

Tuesday, May 21.—Sutro School, Thirteenth Ave., bet. Clement and California; What the Microscope Reveals in Our Bodies, Dr. A. A. D'Ancona.

Wednesday, May 22.—Spring Valley School, Jackson, bet. Hyde and Larkin; R. L. Stevenson in the South Seas, Mrs. Lloyd Osbourne.

Wednesday, May 22.—Adams School, Eddy, near Van Ness; History of Music: Romantic Period, Albert Elkus.

Thursday, May 23.—Laguna Honda School, Seventh Ave., bet. Irving and Judah; London and its Environs, Jas. E. Rogers.

Friday, May 24.—James Lick School, Twenty-fifth and Noe; New York City, Chas. L. Jacobs.

SCHEDULE FOR JUNE.

Monday, June 3.—Portola School, Bacon and Girard; Bird Life in California, Gretchen L. Libby.

Tuesday, June 4.—Hancock School, Filbert, near Taylor; Yosemite and Hetch Hetchy, C. W. Reed.

Wednesday, June 5.—Frank McCoppin School, Seventh Ave., bet. Balboa and Cabrillo; A Trip to Mexico, J. Emmet Hayden.

Thursday, June 6.—Jean Parker School, Broadway, near Mason; From the Alps to the Adriatic, Dr. A. H. Giannini.

Friday, June 7.—Lincoln School, Harrison, near Fourth; The History of Lincoln School, Chas. B. Turrill.

Monday, June 10.—Adams School, Eddy, near Van Ness; A Journey Across Siberia, F. S. Rosseter.

Tuesday, June 11.—Jean Parker School, Broadway, near Mason; Poverty and Criminality (in Italian), Salvatore Schiro, M. D.

Tuesday, June 11.—Bryant School, Bryant, near Twenty-second; Seven Vacation Trips of the Columbia Park Boys' Club, Sidney S. Piexotto.

Wednesday, June 12.—McKinley School, Castro and Fourteenth; A Summer in Mexico, Mrs. Mary Dickson.

Thursday, June 13.—Mission High School, Dolores and Eighteenth; Robert and Elizabeth Barrett Browning, John D. Barry, Mrs. Lillian Quinn Stark, Mrs. M. E. Blanchard, Miss Edna M. Wilcox.

Friday, June 14.—Madison School, Clay, near Cherry; The Pearl on India's Brow, Henry Payot.

The Lectures will be discontinued during the school vacation in July and August, recommencing in September.

DEPARTMENT OF EDUCATION, CITY AND COUNTY OF SAN FRANCISCO, CALIFORNIA.

BOARD OF EDUCATION.

D'ANCONA, DR. A. A., President	Term expires Jan. 8, 1916	$3,000.00
POWER, JAMES E., Member	Term expires Jan. 8, 1915	3,000.00
KINCAID, Mrs. M. W., Member	Term expires Jan. 8, 1913	3,000.00
JONES, Miss S. J., Member	Term expires Jan. 8, 1914	3,000.00

SUPERINTENDENT OF SCHOOLS.

RONCOVIERI, ALFRED	Term expires Jan. 8, 1915	$4,000.00

(Ex-officio member of the Board of Education without right to vote).

DEPUTY SUPERINTENDENTS OF SCHOOLS.

Webster, R. H.	Term expires May 1, 1916	$3,000.00
Cloud, A. J.	Term expires Dec. 1, 1912	3,000.00
Heaton, T. L.	Term expires Mar. 1, 1914	3,000.00
Howard, W. B.	Term expires Mar. 1, 1914	3,000.00

EMPLOYES.

Dodge, M. G.	Secretary, Board of Education	Term at pleasure of Board of Education	$2,400.00
Berliner, C. A.	Financial Secretary, Board of Education	Term at pleasure of Board of Education	2,160.00
Collier, A. M., Mrs.	Assistants to Secretary	Term at pleasure of Board of Education	1,020.00
Norris, M. R., Mrs.	Assistants to Secretary	Term at pleasure of Board of Education	1,020.00
Walsh, E. A., Miss	Stenographer, Board of [illegible]cation	Term at pleasure of Board of E[illegible]cation	1,260.00
O'Rourke, J., Miss	Stenographer, Board of Education	Term at pleasure of Board of Education	1,260.00
[illegible]r, T. S., Miss	Stenographer, Office Supt. of Schools	Term at pleasure of Board of Education	1,260.00
Holden, S. A., Miss	Phone Exchange Operator	Term at pleasure of Board of Education	1,080.00
Harris, J.	[illegible]r, Board of Education	Term at pleasure of Board of Education	1,200.00
[illegible], R.	Messenger, Supt. of Schools	Term at pleasure of Board of Education	1,140.00
Sweeney, E.	Truant Officer	Assigned by Chief of Police.	
Dugan, T. J.	Truant Officer	Assigned by Chief of Police.	
Nolan, E.	Truant Officer	Assigned by Chief of Police.	
Foley, James	Store Keeper	Term at pleasure of Board of Education	$1,800.00
Hunt, John	Assistant Store Keeper	Term at pleasure of Board of Education	1,080.00
Whitney, S. E.	Bookkeeper	Term at pleasure of Board of Education	1,500.00
[illegible]h, C. W.	Building and Repairs	Term at pleasure of Board of Education	2,100.00
Alford, T.	Clerk	Term at pleasure of Board of Education	1,500.00
Schuck, E.	Chauffeur	Term at pleasure of Board of Education	1,500.00

SCHOOLS AND TEACHERS.

Name.	Grade of Class.	[illegible]en El[illegible]ed.	Grade of Certificate	Salary per [illegible]r.
Adams [illegible]olitan Grammar School—				
McFarland, Miss H. F.	Principal	Nov. 30, 1877	High	2,160.00
Levison, Miss E.	V. P., 8th	Aug. 17, 1891	Grammar	1,500.00
Fairchild, Miss M. E.	Third	July 1, 1874	High	1,164.00
Doughty, Mary A.	Seventh	April 2, 1881	Grammar	1,284.00
Dolan, Mrs. C. M.	Fifth	Aug. 16, 1898	Grammar	1,164.00
Hesselmeyer, Miss C. A.	F[illegible]st	Feb. 11, 1892	Grammar	1,224.00
[illegible]r, Miss A. M.	French	Sept. 29, 1892	Grammar and Special	1,200.00
[illegible]field, Eleanor A.	Sixth	June 15, 1866	Grammar	1,164.00
Hurley, Mamie E.	Seventh	Sept. 10, 1884	Grammar	1,224.00
Jacobs, Miss E.	[illegible]n	Aug. 20, 1907	High	1,200.00
[illegible]bs, Margaret E.	Fourth	[illegible] 17, 1907	Grammar	1,164.00
Grace, Miss K. L.	Second	[illegible]g. 3, 1908	High	1,164.00
Duffy, Miss E. A.	First	July 23, 1902	Grammar	1,224.00
Agassiz Primary—				
Hart, Miss P.	Principal	July 6, 1870	High	1,944.00
Harney, Miss A.	First	July 31, 1889	[illegible]ar	[illegible]
Brown, Miss R. F.	Ungraded	July 18, 1902	Grammar	1,224.00
[illegible]n, Miss C. A.	F[illegible]th	July 9, 1877	Grammar	1,164.00
Josselyn, Ada M.	F[illegible]th	[illegible]t. 9, 1883	[illegible]ar and Special	1,224.00
Clausen, [illegible]ss E. A.	Fourth	Jan. 31, 1894	Grammar	1,164.00
Bartlett, Miss O. S.	[illegible]th	Jan. 31, 1894	Grammar	1,164.00
Boyle, Miss O. C.	Third	Oct. 1, 1905	[illegible]ar	1,164.00
Rixon, Miss A. E.	Second	Feb. 28, 1898	Grammar	1,164.00
Fredericks, Miss E. L.	Third	Feb. 16, 1891	Grammar and Special	1,164.00
Hanson, Miss L.	Second	July 20, 1903	Grammar	1,164.00
Wright, Miss H.	Second	Dec. 1, 1890	Primary	1,284.00
[illegible]n, Miss A. M.	First	Jan. 6, 1902	Grammar	1,224.00
Ellis, Miss M. R.	Fifth	Feb. 3, 1908	Grammar	1,140.00

Schoof, Miss L.	Fourth	July 27, 1908	Grammar	900.00
Walters, Miss T.	Second	Jan. 8, 1906	Grammar	1,140.00
Maloney, Miss K. A.	First	Jan. 10, 1881	Grammar	1,224.00
Sankey, Miss M. F.	First	Sept. 15, 1888	Grammar	1,224.00
Knowlton, Grace W.	Third	Mar. 9, 1903	Grammar	1,164.00
Bay View Grammar—				
Prior, Philip	Principal	June 14, 1865	High	2,160.00
McGuire, Miss B. A.	V. P., Eighth	Oct. 16, 1883	Grammar	1,620.00
Stolz, Miss R. C.	Seventh ard Eighth	Dec. 28, 1892	Grammar	1,224.00
Hanford, Miss E. V.	Seventh	Sept. 1, 1886	Grammar	1,224.00
Fitzgerald, Mrs. M. T.	Fifth	Aug. 19, 1907	Grammar	1,164.00
[illegible]ey, Miss A. A.	First	Sept. 15, 1882	Grammar	1,224.00
Sleeper, Miss May	First	Nov. 18, 1873	Grammar	1,164.00
Piper, Miss L. K.	Feurth	July 19, 1885	Grammar	1,164.00
Judson, Miss A. A.	Sixth	Jan. 16, 1903	Grammar	1,164.00
Boylan, Miss M. L.	Fourth	Jan. 12, 1898	Grammar	1,164.00
North, Mrs. E.	Fifth	Jan. 14, 1910	Grammar	840.00
Bernal Grammar—				
Regan, Miss A. G.	Principal	Oct. 5, 1887	Grammar	2,340.00
McGivern, Miss K. A.	V. P., 8th	Oct. 13, 1892	Grammar	1,620.00
Quinn, May	Sixth	Nov. 16, 1905	Grammar	1,164.00
Scott, Mrs. E.	Ungraded	July 15, 1897	Grammar	1,224.00
Schendel, Miss A.	Eighth	Sept. 27, 1880	Grammar	1,224.00
Neppert, Miss L. C.	Sixth	Dec. 29, 1892	Grammar	1,164.00
McQuade, Miss M.	Fifth	Feb. 9, 1892	Grammar	1,164.00
Powell, Mrs. O. T.	Fourth	Jan. 26, 1906	Grammar	1,164.00
Maxwell, Miss E.	Eighth	April 26, 1907	High	1,224.00
Benjamin, Miss M. O.	Seventh	Aug. 26, 1903	Grammar	1,224.00
Elmes, Miss K.	Fourth	Mar. 5, 1909	Grammar	840.00

SCHOOLS AND TEACHERS—Continued.

Name.	Grade of Class.	When Elected.	Grade of Certificate.	Salary per Year.
Bernal Grammar—Continued				
Simpson, Sarah S.	Fourth	July 2, 1889	Grammar	1,164.00
Gilchrist, Miss C. H.	Seventh	Sept. 15, 1901	Grammar	1,284.00
Senter, Miss K. G.	Fifth	Aug. 5, 1907	Grammar	1,164.00
Bliss, Miss M. F.	Sixth	Aug. 3, 1910	Grammar	900.00
Millhone, Miss B.	Sixth	July 27, 1898	Grammar	1,164.00
Powell, Mrs. O.	Fourth	Jan. 26, 1906	Grammar	1,164.00
Gibson, Miss A.	Fifth	Aug. 25, 1910	Grammar	840.00
Bryant Cosmopolitan School—				
Kelly, Miss E. E.	Principal	Oct. 5, 1887	Grammar	1,800.00
Stanford, Miss B. M.	Fifth	Jan. 11, 1877	Grammar and Special	1,224.00
Rutherford, Miss H. M.	Fifth	Nov. 6, 1888	Grammar	[illegible]
Kulmuk, Miss L.	First and German	July 22, 1886	Grammar	1,224.00
Harvey, Miss M. A.	Third	Aug. 29, 1892	Grammar	1,164.00
White, Miss G. M.	Third	Jan. 24, 1910	Grammar	840.00
Curry, Miss M. E.	Second	Feb. 5, 1878	Grammar	1,164.00
[illegible], Miss F. C.	First and French	Aug. 28, 1883	Grammar and Special	1,404.00
Heineberg, Miss L.	First	Aug. 15, 1873	Grammar and Special	1,284.00
Roberts, Miss M. E.	First	July 14, 1871	Grammar	1,224.00
Koch, Miss L. H.	Second	Oct. 31, [illegible]	Grammar	1,164.00
Unger, Miss A. N.	First	Aug. 20, 1878	Grammar and Special	1,284.00
Duffy, Miss H. M.	Fourth	July 1, 1903	Grammar	1,184.00
Cassamayou, Miss A.	Fourth	Aug. 3, 1908	Grammar	960.00
Hitchcock, Miss H. M.	French	July 29, 1876	Grammar and Special	1,200.00
Buena Vista Primary—				
Catlin, Miss A. G.	Principal	Mar. 5, 1878	Grammar	1,560.00
Hunt, Charlotte F.	Fourth	Oct. 28, 1892	Grammar	1,164.00

Hilderth, [illegible] O.	[illegible]	Nov. 11, 1896	Grammar	1,164.00
[illegible], [illegible] M. T.	[illegible]	Nov. 24, [illegible]	[illegible]	900.00
McFadden, Emma	Second	[illegible] 1, 1887	[illegible]	1,164.00
[illegible], Miss M. R.	Second	[illegible] 14, 1896	[illegible]	1,164.00
Rollins, Miss M. A.	[illegible]	Oct. 8, 1879	[illegible]	1,224.00
[illegible], Rose M.	First	Feb. 23, 1898	[illegible]	1,224.00
Crocker, Miss B. H.	First	Aug. 5, 1888	[illegible]	1,224.00
Lewis, Mss R. P.	Fifth	Mar. 14, 1886	[illegible]	1,164.00
Burnett Primary—				
[illegible], Miss L.	Principal	Dec. 6, 1891	[illegible]	1,800.00
Flynn, Miss M. E.	Fourth	Nov. 20, 1877	Primary	1,164.00
Schroeder, Miss S.	Fourth	Aug. 26, [illegible]	High	1,080.00
Curtis, Miss C. M.	First	July 6, 1882	[illegible]	1,224.00
Hopkins, [illegible] J. M.	Third	May 15, 1905	[illegible]	1,164.00
[illegible], [illegible] M. F.	First	July 6, 1877	Grammar	1,224.00
[illegible], Miss S.	Second	Feb. 12, 1890	[illegible]	1,164.00
[illegible], Miss E.	Second	Aug. 3, 1908	Grammar	1,164.00
[illegible], Miss J.	[illegible]	Aug. 25, 1904	[illegible]	1,152.00
[illegible], Miss J. I.	First	Aug. 7, 1888	[illegible]	1,224.00
Reichling, [illegible] Wanda L.	Second	Jan. 6, 1902	[illegible]	1,164.00
[illegible] Primary—				
[illegible], [illegible] E. L.	Principal	Jan. 16, 1884	Grammar	1,560.00
Cove, Miss E. A.	Second	Dec. 28, 1880	[illegible]	1,164.00
Ward, [illegible] S. A.	First and Music	Oct. 30, 1894	Grammar	1,284.00
McArthur, Miss [illegible] A.	[illegible]	Feb. 3, 1908	[illegible]	1,164.00
Curley, [illegible] Alice G.	First	April 1, 1903	Grammar	1,224.00
Harrigan, Miss [illegible] A.	[illegible]	Aug. 2, 1871	[illegible]	1,164.00
de Sousa, Miss Sadie	Fifth	Jan. 23, 1911	[illegible]	[illegible]
Blackman, [illegible] Ruby E.	Second	June 1, [illegible]	[illegible]	1,224.00
Heaney, Miss Beatrice E.	Third	July 24, 1911	[illegible]	840.00
Brunk, [illegible] J. H.	Fourth	July 24, [illegible]	Grammar	840.00
Rosenthal, Miss Esther	Fourth	Jan. 25, [illegible]	Grammar	840.00

SCHOOLS AND TEACHERS—Continued.

Name.	Grade of Class.	When Elected.	Grade of Certificate.	Salary per Year.
Columbia [illegible]—				
Burke, Mrs. L. K.	Principal	Jan. 23, 1857	High	2,460.00
[illegible], Mr. L. M.	V. P., 6th	July 10, 1889	High	1,620.00
[illegible], Miss A. M.	Fifth	Dec. 14, 1892	Grammar	1,164.00
Dunn, Miss M. L.	Eighth	Aug. 13, 1892	Grammar	1,224.00
Krauss, Miss L. H.	Seventh	Sept. 4, 1890	Grammar	1,224.00
Greathead, Mrs. A. L.	Eighth	June 24, 1884	Grammar	1,224.00
[illegible], Mrs. M.	Seventh	Jan. 29, 1871	Grammar	1,224.00
[illegible], Miss M.	Sixth	Aug. 2, 1909	Grammar	900.00
Canar, Mrs. E. R.	Seventh	Nov. 5, 1897	Grammar	1,224.00
Doherty, Miss M. E.	Sixth	Oct. 29, 1891	Grammar	1,164.00
[illegible], Miss Maud L.	Fourth	Nov. 1, 1904	Grammar	1,164.00
[illegible], Miss M.	Fifth	July 14, 1895	Grammar	1,164.00
Stewart, Miss V.	Third and Fourth	Mar. 15, 1884	Grammar	1,164.00
Lyons, Miss K. G.	Fifth	Dec. 20, 1896	Grammar	1,164.00
[illegible], Eva M.	First	Sept. 14, 1892	Grammar	1,224.00
Boland, [illegible] M.	First	Sept. 18, 1875	Grammar	1,224.00
[illegible], Mary I.	Second	Mar. 11, 1873	Grammar	1,164.00
Brown, Mrs. [illegible] M.	First	Feb. 13, 1871	Grammar	1,224.00
Blument[illegible], Miss A. A.	Sixth	Jan. 13, 1892	Grammar	1,164.00
[illegible], Miss [illegible]	Third	Jan. 10, 1910	Grammar	840.00
Haslan, Mrs. J. Pearl	[illegible]	June 14, 1903	Grammar	1,224.00
Manning, Miss F. E.	Second	July 24, [illegible]	Grammar	840.00
Cooper Primary—				
Brogan, Mrs. K. E.	Principal	Nov. 15, 1882	Grammar	1,800.00
Murray, Miss M. G.	Second	Nov. 11, 1907	Grammar	1,020.00
Eager, Miss N. V.	Second	Mar. 21, 1909	Grammar	900.00
Boukofsky, Miss S.	Fourth	Feb. 11, 1891	Grammar	1,164.00
Paterson, Miss M.	First	Aug. 14, 1905	Grammar	1,224.00

Name	Class	Date of Appointment	Grade	Salary
[illegible]n, Miss I.	First	Jan. 18, 1888	[illegible]	1,344.00
[illegible]n, Miss L.	First	Aug. 1905	[illegible]	1,224.00
[illegible]ks, Miss A. [illegible]	Second	Aug. 16, 1888	Gr[illegible]mar	1,164.00
[illegible]l, Miss M. K.	First	Aug. 10, 1882	G[illegible]mar	1,224.00
[illegible]n, Miss Florence	Third	July 27, 1898	[illegible]	1,164.00
[illegible]s, Miss L. B.	Second	Sept. 3, 1883	Grammar	1,164.00
Duncan, Miss C. L.	First	Aug. 4, 1882	[illegible]	1,224.00
Woodl[illegible], [illegible] I. C.	First	Dec. 1, 1882	[illegible]	1,224.00
Crocker [illegible]—				
[illegible]k, [illegible] C. W.	Principal	July 10, 1893	High	2,460.00
Murphy, [illegible]tte	Seventh	Dec. 20, 1890	[illegible]ar	1,224.00
[illegible]a, Miss [illegible]	V. P., Eighth	July 10, 1876	[illegible]	1,[illegible]00
[illegible]n, Miss S. A.	Eighth	Aug. 23, 1880	[illegible]	1,224.00
[illegible]h, Miss E. E.	Seventh	Jan. 7, 1895	[illegible]ar [illegible] Special	1,284.00
Durkin, Miss J. L. [illegible]	Seventh	Aug. 1, 1882	[illegible]	1,224.00
[illegible]tt, Miss Mary A.	Seventh	Sept. 2, 1896	[illegible]	1,224.00
[illegible]aw, Miss [illegible] M.	Seventh	Nov. 29, 1896	[illegible]	1,224.00
Armstrong, Miss N.	Seventh	Dec. 26, 1877	[illegible]	1,224.00
Burke, Miss Elizabeth T.	Eighth	April 3, 1892	Grammar	1,224.00
[illegible]y, [illegible]ie L.	Seventh	Nov. 4, 1886	[illegible]ar	1,224.00
[illegible], Miss E.	Fifth	July 6, 1905	[illegible]	1,164.00
[illegible]n, Frances E.	Sixth	Dec. 14, 1877	[illegible]	1,164.00
[illegible]er, Miss [illegible] L.	Sixth	June 23, [illegible]94	Grammar	1,224.00
Hefron, Miss Helen	Sixth	April 2, 1886	Gram[illegible]mar	1,164.00
[illegible]g, Miss B.	Sixth	June 23, 1904	[illegible]	1,224.00
[illegible]n, Miss Mary T.	Fifth	Dec. 10, 1890	[illegible]	1,164.00
English, [illegible]ia L.	Ungraded	Aug. 11, 1897	Grammar	1,224.00
[illegible]e, Mrs. J. E.	Fifth	Dec. 5, 1889	[illegible]	1,164.00
Daniel Webster—				
Coffey, Miss J. C.	Principal Third	Sept. 11, 1895	Grammar	1,560.00
Loewi, Miss M.	First	Jan. 26, 1898	Grammar	1,224.00

SCHOOLS AND TEACHERS—[illegible].

Name.	Grade of Class.	When [illegible].	Grade of [illegible].	Salary [illegible] Year.
[illegible] [illegible]— [illegible]tinued				
[illegible]k, [illegible]ss C. R.	First	Sept. 1, 1895	Gramm[illegible]r	1,224.00
Doran, [illegible]ss [illegible]e E.	F[illegible]rst	Sept. 4, 8[illegible]1	[illegible]	1,224.00
Carson, Alice M.	Second	Feb. 12, 1906	[illegible]	1,140.00
[illegible]n, Miss [illegible] G.	[illegible]	Aug. 20, 1907	[illegible]	1,080.00
[illegible]y, Miss [illegible]	Second	[illegible]. 10, 8[illegible]		1,164.00
[illegible], Miss [illegible] C.	[illegible]	[illegible]ril , [illegible]2	[illegible]	1,164.00
Anderson, [illegible]ss [illegible] E.	Third	[illegible]. 3, 1908	[illegible]	900.00
Hurley, [illegible]ss [illegible] [illegible]	Fourth	Jan. 19, 1910	Grammar	840.00
Gray, Miss [illegible] [illegible]	First	Sept. 2, 9[illegible]7	Grammar	1,224.00
[illegible] Grammar—				
[illegible]il[illegible], [illegible]	Princi[illegible]al	May 13, 1873	[illegible]	1,800.00
[illegible], J[illegible]ssie	E[illegible]hth	[illegible]. 10, 1863	High	1,224.00
D'Arcy, [illegible]ss [illegible] [illegible]	Fifth	July , 8[illegible]	[illegible]ar	1,164.00
[illegible]ell, [illegible]se A.	Eighth	Aug. 1, [illegible]4	Grammar	1,224.00
Lahaney, Katharin	[illegible]	[illegible]ril 2, [illegible]06	[illegible]	[illegible]
Fairweather, Eva	[illegible]	[illegible] 15, 1[illegible]	[illegible]	1,164.00
Harby, [illegible]ie	[illegible]	May 5, 1879	Gramm[illegible]r	1,224.00
Muldrup, [illegible] L.	Second	July 25, 910	[illegible]	840.00
Barrett, [illegible]	Second	April [illegible], [illegible]10	[illegible]	[illegible]
[illegible]sti[illegible], Miss J.	[illegible]	April 2, [illegible]	[illegible]	1,224.00
Douglass Primary—				
Tarpy, Miss W. L.	Principal	Aug. 19, 1884	Grammar	1,800.00
Hetzer, Miss M.	Fourth	Sept. 12, 1894	Grammar	1,164.00
Bishop, Louise M.	Fourth	Sept. 8, 1897	Grammar	1,164.00
Houghton, Miss E.	Third	Nov. 11, 1896	Grammar & Special	1,224.00
Doherty, Miss M. A.	Second	June 9, 1897	Grammar	1,164.00
Bush, Miss E. S.	First	Oct. 1, 1905	Grammar	1,224.00

Name	Grade	Date	Certificate	Salary
Parks, Miss M. R.	First	Sept. 15, 1891	Grammar & Special	1,224.00
Grafe, Miss L.	First	July 15, 1902	Grammar	1,224.00
Stewart, Miss A. R.	Third	Aug. 6, 1909	Grammar	900.00
Dowling, Miss E. P.	Second	Jan. 10, 1910	High	840.00
Mollett, Miss M. M.	Third	July 24, 1911	Grammar	840.00
Hill, Mrs. M. E.	First and Second	Feb. 21, 1872	Grammar	1,164.00
[illegible] Stone [illegible]—				
Earle, [illegible]ss S. [illegible]	[illegible]rincipal	July 20, [illegible]69	Grammar	1,800.00
Newman, Bertha [illegible]	Third	[illegible] 1, 1[illegible]04	[illegible]	1,164.00
[illegible], Miss [illegible]	First	Sept. 20, 8[illegible]4	[illegible]	1,344.00
[illegible]re, [illegible]ss F.	[illegible]	Oct. 21, 8[illegible]3	[illegible]	1,164.00
[illegible]n, [illegible]ss M. L.	Fourth	Sept. 16, [illegible]85	Primary & Special	1,224.00
[illegible]h, Miss L.	Third	[illegible] 11, 1903	Grammar	[illegible]
Gambitz, Miss Natalie	Second	Nov. 11, 1[illegible]	[illegible]	1,164.00
[illegible], Miss [illegible] C.	Second	Sept. 1, 8[illegible]7	[illegible]	1,164.00
[illegible]abitz, Miss L. [illegible]	Third	[illegible] [illegible], 1898	[illegible]	1,164.00
[illegible], Miss L. [illegible]	Second	July 1, 9[illegible]3	[illegible]	1,164.00
Cullen, Miss [illegible] A.	First	[illegible] 1, 8[illegible]3	[illegible]	1,224.00
[illegible]h, Miss R.	First	[illegible] [illegible], [illegible]4	[illegible]	1,224.00
Edison Primary—				
Saunders, Miss [illegible]	Principal	April 23, [illegible]87	[illegible]	1,800.00
[illegible]lly, Miss [illegible] C.	Fifth	[illegible] 8, 8[illegible]1	[illegible]	1,164.00
Barry, Miss [illegible]	Fifth	April 1, 1884	[illegible]	1,164.00
[illegible]r, Miss A. [illegible]	First	[illegible] 24, 1[illegible]8	[illegible]	1.224.00
Wilson, Miss [illegible] N.	Third	July [illegible], 1902	[illegible]	1,164.00
[illegible]n, Miss A. [illegible]	[illegible]	Sept. 19, 8[illegible]1	[illegible]	1,224.00
McDermott, Miss C. M.	[illegible]	Nov. 30, 8[illegible]2	[illegible]	1,164.00
Serex, Mrs. [illegible]	Third	Aug. 7, [illegible]83	[illegible]	1,164.00
Flanagan, Miss [illegible] A.	Fourth	Jan. 13, 1910	[illegible]	840.00
Porter, Miss [illegible]	Second	Jan. 28, 1907	Grammar	1,020.00
Egan, Mrs. K. T.	First	Mar. 1, 1897	Gr[illegible]	1,224.00

Name.	Grade of Class.	When Elected.	Grade of Certificate.	Salary per Year.
Emerson [illegible]—				
[illegible], [illegible] T. F.	Principal	July 17, 1901	[illegible] & Special	1,800.00
[illegible], [illegible] E.	First	Dec. 5, 1888	[illegible]	1,344.00
L[illegible]n, Miss A. M.	First	[illegible] 8, [illegible]	[illegible]	1,224.00
T[illegible]g, [illegible] A.	Second	Sept. 8, [illegible]	[illegible]	1,[illegible]4.00
[illegible], [illegible] M. L.	Third	Nov. 18, [illegible]	[illegible]	1,[illegible]4.00
[illegible], [illegible] [illegible] G.	Third	Sept. 10, [illegible]	[illegible]	1,164.00
Bailey, [illegible] C. B.	Third	Sept. 13, [illegible]	Grammar	1,[illegible]4.00
[illegible], [illegible] M. F.	[illegible]	[illegible] 13, [illegible]	Grammar	1,[illegible]4.00
[illegible]itz, [illegible] L. B.	[illegible]	[illegible] 27, [illegible]	[illegible]	1,[illegible]4.00
[illegible], [illegible] [illegible] A.	[illegible]	[illegible] 12, 1890	[illegible]	1,224.00
[illegible], [illegible] R.	First	[illegible] 22, 1884	[illegible]	1,224.00
Spafford, [illegible] [illegible] B.	Second	Jan. 8, [illegible]	[illegible]	1,[illegible]4.00
[illegible], Miss C.	Second	[illegible] 25, 1905	[illegible]	1,164.00
Estes, Miss C.	Fourth	Oct. 14, [illegible]	[illegible]	1,020.00
[illegible], Charlotte S.	Third	Oct. 30, [illegible]	[illegible]	840.00
Ethan Allen—				
Alexander, Miss R.	Principal	Oct. 5, 1888	[illegible]	1,680.00
Levy, Miss A.	Second	Jan. 5, 1891	[illegible]	1,320.00
Classen, Miss L. M.	Ungraded	April 9, 1875	[illegible]	1,320.00
Everett [illegible]—				
[illegible], Selden	Principal	[illegible] 6, [illegible]	[illegible]	2,340.00
[illegible], Miss A. J.	Eighth	[illegible] 20, [illegible]	[illegible]	1,224.00
Devine, [illegible] M. E.	Seventh	[illegible] 14, [illegible]	[illegible]	1,164.00
[illegible], Marie J.	Seventh	Feb. 1, 1876	[illegible]	1,2[illegible]4.00
[illegible], [illegible] A. L.	Sixth	[illegible] 14, [illegible]	[illegible]	[illegible]
[illegible], Miss R. I.	Fifth	[illegible] 27, [illegible]	[illegible]	1,164.00
Sullivan, [illegible] F.	[illegible]	Aug. 1, [illegible]	[illegible]	1,164.00
Perl, [illegible] May	Fifth	Nov. 1, [illegible]	[illegible]	1,164.00

Name	Grade	Date	Training	Salary
[illegible], [illegible] [illegible] R.	Third	July 27, [illegible]	[illegible]	1,164.00
Spafford, [illegible] E.	Second	Jan. 6, [illegible]	[illegible]	1,164.00
[illegible], [illegible] N. A.	[illegible]	July 30, [illegible]	[illegible]	1,164.00
Gracier, [illegible] A. J.	First	[illegible] 6, 1877	[illegible]	1,224.00
[illegible], Mrs. [illegible] W.	First	Jan. 3, [illegible]	[illegible]	1,224.00
[illegible], Mrs. K. J.	[illegible]	April 3, 1887	Grammar	1,224.00
[illegible], [illegible] M.	V. P., 8th	[illegible]	Gramm[illegible]	1,620.00
Moore, [illegible] M.	[illegible]	April 5, [illegible]	[illegible]	1,224.00
[illegible], [illegible]	[illegible]	Mar. 30, [illegible]	L. D. Grammar	1,164.00
[illegible], Miss E. M.	Fifth	[illegible] 24, [illegible]	[illegible]	840.00
Erb, Miss N. V.	Third	[illegible] 28, [illegible]	High	1,164.00

Fairmount Grammar—

Name	Grade	Date	Training	Salary
De Bell, [illegible] W. H.	Principal	July [illegible], [illegible]	[illegible]	2,460.00
[illegible], Miss Kathryn	V. P., 8th	Jan. [illegible], [illegible]	[illegible]	1,620.00
[illegible], [illegible] E. [illegible]	[illegible]	Dec. 1, [illegible]	Grammar	1,224.00
Berard, Miss [illegible]	Eighth	Sept. 30, [illegible]	[illegible]	1,[illegible]24.00
[illegible], Miss M. A.	Fifth	Aug. 1, 1897	Grammar	1,164.00
Fall[illegible], [illegible] D. A.	[illegible]	[illegible]	[illegible]	1,[illegible]24.00
Chandler, [illegible] G.	Second	Mar. 1, [illegible]	[illegible]	1,[illegible]64.00
Provost, [illegible] C. E.	[illegible]	[illegible] 14, 1875	[illegible]	1,[illegible]64.00
O'Brien, [illegible]	Fourth	Nov. 19, [illegible]	[illegible]	1,[illegible]64.00
[illegible], [illegible] Mary [illegible]	First	[illegible] 27, [illegible]	[illegible]	1,224.00
[illegible], [illegible]	Fourth	[illegible] 10, [illegible]	[illegible]	840.00
[illegible], Mrs. [illegible] F.	[illegible]	Sept. 16, 1879	[illegible]	1,284.00
Smith, Mrs. [illegible]	[illegible]	Sept. 2, [illegible]	[illegible]	840.00
King, Miss [illegible] A.	Sixth	Sept. 6, [illegible]	[illegible]	840.00
[illegible], Miss K. [illegible]	Sixth	April 4, [illegible]	[illegible]	840.00
Burke, [illegible] A.	Sixth	[illegible] 10, [illegible]	[illegible]	840.00
O'Connor, Miss N. [illegible]	Third	[illegible] 23, [illegible]	[illegible]	1,164.00
[illegible], Miss [illegible]	Sixth	[illegible] 28, [illegible]	[illegible]	1,140.00
[illegible], Miss [illegible] G.	First	[illegible] 23, [illegible]	[illegible]	1,224.00
Bai[illegible], Miss [illegible] J.	Seventh	June [illegible], [illegible]	[illegible]	840.00

Name.	Grade of Class.	When Elected.	Grade of Certificate.	Salary per Year.
Fairmount Grammar—Continued				
Traynor, Miss M. E.	First	Jan. 3, 1876	[illegible]	1,224.00
Flanagan, Miss I. R.	Fifth	Jan. 31, 1910	[illegible]	900.00
Marsh, Miss A. G.	Fifth	Aug. 26, 1903	[illegible]	1,164.00
Farragut Primary—				
[illegible], Miss T. E.	Principal	Jan. 3, [illegible]	[illegible]	1,560.00
[illegible], Miss J.	First	Jan. 21, [illegible]	[illegible]	1,224.00
[illegible], Miss G. A.	First	June 25, 1904	[illegible]	1,224.00
[illegible], Miss J.	Third	Aug. 3, 1[illegible]98	[illegible]	960.00
[illegible], Miss H. R.	Fourth	Aug. 3, [illegible]	[illegible]	960.00
Caswell, Miss A. E.	Second	Jan. 13, [illegible]	[illegible]	840.00
[illegible], Miss M. T.	Third	Aug. 21, [illegible]	[illegible]	1,164.00
Frank [illegible]—				
[illegible], Miss S. B.	Principal	Oct. [illegible], [illegible]	[illegible]	2,160.00
[illegible], Miss E. J.	First	Mar. 1, 1884	[illegible]	1,2[illegible]
Jacobs, Miss [illegible]	Fifth	Sept. 1, 1905	High	[illegible]4.00
O'Neil, Miss [illegible]	Second	Sept. [illegible], 1898	[illegible]	1,164.00
Hart, Miss E. I.	[illegible]	July 18, [illegible]	[illegible] Special	1,164.00
[illegible], Miss L. M.	First	July 30, 1886	[illegible]	1,224.00
Irwin, Miss [illegible]	Fourth	Nov. 4, 1891	Gram. [illegible] Spec.	1,164.00
Fay, Miss M. A.	First	Mar. 11, [illegible]	[illegible]	1,284.00
Brierton, Miss Mary	Eighth	Jan. 2, 1897	[illegible]	1,224.00
[illegible], Miss E.	Second	Aug. 3, 1908	[illegible]	900.00
Love, Mrs. J. S.	Fourth	Oct. 19, 1875	[illegible]	1,164.00
[illegible], Miss L. B.	[illegible]	Aug. 1, 1888	[illegible]	840.00
[illegible], [illegible] C. B.	[illegible]	Aug. 1, [illegible]	Grammar	1,224.00
[illegible], Miss N. C.	[illegible]	Mar. 22, 1907	[illegible]	1,080.00
[illegible]all, Miss [illegible] S.	Seventh	May 2, [illegible]	[illegible]	840.00
Meek, Miss [illegible]	Sixth	July 25, [illegible]	[illegible]	840.00
Bailie, Miss [illegible]	Fifth	June 9, [illegible]	[illegible]	1,164.00

Franklin Grammar—

Name	Grade	Date			Certificate	Salary
[illegible], [illegible]s. N. A.	[illegible]al	Nov.	13,	[illegible]	[illegible]h	[illegible]
Harris, [illegible] R. S.	h[illegible]h	[illegible]	30,	[illegible]	Grammar	1,344 [illegible]
[illegible]d, Miss [illegible] [illegible]	[illegible]	[illegible]	3,	[illegible]	Grammar	1,164.00
McCullough, Miss [illegible] J.	[illegible]th	Aug.	22,	1907	[illegible]	1,224.00
[illegible]r, [illegible] B.	First	Nov.	23,	[illegible]	[illegible]	1,224.00
[illegible]n, [illegible]iss C. [illegible]	F[illegible]	[illegible]t.	22,	1884	[illegible]	1,224.00
Parker, [illegible] A. A.	[illegible]	[illegible]t.	27,	[illegible]	[illegible]	900.00
Miller, Miss [illegible]tta F.	Fourth	[illegible]	15,	[illegible]	[illegible]	1,080.00
[illegible]n, Miss [illegible] A.	Fourth	[illegible]	[illegible]	[illegible]	[illegible]	840.00
[illegible]s, Miss E. G.	Third	[illegible]il	4,	[illegible]	[illegible]	840.00
Kellogg, [illegible] A.	[illegible]	Aug.	3,	[illegible]	[illegible]	1,056.00
[illegible] [illegible] [illegible] A.	Fourth	[illegible]	[illegible]	[illegible]	[illegible]	840.00
La[illegible]g, Miss F.	Third	[illegible]	[illegible]	[illegible]	[illegible]	840.00

Fremont Grammar—

Name	Grade	Date			Certificate	Salary
[illegible]ldsmith, Miss R.	[illegible]	[illegible]	6,	[illegible]	Grammar	2,340.00
Ostrom, Mrs. I. D.	V. P., [illegible]hth	[illegible]	10,	[illegible]	Grammar	1,620.00
Moran, Miss [illegible] F.	[illegible]	[illegible]	1,	1898	Gram. and Special	1,164.00
Hanley, Nora B.	[illegible]d	[illegible]t.	30,	[illegible]	Grammar	1,224.00
Rosenfeld, Miss F.	First	Aug.	1,	[illegible]	[illegible]	1,224.00
Mount, Miss S. F.	[illegible]	[illegible]	31,	[illegible]	Grammar	1,224.00
Luis, [illegible] R.	[illegible]	[illegible]t.	27,	[illegible]	[illegible]	1,[illegible]4.00
[illegible]Nichol, Mrs. [illegible] E.	Second	[illegible]t.	27,	[illegible]	[illegible]	1,[illegible]4.00
[illegible]is, [illegible]e F.	[illegible]	[illegible]	28,	[illegible]	[illegible]	1,[illegible]4.00
Shorb, Mrs. [illegible] [illegible]	Fourth	[illegible]t.	21,	[illegible]	[illegible]	1,[illegible]4.00
Grant, Mrs. K. [illegible]	[illegible]th	June	3,	[illegible]	[illegible]	1,[illegible]24.00
Ramage, Miss E. [illegible]	Fifth	[illegible]t.	17,	[illegible]	[illegible]	1,[illegible]4.00
[illegible]h, Miss R. [illegible]	Third	[illegible]	[illegible]	[illegible]	[illegible]	1,164.00
Macks, [illegible] J. A.	Seventh	[illegible]	[illegible]	[illegible]	[illegible]	840.00
Wil[illegible], Miss [illegible]	Fifth	Jan.	9,	[illegible]	[illegible]ar	840.00
Greenwo[illegible]d, Miss V.	Sixth	[illegible]	[illegible]	[illegible]	[illegible]	840.00
Robinett, Miss M. C.	Third	[illegible]	5,	[illegible]	Grammar	1,164.00

SCHOOLS AND TEACHERS—Continued.

Name.	Grade of Class.	When Elected.	Grade of [illegible]te	Salary pr Year.
Garfield Primary—				
Scherer, [illegible]s M. A.	[illegible]al	Ag. 7, [illegible]9	Grammer	2,160.00
[illegible], Mrs. E.	[illegible]	Jan. 17, [illegible]0	[illegible]r	840.00
Barkley, [illegible]s A.	[illegible]	[illegible]t. 27, [illegible]9	[illegible]h	900.00
[illegible]n, Mrs. I.	F[illegible]st	[illegible]y 28, [illegible]8	[illegible]r	1,224.00
Lynch, [illegible]s F. C.	First	Spt. 22, [illegible]5	[illegible]r	1,224.00
Wehrli, Miss E.	[illegible]t	[illegible]. 29, [illegible]5	[illegible]r	1,284.00
[illegible]r, Mary E.	First	[illegible]b. 1, [illegible]5	Life Dipl[illegible]ma	1,224.00
[illegible]s, Teresa	First	Oct. 17, [illegible]4	[illegible]h	1,344.00
B[illegible]h, [illegible]s [illegible] E.	Fourth	Aug. 27, 1907	[illegible]h	1,164.00
[illegible]w, [illegible]s [illegible]	Fourth	Jan. 29, 1906	L. D. [illegible]r	1,164.00
[illegible]n, [illegible]s M. R.	[illegible]d	April [illegible], [illegible]08	[illegible]h	[illegible]0.00
[illegible]s, [illegible]s [illegible]	Third	Nov. 3, [illegible]64	[illegible]h	1,164.00
Carroll, [illegible]s L. A.	First	Dec. 27, 1896	[illegible]r	1,224.00
Haussler, Miss M.	First	Dec. 28, 1885	[illegible]r	1, 24.00
[illegible]e, [illegible]s M.	[illegible]l	July 22, 1896	[illegible]cial	1, 24.00
Von [illegible]r [illegible]th, Miss O.	[illegible]	April 18, [illegible]0	[illegible]r	[illegible]0.00
Kelly, [illegible]s J. G.	Third	Oct. 19, [illegible]0	[illegible]r	840.00
Le Fevre, [illegible]s S.	[illegible]h	June 12, [illegible]1	Grammar	840.00
Grover, Mrs. E. J.	Third	Aug. 27, [illegible]7	[illegible]r	1,140.00
King, Miss S. A.	Third	July 24, [illegible]1	[illegible]r	840.00
Glen Park Grammar—				
Wade, Miss Janet	Principal	Jan. 2, [illegible]8	Grammar	2,160.00
Ganter, Miss C.	Fourth	Nov. 6, [illegible]9	Grammar	900.00
Doran, Julia A.	Sixth-Eighth	[illegible]. 7, 89	Grammar	1,500.00
McCarty, Miss A.	Seventh	Oct. 4, [illegible]7	Grammar	1,224.00
Crowley, Miss A. T.	First	[illegible]y 6, [illegible]7	Grammar	1,224.00
Glennon, Miss I. T.	Sixth	[illegible]t. 2, [illegible]3	Grammar	1,164.00
Crowley, Miss Mary E.	Third	Mar. 5, [illegible]8	Grammar	1,164.00

McGuire, [illegible] Mary	[illegible]	[illegible]il 7, [illegible]	[illegible]	1,164.00
Barron, Miss C. [illegible]	First	[illegible]. [illegible], [illegible]	[illegible]	1,224.00
[illegible], Mrs. J. H.	First	[illegible]. 20, 1877	Grammar	1,224.00
Gray, Mrs. O. P.	Fifth	July [illegible], [illegible]	[illegible]	840.00
[illegible]tt, Miss L.	Third	[illegible] 1, [illegible]	[illegible]	1,164.00
[illegible], Mrs. V. E.	Sixth	April [illegible], [illegible]	[illegible]	1,164.00
[illegible], Miss F. A.	Fifth	[illegible]. [illegible], [illegible]	[illegible]	900.00
Bruce, [illegible] C. B.	Sixth	Aug. [illegible], [illegible]	[illegible]	840.00
Gol[illegible] Gate [illegible]—				
[illegible], Miss M.	Principal	[illegible]. 16, [illegible]	[illegible]	1,800.00
[illegible], Mary L.	[illegible]	[illegible]. 20, [illegible]	[illegible]	1,164.00
[illegible], Mary A.	Fourth	[illegible]. 15, [illegible]	[illegible]	1,[illegible]
Bonnelli, Mrs. E. M.	Fourth	[illegible]. 5, [illegible]	Grammar	1,[illegible]
Ryan, Miss E. [illegible]	Third	[illegible]. 4, [illegible]	[illegible]	1,164.00
[illegible], Miss [illegible] E.	Third	Nov. 8, [illegible]	Grammar	1,[illegible]
Cashin, [illegible] G.	[illegible]	April 4, [illegible]	[illegible]	1,[illegible]
Hare, Mrs. K. [illegible]	First	[illegible]. 2, 1873	[illegible]	1,224.00
[illegible], Miss A. [illegible]	First	Mar. 1, 1879	[illegible]	1,224.00
Oral School for Deaf—				
Holden, Mrs. J. B.		Aug. 15, 1901	[illegible]cial	1,260.00
Holden, Mr. A. N.		Aug. 1, 1902	[illegible]cial	1,164.00
[illegible] Primary—				
Shaw, [illegible] I. E.	Principal	May 30, 1882	Grammar	1,800.00
[illegible], [illegible] B. C.	[illegible]	Nov. 1, [illegible]	[illegible]	1,224.00
Ryder, Miss V.	Seventh	Aug. 9, [illegible]	G[illegible]	1,224.00
[illegible], [illegible] A. B.	Fifth and Sixth	Jan. 12, 1898	[illegible]	1,164.00
B[illegible], [illegible] Cleva	Fourth-Fifth	Mar. 8, 1[illegible]	[illegible]	900.00
[illegible], [illegible] T.	[illegible]	Aug. [illegible], [illegible]	Grammar	1,164.00
Davidson, Miss E.	Third	Aug. [illegible], [illegible]	[illegible]	1,164.00
[illegible], [illegible] H. F.	First	Jan. 19, [illegible]	Grammar	840.00
Upchurch, Miss L. C.	[illegible]rth	Oct. 26, [illegible]	[illegible]	840.00

SCHOOLS AND TEACHERS—Continued.

Name.	Grade of Class.	When Elected.	Grade of Certificate.	Salary per Year.
Grattan Primary—				
Butler, Mrs. E.	Prin. [illegible] Second	Aug. [illegible], [illegible]	Grammar	1,560.00
[illegible], Miss E. A.	Third and Fourth	Oct. 1, 1877	Grammar	1,224.00
Sprague, Miss A. [illegible]	Fourth	Sept. [illegible], [illegible]	[illegible]	1,164.00
[illegible], M[illegible]s M.	Second	Feb. [illegible], [illegible]	Grammar	1,224.00
[illegible], Miss [illegible]	[illegible]	July [illegible], 1873	[illegible]	1,224.00
Maccord, Miss L.	Second	Feb. 5, [illegible]	Primary	1,164.00
[illegible], Miss A.	Third	July [illegible], [illegible]	Grammar	1,164.00
Drake, Miss [illegible]	Second	Aug. [illegible], [illegible]	[illegible]	1,164.00
Di[illegible]gs, Miss A. B.	First	July [illegible], [illegible]	[illegible]	1,164.00
Haight Primary—				
Haswell, M[illegible]s M. A.	Principal	June [illegible], 1867	High	1,800.00
[illegible], Stella M.	Fourth	Feb. [illegible], [illegible]	High	900.00
[illegible], [illegible] T.	Second	Aug. 3, [illegible]	[illegible]	900.00
[illegible], M[illegible]s C. L.	Fifth	Jan. 6, [illegible]	[illegible]	1,[illegible].00
Gilmore, M[illegible]s E. M.	Fourth	Nov. [illegible], 1897	[illegible]	1,164.00
Donovan, M[illegible]s E.	Fourth	July 14, [illegible]	Primary	1,164.00
Neppert, Miss F. E.	Third	July 25, 1904	[illegible]	1,164.00
Davidson, Mrs. T.	Second	Oct. 26, 1880	Primary	1,[illegible].00
McDevitt, Miss J.	First	July 20, 1903	[illegible]	1,224.00
Miller, Miss S. [illegible]	[illegible]	Nov. 5, 1866	High	1,224.00
Forsyth, M[illegible]s L. M.	First	Jan. 6, 1902	Gram. and S[illegible]al	1,284.00
[illegible], Miss R. C.	S[illegible]ond	July 29, 1889	Primary	1,164.00
[illegible], M[illegible]s J.	First	Aug. 3, 1905	[illegible]	1,224.00
Grace, Miss J. G.	Third	Aug. 19, 1907	[illegible]	1,140.00
[illegible], Miss G. M.	Third	Aug. 3, 1908	Grammar	1,140.00

Hamilton Grammar—

Name	Grade	Date	Certificate	Salary
Kellogg, Mr. A. E.	Principal	Sept. 1, [illegible]	[illegible]	2,340.00
Manley, [illegible] I. M.	Sixth	Aug. 12, [illegible]	[illegible]	1,164.00
Allen, Miss S. H.	Fifth	Oct. 24, [illegible]	[illegible]	1,164.00
[illegible], Mrs. [illegible] C.	[illegible]	Sept. 1, 1886	Grammar	1,224.00
Sheppard, Miss V.	Typewriting	Aug. 7, 1911	[illegible]	540.00
Hauselt, Miss [illegible] E.	[illegible]	July 18, 1902	Grammar	1,224.00
Brown, [illegible]	[illegible]	Aug. 5, 1885	[illegible]	1,224.00
Morton, [illegible] E. J.	Seventh, V.-Prin.	July 23, 1875	[illegible]	1,620.00
Strauss, [illegible] I. R.	Seventh	July 6, 1873	[illegible]	1,224.00
French, [illegible] I. B.	Seventh	Jan. 31, 1889	Grammar	1,224.00
Shaw, [illegible] L. A.	[illegible]	Aug. 14, 1895	Grammar	1,224.00
[illegible], Mary T.	[illegible]	Dec. 7, 1905	[illegible]	1,164.00
Brittan, [illegible] A. C.	Fifth	Sept. 30, [illegible]	Grammar	1,164.00
Martin, Miss I. C.	Sixth	July 25, 1901	High	1,164.00
Whitley, Miss A.	Seventh	Sept. 29, [illegible]	High	1,224.00
Silverberg, Miss [illegible]	[illegible]	Oct. 2, 1903	High	1,224.00

Hancock Grammar—

Name	Grade	Date	Certificate	Salary
[illegible], Miss N. G.	Principal	May 14, 1896	[illegible]	2,160.00
[illegible], Miss J.	Italian	Feb. 14, [illegible]	[illegible]	1,200.00
O'Neil, Miss [illegible]	Fourth	Oct. 14, 1905	[illegible]	1,164.00
Martini, Mrs. [illegible] G.	Eighth	Nov. 24, 1889	Grammar	1,560.00
Scanlan, Miss [illegible]	Seventh	Aug. 14, 1905	[illegible]	1,224.00
Burke, [illegible] C.	Third	Jan. 4, 1905	[illegible]	1,164.00
[illegible], [illegible] L. M.	[illegible]	Mar. 30, 1905	High	1,224.00
[illegible], [illegible] N. C.	Fourth	Aug. 14, 1905	High	1,140.00
[illegible], Miss [illegible] W.	Fifth	April 5, [illegible]	Grammar	1,164.00
[illegible], Mrs. N. [illegible]	[illegible]	Jan. 21, 1907	Grammar	1,224.00
Barry, [illegible] D.	Fifth	Mar. 3, 1910	[illegible]	840.00
Leibold, Mrs. [illegible]	Sixth	Mar. 23, 1911	[illegible]	1,164.00
Hartrick, Miss L.	Fifth	Aug. 22, [illegible]	[illegible]	1,164.00
McWilliams, Miss B.	[illegible]	Jan. 16, 1908	[illegible]	1,164.00

SCHOOLS AND TEACHERS—[illegible]

Name.	Grade of Class.	When Elected.	Grade of Certificate.	Salary per Year.
Hancock Grammar—Continued				
O'Connor, Miss V.	Third	Jan. 6, 1903	Grammar	1,164.00
Kurtz, Miss A.	Third	July 24, 1911	Grammar	840.00
Smith, Miss M. A.	Fifth	Jan. 16, 1911	Grammar	840.00
Harrison Primary—				
Moran, Miss M. R.	Principal, 3d & 4th	Aug. 9, 1890	Grammar	1,560.00
Dolan, Miss Mary J.	First	Feb. 3, 1888	Grammar	1,224.00
Griffin, Miss E. F.	Second	July 24, 1911	Grammar	840.00
Bonnell, Mrs. G. B.	Fourth	Oct. 29, 1894	Grammar	1,164.00
Hawthorne Primary—				
M[illegible], Mrs. S. J.	[illegible]	[illegible] 1, [illegible]	[illegible]	[illegible]
Curran, Mrs. [illegible] W.	[illegible]	[illegible] 1, [illegible]	Grammar	1,164.00
[illegible], Mrs.	[illegible]	Feb. 5, [illegible]	[illegible]	1,164.00
Barrett, [illegible]	Third	[illegible] 14, [illegible]	[illegible]	1,164.00
Simon, [illegible] F.	Second	[illegible] 1, [illegible]	[illegible]	1,164.00
[illegible], [illegible] N. [illegible]	First	[illegible] 12, [illegible]	[illegible]	1,224.00
Love, [illegible] M. L.	First	Sept. 8, [illegible]	[illegible]	1,224.00
[illegible], Mrs. [illegible]	[illegible]	Aug. 1, [illegible]	Grammar	840.00
[illegible]	[illegible]	Jan. [illegible], [illegible]	Grammar	840.00
[illegible], Miss [illegible]	Third	[illegible] 1, [illegible]	Grammar	1,164.00
[illegible], Miss [illegible]	First	[illegible] 1, [illegible]	[illegible]	1,008.00
Hinds, Miss [illegible]	First	[illegible] 3, [illegible]	[illegible]	1,224.00
Hearst Grammar—				
Sullivan, Miss N. F.	Principal	Aug. 13, 1876	Grammar	2,340.00
Franklin, Miss F. M.	V. P., Eighth	Dec. 28, 1880	Grammar	1,620.00
Haynes, Miss R. H.	Second	July 23, 1905	Grammar	1,164.00

Name	Grade	Date	Certificate	Salary
[illegible]mel, [illegible]	[illegible]h	Oct. 15, 1885	Grammar-Special	1,284 00
Bray, [illegible]s L. F.	Seventh	Jan. 5, [illegible]5	[illegible]r	1,224.00
Torpey, Miss [illegible] C.	S[illegible]h	Sept. 6, [illegible]7	[illegible]r	1,164.00
[illegible]s n, Miss [illegible] W.	Seventh	Jan. 2, [illegible]7	G [illegible]r	1,224.00
e[illegible]n, [illegible]s C. L.	Si[illegible]h	Sept. 2, [illegible]4	[illegible]r	1,164 00
Humphrey, [illegible]ss K. [illegible]	Fif[illegible]h	May 1, [illegible]6	[illegible]r	1,164.00
[illegible]n [illegible]n Bergh, [illegible]s F.	Fif[illegible]h	Aug. 9, [illegible]0	Grammar	1,164.00
[illegible]n, [illegible]s R.	Fif[illegible]h	Jan. 12, 1898	[illegible]r	1,164.00
[illegible], Mrs. B. [illegible]	[illegible]	July 1, [illegible]3	[illegible]y	1,164.00
Martin, [illegible]s [illegible]	Fourth	Sept. 1, [illegible]8	[illegible]r	1,164.00
[illegible]y, [illegible]s E. [illegible]	[illegible]	Oct. 29, 1877	[illegible]r	1,224.00
Haynes, Mrs. [illegible] S.	First	May 1, [illegible]6	[illegible]r	1,224.00
Grace, [illegible]s [illegible] M.	[illegible]	Dec. 29, 1896	High	1,224.00
[illegible], Miss [illegible] C.	First	Aug. 1, [illegible]2	[illegible]r	1,224.00
O'Neil, Mrs. N.	[illegible]urth	Dec. [illegible], [illegible]2	[illegible]r	1,164.00

Henry Durant Primary—

Name	Grade	Date	Certificate	Salary
[illegible], Mrs. M. [illegible]	Princi[illegible]al	Jan. 3, [illegible]7	[illegible]r	1,800.00
[illegible], [illegible]s R. A.	Fif[illegible]h	Jan. 3, 1877	[illegible]r	1,224.00
[illegible]l, Miss [illegible]	[illegible]h	April 29, 1886	[illegible]r	1,164.00
[illegible]s, [illegible]s L. F.	[illegible]h	Nov. 1, [illegible]7	[illegible]r	1,164.00
Ambrose, [illegible]s [illegible] R.	Third	July 15, 1895	[illegible]r	1,164.00
Loud, Mrs. E. S.	First	Nov. 2, [illegible]9	[illegible]r	1,224.00
[illegible]s, Miss C.	Second	July [illegible], [illegible]1	Grammar	1,164.00
[illegible]s, [illegible]s [illegible]	Second	May 14, 1890	[illegible]r	1,164.00
Hill, Mrs. M. E.	[illegible]rst	April 15, 1885	[illegible]r	1,224.00
Boukofsky, M[illegible]s R.	First	Sept. 1, [illegible]6	[illegible]r	1,224.00
[illegible]n, [illegible]s S. R.	First	Nov. 5, [illegible]5	[illegible]r	1,224.00
Smith, Mrs. [illegible] I.	Third	Jan. 10, [illegible]0	[illegible]y	900.00
[illegible]y, [illegible]s E. G.	[illegible]h	Nov. 17, [illegible]1	Gr[illegible]r	840.00
Mooney, Miss M. F.	Seventh	Jan. 26, 1898	[illegible]r	1,224.00
Clendenin, Miss M. G.	Fifth	July 24, 1911	[illegible]r	840.00

SCHOOLS AND TEACHERS—Continued.

Name.	Grade of Class.	When Elected.	Grade of Certificate	Salary per Year.
Horace Mann Grammar—				
Faulkner, Mr. Richard D.	Principal	Oct. 2, [illegible]88	High	2,460.00
Elliott, Mary	Seventh	Mar. [illegible], [illegible]89	Grammar and Special	1,224.00
Hatch, Mrs. L. [illegible]	[illegible]th	[illegible] 2, [illegible]81	Grammar	1,224.00
Carson, Miss [illegible]	[illegible]	Jan. 9, [illegible]84	Grammar	1,224.00
Grant, Miss [illegible] C.	Seventh	Jan. 16, [illegible]90	Grammar	840.00
[illegible]ll, Miss B.	Sixth	Aug. 6, [illegible]82	Grammar	1,164.00
Clary, Miss E.	Eighth	Mar. 11, [illegible]96	Grammar	[illegible]
Neppert, Miss J. M.	Eighth	Jan. 2, [illegible]95	Grammar-Special	1,284.00
[illegible], Mary E.	Eighth	July 26, [illegible]88	Grammar	1,224.00
O'Laughlin, Miss N.	Eight [illegible] V.-P.	June [illegible], [illegible]89	Grammar	1,620.00
[illegible], Miss N. F.	[illegible]th	July [illegible], [illegible]91	Grammar	840.00
[illegible], Miss N. E.	Eighth	Jan. [illegible], [illegible]91	Grammar	840.00
[illegible], Miss L.	[illegible]th	Jan. 21, [illegible]91	Grammar	840.00
Toland, Miss M.	Seventh	Feb. 19, 1906	Grammar	1,224.00
[illegible], Miss M. E.	[illegible]th	April 6, [illegible]85	Grammar	1,224.00
[illegible], Miss L.	Seventh	Sept. 30, [illegible]91	Grammar	1,224.00
[illegible], Miss E. D.	Seventh	Jan. 29, [illegible]91	Grammar	1,224.00
Cooney, Miss K.	Fifth	Jan. [illegible], [illegible]90	Grammar	840.00
Hunters Point School—				
Itsell, Mr. A. J.	Principal	July 10, 1871	High	1,500.00
Irving M. Scott Grammar—				
[illegible]ell, Miss A. T.	Principal	Jan. 8, [illegible]91	Grammar	2,340.00
[illegible], Miss M.	Seventh	Sept. 1, [illegible]86	Grammar	1,500.00
[illegible]t, Mary A.	Fourth	Feb. 23, [illegible]88	Grammar	1,164.00
Bryan, Miss E. M.	Fifth	Feb. 5, [illegible]96	Grammar	1,164.00
Gaffney, Miss A. M.	Third	Oct. 6, [illegible]94	Grammar	1,164.00
[illegible], Miss K. M.	Fifth-Sixth	Aug. 21, [illegible]97	Grammar	1,164.00
Kincaid, Miss May	Second	Mar. 30, [illegible]95	Grammar	1,164.00

Name	Grade	Date	School	Salary
Edwards, Frances M.	First	Nov. 30, 1892	Grammar	1,224.00
Stack, Miss C. M.	First	Sept. 12, 1887	Grammar	1,224.00
Huntley, Miss A. M.	First	Oct. 21, 1873	Grammar	1,224.00
Schoenitzer, Miss M.	Sixth	Mar. 7, 1912	High	840.00
Rothke, Miss I. A.	Third	July 24, 1911	Grammar	840.00
Staples, A. L.	Fifth	Aug. 4, 1911	Grammar	1,164.00
Boyle, Miss M.	First	July 23, 1875	Grammar	1,224.00
James Lick Grammar—				
Timmons, N. M.	Seventh	July 24, 1911	Grammar	840.00
Lewis, H. C.	Fifth	Jan. 2, 1911	Grammar	840.00
Strahle, H. A.	Sixth	[illegible] 9, 1911	Grammar	840.00
Graham, Miss E. M.	Principal	Oct. 8, 1879	High	2,223.00
Lewis, Miss F. R.	V. P., 8th	June 10, 1879	Grammar	1,908.00
Torpey, Miss M. M.	Seventh	[illegible] 19, 1892	Grammar	1,224.00
[illegible], Miss I. M.	Eighth	Sept. 1, 1886	Grammar	1,382.00
Kilpatrick, Grace S.	Seventh	June 21, 1904	[illegible] [illegible] Special	1,224.00
[illegible], Miss M.	Fifth	Nov. 18, 1893	[illegible]	840.00
[illegible], Miss P.	Fifth	Aug. 13, 1872	[illegible]	1,164.00
Johnson, Miss E. M.	Sixth	Mar. 30, 1905	Grammar	1,224.00
Kennedy, [illegible]	First	Mar. 1, 1895	Special	[illegible]
[illegible], Miss C. V.	Sixth	Jan. 19, 1905	[illegible]	1,164.00
Hogan, Miss H. M.	[illegible]	Sept. 30, 1900	Grammar	1,224.00
[illegible] Parker Grammar—				
Pechin, Mrs. C. R.	Principal	Sept. 12, 1871	[illegible]	2,160.00
[illegible], Miss I. C.	V.-P., 7th & 8th	April 10, 1874	Grammar	1,620.0.0
McCorkell, Miss L.	Eighth	Aug. 3, [illegible]	Grammar	1,224.00
Anderson, Miss J.	Fifth	July 23, 1[illegible]	Grammar	1,164.00
[illegible], Miss J. M.	First	Oct. 1, [illegible]	Grammar	1,224.00
[illegible], Miss Anna	First	July 22, 1882	Grammar	1,224.00
Heath, Miss R. E. L.	First	Aug. [illegible], [illegible]	Grammar	1,224.00
Beardsl[illegible], Miss E. F.	Ungraded	Mar. 3, [illegible]	Grammar	1,224.00

SCHOOLS AND TEACHERS—Continued.

Name.	Grade of Class.	When Elected.	Grade of [illegible]e.	Salary [illegible] [illegible]r.
Jean Parker Grammar—Continued				
Dworzarek, Miss B. E.	Second	Jan. 3, [illegible]	[illegible]	1,164.00
[illegible], Miss E.	[illegible]	[illegible] 2, [illegible]	High	1,224.00
[illegible], Sarah E.	Third	Sept. 1, [illegible]	Grammar	1,164.00
[illegible], Miss R. V.	S[illegible]ond	[illegible] 7, [illegible]	Grammar	960.00
[illegible], Miss [illegible]	Fifth	Mar 10, [illegible]	[illegible]	840.00
Casey, Miss M.	[illegible]	June 6, [illegible]	[illegible]	1,164.00
[illegible], Mrs. L. D.	Fifth	Jan. 6, [illegible]	[illegible]	1,164.00
[illegible], Miss I. M.	[illegible]hth	[illegible] 24, [illegible]	[illegible]	840.00
Carroll, Miss [illegible]	Fourth	June 25, [illegible]	[illegible]	1,164.00
McBoyle, Miss A. B.	F[illegible]rth	Sept. 30, [illegible]	[illegible]	1,164.00
Jefferson Primary—				
McDonald, Miss A. A.	Fifth	Aug. 3, 1908	Grammar	900.00
Jones, E. A.	Sixth	July [illegible], 1911	Grammar	840.00
Roberts, Miss B. E.	Prin. & Fifth	Jan. 2, 1902	Grammar-Special	1,320.00
Carmichael, Miss B.	Third	[illegible] [illegible], 1910	Grammar	840 00
Brown, Miss M. L.	Seventh	[illegible] [illegible], 1908	Grammar	1,224.00
[illegible]n Swett Grammar—				
Dazy, A. D.	[illegible]rth	Mar. 8, [illegible]	[illegible]	840.00
Duggin, Mrs. M. E.		[illegible] 4, [illegible]	Grammar	1,164.00
[illegible], Mrs. M. M.	[illegible]ci[illegible]al	[illegible]r. 4, [illegible]	[illegible]al	2,160.00
Scherin, Mrs. L. B.	Third	July 10, [illegible]	Gramm[illegible]r	1,164.00
[illegible], Miss K.	[illegible]	Aug. 10, [illegible]	Grammar	1,224.00
McCarty, Mrs. E. B.	[illegible]	[illegible] 27, [illegible]	[illegible]	1,224.00
Carroll, [illegible]	[illegible]	[illegible] 9, [illegible]	Grammar	1,224.00
Horgan, Miss K.	Fourth	[illegible] 26, [illegible]	[illegible]	1,164.00
Erkson, Mrs. J. H.	[illegible]	Sept. 1, [illegible]	Grammar	1,164.00
[illegible], Mrs. E. M.	First	[illegible]ec. [illegible], [illegible]	[illegible]	1,224.00

Name	Grade	Date		Certificate	Salary
Alderson, Mrs. A. E.	First	Mar. 3, 1888		Grammar	1,224.00
Williams, Mrs. M. C.	Fifth	Nov. [illegible], 1877		Grammar	1,164.00
Walsh, Miss M. U.	Eighth	June [illegible], 1895		Grammar	1,224.00
Lalande, Miss A. H.	Eighth & V.-P.	July 5, 1878		Grammar and Special	1,500.00
Corbett, Miss L.	Third	Feb. 8, 1911		Grammar	840.00

Junipero Serra—

Name	Grade	Date		Certificate	Salary
Sullivan, Miss N. M.	Principal	[illegible] [illegible], 1877		Grammar	2,160.00
[illegible], [illegible] [illegible] L.	Second	Aug. [illegible], 1867		Grammar	1,164.00
[illegible], [illegible] May	First	[illegible] 2, 1904		[illegible]	1,224.00
Foley, El[illegible] [illegible]	Second	Nov. [illegible], 1896		[illegible]	1,164.00
Cohen, [illegible] G. J.	First	Jan. 1, 1895		[illegible]	1,224.00
Laven, Mrs. S. [illegible]	First	[illegible] 1, 1879		[illegible]	[illegible]224.00
O'Reilly, [illegible] J. F.	First	[illegible] [illegible], 1897		[illegible]	1,224.00
[illegible], [illegible] P. A.	[illegible]	[illegible] 2, 1897		[illegible]	1,224.00
[illegible], Clara A.	First	Jan. 2, 1871		[illegible]	1,224.00
Parker, [illegible] M.	Third	Nov. [illegible], 1907		[illegible]	1,104.00
[illegible], Miss M. E.	Third	[illegible] 25, 1908		[illegible]	[illegible]
[illegible], Miss M.	Second	Jan. [illegible], 1906		[illegible]	1,164.00
[illegible], Miss [illegible] E.	[illegible]	[illegible] [illegible], 1909		[illegible]	900.00
[illegible], [illegible] M. [illegible]	Third	[illegible] 30, 1905		[illegible]	1,164.00
[illegible]ell, Miss A. C.	Third	Jan. 11, 1910		High	[illegible]
Frank, [illegible] J.	Second	[illegible] 13, 1896		[illegible]	1,164.00
[illegible], [illegible] [illegible] A.	Second	[illegible] 1, 1911		Grammar	840.00
Hill, Miss [illegible] [illegible]	Third	July [illegible], [illegible]		Grammar	840.00

Kate Kennedy Primary—

Name	Grade	Date		Certificate	Salary
Quinlan, Mrs. F. L.	Principal	Aug. 1, 1884		Grammar	1,300.00
Bronson, Mrs. F. P.	First	Sept. 1, 1884		High	1,224.00
Mayers, Miss Eliz.	Third	Jan. 20, 1886		Grammar	1,164.00
Cooke, Edith A.	First	Mar. 1, 1903		Grammar	1,224.00
O'Connell, Miss A.	Fourth	July 6, 1905		Grammar	1,224.00
Hansell, Mrs. M.	First	Aug. 9, 1897		Grammar	1,224.00

SCHOOLS AND TEACHERS—[illegible]d.

Name.	Grade of Class.	When Elected.	Grade of Certificate	Salary per Year.
Kate Kennedy Primary—Continued.				
O'Connor, Miss E.	Second	Jan. 6, 1908	Gr	[illegible]80.00
D'Or, Miss M.	First	Sept. 6, 1901	Gr	1,224.00
Young, Miss M.	Fourth	July 6, 1905	Gr	1,164.00
O'Connell, Miss Mary C.	Second	July 8, 1902	Grammar	1,164.00
Cashman, Miss M.	Third	July 2, 1911	Gr	840.00
Orr, Miss A. C.	Third	Jan. 2, 1910	Gr	840.00
Lafayette Primary—				
Kervan, Miss I. M.	Principal	Sept. 9, 1872	Gr	1,560.00
Lissak, Miss M.	Kindergarten	Oct. 1, 1909	[illegible]rten	840.00
Bigelow, Mrs. S. H.	Second and Third	Sept. 1876	Gr	1,164.00
Sullivan, Miss H.	First	Aug. 2, 1905	Gr	1,224.00
Livingston, Miss N.	6th, 7th & 8th	Nov. 29	Grammar	840.00
Allen, Miss E.	Third	July 2, 1911	Gr	840.00
Longfellow Primary—				
Chalmers, Miss A.	Principal	Jan. 2, 1902	Gramm[illegible]r	1,560.00
Dwyer, Miss A. C.	Second	Mar. 2, 1905	[illegible]h	1,164.00
Meaney, Miss M. E.	Fifth	Aug. 7, 1893	Gr	1,164.00
O'Connor, Miss A. M.	First	Jan. 2, 1898	Gr	1,224.00
Wilcox, Miss M. A.	Third	Mar. 1, 1909	Gr	900.00
Laguna Honda School—				
O'Neal, Mrs. M. L.	Principal	Jan. 20, 1874	Grammar	2,340.00
Donnelly, Miss M. L.	Vice-Principal, 8th	July 2, 1875	Grammar	1,620.00
Carson, Mrs. N. E.	Seventh	July 14, 1898	High	1,224.00
Croughwell, Miss M. V.	Second	Aug. 1, 1904	Grammar	1,164.00
Lynch, Miss E.	Sixth	Feb. 25, 1905	Grammar	1,164.00
Holmes, Miss E. T.	Fifth	July 27, 1898	Grammar	1,164.00

Name	Grade	Date of Election	Certificate	Salary
[illegible]n, M[illegible]s M.	Fourth	July 6, 1905	[illegible]r	1,164.00
S[illegible]k, [illegible]s K.	Third	Jan. 3, [illegible]05	[illegible]h	1,164.00
[illegible]ff, Miss H. L.	Second	Feb. 1, [illegible]05	[illegible]r	1,164.00
[illegible]d, Miss [illegible] [illegible]	First	Sept. 30, [illegible]91	Grammar	1,224.00
[illegible], [illegible]s J.	First	Jan. [illegible] [illegible]87	[illegible]r	1,224.00
[illegible]s, [illegible]s B. E.	Third	Nov. [illegible], [illegible]95	[illegible]r	1,164.00
McKown, Mrs. M. E.	[illegible]th	April 14, [illegible]89	[illegible]h	1,164.00
[illegible]a, M[illegible]s L.	[illegible]h	Jan. 11, [illegible]90	[illegible]r	840.00
M[illegible]s, Mrs. A. F.	[illegible]	Sept. [illegible], [illegible]97	High [illegible]d Special	1,224.00

Lincoln Grammar—

Name	Grade	Date of Election	Certificate	Salary
S[illegible]e, Mr. [illegible] W.	Principal	[illegible]b. 11, 1873	High	1,800.00
Backman, Mrs. [illegible] L.	[illegible]h [illegible]d Eighth	Sept. 3, 1883	[illegible]r & Special	1,284.00
[illegible]d, M[illegible]s J.	Fourth	Jan. 21, 1907	[illegible]r	1,164.00
[illegible]d, Mrs. B. L.	First	[illegible] 29, 1884	[illegible]r	1,224.00
[illegible]r, M[illegible]s [illegible] E.	S[illegible]h	Feb. [illegible], [illegible]96	[illegible]r	1,224.00
[illegible]lly, Mr. [illegible] P.	[illegible]	M[illegible]r. [illegible], [illegible]90	[illegible]r	840.00
Barry, Miss Mary C.	[illegible]h	Feb. [illegible], [illegible]82	[illegible]	1,164.00
Drewry, Miss [illegible]	Second	Aug. 3, [illegible]98	[illegible]r	900.00

Madison Primary—

Name	Grade	Date of Election	Certificate	Salary
[illegible]t, [illegible]s E. F.	Principal	Aug. 5, 1885	[illegible]r	1,800.00
[illegible]b, Miss [illegible] S.	Second	Nov. 18, 1901	[illegible]r	1,164.00
Howard, M[illegible]s F. G.	[illegible]h	Dec. 30, 1892	[illegible]r	1,224.00
[illegible]s, M[illegible]s I. C.	[illegible]h	July 30, 1876	[illegible]r	1,164.00
[illegible]d, [illegible]s. A. E.	Third	July 27, 1898	[illegible]r	1,164.00
B[illegible]e, [illegible]s A. A.	F[illegible]st	Oct. 29, 1897	[illegible]r	1,224.00
Bannon, [illegible] F.	First	Jan. 3, 1873	[illegible]r	1,224.00
[illegible]n, M[illegible]s D. [illegible]	Seventh [illegible]d Sixth	Sept. 1, 1905	H[illegible]h	1,224.00
Tobriner, Miss E.	Fifth	Aug. 3, 1908	[illegible]h	960.00
[illegible], Miss [illegible] [illegible]	[illegible]h	Nov. 13, 1899	Gram. & Spec.	1,164.00
[illegible]ihy, Mrs. L.	Sixth	Feb. 12, 1906	Grammar	1,224.00

SCHOOLS AND TEACHERS—Continued.

Name.	Grade of Class.	[illegible] El[illegible]	Grade of Certi[illegible]	Salary [illegible]
[illegible]				
Bryan, [illegible] J.	Fourth	[illegible] [illegible], [illegible]	[illegible]	840.00
Kearns, Miss M.	First	July [illegible], [illegible]	Grammar	1,224.00
Martin, [illegible] F.	Principal	Aug. [illegible], [illegible]	[illegible]	1,800.00
[illegible], Miss M. C.	Third	Aug. 5, [illegible]	[illegible]	900.00
[illegible], [illegible] M. H.	Third	April [illegible], [illegible]	Gram. & [illegible]ec.	1,224.00
[illegible], [illegible] J.	[illegible]	[illegible] 1884	[illegible]	1,164.00
[illegible], [illegible]. L.	Third	Aug. 3, [illegible]	Grammar	[illegible].00
[illegible], [illegible] C.	Fourth	Oct. 19, [illegible]	[illegible]	1,164.00
Belding, Mrs. M. L.	Second	Nov. 21, [illegible]	[illegible]	1,164.00
[illegible], [illegible] C.	[illegible]	Dec. [illegible], [illegible]	[illegible]	1,224.00
[illegible], [illegible] F.	[illegible]	[illegible] [illegible], [illegible]	[illegible]	840.00
Elliot, [illegible] F.	First	[illegible]. 18, 1885	[illegible]	1,224.00
[illegible], [illegible] C. J.	F[illegible]	[illegible]. [illegible], [illegible]	[illegible]	1,224.00
Gray, Mrs. [illegible] W.	[illegible]	July [illegible], [illegible]	Primary	1,164.00
[illegible], Mary J.	First	July 9, 1895	[illegible]	1,224.00
[illegible]				
[illegible], [illegible] Cora	Principal	Aug. 6, [illegible]	[illegible]	1, [illegible]0.00
[illegible], [illegible] A. E.	Third	Aug. 2, [illegible]	[illegible]	1, [illegible]0.00
[illegible], [illegible] S.	[illegible] and Fifth	[illegible]. 3, [illegible]	[illegible]	1, [illegible]0.00
[illegible], [illegible]	Fifth	July 7, 1877	[illegible]	1, [illegible]4.00
Gurry, [illegible] Mary E.	[illegible]	April 2, [illegible]	Grammar	1, [illegible]4.00
[illegible], [illegible] M. J.	Ei[illegible]	Ja. [illegible], [illegible]	[illegible]	1,224.00
[illegible], [illegible] M. C.	Seventh	June 21, [illegible]	[illegible]	1,164.00
[illegible], [illegible] K.	F[illegible]	[illegible]. [illegible], [illegible]	[illegible]	1, [illegible]4.00
McKinney, Mary C.	Third	Nov. 7, [illegible]	[illegible]	1, [illegible].00
[illegible], [illegible] E.	[illegible]	[illegible]. 1, [illegible]	[illegible]	1, 24.00
Sarles, Mrs. [illegible]	First	[illegible] 7, [illegible]	[illegible]	1, 24.00
[illegible], Mary	[illegible]	June 6, [illegible]	[illegible]	1,164.00
Smith, [illegible] M. A.	Sixth	[illegible]. 3, [illegible]	[illegible]	1,164.00

Mission Grammar—

Name	Grade	Date	School	Salary
Onyon, [illegible] J.	Eighth	Jan. 31, 1889	[illegible]	1,224.00
Crowley, Miss [illegible] H.	[illegible]	Aug. 1, 1880	[illegible]	2,160.00
[illegible], [illegible] J. C.	V. P., 8th	Feb. 13, 1879	[illegible]	1,620.00
Doyle, [illegible] E.	High	Oct. 30, 1889	[illegible]	1,024.00
[illegible], Miss R. A.	Seventh	Aug. 15, 1888	[illegible]	1,024.00
[illegible], Mrs. M. A.	Fifth	Aug. 11, 1897	[illegible]	1,164.00
N on,e [illegible] A.	Seventh	Sept. 30, 1901	[illegible]	1,284.00
[illegible] G.	Sixth	May 15, 1883	[illegible]	1,224.00
Horn, [illegible] L. J.	Sixth	July 14, 1872	[illegible]	1,164.00
O'Brien, [illegible] A.	Sixth	Aug. 11, 1897	[illegible]	1,164.00
Doyle, [illegible] J.	Sixth	July 28, 1898	[illegible]	1,164.00
Harvey, [illegible]	Fifth	Oct. 30, 1890	[illegible]	1,164.00
[illegible], [illegible] S.	Sixth	July 18, 1902	Grammar	1,164.00
[illegible], Miss [illegible]	Fifth	July 24, 1911	Grammar	840.00

Monroe Grammar—

Name	Grade	Date	School	Salary
[illegible] A. [illegible]	Principal	Feb. 20, 1883	[illegible]	2,460.00
Harrower, [illegible] W.	V.-P., Eighth	Sept. 30, 1901	[illegible]	1,620.00
[illegible] M. R.	High	[illegible] 28, 1891	[illegible]	1,224.00
[illegible] E.	Fifth	Sept. 1, 1872	[illegible]	1,164.00
Curtin, Ella J.	Seventh	[illegible] 14, 1905	[illegible]	1,224.00
[illegible] J.	Seventh	Sept. 12, 1904	High	1,224.00
Maher, [illegible] J. G.	Sixth	[illegible] 2, 1884	[illegible]	1,384.00
—El [illegible], Miss L.	[illegible]	[illegible] 3, 1889	[illegible]	1,164.00
Fleming, Miss J.	First	[illegible] 13, 1890	[illegible]	1,224.00
Murphy, Miss J.	Fifth	[illegible] 9, 1911	[illegible]	840.00
Moran, [illegible] U.	Fourth	[illegible] 24, 1911	Grammar	840.00
Inglis, Mrs. [illegible]	[illegible]	[illegible] 24, [illegible]	Grammar	840.00
O'Brien, [illegible]	First	Nov. 30, 1881	[illegible]	1,224.00
Rahilly, Ella [illegible]	[illegible]	[illegible] 7, 1907	Grammar	1,224.00
[illegible], Miss N. E.	[illegible]	Aug. 22, 1907	High	1,224.00
O'Fl[illegible], Miss [illegible] E.	[illegible]rth	Oct. 28, 1907	[illegible]	1,164.00

SCHOOLS AND TEACHERS—Continued.

Name.	Grade of Class.	When Elected.	Grade of Certificate.	Salary per Year.
Monroe [illegible]—Continued.				
[illegible], [illegible] M [illegible]	First	Aug. 3, 1908	Grammar	1,080.00
Morgan, Miss L. V.	First	[illegible] [illegible], [illegible]	[illegible]	1,224.00
[illegible], [illegible] M.	Ungraded	[illegible] [illegible], [illegible]	[illegible]	1,224.00
[illegible], [illegible] C. N.	Fifth	[illegible] [illegible], [illegible]	[illegible]	840.00
[illegible], Miss G. E.	Third	[illegible] [illegible], [illegible]	[illegible]	840.00
[illegible], Mrs. K.	Second	[illegible] [illegible], 1884	[illegible]	1,164.00
[illegible], Miss N. C.	Second	Feb. [illegible], 1896	[illegible]	1,164.00
Moulder Primary—				
O'Connell, Miss A. M.	Principal	Sept. 7, 1884	Grammar	1,560.00
McGinnis, Miss G.	Third	Feb. 4, 1907	Grammar	1,164.00
Miel, Mrs. S. M.	Second	Mar. 1, 1900	Primary	1,164.00
Cadwalder, Edna	Fourth	June 21, 1895	Grammar	1,164.00
Deal, Miss V. V.	First	Dec. 30, 1892	Grammar	1,224.00
Hackett, Mrs. E. S.	First	Oct. 2[illegible] 1873	Grammar	1,224.00
[illegible]—				
[illegible], Mrs. E. H.	[illegible]	[illegible] 1, 1882	[illegible]	2,160.00
[illegible], Mrs. [illegible] V.	First	[illegible] [illegible], 1887	[illegible]	1,344.00
[illegible], Mrs. L.	First	[illegible] 1, 1903	Grammar	1,[illegible]24.00
[illegible], [illegible] E. D.	Second	[illegible] 12, 1903	[illegible] and Special	1,[illegible]84.00
[illegible], Miss L. M.	Second	[illegible] 23, 1907	Grammar	1,[illegible]00.00
[illegible], [illegible] G. S.	Second	[illegible] 23, 1907	[illegible]	1,020.00
[illegible], Elizabeth R.	Third	May 1, 1905	[illegible]	1,[illegible]64.00
Nolan, [illegible] [illegible] L.	Third	June 21, 1904	[illegible]	1,[illegible]64.00
Gray, Mrs. J. E.	Second	Dec. 15, 1890	[illegible]	1,[illegible]64.00
Lewis, Miss A.	Fourth	Jan. [illegible], 1910	Grammar	840.00
Torpey, [illegible] K. L.	Third	[illegible] 23, 1898	[illegible]	1,164.00
[illegible], Miss M. A.	[illegible]rth	[illegible] 30, 1901	[illegible]	1,164.00

Name	Grade	Date		Certificate	Salary
Gaffney Miss S. A.	Fourth	July	21, 1903	[illegible]	1,224.00
McLane, Miss H. E.	First	Dec.	14, 1892	Grammar	1,224.00
Conroy, Miss M. A.	Third	July	1898	[illegible]	1,164.00
Mulgrew, Miss A. M.	Fourth	Jan.	16, 1911	[illegible]	840.00
Francis Scott Key—					
Love, Miss M. L.	Principal	Sept.	8, 1897	Grammar	1,560.00
Hawkins, Miss B. C.	First	July	25, 1902	[illegible]	1,284.00
DeForest, Mrs. J. J.	Third	Feb.	25, 1904	[illegible]	1,164.00
Bartlett, Miss A. G.	Eighth	Oct.	27, 1904	High	1,224.00
Ashley, Miss B.	Seventh and Eighth	Jan.	11, 1910	High	840.00
Paul Revere—					
Delay, Mr. D. J.	Principal	July	8, 1882	High	1,320.00
Oriental Public—					
[illegible], Mrs. C. C.	Principal	Feb.	13, 1870	[illegible]	1,560.00
Greer, Jane E.	Second	June	10, 1868	High	1,164.00
Griffith, Miss A. C.	First	July	27, 1898	[illegible]	1,224.00
[illegible], Miss V. E.	Fourth	June	30, 1902	Grammar	1,164.00
[illegible], [illegible] F. R.	First	Sept.	12, 1904	High	1,164.00
Barrett, Miss K. C.	Sixth	Aug.	5, 1907	High	1,020.00
[illegible], Miss M. V.	First	Nov.	9, 1891	[illegible]	1,224.00
[illegible], Miss J. A.	Seventh and Eighth	Aug.,	10, 1904	Grammar	1,320.00
[illegible], Miss H. A.	Fifth	Feb.	12, 1906	[illegible]	1,080.00
O'Brien, Miss L.	First	Mar.	12, 1890	[illegible]	[illegible]
Pacific Heights Grammar—					
Belvel, Miss M. J.	Fifth	July	24, 1911	Grammar	840.00
Dugan, Miss T.	Fourth	July	24, 1911	Grammar	840.00
Stincen, Miss A. M.	Principal	June	[illegible], 1868	High	2,340.00
Stincen, Miss Ella E.	Second	April	16, 1907	[illegible]	1,080.00
Bliven, Miss F. M.	Eighth	Sept.	3, 1880	[illegible]	1,224.00
Earle, Miss C. B.	Eighth	Feb.	21, 1872	[illegible]	1,224.00

SCHOOLS AND TEACHERS—[illegible]ti[illegible]ed.

Name.	Grade of Class.	When El[illegible]ed.	Grade of Certificate	Salary [illegible]r Year.
a[illegible]ic [illegible]ts Grammar—Continued.				
Cook, Miss F. G.	Fifth	Dec. 4, 1904	Grammar	1,224.00
[illegible], [illegible]ne	Fifth	May [illegible], 1905	Grammar	1,224.00
Dreyfus, Miss R. E.	Sixth	Aug. 5, 1905	Grammar	1,224.00
[illegible]h, Emma F.	Sixth	Jan. 21, 1883	[illegible]r	1,164.00
[illegible]is, Mss A. C.	Sixth	April 18, 1883	[illegible]r	1,164.00
[illegible]i, Mss F. C.	Fourth	Jan. 3, 1905	Grammar	1,224.00
[illegible]r, Mss M.	Third	Jan. 4, 1902	High	1,164.00
Donohue, [illegible]s M. F.	Third	June 21, 1904	[illegible]r	1,164.00
[illegible]h, Mss G. M.	First	Nov. 2, 1878	[illegible]r	1,[illegible]4.00
Robertson, Miss A. C.	V. P., Eighth	July 16, 1867	High	1,620.00
Burnham, Miss C.	Fourth	Aug. 1, 1885	Grammar	1,164.00
Dowling, Mss A. C.	First	Sept. 5, 1897	Grammar	1,224.00
Ram, Dr. H.	German	Jan. 13, 1911	Hi[illegible]h	1,200.00
Peabody Primary—				
[illegible]r, Mss A. M.	Principal	[illegible]r. 17, 1879	[illegible]ar	1,560.00
[illegible]e, Mrs. M. E.	Fourth	[illegible]r. 1, 1880	Grammar	1,164.00
Harris, Miss E. L.	Third	[illegible]g. 3, 1908	Grammar	9[illegible]00
Watson, [illegible] M. G.	First	Jan. 12, 1898	Grammar	1,224.00
Duffy, Miss A. A.	[illegible]	Aug. 18, 1884	[illegible]r	1,164.00
[illegible]an, Miss N. E.	Second	Sept. 7, 1897	Grammar	1,164.00
Cavanagh, Mary E.	[illegible]rd	Aug. 3, 1908	[illegible]r	900.00
Ephriam, Miss A.	First	Dec. 2, 1882	Grammar	1,224.00
Parkside—				
Code, Mrs. E. S.	Primary	July 18, 1871	[illegible]igh	1,320.00
Portola—				
Mills, Mrs. I. E.	Principal	Nov. 20, 1877	[illegible]r	1,800.00
Gillespie, Miss J. H.	Sixth	Aug. 1, 1888	[illegible]	1,164.00

Name	Grade	Date	Certificate	Salary
[illegible]r, Miss E. H.	Fourth	July 20, 1903	Grammar	[illegible]0
Laverene, M[illegible]s C. J.	Third	[illegible] 28, 1907	Grammar	1,140.00
[illegible]n, Miss A. E.	First	April 29, [illegible]1	Grammar	1,224.00
Sullivan, Miss M.	First	[illegible]pt. 25, [illegible]5	Grammar	1,344.00
Ruff, Miss M.	Second	Feb. 2, [illegible]5	Grammar	1,164.00
[illegible]elland, Mrs. M.	Third	June 8, [illegible]8	Grammar	900.00
Ames, M[illegible]s I.	Third	Jan. 10, [illegible]1	Grammar	840.00
[illegible]s Roches, P.		J[illegible]n. 21, [illegible]1	[illegible]r	840.00
Davis, Miss F. V.	Second	[illegible]n. 15, [illegible]84	[illegible]r	1,164.00
[illegible]s, M[illegible]s E.	First	July 24, [illegible]1	[illegible]r	840.00
Ward, H.	Fifth	[illegible]g. 3, [illegible]1	[illegible]r	840.00
Bailey, Miss H.	Sixth	Aug. 29, 1911	[illegible]r	840.00
Lloyd, Miss E. L.	Eighth	Aug. 3, 1909	High	960.00

Redding—

Name	Grade	Date	Certificate	Salary
Heath, Miss V. D.	Principal	Jan. 4, 1894	Grammar	2,160.00
Erikson, Miss A. M.	Third	Mar. 20, 1909	Grammar	900.00
Sullivan, Miss T.	[illegible]h	Jan. 15, 1903	Grammar	1,224.00
[illegible]ry, Miss [illegible] E.	[illegible]d	Aug. 12, 1903	Gr[illegible]mm[illegible]r	1,224.00
May, Miss H. M.	Third	Sept. 23, 1909	[illegible]r	900.00
[illegible]r, Miss S. A.	First	Aug. 14, 1881	[illegible]r	1,224.00
White, Mrs. E. B.	Sixth	June 3, 1905	[illegible]r	1,164.00
[illegible]e, Mrs. L. E.	First	Dec. 23, 1885	[illegible]r	1,224.00
Sullivan, Miss E. G.	Second	[illegible]n. 12, 1898	Grammar	[illegible]0
Grilo, Mrs. C. M.	Fourth	July 23, 1902	Grammar	1,164.00
[illegible]lmes, Mrs. M. B.	Fifth	[illegible]n. 2, 1911	[illegible]r	1,164.00
Jones, Miss M. M.	Sixth	June 11, 1912	Grammar	840.00

Rincon (In charge of Principal of Lincoln)—

Name	Grade	Date	Certificate	Salary
Coyle, Mrs. Mary G.	Fourth	[illegible]. 5, 1892	[illegible]r	1,164.00
Barry, Miss A. P.	First	Sept 21, 1886	Grammar	1,344.00

Rochambeau Primary—

Name	Grade	Date	Certificate	Salary
McIntyre, Miss J. L.	Fifth	Oct. 2, 1905	Gr[illegible]mar	1,164.00
Gavigan, Miss A. E.	Principal	July 20, 1875	Gr[illegible]mar	1,800.00

SCHOOLS AND TEACHERS—[illegible]

Name.	Grade of Class.	When [illegible]	Grade of Certificate.	Salary [illegible]
[illegible] Primary—Continued.				
[illegible], Miss E.	Eighth	April 5, [illegible]	[illegible]	1,284.00
[illegible], [illegible] M. D.	Seventh	June 26, [illegible]	[illegible]	1,224.00
[illegible], [illegible]	[illegible]	June [illegible], 1904	High	1,164.00
[illegible], Mrs. J. D.	Third	[illegible] 27, [illegible]	[illegible]	1,164.00
[illegible], Miss L. R.	First	Oct. 1, 1884	[illegible]	1,224.00
[illegible], Miss A. F.	Third	[illegible] 1, 1897	Grammar	1,164.00
Savage, Miss D. A.	Si[illegible]th	[illegible] 21, [illegible]	[illegible]	1,164.00
Powers, Miss M. V.	First	[illegible] 2, [illegible]	Grammar	1,224.00
Bell, Miss L. V.	Fifth	[illegible] 10, [illegible]	Grammar	840.00
Wilbur, Mrs. V.	Second	Aug. 10, 1897	Grammar	1,164.00
Roosevelt Grammar—				
L[illegible], Mr. Albert	Principal	[illegible]	[illegible]	2,340.00
Browning, Miss E. F.	[illegible]	[illegible]	High	1,224.00
Ryan, Miss B.	Second	Sept. [illegible]	Grammar	1,164.00
Hitchens, Florence J.	Fourth	[illegible]	Grammar	1,164.00
[illegible], Miss A.	Second	[illegible]	[illegible]	1,164.00
[illegible], Miss M. T.	[illegible]	[illegible] 1, [illegible]	[illegible]	1,224.00
Hinds, Miss J. B.	[illegible]	[illegible] 9, [illegible]	[illegible]	[illegible]
Stark, Miss L. M.	First	[illegible] 7, 1887	[illegible]	1,224.00
Cotrel, Edna	Fif[illegible]h	[illegible] 5, [illegible]	[illegible]	1,164.00
Hurley, Miss A. F.	[illegible]	April 27, [illegible]	Primary	1,164.00
Horton, Miss M.	First	[illegible] 14, [illegible]	[illegible]	1,224.00
Levy, Miss M. A.	Eighth	[illegible]	Grammar	1,224.00
Kedon, Mrs. A. E.	Eighth	[illegible] 9, [illegible]	[illegible]	1,224.00
Kelly, Margery F.	Fifth	Sept. [illegible]	[illegible]	900.00
McEachern, Miss M. V	Thi[illegible]d	July 25, 1910	Grammar	840.00

Cohen, Miss D.	German	Jan. 7, 1908	High	1,200
Kurlandzek, Miss R.	French	[illegible] 14, 1903	[illegible]	1,200.00
Boukofsky, Miss R. M.	Seventh & V.-P.	April 1, 1884	[illegible]	1,500.00
[illegible]—				
Riordan, [illegible] C. F.	Principal	Dec. 10, 1890	[illegible]	2,340.00
[illegible], Miss J.	[illegible]	Aug. 26, 1891	[illegible]	1,620.00
Everett, Miss E. B.	Seventh	Jan. [illegible], [illegible]	[illegible]	1,224.00
Hussey, [illegible] E. G.	[illegible]	Feb. 11, [illegible]	High	1,224.00
Tierney, [illegible] E. A.	Fifth	Oct. 13, [illegible]	[illegible]	1,164.00
[illegible], [illegible] M.	Fifth	Sept. 14, [illegible]	[illegible]	1,164.00
Ehat, Mrs. M. I.	[illegible] Fifth	July 7, [illegible]	Grammar	1,224.00
Brignardello, Miss H.	Third	Sept. 8, [illegible]	[illegible]	1,164.00
[illegible], [illegible] A. J.	Second	Sept. 3, [illegible]	Grammar	1,224.00
[illegible], Miss M. W.	First	April 29, [illegible]	[illegible]	1,224.00
[illegible], Miss M. [illegible]	[illegible]	Jan. 6, [illegible]	[illegible]	1,224.00
Kyne, [illegible] E. M.	Second	Aug. 3, [illegible]	Grammar	960.00
Harte, Mrs. S.	Fourth	Mar. 4, 1903	[illegible]	1,164.00
[illegible], [illegible] G. A.	Fourth	July [illegible], [illegible]	[illegible]	840.00
Harrington, [illegible] E. F.	Eighth	April 10, 1911	[illegible]	840.00
[illegible] Primary—				
Hurl[illegible], Miss [illegible] A.	Principal	Jan. 2, [illegible]	[illegible]	1,800.00
Millar, Mrs. S. H.	Fourth	July 6, [illegible]	[illegible]	1,164.00
[illegible], [illegible] J. T.	Second	May 17, [illegible]	[illegible]	1,164.00
Unger, [illegible] R.	[illegible]	Aug. 20, [illegible]	[illegible]	1,224.00
[illegible], Miss [illegible]	Second	Aug. 15, [illegible]	[illegible]	1,164.00
Lyons, Miss E. H.	Second	Sept. 30, [illegible]	Grammar	1,164.00
Hitchens, Eli[illegible]	First	Nov. 25, [illegible]	Grammar	1,224.00
Erb, Miss F. M.	Third	Aug. 3, [illegible]	[illegible]	900.00
Kinsey, Miss L.	[illegible]	Jan. 3, [illegible]	[illegible]	900.00
Gull, Mrs. M.	First	July 7, 1877	Grammar	1,224.00
Fleming, Miss L. M.	[illegible]	Sept. [illegible], [illegible]	Grammar	900.00
Russell, Miss A. C.	Sixth	Jan. [illegible], [illegible]	[illegible]	840.00

SCHOOLS AND TEACHERS—[illegible]

Name.	Grade of Class.	When Elected.			Grade of Certificate	Salary per Year.
Spring Valley [illegible]—						
[illegible], Miss M. E.	Principal	July	[illegible],	[illegible]	Grammar	2, [illegible]0.00
Gregg, Miss A. C.	V. [illegible], 8th	[illegible]	[illegible],	[illegible]	[illegible]	1, [illegible]0.00
Murphy, Miss A. [illegible]	Seventh	Mar.	2,	[illegible]	[illegible]	1, [illegible]24.00
Hause Miss E. N.	Fifth	Mar.	9,	[illegible]	[illegible]	[illegible]0.00
[illegible], Miss [illegible]. B.	Seventh	[illegible]	[illegible],	[illegible]	[illegible]	1,224.00
Hoggs, Mrs. M. A.	Eighth	Jan.	[illegible],	[illegible]877	[illegible]	1,224.00
Davis, Mrs. F.	[illegible]	Sept.	8,	[illegible]	[illegible]	1,164.00
Grozelier, Miss C. B. S.	Fifth	Sept.	[illegible],	[illegible]	High	1,164.00
Gallagher, Miss E. R.	Sixth	Oct.	[illegible],	[illegible]	[illegible]	1,164.00
Dittenhoefer, Miss M. B.	[illegible]	Sept.	[illegible],	[illegible]	High	840.00
Bradley, Mrs. A. B.	First	Oct.	7,	[illegible]	[illegible]	1,224.00
[illegible], Miss M. C.	Second	July	[illegible],	[illegible]	Primary	1,164.00
[illegible], Miss F. R.	First	July	[illegible],	[illegible]	[illegible]	1,124.00
Starr King Primary—						
McGrath, [illegible]. [illegible]. C.	Principal	[illegible]	[illegible],	[illegible]	[illegible]	1,560.00
[illegible], Miss K. F.	Fourth	Oct.	[illegible],	[illegible]	[illegible]	1,164.00
O'Sullivan, Miss [illegible]	First	April	[illegible],	[illegible]	Gram.-Spec.	1,284.00
Foley, K[illegible] J.	Third	July	[illegible],	[illegible]	[illegible]	[illegible],164.00
[illegible], Miss E. S.	First	Nov.	[illegible],	[illegible]	[illegible]	[illegible],[illegible]224.00
[illegible], Miss J. E.	Third	Sept.	[illegible],	[illegible]	[illegible]	1,164.00
Keegan, Miss M. E.	Third	[illegible]	[illegible],	[illegible]	Grammar	840.00
Dunn, Mrs. M. C.	Fourth	[illegible]	3,	[illegible]	[illegible]	1,164.00
Fosberg, Miss C. J.	Third	July	24,	[illegible]	Grammar	840.00
Sunnyside Primary—						
Moore, Miss K.	First	June	[illegible],	1903	Grammar	1,224.00
Eprhaim, Miss J.	1st, 4th and 3d	July	23,	1876	Grammar	1,560.00
Mitchell, Mrs. G. D.	Seventh	Feb.	11,	1879	[illegible]	1,224.00
Papina, Miss J. A.	Third	Feb.	17,	1910	[illegible]	840.00

Columbus—				
Tiernan, Mrs. A. E.	Principal 3d & 4th	July 6, 1869	High	1,320.00
Rowe, Miss M. M.	Second	Aug. 3, 1871	High	1,224.00
Sutro Grammar—				
[illegible]r, M[illegible]s M.	Principal	July 25, 1876	[illegible]r	2,160.00
Duraind, M[illegible]s M. R.	V. P., 8th	Dec., 5, 1875	[illegible]r	1,620.00
Smullen, Miss A. M.	E[illegible]th	Feb. 18, 1903	Grammar	1,284.00
Karatar, M[illegible]s A. C.	Fifth	Oct. 14, 1883	G[illegible]r	1,164.00
Read, Miss M. I.	[illegible]d	July 18, 1902	G[illegible]r	1,080.00
Curran, Miss M. M.	Seventh	Mar. 14, 1906	[illegible]r	1,224.00
C[illegible]or, Miss E. L.	Third	Aug. 3, 1908	G[illegible]r	1,020.00
F[illegible]pe, Miss I. E.	[illegible]ixth	Nov. 18, 1886	Grammar	1,164.00
Maguire, Miss H. E.	Second	Oct. 27, 1892	Grammar	1,164.00
O'Brien, Miss M. J.	First	Aug. 3, 1892	G[illegible]r	1,224.00
[illegible]n, Miss A. B.	First	May 13, 1896	G[illegible]r	1,224.00
[illegible]a, M[illegible]ss K. L.	[illegible]	Sept. 10, 1904	G[illegible]r	1,224.00
Hart, Miss A. P.	Fourth	Aug. 19, [illegible]07	[illegible]r	1,020.00
[illegible]lly, M[illegible]s M. J.	Third	Aug. 3, 1908	G[illegible]r	900.00
Gordon, Miss H.	Sixth	April 18, 1910	G[illegible]r	840.00
[illegible]an, Miss A. J.	Fi[illegible]th	Sept. 1, 1907	G[illegible]r	1,080.00
[illegible], Mrs. J.	Sixth	Aug. 3, 1908	G[illegible]r	960.00
Ungraded School—				
Blum, Josie L.	Ungraded	July 27, 1897	Grammar	....
Visitacion Valley—				
Iredale, Mrs. E. B.	Principal	[illegible]c. 1, 1876	Grammar and Special	1,620.00
Nolan, Miss M. A.	Eighth	[illegible]. 21, 1901	Grammar	1,224.00
Dailey, Miss Alice	Fifth	Mar. 14, 1907	Grammar	1,164.00
Kenny, Miss M.	First	April 8, 1907	Grammar	1,152.00
Mack, Miss A.	Fourth	Aug. 5, 1908	Grammar	1,020.00
Corbett, Miss A. M.	First	Oct. 12, 1905	Grammar	1,224.00

SCHOOLS AND TEACHERS—Continued.

Name.	Grade of Class.	When Elected.	Grade of [illegible]e.	Salary per Year.
Visitacion Valley—Continued.				
McIlvain, Miss M.	Second	[illegible]n. 9, 1911	[illegible]r	840.00
Sawyer, Miss L. M.	Third	[illegible]n. 24, 1911	[illegible]r	840.00
Friedman, Miss F.	Fifth	July 24, 1910	[illegible]r	840.00
[illegible]h Grammar—				
[illegible]r. T. [illegible]	Principal	[illegible]r. [illegible], [illegible]1	[illegible]h	2,160.00
[illegible]y, [illegible] A.	[illegible]	[illegible]. 2, [illegible]7	[illegible]h	1,224.00
[illegible]her, [illegible]s [illegible] G.	[illegible]th	[illegible]y 1, [illegible]8	[illegible]r	1,224.00
[illegible]tt, M[illegible]ss J.	First	[illegible]t. 5, [illegible]1	[illegible]r	1,224.00
[illegible]d, [illegible]r. W. H.	Seventh	[illegible]. 19, [illegible]7	[illegible]r	1,224.00
[illegible]d, Mrs. [illegible] A.	[illegible]d	[illegible]y 20, [illegible]3	[illegible]r	1,164.00
[illegible]y, M[illegible]s [illegible] E.	Six[illegible]h	[illegible]e 18, [illegible]8	[illegible]r	1,164.00
[illegible]key, [illegible]r. F. G.	V. P., 8th	[illegible]y 27, 1897	[illegible]r	1,620.00
[illegible]on, [illegible]s [illegible] [illegible]	[illegible]rth	April 18, 1910	[illegible]r	900.00
Zulberti, Mr. C.	[illegible]talian	[illegible]y 24, [illegible]0	[illegible]h	1,200.00
[illegible]g, M[illegible]s D.	First	[illegible]t. [illegible], 1902	[illegible]r	1,224.00
Butler, [illegible]s [illegible] M.	Sixth	Sept. 27, [illegible]0	[illegible]r	840.00
Jordi, Mrs. S. J.	[illegible]d	[illegible]e [illegible], [illegible]5	[illegible]r	1,164.00
Ludke, M[illegible]s E.	S[illegible]h	[illegible]n. 9, [illegible]1	[illegible]r	840.00
[illegible]h, [illegible]s C.	[illegible]d	July [illegible], [illegible]1	[illegible]r	840.00
Price, [illegible]E.	[illegible]h	[illegible]y [illegible], [illegible]1	[illegible]r	840.00
[illegible]al[illegible], Mrs. M. A.	Third	July 29, 1903	[illegible]r	1,164.00
Washington Irving Pr.—				
Barlow, Miss C. B.	Principal	[illegible]ug. 1, 1868	Grammar	1,560.00
Miller, Miss J. G.	Fifth	[illegible]r. [illegible], 1895	Grammar	1,164.00
McVerry, Miss M.	First	Sept. 2, 1884	Grammar	1,224.00
Fleming, Miss H.	Second	Feb. 1, 1907	Grammar	1,164.00
Laurent, Miss S. E.	First	Jan. 7, 1908	Grammar	1,224.00
McEwen, Miss E. G.	Second	Oct. 12, 1895	Grammar	1,196.00

Name	Grade	Date	Certificate	Salary
O'Rourke, Miss E.	Third	Jan. 16, 1911	[illegible]ar	840.00
Eichen, Miss P. M.	Fourth	July 24, 1911	Grammar	840.00
Koller, Miss S. E.	Third	July 24, 1911	Grammar	840.00
[illegible]ld [illegible]tt Primary—				
Thomas, Miss [illegible] E.	Principal	July [illegible], 1887	Grammar	[illegible]
Horgan, Miss E. E.	[illegible]d Eighth	Sept. [illegible] [illegible]	Grammar	1,224.00
Wright, Miss A. B.	[illegible]nd	[illegible] 6, [illegible]	High	1,164.00
[illegible]s, [illegible]s A. G.	First	[illegible] [illegible], [illegible]	Grammar	1,224.00
[illegible]k, Mrs. M. F.	First	Dec. [illegible], [illegible]	Grammar	1,224.00
Birch, [illegible]rs. Lily	Fifth	[illegible]r. [illegible], 1907	[illegible]ar	1,164.00
[illegible]in, Miss M. L.	Fourth	Jan. 22, 1908	Grammar	1,140.00
Lindberg, Miss Emily	[illegible]	Sept. 6, [illegible]74	[illegible]m. & French	1,164.00
Wol[illegible], Miss H. F.	Sixth	[illegible]b. 7, [illegible]	Grammar	840.00
Yerba [illegible] Primary—				
[illegible], [illegible]s K. F.	Princi[illegible]l	[illegible]n. [illegible], [illegible]	Grammar	1,800.00
Klaus, Miss [illegible]. J.	Seventh	[illegible] 9, [illegible]	[illegible]ar	1,224.00
[illegible]t, Miss J. M.	Third	Oct. [illegible], [illegible]	Grammar	1,164.00
Bloch, Miss B. B.	Third	[illegible]ly 1, [illegible]	[illegible]ar	1,164.00
[illegible]el, Miss M. C.	Third	Aug. 3, [illegible]	[illegible]ar	1,164.00
[illegible]s, Miss N. A.	First	Sept. 5, [illegible]	[illegible]r	1,224.00
[illegible]h, Miss M.	First	Nov. 1, [illegible]	Grammar	1,224.00
Hochheimer, Miss J.	First	[illegible]n. [illegible]77	[illegible]ar	1,224.00
[illegible]u, M[illegible]s M. G.	First	[illegible]g. [illegible], [illegible]	Grammar	1,224.00
[illegible]e, Alice	[illegible]rth	April [illegible]	Grammar	900.00
[illegible]n, Miss A. [illegible]	Fifth	Feb. [illegible], [illegible]	Grammar	1,164.00
[illegible]n, Miss J. W.	Sixth	[illegible]g. [illegible], [illegible]	Grammar	960.00
Clauss, Miss R. E.	Sixth	July [illegible], [illegible]11	[illegible]ar	840.00
Klein, Miss M. G.	First	[illegible] 6, [illegible]	Grammar	1,224.00
San Francisco Commercial—				
Murphy, Chas. H.	Principal	Nov. 27, 1890	High	3,000.00
Deacon, Mrs. E. S.	Bookkeeping	Sept. 1, 1887	Special	1,620.00

SCHOOLS AND TEACHERS—[illegible]

Name.	Grade of Class.	When Elected.	Grade of Certificate.	Salary per Year.
San Francisco [illegible]—Continued.				
Sykes, [illegible] B.	[illegible], Gov.	Dec. 16, [illegible]	[illegible]	2, 16.00
[illegible], Mrs. S. W.	Arith.	July 20, [illegible]	[illegible]	1, 60.00
[illegible], [illegible] M. G.	[illegible]	July 30, [illegible]	[illegible]	1, 60.00
[illegible], [illegible] S. A.	Typewriting	July 20, [illegible]	Grammar and Special	1, 60.00
[illegible], Miss Mary L.	[illegible]	Aug. 15, [illegible]	Special	1, 60.00
[illegible], Miss M. I.	[illegible]	Jan. 14, [illegible]	[illegible]	1, 60.00
Freese, [illegible]	[illegible]	Mar. 8, [illegible]	[illegible]	1, 60.00
Reeves, Mrs. I. D.	[illegible]	Jan. 10, 1897	[illegible]	1, 60.00
Garbarino, Miss I.	[illegible]	Nov. [illegible]	Special	1, 60.00
[illegible], Miss M. L.	[illegible]	Sept. 1, [illegible]	[illegible]	1, 60.00
[illegible], [illegible] H. E.	Bookkeeping	May [illegible]	[illegible]	1, 60.00
[illegible], Miss [illegible] G.	[illegible]	Oct. 10, 1901	[illegible]	1, 60.00
[illegible], [illegible]	[illegible]	Jan. 4, [illegible]	[illegible]	1, 60.00
[illegible], [illegible] S. G.	[illegible]	Jan. [illegible]	Grammar [illegible]	1, 60.00
Cameron, M. E. M.	[illegible]	Aug. 9, [illegible]	Special	1, 60.00
[illegible], Mr. M. A.	Bookkeeping	Jan. 2, [illegible]	[illegible]	1, 60.00
Martin, [illegible] M. P.	[illegible]	[illegible] 2, 1912	[illegible]	1, 60.00
Pendergrass, Mrs. G. W.	[illegible]	Aug. [illegible]	Gramm[illegible]	1, 60.00
Murray, Miss B. M.	[illegible]	Aug. [illegible]	[illegible] Special	1, 60.00
Barnes, Mr. J. E.	[illegible]	Aug. 18, 1910	[illegible]	1, 60.00
[illegible], Miss C. A.	English	Aug. 2, [illegible]	High	1, 60.00
Girls' [illegible]—				
Greer, Y. C. C.	Domestic Science	Sept. 11, [illegible]	Special	1,200.00
Scott, Dr. A. W.	Principal	[illegible] 5, [illegible]	High	3,000.00
Prag, Mrs. M.	History	[illegible] 27, [illegible]	High	2,160.00
[illegible], [illegible] O.	Science	[illegible] 23, [illegible]	High	2,520.00
Dupuy, Mr. E. J.	French	May 15, [illegible]	Special	2,040.00
[illegible], [illegible] M.	Drawing	Mar. 1, 1887	High	2,040.00
Roth, [illegible] N. E.	English	Jan. 10, [illegible]	High	1,680.00

Name	Subject	Date	School	Salary
[illegible]cle, [illegible]s B.	French	Mar. 13, [illegible]5	High	1,[illegible]60.00
[illegible]l, Miss L.	[illegible]t. [illegible]e	Dec. 17, 1890	High	2,[illegible]0.00
[illegible]r, Miss [illegible] D.	English	Aug. 15, [illegible]8	High	1,[illegible]60.00
Croyland, [illegible]s A. B.	[illegible]h	July 20, [illegible]1	High	2,[illegible]0.00
[illegible]k, Miss C. M.	[illegible]in	July 21, [illegible]2	H[illegible]h	1,[illegible]60.00
[illegible]n, [illegible]s E. L.	[illegible]atics	Sept. 30, [illegible]1	High	1,[illegible]60.00
[illegible]n, Mr. Wm.	German	Jan. 4, 1871	H[illegible]h	1,[illegible]60.00
[illegible]n, Miss E. R.	English	Jan. 3, [illegible]3	[illegible]h	1,[illegible]60.00
[illegible]r, Martin A.	[illegible]in	Aug. 19, 1907	H[illegible]h	2,[illegible]0.00
[illegible], [illegible]s M.	[illegible]g	July 23, [illegible]8	Special	1,[illegible]60.00
[illegible]s, [illegible]s [illegible]e M.	t[illegible]y	Aug. 7, [illegible]9	High	1,[illegible]80.00
[illegible]e, [illegible]s S. A.	[illegible]atics	July 21, [illegible]1	High	1,[illegible]80.00
Flynn, Miss H. A.	[illegible]h	July 24, [illegible]1	High	1,[illegible]60.00

Lowell High—

Name	Subject	Date	School	Salary
Morton, Mr. [illegible]k	[illegible]al	Aug. 1, 1886	High	3,300.00
[illegible]k, Mr. F. H.	Head [illegible]istory	July 8, [illegible]9	[illegible]h	2,160.00
Crofts, [illegible]s E.	[illegible]d [illegible]atics	Nov. 28, 1891	[illegible]h	2,040.00
Schmit, [illegible]r. J. J.	[illegible]d [illegible]g	Dec. 26, 1894	[illegible]h	1,980.00
[illegible]e, Mr. J. [illegible]	[illegible]d [illegible]c. [illegible]g.	Jan. 14, 1901	Hi[illegible]h	1,980.00
Duffy, [illegible]s A. G.	Head [illegible]h	[illegible]. 24, 1897	[illegible]h	2,040.00
[illegible]d, [illegible]r. F. W.	[illegible]s	Jan. 3, [illegible]1	High	1,500.00
Bowman, Elsie	Latin-Mat[illegible]atics	[illegible]e 17, [illegible]3	[illegible]h	1,680.00
[illegible]y, Mr. J. A.	t[illegible]y	[illegible]ly 20, [illegible]1	[illegible]h	1,680.00
[illegible], Mr. F. E.	[illegible]glish	[illegible]. 4, [illegible]1	[illegible]h	1,680.00
[illegible]s, Mr. T. H.	[illegible]atin [illegible]d [illegible]h	Nov. 15, [illegible]6	[illegible]h	1,680.00
[illegible]e, Miss C. B.	English	[illegible]ril 4, [illegible]7	High	1,680.00
Cox, Mary M.	[illegible]ead [illegible]n [illegible]g.	[illegible]g. 20, [illegible]5	High	2,046.00
[illegible]e, [illegible]s E. A.	[illegible]ry	[illegible]. 1, [illegible]7	High	1,680.00
[illegible]n, Miss F.	t[illegible]y	May 27, [illegible]5	High	1,680.00
Smith, Mr. Thos. A.	[illegible]istry	[illegible]g. 2, [illegible]9	High	1,680.00
Altmann, Mr. A.	Drawi[illegible]g	July [illegible], [illegible]3	Special	1,680.00
Koch, Mr. [illegible] W.	Science	July [illegible], [illegible]1	High	1,680.00
[illegible]r, Mr. F. B.	Latin [illegible]d Greek	July 25, 1910	High	1,500.00

SCHOOLS AND TEACHERS—Continued.

Name.	Grade of Class.	When Elected.	Grade of [illegible]	Salary per Year.
Lowell High—Continued.				
Downey, Mr. A. D.	Science	Jan. 21, 1907	High	2,040.00
Rogers, Mr. J. E.	English	July 24, 1911	[illegible]	1,500.00
Fender, Mr. C. W.	Biology	Jan. 2, 1912	High	1,500.00
M[illegible] [illegible]—				
[illegible]r, [illegible]ph.	[illegible]al	Oct. 1, [illegible]	[illegible]	3, [illegible]00.00
[illegible]y, [illegible] M. E.	Engl[illegible]sh	[illegible] 9, [illegible]	[illegible]	2, [illegible]60.00
[illegible]th, Miss A.	[illegible]	Feb. 19, [illegible]	[illegible]	2, [illegible]00.00
Blanchard, Dr. M. E.	[illegible]	Jan. 5, [illegible]	[illegible]	2, [illegible]60.00
Kelly, Miss A. G.	[illegible]	[illegible] 10, [illegible]	[illegible]	2, [illegible]00.00
[illegible]e, Miss E.	[illegible]	July 20, [illegible]	[illegible]	1, [illegible]60.00
Cerf, Miss [illegible]	French-Latin	[illegible] 21, [illegible]	[illegible]	1, [illegible]60.00
[illegible]r, Miss M.	[illegible]	[illegible] 28, [illegible]	[illegible]	1, [illegible]60.00
Van Gorder, Mr. [illegible] G.	[illegible]	[illegible] 1, [illegible]	[illegible]	2, [illegible]00.00
[illegible]h, Mr. R. E.	[illegible]	Jan. 2, [illegible]	[illegible]	1, [illegible]60.00
[illegible]y, Mr. C. S.	Drawing	[illegible] 27, [illegible]	Special	2, [illegible]00.00
[illegible]nell, [illegible] M.	Drawing	Dec. 6, [illegible]	Special	1, [illegible]50.00
Gray, Miss [illegible] E. [illegible]	[illegible] and English	Sept. 20, [illegible]	[illegible]	1, [illegible]60.00
Kendrick, [illegible] N. K.	[illegible]	[illegible] 29, [illegible]	[illegible] & Spec.	1, [illegible]60.00
Harrison, Mrs. E. C.	[illegible]	[illegible] 3, [illegible]	[illegible] Special	2,040.00
[illegible]g, [illegible] C.	[illegible]	[illegible] 20, [illegible]	[illegible]	1, [illegible]60.00
[illegible]un, [illegible] E.	[illegible] & [illegible]	April 4, 1887	[illegible]	1, [illegible]60.00
Durham, [illegible] R. L.	[illegible]	Nov. 2, [illegible]	[illegible]	1, [illegible]50.00
Polytechnic High—				
Ferguson, James	Principal	Aug. 21, 1905	High	3,000.00
Jordan, Mr. A. L.	Head Science	Jan. 26, 1899	High	2,040.00
Van Vleck, Miss M.	Head Ind. Arts	July 22, 1889	[illegible]	2,040.00
Carniglia, Mr. E. S.	Head Mach. Shop	Mar. 25, 1905	High	2,160.00

Name	Subject	Date			Grade	Salary
Watson, [illegible] R.	[illegible]h & English	April	30,	[illegible]98	High	1, [illegible]60.00
Mohr, [illegible]r. [illegible] J.	[illegible] [illegible]cs	[illegible]	21,	[illegible]93	High	2, [illegible]00.00
[illegible]h, Mr. I. C.	[illegible] [illegible]. [illegible]g.	Aug.	12,	[illegible]95	[illegible]h	2, [illegible]00.00
[illegible]e, Etta	[illegible]atics	[illegible]c.	1,	1897	[illegible]h	1, 60.00
[illegible]h, Miss R.	Drawing	Nov.	18,	[illegible]93	[illegible]al	1, 60.00
[illegible]l, Miss N. L.	[illegible]g	Sept.	21,	1907	[illegible]al	1, [illegible]00.00
Drew, Mr. [illegible]. J.	[illegible] M[illegible]h. Draw.	[illegible]r.	28,	[illegible]98	High	2, [illegible]00.00
[illegible]f, Miss C.	[illegible]h	Feb.	3,	[illegible]98	High	1, 60.00
Kelly, Miss M. E.	[illegible] English	[illegible]y	20,	1902	High	2, [illegible].00
McTiernan, Mr. [illegible] J.	Asst. Forge	[illegible]pt.	14,	[illegible]98	Special	1, 60.00
Ostrom, Carmel	Drawing	[illegible]	10,	[illegible]01	[illegible]cial	1, 60.00
Carne, Harry L.	[illegible]h [illegible]r	[illegible]	2,	[illegible]99	Special	1, [illegible]00.00
[illegible]tt, [illegible]s [illegible]y	English	[illegible]y	18,	[illegible]02	[illegible]cial	1, 60.00
[illegible]r, [illegible]r. C. C.	[illegible]h. Drawing	[illegible]t.	30,	[illegible]97	Special	1, 60.00
Carlson, [illegible]r. C. L.	[illegible]y	[illegible]	2,	[illegible]99	[illegible]h	1, 60.00
[illegible]e, Mrs. E.	[illegible]g	[illegible]y	26,	[illegible]01	[illegible]al	1,200.00
Carey, [illegible]r. [illegible] P.	Sci[illegible]ce	[illegible]b.	3,	[illegible]98	[illegible]h	1,680.00

Bernal Evening—

Name	Subject	Date			Grade	Salary
Nolan, Mr. W. C.	Principal and 8th	Jan.	24,	1910	Grammar	900.00
Paulson, Mr. A. J. R.	Commercial	Aug.	29,	1911	High	780.00
Harris, Miss M. E.	Fourth	July	24,	1911	Grammar	660.00
Egan, Miss A. M.	5th, 6th, 7th	July	28,	1911	Grammar	660.00

Commercial Evening—

Name	Subject	Date			Grade	Salary
Riley, Mr. [illegible] T.	Principal	July	[illegible],	[illegible]01	High	1,320.00
Davidson, Mr. W. W.	Bookkeeping	[illegible]y	5,	[illegible]04	[illegible]r and Special	780.00
Kozminsky, [illegible]ss D.	[illegible]	[illegible]t.	9,	[illegible]02	[illegible]l	780.00
O'Malley, Miss [illegible]. W.	e[illegible]g	[illegible].	[illegible],	1897	[illegible]l	780.00
Delaney, Mrs. K. F.	Bookkeeping	Mar.	3,	[illegible]06	[illegible]r	780.00
Kelleher, Mr. J. B.	Eng. & Com. Arith.	[illegible]	8,	1908	Grammar, L. D.	780.00
Di[illegible]n, Mrs. Mary	Penmanship	April	7,	[illegible]00	High	780.00
Bodkin, Miss A. J.	Seventh	[illegible]c.	8,	[illegible]98	[illegible]r and Special	780.00
Alexander, Mrs. M. E.	Stenography	Nov.	[illegible],	[illegible]00	Special	780.00

SCHOOLS AND TEACHERS—Continued.

Name.	Grade of Class.	When El[illegible]ted.	Grade of Certificate.	Salary per Year.
Commercial Evening—Continued.				
Nelson, Mr. D. A.	Bookkeeping	Nov. 15, 1909	Grammar	780.00
Tobin, Miss Alma	Spanish	Feb. 3, 1910	High	780.00
Kendrick, Mr. J. A.	Bookkeeping	Aug. 8, 1911	Special	780.00
Daniels, Mr. J. R.	Bookkeeping	Sept. 1, 1891	Special	780.00
Stokes, Mr. G. H.	Bookkeeping	Aug. 1, 1901	High	780.00
Hickey, Mr. D. J.	Stenography	Sept. 26, 1911	Special	780.00
Ham[illegible] [illegible]—				
Lenahan, Mr. J. A.	Princi[illegible]al	[illegible] [illegible], [illegible]	[illegible]	1,020.00
Israel, [illegible] D. T.	S[illegible]th and Eighth	[illegible]. [illegible], [illegible]	[illegible]	660.00
Burnett, Miss S. C.	Foreign	Oct. [illegible], [illegible]904	[illegible]	660.00
Livingst[illegible], Miss B.	Sten.	[illegible]	Special	780.00
Cronin, [illegible] K. F.	[illegible]riting	[illegible] 2, [illegible]	[illegible] and S[illegible]cial	780.00
Wirt, [illegible]	[illegible]	[illegible] 9, [illegible]	H[illegible]h	660.00
[illegible], [illegible] F.	Foreign	Nov. [illegible], [illegible]	[illegible]h	660.00
Clark, [illegible] Mary	Stenography	July [illegible], [illegible]	S[illegible]al	780.00
Morse, Mr. A. G.	Seventh	[illegible] 4, [illegible]	High	660.00
McDonough, [illegible] M. M.	Sixth	[illegible]ly 24, [illegible]	[illegible]	660.00
[illegible], Miss M. L.	Foreign	[illegible]t. 20, [illegible]	[illegible]h	660.00
Dunkley, [illegible] [illegible] P.	S[illegible]th	[illegible] 9, [illegible]	Grammar	660.00
[illegible], [illegible] M. [illegible]	[illegible]	[illegible]g. 1, [illegible]	[illegible]	660.00
[illegible], Mrs. C.	[illegible]	M[illegible]y 17, [illegible]	[illegible]	660.00
Horace Mann Evening—				
Kratzer, Mr. D. W.	Principal	[illegible]. [illegible], 1897	Grammar	960.00
Murphy, Mrs. C. L.	Ninth	[illegible]. [illegible], 1897	Grammar and Special	660.00
Tobin, Miss B.	[illegible]	[illegible]y [illegible], 1911	Grammar	660.00
McCord, Miss C. E.	Foreign	[illegible]y [illegible], 1911	Grammar	660.00
Rockwell, Mr. W. J.	Seventh	July [illegible], 1910	Grammar	660.00
Kelly, Eliz. F.	E[illegible]ghth	Aug. [illegible], 1904	Grammar	660.00

Name	Subject	Date		Year	School	Salary
Lane, Miss H. F.	Eighth	Sept.	1,	[illegible]5	Grammar	660.00
Martin, Miss A. G.	Seventh	July	8,	[illegible]8	Grammar	660.00
Marshall, Mrs. M. L.	Sixth and Seventh	Sept.	1,	[illegible]7	Grammar	660.00
McManus, Mr. F. A.	Seventh	Oct.	7,	[illegible]7	Grammar	660.00
Kozminsky, Miss B.	Fifth and Sixth	[illegible]	[illegible],	[illegible]2	Grammar	660.00
Dwyer, Mrs. M.	First and Fourth	Feb.	2,	[illegible]8	Primary	660.00
O'Neil, Miss L. C.	Foreign	Sept.	8,	[illegible]8	Grammar	660.00
[illegible]oldt E[illegible]g High—						
[illegible]e, M[illegible] L. A.	Principal	[illegible]c.	2,	[illegible]6	[illegible]h	1,320.00
[illegible]rts, M[illegible] A. E.	[illegible]d. of [illegible]g [illegible]pt.	[illegible]c.	[illegible],	[illegible]2	Grammar and Special	1,260.00
Riley, Mr. G. E.	[illegible]igh [illegible]ol	Sept.	1,	[illegible]2	[illegible]h	780.00
[illegible]d, [illegible]r. [illegible] M.	[illegible]h [illegible]	Aug.	[illegible],	[illegible]5	[illegible]h	780.00
[illegible]y, Miss [illegible] J.	[illegible]h [illegible]ol	[illegible]	4,	[illegible]5	High	780.00
[illegible]ry, Mr. [illegible]n	[illegible]g	April	2,	[illegible]8	[illegible]al	[illegible]0.00
Walsh, Mr. C. F.	Latin	[illegible]t.	[illegible],	[illegible]8	[illegible]h	[illegible]0.00
[illegible]e, [illegible]r. L. C.	Drawing	[illegible]	3,	[illegible]2	[illegible]al	[illegible]0.00
r[illegible]s, Mr. [illegible] E.	[illegible]wing	[illegible]t.	4,	[illegible]2	[illegible]al	[illegible]0.00
Harvey, Mr. [illegible] W.	[illegible]y	[illegible].	8,	[illegible]5	[illegible]al	[illegible]0.00
Carroll, Mr. [illegible] E.	[illegible]g	[illegible]il	[illegible],	[illegible]5	[illegible]al	[illegible]0.00
[illegible], [illegible] F. K.	[illegible]g	[illegible]	5,	[illegible]1	[illegible]al	[illegible]0.00
[illegible]ll, Mr. [illegible] C.	[illegible]riting	July	1,	[illegible]3	[illegible]h	780.00
[illegible]h, [illegible]r. [illegible] P.	Drawing	Aug.	8,	[illegible]0	[illegible]al	780.00
Little, [illegible]n W.	[illegible]awing	Oct.	[illegible],	[illegible]0	[illegible]al	780.00
Tertzen, Miss A. M.	[illegible]h [illegible]ol	Jan.	9,	[illegible]1	High	780.00
Trefts, Mr. W. E.	Stenog'y & Typ'g	Aug.	1,	[illegible]3	[illegible]d Special	780.00
[illegible]len, Mr. A. [illegible]	[illegible]cial	Aug.	2,	[illegible]1	[illegible]al	[illegible]0.00
[illegible], Mr. J. A.	Commercial	Aug.	1,	[illegible]1	S[illegible]al	[illegible]0.00
Welch, Mr. [illegible] [illegible]	[illegible]rcial	Aug.	14,	[illegible]1	[illegible]al	[illegible]0.00
[illegible]h, Mrs. M. E.	[illegible]rcial	Sept.	8,	1911	S[illegible]al	[illegible]0.00
G[illegible]y, Mr. T. [illegible]	D[illegible]g	Jan.	17,	[illegible]2	[illegible]al	[illegible]0.00
[illegible]t, Mr. G. [illegible]	Drawing	Jan.	26,	[illegible]2	e[illegible]ial	[illegible]0.00
[illegible]ill[illegible]n, Mr. [illegible] T.	Navigation	[illegible]	[illegible]	[illegible]	e[illegible]al	[illegible]0.00

SCHOOLS AND TEACHERS—Continued.

Name.	Grade of Class.	When Elected.	Grade of Certificate.	Salary per Year.
Humboldt Evening High—Continued				
Cuthbertson, Mr. G. W.	Science	Dec. 1, 1905	High	780.00
Drew, John S.	Science	Feb. 25, 1897	High	780.00
Irving M. Scott Evening—				
Hoagland, Miss G. D.	All	[illegible] 24, 1911	[illegible]	660.00
Jean Parker—				
Kean, Mrs. L. R.	All	Aug. 1, 1911	Special	1,200.00
Hanlon, Miss F. M.	All	Aug. 15, 1911	Special	$3.50 per day
Lagunda Honda—				
Telfer, Dr. G. J.	All	[illegible] 20, 1903	Grammar	660.00
Lincoln [illegible]—				
[illegible], Mr. A. [illegible]	[illegible]	Sept. 2, 1880	High	960.00
[illegible], Miss M. R.	[illegible]	Aug. 14, [illegible]	[illegible]	660.00
Parlin, Mrs. A. E.	[illegible]	Aug. 31, 1892	[illegible]	660.00
[illegible], Mr. P. S.	Seventh	July 11, 1870	High	660.00
Rich, Mrs. L. A.	Vice Principal	Dec. 23, 1885	[illegible]	960.00
[illegible], Mrs. S. S.	Foreign	Dec. 27, 1890	[illegible]	660.00
[illegible], Mrs. E.	[illegible]	Oct. 23, 1901	[illegible]	660.00
[illegible], Miss E. L.	[illegible]	Aug. 30, 1896	Primary	660.00
[illegible], Miss C. E.	Seventh	July 24, 1911	[illegible]	660.00
[illegible], Miss J. C.	Fifth	July 29, 1908	[illegible]	660.00
Monroe Evening—				
Munday, Mr. C.	All	Nov. 22, 1909	[illegible]	780.00
Sheridan—				
Woodcock, Mr. E.	All	Aug. 7, 1911	[illegible]	660.00
Portola Evening—				
Prusch, Mr. N. H.	All	Feb. 1, 1906	Grammar	660.00

Name	Grade/Subject	Date		Certificate	Salary
Roosevelt Evening—					
Dougherty, Wm. J.	Seventh and Eighth	Aug. 19, 1907		Gr[illegible]	780.00
Wheeler, Miss C. F.	Foreign	Nov. 1, 1900		[illegible]	660.00
Sherman Evening—					
Fenton, Mr. F. L.	Principal	Feb. 11, 1904		High	900.00
Williams, Mr. W. J.	Foreign	July 15, 1868		High	660.00
Reed, Miss C.	6th, 7th, 8th	Aug. 4, 1908		Gr[illegible]	660.00
Cella, Miss E. L.	Italian	Aug. 2, 1909		Gramm[illegible]r	600.00
Fiala, Miss A. M.	Ninth	May 9, 1886		Gr[illegible]	600.00
Faure, Mrs. E. S.	Commercial	April 13, 1908		Gr[illegible]	780.00
Washington Evening—					
[illegible], Mrs. P.	Principal	Dec. 4, [illegible]6		Gr[illegible]	960.00
Roden, Miss L. A.	Foreign	June 9, [illegible]7		[illegible]	660.00
Caglieri, Mrs. V.	[illegible]h	Nov. 19, [illegible]9		[illegible]	660.00
[illegible], M[illegible]s M. C.	Seventh	Dec. 10, [illegible]6		[illegible]	660.00
Grosjean, Mrs. E. S. M.	Foreign	May 17, 1[illegible]83		Gr[illegible]	660.00
Taylor, Ella B.	[illegible]h	Sept. 1, [illegible]7		[illegible]	660.00
[illegible]y, [illegible]r. M.	Foreign	Sept. 30, [illegible]9		[illegible]	660.00
Bretz, M[illegible]s B.	Foreign	Sept. 16, [illegible]6		[illegible]	660.00
[illegible]n, Miss A.	Foreign	July [illegible], [illegible]84		Gra[illegible]mr	660.00
[illegible]e, M[illegible]s M. M.	Foreign	Mar. [illegible], [illegible]1		Gr[illegible]	660.00
McDermott, M[illegible]s K.	Fourth	Aug. [illegible], [illegible]8		Gr[illegible]mar	660.00
[illegible]n, Miss G. G.	Fifth	July [illegible], [illegible]1		[illegible]	660.00
[illegible]y, M[illegible]s M.	[illegible]h	July 9, [illegible]0		Gr[illegible]	660.00
[illegible]y, M[illegible]s M. C.	[illegible]d	July 21, [illegible]1		Primary	660.00
Washington Evening High—					
Fischer, Dr. F.	All	July 6, 1886		High	780.00
Department at Large—					
Cook, M.	Cooking	Oct. 11, 1911		Special	1,020.00
Barthel, Mr. F. K.	Supt. Manual Trng.	Jan. 15, 1904		Grammar and Special	1,920.00

SCHOOLS AND TEACHERS—[illegible]

Name.	Grade of Class.	When Elected.	Grade of Certificate.	Salary per Year.
Davidson, Mr. L. E.	[illegible]	[illegible] 1, 1901	Special	1,[illegible]0.00
Bagot, Mr. H. C.	[illegible]	[illegible] 15, 1903	[illegible]	1,[illegible]0.00
[illegible], [illegible] P. F.	[illegible]	[illegible] 10, 1905	Special	1,[illegible]0.00
[illegible], Mr. D. E.	[illegible]	[illegible] 4, 1906	Special	1,[illegible]0.00
Silvia, Mr. A. M.	[illegible]	[illegible] 11, 1905	High [illegible]	1,[illegible]0.00
Doyle, [illegible] M. J.	[illegible]	[illegible] 5, 1897	Special	1,[illegible]0.00
[illegible], Mr. M. A.	[illegible] Trai[illegible]	[illegible] 30, 1902	[illegible] Special	1,[illegible]0.00
Denver, W. J.	[illegible] Trai[illegible]	[illegible] 24, 1911	[illegible]	1,[illegible]0.00
[illegible], [illegible] E.	[illegible]	[illegible] 28, 1908	[illegible]	1,[illegible]0.00
[illegible], [illegible]	[illegible]	Sept. 3, 1903	[illegible]	1,620.00
[illegible], Mrs. A. W.	[illegible]	[illegible] 1, 1910	[illegible]	1,620.00
[illegible], [illegible] M.	Drawing	[illegible] 1, 1894	Special	1,920.00
[illegible], [illegible] A. B.	Drawing	Aug. 3, 1908	Special	1,[illegible]0.00
Martin, [illegible] E. H.	[illegible]	Aug. 3, 1908	Special	1,[illegible]0.00
[illegible], [illegible] O. S.	[illegible] [illegible]ulture	Aug. 1, 1897	[illegible]	1,[illegible]0.00
[illegible], Mrs. N. J.	Physical [illegible]ulture	Jan. 1, 1910	Special	1,[illegible]0.00
Bartlett, [illegible] E. M.	[illegible]	July 1, 1901	Special	1,[illegible]0.00
[illegible], [illegible] C. A.	[illegible]	July 20, 1905	Special	1,020.00
[illegible], [illegible] L. G.	[illegible]	Aug. 2, 1909	[illegible]mar and Special	1,020.00
Fenton, Mrs. M. N.	[illegible]	Sept. 1, 1909	[illegible]	1,020.00
Tobriner, [illegible] A.	[illegible]	Aug. 18, 1910	Special	1,020.00
Congdon, [illegible] M.	Cookery	Aug. 19, 1905	[illegible]	1,020.00
Gerhardt, Mrs. M.	Cookery	Oct. 25, 1909	Special	1,020.00
Gray, [illegible] E.	[illegible]	Aug. 19, 1907	[illegible]	1,020.00
Ball, [illegible] L.	[illegible] Read'g Pr. [illegible]	April 1, 1908	[illegible]	2,040.00
Espina, Mr. P. A.	Penmanship	Sept. 13, 1887	Special	1,800.00
[illegible], Mrs. M.	[illegible]	Sept. 25, 1911	[illegible]	1,020.00
Riley, [illegible]	[illegible]	Feb. 28, 1912	Special	1,020.00
Clary, M.	[illegible]	Jan. 8, 1912	Special	1,020.00
Deneen, C.	Drawing	Jan. 19, 1911	Special	1,200.00

Davidson, W. C.	Manual Training	Feb. 23, 1912	Special	1,260.00
McCarthy, L.	Physical Culture	Nov. 22, 1911	Special	1,200.00
Peixotto, E. M.	Physical Culture	Nov. 8, 1911	Special	1,200.00
Powers, B. M.	Physical Culture	Nov. 1, 1911	Special	1,200.00
Murray, A.	Ind. Work	Aug. 7, 1911	Special	1,620.00
Sullivan, G.	Ind. Work	Feb. 14, 1912	Special	1,020.00

JANITORS.

SCHOOL.	NAME.	SALARY. per Month.		per Annum.
Adams	Sample, R.	$50.00	=	$600.00
Adams	O'Leary, N. G.	75.00	=	900.00
Agassiz	Foley, M. A.	60.00	=	720.00
Agassiz	Dempsey, P.	60.00	=	720.00
Bernal	Murphy, J.	90.00	=	1,080.00
Bay View	Jacobs, J. *	85.00	=	960.00
Bay View	Gorman, A.	45.00	=	540.00
Bryant	O'Donnell, A.	60.00	=	720.00
Bryant	Foster, Wm. *	80.00	=	960.00
Buena Vista	McQuaide, J.	55.00	=	660.00
Burnett	Davis, S.	75.00	=	900.00
Columbia	McCarthy, M.	60.00	=	720.00
Columbia	Adams, M.	60.00	=	720.00
Columbus	Aubertine, G.	25.00	=	300.00
Cleveland	Lee, K.	40.00	=	480.00
Cleveland	Hancock, A.	75.00	=	900.00
Cooper	Spinetti, M.	62.50	=	750.00
Crocker	Creegan, C.	55.00	=	660.00
Crocker	Brennan, T.	55.00	=	660.00
Daniel Webster	Hayes, A.	55.00	=	660.00
Denman	Fordyce, M.	75.00	=	900.00
Denman	Horgan, E.	45.00	=	540.00
Douglass	Carter, K.	72.50	=	870.00
Dudley Stone	Byrne, B.	70.00	=	840.00
Edison	Swanson, A.	60.00	=	720.00
Emerson	Dunn, G. *	85.00	=	1,020.00
Ethan Allen	Rankin, M.	40.00	=	480.00
Everett	Cormack, W. *	90.00	=	1,080.00
Farragut	Bassett, Mrs.	75.00	=	900.00
Fairmount	Cuddy, J.	60.00	=	720.00
Fairmount	Kellerher, N.	60.00	=	720.00
Frances Scott Key	Benson, M.	50.00	=	600.00
Franklin	Kelly, B.	75.00	=	900.00
Franklin	Caveney, M.	60.00	=	720.00
Fremont	Gunn, S. *	80.00	=	960.00
McCoppin, Frank	Ferguson, E.	50.00	=	600.00
McCoppin, Frank	Tully, T. J.	75.00	=	900.00
Garfield	Stoermer, M.	60.00	=	720.00
Garfield	Garibaldi, J.	85.00	=	1,020.00
George Peabody	Bole, N.	45.00	=	540.00
George Peabody	Brennan, J.	75.00	=	900.00
Glen Park	O'Connor, E.	45.00	=	540.00
Glen Park	Skinner, M.	45.00	=	540.00
Golden Gate	Dehoney, E.	75.00	=	900.00
Grant	McAdams, J. W	55.00	=	660.00
Grattan	Dawson, M.	45.00	=	540.00
Grattan	Woods, H.	75.00	=	900.00
Haight	Lavelle, M.	70.00	=	840.00
Hamilton	Creighton, J.	47.50	=	570.00
Hamilton and Eve	Hanley, J.	85.00	=	1,020.00
Hancock	Heine, J.	60.00	=	720.00
Hancock	Costello, L. *	75.00	=	900.00

Harrison	Cavanagh, M.	35.00	=	420.00
Hawthorne	Allen, R.	50.00	=	600.00
Hearst and Lincoln Eve	Ferbeck, H. *	140.00	=	1,680.00
Henry Durant	McQuaide, E. *	65.00	=	780.00
Horace Mann and Eve	McGowan, J. *	72.50	=	870.00
Horace Mann and Eve	Herring, D. T. *	72.50	=	870.00
Hunter's Point	Koch, A.	15.00	=	180.00
Irving M. Scott	Rollins, E.	50.00	=	600.00
Irving M. Scott	Clark, M. E.	60.00	=	720.00
Jackson	Dolan, M.	35.00	=	420.00
James Lick	Foley, J.	85.00	=	1,020.00
Jean Parker	Kennedy, J.	72.50	=	870.00
Jean Parker	Woods, H.	75.00	=	900.00
Jefferson	Baker, A.	32.50	=	390.00
John Swett	Kaskell, A. *	75.00	=	900.00
John Swett	McHugh, M.	55.00	=	660.00
Junipero Serra	Murphy, E.	50.00	=	600.00
Junipero Serra	Staff, G. F. *	75.00	=	900.00
Kate Kennedy	McHugh, M.	55.00	=	660.00
Kate Kennedy	Linstrom, E.	75.00	=	900.00
Lafayette	Hemenez, D. F.	40.00	=	480.00
Laguna Honda	Cavanagh, M. R.	50.00	=	600.00
Laguna Honda	Nolan, D. A.	80.00	=	960.00
Lincoln	McShea, S.	40.00	=	480.00
Lincoln	Stanton, E.	75.00	=	900.00
Longfellow	Cook, J. F. *	75.00	=	900.00
Madison	Powers, P. F.	75.00	=	900.00
Madison	Devine, M.	40.00	=	480.00
Marshall	Kelly, E.	55.00	=	660.00
Marshall Annex	Keslin, C.	30.00	=	360.00
McKinley	Langan, R.	75.00	=	900.00
McKinley	McCullough	50.00	=	600.00
Mission Grammar	Belden, A.	50.00	=	600.00
Mission Grammar	Whiting, C. E. *	75.00	=	900.00
Monroe	Vannucci, O.	85.00	=	1,020.00
Monroe	Savage, O.	52.50	=	630.00
Moulder	Jones, J.	45.00	=	540.00
Noe Valley	Kelly, J. *	75.00	=	900.00
Noe Valley	Keohane, N.	40.00	=	480.00
Ocean House	Davis, M.	20.00	=	240.00
Oceanside	Benson, M.	50.00	=	600.00
Oriental	Naughton, J.	50.00	=	600.00
Pacific Heights	McDonald, J.	55.00	=	660.00
Pacific Heights	McMahon, K.	55.00	=	660.00
Parental	McQuaide, J.	35.00	=	420.00
Parkside	Jileck, M.	25.00	=	300.00
Paul Revere	Davis, M.	20.00	=	240.00
Potrero	Hayes, A.	45.00	=	540.00
Redding	Curran, D.	60.00	=	720.00
Rochambeau	Stelljes, H.	72.50	=	870.00
Roosevelt and Eve	Fevrier, I.	62.50	=	750.00
Roosevelt and Eve	Lillis, M. B.	62.50	=	750.00
Rincon	Hogan, J.	35.00	=	420.00
Sheridan	Moran, A.	55.00	=	660.00
Sheridan	Arnold, S. T. *	75.00	=	900.00
Sherman and Eve	Kelly, M.	85.00	=	920.00
Portola	Holmes, B.	65.00	=	780.00

SCHOOL.	NAME.	SALARY. per Month.		per Annum.
Portola	Reid, W.	75.00	=	900.00
Spring Valley	Branley, A.	50.00	=	600.00
Spring Valley	Madin, G. H.	75.00	=	900.00
Starr King	Neary, J.	45.00	=	540.00
Sunnyside	Morris, K.	50.00	=	600.00
Sutro	Ganzert, W.	50.00	=	600.00
Sutro	Rossiter, J. J. *	75.00	=	900.00
Ungraded and Cooper	Fitzpatrick, A.	32.50	=	390.00
Visitacion Valley	Freelond, R. I.	70.00	=	840.00
Washington Eve	Tierucinis, W.	55.00	=	660.00
Washington	Kane, D. *	100.00	=	1,200.00
Washington Irving	McMahon, B.	50.00	=	600.00
Winfield Scott	McEvoy, E. *	75.00	=	900.00
Yerba Buena	Hill, A.	70.00	=	840.00
Yerba Buena	Andrews, A.	40.00	=	480.00
Girls' High	Connors, M.	70.00	=	840.00
Girls' High	Nellman, E. *	90.00	=	1,080.00
Lowell High	Ackerson, K.	50.00	=	600.00
Lowell High	Power, P. *	100.00	=	1,200.00
Mission High & Humboldt Evening High	Boyd, E. *	125.00	=	1,500.00
Mission High & Humboldt Evening High	Norton, K. *	80.00	=	960.00
Polytechnic High	Majnussen, G. *	110.00	=	1,320.00
S. F. Commercial	Mahoney, J. F. *	100.00	=	1,200.00
S. F. Commercial	Cohen, J. *	100.00	=	1,200.00

*Names starred (*) are men.
All others are women.

NAMES AND LOCATION OF SCHOOLS AND DESCRIPTION OF SCHOOL PROPERTY.

CLASS "A"

Designates a strictly fireproof building with steel frame, concrete or tile floors or partitions, brick or stone or concrete walls.

"SPECIAL CONSTRUCTION"

Designates a building with fireproof stairways, concrete basement walls with concrete first floor, wood frame above with metal lath and plaster interior and exterior, metal frame and sash.

"CLASS C"

Designates a steel frame with exterior brick walls, fireproof stairways and wooden joists and partitions.

Adams Grammar School—Eddy street, between Van Ness avenue and Polk street, 2-story, 14-room and basement Class "C" building. $94,739.36, was cost. Lot in Western Addition, Blk. 62, 120 x 137½ feet.

Agassiz School—Frame building; cost $31,500; eighteen rooms; Bartlett street, between Twenty-second and Twenty-third streets; lot in Mission Blk. 136, 150 x 250 feet, occupied also by Horace Mann Grammar School. On May 9, 1902, additional lot, southwest corner Twenty-second and Bartlett streets, S. 55 feet by W. 85 feet, was purchased from S. J. Hendy, December 28, 1908, from H. J. Koepke, a lot in Mission Block 136, $5,000; March 19, 1909, from Johanna Sheehan, W. line of Bartlett street 255 feet S. to Twenty-second street, S. 25 feet by W. 125 feet Mission Block 136, $4,500; December 6, 1909, from G. W. Wepfer, lot W. line of Bartlett street, 205 feet S. of Twenty-second street, S. 25 by W. 125 in Mission, Block 136, $7,000.

Bay View School—New building of 18 rooms and assembly hall, Class "A." Costing nearly $117,000.00. On July 10, 1905, lot in Silver Terrace tract, block C, was purchased from Allen Riddell for $10,250. Commencing at the corner formed by the intersection of the southerly line of Bay View avenue and the easterly line of Flora street, and running thence easterly along said southerly line of Bay View avenue 200 feet to the westerly line of Pomona street; thence at a right angle southerly 350 feet; thence at a right angle westerly 200 feet to the easterly line of Flora street; thence northerly along said line of Flora street 350 feet to the southerly line of Bay View avenue and point of commencement. Recorded in Book 2, 124 of Deeds, page 60. School located on Bay View avenue and Flora street.

Bernal School—Frame building, 16 rooms; cost $30,560; Courtland avenue, between Andover avenue and Moultrie street. Lot in Gift Map No. 2, 140 x 148 feet 8½ inches. October 17, 1908, from Elizabeth S. Ford, lots Nos. 17, 19, 21 and 23, Gift Map No. 2, $2,600. January 15, 1909, lot on corner of Andover and Jefferson avenues, $2,600. October 2, 1911 from L. Depaoli, lot in section S. line S. Jarboe avenue with W. line Moultrie street S. 62 ft. 6 in., W. 70 ft., N. 62 ft. 6 in., E. 70 ft. (bonds 1904) $3300. October 2, 1911 from Joseph S. Lemos, lot W. line Moultrie street 62 ft, 6 in. from Jarboe avenue S. 37 ft. 6 in. x W. 70 ft. (bonds 1904) $3300.

Bryant Cosmopolitan School—Bryant street, between Twenty-second and Twenty-third; 2-story, eighteen rooms and basement; "Special Construction" building. Occupied by Board of Education June 9, 1910; cost $106,306.15. Lot in Mission block 147, between Twenty-second and Twenty-third streets, Bryant and York streets, 150 x 200 feet.

Buena Vista School—Frame building, thirteen rooms; costing $21,867.00. Bryant street, between Eighteenth and Nineteenth streets. Lot on Potrero, block 39, 100 x 200 feet.

Burnett School—Fourteenth avenue, south, near Railroad avenue, 2-story, twelve-room and basement "Frame—Cement and Plaster" building. Cost $54,372.92. Lot in South San Francisco Homestead, block 289. Lot 1, 75 x 100 feet, and additional lot purchased from Cecilia Wright, August 26, 1903, for $500, South San Francisco Homestead. Commencing at a point on the southwest line of Fourteenth avenue, south; distant 150 feet northwesterly along the northwesterly line of L street south; thence northwesterly along Fourteenth avenue south 32½ feet by uniform depth of 100 feet. September 27, 1909, from Martha A. Stapleton; commencing S. W. line Fourteenth avenue S. 182 feet 6 inches, S. W. on L. S. N. W. 42 feet 6 inches by S. W. 100 feet, block 289, S. S. F. Homestead and R. R. Association, $1,750. August, 1910, lot in Homestead Association, block 189, $5,500. October 23, 1911, from Isabella Sprague, Trustee. lot N. E. line Oakdale avenue 75 feet N. W. from Lane street N. W. 75 feet x N. E. 100 feet in block 289 South San Francisco Homestead (bonds 1908) $2,250.

Clement Cooking and Manual Training Center—(Suspended)—Temporary frame building, six rooms. Geary near Jones street. Lot in block 253, 77½ x 137½ feet; additional lot commencing at a point on the southerly line of Geary street, distant 137 feet 6 inches westerly from the southwest corner of Geary and Jones streets; thence northerly along said line of Geary street, 25 feet by south 137 feet 6 inches in depth, being a portion of 50 vara block 253. Purchased from S. L. and Mabel V. Starr, August 14, 1905, for $27,000. Recorded in Book 2, 134 of Deeds, page 98.

Cleveland School—Persia, between Moscow and Athens; 2-story, fourteen-room and basement "Special Construction" building. Cost $64,782.24. January 11, 1909, from Annie M. Creighton, lot northwest corner of Moscow street and Persia avenue, 100 feet by 300 feet, $6,500. February 15, 1909, from William McCall, lot in Excelsior Homestead Association, block 73, northeast corner Persia avenue and Athens street, 100 feet on Persia avenue by 300 feet on Athens street, $6,750.

Columbia School—Cost $30,300; frame building, eighteen roms and three portable roms. Florida street, between Twenty-fifth and Twenty-sixth streets. Lot in Mission, block 178. Lot No. 1, 100 x 200 feet; lot No. 2, 50 x 100 feet.

Columbus School—Temporary frame building, six rooms. Thirteenth avenue and Kirkham streets. Block No. 780. West of First avenue; 150 feet x 240 feet.

Cooper School—Temporary frame building, fifteen rooms. Greenwich street, between Jones and Leavenworth streets, lot in block 237, 137½ x 137½ feet.

Crocker School—Frame building, twenty rooms; cost $26,547; Page street, between Broderick and Baker streets. Lot in block 523, W. A., 137½ x 137½ feet. Additional lot purchased from W. J. Hawkins, May 16, 1905, for $2,750. Commencing at a point on the southerly line of Page street, distant 96 feet 10½ inches, easterly from the easterly line of Baker street; thence easterly 25 feet by uniform depth of 110 feet.

Daniel Webster **School**—Temporary frame building; Potrero Nuevo block 231, west line of Connecticut street; 125 feet north from Twentieth street, thence 150 feet x 200 feet from the Western Pacific R. R. Co., January 25, 1909; agreement in condemnation suit.

Denman School—Pierce street, between Fell and Hayes; 2-story, eighteen-room and basement Class "A" building. Cost $158,494.85. May 17, 1909, from the Edwin Barron estate, lot northeast corner Fell and Pierce streets, 137 feet 6 inches on Fell street, by 137 feet 6 inches on Pierce street, Western Addition, block 379, $29,118. October 18, 1909, from P. J. Stuparich and H. Adams, lot southeast corner Pierce and Hayes streets, 137½ by 137½, $37,125. June 13, 1910, from Emery B. Hopkins, lot N. side of Fell street, 137 feet 6 inches E. from E. line of Pierce street, 55 feet by 137½ feet, W. A. block 379, $9,500. September, 1910, two lots in W. A. block 379, $13,100.

Douglass School—Cost $28,787; frame building, eleven rooms. Corner Nineteenth and Collingwood streets. Lot in Horner's Addition, 135 x 113 feet. June 27, 1910, from Alfred H. Grant, lot east line of Nineteenth street, 113 feet west of Collingwood street, west 30 feet by south 135 feet, Horner's Addition block 194, $4,500. On Nineteenth street, 143 feet west of Collingwood street. West 40 feet by south 135 feet, Horner's Addition block 194, $6,250.

Dudley Stone School—Frame building, sixteen rooms; cost $28,755; Haight street, between Lott and Masonic avenues, lot in block 657, W. A., 137½ x 137½ feet. August 12, 1908, from E. L. Pritchard; consideration $6,000. Lot on south line of Haight street 112 feet 6 inches west of Central avenue, west 25 feet by 137 feet 6 inches being a part of Western Addition, block 657. August 12, 1908, from J. L. Pritchard, out of School Fund, lot south line Haight street 112 feet 6 inches west of Central avenue, west 25 feet by 137 feet 6 inches, Western Addition block 657, $6,000.

Edison School—Frame building, ten rooms; cost $27,936; Church and Hill streets. Lot in Mission, block 90, 101 feet 9 inches by 114 feet. August 21, 1911 from J. H. Attell intersection N. line Twenty-second street with W. line Church street; along N. line Twenty-second street 50 feet 10 inches by N. 114 feet, E. 50 feet 10 inches to W. line of Church. S. along Church to commencement. Mission block 90. $9,100. August 28, 1911, from Patrick Coleman N. line Twenty-second street 50 feet 10 inches W. of Church street, W. 25 feet x 114 N. Mission block 90, (bonds 1904), $4,500. August 28, 1911 from Anna Martin lot N. line Twenty-second street 75 feet 10 inches W. of Church street, W. 25 x N. 114 feet Mission block 90 (bonds 1904), $3,800.

Emerson School—Frame building, twenty rooms; cost $28,155; Pine street, between Scott and Devisadero streets. Lot in block 460, W. A., 137½ x 137½ feet.

Everett School—Frame building, sixteen rooms; cost $24,132. Sanchez street, between Sixteenth and Seventeenth streets. Lot in Mission, block 95, 125 x 160 feet. A lot of land 28 x 160 feet on Sanchez street north of and contiguous to the present site of the Everett Grammar School, $10,000. November 29, 1909, from Frank L. Roseneau, lot east line of Sanchez street 202 feet south of Sixteenth street south 28 feet by east 80 feet, in Mission block 95, $6,900. A Manual Training and Cooking Laboratory has been built. July 17, 1911, from Michael McHugh lot W. line Dehon street 290 feet N. of Seventeenth street, N. 28 x W. 100 Mission block 95, (bonds of 1908) $3,500.

Ethan Allen School—Temporary frame building, three rooms. Bryant street, near Sixth street.

Fairmount School—Frame building, twelve rooms. Chenery street, near Randall street, five portable rooms on premises. Lot in Fairmount tract, block 29, lot 1, 112 x 125 feet; lot 2, 62 x 175 feet.

Farragut School—Holloway avenue, between Capitol and Faxon; 2-story, eighteen-room and basement "Special Construction" building. Occupied by Board of Education, March 29, 1911. Cost $101,914.91. April 25, 1909, from John and Belle McCaffery, lot east line of Faxon avenue, 100 feet south from Halloway avenue, south 37½ feet by east 112½ feet, lot 25, lot 19, Lake View, $1,025. April 26, 1909, from Spaulding & Neff, lots 19, 20, 21, 22, 23, half of lot 24, and lots from 26 to 41, inclusive, block 19, Lake View, $11,512.50.

Francis Scott Key School—New frame building, eight rooms, $38,000. Forty-second avenue and I street. Lot in block No. 714. 150 feet by 240 feet.

Frank McCoppin School—Seventh avenue, between B and C; 2-story, eighteen-room and basement "Special Construction" building. Occupied by Board of Education, October 24, 1910. Cost $106,294.69. Lot in block 375, west of Sixth avenue, 150 x 240 feet. April 5, 1909, from Elizabeth M. Strand, lot west line Sixth avenue 200 feet south of B street, south 25 feet by west 120 feet O. L. block 375, $2,000. April 16, 1909, from Robert Bennett, lot east side Seventh avenue 200 feet south of B street, south 25 feet by east 100 feet O. L. block 375, $7,500.

Franklin School—Eighth, between Bryant and Harrison; 2-story, fourteen-room and basement "Special Construction" building. Cost $75,926.83. Lot in vara block 410, 140 x 275 feet.

Fremont School—Frame building, sixteen rooms; cost $35,873; McAllister street, between Broderick and Baker streets. Lot in block 530, W. A., 137½ x 137½ feet. Additional lot (No. 1) purchased from Herman Murphy, January 3, 1902, for $3,250. Commencing at a point on the northerly line of McAllister street, distant 112½ feet westerly from the westerly line of Broderick street; thence westerly 25 feet by uniform depth of 137 feet 6 inches. Recorded in book 1, 947 of Deeds, page 102; additional lot (No. 2) purchased from Owen McHugh, July 1, 1902. Commencing at a point on the northerly line of McAllister street, distant 96 feet 10½ inches easterly from the easterly line of Baker street, running thence easterly 25 feet, by uniform depth of 137 feet 6 inches. Recorded in book 1, 692 of Deeds, page 138.

Garfield School—Filbert and Kearny; 2-story, nineteen-room and basement "Special Construction" building. Occupied by Board of Education, November 21, 1910. Cost $111,188.18. Lot in block No. 82. Corner Filbert and Kearny streets; 137½ x 137½ feet. Additional lot adjacent in litigation. July 28, 1908, from Annie M. Gallagher and Mary B. Waller, lot on north line of

Filbert street, distant 137 feet 6 inches west from Kearny street; thence west on Filbert street 68 feet 9 inches by 137 feet 6 inches, being a part of 50 vara lot No. 461 and 50 vara lot No. 82, $8,000. From Charles Huth, November 2, 1908, south line of Greenwich street, between Kearny and Dupont streets, 25 feet square, block 82, $750. November 2, 1908, from Charles Kosta, rear portion of lot adjoining above 25 feet square, $550. West line of Kearny street 112 feet 6 inches south from Greenwich; thence south along west line of Kearny street 25 feet; thence at right angles west 87 feet 6 inches, thence at right angles north 25; thence east 87 feet 6 inches, purchased from the Hibernia Savings and Loan Society July 10, 1908, $850.

George Peabody School—Sixth avenue, between California and Clement streets; 2-story, fourteen-room and basement "Special Construction" building. Now in course of construction. Cost $80,545.02. Lot in block No. 176; 150 x 240 feet.

Girls' High School—Scott street, between Geary and O'Farrell; 2-story, twenty classrooms and basement, Class "C" building. Appropriation $350,000, spent to date $225,502.60. Temporary frame building completed at a cost of $16,000 Scott street, near Geary street. This school is not built on school property, but on property belonging to the City, and which originally formed a part of Hamilton Square. In 1870 the Board of Education obtained permission to use a portion for the erection of school buildings. Lot 275 feet front on Scott street, 341 feet 3 inches on Geary and O'Farrell streets.

Glen Park School—New frame building, twelve rooms, costing $42,500, San Jose and Joost avenues. Additional lot purchased from the estate of John Pforr, May 20, 1905, for $5,600. Mission and Thirtieth Extension Homestead Union. Beginning at the corner formed by the intersection of the southwesterly line of Berkshire street with the southeasterly line of Lippard avenue; thence southwesterly along Lippard avenue 400 feet; thence at right angles southeasterly 200 feet to the northwesterly line of Fulton avenue; thence at right angles northeasterly 400 feet along Fulton avenue to the southwesterly line of Berkshire street; thence at a right angle northwesterly along Berkshire street to the point of beginning, being all of block 3, Mission and Thirteenth Street Extension Homestead Union. Recorded in Book 2, 125 of Deeds, page 76.

Golden Gate School—New building; twelve rooms, Class "C" costing $73,533. Golden Gate avenue, between Pierce and Scott streets. Lot in block 433 W. A., 100 x 137½ feet. Additional lot purchased from Fred H. Hansen, July 20, 1905, for $4,375. Commencing at a point on the northerly line of Golden Gate avenue, distant thereon 68 feet 9 inches, westerly from the westerly line of Pierce street; thence westerly 25 feet, by uniform depth of 137 feet 6 inches. Additional lot (No. 2) purchased from Margaret Poyelson, June 28, 1905, for $8,856. Commencing at a point on the northerly line of Golden Gate avenue, distant thereon 93 feet 9 inches, westerly from the westerly line of Pierce street; thence westerly 43 feet 9 inches, by uniform depth of 137 feet 8 inches. Additional lot (No. 3) purchased from Gustave A. DeManiel, June 14, 1905, for $12,462. Commencing at a point on the northerly line of Golden Gate avenue, distant 137 feet 6 inches, westerly from the westerly line of Pierce street; thence westerly 37 feet 6 inches, by uniform depth of 137 feet 6 inches.

Grant School—Frame building, 8 rooms; cost $18,499; Pacific Avenue, between Broderick and Baker streets. Lot in block No. 546, W. A., 137½x137½ feet. January 8, 1912, from Cornelia M. Stafford lot S. line Broadway, 150 ft.

W. Broderick St. W. 60 x S. 127 ft. 8¼ in. W. A. Blk. 546. (Bonds 1904) $22,000; also from John Lee, Jr. lot S. line Broadway 210 W. of Broderick St. W. 65 ft. x S. 89 ft. 1⅝ in. x S. E. 39 ft. 7½ in. E. 55 ft. 9 in. N. 127 ft. 8¼ in. W. A. Blk. 546 (1904 bonds) $22,500.

Grattan School—Shrader street, between Alma and Grattan; 2-story, 16-room "Frame" building. Cost $68,579.17. Additional lot purchased from the Pope Estate Co. for $28,500. Recorded in Book 2, 130 of Deeds, page 204. Western Addition, block 874. Commencing at the point of intersection of the southerly line of Grattan street with the easterly line of Shrader street; thence easterly along Grattan street 203 feet 7¾ inches; thence at a right angle southerly 249 feet to the northerly line of Alma street; thence at a right angle westerly and along said line of Alma street 203 feet 7¾ inches to the easterly line of Shrader street; thence at a right angle northerly 249 feet 11 inches to the southerly line of Grattan street, and point of commencement.

Haight School—Frame building, 13 rooms; cost $23,488; Mission street, between Twenty-fifth and Twenty-sixth streets. Lot in Mission block 183; 150x117½ feet.

Hamilton School—Frame building, 17 rooms; cost $27,650; Geary street, between Scott and Pierce streets. (See Girls' High School).

Hancock School—Filbert street, between Jones and Taylor; 2-story, 18-room and basement Class "A" building. Now occupied by Board of Education. Cost $166,321.20. Lot in block 208, 100x120 ft. December 21, 1908, from R. H. McColgan and Mary E. Russell, north line Filbert street, 110 feet west from Taylor, west 60x120 feet, 50 vara lot No. 208, $10,800.

Harrison School—Jamestown Avenue, between Railroad and Jennings; 1-story, 6-room and basement "Special Construction" building. Occupied by Board of Education, May 15, 1911. Cost $22,435.41. All of block 584, Bay View Tract, Sub. 2, bounded by Railroad Avenue, J. street South, Thirty-fourth Avenue South, and Thirty-fifth Avenue South, except lot south line of Thirty-fourth Avenue South, 100 feet west of J street, S. W. 50 x S. 100 feet, $10,000.

Hawthorne School—Frame building, 11 rooms; cost $11,500; Shotwell street, between Twenty-second and Twenty-third streets, lot in Mission block 138, 122½x122½ feet.

Hearst School—Frame building, 25 rooms; cost $25,007; corner Fillmore and Hermann streets, lot in block 374 W. A., 137½x137½ ft.

Henry Durant School—Frame building 12 rooms; cost $18,294; Turk street, between Buchanan and Webster streets, lot in block 281 W. A., 137½x120 feet.

Horace Mann School—Frame building, 20 rooms; cost $33,149; Valencia street, between Twenty-second and Twenty-third streets. (See Agassiz School). December 28, 1908, from Moore Investment Company, commencing 205 feet south from Twenty-second street, thence south on Valencia street 37½ feet by 125 feet, Mission block No. 136, $15,000.

Hunter's Point School—Temporary frame building of 2 rooms. Eighth Avenue, between C and D streets. (Lot is leased).

Irving M. Scott School—Frame building, 20 rooms; cost $35,360; Tennessee street, near Twenty-second. Lot in Potrero, block No. 373, 150x200 feet.

James Lick School—Frame building, 14 rooms; cost $21,877; Noe and Twenty-fifth streets. Lot in Horner's Addition, block No. 163, 114x116 feet. November, 1910, additional lot, $5,600.

Jean Parker School—Broadway, between Powell and Mason streets; 2-story, 18-room and basement Class "A" building. Now in course of construction. Cost $173,355.57. Lot in block No. 157. Lot 1, 65 feet 2 inches by 137½ feet; lot 2, 30x91 feet 8 inches; lot 3, 39 feet 9 inches by 91 feet 8 inches, December 28, 1908, from Fannie Galloway, 227 feet 11 inches by 69 feet 7 inches of lot in 50 vara, block 157, 91 feet 8 inches perpendicularly distant from north line of Broadway, $2,000. January 4, 1909, from the estate of Jose M. Jininez, north line of Broadway, 137 feet east from east line of Mason street; thence east on Broadway 34 feet 4 inches by 137 feet 6 inches deep, 50 varas, lot No. 167, $8,925. November 15, 1909, from Bernardo Fernandez, lo tnorth of Broadway 171 feet 10 inches east of Mason, east 38 by north 137 feet 6 inches, 50 vara, block 167, $9,750.

Jefferson School—Temporary frame building, 4 rooms. Lot in block 690 Nineteenth Avenue between I and J streets, $3,000, 150x240 feet.

John Swett Grammar School—McAllister street, between Gough and Franklin streets; 2-story, 16-room and basement Class "C" building. Cost $91,156.74. Lot in block No. 136, W. A., 137½x137½ feet. June 27, 1910, from Elizabeth M. Kreuz, lot south line of Golden Gate Avenue 169½ feet west of Franklin street, west 27½ by south 120 feet, W. A. block 136, $11,000. From Sara Patek, lot south line of Golden Gate Avenue, 197 feet west from Franklin street, west 25 feet by south 120 feet, W. A. block 136, $9,750. From Mary Mocker, lot south side of Golden Gate Avenue, 222 feet west from Franklin street, 28x120 feet, W. A. block 136, $12,000. July 5, 1910, from Veronica J. Porcher, lot on the south line of Golden Gate Avenue, 137½ feet west from Franklin street, west 32 feet by south 137½ feet, W. A. block 136, $14,000. July 25, 1910, west 32 feet x south 137½ feet, W. A. block 136, $14,000. August 15, 1910, from 137½ feet east from Gough street, east 25 feet x south 137½ feet, W. A. block No. 136.

Junipero Serra School—Holly Park Avenue, between Highland and West Park; 2-story, 18-room and basement "Special Construction" building. Occupied by Board of Education, January 5, 1911. Cost $91,603.59. July 12, 1909, from A. B. Ruggles, lots 31, 32, 33, 34, 35, 36, 37, 38, 39, 40. Block 3, Holly Park Tract, $13,700. October 9, 1911, from Anita P. C. T. Shelby lot 29, Block 3 Holly Park Tract 25 feet. x 100 ft. (School Bonds 1908) $3,255, also in same block from Cayetano Arellano lot 30, 100 ft. x 25 ft. (Bonds 1908) $2,700.

Kate Kennedy School—Noe and Thirtieth streets; 2-story, 15-room and basement "Special Construction" building. Occupied by Board of Education, March 20, 1911. Cost $102,370.57. May 3, 1909, from Ellen S. McGowan and E. Connors, lot west line of Noe street 26½ feet north of 30th street, north 25 feet by west 105 feet in Horner Addition, block 172, $1,500. April 5, 1909, from Ellen S. McGowan and Delia Williams, lot southwestern corner Noe and Day streets, 105 feet by south on Noe street 26½ feet in Horner Addition, block 172, $6,000. April 12, 1909, from Ellen S. McGowan, west line Noe street, 25½ feet south of Day street, south 150 feet by west 105 feet, south 51½ feet; by west 50 feet by north 228 feet by east 50 feet by south 26½ feet; thence east 105 feet, Horner Addition, block 172, $16,600. May 24, 1909, from W. E. Smith and Ellen McGowan, lot northwest corner Noe and 30th streets. North 26½ feet by west 105 feet, Horner Addition, block 172, $2,150. June 1, 1909, from Ellen S. McGowan and Joe Gottwald, lot south line of Day street 155 feet west of Noe street, west 25 feet by south 228 feet to the north line of 30th street in Horner Addition, block 172, $5,400.

Lafayette School—Thirty-seventh Avenue, near Point Lobos.

Laguna Honda School—New building; cost $91,418.99; 14 rooms; brick, class B. Seventh Avenue, between I and J streets. Lot in block No. 678, 150x240 feet.

Lincoln School—Harrison street, near Fourth street; 1-story, 12-room "Frame-Cement-Plaster" building. Cost $74,650.96. Lot in block No. 374, 195x160 feet. Additional lot (1) purchased from Bertha Gunnison, February 9, 1906, for $4,250. Commencing at a point on the northwesterly line of Harrison street, distant thereon 275 feet, southwesterly on the southwest line of Fourth street, running thence southerly along said line of Harrison street; thence at a right angle northwesterly 85 feet; thence at a right angle northwesterly 85 feet to the north line of Harrison street from the point of commencement. Additional lot (2) purchased from Herman Scholten, December 18, 1905, for $2,800. Commencing at a point on the southeasterly line of Clara street, distant 275 feet southwesterly from the point of intersection of said southeasterly line of Clara street with the southwesterly line of Fourth street, running thence southwesterly along said southeasterly line of Clara street 25 feet; thence at a right angle southeasterly 75 feet; thence at a right angle northeasterly 25 feet; thence at a right angle northwesterly 75 feet to the southeasterly line of Clara street and point of commencement.

Longfellow School—Corner Morse and Lowell streets; 2-story, 14 rooms and basement, "Special Construction." Occupied January 3, 1911. Cost $78,675.38. Lot in West End Map. Block 23; 80x165 feet. March 1, 1909, from D. A. Helbing et al., lot southwest corner Lowell, Mission and Morse, 267 by 213, being lots 49, 50 and 51, West End Homestead, $9,250.

Lowell High School—Frame building, 21 rooms. Sutter street, between Octavia and Gough streets. Lot in block No. 158, W. A., 137½x120½ feet. July 1, 1912 from Trustees of Centennary M. E. Church S. side Bush street 137 ft. 6 in. E. of Octavia, E. 68 feet 9 in. x 137 ft. 6 in. W. A. Blk. 158 (Bonds 1904) $22,000. November 29, 1909, from Ivan Treadwell, et al., the whole of Western Addition Block 667 bounded by Masonic Avenue, Hayes, Ashbury and Grove streets, $116,500, on which will be built a 3-story, 60-room and basement Class "C" building. Now in course of construction. Spent to date.

McKinley School—Fourteenth and Castro; 2-story, 18-room and basement "Special Construction" building. Occupied by Board of Education, November 21, 1910. Cost $111,018.18. Lot purchased from Jas. Irvine, August 14, 1905, cost $35,000. Mission block No. 121, commencing at the southwesterly corner of Fourteenth and Castro streets; thence westerly along the southerly line of Fourteenth street 320 feet; thence at right angles southerly 230 feet to the northerly line of Henry street; thence easterly along said last named line 320 feet to the westerly line of Castro street; thence northerly along said last named line 230 feet to the point of commencement.

Madison School—Clay street, between Cherry and First Avenue; 2-story, 14-room and basement "Special Construction" building. Occupied by Board of Education, May 24, 1910. Lot in block No. 848, Western Addition, 137½x137½ feet. Cost $87,945.72.

Marshall Primary School—Temporary frame building, 15 rooms. Julian Avenue, between Fifteenth and Sixteenth streets. Lot in Mission, block No. 35, 200x182 feet. (Also occupied by the Mission Grammar school). July 13, 1908; from R. A. Archbishop of San Francisco, lot corner Nineteenth and Angelica streets (resolution 1426 and 1757, Board of Supervisors). Commencing intersection south line Nineteenth street with east line Angelica street, south 205 feet to Cumberland Place; thence east 183 feet by north 114 feet west 50 feet N. W. 118 feet 2½ inches to Nineteenth street, west 102 feet to point of commencement. Mission, block 72, $33,625. Spent on plans for new building $3,419.70. Commencing at point of intersection of the south line of Nineteenth street with the east line of Angelica street, thence south along Angelica street 205 feet to the north line of Cumberland Place, thence east 183 feet, thence north 91 feet, thence at right angles west 50 feet, thence northwest 118 feet 2½ inches to a point in the south line of Nineteenth street, which is distant east 102 feet from the southeast corner of Nineteenth and Angelica streets; thence west on south line of Nineteenth street 102 feet to point of commencement, being a portion of Mission block 72 purchased from Rev. P. W. Riordan, Roman Catholic Archbishop of San Francisco, a corporation sale for $33,625, as alternative site for the Marshall Primary authorized by the bond issue September 29, 1903.

Mission Grammar School—Mission, between Fifteenth and Sixteenth; 2-story, 19-room and basement Class "A" building. Occupied by Board of Education, January 26, 1910. Cost $171,836.66. Land (See Marshall School).

Mission High School—Brick building, 25 rooms; costing about $173,000. 18th and Dolores streets. Mission block No. 85, 398x194 feet. Purchased in 1896 for $52,500. April 19, 1909, from Owen M. V. Roberts, lot in Mission block 85, south line of Dorland street 88 feet east of Church street, east 25 feet by south 100 feet $3,500. April 19, 1909, from J. and Winifred O'Donnell, lot south line Dorland street 138 feet southeast of Church street, southeast 25 feet by south 100 feet in Mission block 85, $5,225. April 19, 1909, from the Catholic Apostolic church, or north line of Eighteenth street 112 feet east of Church street, east 25 feet by north 114 feet, $7,800. June 1, 1909; from Amelia Dorland and Leonora Son, lot in Mission block No. 85, southeast corner Dorland and Church streets, south 35 feet 8 inches by east 88 feet, $6,300. June 1, 1909, from Herman D. Junck, lot in Mission block 85 south line Dorland street, 138 feet east from Church street; thence 100 feet east, 25⅝ feet by north 100 feet; thence west 25⅝ feet, $17,000. June 1, 1909, from Jessie Hauser, lot east line of Church street 168 feet north of Eighteenth street, north 27 feet by east 88 feet, $10,000; also northeast corner Church and Eighteenth streets, 62 feet on Eighteenth street by 114 feet on Church street, Mission block No. 85, $17,000, June 28, 1909, from Eva Topper, lot east line Church street 141 feet north Eighteenth street, north 27 feet by east 88 feet Mission block 85, $11,085. October 4, 1909, from Ida G. Shade, lot north line Eighteenth street, 137 feet east of Church, east 25 by north 114 feet, $9,000. From James A. Symon, lot north line Eighteenth street, 62 feet east from east line of Church, east 25 by north 114 feet in Mission block 85, $8,500. November 1, 1909, from David Dorward, lot south line of Church street, 114 feet north of Eighteenth street north 27 by east 88 in Mission block 85, $9,100. November 15, 1909, from James A. Symon, exec., north line of Eighteenth street, 87 feet east of Church street, east 25 feet by north 114 feet, $8,500.

Monroe School—New building; Class "C", costing $83,500. China Avenue and London street. Lot in block 14, Excelsior Homestead, 150x100 feet. Additional lot purchased from Thomas Shewbridge, August 30, 1902, Excelsior Homestead, block No. 14. New lot, corner China Avenue and Paris street, northwest 100 feet by northeast 150 feet, lot 4, block 14, Excelsior Homestead. September 5, 1911, from George Somers lot E. side London street 150 ft. N. E. from N. E. line Excelsior Avenue N. E. 75 ft. along S. E. line London street x S. E. 100 feet Excelsior Homestead Block 14. (Bonds 1904) $4,300. September 11, 1911, from Margaret Richter lot S. E. line London street 225 feet N. E. from N. E. line Excelsior Ave. thence 75 ft. N. E. x 100 ft. S. E. Excelsior Homestead Block 14. (Bonds 1904) $4,750.

Moulder School—Frame building, 10 rooms, cost $21,000; Page and Gough streets, lot in block No. 145, W. A., 137½x120 feet.

Noe Valley School—Frame building, 15 rooms, cost $29,474. 24th. and Douglass. Additional lot (No. 1) purchased from George and Christina Gies. Deed dated October 5, 1901. Horner's Estate, block 244. Commencing at a point on the west line of Douglass street, 139 feet north to Twenty-fourth street; thence north on the west line of Douglass street 25 feet by west 125 feet in depth. Additional lot (No. 2) purchased from Mary E. Gies. Deed dated October 7, 1901. Commencing at a point on the west line of Douglass street 114 feet north of Twenty-fourth street; thence north on the west line of Douglass street 25 feet by west 125 feet in depth. Additional lot (No. 2) purchased from Mary E. Gies. Deed dated October 7, 1901. Commencing at a point on the west line of Douglass street 114 feet north of Twenty-fourth street; thence north on the west line of Douglass street 25 feet by west 125 feet in depth. Additional lot (No. 3) commencing at a point on the west line of Douglass street, 64 feet north of Twenty-fourth street; thence north on Douglass street, 50 feet, by west 125 feet in depth from Mary Tobener, Sept. 6, 1901. Additional lot (No. 4) purchased from James M. Curtin, deed dated September 6, 1901. Commencing at a point on the northwest corner of Twenty-fourth and Douglass streets; thence north 64 feet, west 125 feet, north 50 feet, west 51 feet 8 inches, south 114 feet, east 176 feet, 8 inches. Additional lot (No. 5) purchased from Eliz. Overend for $2,050. Commencing at a point on the south line of Elizabeth street, 125 feet west of Douglass street; thence west on Elizabeth street, 51 feet 8 inches, by south 114 feet, in depth.

Oral School for Deaf—Located in a classroom of the Golden Gate School.

Oriental Public School—Temporary frame building, 5 rooms. Clay street, near Powell street, 50 vara block, No. 137.

Pacific Heights School—Frame building, 19 rooms; cost $31,270; Jackson, between Fillmore and Webster streets. Lot in block 318, W. A., 137½x137½ feet. May 17, 1909, from Mary W. Shannon, lot west line of Jackson street, 113 feet west from Webster street, west 24½ feet by north 90 feet, Western Addition, block 318, $11,500. June 1, 1909, from Lillie E. Lincoln, north side of Jackson street 112 feet east of Fillmore street, east 25½ feet by north 127 feet 8¼ inches, Western Addition, Block 318, $12,000.

Parkside School—On Taraval street, near Thirteenth Avenue. Lot in O. L. block 1114, 150x240 feet; 1 room, frame building; value $1,700.

Paul Revere School—Frame building, 2 rooms; cost $1,401.58; corner Corbett Road and Ocean Avenue. Cost $1,401.58. Lot in San Miguel, 100 feet by 240 feet.

Polytechnic High School—Temporary frame building, 16 rooms. Frederick street, near First Avenue. Lot purchased from the City Realty Company, July 31, 1905, for $65,000. Western Addition, block No. 740. Commencing at a point on the south line of Frederick street 121½ feet east from First Avenue; thence in a southerly direction 175 feet; thence at a right angle easterly 1 foot 6 inches; thence at a right angle southerly 100 feet to a point in the north line of Carl street 151½ feet of First Avenue; thence easterly along Carl street 464 and 8-12 feet to a point 269 4-12 feet west of Willard street; thence northerly 278 5-12 feet to a point on the south line of Frederick street 226 11-12 feet West of Willard street; thence west along south line of Frederick street 505 10-12 feet to point of commencement.

(Main building) 3-story, 61-room, attic and basement. Class "C" building;

(Shop building) 2-story, 13-room, shops and drafting rooms, Class "A" building.

Appropriation $600,000. Contracts for construction of shop buildings awarded. Spent to date $202,919.22.

Portola School—Bacon street, between Berlin and Girard streets; 2-story, 18 rooms, "Special Construction" building. Occupied April 22, 1910. Cost $97,042.23. Lot in University Mound survey, 50 feet by 120 feet. Additional block purchased from P. J. Kennedy, August 22, 1905, for $5,000. University Mound survey, block 12. Commencing at a point formed by the intersection of the northwesterly line of Bacon street, in the southwesterly line of Girard street, running thence northwesterly along Girard street 200 feet and thence at a right angle 240 feet to Berlin street; thence at a right angle southeasterly and along Berlin street 200 feet to the northwesterly line of Bacon street; thence at a right angle 240 feet to the southwesterly line of Girard street and point of commencement, being the southerly half of block No. 12, University Mound Survey.

Redding School—Temporary frame building, 12 rooms. Pine street, between Polk and Larkin streets. Lot in block 14, W. A., 200x120 feet.

Rincon School—Temporary frame building, two rooms. Lots in 100 vara block 358; Silver street, between Second and Third streets. Lot No. 1, 88x70 feet; lot No. 2, 100x185 feet.

Rochambeau School—New building, 12 rooms; cost $37,000; Twenty-fifth Avenue and California street, block 95, 150x240 feet.

Roosevelt School—Frame building, 17 rooms, costing $31,216. First Avenue, near Point Lobos Avenue. Lot in Academy of Science block W. A. block No. 647, O. L. R. 157 feet 7 inches by 240 feet. The Board of Education has permission to use this lot for school purposes.

San Francisco Commercial High School—Grove street, between Polk and Larkin streets; 3-story, 31-room and basement Class "A" building. Occupied by Board of Education, December 14, 1910. Cost $261,635.28. Lot in block 3, W. A., 137½x120 feet. January 18, 1909, from F. Siefke, north line Grove street 100 feet west of Larkin street, 37½ feet by 120 feet, Western Addition, block No. 3, $15,000. February 8, 1909, from Dorothea Fassman, west line of Grove street 112½ feet east from east line of Polk street, east 25 feet by 137½ feet, Western Addition, block No. 3, $9,800. June 21, 1909, from Chas. Worth, lot north line Grove street, 82½ feet east of Polk street, east 30 feet by north 120 feet, Western Addition, block No. 3, $12,000.

Sheridan School—Capitol Avenue, between Farallones and Lobos; 2-story, 18-room and basement "Special Construction" building. Occupied by Board of Education, December 12, 1910. Cost $105,749.60. Lot in block S, Railroad Homestead Association 100 feet by 125 feet. Lot 7' May 10, 1909, from W. S. Benthame, lot northwest corner of Farallones and Capital Avenue in block L, Railroad Homestead Association, $3,450. September 23, 1908, from Welthy and Wm. S. Stafford, north side of Minerva street 150 feet west of Plymouth street; thence west on Minerva street 50 feet by north 125 feet. November 29, 1909, from Adolph Mueller, Caroline Bauer, admx. Wm. T. and Edward Bauer, interest and improvement in lot southwest corner of Capitol Avenue and Lobos street, 50 feet by 125 feet, in R. R. Homestead Association, block L, $6,300.

Sherman School—Frame building, 14 rooms. Union street, near Franklin. Lot in block No. 117, W. A., 137½ feet by 137½ feet.

Spring Valley School—Washington street, between Hyde and Larkin streets; 2-story, 14-room and basement "Class "A" building. Now in course of construction. Cost $118,595.67. Temporary frame building, 9 rooms, Broadway, near Polk street. Lot in block 21, W. A., 137½ feet by 137½ feet. May 24, 1909, from Margaret and Catherine Matthews, lot south line of Jackson street 137 feet 6 inches east from Larkin street, east 68 feet 9 inches by 137½ feet, $15,250. From Samuel Polack, lot south line of Jackson street 137 feet 6 inches west of Hyde street, west 34 feet 4½ inches by 137 feet 6 inches, 50 vara block 302, $6,975. July 19, 1909, from Edward P. McGeeney, et al., lot south line Jackson, 171 feet 10½ inches, west of Hyde west 34 feet 4½ inches, by south 137 feet 6 inches, $9,100.

Starr **King** School—Temporary frame building, 9 rooms, San Bruno Avenue, near Twenty-fifth street. Commencing on the east line of Utah street 100 feet south from Twenty-fifth street, thence south on Utah street 100x200 feet in depth to San Bruno Avenue, being lots 13, 14, 15, 16, 25, 26, 27, 28, in Potrero block No. 85. January 8, 1912 from Margaret Hayden et al. lot S. E. corner 25th and Utah streets 125 ft. on 25th and 100 ft. on Utah street (Bonds 1904) $4,500.

Sunnyside School—New class C building. Cost $30,000. Sunnyside block No. 219. Additional lots 10 and 24, inclusive, Sunnyside tract. Purchased from the Sunnyside Land Company, July 9, 1902. June 22, 1908, bought from Monarch Mutual Building and Loan Association sewer right of way for Sunnyside School portion of lot 23, Sunnyside, block 47, $400.

Sutro **School**—Thirteenth Avenue, between California and Clement streets; 2-story, 18-room and basement "Special Construction" building. Occupied by Board of Education, July 25, 1910. Cost $101,341.49. Lot in block 179; west of First Avenue; 150x240 feet. January 18, 1909, from F. C. Fish and J. J. Higgin, lot on west line Twelfth Avenue 200 feet south from California street, 25 feet by 140 feet, in block 170, $7,100.

Ungraded School—Temporary frame building. 10 rooms. Union street, near Kearny street. Lot in 50 vara block 62, 137½x137½ feet.

Visitacion Valley School—Visitacion Avenue, between Leland and Schwerin streets; 2-story, 12 rooms, "Frame" building. Cost $46,623.88.

Washington Grammar School—New steel-brick building; 20 rooms and auditorium. Cost approximates $118,944. Washington and Mason streets. Lot in 50 vara block No. 188; 137½x137½ feet. Additional new lot No. 1; purchased from the estate of Louise C. Kauffman, March 10, 1905, for $7,500. Commencing at a point on the southerly line of Washington street, 137 feet 6 inches northerly from the southwest corner of Mason and Washington streets; thence southerly 137 feet 6 inches by west 34 feet 4½ inches, being a portion of 50 vara, lot 188. Additional new lot No. 2, purchased from Julie Dunnier and others, July 12, 1905, for $9,500. Commencing at a point on the southerly line of Washington street, distant 170 feet 10½ inches from the southwest corner of Mason and Washington streets; thence northerly 34 feet 4½ inches by south 137 feet 6 inches in depth, being a portion of 50 vara, lot 188.

Washington Irving School—Temporary frame building, 6 rooms. Broadway, between Montgomery and Sansome streets. Lot in 50 vara block No. 47, 68¾ x137½ feet.

Winfield Scott School—Building cost $42,206.43. Lombard street, between Broderick and Baker streets. Lot in block No. 553, W. A.; 137½x137½ feet.

Yerba Buena School—Building cost $59,206.43. Greenwich street, between Webster and Fillmore streets. Lot in block No. 325, W. A.; 137½x120 feet. February 23, 1909, from McEwen Bros. lot Webster and Greenwich streets west 137½ feet by 120 feet in Western Addition, block No. 235, $17,000. $30,000 of the above cost were contributed by the school children of the United States immediately subsequent to the Great Fire of 1906.

LIST OF UNOCCUPIED PROPERTIES BELONGING TO SCHOOL DEPARTMENT.

Lot in 50 vara block No. 220; northwest corner Bush and Taylor streets; 137½x137½ feet.

Lot in 50 vara block No. 286; Golden Gate Avenue, near Hyde street; 110x137½ feet.

Lot in 100 vara block No. 348; Tehama street, between First and Second streets, irregular in size; about 118x155 feet.

Lot in 50 vara block No. 160; Powell street, between Washington and Jackson streets; 68¾x137½ feet.

Lot in Mission Block No. 8; 137½ feet x 137½ feet.

Lot on Bush street, between Larkin and Hyde streets.

Precita Valley School, August 21, from George Miller, commencing W. line Alabama street 90 ft. S. from Norwich, S. 25 ft. x 110 ft., lot 168, Precita Valley lands. (Bonds of 1904), $3,700.

Precita Valley School, August 21, from Roger R. Vair, Lot commencing S. W. corner Alabama and Norwich streets, S. 90, W. 110 ft., S. 50 ft. W. 110 ft. North 140 ft. E. 220, lots 166, 167, 168, Precita Valley lands. (Bonds 1904), $10,300.

Precita Valley School, November 6, 1911, from Frances A. Curran, Lot W. line Alabama street, 115 ft. S. Norwich street. S. 25 ft. x 100 ft. (Bonds 1904), $4,300.

December 4, 1911 (Jackson Primary) from C. W. Moores, agent, N. line Hayes, 140 ft. 6 inches W. from W. line Clayton street, W. 122 ft. x 275 ft. W. A. block 685. (Bonds 1904), $37,500.

Lot in 100 vara block 371; Fifth street, near Market; 275x275 feet. Leased to Wise Realty Company (later merged into the Lincoln Realty Company) for thirty-five years, at a total rental of $2,835,000, as follows: for the first five years, a rental of $3,780 per month, and for the remaining thirty years, a rental of $7,245 per month.

Lot in Mission block No. 21; West Mission street, between Herman and Ridley streets; 133¾x137½ feet.

Lot in 50 vara block No. 118; corner Bush and Stockton streets; 137½x137½ feet; 50 vara, lot 301.

Lot in Mission Block No. 72. Commencing at a point formed by the intersection of the southerly line of Nineteenth street with the easterly line of Angelica street, running thence southerly along said easterly line of Cumberland Place; thence easterly along said northerly line of Cumberland Place and Cumberland Place Extension 183 feet; thence at a right angle northerly 91 feet; thence at a right angle northerly 50 feet; thence in a northwesterly direction 118 feet 2½ inches to a point in the southerly line of Nineteenth street, which point is distant easterly 102 feet from the southeasterly corner of Nineteenth and Angelica streets; thence westerly along said southerly line of Nineteenth street 102 feet to the point of commencement. Purchased from His Grace P. W. Riordan, Roman Catholic Archbishop of San Francisco, for $33,625, as an alternate site for the Marshall Primary school. Recorded in Book 128 of Deeds, page 251, new series.

Lot in 50 vara block No. 119; Post street, between Grant avenue and Stockton streets; 70x122½ feet. Leased at an average of $911.42 per month.

Total rental, 35 years	$382,800.00
Average rental, per month	911.42
Graduated Rentals—Leases commenced December 16, 1908:	
First 4 months of lease, per month	$ 250.00
Second 4 months, per month	300.00
Third 4 months, per month	350.00
Second year, per month	400.00
Third year, per month	450.00
Fourth year, per month	500.00
Fifth year, per month	550.00
Sixth year, per month	650.00
Seventh year, per month	700.00
Eighth year, per month	750.00
Ninth year, per month	800.00
Tenth year, per month	850.00
Eleventh year, per month	900.00
Twelfth year, per month	900.00
13th and 14th years, per month	950.00
15th year, per month	1,000.00
16th to 25 years, inc., per month	1,000.00
26th to 35th years, inc., per month	1,125.00

Lot in 50 vara block No. 182, on northeast corner Taylor and Vallejo streets; 137½x137½ feet.

Lot in 50 vara block No. 302, on Washington street, between Hyde and Leavenworth streets; 137½x137½ feet. (Site of new Spring Valley School.)

Lot in Mission Block No. 61, on Nineteenth street, between Mission and Howard streets; 137½x137½ feet, less 60 feet included in Capp street. Title in litigation.

Lot in block No. 29, W. A., on south side of Francisco street, between Larkin and Polk streets; 137½x137½ feet.

Lot in block No. 111, W. A., on south line of Bay street, between Franklin and Gough streets; 137½x137½ feet. In litigation.

Lot in block No. 123, W. A., on south line of Washington street, between Franklin and Gough streets; 137½x137½ feet.

Lot in block No. 253, W. A., on south line of Geary street, between Jones and Leavenworth streets; 102½x137½ feet. (Present location of school repair shop.)

Lot in block No. 465, W. A., on north line of Jackson street, between Scott and Divisadero streets; 137½x137½ feet.

West of First Avenue and north of the Park, the School Department owns property as follows.

(All not otherwise stated are 150x250 feet.)

Block 152; Thirty-first avenue, between California and Clement streets, $10,000.

Block 164; Nineteenth Avenue, between California and Clement streets, $17,000.

Block 242; Forty-third avenue, between Point Lobos avenue and A street, $7,000.

Block 248; Thirty-seventh avenue. between Point Lobos avenue and A street, $8,000.

Block 254; Thirty-first avenue, between Point Lobos avenue and A street. $8,000.

Block 260; Twenty-fourth avenue, between Point Lobos avenue and A street, $10,000.

Block 266; Nineteenth avenue, between Point Lobos avenue and A street, $15,000.

Block 272; Thirteenth avenue, between Point Lobos avenue and A street, $18,000.

Block 278; Seventh avenue, between Point Lobos avenue and A street, $22,000.

Block 339; Forty-third avenue, between B and C streets, $3,000.

Block 345; Thirty-seventh avenue, between B and C streets, $4,000.

Block 351; Thirty-first avenue, between B and C streets, $4,000.

Block 357; Twenty-fifth avenue, between B and C streets, $3,500.

Block 363; Nineteenth avenue, between B and C streets, $18,000.

Block 369; Thirteenth avenue, between B and C streets, $12,000.

Block 395; Sixteenth avenue, between C and D streets, $8,000.

Block 407; Twenty-eighth avenue, between C and D streets, $6,000.

Block 418; Twenty-ninth avenue, between C and D streets, $6,000.

Also west of First avenue and south of the Park, as follows:

(All not otherwise stated are 150x240 feet.)

Block 673; First avenue, between I and J streets; 107x178 feet. $10,000.

Block 690; Nineteenth avenue, between I and J streets, $10,000.

Block 696; Twenty-fifth avenue, between I and J streets, $7,000.

Block 702; Thirty-first avenue, between I and J streets, $7,000.

Block 708; Thirty-seventh avenue, between I and J streets, $4,000.

Block 775; Eighth avenue, between K and L streets, $15,000.

Block 786; Nineteenth avenue, between K and L streets, $12,000.

Block 792; Twenty-fifth avenue, between K and L streets, $6,000.

Block 798; Thirty-first avenue, between K and L streets, $4,000.

Block 804; Thirty-seventh avenue, between K and L streets, $4,000.

Block 810; Forty-third avenue, between K and L streets, $4,000.

Block 872; Thirteenth avenue, between M and N streets, $7,000.

Block 878; Nineteenth avenue, between M and N streets, $9,000.

Block 884; Twenty-fifth avenue, between M and N streets, $4.000.

Block 890; Twenty-first avenue, between M and N streets, $4,000.

Block 896; Thirty-seventh avenue, between M and N streets, $4,000.

Block 902; Forty-third avenue, between M and N streets, $2,000.

Block 952; Ninth avenue, between O and P streets; irregular, 147½x182 feet, $4,000.

Block 957; Thirteenth avenue, between O and P streets, $3,000.

Block 963; Nineteenth avenue, between O and P streets, $6,000.

Block 969; Twenty-fifth avenue, between O and P streets, $5,000.

Block 975; Twenty-first avenue, between O and P streets, $4,000.

Block 981; Thirty-seventh avenue, between O and P streets, $3,500.

Block 987; Forty-third avenue, between O and P streets, $3,500.

Block 1,038; Thirteenth avenue, between Q and R streets, $3,000.

Block 1,044; Nineteenth avenue, between Q and R streets, $7,000.

Block 1,050; Twenty-fifth avenue, between Q and R streets, $3,000.

Block 1,056; Thirty-first avenue, between Q and R streets, $3,000.

Block 1,062; Thirty-seventh avenue, between Q and R streets, $3,000.

Block 1,068; Forty-third avenue, between Q and R streets, $4,000.

Block 1,120; Nineteenth avenue, between S and T streets, $6,000.

Block 1,126; Twenty-fifth avenue, between S and T streets, $5,000.

Block 1,132; Thirty-first avenue, between S and T streets, $4,000.

Block 1,138; Thirty-seventh avenue, between S and T streets, $5,000.

Block 1,144; Forty-third avenue, between S and T streets, $4,000.

Block 1,186; Fourteenth avenue, between U and V streets; irregular 161x 92½ feet, $3,000.

Block 1,191; Nineteenth avenue, between U and V streets, $6,000.

Block 1,197; Twenty-fifth avenue, between U and V streets, $5,000.

Block 1,203; Twenty-first avenue, between U and V streets, $5,000.

Block 1,209; Thirty-seventh avenue, between U and V streets, $4,000.

Block 1,215; Forty-third avenue, between U and V streets, $4,000.

Block 1,258; Nineteenth avenue, between W and X streets, $4,000.

Block 1,264; Twenty-fourth avenue, between W and X streets, $3,000.

Block 1,276; Thirty-seventh avenue, between W and X streets; irregular; 125 feet 10 inches by 240 feet, $4,000.

Block 1,282; Forty-third avenue, between W and X streets; irregular; 11 feet 2 inches by 240 feet, $300.

LOTS IN POTRERO.

Block 46; York street, between Fifteenth and Alameda streets; 100x200. Rented at $2 per month.

Block 127; Vermont street, between Eighteenth and Nineteenth streets; 120x 200 feet.

Block 149; Kansas street, north of Army street; 150x200 feet, $1,663.

Block 163; Rhode Island street, between Mariposa and Eighteenth streets; 100x200 feet. Rented $2 per month.

Block 226; Arkansas street, south of Twenty-third street; 150x200 feet, $832.

Block 287; Texas street, between Twenty-third and Twenty-fourth streets; 150x200 feet.

Block 391; southwest corner Kentucky and Twentieth street; 150x200 feet.

Potrero block 254, O. L. R., also Potrero block 265, O. L. R., condemned and acquired by Western Pacific Railroad Company for $14,000.

OTHER OUTSIDE LOTS.

Precita Valley lands; Eve street, between Army and Adam streets; 150x32 feet.

Paul Tract Homestead; Berlin street, between Ordway and Ward streets; 85 feet and 2 inches by 120 feet.

December 21, 1908, from Joseph B. and Carlotta L. Keenan, all of block No. 132 of University Mound Homestead Association, excepting one lot 25 feet by 100 feet on Pioche street, and one on Cambridge street, 25x120 feet, $8,250.

WITHIN THE PRESIDIO WALL.

Block 553, W. A. Commencing on the north line of Lombard street, 137½ feet west from Broderick street; thence west on Lombard street, 137½ feet by 137½ feet in depth. Lot 2. Outside Land Reservation.

Block 810, W. A. Commencing on the north line of Broadway, 137½ feet west from Walnut street; thence west on Broadway, 137½ feet by 137½ feet in depth. Lot 2. Outside Land Reservation.

Block 841, W. A. Commencing on the north line of Pacific avenue, 137½ feet west from Maple street; thence west on Pacific avenue, 137½ feet by 137½ feet in depth. Lot 2. Outside Land Reservation.

REPORT ON CHILDREN'S SAVINGS BANK SYSTEM, BY SCHOOL DIRECTOR, JAMES E. POWER.

San Francisco, July 1, 1912.

To the Honorable,
The Board of Education.

Ladies and Gentlemen:—It is with extreme pleasure that I have the honor to herewith submit the first annual report on the School Children's Savings Bank System. It is very gratifying indeed to be able to report to this Board that as a result of the hearty cooperation and support of the principals and teachers of this department the system has had a greater success in San Francisco than in any other city of the world, of similar size.

REPORT.

1. INTRODUCTION OF SYSTEM.

In February 1911, upon the recommendation of the undersigned, the members of the Board of Education expressed themselves in favor of the School Children's Savings Bank and advised me to submit a plan of operation to the Board. Shortly after this expression of opinion from the members of the Board, a communication on the subject was received from the Social Science Department of the California Club and said communication was referred to me. Shortly thereafter a conference was held with the Social Science Committee of the California Club. There were also several conferences with Miss Fannie Stockton, a teacher in the department, who had given considerable thought to this work. In addition to these, I conferred with bankers and found that Mr. John Drum of the San Francisco Savings Union had spent considerable time in gathering data and statistics from other cities.

As a result of the above the Board on April 5th, 1911 adopted a resolution ordering the Savings Bank System established in the schools and authorizing the undersigned to submit plan of operation. On May 19th, 1911, partial report on plan of operation was submitted and the Bank of Italy of San Francisco selected as the official depository. On July 19th, 1911, the following report was adopted by the Board:

2. PLAN OF OPERATION.

To the Honorable,
The Board of Education.

Mrs. Kincaid and Gentlemen:—I herewith submit the following report on plan of operation for School Savings System, the same being agreeable to the official depository (Bank of Italy) as follows:

Stamps of the denomination of one cent will be provided; also folders which will hold fifty stamps. When a pupil presents at the bank two of these folders, with fifty stamps affixed to each folder, the bank will issue a pass book showing a deposit of One Dollar. The bank will then accept any further deposits of fifty cents or more that the pupil may desire to make, either with folders or in coin.

All deposits will bear interest at the regular rate of interest allowed by the bank and under the same conditions governing savings deposits.

Folders should not be presented at the bank until they are filled.

Upon opening an account with the bank the pupil should be accompanied either by the parent or guardian, who should act as trustee. To withdraw money from the bank the signature of the trustee will be required. The account is thus placed entirely within the control of the parent or guardian of the pupil.

No withdrawals should be made for less than One Dollar.

When pupils are removing from the city and have folders partially filled with stamps, the folders will be redeemed by the bank upon an order from the principal of the school.

Neither the School Department nor the Bank will be responsible for filled or partially filled folders which may be lost, stolen or destroyed.

RECEIVING DEPOSITS FROM PUPILS AT SCHOOL.

The pupils' savings will be collected by the teacher once a week, during the first half hour at school, on a day to be designated.

The teacher's report of these collections will be made in duplicate on blanks furnished for the purpose, and will show the name of each pupil depositing and the amount deposited. The report in duplicate, together with the total amount called for, will be handed at once by the teacher to the principal of the school.

During the day on which collections are made a representative of the bank will call upon the principal of the school, will check up the reports of the teachers with the amount of money turned over by the principal, and receipt for same, at the same time handing to the principal the equivalent in stamps. The principal will then return to the teacher the latter's duplicate report receipted, accompanied by stamps to the amount called for. The teacher will then distribute the stamps to the pupils to be affixed by them to their folders. By this method both principal and teacher will avoid the responsibility of keeping pupils' money in their possession and accounting for stamps.

I would respectfully recommend that the system be put in effect at the opening of the fall term, the first week of school to be taken up with instruction by myself and representative from the bank on the plan of operation, and deposits to be taken commencing August 1st.

Very respectfully yours,

JAMES E. POWER.

In carrying out this plan the schools were districted and collections are made from sixteen to eighteen schools daily, thus all day schools are visited by the collector once a week. In order to carry out this system the Bank of Italy has to engage an automobile, a chauffeur and a collector, which cost approximately $300 a month.

The system has worked perfectly and it is gratifying to report the following results.

Total Deposits in School Savings Department in accounts of $1.00 and over	$54,557.86
Total Amount of Stamps outstanding same date	13,629.51
Total	$68,187.37

Total amount of accounts same date	7,604
Approximater number of pupils having stamps who have not as yet opened an account	2,000
Total number of pupils with school savings acct.	9,604

Average daily enrollment of pupils in schools where the system is in effect June 30, 1912--39,257.

The above figures show practically one out of every four pupils has commenced to acquire a bank account and thus realized the value of thrift and saving as a result of the introduction of this system.

We can probably go further and estimate that perhaps 5,000 of our pupils had a savings account before the adoption of this system. These did not necessarily open new accounts so that we would probably be safe in saying that one out of every three children attending our schools is now blessed with a savings account.

4. SUMMARY.

The above figures speak volumes for the future welfare and comfort of thousands of our rising generation and they show further that the children of San Francisco are second to none in the world in appreciating the value of thrift and saving.

No small amount of credit is due our good principals and teachers for the manner in which they have instilled into the minds of those in their charge the value of saving.

The Board of Education as well as all of those that were in any way interested in the introduction of this system into the schools may be proud of its success.

In conclusion I wish to say that the Bank of Italy has carried on the work of collecting deposits and keep the proper accounts of same at considerable cost to themselves, as the difference in the rate of interest, 4%, paid to the pupils on deposits and the rate they may be able to place the money at cannot be more than 2 or 3%. Thus on $70,000 they would net 2½ per cent $1.750 a year whereas their expenses amount to approximately $4,000 a year. Thus it will be seen that they handle this business at a loss, which will not be overcome until the present deposits have more than doubled. Therefore I must say that the officials of this bank have shown an excellent spirit and an interest in the future welfare of the youth of this city by continuing to make this sacrifice.

Respectfully submitted,

JAMES E. POWER,
Member Board of Education.

REPORT OF THE SUPERVISOR OF DOMESTIC SCIENCE.

San Francisco, June 28, 1912.

Mr. Alfred Roncovieri,
Superintendent of Schools,
San Francisco, Cal.

Mr. dear Mr. Roncovieri:—I beg to submit the report of the domestic science department for the school year 1911-1912.

The following is a brief summary of the principal data about the department:

Fall Term:—Teachers: One supervisor, ten teachers. Equipment: Thirteen cooking laboratories, one lunch kitchen.

Average monthly enrollment in cooking classes 2,731.27.

Cost of supplies and laundry for cooking classes, $1,422.53.

Cost of supplies for lunch kitchen, $170.265.

Total cost of supplies for domestic science department $1,492.795.

Average number of meals served daily at Ethan Allen lunch kitchen, 49.

Average cost of supplies per meal $0.026.

Average number of baths supervised daily by domestic science teacher at Ethan Allen School, 14.

Number of visits to cooking laboratories and lunch kitchen; from officials 94; from other 1,594.

The School Board has equipped the cooking laboratories during the past year. We have now twenty-three laboratories or centers, and, at the end of the spring term, had an enrollment of 2,671 Seventh and Eighth Grade girls, 79.6% of whom we taught in their own school buildings.

In the fall term 1908 we had an enrollment of 1,635 pupils, 39.1% were taught in their own schools. The rest had to travel to distant centers. There were also at that time, 917 girls entitled to lessons who were not getting them because we lacked room.

The new centers were opened one at a time when the equipment was ready. This has been a hardship for both domestic science and grade teachers. Indeed, reorganizing a class schedule in mid-term is much like swapping horses while crossing a stream.

However, these changes have been effected with little friction, and excellent proof, I think, of the spirit of co-operation that exists between the different branches of the service.

The new centers are satisfactory to us and have been admired and copied by visiting teachers and superintendents.

During the past year several firms have made valuable gifts to the domestic science department. Some of these have been food stuffs for use in the cooking classes, and others have been educational exhibits, showing food production and manufactures.

We have received almost three thousands pounds of flour from the Globe Grain and Milling Co., four cases of Royal Baking Powder from the Johnson-Locke Mercantile Company, a case each of baking powder, baking soda, spices and extracts from A. Schilling Company, a case of dry milk from the 3 C Dry Milk Company, about two cases of Califene from the Western Meat Co., four cases of Cottolene from N. K. Fairbanks Co., and about one thousand yeast tickets from the Golden Gate Yeast Co.

We have received educational exhibits from seventeen firms, and have, in several centers, the beginnings of food museums that promise to be notably good.

The following is a brief outline of the course given in the cooking classes:

A-SEVENTH.

I. Study of the five food principles, proteids, carbohydrates, fats and oils, mineral matter and water.

II. Study of carbohydrates, sugars and starches. Practical work; (a) cooking of fruit, fresh and dried, (b) cooking of potatoes, cereals, sago, vegetables and macaroni.

III. Study of flour, leavens and leavening agents. Practical work: Making of quick breads.

B-SEVENTH.

IV. Study of yeast. Practical work, bread-making.

V. Study of proteid foods, eggs, fish, meat and legumes. Practical work; (a) soft and hard cooked eggs, omelets, custards. (b) Cooking of tender meat, broiling and roasting, cooking of tough meats, scrip-stock, stews. (c) Broiling, frying and baking of fish. (d) Bean, pea and lentil soups.

VI. Invalid Cookery (a) Liquid, soft and light diet, (b) Preparing a tray for an invalid.

VII. Salads. Practical work, French and cooked dressing, potato salad.

VIII. Cake making. Practical work; Cookies, cup-cakes and sponge cakes.

IX. Pastry. Practical work: Apple and lemon pies.

X. Beverages. Practical work: Tea, coffee, cocoa.

In the Eighth Grade the same food principles are studied, and the same principles of cookery are demonstrated in a more extended form.

The pupils are also taught something of the many things that go to make up the art and the science of home making.

At the end of each term the girls of the graduating classes give "teas" to their parents and teachers. This gives them the opportunity for "group work" so highly commended by school people, and brings teachers and parents together pleasantly.

In conclusion I would like to thank you and your deputies and the members of the present Board of Education for the courtesies that I have received.

I would also like to express my appreciation for the loyal and friendly co-operation that I have always received from my fellow teachers.

Respectfully yours,

(Signed) ELLEN M. BARTLETT,
Supervisor of Domestic Science.

REPORT OF MRS. AMY WATERS DEANE, DIRECTOR OF MUSIC IN HIGH SCHOOLS.

Honorable Alfred Roncovieri,
Superintendent of Common Schools,
San Francisco, Cal.

Dear Sir:—It affords me great pleasure to inform you in this my second official report, that two very important and radical advancements have been made in the past year in the Musical Curriculum of the High Schools. The first, allowing credits for work done outside of school hours. The Board of Education passed a resolution to this effect and after a number of conferences when the subject was given careful and earnest consideration, the Committee, consisting of Superintendent Roncovieri, Deputies Cloud and Heaton, Dr. Scott, Principal of Girls' High School and Mrs. Deane, a system of crediting was adopted which has proven eminently satisfactory. Although from time to time adverse criticism has been made on the comparative limitation of music done in the High Schools in our city, yet I think that I am safe in asserting that San Francisco is the first to find a practical solution of the outside music marking. Briefly, a card is sent monthly to both parent and private teacher with blanks to be filled in as to time given to lessons and practice and general remarks as to advancement. These cards in conjunction with a careful examination by a specially appointed teacher, form the basis of this report of musical standing.

The second step of great musical value to the young artistic aspirant of our High School was the forming in the early days of April of a High School Orchestra under the leadership of Hon. Alfred Roncovieri. This orchestra is formed from the musical executants of the five High Schools. Although each High School has its absolutely separate ambition to excel, in this subject alone, consistently and logically, harmony prevails, it being a thoroughly interscholastic pride that prompts the effort to make this Orchestra a credit to the High Schools of San Francisco. Although there had been but six rehearsals at the time of graduation the work done at the closing exercises of the different schools was up to a positively professional standard. The members of the orchestra are both talented and enthusiastic and unmistakably devotedly gratified to Mr. Roncovieri who has so kindly and generously given his time to their advancement. On his arrival each Friday nothing short of an ovation is tendered him, the young executants being keenly aware of the professional and musicianly leadership afforded them gratis. I doubt that in the United States there is another Superintendent of Public Instruction who can bestow this great and far-reaching privilege on any class of students under his jurisdiction. In closing my report I wish to express my thanks to the members of the Board of Education who have so unfailingly supported me in my efforts to make my department a success and to the Principals and Teachers of the five High Schools who have helped to smooth the path in this hitherto untrodden road, Music in the High Schools.

Respectfully submitted,

(Signed) AMY WATERS DEANE.

August 4th, 1912.

REPORT OF THE SUPERVISOR OF MUSIC.

San Francisco, June 30, 1912.

Mr. Alfred Roncovieri,
Superintendent of Schools,
San Francisco, Cal.

My dear Sir:—In reply to your request for a report from the Music Departemnt of the City Schools I submit the following:

I am pleased to inform you that there has been a progression in the work during the past year.

There has been a growth in musical feeling and musical power.

I find that the class work has grown more systematic, and shows intelligent unedrstanding on the part of the teachers.

Many teachers have a genuine musical interest which creates a response in the child, and lends an artistic charm to the work.

Considering the very limited time allowed for Music in each grade, and considering how few children enter school with acute tone perception and good voice production, the results are remarkable.

I often ask myself these questions: "Do parents realize what is being done for their children in a musical way? Do they realize how many children come to school with no knowledge of tone? Do they appreciate the patient endeavor and skill that is put forth daily by the teachers to accomplish results?"

The greatest forethought is given to the subject of the musical development of the child in the Public Schools, and thus the child is helped physically, mentally and spiritually.

To produce and appreciate good tone, to perceive quickly correct tone, to be capable of expressing emotion through tone, to create a genuine love of good music this is the aim, always remembering that through such Music Study we have a great means for deepening and enriching the spiritual nature of the child.

The history of the race development becomes the history of the Child development. The ancients expressed themselves through song and dance and in the lowest grades the child is given the motion song—"rythm and expression" to arouse the Elemental Emotions.

Upon this foundation we build our structure,—songs of interest, Home, Nature, God, always remembering that sweet voices should be used, produced by natural breathing and good vocal habits. Thus through the pure voice, the heart of the child can speak, and through the great and good songs of the Nations, the child feels deeply the various emotions.

Ear training and sight singing provide mental drill and give delight in part singing, and the great works in Music, while the oral and written dictation are steps in the development of creative power and give an impetus toward composition.

At the graduations, have been given in part, such songs as "The Two Grenadiers" by Schumann; "Intermezzo" Cavelleria Rusticana; "Sextette", Lucia; "Pilgrims' Chorus", "Soldiers' Chorus", Faust; "Lift Thine Eyes"; "Miserere" and other selections from Il Trovatore; "Thou'rt Like A Flower", Liszt; "Spring Song" by Mendelssohn; Handel's "Largo". Besides these, the folk songs and patriotic songs have been given. In the Cosmopolitan Schools the songs are sung in French, Spanish, German and Italian.

An audience of twenty thousand were delighted when three hundred little children of the second, third and fourth grades of the Garfield School marched from Telegraph Hill and sang under my direction at Kearny and Market Streets in honor of placing a tablet on Lotta's Fountain in memory of the songs sung by Madame Tetrazzini on the same spot Christmas Eve.

The children sang "Anvil Chorus", "Intermezzo" and patriotic selections. The sweetness and clearness of the childrens' voices were remarked by all, and the children followed my slightest gesture. Madame Tetrazzini sent for me at the Palace Hotel and said, "No where in the world do the children sing so sweetly as they do in San Francisco."

Dedications of a number of new school houses have taken place on Sundays and the songs on these occasions have been led by the Supervisor or Assistant Supervisor.

A number of Mothers' Clubs have been addressed by me on the subject of School Music.

In January the work was outlined for the year to the one thousand teachers in a series of eight meetings.

One of the most interesting phases of the work this year has been a study of the recognition of well known melodies such as "Anvil Chorus" and "Home to Our Mountains" from Il Trovatore; "Toreador", Carmen; "Pilgrims' Chorus"; Sextette", Lucia; "Who is Sylvia", Schubert; and Schubert's "Serenade", "Traumeri", Schumann, etc.

In every way the Study of Music is encouraged and all children are asked to attend concerts, to study piano or other instruments, and to cultivate the voice.

The Henry Hadley Symphony Concerts were talked of and introduced by using two of Henry Hadley's songs in the Eighth Grade.

Talks of the orchestral instruments were given as well as simple sketches of lives of composers.

In a large department some schools need to be helped more than others, consequently some schools have been visited frequently, others not so often. Where the regular teacher does the work systematically, then the work speaks.

In some places where teachers cannot do the work, Principals see that teachers who are musical teach the classes.

In a number of schools special teachers take charge of classes where teachers are not capable. There are about thirty such teachers in the various schools.

I am grateful that new pianos have been installed in the new schools.

I wish to recommend the following:

(a) That two pianos be given to each large school.

(b) That in transferring and assigning teachers, that the musical ability of the teacher be taken into consideration with the musical need of the school.

(c) That a piano be bought for the office of the Supervisor of Music, as one is needed for the instruction of teachers.

(d) That special notices be sent to the children about the Symphony Concerts for the coming season by the Board of Education.

(e) That the Superintendent send to schools supplementary books, "Stories of Great Musicians" by Hurne and Scobey.

(f) That some octavo music be allowed the schools for Supplementary work to be selected by the Supervisor.

I wish to mention the good work of the regular teachers, and the cordial support given to me and the Music Department by the Principals, of the excellent work done by the Assistant Supervisor, Mrs. McGlade, and the special teachers of the various schools.

Thanking the Superintendent, the Deputy Superintendents and the Board of Education for their co-operation and kindness, I am,

Sincerely yours,

(Signed) ESTELLE CARPENTER,
Supervisor of Music.

ANNUAL REPORT OF THE SUPERVISOR OF LECTURES TO THE BOARD OF EDUCATION FOR THE SCHOOL YEAR ENDING JUNE 30, 1912.

San Francisco, July 1, 1912.

To the Board of Education of the City of San Francisco.

Ladies and Gentlemen:

Herewith I respectfully submit my second annual report on Public Lectures, for the school year ending June 30, 1912. During this year 209 public lectures have been given in school halls to audiences aggregating 47,460 persons; an average of 227 per lecture; 33 schools are now equipped with stereopticons and screens. The school department owns over 3,000 slides which are used for stereopticon lectures, and the lecture bureau enjoys cordial relations with a large number of public-spirited lecturers owning slides, and with institutions, such as the Affiliated Colleges of the University of California and the San Francisco Association for the Study and Prevention of Tuberculosis, willing to provide both slides and lectures gratis.

As heretofore, the fields of geography and travel, history and biography, science, hygiene, social topics, music and literature have been touched; the stereopticon and music, vocal and instrumental, have been liberally employed in illustration. These lectures and this music, almost without exception, have generously been given gratis to the people of San Francisco; a list of the volunteers to whom grateful acknowledgment is due would include practically every name on the year's program. Pianos have also, on occasion, been supplied free by Sherman, Clay & Co. The newspapers have regularly announced the lectures as news items, without charge. All this has meant a great saving to the city; so that the total expense of the lecture system for the year—excluding electric current and increased equipment, but including lectures, supervision, operating of lanterns, printing, postage, and the nominal expense fees of lecturers residing outside the city—has been less than $1,500.

The size of the audiences, as well as numerous expressions of approval, would seem to justify this outlay. The value of the lectures on science, geography, and hygiene, merely as information, must have been considerable; even higher should be rated the broadening instruction offered by evenings devoted to travel or to excursions in the high realms of literature, music, and art. Incidental benefits of the work have been, the awakening facilitation of public interest and cooperation in matters of civic concern; the freer meeting of parent, teacher, and pupil; the discovery of several excellent lecturers among our teachers, with consequent reaction upon the school work; and lastly, a beginning in the use of the lecture equipment by the schools in the day time.

The principals of several schools have spoken for the use of lanterns and slides to supplement the course of study; the present working arrangement, however, forbids this in anything like systematic form, and indeed permits only 3 or 4 evening lectures per annum, on an average, in each of the centers already established and equipped. Wise economy would suggest that the equipment, particularly the slides, be increased, and be used in the regular instruction of pupils by day, as well as in the occasional public lecture at night, thus increasing the educational efficiency of the plant ten-fold. This would cost more, but considering the population of the city, not nearly in proportion to what New York City is spending for evening lectures alone; if San Francisco with a population of one-tenth that of New York, should appropriate one-twentieth of the amount annually spent by the latter city on evening lectures alone ($125,000), the resulting sum ($6,000) would enable the Lecture Bureau to continne the evening lectures, opening new centers as required; to acquire a larger stock of slides and a collection of select photographs of art subjects for visual instruction; and in addition to extend the lecture system into the schools, where it could be made a highly useful auxiliary in the teaching of history, civics, geography, literature and elementary science.

Perhaps use can also be made of the motion picture in the both schools, and evening lectures, provided really educational films can be secured and the practical difficulties of operation overcome. Here is a new field with large, but as yet undefined possibilities.

These, then, are the next steps; and this policy I respectfully and earnestly recommend.

MILTON E. BLANCHARD,

Supervisor of Lectures.

EARLY HISTORY OF THE SAN FRANCISCO SCHOOL DEPARTMENT

In 1854 Frank Soule, John H. Gihon and James Nisbet compiled and had published through D. Appleton & Co., a book of 824 pages entitled "The Annals of San Francisco" containing a summary of the history of the first discovery, settlement, progress, and condition of California and a complete history of its great city, San Francisco. This is a most valuable fund of information excellently written and very interesting to any reader especially to one who is a resident of San Francisco. As the book is now difficult to obtain it may be well to incorporate in this report some excerpts from it relating to the origin of the public schools of this City and County.

"The first American school in San Francisco, and we believe in California, was a merely private enterprise. It was opened by a Mr. Marston from one of the Atlantic states, in April, 1847, in a small shanty which stood on the block between Broadway and Pacific Street, west of Dupont St., (Grant Avenue). There he collected some twenty or thirty pupils whom he continned to teach for almost a whole year, his patrons paying for tuition. * * *"

The people of the town at length saw the necessity of some public movement to secure for their children a fit education, and late in 1847, they built a school-house, on the southwest corner of Portsmouth Square, fronting Clay Street, where it is now joined by Brenham Place. Insignificant as the building appears it was destined to subserve more useful purposes than any other than has been erected in the city, and should have been preserved as one of its most valuable relics. Its history was almost an epitome of that of the curious people who built it. Every new enterprise found here a heating oven to warm the egg into successful hatching. Here churches held their first meetings; and here the first public amusements were given. It was the assembly room of early gatherings of Odd Fellows and other benevolent associations; and a universal public hall for political, military, and almost every other description of meeting. It was dignified as a Court House under Judge Almond, designated as an Institute at another period, and at length degraded to a police office and a station house. Its site is only recognized by the thousand cherished associations that hover like spirits around its unmarked grave.

On the 21st of February, 1848, a town meeting was called for the election of a Board of School Trustees, and Dr. F. Fourgeaud, Dr. J. Townsend, C. L. Ross, J. Serrine and William H. Davis, Esquires, were chosen. On the third of April following, these Trustees opened a school in the building just erected under the charge of Mr. Thomas Douglas, A. M., a graduate of Yale College, and an experienced teacher of high reputation. The Board pledged him a salary of $1 000 per annum, and fixed a tariff of tuition to aid toward its payment; * * *. Soon after this, Mr. Marston discontinued his private school, and Mr. Douglas collected some forty pupils. Prior to the opening of the school, the Trustees had taken a census of the town, and ascertained that the population was something over 800 including Indians of which 473 were males, 177 females and 60 children of suitable age for school. Eight months previously the population numbered 375.

The public school prospered and increased for eight or ten weeks when it received a sudden and unforseen check * * *. Rumors of immense and rapidly acquired fortunes, but above all, the exhibition of specimens of the precious ore, drove the whole population to such an intensity of excitement, that it resulted in a general stampede of men, women, and children for the "mines", leaving the teacher minus pupils, minus trustees and town council and minus tuition salary. He, therefore, locked the school-house, and, shouldering his pick and pan, himself started for the "diggins". * * * April 23, 1849 Reverend Albert Williams, Pastor of the First Presbyterian Church, obtained the use of the public school-house and opened a private school, charging tuition. He gathered some 25 pupils, and continued teaching until Sept. 20, when on account of the increased demand upon his ministerial service, the school was suspended.

Late in the autumn of 1849 Mr. J. C. Pelton arrived from Maine and Massachusetts and on December 26 opened a school with three pupils in the Baptist Church, on Washington Street, which was generously furnished to him by that society, free of rent. He fitted up the church with the necessary writing tables at his own expense, made no charge, but, for several months depended upon voluntary subscriptions and donations, and the profits on the sale of school books (a lot of which he had brought with him and which he furnished to the pupils), for his compensation, and that of Mrs. Pelton who assisted him."

At this point the history of the First Baptist Church written by John F. Pope, a member from 1849 will be quoted as far as it pertains to the work of Mr. Pelton. "On December 26, 1849, the first free public school was opened in the Church conducted by John C. Pelton and his wife; only three children were present, but by April 1, 1850, 130 children had received instruction.

On March 25, 1850, the following resolution was unanimously adopted by the Council of San Francisco: "Resolved, that from the 1st day of April, 1850, John C. Pelton and Mrs. Pelton, his wife, be employed as teachers for the public school, at the Baptist Church, which has been offered to the Council free of charge, and that the average number of scholars shall not exceed 100; and that they shall be entitled to a monthly salary, during the pleasure of the Council, of $500 per month, payable each and every month."

The school continued to increase, having at one time nearly three hundred pupils in attendance. It continued to occupy the church building until the fire of June 28, 1851. Thus the first Protestant house of worship was the birthplace of the first free public school of California."

To continue the quotation from the annals of San Francisco. "In 1850, the original public school on Portsmouth Square was Vandalised * * *.

In the meantime several other schools were started among them Mr. Osborn's Select School, which was patronized particularly by the Presbyterian Church; Rev. Mr. Preveaux's San Francisco Academy under the management of persons belonging to the Baptist Church; Dr. Ver Mehr's Episcopal Parish School; and several small primary schools in different portions of the city. In June, 1850, Col. T. J. Nevins, then agent of the American Tract Society for this Coast, applied to Messrs. Mellus and Howard, and obtained the free use of a building in Happy Valley at the corner of Mission and Second Sts. for school purposes, employing Mr. Samuel Neuton from Connecticut, as teacher, who opened, July 13, and conducted a school for a few months when his place was, for a short time, supplied by Mr. L. Rogers, and subsequently by Mr. Cooley and Hyde and who took charge of it until the Spring or Summer of 1851 at which time it was suspended * * *. It was called the Happy Valley public school. From a small beginning it had increased to nearly 200 pupils. In January, 1851, Colonel Nevins procured a fifty vara lot at Spring Valley, on the Presidio Road, and erected, principally at private expense, a large and convenient building, employed a teacher and opened a free school, which during the first quarter was sustained wholly by voluntary contributions * * *. The house and lot were leased to the city for free school purposes for ninety-nine years, for a rent of not less than $700 for the entire time or about 57 cents per month. The situation is delightful being shaded by a grove of evergreens on a magnificent road, and sufficiently removed from the noise and bustle of the living mass, to prevent their interference with useful study. Until the spring of 1854 it was the only school-house owned by the city * * *. In the summer of 1851 the Boards of Aldermen appointed a Committee on Education, at whose request Colonel Nevins prepared a bill for "The establishment, regulation, and support of free common schools in the city," which without alteration, was passed by the Common Council and became a law on the 25th of Sept., 1851. This ordinance divides the city into seven school districts and provides for the erection and establishment of a free school in each district, making these schools public and free to all children and youths between the ages of four and eighteen years within their respective districts, and forbids in their control all sectarian influence or interference. It makes provision for raising a common school fund; for the annual election by the Common Council, of a Board of Education, to consisit of one Alderman, one Assistant Alderman, two citizens and the Mayor who is ex officio a member and President of the Board. It gives to the Board of Education the power to elect a Superintendent of Schools and to provide for necessary buildings for school purposes; defines the duties of the Superintendent; constitutes the Superintendent and two members of the Board a committee for the examination of teachers; exacts a quarterly report from the Superintendent to the Board, and an annual report from the Board to the Common Council; and requires a quarterly meeting of the Superintendent and teachers to examine and discuss the best methods of imparting instruction and of conducting the schools to the greatest advantage. in San Francisco & California

The first Board of Education consisted of Hon. Charles J. Brenham, Alderman Chas. L. Ross, Asst. Alderman Joseph F. Atwill, General John Wilson and Henry E. Lincoln, Esq. On the 21st of October they appointed Col. T. J. Nevins Superintendent of Schools * * *. These were the schools and teacher May 1, 1854.

District No. 1 Rincon Point established Jan. 8, 1852, 1st and Folsom Sts., teachers, Mr. J. Swett and Miss Rebecca W. Foster.

District No. 2, Happy Valley, Nov. 17, 1851, Bush and Stockton Sts., Mr. James Denman, Miss Anna E. Sanford, Mrs. E. Wright, Mrs. J. A. Hazelton and Miss Kennedy.

District No. 3, Central, Dec. 22, 1852, Washington between Stockton and Dupont, Mr. E. H. Holmes, Miss A. C. Park, Miss Harriet A. Hancke and Miss Mary S. Haynes.

District No. 4, Clark's Point, June 7, 1852, corner Broadway and Montgomery, Mr. Ahira Holmes, Miss Sophronia Allyne and Miss E. A. Pomeroy.

District No. 5, North Beach, Nov. 19, 1851, Washington Square, Mr. H. P. Carlton, Mrs. Olive P. Cudworth.

District No. 6, Spring Valley, Feb. 9, 1852, Mr. Jos. C. Morrill.

District No. 7, Mission Dolores, Feb. 10, 1852, Miss Clara B. Walbridge.

* * * Male teachers receive $150 a month; females $100. During the first year the Superintendent was paid $1,200 per year, but since then his salary has been $2,400.

On Feb. 1, 1852, Supt. Nevins made his first quarterly report from which it appeared that 485 pupils had attended the five schools then organized. On Nov. 1st, 1852, 791 were at school while the census showed 2,050 between the ages of 4 and 18 residing in the city. August, 1853, there were 1399 at school, the number of children in the city being 2,730.

Mr. William H. O'Grady succeeded Col. Nevins as Superintendent in October, 1853. On May 1, 1854, 1,574 pupils were in the school, 901 boys and 673 girls * * *. Besides the seven public schools there are in San Francisco (1854) 27 private school with an attendance of 947 pupils. Therefore the aggregate number of schools in the city is now 34; the whole number of teachers 62, 30 being men and 42 women; and the total number of scholars

1,305 boys and 1,216 girls or in all 2,521. In 1854 the friends of the San Francisco Academy, now called the English and Classical High School, dedicated a new school building on Powell Street south of Jackson which was the first substantial structure in this city built expressly for educational purposes. Its teachers are Mr. F. E. Prevaux, Prof. A. J. Segueria, Mrs. I. H. Purkitt, Miss H. R. Barlow and Miss S. L. Larkin and Miss W. E. Stowe * * *. The floating population has hitherto much embarassed public school enterprise * * * Those who have steadily attended have made rapid and commendable improvement. Their teachers are proficient, liberal, benevolent, zealous and indefatigueable in the discharge of their duties. The climate is the most salubrious in the world and well adapted for the highest mental exertion and efficiency. The school bell now echoes through the streets of the busy city and the astonished stranger meets groups of bright and smiling faces merrily trudging to their daily task and ere long may listen to learned professors expounding to classes of intelligent students, art, literature and science as completely and perfectly as can be heard in the most time honored institutions of the world.''

(For statistics of school attendance, population, expenditures from the year 1850, see page 20 and 21 of this report.)

NECROLOGY.

Miss Effie Douglas, Hamilton school; died April 23, 1906.

Miss Barbara Bannon, Emerson school; died June 5, 1906.

Mr. J. W. Gorman, Lincoln Evening school; died July 31, 1906.

Miss A. L. Hornsby, Laguna Honda school; died October 24, 1906.

Miss M. M. Murphy, principal Irving M. Scott school; died Dec. 24, 1906.

Mr. Madison Babcock, vice-principal Hancock school, ex-superintendent public schools; died December, 1906.

Miss Emma Stincen, principal Grattan school; died January 29, 1907.

Miss Leah C. Peckham, Laguna Honda school; died February 11, 1907.

Mr. J. B. Clarke, Polytechnic High school; died March, 1907.

Miss Helen Thompson, Girls' High school; died December 17, 1907.

Miss Josephine C. Evans, McKinley school; died February 5, 1908.

Mrs. M. E. Steele, Hearst school; died June, 1908.

Miss Margaret O'Brien, Sherman school; died August 13, 1908.

Miss L. R. Cullen, Burnett school; died September 3, 1908.

Miss Katherine Gaines, Winfield Scott school; died October 2, 1908.

Miss Adelaide C. Cherry, Redding school; died October 26, 1908.

Miss Rose Prince, Portola school; died October 31, 1908.

Mrs. Anne Armstrong, Noe Valley school; died November 20, 1908.

Miss S. M. Boniface, Hamilton school; died March 25, 1909.

Miss Mary Phillips, Agassiz school; died April 11, 1909.

Mrs. Georgia Washburn, principal Henry Durant school; died April 17, 1909.

Mrs. Anna M. Kortick, Burnett school; died May 3, 1909.

Miss Nell O'Hara, Marshall school; died May 27, 1909.

Mrs. M. B. Thompson, Starr King school; died June 25, 1909.

Mme. Ernestine Giffard, Bryant school; died July 24, 1909.

Mr. Leslie A. Jordan, ex-Deputy Superintendent of Schools, Lincoln Evening school; died July 30, 1909.

Mrs. Ellen R. Kenzla, Washington Evening school; died August 4, 1909.

Mrs. Lucy McNear, Bryant Cosmopolitan Primary; died January 21, 1910.

Mrs. V. C. Ingram, Peabody school; died March 10, 1910.

Miss Minnie R. Bley, Agassiz school; April 1, 1910.

Miss Mary L. Marks, Bernal school; died April 20, 1910.

Mrs. M. A. Steele, Edison school; April 25, 1910.

Mr. George Foulks, principal Hamilton Evening school; died June 7, 1910.

Mrs. J. B. Levey, Hearst Grammar school; died July 25, 1910.

Mrs. Cora B. Tompkins, Moulder school; died October 8, 1910.

Miss Katherine E. Meighan, Fairmount school; August 31, 1910.

Mr. A. C. Kinne, Lincoln Evening school; died October 6, 1910.

Miss Laura C. Perry, Lincoln school; died October 26, 1910.

Mrs. Clara Bigelow, vice-principal John Sweet Grammar school; died December 6, 1910.

Mr. Azro L. Mann, principal Denman Grammar, Superintendent of Schools 1878-1879; died February 28, 1911.

Mr. Ebenezer Knowlton, formerly principal of Rincon Grammar school, vice-principal of Lincoln Grammar and teacher in Boys' High, Commercial and Roosevelt Evening schools; died February 9, 1911.

Mr. John C. Pelton, founder of the first free public school in San Francisco or California, December, 1849; principal grammar schools, Superintendent of Schools 1856, 1857, 1865, 1866, 1867; died March 5, 1911.

Mr. William A. Leggett, vice-principal Franklin school; died March 31, 1911.

Miss Martha Galloway, principal Visitacion Valley school; April 5, 1911.

Mrs. Rebecca Greenan, Lincoln Evening school; died April 12, 1911.

Mr. W. N. Bush, formerly teacher Lowell High and principal Polytechnic High schools; died May 21, 1911.

Mrs. M. S. Wright, Frank McCoppin school; died March 9, 1911.

Miss Emily Wickman, Jackson school.

Miss A. Weed, Washington school; died October, 1911.

Miss E. J. Moynihan, Horace Mann school; died December 31, 1911.

Mrs. M. J. Parolini, principal Cleveland school; died January 10, 1912.

Mrs. M. H. Walker, principal Marshall school; died January 22, 1912.

Miss G. F. Libby, Bernal school; died February 7, 1912.

Miss M. K. Gavigan, Portola school; died March 9, 1912.

Miss M. A. Deane, formerly principal Redding School, member Board of Education; died March 20, 1912.

Mrs. A. M. Sechrist, Laguna Honda school; died April 24, 1912.

Miss H. B. Fairweather, Rochambeau school; died May 23, 1912.

DECEASED ANNUITANTS.

Miss E. A. Cleveland, April, 1906; Miss H. M. Fairchild, May 14, 1906; Miss Flora McDonald Shearer, February 12, 1907; Mrs. C. M. Sisson, June 16, 1907; Mrs. L. G. Webster, November 17, 1907; Miss Helen Thompson, December 7, 1907; Mrs. E. M. Steele, June 15, 1908; Mrs. E. M. Poole, November 23, 1908; Miss Margaret J. Gallagher, November 30, 1908; Miss C. A. Templeton, January 1, 1909; Mrs. M. E. Caldwell, March 9, 1909; Miss L. C. McNear, January 24, 1910; Miss L. E. Ryder, February 18, 1910; Miss M. J. Bragg, June 15, 1910; Mrs. S. A. Miles, April 12, 1912; Mrs. Mary A. Hogan, April 21, 1912; Mrs. Christine Chalmers, June 26, 1912; Professor Adolph Herbst, October 2, 1912; Mr. Paul A. Garin, November 30, 1912.

Australian Reports and Legal Periodicals	130.90
Australian Textbooks	7.80
Scotch and Irish Publications	198.00
Collected Cases	128.15
Trials	403.85
Citations	213.70
Dictionaries	76.25
Encyclopedias, Legal	24.00
Other Foreign Statutes and Publications	117.25
Directories	93.96
General Literary Works	115.70
Supreme Court Records	550.00
Postage	31.18
Newspapers	44.30
Maps	10.00
Express, Cartage and Freight	137.63
Insurance	441.95
Binding	1,738.85
Printing	44.00
Miscellaneous expense	111.34
Salaries	2,950.00
Total	$15,063.92

The income for the year was:

Dollar Tax and Miscellaneous	$16,162.76
Expenses for the year	15,063.92

During the year there was lost from the membership of the Library by death:

JOHN CURRY.
AYLETT R. COTTON.
LESTER H. JACOBS.

The Library is now in a very satisfactory condition from the standpoint of the practicing attorney. From the standpoint of the historian and writer it is still lacking in many important particulars. Necessarily in the future the accessions will lie along the lines of the more unused departments of legal literature. It was in these departments that the old library was so rich. The important fields yet to be covered are statutes and British Colonial Reports. It is hoped that much progress will be made in these particulars the coming year.

Commodious quarters have been set apart for the Library in the permanent City Hall. The architects of the building have shown a disposition to treat the Library as generously as the circumstances would permit. The plans are on file in the office of the Secretary and will be shown to any one who wishes to see them.

Respectfully yours,

JAMES H. DEERING,
Secretary and Librarian

Report of Board of Education

San Francisco, August 28, 1913.

Hon. James Rolph, Jr.,

Mayor City and County of San Francisco.

Dear Sir:—By order of the Board of Education I have the honor to transmit herewith the Annual Report of this Board for the fiscal year 1912-1913, as required by Article VII, Chapter III, Sec. 3, of the Charter of the City and County of San Francisco.

Respectfully yours,

M. R. NORRIS,
Acting Secretary Board of Education.

DEPARTMENT OF EDUCATION, CITY AND COUNTY OF SAN FRANCISCO, CALIFORNIA.

BOARD OF EDUCATION.

D'ANCONA, DR. A. A., President	Term expires Jan. 8, 1916	$3,000.00
POWER, JAMES E., Member	Term expires Jan. 8, 1915	3,000.00
KINCAID, Mrs. M. W., Member	Term expires Jan. 8, 1917	3,000.00
JONES, Miss S. J., Member	Term expires Jan. 8, 1914	3,000.00

SUPERINTENDENT OF SCHOOLS.

RONCOVIERI, ALFRED	Term expires Jan. 8, 1915	$4,000.00

(Ex-officio member of the Board of Education without right to vote).

DEPUTY SUPERINTENDENTS OF SCHOOLS.

Webster, R. H.	Term expires May 1, 1916	$3,000.00
Cloud, A. J.	Term expires Dec. 1, 1916	3,000.00
Heaton, T. L.	Term expires Mar. 1, 1914	3,000.00
Howard, W. B.	Term expires Mar. 1, 1914	3,000.00

EMPLOYES.

Norris, [illegible] M. R.	Acting Secretary Board of Education	Term at pleasure of Board of Education	$1,800.00
[illegible], C. A.	Financial Secretary, Board of Education	Term at pleasure of Board of Education	2,[illegible]60.00
[illegible], A. M., Mrs.	Assistants to Secretary	Term at pl[illegible]sure of Board of Education	1,020.00
Anderson, Miss L. E.	Assistants to Secretary	Term at pleasure of Board of [illegible]ation	1,020.00
[illegible]h, E. A., Miss	Stenographer, Board of [illegible]	Term at pleasure of Board of Education	1,260.00
[illegible]e, J., [illegible]s	Stenographer, Board of Education	Term at pleasure of Board of Education	1,260.00
O'Connor, T. S., Miss	Stenographer, Office Supt. of Schools	Term at pleasure of Board of Education	1,260.00
Holden, S. A., Miss	Phone Exchange Operator	Term at pleasure of Board of Education	1,080.00
[illegible]is, J.	Messenger, Board of [illegible]	Term at pleasure of Board of Education	1,200.00
Larkin, R.	[illegible]r, Supt. of Schools	Term at pleasure of Board of Education	1,140.00
Sweeney, E.	[illegible]nt Officer	Assigned by Chief of Pol[illegible]e.	
Dugan, T. J.	Truant Offi[illegible]er	Assigned by Chief of Pol[illegible]e.	
Nol[illegible], E.	[illegible]nt Offi[illegible]er	[illegible]d by Chief of Pol[illegible]e.	
Foley, James	Store Keeper	Term at pl[illegible]sure of Board of [illegible]cation	$1,800.00
Hunt, John	Assistant Store Keeper	[illegible]m at pl[illegible]sure of Board of Education	1,080.00
Whitney, S. E.	Bookkeeper	Term at pleasure of Board of [illegible]cation	1,500.00
[illegible], C. W.	Building and Repairs	Term at pleasure of Board of Education	2,100.00
[illegible]y, M. J.	Water and [illegible]s Inspector	[illegible]m at pleasure of Board of Education	1,500.00
Schuck, E.	Chauffeur	Term at pleasure of Board of [illegible]cation	1,500.00

Total Number of Schools		103
Number of days school were kept open		174½

Average daily attendance:

Secondary	3,757	
Elementary	39,044	
Total		42,801

Number of Teachers employed (including substitutes)	1,409
Number of Teachers on leave during 1912-1913	42
Number of Teachers on pay roll June, 1913	1,367

Total appropriation 1912-1913		$1,812,500.00
Total amount drawn from Treasury, 1912-1913		1,811,287.71
Surplus	$	1,212.29
Receipts from State		690,396.79

Disbursed for:

Administration	$ 54,358.64
Salaries of Teachers	1,532,256.25
Wages, Janitors and Labor	114,185.00
Rents	2,167.55
Maintenance, Supplies, etc.	108,320.27
	$1,811,287.71

DISBURSED FOR FISCAL YEAR 1912-1913.

Board of Education	$ 11,988.00
Superintendent and Deputies	15,975.96
Secretary and Attaches	12,783.00
Storekeeper and Attaches	4,380.00
Scavenger	4,140.00
Superintendent Building and Repairs	2,100.00
Water and Gas Inspector	1,491.65
Chauffeur	1,500.00
Teachers P. and G.	1,320,448.55
Teachers High	211,807.70
Janitors	100,556.00
Rents	2,167.55
Wages in Supply Department	13,629.00
Stationery	14,900.62
Incidentals	6,523.25
Furniture	16,014.37
Manual Training	3,164.56
Janitorial	4,306.86
Printing	5,138.47
Books	5,763.01
Fuel	17,535.38
Telephone and Telegraph	40.94
Water	11,454.93
Light	7,018.48
Cartage	1,617.00

Cooking	1,774.63
High School	3,606.06
Advertising	284.60
Athletics	2,636.40
Lectures	1,892.42
Home Economics	878.56
Industrial Work	1,789.46
President's Incidental Fund	468.22
Teachers' Institute	1,512.00
Total	$1,811,287.71

RECAPITULATION.

Appropriation 1912-1913	$1,812,500.00
Disbursed as above	1,811,287.71
Surplus	$ 1,212.29

Resolved: That the rule requiring teachers of the department residing outside of the City and County limits to move to San Francisco be recinded.

Resolved: That all oiling of school floors be ordered done by Union painters.

Resolved: That a division of the school year into four teaching periods of ten weeks each be followed as far as possible.

Resolved: That protest against the establishment of stable in the rear of the Golden Gate School be sent to the Board of Supervisors.

Resolved: That a four-year course be added to the course in the High School of Commerce.

Resolved: That a class be formed at the Detention Home.

Resolved: That permission be granted to the Department of Education of the University of California to give a course of lectures on educational topics before the teachers of the department on consecutive Saturdays.

Resolved: That an evening class for foreigners be established in the Portola School building.

Resolved: That this Board approves transfer of lease covering school lot at Taylor and Vallejo Streets from G. F. Bernard to the Russian Hill Improvement Company and further grants an extension of time in which to construct building on said lot to Feb. 24, 1914.

Resolved: That the sum of $3000 be set aside to cover expenses of school athletics.

Resolved: That the Board of Supervisors be formally requested to submit charter amendment for consideration of voters by which control of construction of and repairs to all school buildings, as well as control of all funds for such repairs and construction, shall be in the hands of the Board of Education.

Resolved: That two new manual training centers be opened, one at the Irving M. Scott and one at the Glen Park School.

Resolved: That the following named ladies and gentlemen be and are hereby appointed to act as an Advisory Commission on Vocational Training and Guidance in the Public Schools: Raphael Weill, John A. Britton, Jesse Lilienthal, Mrs. Louis Hertz, Miss Katherine Felton, Walter McArthur, Henry Payot, Alexander Russel, Andrew J. Gallagher, Superintendent of Schools Alfred Roncovieri and President of the Board of Education, Dr. A. A. D'Ancona.

Resolved: That the Board of Supervisors be requested to disburse the fund remaining in the 1904 bond issue money for the Glen Park annex, 6 room building for the Columbus school and a 4 room annex for the Edison school.

Resolved: That the recommendations offered by Director Jones relative to simplicity in graduation exercises be and are hereby adopted.

Resolved: That teachers be instructed to advise children relative to the throwing of papers on sidewalks, etc.

Resolved: That an evening class for Russians and other foreigners be established in the vicinity of 20th and Rhode Island St.

Resolved: That principals shall be allowed to permit their teachers, with their classes, to make appointments for attending lectures under the direction of the Museum of Anthropology, University of California.

Resolved: That the corner-stone of the Franklin School be set in place with suitable exercises on Sunday, November 24, 1912.

Resolved: That the Board of Supervisors be requested to purchase additional area for the Daniel Webster school site.

Resolved: That the sum of $1000 be expended from the equipment fund of the Girls' High School and a similar amount from the fund of the Lowel High School for equipment of the gymnasia of said schools.

Resolved: That the Commercial High School be hereafter known as the "High School of Commerce."

Resolved: That grammar grades be established in the Grattan School.

Resolved: That the High School of Commerce building be vacated to expedite the work of the Civic Center, said building to be moved to the Library site.

Resolved: That the offer of the Remington Typewriter Company, for the furnishing of typewriting machines for use of this department be accepted.

Resolved: That a cookery department be installed in the Bernal School.

Resolved: That immediately after the beginning of the spring term 1913 arrangements be made for the establishment of first and second grade classes in the temporary building on the Andrew Jackson school lot, Hayes Street, near Cole Street.

Resolved: That an Italian class be re-established in the Sherman Evening School.

Resolved: That lecture centers be established at the Rochambeau, Farragut and Irving M. Scott schools.

Resolved: That the Board of Education hereby approves the Pension Bill known as the "Flat Rate Pension Bill."

Resolved: That the Board of Education inform the Board of Supervisors that it is agreeable to the transfer to the Trustees of the Public Library of school lot situated in block 190, Richmond District, between 9th and 10th Avenues and Clement and Pt. Lobos Avenue.

Resolved: That the Board of Supervisors be requested to provide for the construction of the Glen Park School and yard, Edison School and yard and Columbus School out of the 1904 bond issue.

Resolved: That no deduction shall be made from the summer vacation salary of any teacher in regular status at the close of the school year, whether in actual attendance or on leave of absence, provided said teacher shall have been in reasonably regular attendance, in the judgment of the Board, throughout either the spring or fall term, and provided further that the absence has been for purpose of travel or study or rest or has been due to illness and has been excused by resolution of the Board of Education.

Resolved: That the resignation of Mrs. J. B. Holden and of Mr. A. V. Holden, as teachers of the Oral-Deaf classes, be accepted.

Resolved: That the Board of Public Works be requested to furnish an estimate of the cost of yard work at the Junipero Serra School.

Resolved: That the Board of Supervisors be requested to set aside out of the 1908 bond issue the sum of $2500 for equipment of the Girls' High School.

Resolved: That the Board of Supervisors be requested to set aside from the bond construction fund for the Girls' High School the sum of $1000 for the completion of the stage in the auditorium of said school.

Resolved: That the Board of Public Works be requested to furnish this Board estimates of cost of paving and placing in order the yard of the Roosevelt School.

Resolved: That the Board of Supervisors be requested to set aside $1000 out of the 1904 bond issue for the installation of blackboards for the Patrick Henry School not covered by contract.

Resolved: That Feb. 22, 1913, be set as the date for the dedication of the new Lowell High School building.

Resolved: That the Board of Education approves the transfer by the Board of Supervisors of lands situated on the northerly line of Grove Street, between Polk and Larkin (High School of Commerce) in exchange for the westerly half of block bounded by Fell, Franklin, Van Ness Avenue and Hayes Street.

Resolved: That the Board of Public Works be requested to prepare plans and specifications for the Oriental School.

Resolved: That the Board of Public Works be requested to furnish the Board of Education with present plans of the Polytechnic High School and with an itemized statement of construction up to date and amount remaining in fund.

Resolved: That the claim of M. Alice King for payment of $400.00, claimed to be due as unpaid salary, be denied.

Resolved: That the Board of Education hereby approves the plans for the Polytechnic High School recently submitted by the Board of Public Works.

Resolved: That the Board of Supervisors be requested to make an investigation and make changes in construction of the Lowell High School on account of a cafeteria in said school.

Resolved: That the Board of Supervisors be requested to pave the block on Hayes Street between Masonic Avenue and Ashbury Street, same being site of the Lowell High School.

Resolved: That C. Siverson, now occupying school lot on Grove Street, between Cole and Clayton Streets, be charged rental at $10 per month, such occupancy to be at pleasure of Board; rental to date from March 1st.

Resolved: That the Board of Public Works be requested to consider the following details when making plans for the new Washington Irving School: (1) Complete yard and fence work; (2) $4000.00 for equipment.

Resolved: That the balance of 1904 bonds not appropriated for the work at the Glen Park, the Edison and the Columbia schools be set aside for the construction of incomplete bond school yards and other improvements.

Resolved: That the Board of Supervisors be requested to set aside for the equipment of the following named schools the sum of $25,000.00: Cooper, Oriental, Washington Irving, Patrick Henry, Glen Park addition, Edison addition.

Resolved: That the Crown Realty Co. be allowed to make certain alterations on building located on School lot No. 244 Post Street as approved by this Board and noted in the records of this office.

Resolved: That the estimate of the City and County funds required for the conduct and maintenance of the School Department for the fiscal year 1913-14 as prepared under the supervision and direction of the Board of Education and Superintendent of Schools and as shown in schedule on file in this office, be and the same is hereby approved.

Resolved: That the Board of Supervisors be requested to authorize the Mayor to sell at public auction building adjoining the Mission High School.

Resolved: That a modification of the course of study for the advanced grammar grades in the Hamilton, Horace Mann and Crocker Schools to include vocational training, be adopted.

Resolved: That the Board of Public Works be requested to furnish estimate of the cost of installing fire escapes at the Laguna Honda School.

Patrick Henry School completed.

Notice of acceptance of Girls' High School building by Board of Public Works.

Resolved: That teachers in the elementary schools be allowed for outside experience one-half of what is now allowed in the various grades for experience in San Francisco.

Resolved: That Dr. M. E. Blanchard be assigned for duty as supervisor of lectures and lecturer on Morals and Civics for the ensuing school year.

Resolved: That cooking be introduced in the 6th and 7th grades and sewing in the 8th grade for girls and manual training (wood work) in the 6th and 7th grades and wood work with iron in the 8th grade for boys.

Resolved: That cooking class be established in the Bernal Evening School and millinery class in the Irving M. Scott Evening School.

Resolved: That such foundry subjects as may be deemed advisable shall be taught in the Polytechnic High School.

Resolved: That Mr. Thaddeus H. Rhodes of the Lowell High School be appointed to the principalship of the Laguna Honda School.

Resolved: That prevocational courses be established in the Jean Parker School in accordance with the reports of Professor Richard G. Boone and of Mme. Pechin, principal of the school.

Resolved: That as mechanical drawing will form two-thirds of the course of drawing in the Hamilton, Crocker and Horace Mann schools, the drawing in said schools be not subject to the supervision of the Supervisor of Drawing in the elementary schools.

Resolved: That the Board of Supervisors be requested to set aside the sum of $3000 for the equipment of the Patrick Henry School out of the 1908 bond issue.

Resolved: That the representatives in Congress be requested to vote for the passage of Senate Joint Resolution No. 5.

Resolved: That the Hamilton, Horace Mann and Crocker schools be hereafter designated as the Hamilton Intermediate School, Horace Mann Intermediate School and Crocker Intermediate School.

Resolved: That James Edwin Addicott be appointed to the principalship of the Polytechnic High School.

Resolved: That a temporary building similar to the Andrew Jackson School be placed on the Le Conte site.

Resolved: That kindergarten classes be established in the Noe Valley, Bernal and Bryant schools and that the salaries of the teachers thereof be the salaries of the second grade teachers according to the salary schedule; such kindergarten teachers to be available in the afternoon for service in primary classes and no compensation to be allowed for outside experience.

Resolved: That no scholarships shall be maintained by the pupils of the Girls' High School.

The Agassiz School kindergarten has been completed and is being occupied.

Respectfully submitted,

M. R. NORRIS,

Acting Secretary Board of Education.

BOARD OF EDUCATION—EXPENDITURES FOR FISCAL YEAR JUNE 30, 1913.

	Budget.	Bond.
Secondary.		
High—		
1. Galileo		
2. Girls	$ 1,357.71	$22,530.65
3. Lowell	2,594.37	24,415.34
4. Mission	1,535.62	
5. Polytechnic	3,262.89	21,646.52
Technical—		
6. S. F. Commercial	1,313.56	
	$10,065.15	$68,592.51
Elementary.		
7. Adams	755.87	
8. Agassiz	972.37	
9. Bay View	626.02	
10. Bernal	1,323.31	
11. Bryant	886.60	
12. Buena Vista	408.87	
13. Burnett	692.89	
14. Cleveland	602.66	
15. Columbia	1,006.48	
16. Columbus	168.10	
17. Cooper	501.07	
18. Crocker	1,960.09	
19. Daniel Webster	403.35	
20. Denman	646.51	
21. Detention Home	17.72	
22. Douglass	346.84	
23. Dudley Stone	481.63	
24. Edison	415.51	
25. Emerson	964.43	
26. Everett	873.60	
27. Fairmount	1,009.79	
28. Farragut	1,144.62	
29. Francis Scott Key	288.26	
30. Frank McCoppin	1,269.06	
31. Franklin	719.93	
32. Fremont	727.80	
33. Garfield	1,096.38	
34. George Peabody	629.27	

		Budget.	Bond.
35.	Glen Park	727.73	
36.	Golden Gate	600.57	
37.	Grant	416.43	
38.	Grattan	531.12	1,120.25
39.	Haight	564.23	
40.	Hamilton	919.10	
41.	Hancock	960.26	
42.	Harrison	371.88	
43.	Hawthorne	447.87	
44.	Hearst	523.50	
45.	Henry Durant	480.53	
46.	Horace Mann	2,253.87	
47.	Hunter's Point	111.71	
48.	Irving M. Scott	810.08	
49	Jackson	153.00	
50.	James Lick	428.74	
51.	Jean Parker	1,098.15	
52.	Jefferson	319.21	
53.	John Swett	782.97	894.71
54.	Junipero Serra	804.92	
55.	Kate Kennedy	625.51	
56.	Lafayette	261.40	
57.	Laguna Honda	1,138.97	
58.	Le Conte	....	
59.	Lincoln	349.17	195.00
60.	Longfellow	563.18	
61.	McKinley	872.05	
62.	Madison	648.35	
63.	Marshall	432.96	
64.	Marshall Annex	173.75	
65.	Mission	1,161.10	
66.	Monroe	971.34	
67.	Moulder	290.45	
68.	Noe Valley	614.77	
69.	Oral School for Deaf	.60	
70.	Oriental	422.19	
71.	Pacific Heights	1,688.61	
72.	Ethan Allen	176.19	
73.	Parkside	114.47	
74.	Patrick Henry	29.50	2,987.24
75.	Paul Revere	81.56	
76.	Portola	890.75	
77.	Redding	364.46	
78.	Rincon	106.24	
79.	Rochambeau	397.78	
80.	Roosevelt	1,241.74	
81.	Sheridan	809.30	
82.	Sherman	990.06	
83.	Spring Valley	906.28	156.00
84.	Starr King	343.35	
85.	Sunnyside	412.16	
86.	Sutro	916.45	
87.	Ungraded Primary	97.19	
88.	Visitacion Valley	465.71	
89.	Washington	921.37	

	Budget.	Bond.
90. Washington Irving	290.76	
91. Wingfield Scott	282.29	
92. Yerba Buena	976.16	
	$55,273.07	
Evening.		
93. Bay View	48.07	
94. Bernal	336.00	
95. Commercial	109.90	
96. Hamilton	119.43	
97. Horace Mann	114.68	
98. Humboldt High	190.96	
99. Irving M. Scott	40.34	
100. Jean Parker School of Home Economics	279.35	
101. Laguna Honda	131.66	
102. Lincoln	78.46	
103. Monroe	....	
104. Navigation	10.77	
105. North Beach High	74.56	
106. Portola	43.46	
107. Roosevelt	53.86	
108. Sheridan	71.45	
109. Sherman	146.23	
110. Washington	38.00	
	$ 1,887.18	
	$67,224.30	$73,945.71

Water	$11,261.13
Gas and Electricity	6,880.75
Department—At Large	2,505.15
Secretary—Postage, Advertising, etc.	1,917.99
A. Roncovieri	2,112.78
Automobile	1,020.74
Payroll—Labor	15,019.25
Golden Gate Shop—Material for desks, etc.	528.52
Lectures—Slides, Printing	838.00
Repair Shop—Horse Hire Superintendent Repair Shop	540.00
Penmanship—Engrossing Diplomas	501.41
Music	235.98
Drawing—Material, etc.	521.86
Domestic Science—Groceries and Utensils	1,905.41
Manual Training—Lumber, Tools, Superintendent	2,503.56
Athletics—Printing, Medals	633.03
	$48,925.56

SUMMARY.

2,416	Desks and Rears	$11,600.27
1,404	Chairs	2,221.42
76	Teachers' Desks	1,510.20
5	Pianos	2,389.00
1,582	Assembly Chairs	2,531.20
988	Opera Chairs	2,588.56
207	Tables	2,565.64
751	Stools	1,181.60
38	Settees	228.60
	Fuel—Wood and Coal	16,567.01
		*$43,383.50

RECAPITULATION.

Budget	$67,224.30	
Bond	73,945.71	
		$141,170.00
Water	11,261.13	
Gas and Electricity	6,880.75	
Department	2,505.15	
Secretary	1,917.99	
Superintendent of Schools	2,112.78	
Automobile	1,020.74	
Pay Roll	15,019.25	
Golden Gate Shop	528.52	
Lectures	838.00	
Repair Shop	540.00	
Penmanship	501.41	
Music	235.98	
Drawing	521.86	
Domestic Science	1,905.41	
Manual Training	2,503.56	
Athletics	633.03	48,925.56
		$190,095.57
* Charged in Budget		43,383.50
		$146,712.07

MARY W. KINCAID,
Chairman Com. on Supplies.

S. G. WHITNEY,
Accountant.

ANNUAL REPORT OF THE SUPERVISOR OF LECTURES TO THE BOARD OF EDUCATION FOR THE SCHOOL YEAR ENDING JUNE 30, 1913.

San Francisco, July 1, 1913.

To the Honorable Board of ducation,
City and County of San Francisco.

Ladies and Gentlemen:—

Herewith I respectfully submit my third annual report on public lectures, for the school year ending June 30, 1913. During this year, the total attendance at 111 lectures was 23,757, an average of 214 to each lecture; 4 more schools, making 37 in all, have been made lecture centers and equipped with streopticon and screen; the department's stock of slides has been added to, and one moving picture film, illustrating the circulation of the blood, has been purchased. With this film the moving picture was given its first use in regular school work in San Francisco by Dr. A. A. D'Ancona, President of the Board of Education, in a lecture to a Girls' High School class in Biology.

The free lectures for adults have proceeded on the same general lines as heretofore; and again it is a pleasure to make grateful acknowledgment to the press, and to the lecturers who, in almost every case, have cheerfully tendered their services to the cause, without pay. This generosity, coupled with strict economy in expenditures, has enabled the lecture bureau to keep well within its allowance for the year.

The death of George Otis Mitchell, director of the bureau of lectures, is recorded with much regret. As operator and as maker of slides, Mr. Mitchell has been with the bureau from its formation; his place will be most difficult to fill.

Your honorable body has seen fit to adopt a recommendation, made in my last annual report, that the lecture system and use of the stereopticon and moving picture be extended into the day schools; the work of the bureau to include: 1. Free evening lectures for adults, as heretofore; 2. School lectures for pupils; 3. Organization of school work in morals and civics, including literature, debates, lectures, and certain investigations into child life and conduct. This is a large plan and a serious undertaking; no one can guarantee its success; but if it shall reasonably succeed, it will fairly introduce the lecture method into school practice, and, what is more, will contribute toward the emphasis, in our San Francisco schools, of personal character and social service as the aim of education conducted by the State.

Respectfully,

MILTON E. BLANCHARD,
Supervisor of Lectures.

Report of Superintendent of Schools

San Francisco, August 18, 1913.

To the Honorable James Rolph, Jr.,
Mayor of the City and County of San Francisco.

Dear Sir:—I have the honor to submit herewith the annual report on the condition of the public schools of this City and County, as required by the Charter for the sixtieth fiscal year of the School Department, ending June 30, 1913.

ALFRED RONCOVIERI,
Superintendent of Common Schools, in and
for the City and County of San Francisco.

REPORT OF THE SUPERINTENDENT OF SCHOOLS.

PREFACE.

The last year in the San Francisco school department has been one of steady, but unsensational progress. The daily average attendance, which was 41,931 in 1905-06, and which after the fire fell to 29,929 in 1906-07, has now increased to 42,830 for the year ending July 1, 1913. This figure has, therefore, now passed the totals of the year 1905-06, heretofore the maximum in our school history.

In material advancement—new buildings, equipment, etc.—the most striking manifestation is to be found in the high school rather than in the elementary domain. Two new buildings, those of the Lowell High and the Girls' High, have been completed and are now occupied; a third, that of the Polytechnic High, has one wing completed and occupied and the second wing well under way. These are thoroughly modern structures, and of sufficient size to accommodate our high school poulation for several years to come.

The plant of machinery and other apparatus for industrial courses at the Polytechnic high school has been greatly extended and enlarged during the year.

Last August the San Francisco Commercial School was reorganized upon a four years' basis (having theretofore had courses of two years' duration only), being now entitled the "High School of Commerce."

The course of study of this school was completely revised and permits of much more complete preparation than formerly, either for a business career or college. That these advantages are appreciated by the young men and women of the community is reflected in the fact that the enrollment in this school has grown with exceeding rapidity, until now it is the largest high school in point of numbers in San Francisco.

Commercial work (stenography, typewriting and bookkeeping) has been installed in the Humboldt Evening High school besides that given in the commercial evening school. As the former institution is located in the Mission High School building, and is, therefore, convenient to the homes of many who found it difficult to go to the other school at night, the attendance has been very gratifying from the start. It is the largest evening High school west of Chicago. It should be noted that the evening schools of San Francisco are in operation from 175 to 204 evenings of each year, while in many of the largest cities of the United States they are in session from 60 to 90 evenings.

A number of additional manual training and cooking centers have been opened in the twelvemonth. Facilities in this respect are now adequate, but the number of teachers required to operate the laboratories is insufficient; hence many of the centers are unused a considerable part of the time.

Manual work has been introduced in the grades much more extensively than at any previous time. In several of the evening schools courses in cooking, dressmaking, and millinery have been established and have proved very popular.

It will be of interest to know that there is a phase of our school work that has made wonderful strides forward in the last several years—viz., the teaching of beginners to read. Formerly, when all lessons meant drudgery to the little child, results were slow in coming. Now the efficient primary teacher recognizing the wisdom of following the interests of the child, brings childlike devices into the primary schoolroom and results come more quickly.

This change is shown in our present plan of teaching children to read. Those of us who went to primary school during the '70s and even into the '80s recall that the important first step in the learning to read process was the memorizing of the letters of the alphabet. Quite in contrast to this is the present way. Now the children take their toys and games into the schoolroom, and the skillful teacher draws from the children's world, the play world, for their first reading lessons.

In the old way the alphabet came first, single letters, double letters, capitals and small letters, then combinations of letters into meaningless syllables, from syllables to short words, from short words to long, taking two years to reach the point where children knew what they were reading about. By the new method the child reads entire sentences at first, then recognizes individual words, and finally gets to the letter when he needs to use them in spelling. Today the child can read more at the end of the first year than formerly at the end of the second or third year, and all this done while the child is having a good time, without care, without drudgery.

Public lectures for adults in the evenings now form a definite part of our school program. This is in keeping with the modern idea of the "Wider Use of the School Plant" to which our people are becoming alive.

A good beginning has been made and some of our buildings are now used for evening schools, lecture centers and meeting places for parents' associations and improvement clubs. We must open all our buildings and lands to the various kinds of recreational and educational activities for the oncoming citizens, such as school playgrounds under proper athletic and play supervision, school gardens and vacation schools.

In the evenings the plant can be utilized for social centers, wherein home and neighborhood associations and other organizations of a civic, educational or philanthropic character shall find auditoriums and general meeting rooms. The public school buildings should become the all inclusive social and civil centers of the various districts of our great city.

The illustrated lecture method has been followed more successfully in the schools during this year than ever before. Its application to lessons in geography, history, etc., is surprisingly effective. A series of lectures under the direction of Doctor Kroeber, curator of the museum of anthropology, Affiliated Colleges, has been conducted and our classes have greatly benefited therefrom.

In point of administration the civil service rules of the department have been faithfully observed. In particular, expert supervision has been had of the teaching capacity of "probationers," viz., those teachers who, having but recently entered the department, must serve a trial period of two years before being elected to regular standing. Thus the interests of the children have been carefully safeguarded. The state compulsory education law has been rigorously enforced. The truant officers report relatively few cases of delinquencies.

The superintendent's office has made vigorous effort to raise the standard of certification of the teachers of the department, particularly in cases of appiicants of the semi-annual teachers' examination. It is felt that much good has been accomplished in this direction.

Monthly principals' meetings have been continued during the last year under the direction of Mr. Heaton. At these the most important school questions have been discussed and means devised to improve the daily work of the schools. We are still working on the great problem of retardation, trying to keep the children in school until they have completed the eighth grade.

A very large per cent of our grammar school graduates are attending the high schools and the per cent of our pupils in the upper grammar grades is constantly increasing. Departmental work in the grammar grades, which was first taken up in the Horace Mann and the Hamilton Schools, has little by little won its way among our teachers, and at the present time ten grammar schools are doing departmental work. This enables each teacher to specialize on a group of subjects instead of trying to cover the whole range, and enables children to get the best teaching from each of three or four teachers. This work will be gradually extended in the department.

Ungraded classes have been continued in the schools to take care of those children who for any reason have fallen behind in their work.

The greatest need of our schools is more money, in order that we may do some new lines of work demanded by modern education in as thorough a manner as we are teaching the old and well established subjects. Many of our manual training and cooking laboratories are standing idle because we have not enough teachers to run them full time. This work should be given to all grammar grades and should be open both day and evening.

We need money to turn vacant lots and vacant school property into gardens where children may get useful instruction, combined with healthful out of door exercise. We need an agricultural high school embracing the seventh, eighth, ninth and tenth grades on a ten acre tract of land in the southern part of the city. Many of the large cities of our country are establishing agricultural high schools. The work will attract many pupils who could not be kept in the old line schools. We need a manual arts school embracing the same grades in the northern portion of our city.

These schools would take boys and girls who have no taste for history, literature, geography and grammar and who drop out of school at the earliest period the law will permit. These schools would give such boys and girls an insight into vocations and at the same time hold them to an account of academic training which will be of value to them in any calling of life. These schools will not teach vocations, but will open their eyes to vocations, awaken latent tastes and direct their choice of work.

We need intermediate schools consisting of the seventh and eighth grades, where modern languages, elementary science, home economics and manual training may be offered as elective and the academic work be reduced in quantity. Several of our large grammar schools should be equipped for this work, but it will require money. Such schools are being established in other cities and we should not be behind the times.

We are very desirous of having "vacation schools" organized and conducted in the summer months in our department. Pupils who had failed of promotion would thus be enabled to recover lost ground so that upon entering school at the opening of the fall term they may be put ahead regularly into the next grade; children regularly promoted but over age for their grade, would have an opportunity to devote their time to the fundamentals during the vacation school and by the aid of the ungraded class during the next term, be able to skip a grade.

These vacation schools should continue for five or six weeks of the summer and should be located in eight or ten buildings selected to meet best the needs of the community. Their cost would be about $7000, but, in my opinion, it would be money well spent, for a month or five weeks of work from 9 to 12 —half day sessions—would overcome the malady known technically as "retardation" in perhaps hundreds of cases.

We need a large amount of money to equip our schools with supplementary books, maps and globes and simple apparatus for teaching elementary science. We need better equipment for our school playgrounds. Most of all we need to let our people know that they can make no investment which will bring as large returns as investment in the best modern up to date school. Such schools will attract both capital and population. The best schools in the best city in the best country in the world—that is our ambition.

ANNUAL REPORT OF THE SUPERINTENDENT OF SCHOOLS FOR THE FISCAL YEAR ENDING JUNE 30, 1913.

GENERAL STATISTICS.

Population of the City and County (estimated on school attendance) 42,830x11.2		479,696
Municipal Assessment—		
Real Estate and Improvements	$447,780,237.00	
Personal Property	62,651,864.00	
Total	$510,432,101.00	
State Assessment	94,293,628.00	
Total Assessable		$604,725,729.00
Assessment just completed on which taxes will be collected for year 1913-14—		
Municipal	$526,244,423.00	
State	97,600,193.00	
Total		$623,844,616.00

City and County School Tax (includes Day and Evening Elementary and High Schools) on each 100.00, 1912-13, 22-4/10 cts.

Total rate (including Panama Pac. In. Ex. Co. 5c.) $2.10, 1912-13.

City and County School Tax on each $100.00, 1913-14, 20.8 cts.

City and County Taxes for School Purposes		$ 1,146,051.84
Apportionment of State School Funds—		
High School	$ 28,533.75	
Elementary Schools	608,363.04	
Total		$ 638,604.13

ESTIMATED VALUE OF SCHOOL PROPERTY.

Sites occupied by Elementary Schools	$2,682,000.00	
Sites occupied by Secondary Schools	625,000.00	
Sites not occupied by schools	2,650,000.00	
Total value of land		$ 5,957,000.00
Buildings—		
Elementary Schools	$4,241,000.00	
Secondary Schools	1,363,000.00	
Administration	15,000.00	
Total value of Buildings		$ 5,619,000.00
Furniture—		
Elementary Schools	$ 251,000.00	
High Schools	59,500.00	
Administration	3,500.00	
Total value of Furniture		$ 314,000.00
Apparatus and Laboratories—		
Elementary Schools, including Manual Training and Cooking	$ 16,000.00	
High Schools	52,000.00	
Total value of all Apparatus and Laboratories		$ 68,000.00
Library—		
Elementary Schools (including State texts)	$ 39,500.00	
High Schools	4,500.00	
Teachers'	1,000.00	
Storeroom	2,000.00	
Total value Libraries		$ 47,000.00
Total Value (Estimated) of all School Property		$12,005,000.00

FINANCIAL STATISTICS.

DISBURSEMENTS.

Salaries—		
Administration or General Control—		
Board of Education (4)	$ 11,988.00	
Secretary and Attaches	12,783.00	
Chauffeur	1,500.00	
Department Scavenger	4,140.00	
Storekeeper and Attaches	4,380.00	
Superintendent of Buildings and Repairs	2,100.00	
Supply Department Wages	13,629.00	
Water and Gas Inspector	1,491.65	
Superintendent of Schools	4,000.00	
Deputy Supts. of Schools (4)	11,975.96	
Total salaries (Administration)		$ 67,987.61
Teachers—		
High School—		
(a) Principals	$ 15,300.00	
(b) Teachers	174,667.70	
Grammar and Primary—		
(a) Principals	145,980.00	
(b) Teachers	1,075,408.55	
Kindergarten	840.00	
Specials—		
(a) Supervisors	11,840.00	
(b) Teachers	34,000.00	
Evening Schools—		
Humboldt High and North Beach—		
(a) Principals	2,100.00	
(b) Teachers	19,740.00	
Elementary—		
(a) Principals	6,120.00	
(b) Teachers	44,760.00	
Sewing, Millinery and Dressmaking	1,500.00	
Total Teachers' salaries		$1,532,256.25
Janitors—		
High School	$ 12,660.00	
Elementary	84,446.00	
Evening—		
Humboldt and North Beach High—	450.00	
Elementary	3,000.00	
Total Janitors' salaries		$ 100,556.00
Grand Total of all Salaries		$1,700,799.86
Advertising	$ 284.60	
Athletics	2,636.40	
Books	5,763.01	
Cartage	1,617.00	
Cooking	774.68	

DISBURSEMENTS—Contd.

Fuel	17,535.38	
Furniture	16,014.37	
Home Economics (Sewing, Dressmaking, Millinery)	878.59	
Incidentals	6,523.25	
Incidentals (President's)	468.22	
Industrial Work	1,789.46	
Janitorial Supplies	4,306.86	
Laboratory Supplies (High School)	3,606.06	
Lectures	1,892.42	
Light and Power	7,018.46	
Manual Training Supplies	3,164.56	
Printing	5,138.47	
Rents	2,167.55	
Stationery	14,900.62	
Teachers' Institute	1,512.00	
.Telegraph and Telephone	40.94	
Water	11,454.93	
Grand Total of Budget Expenses		$1,811,287.71

DISTRIBUTION OF BUDGET EXPENSES AMONG THE DIFFERENT CLASSES OF SCHOOLS.

(Items marked * are prorated on basis of average daily attendance).

	High	Elementary	Hdt. Eve. High	Other Evening	Total
*Expenses of [illegible] Control on Administration (overhead charges)	$ 4,711.57	$ 59,009.71	$ 1,250.70	$ 3,015.63	$ 67,987.61
*Advertising	17.90	248.98	5.20	12.52	284.60
Athletics—Salaries		2,003.35			
Supplies		633.05			2,636.40
Books	490.01	5,252.00		21.00	5,763.01
Cartage	112.07	1,404.15	29.00	71.78	1,617.00
Cooking	3.20	1,771.48			1,774.68
Fuel	1,396.20	15,814.48		324.70	17,535.38
Furniture	8,064.15	7,776.02		174.20	16,014.37
Home Economics (Sewing, Millinery, Dressmaking)	224.20	153.19		501.20	878.59
i [illegible]s	456.40	5,658.26	119.63	288.96	[illegible]
Incidentals (President)	50.00	418.22			[illegible]
Industrial Work		1,789.46			1,789.46
Janitorial Supplies	298.41	3,738.57	[illegible]	190.80	[illegible]
Laboratory Supplies	[illegible]				[illegible]
High School Light and Power	1,135.84	72.16	721.28	5,089.20	[illegible]
*Lectures	[illegible]	[illegible]	34.12	83.95	1,892.42
[illegible] Training (supplies)	[illegible]	[illegible]			3,164.56
*Printing	[illegible]	4,460.20	94.47	227.64	5,138.47
Rents		2,167.55			2,167.55
*Stationery	1,032.57	12,937.55	269.00	661.50	14,900.62
*Teachers' Institute	104.26	1,313.17	27.50	67.07	1,512.00
*Telegraph and [illegible]	2.85	35.49	.78	1.82	40.94
[illegible]	793.77	10,389.62	78.00	193.54	11,454.93
Principals' or Supervisors' Salaries	15,300.00	157,280.00	1,320.00	6,900.00	181,340.00
Teachers' Salaries	174,667.70	1,110,248.55	19,740.00	46,260.00	[illegible]
Jani[illegible]' Salaries	12,660.00	84,446.00	[illegible]	3,000.00	[illegible]
Totals	$226,275.44	$1,493,707.00	$24,218.76	$67,086.51	$1,811,287.71

RECEIPTS (BUDGET OR ANNUAL APPROPRIATION.)

City and County Taxes		$1,146,051.84
State Apportionment (High Schools)	$ 28,533.75	
State Apportionment (Elementary Schools)	608,363.04	
Total		636,896.79
Rents derived from School Property		56,389.05
Money from Sale of Old Material		644.63
Total Receipts (on Budget Account)		$1,839,982.31

RESUME.

Receipts	$1,839,982.31
Expenditures	1,811,287.71
Surplus	$ 28,694.60

(This surplus should nearly pay deficit existing at end of year 1911-12.)

STATEMENT OF ALL RECEIPTS AND EXPENDITURES FOR YEAR 1912-1913.

Receipts—	
Budget (as already set forth)	$1,839,982.31
Special Appropriation for Repairs	97,510.56
Sale of Bonds	611,217.25
Grand Total	$2,548,710.12

RECEIPTS AND EXPENDITURES OF MONEY DERIVED FROM SALE OF BONDS, YEAR 1912-13.

Schools.	Sites.	Buildings.	Equipment.	Total.
Girls' High		$145,614.90	$ 22,530.65	$168,145.55
Lowell		136,059.89	24,415.34	160,475.23
Polytechnic		50,842.16	21,646.52	72,488.68
Total High Schools		$332,516.95	$ 68,592.51	$401,109.46
Cooper	$ 37,050.00			
Grattan			1,120.25	
Holly Park (yard)	1,319.00			
John Swett			894.71	
Lincoln			195.00	
Marshall	33,000.00	1,695.85		
Oriental	24,000.00			
Patrick Henry		61,380.99	2,987.24	
Starr King		30,183.75		
Spring Valley			156,00	
Washington Irving	16,125.00			
	$111,494.00	$ 93,260.59	$ 5,353.20	$210,107.79
Grand Total	$111,494.00	$425,777.54	$ 73,945.71	$611,217.25

There was levied by the Board of Supervisors a special appropriation for the repair of school buildings of $97,510,66 which was expended by the Board of Public Works on elementary schools.

STATEMENT OF ALL RECEIPTS AND EXPENDITURES FOR YEAR 1912-13.

RECEIPTS.

Budget (as already set forth)	$1,839,982.31
Special Appropriation for repairs	97,510.56
Sale of Bonds	611,217.25
Grand Total Receipts	$2,548,710.12

EXPENDITURES.

Schools.	Budget.	Special App. to Board of Public Works for Repairs.	Bonds.	Total.
High	$ 226,275.44	$	$401,109.46	$ 627,384.90
Elementary	1,493,707.00	97,510.56	210,107.79	1,801,325.35
Humboldt	24,218.76			24,218.76
Other Evening	67,086.51			67,086.51
Grand Totals	$1,811,287.71	$ 97,510.56	$611,217.25	$2,520,015.52

RESUME.

Receipts	$2,548,710.12
Expenditures	2,520,015.52
Surplus	$ 28,694.60

COST PER PUPIL, 1912-13.

	Per Pupil Enrolled.	Per Pupil Ave. Daily Attendance.	Ave. Daily Att. Year 1911-1912
(a) For Instruction Only—			
High Schools	$ 54.90	$ 63.97	$ 64.35
Primary and Grammar Schools	29.18	34.03	35.70
Evening Schools	8.07	20.62	27.73
Average	$ 28.50	$ 34.36	
(b) For all Expenditures (not including buildings and sites)—			
High Schools	$ 65.39	$ 76.19	$ 69.16
Primary and Grammar Schools	34.38	40.72	44.52
Evenings Schools	13.30	34.03	37.15
Average	$ 35.51	$ 44.57	
(c) For all Expenditures—			
High Schools	$181.33	$211.24	
Primary and Grammar Schools	41.47	45.83	
Evening Schools	13.30	34.03	
Average	$ 46.80	$ 58.84	

STATEMENT SETTING FORTH THE EXPENDITURE OF MONEY DERIVED FROM SALE OF BONDS (ISSUES OF 1904, 1908 AND 1909), TO JUNE 30, 1913.

School.	Site.	Buildings.	Furniture or Equipment.
Girls' High	$	$ 371,117.50	$ 22,530.65
Lowell High	138,500.00	343,865.09	24,415.34
Mission High	103,910.00		
Polytechnic High	65,000.00	253,761.38	21,646.52
S. F. Commercial	36,800.00	261,635.28	15,462.43
Adams		94,739.36	4,159.98
Agassiz	16,500.00		
Bay View	10,250.00	116,892.00	5,296.00
Bernal	11,800.00		
Bryant		106,306.15	4,545.89
Burnett	10,000.00	54,372.92	3,800.08
Cleveland	13,250.00	64,782.24	3,566.44
Cooper	37,050.00		
Crocker	2,750.00		
Denman	88,843.00	158,494.85	3,502.02
Douglass	10,750.00		
Dudley Stone	12,000.00		
Edison	17,400.00		
Everett	20,400.00		
Farragut	12,537.50	101,914.91	2,474.30
Francis Scott Key		38,904.00	2,869.40
Frank McCoppin	9,500.00	106,294.69	4,085.56
Franklin		75,926.83	4,284.62
Freemont	6,750.00		
Garfield	10,150.00	111,188.18	4,884.99
George Peabody		80,545.02	2,951.80
Glen Park	5,600.00	45,750.00	3,762.00
Golden Gate	25,693.00	73,533.00	4,200.00
Grant	44,500.00		
Grattan	28,500.00	68,579.17	4,605.13
Hancock	10,800.00	166,321.20	5,233.72
Harrison	10,000.00	22,435.41	441.39
Holly Park	1,319.00		
Horace Mann	15,000.00		
Jackson	37,500.00		
James Lick	5,600.00		
Jean Parker	20,675.00	173,355.57	5,720.17
John Swett	56,750.00	91,156.74	3,904.73
Junipero Serra	21,815.00	91,603.59	4,545.89
Kate Kennedy	31,650.00	102,370.57	3,697.44
Laguna Honda		91,418.99	4,283.28
Le Conte	14,000.00		
Lincoln	7,050.00	74,650.96	4,215.76
Longfellow	9,250.00	78,675.38	2,645.83
McKinley	35,000.00	111,018.18	3,523.33
Madison		87,945.72	3,500.00
Marshall	100,250.00	5,115.55	
Mission Grammar		171,836.66	4,053.10
Monroe	13,800.00	84,296.00	3,600.00
Noe Valley	13,250.00		

School.	Site.	Buildings.	Furniture or Equipment.
Oriental	24,000.00		
Pacific Heights	23,500.00		
Patrick Henry		61,380.99	2,987.24
Portola	5,000.00	97,042.23	3,700.00
Rochambeau	39,489.00	38,900.00	3,891.00
Sheridan	9,750.00	105,749.60	4,991.58
Spring Valley	31,325.00	118,595.67	5,389.72
Starr King	14,500.00	30,183.75	
Sunnyside	2,000.00	31,000.00	
Sutro	7,100.00	101,341.49	4,448.78
Visitacion Valley		46,623.88	2,918.53
Washington	17,000.00	118,944.00	4,988.00
Washington Irving	16,125.00	26.62	
Winfield Scott		42,206.43	3,590.58
Yerba Buena	17,000.00		
Miscellaneous Plans		57,656.08	
Lot on Geary St. (old Clement School Site)	27,000.00		
	$1,375,931.00	$4,730,796.19	$229,220.86

Grand Total Expended..........$6,335,948.05

SCHOOLS.

Number of High Schools, including Humboldt Evening High School	6
Number of Grammar	29
Number of Primary Schools	51
Number of Special Schools	2
Number of Evening Schools	16
Total Number of Schools	104

SCHOOL BUILDINGS.

Number of concrete school buildings owned by the department Class "A"	9
Number of brick school buildings owned by the department, "Special Construction"	19
Number of concrete school buildings owned by the department	8
Number of wooden school buildings owned by the department	53
Number of buildings rented by the department	2
Total number of buildings used by the department	91

"STATE ENROLLMENT" BY GRADES AND SEX.

(STATE ENROLLMENT ADMITS NO DUPLICATION. PUPILS PROMOTED DURING THE YEAR ARE ENUMERATED ONLY IN THE GRADES FROM WHICH THEY WERE PROMOTED.)

DAY SCHOOLS.

	Boys.	Girls.	Total.
Kindergarten	25	41	66
First Grade	5,763	4,950	10,713
Second Grade	3,193	2,801	5,994

	Boys.	Girls.	Total.
Third Grade	3,012	2,931	5,943
Fourth Grade	2,751	2,721	5,472
Fifth Grade	2,661	2,549	5,210
Sixth Grade	2,021	2,108	4,129
Seventh Grade	1,549	1,675	3,269
Eighth Grade	1,297	1,347	2,644
Totals Elementary and Kindergarten	22,317	21,123	43,440
High Schools—			
*First Year	632	976	1,608
Second Year	371	622	993
Third Year	170	302	472
Fourth Year	134	253	387
Total High	1,307	2,153	3,460
Grand Totals (Day Schools)	23,624	23,276	46,900

EVENING SCHOOLS.

	Boys.	Girls.	Total.
Humboldt High—			
First Year	933	276	1,209
Second Year	258	105	363
Third Year	110	7	117
Totals	1,301	388	1,689
North Beach High, Humboldt Evening High and Evening Technical Schools—			
First Year	499	606	1,109
Second Year	151	173	324
Third Year	4	3	7
Fourth Year	6	1	7
Totals	660	779	1,439
	Boys.	Girls.	Total.
Elementary Evening Schools—			
First Grade	521	193	714
Second Grade	182	30	212
Third Grade	461	72	533
Fourth Grade	334	24	358
Fifth Grade	211	97	308
Sixth Grade	308	97	405
Seventh Grade	509	175	684
Eighth Grade	475	40	515
Totals	3,001	728	3,729
Grand Totals Evening Schools	4,962	1,895	6,857
Grand Totals Day School	23,624	23,276	46,900
Grand Totals (Day and Evening)	28,586	25,171	53,757

* These figures EXCLUDE those enrolling in January and who, during the year, were enrolled in the grammar (8th grade) by order of the State Superintendent of Public Instruction.

STATE ENROLLMENT AND ATTENDANCE STATISTICS FOR THE YEAR ENDING

	Enrollment June 30, 1913	Increase (I) over or decrease (D) from 1912	Enrollment June 30, 1912
High Schools	3,460*	I. 122	3,338*
Elementary	43,374*	I. 1,400	41,974
Kindergarten	66	D. 4	70
Humboldt Evening High	1,689	I. 185	1,504
Other Evening Schools	5,168	D. 1,106	6,274
	53,757	I. 597	53,160

AVERAGE DAILY ATTENDANCE.

High Schools	2,970	I. 132	2,838
Elementary	37,148	I. 2,269	34,879
Kindergarten	29	I. 4	25
Humboldt Evening High	787	I. 98	689
Other Evening Schools	1,896	D. 121	2,017
Totals	42,830	I. 2,382	40,448

GRADUATES.

Number of graduates from the grammar schools for the year—

Boys	Day 810,	Evening 151	961
Girls	Day 879,	Evening 25	904
Total			1,865

Number of graduates from the high schools for the year—

Boys	Day 148,	Evening 83	231
Girls	Day 305,	Evening 27	332
Total			563

*All pupils entering high schools, who were enrolled at any time during the year in a grammar school, are omitted in high school enrollment by order of the State Superintendent.

ENROLLMENT OF PUPILS FOR THE FIRST AND FIFTH DAYS OF SCHOOL YEAR.

Year	First Day High	First Day Elementary	First Day Evening	First Day Total	Fifth Day High	Fifth Day Elementary	Fifth Day Evening	Fifth Day Total
1906	1 59	22,790	Not Open	24,549	1964	25,585	Not Open	27,549
1907	2275	29,012	1841	3128	2306	30,210	1970	34,486
1908	2463	31,014	2006	35,483	2465	32,144	2371	36,980
1909	2681	32,115	2089	36,885	2702	188	2389	38,259
1910	2600	32, 63	2198	37,471	2798	34,390	2542	9,330
1911	2687	33,403	2255	38,345	2888	35,056	2581	525
1912	3060	36,236	2612	41,908	3186	37,595	3054	43,835
1913	3124	37,991	2546	4661	3306	303	3451	46,160

ENROLLMENT AND AVERAGE DAILY ATTENDANCE BY YEARS.

Year	Enrollment *High	Enrollment *Elementary	Enrollment *Evening	Enrollment Total	Average Daily Attendance High	Average Daily Attendance Elementary	Average Daily Attendance Evening	Average Daily Attendance Total
1906	5188	47,661	4933	57,782	3211	35,753	2967	41,931
1907	2823	37,923	4887	45,633	1762	26,765	1402	29,929
1908	2990	37,866	7189	48,045	2023	29,812	2096	33,931
1909	3224	39,940	5345	48,509	2306	0,954	2281	35,541
1910	3545	39,610	7057	50,212	2416	31,967	2391	36,774
1911	3789	40,190	483	51,462	2707	32,545	2484	37,736
1912	3338	42,044	7778	3,560	2838	4,904	2706	40,448
1913	3460	43,440	6857	53,757	2970	37,177	2683	42,830

* This represents "SCHOOL" enrollment, not "STATE" enrollment. Subsequent figures represent "STATE" enrollment.

TEACHERS EMPLOYED DURING THE YEAR ENDING JUNE 30, 1913.

	Principals or Supervisors of Special Subjects		Teachers	
	Men	Women	Men	Women
(5) High Schools (Day)	5	0	A44	AA63
Humboldt Evening High	1	0	25	3
North Beach Evening High	1			
(29) Elementary (Day) Grammar including Detention, Ethan Allen and Ungraded	8	21	B 4	C363
(54) Elementary (Day) Primary	3	52	1	602
Oral for Deaf		1	1	
Special Subjects	3	5	9	19
Elementary Evening	7	4	11	38
Commercial Evening	1		5	8
Jean Parker Evening School of Home Economics				5
Substitutes (Emergency June, 1913)			1	63
Teachers on leave who are employed some time during the year (eight of these in evening service)			3	10
Totals	29	84	104	1,174
Grand Total (employed)	Men 133	Women	1,258 =	1,391
Less Leaves	Men 3	Women	10 =	13
Net number on the Pay Roll June, 1913	Men 130	Women	1,248 =	1,378

A=3 Vice Principals.
AA=2 Vice Principals.
B=2 Vice Principals.
C=27 Vice Principals.

SCHOLASTIC TRAINING AND CERTIFICATION OF TEACHERS.

Number of Teachers (including Principals).

	Men	Women
Who are graduates of University of California	42	111
Who are graduates of Leland Stanford Jr. University	11	16
Who are graduates of other universities	19	9
Who are graduates of other colleges	20	18
Who are graduates of S. F. City Normal School	2	363
Who are graduates of Chico State Normal School	1	16
Who are graduates of the Los Angeles State Normal	1	8
Who are graduates of the San Diego State Normal		4
Who are graduates of the San Francisco State Normal		161
Who are graduates of the San Jose Normal	3	106
Who are graduates of Normal Schools of other States	9	43

CERTIFICATES.

No. holding certificates of High School Grade	215
No. holding certificates of Grammar School Grade	1,027
No. holding certificates of Primary School Grade	20
No. holding Special Certificates	116
Total	1,378

VOLUMES IN SCHOOL LIBRARIES AND STOREROOM (INCLUDING BOOKS FOR USE OF INDIGENTS).

	Volumes	Estimated Value
High Schools, including Humboldt Evening and Commerce	5,246	$ 4,505.00
Primary and Grammar Schools	101,246	38,300.00
Evening Schools	3,529	1,200.00
In Storeroom	7,253	2,000.00
	117,271	$46,005.00

SCHOOL VISITATION.

Official Visits of Superintendent and Deputies	3,796
Official Visits by members of Board of Education	1,827
Visits by other persons	55,269

SOME SCHOOL STATISTICS FROM THE OPENING OF THE FIRST

Year Ending Oct. 31.	No. of Schools.	Teachers.	Pupils Enrolled.	Average Daily Attendance.	Po
1850	1	2	150	......	
1851	1	4	325	......	
1852	7	15	700	445	
1853	....	16	2,870	1,182	
1854	....	19	4,199	1,727	
1855	....	29	4,694	1,638	
1856	9	61	3,347	2,516	
Year Ending June 30.					
1857	....	60	2,821	2,155	
1858	....	67	5,273	2,521	
1859	11	75	6,201	2,829	
1860	....	68	6,180	2,837	
1861	13	73	6,617	3,377	
1862	17	82	8,204	3,786	
1863	....	94	8,177	4,389	
1864	20	108	7,075	5,470	
1865	....	138	8,000	6,718	
1866	32	206	10,152	8,131	
1867	37	253	13,385	10,177	
1868	39	285	17,426	11,871	
1869	42	326	19,885	13,113	
1870	55	371	22,152	15,394	
1871	56	416	26,406	16,978	
1872	56	480	27,664	18,272	
1873	58	506	27,722	18,550	
1874	64	510	29,449	19,434	
1875	64	552	31,128	21,014	
1876	66	574	34,029	22,761	
1877	66	632	37,268	24,899	
1878	65	672	38,672	26,292	
1879	64	696	38,129	27,075	
1880	59	685	38,320	28,150	
1881	62	719	40,187	29,092	
1882	65	675	40,752	29,435	
1883	63	687	40,722	30,827	
1884	64	714	41,942	31,578	
1885	65	734	43,265	32,183	
1886	65	773	43,140	32,146	
1887	68	799	43,311	31,316	
1888	68	806	42,330	30,191	
1889	71	838	42,626	31,609	
1890	72	859	42,926	31,352	
1891	73	879	43,626	31,809	
1892	75	897	46,172	32,431	
1893	76	929	45,775	32,799	
1894	73	866	44,349	32,939	
1895	75	904	44,822	32,974	
1896	76	927	45,435	33,508	
1897	77	974	46,564	33,531	
1898	92	1,070	50,101	35,116	
1899	90	1,074	48,972	36,830	
1900	86	1,061	48,058	35,004	
1901	82	1,017	48,517	34,771	
1902	84	1,052	48,893	35,691	
1903	84	1,086	48,345	37,077	
1904	85	1,121	49,600	37,700	
1905	85	1,181	55,067	40,920	
1906	86	1,115	57,782	41,932	
1907	83	971	45,633	29,929	
1908	89	1,095	48,045	33,931	
1909	92	1,195	48,509	35,541	
1910	95	1,198	50,212	36,774	
1911	100	1,227	51,462	37,736	
1912	105	1,308	53,160	40,448	
1913	103	1,378	53,757	42,830	
		Total			

OL BY J. C. PELTON, DECEMBER, 1849, TO JUNE 30, 1912.

Cost per Capita on Average Daily Attendance.	School Census Children 4 to 18 Years.	Value of School Property.	Assessment of City and County Property.
....	500	....	....
....	1,510	....	....
51.96	2,132	....	....
296.5	2,730	....	....
125.19	3,268	....	....
83.38	4,531	....	....
49.71	4,751	....	....
43.14	4,755		....
41.57	6,375		....
47.62	7,767	....	....
55.13	9,025	....	....
47.04	13,316	....	....
35.58	13,358		....
47.67	16,501		....
41.76	18,748		....
50.15	21,013		....
	5 to 15 Years.		
44.48	17,369	....	$70,202,000
49.89	20,253	$1,057,000	74,976,000
35.09	23,306	1,368,000	84,689,000
30.34	24,817	1,531,000	95,700,000
33.56	27,055	1,729,800	114,759,500
41.53	28,971	1,786,400	....
36.02	31,936	1,810,000	(?)97,000,000
35.45	34,676	....	....
	5 to 17 Years.		
35.40	38,084	2,227,620	212,407,505
33.71	41,029	2,367,000	264,000,000
38.12	46,238	2,505,500	269,105,141
29.41	53,210	2,585,000	260,576,978
37.62	55,899	2,711,000	254,702,960
32.37	62,105	3,047,303	244,477,360
28.74	58,492	3,073,000	217,487,074
28.44	55,115	3,137,000	253,545,476
24.98	55,880	3,137,000	222,336,400
25.66	58,061	3,137,000	201,992,152
25.25	63,029	3,137,000	201,763,762
25.80	69,000	3,137,000	223,509,560
25.37	74,079	3,189,000	230,386,325
26.93	78,246	3,184,575	230,151,009
30.69	59,517	3,230,598	251,746,111
28.99	60,642	4,772,180	273,389,616
31.35	61,144	4,757,724	306,041,440
33.12	62,456	4,798,427	301,444,140
33.88	63,933	4,932,754	311,566,079
34.59	65,317	5,019,317	346,224,706
30.05	68,390	5,063,364	342,644,179
26.09	70,006	5,140,258	325,108,898
32.42	71,822	5,284,000	327,805,147
36.52	74,840	5,354,859	330,401,154
37.58	76,336	5,474,739	351,784,094
40.92	75,292	5,514,200	405,111,615
36.41	78,554	5,514,200	410,155,304
30.27	82,173	5,207,600	413,417,241
36.88	82,391	5,334,000	413,338,420
35.67	91,386	5,649,651	420,555,541
37.09	97,353	5,702,001	564,070,301
34.29	98,127	5,800,000	583,056,457
35.73	101,836	6,984,000	524,392,047
44.28	77,367	6,207,010	375,932,477
57.01	87,696	6,379,000	429,632,843
47.86	88,058	7,206,573	454,334,160
89.98	74,729	8,733,285	492,867,374
83.18	abolished	10,161,492	545,057,591
92.54		11,536,929	605,488,153
59.60		12,005,000	623,844,616

REPORT OF THE BOARD OF EXAMINATION.

The Board of Examination for the issuance of teachers' certificates is composed of: Superintendent Alfred Roncovieri, Chairman; Deputy Superintendent W. B. Howard, Secretary; Deputy Superintendent T. L. Heaton, Deputy Superintendent A. J. Cloud, Deputy Superintendent R. H. Webster.

The Board of Examination has conducted two examinations (October, 1912, and May, 1913), according to law, of persons desirous of securing certificates. It has met monthly and forwarded the recommendations to the Board of Education.

Herewith is a resume of its work:

CERTIFICATES GRANTED ON CREDENTIALS.

HIGH SCHOOL.

Men	12
Women	28
	40

GRAMMAR.

Men	4
Women	153
	157

SPECIALS.

Men	4
Women	35
	39

RENEWALS.

Men	6
Women	26
	32

ON EXAMINATION.

GRAMMAR.

Men	0
Women	2
	2

REJECTED.

GRAMMAR.

Men	0
Women	2
	2

SPECIALS.

Men	3
Women	28
	31

Number of Certificates issued	238
Number of Certificates renewed	32
Number of Applicants rejected	33
Amount fees collected of applicants, including renewals	$584

REPORT OF THE PUBLIC SCHOOL TEACHERS' ANNUITY AND RETIREMENT FUND COMMISSIONERS.

RECEIPTS.

Balance in Fund July 1, 1912, not deducting sinking fund for Fire Protection Bonds to replace premium paid for them	$ 2,738.94	
Contributions by teachers under provisions of Annuity Law	13,656.50	
Absence money granted by Board of Education	3,000.00	
Interest on Permanent Fund ($50,000 invested in 44 $1,000 Bonds S. F. Fire Protection	2,200.00	
Interest on funds in bank	307.45	
Amount received from teachers retiring during the year..	728.25	
Total receipts		$22,631.14

DISBURSEMENTS.

Annuities to retired teachers.

1912—		
October 1	$ 5,152.90	
1913—		
January 1	5,328.75	
April 1	5,318.75	
July 1	5,193.60	
Total	$20,994.00	
Clerical Services	120.00	
Sinking Fund ($142.86 semi-annually commencing July, 1909) to pay premium paid on Fire Protection Bonds ($44,000 par)	1,207.29	
Total disbursements		22,321.29
Balance June 30, 1913, E. & O. E.		$ 309.86

LIST OF ANNUITANTS.

Limited revenue admits the payment of but fifty per cent (50%) of these annuities.

Date of Retirement.	Name.	Maximum or Fraction Thereof.	Annuity Per Month.	Annuity Per Quarter.
1895.				
Nov. 27,	Mrs. L. T. Hopkins	Max.	$50.00	$150.00
1896.				
Jan. 22,	Mrs. M. H. Currier	Max	50.00	150.00
April 24,	Miss V. M. Raclet	9/10	45.00	135.00
1897.				
Sept. 11,	Miss M. Solomon	Max.	50.00	150.00
Dec. 8,	Miss F. L. Soule	Max.	50.00	150.00
1898.				
Sept. 14,	Miss Kate Kollmyer	8/15	26.66⅔	80.00
1900.				
July 18,	Mrs. A. Griffith	Max.	50.00	150.00
July 25,	Miss K. F. McColgan	Max.	50.00	150.00
Aug. 1,	Miss L. M. Barrows	13/15	43.33⅓	130.00
Aug. 1,	Miss Annie A. Hill	Max.	50.00	150.00
Oct. 15,	Miss M. J. Canham	14/15	46.66⅔	140.00
1901.				
July 20,	Miss J. B. Gorman	Max.	50.00	150.00
Oct. 4,	Miss E. Murphy	9/10	45.00	135.00
1902.				
Jan. 2,	Miss R. B. Campbell	Max.	50.00	150.00
Jan. 2,	Miss L. S. Templeton	Max.	50.00	150.00
Jan. 2,	Mr. A. T. Winn	Max.	50.00	150.00
Sept. 28,	Miss Emma J. Miller	11/15	36.66⅔	110.00
1903.				
Feb. 17,	Mrs. B. A. Chinn	Max	50.00	150.00
Feb. 17,	Miss Lydia Hart	11/15	36.66⅔	110.00
Feb. 17,	Miss Christine Hart	Max.	50.00	150.00
Aug. 1,	Mr. T. B. White	Max.	50.00	150.00
Sept. 1,	Miss A. E. Slaven	Max.	50.00	150.00
Oct. 15,	Miss L. Burnham	¾	37.50	112.50
1904.				
Aug. 1,	Mr. Elisha Brooks	Max.	50.00	150.00
Aug. 1,	Miss I. Patterson	Max.	50.00	150.00
Sept. 1,	Mrs. E. M. Whitcomb	Max.	50.00	150.00
1905.				
Jan. 16,	Miss E. G. Grant	Max.	50.00	150.00
March 1,	Miss M. A. Smith	⅔	33.33⅓	100.00
March 1,	Miss Jean Parker	Max.	50.00	150.00
March 1,	Mrs. T. C. Nicholl	Max.	50.00	150.00
March 1,	Mr. Charles Ham	Max.	50.00	150.00
March 1,	Miss R. Jacobs	Max.	50.00	150.00
March 1,	Mr. D. Lambert	Max. (Even)	25.00	75.00
1906.				
Feb. 1,	Miss M. E. Carson	Max.	50.00	150.00
Feb. 1,	Mrs. A. C. Taylor	Max.	50.00	150.00
Aug. 1,	Miss E. R. Elder	Max.	50.00	150.00
Oct. 1,	Miss H. E. Whirlow	Max.	50.00	150.00
Dec. 1,	Mrs. V. Troyer	Max.	50.00	150.00
1907.				
April 1,	Miss Madge Sprott	½ (Even)	25.00	75.00
April 1,	Miss A. D. Miley	14/15	46.66⅔	140.00
April 1,	Miss Q. O. McConnell	Max.	50.00	150.00
July 1,	Mr. C. W. Moores	Max.	50.00	150.00
Sept. 1,	Miss V. E. Bradbury	Max.	50.00	150.00
Sept. 1,	Miss Martha Stone	Max.	50.00	150.00
Sept. 1,	Miss N. C. Stallman	Max.	50.00	150.00
Sept. 1,	Mr. W. H. Edwards	Max.	50.00	150.00

1908.				
Jan. 1,	Miss R. V. Claiborne	⅔	33.33⅓	100.00
Feb. 15,	Mrs. F. A. Banning	Max.	50.00	150.00
March 1,	Miss Rose Fay	11/15	36.66⅔	110.00
May 1,	Miss Julia A. Danks	Max.	50.00	150.00
July 1,	Miss Laura T. Fowler	Max.	50.00	150.00
Sept. 1,	Miss Ruby A. Jewell	Max.	50.00	150.00
Sept. 1,	Miss Regina Hertz	4/5	40.00	120.00
1909.				
Jan. 1,	Miss A. T. Campbell	Max.	50.00	150.00
Jan. 1,	Mrs. Mary J. Mayborn	Max.	50.00	150.00
Jan. 1,	Miss C. M. Johnston	Max.	50.00	150.00
Aug. 1,	Mrs. N. Seabrook	7/10	35.00	105.00
Aug. 1.	Miss Rose E. Morgan	Max.	50.00	150.00
Aug. 1,	Miss Jessie I. King	Max.	50.00	150.00
1910.				
Jan. 1,	Miss E. R. Pettigrew	3/5	30.00	90.00
Jan. 10,	Miss Anne B. Campbell	Max.	50.00	150.00
July 1,	Miss E. S. Heney	Max.	50.00	150.00
Aug. 1,	Mrs. R. H. Hazelton	Max.	50.00	150.00
1911.				
July 1,	Miss Emily M. Goggin	29/30	48.33⅓	145.00
July 1,	Miss Caroline L. Hunt	Max.	50.00	150.00
July 1,	Miss E. A. Sutherland	18/30	30.00	90.00
Sept. 1,	Mrs. Kate Waters	Max.	50.00	150.00
Nov. 1,	Mr, Jas. T. Hamilton	Max.	50.00	150.00
1912.				
Jan. 2,	Miss K. B. Childs	Max.	50.00	150.00
March 1,	Miss Bertha Goldsmith	Max.	50.00	150.00
April 1,	Mrs. Katherine Turney	2/3	33.33⅓	100.00
Oct. 1,	Miss L. M. Brooks	21/30	35.00	105.00
Oct. 1,	Mrs. Margaret Dwyer	Max.	50.00	150.00
Oct. 1,	Mrs. Josephine S. Love	Max.	50.00	150.00

NECROLOGY.

Miss Effie Douglas, Hamilton school; died April 23, 1906.
Miss Barbara Bannon, Emerson school; died June 5, 1906.
Mr. J. W. Gorman, Lincoln Evening school; died July 31, 1906.
Miss A. L. Hornsby, Laguna Honda school; died October 24, 1906.
Miss M. M. Murphy, principal Irving M. Scott school; died December 24, 1906.
Mr. Madison Babcock, vice-principal Hancock school, ex-superintendent public schools; died December, 1906.
Miss Emma Stincen, principal Grattan school; died January 29, 1907.
Miss Leah C. Peckham, Laguna Honda school; died February 11, 1907.
Mr. J. B. Clarke, Polytechnic High school; died March, 1907.
Miss Helen Thompson, Girls' High school; died December 17, 1907.
Miss Josephine C. Evans, McKinley school; died February 5, 1908.
Mrs. M. E. Steele, Hearst school; died June, 1908.
Miss Margaret O'Brien, Sherman school; died August 13, 1908.
Miss L. R. Cullen, Burnett school; died September 3, 1908.
Miss Katherine Gaines, Winfield Scott school; died October 2, 1908.
Miss Adelaide C. Cherry, Redding school; died October 26, 1908.
Miss Rose Prince, Portola school; died October 31, 1908.
Mrs. Anne Armstrong, Noe Valley school; died November 20, 1908.
Miss S. M. Boniface, Hamilton school; died March 25, 1909.
Miss Mary Phillips, Agassiz school; died April 11, 1909.
Mrs. Georgia Washburn, principal Henry Durant school; died April 17, 1909.
Mrs. Anna M. Kortick, Burnett school; died May 3, 1909.
Miss Nell O'Hara, Marshall school; died May 27, 1909.
Mrs. M. B. Thompson, Starr King school; died June 25, 1909.
Mme. Ernestine Giffard, Bryant school; died July 24, 1909.
Mr. Leslie A. Jordan, ex-Deputy Superintendent of Schools, Lincoln Evening school; died July 30, 1909.
Mrs. Ellen R. Kenzla, Washington Evening school; died August 4, 1909.
Miss Lucy McNear, Bryant Cosmopolitan Primary; died January 21, 1910.
Mrs. V. C. Ingram, Peabody school; died March 10, 1910.
Miss Minnie R. Bley, Agassiz school; April 1, 1910.
Miss Mary L. Marks, Bernal school; died April 20, 1910.
Mrs. M. A. Steele, Edison school; April 25, 1910.
Mr. George Foulks, principal Hamilton Evening school; died June 7, 1910.
Mrs. J. B. Levey, Hearst Grammar school; died July 25, 1910.
Mrs. Cora B. Thompkins, Moulder school; died October 8, 1910.
Miss Katherine E. Meighan, Fairmount school; August 31, 1910.
Mr. A. C. Kinne, Lincoln Evening school; died October 6, 1910.
Miss Laura C. Perry, Lincoln school; died October 26, 1910.
Mrs. Clara Bigelow, vice-principal John Swett Grammar school; died December 6, 1910.
Mr. Azro L. Mann, principal Denman Grammar, Superintendent of Schools 1878-1879; died February 28, 1911.
Mr. Ebenezer Knowlton, formerly principal of Rincon Grammar school, vice-principal of Lincoln Grammar and teacher in Boys' High, Commercial and Roosevelt Evening schools; died February 9, 1911.
Mr. John C. Pelton, founder of the first free public school in San Francisco or California, December, 1849; principal grammar schools, Superintendent of Schools 1856, 1857, 1865, 1866, 1867; died March 5, 1911.
Mr. William A. Leggett, vice-principal Franklin school; died March 31, 1911.
Miss Martha Galloway, principal Visitacion Valley school; April 5, 1911.
Mrs. Rebecca Greenan, Lincoln Evening school; died April 12, 1911.

Mr. W. N. Bush, formerly teacher Lowell High and principal Polytechnic High schools; died May 21,, 1911.

Mrs. M. S. Wright, Frank McCoppin school; died March 9, 1911.

Miss Emily Wickman, Jackson school.

Miss A. Weed, Washington school; died October, 1911.

Miss E. J. Moynihan, Horace Mann school; died December 31, 1911.

Mrs. M. J. Parolini, principal Cleveland school; died January 10, 1912.

Mrs. M. H. Walker, principal Marshall school; died January 22, 1912.

Miss G. F. Libby, Bernal school; died February 7, 1912.

Miss M. K. Gavigan, Portola school; died March 9, 1912.

Miss M. A. Deane, formerly principal Redding school, member Board of Education; died March 20, 1912.

Mrs. A. M. Sechrist, Laguna Honda school; died April 24, 1912.

Miss H. B. Fairweather, Rochambeau school; died May 23, 1912.

Mr. Lawrence Taaffe, Humboldt Evening school; died July 20, 1912.

Mrs. K. D. Grant, Fremont school; died September 9, 1912.

Mr. P. T. Riley, Commercial Evening school; died September 23, 1912.

Mrs. A. E. Kedon, Roosevelt school; died October 1, 1912.

Miss L. C. Cole, Hearst school; died December 22, 1912.

Miss M. M. Robinett, Fremont school; died January 24, 1913.

Miss C. B. Earle, Pacific Heights school; died February 4, 1913.

Miss E. L. West, Unassigned; died March 1, 1913.

Miss C. Deneen, Drawing Department; died April 16, 1913.

Miss F. Erb, Sherman school; died June 13, 1913.

Mrs. M. L. O'Neal, Laguna Honda school; died June 16, 1913.

Mr. Geo. O. Mitchell, Girls' High school; died June, 1913.

Miss M. C. Robinson, Washington Evening school; died August 3, 1913.

Miss Deane Mrs Kinkaid etc

DECEASED ANNUITANTS.

Miss E. A. Cleveland, April, 1906.
Miss H. M. Fairchild, May 14, 1906.
Miss Flora McDonald Shearer, February 12, 1907.
Mrs. C. M. Sisson, June 16, 1907.
Mrs. L. G. Webster, November 17, 1907.
Mrs. Helen Thompson, December 7, 1907.
Mrs. E. M. Steele, June 15, 1908.
Mrs. E. M. Poole, November 23, 1908.
Miss Margaret J. Gallagher, November 30, 1908.
Miss C. A. Templeton, January 1, 1909.
Mrs. M. E. Caldwell, March 9, 1909.
Miss L. C. McNear, January 24, 1910.
Miss L. E. Ryder, February 18, 1910.
Miss M. J. Bragg, June 15, 1910.
Mrs. S. A. Miles, April 12, 1912.
Mrs. Mary A. Hogan, April 21, 1912.
Mrs. Christine Chalmers, June 26, 1912.
Professor Adolph Herbst, October 2, 1912.
Mr. Paul A. Garin, November 30, 1912.
Mrs. M. E. Michener, March 15, 1913.
Miss Alice D'Arcy, April 26, 1913.
Miss Ellen A. Sleator, June 14, 1913.

Electricity Department

FINANCIAL STATEMENT—1912-1913.

Appropriations.		Expenditures.	Surplus.
$ 72,546.00	Salaries	$ 72,278.85	$267.15
15,000.00	Expense and Equipment	14,715.41	284.59
15,000.00	Reconstruction	14,967.77	32.23
1,380.00	Motor Runabout	1,380.00	
$103,926.00		$103,342.03	$583.97

SPECIAL APPROPRIATIONS.

Resolution Number.		Appropriation.	Expenditure.	Surplus.
9125	Installation of Police Boxes (Central District)	$12,274.70	$12,222.87	$51.83

INTERIOR INSPECTIONS.

Applications on file June 30, 1912 (Corrected)	3,418
Applications received for inspection during year	7,417
	10,835
Installations approved	8,417
Applications on file June 30, 1913	2,418
Inspections made during year	17,042
Installations found defective	3,791
Installations disconnected from service	100
Non-record installations detected	902

DOCUMENTS ISSUED.

Contractors' licenses	223
Complaints on defective wiring	3,791
Certificates of approval	7,538
Electric sign permits	342
Housemovers' permits	46
Receipts for fees	2,463

MONEYS RECEIVED.

Fees for wire inspection, Ordinance No. 1008	$14,619.05
Fees for electric sign permits, Ordinance No. 1009	618.65
Fees for fire tapper service, Ordinance No. 698	809.85
Total	$16,047.55
Housemovers' deposits, Ordinance No. 1026	1,150.00
Housemovers' refundment	946.25

Report of Board of Education

September 2, 1914.

To the Honorable Board of Supervisors,
San Francisco.

Gentlemen:—I have the honor to submit herewith the annual report of the Superintendent of Common Schools, to the Board of Education, covering the condition of the public schools of this City and County for the sixty-first fiscal year of the School Department ending June 30, 1914.

Respectfully yours,

M. R. NORRIS,
Secretary Board of Education.

DEPARTMENT OF EDUCATION, CITY AND COUNTY OF SAN FRANCISCO, CALIFORNIA.

BOARD OF EDUCATION.

GALLAGHER, GEORGE E., President	Term expires Jan. 8, 1918	$3,000.00
D'ANCONA, DR. A. A., Member	Term expires Jan. 8, 1916	3,000.00
KINCAID, Mrs. M. W., Member	Term expires Jan. 8, 1917	3,000.00
JONES, Miss S. J., Member	Term expires Jan. 8, 1915	3,000.00

SUPERINTENDENT OF SCHOOLS.

RONCOVIERI, ALFRED	Term expires Jan. 8, 1915	$4,000.00

(Ex-officio member of the Board of Education without right to vote).

DEPUTY SUPERINTENDENTS OF SCHOOLS.

Webster, R. H.	Term expires May 1, 1916	$3,000.00
Cloud, A. J.	Term expires Dec. 1, 1916	3,000.00
Heaton, T. L.	Term expires Mar. 1, 1918	3,000.00
Howard, W. B.	Term expires	3,000.00

EMPLOYES.

Norris, [illegible] M. R.	Acting Secretary Board of Education	Term at pleasure of Board of Education	$1,800.00
Berliner, C. A.	Financial Secretary, Board of Education	Term at pleasure of Board of Education	2,160.00
[illegible], Mrs. A. M.	Secretary Board of Education	Term at pleasure of Board of [illegible]	[illegible]
Anderson, Miss L. E.	[illegible] to Secretary	Term at pleasure of Board of Education	1,020.00
[illegible], [illegible] Irene S.	Stenographer, Board of Education	Term at pleasure of Board of Education	1,260.00
O'Rourke, J., Miss	Stenographer, Board of [illegible]	Term at pleasure of Board of Education	1,260.00
O'Connor, T. S., Miss	Stenographer, Office Supt. of Schools	[illegible] at pleasure of Board of Education	1,260.00
Holden, S. A., Miss	Phone Exchange Operator	Term at pleasure of Board of Education	1,080.00
Harris, J.	Messenger, Board of [illegible]	Term at pleasure of Board of Education	1,200.00
[illegible], R.	[illegible], Supt. of Schools	Term at pleasure of Board of Education	1,140.00
Sweeney, E.	Tru[illegible] Officer	[illegible] by Chief of Pol[illegible]	
[illegible], T. J.	Truant Officer	Assigned by Chief of Police.	
Nolan, E.	Truant Officer	[illegible] by Chief of Police.	
Foley, James	Store Keeper	Term at pleasure of Board of E[illegible]	$1,800.00
Hunt, John	[illegible] to [illegible] Keeper	Term at pleasure of Board of E[illegible]dcation	1,080.00
Whitney, S. E.	Bookkeeper	[illegible] at pleasure of Board of Education	1,500.00
[illegible], M. J.	Building and Repairs	Term at pleasure of Board of Education	2,100.00
Dempsey, T.	Water and Gas Inspector	Term at pleasure of Board of Education	1,500.00
[illegible], E.	Chauffeur	Term at pleasure of Board of Education	1,500.00

Total Number of Schools	101
Number of days Schools were kept open	193½

Average daily attendance:

Secondary	3,642
Elementary	39,245
	42,887

Number of teachers employed	1,436
Number of teachers on leave during 1913-1914	68
Number of teachers on pay roll 1914	1,407
Total appropriation 1913-1914	$1,868,280.00
Total amount drawn from Treasury, 1913-1914	1,879,187.76
Receipts from State	683,766.48

Disbursed for:

Administration	$ 50,792.96
Salaries and Rents	1,735,517.80
Scavenger	3,600.00
Lectures	1,030.81
President's Incidental Fund	318.25
Maintenance	87,927.94
	$1,879,187.76

DISBURSED FOR FISCAL YEAR 1913-1914.

Board of Education	$ 11,988.00
Superintendent and Deputies	15,975.96
Secretary and Attaches	13,349.00
Storekeeper and Attaches	4,380.00
Scavenger	3,600.00
Superintendent Building and Repairs	2,100.00
Water and Gas Inspector	1,500.00
Chauffeur	1,500.00
Teachers P. & G.	1,380,820.20
Teachers High	233,295.55
Janitors	107,133.35
Rents	2,816.20
Wages in Supply Department	17,666.25
Stationery	11,638.78
Incidentals	7,698.42
Furniture	10,964.67
Manual Training	5,311.61
Janitorial	4,894.76
Printing	1,600.94
Books	3,030.15
Fuel	7,866.52
Telephone and Telegraph	91.85
Water	8,236.23
Light	5,198.90
Cartage	2,000.25
Cooking	1,691.97
High School	7,041.88

Advertising	23.97
Athletics	363.54
Lectures	1,030.81
Home Economics	1,171.09
Industrial Work	1,390.66
President's Incidental Fund	318.25
Teachers' Institute	1,498.00
	$1,879,187.76

RECAPITULATION.

Appropriation 1913-1914	$1,868,280.00
Surplus 1911-1912	9,695.47
Surplus 1912-1913	1,212.29
Total	$1,879,187.76
Disbursed as above	1,879,187.76

Report of Superintendent of Schools

STATE ENROLLMENT.

Day Schools—Kindergarten and Elementary	46,843	
High Schools—Day	3,843	
Total Day School Enrollment		50,686
Elementary Schools—Evening	5,009	
High Schools—Evening	2,157	
Total Evening School Enrollment		7,166
Grand total Day and Evening Enrollment		57,852

AVERAGE DAILY ATTENDANCE.

Elementary Schools	40,154	
High Schools	4,085	
Total		44,239

"STATE ENROLLMENT" BY GRADES AND SEX.

(STATE ENROLLMENT ADMITS NO DUPLICATION. PUPILS PROMOTED DURING THE YEAR ARE ENUMERATED ONLY IN THE GRADES FROM WHICH THEY WERE PROMOTED.)

DAY SCHOOLS.

	Boys.	Girls.	Total.
Kindergarten	155	150	305
First Grade	6,181	5,371	11,552
Second Grade	3,679	3,192	6,871
Third Grade	3,117	2,756	5,873
Fourth Grade	3,020	2,819	5,839
Fifth Grade	2,734	2,653	5,387
Sixth Grade	2,253	2,273	4,526
Seventh Grade	1,745	1,931	3,676
Eighth Grade	1,353	1,461	2,814
Totals Elementary and Kindergarten	24,237	22,606	46,843
High Schools—			
First Year	*679	*1,179	*1,858
Second Year	409	656	1,065
Third Year	209	330	539
Fourth Year	139	242	381
Total High	1,436	2,407	3,843
Grand Total (Day Schools)	25,673	25,013	50,686

* These figures EXCLUDE those enrolling in January and who, during the year, were enrolled in the grammar (8th) grade.

EVENING SCHOOLS.

Humboldt and North Beach Evening High Schools—			
First Year	1,225	462	1,687
Second Year	272	20	292
Third Year	126	18	144
Fourth Year	32	2	34
Totals (Evening High Schools)	1,655	502	2,157
Elementary and Technical Evening Schools—	Boys.	Girls.	Total.
First Grade	504	301	805
Second Grade	420	223	643
Third Grade	295	90	385
Fourth Grade	303	113	416
Fifth Grade	164	73	237
Sixth Grade	431	158	589
Seventh Grade	531	252	783
Eighth Grade	778	373	1,151
Totals	3,426	1,583	5,009
Grand Totals Evening Schools	5,081	2,085	7,166
Grand Total Day Schools	25,673	25,013	50,686
Grand Totals (Day and Evening)	30,754	27,098	57,852

	Enrollment June 30, 1914.	Increase (I) over or decrease (D) from 1913	Enrollment June 30, 1913.
High Schools	*3,843	I. 383	*3,460
Elementary	46,538	I. 3,164	43,374
Kindergarten	305	I. 239	66
Humboldt and North Beach Evening High	2,157	I. 448	1,689
Other evening schools	5,009	D. 159	5,168
Totals	57,852	I. 3,164	53,757

AVERAGE DAILY ATTENDANCE

High Schools	3,198	I. 228	2,970
Elementary	38,336	I. 1,188	37,148
Kindergarten	149	I. 120	29
Humboldt and North Beach Evening High	887	I. 100	787
Other Evening Schools	1,818	D. 78	1,896
Totals	44,388	I. 1,558	42,830

GRADUATES

Number of graduates from the grammar schools for the year—

Boys	Day 1,034,	Evening 265	1,299
Girls	Day 1,243,	Evening 147	1,390
Total			2,689

Number of graduates from the high schools for the year—

Boys............Day 169,	Evening 128	297
Girls............Day 325,	Evening 63	388
Total		685

GRADE ENROLLMENT.

(These figures indicate the pupils taught in each grade. Unlike "State" enrollment it admits duplication, e. g. If 2,900 are promoted from the first to the second grade in December they are taught, hence counted in both grades. State enrollment places them in the first grade only.)

Elementary	Day School	Evening (including Technical)
First Grade	11,582	825
Second Grade	9,012	689
Third Grade	8,793	420
Fourth Grade	8,227	433
Fifth Grade	7,889	242
Sixth Grade	6,308	655
Seventh Grade	4,927	825
Eighth Grade	4,237	1,169
High Schools		
First Year	2,902	2,480
Second Year	1,501	413
Third Year	674	158
Fourth Year	486	34

AVERAGE DAILY ATTENDANCE IN DETAIL.

Elementary Schools—Day	38,336	
Elementary Schools—Evening	1,818	
Total Elementary Schools		40,154
High Schools—Day	3,198	
High Schools—Evening	887	
Total High Schools		4,085
Grand Total		44,239

(NOTE—On the State records at Sacramento the average daily attendance total appears as 42,887 owing to the rule of the State Board of Education, followed in the apportioning of State school funds, that only half-time credit shall be allowed for evening school attendance. The figures given above, however, are those which state the actual fact as to the number of individual pupils attending school.)

*All pupils entering high schools, who were enrolled at any time during the year in a grammar school, are omitted in high school enrollment by order of the State Superintendent.

	Principals or Supervisors of Special Subjects Men	Women	Teachers Men	Women
(5) High Schools (Day)	5	0	*50	†68
Humboldt Evening High	1	0	28	3
North Beach Evening High	1			
(29) Elementary (Day) Grammar	8	21	‡6	§426
(54) Elementary (Day) Primary, including Ethan Allen, Ungraded and Detention	2	52		481
Oral for Deaf				2
Kindergarten				4
Special Subjects	3	5	14	31
Elementary Evening	5	2	7	29
Commercial Evening	1		6	7
Jean Parker Evening School of Home Economics				5
Substitutes			1	49
Substitutes (Emergency June, 1914)			5	53
Totals	26	81	118	1,158

Men 107 Women 1,276 = 1,383

SCHOLASTIC TRAINING AND CERTIFICATION OF TEACHERS.

Number of Teachers (including Principals)	Men	Women
Who are graduates of University of California	39	109
Who are graduates of Leland Stanford Jr. University	15	8
Who are graduates of other universities	18	6
Who are graduates of other colleges	14	14
Who are graduates of San Francisco City Normal School	2	353
Who are graduates of San Francisco State Normal School	2	203
Who are graduates of Chico State Normal School	1	13
Who are graduates of the Los Angeles State Normal School	1	4
Who are graduates of the San Diego State Normal School	2	3
Who are graduates of the San Jose Normal School	4	82
Who are graduates of the Santa Barbara Normal School		2
Who are graduates of Normal Schools of other States	7	17

CERTIFICATES.

No. holding certificates of High School Grade	227
No. holding certificates of Grammar School Grade	1,032
No. holding certificates of Primary School Grade	18
No. holding Special Certificates	106
Total	1,383

SCHOOL VISITATION.

Official Visits of Superintendent and Deputies	3,557
Official Visits by members of Board of Education	1,603
Visits by other persons	62.519

* 3 Vice Principals.
† 2 Vice Principals.
‡ 2 Vice Principals.
§ 26 Vice Principals.

VOLUMES IN SCHOOL LIBRARIES AND STOREROOM (INCLUDING BOOKS FOR USE OF INDIGENTS).

	Number	Estimated Value.
In libraries of High Schools	6,810	$ 6,630.00
In libraries of Elementary Schools	96,569	35,021.00
In libraries of Evening Schools	2,897	1,000.00
In San Francisco Teachers' Library	878	1,589.00
	107,154	$44,240.00

Statement of Free Elementary State Text-Books given by the State of California for the use of pupils of public schools of San Francisco. Received from State from March 1, 1913, to Jun 30, 1914:

Text-Books		183,675
In good condition in schools	156,446	
In storeroom for distribution in July, 1914	24,760	
Lost or mutilated by pupils	2,143	
Worn out or destroyed because of contagious diseases	326	183,675

Pupils have contributed for 1,490 books lost or destroyed by them, $406.57, which sum has been deposited with State Treasurer Roberts, to the credit of the State Free Text-Book Fund.

Writing Books received from State		78,267
Used	41,420	
Unused in schools	17,162	
Unused in storeroom	19,685	78,267

Value of State Text-Books in Schools and Storeroom	$52,908.37
Value of Writing Books	1,473.88
Total	$54,382.25

RECEIPTS AND EXPENDITURES.

Elementary Schools—Receipts:	
State Apportionment	$ 644,899.76
Tax Revenue	861,847.64
Bond Sale Receipts	249,101.50
From Miscellaneous Sources	135,807.82
Total	$1,891,656.72
Elementary Schools—Expeditures:	
Teachers' Salaries	$1,380,820.20
Repairs, Rent, etc	274,969.47
Sites, Buildings, etc	248,901.50
Library, Books, Apparatus, etc	5,042.48
Total	$1,909,733.65
High Schools—Receipts:	
State Apportionment	$ 38,866.72
Tax Revenue	231,246.40
Bond and Building Funds	209,463.93
Total	$ 479,577.05

High Schools, Expenditures:

Teachers' Salaries	$ 233,295.55
Current Expenses, Supplies, etc.	33,835.65
Buildings	209,463.93
Total	$ 479,577.05

KINDERGARTEN WORK.

Number of Schools Under City Control	4
Number of Teachers Employed (women)	4
Number of Pupils Enrolled	305
Number of Days' Schooling given during year	703
Total amount paid teachers	$3,528

GENERAL STATISTICS.

Population of the City and County (estimated on average daily school attendance of 44,239 by multiplying same by 11.2)	495,477
Municipal Assessment, 1913-14—	
Real Estate and Improvements	$461,282,132.00
Personal Property	64,965,404.00
Total	$526,247,536.00
State Assessment, 1913-1914	97,600,193.00
City and County School Tax Rate on each $100 of property assessed for municipal purposes	.208
Amount of City and County taxes collected for school purposes	1,868,280.00
State School Fund apportionment, 1913-1914	683,766.48

NUMBER OF SCHOOL HOUSES.

	Composite	Concrete and Steel	Brick and Steel	Wood	Total
High School	1	1	3	2	7
Elementary	19	4	9	52	84
Grand Total					91

ESTIMATED VALUE OF SCHOOL PROPERTY.

Sites occupied by Elementary Schools	$2,747,000.00	
Sites occupied by Secondary Schools	630,000.00	
Sites not occupied by schools	2,693,000.00	
Total value of land		$ 6,070,000.00
Buildings—		
Elementary Schools	4,453,000.00	
Secondary Schools	1,620,715.00	
Administration	12,435.00	
Total value of buildings		6,086,150.00
Furniture—		
Elementary Schools	250,000.00	
High Schools	70,110.00	
Administration	3,500.00	
Total value of furniture		323,610.00

Apparatus and Laboratories—		
Elementary Schools, including Manual Training and Cooking	17,500.00	
High Schools	76,326.00	
Total value		93,826.00
Library—		
Elementary Schools, Free State Texts	54,382.00	
Library and Supplemental	36,021.00	
High Schools	6,630.00	
Teachers'	1,589.00	98,622.00
		$12,672,208.00

SCHOOL PROPERTY—NAMES AND LOCATIONS OF SCHOOLS AND DESCRIPTIONS OF SCHOOL PROPERTY.

(a) Estimated value of school property.

Land	$ 6,070.000.00
Buildings	6,086,150.00
Furniture	323,610.00
Apparatus and Laboraties	93,826.00
Libraries	98,622.00
Total	$12,672,208.00

(b) School lots leased by Board of Education.

1. Lot in 100 vara block 371, Fifth street, near Market, known as Lincoln block, 275x275 ft. Leased to Wise Realty Company (later merged into the Lincoln Realty Co.) for thirty-five (35) years at a total rental of $2,835,000, as follows: For the first five years to June 30, 1913, a rental of $3,780.00 per month, and for the remaining thirty (30) years a rental of $7,245.00 per month.

2. Lot in 50 vara block 119, Post street, between Grant avenue and Stockton street 70x122½ ft. Leased at an average of $911.42 per month.

Graduated Rentals—	
First four months, per month	$ 250.00
Second four months, per month	300.00
Third four months, per month	350.00
Second year, per month	400.00
Third year, per month	450.00
Fourth year, per month	500.00
Fifth year, per month	550.00
Sixth year, per month	650.00
Seventh year, per month	700.00
Eighth year, per month	750.00
Ninth year, per month	800.00
Tenth year, per month	850.00
Eleventh year, per month	900.00
Twelfth year, per month	900.00
Thirteenth and fourteenth, per month	950.00
Fifteenth year, per month	1,000.00
Sixteenth to twenty-fifth year, per month, inc	1,000.00
Twenty-sixth to thirty-fifth year, per month, inc	1,125.00

3. Lot in 100 vara lot 348, Tehama street, between First and Second, 118x 155 ft. Leased June 29, 1911, thirty-five (35) years; December 1 to November 30, 1946, at $103.00 per month.

4. Old Denman School lot, Bush and Taylor streets, leased March 24, 1911, to Mary L. Burns.

September 1, 1911, to August 31, 1921.....................at $60.00 per month
September 1, 1921, to August 31, 1936.....................at 100.00 per month
September 1, 1936, to August 31, 1946.....................at 160.00 per month

5. Lot on Turk street at $3.00 per month to Hann Bjorn.

6. Lot on Jackson street, between Scott and Divisidero, leased to the Sacred Heart Academy, at $50.00 per month, during the pleasure of the Board of Education.

7. Paul Revere lot, Corbett road and Ocean avenue, rented to T. Varni, at $2.50 per month, during the pleasure of the Board of Education.

8. Lot at Rhode Island and Mariposa streets to Mahoney, at $2.00 per month, during the pleasure of the Board of Education.

9. Lot at Thirty-first avenue and Geary street, leased to Owen McHugh, during the pleasure of the Board of Education, at $10.00 per month.

ALFRED RONCOVIERI,
Superintendent of Schools.

REPORT

OF THE

SUPERINTENDENT OF SCHOOLS

OF

SAN FRANCISCO, CAL.

FOR THE FISCAL YEAR ENDING JUNE 30, 1915

(Sixty-Third Fiscal Year of the School Department)

TO

His Honor, the Mayor; the Board of Supervisors, and the Board of Education in and for the City and County of San Francisco

---

SUPERINTENDENT OF SCHOOLS

ALFRED RONCOVIERI

DEPUTY SUPERINTENDENTS OF SCHOOLS

T. L. HEATON W. B. HOWARD A. J. CLOUD

W. H. DeBELL MARY MAGNER

FINANCIAL AND STATISTICAL*

GENERAL STATISTICS.

FISCAL YEAR ENDING JUNE 30, 1915.

Population of the City and County....521.494
(Estimated by multiplying the total average daily attendance of 46,562 by 11.2.)

Municipal Assessment	$541,894,443	
State Assessment	105,313,071	
Total		$647,207,514

Assessment just completed on which taxes will be collected for year 1915-1916.

Municipal Assessment	$538,703,750	
State Assessment	117,640,479	
Total		$656,344,229

City and County School Tax rate on each $100.00 for 1914-1915.... .222c
City and County School Tax rate on each $100.00 for 1915-1916.... .255c

Data secured from City and County Assessor (E. and O. E.).

* The financial data presented in this report were secured from various departments of the city and county government as herein specified in foot-notes, and are here presented without further verification by the Superintendent of Schools.

ESTIMATED VALUATION OF SCHOOL PROPERTY.

Sites occupied by Elementary Schools	$2,672,527	
Sites occupied by Secondary Schools	600,000	
Sites not occupied by Schools	2,600,000	
Total valuation of land		$ 5,872,527
Buildings—		
Elementary Schools (including $2550 for Kindergartens)	$5,991,439	
Secondary Schools	1,317,753	
Administration	16,000	
Total Valuation of Buildings		$ 7,325,192
Furniture—		
Elementary Schools	$ 360,000	
High Schools	30,500	
Administration	3,700	
Total Valuation of Furniture		$ 394,200
Apparatus and Laboratories—		
Elementary Schools, including Manual Training and Cooking	$ 40,777	
High Schools	42,223	
Kindergartens	100	
Total Valuation of all Apparatus and Laboratories		$ 83,100
Libraries—		
Elementary Schools	$ 36,050	
High Schools	9,080	
Teachers	1,020	
Total Valuation of Libraries		$ 46,150
Total Valuation (Estimated) of all School Property		$13,721,169

Data prepared with advice of Assessor (E. and O. E.) and set forth in annual report by San Francisco Superintendent of Schools to State Superintendent of Public Instruction.

RECEIPTS.

City and County Taxes		*$1,529,823.34
Divided as follows:		
Elementary Schools	$1,134,142.18	
High Schools	388,613.47	
($240,980.97 regular, $147,632.50 special appropriation of Board of Supervisors)		
Kindergartens	7,067.69	
Total		$1,529,823.34
State Apportionment:		
Elementary Schools	$ 631,986.35	
High Schools	43,015.73	
Total		$ 675,002.08
Rents derived from School Property		97,614.69
School bonds sold		457,020.82
Elementary Schools $366,385.00		
High Schools 90,635.82		
Total $457,020.82		
Amounts for Medical Inspection and Truant Officers		31,723.41
Total Receipts		$2,791,184.34

Data secured from City Asessor, City Auditor, Financial Expert Board of Supervisors, and set forth in annual report of Superintendent of Schools of San Francisco to State Superintendent of Public Instruction.

* $1,201,614.25 derived from City and County tax levy of $.222 on each $100.00 assessed valuation of property. $328,209.08 derived from special resolutions of appropriations by Board of Supervisors.

DISBURSEMENTS.

(A) Salaries—

(I) Teachers—

Day High Schools (5)	$ 217,334.20	
Evening High Schools (2)	26,820.00	
Day Elementary Schools	1,283,753.45	
Evening Elementary and Special Schools	107,537.50	
Kindergartens	6,120.00	
Total of Teachers' Salaries		$1,641,565.15

(II) Janitors—

Day High Schools	15,840.00	
Evening High Schools	360.00	
Day Elementary and Kindergarten Schools	92,545.60	
Evening Elementary and Specials	2,190.00	
Total of Janitors' Salaries		$ 110,935.60

Data secured from City and County Auditor, and the Financial Expert of the Board of Education, and set forth in Annual Report of San Francisco Superintendent of Schools to State Superintendent of Public Instruction.

(III) Administration and Miscellaneous—

Board of Education (4 members)	$ 11,976.00	
Chauffeur	1,500.00	
Inspector (Gas and Water Supply)	1,500.00	
Scavenger	3,600.00	
Secretary and Attaches (10 persons)	13,260.00	
Storeroom-Bookkeeper	1,680.00	
Storekeeper and Assistant	2,880.00	
Superintendent of Buildings	2,100.00	
Superintendent of Schools (including 5 Deputies and Clerk)	18,980.00	
Wages, Mechanics	15,200.25	
Total Administration and Miscellaneous Salaries		$ 72,676.25
* Grand Total of Salaries		$1,825,177.00

(B) New Buildings and Sites—

Elementary	$ 464,467.10	
Secondary	194,954.90	
Total		$ 659,422.00

Data secured from City and County Auditor, the Financial Secretary of the Board of Education and from the Board of Public Works.

* Including $15,959.00 paid into Teachers' Retirement Fund.

(C) Expenses of Administration—

Advertising	$ 133.51	
Athletics	7,150.31	
Books and Charts	3,009.51	
Cartage	1,522.25	
Deficit (1913-1914)	18,076.93	
Fuel	26,708.49	
Furniture	18,395.02	
Home Economics	522.99	
Lectures, Free Public	357.23	
Light	9,484.52	
Printing	2,888.80	
Rents	2,407.95	
Social Centers	1,845.47	
Stationery	19,960.19	
Teachers' Institute	1,235.00	
Telephone and Telegraph	65.66	
Water	15,516.99	
Total		$ 129,280.82

(D) Supplies—

Cooking	$ 3,701.08	
Incidental (including President's Incidental $540.60)	9,779.38	
Kindergartens	947.69	
Primary Industrial	1,122.27	
Janitorial	8,959.15	
Manual Training	5,732.05	
Total		$ 30,241.62

(E) Expenditures by other City Boards for School Purposes—

* Medical Inspection	$27,403.41		
† Truant Officers	4,320.00	$ 31,723.41	
‡ Repairs		109,384.36	
Total			$ 141,107.77

Data secured from City and County Auditor, the Financial Secretary of the Board of Education, the Boards of Health and of Public Works, and the Police Commission.

GRAND TOTAL OF DISBURSEMENTS.

(A) Salaries	$1,825,177.00	
(B) New Buildings and Sites	659,422.00	
(C) Expenses of Administration	129,280.82	
(D) Supplies	30,341.62	
(E) By other Boards	141,007.77	
Grand Total		$2,785,229.21
Grand Total of Receipts		2,791,184.34
Balance		5,955.13

* Expended by Board of Health.

† Expended by Police Commission.

‡ Expended by Board of Public Works.

DISTRIBUTION OF EXPENDITURES AMONG SCHOOLS.

(Not including Sites and Buildings)

High Schools—		
Equipment (Polytechnic)	$ 19,040.94	
Instruction	217,334.20	
Janitors	15,380.00	
Light and Electricity	688.00	
Supplies	23,227.75	
* Share of Department Expenditures prorated	14,718.64	
		$ 290,389.53
Elementary Schools (Day)—		
Buildings (additions to)	$ 82,519.18	
Cooking Center Equipment	3,701.08	
Instruction	1,283,753.45	
Janitors	92,545.60	
Supplies	27,416.92	
Rents	2,407.95	
* Share of Department Expenditures prorated	174,597.81	
		$1,666,941.99
Humboldt and North Beach Evening High Schools—		
Instruction	$ 26,820.00	
Janitors	360.00	
Light	3,061.04	
Supplies	280.65	
* Share of Department Expenditures prorated	3,986.25	
		$ 34,507.94
Other Evening and Special Schools—		
Home Economics	$ 522.99	
Instruction	107,537.50	
Janitors	2,190.00	
Light	5,735.48	
Supplies	2,631.01	
* Share of Department Expenditures prorated	7,475.85	
		$ 126,092.83
Kindergarten Schools—		
Instruction	$ 6,120.00	
Supplies	947.69	
* Share of Department Expenditures prorated	807.23	
		$ 7,874.92

Compiled from data in various departments as heretofore stated (E. and O. E.)

---

* The "Share of Department Expenditures prorated" was gained by adding the total sums found under Schedules (A III) and (C) above, viz.: $72,676.25 and $129,280.82, dividing the same by the daily average attendance 46,562, and multiplying by the daily average attendance of each group of schools set forth above.

STATEMENT CONCERNING THE ISSUANCE OF SCHOOL BONDS.

1. 3½% School Bonds Dated July 1, 1904.

Authorized at a special election Sept. 29, 1903. Total vote, 27,308; two-thirds of the vote necessary to carry, 18,206. Votes in favor, 23,327; excess over number of votes necessary, 5,121.

Receipts:		
Bonds sold	$1,616,400.00	
Premiums	80.00	
Sales buildings	1,181.92	
		$1,617,661.92
Payments:		
Lands	$ 446,376.75	
Miscellaneous	3,504.12	
Appropriations	1,162,338.49	
		$1,612,219.36
Available July 1, 1915		$ 5,442.56

2. 5% School Bonds Dated July 1, 1908.

Election May 11, 1908. Total vote cast, 23,560; two-thirds necessary to carry, 15,707. Votes in favor, 21,397; excess over number of votes necessary, 5,694.

Receipts:		
Bonds sold	$5,000,000.00	
Premiums	301,290.40	
		$5,301,290.40
Payments:		
Appropriations	$4,370,327.40	
Miscellaneous	6,822.95	
Lands	891,236.20	
Liabilities	3,985.84	
		$5,272,372.39
Available July 1, 1915		$ 28,918.01

3. Polytechnic High School 4½% Bonds Dated Jan. 1, 1910.

Authorized by election June 22, 1909. Total vote, 24,058; two-thirds of vote necessary to carry, 16,038. Votes in favor, 17,979; excess over number of votes necessary, 1,940.

Receipts:		
Bonds sold	$ 600,000.00	
Premiums	1,758.00	
		$ 601,758.00
Payments:		
Appropriations	$ 583,243.84	
Miscellaneous	425.74	
Liabilities	13,750.45	
		$ 597,420.03
Available July 1, 1915		$ 4,337.97

Data taken from Report of Finance Committee Board of Supervisors, Dec. 31, 1915.

STATEMENT OF EXPENDITURE OF SCHOOL BOND MONEY 1914-15.

$1,767,280.98 of Bond Money was spent for Buildings, Equipment, Sites; $2,370,300 for redemption and interest on Bonds, from date of last Report, June 30, 1912, to June 30, 1915; making a total of $4,137,780.98.

Redemption and interest, 1912-1913	$ 808,200	
Redemption and interest, 1913-1914	1,123,000	
Redemption and interest, 1914-1915	439,300	
		$2,370,500

Data secured from the Financial Expert of the Board of Supervisors.

TEACHERS EMPLOYED DURING THE YEAR ENDING JUNE 30, 1915.

	Principals or Supervisors of Special Subjects		Teachers	
	Men	Women	Men	Women
(5) High Schools (day)	5	0	53	76
Humboldt Evening High	1	0	26	5
North Beach Evening School	1	0	0	0
(35) Elementary (day) Grammar	7	28	6	590
(49) Elementary (day) Primary	2	47	1	433
Oral for Deaf	0	1	0	1
Special Subjects	1	3	10	16
Elementary Evening School	9	2	3	52
Jean Parker and Irving M. Scott Schools of Home Economics	0	1	0	5
Kindergarten	0	0	0	7
Substitutes	0	0	6	87
Totals	26	82	105	1272

Net number on pay roll for year ending June 30, 1916—

Men	131
Women	1354
Total	1485

Compiled from records of City Board of Examination.

SCHOLASTIC TRAINING AND CERTIFICATION OF TEACHERS.

Number of teachers (including Principals.)

	Men	Women
Who are graduates of University of California	33	100
Who are graduates of Leland Stanford Jr. University	13	8
Who are graduates of other Universities	23	5
Who are graduates of other Colleges	9	18
Who are graduates of S. F. City Normal School or Class	4	373
Who are graduates of Chico State Normal School	2	15
Who are graduates of Los Angeles State Normal School	1	4
Who are graduates of S. F. State Normal School	2	209
Who are graduates of San Jose State Normal School	7	112
Who are graduates of Normal Schools of other States	8	23
Who are graduates of Santa Barbara Home Economics	0	10
Who are graduates of Lux School of Home Economics	0	2

Compiled from reports of Principals.

CERTIFICATES.

	Men	Women
No. holding High School Grade	85	139
No. holding Grammar School Grade	16	1033
No. holding Primary School Grade	0	16
No. holding Special Grade	53	143

Compiled from records of "Board of Examination".

	Resigned	Died	Dropped from Roll	Total	Total No. of Teachers appointed Day and Evening High and Elementary
1911-12	33	9	10	52	116
1912-13	38	9	4	51	86
1913-14	38	14	7	59	83
1914-15	38	4	4	46	107
1915-16 to Mch. 1, 1916	36	10	2	48	103

Serving in Department on March 1, 1916, 100 Emergency Substitutes.

There are on March 1, 1916, 60 regular Vacancies in Day Elementary Schools.

NECROLOGY.

Name	School	Date
Miss M. C. Barry	Lincoln	Sept. 29, 1913
Mary A. Kenny	Visitacion Valley	Sept. 30, 1913
Mrs. Julia J. Sarles	McKinley	Dec., 1913
M. E. Walsh	Longfellow	Feb., 1914
Mrs. K. T. Egan	Edison	April 6, 1914
Miss E. Richardson	Horace Mann	April 17, 1914
Mr. J. A. Dailey	Humboldt Evening	May 3, 1914
Mr. C. J. Couchot	Humboldt Evening	May 7, 1914
Miss Belinda Roper	Franklin	Jan. 4, 1915
Miss A. Lewis	Franklin	Aug. 1, 1914
Miss M. E. Devine	Everett	Jan. 14, 1915
Miss M. Haswell	Haight	April 6, 1915
Mr. Hudson Sheldon	Lowell High	July 20, 1915
Miss E. R. Stevenson	Girls' High	Aug. 8, 1915
Miss Ida R. Strauss	Hamilton	Aug. 19, 1915
Mr. J. A. Longley	Lowell High	Aug. 19, 1915
Mrs. E. M. Doud	John Swett	Aug. 25, 1915
Miss Josephine A. McIntyre	Rochambeau	Sept. 25, 1915
Mr. D. J. Delay	Paul Revere	Nov. 22, 1915
Miss C. S. Sweeney	Haight	Dec. 27, 1915
Mrs. M. Gerhardt	Cookery	Jan. 4, 1915
Mrs. A. E. Tiernan	Rincon	Jan. 16, 1916

ANNUITANTS—DIED 1915.

Miss E. Williamson	Miss M. E. Carson
Miss A. E. Slavan	Miss N. F. Sullivan

SCHOOL STATISTICS FOR YEAR ENDING JUNE 30, 1915.

From the Report of Mr. Job Wood, Jr.

Statistician of the office of the State Superintendent of Public Instruction.

In the Elementary School the average daily attendance for the year was 333,834, which is a gain of 14,605 over last year. Taking into consideration the fact that the year before showed a gain of 91,354, it shows that the taking away of the census report and the substituting of the average daily attendance has caused a marked increase and that school officers and teachers have done all in their power to get and hold all the children in the schools. The ratio of the population to the attendance child is less than in 1910.

In the High Schools the average daily attendance has been raised in every county of the state where there is a high school (Alpine and Mono Counties having no high schools). The gain has been 5,085, which totals a gain of 22,504 for the last five years. If the same ratio of attendance is kept for the next six years as in the last the high schools will double their average attendance, which has been almost done since 1910. All of this leads to the fact that the state has for several years based its apportionment of state aid on the attendance. The last legislature passed a law providing a county tax for high schools at $60 per pupil on the property of the entire county for the maintenance of the high schools. Thus a high school pupil means at least $75 of state and county money per year, and the result will be the holding the pupils to higher standards of work so that the record of dropping pupils will be lowered.

The per cent of attendance in the high schools of the state is 73, which, although it seems low, is due in great part to the fact that the evening high school cut the attendance by having a large number enrolled and a small average daily attendance. The per cent of the elementary school average daily attendance is 81. From this it is seen that any city or county that makes a percentage of attendance of over 80 on the enrollment is up to the average of the state.

The greatest gain in attendance by county is noted in Los Angeles of 1,739, Alameda being second with a gain of 598. For the high schools San Francisco leads with a gain of 1,878, Los Angeles 1,867, and Alameda 1,723. The entire gain being 5,065 in the high schools of the entire state, and 11,771 in the elementary schools.

SOME SCHOOL STATISTICS FROM THE OPENING OF THE FIRST F

Year Ending Oct. 31.	No. of Schools.	Teachers.	Pupils Enrolled.	Average Daily Attendance.	Populat
1850	1	2	150	......	
1851	1	4	325	......	
1852	7	15	700	445	
1853	....	16	2,870	1,182	
1854	....	19	4,199	1,727	
1855	....	29	4,694	1,638	
1856	9	61	3,347	2,516	
Year Ending June 30.					
1857	....	60	2,821	2,155	
1858	....	67	5,273	2,521	
1859	11	75	6,201	2,829	56,
1860	....	68	6,180	2,837	
1861	13	73	6,617	3,377	
1862	17	82	8,204	3,786	
1863	....	94	8,177	4,389	
1864	20	108	7,075	5,470	
1865	....	138	8,000	6,718	
1866	32	206	10,152	8,131	
1867	37	253	13,385	10,177	
1868	39	285	17,426	11,871	
1869	42	326	19,885	13,113	
1870	55	371	22,152	15,394	150,
1871	56	416	26,406	16,978	
1872	56	480	27,664	18,272	
1873	58	506	27,722	18,550	
1874	64	510	29,449	19,434	
1875	64	552	31,128	21,014	
1876	66	574	34,029	22,761	
1877	66	632	37,268	24,899	
1878	65	672	38,672	26,292	
1879	64	696	38,129	27,075	
1880	59	685	38,320	28,150	234,
1881	62	719	40,187	29,092	
1882	65	675	40,752	29,435	
1883	63	687	40,722	30,827	
1884	64	714	41,942	31,578	
1885	65	734	43,265	32,183	
1886	65	773	43,140	32,146	
1887	68	799	43,311	31,316	
1888	68	806	42,330	30,191	
1889	71	838	42,626	31,609	
1890	72	859	42,926	31,352	298,
1891	73	879	43,626	31,809	
1892	75	897	46,172	32,431	
1893	76	929	45,775	32,799	
1894	73	866	44,349	32,939	
1895	75	904	44,822	32,974	
1896	76	927	45,435	33,508	
1897	77	974	46,564	33,531	
1898	92	1,070	50,101	35,116	
1899	90	1,074	48,972	36,830	
1900	86	1,061	48,058	35,004	342,
1901	82	1,017	48,517	34,771	
1902	84	1,052	48,893	35,691	
1903	84	1,086	48,345	37,077	
1904	85	1,121	49,600	37,700	
1905	85	1,181	55,067	40,920	
1906	86	1,115	57,782	41,932	
1907	83	971	45,633	29,929	
1908	89	1,095	48,045	33,931	
1909	92	1,195	48,509	35,541	
1910	95	1,198	50,212	36,774	416,
1911	100	1,227	51,462	37,736	
1912	105	1,308	53,160	40,448	
1913	105	1,423	53,757	42,820	
1914	104	1,478	57,852	44,388	
1915	104	1,485	61,941	46,562	

Compiled from the Report of San Francisco Superintendent of Schools of June

'BLIC SCHOOLS BY J. C. PELTON, DECEMBER, 1849, TO JUNE 30, 1915.

Expenses for All Purposes. (Inc. Bonds)	Cost per Capita on Average Daily Attendance.	School Census Children 4 to 18 Years.	Value of School Property. (Estimated)	Assessment of City and County Property.
....	....	500		....
....	....	1,510	....	....
$23,125	51.96	2,132	....	....
35,040	296.5	2,730	....	....
159,249	125.19	3,268	....	....
136,580	83.38	4,531	....	....
125,064	49.71	4,751	....	....
92,955	43.14	4,755	....	....
104,808	41.57	6,375	....	....
134,731	47.62	7,767	....	....
156,407	55.13	9,025	....	....
158,855	47.04	13,316	....	....
134,576	35.58	13,358	....	....
178,929	47.67	16,501	....	....
228,411	41.76	18,748	....	....
346,862	50.15	21,013	......	....
		5 to 15 Years.		
361,668	44.48	17,369	....	$70,202,000
507,822	49.89	20,253	$1,057,000	74,976,000
416,654	35.09	23,306	1,368,000	84,689,000
397,842	30.34	24,817	1,531,000	95,700,000
526,625	33.56	27,055	1,729,800	114,759,500
705,116	41.53	28,971	1,786,400	....
668,262	36.02	31,936	1,810,000	(?)97,000,000
611,818	35.45	34,676	....	....
		5 to 17 Years.		
689,022	35.40	38,084	2,227,620	212,407,505
707,445	33.71	41,029	2,367,000	264,000,000
867,755	38.12	46,238	2,505,500	269,105,141
732,324	29.41	53,210	2,585,000	260,576,978
989,259	37.62	55,899	2,711,000	254,702,960
876,489	32.37	62,105	3,047,303	244,477,360
809,133	28.74	58,492	3,073,000	217,487,074
827,324	28.44	55,115	3,137,000	253,545,476
735,435	24.98	55,880	3,137,000	222,336,400
791,175	25.66.	58,061	3,137,000	201,992,152
797,452	25.25	63,029	3,137,000	201,763,762
840,367	25.80	69,000	3,137,000	223,509,560
815,778	25.37	74,079	3,189,000	230,386,325
843,297	26.93	78,246	3,184,575	230,151,009
926,662	30.69	59,517	3,230,598	251,746,111
916,644	28.99	60,642	4,772,180	273,389,616
983,014	31.35	61,144	4,757,724	306,041,440
1,053,610	33.12	62,456	4,798,427	301,444,140
1,098,839	33.88	63,933	4,932,754	311,566,079
1,134,757	34.59	65,317	5,019,317	346,224,706
989,009	30.05	68,390	5,063,364	342,644,179
1,043,067	26.09	70,006	5,140,258	325,108,898
1,086,571	32.42	71,822	5,284,000	327,805,147
1,222,941	36.52	74,840	5,354,859	330,401,154
1,319,829	37.58	76,336	5,474,739	351,784,094
1,507,163	40.92	75,292	5,514,200	405,111,615
1,274,696	36.41	78,554	5,514,200	410,155,304
1,152,631	30.27	82,173	5,207,600	413,417,241
1,316,170	36.88	82,391	5,334,000	413,099,993
1,322,585	35.67	91,386	5,649,651	419,968,644
1,398,296	37.09	97,353	5,702,001	545,866,446
1,403,349	34.29	98,127	5,800,000	502,892,359
1,498,275	35.73	101,836	6,984,000	524,230,946
1,325,433	44.28	77,367	6,207,010	375,932,447
1,934,355	57.01	87,696	6,379,000	429,632,592
1,701,236	47.86	88,058	7,206,573	454,334,160
3,307,948	89.98	74,729	8,733,285	492,867,037
3,137,825	83.18	abolished	10,161,492	515,028,064
3,744,073	92.54		11,536,929	461,855,781
3,329,054.50	77.70		11,983,657	510,432,101
3,504,838.65	78.95		12,600,202	526,247,536
3,224,429.19	69.25		16,929,218	541,894,443

1912, and data from Auditor's Office, Assessor's Office, etc.

SCHOOLS.

Number of High Schools, including Humboldt and North Beach Evening High Schools	7
Number of Grammar	35
Number of Primary Schools	49
Number of Special Schools	2
Number of Evening Schools	11
Total Number of Schools	104

Number of concrete school buildings owned by the department, "Class A"	1
Number of brick and steel school buildings owned by the department, "Special Construction"	19
Number of concrete and wooden school buildings owned by the department, "Class C"	68
Number of rooms rented by the department	9

Data secured from Board of Public Works.

"STATE ENROLLMENT" BY GRADES AND SEX.

(State Enrollment ADMITS NO DUPLICATION. PUPILS PROMOTED DURING THE YEAR ARE ENUMERATED ONLY in the grades from which they were promoted.)

ELEMENTARY AND KINDERGARTEN DAY SCHOOLS.

	Boys	Girls	Totals
Kindergarten	271	304	575
First Grade	6,071	5,355	11,426
Second Grade	3,725	3,254	6,979
Third Grade	3,406	3,171	6,577
Fourth Grade	3,149	3,834	6,983
Fifth Grade	2,889	2,747	5,636
Sixth Grade	2,381	2,349	4,730
Seventh Grade	1,971	2,124	4,095
Eighth Grade	1,506	1,612	3,118
Total Elementary and Kindergarten	25,369	24,750	50,119

Data from Reports of Principals.

SECONDARY DAY SCHOOLS.

	Boys	Girls	Total
First Year	777	1,003	*1,780
Second Year	494	638	1,132
Third Year	203	320	523
Fourth Year	178	282	460
Total	1,652	2,243	3,895
Total Secondary and Elementary Day Schools	27,021	26,993	54,014

* These figures EXCLUDE those enrolling in January and who during the year were enrolled in the Grammar (8th) grade.

SECONDARY EVENING SCHOOLS.

Humboldt and North Beach Evening High Schools—

	Boys	Girls	Total
First Year	1,249	403	1,652
Second Year	291	158	449
Third Year	113	13	126
Fourth Year	3	1	4
Totals	1,656	575	2,231

ELEMENTARY EVENING SCHOOLS.

	Boys	Girls	Total
First Grade	424	107	531
Second Grade	305	72	377
Third Grade	307	65	372
Fourth Grade	224	51	275
Fifth Grade	303	48	351
Sixth Grade	380	79	459
Seventh Grade	1,061	442	1,503
Eighth Grade	1,037	791	1,828
Totals	4,041	1,655	5,696
Grand Totals	32,718	29,223	61,941

(Secondary and Elementary Day and Evening Schools)

Data from Reports of Principals.

STATE SCHOOL ENROLLMENT AND ATTENDANCE STATISTICS FOR THE YEAR ENDING JUNE 30, 1915.

STATE ENROLLMENT.

High Schools	3,895
Elementary Schools	49,544
Kindergarten	575
Humboldt and North Beach Evening High Schools	2,231
Other Evening Schools	5,696
Total	61,941

AVERAGE DAILY ATTENDANCE.

High Schools	3,392
Elementary Schools	40,256
Kindergarten	270
Humboldt and North Beach Evening High Schools	922
Other Evening Schools	1,722
Total	46,562

GRADUATES.

Number of graduates from the grammar school for the year—

Boys	Day, 1,204	Evening, 322	1,526
Girls	Day, 1,373	Evening, 375	1,748
Total			3,274

Number of graduates from the high schools for the year—

Boys	Day, 149	Evening, 144	293
Girls	Day, 337	Evening, 79	416
Total			709

Data compiled from Principals' reports.

REPORT OF THE BOARD OF EXAMINATION.

The Board of Examination is composed of: Superintendent Alfred Roncovieri, Chairman; Deputy Superintendent W. B. Howard, Secretary; Deputy Superintendent T. L. Heaton, Deputy Superintendent A. J. Cloud, Deputy Superintendent W. H. DeBell, Deputy Superintendent Miss M. Magner.

The Board of Examination has conducted two examinations (October, 1914, and May, 1915) according to law, of persons desirous of securing certificates. It has met monthly and forwarded its recommendations to the Board of Education.

Herewith is a resumè of its work:

CERTIFICATES GRANTED ON CREDENTIALS.

HIGH SCHOOL.

Men	15
Women	11
	26

GRAMMAR.

Men	4
Women	113
	117

SPECIALS.

Men	13
Women	24
	37

RENEWALS.

Men	6
Women	24
	30

ON EXAMINATION.

GRAMMAR.

Men	0
Women	2
	2

REJECTED.

Men	5
Women	29
	34

SPECIALS.

Men	5
Women	25
	30

Number of Certificates issued	212
Number of Certificates renewed	30
Number of Applicants rejected	34
Amount fees collected of applicants, including renewals	522

COST PER PUPIL 1914-1915.

	Per Pupil Enrolled	Per Pupil Average Daily Attendance
(a) For instruction only—		
Secondary Schools	$55.79	$64.07
Elementary Schools	25.91	31.88
Evening Schools, including Humboldt and North Beach	16.94	50.81
(b) For all Expenditures (not including buildings and sites)—		
Secondary Schools	74.55	85.61
Elementary Schools	33.64	41.40
Evening Schools, including North Beach and Humboldt	20.25	60.74

MEDAL FUNDS.

Name of Fund	Deposited in	In Fund June 30, 1915
Bridge Silver Medal	Hibernia Savings & Loan Society	$2158.75
Denman Grammar School	" " " "	839.20
Denman Silver Medal	German " " "	1747.64
Hancock Grammar School	" " " "	367.86
Jean Parker Grammar School	" " " "	350.29
John Swett Grammar School	Hibernia " " "	179.78
Lincoln Grammar School	" " " "	3935.18

STATEMENT SETTING FORTH THE EXPENDITURE OF MONEY DERIVED FROM SALE OF BONDS (ISSUE OF 1904, 1908 AND 1910), TO JUNE 30, 1915.

Schools	Buildings	Equipment	Sites
Girls High	$ 408,405.79	$ 21,128.95	
High School Commerce	261,635.28	15,792.83	$ 36,800.00
Lowell High	346,703.59	25,000.00	138,500.00
Mission High			103,910.00
Polytechnic High	581,797.93	26,135.67	65,000.00
Adams Cosmopolitan	94,739.36	4,592.72	
Agassiz			16,500.00
Andrew Jackson			37,600.00
Bay View	124,605.02	5,296.00	10,250.00
Bernal			11,800.00
Bryant Cosmopolitan	106,306.15	5,888.75	
Burnett	54,372.92	673.84	10,000.00
Cleveland	64,782.24	3,566.44	13,250.00
Columbus	74,442.75	1,949.51	
Crocker Intermediate	19,856.39		22,750.00
Denman	181,009.84	4,274.17	88,843.00
Douglass			10,750.00
Dudley Stone			12,000.00
Edison	56,624.33	1,933.75	17,400.00
Everett	7,942.26		20,400.00
Farragut	103,276.16	2,533.00	12,537.50
Francis Scott Key	56,115.04	2,869.40	
Frank McCoppin	106,294.69	5,739.20	9,500.00
Franklin	76,214.83	4,799.98	
Fremont			6,750.00
Garfield	111,034.03	4,884.99	10,150.00
George Peabody	80,693.02	2,951.80	
Glen Park	136,259.60	2,909.56	5,600.00
Golden Gate	72,243.94	4,200.00	25,692.25
Grant			44,500.00
Grattan	69,786.17	4,229.13	28,500.00
Hancock	166,321.20	6,492.86	10,800.00
Harrison	22,435.41	441.39	10,000.00
Hawthorne			2,750.00
Horace Mann Intermediate			15,000.00
James Lick			5,600.00
Jean Parker	174,491.51	5,968.19	20,675.00
John Swett	105,354.22	6,271.32	56,750.00

Schools	Buildings	Equipment	Sites
Junipero Serra	92,922.59	4,545.89	21,815.00
Kate Kennedy	127,978.52	3,697.44	27,000.00
Lafayette	9,692.00		8,000.00
Laguna Honda	95,133.04	4,283.28	
Le Conte			18,393.00
Lincoln	75,537.96	3,205.52	7,050.00
Longfellow	78,675.38	2,645.83	9,250.00
Madison	87,945.72	3,500.00	
Marshall	83,837.14	5,476.15	33,625.00
McKinley	111,388.18	3,523.33	35,000.00
Mission Grammar	173,503.16	4,053.10	
Monroe	86,063.98	3,600.00	9,110.00
Noe Valley			13,250.00
Oriental	101,172.34	11,528.83	
Pacific Heights			23,500.00
Patrick Henry	61,380.49	2,987.24	
Portola	97,042.23	3,700.00	5,000.00
Redding			22,000.00
Rochambeau	48,525.62	3,891.00	39,489.00
Roosevelt	11,601.56		
Sarah B. Cooper	91,301.52	10,452.20	
Sheridan	107,699.60	4,991.58	9,750.00
Sherman			1,500.00
Spring Valley	119,722.67	5,362.43	31,325.00
Starr King	65,811.76	3,124.38	14,575.00
Sunnyside	39,056.25		400.00
Sutro	108,346.49	4,448.78	7,100.00
Visitacion Valley	52,509.73	2,918.53	
Washington Grammar	104,887.27	4,988.00	17,000.00
Washington Irving	77,975.86	5,024.75	17,000.00
Winfield Scott	42,206.43	3,590.58	
Yerba Buena			17,000.00
Lot on Geary St.			27,000.00
Miscellaneous, Plans, Specifications, and Titles	121,658.58		
Totals	$5,936,959.74	$276,062.29	$1,278,989.75

Grand Total $7,492,011.78

Data secured from records of Board of Supervisors.

VISITS TO THE PANAMA-PACIFIC INTERNATIONAL EXPOSITION AND THE COURSE OF STUDY.

The wonderful educational possibilities of the great Exposition were recognized, as a matter of course, from the very inception of the enterprise by those interested in the welfare of the School department and school children of San Francisco. The exhibits were no sooner in place in the Wonder Palaces of the Great Show than the Superintendent of Schools, with the hearty support of his deputies, the members of the Board of Education and the teachers of the Department, put on foot the plans designed to insure the best possible use being made, on behalf of the many thousands of pupils under their joint charge, of the splendid opportunities at hand. At the request of the Superintendent, hundreds of teachers, in their own time and at their own expense, paid visit after visit to the Exposition for the purpose of searching out and classifying such exhibits as, in their judgment, would prove most valuable as aids to the mental development of their youthful charges. As the result of days and weeks of painstaking investigation hundreds of lists were turned over to the Superintendent. With the efficient aid of a special committee of 50 teachers appointed for the purpose this mass of valuable material was carefully gone over, all eliminations necessary because of duplications or for other reasons were made, a world of segregation and classification work was done, and the final result was an "Exposition Course of Study" both compact and comprehensive. It was in accordance with this that 30,000 pupils, members of grades from the third to the eighth inclusive, were conducted through the Exposition in "groups"—"armies" rather— of 6,000 each on the five school days of each week, and under conditions and arrangements which insured a most admirable combination of pleasure and profit to the youthful visitors.

The preparing of the "Exposition Course of Study", important and arduous as was this branch of the work, was only a part of that which had to be done. There remained the arrangement of the 30,000 pupils into groups and sections such as could be successfully and safely handled on the way to and from the Exposition and within the grounds and buildings; the "routing" of the visiting parties through the maze of exhibits in such a manner as not to cause congestion and to allow the best opportunity for the lessons to be learned therefrom to be impressed upon the pupils: the negotiations with the Exposition management as the result of which the charge for admission was reduced to five cents for each pupil and attendant teacher; also others with the Municipal Railway and United Railroads officials to insure half-rate carfare charges to and from the Fair grounds; the securing of the formal consent of the parents or guardians of all pupils for their attendance at the Exposition under these special circumstances.

All these and a host of other details, some of minor character and some nearly if not quite as important as those which have been mentioned, were taken in hand and successfully arranged by the Superintendent and his deputies, Miss Magner, Mr. De Bell, Mr. Heaton, Mr. Cloud and Dr. Howard. Under the arrangements made the pupils assembled at specified hours, in the majority of cases about a quarter to nine o'clock, at their respective schools, where, each class under charge of its special teacher and an assistant, took the cars to the Exposition grounds. At the gates they were joined by Exposition Guards, one for each class, who assisted the teachers in charge in guiding the youthful visitors through the grounds and the various Industrial Palaces, in keeping them together and in preventing accident of any kind. There was no scattering necessary even at noontime, since all pupils brought their lunches, and were therefore enabled to remain together from the time they assembled in the morning until, still under care of their teachers, they left the grounds between 2:30 and 3:30

in the afternoon, to return to their school houses, where they were dismissed as usual. It should not be lost sight of that the days spent at the Exposition by the classes were not devoted to sight-seeing pleasure excursions merely, but were school days dedicated to the very highest class of practical instruction, though the greater the amount of enjoyment combined therewith for the pupils the better those in charge were pleased.

The plan consisted of not merely one or two visits by the various classes to the Jewel City and its wonders—quite the contrary. A glance through the "Exposition Course of Study" makes evident that no single visit or short series of such would have been sufficient for all its educational possibilities to be availed of. Therefore the plan provided for one visit for each of the five school groups during each week of the continuance of the Exposition except those of the vacation period. The 26 schools composing Group One sent their 6th, 7th and 8th grade pupils, 6,000 in number, on Friday, May 14th; the pupils of the corresponding grades of the 25 schools in Group Two came next on Monday, the 17th; Tuesday, the 18th, was the day set apart for the 3d, 4th and 5th grade pupils of the 30 schools in Group Three, while the corresponding grades of the 25 schools in Group Four followed on Wednesday the 19th, and the same grades in the 24 schools of Group Five on Thursday, May 20th. The next school day was that for the second visit of Group One, after which the succeeding groups renewed their excursions in the regular order, the same system being followed on succeeding weeks until the final completion of the elaborate and effective plan. That it was carried out, first and last, virtually without a hitch, though at the cost of much tiring labor on the part of the teachers of the Department, affords strong testimony to the care with which it was arranged and the unselfish zeal of those earnest workers who had charge of the almost innumerable details. As to the practical results, it is, of course, impossible to set forth in words and figures the unquestionably great educational value that has accrued to our children, and through them to our community, because of the successful carrying out of the plans under which the great Exposition, with its myriad wonders, was made a part of the course of instruction of the schools of San Francisco. But, like all properly directed study, whether of childhood or maturity, it will serve its splendid purpose in building up for the future of our city, state and country that broader, greater, nobler citizenship to which all true education tends.

To bring the schools back to the regularly prescribed grade work the following circular was issued January 5, 1916:

To Principals and Teachers,

Ladies and Gentlemen:

I.

In order to get the greatest educational value from the Exposition it has been necessary to handle in a less thorough manner than hitherto some portions of our Course of Study. We wish now to resume thorough, earnest work on every phase of the regular work. We look to Principals to bring their schools to the highest degree of efficiency. We regret that it has been impossible to put into your hands a Course of Study all within one cover. We are obliged to refer you to the course of 1911 and the outline of January, 1915. We cannot supply each teacher with the course of 1911, but there are enough in each school so that copies may be passed around. We expect at the opening of the fall term to have the course prepared and based on the new State texts.

We wish to call attention to some features which need special emphasis:

1. Out-of-door geography including simpler forms of division of labor.

2. Relief maps on sand table in the lower grades and product maps from the Fourth Grade up.

3. Cumulative reviews. A cumulative review of the preceding term's work should be fresh in hand at the end of the sixth week. We will not go back of one term's work at present.

4. Minimum Course of Study, supplementary work, and honorary promotion as indicated in the Course of 1911.

5. Use of Number Cards for combinations in primary grades. Use of units, bundles of ten, bundles of 100, to aid in comprehending reading and writing numbers in first, second and third grades.

6. Enunciation, syllabification in spelling.

7. Teaching the use of dictionary in proper grade. Every child required to use dictionary must be provided with one. In case child is unable to purchase one, application must be made to the Board of Education.

8. Compositions corrected and put in composition book as directed in Course of Study.

9. Sentences for grammar and language must be made to mean something as a fact in history, or geography, or current events, or a statement about the Exposition.

10. Not too much writing in the lower grades; but all writing carefully supervised with reference to position and movement.

11. Nature Study and Elementary Science lessons.

12. Inform your local dealer in time, so that the work you wish the children to buy for literature may be on hand.

13. In the primary grades be thorough in the Number Work but do not give difficulties beyond those laid down in the Course of Study and Outline. Emphasize concrete work.

14. Give to each special subject only the amount of time indicated by the Course of Study.

II.

There will be a meeting of Principals at the High School of Commerce on Thursday, January 13th, at 2:30 P. M.

Respectfully yours,

ALFRED RONCOVIERI,

Superintendent of Schools.

PRINCIPALS' AND TEACHERS' MEETINGS.

Principals' and teachers' meetings have been held less frequently the past year on account of the time devoted to the Exposition.

Teachers' meetings are held grade by grade at frequent intervals during the term, the work discussed and instructions given concerning the teaching. Principals' meetings have been held monthly for the discussion of all matters pertaining to the welware of the schools. Subjects for discussion have been assigned to principals to discuss or referred to committees for investigation and report. The results of such discussion have been reported to the Board of Education for their consideration. Sometimes the program of the meeting has been "The Good of the Department". Any principal could have five minutes for discussion on a subject of his own choosing. If the topic seemed of sufficient importance, it was referred to a committee to report at a future meeting. Sometimes the program of the meeting was a book or chapters from a book. Sometimes it was a change in the Course of Study. Each principal holds a meeting of his teachers monthly and any results of the principals' meeting are then communicated to the teachers at large.

SCHOOL MUSEUM.

The suggestion was made at one of our Principals' meetings that an effort be made to secure as much material as possible from the Exposition to form the nucleus of a School Museum. A committee was at once named to confer with the Board and the work was organized. The various sub-committees of this body worked strenuously throughout the Exposition.

"The San Francisco 1915 Schools Committee is composed of a representative of each school and department of the San Francisco Public School System and has been organized to take advantage, in a systematic way, of the many educational opportunities offered by the great Exposition now being held in our city and to endeavor to secure for the school children of San Francisco all possible benefits.

One important activity of this Committee will be to secure material for a Public School Museum.

St. Louis has a notable example of such an institution, the nucleus of which was obtained through the generosity and by the active co-operation of the exhibitors at the great exposition held in that city.

This Committee believes that the exhibitors at the Panama-Pacific International Exposition will deal no less generously and cordially with the children of San Francisco.

At the close of the Exposition period, exhibitors will have on hand exhibit material of great educational value, which can be devoted to no higher purpose than to the education of the children of this great and growing city by the Golden Gate, and, furthermore, its installation in a School Museum will but perpetuate the original purpose for which it has been brought to San Francisco.

An Educational or School Museum consists of collections of material properly arranged, and sent from school to school as required, to supplement in a concrete manner other forms and methods of instruction. It comprises pictures, books, pamphlets, maps, charts, reliefs, slides and films; specimens of rocks, ores and minerals; examples of animal and vegetable life and products; models of tools, machinery and buildings; exhibits of raw and manufactured products and their processes of manufacture—any material illustrative of the geography, history, government, arts and industries, products and resources, manners and customs of the peoples and countries of the earth.

Such is the kind of material desired and it is the hope of this Committee that every exhibitor at the Panama-Pacific International Exposition will give this subject due consideration and co-operation to the extent that his exhibit may be well represented among the Museum collections and thus become a permanent part of the educational plant of this city.

Mr. F. K. Barthel was Chairman of the Committee.

The material has been taken to the old Lowell High School building. We hope in the next budget to secure the money to have this material put in shape for transportation from school to school for study purposes. We shall have excellent co-operation from the California Academy of Sciences and the Park Museum. The Museum thus started from the Exposition should grow rapidly and thus make a large part of our teaching very concrete.

We have had fine co-operation from the Museum at the Affiliated Colleges. Courses of lectures have been given there each term for children of the 6th, 7th and 8th grade. The children have been taken by their teachers to these lectures which are adapted to the Course of Study and abundantly illustrated with pictures and specimens from the Museum.

MINIMUM COURSE.

To provide for differing abilities of pupils a minimum and maximum course of study have been prepared. The minimum is within the grasp of from 90 to 95% of pupils. This is required of all. For those of larger capacity a supplementary amount of work is outlined, and for encouragement to do such work an honorary promotion certificate is provided. The additional work may be recited before the entire class by those who are doing the extra work. This gives good practice in oral English for the abler pupil, and those of less ability may learn much by listening to the recitation. If a teacher has two or more grades there will not be time to go over the supplemental work in class, but the teacher may assign it and may test it in every class examination. She has only to add to the minimum test three or four questions taken from the supplemental work upon which the pupils have made their own preparation. In the hands of a skillful teacher this gives each pupil as much work as he can accomplish, and an incentive for doing it. The 5 or 10% of pupils for whom the minimum is too difficult should find their place in classes for the mentally defective or special ungraded rooms for backward pupils. The carrying out of the above plan requires that the schools should be well equipped with supplementary books.

ARITHMETIC.

No formal number work is given during the first year but much attention is given to developing the number sense. We aim to complete the fundamental operations in the first four years, common fractions in the fifth year and begin decimals in the sixth. We believe accuracy and rapidity should be the special drill of the primary grades. When the tools are thus sharpened, we are able to apply them to the solution of problems in the grammar grades. Our self-testing cards for the number combinations make a game of the fundamental operations and enable pupil and teacher to drill on the weak points and not distribute attention over the entire series. It gives an opportunity for pupils to drill each other and for children who are backward to receive additional and proper help at home. This system has been in operation for over a year and its results are very satisfactory.

In problem work emphasis is put on selecting practical problems. Much drill is given in the correct reading of problems. An example well read is half solved.

READING.

Reading is taught in connection with every text. In Literature we believe the use of the voice helps the child not only to express but to get the thought. As in music the finest interpretation of a master can be secured only through the instrument or the voice, so in literature the finer shades of meaning must be tried out by the living voice. The audible voice cultivated in the young becomes the silent reading voice of the high school and college student. We therefore read literature.

We apply the principle of reading to arithmetic, geography, science, physiology. The child who cannot with the open page before him express the thought with his voice cannot silently study and master the lesson. Wherever necessary, therefore, we give reading lessons from all text-books. Less attention is given to this as children master the art of reading, but the time does not come in the grammar school when oral reading can be dispensed with. We believe in silent supervised study periods when the child is left to test his strength on the printed page.

Pupils of the grammar grades are trained in the constant use of the dictionary, not forgetting that frequently the best dictionary is a close study of the context. When the dictionary has been used, its meanings must be applied to the context. Word formation is of great value both in the spelling of words and in the enrichments of their meaning.

GEOGRAPHY.

According to our Course of Study physical, industrial and commercial geography form three strands of this great subject extending through all grades.

The work begins with out-of-door geography observing land forms in the vicinity of the school. Stream erosion furnishes interesting nature study lessons and shows the great power of running water within the compass of a small stream. Magnify this small stream in the imagination and we have a great river system. From the out-of-door study children may comprehend relief maps. Observation of common industries illustrates the division of labor. Trace foods on the dinner table back to the place of their production. We find soil and climate adapted to particular products. This gives us division of labor and production of articles on a large scale according to the soil and climate of the particular region. This leads to exchange of goods and transportation. Picture this in color on a product map. This principle of the division of labor is applied to the parts of a county, to portions of the State, to sections of the country, or is made applicable to the countries and continents of the globe. The physical geography is applied in similar manner to an understanding of soil, climate and products of every geographical division. Thus we do not complete descriptive geography before taking up physical, nor do we make commercial geography a separate study for the high school. All the elements are bound tightly together and strengthen each other.

NATURE STUDY AND ELEMENTARY SCIENCE.

Two years ago Nature Study and Elementary Science were introduced into all grades. The work was based on Merchè's Science Readers. The grammar schools were supplied with a limited amount of apparatus for the purpose. The work was received with much enthusiasm by the children, and has been productive of good results in cultivating their powers of observation and making them familiar with common objects and phenomena. The purpose is not to give systematic science, but to familiarize the child with the object and forces which surround his daily life. We call it the science of common things. This awakens the interest and lays the foundation for more systematic science in the high school, or for continued observation and reading on the part of those who do not go to high school. During the past year the time given to Elementary Science has been greatly reduced owing to the large opportunities for observation afforded by the Exposition. We wish now to take up the subject with renewed vigor and give the schools a thorough equipment as soon as school funds will permit.

GARDENING.

Lacking the money we have been unable to establish many regular school gardens. The children, however, have been encouraged in home gardening and the work has been carried on in many schools with much success. We have many vacant school lots and believe that these should be turned into gardens because of the healthful exercise, the knowledge of nature, and the useful information which school gardening affords. The school garden should be the demonstration which will lead to home gardening and establish the garden as part of the home for the boy and girl grown to manhood and womanhood. The garden is a pleasure, a profit, a recreation and a preventive of bad associations and habits.

SPELLING.

We teach spelling by a combination of the oral and written method. On the assignment of a lesson children are drilled on clear distinct pronunciation and syllabification. We lay stress upon division into syllables, because proper division of the word at the end of a line is an essential part of the spelling. The pronunciation of a word often depends upon correct grouping of the letters in syllables. Giving to each vowel and consonant its proper sound is essential to good pronunciation and a great aid to correct spelling. Most words in our language are spelled as pronounced, if pronounced properly. In assigning a spelling lesson children are taught to observe the words which spell themselves when properly pronounced, to observe the parts of unphonetic words requiring special study. They thus focus their attention on the parts requiring drill.

The use of the dictionary is begun in the Fourth Grade. Children are trained to its use through their desk copies and the constant reference to the dictionary is emphasized throughout the grades. Children are urged to write no word whose spelling is in doubt. In the lower grades words used in composition are written upon the board, or the child may raise his hand and ask for the spelling. In the higher grades the child may use his dictionary at all times except in a spelling test. We teach by column spelling and by using words in sentences. In the upper grades we give much attention to word formation. We train children to study the meaning of words by aid of the context as well as from the dictionary.

HISTORY AND CIVICS.

Under the Course of Study, while pupils in the earlier grades read largely from historical material and are thus put in touch with the lives of great men and women and imbibe the atmosphere of historical happenings, yet the careful study of historical narrative, in its manifold relations, is not undertaken until the Sixth Grade. Virtually the same statement holds for the study of Civics.

The B-Fifth and A-Sixth Grade course in History is intended to give the background or European beginnings, of American history. The text used is Wallach's 'Historical and Biographical Narratives''. This text furnishes a skeleton outline on which teacher and child build by readings and oral and written discussions and papers from varied sources. The installation of this particular line of work five years ago had almost immediate fruitage in producing a renewed interest in historical study. It has had a splendid result in giving life to this branch of instruction.

The remainder of the work in History is devoted to U. S. History, to the end of the A-Eighth Grade, from the State text, with special emphasis upon California History toward the close of the course. It is thought that this work is now well graded. Supplementary books are used wherever possible.

The study of Civics, as a definite classroom subject (as distinguished from its consideration as a part of the History course), is confined to the B-Eighth Grade, at which time it displaces U. S. History in time allotment. The text used is Dunn's ''The Community and the Citizen'' (State text). This subject is made very concrete, with constant reference to activities of citizens in Local, State and National affairs.

The study of Current Events, from the lower grades to the highest, furnishes much material for use in the history classes. Much progress has been made in recent years in the handling of this material. It is especially valuable for Oral Expression.

LITERATURE.

As distinguished from Reading in the technical sense, the course in Literature commences in the A-Sixth Grade.

The Course of Study in this subject, as revised in the outline of January, 1915, provides six literary selections for each grade, of which one is marked ''required'' and is to be studied carefully; while, from the remainder, two or three are to be chosen for more rapid reading. The ''required'' selection is not to be studied in the classroom for a period of time exceeding one-half of the term. The end and aim of the course is to limit close analytical study, and to encourage extensive reading for enjoyment, as well as for understanding. English Literature is to be treated from the viewpoint of the study of an art, and not from that of the study of a science.

In our belief considerable progress has been made in the last year by teachers in presenting Literature to their pupils in such a way as to arouse artistic appreciation in them. In many schools lists of library books have been drawn up by principals and teachers, with great care and skill, and much has been accomplished in inducing pupils to secure such books and read them. Frequent reports on such readings have become a regular part of the literature course in many classes.

Oral Expression, as a phase of English, has been given very much more attention in the past several years in our schools than at any former time. Boys and girls are encouraged to "think on their feet", and frequently gain remarkable ability in that regard.

PENMANSHIP.

Written work in the lower grades is confined very largely to the blackboard. The first work at the seats is done with the pencil using light lines for the purpose of getting good movement. We have greatly cut down the amount of required written work so that the largest amount of supervision can be given to all exercises involving writing. It is not desired that the lower grades show pretty writing but rather that they should acquire correct posture and mastery of the muscular movement. In many schools we are getting good results in penmanship.

The best results in the department, however, cannot be secured until we have a supervisor and two assistants to supervise the work and drill teachers who have not themselves been trained in correct movement.

Excellent results are obtained in penmanship in the Hancock School where the subject is in charge of a trained teacher who devoted about four and a half hours a week to giving lessons in the different classes. Through her inspiration, and the earnest co-operation of the principal and the other class teachers, penmanship throughout the school has reached rank I in efficiency, according to a test made by the Committee on "Economy of Time in Education", National Council of Education.

OVERCROWDED CONDITIONS.

The rapid growth of our city in some sections has caused much overcrowding in many of the schools, necessitating a number of very large classes. In some schools this condition has been relieved by the formation of half-day classes. In some cases substitute teachers are assigned to assist teachers having very large classes. Wherever circumstances have permitted, portable schoolrooms have been built on or adjacent to the school premises to relieve the overcrowding.

During the past term 23 new classes were established and so far this term 30 more have been formed. As soon as suitable arrangements can be made, additional classes should be established to relieve the most urgent needs. At present in the elementary schools out of a total of 1081 classes, there are 714 with an enrollment of 40 or over; of these 166 have an enrollment of 50 or over.

INDIVIDUAL INSTRUCTION.

The best education results from a combination of class teaching with individual instruction. Coaching or individual teaching used as the only method lacks the enthusiasm of numbers and the social contact. It is the experience of most successful teachers and institutions that it is as difficult to kindle enthusiasm in the solitary pupil as to make a camp-fire with a single stick of wood. Even if individual coaching were a success, it would be extremely expensive. No teacher could so instruct from 35 to 40 children. Individual teaching, however, should be combined with class-teaching. The day should be divided into half-hour periods, recitation and silent supervised study periods succeeding each other. Thirty minutes is long enough for recitation in the elementary schools. During this period instruction is given to the class as a whole; during the study period which follows the teacher gives individual help to pupils who have not found the class instruction adequate. Pupils come quietly to the desk, sit by the teacher and receive the necessary aid; or the teacher passes around the room giving a word here and pointing out a better method there. During this study period the room should be quiet and the pupils be encouraged in close concentration.

HOW THE PUPIL'S INDIVIDUALITY MAY BE PRESERVED IN REGULAR CLASS TEACHING.

Individual instruction was the method of the schools up to the 19th century. The number of pupils per teacher was generally small, and each received attention individually and in order. The number of pupils one teacher could instruct was very limited. As time went on and schools increased, the number of teachers required was proportionately heavy, and from the standpoint of economy in expense, rather than increase in school efficiency, the plan of grouping the pupils and instructing all of a group simultaneously was introduced. The plan seemed so attractive and the educational results so satisfactory, that there seemed to be no limit but that of space to the number of pupils a teacher could properly instruct. The results, however, proved the fallacy of such an assumption, and an effort was made to modify the size of the classes. But the group system, which was introduced for purely economic reasons, proved so popular, not only in the way of meeting the purpose for which it was introduced but also for many virtues inherent in itself, that the "class" system came to dominate formal education. And now in our city school systems it is possible to give a single grade to a teacher, and such a grade becomes the present day unit in school administration, without due attention to variation in individual capacities. In consequence of this fact, the class method is receiving much severe criticism.

The schools are characterized as "machines", aiming their teaching at an "ideal or a "myth", and causing over-strain to some while not sufficiently taxing the capacities of others, and by overlooking individual needs, produce the condition characterized as the "lock-step"; and in all of these ways through disheartening the pupils cause great numbers to withdraw from the schools.

This seems a strong bill of indictment against the "class system" of instruction, despite the fact of its recognized virtues of economy, effectiveness in social discipline, and the generally recognized advantages gained through emulation, competition, and the conditions most favorable to mental growth.

Each system has its virtues; and if the end of the school is "to fit the child for life in civilized society", that purpose cannot be met through treating the individual, as such, nor through causing him to lose his identity in the "class" or "group", but through such a compromise or modification of the present system as will preserve its virtues and eliminate its vices. To meet this condition the following is submitted:

Every class of forty-five pupils consists usually of three distinct groups, however carefully the grading may have been done—a small group at the top, of pupils of greater capacity than the rest; a small group at the bottom, of less capacity than the rest; and a third group comprising approximately two-thirds of the class, who, while varying in some respects, are, upon the whole, able to show a uniform result in their class work, although it may have been reached through somewhat different means. This two-thirds, or middle section, is the steady strength of the room, able to appreciate the instruction of the teacher as presented to the class, and to show the proper reaction therefrom. This section receives inspiration from the leading group, and in its turn may encourage, but not dazzle, the group of which they are the leaders. Evidently the interests of the first group, as well as that of the third group, will not be fully met through the regular class-teaching.

The mere giving of information to a pupil does not necessarily educate him. There is something for him to do. He must reflect. He must study. He must bring his attention to his work in a way that will cause him to appropriate, digest what he has received, correlate, and so develop his mental processes. For this important work he needs a daily program making provision for such opportunity.

The teacher's program should consist of alternate study and recitation periods.

During the recitation period, she addresses herself to the entire class.

During the "study period", the teacher, having given specific directions in her assignment of the lesson, is free to devote her time to the assistance of the third division. She will not have them come to her desk for assistance. She will pass around amongst them. She will observe their methods of work. She will, by a few questions, find their troubles and judiciously give suggestions, always endeavoring to encourage them to put forth the desired effort. In all of this, she should be so quiet as to reach only the individual pupil addressed. Thus she will encourage the pupil to be free in exposing his weaknesses—a pre-requisite to her successful assistance.

But most slow or backward pupils are proficient in certain subjects—need special help in others. The teacher may sometimes, by grouping three to five such pupils, say to them: "During the study period for Geography to-morrow, I would like to give you some special assistance in your arithmetic. Could you not prepare your Geography at home this evening, so you will not fail on that if I occupy your study period?" The answer invariably is—"We will do so." In these ways the teacher of a single grade has great opportunity to reach the slow or weak pupil—in fact, any pupil needing her assistance.

But this is not the only means of meeting this important condition. An ungraded teacher is needed in every primary and grammar school.

But the brightest section of the class is deserving of the most serious attention. One of the most active advocates of individual instruction was P. W. Search, who not only sought to introduce this method in the schools under his supervision, but in 1901 wrote a book on the subject—"An Ideal School"—setting forth the means of providing for individual differences in capacity. The work of Prof. E. L. Thorndike and Dr. Leonard Ayers has proved, on a statistical basis, what has always been apparent to every reflecting teacher, the great difference in capacity between the fast and the slow members of each class. It is in dealing with them that the Ungraded Class teacher proves most helpful.

It has been the writer's habit, at the opening of a term to allow those whose age and grade showed retardation, to skip one term, provided the quality of the previous term's work would justify it. As many as fifty-five pupils out of six hundred have been so promoted in a single term, and of that number all but two succeeded, and many of the others took leading places in the grades they entered.

During the first half of the term, these pupils skipping a grade, were allowed to take up the regular work of the grade to which they skipped, but during their study periods, were scheduled for two or three subjects with the Ungraded Class. By the expiration of that time, and with the co-operative work of the regular class teacher, these pupils were able to do independent work.

During the second half of the term, those deficient pupils first mentioned above, together with those whose present reports showed need of assistance, composed the classes of the Ungraded Teacher.

The Ungraded Class is instrumental in firmly establishing in their grades those who skip (and there are many capable of doing this, particularly if age in years is not a pre-requisite, and it does not seem that it should be), as well as in preventing very many of the poorer pupils from failing of promotion.

In addition to the direct assistance given by the class teacher and by the Ungraded Class teacher, there are other means of special consideration for the most capable pupils.

1. They may profit by assisting other pupils.

2. They may do supplementary work in another text.

3. The teacher should be furnished with standardized, mimeographed, supplementary assignments for bright pupils.

4. Specially selected readings should be assigned and reports of same be made, where work is not systematized and outlined as suggested above.

The bright pupils of to-day are the main dependence for the future leadership in business, as well as for shaping thought and action in State and Nation. They should be given such opportunity as will insure their highest development.

It is not true, therefore, in our graded school system, that ample opportunity may not be provided to meet the needs of all, if the methods indicated herein are followed. No doubt these might be improved. But if systematically followed, the discipline of the school will become easier, because all will be receiving the sympathetic assistance they need, each will prove willing to do his part, and through such mutual good feeling and co-operation, retardation will be largely eliminated and our pupils will be saved to the schools.

UNGRADED CLASSES.

The Ungraded Class furnishes instruction for pupils unable to keep up the minimum classroom work. In this class pupils receive much individual attention together with group teaching. Groups are not permanent, but are rearranged as the needs of the children require. Pupils who are falling behind in any one subject may be sent to the ungraded class for additional instruction in this topic. This help prevents them from falling behind. 95% of children have the mental capacity for pursuing their subjects pari passu. It is not necessary that the child should run ahead of his class in the thing which he happens to like and consequently lag back in the subject less pleasing to him. A little help and a little urging will bring him up with the rest of his class in the subject which has less attraction, or is more difficult. As at the dinner table he is not permitted to follow his own whim or fancy, so at the educational board his work should be directed, restrained, or stimulated as the special case demands. The time of the ungraded teacher should be divided into half-hour periods, children coming from different classes to her in groups for instruction in the studies in which they are weak. No pupil should go to the ungraded teacher who doesn't have a lesson in the same subject from his class teacher. It should not be the substitution of one teacher's work for that of another, but a double dose for the pupil who is weak. These groups will change from time to time as pupils make up their back work and others for various reasons, such as sickness, fall behind. . Our Ungraded Classes when in operation have saved hundreds of pupils from retardation. They have enabled large numbers of pupils moving to our City to even up their work with our Course of Study and fall into regular grades.

The Ungraded Class is established not for the backward or retarded pupil alone. It is equally for the bright or mature pupil who desires to skip a grade. Such a pupil may omit subjects which are taken up more fully in higher grades from the advanced text. Thus a pupil may omit entirely some of the primary history and geography, since he will get them from the grammar school text. Some subjects, however, such as his arithmetic and language, he cannot well omit, but he may be promoted and make these up in the ungraded class. The Ungraded Class thus enables us to promote a pupil whenever he is able to do the work of the higher grade, at the same time preventing serious omissions in his education. Our Ungraded Classes were discontinued some two years ago for lack of funds. They should be re-established and their number greatly increased.

In the large primary schools where there are several classes of the same grade, we have accomplished much by grading the grade. Thus, if there are three classes in the A-1st grade, we put into the lowest class pupils backward in maturity and mentality and let them take a year for the term's work. Into the second class we put pupils of ordinary ability who will accomplish the year's work in a year. Into the third class we put mature and bright pupils who may accomplish the year's work in a term. Into this class we will put foreign pupils who are much beyond the six year age and have had some education in their own language. Pupils are changed from time to time from one of these classes to another. The same method may be applied to the second year's work if there are two or more classes. It may be applied in a measure where there is but a single class to the grade, the pupils being divided into sections according to their ability.

THE PROBLEM OF THE UPPER GRAMMAR GRADES AND ITS PARTIAL SOLUTION.

The function of the elementary schools is not merely to prepare for the high school, but to put the pupil in possession of the tools of knowledge, and, incidentally, to give him such information and general culture as time and the pupil's capacity will admit. But the opportunity of the school is lost if the pupil drops out. A comparison of the number who enter the first grade with the number who complete the eighth, shows a startlingly great number lost by the way, a very heavy part of such mortality being in the upper grammar grades. In general, elimination takes place as follows: From the 7th grade to the 8th, 26%; from the 8th to the 9th, 32.5%, and from the 9th to the 10th, 37%. Doubtless, there are economic reasons why many pupils fail to enter the high school, and in other instances lack of confidence in capacity to meet the high school requirements probably deters. But of those great numbers—37%—who do enter the high school and during the first year drop out, the main reason for their leaving is the fact that their preparation has not been satisfactory. So that in considering the needs of the upper grammar grades one must keep in mind the great number who fail to complete the grammar school and so go into the world poorly prepared, and also the great number who, finishing the grammar school, either do not enter the high school at all, or else drop out within the first year.

In most instances the parents are very anxious to have their children continue in school, but despite the combined efforts of the school and the home, the indifference of the student toward his work, and his persistent demand to withdraw overcome parental objection and he leaves school. Lack of interest on the part of the pupil is the chief reason for the great defection in the school ranks.

Nor is this strange to one who has been associated with the upper grammar grades and has observed the attitude of the rapidly developing boys and girls in the 6th, 7th and 8th grades.

It seems a little remarkable, considering how much has been said of the problem of "Adolescence" as pertaining to the High School, that so little attention has been given to a similar condition in the upper grammar grades.

Statistics compiled from eight of our representative grammar schools show that only 2% of the pupils of the seventh and eighth grades are under thirteen years of age, while the great majority are fourteen or fifteen, and not a few are sixteen yeares of age. In the sixth grades, A and B, over seventy-five percent are above twelve years of age—many being 13 past.

Accepted authorities fix the period of adolescence at twelve to sixteen for girls and fourteen to eighteen for boys. According to this and the statistics given above, this period of adolescence is not a high school problem in the high school only, but indeed a very serious high school problem in the grammar school, where conditions are least favorable to meet its demands.

The early adolescent period is one of the most trying as well for the pupil as for the school, and should be of grave concern to both. Twelve to fourteen for girls and fourteen to sixteen for boys are periods of greatest physical growth and development—the time of actual growing pains. The heart increases in size and contractible power, blood pressure is tremendously augmented, and the temperature of the body rises. Lungs and chest have a large part in this extraordinary growth. The voice changes, and most of all, there is perfected development of those parts that mark sex differences. The growth of the body and its parts is accompanied by a corresponding increase in its powers. The boy needs active and systematic exercise—the girl proper periods of rest and relaxation as well as of judicious, active exercises.

Along with the physical ones of increased energy and activity, alternating with depression, inactivity, and apparent laziness, there are great mental tracts developing. There are new sensations, greater and more prolonged attention, keener perception, finer discrimination, saner judgment, and more logical reasoning. Imagination becomes active. Interest broadens but persistence is weak. The boy demands reasons. He grows self-assertive and self-sufficient, careful of self-comfort and adornment. It is a period of stresses, superlatives, strong likes and dislikes. The will strengthens as do the impulses. Fortunately, the judgment develops as well. The social instinct is apparent. The "square deal" is demanded. Athletic sports are attractive and desire to excel in them is great. This is the age of adventure—the "runaway" age. This is the age that demands recognition proportionate to the pupil's own self-esteem, and one which should elicit from the teacher all the sympathy and studied interest in the pupil that this future citizen and member of society demands.

It is in the grammar school that all of these characteristics are observed in some and many of them in each of these children in early adolescence, and it is in these grades that little is being done to allow these boys and girls to develop along the lines of their natures and instincts, but a great deal is being done—much necessarily—to suppress, dishearten them, and to hinder the development of their individualities. The association of the adolescent boy and girl with the elementary grades is wrong in theory, and the effort to subject them to the same methods of discipline at a time when their very natures cry out for change and a greater freedom, is responsible for much of the discontent that drives many of them from the schools.

This same inherent feeling for change, for something new—is responsible for lack of interest in subjects begun in the elementary grades, repeated in more advanced books in grammar grades, and are the constant regimen for eight years. Thinking of life, they question the practicability of the school course. The thinking public is of much the same mind and educators are practically agreed that:

1. The time spent in the elementary school is out of proportion to the results accomplished.

2. Too much time is devoted to arithmetic, grammar, and certain phases of history, and that more time could be spent to advantage upon composition and literature.

3. Elementary general science, manual training, and domestic science should receive considerable attention, and that some attention might be given to elements of algebra and concrete geometry.

4. A foreign language, and some phase of what would seem to the pupil more directly practical work, such as stenography, typewriting, or bookkeeping should be included.

5. Special attention should be given to oral and written expression and music, as well as to physical education, and social affairs.

6. The course of study for these grades has a true psychological basis for variation from that of the primary grades.

The same feeling and longing for change craves association with men teachers. From the infant class their teachers have been women whom they loved and respected. They have been tenderly cared for and skillfully taught. And it is not that women are not as good teachers as men—no doubt they are better and more capable for the pre-adolescent period—and for the adolescent have the lessons of womanly grace and tenderness along with excellent teaching ability—yet they do not represent all that seventh and eighth grade pupils need in rounding out and developing perfect characters. They need as well the companionship of the man in the school as of the father in the home. They should be taught by both men and women. To quote John Franklin Brown "Boys need virile qualities to initiate, and manly strength as well as womanly grace to restrain them. Girls need womanly ideals set before them, but they need also the influence of the critical virility of the masculine mind and character."

Another change that would be most agreeable to the pupil of the upper grammar grade would be the departmental system of instruction. This would afford a modified method of work, change of room and of teacher, and a freer, less restrained feeling than is experienced under the regular system.

And still another opportunity that should be offered to these pupils of rapidly developing minds is provision for regular study in each subject, under the supervision of the teacher of that subject. Many a pupil is lost to the high school simply through lack of knowledge to how to study. His preparation in the grades did not properly provide for the changed conditions in the high school where the pupil is thrown upon his own resources. The High School unfortunately assumes that the pupil has such ability, and does not endeavor systematically to strengthen or develop it. The pupil flounders and soon withdraws. It is to meet the ability to do independent study and thinking, that special attention should be given to the matter in the grades. The pupils can do exactly the same kind of logical reasoning in the grades that they can in the High School—the main difference being in quality due to wider experience and greater development. The teacher's main duty is to help the pupil to help himself. Unless the proper reaction takes place, mental indigestion will result, rather than true education. Information for the present is desirable, but power and discipline of mind the necessary guarantee for the future.

The claims of the children in these grades for treatment more in accord with their ages and physical and mental development seem well founded. They are entitled to be treated with greater consideration and with that confidence and liberality that will really qualify them for greater possibility of success in life, as well as in the high school. The gap between the grammar school and the high school is too wide. It can and should be made the easiest and most inviting step in the entire school life. And to accomplish this a definite school policy should be agreed upon and gradually instituted including, amongst others, the following policies:

1. The establishing of the Grammar Schools by concentrating the 6th, 7th and 8th grades at convenient centres, and not in association with children of primary grades.

2. Reorganization of the Course of Study.

3. Introduction of departmental teaching.

4. Introduction of approximately as many men as women teachers.

5. Extension of the school day for all grades from sixth grade to the twelfth to 3:30. This would enable nearly all preparation to be made in school.

6. Requirement of regularly supervised study periods in which pupils would be taught proper methods of study.

7. One Ungraded Class teacher should be provided for each school.

Already in the city there are three distinctly grammar schools, all of which could easily conform to this scheme; and three Intermediate Schools, which need but slight modification.

It would not be possible to carry out this plan in every section of the city, but in many instances it could be done at once. And where it would not be practicable to carry out the entire policy, it would be entirely so to make several of the suggested modifications, to advantage.

Any such scheme as this would somewhat increase the cost of the schools. But should this be a matter of great objection, if it would be instrumental in holding the pupils in school and making of them better and more capable men and women, the future citizens of to-morrow?

SPECIAL UNGRADED SCHOOLS.

We have a large number of overgrown boys 14 or 15 years of age who are still in grades with younger children. The law compels these boys to be in school until they are sixteen. For many reasons the grade work, while suited to the ordinary child, makes little appeal to these boys and will be of comparatively little use to them. They will drop out of school as soon as the law permits. For such boys we ought to have a number of special ungraded schools. The work in these schools should be largely industrial. The book work should grow in a great measure out of the interest awakened by the hand work. The Moulder School has a small attendance and could be dispensed with as a primary school. It is centrally located for a school of the type above-mentioned. It is within easy reach of a very large number of our primary and grammar schools. I believe we should make arrangements to start such an industrial ungraded school at the Moulder next year. In fact there is room enough there for a beginning to be made at the present time. The annex contains a large manual training room unused, and there are several unoccupied classrooms in the main building.

ETHAN ALLEN SCHOOL.

For the past ten years the city has maintained a day parental school called the Ethan Allen. To this school are sent, by order of the Superintendent's office, children found exceedingly troublesome, incorrigible or habitual truants. The work in this school is largely individual, there being not more than twenty pupils to the teacher. A large amount of manual work is given. Hot lunches are supplied to the pupils and they assist in preparing and serving them. A vegetable garden cultivated by the children makes a large contribution to the noon-day meal. Many children sent to this school are simply unfortunate in their home conditions, or need that individual help which our crowded classrooms cannot give them. In some cases the defect in school work is due to the poor foundation laid in an earlier grade. This by individual instruction may be built up and the child put on the road to steady progress. Much of the same work was accomplished in our Ungraded Classes before they were abolished. When pupils are evened up in their scholarship, and deportment corrected, they are sent on probation to one of the regular schools.

This school has been doing excellent work as a day parental, but it does not take the place of the boarding parental for those children who should be kept from bad surroundings of home, street, and companionship, for 24 hours out of the day. We hope for a boarding parental school, on a ten acre tract of land, where children may work four hours a day at books and four hours a day in the shops or on the soil.

OPEN AIR SCHOOLS.

Open air classes at the Buena Vista and the Edison Schools have been recently opened and are rendering valuable service to the community. There should be many more of these and provision should be made to furnish the children with warmer clothing in cold weather and more nutritious food to keep up the warmth from within.

SUBNORMAL CLASSES.

The Superintendent's office has been recommending for the past ten years that adequate provision be made for sub-normal children. Under the State law they are entitled to places in the regular schools unless special classes are provided for them. They get little or no help from regular school instruction and are a hindrance to the normal children in the classes. There is a State institution for these children which has a long waiting list, and therefore cannot take care of the subnormal in our own schools. Even if the State made ample provision for this class of children, there is no law by which they can be sent to this school without the consent of their parents. It is, therefore, an imperative necessity that San Francisco should provide classes for exceptional children.

For several years we have had an "Ungraded Primary School" at Union and Kearny Streets. This is a class for the mentally defective. It has an attendance of about twenty pupils, and is under the care of a highly trained and skillful teacher.

Recently a class was established in the Buena Vista School, Bryant and 18th Streets.

There is need for at least three such classes, and a building adequate for their accommodation is a crying need of this department.

Provision should be made not only for regular classrooms, but for various forms of manual work, physical education, properly equipped playground, and for gardening.

DEAF SCHOOL.

We employ three teachers for instructing the deaf. The work is done in large measure by the oral method. Children are taught to speak and to read the lips. They are given the regular Course of Study together with much manual training. A separate building should be erected for this school.

HEALTH.

We have had the best of co-operation from the Health Department, from the Children's Clinic at the Affiliated Colleges and from the school nurses in caring for the health of the children. More could not be done with the present means at our command. Much more, however, ought to be done to send the children into life with the healthiest bodies and soundest minds. We need to organize, as part of the educational system, a department of child study. This should include an educational psychologist to determine the mentality and educational needs of children in any respect below par. This department should have experts on the special senses. Children frequently come to our notice who are in whole or in part unteachable because of enlarged tonsils, adenoids, or defective eyesight. These defects are not discovered by the class teacher and cannot be remedied by a school nurse. A department of child study would cost from ten to sixteen thousand dollars a year for proper equipment and maintenance. It would cost as much more to provide special teachers for defective children. This branch of work is not less important than the physical development of the child who is all there.

VACATION SCHOOLS.

We have several times recommended Vacation Schools for the Summer weeks but have always met the same reply, "No money"! Such schools would often prevent a pupil from becoming retarded or aid an advanced pupil in skipping a grade. Frequently, students in perfect health are prevented from going to school, because of contagious diseases in the family,—contact-cases. A vacation school would keep such pupils from falling behind in the term's work. Most families are unable to take their children from the city during the Summer, the Labor Law prevents them from working, and time, during a long summer vacation, hangs heavily upon their hands. Attendance during the forenoon at a Vacation School, with supervised play for the afternoon, would fill time pleasantly and profitably. We shall ask money for Vacation Schools in the next Budget. We need $15,000 to make a beginning.

DEPARTMENTAL WORK.

Departmental work in grammar grades has been tried many times in many places and failed. The advantages are that it gives a teacher the subject in which she is best prepared or which she likes best to teach. If she is not already so, she may become an expert in that subject. The pupils are relieved by different voice and personality. It accustoms the pupil to more than one teacher and thus makes a transition to high school methods. Departmental work has failed by bringing too many teachers into the departmental group, thus breaking up the unity of the pupil's instruction and loosening the teacher's moral control of the class. The first of these difficulties is overcome by frequent conference of the principal with the group of teachers working together. Each teacher is thus made acquainted with what the others are doing, and the work is correlated. Only four teachers should work together in a departmental group. Each teacher takes one subject in which she instructs the four classes. The remaining subjects are taught by the class-teacher. Thus the class is with its own teacher three hours of the day and with the other teachers of the group two hours out of each day. Each teacher of the group retains the same class for two years, thus giving her a stronger moral hold upon them. The four main subjects of instruction are for two years in the hands of an expert teacher, giving unity to each subject. Thus grammar, for instance, is handled through the seventh and eighth years by the same teacher.

A large number of our schools have now adopted the departmental system. The seventh and eighth grades are put into the departmental groups, and occasionally the sixth. A school may have one, two, or three departmental groups. It is best to have the classes, rather than the teachers, change rooms. It gives a little relief to the children to make the change and the room may be equipped for its special subject. We hope to have money enough to equip our grammar schools. The departmental method has been left optional with the schools, but the results have been so satisfactory that the number of schools so organizing has increased greatly.

INTERMEDIATE SCHOOLS.

The success of the departmental schools was so great that it seemed wise, two and one-half years ago, to give three of them a modified Course of Study and designate them as Intermediate Schools. The work being so thoroughly systematized under the departmental system, it was found possible to add to the ordinary Course of Study a larger amount of Elementary Science, Manual Training, and Domestic Arts, and to give the pupils a choice between typing and a modern language. After two years of experimenting we were able during the summer vacation to formulate a time schedule for these schools. The schools are a marked success, and we wish to extend this new type of school so that pupils in every part of the city may be within easy reach of an Intermediate School. We give below the time schedule of these schools:

	Minutes Per Week	
	Sixth Grade	Seventh and Eighth Grades
Writing	50	
Arithmetic	250	160
Language (Composition, Grammar)	200	160
Spelling	75	80
Literature and Oral Expression	200	160
Geography and History (alternating)	300	240
Music	60	80
Drawing	60	120
Modern Language or Typing		120
Manual Training or Domestic Science	80	160
General Science including Physiology	80	120
	1355	1400

THE JEAN PARKER PREVOCATIONAL SCHOOL.

In the Jean Parker, a school exclusively for girls, a systematic course in domestic science is given which enables any girl going through the school and graduating to cook a good, hygienic, well-balanced meal and serve it—to make any garment she wishes for herself or those about her, and make a hat fit to wear. She has the rudiments of three occupations, if she wishes to follow any of those for a living.

Pupils of grades I through V have from an hour to an hour and ten minutes of manual work a week; those of grades VI through VIII A have three hours a week; and those of the VIII B have four and one-half hours. Sewing is taught by the class teachers under the supervision of the principal; cooking and millinery by the Domestic Science teacher. A synopsis of the course follows:

HAND WORK.

Grades I, II and III—Paper tearing, cutting, pasting; slat and raffia weaving; cardboard construction, etc.

SEWING.

Grade IV **A**—Sampler-unbleached muslin with red stitches. Doll's sheet for model bed. Hemming, soft-finished material.

Grade IV **B**—Wash-cloth or dust-cloth—cheese-cloth with red stitches. Doll's blanket—white tennis flannel bound with ribbon (back stitching). Doll's pillow-case—soft finished muslin (French seam and hem).

Grade **V A**—Doll's tufted quilt—figured quilting goods, yarn to match. Tea towel—model size (napery stitch). Belt apron— striped gingham (felling, hemming, gathering, belt, etc.).

Grade **V B**—Patching—large-checked gingham. Linen hand-bag with cord. A strap apron, model size.

Grade VI **A**—Darning. Tennis flannel skirt with bodice, cut from pattern by girls. Night gown (putting on edging and beading), cut from pattern by girls.

Grade VI **B**—Doll's rompers, bloomers, and overdress—gingham or chambray.

Grade VII **A**—Doll's sailor blouse, skirt, and cap—gingham or chambray (putting on sailor collar, cuffs pocket, etc.).

Grade VII **B**—Button holes. A set of doll's underwear (drawers, chemise, underskirt and slip)—soft-finished muslin (scalloped edge).

Grade VIII **A**—A doll's lawn one-piece dress with insertion, edging, gathered pleated skirt, belt, etc. Figured lawn preferred.

Grade VIII B—Graduation suit—blouse and skirt. Use of Butterick patterns and sewing machine.

EXTRA.

A supply of cross-bar lawn and lace edging is kept on hand for tea-aprons for pupils getting through the regular course and requiring more work. After completing the grade work a girl may bring additional work from home.

COOKING.

Grades VI B, VII A and B, VIII A, VIII B—Time, one hour and a half a week.

MILLINERY.

Grade VIII **B**—Time, one hour and a half a week, from 3 to 4:30 P. M.

MONROE SCHOOL.

In the Monroe School, one of the largest in our department, considerable attention is given to manual work. The pupils of the Second, Third, and Fourth Grades are instructed in weaving, bead-making, and raffia work; the Fifth Grade pupils are now drawing designs which will be used later in making rugs.

The grammar grade pupils of this school have done some excellent work in rug making. The designs are drawn by the pupils, enlarged to a working scale, and the work executed either on the large loom by individual pupils, or, as community work, in sections on small pasteboard looms; these sections are then sewed together to make the finished product.

Once a week lessons in sewing are given to the girls of the Sixth Grade classes by student-teachers from the Lux School of Industrial Training.

COSMOPOLITAN SCHOOLS.

There are four Cosmopolitan schools in our department; the Adams, the Bryant, the Columbia and the Roosevelt. French, German and Spanish are taught in two of these schools, each pupil being allowed to select the language he or she wishes to study. In the Adams School pupils studying French or German receive five lessons a week; those studying Spanish receive but two lessons; while in the Columbia three lessons in each language are given weekly. In the Bryant School, French and German are taught in the First and Second grades by the regular grade teachers and in the other grades by special teachers, each pupil receiving two lessons a week. In the Roosevelt School, French and German are taught, pupils taking either language receiving five half-hour lessons a week.

In addition to the above, German is taught in the following Elementary schools: Pacific Heights, Crocker Intermediate, Hamilton Intermediate, and Horace Mann Intermediate; and Italian in the Hancock, Sherman, Monroe and the Horace Mann Intermediate.

Great interest is manifested in the study of the foreign languages and the results in the main are satisfactory. Credit is given in the High Schools for the work accomplished in the Elementary Schools.

In several schools where foreign languages do not form a part of the regular course, classes are conducted after school hours by teachers from the Alliance Francaise and the Schule Bund, those organizations having received from the Board of Education permission to use classrooms for that purpose. A nominal sum is charged the pupils for this tuition.

SUBSTITUTE TEACHERS.

At the beginning of the last term, a conference with the Substitute Teachers was held by the Superintendent and his Deputies, the object being to discuss the general problem of the Substitute Teacher and her relationship and duties to the school, as well as the duties of the school to the Substitute Teacher. The conference was most satisfactory and led to the following directions which were endorsed by the Board of Education, and which have been in effect since that time.

1. Principals requiring substitutes in their schools shall notify the Secretary of the Board of Education, by 2 o'clock of any day, as to the number of substitutes and the grades for which such substitutes shall be needed on the following day. The Secretary shall at once direct substitutes to report to such Principal by 8:45 next morning.

2. Regular teachers in EMERGENCY cases, finding themselves unable to meet their classes, shall so notify the Secretary sufficiently early to enable substitutes to reach the school by 8:45 A. M.

3. Regular teachers shall keep in their registers, a loose copy of the program, and a diagram of the room showing the names of the pupils as seated; also a set of name-cards,—one card for each pupil.

4. Every regular teacher shall post in a conspicuous place a note of the lessons in each subject assigned for the following day.

5. It shall be the duty of every substitute to follow the program arranged for the day, unless otherwise directed by the Principal. Each substitute shall place the diagram of the room on the teacher's desk so that the names of the pupils may be called without the children knowing how their names are obtained.

6. (a) Substitutes sent out for one day shall telephone at the close of the day's work to the Secretary, whether or not they will be needed in the same school on the following day.

(b) Substitutes sent out for definite periods of more than one day shall likewise telephone to the secretary at the close of the last day of such period.

(c) Substitutes shall not leave the school before three o'clock on the last day of their assignment, in order that the Secretary may direct them by telephone where to report on the next day.

With these conditions met, the substitute teachers will be enabled to prepare themselves better to meet and interest their classes.

There is nothing more disconcerting to a school, however well regulated, than the absence of the teacher, nor few positions more trying than that of the substitute, particularly should she be young and inexperienced. These directions tended to systematize the work and provide for desired co-operation, but with all this the question is a serious one.

The present method although an improvement, is not as satisfactory as it should be to the schools for the following reasons:

1. The substitute teachers are ordinarily young and inexperienced.

2. Serving in every part of the city, they do not visit the same school often enough to make an acquaintance.

3. Being inexperienced, they are not sufficiently familiar with the work of the various grades.

4. The term of service as substitute is very short.

5. It is only in the case of the long calls that the school gets any real satisfaction from the substitute teacher.

The matter assumes a very serious aspect for at least three reasons:

1. That the absence of a teacher should not cause a serious break or demoralization in the work of the class.

2. The inexperienced teacher who composes the list could be most helped by assignment to regular work in a well regulated school, and thus be getting the kind of experience most needed. They should be given positions of responsibility and should be expected to try to meet it.

3. The substitute teacher in a school system offering "life tenure" should be given every opportunity to demonstrate her ability as a teacher, and the School Department should have equal opportunity in really forming an acquaint-

ance with her work to the end that, if she proves worthy, she may be advanced to the grade of regular teacher.

All of these conditions could be met most satisfactorily by the following plan:

1. The substitute list should comprise the requisite number of teachers chosen from the personnel of the School Department on the basis of excellence in instruction and discipline, and for attractiveness and forcefulness in general character. They should be teachers familiar with the work in all the grades, or those having the ability and disposition to so prepare themselves.

This list should be regarded as a kind of "honor roll". It should offer no greater inducement than this fact. Each such substitute should be reimbursed, however, for traveling expenses, and (at the expiration of one year of substitute work) should be given the privilege of returning to the grade position from which she had been taken.

2. As these substitute teachers would be paid full salary, they should serve full time. Therefore, each should be assigned to a particular school for substitute service in that or a neighboring school; and, provided she should not be needed in that particular group, she would be subject to call to any other point in the city. In her school headquarters, she should have a program for regular assistance such as an Ungraded Class teacher generally gives, and whenever her services are not needed in any school as substitute, she should follow the program above-mentioned.

3. The teacher now designated "Substitute Teachers", should be used to fill the vacancies caused by the withdrawal of the regular experienced teachers for substitute work.

The plan as outlined, if instituted, would entail some expense, but it would carry with it more than a proportionate educational return.

See topic "Method of Assignment of Probationary Teachers", beyond, in this report.

ENFORCED ATTENDANCE.

The Compulsory Education Law requires that every child shall be in school until the completion of the grammar grades or to the age of 16. It is our duty to enforce this law because the child upon reaching majority should be possessed of a common school education. The child may not see the future value of this education and we therefore are made his educational guardians. We cannot permit him to suffer from his own neglect or that of his parents. The law provides all means necessary for its enforcement. Three truant officers are inadequate to the enforcement of this law. They are not enough even to compel the attendance enrolled in the schools, but there are many children not enrolled in the schools at all. The families move into the city and the children may for months or years elude the vigilance of school authorities and truant officers. Cases are constantly coming to our attention of children who have been in our midst for a long time but not in school.

Compulsory education is a State law and should be enforced by the Police Department just as should any other law of the city or state. Several years ago an order was issued that every policeman should be a truant officer on his beat between 9 and 3 o'clock. The work was taken hold of in good earnest, but after a short time the department lost interest and enthusiasm because every child questioned on the street by a policeman gave reasons for being there which the officer had no power to refute. "It's a holiday at our school". "I go to a private school and we are excused to-day". "The teacher excused me to go on an errand". "My little brother has measles and I cannot go to school". "The Board of Health wont let me go to school because of contagious disease". "My mother is sick and I have to mind the baby". "I am going for some medicine". Other children soon picked up these cues by which the policeman could be dodged. The order from the Chief of Police soon became a dead letter because it could not be enforced.

We have already recommended a system of absence cards to be signed by the principal permitting the child to be on the street during school hours. If a child expects for any reason to be absent, the Principal can issue the card before the pupil leaves school. This card is a permit from the Principal for the child's absence. The card may be carried in the pocket and must be shown to the officer who finds the child on the street. Failure to produce the card justifies the officer in phoning to the school nearest the child's home or turning the child over to the nearest school. If the child is taken sick suddenly and not able to go to school he can send by some companion to the school and receive his card before he is convalescent enough to be out of the house. If the child is sent home by order of the Board of Health the card is given to the child before he leaves the school. In case of contagious diseases where the child should not be on the street the card will be refused and the Health Office thus greatly aided in enforcing quarantine and preventing the spread of contagious diseases. Cards should be provided for pupils of public schools, private schools and pupils with working permits who must return to school when out of employment. These cards will be printed on different color paper so that they may be distinguished at a glance. We have had a conference with the Chief of Police, who has promised most hearty co-operation. Archbishop Hanna strongly approved of the plan and confidently believed that the parochial schools would co-operate. Mr. Astredo, Chief Probation Officer, considers it one of the best plans ever devised. Chief White asked to have a report from prepared so that each policeman could report the work he accomplished as a truant officer. This would stimulate every policeman to his best efforts. Samples of the cards to be used are herewith presented.

ABSENCE CARD.

(Public School)

.... School

.... Date

....Name of Child

is permitted to be absent from

.... to ....

on account of ....

....Principal.

ABSENCE CARD.

(Private School)

.... School

.... Date

....Name of Child

is permitted to be absent from

.... to ....

on account of ....

....Principal.

ABSENCE CARD.

(Working Certificate)

.... Date

....Name of Child

is permitted to be absent while working at

....

(This child must attend school when out of employment)

....(Name of Employer)

....(Name of Principal)

The official records of the Truant Officers of the San Francisco School Department for the fiscal year ending June 30, 1915, showed that 4,024 truancy complaints made by school principals were investigated and in each case followed to a definite conclusion during the 12 months covered by the report. In addition 2,219 cases of children of school age found on the street during school hours without apparent warrant to be there were also investigated, while 160 truants, with whom milder means failed, were brought before the Juvenile Court. In 149 instance parents, who were considered at fault as well as, or more than, their children, were cited before the same tribunal, where their cases were variously disposed of.

The figures quoted show a steady and material decrease in truancy from the records of previous years.

Three truant officers—policemen especially detailed for this duty—are active agents, as has been stated, in the daily enforcement of the Compulsory Education Law, combining with this kindred duties in support of the Child Labor Law. All their time is devoted to the work, and it is inadequate for the labors to be performed. The fact that much of the dereliction of school pupils in the matter of attendance is due to a desire to go to work without proper authorization makes it absolutely necessary that the truant officers shall combine with their efforts to suppress truancy others directed to the support of the law regulating Child Labor. Aside from this important but, in a manner, incidental work of this character done by them, they are also charged directly with such special inquiries as have to be made in connection with the issuing of working permits, or "Age and schooling certificates," to give them their technical name. Outside investigations are necessary in virtually all cases where "special" permits are applied for, and in this work the aid of the truant officers is necessary and invaluable. It is the truant officer detailed to that section of the city in which the family concerned resides who visits the home and the child's school, and assures himself by personal investigation that the hardships of the case are as stated, also that there are no incidental or other reasons why the permit should not be granted. Without the investigating truant officer's approval, and that of the school principal especially concerned, the so-called "special" permits are never granted. These permits are such as are issued for a limited time to the children of widows or of fathers physically unable to work and in certain other cases where to do so seems the only means of relieving extreme privation.

The position of truant officer in a cosmopolitan seaport city such as San Francisco is in no sense to be considered as a "snap". With a population speaking just about every known language—and a few that it would be no particular strain upon the facts to class as unknown—such an official's duties at times become as onerous as they are important. In many cases—perhaps the majority—they lead him to foreign quarters where his own native tongue is wholly unknown, and where the denizens' real or affected ignorance of the laws as to Compulsory Education and Child Labor stands up like a seemingly impenetrable wall to defeat his efforts at inquiry, explanation, persuasion or compulsion. But always he breaks the wall down, and the child goes back to school. In extreme cases radical measures have to be taken. Arrests are made, parents or children, more frequently both, are taken to the Juvenile Court, but, in one way or another, the desired and desirable result is accomplished.

Nor is the duty of the truant officer without distinct elements of danger at times. Witness the experience of Policeman Eugene Sweeney, when a young vagabond who had coaxed a colored girl away from school and home, in his rage at the foiling of his plans, suddenly drew a pistol and attempted to shoot the officer. The latter was the more prompt with his weapon, and the would-be bad man went down with a bullet in the leg. Then the truant officer, casually remarking, "You want to be quicker than that, my boy, when you pull a gun," tied up the fellow's limb, sent him to the lock-up—and took the girl back to school.

Incidents such as this, fortunately and as a matter of course, are extremely rare, but the difficulties to be met and overcome by the truant officer through the ignorance of some parents, the unreasonableness and obstinacy of others, are many and various. Not all his troubles are encountered in the homes of the poor by any means. Parents well off in a material sense often insist that they have the right "to do as they please with their own children". Especially is this the case among people who desire to employ their offspring at too early an age as assistants in the conduct of business enterprises. With all these the truant officers have to deal in such manner as shall insure the carrying out of the law, while at the same time avoiding, if possible, the creating of bad feeling between the parents and the school or other civic authorities. All in all, the lot of the truant officers is not particularly to be envied, and it would be well if their ability to enforce the educational and labor laws in this city could be strengthened by the addition of more members to their at present very small but active corps.

CHILD LABOR LAW AND SUGGESTED MEANS OF NEEDED CO-OPERATION.

The Child Labor Laws, as amended, show great concern for the child's schooling. They raise the compulsory age to fifteen years, and the educational qualification for Age and Schooling Certificate to completion of "the equivalent of the seventh grade of the regular grammar school course" (as a minimum), and require that the minor be "a regular attendant for the then current term at a regularly conducted night school". Provision is made for the following permits or certificates to work:

First, a "vacation permit" allowing a minor over twelve but under the age of fifteen years to work "on regular weekly school holidays and during the regular vacation of the public schools".

Second, any minor fourteen years of age shall, upon application to the school authorities and upon compliance with all the requirements for the issuance of an age and schooling certificate, be entitled to receive "a permit to work outside of school hours".

Third, the Superintendent of Schools shall have authority to issue a permit to work to any minor over the age of fourteen years, in any of the following circumstances:

(1) When the minor has completed the Grammar School Course.

(2) When the minor is "past the age of fourteen" and the parent or guardian, under oath, declares that sufficient aid for support of the family cannot be secured but through the assistance of said minor. The person authorized to issue such permit shall investigate the conditions, and finding them as reported shall make a signed statement to that effect, and issue the permit

to work, but only upon **written evidence** that suitable work **is waiting** for such minor, and **such permit** shall specify the **kind of labor.** Such permit shall in no case be issued for more than **six months.**

Fourth, no minor of the age of fifteen years shall be permitted to work during the hours the public schools are in session unless "provided with an age and schooling certificate as herein provided", and secured in the manner prescribed.

To secure this certificate the minor, accompanied by parent or guardian, shall make personal application, and the person authorized to issue age and schooling certificates shall not issue such certificate "until he has received, examined, approved and filed the following papers duly executed":

(1) The school record of such minor duly signed by the principal or teacher.

(2) Convincing evidence of true date of birth of such minor.

(3) Written statement from prospective employer that he intends to employ the minor, and the nature of the occupation for which such minor is to be employed.

(4) Certificate of a physician appointed by the school board, or other public medical officer that the minor is physically and mentally able to be employed in the work which he intends to do.

(5) Evidence that the minor applying for the age and schooling certificate is a regular attendant for the then current term at a regularly conducted night school.

Section 12 prescribes the penalty for violation of these laws. It, therefore, is important that the employers of minors should be thoroughly informed as to the law, and that the schools should endeavor to get their hearty co-operation, as well as that of all other parties concerned. To this end the following recommendations are offered:

First. A copy of "Laws Pertaining to the Employment of Children", together with a copy of a circular letter (a form of which is attached) should be mailed to each prospective employer.

Second. All evening school principals should be furnished with postal cards on which to report to the attendance officer the absence from school of pupils whose excuses are not satsfactory.

Third. Whenever a permit to work is about to be given to a pupil belonging to any school, the school concerned should be first notified by telephone, if during the session of school; else by postal card.

If the provisions of the Child Labor Laws as touching the schools are carefully enforced, great and unlimited good will accrue to the children, their employers, and the future of society. Great evil has resulted in times past through the "gang" influence of those who, having entered evening school, received permits to work, and then in a short time were idle upon the streets.

The co-operation that reasonably may be expected will be sufficient to render effective the excellent provisions of the Child Labor Laws pertaining to the schools.

The following Age and Schooling Certificates were issued during the fiscal year 1914-1915:

	Boys	Girls	Total
Certificates issued to children between 15 and 16 years (not graduates)	359	121	480
Certificates issued to children between 15 and 16 years (graduates)	54	16	70
Temporary permits issued to children between 12 and 15 years	116	29	145
Certificates issued to graduates under 15 years	41	9	50
Grand Total			745

IMMIGRANTS.

The classes of our evening schools are doing much for young men and women who have recently come to our country and are preparing to become citizens. These people have had the hardihood and courage to leave home, friends and relatives and take up their abode in a strange land. They are among the most progressive among their countrymen. Just as it required courage for our own pioneers to brave the dangers of the wilderness in reaching California, so have these young people shown fortitude in coming to a new land. They give promise of useful citizenship. We should have special classes to teach them our language, our history and our government. Such we would call citizenship classes, or schools. The United States Bureau of Immigration is prepared to furnish us data regarding immigrants, so that we may find them and make the offer of education that will prepare them to pass citizenship tests and to become good citizens among us. We have not now the money necessary for this purpose. We should have from $20,000 to $50,000 in our next School Budget.

VISUAL EDUCATION.

Concreteness has long been recognized as a fundamental principle in the educative process. In the earlier years we think best with objects, later with graphic representation and finally reach the process of abstract symbols. Omitting the first or second step greatly retards the attainment of the third. Continning too long the first or second step may retard abstract thinking. These three processes are intermingled in the thought process through all periods of mental growth. They are dominant factors in the order given above. Recent invention has given us a new aid to concrete thinking, namely the projection of pictures. Many of our schools are equipped with stereopticons and the department possesses a large number of slides. Large numbers of motion pictures are now being prepared for the schoolroom. The stereopticon and the moving picture should be brought into constant use in presenting Nature Study and Elementary Science, History, Geography, Industry, Commerce and Literature. The University of California has a Bureau of Visual Instruction which furnishes to schools at very small cost films and slides for educational purposes. We should take advantage of this offer and put motion picture apparatus in many of our schools. For this purpose we should have an appropriation the coming year of from $5,000 to $10,000.

We must bear in mind, however, that carrying the visual process too far may retard or prevent the formation of abstract thinking through symbols and great care must be taken that the child be trained to gather thought properly organized and arranged from the printed page and return that thought through written composition, or oral expression. It would be easy now to swing too far toward Visual Education and forget that the end of all training is the power to handle abstract symbols. Thus all the sciences and mathematics deal in symbols. Words are symbols. All concrete teaching has for its aim and end the power of abstract thinking. Thus far we have given too little attention to concreteness of teaching in the earlier years.

ELEMENTARY CERTIFICATION ON EXAMINATION.

As an indication of the high standard of preparation required for the securing of the elementary teacher's certificate on examination, the following extract from the State law is given:

Section 1772a State School Law reads:

"Candidates (for the elementary school certificate on examination) shall present satisfactory written or documentary evidence that they have completed a four-year high school course or the equivalent hereof, or give evidence of four years of successful experience in teaching. In determining such equivalent, the Board may take cognizance of any adequate evidence of preparation a candidate may present."

METHOD OF ASSIGNMENT OF PROBATIONARY TEACHERS.

In dealing with probationary teachers two considerations should be kept constantly in mind—first, that the probationary teacher shall have the best possible opportunity to demonstrate his or her ability, and second, that the department may have the best and fairest basis for estimating the desirability of making of the probationary teacher a regular teacher entitled to "life tenure". Both considerations are important—the first, from the standpoint of humane, considerate treatment of the young and inexperienced teacher—the second, from the standpoint of the thousands of pupils who in the years to follow must pass under the instruction and influence of every regular teacher. The future personnel of the teaching force of this city is being determined through such teacher annually added to our lists. The method therefore by which our selection is made becomes a most serious matter.

We submit the following as a plan by which the general conditions in this regard may in our judgment be greatly improved, and recommend the adoption of the following rule:

"Each probationary teacher should serve in not less than three schools during the probationary period. This rule shall be effective January 3, 1916."

Advantages of the above plan:

1. Safeguarding the pupils' interests by giving an extended period of service in each school.
2. Acquaints the probationary teacher with methods of different schools.
3. Makes transferring of probationary teachers a systematic and uniform procedure.
4. Causes schools to have equal opportunities in assignments of probationary teachers.
5. Gives like chances to each probationary teacher to prove her ability.
6. Secures judgment upon her from at least three Principals.
7. Assures a comprehensive report at end of two years by the Superintendent's office.

San Francisco, January 28, 1916.

Hon. Alfred Roncovieri,
Superintendent of Schools.

My Dear Sir:—

I respectfully submit the following report upon Kindergartens and Primary Grades:

KINDERGARTENS.

In consideration of the present movement towards the wider establishment of Kindergartens, I beg to present this recapitulation of their organization as part of the San Francisco school system.

The first of the group of Kindergartens now in our schools was opened in the Lafayette School in October, 1909. As there was no fund for this purpose, no others were opened until 1913, although the success of the first one, and the importance of extending this work was recognized. In 1913 a special appropriation was granted for the maintenance of three, although an appropriation for five had been asked for. Again, in 1914, the school budget included an appropriation for three new ones. This was at first denied, but at the last moment was granted through the urgent request of a Kindergarten committee. In 1915, again the Kindergarten item was included in the budget, and was granted, providing for the maintenance of four additional classes and bringing the number to eleven in all. They are located in the following schools.

Lafayette	established	in	October,	1909
Bernal	"	"	July,	1913
Bryant	"	"	"	"
Noe Valley	"	"	"	"
Agassiz	"	"	"	1914
Glen Park	"	"	"	"
Washington Irving	"	"	"	"
Golden Gate	"	"	"	1915
Lincoln	"	"	"	"
Patrick Henry	"	"	"	"
Starr King	"	"	"	"

In all schools were they are located, these Kindergartens are in great favor, and there is an increasing demand for many more. It is important that more may be opened from year to year as an appropriation is obtained for this purpose. Towards this end, unfailing support has been given by the Superintendent of Schools and Board of Education.

The Kindergartners in charge of these classes are graduates of a State accredited Kindergarten Normal Training School, and are teachers of experience. They are assisted by students from the Kindergarten Training Department of the State Normal School.

The children of the Kindergartens remain during the morning hours only; the teacher remains for the afternoon session of the primary grades. In the afternoon, her time is given to the first grade children, teaching those subjects in which she is specially trained—hand-work, story-telling, singing and rhythmic games. In co-operation with the primary supervisor, with principals and teachers, the work for the term is systematized and programmed. Since, in the various schools there is a difference in the number of first grade classes, these programmes are not uniform.

PRIMARY HAND WORK.

In all schools, various forms of handwork are carried on in the first and second grades. In our present plan, the chief purpose of this work is to furnish a profitable and an interesting employment for the children that are not in the group reciting to the teacher. Therefore, the outlines and directions which have been given at teachers' meetings do not form a course of study to be followed in consecutive order. They suggest, rather, types of work that may be adapted to regular class-room conditions. More and more, this construction work is being used as a medium of expression, while the formal work is developing something of hand skill.

The common materials are furnished to all schools—papers of various kinds for cutting and folding, scissors and paste, raffia for weaving and basketry. All Kindergartens and a few primary classes have clay or a modeling composite. Many classes now use sand boxes. All these materials are selected, because, while relatively inexpensive, they lend themselves to a variety of uses without special laboratory care and preparation.

PRIMARY READING.

In the lower primary grades, a uniform method of teaching reading is used. The teachers of these grades are skillful in the handling of this subject, and good results are being obtained.

While there is uniformity of method, there is flexibility in its application, and great variation in the devices employed. The fundamental points of this method are (1) the teaching of sight words in groups of sentences so as to make the words learned a real expression of thought, (2) the developing the power to read new words through their form similarity to those that are already known. It is an analytical method. In the early stages, the children deal with sentences and whole words only. Later, phonic symbols are derived through analysis of familiar words. It is, therefore, a sentence word and phonic method.

The words of the first reading vocabulary are selected because of their possibilities in lending themselves to sentences and phrases whose meaning all children can understand. There are sentences which direct the children to games and actions; sentences about playthings, flowers, animals, color; rhymes and jingles. There is a maximum number of concrete words, a minimum number of abstract words. These words are found, in a large measure, in the first pages of many primers. From the first blackboard sentence, reading is thought getting.

The Teachers' Manual and the supplementary leaflets are in the hands of all teachers of the first and second grades. This gives in full the work of the first steps in reading, and outlines the work of the following stages. The lists of words and sentences are arranged to guide and suggest to the teacher, who supplements and varies as her work requires. It is hoped that, with the granting of money for this purpose, printed slips and leaflets may be supplied which will add to the efficiency of the work.

We are most appreciative of the new sets of supplementary readers which have been purchased for all schools. These books are of inestimable value. They are in constant use. They have added to the possibility of arousing genuine interest in reading.

A new series of readers has been adopted by the state to come into use with the opening of the fall term. With this change there should come modifications of our present method which have been in contemplation. Investigations are establishing more and more definitely knowledge of the psychology of reading.

The function of reading is to master the thought of the printed page. Until the child is master of the mechanics of the printed page, however, the mastery of the thought is beyond his power. All reading methods seek to give to the child an early mastery of the mechanics of reading. This is sometimes accomplished at too great a sacrifice, without considering the final test of a good reading method,—what habits of reading are being established. So well is this discussed in a recent article by Dr. Thomas M. Balliet that I beg to quote here—"The well-trained adult in reading recognizes words as wholes and not as composed of separate letters. The eye perceives the printed word, not by perceiving all its letters or parts, but by perceiving the word as a unit, as a whole, either by its form or by certain so-called dominant letters. Adults, therefore, do not read by spelling or by letters; with them the units of perception are words and groups of words. However, when the adult meets with an unfamiliar word he resolves it into its letters. In addition to the habit of perceiving familiar words as wholes, he has also the power of analyzing unfamiliar words into their letters. From this point of view the question of method is, which method will develop in the child this habit of perceiving words, and even phrases. as wholes? As the perception of words as wholes is the predominant or almost universal need, and the analysis of words into letters occurs only occasionally, the habit of word perception as wholes should be developed first, since the habit first formed, in accordance with a familiar psychological law, tends to prevail, other things being equal. After the child has formed this habit, he must learn letters and sounds so as to be able to resolve unfamiliar words into their component parts.

This would suggest that the first methods to be used are the sentence and word methods, to be followed later * * * by some phonic method which is not too analytic."

With appreciation of the cordial support which is unfailingly given in our efforts to render efficient service, I am, Respectfully yours,

LEW ANNA BALL,
Supervisor of Primary Grades.

Department of Music,
San Francisco, August 3, 1915.

Report of Miss Estelle Carpenter.

Mr. Alfred Roncovieri,
Superintendent of Schools,
San Francisco, California.

My Dear Sir:—

In reply to your request, I herewith submit the following report of the work done in the Music Department of the City Schools ending June, 1915.

Many sides of the study of Music have been brought forward. An all round development of the child through the subject has been maintained

In certain classes and schools, some remarkable specialization has been developed, but on the whole, the work has progressed uniformly.

In the school, a relation has been established through Music toward the community, which undeniably will refine, deepen, and unify social relations. Few educational activities make more directly for the higher social life than Music, if it be carried over into the doings of after school life.

And even during school years, the songs of the Graduation Exercises where the parents congregated, the songs of the children at the Mothers' Meetings where the singing was appreciated, the songs given at the dedications and at various school functions, welded the spirit of the school and home together in a common interest.

The Patriotic Songs on patriotic occasions have untold value. No teaching of history will do for patriotic sentiment what a daily school song can do. Patriotism is devotion with the human christening. It idealizes, almost deifies one's country. This feeling intensified by songs, given to the children, weaves better citizenship into the fibre of any community.

From the earliest ages the peoples have expressed their elemental emotions through song and instruments. Music is a universal language and has become an actual necessity in the life of the community, and in the life of the individual. Music inspires and comforts and uplifts and restores the spirit. It brings with it the dewy freshness of the land of Early Youth. It makes vivid impressions and draws on the imagination. It is a vital force through which its beauty and power can lift each soul that comes under its influence into the realm of Art and into a life of nobility and strength for good.

It is no longer a question if we shall include Music in the school curriculum. It is the inherent right of the individual child to obtain an insight into that Art which will undoubtedly enrich his mind and heart.

"The inclination toward Art is universally innate in every human being, just as a perception of truth and love of goodness is a widespread human quality. Certain incipient steps leading toward achievement are taken by every one, and the fact that he can take these, proves that he can perfect himself if he has the opportunity, and can at least appreciate the highest." So in the work I have prepared for the schools, an immense amount of thought has been given to bringing this wonderful Art to the child. Simply at first, and within the comprehension of the immature mind, yet within the activities and enjoyments of the little body and soul, the steps have been measured out that bring into realization the giving of the very best to each one."

Ruskin says: "It is only by Labor that Thought can he made healthy, and only by Thought that Labor can be made Happy." So the Healthy Thought and the Happy Labor have created the various outlines of instruction, so that the most can be obtained from the time allotted. Each moment I have hoped would be used as a royal opportunity.

During the last year well defined outlines were planned and given out by the Supervisor covering all sections of the work. At the regular grade meetings, minute instruction were given to the teachers as to methods and as to subject material. Consideration was given to the Sensory period of the child life, and beautiful songs adapted to the ability of the child were selected and sung to give the interpretation to the teachers.

The child's earliest musical experience is gained by imitation, and from the beginning the choicest material was given. A love of Music was developed, and a love of singing created. The child learned by doing the thing himself. William Harris says: ''Education, in order to be a preparation for Life, should be a Participation in Life.''

During the Sensory period it is a time for concrete experiences. Suggestion, imagination, and imitation fill a large part of the child's life, therefore many songs have been given which induce action, and they have become a part of the child's experience and thus build the beginning of his educational structure. With the songs much rhythm and ear-training have been given. The Ancients expressed themselves through song and dance, therefore steps, motions, and beats have been given through the use of the body. By means of artistic singing and by action, a feeling for tonality and rhythm is developed.

During the past two years, in the beginning stage, an important side of the instruction has been strengthened. The child that could not perceive pitch of tones was carefully helped. The monotone is produced by wrong use of vocal organs caused by disease or carelessness, and lack of concentration and practice. These cases have been treated, and remarkable results effected in many instances.

In the Associative Period strength of endurance, quick sure memory, drill, and discipline come easily. There is interest in result of the activities, thus definite problems were taken with interest. Voice and ear-training, rhythm, oral and written dictation, phrasing and sight-singing were handled so that the capacity of the child was strengthened by drill. Careful training in phrasing made rapid sight reading and correct expression possible. Improvements in the above mentioned lines are noticeable.

Ear-training and sight-singing provide mental drill and through their use give an introduction to great works in music. Oral and written dictation are steps in development of creative power and form impetus towards composition. Appreciation during the last year has been given through recognition of various airs such as: "Anvil Chorus", "Wedding March", "Old Folks' Songs", "Toreador", "Soldiers' Chorus", and other classics. This work should be materially aided by the use of phonographs. In each school there should be a Victrola or grapophone of some kind, and records should be supplied so that the worlds great airs could be recognized.

Into the Adolescent period the above elements are carried in such preportion as to contribute to the interest at this time. The Adolescent period is characterized by physical development, and is the time the child matures into young manhood or womanhood. The emotions are predominant and through Music an appeal can be made to the heart with such strength, and to the artistic nature with such discrimination that a permanent effect will be made toward high ideals in character building, and good taste for life. Beauty of melody and harmony appeal, and through singing there will be an impress towards the higher social and spiritual life.

During the last year the upper grades have been stimulated by productions of the best songs. In regular work and at the graduations the following songs have been given:—"The Two Grenadiers", "Intermezzo Cavalleria Rusticania", "The Sextette" from "Lucia", "Pilgrims' Chorus", Verdi; "Pilgrims' Chorus", Wagner; "Soldiers' Chorus", Gounod; "Lift Thine Eyes", Mendelssohn; "Miserere" and other selections from "Il Trovatore", "Handel's Largo", "Toreador" from Carmen, "The Heavens Resound" by Beethoven, "Serenade" by Gounod, selections by Schubert and Schumann, "Lost Chord" by Sullivan, "Blue Danube", Strauss; Mendelssohn's "Spring Song", "Stars and Stripes", by Sousa, and many other beautiful part songs, folk songs and patriotic songs. Songs from our modern composers have been used and California's composers have been given prominence through use of songs. Dr. H. J. Stewart's "Pohono" and "California", Oscar Weil "Spring Song", Metcalf's "Absent' and "Land of Dreams", Pasmore's "Hail California", Pickenscher's "Brass Band", and Savannah's and McCurrie's "Songs of Child Life" have been studied.

Through all the work the sweet tone of the child voice has been preserved and developed. There has been a steady devotion to the ideal of beautiful tone. The voices are helped and during the time of mutation the voices are watched and treated. During the past year the tone quality has been greatly improved.

In the regular meetings with the grade teachers, guidance as to methods was suggested. The regular teacher is by training and experience expert in developing the child. With a knowledge of methods in the Music teaching, and with some knowledge of the subject, the teacher becomes the medium through which the Supervisor reaches the individual child.

There has been an improvement along the line of endeavor amongst the teachers. This is partly due to the instruction given in classes to a number of the regular teachers and to the instruction given at the headquarters of the Music Department after school hours. There is also an evident responsibility on the part of the teachers towards the teaching of Music, and there is a growing love toward the subject. Many of the teachers are musical, and attend concerts. and are keenly alive to the necessity of helping the child in the music lesson.

Whenever a teacher is capable of doing her own work, the work is exacted. If she is not capable, an exchange of work is made. In some schools if there are a number of teachers who are not capable in Music, the work is given to one teacher who is certificated and appointed by the Board of Education, as special teacher, and is given extra compensation. There are thirty-two such teachers in the Music Department besides a number who take the singing of their schools without the extra compensation. They have formed a power in the Music work as their systematic instruction has been most helpful. I recommend that a few of these teachers be appointed during the next year.

In a large department such as this, some schools have required more attention and inspection than others, as some schools have been visited more often than others. Where the principal has organized the work carefully and where the teachers have followed directions of the Supervisor, the work has been excellent.

These directions were given for the year during February in a series of meetings at which one thousand teachers were addressed, and at which one hundred songs were sung. The guidance and experience of the Supervisor is multiplied through the meetings and through the co-operation of the teachers. The teachers are a vital factor in carrying out the work. I commend highly the faithful, skillful work of our teachers and I appreciate intensely the spirit of their earnest co-operation.

There have been a number of people who have visited the music work and they have freely expressed their pleasures at the results shown them. Some have even said that they have not anywhere enjoyed Public School music more, and they were particularly impressed with the co-operation that exists between the teachers and the Supervisor.

During the spring and summer of 1914, I took an extended trip through the East to address the Music Supervisors' National Conference, and to inspect school systems throughout the United States and to observe the music work. Schools were visited in twenty cities with interest and profit. Nowhere did I hear the equal of the tone quality or expression secured by the best classes here. The recollection comes to mind that Madame Tetrazzini sent for me after the singing of the Garfield children at Lotta's Fountain and said, "Nowhere in the world do the children sing as sweetly as they do in San Francisco".

Children were encouraged to attend the concerts of the San Francisco Symphony Orchestra while studying some of Henry Hadley's songs. Simple lessons in biography and talks on orchestral instruments were given. The People's Philharmonic Orchestra under Mr. Herman Periet has given concerts and amongst the audience many public school children were present.

A number of small orchestras have been formed during the past years in the various schools. Time after school has been given to practice with a teacher of music in charge.

During the past two years on a number of occasions the children have sung under my direction at dedications, Mother Clubs, Playground affairs, and graduations. Some of these events have frequently occurred on Sundays, Saturdays, and holidays. Among this number a chorus of volunteer children sang at a dedication of the monument to Verdi on the date of his birth, 1914. This took place at the bandstand at Golden Gate Park accompanied by Mr. Cassasa's band. The songs from Italian opera and Italian folk selections lent pleasure and enthusiasm to the event. At the close of the ceremonies the audience was kept waiting by the Committee, and to prevent restlessness, I suggested that the children sing the old folk songs and invited the audience to join with them. The effect was wonderful as 8,000 people standing closely together were singing in perfect time, with expression and keen enjoyment. The singing became a part of the city, joining all classes in community interest.

Madame Schumann Heink in Festival Hall at the Panama Exposition gave a free concert on Saturday afternoon to the children. Through the diva's invitation I directed the four thousand young voices in patriotic songs and the event was memorable for the splendid singing, the behavior, and the attention the children gave the great singer, who was delighted. I cannot let this opportunity pass without expression of my deep appreciation for the wonderful kindness of Madame Schumann Heink in giving us such inspiration through her marvelous songs. This is the second time she has bestowed upon San Francisco's children her precious gift of song. In the spring of 1914, eight thousand seventh and eighth grade children were invited by her to a free concert at the Pavilion Rink. The occasion was a memorable event; generously the Madame poured out her glorious tones, and the children will ever remember them and be inspired by the recollection of that Saturday afternoon.

In the Cosmopolitan schools variety has been given to the work by the study of the songs of the different countries in the native languages.

In the three intermediate schools the work is carried on departmentally with good results. In these schools some remarkable singing has been developed as they have more time for the subject than the other schools. All the schools should have more time for the study of singing and music.

The graduation exercises of the Horace Mann School were interesting as one thousand children sang together sustained by the orchestra made up by the pupils from the school.

The Panama Exposition has brought tremendous opportunities to all in a musical way. The teachers and many of the children are gaining much inspiration from this source. I trust that the pupils when they visit the Fair will take the time to listen to the splendid band concerts throughout the grounds.

There have been many events during the past five years when the children's singing has contributed in some measure to the unbuilding of the Panama Expositiou. At the first tree planting in the Exposition grounds the children sang some patriotic songs. The Chinese from the Oriental school sang at the ground breaking exercises of the Chinese site. The Chinese band played at this occasion also. At the ground breaking exercises of the Machinery Hall a chorus of children took part. When the Liberty Bell was asked for from Philadelphia, songs were sung in every school to arouse enthusiasm. The Madison school children sang in two public performances for the Liberty Bell. There was a chorus of three hundred children taken from ten schools which sang at the ground breaking exercises of the City Hall and Auditorium given by the Exposition.

I received an invitation for the San Francisco school children to sing in the Welsh Festival known as the Eisteddfod held under the auspices of the International Exposition, but on account of the vacation it was not considered.

The children's singing has greatly entered into the life of the city, and has been a part of the foundations of the growth of San Francisco after the calamity. From the chorus given June 2, 1906; through the many choruses given at school dedications, about thirty in all; through the great choruses such as Fleet, Portola, Admission, Tetrazzini, Park Dedications, and school functions, the singing of the children has occupied an unique place in the history of our city, and has been a factor in the community.

At the beginning of the last school year, the assistant, Mrs. Mary D. McGlade, was promoted to the High Schools to take charge of the music in those schools, where she is obtaining excellent results.

During the last month my headquarters have been moved from the Golden Gate School to the Moulder school. I wish to thank the Board of Education for establishing me in such comfortable and convenient quarters.

In every way the study of music is encouraged, and all children are asked to join concerts, to play piano or the other instruments, and to cultivate the voice.

Constantly I have striven to keep before all, the thought that music in the public schools is one of the greatest needs of the child. Through it, not only enjoyment and skill are obtained for the individual, but it is a leavening power that reaches the innermost recesses of the soul, and through its practice the use of the higher emotions are brought into play and thus it uplifts the mind and spirit. To this process pure motives inspire noble deeds and actions and produce good citizenship.

I wish to recommend the following:

(a) That two pianos be given to each large school.

(b) That in transferring and assigning teachers, the musical ability be taken into consideration with the musical need of the school.

(c) That special notices be sent to the children about the Symphony Concerts for the coming season by the Board of Education.

(d) That the Superintendent send to schools supplementary books "Stories of Great Musicians" by Hurne and Scobey.

(e) That supplementary books be allowed for the teachers of the second and third grades to be selected by the Supervisor.

(f) That supplementary octavo material to be selected by Supervisor be given to each school for upper grade use.

(g) That Supervisor of Music be allowed to select an assistant when funds afford it.

(h) That a Victrola or phonograph be given to each school, and traveling library of records be used.

(i) That a typewriting machine be sent to the office of Supervisor.

(j) That music books, destroyed by the fire, be restored to the schools.

I wish to thank the teachers for their good work, and the principals for their support of the music department.

I am appreciative of the help given by the Assistant and the co-operation of the special teachers of the various schools.

I am deeply grateful to the Superintendent and to the Deputy Superintendents and to the Honorable Board of Education for their assistance and kindness.

I am,

Sincerely yours,

ESTELLE CARPENTER,

Supervisor of Music.

San Francisco, June 6, 1915.

Honorable Alfred Roncovieri,
Superintendent of Schools.

My Dear Sir:—

I take pleasure in submitting the following as my report from the department of Drawing and Art of the elementary schools, and for the four years ending June 6, 1915.

I am pleased to inform you that the proportion of successful achievement in our schools is greater than in any preceding period, and the interest on the part of both the pupils and teachers is constantly increasing.

While the results as a whole are good, considering that but one hour a week is given to the subject, there are places in the department—particular classes, taught by teachers eminently qualified to teach the subject—where the work is of exceptional quality, which we are frequently told is comparable not only to similar grade work in other cities, but to that of the higher schools.

Our foreign visitors, particularly those of the profession, are more than enthusiastic regarding the character and quality of our design. One gratifying appreciation came from Mr. and Mrs. Albert Herter of the Herter Studios of New York City, who visiting San Francisco a year ago, were so impressed by the designs of the pupils of the grammar schools, that they agreed to buy from the children any of their designs I should submit, for the purpose of reproduction in their textile industries.

Learning to draw and design is largely dependent upon sympathetic and scientific teaching, hence if it were possible to departmentalize the subject and designate to teachers—who by natural fitness and necessary training are qualified to teach the subject, the results would be more uniform than is possible under existing conditions.

In every corporation the wise administrators see the economic value of assigning each kind of work to the particular individual who is best qualified to perform it. If we could follow this example in our schools, particularly for the teaching of the special subjects, by arranging for an interchange of teachers and classes, it would tend to equalize the opportunities of our pupils and advance their development to a surprising degree.

The value of drawing as a medium of expression, its actual necessity as an adjunct to technical and industrial accomplishment, is practically a settled question, and while we in California are not as yet a manufacturing people, and there is at present only a limited demand for talented and trained workmen, we cannot ignore the fact that among our young there are many who have the right to demand of the public school system at least the chance of being discovered and directed to institutions, where they may be trained for expert service.

It is only a question of time when the Pacific Coast will rival the East in industries, and until then our pupils—talented in the arts—may pursue their vocations in other localities of our country and thereby be saved as a valuable industrial asset to the nation.

To the art supervisor of a large city, constant opportunity affords itself for the full realization of the pitiful waste of native and creative ability due to the inadequate facilities for its development and preservation.

We hear and read a great deal today about vocational guidance and the question naturally arises "What do the different vocations demand of the worker that can be supplied by our schools"? Is it not a training in the fundamentals of craftsmanship coupled with the development of the human faculties, that makes the pupil adaptable to the demands of a vocation? Or is it expected that the school shall equip him with a technical training that will enable him to compete with the experienced workman?

Can the typical elementary or high school, in the limited time at its disposal, hope to give a training for any vocation that is the equivalent of an apprenticeship, and simultaneously accomplish all that is required by the literary and scientific courses?

Has the capacity for achievement in art and artifice, of the average grammar and high school pupil, as yet been determined, beyond the mere working out of a problem from dictation or the following of a formula?

Is it possible for a school to do more for technical and industrial training than lay a foundation upon which later a superstructure may be built, unless it be a technical school devoted to but one trade, and giving a lengthy and comprehensive course of instruction in all the ramifications of the craft?

Do we fully realize how much time it requires to become proficient as an artisan? How much training is necessary to draw technically and design artistically; to weave a patterned textile; to model a vase or turn it on the potter's wheel; to do a piece of artistic painting—illuminating the text, binding the book and tooling the leather of its cover; to produce any of the many articles of use or beauty made of brass, bronze, iron or wood; to create a beautiful costume including millinery and jewelry?

There is a vast difference between educational art and artifice and technical art and artifice.

With an investment of an hour a week, we can give our children an appreciation of the beauties of nature and of art, but only in a limited degree, teach them some of the fundamental principles of design and instruct them regarding standards of excellence which govern skilled workmanship; but no more.

If our graduates from the grammar schools are expected to have trained eyes and skilled hands, it will be necessary to double, treble, yea quadruple, the time now given to the subject.

For some years there has been a demand upon the Drawing and Art Department to correlate the work with the manual training and domestic arts. In every instance it has meant that the particular drawing related to those two special deparments should be substituted for the fundamentals of freehand drawing and the elements of design which constitute the general training of the subject. With an additional period and the departmentalizing of the work in the grammar schools, such correlation would be possible, but not under existing conditions.

During the past four years the Drawing Department has prepared two exhibitions. The first was shown at the San Francisco Institute of Art during the meeting of the National Education Association in July, 1911. Upon this occasion we received many gratifying expressions of appreciation from visiting experts, and for weeks following the great convention, our office was kept busy sending our outlines, course of study and samples of pupils' work, to art teachers and art supervisors in this country and in Europe.

One notable instance of this appreciation came from Miss Kate Stevens, the delegate from Great Britain to the convention. Miss Stevens was so impressed by the work, that she wrote a letter to the Board of Education, commenting most favorably upon the exhibition and requesting a contribution of our drawings for the London schools.

The second exhibition we prepared was shown at the Fourth International Congress for the Promotion of Art Education held in Dresden, August, 1912. It was a great honor for the city, that the American Committee for the Dresden Congress, included San Francisco in the group of metropolitan cities selected to represent the educational art of the United States. The other cities being favored were Boston, Chicago, Cleveland, St. Louis and Denver.

In addition to these cities several Art Normal schools and a rural district were invited to show their work. The former included Columbia University, Pratt Institute, Boston Art Normal, Chicago Art Institute, Miss Emma Church's School, Chicago and Newcomb College; and the latter, one of the sections of the State of New York.

The Dresden exhibition was designed to give the clearest possible survey of the art teaching of the present day and the methods adopted in the different counties, showing typical sequential examples of all stages of the work of schools of various grades. The advance sheets of directions from the administrative committee to exhibitors stated:

"It is highly desirable that the selected work shall clearly show the method of teaching and its results. Great importance will be attached to new experiments in teaching will show deviation from existing syllabus and methods, and indicate new ways and aims." With this end in view, the committee sought such cities and institutions, which represented individual effort and stand for the working out of local problems under local conditions.

It was a great privilege to attend this great convention and most interesting to see how the work of each nation expressed its local characteristics and ideals of life.

Three months preceding the Dresden Congress, I saw the exhibitions of Art and Manual Training shown in connection with the two great conventions of Art and Manual Training, which included representative work from the principal cities and institutions of the Middle West and the Atlantic Coast. These conventions I had the honor of addressing, one convening in Cincinnati and the other in Baltimore, during the early part of May.

In comparing the work of the European and American schools, I felt that the latter excelled in the primary and grammar grades, but in the high schools, Europe is considerably in advance of us, and it was the opinion of everyone present, that the technical schools of the latter have no parallel in our country.

The particular exhibit which attracted the greatest attention among attendants at the Congress was that of the Kunstgewerbe Schule of Vienna. In the Sonderkurs fur Jugendkunst—the experimental school for children—under the direction of Prof. Cizek, we found the demonstration of the problem of dealing with the talented child in a technical school. For this school, we were told, is restricted to pupils who in the common schools have shown exceptional ability in some particular line of artistic endeavor.

The children enter at the age of eight and remain six years. There appear to be three separate courses of instruction: one devoted exclusively to graphic illustration, another to design in its application to construction and decoration, and the third to modeling in its different forms.

Each pupil is given the particular course which meets his individual needs.

Prof. Cizek has discovered that it takes time to learn an art, for half of the pupil's time of six year's attendance at the school is given exclusively to but one of these three courses, the remaining half being given to the academic subjects.

Other exhibits that impressed me favorably were those from Leipzig, Hamburg, Prague, Buda-pest, Plauen and Weimar.

The design of all the Austrian and German products commanded our admiration for its sincerity. It was most apparent that the mastery of technique in drawing and a knowledge of the abstract principles of design are a fundamental necessity for advancement in any kind of industrial work.

In investigating the conditions which led to such successful achievement, I find that the preparation of the teachers—grade as well as special—is an important factor. In a number of places, the grade teacher is compelled to devote the major part of two years out of six, given to normal training, to art and handcraft, while the special teacher is obliged to give in addition to the above, two years exclusively to the study of the special subject.

I also find that not only are the schools well equipped with tools, materials, models, charts and helpful publications, but the art and industrial museums, which abound in Europe, are as potent an educational factor as are the libraries; and every municipality encourages in many ways every kind of art and industrial achievement.

In addition to the great exhibition shown at Dresden, the attendants enjoyed the great congress which offered addresses, papers and discussions on the following topics:

The Underlying Principles of Elementary Art Teaching
Drawing the Universal Language
Drawing, Manual Work and Language as a Means of Expression
The General Raising of Graphic Expression as a Cultural Necessity
The Relation of Drawing and Manual Training
National Art in Primary Schools
Ornamental Art of the Child
Ornamental Design
Colors and Their Significance
Aesthetic Lettering as a Means of Art Education
The Cultivation of Taste Through Drawing and Manual Work
The Training of Teachers and Supervisors of Drawing, Art and Manual Training
The Necessity for Special Colleges for the Training of These Teachers
Special Normal Art Courses
Art Training a Necessity in Universities
Museum Co-operation in Art Training

These addresses were given in German, French and English. There were also special meetings for Esperanto and Ido.

The attendance at such a congress was a great privilege—an epoch in a professional life. I appreciate, to the fullest extent, the value of this experience. My only regret is that I could not share it with my co-workers, my assistants and the grade teachers who rendered such valuable service in the production of the work we exhibited. I returned to my work recuperated and renewed, full of inspiration and enthusiasm, which I trust may prove to be a source of profit to the department I direct and a benefit to the children of our city.

During the past two years, the pupils of the Grammar and High Schools have been given an opportunity to see a very interesting collection of pictures—reproductions of masterpieces—suitable for schoolroom decoration. The exhibition is the property of the firm of Sanborn Vail & Co., who not only generously loaned it to the department, but bore all the expense of transportation to and from the school buildings. The interest and delight in these pictures was so great with both pupils and teachers, that it was generally felt that our department should own a permanent traveling picture exhibition which could be sent annually to each school.

Picture study is valuable educationally and culturally, for while it can be beneficially correlated with history and geography, it also offers a training of the eye for the appreciation of the beautiful. Every school should be decorated with pictures suitable to the children of the classroom. In some localities the Mothers' Clubs organized in connection with the schools,—feeling the need for some such decoration,—have presented their respective schools with such collections.

Of the recommendations, which you request me to make regarding any improvements pertaining to my department, I desire to say, that in addition to departmentalizing the work in the grammar grades, I feel that every school building should be provided with a specially equipped drawing room, where the classes may be taught and where not only the models may be kept and all illustrative exhibits may be installed, but where the work of the subject may be permanently placed on exhibition.

I conclusion I wish to express my appreciation of the courtesy of yourself and your staff, as well as of that of the Board of Education, for the kindly consideration of our needs, and particularly desire to thank the Board most sincerely for housing the office of the drawing department in its present comfortable quarters at the Moulder School.

I further wish to thank the principals and teachers of the department for their sympathetic co-operation in carrying out our plans, and give full recognition to my three assistants, who not only are faithful but able. Their interest, professional spirit and industry constitutes one of the important factors in the success of our work.

Respectfully yours,

KATHERINE M. BALL,
Supervisor of Drawing.

REPORT OF SUPERVISOR OF MANUAL TRAINING.

San Francisco, June 30, 1915.

Hon. Alfred Roncovieri,
Supt. of Schools,
San Francisco, Cal.

Dear Sir:—

Pursuant to your request, I submit the following report for the school year ending June 30, 1915:

The following is a list of the Manual Training teachers and of the laboratories in which they teach:

H. C. Bagot	Mission Grammar
R. C. Bowman	Fairmount
H. Carne	Hamilton Intermediate
E. Carmichael	Hamilton Intermediate
L. E. Davidson	Pacific Heights
W. C. Davidson	Hancock and Washington
P. F. Dailey	Crocker Intermediate
W. C. Denvir	Crocker Intermediate
D. W. Dowling	Horace Mann Intermediate
M. J. Doyle	Bay View, Glen Park, Sheridan
M. A. Felton	Bryant, Irving M. Scott, Oriental
G. FitzGerald	Everett, Roosevelt
J. Hedge	John Swett
D. Richards	Horace Mann Intermediate
W. Stillwell	Ethan Allen, Monroe, Spring Valley
T. Stevens	Franklin, Laguna Honda
A. M. Sylvia	Frank McCoppin, Sutro

ELEMENTARY SCHOOLS.

In the Elementary Schools, boys of the Seventh and Eighth Grades receive one lession of from 90 to 120 minutes per week in Manual Training. Immediate provision should be made to extend the work to include boys of the Sixth Grades.

During the past year an occasional free teaching period has afforded opportuntiy to give instruction in this subject to selected groups of "retarded" boys, such boys being twelve years or older and enrolled below the Sixth Grade.

The beneficial effect of this kind of instruction upon this type of boy is very marked. A definite policy regarding this element of our school population should be inaugurated to the end that every "retarded" boy of proper age receives at least one lesson per week in the Manual Training Laboratory.

During the year the laboratory at the Oriental School was equipped and occupied. It is well furnished and in the main quite satisfactory.

The laboratory at the Adams School was taken over for classrooms, the boys going to the John Swett laboratory instead.

This is the second one of our new laboratories to be taken over for classroom purposes, the other being at the James Lick School.

It might be of interest in this connection to note that the only laboratory remaining from pre-conflagration days is at the Crocker Intermediate School.

INTERMEDIATE SCHOOLS.

In each of three Intermediate Schools are two woodworking laboratories and also, except in the Crocker School, a laboratory for metal work.

The time allotted to Manual Training in these schools is as follows: Sixth Grade, 80 minutes; Seventh Grade, 160 minutes; and Eighth Grade, 160 minutes per week.

This is a reduction of from 30 to 50 per cent under the time allowed during the past two years and includes a similar reduction in the time given to sewing and cooking by the girls.

A motor and lathe has recently been ordered for the Crocker School, being the first power machinery furnished for the use of grammar school pupils. Every laboratory should have a motor and some power machinery.

MECHANICAL DRAWING.

Mechanical Drawing has a specific time allotment in the three Intermediate Schools and is taught partly by Manual Training teachers and partly by others.

The teacher of Mechanical Drawing in schools of this kind should be one who has had considerable mechanical experience and training in practical construction and handling of materials.

Drawing fancy lines in fantastic combinations has no place in the elementary stage of this work. The work should embrace problems of practical application and importance and should be subordinate to the work of the laboratory.

In the Seventh and Eighth Grades of the elementary schools there is no definite time set apart for this subject. A portion of the Manual Training time, just sufficient to teach the pupil to make simple working plans, is taken for this purpose.

It might be well to consider giving all Seventh and Eighth Grade boys a lesson in Mechanical Drawing per week in addition to their present work in Freehand Drawing.

EXPOSITION.

At the invitation of the Director of the Department of Education of the Panama-Pacific International Exposition, we placed a small exhibit of Sixth Grade work in the Palace of Education. The jury awarded gold medals to the two schools furnishing the exhibit.

Respectfully,

F. K. BARTHEL,
Supervisor.

REPORT OF SUPERVISOR OF HOME ECONOMICS, JUNE 5, 1915.

Mr. Alfred Roncovieri,
Superintendent of Schools,
San Francisco, Cal.

Dear Sir:—

I beg to submit the following report of the Home Economics Department for the fiscal year 1914-15.

Personnel.

Supervisor	1	
Teachers, in Intermediate Schools	3	
Teachers, in other elementary schools	10	
Part-time teacher, emergency substitutes	1	15

Plant.

Domestic science laboratories, Intermediate Schools	3	
Domestic Science laboratories, other elementary schools	24	27
Dining-rooms, Intermediate schools		2

Enrollment and Cost.

Average monthly enrollment	3,956.8
Cost of cooking supplies and laundry	$2,153.31
Cost of cooking supplies and laundry, per pupil	0.656

Visits to Domestic Science Laboratories.

By school officials	60
By supervisor	331
By others	1206
Total	1597

A two years' course in elementary domestic science is given to all the girls of the 7th and 8th grades. Each class has one lesson a week, the lessons varying in length from eighty minutes to two hours.

In the Crocker and Hamilton Intermediate schools, cooking is taught to the girls of the B-6th grade also, and the girls of the 7th and 8th grades have six lessons a month. In the Horace Mann Intermediate school, it has not been possible to give the girls more than one laboratory period a week, but in this school special effort has been made to correlate other studies with domestic science. The arithmetic teachers have given the girls a special course in household accounts, and the art and domestic art teachers have helped in the planning and furnishing of the dining-room.

The lessons given to all our 7th and 8th grade girls are essentially the same. It is a course of lessons in elementary domestic science, and treats of the selection and preparation of food. However, as we have a varied and cosmopolitan school population, some of our recipes and the method of presenting certain subjects are adapted to meet special tastes and needs. We use, as text-book, a series of forty leaflets, prepared by me. We have also a printed outline of lessons.

In addition to the work with foods, we began last term, a series of short lessons on the house, its equipment and care. This was given to the 8th grade girls. As a preparation for this course, our home economics teachers made a survey of the housing conditions in the neighborhoods of their schools and studied prices and quality in local firms dealing in household effects. During the spring term our laboratories have been used for practice teaching by both the University of California, and the Lux School, of San Francisco. While there are still some details to be worked out, the plan has worked well. Four cadet-teachers from the University and one from the Lux School have taught cooking, and two from the Lux school have taught sewing. The Lux students have substituted for my teachers, allowing them to visit schools.

During the months of April and May, the Home Economics teachers have taken all the pupils of our classes, some four thousand, to the Exposition, to learn about milling at the Sperry Flour Exhibit in the Food Products Palace. Two teachers went each day, each teacher being responsible for about sixty pupils. The Supervisor accompanied one teacher, and the other was assisted by a cadet-teacher kindly detailed for the purpose by the San Francisco State Normal School. The girls were given an interesting talk on milling by a representative of the Sperry Flour Co., after which they were divided into small groups and given competent guides who took them through the mill, bakery, laboratory and cooking booths, and let them sample foreign and other cookery. The morning so spent seemed of real educational value, and the girls were returned to their respective schools in time for the afternoon session.

seeing others succeeding where he fails and realizes that little is expected of him and settles down to morose inertia or becomes incorrigible. In the special class he finds he can do as well as others and possibly better than some and is allowed to work along some line of manual or industrial work for which he has special aptitude.

He begins to feel the spur of being able to accomplish something for himself and though the progress may be slow he is almost sure to make material gain.

In San Francisco no general survey of the schools has been made but certain districts have been examined and enough of these subnormal children found out to prove the necessity for the organization of several of these classes.

At present the work is limited to two classes in the Ungraded Primary school and one which is being organized in the Buena Vista School.

In the Ungraded Primary School thirty-three subnormal and backward children have been cared for in the past two years.

These children range in physical age from seven to seventeen years and mentally from four to nine years. Five backward children have been brought up to normal grade work and sent back to regular classes. Two boys of fourteen and sixteen years were taken to Sonoma State Home and there are three cases which should receive institutional care. The remaining members of the class are trainable along simple vocational lines and able to receive simple academic instruction. It would seem advisable on account of the crowded condition of schools in this part of the city to make of the Ungraded School property a subnormal center. It is near enough several large schools to relieve them of their special cases and still segregate these children in their own district which is the best policy. There is also plenty of room for the outdoor activities which are so necessary in this work.

There are no doubt other congested districts where public schools are near together and two or three special classes needed. These schools might find it almost impossible to give up one room for fifteen pupils. Often an old school building is left unoccupied when a new one is built and can be utilized at little expense. Here would be found room for shops for boys and rooms where girls could be trained in simple home duties and industries. This plan has been carried out successfully in some cities.

These unfortunate children form a portion of the material furnished by the community for instruction in the schools. The schools have now to a certain degree adapted themselves to the need of all children and undertaken the task of training and educating all classes. All this tends toward making the public schools a more efficient instrument for the education of all the children of the State, and is but another upward step in the cause of education and the uplifting of mankind.

LOUISE M. LOMBARD.

REPORT OF ETHAN ALLEN PARENTAL SCHOOL.

On July 27, 1914, we opened our school with 56 boys; on that day we paroled 14. On January 3, 1915, we paroled 16 boys. In addition to paroling 30 boys, we allowed 12 to go to work. Of the 30 paroled boys, 3 were compelled to return; the rest keeping up with the class work, in many cases having been promoted, during the term advancing a grade or two. Several boys are attending High School and making good records. The boys sent to work have proven satisfactory and all have been able to advance in the places we sent them.

During the term we received 93 boys. They are either truants or incorrigibles sent by Superintendent's office or through the Juvenile Court. The purpose of the school is to receive chronic truants and school-room incorrigibles, who cannot be profitably handled in the regular schools (for a short period of training) and then return them to the home school. They are trained in habits of obedience and application; the idea of punishment is subordinate to training. Watchfulness and a spirit of co-operation among the boys are relied upon to hold the boys. Each is made to feel that there is fairness in the treatment to all and that each boy is in a measure responsible for the conduct of the school. In attendance the school has ranked among the highest and much is due to the boys themselves; they acting as truant officers. If a boy has been a truant or in the habit of running away from home, he is brought back by one of the boys and made to feel that it is his duty to do right.

The school contains 4 regular classrooms, that can be thrown into one and used as an assembly hall, a workshop, a manual training room, a reading and game room for the boys, a dining room, a kitchen, laundry and wash-room that contains 5 shower-baths, 3 bath-tubs and 5 wash-stands. Each boy has two baths a week, he has his own locker in which is kept 2 towels, tooth brush, comb and change of underwear if necessary.

Our school work is ungraded, consisting of grades from 1st to 8th. We follow the regular course of study, slightly modified to meet the special, individual conditions, so that a boy may fit in readily when paroled.

In addition to the regular curriculum we have established and are carrying on successfully rug-weaving, making of stockings, shawls, runners, towels, brush-work, wood-work, cobbling and gardening. Each boy is assigned a garden of his own. He is taught to care for the veegtables commonly grown. He derives no pecuniary benefit from his garden, but all the boys become much interested in this work. An effort is made to plan crops so that all produce can be used in the kitchen. Enough vegetables are raised to supply 100 boys with a luncheon daily. The work in manual training and gardening have proved valuable in developing habits of control and inspiring interest.

In industrial work our boys are given assignments by turn to assist in the various activities of the school and thus encourage "Vocational Discovery". Nearly all the boys become greatly interested in wood-work, gardening and the other industries. Many opportunities for correlating the manual and school work occur.

Boys are not consulted as to what or how much they wish to do, as they are immature in judgment and have no experience on which to base a choice; moreover boys of this type need training and continued application to break up the habits of shifting from one thing to another as fancy directs. This training becomes valuable to them when they attempt to fill positions later.

The Ethan Allen Parental School has endeavored to keep the school system by being prepared to take boys who need its corrective influence with as great promptness as possible. The truant is often the graduated incorrigible. His absence from school is a sequel to his trouble in school. Occasionally a boy is simply nomadic or migratory—will not stay at home or in school. A boy who answers the call of the street and the gang, becomes addicted to cigarettes, gambling and other vices of the alley, cannot long remain good. The temptation to vandalism and thievery is strong. Delinquents begin as truants and many a criminal has taken his first lesson on the streets when he should have been in school. The lack of "team-work" on the part of the parents accounts for many of the lapses of childhood. The death of a parent is serious to the child; disagreement of parents, the influence of drunkenness, crime, vice and abuse on the part of the parent is tragic. Misdemeanors are hidden from the father, deception is a common thing, and too often the responsibilities of parenthood are regarded lightly and through it all the child is the loser.

On account of the varied manual training habits of industry are established which are strong enough to lure the boy away from the street life which has had such a strong hold on him. Boys of this type under the school environment of this school develop habits of conduct, concentration, cleanliness and character which enables them to take their places by the side of normal children in regular schools.

A playground furnished with necessary appliances is provided for the school. The supervision of play is considered as important as that of work or study and every effort is made to cultivate an attitude of cheerful co-operation among the boys. It is remarkable that boys who have always been against the established order of things should so soon show a spirit of loyalty, and assume so much responsibility in its management. They have great admiration for firmness and precision and corresponding contempt for sentimentality and "gush", or for one who is easy. The new boy who has passed as a hero at home in his misdemeanors is soon disappointed in the results of his efforts here.

On Tuesday, Thursday and Friday morning the entire school assembles for patriotic exercises and singing.

The time of detention varies. It is very necessary to have a definite system in determining when a boy shall be paroled. Many of the boys received are in poor physical condition. The use of cigarettes, exposure and staying out at night, and other bad practices usually bring about a state of poor vitality. Before corrective influences can be effective, the physical conditions must be improved, therefore a weekly dietary has been prepared with a view to supplying a right amount of each of the food elements necessary to the proper nourishment of these boys. This means that the menu for every Monday is practically the same, varied of course by the market conditions and the season. During the summer we have so many vegetables that vegetables enter largely in the diet. The boys are taught to set a table, wash dishes, clean the kitchen and how to behave properly at the table.

As it is necessary to improve the physical condition of the boys, I recommend that a physician be appointed to make weekly or semi-weekly visits to the school examining the boys for physical defects as well as to general condition.

We have a Patrons' and Mothers' Club in connection with the school, and we find that these are great factors in drawing closer bonds between home and school; very often boys misunderstood at home are readjusted in their home relations, through the closer relation established between the teacher and the child.

During the regular vacation it has been our custom to send many of the boys berry picking under the guidance of the Boys' and Girls' Aid Society. Their industry has enabled them to pay for the summer outing and a little money besides. The boys remaining in the city are looked after by three trained women from the Juvenile Protective Association (patrons of our school). They visits the homes upon friendly relations, at least 4 or 5 times during the vacation, getting a full account of conduct. This is kept on record. By this means we keep in touch with all the boys during vacation which in my mind is far more important than regular school time. Very few, if any, of our boys get in trouble during the vacation.

We have a circulating library in connection with the school in order to cultivate a taste for good reading. We also have a Balopticon and Stereopticon used for illustrated lectures and teaching of Geography and History. During the school term from 1914 to 1915, we sold enough rugs, shawls, etc., to pay for material for the succeeding term. We also paid $25 for an extra rug loom, $90 for a stocking machine and enough money left to buy four sets of stereographs to be used in the study of geography. Each boy is encouraged to save money and nearly all the boys have a bank book. I act as guardian for the boy.

I recommend that the curfew law be strictly enforced; boys not allowed to attend mevies at night unless accompanied by parents. and particularly see that the boys are not allowed to peddle on wood wagons or act as caddy at the golf links, as the little money they earn, together with the vast amount of liberty, gives them a desire to leave home and under these conditions they come under very evil influences.

As many of these boys have a tendency to gamble, I recommend that a very strict supervision by the police by established over the city.

I suggest that a special fund be set aside by the Supervisors to provide for additional equipment to be used in the school.

The school has been much encouraged by the Board of Education, the Superintendent's office, Juvenile Court, Mothers' and Patrons' Club of Ethan Allen School, as well as by the cheerful co-operation of principals.

Respectfully,

RAE ALEXANDER,
Principal.

REPORT ON DETENTION HOME SCHOOL.

San Francisco, June 14th, 1915.

To the Board of Education,
San Francisco, Cal.

Ladies and Gentlemen:

I herewith submit a synopsis of the records I have kept in the Detention Home. I feel impelled to do so by the knowledge that there is some misunderstanding in regard to the ages and grades of the children. I hope the report will be of interest and use to you.

Very sincerely yours,

(Signed) AGNES E. CLARY.

SPECIAL REPORT OF DETENTION HOME SCHOOL FROM NOV. 23, 1914, TO JUNE 4, 1915.

Pupils under compulsory age	176
Pupils over compulsory age	199
Total	375

ENROLLMENT UNDER COMPULSORY SCHOOL AGE.

	Boys	Girls	Total
Between 6 and 7 years	7	8	15
Between 7 and 8 years	6	2	8
Between 8 and 9 years	12	0	12
Between 9 and 10 years	6	3	9
Between 10 and 11 years	12	3	15
Between 11 and 12 years	15	1	16
Between 12 and 13 years	15	0	15
Between 13 and 14 years	27	7	34
Between 14 and 15 years	44	8	52
Under age	144	32	176

OVER COMPULSORY SCHOOL AGE

	Boys	Girls	Total
Between 15 and 16 years	41	9	50
Between 16 and 17 years	42	17	59
Between 17 and 18 years	47	16	63
Between 18 and 19 years	8	9	17
Between 19 and 20 years	2	7	9
Between 20 and 21 years	0	1	1
Over age	140	59	199
Total enrollment for 6 months	284	91	375
Grade			
1st	20	8	28
2nd	12	3	15
3d	24	8	32
4th	34	15	49
5th	46	8	54
6th	50	12	62
7th	44	17	61
8th	27	8	35
8th grade finished and pupils stopped	12	6	18
	269	85	354
1st year High School	10	5	15
2nd year High School	4	1	5
3rd year High School	1	0	1
4th year High School	0	0	0
	15	6	21
8th grade finished in San Francisco Public Schools	8	6	14
8th grade finished in San Francisco Private Schools	3	3	6
8th grade finished in outside of San Francisco Public Schools	15	1	16
8th grade finished in outside of San Francisco Private Schools	1	2	3
Pupils who had finished 8th grade	27	12	39
Pupils who came to the Detention Home from school	175	29	204
Pupils of school age, never in school	0	4	4
Pupils who had left school before coming to Detention Home	109	58	167
			375
Pupils who left school before reaching 13 years	3	4	7
Pupils who left school before reaching 14 years	6	9	15
Pupils who left school before reaching 15 years	21	11	32
Total number leaving school before reaching 15 years	30	24	54
Pupils who had completed 8th grade under 15 years	2	2	4
Truants (including those who ran away from home and school)	81	2	83
"Floaters" (pupils who have moved from school to school) no record at first	134	38	172
"Repeaters" counted but once in total—have been back more than once	41	21	62

RETARDATION.

	Boys	Girls	Total
Retarded from 2 to 4 terms	117	38	155
Retarded from 4 to 8 terms	78	20	98
Retarded from 8 to 12 terms	14	3	17
Retarded over 12 terms	3	1	4
Foreign children not counted as retarded	16	3	19
			293
Normally advanced	55	24	79
Advanced beyond years	1	2	3
			82
Average daily attendance (half days)			27

SUMMARY OF THE WORK OF THE SAN FRANCISCO JUVENILE PROTECTIVE ASSOCIATION IN THE SUPERVISION OF THE BOYS OF THE ETHAN ALLEN SCHOOL IN THEIR HOMES DURING THE SUMMER VACATION, JUNE 7—JULY 26, 1915.

Number of boys referred by the Principal of the Ethan Allen School for care during the Vacation Period, June 7—July 26, 1915	34	
Not seen on account of Diphtheria in district though an attempt was made to have them report elsewhere	3	
Dropped from list on account of residence, removed to country	6	
Under supervision so "personal touch" could be considered a factor	25	
Stopped "craps", fighting, running away, smoking, idleness and disobedience to parent	10	40%
Ran away and did not return until end of vacation	1	4%
Brought before Juvenile Court	2	.8%
Court unable to capture	1	4%
Stealing but not caught (own confession)	1	4%
Perceptibly deteriorated though closely supervised	1	4%
Kept out of trouble but cause not obviously attributable to visits	9	36%
Telegraph Hill contributed	10	40%
Poverty positively not a predisposing cause	10	40%
Selling papers at Ferry	7	28%
Low mentality (obvious without tests)	4	16%
Obtained permanent work	1	4%
Total number of visits made in case of 34 boys	140	
Total number of visits made in case of 25 boys	124	
Greatest number of visits made to a boy	10	
Least number of visits made to a boy	3	
Average number of visits made to a boy	5	
Age of the youngest boy	11	years
Age of the oldest boy	16	years

The majority of these boys worked, so a postal was sent in advance as to time and place of visit, though many visits were made in the homes unannounced.

A large number of parents expressed appreciation for the interest shown in the boys. Only one parent objected to the visits. This was a mother who said she "had seven children and something was the matter was every one of them".

The principal of the Ethan Allen School reports the undertaking returned beneficial results. One of the teachers reported the prompt return of more boys than usual at the opening of the school after vacation.

CHARLOTTE W. FARNSWORTH,
Chairman Social Service Committee.

HEALTH AND MEDICAL INSPECTION.

Department of Public Health,
Central Office.

July 2, 1915.

Mr. Alfred Roncovieri,
Superintendent of Schools,
San Francisco, Cal.

Sir:

In compliance with request contained in yours of May 26th, I herewith enclose a tabulated statement showing exclusions from schools on account of communicable diseases during the past five months; also furnishing the periods of exclusions in the various diseases.

Trusting that this will prove satisfactory, I beg to remain,

Respectfully,
(Signed) WILLIAM C. HASSLER,
Health Officer.

COMPULSORY EXCLUSIONS BY ORDER OF BOARD OF HEALTH FROM SCHOOL FOR COMMUNICABLE DISEASES DURING PAST FIVE MONTHS.

	Jan.	Feb.	Mch.	Apr.	May	Periods of exclusion
Chickenpox	65	82	142	91	61	2 weeks
Diphtheria	68	51	106	44	62	(2 negative swabs 5 days apart from patient and contacts must be obtained)
Measles	276	239	119	56	13	2 weeks
Mumps	0	7	13	16	35	2 weeks
Scarlet Fever	13	8	20	10	3	4 weeks
Tonsilitis (Acute)	11	23	13	2	6	during illness
Whooping Cough	22	14	25	56	30	2 weeks after coughing stops
Contacts	489	358	449	265	261	Contacts are kept out of school during period of disease
Chorea		2	2			during illness
Total	944	784	889	540	471	

July 1st, 1915.

Mr. Alfred Roncovieri,

Superintendent of Schools,
San Francisco, Cal.

My Dear Mr. Roncovieri:

Replying to your inquiry of July 6th, will state that the average period of exclusion in all cases of Diphtheria is approximately 21 days; Tonsilitis, 10 days; and for Contacts of Diphtheria it would be safe to say four weeks of all cases. For Chorea we have no data.

The above periods have been estimated from approximately 250 cases.

It is very difficult to estimate accurately the time of exclusion in these cases, because our records have not been kept with that obect in view. During the coming year we will bear this in mind and perhaps give you a more definite time for the next report.

Thanking you for your kindly sentiment and good wishes, I am,

Respectfully,

(Signed) WILLIAM C. HASSLER,
Health Officer.

Department of Public Health,
Central Office.

August 2d, 1915.

Mr. Alfred Roncovieri,

Superintendent of Schools,
San Francisco, Cal.

Sir:

In compliance with request contained in your communication of July 6th, 1915, I am transmitting herewith a copy of the report of Chief Medical Inspector of Schools in regard to the development of School Medical Inspection.

Trusting this will meet with your requirements, I am,

Respectfully,

(Signed) WILLIAM C. HASSLER,
Health Officer.

August 2, 1915.

To the Health Officer:

Sir: The past fiscal year has witnessed further development of School Medical Inspection in San Francisco.

The three important functions of school inspection are:—

1st. The detection and correction of physical defects in school children.

2nd. The detection and exclusion of cases of communicable diseases and parasitic skin disease.

3rd. The maintenance of proper hygienic conditions in the schools, and in the environment of the schools.

The number of physical defects in children corrected during the year shows an increasing interest of parents in the real constructive work of school medical inspection.

We are in constant receipt of letters from parents who express appreciation to the Department for having called attention to the remediable defects in their children.

The sanitary condition of our schools is excellent, and recommendation has recently been made to the Board of Education with a view of improving certain phases in the janitorial service.

I can safely say that the number of cases of pediculosis capitis and parasitic skin diseases have been appreciably decreased under the vigilant eye of our school nurses.

The value of school inspection in dealing with communicable disease was recently demonstrated in handling diphtheria. Following the taking of swabs in the schools, and the exclusion and isolation of over four hundred diphtheria carriers, the number of cases of clinical diphtheria was markedly decreased.

It is my earnest recommendation that future outbreaks of communicable disease outside of the schools be controlled by the Division of Sanitation and if necessary by graduate nurses obtained from the accredited Civil Service list. The removal of a nurse from her school district where she is familiar with her duties, and conversant with the social condition of the children under her care, is a blow at the very fabric of school medical inspection, with consequent loss of efficiency and irreparable harm.

I look forward to the coming year for the consummation of the following important plans; the establishment of additional classes for subnormal children, particularly in the Mission district; the establishment of numerous open-air classrooms throughout the city, not only for children who present evidence of malnutrition, but also for those who are physically well.

Under separate cover I have submitted a purely statistical report of the Division of School Medical Inspection.

Respectfully,

(Signed) THOS. D. MAHER,
Chief Medical Inspector of Schools.

Department of Public Health,
General Office. February 25th, 1915.

Mr. Alfred Roncovieri,
Superintendent of Schools,
San Francisco, Cal.

Sir:

Pursuant to your request for a copy of the duties of school medical inspection and the methods employed, I am forwarding you a copy of the report submitted by Chief Medical Inspector of Schools T. D. Maher.

Respectfully,

(Signed) WM. C. HASSLER,
Health Officer.

Feb. 25, 1916.

To the Health Officer.

Sir:—In reply to the communication of Alfred Roncovieri, Superintendent of Schools, of January 29, 1916, bearing on the subject of School Medical Inspection the following data is submitted:—

The Division of School Medical Inspection of the Department of Public Health is composed of a Chief Medical Inspector of Schools and two assistant medical inspectors, the Chief receiving a salary of one hundred and fifty dollars a month, the assistants one hundred dollars a month each, all three of whom are appointed by and hold office at the pleasure of the Board of Health.

There are in addition fourteen graduate nurses who received their positions as a result of competitive Civil Service examination, and whose salaries have been apportioned to seniority in service, three receiving a monthly salary of eighty-five dollars, six eighty dollars, and five seventy-five dollars, respectively.

The Assistant School Medical Inspectors are under the control and supervision of the Chief Medical Inspector of Schools, who on Saturday of each week assigns to them a schedule of schools for the coming week in which schools they are to make physical examinations of pupils. Upon finding correctible physical defects in children, defect cards are mailed to the parents or guardians of such children.

School nurses are under the supervision of the Chief Medical Inspector of Schools, who assigns to them the district and schools to be visited by them.

The hours of School Nurses in the schools are from 9 A. M. to 3 P. M., after which time home visits are made to the homes of children who have been absent from school for three or more days.

Within the school, the school nurse inspects all children isolated by teachers as ailing, or as suspected cases of communicable disease.

All children returning after a previous exclusion from school.

She treats, and if necessary, excludes all children suffering with parasitic skin diseases.

The school nurse reports to the Chief Medical Inspector of Schools any insanitary condition in and about the school.

A most important function of the school nurse is to visit homes following the issuance of defect cards with a view to having parents act quickly in such important matters.

On Saturday of each week from 10 to 12 M. the whole division of School Medical Inspection assembles at the office of the Board of Health to report on the work of the past week and discuss all questions bearing on the subject of school medical inspection.

The following is a recapitulation of work accomplished by the Division of School Medical Inspection for the six months ending with December, 1915:

General examinations by School Nurses	101,416
Dressings by School Nurses	2,175
Treatments by School Nurses	3,897
Home visits by School Nurses	4,301
Examination by School Medical Inspectors	4,762
Defect cards issued to parents	683
Treated by operation	311
Treated without operation	49
Vision corrected by glasses	106
Referred to clinics	87

(Signed) THOMAS D. MAHER,
Chief Medical Inspector of Schools.

The following circular letter of general information was prepared by the Superintendent and distributed widely for the benefit of parents and prospective pupils just previous to the opening of the Fall Term of 1914:

Department of Public Instruction
Office of the Superintendent of Schools

San Francisco, June 5th, 1914.

To Parents and Guardians:

Vacation is about to begin. Schools will reopen Monday, July 27th, 1914. Let us begin the opening of the fall term with a full attendance. Do not deprive your child of a single day of the education to which he is entitled. Our school buildings will have been overhauled, scrubbed and cleaned. Our teachers will be back at their posts of duty refreshed from the vacation, and ready to take up the work without delay. Lessons will begin on the very first day. If your child is not present, his class will be one day ahead of him. If he is absent for any length of time, he will fall behind the educational procession by that much, and possibly lose his promotion at the end of the term. The full responsibility for the child's regular daily attendance is upon the HOME.

Parents should see to it that their children do not fall behind their classes through avoidable causes. Nothing so discourages a child as to fail of promotion. Our teachers are faithful to their trust. They are only too willing and anxious to help your children, but they must have the sympathetic help of the HOME for complete success.

We have been investigating the problem of "RETARDATION" in the Public Schools. This problem causes school authorities the greatest concern. By "retardation" we mean that children are often found in classes one or more years behind the classes in which they should be. We frequently find children one, two, three and even four years older than they ought to be for the grade in which they are enrolled. As the result of this, they are often humiliated at being placed with younger pupils, become discouraged, lose interest in their work, and drop out of school at the earliest opportunity that the law will allow, with only a partial education. Thus they enter life poorly prepared for its strenuous competition. If such pupils, however, have the courage to continue their school work, they complete their education at an age older than their fellows, and lose the time which should have been used in learning their trade or profession. The course of study is being revised and readjusted so that it is expected that ninety per cent of the children with reasonable application can accomplish the work and be promoted from term to term completing the elementary school work in eight years. There will probably be ten percent of slower pupils; but these will get additional help in our ungraded classes. Pupils who are able to do more than the minimum amount required by the course of study will be encouraged to take more work, supplemental to the regular course, and will be given an honorary certificate to encourage their efforts. Supplementary books, shop work, nature study and gardening will be provided for such pupils. Thus the strongest will be given all they can possibly bear, while the weakest will not be over-burdened, left behind and discouraged in the race.

There are several causes for retardation that are under the direct control of the home. Irregular attendance, when avoidable, is the very worst. The home is solely responsible for this. Another of these avoidable causes is late entrance into school. Children entered at 7, 8 and 9 instead of at six usually lag behind the grade in which they should be. Our Principals all say that in comparatively few cases is this time ever made up. Our Primary work is carefully graded to the age and capacity of the child. It is not, as in former times, six hours per day on a straight-back bench with feet dangling in mid-air, but is a constant change of work, with music, drawing, recreation, nature study, reading, spelling, pictures, number work, in simple and concrete form. Every healthy child of six years can easily pursue the work without taxing his strength or interfering in any way with his development. The years between 6 and 8 may seem unimportant, but if these are lost from the school, they may mean the loss from 18 to 20, or 22, which are the most important years in preparing for trade, business or profession. We would therefore urge parents to enroll their children, when they are 6 years of age.

Under the State law no child can be enrolled in a first grade after the first 30 days of any new term. There are two such terms in each school year. The first or "Pall Term" will begin this year on Monday, July 27. The second or "Spring Term" will begin shortly after the first of January, 1915. The schools will do all in their power to assist retarded children in making up lost time. We promote a child whenever he is able to do the work of the next grade. Mature and capable children may do two terms' work in one. Programs will be arranged so that children who have the ability may do work in two different classrooms. We are urging the establishment of Vacation Coaching Schools, and Ungraded Classes, in which children may receive individual instruction and make up lost time. Our class teachers do all that they can to assist earnest pupils who have fallen behind in their work; but the best results cannot be accomplished, nor the discipline of self-control be taught to the children of indulgent or indifferent parents.

The education of children is a most sacred work in which parents and teachers should act as partners. Do you wish your child to play his or her part in the new San Francisco? If so, then must you accept your responsibilities and co-operate with the schools. You must second the efforts of the teachers. **Send your children to school regularly!** See that home conditions favor study for the advanced pupils. Children need proper nutrition for school work, regular meals with wholesome food, stomachs not weakened by confections and sweetmeats, eaten at all hours. They should attend school after a night of restful sleep, refreshed in body and mind. The adult is not fit for a good day's work without a good night's rest. This is still more true of children. Recreation and amusements are essential; but no child should keep late hours preceding a school day. Children must come to school in proper condition of mind and body, in order that teachers may do their best work. The **Home** and the **School** must co-operate with unselfish zeal, at a sacrifice when necessary, in the interest of the children. Let us discharge our high, partnership duty, both as teachers and parents, by giving to our children more than we have received, and thus gain the benediction bestowed on good and faithful stewards when life's work is done. We ask your hearty co-operation and support in all that is good and great for our schools, in order that we may do the best work for your children, and through them for the greater San Francisco.

Respectfully yours,

ALFRED RONCOVIERI,
Superintendent of Schools.

February 26, 1916.

Mr. Alfred Roncovieri,
Superintendent of Schools,
City and County of San Francisco.

My dear Mr. Roncovieri:

Pursuant to your request, I herewith hand you material which I submit as a report concerning the work of my department. One part of the material submitted (Folder A) shows the method of procedure in establishing the work of my department during the months of February and March, 1915. The remainder of the material (Folder B) shows the present status of the work as reported to the Board of Education January 19th, 1916. My work of this first year has been deliberately experimental in some of its phases, with the end in view of ascertaining certain facts upon which I might base recommendations for a more final plan of physical education, school athletics, social and lecture centers.

I am now engaged in the development of a report which will contain budget estimates and my final recommendations.

The date of rendering the material attached herewith is too early to enable me to include final recommendations. However, I trust that the material here submitted will answer your present need.

Respectfully,

(Signed) E. B. DeGROOT.

DEPARTMENT OF PHYSICAL EDUCATION, ATHLETICS, SOCIAL AND LECTURE CENTERS.

BUDGET ESTIMATE FOR SCHOOL YEAR 1915-1916.

BUDGET—PHYSICAL EDUCATION IN ELEMENTARY SCHOOLS, 1915-16.

District Supervisor of Physical Education in Elementary Schools (Woman), per month	$ 80.00

Summary:

4 District Supervisors of Physical Education (Women) 12 mos.	$ 3,840.00
Pro rata salary office clerk ($600 per year) 1/5	120.00
Pro rata salary Director of Dept. ($3,000 per year) 1/5	600.00
Special Printing	150.00
Equipment, Supplies and Incidentals	348.00
Total	$ 5,058.00
George S. Miehling (carried over)	1,224.00
Total	$ 6,282.00

BUDGET—ATHLETIC, PLAY AND ACHIEVEMENT LEAGUE.

Supervisor of Athletic, Play and Achievement League, per month	$ 150.00
Play and Achievement Leader, per month	20.00
Athletic Leader, per month	20.00

Summary:

1 Supervisor of Athletics, Play and Achievement	$ 1,800.00
20 Play and Achievement Leaders (10 mos.)	4,000.00
16 Athletic Leaders (10 mos.)	3,200.00
Printing	300.00
Equipment and Supplies	500.00
Pro rata salary office clerk ($600 per year) 1/5	120.00
Pro rata salary Director of Dept. ($3,000 per year) 1/5	600.00
Total	$10,520.00

BUDGET—SOCIAL CENTERS.

Social Centers to be operated 5 nights each week, 10 months the year, August to June.

Principal (or teacher) in charge, per month	$20.00
Leaders of special activities, $2.50 per night each, per month	40.00
Janitor, per month	10.00
Equipment, Supplies and Incidentals, per month	18.00
Total Each Center	$88.00

Summary:

10 Social Centers at $88.00 per mo. each, $800 per mo., 10 mos.	$8,800.00
Pro rata salary office clerk ($600 per year) 1/5	120.00
Pro rata salary Director of Dept. ($3,000 per year) 1/5	600.00
Total	$9,520.00

BUDGET—LECTURE CENTERS.

20 Lecture Centers—2 Lectures each month at each center, October to March, inclusive.

Principal (or teacher) in charge, per month	$5.00
Janitor in charge, per month	2.50
Printing, advertising and incidentals (each center) per month	5.00
Summary:	
20 Principals, or teachers, per year	$600.00
20 Janitors, per year	300.00
Printing, advertising and incidentals, per year	600.00
Equipment and supplies, per year	100.00
Pro rata salary office clerk ($600 per year) 1/5, per year	120.00
Pro rata salary Director of Dept. ($3,000 per year) 1/5, per year	600.00
Total	$2,320.00

BUDGET—PHYSICAL EDUCATION, PLAY AND ATHLETICS IN HIGH SCHOOLS.

Lowell High—	
Man teacher employed for service after school hours, $20 per mo	$ 240
Woman teacher employed for service after school hours, $20 per mo	240
Polytechnic High—	
Man teacher employed for service after school hours, $20 per mo	240
Woman teacher employed for service after school hours, $20 per mo	240
High School of Commerce—	
Man teacher employed for service after school hours, $20 per mo	240
Woman teacher employed for service after school hours, $20 per mo	240
Mission High—	
Man teacher employed for service after school hours, $20 per mo	240
Woman teacher employed for service after school hours, $20 per mo	240
Girls High—	
Special teacher (Mrs. Tharp carried over) $115 per mo	1,380
Equipment and supplies—all high schools	250
Pro rata salary office clerk ($600 per year) 1/5	120
Pro rata salary Director of Dept. ($3000 per year) 1/5	600
Total	$4,270

SUMMARY OF BUDGET ESTIMATES.

1.	Physical Education in Elementary Schools	$ 6,282.00
2.	Athletic, Play and Achievement League	10,520.00
3.	Social Centers	9,520.00
4.	Lecture Centers	2,320.00
5.	Physical Education, Play and Athletics in High Schools	4,270.00
	Total	$32,912.00

APPROPRIATIONS FOR CURRENT SCHOOL YEAR.

Athletics	$7,000.00	
Social Centers	5,000.00	
Lectures	2,500.00	
Total		$14,500.00
Balance February 1, 1915		$12,260.10

Respectfully submitted,

(Signed) E. B. DeGROOT.

Approved Board of Education, March 2, 1915.

APPLICATION OF ORGANIZATION CHART.

DEPARTMENT OF PHYSICAL EDUCATION, ATHLETICS, SOCIAL AND LECTURE CENTERS.

(Note: The chart and the following statement represent recommendations for a complete scheme, the full operation of which may have to await larger appropriations. A conference with the Board is requested concerning the details recommended and to determine to what extent the scheme may be put into operation at this time.)

EXPLANATORY.

DEPARTMENT: Responsible to the Board of Education for all duties, responsibilities and activities indicated in the organization chart and for all other duties and responsibilities imposed upon the department by the Board.

TITLE OF DEPARTMENT: Department of Physical Education, Athletics, Social and Lecture Centers.

TITLE OF HEAD OF DEPARTMENT: Director of the Department of Physical Education, Athletics, Social and Lecture Centers.

FUNCTION OF THE HEAD OF THE DEPARTMENT: To give general direction and supervision to the work of the entire department and to all workers therein. To outline suitable courses of physical education for the various schools and grades. To formulate and enforce rules, regulations and methods in school athletics. To organize, guide and direct social and lecture center developments. To call and conduct meetings, study-courses and institutes among workers in the department. To take charge of planning and equipping gymnasiums, playgrounds and social centers. To check all requisitions for supplies, tools and implements called for and distributed among workers in the department. To maintain an inventory of all tools and implements entrusted to the department. To represent the department and the Board of Education in all matters outlined herein. To render regular and special reports to the Board. To respond to any service imposed by the Board of Education.

AIDS TO THE HEAD OF THE DEPARTMENT.

One Supervisor (man) of the "Athletic, Play and Achievement League". Salary $1,800.00 per year.

Four District Supervisors (women) of the Physical Education in Elementary Schools. Salary, $960.00 to $1,224.00 per year.

One Special Instructor (man) in physical training work. Salary $102.00 per month. One Office Clerk. Salary $600.00 per year.

DIVISION OF PHYSICAL EDUCATION, ATHLETICS, PLAY AND ACHIEVEMENT.

This division represents a logical grouping of subjects and activities related to all schools below the high schools. For convenience and efficiency in operation and supervision, all schools have been grouped according to certain geographical divisions of the City. Four divisions are proposed as shown in the accompanying map and list of schools. It is proposed that the work of this division be carried on under the general supervision of four women and one man, as follows:

One woman in each division styled "DISTRICT SUPERVISOR OF PHYSICAL EDUCATION IN ELEMENTARY SCHOOLS".

To supervise the work of physical education treated as a subject in the regular school program. She will guide the principal and regular teacher in carrying out the prescribed course of physical education. To establish in her respective division a free, voluntary, after-school training course for. teachers. The course will be principally a practice course in gymnastics, folk dancing, school-room and school-yard methods. (The course will also aim to improve the health of all teachers who participate.) To supervise the social dancing and girls' gymnastics conducted in social centers in her respective division.

One man styled "SUPERVISOR OF ATHLETICS, PLAY AND ACHIEVEMENT''.

To supervise the work of the ''Play and Achievement Leaders'' and the work of the ''Athletic Leaders''. To conduct a training course of Athletic Leaders. To arrange and conduct all athletic meets, leagues and tournaments of the elementary schools. To maintain the records in all matters pertaining to Athletics, Play and Achievement in elementary schools.

LOCAL WORKERS IN THIS DIVISION.

''ATHLETIC LEADERS.''

One leader for each group of five schools.

To take charge, after school hours, under the direction of the Supervisor and approval of the Principals of the schools involved, of organizing, coaching and preparing individuals and teams (boys only of grades 5 to 8) for competition in the meets and tournaments of the Athletic League. To take charge of and be responsible for all movable athletic equipment in the possession of the five schools in his charge. To attend the training course, conducted by the Supervisor, once each week. Salary, $20.00 per month, 10 months.

''PLAY AND ACHIEVEMENT LEADERS''

One regular school teacher, in each school selected, employed for after-school service. To organize and lead, under the direction of the Supervisor and approval of the Principal, the play of both boys and girls in the school yard or school building, after regular school hours. To promote, and keep the records of, the ''Achievement League''.

To attend the training courses conducted by the District Supervisors of Physical Education. Salary, $20.00 per month, 10 months.

(Note: The meaning of the words ''Play and Achievement'' as distinct from physical education and athletics will be set forth in a special report concerning the re-organization and functions of the Public Schools Athletic League. Briefly, the words ''Play'' and ''Achievement'' here represent a scheme of credits and honors to be given for the mastery of certain good games, and for the performance of work in connection with the home; for superior rank in school, and for social, mechanical and industrial accomplishments. The central idea is to give encouragement and educational direction to the leisure time of the child and to include not only boys who are eligible for athletic competition, but girls and boys of all ages and conditions.)

DIVISION OF HIGH SCHOOL PHYSICAL EDUCATION, PLAY AND ATHLETICS.

It is here proposed that the high schools be regarded as a logical group to be treated apart from the type of operation proposed for the lower schools. It is proposed that the supervision of physical education, play and athletics in the high schools come directly under the head of the department, with one man or one woman (or both) in charge of the activities in each school. The person engaged in each school may be either one of the regular high school teachers or a specialist, acording to the conditions to be met in each school. Salary for regular teacher on part time: $20.00 per month, 10 months. Salary for special teacher giving full time: $960.00 to $1,224.00 per year.

DIVISION OF SOCIAL AND LECTURE CENTERS.

This division represents a logical grouping of activities related to the use of school buildings at night. It is proposed that certain school buildings be used as lecture centers and that certain other schools be used as social centers. It is proposed that both the lecture and social centers be supervised by the head of the department and that the principal or a teacher be placed in direct charge of each of the lecture and social centers. Lecture centers should be operated two nights each month and the social centers should be operated, in most cases, five nights each week. When the social center work seems too heavy for teacher or principal, persons from outside of the school system may be employed to take charge. Salary Principal or Teacher at Lecture Center: $5.00 per month, 6 months. Salary Principal or Teacher at Social Center: $20.00 per month, 10 months.

The activities of each social center will be determined to a large extent by the physical facilities at hand and the character of the neighborhood involved. In general it is proposed that our social center program aim to establish the following:

(1) Community Singing.

(2) Hand work exchange.

(3) Civic forum.

(4) Recreational activities—dancing, dramatics, gymnastics, etc., according to facilities at hand.

The lecture center will aim to present to the neighborhood people, twice each month, a lecture from one of the following groups:

(1) A group of lectures dealing with the business and industrial life, opportunities and possibilities of San Francisco.

(2) A group of lectures dealing with the structure and operation of government—town, city, county, state and federal.

(3). A group of lectures dealing with health, individual and community.

(4) A group of lectures dealing with science, literature and travel.

The program and leadership of the various activities of the social center will be secured as far as possible, out of the community. The more the social center is one of self-expression on the part of the community, the better. Special workers, however, will be employed to lead special activities. Lecturers for the lecture centers will, in most cases, be secured with pay.

Salary for Special Workers in Social Centers: $2.50 per night.

Salary for Janitors at Lecture Centers: $2.50 per month, 6 months.

Salary for Janitors at Social Centers: $10.00 per month, 10 mos.

Respectfully submitted,

(Signed) E. B. DeGROOT.

Approved by Board of Education, March 2nd, 1915.

REPORT ON HIGH SCHOOLS.

San Francisco has five day high schools, one evening high school, one advanced evening commercial school, and an evening continuation school. These are the Girls High School, the High School of Commerce, Lowell High School, Mission High School, Polytechnic High School, Humboldt Evening High School, Evening Commercial School, and North Beach Evening Continuation School.

The five day high schools were originally separately organized as specialized or type schools.

For historical purposes, we may select the year 1910 as the approximate date when the San Francisco school officials became thoroughly awakened to the fact that while, elsewhere, a constantly increasing proportion of young men and women were receiving their final training for the world's work and for social and civic usefulness, in high school, such was not the case in San Francisco. These officials realized that the high schools of San Francisco were not prospering to the degree that they were in other parts of the state and country.

Attention was drawn to the general condition, in an address before the Teachers' Institute of San Francisco in 1912, by Deputy Superintendent A. J. Cloud. A careful and exhaustive study of the local situation, followed by a comprehensive examination of administration, courses of study, methods and results in other cities, was made.

In the middle of the year 1912, the Board of Education acceded to the urgent representations of the Superintendent of Schools that the high school courses of study be revised, and the task of making such modifications was definitely undertaken. The Superintendent assigned this work in the main to Deputy Superintendent A. J. Cloud, who was ably assisted by Deputy Superintendent T. L. Heaton, and by Mr. C. L. Carlson, a teacher of the Department.

A year later (July 2, 1913), the Board approved the high schools' Course of Study so prepared—a Course which, in many respects, called for radical readjustments—and ordered that it go into effect at the opening of the fall term, 1913.

In this course, an endeavor was made to give these type-schools a greater trend toward the cosmopolitan, or inclusive, form of high school. The philosophy of President Nicholas Murray Butler was adhered to that "The wise policy for a community to pursue is to make itself familiar with the function and the problems of the secondary school, or of so many secondary schools of differing types, as will best meet the individual, social, and industrial needs of the children of its own population," and, again, that "The secondary school must exist in sufficiently diverse forms and must be administered with sufficient elasticity of method to enable it to adapt itself to the needs of a complex social organism". An endeavor was made so to reconstruct the character of the appeal of the high schools as to minister more adequately to the capacities and abilities of individual students, and, further, to utilize the materials and modes of work of industrial and social life in such reorganization.

The High School Course of Study gives an outline of a central trunk line, or general plan of work. This trunk-line, however, has branches in many directions, forming "Groups" or sections of the main course, designed to conform to the varying aims and life objects of the students. The "Groups" are planned to meet the needs, so far as possible, of all who are ready to share the opportunities a high school affords. The Groups are guides only, and may be multiplied many times over to allow of almost a countless number of possible combinations of school-work. In fact, so far as the number of such possible combinations is concerned, it is limited only by facilities of instruction, and other administrative requirements. The Course, in this respect, is exceedingly elastic. Not one Course, but literally hundreds, may readily be constructed from it. Yet, while the Course permits the student's individuality, his personal aptitudes, to develop freely under safe guidance, and provides both scope and material for the development of his talents, at the same time, its provisions are sufficiently rigorous to insure against dawdling and superficiality. "Hard work is to be secured not by insistence upon uniformity of tastes and interests, but by the encouragement of special effort along lines that appeal to the individual."

The Course provides for "fundamental" work in the first and second years, and "intensive", or "specialized", work in the third and fourth. It gives the student a full opportunity to find his (or her) bearings before coming to a final decision in respect to his (or her) life-occupation. By a novel "interlocking plan", it is possible for students registered in one high school to take, in any other high school, any work they may desire if such work is not offered in the school in which the student is enrolled. Two-year "Groups", and one-year "Groups", in commercial and industrial branches of instruction, may be taken by those students who cannot attend high school beyond the length of time so specified.

The Course of Study fixes a standardized, or uniform, program for four-year regular students, as follows:

Distribution of Work	Years	Hours	"Advanced" Hours
Prescribed Major—English and United States History and Civics	3	24	8
	1	8	8
Elective Major—Four "Subjects" in any single "Department"	4	32	0 to 16
Alternative Language or Mathematics Minor	2	16	0
Elective Minor—two "Subjects" in any single "Department"	2	16	0
Electives—Six "Subjects"		64	8 to 24
Totals	4	160	40

"Hour" is the expression used to designate one class-exercise period per week for a half year in subject-matter which requires preparation outside of the scheduled periods of instruction. For work not requiring the preparation just stated, the number of periods of classroom or laboratory exercise must be doubled to be allowed full "Hour" value.

(Note: To express high school "Hours" in terms of matriculation "Units" (University of California Entrance Requirements), multiply by three-eights, i. e., eight high school "Hours" equal three matriculation "Units".)

A sufficient number of "Advanced Hours" must be included among the "Electives" to make a total of forty "Hours" for all "Advanced Subjects".

This five subject four period plan was decided upon, after mature study, in accord with the theory that the youth entering high school should be given the widest possible opportunity to test himself in all the major branches of instruction. Each subject, it will be seen, being given four times a week (with few exceptions) constitutes approximately a quarter of the student's work per semester—or four "Hours". The length of the school year in San Francisco is forty weeks. A period is usually forty-five minutes in length—laboratory periods double.

In planning this Course, great care was taken that students should do solid work, but not that which would overtax their strength or capacity. Also, because the student at the time of entrance is less mature, and his or her vital interest not so fully aroused then as later, fewer "electives" are allowed in the earlier than in the later years of the Course.

To graduate from the four-year Course, the student must have a satisfactory record, both in scholarship and conduct, in one hundred sixty "Hours" of work (the equivalent of twenty class-exercise periods per week for four years), distributed according to the valuations given in the table immediately above.

To summarize the program of studies for regular four-year students:

(1) The number of elective "Subjects" is fourteen out of twenty. Freedom of election may be partially limited by the choice of "Group"; also, a "Major" and a "Minor" must be provided for.

(2) Of the remaining six "Subjects", four are prescribed, and two must chosen from either a Language (other than English) or Mathematics.

(3) Five "Advanced Subjects" are required.

''Major'' is the expression used to designate general subject-matter in which a student specializes, and to which he must devote four consecutive years of work.

''Minor'' is the expression used to designate general subject-matter in which a student must accomplish two consecutive years of work.

(1) The ''Prescribed Major'' is a combination of English, to be studied for at least three years, and United States History and Civics in the Fourth Year. ''There is at the present time also unanimous agreement among high school and college authorities that three or four (years) of English should be required of all . . . Every high school student should be given a practical knowledge of affairs in his own community . . . of the basic principles of state and national politics.'' (N. E. A. Report, 1911.)

(2) The ''Elective Major'' provides an opportunity for the student to specialize at will. It is assumed that students entering high school have a serious motive. Proficiency in this ''age of specialization'' can be attained only by intensive foundational study, and it is thought that four consecutive years of application along a main line, under the direction of skilled teachers, should result in the acquisition of thorough knowledge and practical training on the part of the student.

(3) The ''Alternative Language or Mathematics Minor'' fixes a choice between the two ''Subjects'' which are most frequently needed to re-enforce an ''Elective Major''. While the majority of students will elect both of these ''Subjects'', some students seem to lack the faculty of grasping one, although they acquire the other readily. The concession of this ''Minor'' is a distinct, liberal departure from conventional high school programs.

(4) The ''Elective Minor'' permits a student to choose a ''Department'' intimately related to his ''Elective Major'' and essential to complete equipment in the latter. In selecting this ''Minor'' the guidance and advice of the principal should be sought.

(5) The ''Electives'' permit a student to choose such ''Subjects'' as will complete other ''Majors''; or enable him to gain intensive knowledge of two allied branches of work; or allow him to increase his specialized qualifications in any province of instruction. This is a margin to be used for any ''kind of work that the best interests of the student appear to require''. That the ''Subjects'' should be left unspecified ''appears to be vital to the progressive development of secondary education''.

The original selection of a Group is not necessarily final, but may be provisional only. Students may change from Group to Group, with the approval of the Principal in certain clearly defined ways. Great flexibility is then secured, without the loss of efficiency.

Graduation requirements from the Two-Year Course are eighty ''Hours'' of work; from the One-Year Course, forty ''Hours''. A Certificate of Proficiency (as distinguished from a Diploma) is granted to those fulfilling the above requirements.

THE DIFFERENT DAY HIGH SCHOOLS.

GIRLS HIGH SCHOOL.

The GIRLS HIGH SCHOOL (established separately in 1862) occupies the beautiful and commodious new building at the corner of Scott and O'Farrell Streets. There are in the building 20 class-rooms, 5 laboratories, 2 sewing rooms, 1 dress-fitting room, 1 cooking room, 2 drawing rooms, 2 large study halls, a library, an auditorium seating 1050 people, a gymnasium, a recreation room and a cafeteria. The building and equipment cost approximately $430,000. It was erected in 1912.

For the school year ending June 2, 1911, the average daily attendance in this school was 606; the total number enrolled was 836. For the school year ending June 4, 1915, the average daily attendance was 540; the enrollment was 758. The actual attendance in January, 1916, is 577. This shows an actual decrease in enrollment in four years of 78, and a percentage decrease of 9.3%. The number of graduates in 1911 was 84; in 1915, 110. In 1911 the number of teachers was 22, including the Principal. In 1916, the number is 25, including the Principal. The increase in the number of teachers is the direct result of the inauguration of a sewing course, and the development of gymnasium work, as called for under the 1913 Course of Study. The number of students per class runs from 15 as a minimum to 35 as a maximum (January, 1916). The average number of recitations per teacher per week is 25.

Although it is a liberal culture school, the aim of which is to prepare its students for the ethical, social, intellectual and civic responsibilities of life, yet it does not neglect the vocational training so necessary for the domestic requirements of today. It gives full preparation for entrance to the Universities and Normal Schools of California, and the principal Women's Colleges of the East, but its main purpose is to give a generous education to that large number of girls (who, indeed, form the majority) whose formal training goes no farther than the high school.

In English, in addition to the usual work in literary appreciation and interpretation, special emphasis is placed on developing the habit of using good English, both in written and in oral speech. A language (Latin, French, or German) may be begun either on entering school or at the beginning of the third year. This gives the following possibilities in linguistic work: four years of one language or two years of one language and two years of another one. Four years of History are given, including Ancient, Medieval and Modern, English and American; also Civil Government and Economics. In Science, courses are given in Biology, Physiology and Sanitation, Domestic Chemistry (including the chemistry of Cooking, Dietetics, Cleaning, Dyeing and Household Arts), Physics, Geology and Astronomy. In Mathematics a three years' course in Algebra and Geometry is given. The Course in Art is one of four years, including Freehand Drawing, Perspective, work in Charcoal, Pen-and-Ink, Water Color, Applied Design, Tiling, Leather and Metal Work, etc., and, in the Senior year, History of Art. A Two Year Course in Sewing is given, including Millinery. All first and second year girls are required to take the courses in Physical Culture and Gilbert and Folk Dancing. Educational guidance is conducted by a thoroughly prepared and sympathetically-minded teacher.

The school is equipped with a cafeteria, where wholesome lunches may be had at very reasonable prices.

RECOMMENDATIONS.

The Superintendent has from time to time called attention emphatically to the fact that, while this school is distinctively established for girls, yet its educational facilities at present differ very slightly from those in mixed high schools in this city. The 1913 Course of Study made provision, in addition to the regular academic courses, for the organization of a complete Home Economic Course, including Plain Sewing, Dressmaking, Millinery, Cooking, Household Chemistry and the Household Arts; but, to date (January, 1916), the course in Cooking, etc., has not been begun, while only incomplete courses are given in Sewing, etc. A partial explanation of the decrease in attendance noted above, is found in the desire of young women to enter schools, such as the Lux, where home-making courses may be had. Inasmuch as the Girls High School is the only public one in the city set aside entirely for girls, it should be made peculiarly a Home Culture High School. We cannot insist too strongly on the installation and equipment in this school of courses in Cooking, Sewing, and Dressmaking, Millinery and Home Decoration.

Furthermore, we recommend that a course in Spanish be added to the program of studies of this school to meet the growing demand, and, in the fourth year, courses in the commercial branches of instruction (Stenography, Typing and Bookkeeping, and their correlated studies). The latter should have the motive of preparing young women for secretarial positions.

HIGH SCHOOL OF COMMERCE.

The HIGH SCHOOL OF COMMERCE, historically speaking, is in its swaddling clothes as a four-year school, for, not until the installation of the 1913 Course of Study, had it had a course of more than two years' duration. It was then known as the San Francisco Commercial School; the Course was restricted to Commercial Subjects, English, and the Spanish language.

This school is located at Fell and Franklin Streets in a three-story steel-frame brick building erected in 1907, at an approximate cost of $265,000. There are in the building 23 recitation rooms, 1 study hall (capacity 100), 1 laboratory, a gymnasium, and an auditorium (capacity 350). The equipment of the Commercial Department consists of 150 Remington Typewriters, 4 dictaphones, I Underwood revolving duplicator and 1 Burrough's Adding Machine.

For the school year ending June 2, 1911, the average daily attendance in this school was 581; the total number enrolled, 917; 280 boys and 637 girls. For the school year ending June 4, 1915, the average daily attendance was 825: the enrollment was 1211; 433 boys and 778 girls. The actual attendance in January, 1916, is 1176; 372 boys and 804 girls. This shows an actual increase in enrollment in four years of 294 and a percentage increase of 38%. In 1911 the number of teachers was 19, including the Principal. In 1916 the number is 27, including the Principal, an increase of 8 in five years. Notwithstanding this increase, at present (January, 1916), the teachers in this school are carrying heavier burdens than will assure the best results. The average number of recitation periods per teacher per week is 28, the maximum being 35 (commercial work), and the minimum 21. The average number of students per recitation class (January, 1916) is 35, but the maximum runs in a few commercial classes as high as 51.

For the year 1911, the number of graduates was 124 (two year course at that time); 19 boys, 105 girls. In 1915, the number of graduates was 21 (four year course); 7 boys and 14 girls. Two year graduates numbered 88; 13 boys and 75 girls. The grand total of graduates was therefore 109.

While the present Course of Study emphasizes the work in the fundamental commercial subjects—stenography, typewriting, bookkeeping, commercial arithmetic and penmanship—it also makes provision for work in Modern Languages (Spanish, French and German), Chemistry, Mathematics, History and Economics, and English.

The Four-year Course is designed to prepare for general executive positions in the business world. Admission to the Universities, particularly the College of Commerce of the University of California, is one of the ideas back of the Course.

The Two-year Course is designed to meet the wants of these pupils who do not intend to prepare for college entrance, and who can continue in school but a limited time. This course prepares particularly for the positions of stenography, typist, assistant bookkeeper and general secretary.

The One-year Course, in which a limited number of subjects may be pursued in an intensive manner, is particularly adapted to the wants of pupils who find it necessary to earn their own livelihood in as short a time as possible.

RECOMMENDATIONS.

It is remarkable that this school has accomplished so much when we consider the handicaps under which it has labored in being deprived of its own building for a great part of the time in the past nine years, from lack of equipment, from an insufficient teaching force, and from the present overcrowding of the building.

The Superintendent has pointed out from time to time the imperative need for complete modern equipment of office appliances and commercial furniture, and devices for use in the Business Department. In a report to the Board a year ago, he stated that $10,000 was required to equip this school properly. The first steps have been taken in this direction during the present year as is seen from the listing of the commercial equipment above, but much still remains to be done to put this school on a proper footing in respect to equipment. As the Superintendent said a year ago, "In competition with other business and commercial schools, we can only expect our boys and girls to suffer in the way of gaining and holding positions, unless that for the benefit of the best training; and that training cannot be had in the High School of Commerce until it is adequately equipped."

We are glad to note that the pressure on the teaching force has been considerably reduced during the past year. The Board of Education has followed the recommendations of the Superintendent, and by adding four teachers to the faculty, has relieved greatly the strain. An improvement, however, in the strictly administrative system still remains to be accomplished by establishing the departmental system in this school, as recommended by the Superintendent for the past several years. This school should be organized on the plan common to all high schools, that is, the departmental system.

The rapid growth of this school has led to such a degree of overcrowding that the Board of Education has this term (January, 1916), in line with the recommendations of the Superintendent, been forced to place two portable temporary classrooms on the school property, and these are being continuously occupied. Furthermore, two basement rooms and the auditorium are being used as classrooms. In all, there are at present 29 classes in the school, with only 23 regular classrooms to hold them. It has been thought for some time past that a necessary item in the proposed forthcoming bond issue for school purposes should be a new building for the High School of Commerce, and the urgency of this need is more apparent every day. The City owns the land on which a twin building to the present one, in size and appearance, could be erected. An auditorium, of sufficient seating capacity to hold the teaching corps of the City Schools, could well be placed on this ground, which is in a very central location. The cost, with the classroom building and the auditorium, might be figured in the neighborhood of $500,000.

Readjustments have been made in the Course of Study as experience warranted. While it is true that, in general, the commercial branches of instruction prepare for clerical rather than true commercial positions, and that, in small communities, an overplus of stenographers and office clerks is thus supplied, yet, in a great business center such as San Francisco, a constant demand is found to exist for well trained young men and young women to fill these clerical and office positions, and the avenues of promotion are many and varied. That the commercial studies in this High School are serving a distinct vocational need is testified to by the fact that the High School of Commerce graduate has small difficulty in finding employment. However, it is most important that the youth of our city be offered every educational opportunity to be trained for the wider business occupations in the great mercantile world, and not be limited to the narrower field of office employment. With such an end in view, considerable progress has been made in the past several years in this school in the development particularly of the English course and of the

Modern Languages, beginnings have been made in instruction in advanced accountancy, in the operation of office machines, appliances and time-saving devices, and work has been begun upon a plan for a course in salesmanship.

Writing of this school, Dr. E. R. Snyder, Commissioner of Vocational Education of the California State Board of Education, states:

"I * * * was tremendously impressed with the enthusiasm and interest in their work shown by the Principal and teachers of that institution". (High School of Commerce.)

"The thing that appealed to me the most strongly was the fact that the teachers of your Commercial High School make it a business to keep up with the demands of the commercial world. In every class that I visited I found the teacher using forms secured from business offices in San Francisco rather than from text-book, and these teachers seemed to know what the forms which they were teaching meant.

"In my judgment San Francisco has a Commercial High School of which it can be justly proud."

LOWELL HIGH SCHOOL.

The LOWELL HIGH SCHOOL (established in 1856 as the "Boys High School") is located in a fine, well-equipped building on Hayes Street, near Masonic Avenue, occupied in 1912. There are in the building 24 classrooms, 8 laboratories, 2 drawing rooms, 3 study halls, holding respectively, 80, 120, and 140 students, an auditorium with a seating capacity of 500, a gymnasium for boys and one for girls, and a Cafeteria. The cost of the building is approximately $350,000; that of the land approximately $100,000.

For the school year ending June 2, 1911, the average daily attendance in this school was 742; the total number enrolled 1032; 595 boys and 437 girls. For the school ending June 4, 1915, the average daily attendance was 991; the enrollment was 1322; 768 boys and 554 girls. The actual attendance in January, 1916, is 1260. This shows an actual increase in enrollment in four years of 290, and a percentage increase of 29%. In 1911 the number of teachers was 23, including the Principal. In 1916 the number is 38, including the Principal, an increase of 15 in five years. Notwithstanding this liberality on the part of the Board of Education in an endeavor to supply teachers to meet the most urgent needs, at present (January, 1916) the average number of recitation periods per teacher per week is 25 for teachers of academic subjects and 30 for laboratory subjects. This is still too heavy an allotment for the attainment of the best results, particularly in such subjects as English and Mathematics. The average number of students per class is (January, 1916) 40. There are about eight classes having 45 pupils, but none over 55. In this respect, also, improvement is shown over former years, but there is still considerable room for improvement. All of the classes should be brought down to the 40 level.

In 1911 the number of graduates was 93; 43 boys and 50 girls. In 1915 the number of graduates was 139; 76 boys and 63 girls.

This school prepares not only for Normal Schools, Colleges, Universities and Professional Schools, but also for life in general. The traditional "classics", which are still required by the colleges for the A. B. degree, are given, although not prescribed. Of foreign Modern Languages,—Spanish, French and German are taught. In English more work is offered and required than in any other branch. In the Sciences are offered Physical Geography, Botany, Zoology, Chemistry, Physics; in Mathematics,—Algebra, Geometry (plane and solid), Trigonometry; in History,—Ancient, Medieval, Modern, English, United States; also courses in Government and Economics; courses in

Drawing (Freehand and Mechanical), in History of Art, and in Physical Education.

Girls are admitted on the same terms as boys to all courses.

The school is provided with a Cafeteria, where warm lunches are served at cost.

MISSION HIGH SCHOOL.

The Mission High School is located in a brick building erected in 1896. There are in the building 25 classrooms; also an auditorium holding about 1200 people, and a gymnasium. The cost of the building was about $175,000.

For the school year ending June 2, 1911, the average daily attendance in this school was 478; the total number enrolled 663; 279 boys and 384 girls. For the school year ending June 4, 1915, the average daily attendance was 445; the total number enrolled 643; 292 boys and 351 girls. The actual attendance is (January, 1916) 560. This indicates a slight falling off in the attendance in this school in the past four years.

In 1911 the number of teachers was 22, including the Principal. In 1916 the number of teachers is 21, including the Principal. The average number of pupils per class is (January 1916) 37. The teachers have reasonable allotments of recitation periods.

The number of graduates in 1911 was 73; 24 boys and 49 girls. The number of graduates in 1915 was 69; 26 boys and 43 girls.

In addition to the regular courses leading to all the University Colleges, the Mission High School provides instruction during the first and second years in all the Commercial Subjects, in Physical Education, Applied Arts and Sewing. It approaches more nearly to an "inclusive" Course of Study than is true in any other San Francisco High School.

In the third year, History is made elective with Economics, Drawing is broadened out under the captions "Mechanical", "Architectural", "Civil Engineering", "Mining and Marine", and the subject of Mathematics becomes "Applied".

The Commercial Subjects being completed in the second year, Oral Expression is developed in the third and fourth years, and Arithmetic and Grammar, with methods of teaching these and other subjects, are taken up for the benefit of prospective teachers.

In the fourth year of the 1913 Course the new subjects provided are:—Mechanical, Architectural, Engineering, Mining and Marine Design; Surveying; Industrial Chemistry; and Recreational Activities.

The Household Arts Course outlined in the 1913 Course of Study has been realized only in part. A basement room has been used since 1914 for a sewing room, and a teacher appointed for that line of work. Very little equipment, however, has been furnished. Furthermore, the Superintendent and the Principal have at various times recommended the installation of a cooking course in this school, but without success to date.

The 1913 Course of Study strengthened the connection between the commercial department and other departments of the school. However, the equipment in modern office appliances for the use of the commercial students is inadequate. Recommendations asking for money allowances for this purpose by the Superintendent have not availed, because of the financial stringency of the Department.

The daily session in this school begins at 8 a. m. and runs to 1:20 p. m.

The Mission High School should develop into one of the largest if not the largest, in the city. By reason of its location, it would be a magnet to attract both boys and girls if courses of the polytechnic and household arts description were afforded in it. This should be the ideal towards which to strive in the administration of this school.

POLYTECHNIC HIGH SCHOOL.

The Polytechnic High School is situated south of Golden Gate Park, near First Avenue on Frederick St. It occupies a magnificent structure consisting of two buildings, one used as the main academic building and the other for the shops. The cost of the building was approximately $675,000; of the land $65,000; and of the equipment nearly $100,000. The Industrial wing was occupied in 1911; the academic wing in the Fall of 1915.

In the Academic wing, there are six rooms in the science department, two rooms for cooking, two for sewing, one for dress-making, one for millinery, eight for drawing and art, one for art leather, three for clay modeling and ceramics, fourteen recitation classrooms, and two study halls seating 100 each. In the Industrial wing there are four very large rooms devoted to the wood-working plant, machine shop and forge; a foundry; an assembly hall seating 500 people; three drawing-rooms; and two recitation classrooms.

The gymnasium includes showers, dressing rooms and lockers for both boys and girls.

The Cafeteria accommodates 320 students at one time. It includes dining room, kitchen, pantry and storeroom.

The lecture rooms are fitted with stereopticons and slides for modern educational work in art, literature, science and industry.

For the school year ending June 2, 1911, the average daily attendance in this school was 300; the total number enrolled 464; 303 boys and 161 girls. For the school year ending June 4, 1915, the average daily attendance was 590; the enrollment was 753; 468 boys and 285 girls. The actual attendance in January, 1916, was 956. This shows an actual increase in enrollment in four years of 289, and a percentage increase of 62%. In 1911 the number of teachers was 22, including the Principal. In 1916 the number is 34, including the Principal, an increase of 12 in five years. Notwithstanding this liberal treatment, at present (January, 1916) the teachers are carrying heavier burdens than they should be expected to do to gain the best results. The average number of recitation periods per teacher per week is 28 for teachers of academic subjects and 36 for teachers of shop subjects. The average number of students per class (January, 1916) is 35 in academic work and 28 in shop work, but the maximum in the academic classes is slightly over 50 and in shop classes the maximum is 33. These maxima are considerably above the level, if the best results are to be had.

For the year 1911 the number of graduates was 24; 13 boys, 11 girls. In 1915 the number of graduates was 62; 34 boys and 28 girls.

The Polytechnic High School offers a modern progressive education leading either to the university or more directly to practical life work. Courses are offered in Household Arts for girls, including elementary hand and machine work, dressmaking, millinery and tailoring. Design and color are important features of this work. Courses in cooking and household management will be offered in the newly equipped domestic science rooms. The management of the school cafeteria constitutes a part of the practical training offered. The graphic arts department includes college preparatory work, as well as practical courses in design, which prepare for art industries. The clay modeling course ranges from elementary antique to architectural design, pottery and portrait studies from life. These departments are now fully equipped and in operation.

Besides the regular college preparatory work in science, advanced courses are offered in industrial chemistry and industrial physics. This practical work in physics includes direct currents, alternating currents, practical mechanics, strength of materials, steam and gas engines and automobile construction. Advanced manual courses are offered in carpentry, blacksmithing, foundry work, machine shop practice and advanced mechanical drawing. The plant is equipped with the best modern machinery and appliances for woodwork, for cabinet making, for wood-turning, for pattern-making, for forging, for foundry practice, for machine shop work and for mechanical and architectural drawing.

Under the immediate direction of the Principal a course in Educational Guidance or life career study is given to all first year students. Thus they are given a survey of the world's work and are led to give earnest and serious attention to their own life careers. The work of this Course is closely correlated with that in oral and written expression.

The average program of the Polytechnic student includes four periods spent in laboratories and three academic subjects requiring home study. The Course of Study of this school has been expanded in the past year in the Department of History, a four years' course in that department now being given instead of a two year course. General History is offered in the first and second years, United States History (industrial and economic) in the third year, and United States History and Civics in the fourth year. The last year's work only in this subject is prescribed. The first year is devoted to a general outline of Ancient History and English History, and the second year principally to Modern and Recent History. Physical Education is being well looked after by a skilled instructor, a military company has also been organized.

Courses in printing and book-keeping, and possibly in Latin (third and fourth year) are in prospect.

At the present time (January, 1916) the foundry is not being run. This is due to conditions that seem to make it better at this time to put the money needed for the securing of an additional teacher into employing one for the mathematics and science departments, rather than for the Industrial work. It is thought that by the opening of the Fall Term of 1916 this condition will have been remedied.

To give full equipment to this school about $35,000 in additional funds, it is estimated, will be required. This amount of money should be expended chiefly in equipping a school library, and in completing the equipment of the auditorium stage and dressing rooms.

The program of the school is arranged upon the so-called X Y plan. This is found to work very satisfactorily.

ADVANCED EVENING SCHOOLS.

For industrious and ambitious students beyond the average grammar school age, who are prevented by circumstances from entering the day high schools, the city has provided the "Commercial Evening School", the "Humboldt Evening High School", and the "North Beach Evening Continuation School", in which courses may be had that meet their peculiar needs. Sessions hold from 7:15 to 9:15 p. m.

COMMERCIAL EVENING SCHOOL.

The Commercial Evening School is located in the High School of Commerce Building, Fell and Franklin Streets. This school prepares students for business careers. The entire equipment of the High School of Commerce is put into use in this evening school.

When the present Principal, Mr. John A. Lenahan, took charge in 1912, the enrollment was approximately 320; in January, 1916, it is 691, or more than double. In 1912, the school had 13 teachers, including the Principal; in 1916 it has 18 teachers, including the Principal.

The Course of Study has been amplified and enriched in the period covered by the above dates, and the length of time devoted thereto increased from one and one-half to two years. Thorough instruction is given in stenography, type-writing, bookkeeping and accounting. Special attention is given to correlative subjects, such as Commercial Arithmetic, Commercial Law, Spelling, Commercial English (including correspondence), Penmanship and Spanish. Special teachers supervise the work in Penmanship, English and Spanish. There are two main departments, viz., the Bookkeeping Department and the Department of Stenography.

One of the interesting developments in this school has been the organization of classes for foreigners who are preparing themselves for naturalization as citizens of the United States. They are given instruction principally in the English language and Civics. There are three such classes in existence in this school at the present time (January, 1916), consisting of 95 students, presided over by three teachers.

The text-books in use in the various subjects are: Rogers & Williams Modern Illustrative Bookkeeping; Bennett's Accountancy; Van Tuyl's Essentials of Commercial Arithmetic; the Palmer Method of Penmanship; Kimball's Business Speller; Sherwin Cody's How to do Business by Letter and Training Course in Conversational English; Gallagher & Marsh Stenography text-book; Nichols & Rogers' Commercial Law; Rational Typewriter Course; Spanish Grammar and Classics.

Sessions hold from 7:15 to 9:15 p. m.

RECOMMENDATION.

Much of the work now being given in this school is of real secondary rank, and, as opportunity offers, the course should be still further expanded, until the school is placed upon a footing similar to that of our secondary schools.

HUMBOLDT EVENING HIGH SCHOOL.

In the Humboldt Evening High School (located in the Mission High School Building) there are three Departments: the Academic, the Technical, and the Commercial.

The Academic Department furnishes instruction to those students whose daily employment affords them opportunities of entering professional, literary or business careers, and to those also who intend entering a Day High School at some future time. Many students have in this manner successfully prepared themselves for college, spending three years at Humboldt and one at a day high school. The course in this department includes English Literature and Composition, Latin and German, Mathematics, History and Science. This Course extends over four years.

The Technical Department offers instruction in Drawing in its practical application to the various mechanical and building trades, as well as the several departments of Engineering. This is supplemented by courses in Mathematics and Science, especially adapted to the needs of the technical students. Through this specialized training under teachers who are themselves professionally engaged in the practical work in which they are giving instruction, the students, while going through their apprenticeship, receive a substantial technical training, which enables them to become leaders in their chosen lines. The full outlined course, leading to a diploma, covers three years, and, in addition, post-graduate instruction is provided for those who desire to do advanced work.

The Commercial Department gives instruction in Shorthand and Typewriting, and in Bookkeeping. The Shorthand and Typewriting Course covers a period of one year. In connection with this course, one and one-half hours of each week are devoted to the study of Commercial English, Grammar and Spelling. The first term is devoted to the study of the elementary principles in Shorthand and prepares the student for dictation. The second term in Shorthand consists of practical matter for dictation, covering both commercial and legal work thoroughly. In Typewriting the student is taught during the first term the mechanism of the machine, typewriting technique, and a complete mastery of touch, thus preparing him for advanced work. The second term in

Typewriting is devoted to the teaching of business and legal forms and to the attainment of speed with accuracy. In both Shorthand and Typewriting individual instruction is given and all work corrected nightly. The Bookkeeping Course may be taken instead of the complete course in Shorthand and Typewriting, and requires a period of one year for completion. This course is so arranged as thoroughly to familiarize the student with all branches of business. In connection with the Bookkeeping Course one and one-half hours of each week are devoted to the study of commercial law and commercial arithmetic.

For the school year ending June 2, 1911, the average daily attendance in this school was 451; the total number enrolled was 1032; 948 boys and 84 girls. For the school year ending June 4, 1915, the average daily attendance was 890; the enrollment was 2159; 1606 boys and 553 girls. The actual attendance in January, 1916, is 990. This shows an actual increase in enrollment in four years of 1127, and a percentage increase of 52%. In 1911 the number of teachers was 21, including the Principal. In 1916 the number is 37, including the Principal. The increase in the number of teachers has come from expansions in the Commercial and Technical Courses and from the gain in numbers of students. For the year 1911 the number of graduates was 67; 52 boys and 15 girls. In 1915 the number of graduates was 220; 141 boys and 79 girls.

This school is so crowded that four overflow classes have been placed, of necessity, in the Horace Mann School Building.

The Course in Science should be strengthened by furnishing opportunity to the students to have laboratory practice.

Writing of the Humboldt Evening High School, Dr. E. R. Snyder, Commissioner of Vocational Education of the California State Board of Education, states:

"I am sure that few people, even around the Bay region, appreciate the fact that San Francisco has for many years maintained at least one thoroughly efficient evening vocational high school.

"The thing that appealed to me in this Institution was the fact that the pupils in the school were being given the work which they desired rather than the work which some one else thought they desired. The teachers were men from the practical walks of life and they were instructing these young people largely in the technical subjects which supplemented their daily work.

"I am free to say that I consider the Humboldt Evening High School one of the most effective institutions in the State of California."

THE NORTH BEACH EVENING CONTINUATION SCHOOL.

In 1915 the daily average attendance in this school was 31; the enrollment was 81; 59 boys and 22 girls. There is but one teacher. This school occupies the building of the Hancock Grammar School.

The number of graduates in 1915 was 3; all boys.

In connection with this school the Superintendent has recommended that instruction be given to improve the educational status of immigrants, in support of the efforts of the Bureau of Naturalization of the United States Department of Labor in that direction, and that classes be organized in such school for instruction in advanced English and Commercial Subjects.

ENTRANCE TO HIGH SCHOOL.

Beginning pupils enter high school upon the basis of a diploma of graduation from the elementary public schools, or from private schools when the same are placed upon an accredited list by the Superintendent, such accrediting being evidence that the school in question follows a course of study equivalent to that in the public elementary school.

For pupils of the highest elementary grade who have failed of graduation, and for pupils of the next lower grade who are specially recommended by the principal and teachers, and for pupils of corresponding gradès of unaccredited private schools, the Superintendent's staff has semi-annually, for a number of years past, conducted entrance examinations to high schools. The subjects given in the examinations are the common branches of the elementary school curriculum. The numbers taking these examinations have varied from 15 to 30 or 40. Very few have passed these examinations; in fact, out of 15 applicants, none passed the last examination (January, 1916).

The Superintendent and Deputies have bent their energies for the past several years towards increasing the attendance in the high schools. This they have done by impressing the importance of further education upon the minds of grammar school pupils (particularly of 8th grades), teachers and parents, through the media of addresses to 8th grade classes, and the distribution of printed circulars.

That this propaganda has been at least partially successful is indicated by the steady increase of grammar school graduates in attendance at high school. Thus, of 1449 graduates of San Francisco grammar schools in June, 1915, 896, or 62%, entered San Francisco high schools in July, 1915; and, of 1334 graduates of San Francisco grammar schools in December, 1915, 896, or 67%, entered San Francisco high schools in January, 1916 (See table below).

(Note: Graduations are held semi-annually. It is the invariable rule that June classes are larger than December classes.)

TABLE.

Number of graduates of San Francisco Public Grammar Schools for the term ending June, 1915	1449
Number entering San Francisco Public High Schools from above schools July, 1915	896
Percentage	62%
Total enrollment entering classes San Francisco Public High Schools July, 1915	1064
Number of graduates San Francisco Public Grammar Schools for the term ending December, 1915	1334
Number entering San Francisco Public High Schools from above schools January, 1916	896
Pencentage	67%
Total enrollment entering classes San Francisco Public High Schools January, 1916	1028

QUALIFICATIONS OF HIGH SCHOOL TEACHERS.

The State law requires that regular high school teachers be certificated. The standard of this certification is the highest in the United States, the requirement calling for five years' preparation beyond high school, including one year of graduate work in a university of recognized standing (embracing both education theory and teaching practice). In addition, teachers of regular subjects in the San Francisco High Schools have been appointed on the basis of their fitness to teach the particular subject, or subjects, to which they have been assigned.

Teachers of special subjects in California Secondary Schools may be certificated on credentials, or examinations. For the past six years the standard fixed by the San Francisco County Board of Examination for the granting of special secondary certificates on credentials has been the highest and most rigid in the State, and has served as the basis for the regulations on that subject recently adopted by the State Board of Education under an act passed by the last legislature. The standard so set by the San Francisco authorities had as its governing idea the effort to require teachers of special subjects to prove as high a degree of preparation as teachers of regular subjects. The certification of teachers of special subjects, by examination, has also been conducted upon the most rigid standards.

INDIVIDUAL RECORDS OF CALIFORNIA PUBLIC HIGH SCHOOLS.

(As shown by official reports of the examiner of High Schools of the University of California.)

	Index and Number of Students (See note below)		
	1912-13	1913-14	1914-15
S. F. Girls High	2.02 (6)	2.10 (10)	2.06 (17)
S. F. Lowell	2.26 (38)	2.14 (39)	2.19 (59)
S. F. Mission	2.20 (10)	1.89 (3)	2.25 (5)
S. F. Polytechnic	2.68 (6)	2.02 (7)	2.17 (8)
Alameda	2.38 (17)	2.21 (17)	2.14 (18)
Berkeley	2.57 (104)	2.36 (120)	2.28 (138)
Oakland High	2.24 (57)	2.19 (43)	2.22 (64)
Oakland Fremont	2.56 (28)	2.23 (23)	2.08 (24)
Oakland Technical	1.99 (4)	2.19 (8)	1.92 (6)
Sacramento	2.42 (12)	2.15 (29)	2.37 (41)
Santa Rosa	2.51 (9)	2.54 (8)	2.45 (14)
Fresno	2.39 (5)	2.36 (6)	2.13 (6)
Stockton	2.64 (7)	2.70 (17)	2.17 (8)
San Jose	2.29 (11)	2.44 (9)	2.11 (13)
Los Angeles High	2.66 (35)	2.43 (32)	2.43 (30)
Los Angeles Polytechnic	2.41 (8)	2.24 (19)	2.42 (20)
Los Angeles Hollywood	2.52 (3)	1.94 (6)	2.10 (13)
Los Angeles Manual Arts		2.42 (3)	2.52 (18)
Redlands High	2.13 (5)	2.17 (1)	2.61 (3)
Long Beach	2.54 (6)	1.84 (7)	2.44 (9)
Pasadena		2.03 (7)	2.19 (5)
San Diego	2.06 (11)	1.97 (14)	2.11 (13)
Santa Barbara	1.86 (8)	2.42 (10)	2.47 (8)

Notes: The index number gives the general average scholarship of a school's membership in the freshman class of the University for the given year; or, in other words, the general efficiency of the school for college purposes in terms of scholarship grades of the University. The index figure is obtained by multiplying the number of units of work in each grade of scholarship by the numeral representing that grade; adding the products so obtained; and dividing this total by the number of units of work taken. The lower or smaller numerically the index figure is, the higher the scholarship ranking of the school under consideration. When the number of students from a school is large, and the index figure low, such school has attained the highest record.

The above table demonstrates the fact that the San Francisco High Schools stand well at the top of the list in respect to the records of their graduates in the University of California.

(The San Francisco High School of Commerce is not represented in the above table, for the reason that it had sent no graduates to the University up to the time of the last report of the University examiner. The Four Year Course of the High School of Commerce had not been in operation long enough to permit of completion of the work by any students up to that date (1914-15).

GENERAL RECOMMENDATIONS.

GALILEO HIGH SCHOOL—PROPOSED.

It has been felt that the day high schools of San Francisco are located within a comparatively close range of each other when the whole extent of the city's area is taken into account. The whole northern end of the City is stripped of high school accommodation and the youth living therein must travel very long distances to reach high school.

To remedy that situation, and also to provide for the life needs of boys and girls of the northern end of the city, the Superintendent has recommended the establishment of a two year high school, to be known as the Galileo High School. Though the urgent need for such a school has been recognized, yet funds have not so far been available for that purpose. We should continue to renew this recommendation until we meet with success.

BURBANK AGRICULTURAL HIGH SCHOOL—PROPOSED

As long ago as 1911 the Superintendent recommended that a high school be established in the far southern portion of the city, on city land, for practical instruction in the arts of agriculture, horticulture and related subjects. This rocommendation has so far not been carried into effect. We should continue to renew this recommendation, also, until we meet with success.

CLERICAL ASSISTANCE.

One of the most urgent requirements of the situation in the San Francisco high schools is that of employing clerks as assistants to the Principal. The number of students now attending each one of our high schools is so large so to demand that the full time of the Principal be devoted to his supervisorial and purely administrative duties. Principals and teachers are now doing a large amount of detail work which should be done by a secretary or clerk. Practically all the large high schools of the State employ a secretary. It is decidedly uneconomical to pay Principals $3000 a year, or upward, to do work which a clerk at $1200 a year can do just as well.

LIBRARY FACILITIES.

The supply of books for reference purposes in our high schools is wholly inadequate. At different times during the past several years the Superintendent has endeavored to enlist the interest of the public library officials of San Francisco in this subject in the hope that branch public libraries might be established in some or all of the high school buildings, but such efforts have been unavailing. Probably the best plan, of co-operation, would be to have the schools supply the necessary space and equipment while the Public Library should supply the books. The librarian should, however, be at one and the same time a teacher and a librarian, that is, be trained in both directions. A school library so conducted has come to be of vital importance to efficiency in high school work. Without it, supervised study cannot go very far. This is particularly true in social science studies such as English, History, Economics, etc. Either the School Department should spend a large amount to rehabilitate our high school library and employ the necessary quota of teacher-librarians, or else renewed efforts should be made to have branch public libraries installed in high school buildings. These libraries should include maps, globes, dictionaries of the English and foreign languages, reference books, and supplementary reading books.

MUSIC.

One of the most immediate needs of the high schools is to be furnished with a corps of instructors in music, one for each day high school. At present (January, 1916) one teacher only is assigned to the high schools in this subject. The Superintendent has stoutly advocated for a number of years past that music should be given its rightful place in the high schools.

PHYSICAL EDUCATION.

More attention has been devoted in the past two or three years to physical education training and supervised athletics in our high schools, both for boys and girls, than ever before. The half-day time of five teachers, and the full time of one teacher, is being devoted to this subject. This plan is highly commendable. We recommend its extension so that each day high will be provided with at least one instructor in Physical Education and Athletics, on full time.

Following is a copy of a pamphlet designed for the guidance of Grammar Grade graduates and issued from the office of the Superintendent of Schools: To Eight Grade Pupils, and to Their Parents and Guardians:

We urge you most strongly to give at this time your very best thought to the subject of further and higher education. Graduation from grammar school means that the individual has come to the educational cross-roads of life, and a wise decision at this point will have a most important bearing upon his or her future career.

We are confident that you will find a high school education of inestimable value in the great struggle for success that is going on in the highly organized society of to-day. The value of a high school course may be summarized as follows: (1) The student receives the best moral and cultural training; (2) his mental powers are developed; (3) he is afforded an opportunity to acquire certain practical knowledge and skill which may be instrumental in gaining a livelihood for him, and (4) he gains an opportunity of developing qualities of leadership and executive ability which in after life may be the basis of promotion and advancement. That a high school course is a good financial investment aside from its acknowledged cultural values is shown by figures recently compiled by the United States Department of Education. These figures show that uneducated help, on an average, earns about $500 per year throughout a working lifetime of forty years, or $20,000. High school graduates earn, on an average, $1000 per year throughout a working period of forty years, or $40,000. These figures should convince you that pupils cannot afford to drop out of school before completing a High School education.

The selection of a high school should not be based on sentiment alone. The training had in the grammar school is designed to lay the foundations of useful citizenship, and the boys and girls who are to enter the high schools should choose, with the advice and consent of their parents, the schools which will give them the largest return in educational advantage for the time expended in obtaining it.

With the above facts in mind we are issuing this circular of information concerning the work that is being carried on in the public high schools of San Francisco.

In the five Day High Schools is organized a course of study which may be compared to a central trunk-line, or general plan of work. This "trunk-line" course of study is formed into "Groups," planned to meet the needs, as far as possible, of all those who are willing to share the opportunities that our High Schools afford.

This Course provides for "foundational" work in the first and second years, and "intensive" or "specialized" work in the third and fourth. It gives the student a full opportunity to test himself (or herself) before coming to a final decision in respect to his (or her) life-occupation. By a novel "inter-locking plan", it is possible for students registered in one high school to take, in any other high school, any work they may desire if such work is not offered in the school in which the student is enrolled. Two-year "Groups", and one-year "Groups", in Commercial and Industrial branches of instruction, may be taken by those students who cannot attend high school beyond one or two years.

Great elasticity and a Guarantee of Thoroughness are the salient features of this high school course. It permits the student's individuality, and personal aptitudes, to develop freely under safe guidance; it provides both scope and material for the development of his talents. At the same time, its provisions are sufficiently rigorous to insure against dawdling and superficiality. "Hard work is to be secured not by insistence upon uniformity of tastes and interests, but by the encouragement of special effort, along lines that appeal to the individual."

In planning this Course, great care has been taken that students shall do solid work, but not that which will overtax their strength or capacity. Also, because the student at the time of entrance is less mature, and his or her vital interest not so fully aroused then as later, fewer "electives" are allowed in the earlier than in the later years of the Course. The expectation is that the amount of preparation outside of the class-exercise period, necessary to enable a student to carry on his work successfully, will be approximately two hours a day in the First and Second Years, and approximately three hours a day in the Third and Fourth Years. It is thought that this is a moderate requirement for the attainment of good results in school. The effort has been made to adjust both the quantity and the quality of the work, in such a fashion as to place emphasis rather upon quality than upon quantity.

In many cases, particularly of students in delicate health, or of those who find unusual difficulty with certain branches of instruction, provision is made for extending the time for graduation one or more "terms". A "term" is a period of six months. Permission for such extension will be granted on petition to the principal by the student, attested by the parent. On the other hand, students who have shown unusual aptitude for the work may, with the permission of the principal, meet the requirements for graduation in less than four years' time.

THE DIFFERENT DAY HIGH SCHOOLS.

The Girls High School occupies the beautiful and commodious new building at the corner of Scott and O'Farrell Streets. Although it is a liberal culture school, the aim of which is to prepare its pupils for the ethical, social, intellectual and civic responsibilities of life, yet it does not neglect the vocational training so necessary for the domestic requirements of today. It gives full preparation for entrance to the Universities and Normal Schools of California, and the principal Women's Colleges of the East, but its main purpose is to give a generous education to that large number of girls (who, indeed, form the majority) whose formal training goes no farther than the high school.

In English, in addition to the usual work in literary appreciation and interpretation, especial emphasis is placed on developing the habit of using good English, both in written and oral speech. A language (Latin, French, Spanish or German) may be begun either on entering school or at the beginning of the third year. This gives the following possibilities in linguistic work: Four years of one language or two years of one language and two years of another language; or four years of one language and two years of another one. Four years of History are given, including Ancient, Mediaeval and Modern, English and American; also Civil Government and Economics. In science, courses are given in Biology, Physiology and Sanitation, Domestic Chemistry (including the chemistry of Cooking, Dietetics, Cleaning, Dyeing and the Household Arts), Physics, Geology and Astronomy. In Mathematics a three years' course in Algebra and Geometry is given. The Course in Art is one of four years, including Freehand Drawing, Perspective, work in Charcoal, Pen-and-Ink, Water Color, Applied Design, Tiling, Leather and Metal Work, etc., and, in the Senior year History of Art. The Domestic Science Course is planned to include Sewing, Cooking, Household Chemistry and the Household Arts.

All first and second year girls are required to take the course in Physical Culture and Gilbert and Folk Dancing.

The school is equipped with a Cafeteria, where wholesome lunches may be had at very reasonable prices.

The High School of Commerce centralizes its work around the fundamental commercial subjects. It is housed in a modern building on Fell Street, corner of Franklin Street. In addition to the commercial subjects, this school offers work in Modern Languages, Science, Mathematics, History, Economics and English.

The One-year Course, in which a limited number of subjects may be pursued in an intensive manner, is particularly adapted to the wants of pupils who find it necessary to earn their own livelihood in as short a time as possible.

The Two-year Course is designed to meet the wants of those pupils who do not intend to prepare for college entrance, and who can continue in school but a limited time. This course prepares particularly for the positions of stenographer, typist, assistant bookkeeper and general secretary.

The Four-year Course is designed to prepare for college entrance and admission to our State Normal Schools and for general executive positions in the business world. We strongly recommend that pupils, wherever possible, should take the complete four-year course.

The Lowell High School is located in a fine, well-equipped building on Hayes Street, near Masonic Avenue. This school prepares not only for Normal Schools, Colleges, Universities and Professional Schools, but also for life in general.

The traditional "classics", which are still required by the colleges for the A. B. degree, are given, although not required. Of foreign Modern Languages, Spanish, French, and German are offered. In English more work is offered and required than in any other branch. In the Sciences are offered Physical Geography, Botany, Zoology, Chemistry, Physics; in Mathematics, Algebra, Geometry (plane and solid), Trigonometry; in History, Ancient, Mediaeval, Modern, English, United States; also courses in Government and Economics;

courses in Drawing (Freehand and Mechanical), in History of Art, in Physical Culture.

Girls are admitted on the same terms as boys to all courses.

The school is provided with a Cafeteria, were warm lunches are served at cost.

The Mission High School is situated at the corner of Eighteenth and Dolores Streets. In addition to the regular courses leading to all the University Colleges, the Mission High School provides instruction during the first and second years in all the Commercial Subjects in Physical Education, Applied Arts and Domestic Science.

In the third year, History is made elective with Economics, Drawing is broadened out under the captions "Mechanical," "Architectural," "Civil Engineering," "Mining and Marine," and the subject of Mathematics becomes "Applied."

Under Domestic Science in the third year are to be found Domestic Chemistry and Chemistry of Foods; Home Economics and Management; Advanced Dressmaking, Millinery and Art Sewing. Under Applied Arts, instruction will be given in Color and Wash-Work, Applied Design, Sketching, Tiling, etc.

The commercial subjects being completed in the second year, Oral Expression is developed in the third and fourth years. and Arithmetic and Grammar, with methods of teaching these and other subjects, are taken up for the benefit of prospective teachers.

In the fourth year of the Course the new subjects are: Mechanical, Architectural, Engineering, Mining and Marine Design; Surveying; Industrial Chemistry; Dietetics and Sanitary Chemistry, and Recreational Activities.

With an anticipated enlargement of facilities—faculty, building and equipment—the Mission High School will, under the Course of Study herein briefly set forth, be able to make unusual provision both for students who can, and those who cannot, extend their education beyond the secondary school.

The daily session in this school begins at 8 a. m. and runs to 1:20 p. m.

The Polytechnic High School is situated south of Golden Gate Park, near First Avenue on Frederick Street. It is a fine new structure magnificently adapted for classroom studies, for electrical courses, for household arts, for arts and crafts and for the graphic arts. It is equipped with the best modern machinery and appliances for woodwork, for cabinet making, for wood turning, for pattern making, for forging, for foundry practice, for machine shop work and for mechanical and architectural drawing.

The Polytechnic High School offers a modern progressive education leading either to the university or more directly to practical life work. Courses are offered in Household Arts for girls, including elementary hand and machine work, dressmaking, millinery and tailoring. Design and color are important features of this work. Courses in cooking and household management will be offered in the newly equipped domestic science rooms. The management of the school cafeteria constitutes a part of the practical training offered. The graphic arts department includes college preparatory work, as well as practical courses in design, which prepare for art industries. The clay modeling course ranges from elementary antique to architectural design, pottery and portrait studies from life.

Besides the regular college preparatory work in science, advanced courses are offered in industrial chemistry and industrial physics. This practical work in physics includes direct currents, alternating currents, practical mechanics, strength of materials, and steam and gas engines.

Students wishing to enter the college of natural science, of commerce, of agriculture, or of engineering in the State University, will find in the Polytechnic High School complete preparatory courses. Boys not preparing to attend the university may take vocational courses at the Polytechnic in carpentry, blacksmithing, foundry work, machine shop practice and advanced mechanical drawing. For girls who are not preparing for college special courses in sewing, millinery, tailoring, cooking, and other household arts are offered.

The average program of a Polytechnic student includes four periods spent in laboratories and three in academic subjects requiring home study. Regular home study and close application to scientific methods in the laboratories are essential to successful work.

This school is equipped with a first class up-to-date Cafeteria where warm lunches are served at cost.

ADVANCED EVENING SCHOOLS.

For the graduates of the grammar schools who are prevented by circumstances from entering the day high schools, the city has provided the "**Commercial** Evening School," the "Humboldt **Evening** High School," and the "North **Beach Evening** High School," in which courses may be had by industrious and ambitious students who are engaged in daily toil. Sessions hold from 7:15 to 9:15 p. m.

The **Commercial Evening** School is located in the High School of Commerce Building, Fell and Franklin Streets. This school prepares students for a business career. The entire equipment of the High School of Commerce is put into us in this Evening School. Thorough instruction is given in stenography, typewriting, bookkeeping and accounting. Special attention is given to correlative subjects, such as Commercial Arithmetic, Commercial Law, Spelling, Commercial English, Penmanship and Spanish. Special teachers supervise the work in Penmanship, English and Spanish. The complete course in either the Bookkeeping or Stenographic Department covers one and one-half years.

In the Humboldt **Evening High** School (located in Mission High School building) there are three departments: The Academic, the Technical and the Commercial.

The Academic Department should be of interest to those pupils whose daily employment affords them opportunities of a professional, literary or business career, and to these also who intend entering a Day High School at some future time. Many pupils have in this manner successfully prepared themselves for college, spending three years at Humboldt and one at a Day High School.

The course includes English Literature and Composition, Foreign Languages, Mathematics, History and Science.

The Technical Department offers instruction in Drawing in its practical application to the various mechanical and building trades, as well as the several departments of Engineering. This is supplemented by courses in Mathematics and Science, especially adapted to the needs of the technical students. Through this specialized training under teachers who are themselves professionally engaged in the practical work in which they are giving instruction, the students, while going through their apprenticeship, receive a substantial technical training, which enables them to become leaders in their chosen lines. The full outlined course leading to a diploma, covers three years, and, in addition, post-graduate instruction is provided for those who desire to do advanced work.

The Commercial Department gives instruction in Shorthand and Typewriting, and in Bookkeeping. The Shorthand and Typewriting Course covers a period of one year. In connection with this course, one and one-half hours of each week are devoted to the study of Commercial English, Grammar and Spelling. The first term is devoted to the study of the elementary principles in Shorthand and prepares the student for dictation. The second term in shorthand consists of practical matter for dictation, covering both commercial and legal work thoroughly.

In Typewriting the student is taught during the first term the mechanism of the machine, typewriting technique, and a complete mastery of touch, thus preparing him for advanced work. The second term in Typewriting is devoted to the teaching of business and legal forms and to the attainment of speed with accuracy.

In both Shorthand and Tyepwriting individual instruction is given and all work corrected nightly.

The Bookkeeping Course may be taken instead of the complete course in Shorthand and Typewriting, and requires a period of one year for completion. This course is so arranged as thoroughly to familiarize the student in all branches of business. In connection with the Bookkeeping Course one and one-half hours of each week are devoted to the study of commercial law and commercial arithmetic.

The "North Beach Continuation School", in the Hancock School Building, on Filbert Street, near Jones, offers work for those who are unable to attend the day schools.

The student's school work is his or her most important employment during the year of attendance. Each school needs and greatly desires the earnest co-operation of the home. That this may be secured, parents are cordially invited to visit the school which their children attend, and to become acquainted with its plan in general, and with the teachers of their children in particular. In that way you will learn at first hand what the school is doing for your child, and you will see for yourselves that, although the school work is well done, it must be supplemented by your own efforts at the hearthside. With the home in sympathy with the school, differences between the pupil and teacher rarely occur. When school management, school aims and school studies are appreciated by the parents at the table and around the fireside, the student puts a value upon school activities which can never be imparted by the teacher's sole endeavor.

Since the parent was a pupil in school, old subjects are taught in new ways, new material is added to once familiar studies, and subjects new to the parent find a place in the school. To achieve the maximum of results, the home must enter into partnership with the school. Teachers and school officials need to feel that the two great agencies—home and school—are bound by close and sympathetic ties.

Information in greater detail, outlining the courses of study of these high schools, may be obtained on application to the Principals, teachers and other officials of the department.

I earnestly request that you, as parents, give serious thought to this most vital subject, realizing that now has come a turning-point in the life of your boy or girl, and that in the world of today no man or woman can have too much education of the right kind. May I also urge upon these young people that they remember the school from which they have been graduated, and that they return frequently, to see and to consult with their former teachers and principals, whose friendship for them is strong and whose advice will be helpful at all points of life. We, as educators, have only the good of the child at heart.

Give this matter your best thought!

Respectfully,

ALFRED RONCOVIERI,
Superintendent of Schools.

MILITARY SCIENCE AS TAUGHT IN THE SAN FRANCISCO HIGH SCHOOLS.

There are some twenty-five companies of high school cadets in the State of California authorized by the Act of the Legislature approved in 1911 and amended in 1915. Six such companies are located in this city, and in the Mission High School, Lt. Charles S. Hendry, California Naval Militia, Military Instructor; two in the San Francisco Polytechnic High School, Major James Reade Watson, Commandant of Cadets in charge; one in the High School of Commerce, under the immediate supervision of Col. Charles H. Murphy, Principal; two companies at Lowell High School under direction of Mr. J. P. Nourse. The instructors are in immediate charge of the cadets and are responsible for the discipline, care of state property, and the general proficiency of the companies in their particular school. The actual work of drilling is done by the cadet officers. The various "Manuals" of the United States Army have been generously provided by the Adjutant General's office and are used as reference books. The text books on Military Science are the "Rules and Regulations for High School Cadets" issued by the Adjutant General's office, and "Manual of Military Training" by Capt. A. Morse, U. S. A.

Our school department has been fortunate indeed in securing the gratuitous services of Lt. Burnett, First Cavalry, U. S. A., on detached service, who spends much of his valuable time in instructing the various cadet companies. One evening of the week he conducts a school for commissioned and non-commissioned officers. The work is practically a military normal school where the young officers learn that which they in turn must teach to the other cadets in their commands.

Lt. Burnett is rated as one of the best instructors in the United States Army. He is an ex-star on a winning all-American football team, graduate of West Point Military Academy, spent seven years in Japan as attache to the American Embassy and is a Government Specialist in the Japanese language. The Adjutant General recently appointed Major John P. Ryan, U. S. A., retired, military instructor of all of the cadet companies of the state. The law requires that each company shall be inspected annually by an officer detailed from the Adjutant General's office.

The following paragraphs are from a circular letter prepared for the benefit of parents of boys attending the Polytechnic High School and give an idea of the ground covered in military science. The course does not differ particularly from that given in the other High Schools:

"The purpose of the battalion of High School cadets is to unite the boys of the various classes of the school in a common interest and promote good fellowship among them; to support, inculcate and promote the principles upon which the American Government is founded and to encourage and sustain absolute and unqualified loyalty to the national, the state, and the school government. To teach prompt and willing obedience. To develop initiative and willingness to assume responsibility. To be thorough, accurate and methodical and to do whatever attempted with vigor and dispatch. Formal drills are held every Wednesday from 3:15 to 4:45 p. m. Besides the usual Manual of Arms and Closed Order drill work is given in extended order and skirmish drill in Golden Gate Park where actual field problems are worked out. There is rifle practice with sub-calibre Springfields on the school indoor rifle range, according to United States Army regulations and on Saturdays and holidays similar practice is given with a regulation United States Army Springfield at the state rifle range at Manzanita.

"A systematic course in signal work is offered, including wigwagging, semaphore, and wireless telegraphy in connection with the Science Department. A competent athletic officer and staff of assistants give a course in physical culture, using Capt. Butt's 'Manual' as a basis of their work. The course includes setting up exercises, rifle calisthenics, dancing, gymnasium and track athletics. School credit is given for the work done on the same basis as for manual training. Drills, rifle shooting, school for commissioned and non-commissioned officers and signal drills are all conducted out of regular school hours, and in no way interfere with the regular academic studies."

The work in Military Science in this particular High School is divided as follows:

Rifle practice under a competent instructor every afternoon from three until five p. m. that school is in session except Wednesday, and from nine until twelve a. m. on Saturdays.

Tuesday after school, officers' meeting, where military problems are discussed and plans worked out for the formal drill on the following day.

Wednesday, after school, weekly drill. All cadets must appear in uniforms; manual of arms, closed order and extended order work generally in Golden Gate Park.

Thursday, after school, signal drill and school for musicians.

From time to time on Saturdays and holidays the cadets are taken to the state rifle range at Manzanita for practice with United States Army rifles, State Range Officer, Capt. Charles F. Armstrong, generally acting as instructor, assisted always by the teacher in charge of cadets.

The law provides that High School cadets shall wear a uniform similar to that prescribed for the infantry of the National Guards of California, except that instead of shoulder straps, cadet chevrons indicating rank and distinctive collar ornaments shall be worn. The cadets provide themselves with discarded olive drab cotton uniforms of the United States Army, including cap, blouse, breeches and leggings at a cost not to exceed $1.50 for private; officers generally wear the same uniform of woolen material, which costs about $3.00. The state provides collar and cap ornaments and officers' chevrons.

At no expense to the local school department, the state has installed in our High Schools gallery rifle ranges and furnishes sub-calibre Springfield rifles for work on the State rifle range. Also a generous supply of ammunition for all target practice, obsolete rifles for drill guns and officers' side arms. The cadets are all members of the National Rifle Association and receive from the War Department proficiency medals when they qualify as marksmen, sharpshooters or expert rifle men.

At the last Junior Exposition the signal detachment from one of our schools transmitted a message which was returned at the rate of eight words per minute without an error. The same school at present is even more proficient, a squad having spent a recent afternoon signaling between Lone Mountain and Twin Peaks. Within its limits they are equally proficient with the semaphore. In the manual training department of the Polytechnic they have a heliograph set under construction which they expect soon to have in commission.

The cadets have one annual official State camp of instruction for one week open to all, besides the annual Summer Students' Camp maintained by the War Department, to which only cadet commissioned officers are eligible. The official state encampments are under the direction of officers of the United States Army and National Guard of California, and the work consists in drill in larger units than is possible in an organization from a single school. Lectures are given by eminent specialists on military subjects including camp sanitation, personal hygiene, et cetera. All expenses of official encampments and State rifle matches are at the cost of the State. The various schools have their own practice marches, encampments and tours of reconnaissance in charge of the school military instructor, a favorite camping place being the Manzanita rifle range and Bolinas Bay.

In the national matches held under the auspices of the National Rifle Association last summer at the Students' Summer Camp, the High School Cadet rifle team under Cadet Captain Mark A. Devine, of Mission, won the national championship, although the cadet team had had no previous training or coaching to prepare them for this particular match. Their score was 929 points out of a possible 1,000. In shooting contests with our local National Guardsmen, the cadets beat them not only in the aggregate but in the individual scores.

The real purpose of the entire "movement" is admirably summed up in the cadets' "Rules and Regulations", Article XII, Sec. 61, and entitled "A Cadet's Glory":

"A high school cadet is a true gentleman. He stands for the high ideals of life. He loves peace and deplores war, but is always ready to defend his country in its hour of need. He respects authority. He obeys the law. He cultivates filial love, and strives earnestly to be an honor to his father and mother. He honors the Supreme Being in thought, word, and deed."

Over four hundred high school boys of this city have voluntarily assumed these additional duties and responsibilities. The military work in no way interferes with the routine work of the school, but acts as a stimulant to good scholarship and deportment.

The high school cadets should be encouraged in their work, the patriotic teachers who do this work should be compensated therefor. They should receive better recognition from the press and the community.

The great and ever-generous city of San Francisco should do her part as do the other cities throughout the State. If Los Angeles and Sacramento, Marysville and San Mateo can afford to encourage cadet companies and assist in their maintenance, why should not we be equally appreciative?

To offer a course in military training in our High Schools is not a startling innovation. In Boston they have had High School Cadets for the last fifty years, and for thirty-two years in Washington, D. C. The training is universal in Salt Lake, and this work is done by 90% of the High School boys in the State of Wyoming. Prior to the Spanish-American War the old organization of Lowell High School Cadets acquired a national reputation. Switzerland, the most democratic country of Europe, has maintained such a system in her schools since the days of Pestalozzi. Argentina, Australia and New Zealand, the world's newest and most democratic governments, have developed a similar system, each modified slightly to suit local conditions and needs. In Japan, the system is carried out with an even greater thoroughness and proficiency.

Captain H. A. Hanigan, U. S. A, Inspector of Infantry, in his official report last year to Adjutant General Thomas, after a careful inspection of eight cadet companies from various parts of the state (three of them being in San Francisco) said: "I find the work accomplished by them very satisfactory indeed. Great benefit has been derived from the military instruction. The discipline of the schools has been improved remarkably as a result of this training. The cadets have proven a wholesome influence for good in the communities in which they have been organized. In one school in particular in the state the High School boys made themselves a public nuisance by repeated acts of disturbing mischief. The introduction of military training in the District High School resulted in a total disappearance of such acts of mischief. The cadets are looked upon as keepers of good order. The training in organization and team work enabled one cadet company to successfully handle a serious forest fire."

After four years' experience with High School Cadet Companies in this city, I am certain that there is no other work in our schools so conducive to true patriotism, integrity, courage, stability, self-control and old-fashioned American manhood. The cadet Captain voluntarily assumes almost as much responsibility as a teacher in the school. The Corporal is responsible for his squad, the Cadet Major for the entire battalion, and every boy in the ranks realizes that the success of the entire organization depends on his individual efforts. The esprit de corps developed in some of these companies is astonishing. Last year in the Annual Inspection one battalion turned out every man whose name was on the muster roll. In one school 20% of the cadets were awarded ribbon pins and given the title of "Honor Cadets". These boys were present at every drill during the term and their academic work was such as would secure recommendation for college. Their deportment at all times was above reproach. In another school a careful investigation of the academic standing of the cadets and of the track, baseball and football teams, showed a remarkable superiority in favor of the cadets, although many of the boys that took Military Science also took part in athletic activities and their same record appeared on both lists.

This great commercial city will need these citizens of tomorrow who have been trained to give orders and to receive them, who in their boyhood are willing to join voluntarily a school military organization, not for what they can get out of it but for what they can put into it; who are taught from their text book on Military Science "Whatever you do, it matters not how unimportant, do it with all your might, and all your soul, as if your very life depended on it, and when you get through with that, look for something else to do".

And lastly, the training of these boys may be of inestimable value to our country. When our cadet officers have attended the United States Students' Summer Camp they are recommended to the War Department as qualified to receive a commission in the United States Volunteer Army.

When the steamer "Titanic" was launched we thought that human ingenuity had triumphed over the laws of physics and that the vessel was unsinkable. In her maiden voyage her sides merely grazed an iceberg and the passengers were delighted at the novel experience. Life-boats were lowered, passengers were ordered into them, at first they refused to embark in such an antiquated device. Why should they leave the deck of the "Titanic", the unsinkable? But she went down and only those in the old-fashioned life-boats remained to tell the story.

We all hope and pray that there will never be another call for volunteers, but who knows what the future has in store for us? A few years ago eminent authorities told us that the world would never see another great war; that a general European conflict was unthinkable, and yet it came.

Yet it matters not whether in after years these cadets be called upon to serve as the leaders of martial hosts or as captains of industry, this military training in their youth will be of equal value to the individual, to the community, the state and the nation; for this form of education stands for efficiency.

TEACHERS' COMPETITIVE EXAMINATION, S. F., JUNE 12, 1915.

Following are the questions made use of at the annual competitive examination of teachers held for the creation of the eligible list from which vacancies on the elementary grades are filled:

ARITHMETIC.

1. For what sum must I give my note at a bank for 90 days at 6% in order to secure $675.00 cash? (Omit days of grace)

2. A merchant sells 75 pairs of shoes for what 100 pairs cost him. Find his gain per cent.

3. A hot air flue is 12 inches by 24 inches. Find the diameter and circumference of a circular flue having the same area.

4. Wabash 5's are quoted at 107½. How much must be invested in them to yield an annual income of $1200?

5. The difference between two numbers is 5 and the difference between their squares is 95. Find the numbers by algebra.

6. Is it desirable for a pupil to analyze every problem he solves? Should he analyze any? Reasons for answer.

7. (a) Two girls receive $2.10 for making button-holes. One makes 42, the other 28. How shall they divide the money?

(b) Mr. Brown paid one-third the cost of a building and Mr. Johnson one-half. Mr. Johnson's share of the rent is $500 per year more than Mr. Brown's. How much did each receive?

8. Indicate which of the following topics in a course in arithmetic should receive little emphasis, which moderate emphasis, and which great emphasis:

Cube root	Speed in fundamentals
Complex fractions	Least common multiple
Accuracy in fundamentals	Compound proportion
"Cases" in percentage	Insurance
Taxes and public expenditures	Apothecaries' weight
Greatest common divisor	Savings and investments.

TEACHERS' EXAMINATION, S. F., JUNE 11, 1915.

HISTORY AND CIVICS.

1. If history be regarded as concerned with the actions and achievements of the people,

(a) in founding and managing a stable government;
(b) in framing moral standards and acquiring practice in following them;
(c) in developing and regulating their industries; and
(d) in stimulating and conserving wholesome family and neighborhood customs and institutions;

what can the school do to help on right practice in these several ways?

2. If you could discuss but one of these two problems in our history:

(a) the struggle for and winning our independence as a nation (culminating in the Revolution and the war of 1812-15); or
(b) the achieving of national unity (through the rise and fall of slavery, and the multiplication of common interests between the north and south, between the east and west),

which would you select and why?

3. What effect does or should elementary history studies have upon the ideals and practice of citizenship?

Discuss along with this the methods of teaching history to accomplish these results.

4. For pupils who do not reach high school which part of American history is more valuable—the 150 years of pre-revolutionary colonial life, or the 50 years since the Civil War? Why?

Your answer will depend upon what you conceive to be the purpose of history studies to such youth.

Answer either the first or second and either the third or fourth.

TEACHERS' EXAMINATION, S. F., JUNE 11, 1915.

METHODS OF TEACHING.

1. Discuss the teacher's responsibility toward

(a) the alert, capable, willing pupil;
(b) the willing and studious, but slow pupil of only average ability;
(c) the capable, but indifferent or unwilling pupil; and
(d) the well-disposed, but born-short pupil.

How does the organization of the school help or hinder you in accomplishing these purposes?

2. In your teaching, what difference do you, or in your proposed teaching, would you make in your treatment of boys and girls just entering their teens, as to

(a) instruction and (b) discipline?

3. Of the several studies in the most progressive elementary schools, which ones do you consider the most important for children who are destined to leave school before the high school? Why?

4. Give the educational argument for the introduction of hand and constructive exercises into the elementary schools. Into what grades should they go?

Give the argument from the industrial or economic situation, for including industrial and vocational work in the school course. In what grades does this belong?

Answer No. 4, and one of the other three questions.

TEACHERS' EXAMINATION, JUNE 12, 1915.

GENERAL SCIENCE AND HYGIENE.

(Answer three out of four in each list.)

I. General Science.

1. Select one of the following, and give a brief account of its life history and its uses or dangers to man:
   - (a) The common house-fly
   - (b) The common toad
   - (c) Some bird (to be selected).

2. (a) What are the functions of the root, leaf, and flower of a plant?
   (b) Explain how you would teach these functions to a class of fifth or sixth grade children.

3. What are the main purposes of nature study in grades below the high school?

4. Explain the composition of air, water and coal.

II. Hygiene.

1. Discuss decay of the teeth under the following heads:
   - (a) Prevalence among children of school age.
   - (b) Causes.
   - (c) Means of prevention.

2. In about 150 or 200 words set forth some of the most important requirements of school sanitation.

3. (a) How is the temperature of the body regulated?
   (b) What does heat regulation of the body have to do with health?

4. Explain the most important effects of exercise on the health.

The following circular of information explains the plan of the examination and how appointments are made thereunder:

CITY AND COUNTY OF SAN FRANCISCO, DEPARTMENT OF EDUCATION. TEACHERS' COMPETITIVE EXAMINATION.

Teachers are appointed to this department solely on merit as determined by competitive examinations of applicants who already hold regular teachers' certificates. The object of these examinations is to enable the Board of Education to select the best of those already certified as teachers.

Requirements:

(1) Applicants must be well-educated, of good character and sound bodily health.

(2) Applicants are required:

(a) To have been graduated from a State Normal School; or

(b) To have been in attendance as regular students for two years in an institution of collegiate grade; or

(c) To have had two years' actual teaching experience subsequent to graduation from an institution of high school grade.

(3) Married women are not eligible for the competitive examinations unless their husbands are totally incapacitated through disease or infirmity.

(4) Applicants must not be over thirty-five years of age.

The written examinations are upon the following subjects:

(1) United States History, American Institutions and current events.
(2) Arithmetic.
(3) General Science.
(4) Personal and public hygiene.
(5) Methods of teaching and school management.

The examinations are not based upon any particular books. The following books, however, indicate the scope and range of the subjects covered by the examination:

United States History and American Institutions:

Epochs of American History Series, three volumes (Longman's).
Government in State and Nation, James & Sanford (Scribner's).
Government in the United States, Garner (American Book Co.).

Arithmetic:

Complete Arithmetic, Hamilton (American Book Co.).
Robinson's Arithmetic with Supplement of Fish's Problems.
Packard's Commercial Arithmetic.

General Science:

Rowell's General Science.
Clark's (American Book Co.).
Nature Studies by Hodge.

Personal and Public Hygiene:

The Human Mechanism, Hough & Sedgwich (Ginn & Co.).
Human Body and Health, Davison (American Book Co.).
Primer of Hygiene, Ritchie—Caldwell.
Primer of Sanitation, Ritchie.

No formal examination in English is given; the ability to write and speak correct, forceful English is determined from a consideration of the examinations in general.

Applicants must obtain at least seventy-five per cent (75%) in each subject. If, however, an applicant falls below seventy-five per cent (75%) but not below sixty-five per cent (65%) in one subject only, and the average in the other subjects is at least eighty-five per cent (85%), the applicant is considered to have passed the written examination successfully but is required to take an examination in that subject at the teachers' competitive examination given the following year.

Applicants who pass the written examinations appear before the Board of Education for an oral examination, designed to test their fitness and technical training for teaching, their general intelligence, their information upon matters of world importance and present-day interest known to all educated persons who keep abreast of the times.

Each of the five members of the Board of Education, without conferring with his fellow-members, marks the applicant, the average constituting the mark for the oral examination. Applicants must obtain an average of at least seventy-five per cent (75%) in the oral examinations. Applicants receiving less than seventy-five per cent (75%) from three of the members of the Board are rejected regardless of the marks obtained in the written examination and of the average in the oral. The average of the marks in the written examination, plus the average in the oral, determines the applicant's rank.

Applicants passing the next competitive examination will be divided into Classes A and B; Class A will consist of those who have been graduated from State Normal Schools or from the pedagogic departments of recognized colleges and who after such graduation have had at least two years of successful experience. Of this class the first fifty (50) will be assured appointment to vacancies or to new positions in the elementary schools on the opening day of the school year 1916-17 and their salary will be the usual amount paid probationary teachers, Seventy Dollars ($70.00) per month, plus allowance for experience in teaching. All the other applicants passing the competitive examination successfully will constitute Class B. Class B will be the eligible list of substitutes and such eligible substitutes, as heretofore, will be appointed to vacancies and to new positions in the elementary schools in the order of their rank as they may be needed.

The competitive examinations are held during the summer vacation about June 10th. When necessary, a second examination for the year is set for the Christmas vacation. Application blanks will be furnished all those asking for them, during the two months preceding the dates set for an examination. They should be filled out and forwarded to the Secretary of the Board of Education not later than one week prior to the examination. Applicants must furnish full information relative to their academic preparation, their professional training, and their experience in teaching. Applicants must give references to at least three persons competent to speak of their fitness for teaching. Such references must include the persons whose official position enables them to give the most exact information regarding the applicant's scholarship, training, experience and efficiency. The Board of Education will not consider general letters of recommendation but will request from the persons referred to by the applicant confidential statements regarding the applicant's qualifications. In case of doubt the Board will call for and use supplementary information from other persons who may be deemed competent to speak intelligently of the candidate's qualifications.

Before appointment to the eligible list the successful applicant must obtain from one of several physicians designated by the Board of Education a statement certifying that the applicant is in sound physical and mental health. The expense of the medical examination is born by the applicant. The fee is $2.50.

Before election as regular teachers in the department applicants must serve at least two years after assignment as probationary teachers. They will be assigned for one year and if reported as successful will be re-elected for a second year. At the close of the second year if still deemed successful they will be elected regular teachers and will hold teaching positions for life, provided they comply at all times with the rules of the Board of Education, the laws of the State of California and the Charter of the City and County of San Francisco so far as they relate to the school department.

GENERAL PROVISIONS GOVERNING THE COMPETITIVE EXAMINATIONS

Announcement of dates is made in San Francisco's official daily newspaper (Daily Journal of Commerce) and in the Western Journal of Education, as well as in some of the leading newspapers of the State.

A number system is used by which the identity of the examination papers of the candidate is lost.

At each of the sessions the envelope and the sheets containing the answers of each candidate are stamped with the same number. This number stamping does not begin, however, until all the examination papers of each session have been turned in by the candidates. The envelope and the set of answers of each candidate have a different number from those of every other candidate. In order to avoid confusion the same number is never used twice. The sets of envelopes, after having been numbered, are all placed in a box which is sealed and deposited in the safe of the Board of Education. After the answers have been examined and marked the seal is broken from the box containing the numbered envelopes. This is done in the presence of representatives of the Board of Education and of the Superintendent's office. The envelopes are opened and the identity of the candidate is then disclosed for the first time.

The oral examination is held in the offices of the Board of Education and continues in morning and afternoon sessions until all applicants successful in the written examination have been examined. Each candidate receives notification when to appear.

"SCHOOL BOND ISSUES."

By Alfred Roncovieri, Superintendent of Schools, San Francisco.

For a number of years past, in official reports to the Board of Supervisors and the Board of Education, I have urged the adoption of the "pay-as-you-go" policy for the keeping up of our existing school buildings and the construction of such new buildings as become necessary from time to time to accommodate our steadily increasing attendance. My recommendations have not been adopted, but I regard the "pay-as-you-go" policy as being of such great importance in the matter of school construction that I desire now to call upon the people of this City and County, with all the power and earnestness at my command, to give serious consideration to my arguments in favor the plan and against the extravagantly wasteful and otherwise unsatisfactory bond issue system. After an experience of fifteen years in the administration of the public schools of this City and County, and having given to my work the deepest thought and study of which I am capable, I feel that my arguments should be entitled to consideration.

Attendance in the San Francisco public schools has been steadily increasing since the calamity of 1906. This increase has been regular and continuous, and it goes without saying that, in a great city like San Francisco, it must continue for an extent of time to which we have neither reason nor means to place a limit.

The total number of pupils enrolled in 1908 was 48,045. The enrollment for the fiscal year ending June 30, 1916, was 64,040—an increase in eight years of 15,995 pupils, or an average annual increase of 2,000.

As a result our accommodations have proved inadequate, and our school houses are overtaxed in many parts of the city—this notwithstanding the fact that over fifty buildings have been constructed during the last decade. The greater number of these structures, however, were needed to replace those destroyed by the calamity of 1906, and our present overflow classes are the result of the failure of the people to provide money annually for the additional school accommodations needed for the natural—and highly gratifying—increased demands of our steadily growing attendance. The effort to meet these conditions has—up to the present date, November, 1916—compelled the use of auditorium, library rooms and other unsuitable apartments as classrooms, also the placing of fifty more or less unsightly temporary or portable buildings in the yards of nearly twenty schools, cramping the already insufficient playground space. It was thought that the buildings for those particular schools had been so planned as to meet the requirements of their respective districts for many years to come, but in every case the school population increased beyond expectation. Furthermore, it has been found necessary in several instances to establish "part-time" or "half-time" classes, meaning thereby that the pupils of two classes use the same room, the members of one in the morning, the pupils of the other in the afternoon. This "part-time practice—a direct result of the failure to provide additional school accommodations immediately upon the discovery that they were needed—is an educational evil which with the school and other civic authorities of New York has grown to be a most serious and embarrassing problem. I trust that it may never become so serious in San Francisco, and I feel that it cannot when once our people shall realize the necessity for, and the wisdom and simplicity of, the plan of building as our need develops. It must not be forgotten that the children are the real sufferers from the use of portable buildings, which mean make-shift accommodations and the taking up of yard space, and from the maintaining of "part-time" classes, which, to a certain degree, deny to the children their full educational opportunities. All of these facts, backed by others which I shall shortly cite, go to emphasize the necessity for providing school accommodations step by step and year by year in accordance with the constantly increasing demands caused by the growth of the city and the shifting of centers of population, and also prove the wisdom, as I propose to make clear, of doing so on the "pay-as-you-go" system.

Two methods may be employed to provide adequately for the financial needs of our school-building service:—First, the present plan, by which I mean that heretofore pursued, of issuing long-term bonds; second, by the levying of an annual school-building tax, provided for under our State School Law, and which will permit us to build on the "pay-as-you-go" system, and to build at the time when we most need the buildings, instead of waiting an indefinite number of years for a bond issue, and in the meantime subjecting our children to inconvenience more or less serious and to an actual lack of educational necessities. Of these two methods I advocate the second.

I do not favor long-term school bond issues except as a last resort, and only to meet great emergencies. To provide for the necessities arising from ordinary conditions of growth I favor levying the annual school building tax permitted by the State School Law, and already levied in every county in the State except our own.

As an illustration of the wasteful business policy and the great wrong done to taxpayers and school children alike by neglecting to build school houses annually as they are needed, let us note the results of issuing bonds for school-building purposes after a few years of neglect. As a concrete example, consider the cost to our San Francisco taxpayers of the $5,000,000 of 5 per cent school bonds of 1908, the redemption of which began in July, 1914, and is to continue at the rate of $200,000 per annum until 1938. I cite this case merely to make clear my objections to the financial methods which it has become the custom to employ, and with no purpose of criticising the wisdom of this particular issue of bonds. It was entirely justifiable, the money to be raised being absolutely necessary to replace the many building destroyed by the fire of 1906. But note, and consider carefully, what it has meant, and still means, to the taxpayers of this City and County:

The amount of the bond was	$5,000,000.00
The interest coupons called for a total of	4,500,000.00
If all the bonds had been sold at par on the day of issue the people would have had to provide for interest and redemption funds during the 30 years of the life of the bonds a total of	9,500,000.00
But sales were not effected until a number of interest coupons had become void, such coupons aggregating in value $447,950. Also the bonds were sold at an aggregate premium of $301,-290.40. Making a total to be deducted of	749,240.40
Leaving the net amount to be paid by the people for interest and redemption during the 30 years of life of the bond issue	8,750,759.60
Or an average of $291,692 per year for 30 years	
Deducting from this one-thirtieth of $5,000,000 for redemption payments, $166,667, shows the average annual payments for interest alone to be	125,025.00

We observe that this average annual interest payment alone would construct each year a handsome and commodious school building; therefore the interest which the taxpayers will have paid on this bond issue, at its maturity, would construct thirty or more school buildings.

To think that this vast sum should be expended, and that our taxpayers and our children should have nothing to show for such expenditure, seems appalling, and the facts lose nothing of their unpleasant significance when summarized. For example:

Total net cost of the $5,000,000 of bonds to the people after deducting premiums, etc.	$8,750,759.60
Total value of school buildings obtained for this expenditure	5,000,000.00
Actual cost to the taxpayers of each dollar's worth of improvements	1.75

In other words, a school building actually costing only $100,000 to construct costs the taxpayers in the end just $175,000.

If our citizens can afford to tax themselves to pay $8,750,759.60 in thirty years to buy only $5,000,000 worth of improvements, surely it would be far better business to levy for 15 or 16 years, under the State laws or the emergency clause of the Charter, an annual tax of $325,023—the amount that is now being paid for the redemption of and interest upon these bonds—and thus at the end of the 15 or 16 years to secure $5,000,000 worth of improvements for the $5,000,000 so paid in taxes, or a dollar's worth of school property for each dollar expended.

As a further illustration of the wastefulness of building school houses by means of bond issues, let me remind you that, due to financial conditions in the past, our bonds did not always find a ready market, and some were quoted below par—which may very possibly happen again, owing to the fluctuations of the bond market, a lowering of the rates of interest or other causes. Our Charter provides that bonds shall never be sold below par, but this provision it was found easy to evade. The contractors simply accepted school bonds instead of cash—and protected themselves by adding to the proper cost of the work performed or material furnished the discounts on the bonds. In this indirect manner our taxpayers have been obliged at times to pay premiums upon the actual cost of the work done, such premiums amounting in certain instances to as much as ten per cent, which means, of course, that $1,100 must be paid for each $1,000 worth of service rendered or material furnished. In such instances, therefore, the proper proportion of this extra cost, also of the interest thereon, must be added to the $1.75, which, as already has been shown, has to be paid, under bond—issue methods, for every dollar's worth of new school accommodations. Obviously, in view of the figures just quoted—figures which cannot be disputed—under bond issue conditions less favorable than those attending the issue of 1908, each dollar of labor and material represented in the building done might easily cost the taxpayers $2.

Therefore I contend that school bonds should be issued only in cases of great and sudden emergency, or for the purchase of land—the reason for the exception in the latter case being that it is good business to provide against the inevitable increase in realty values. The great calamity of 1906 justified the issuance of bonds to meet imperative demands for rehabilitation, but these demands have been satisfied, and no real emergency now exists, no need for extensive construction work, except such as has been brought about by a few years of neglect. It is a fact—a most regrettable fact—that certain sections of our city are very poorly supplied with school accommodations, or have school buildings which are crowded far beyond the point of propriety and efficiency, almost beyond endurance, but these conditions are due wholly to the fact that there has been no annual appropriations for new construction since the last bond issue. The results of the neglect of the past eight years are now upon us, but to attempt to remedy them by the issuance of more bonds I hold to be neither wise nor justifiable.

To fail to provide for natural and steadily increasing school needs during eight years, so rendering it necessary, when conditions finally become intolerable, to call upon the people for a bond issue, is bad policy and bad business. Right here, basing my action on the experience gained during fifteen years of service as a school official, and as a matter of simple justice to our children and our taxpayers, I wish to protest against such a system and to do my best to arouse public opinion to the point of demanding its abolishment.

Let it be remembered, and emphasized, that, however often bad conditions may be removed by bond issues, they must inevitably recur, unless, as I have endeavored to point out, provision is made to keep the Department abreast of its needs by means of moderate annual appropriations for new construction. Failing the adoption of this simple, economical and business-like "pay-as-you-go" plan, we must, also inevitably, find ourselves authorizing new bond issues every few years even while the very first issue is still unredeemed. This system of "progressive borrowing" amounts to a piling up of mortgage upon mortgage such as must ultimately lead any business concern to bankruptcy, and the fact that this rich and splendid city of ours is one that simply cannot be placed in such a position is no excuse for the pursuance of methods which, were we less fortunately situated, would mean financial ruin.

For the acquisition or creation of income-earning public utilities, the profits from which provide for the interest upon their cost and at least assist toward the ultimate redemption of the securities, the issuing of bonds is, of course, justifiable; but for school purposes, after the Department needs once have been fully provided for, it is business folly of the worst kind. It is not fair to the next generation to pass along a debt incurred for the housing of children of the present generation—a debt which will then have no other visible evidence of "value received" except a number of old buildings, out of date and behind the times. The next generation will have even larger problems than ours to solve in the housing of its own children. Our fathers left us no such debt. They paid cash for the school structures that housed us, and it is only right that each generation should pay for the school buildings actually needed by its own children. That which follows ours will have more pupils to provide for than we have. For the year ending June 30, 1916, there were 7042 new children enrolled in the First Grade classes—the receiving classes—who had never attended school before. They were the new "crop" of "babies," just arrived at "school age." With every year this "new crop" increases. Where, then, can we find justification for adding to the troubles of those who shall come after us in the management of the School Department by passing on to them so large a share of our own financial burdens?

But, aside from considerations such as this, is it not obviously folly to allow our children and our teachers to suffer for years the inconvenience of—not to say actual injury arising from—insufficient accommodations and overcrowded conditions, and then seek to "catch up" by a wastefully expensive bond issue, when, by a judicious annual expenditure, all of our needs may be amply supplied, as we go along, and without the payment of any interest? In no other way, let it be remembered, can we successfully solve the problem of having always "a seat waiting for every child" rather than that any of our school children, however small the number, should ever be obliged to wait for seats. And we absolutely know that to obtain the best results in construction work school houses must be built one—or a very few—at a time, since under this plan they are always built more practically, carefully and economically than is ever done when a "blanket job" involving the expenditure perhaps of millions, to be spent in many different sections of the city, is rushed through to completion. (Evidence of this, if evidence is needed to support this almost axiomatic fact, may be obtained by an inspection of some of the buildings recently constructed.) Neither is it good policy to buy land in a rush, or to pass upon plans and specifications in haste, because many minor and even major details may so be overlooked.

Bear in mind that I am in favor of bond issues for emergency school purposes, provided the money cannot be raised by a direct tax, but I wish to make the distinction clear between real emergencies and conditions which, while not satisfactory, do not constitute such in the strict sense. I should object, and object strenuously, for example, to the issuing of bonds to provide for the replacement of all of our old school buildings at one time. No sensible corporation manager would think of borrowing millions in order that he might replace all of his old buildings with new ones at one time, while some at least of the old structures were still capable of being put to good and efficient use, even though not entirely up to date. The present is not an opportune time for the wholesale replacement of our old school buildings. I stand firmly on the proposition that no bond money should ever be expended for replacements or for the purchase of anything that will not be in existence beyond the term of the bonds. If bonds are issued at all it should be done only for the purchase of land and for permanent improvements—never for temporary structures or for furnishings which will be worn out before the expiration of the life of the bonds.

In assuming this position I do not wish to invite the charge that I seek to obstruct the progress of our School Department. I simply do not believe in school bond issues except in extreme cases, and as a last measure. As I have said, I believe in bond issues to provide for great public utilities, the income from which helps to pay the interest and the first cost of the investment, but it is quite different with school bonds, which are non-producing in a financial sense, and, as has already been demonstrated, a heavy drain on the resources of our people. The system is not only extravagant, but it also results in an unwarranted waste of our resources.

These resources, by which I mean, in this connection, our bonding power, we should conserve for the great income-producing utilities. We must not forget that in 1909-10 the fear that we would pass our bonding limit if the Water Supply bond issue should be successful caused our Supervisors to cancel over $9,000,000 of bonds previously authorized. Let us not overlook the fact that, under the law, the bonding limit of the municipality of San Francisco is 15 per cent of the assessed value of the real and personal property of the City and County. Consider the following figures:

In 1915 the total assessment was, approximately		$600,000,000
15 per cent of $600,000,000 is		90,000,000
Aggregate of bond issued authorized by the people up to June 30, 1915	$102,594,000	
Bonds remaining unsold as of that date	45,014,200	
	$ 57,579,800	
Bonds cancelled by Supervisors 1909-1910 in fear that if the Hetch-Hetchy issue proved successful the bonding limit might be passed	9,060,000	
Bonds sold	$ 48,519,800	
Redemptions to June 30, 1915	5,881,000	
Outstanding bonded indebtedness June 30, 1915		42,635,800
The remainder of		47,364,200
is represented by unsold bonds authorized by the people amounting to		45,014,200
and by a bonding margin of only		$ 2,350,000

It is, of course, assumed in the above tabulation that the authorization of a bond issue by the people pre-supposes that the bonds will be sold. When we remember that our people have in view the further development of that great public utility, the Municipal Street Railway System, also a further expansion of the city's water supply by the purchase of the Spring Valley Company's properties, this latter project in itself necessitating a bond issue of more than $40,000,000, we may readily understand why real estate values are not increasing. And it should need no argument to convince our people that if our City and County is to be able to carry out these great income-producing public utility plans the bonding limit must be protected.

I repeat that I shall advocate a bond issue for school purposes only as a last resort, and after the people have been shown that there is a better, a less expensive, a more business-like and a more righteous way of providing for the interests of the children—a way which, while so providing for such interests, will also safeguard the rights of the taxpayers.

This better way is the levying of an annual tax for school-building purposes. This may be done under the State laws, which permit the school district of San Francisco to levy such taxes annually in sufficient amount to build all the schools we shall ever need without going through the expensive process of issuing bonds. Following are the Statutes referred to, now in full force and effect in every county of this State:

Section 1755 of the Political Code, which permits a maximum tax for high school purposes of 75 cents on each $100 of assessed valuation.

Section 1756 of the Political Code, which defines the method of preparing the estimate of high school needs within the maximum of the 75-cent rate for such schools.

Section 1757 of the Political Code, which specifies the procedure under which the Board of Supervisors shall levy this tax rate, and also makes it compulsory for the Auditor to levy the tax rate for high school purposes, should the Board of Supervisors fail to do so.

Section 1818 of the Political Code, which provides that the maximum tax rate levied by the Supervisors for the support of the elementary schools of this City and County shall be 50 cents on each $100 of taxable property in this City and County.

Section 1839 of the Political Code, which provides that the maximum rate of tax levied for building purposes upon the "School District of San Francisco" must not exceed 70 cents on each $100, and that the maximum rate levied for other school purposes shall not exceed 30 cents on each $100 in any one year.

Section 1840 of the Political Code, which provides the method of preparing the estimate of the needs of the "School District of San Francisco" and of the "City and County of San Francisco."

Section 1830 of the Political Code, which provides the procedure for calling an election for a "school district" tax, the maximum rate of which must not exceed the 70 cents for building purposes and 30 cents for maintenance prescribed in Section 1839.

We learn from these sections of the State Law that several plans are provided for the levying of special school taxes. If, however, it is argued that the Charter has precedence over the State Law, which is very doubtful, then let us take all the income from the rental of school property—such rental now amounting to nearly $100,000 per annum—and set it aside to be used solely as a "School Building Fund" for new construction. To secure the additional money that may be needed, let us so amend our Charter as to provide for an annual school-building tax, the rate not to exceed the limitations provided by the State Law. But the sections of the State Law quoted in the preceding paragraphs are in force, and are made use of, in the great majority of the school districts and the cities of the State of California, and I firmly believe that they are applicable to San Francisco, which, under the educational system of the State, is a school district. The courts have held in several decisions that education is a State affair, and that the State laws take precedence over Charters in respect to school affairs.

As I have already pointed out, the interest which we are now paying on school bonds would be sufficient in itself to build all the school houses that will be needed, **and as they are needed**, if the Department were once brought to a condition equal to the requirement of pupil attendance. We are now paying in interest on all outstanding school bonds over $250,000 annually (issues 1904-1908 and 1910)—money virtually thrown away, in view of what might be done under the better plan suggested, with the School Department brought up to standard. Instead of postponing the building of needed schools to an undetermined future date, and then raising millions of dollars by the sale of bonds—a method not only extravagant but also such as must continually tend to impair our municipal credit—why not levy annually a small building tax—say 10 cents on each $100 of assessed valuation—within the provisions of the State laws already cited, **and so build our new buildings** just **when we need them**, at an expense to the taxpayer which he will not feel, and which in any case, as has been shown, will be 50 per cent less than he would have to meet to secure the same new structures under the bond-issue system?

The tax rate in this City and County for all school purposes has in late years varied from 20 to 27 cents for each $100 of assessed property valuation. It has even been as low as 6 cents—a ridiculous figure when compared with the allowance provided for in other cities of the Coast and elsewhere. A rate of 10 cents would yield, on the present assessed valuation of San Francisco's real and personal property, approximately $600,000 a year, a sum more than sufficient to provide for all necessary increased school accommodations on the "pay-as-you-go" plan. As the city, its population and its school attendance, grow, so will grow the assessed valuation, and the amount produced by a ten-cent tax levy will increase correspondingly. First and last, the adoption of this system will save millions to the taxpayers, and will enable us to bequeath to posterity substantial assets instead of a load of debt.

After an experience of 15 years in school affairs, I will stake my reputation that, starting with accommodations sufficient to meet existing needs, and barring great emergencies and calamities, all the new schools that will ever be needed in this City and County may be built—**and built as they are needed**—under a "pay-as-you-go" plan based on a special school-construction tax levy **not to** exceed 10 cents on each $100 of assessed property valuation. Therefore I hope and urge that such special tax rate for school-building purposes may be provided for by the Board of Supervisors with the approval and upon the recommendation of the Board of Education.

Report of the Public Pound

To his Honor the Mayor of the City and County of San Francisco:

As per requirements of the Charter, we herewith submit our annual report for the fiscal year ending June 30, 1915.

Dogs on hand July 1st, 1914		56
Impounded during the year		4,139
Redeemed	499	
Released on licenses	302	
Sold	338	
Destroyed	3,004	
On hand June 30, 1915	52	
	4,195	4,195

LARGE STOCK.

Impounded		232
Redeemed	204	
Sold	1	
Destroyed	27	
	232	232

SMALL STOCK.

Impounded		253
Redeemed	236	
Sold	12	
Destroyed	5	
	253	253

CATS.

Impounded		5,936
Destroyed	5,936	
	5,936	5,936

CASH STATEMENT.

Received for dogs redeemed and released on licenses	$ 1,453.30
Received for dogs sold	1,014.00
Received for large stock redeemed	654.00
Received for large stock sold	5.00
Received for small stock redeemed	371.50
Received for small stock sold	30.25
	$ 3,528.05

All the above cash was paid into the City Treasury, as per receipts attached to monthly reports on file in the Board of Supervisors' and Auditor's Offices.

[64th]

REPORT

OF THE

UPERINTENDENT OF SCHOOLS

OF

SAN FRANCISCO, CAL.

FOR THE FISCAL YEAR ENDING JUNE 30, 1916

Superintendent of Schools

ALFRED RONCOVIERI

Note.—The financial data presented in this report were secured from various departments of the city and county government as herein specified in foot-notes, and are here presented without further verification by the Superintendent of Schools.

SCHOOL CALENDAR FOR BOTH DAY AND EVENING SCHOOLS 1915-1916.

Fall Term, 1915—

July 26 to August 27 (Aug. 16-20, N. E. A. vacation)	20	days
Aug. 30 to Sept. 24 (Sept. 6, Labor Day; Sept. 9, Admission Day; Sept. 10, Holiday)	17	"
Sept. 27 to Oct. 22 (Oct. 12, Columbus Day; Oct. 11, Education Day)	18	"
Oct. 25 to Nov. 19 (Oct. 25, ½ day, Edison day P. P. I. E.; Nov. 2, S. F. Day)	18½	
Nov. 22 to Dec. 17 (Nov. 25, Thanksgiving; Nov. 26, Holiday; Nov. 29 to Dec. 4, vacation, last week of P. P. I. E.; Dec. 17, ½ day)	12½	"
	86	days

Schools close on Dec. 17th and reopen Jan. 3d, 1916.

Spring Term, 1916—

Jan. 3 to Jan. 28	20	days
Jan. 31 to Feb. 25 (Feb. 22, Washington's birthday)	19	"
Feb. 28 to March 24	20	"
March 24 to May 5 (April 10 to 14, vacation; April 17 to 21, Institute; May 1, May Day)	19	
May 8 to June 9 (May 30, Memorial Day; June 9, ½ day)	23½	"
	101½	days

Schools close June 9 and reopen July 31, 1916.

SCHOOLS.

Number of High Schools, including High School of Commerce, Commercial Evening, Humboldt Evening High School, and North Beach Evening High School	8
Number of Grammar Schools	33
Number of Primary Schools	46
Number of Special Schools	3
Number of Evening Schools	12
Number of Intermediate Schools (Specialized Grammar)	3
Total number of schools	105

Number of school buildings owned by the department, Class "A"	7
Number of brick school buildings owned by the department, "Special Construction"	23
Number of brick and steel school buildings owned by the department Class "C"	14
Number of wooden school buildings owned by the department	44
Number of school buildings owned by the department Class "B"	1
Total number of buildings used by the department	89
Total number of rooms rented by the department	7

PRINCIPALS AND TEACHERS EMPLOYED DURING THE YEAR ENDING JUNE 30, 1916.

	Principals		Teachers			
			Regular		Special	
	Men	Women	Men	Women	Men	Women
Day High Schools	5	0	43	57	17	28
Evening High Schools	3	0	11	6	21	16
Day Elementary Schools	8	75	11	1002		
Evening Elementary Schools	9	2	7	31		5
Kindergartens						11
Schools (Evening) Home Economics						7
Domestic Science						18
Manual Training					18	
Athletics					9	4
Drawing						8
Music						2
Supervisor Primary Grades						1
Substitutes in Day Schools				86		
Substitutes in Even'g Schools				3		

SCHOLASTIC PREPARATION OF TEACHERS.

Number of Teachers (including Principals).

	Men	Women
Who are graduates of University of California	45	119
Who are graduates of Leland Stanford Jr. University	10	15
Who are graduates of other Universities	23	12
Who are graduates of other Colleges	16	29
Who are graduates of S. F. City Normal School or Class	0	376
Who are graduates of Chico State Normal School	2	15
Who are graduates of Los Angeles State Normal	1	4
Who are graduates of San Diego State Normal	0	0
Who are graduates of San Francisco State Normal	0	263
Who are graduates of San Jose State Normal	6	104
Who are graduates of Normal Schools of other States	2	24

CERTIFICATION OF TEACHERS.

	Men	Women
Number holding certificates of High School Grade	85	141
Number holding certificates of Grammar School Grade	17	1112
Number holding certificates of Primary School Grade	0	21
Number holding special certificate in Bookkeeping	7	11
Number holding special certificate in Domestic Science	0	29
Number holding special certificate in Drawing (all departments)	18	15
Number holding special certificate in Languages	2	28
Number holding special certificate in Manual Training (all departments)	26	1
Number holding special certificate in Music	1	51
Number holding special certificate in Physical Culture	10	7
Number holding special certificate in Stenography and Typewriting	6	22
Number holding special certificate Kindergarten	0	11

VOLUMES IN SCHOOL LIBRARIES AND STOREROOM.

(Including Books for Use of Indigents.)

	Volumes	Value
High Schools, including Humboldt Evening and S. F. Com'l....	7,585	$6,070.00
Primary and Grammar Schools	90,659	39,976.00
Evening Schools	1,700	612.00
In Storeroom	2,465	1,232.50

SCHOOL VISITATION.

Official visits of Superintendent and deputies	5,266
Official visits by members of the Board of Education	2,050
Visits by other persons	71,818

"STATE SCHOOL ENROLLMENT" AND ATTENDANCE STATISTICS FOR THE YEAR ENDING JUNE 30, 1916.

ENROLLMENT.

High Schools	4,664
S. F. Commercial (Evening) (See note below)	1,504
Elementary	50,333
Kindergarten	897
Humboldt Evening High	2,298
Other Evening Schools	4,344
	64,040

AVERAGE DAILY ATTENDANCE.

High Schools	3,852
San Francisco Commercial (Evening) (see note below)	*195
Elementary	41,301
Kindergarten	430
Humboldt Evening High	*454
Other Evening Schools	*630
	46,862

Note:—This year, 1915-16, the San Francisco Commercial School is regarded as a high school.

GRADUATES.

Number of graduates from the grammar school for the year:

	Day	Evening	Total
Boys	1334	287	1,621
Girls	1522	228	1,750
Totals			3,371

Number of graduates from the high schools for the year:

	Day	Evening	Total
Boys	179	223	402
Girls	254	82	336
Totals			738

* Average daily attendance in Evening Schools is estimated on 50% basis.

DAY GRAMMAR SCHOOL GRADUATES BY SCHOOLS.

	December, 1915		June, 1916	
	Boys	Girls	Boys	Girls
Adams	19	6	16	16
Bay View	22	15	14	21
Bernal	29	16	26	40
Columbia	20	30	12	23
Crocker	31	33	30	39
Denman	....	15	....	17
Everett	16	25	20	20
Fairmount	26	20	32	43
Farragut	6	10	7	7
Francis Scott Key	....	....	4	6
Frank McCoppin	13	14	18	17
Franklin	7	6	11	8
Fremont	10	8	16	11
Glen Park	9	10	10	17
Grant	7	8	22	12
Grattan	13	12	14	10
Hamilton	44	38	27	36
Hancock	40	34	14	18
Hearst	12	14	14	18
Horace Mann	50	53	63	115
Hunters Point	....	1	....	....
Irving M. Scott	5	5	12	6
John Swett	27	19	21	15
James Lick	20	23	22	36
Jean Parker	....	19	....	22
Jefferson	....	....	1	4
Lafayette	5	6	1	8
Laguna Honda	13	28	25	22
Lincoln	2	3	7	3
Longfellow	7	11	....	....
Madison	23	13	12	18
McKinley	9	11	15	10
Mission	20	11	23	19
Monroe	18	20	20	30
Oriental	11	4	15	7
Pacific Heights	15	18	16	22
Portola	4	12	3	13
Redding	3	6	5	9
Rochambeau	12	8	13	7
Roosevelt	4	23	14	21
Sheridan	9	7	3	4
Sherman	4	5	12	7
Spring Valley	17	16	15	17
Sunnyside	5	2	4	2
Sutro	15	28	20	26
Visitacion Valley	....	....	9	11
Washington	26	....	16	....
Winfield Scott	3	6	5	1
Yerba Buena	4	6	9	10
	646	678	688	814

RECAPITULATION.

	Boys	Girls
December, 1915	646	678
June, 1916	688	844
Total	1334	1522
Total Boys and Girls		2856

* "STATE SCHOOL ENROLLMENT" BY GRADES AND SEX.

(State School Enrollment admits no duplication. Pupils promoted during the year are enumerated only in the grades from which they were promoted.)

DAY SCHOOLS.

	Boys	Girls	Total
Kindergarten	456	441	897
First Grade	5,970	5,250	11,220
Second Grade	3,867	3,644	7,511
Third Grade	3,665	3,298	6,963
Fourth Grade	3,089	3,007	6,096
Fifth Grade	3,032	2,697	5,729
Sixth Grade	2,444	2,517	4,961
Seventh Grade	2,145	2,239	4,384
Eighth Grade	1,637	1,832	3,469
Total Elementary and Kindergarten	26,305	24,925	51,230
High Schools—			
First Year*	1,080	1,407	2,487
Second Year	507	634	1,141
Third Year	219	338	557
Fourth Year	196	283	479
Total High	2,002	2,662	4,664
Grand Totals (Day Schools)	28,307	27,587	55,894

* These figures exclude those enrolling in January and who during the year were enrolled in the Grammar (8th) grade.

STATE SCHOOL ENROLLMENT—Continued.

EVENING SCHOOLS.**

	Men	Women	Total
Humboldt Evening High—			
First Year	1,294	433	1,727
Second Year	281	141	422
Third Year	123	10	133
Fourth Year	16		16
Totals	1,714	584	2,298
North Beach Evening High and Commercial Evening Schools—			
First Year	620	313	933
Second Year	477	154	631
Third Year	10	3	13
Fourth Year	6	1	7
Totals	1,113	471	1,584
Elementary Evening Schools—			
First Grade	306	43	349
Second Grade	115	10	125
Third Grade	452	96	548
Fourth Grade	691	151	842
Fifth Grade	277	65	342
Sixth Grade	483	94	577
Seventh Grade	382	64	440
Eighth Grade	355	680	1,035
Totals	3,061	1,203	4,264
**Grand totals Evening Schools	5,888	2,258	8,146
Grand totals Day Schools	28,307	27,587	55,894
Grand Totals	34,195	29,845	64,040

TEACHERS.

	Resigned	Died	Dropped from Roll	Total	Total No. of Teachers appointed Day and Evening High and Elementary
1911-12	33	9	10	52	116
1912-13	38	9	4	51	86
1913-14	38	14	7	59	83
1914-15	38	4	4	46	107
1915-16	41	13	2	56	105

** Evening Schools enroll only pupils who are over 15 years of age except a few who have been granted a permit to work but who are over 14 years of age. Many adults are enrolled.

REPORT OF THE BOARD OF EXAMINATION.

The Board of Examination is composed of: Superintendent Alfred Roncovieri, Chairman; Deputy Superintendent W. B. Howard, Secretary; Deputy Superintendent T. L. Heaton, Deputy Superintendent A. J. Cloud, Deputy Superintendent W. H. DeBell and Miss Magner.

The Board of Examination has conducted one examination, according to law, of persons desirous of securing certificates. It has met monthly and forwarded its recommendation to the Board of Education.

Herewith is a resume of its work:

CERTIFICATES GRANTED ON CREDENTIALS.

HIGH SCHOOL.

Men	18
Women	41
	59

ELEMENTARY.

Men	5
Women	141
	146

SPECIALS.

Men	6
Women	16
	22

RENEWALS.

Men	2
Women	37
	39

ON EXAMINATION.

GRAMMAR.

Men	0
Women	3
	3

REJECTED.

Men	2
Women	10
	12

SPECIALS.

Men	3
Women	11
	14

Number of Certificates issued	244
Number of Certificates renewed	39
Number of Applicants rejected	12
Amount fees collected of applicants, including renewals	$640

NECROLOGY.

	Lowell High	July 20, 1915
	Girls High	Aug. 8, 1915
	Hamilton	Aug. 19, 1915
	Lowell High	Aug. 19, 1915
	John Swett	Aug. 25, 1915
ntyre	Rochambeau	Sept. 25, 1915
	Paul Revere	Nov. 22, 1915
	Haight	Dec. 27, 1915
	Cookery	Jan. 4, 1916
	Rincon	Jan. 16, 1916
	Franklin	May 2, 1916
	Madison	May 14, 1916
	Lincoln	May 27, 1916
	Manual Training	July 20, 1916

REPORT TO UNITED STATES COMMISSIONER OF EDUCATION.

The following statement of the financial affairs of the Department was prepared in accordance with the request of the United States Bureau of Education.

STATISTICS FOR THE FISCAL YEAR ENDING JUNE 30, 1916.

A.—PAYMENTS.

I.—Expenses (Cost of Conducting School System).

	Total	Salaries	Other Objects
Expenses of General Control (Overhead Charges)—			
Board of Education & Secretary's office	$26,531.83	$24,717.00	$ 1,814.83
Inventory of stores	7,564.06	4,560.00	3,004.06
Offices in charge of buildings	3,765.26	3,600.00	165.26
Office of superintendent of schools	24,531.54	23,259.96	1,271.58
Enforcement of compulsory education and truancy laws	4,080.00	4,080.00	
Other expenses of general control	3,460.49		3,460.49
Total	$76,749.45	$60,216.96	$16,532.49

	Total	Sch Elementary, including Kindergarten	Secondary (High)	Evening Schools Elementary	Evening Schools Secondary	*Special Activities	Unassigned
Expenses of Instruction—							
Salaries of principals and their clerks	$ 178,638.65	$ 156,198.65	$ 15,900.00	$ 3,900.00	$ 2,640.00		
Salaries of teachers	1,544,324.25	1,167,369.30	230,270.65	26,980.15	39,821.90	$15,682.00	$ 64,200.25
Stationery and supplies used in instruction	74,613.15	20,871.15	4,407.64	367.03	166.49	48,800.84	
Total for instruction	1,797,576.05	1,344,439.10	250,578.29	31,247.18	42,628.39	64,482.84	64,200.25
Expenses of Operation of School Plant—							
Wages of janitors and other employes	116,672.10	96,300.60	17,911.50	1,860.00	600.00		
Fuel	17,320.67	15,671.18	1,649.49				
Water	12,247.78						12,247.78
Light and power	8,541.57						8,541.57
Janitor's supplies	11,611.53	6,968.27	3,197.88	136.71	307.25	1,001.42	
Other expenses of operation of school plant	4,680.00						4,680.00
Total for operation	171,073.65	118,940.05	22,758.87	1,996.71	907.25	1,001.42	25,469.35
Expenses of Maintenance of School Plant—							
Repair of buildings and upkeep of grounds	120,635.55	195.27	24.28			16.00	120,400.00
Repair and replacement of equipment	869.99	821.38	48.61				
Insurance	1,225.91						1,225.91
Other expenses of maintenance of of school plant (labor)	14,753.25						14,753.25
Total for maintenance	137,484.70	1,016.65	72.89			16.00	136,379.16

A.—PAYMENTS (Continued).

	Total	Day Schools: Elementary, including Kindergarten	Day Schools: Secondary (High)	Evening Schools: Elementary	Evening Schools: Secondary	*Special Activities	Unassigned
Expenses of Auxiliary Agencies—							
[illegible]s, [illegible] bureau	35.00					35.00	
Teachers' [illegible]stitute	[illegible]					1,162.00	
Salaries, Social [illegible]rs	2,039.00					2039.00	
Supplies, Social Centers	456.99					456.99	
[illegible]s, school museum	232.17					232.17	
Promotion of [illegible]th, salaries and other [illegible]es	18,507.68					18,507.68	
Total for auxiliary agencies	22,432.84					22,432.84	
Miscellaneous Expenses—							
Rent	1,595.60						1,595.60
Total miscellaneous	1,595.60						1,595.60
Total expenses	$2,206,912.29	$1,464,395.80	$273,410.05	$33,243.89	$43,535.64	$87,933.10	$304,393.81

II.—Outlays (Capital Acquisition and Construction).

	Total	Day Schools: Elementary, including Kindergarten	Day Schools: Secondary (High)	Evening Schools: Elementary	Evening Schools: Secondary	*Special Activities	Unassigned
New buildings	$ 235,668.91	$ 150,391.79	$ 85,277.12				
Alteration of old buildings	222.80	222.80					
Equipment of new buildings and grounds	12,535.68		12,535.68				
Equipment of old buildings, exclusive of replacements	3,153.64	1,693.49	1,457.12	$ 3.03			
Classroom equipment	74,034.10	22,577.88	49,668.48	17.79	$ 157.25	$ 1,612.70	
Total outlays	$ 325,615.13	$ 174,885.96	$148,938.40	$ 20.82	$ 157.25	$ 1,612.70	

A.—PAYMENTS (Continued).

III.—Other Payments.

Redemption of bonds	$ 314,800.00
Payment of warrants and orders of preceding year	6,085.35
Payments of interest	285,074.25
Total other payments	$ 605,959.60
Grand total of payments for all purposes	$3,138,487.02
Balance carried forward to next year	$ 550,172.10

B.—RECEIPTS.

Revenue Receipts—	
Subventions and grants from state	$ 706,366.99
Appropriations from city treasury	326,441.79
General property taxes	1,933,507.92
Rents	98,142.50
Total revenue receipts	$3,064,459.20
Non-revenue Receipts—	
Loans and bond sales	$ 8,300.00
Sales of equipment and supplies	64.03
Total non-revenue receipts	$ 8,364.03
Total receipts	$3,072,823.23
Balances at beginning of year	615,835.89
Total receipts and balances	$3,688,659.12

STATISTICS OTHER THAN FISCAL FOR THE SCHOLASTIC YEAR.

	Total	Elementary including Kindergarten	Seconda (High
Superintendents, and associate and assistant superintendents, whose duties are mainly connected with the general control of the system......1 Superintendent 5 Deputy Superintendents			
Supervising principals, principals of groups and districts, and principals of buildings or similar units, including only those persons devoting half or more than half of their time to control or administration, and supervision of instruction..........	84	76	8
Supervisors whose duties are mainly connected with the supervision of instruction of special subjects and grades, including only those who devote half or more than half of their time to supervision................	10	10	0
Number of different individuals employed as teachers:			
Males	162	62	100
Females	1,359	1,252	107
Total teachers	1,521	1,314	207
Number of teaching positions (numbers of teachers necessary to supply the school)....	1,521	1,314	207
Enrollment of pupils (net registration, excluding duplicates):			
Males	34,195	29,366	4,829
Females	29,845	26,128	3,717
Total enrollment	64,040	55,494	8,546
Aggregate attendance (total number of days attended by all pupils)............................	8,786,141	7,940,520	845,621
Average daily attendance.................................	46,862	42,346	4,516
Number of days the public schools were actually in session......................................	187½	*189 †187½	187
Number of schools buildings or units of plant, not including portable or temporary structures operated as part of a permanent building	91	86	5
Number of school rooms..................................	1,455	1,294	160
Number of sittings or seats for study............	54,430	49,861	4,569

* Kindergarten.

† Elementary.

Number of buildings not used for schools or special activities, occupied as office buildings, warehouses, etc., 2.

How many of the public high schools are in buildings not occupied also by elementary grades? 5.

How many public high schools belong to the city system? 8 (5 day and 3 evening). Normal schools? 0. Vocational schools, or schools for the industries? 1. Name any special schools, such as schools for the blind, deaf, feeble-minded, delinquents, dependents, etc. 1 for deaf, 2 for delinquents, 3 for defectives.

Have you any special activities connected with the school system, as lectures, playgrounds, social centers? Yes.

How many librarians and assistants are employed in school libraries? None. Libraries in each school are managed by the Principal.

How many school physicians are employed? 3. How many school nurses? 14.

How many truant officers? 3. What is their average salary? $1,440 each.

How many teachers are employed in the public evening schools? Males 50, females 67, total 117. How many of these are also teachers in the public day schools? Males 5, females 0, total 5.

* How many pupils are enrolled in the public elementary and high evening schools? Males 5,888, females 1,657, total 7,545. How many of these pupils were also enrolled, sometime during the year, in the public day schools? Males 0, females 0, total 0.

How many public kindergarten teachers were employed? 11.

How many children were enrolled in the public kindergartens? Males 456, females 441, total 897.

What is the length of school term provided by law or regulation, not omitting holidays, etc.? 100 school days. We have two terms of 100 days each.

Name of Superintendent for 1915-16, Alfred Roncovieri.

---

* The elementary evening school enrollment was 3,663
The high evening school enrollment was 3,882

7,545

The average daily attendance of the evening elementary schools was actually 1,230, but under our State laws we are required to report only 50% of this number (615) for purposes of State apportionment of State school funds.

The average daily attendance of evening high schools on the basis of 187½ days' attendance was actually 1,328, but under our State laws we are required to report 50% of this number, or 664, for purposes of State apportionment of State school funds.

SOME SCHOOL STATISTICS FROM THE OPENING OF THE FI

Year Ending Oct. 31.	No. of Schools.	Teachers.	Pupils Enrolled.	Average Daily Attendance.
1850	1	2	150	......
1851	1	4	325	......
1852	7	15	700	445
1853	....	16	2,870	1,182
1854	....	19	4,199	1,727
1855	....	29	4,694	1,638
1856	9	61	3,347	2,516
Year Ending June 30.				
1857	....	60	2,821	2,155
1858	....	67	5,273	2,521
1859	11	75	6,201	2,829
1860	....	68	6,180	2,837
1861	13	73	6,617	3,377
1862	17	82	8,204	3,786
1863	....	94	8,177	4,389
1864	20	108	7,075	5,470
1865	....	138	8,000	6,718
1866	32	206	10,152	8,131
1867	37	253	13,385	10,177
1868	39	285	17,426	11,871
1869	42	326	19,885	13,113
1870	55	371	22,152	15,394
1871	56	416	26,406	16,978
1872	56	480	27,664	18,272
1873	58	506	27,722	18,550
1874	64	510	29,449	19,434
1875	64	552	31,128	21,014
1876	66	574	34,029	22,761
1877	66	632	37,268	24,899
1878	65	672	38,672	26,292
1879	64	696	38,129	27,075
1880	59	685	38.320	28,150
1881	62	719	40,187	29.092
1882	65	675	40,752	29,435
1883	63	687	40,722	30,827
1884	64	714	41,942	31,578
1885	65	734	43,265	32,183
1886	65	773	43,140	32,146
1887	68	799	43,311	31,316
1888	68	806	42,330	30,191
1889	71	838	42,626	31,609
1890	72	859	42,926	31,852
1891	73	879	43,626	31,809
1892	75	897	46,172	32,431
1893	76	929	45,775	32,799
1894	73	866	44,349	32,989
1895	75	904	44,822	32,974
1896	76	927	45,435	33,508
1897	77	974	46,564	33,531
1898	92	1,070	50,101	35,116
1899	90	1,074	48,972	36.830
1900	86	1,061	48,058	35.004
1901	82	1,017	48,517	34,771
1902	84	1,052	48,893	35,691
1903	84	1,086	48,345	37,077
1904	85	1,121	49,600	37,700
1905	85	1,181	55,067	40.920
1906	86	1,115	57,782	41,932
1907	88	971	45,633	29,929
1908	89	1,095	48,045	33,931
1909	92	1,195	48,509	35,541
1910	95	1,198	50,212	36,774
1911	100	1,227	51.462	37,736
1912	105	1,308	53.160	40,448
1913	105	1,423	53,757	42,820
1914	104	1,478	57,852	44,388
1915	104	1,485	61,941	46,562
1916	105	1,520	64,040	46,825

...LIC SCHOOLS BY J. C. PELTON, DECEMBER, 1849, TO JUNE 30, 1915.

...penses for ... Purposes. (...nc. Bonds)	Cost per Capita on Average Daily Attendance.	School Census Children 4 to 18 Years.	Value of School Property. (Estimated)	Assessment of City and County Property.
....	....	500	....	$ 21,621,214
....	....	1,510	....	14,016,903
$23,125	51.96	2,132	....	18,481,737
35,040	29.65	2,730	....	28,900,150
159,249	92.21	3,268		34,762,827
136,580	83.38	4,531	....	32,076,572
125,064	49.71	4,751	....	30,368,254
92,955	43.14	4,755	....	35,397,176
104,808	41.57	6,375	....	30,725,950
134,731	47.62	7,767	....	30,019,222
156,407	55.13	9,025	....	35,809,639
158,855	47.04	13,316	....	41,870,811
134,576	35.58	13,358	....	41,870,811
178,929	47.67	16,501	....	66,566,655
228,411	41.76	18,748	....	78,709,337
346,862	50.15	21,013	....	83,197,725
		5 to 15 Years.		
361,668	44.48	17,369	....	88,934,543
507,822	49.89	20,253	$1,057,000	96,740,159
416,654	35.09	23,306	1,368,000	109,360,825
397,842	30.34	24,817	1,531,000	106,414,128
526,625	33.56	27,055	1,729,800	114,759,510
705,116	41.53	28,971	1,786,400	106,391,876
668,262	36.02	31,936	1,810,000	105,025,534
611,818	35.45	34,676	....	288,533,256
		5 to 17 Years.		
689,022	35.40	38,084	2,227,620	212,407,505
707,445	33.71	41,029	2,367,000	264,000,000
667,755	38.12	46,238	2,505,500	269,105,141
732,324	29.41	53,210	2,585,000	260,576,978
989,259	37.62	55,899	2,711,000	254,702,960
876,489	32.37	62,105	3,047,303	244,477,360
809,133	28.74	58,492	3,073,000	217,487,074
827,324	28.44	55,115	3,137,000	253,545,476
735,435	24.98	55,880	3,137,000	222,336,400
791,175	25.66	58,061	3,137,000	201,992,152
797,452	25.25	63,029	3,137,000	201,763,762
840,367	25.80	69,000	3,137,000	223,509,560
815,778	25.37	74,079	3,189,000	230,386,325
843,297	26.93	78,246	3,184,575	230,151,009
926,662	30.69	59,517	3,230,598	251,746,111
916,644	28.99	60,642	4,772,180	273,389,616
983,014	31.35	61,144	4,757,724	306,041,440
053,610	33.12	62,456	4,798,427	301,444,140
098,839	33.88	63,933	4,932,754	311,566,079
184,757	34.59	65,317	5,019,317	346,224,706
989,009	30.05	68,390	5,063,364	342,644,179
043,067	26.09	70,006	5,140,258	325,108,898
986,571	32.42	71,822	5,284,000	327,805,147
322,941	36.52	74,840	5,354,859	330,401,154
119,829	37.58	76,336	5,474,739	351,784,094
507,163	40.92	75,292	5,514,200	405,111,615
374,696	36.41	78,554	5,514,200	410,155,304
52,631	30.27	82,173	5,207,600	413,417,241
316,170	36.88	82,391	5,334,000	413,099,993
322,585	35.67	91,386	5,649,651	419,968,644
398,296	37.09	97,353	5,702,001	545,866,416
03,349	34.29	98,127	5,800,000	502,892,359
98,275	35.73	101,836	6,984,000	5[illegible]4,230,946
25,433	44.28	77,367	6,207,010	375,932,447
84,355	57.01	87,696	6,379,000	429,632,592
01,236	47.86	88,058	7,206,573	454,334,160
07,948	89.98	74,729	8,733,285	49[illegible],867,037
87,825	83.18	abolished	10,161,19[illegible]	545,057,591
44,073	92.54		12,536,929	605,488,153
29,054.50	77.70		11,983,657	604,793,249
04,838.65	78.95		12,600,202	623,847,729
24,429.19	69.25		16,929,218	647,207,514
17,831.00	60.13		14,020,943	749,000,000

FOREWORD.

The Report of the Superintendent for the fiscal year 1914-15 gave a very complete exposition of the condition of the Department to July 1, 1915; and, subsequent thereto, very large supplements were appended, bringing the Report down to approximately March 1, 1916.

It has therefore been considered unnecessary in this Report (annual Report 1915-16) to repeat the content of the former Report in toto. Instead, the period from March 1, 1916, to July 1, 1916, only has been covered herein insofar as educational progress and conditions are concerned, and reference made to the earlier Report for preceding periods. The title-heads herein used are those of the former Report. Statistical matter for the entire fiscal year 1915-16 is, however, herein contained.

PRINCIPALS' AND TEACHERS' MEETINGS.

These meetings, as described in the report of 1914-15 (to which reference is hereby made) were held regularly during the spring term 1915-16. One of the most important discussions was that at the May meeting on the topics "Grading of Review Papers" and "The Basis of Promotion". Deputy Superintendents DeBell and Cloud led the discussion on each of these topics respectively.

SCHOOL MUSEUM.

The immediate opportunity afforded by the presence of the Panama-Pacific Exposition to collect material to form the nucleus of a School Museum, and the function to be exercised by such an institution, are set forth in the report of 1914-15 (to which reference is hereby made).

The Committee of teachers having this matter in charge, headed by Mr. F. K. Barthel, with Mr. Con A. Davis, chief assistant, showed great devotion to the work and accomplished important results. While, as yet, no definite sum has been set aside to put the collected material in shape for concrete use in the schools, it is hoped that the Museum may be organized during the coming year.

GARDENING.

There has been little change in this important phase of school work since the report of 1914-15 (to which reference is hereby made).

In our official recommendations to the Board of Supervisors on the financial needs of the Department, in May, 1916, we asked for an appropriation of $5,000 for the extension of school gardening; but no specific sum was allowed; and no definite action has been had.

We renew our frequent recommendations in this particular.

NATURE STUDY AND ELEMENTARY SCIENCE.

Class-room work in this study (as described in the report of 1914-15, to which reference is hereby made) has progressed favorably, though hampered by lack of equipment. In our official recommendations to the Board of Supervisors on the financial needs of the Department, in May, 1916, we asked for an appropriation of $5,000 for materials and equipment for the extension and improvement of the Science Course; but no specific sum was allowed; and no definite action has been had.

PENMANSHIP.

Owing to the adoption of the Zaner System of Penmanship books by th State Board of Education, to be introduced in all elementary schools of Cal fornia in the Fall Term 1916, it has been necessary to make radical readjustments in the Course of Study in this subject. Teachers throughout the department have been thoroughly advised of the contemplated change. The Superintendent secured the services of Mr. C. P. Zaner, author of the newly adopted series, to lecture before the teachers of the department, in April, and also to give counsel in regard to the new lines of work. It is thus thought that the readjustments will be effected without undue difficulty.

In our official recommendations to the Board of Supervisors on the financial needs of the Department, in May, 1916, we asked for an appropriation of $5,500 for a Supervisor of Penmanship and two assistants; but no specific sum was allowed and no definite action has been had.

OVERCROWDED CONDITIONS.

Realizing the necessity for the establishment of new classes to relieve congestion in the scnools, as described in the report of 1914-15 (to which reference is hereby made), the Board of Education has increased the teaching force for the coming fiscal year by sixty-nine appointments in the elementary schools, and thirty-four in the high schools. We take pleasure in commending this action.

UNGRADED CLASSES.

A thorough-going analysis of the function and value of the Ungraded Class is furnished in the report of 1914-15 (to which reference is hereby made).

During the past term a few classes of this general description, though not specifically so designated, have been established by the Board of Education. We reiterate former recommendations that a much larger number be formed. At least twenty are urgently needed.

In our official recommendations to the Board of Supervisors on the financial needs of the Department, in May, 1916, we asked for an appropriation of $25,000 for this purpose; but no specific sum was allowed.

SPECIAL UNGRADED SCHOOLS.

We renew the recommendations on this subject contained in the report of 1914-15.

SUBNORMAL CLASSES.

We renew the recommendations on this subject contained in the report of 1914-15.

VACATION SCHOOLS.

We have watched with great interest the remarkable success achieved by Vacation Schools in many cities of the Union. In our reports for the past several years we have presented the argument in favor of such schools, and have strongly urged the Board of Education to make a beginning, no matter how modest, in organizing such schools. We regret that we have met with no success in this endeavor.

In our official recommendations to the Board of Supervisors on the financial needs of the Department, in May, 1916, we earnestly asked for the meagre appropriation of $5,000 for this purpose; but no specific sum was allowed, and no action has been had.

We strongly renew our recommendations on this subject, as contained in our last several reports.

HEALTH.

The article under this heading in the Report of 1914-15 (to which reference is hereby made) gives a detailed explanation of conditions in this respect.

In our official recommendations to the Board of Supervisors on the financial needs of the Department, in May, 1916, we asked that an additional sum be allowed the Board of Health for the extension of this work.

INTERMEDIATE SCHOOLS.

In view of the success of the three schools of this type described in the Report of 1914-15 (to which reference is hereby made) we asked in our official recommendations to the Board of Supervisors, in May, 1916, that the sum of $15,000 be appropriated for establishing and equipping three additional Intermediate Schools; but no specific sum was allowed; and no action has been had.

SUBSTITUTE TEACHERS.

To carry into effect the plan for an improved substitute list, as set forth in full in the Report of 1914-15 (to which reference is hereby made), we asked in our official recommendations to the Board of Supervisors on the financial needs of the Department, in May, 1916, that an appropriation of $5,000 be made. No specific sum was so appropriated.

ENFORCED ATTENDANCE.

Referring to the treatment of the subject of Enforced Attendance, in the report of 1914-15 (which see), we desire to repeat our recommendation that a system of absent cards be inaugurated, for the purpose of preventing children of school age from being on the street during school hours, and of requiring their presence at school, in accordance with State law. No action has been had on this recommendation.

The following Age and Schooling Certificates (Working Permits) were issued by the office of the Superintendent of Schools during the fiscal year 1915-16:

AGE AND SCHOOLING CERTIFICATES ISSUED TO CHILDREN FROM JULY 1, 1915, TO SEPTEMBER 10, 1915 (OLD LAW).

Certificates issued to children between 15 and 16 (not graduates)	132
Certificates issued to children between 15 and 16 (graduates)	24
Temporary Permits issued to children between 12 and 15 years	22
Certificates issued to graduates under 15 years	12

AGE AND SCHOOLING CERTIFICATES ISSUED TO CHILDREN FROM SEPTEMBER 10, 1915, TO JUNE 30, 1916 (NEW LAW).

Owing to changes in the law, in operation on and after Sept. 10, 1915, Age and Schooling Certificates cannot be issued to children under 14 years or who have not completed the 7th grade.

Certificates issued to children between 15 and 16 (not graduates)	126
Certificates issued to children between 15 and 16 (graduates)	63
Temporary Permits issued to children 14 years or over	19[illegible]
Certificates issued to graduates over 14 years of age but not 15 years	3[illegible]

THE CURBING OF TRUANCY.

The work of the Truant Officers of the School Department, who are members of the police force especially detailed for this duty, has lost nothing in importance, though, as will be shown by a comparison of figures, the efforts of the officers are bringing about a steady improvement in the conditions which make their services necessary. Their labors continue arduous, however, the more so that there are now but two truant officers available where there were formerly three. The larger number was by no means in excess of the requirements but, owing to the need believed to exist for the strengthening of the ordinary branches of police service, Officer J. H. Duggan was recalled to regular street duty three months ago, leaving the truancy work to be done by Officers Eugene Sweeney and E. J. Nolan. As a result the pressure upon these two officers has been materially increased, but I take pleasure in testifying to my belief that they have made every effort to meet effectively their increased responsibilities.

The following tabulated statement shows, in outline, the work done by the truant officers during the school year (fiscal year) which began July 1, 1915, and ended June 30, 1916:

Number of truancy complaints investigated, reported on to principals and followed up further when necessary	3720
Number of children found on streets during school hours and reported back to principals	1284
Number of children taken before Juvenile Court	115
Number of parents taken before Juvenile Court	114
Total number of cases so disposed of	5233

That the efforts of the Truant Officers have not been without effect, not only in the immediate enforcement of the rules against truancy, but also in a general discouragement of this offense, is made evident by a comparison of the figures given above with the corresponding showing for the previous year. For example, the total number of truancy cases referred to the Truant Officers by principal and others for investigation was 4024 in 1914-1915 as against 3720 in 1915-1916, and this despite an increased enrollment in the latter year. Also, during the former year 2219 school children were found on the streets during school hours, as against 1284 during the latter. Again, the number of children taken before the Juvenile Court was 160 in 1914-1915, and but 115 in 1915-1916, while in the latter year only 114 parents were cited before that tribunal as against 149 in the former.

In addition to the work outlined in the foregoing tabulation for 1915-1916, the Truant Officers were also called upon to investigate numerous cases of boyish mischief or more serious vandalism, their efforts toward the detection of the offenders, the enforcement of reparation, and the bringing about of punishment, where a penalty of such character has seemed necessary, being uniformly successful. In the great majority of cases parents of the children at fault have been promptly made to see the wisdom of replacing broken glass or providing for other necessary repairs. The tendency to petty pilfering from school premises by children lacking in proper impulses and training, likewise by more blameworthy offenders of larger growth, has also been kept well in check by the watchful zeal of the Truant Officers.

IMMIGRANTS.

A clear statement of the value and function of classes for immigrants is made in the report of 1914-15 (to which reference is hereby made.)

That the work actually being carried on in one of our evening schools in this particular direction may serve as an illustration of that being done in several others, we here set forth details of the instruction being given to immigrants at the Lincoln Evening School under the direction of Mr. Frank Fenton, Principal, and Miss Charlotte Wheeler, teacher.

The Lincoln Evening School has three classes devoted to the instruction of foreigners. The course embraces:

(a) Reading by a phonetic system, that is, placing the sounds and increasing the vocabulary, aided by charts, pictures and review cards.

(b) Conversational methods and written composition, a dramatic object method of acting, based on a thorough drill of the verbs in common use.

Example—Lesson 1. Objects—Hands, face, soap, water, towel. Verbs—See, saw, wash, washed, wipe, wiped.

These lessons are so arranged that the work syncronizes.

One term of five months enables the educated foreigner to enter the 6th or 7th grade.

The illiterate student requires at least a year in this drill class.

The pupils are encouraged to enter the graded classes and study the regular grammar grade work as soon as possible, and their work is so arranged that they may do so. In fact, many stay to graduate and receive diplomas.

Lessons in citizenship, civics and history are taught to the advanced pupils nightly.

Emphasis is put upon the necessity of students in the citizenship class spending at least three full months in night school each of the five probationary years before final papers are issued to them.

Patriotism and love of the American flag and institutions is instilled by flag drills, stories of American heroes and public men, and the singing of patriotic songs.

The class teacher attends with each class court proceedings, where final examination for citizenship papers is held.

The principal examines each individual of the class before appearance in court, in order to insure the success of applicant.

We recommend again that an additional number of such classes be established.

VISUAL EDUCATION.

We renew the recommendations on this subject contained in the report of 1914-15.

To endeavor to accomplish such an end, in our official recommendations to the Board of Supervisors on the financial needs of the Department, in May, 1916, we asked for an appropriation of $2,500 for this purpose; but no specific sum was allowed, and no action has been had.

ELEMENTARY CERTIFICATION ON EXAMINATION.

In accordance with a change in the State School Law (Section 1790) the Board of Examination has held no examination for the elementary teachers' certificate since the date of the supplement to the report of 1914-15. The next examination has been set for December, 1916.

CONTINUATION CLASSES.

In our official recommendations to the Board of Supervisors on the financial needs of the Department, in May, 1916, we stated the case for the establishment of Continuation Classes, as follows:

"Continuation Classes—$10,000. A large number of young men and women who have left school and who are employed in wage earning need additional education in academic and technical branches to make their labor most useful to themselves and to the community. For these we should establish morning classes from 8 to 10 a. m. as now carried on at the private expense of some of the large firms of this city. While it is true that we have evening schools it is always better, if possible, for the young people who need additional education to attend these morning classes at the expense of the employer who, in many cases, is willing to grant his youthful employees permission to study at his expense. Morning Continuation Classes would be a God-send to a great many, especially to young girls whose parents do not wish them to attend evening classes. Besides, the minds of these young people are clearer in the morning and not over-burdened with the fatigue of the labors of the day as when they attend evening schools.

In keeping with the idea of the "Wider Use of the School Plant", our Manual Training and Cooking laboratories used by the pupils of the day schools and which are now closed evenings and Saturdays should be opened every evening and Saturdays.

Sewing, Dressmaking, Millinery and Cooking would be largely patronized if all of these laboratories were opened in the evening. At present we have about four such centers and these are not open every evening in the week. Wood and Metal-work, Mechanical and Architectural Drawing in these laboratories would offer means of promotion to large numbers of young men who are working along these lines during the day. $10,000 is a very small sum to start this work, for I feel confident that if such an opportunity is given to our young people that in the near future thousands of serious-minded apprentices in the trades will gladly avail themselves of this opportunity."

No specific sum for this purpose was allowed, and no action has been had. We renew our recommendation on this subject.

SUPPLEMENTARY BOOKS.

In our official recommendations to the Board of Supervisors on the financial needs of the Department, in May, 1916, we said in part: "The schools of San Francisco are in urgent need of supplementary text-books. This is one of the greatest needs of our schools". We asked for an appropriation of $50,000 for this purpose; but no specific sum was allowed.

HIGH SCHOOLS.

An exhaustive report on the Course of Study and the general conditions in the San Francisco high schools is contained in the report of 1914-15 (to which reference is hereby made). The recommendations embodied in that report were later presented in separate form to the Board of Education, and action has been had on a number of them. The recommendations for particular schools that have been accepted are: at the Girls High School funds for the installation of a course in Cooking have been allowed; at the High School of Commerce a General Science course, well equipped, has been established, and provision made to relieve over-crowding; at the Mission High School, the commercial course and the course in drawing have been extended; and readjustments and increases in the teaching corps have been made at the Polytechnic and Lowell. The general recommendations for the high schools that have been accepted are: three additional teachers of music, and a full corps of teachers (8) to carry on a program of physical education for both boys and girls.

In our official recommendations to the Board of Supervisors on the financial needs of the Department, in May, 1916, we asked for the following amounts:

(1) For permanent equipment, $49,500 (including an annex to the Mission High, but exclusive of the sum of $30,000 asked for the equipment of the Polytechnic by the Board of Education and concurred in by the Superintendent).

(2) Supervisor and Assistants of Drawing, $3,000.

(3) Five Music Teachers, $7,500.

While these sums were not specifically appropriated by the Board of Supervisors for the purposes aforementioned, the Board of Education has been able to allow considerable amounts to accomplish these various purposes.

We desire to commend the action of the Board of Education in regard to our high school recommendations.

TEACHERS' INSTITUTE.

The annual institute of the teachers of the City and County was conducted during the four days beginning April 17, 1916, in conjunction with the annual session of the California Teachers' Association-Bay Section. The attendance was very large, the speakers were enthusiastically greeted and attentively listened to, and in all othr respects this Institute was one of the most successful ever held. We were very fortunate in being able to secure the services of the Honorable P. P. Claxton, United States Commissioner of Education, as the chief lecturer on the program.

An outline of the programs of the General Sessions, and of the Elementary and High School Departments follows:

GENERAL SESSIONS.

Monday, April 17, 1916, 9:00 A. M.

Community singing.

Call to Order and Opening Remarks—President Cloud.

Recital of Folk-Lore—Mr. Henry Kendall Bassett, formerly Assistant Professor of English, University of Wisconsin.

Community singing.

Address, "What We Owe the National Red Cross"—Hon. Samuel M. Shortridge, San Francisco.

Lecture. "The Place of the High School in Our Public School System"—Hon. P. P. Claxton. U. S. Commissioner of Education.

Thursday, April 20, 1916, 9:30 A. M.

Lecture, "The Teacher"—Mr. John H. Francis, Superintendent of Schools, Los Angeles.

Soprano solos—Madame Jeanne Gustin-Ferrier. (a) Aria "Madame Butterfly", Puccini; (b) "Old Italian Folk Songs", "La Colomba" arranged by Schindler. Mr. Jno. Tibbets at the piano.

Lecture, "The Civic Education of the Immigrant"—Miss Mary Antin, author of "The Promised Land". "The Knock at Our Gates," etc.

Thursday, April 20, 1916, 1:30 P. M.

Orchestra.

Address—His Honor, James Rolph, Jr., Mayor of San Francisco.

Baritone solos—Mr. William H. Keith. (a) "Sancta Maria", Faure; (b) "Alla Stella Confidente", Robaudi. Violin obligato by Mr. Nat J. Landsberger. George Lerond at the piano.

Lecture, "More Salubrities I Have Met"—Mr. John Kendrick Bangs, author of "A House Boat on the Styx", "The Genial Idiot", etc., etc.

Orchestra.

Regular annual business meeting of the Bay Section C. T. A., same hall. Members only are entitled to participate in the business meeting. Order of business: Reading of Minutes of last Annual Meeting; Report of Board of Directors: Election Returns; Unfinished Business; Reports of Committees; New Business: Installation of President-elect.

Adjournment.

SYNOPSIS OF RECOMMENDATIONS MADE BY THE SUPERINTENDENT OF SCHOOLS SINCE JANUARY, 1913.

(For recommendations for the several years prior to this date see Superintendent's report of 1912.)

March, 1913.

First—That work in Manual Training and Domestic Science be extended, and that these Centers be open on Saturday mornings.

Second—That Vacation Schools be organized (renewal of earlier recommendation).

Third—That Continuation Schools be organized.

Fourth—That work in School Gardening be extended (renewal of earlier recommendation).

Fifth—That a complete course in Music be established in the High Schools, and that one teacher in this subject be appointed for each high school.

May, 1913.

That three designated Elementary Schools be organized as Intermediate Schools, and that suitable modifications of the existing Courses of Study of those schools be made.

July, 1913.

First—That the new High School Course of Study prepared and presented by the Superintendent be adopted and printed.

Second—That the Course of Study for the elementary schools be revised in such a manner as to reduce the amount of academic work and increase the amount of manual and vocational work.

August, 1913.

First—that supplementary books be purchased for Science Work in the grades, and giving a list of such books.

That specific changes in the elementary Course of Study in Geography, History, Nature Study and Science be adopted.

July, 1914.

That Ungraded Classes be established and extended.

November, 1914.

First—That self-testing cards be supplied the primary classes of the department.

Second—That School Gardening be extended (renewing former recommendation).

Third—That a plan formulated to increase the daily attendance in the schools and to enforce compulsory education law be ratified.

December, 1914.

First—That the elementary schools classification be completed by 12 o'clock on the last day of each school term.

Second—That a revised Elementary Course of Study, prepared and presented by the Superintendent, be adopted and printed.

May, 1915.

First—That certain administrative improvements be made in regard to the classification reports, transfers of pupils from primary to grammar schools, and in the organizing of Manual Training and Domestic Science classes at the opening of school terms.

Second—That a Course of Study for visits to the Panama-Pacific International Exposition, prepared and presented by the Superintendent, be ratified.

June, 1915.

That a Time Schedule for the Intermediate Schools, prepared and presented by the Superintendent, be adopted.

July, 1915.

First—That teachers be selected to study under Madame Montessori in classes to be conducted by her in San Francisco.

Second—That the necessary apparatus for inaugurating the Language-Phone Method of teaching foreign languages be supplied the Polytechnic High School.

August, 1915.

That a four year History Course be organized at the Polytechnic High School.

October, 1915.

First—That in high schools no student activities be allowed during regular school hours.

Second—That the Girls High School be equipped for courses in Household Arts, including Sewing, Dressmaking, Millinery and Cooking.

December, 1915.

First—That a course in the education of immigrants, in furtherance of the commendable efforts of the Bureau of Naturalization of the U. S. Department of Labor, be organized at the Hancock School Building at night time, and that the school in that location be hereafter designated as the North Beach Evening Continuation School.

Second—That a course in Physical Education be prescribed for all boys in the first year at Lowell High School.

Third—That, to improve the conditions relative to the assignment of probationary teachers, a detailed plan, prepared and presented by the Superintendent, be ratified.

January, 1916.

That a schedule for inclement days, prepared and submitted by the Superintendent, be adopted.

February, 1916.

First—That Dr. F. B. Dresslar be invited to examine the plans of the Redding School.

Second—That physical education in the high schools including military training and tactics, be more definitely organized.

April, 1916.

That teachers of the department attending the 1916 Summer Session of the University of California be excused from class-work during the first week of the Fall Term, 1916, without loss of pay, and that necessary substitutes be employed to fill temporarily their positions during said first week.

May, 1916.

First—The "Report on high schools and recommendations concerning the same", rendered May 9, 1916, is herein summarized:

(a) That the high school day be extended to a six hour schedule.

(b) That adequate clerical help be provided the principals.

(c) That at least one teacher of Music be assigned to each high school and that Music be accorded full recognition as an elective study.

(d) That supplementary books be provided.

(e) That a "Dean of Girls" be appointed for each high school.

(f) That physical education be extended.

(g) That, in the High School of Commerce, a course in applied Arts be installed; that the Science Course be enriched by the introduction of a practical course in Physics; that a course in Salesmanship be begun; and that Heads of Departments be appointed.

(h) That, in the Mission High School, the Commercial Course be extended and strengthened; that the Household Economic Course be extended and improved, and that a temporary building be constructed to accommodate departments of this school not properly housed.

(i) That, in the Girls High School, a thorough and complete course in Household Economics be organized; that Spanish be introduced as an elective study; that an elective course in typewriting and stenography be placed in the third and fourth years of this school; and that a head of the Science Department be appointed.

(j) That, in the Polytechnic High School, a course in Latin be organized in the third and fourth years, and that the teaching time of teachers of academic subjects be reduced to a basis approximating twenty-eight periods per week.

(k) That, in the Lowell High School, the teaching time of teachers be placed on a basis approximating twenty-eight periods per week; and that a faculty secretary be appointed.

Second—That a one hour course in Vocational Guidance for senior students be organized at the Polytechnic High School.

Third—That the following modifications in the Course of Study of the Lowell High School be approved:

(a) That the Science taught in the second year be Biology in place of the choice of Botany or Zoology as heretofore.

(b) That a course in Physiology (with special attention to Hygiene) be given as an additional elective course in the third year, open to third and fourth year pupils.

(c) That an elective course in Domestic Chemistry be given in the third year, open to the girls in the third and fourth years.

(d) That the modern languages, French, German, Spanish, be made elective in the second year with Greek or Science, thus providing for complete three year courses in each modern language in place of the former two year courses.

Fourth—That afternoon recesses be held in elementary schools with this qualification, that, whenever need for deviation from said rule arise in individual schools, the principal shall present such need to the Superintendent of Schools and he shall thereupon act as he deems best.

Fifth—That a small sum of money be set aside for the purpose of paying transportation expenses of defective children to enable them to attend schools set aside for such pupils, when it appears that the parents of such children cannot afford to pay that expense.

June, 1916.

First—That, at the Humboldt Evening High School, an office assistant and recorder be appointed; and that a teacher of Penmanship be appointed.

Second—That recommendations relative to the high school needs, set forth in the "Report on High Schools and Recommendations" of May, 1916, be reaffirmed, with details as to necessary appointments and assignments.

July, 1916.

First—That thirty-four new classes be organized at specified schools: that overcrowding be avoided by erecting temporary buildings in two specified locations; and that consolidations of classes be effected in specified locations.

Second—That a submitted list of text-books for high schools be adopted.

August, 1916.

That the Board of Education set aside and employ sufficient funds for the purpose of engaging the services of truant officers under its own direction.

THE CIVIL SERVICE PLAN FOR THE APPOINTMENT OF TEACHERS FOR THE CITY AND COUNTY OF SAN FRANCISCO.

By Alfred Roncovieri.

As the real objective of education is the rearing of a perfect citizen, so should it be the purpose of governing educational bodies to adopt and enforce a system through the exercise of which the services of the most competent instructors may be secured. It is not educational qualifications alone which denote the successful teacher, any more than the adoption of an excellent course of study could be said to insure the successful education of a pupil. A teacher must be, aside from the standpoint of academic qualifications, of agreeable disposition, strong personality, good bearing and address, as well as perfectly sound in health and possessed of sufficient bodily vigor to do effective teaching. The importance of a teacher's life work can not be over estimated. To her is entrusted a sacred duty, since the child comes directly under her control during its formative period. None can gainsay the fact that the force of the teacher's example, and the general environment of the classroom, play a most important part at this impressionable stage of a child's career.

The most solemn duty which devolves upon a Superintendent of Schools and a Board if Education is the selection of the best teachers in the United States for the education of the innocent children who are entrusted to their care. All other duties sink into insignificance compared to this one. Therefore, a sound plan for the selection and appointment of teachers is the most important function in the proper administration of public schools. With these ideals in mind, a plan was adopted and a crude beginning was made in the fall of 1901. This was the first attempt ever made in San Francisco to hold a competitive examination of teachers.

In the Spring of 1902 I worked out the details of the present plan and placed it definitely on a practical basis by making many changes and introducing innovations theretofore untried.

After three years of preliminary trial and experimentation with this system, which proved its practical effectiveness and its fairness to the satisfaction of all concerned, I requested the Board of Education formally to adopt the competitive civil service plan which I had prepared. This was done by resolution of the Board in May, 1904, and the system became thereafter permanently fixed in the San Francisco School Department.

This Competitive Civil Service System has been faithfully adhered to ever since its formal adoption, although modifications and improvements have been made from time to time on my recommendation, and the plan has been strengthened until now we believe we have the best system yet devised for the selection and appointment of teachers.

San Francisco, through the sifting process of this Civil Service Plan, has become possessed of a corps of well-prepared, enthusiastic, faithful and efficient teachers unsurpassed in any other school department in the United States.

In preparing the present Competitive Civil Service Plan and in proposing its permanent adoption my object was to eliminate and prevent all political, social, fraternal and religious "Pulls" from exercising their pernicious influences in the conduct of school affairs. Under this system applicants for positions are not obliged to expend their time, energy and money in "seeing" and "influencing" the Superintendent of Schools or the members of the Board of Education, or in importuning their friends to do this for them. Those who are successful in the examination, and who receive appointments in the order of their rank, are relieved from anxiety and worry, and are free to devote all of their time to their work. They are not obliged to keep in touch with politicians or other "influential citizens", or to dance attendance on a too frequently complacent Superintendent of Schools, who is himself the creature of a Board of Education. many members of which are ordinarily controlled by political and other dark considerations.

Annually in the months of May and June many cities drop all their teachers from the roll. The entire teaching force is dismissed in order to "get" one or more teachers who have not been "right". Great injustice is often done in this way. Frequently teachers of excellent character and ability are not re-elected for the sole reason that they are "not politically right."

To dismiss all the teachers of the department, and almost immediately to re-elect all who are "satisfactory" (?), dropping from the new list by omission of their names, those who are "not satisfactory" (?), is a piece of cowardice on the part of the Superintendent who engages in this dirty work, and a disgrace to the Board members who are guilty of taking part in such sharp practice. If a teacher is no longer wanted, owing to good and sufficient reasons, the school authorities should have enough manhood to tell her so, first giving her an opportunity to be heard in a public meeting if she so desires. To drop the teacher in an underhand way attaches dishonesty and shame to any school superintendent or board member who engages in it. It is crooked work, and succeeds only when a superintendent appointed by a Board of Education is of the kind willing to take orders from the Board and to make a door-mat of himself to save his job.

. The San Francisco Competitive Civil Service System for the selection of teachers, if adopted everywhere, would prevent the injustice so often practiced on excellent teachers by removing them from the too-often baneful influence of an appointed superintendent who holds his position by the grace of politicians and a political Board of Education, and who, to retain it, is compelled to play the "trimmer" almost constantly.

I am induced to elaborate thus in explanation of the San Francisco Competitive Civil Service System because at times petty and unjust reflections have been cast upon the teachers of this city and upon the Superintendent of Schools by self-appointed educational critics.

The honest treatment and square deal given to all those who have been candidates in the competitive examinations is evidenced by the fact that in sixteen years not a single complaint against our system has ever been made by any one of the hundreds of candidates who failed to pass the examination.

It is not difficult to account for the eagerness displayed by teachers throughout California and other States to secure positions in San Francisco. Our city offers the most attractive field of labor on the coast, higher salary, permanent tenure, social and educational advantages, and finally, the enjoyment of a pension at the time of retirement.

Private and personal interests, and established custom, at first opposed our Competitive Civil Service system for the appointment of teachers. But, after a trial of sixteen years our system is here to stay, for it rests upon correct principles.

I believe that public sentiment will in due time cause our present Competitive Civil Service Plan to be formulated into a State law making it a compulsory on all Boards of Education to select their teachers impersonally and on merit alone.

In developing and perfecting the present competitive system which I count the most important educational work for which it is my privilege to claim at least a considerable share of responsibility, I had in mind the following statement of principles found in a report addressed to the Board of Education in 1901, by a select committee composed of President David Starr Jordan, President Benj. Ide Wheeler, State Supt. Thomas J. Kirk, Dr. E. P. Cubberley, Dr. Frederic Burk and Dr. Elmer E. Brown:

PRINCIPLES UNDERLYING THE SELECTION OF TEACHERS.

I. The sole purpose of the public schools is education. No consideration whatever, other than educational interests of pupils, can honestly enter into any plan for the appointment of teachers. In no sense do schools exist to provide employment for teachers.

II. No one should be employed as a teacher who does not possess high personal character, liberal education and bodily health and vigor.

III. Successful experience is manifestly the best evidence of fitness for appointment.

IV. Professional training in the principles and practice of teaching is desirable, and is increasingly demanded in systems of public education.

V. The duty of the Board of Education requires that these officers should frequently take the initiative in securing the best possible teachers for the schools under their management. It is not sufficient that they should merely select from the candidates who apply for appointment.

VI. The employment of any sort of personal or political influence to secure appointment to the teaching force, or the urging of any consideration other than fitness for the work of teaching as a ground for such appointment, is held to be an act of unprofessional conduct.

GENERAL PROVISIONS REGULATING THE EXAMINATIONS.

The San Francisco Competitive Civil Service System for the selection and appointment of teachers disregards all questions of personal, social, political, fraternal or religious influences. It is based *solely on merit* as primarily determined by the competitive examination of applicants who already hold regular teachers' certificates issued under the laws of the State of California, and by a successful probationary period of actual teaching covering two years.

The object of the examinations is not primarily to test applicants as to their proficiency in primary and grammar studies, but to select the best of those graduates of Normal Schools and Universities who are already certificated as teachers under our State laws. Applicants must furnish, before the examination, full information relative to their academic preparation, their professional training and their experience in teaching. Each applicant must give the names of not less than three nor more than seven persons who are competent to speak of his or her moral character and fitness for the work of teaching. Such references must include persons whose official positions enable them to give the most exact and pertinent information with regard to the applicant's scholarship, training, experience and general character and efficiency. General letters of recommendation are not considered. Confidential statements are requested from persons competent to speak of the applicants' qualifications. Such statements are made in answer to a uniform list of questions, and in case of doubt supplementary information relating to these questions is called for from other persons who may be deemed competent to speak intelligently of the candidate's qualifications.

These evidences of the qualifications of the applicants are canvassed, and a list is prepared of candidates who are to participate in the competitive examination. No candidate for the Civil Service Examination is included in this list who does not hold a valid California State teachers' certificate of a grade not lower than the grammar grade authorizing such candidate to teach in the schools of the State. Nor is any applicant included in this list if the information obtained indicates that such applicant is not a suitable person to be appointed as a teacher in the schools of San Francisco.

During the oral examination applicants have ample opportunity to demonstrate their fitness and general ability, but no applicant is privileged to call on the

Superintendent, or members of the Board, individually to press his or her claims for appointment, nor must the friend of any applicant endeavor to use any personal, political or social influence with any member of the Board. The employment of any sort of personal, political or social influence to secure appointment to the teaching force, or the urging of any consideration other than fitness for the work of teaching as a ground for such appointment, is held to be an act of unprofessional conduct, and debars the candidate from taking the examination.

It is the duty of the Superintendent and of every member of the Board of Education immediately to report the fact, should any attempt be made by any one to employ improper personal, political, or other influence in connection with these examinations; and the candidate concerned in such attempt would thereafter be considered debarred for appointment, assignment, or election to a teaching position unless such candidate satisfy the Board that he or she was not responsible, either directly or indirectly, for the actions so reported.

All assignments to teaching positions on the schools of San Francisco are made from a Substitute List, and no person is appointed to this list except by a unanimous vote of the Board, and after having successfully passed the regular Competitive Civil Service Examination.

To insure absolute fairness in the examinations the system includes a plan by which the identity of all of the candidates is completely concealed from the examiners and from everyone else, until the percentages attained by all of the candidates in all of the tests have been determined and recorded.

All teachers before being appointed must show that they are under 35 years of age, and must obtain from one of the consulting physicians of the Board of Education a certificate showing that the holder is perfectly sound in health and possessed of sufficient bodily vigor to do effective teaching.

It is not to be understood that the successful passing of the competitive examinations, oral and written, leads immediately and irrevocably to permanent tenure in the San Francisco School Department. The system under which these examinations are held *does* insure to every worthy candidate a fair and open chance to secure admission to the Department strictly upon merit. Once admitted, however, there is yet before her the test of two years' service as "*Probationary* teacher" before the much coveted prize of *life tenure* is finally won. To appoint a teacher for life who, however brilliant in the passing of an examination, has given no sufficient proof the possession of practical teaching ability and a strong personality would obviously be absurd. But if, upon the expiration of the probationary period of two years, the reports of the principals and all of the Deputy Superintendents under whom the probationer has taught are favorable as to her moral and educational qualifications, including, of course, her ability to enforce discipline, she is elected by the Board of Education, on the Superintendent's recommendation, as a regular member of the teaching force. Her tenure in her occupation is now for life, subject still, however, to the condition that her behavior and efficiency continue unimpaired, as also her willingness to observe properly the rules of the Department. She may at any time be dismissed as provided by law for insubordination, immoral or unprofessional conduct, intemperance and evident unfitness for teaching; but she must be given a fair and impartial trial after due notice of any charges made against her. Life tenure, with its accompanying feeling of independence and freedom from doubt as to the chances of the future, is a prize worth winning, but it will be seen from what has been stated as to the conditions attending the securing of admission to the department, and insuring permanency therein, that it is not lightly bestowed.

And it is right and proper that this should be so. The American citizen is ever willing to contribute to the maintenance of the public school system. He does so uncomplainingly and without hesitation or quibble, for to him the very mention of our schools possesses a talismanic power, for is not our public school system the most sacred and jealously guarded of American institutions? The right-thinking citizen regards the taxes paid for the support of our schools as one of the very best of his investments. But he demands for his children the best that is to be had in the way of instruction and instructors, and he is fair enough to ask for such teachers who prove their worth the peace, contentment and permanency of position to which their merit entitles them. This is the true spirit of Civil Service reform. Our citizens realize, as we all should realize, that the effect of the teachers' spiritual contentment is reflected in the lives and the intellectual progress of the pupils.

RESULTS OBTAINED.

Judging by the large and splendid corps of teachers which has been selected during the past 16 years under our system, I can only say that the results obtained have fully justified it. Through its enforcement by an honest and loyal Board of Education, ready and willing to carry out all the provisions governing the examination and other tests, the efficiency of our teachers has been elevated to the highest possible standard. I say, most emphatically, that political pressure, social influence, personal intercession and the exercise of improper and unworthy considerations have been completely done away with in the selection of teachers under our Civil Service system—a system which gives the teachers selected under it dignity, independence and freedom from unnecessary worry by delivering them from the necessity of securing annual re-election. Those who are successful in the examination are relieved from anxiety and are free to devote their time and thought to their proper work. A teacher appointed under our system can truly call her soul her own. I fully believe that our Civil Service plan has resulted in the acquisition by this Department of the best available teaching talent in California; also that it at least approximates the ideal plan for the selection and appointment of thoroughly equipped and competent teachers. There is available, in this connection, the testimony of school officials of other and important cities of the State to the effect that the San Francisco plan, by its obvious fairness, as well as by is promise of immediate recognition of ability and corresponding reward therefor, has had the effect of drawing away a number of the best teachers of other departments. That the plan under which the examinations are conducted works well and effectively is proven by the statements of Normal School officials that those of their graduates who succeed at our competitive examinations are uniformly the same individuals who won deserved success during their course of Normal study. In short, it is merit, and merit only, which wins under the San Francisco system, and it was to insure that this should be so, that the system was organized, and that I have ever labored in season and out of season for its development and permanency.

CANDIDATES EXAMINED DURING THE LAST FIVE YEARS.

The number of candidates taking the examinations and number passing in the last five years was:

Date	Examined	Passed	Failed
June, 1912	117	58	59
June, 1913	140	60	80
June, 1914	190	91	99
June, 1915	167	61	106
June, 1916	242	177	65

The average age of the candidates who successfully passed the examinations referred to above did not exceed 24 years, no one being over 35.

SPECIFIC PROVISIONS.

That fuller knowledge may be had of the exact details of the examination system we publish the following Circular of Information issued for the Teachers' Competitive Examination of 1916:

Examination to be held Friday and Saturday, June 16th and 17th, 1916, at the High School of Commerce building, Fell and Franklin Streets.

Teachers are appointed to this department solely on merit as determined by competitive examinations of applicants who already hold regular teachers' certificates. The object of these examinations is to enable the Board of Education to select the best of those already certificated as teachers.

Requirements:

(1) Applicants must be well-educated, of good character and sound bodily health.

(2) Applicants are required:

(a) To have been graduated from a State Normal School; or

(b) To have been in attendance as regular students for two years in an institution of collegiate grade; or

(c) To have had two years' actual teaching experience subsequent to graduation from an institution of high school grade.

(3) Married women are not eligible for the competitive examinations unless their husbands are totally incapacitated through disease or infirmity.

(4) Applicants must not be over thirty-five years of age.

The written examinations are upon the following subjects:

(1) United States History, American Institutions and current events.

(2) Arithmetic.

(3) General Science.

(4) Personal and public hygiene.

(5) Methods of teaching and school management.

The examinations are not based upon any particular books. The following books, however, indicate the scope and range of the subjects covered by the examination:

United States History and American Institutions:

Epochs of American History Series, three volumes (Longman's).
Government in State and Nation, James & Sanford (Scribner's).
Government in the United States, Garner (American Book Co.).

Arithmetic:

Complete Arithmetic, Hamilton (American Book Co.).
Robinson's Arithmetic with Supplement of Fish's Problems.
Packard's Commercial Arithmetic.

General Science:

Rowell's General Science.
Clark's (American Book Co.).
Nature Studies by Hodge.

Personal and Public Hygiene:

The Human Mechanism, Hough & Sedgwick (Ginn & Co.).
Human Body and Health, Davison (American Book Co.).
Primer of Hygiene, Ritchie—Caldwell.
Primer of Sanitation, Ritchie.

No formal examination in English is given; the ability to write and speak correct, forceful English is determined from a consideration of the examinations in general.

Applicants must obtain at least seventy-five per cent (75%) in each subject. If, however, an applicant falls below seventy-five per cent (75%) but not below sixty-five per cent (65%) in one subject only, and the average in the other subjects is at least eighty-five per cent (85%), the applicant is considered to have passed the written examination successfully but is required to take an examination in that subject at the teachers' competitive examination given the following year.

Applicants who pass the written examinations appear before the Board of Education for an oral examination, designed to test their fitness and technical training for teaching, their general intelligence, their information upon matters of world importance and present-day interest known to all educated persons who keep abreast of the times.

Each of the five members of the Board of Education, without conferring with his fellow-members, marks the applicant, the average constituting the mark for the oral examination. Applicants must obtain an average of at least seventy-five per cent (75%) in the oral examinations. Applicants receiving less than seventy-five per cent (75%) from three of the members of the Board are rejected regardless of the marks obtained in the written examination and of the average in the oral. The average of the marks in the written examination, plus the average in the oral, determines the applicant's rank.

Applicants passing the next competitive examination, to be held in June of this year, will be divided into Classes A and B; Class A will consist of those who have been graduated from State Normal Schools or from the pedagogic departments of recognized colleges and who after such graduation have had at least two years of successful experience. Of this class the first fifty (50) will be assured appointment to vacancies or to new positions in the elementary schools on the opening day of the school year 1916-1917 and their salary will be the usual amount paid probationary teachers, Seventy Dollars ($70.00) per month, plus allowance for experience in teaching. All the other applicants passing the competitive examination successfully will constitute Class B. Class B will be the eligible list of substitutes and such eligible substitutes, as heretofore, will be appointed to vacancies and to new positions in the elementary schools in the order of their rank as they may be needed.

The competitive examinations are held during the summer vacation about June 10th. The next examinations will be held Friday and Saturday, June 16th and 17th, 1916. When necessary, a second examination for the year is set for the Christmas vacation. Application blanks will be furnished all those asking for them, during the two months preceding the dates set for an examination. They should be filled out and forwarded to the Secretary of the Board of Education not later than one week prior to the examination. Applicants must furnish full information relative to their academic preparation, their professional training, and their experience in teaching. Applicants must give references to at least three persons competent to speak of their fitness for teaching. Such references must include the persons whose official position enables them to give the most exact information regarding the applicant's scholarship, training, experience and efficiency. The Board of Education will not consider general letters of recommendation but will request from the persons referred to by the applicant confidential statements regarding the applicant's qualifications. In case of doubt the Board will call for and use supplementary information from other persons who may be deemed competent to speak intelligently of the candidate's qualifications.

Before appointment to the eligible list the successful applicant must obtain from one of several physicians designated by the Board of Education a statement certifying that the applicant is in sound physical and mental health. The expense of the medical examination is borne by the applicant. The fee is $2.50.

Before election as regular teachers in the department applicants must serve at least two years after assignment as probationary teachers. They will be assigned for one year and if reported as successful will be re-elected for a second year. At the close of the second year if still deemed successful they will be elected regular teachers and will hold teaching positions for life, provided they comply at all times with the rules of the Board of Education, the laws of the State of California and the Charter of the City and County of San Francisco so far as they relate to the school department.

Announcement of dates is made in San Francisco's official daily newspaper (Daily Journal of Commerce) and in the Western Journal of Education, as well as in some of the leading newspapers of the State.

A number system is used by which the identity of the examination papers of the candidate is lost.

At each of the sessions the envelope and sheets containing the answers of each candidate are stamped with the same number. This number stamping does not begin, however, until all the examination papers of each session have been turned in by the candidates. The envelope and the set of answers of each candidate have a different number from those of every other candidate. In order to avoid confusion the same number is never used twice. The sets of envelopes, after having been numbered, are all placed in a box which is sealed and deposited in the safe of the Board of Education. After the answers have been examined and marked the seal is broken from the box containing the numbered envelopes. This is done in the presence of representatives of the Board of Education and of the Superintendent's office. The envelopes are opened and the identity of the candidate is then disclosed for the first time.

The written examinations will be held in the High School of Commerce, corner Fell and Franklin Sts., on Friday and Saturday, June 16th and 17th, beginning at nine o'clock a. m. sharp. Applicants will therefore present themselves promptly at 8:45 a. m.

The oral examination is held in the offices of the Board of Education and continnes in morning and afternoon sessions until all applicants successful in the written examination have been examined. Each candidate receives notification when to appear.

The following lists used during various years will give some idea of the general character of the questions:

QUESTIONS GIVEN IN 1902.

1. Interest. How would you rouse it? Is it all sufficient for accomplishing results?
2. State and describe three essential features of the class recitation.
3. State some IMPORTANT defects of a strictly graded system of classes and give one GOOD remedy for each defect mentioned.
4. Since about 70 per cent of the pupils attending the public schools, on an average, are in the primary grades, which three subjects of instruction do you regard as the most important in training the great mass of our pupils who never enter the grammar school? Give your reasons.
5. Do you think the State School Law which forbids teachers to assign any home-work to pupils under fifteen years of age is a wise provision, and give your reasons for or against this law?
6. What would you do to advance a very diffident or backward child?
7. Discuss the Use and Abuse of Text Books.
8. Discuss discipline, its necessity, aim or aims.
9. Discuss helps to memory.
10. Point out specifically some of the uses and common abuses of the memory in geography teaching, making your explanation show your knowledge of the psychology involved.
11. Explain what is meant by visual, auditory and motor types of thinking, and illustrate by reference to corresponding types of spellers.

12. Why is it that pupils who write neatly in their copy books frequently do much inferior work in original composition? Explain the psychological causes.

QUESTIONS GIVEN IN 1903.

1. What is the ultimate end of education? State specifically some of the things education should do for the individual. For society.

2. Considering the limited time at your disposal for the instruction of a large class, what methods would enable you to give maximum attention to the special needs of individuals or groups of individuals that are particularly backward or brilliant?

3. How far can you teach parts of one school subject when you are definitely teaching another subject; for example, how far can you correlate geography with history? Should the attention of the child upon the history material be intensified or lessened by such introduction of geography? Point out some dangers in attempting to correlate subjects.

4. What constitutes an ideal teacher?

5. Discuss the intellectual features particularly active in children and educational significance.

6. Give a description of a model lesson in arithmetic in a primary grade.

7. Discuss the development of the imagination in primary grades—its importance—means to secure it.

8. Discuss maintenance of strict discipline. How it may be tempered and how far relaxation from it may be allowed for the sake of promoting interest, emulation, and fellowship between teacher and pupils?

9. How can you make history teaching contribute directly to training for good citizenship? How far would you require children to learn facts of history, such as dates and names? What importance in history teaching would you give to the ideas and sentiments which have been the causes and results of historical events? What feelings should good history teaching awaken in the pupil?

10. Briefly outline the most approved general methods in use for teaching first grade pupils to read, and show by your explanation your comprehension of the mental process involved.

11. State three advantages and three disadvantages of department teaching in grammar grades.

12. Describe briefly any approved general method of teaching:

(a) Rapid and accurate addition.

(b) Geography.

Justify your methods by psychological reasons.

QUESTIONS FOR 1904.

1. Write a model lesson in geography and tell how you would make use of the following in teaching the same: 1, attention; 2, interest; 3, association; 4, memory; 5, imagination.

2. What standards or principles should guide a teacher in advancing or detaining a child at promotion time? Should all subjects have equal weight? If not, suggest some subjects that should have more weight than others. Give reasons in full for your answers.

3. Describe a remedy for each of the following cases: (a) Poor spellers; (b) faulty grammarians; (c) careless calculators; (d) thoughtless memorizing; (e) poor readers.

4. Why is it important to give special attention to ventilation of the schoolroom? Discuss fully the psychological processes involved.

5. What are your standards of good work in composition? Suggest the most effective way or methods of correcting composition in class. In your suggestion explain the defects as well as the merits of your method.

6. Discuss the method best calculated to secure the friendship and co-operation of a class.

7. How would you make use of the school or public library to the best advantage?

8. In teaching literature what would be your chief aims? What are the defects in the present methods? Would you use the sentences in literature as drills in grammar? Give reasons for answers.

9. How would you make the recitation of each pupil an intellectual activity for every member of the class?

10. Outline an inductive lesson in English grammar.

QUESTIONS FOR 1905.

1. By the history lesson, how may patriotism be best inculcated?

2. (a) What studies taught in school are especially adapted to the cultivation of the perceptive faculties? (b) Give some illustrations.

3. Tell how you would teach a class to add columns of figures with accuracy and rapidity and justify your method by psychological reasons.

4. How would you direct and encourage home reading? Name ten books suitable for Sixth and Seventh grades.

5. Discuss the Art of Questioning with definite suggestions.

6. How would you teach the ready and correct use of the English language to the First, Second, and Third grades of the primary school?

7. How do you teach "pointing off" in division of decimals? Illustrate with examples showing various difficulties that perplex children.

8. Explain the method to be pursued in teaching writing during the first two years of a child's school life.

9. If you had a pupil with a remarkable gift of memory who succeeds but poorly in original work, such as composition and arithmetic, how would you work to correct the deficiency?

10. What devices would you employ to keep up a good standard attendance in your class?

QUESTIONS FOR 1907.

1. What are the purposes of school discipline?

What different ways of disciplining children has the teacher at command?

Suggest how you would vary the use of these means: With incorrigible children as opposed to sensitive children. With boys as opposed to girls.

2. Suggest the various ways by which the teacher may rest a child from mental fatigue resulting from classroom instruction. Discuss the special merits of each way suggested.

3. When you find a pupil of normal mind who does not know how to study, how would you proceed to remedy the condition? Suggest as many detailed ways as you can of giving him desire and power to study by himself.

4. What are the different ways by which you can convey the meaning of an unfamiliar word, phrase, or sentence to a child? Discuss the relative value of each way.

5. What are the different elements which must be associated in the child's mind in order to make him a good speller? Suggest several ways of presenting and associating these elements.

6. What are the main advantages to be derived from nature study? How would you use the school garden and the school excursion in connection with this subject?

7. What are the objects to be kept in view in the teaching of history in the elementary schools? What are the most interesting and valuable kinds of historical facts to be learned in the primary grades? In the grammar grades?

8. In leading a child from home geography to world geography, how would you proceed?

9. State briefly in detail what means you would use in the primary grades to make your pupils speak and write good English.

10. In teaching arithmetic when would you let the child do the work mentally? When have him write it out in full? When mix both methods?

1. There is a growing tendency to abolish corporal punishment as a means of correcting the faults of pupils:

(a) If you had charge of a school in which corporal punishment was not permitted state briefly how you would maintain order in the case of pupils disposed to be unruly.

(b) If you were allowed to inflict corporal punishment at your discretion, in exceptional cases, state some circumstances under which it might, in your opinion, be resorted to as a just and effective mode of correction.

(c) When a teacher decides that a pupil should be punished for wrong doing, what objects should he (the teacher) have in view; that is, what worthy ends would he expect to reach through the infliction of the punishment?

2. What would you do with a pupil who, from absence or other cause, has fallen behind the class?

3. What rules of order would you insist upon to be observed by pupils in passing from the building during fire drill?

4. (a) Tell how you would teach reading to beginners.

(b) Name the important qualities of good reading.

(c) What are the commonest faults which you have found in the reading of children? How would you correct these faults?

5. Our new Course of Study requires an exercise in rapid addition:

Make out a column of figures suited for this exercise, and say how you would best secure speed and accuracy in performing it.

6. (a) What is the main benefit to be derived from the study of general History? Of Geography?

(b) How would you use Geography in connection with History?

7. (a) Describe a good method of teaching the geographical idea of day and night.

(b) What conditions give a country large foreign commerce? Domestic commerce?

8. (a) In what school year would you introduce the regular study of fractions?

(b) With what other rules of Arithmetic would you correlate percentage?

9. Suppose you had charge of an elementary class consisting of pupils of two consecutive grades; make out a program of daily exercises therefor in regular form, showing the grades and divisions taught, the simultaneous work in each, the hour and duration of each subject, and the time for reviews, oral or written.

10. A great many pupils find it extremely difficult to concentrate their attention on the instruction and explanations of the teacher, or to record mentally the most important points set forth in their reading matter. In the case of normal children, what, in your opinion, is the chief cause of this defect, and how would you remedy it?

QUESTIONS IN ARITHMETIC.

1. (a) A pupil writes 425 words in 5 minutes, 3 seconds. At next lesson she writes 521 words in 4 minutes, 5 seconds. At next lesson she writes 593 words in 4 minutes, 17 seconds. At what average rate of speed per minute does she write?

(b) Hale & Co., Stockton, bought of Lamont & Co., San Francisco, 3 doz. plain gold rings at $20.00 per dozen; 4 gold rings, diamond settings, at $50.00

each; 6 gold watches at $15.00 each; 5 sets teaspoons at $6.00 each. Make out the bill allowing a discount of 25%.

2 (a) A commission merchant received $50.00 from a country customer with orders to send him ribbon, worth 6¼c per yard, and to pay himself for his trouble. The merchant charged 2¼%. How many yards of ribbon did the merchant send to his customer?

(b) A ship worth $75,000.00 was insured for three-fifths of its value at 1⅞%. The cargo, valued at $7,500.00, was insured for four-fifths of its value at 2½%. Find amount of premiums.

3 (a) If it cost $312 to fence a piece of land 216 rods long and 24 rods wide, what will it cost to fence a square piece of equal area with the same kind of fence?

(b) Find the interest on $125.50 from January 1st, 1898, to July 7th, 1899, at 7% per annum.

4 (a) What will it cost to dig a cellar 60'x30'x9' at 33 1-3 cents per cubic yard?

(b) A room is 15 feet square and the walls are 9 feet high. What will it cost to paint the four walls at 25 cents per square yard, making no allowance for doors or windows?

5 (a) If four men build 12¼ rods of fence in 3¼ days, how long will it take 18 men to build 237 6-13 rods?

(b) Four persons engage in manufacturing, and invest together $22,500.00. At the end of a certain time A's share of the gain is $2,000.00, B's share $2,800.75, C's share $1,685.25, and D's share $1,014.00. How much capital did each put in?

GRAMMAR.

1. "*In the bosom* of one of those spacious coves which indent the eastern shore of the Hudson, *at that broad expansion* of the river denominated by the ancient Dutch navigators the Tappan Zee, and *where they always prudently shortened sail* and implored the protection of St. Nicholas when they crossed, there lies a small market town or rural port, which by some in called Greensburgh, but *which is more generally and properly known* by the name of Tarry Town.

(a) Draw one line under the *entire* subject, and two lines under the *entire* predicate.

(b) Parse the underlined phrases and clauses in above.

2. "The sun that brief December day
Rose cheerless over hills of gray,
And, darkly circled, gave at noon
A sadder light than waning moon."
Diagram or analyze the above.

3. What is a synopsis?
What is meant by voice?
What is declension?
Give the principal parts of lay, set, go, give and lie (to recline).
Singing birds are silent at this season.
The bird's singing under the window awakened us.
What is the use of "singing" in each of the above sentences?

4. "In the Old Colony days, in Plymouth, the land of the Pilgrim,
To and *fro* in a room of his simple and primitive dwelling,
Clad in doublet and hose, and boots of Cordovan leather,
Strode with a martial air, Miles Standish, the Puritan Captain,
Buried in *thought* he seemed, with his hands *behind* him, and *pausing*
Ever and anon *to behold* his glittering weapons of warfare,
Hanging in shining array along the walls of the chamber."
In the above selection, tell the part of speech of each underlined word.

5. (a) Give sentences illustrating the following uses of clauses. (Underline each clause.)
   1. Adverbial,
   2. Adjective,
   3. As object,
   4. As subject.

   Give an example of an infinitive used as subject.

(b) Give an example of a compound and a complex sentence, and explain the difference between them.

METHODS OF TEACHING.

1. (a) Which study do you consider the most valuable in the ordinary school curriculum, and give several reasons for your choice.

(b) 1. Upon what is the science of teaching based?
   2. What should be the great object of teaching?
   3. What are the characteristics of any good method of teaching?

2. (a) What method would you adopt to prevent tardiness; and to secure regular attendance in school?

(b) What is to be accomplished in teaching English Grammar?

3. (a) What special training is given by Literature, by History?

(b) By Mathematics, by Science?

4. (a) For what definite purpose and to what extent would you use analysis or the diagram?

(b) In teaching composition, in any grade above the fourth, state your method as to choosing subject, writing the composition, or correcting it. Name the grade or class you have in mind.

5. (a) Distinguish between principle, method, device. Which may change?

(b) 1. When is a schoolroom in good order?
   2. What incentive will you put before children for study?

QUESTIONS IN 1910.

1. (a) The longitude of Portland, Maine, is 70 degrees 15 minutes, and that of Chicago is 87 degrees 38 minutes. What is the difference in time between the two places?

(b) How many square inches of tin are there in a dozen tin pails of cylindrical shape, the diameter of each being 8 inches and the height 10 inches? (No top.)

2. (a) A rectangular field having an area of 135 1/5 acres is 3 1/5 times as long as it is wide. Find the length of its diagonal.

(b) If 9 bricklayers can lay a wall 80 ft. long, 20 ft. high, 1½ ft. thick, in 15 days of 9 hours each, in how many days of 10 hours each can 12 bricklayers lay a wall 100 ft. long, 25 ft. high and 2 ft. thick?

3. (a) On $860.56, $149.63 interest was paid for 2 years, 8 months, 3 days. What was the rate?

(b) An agent received $10,200 with which to purchase wheat at $1.25 per cental at a commission of 2%. How many centals did he buy?

4. (a) The distance from San Francisco to San Jose is 50.6 miles. An automobile party leaves San Francisco at 10:35 A. M. and arrives at San Jose at 1:20 P. M. What was the average speed on the trip?

(b) A man owns 3/5 of a ship that is worth $85,000. If the ship is insured for 57½% of its value, how much money would this man receive if the ship were a total loss, and how much would he lose?

5. (a) Subtract 5⅜ from 9.65 and divide the difference by (3⅞—2.65).

What number is that from which if we deduct 3/7 of itself and 2/9 of the remainder, 28 will be left?

(b) A shed is 15 ft. long and 10 ft. wide. It is 12 ft. high in front and 7 ft. high in the back. How much lumber (one inch boards) should be ordered to cover the four sides, adding 10% for waste.

How many full bundles of shingles should be ordered for the roof, if there are 250 shingles in a bundle, and they are laid so that one thousand cover an area 80 square feet?

GRAMMAR.

1. Part of speech of the underlined words, and why?

(a) (b) He is *as* honest *as* he looks.

(c) He came *as* he had promised.

(d) There is little hope, *but* I shall try.

(e) *There* is no lad *but* honors his mother.

(f) The game is not *worth* the candle.

(g) This is the book *that* I prefer.

(h) Not *that* I love Caesar less.

(i) *The* longer we live, the more we learn.

2. Name the principal and subordinate clauses, and tell how subordinate clauses are used:

The drawbridge dropped with a surly clang,
And through the dark arch a charger sprang,
Bearing Sir Launfal, the maiden knight,
In his gilded mail, that flamed so bright
It seemed the dark castle had gathered all
Those shafts the fierce sun had shot over its wall
    In his siege of three hundred summers long,
And, binding them all in one blazing sheaf,

3. In the above selection tell what each participial and prepositional phrase modifies.

4. Give the case of nouns and pronouncs and why, and parse all finite verbs in the following selection:

The investigations and prosecutions initiated by Secretary Hitchcock and carried on by his successor, Secretary Garfield, demonstrated conclusively that land thieves have been for some time getting possession of the public domain, and that they have had sometimes the direct, sometimes the indirect, aid of public officials in and out of Congress.

5. Are the following correct? Give your reasons:

(a) I saw him many times this year.

(b) One of his best friends were accused of the crime.

(c) It looks like it would rain to-day.

METHODS OF TEACHING—SCHOOL MANAGEMENT—HYGIENE.

(Write not more than one page on each lettered division of a question.)

11. (a) Discuss the importance of the personal life and character of the teacher in relation to her profession. Illustrate.

(b) How much time should a teacher spend daily out of school hours in preparation of her work, and how should that time be spent?

12 (a) How would you handle the "topical method" in History, in study and recitation, and what are its advantages over the "question and answer method"?

(b) How may the judgment be trained in History study?

13. (a) What are the causes of impure air in a schoolroom, and what are its effects on the children? How can a room be ventilated by doors and windows without subjecting some to cold air?

(b) Name two books on "Methods," or History of Education, you have read. Give a brief summary of the contents of one of these.

14. (a) Name the most important factors in moral training. Illustrate by suggesting how the different school subjects might contribute.

(b) How do you teach division and pointing off of decimals? How would you secure accuracy in number combinations?

15. (a) How would you give individual aid to backward pupils in a class of 40 to 50 pupils?

(b) How do you estimate a pupil's fitness for promotion?

QUESTIONS IN 1911.

ARITHMETIC.

1. (a) The people of a school district wish to build a new school house which will cost $2,850. The taxable property of the district is valued at $190,000. What will be the rate of taxation?

1. (b) A man had three lots, each containing 6¼ acres, which he re-divided into building lots of ⅝ of an acre each. How many building lots did he have?

2. (a) How many square inches are there in the surface of a cube whose solid contents are 2,744 cubic inches.

2. (b) If 120 bushels of oats last 15 horses 56 days, in how many days will 6 horses consume 90 bushels? (No analysis. To be answered by proportion.)

3. (b) A grocer bought 7 gallons of wine, and lost two gallons by leakage. He sold the remainder for $8.05 a gallon, making 25% on the whole. What was the cost per gallon?

4. (a) Mary bought a piece of silk for $63.50; she found, on measuring the silk, that she had only $61.25 in value. How many inches to a yard were given her?

4. (b) For what sum must a three months note be drawn so that, when discounted at a bank at 6%, the proceeds will pay for 75 barrels of flour at $8.50 per bbl.?

5. (a) Find the difference between the simple and compound interest, computed annually, of $1,200, for three years, three months, at 8%.

5. (b) Berlin is 13° 23′ 53″ east longitude, and San Francisco is 122° 26′ 12″ west longitude. When it is 12 M at San Francisco, what time is it at Berlin?

GRAMMAR.

6. Correct, where necessary, giving reasons:
   - (a) "It is them."
   - (b) "Who will the book be read by?"
   - (c) "Than who none higher sat."
   - (d) "Every man, woman and child lifted their voice in anger."
   - (e) "I do not like those kind of people."

7. Choose the better tense, with reasons:
   - (a) "It had happened before I saw him," or
"It had happened before I had seen him."
   - (b) "I should have liked to have done it," or
"I should like to have done it."
   - (c) "We have met on a great battlefield," or
"We are met on a great battlefield."

8. Give the principal parts of:

Awake, begin, blow, break, do, sing, swim, drink, steal, write, teach, catch, forget, take, fall.

9. Distinguish the adverbs and the adjectives in the following sentences:

He was sick nigh unto death.
The tumult shows the battle night.
How ill this taper burns.
All left the world much as they found it.
Much learning doth make thee mad.

10. Tell the part of speech each italic type word is, and give reason for your classification:

Heaven still guards the *right*.
Be sure you are *right* and then go ahead.
He will *right* the wrongs of the innocent.
And that my soul knoweth *right* well.
He is an *American* and glories in the right of an *American* citizen.
His years *but* young, *but* his experience old.
Quick! *man* the lifeboat.
Man wants but *little* here below.
Nor wants that *little* long.

METHODS OF TEACHING.

(Answer to each question to be limited to one page.)

11. (a) How best may the problem of retardation be met by the class teacher?

11. (b) When, if ever, is corporal punishment justifiable? What are the special dangers in its use?

12. (a) State three ways in which interest may be aroused and facility be developed in the writing of compositions.

12. (b) State the educational justification of the school garden?

13. (a) Discuss the relationship between the personal character of the teacher and its effect upon the moral development of the child.

13. (b) Name five essential qualities for a good teacher to possess.

14. (a) What qualities should characterize the work of a "good disciplinarian"?

14. (b) How would you deal with a restless class of fourth grade children placed indefinitely in your charge?

15. (a) Do you favor the holding of examinations at regular intervals in the grades? State your reasons for or against.

QUESTIONS FOR 1912.

AMERICAN HISTORY AND INSTITUTIONS.

1. What parts of American History should be taught, and during what years, to children before the Seventh Grade?

2. What purposes would you have in mind in teaching the "Revolution Period" to a Seventh Grade class? and how would you use the material?

3. Name 10 characters in American history a study of whose lives and public services would give a fairly connected view of the Nation since 1750.

4. Give your reasons for and against teaching Grammar Grade pupils both sides of the Civil War struggle, fairly.

5. Among "current" happenings since June, 1911, in political, industrial, religious and cultural interests, what do you consider suitable for instruction in the Grammar Grades?

6. Had the Panama Canal been built by private enterprise, would it have been a fact of "history" as much as when built by the Government? Why?

Answer the first, third and fifth questions, and two of the other three.

SCHOOL METHODS AND MANAGEMENT.

(Answer two out of the first four, and five others.)

1. (a) It is often urged that we should teach reading, history, geography and civics in close relation, making each serve the purpose of all. Is this a good plan or should we keep the subjects of the curriculum separate? Explain.

(b) Is it better to teach geography by topics or by countries? Give reasons for your answer.

2. Which is better; to keep the class upon a topic (e. g. alcohol, the Revolutionary War, interest, etc.) until they have mastered it, or to return to the topic at different times and from different points of view? Explain.

3. In the teaching of U. S. History what would be the relative emphasis placed on (1) industrial development, and (2) political and military events? Why?

4. (a) Mention some general principles which ought to govern the selection of topics for nature study.

(b) With what subjects is nature study readily correlated?

5. (a) What should be done with the dull pupil who is over-age for his grade but has not done his year's work satisfactorily?

(b) State some important facts and list some important questions relating to the general problem of retardation.

6. Name as many recent books as you can bearing on the pedagogy of the following subjects: reading, writing, spelling, nature study, arithmetic.

7. (a) State as specifically as possible what you would do to improve the spelling of children who continually miss even the simplest words.

(b) In the teaching of spelling what objection or objections could be raised to the use of such words as the following taken from the State Series Speller? Fillet, timorous, frieze, fuchsia, epaulet, aconite, lapidary.

8. (a) What is the proper temperature for a classroom?

(b) What special considerations should govern the seating of pupils in the classroom?

(c) What are some specific effects of Open Air schools upon pupils?

(d) Will you require home study? If any, how much and in what studies?

9. (a) What is the best method of preventing disorder?

(b) To what extent, if at all, would you permit one pupil to help another with his lessons?

(c) Is it better to punish rarely and severely, or to punish less severely but to exercise great care in calling to account for every offense? Explain briefly.

10. Define or explain each of the following terms: experimental pedagogy, adolescence, school clinic, vocational guidance, Blinet mental tests, social center activities, ungraded class, Batavia teacher, inductive method.

ARITHMETIC—FIRST 6 YEARS.

1. Write out in full all the possible combinations of change one can make for a quarter of a dollar. With what age of children could such problem be used?

2. What common fractional forms (specify) can be taught to children profitably, during the first 3 years? Why should these be taught? Why not others?

3. A newsboy buys nickle papers, three for a dime; how many papers must he sell to clear $1.00? What preparatory teaching would you want to do before giving this problem to a class of Fourth Graders?

4. How early can demical fractions be taught profitably? Is the notion, one tenth, more difficult than one-fifth? Why?

5. In "reduction of fractions" you accustom the pupil to see the given fraction in two or more forms having the same value: as 1-2=2-4=5-10=7-14, etc. What use do you make of this principle in working with integers, as in addition or subtraction?

Answer all five questions.

ARITHMETIC.

(Write legibly. Answer ten.)

1. A man bought a lot for $1,500 and built a house on it costing $3,000. He rented his property for $300 a year. Taxes, repairs and insurance cost him $74.00 a year. What per cent does he make on his investment?

2. There are 48 pupils and a teacher in a room 36 ft. long, 30 ft. wide and 14 ft. high. If fresh air is introduced at the rate of 30 cu. ft. per person per minute how often is the air of the entire room renewed?

3. If a city raises $13,093.75 from a ¼% tax, what is the assessed valuation of the property in the city?

4. The diameter of a circular tank is 8 feet. How high must it be to contain 15,000 gallons.

5. (a) 48.225÷15= ?
   (b) $\frac{.124}{132}$ =?

6. The sum of two numbers is 10, and the sum of their squares is 52. Find the numbers by algebra.

7. What arithmetical knowledge should children entering the seventh grade possess? Answer fully.

8. In seventh and eighth grade arithmetic which is better; to teach the short cuts and abbreviated forms of solution used by accountants and business men, or to require the pupil to make a detailed analysis of his solution by formally setting forth each step in the process? Give reason.

9. If a pupil in the seventh grade is excellent in all his studies save arithmetic, but fails in that branch, should he be promoted? Give reason for your answer.

10. What are some of the newer trends in the teaching of seventh and eighth grade arithmetic as regards:
   (a) The subject matter covered.
   (b) The nature of the problems used in the teaching of a given topic.

11. Does the reasoning ability which is gained through the study of arithmetic enable the pupil to reason better in matters pertaining to history, geography, etc? Defend your answer.

QUESTIONS FOR 1913.

GENERAL SCIENCE AND PUBLIC AND PERSONAL HYGIENE.

1. In what respects, and for what reasons, do the problems of school hygiene and school sanitation differ from those of the home, the church, or the shop?

2. In what ways can the school assist in the fight against tuberculosis and other communicable diseases?

3. What are the arguments for open-air school and open-air sleeping rooms?

4. What wholesome habits of personal hygiene may the schools hope to fix, for children under 12 years of age? For Grammar Grade children?

Answer questions 1 and 4, and either 2 or 3.

5. What are the several purposes of nature study during the first four or five years of schooling? During the later elementary grades?

6. What is meant by the "Science of Common Things"? Name three groups of such studies, and submit an outline of one of them, for a selected grade.

7. What "heat" studies would be appropriate for a Fifth Grade? An Eighth?

8. What "laboratory" or "field" work have you done in any of the sciences?

Answer 5 and 8, and either 6 or 7.

METHODS AND SCHOOL MANAGEMENT.

1. What are the factors involved in deciding upon fitness for promotion? And what is the relative importance of each of these factors?

2. As a room (or class) teacher, what is your responsibility toward pupils of the following groups?

(a) Backward children.
(b) Children of defective hearing.
(c) Children of defective vision.
(d) Morally delinquent children.
(e) Subnormal children.

3. Explain what is meant by "school incentives"; natural and artificial incentives. Name some incentives that are objectionable; why? Some worthy incentives; why?

4. What factors are involved in the arrangement of a daily program? Construct a provisional program for your grade. Explain its provisions.

5. What wholesome function can a parents' association serve for your school? Make a list of possible services.

6. Characterize an effective recitation for your grade, in some one subject.

7. What do you expect from children below the Fifth Grade in "preparing a lesson"? In the Grammar Grades? (Take some selected subject.)

8. Name and explain the uses of supplementary reading and references, below the Fifth Grade; in the Grammar Grades.

9. Discuss the statement: "The arousing of the pupil's interest is both a means and an end in his education."

10. Show how hand-work may be used to re-enforce the academic or book-work, in some one selected subject, in a given grade.

Answer the 2, 3, 6 and 8 and any other two of the remaining six questions.

UNITED STATES HISTORY, AMERICAN INSTITUTIONS AND CURRENT EVENTS.

(Answer ten of the eleven questions. Avoid making your answers unnecessarily long.)

1. The Conservation of Natural Resources.

(a) State what is included in this term.

(b) What problems connected with it have commanded special attention and interest in recent years?

(c) Mention some names prominently associated with the conservation movement.

2. (a) What are some of the main features of the tariff bill now before congress?

(b) Explain what a tariff commission is and why one would (or would not) be desirable.

3. With what accomplishments are the names of the following men connected: S. F. B. Morse, James B. Eads, Cyrus McCormick, Elias Howe, Henry Clay, Commodore Perry, Alexander Hamilton, William Howard Taft, Robert M. La Follette?

4. Mention as many instances as you can in which controversy has arisen over the question of state's rights. Give specific facts.

5. Outline some of the important considerations relating to the content and methods of teaching civics:

(a) In the first five or six grades;

(b) In the last two or three grades.

6. International peace.

(a) Give definite facts showing its desirability.

(b) What are some of the obstacles in its way?

(c) What part should the school play (if any) in regard to this issue?

7. Explain why California is interested in the Panama Canal. In what ways will it probably affect California industries?

8. The Monroe Doctrine.

(a) What is it and what was its origin?

(b) Give instances in which it has influenced the action of the United States.

(c) What is the general attitude of European countries toward the doctrine?

9. What were some of the leading after-effects of the civil war on the South?

10. (a) How is an amendment to the Constitution of the United States brought about? (b) Give as many as you can of the amendments that have been made.

11. What change is being effected in the election of United States senators, and what considerations have led to this change?

ARITHMETIC.

(Answer seven of the first eight and three of the last four.)

1. If a baker's loaf weighs 9 ounces when wheat is worth 90 cents, what should it weigh when wheat is worth $1.50?

2. What will it cost to carpet a room 27 feet long and 13 feet 6 inches wide with carpet 27 inches wide costing $1.87½ a yard—allowing ½ a yard on each strip for matching?

3. In digging a well 5 feet in diameter and 24 feet deep how many cubic yards of earth must be removed?

4. A man who has $7850 out on interest at 6½ per cent (with reliable security) calls in the money and invests it in a manufacturing enterprise. At the end of eleven months he sells his interest in this for $8000 cash. No dividend having been declared and no assessment having been made during the eleven months, to what extent did the man gain or lose by the manufacturing venture?

5. Reduce the following ahe decimals, carrying four places if necessary: (a) 25/36, (b) 15/16, (c) 3.4½, (d) .85 7/11.

6. Make out a bill for the following and receipt the bill:

2 packages of white drawing paper at $1.85.
5 gal. of black ink $4.60.
3 packages of legal-cap paper at $2.00
2 gross lead pencils at 30c per dozen
1 box assorted rubber bands at $2.75.

7. How much less is the distance along a diagonal path across a rectangular field 40 by 80 rods than the distance around two sides of the field?

8. Two logs are "similar solids" but of different size. One of them is 2 feet in diameter at the larger end and contains 1000 board feet. The other log, which is 3 feet in diameter at the larger end, contains how many board feet?

9. What are the Courtiss Standard Tests in Arithmetic and for what purposes are they intended?

10. What factors determine the value of any subject in arithmetic?

11. State, with reasons, your opinion on the following questions:

(a) Keeping a pupil in and having him write the multiplication table one or more times.

(b) Letting children count on their fingers or by the use of objects.

(c) Teaching all possible combinations of numbers below 10 before letting the child deal with larger numbers.

12. (a) Explain the purpose and value of drills in mental arithmetic. (b) About what proportion of the time would you give to mental aritmetic in the fourth, fifth and sixth grades?

QUESTIONS FOR 1914.

GENERAL SCIENCE.

1. What may profitably be included in "Science" studies in the first five grades? In the sixth, seventh, and eighth grades? What are the purpose to be kept in mind in each group?

2. Work out an outline for a series of lessons on "Moisture", for your grade—its constituents, forms, relation to life, relation to industry, relation to landscape beauty.

3. Characterize the respective fields of (1) object lessons, (2) nature study, (3) geography, and (4) systematic science, in the upper grades. In matter, and method of teaching, how are they similar? How different?

4. Describe the work of school gardening for your grade, and the science lessons to accompany it. How would how manage this work in the general program of school exercises? and what educational purposes should it serve?

Answer the first and third questions, and either of the others.

HISTORY AND CIVICS.

1. Tell the story, in 300 or 400 words, of the migration of the peoples across the Alleghenies and into the Mississippi Valley; when, by what routes, why, and a few of the principal frontier settlements—all before 1850.

2. Recount important social, economic, and cultural movements, north, south and west, 1860 to 1900, and trace their relations to the Civil War results.

3. Name the three or four great national political movements in the United States in the last 25 years, and tell why they are significant.

4. If but three civic (citizenship) questions were to be worked upon by your grade for a half year, what ones would you select? How could you treat one of them for your children?

Answer the first and fourth, and either one of the others.

ARITHMETIC.

(Answer 10.)

1. The diagonal of one face of a cube is 162 inches. Find the volume of the cube, and its surface.

2. A tinsmith wishes to make a pattern for the bottom of a pail, the area of the bottom being 164 square inches. If he must allow, in addition, ¼ inch all around for soldering what radius should he use in drawing the circle for the pattern?

3. A certain creamery uses 6400 pounds of milk a week. The skim milk amounts to 80% of the whole and tests 3/5% butter fat. How many pounds of butter fat are lost in the skim in a year?

4. A certain State, whose valuation is $1,800,000,000, has an annual tax of $0.07 on the $100 for the support of its three state colleges. This revenue is divided among the three schools in the proportion of 2, 2 and 1. What income does this provide for each school?

5. Which gives the better rate of income: a 6% bond at 120, or a 5% promissory note, ignoring the brokerage? Explain.

6. (a) 48,255÷15= ?
(b) 120.12÷1.9= ?
(c) $\frac{.124}{132}$ = ?
(d) ⅛ of .69 5/11= ?

7. How long will it take 12 men working full time to do a piece of work which 8 men can do in 54 working days working ¾ time?

A ship at 69 degrees, 4 minutes and 40 seconds W. receives a wireless telegram from a ship at 60 degrees, 12 minutes and 15 seconds W. at 10 a. m. When was it sent?

9. A crew can row nine miles an hour down stream and 6 miles an hour up steam. How far can they row down stream and return in 8 hours. (Solve by algebra.)

10. (a) Approximately how many minutes per week should be devoted to arithmetic in each of the following grades: first, fourth, sixth, eighth?

(b) What fraction of your allotment of time for each of the above grades would you give to mental arithmetic?

11. (a) Give illustrations to show how you would introduce children to the subject of denominate numbers.

(b) Do the same for the subject of common fractions.

METHODS AND SCHOOL MANAGEMENT.

(Answer five in all, not omitting numbers 3, 5 or 6).

1. Discuss tardiness and irregularity of attendance from the point of view of school management.

2. What criteria should rule in the selection of material for class use in the teaching of reading?

3. Give the name of an author who has made an important contribution to the pedagogy of reading. Do the same for writing, spelling, arithmetic and nature study.

4. Discuss the following: "The chief trouble with modern teaching is, that it seeks to get at formal results without regard to the sort of experience the pupil has in reaching the same."

5. What is the value of the recess period?

6. Would you require home work of your pupils? If so, in what grades, in what subjects, and to what extent? (Indicate hours and minutes.)

PERSONAL AND PUBLIC HYGIENE.

1. What is the chief purpose of hygiene teaching in the grades? Mention devices or indicate methods of procedure which will aid the teacher in attaining this end.

2. Describe somewhat fully the work of the State Board of Health in California.

3. (a) Give specific directions for the care of the eyes.
(b) Explain fully how you would detect eye defects in children.
(c) What evils result from defective vision?

4. How is each of the following diseases spread: "typhoid, malaria, tuberculosis, hookworm disease, diphtheria?

5. From the point of view of hygiene, what are the satisfactory and unsatisfactory features of the following described schoolroom:

Height 18 feet, length 34 feet, width 32 feet. Floors 1x6 soft pine boards. Five windows; three to children's left, one to their right, and one at the rear of the room. Windows are 3 feet wide, reaching within 2 feet of floor and within 6 feet of ceiling. Windows at rear and right are at the middle of their respective walls, those at left have 5 feet of space between them and are as nearly as possible at middle of left wall. Children at their desks face directly west. Half of blackboard is on front, half to the children's left. Number of seats 56. Seats and desks arranged with 2 inches "plus distance". Room is for children of a single grade and desks are of two sizes. Cloak rooms open into rear of classroom and not into hall. Furnace-heated, register in the floor at children's left. No exhaust.

QUESTIONS FOR 1915.

ARITHMETIC.

1. For what sum must I give my note at a bank for 90 days at 6% in order to secure $675.00 cash? (Omit days of grace).

2. A merchant sells 75 pairs of shoes for what 100 pairs cost him. Fin his gain per cent.

3. A hot air flue is 12 inches by 24 inches. Find the diameter and circum ference of a circular flue having the same area.

4. Wabash 5s are quoted at 107½. How much must be invested in them to yield an annual income of $1200?

5. The difference between two numbers is 5 and the difference between their squares is 95. Find the numbers by algebra.

6. Is it desirable for a pupil to analyze every problem he solves? Should he analyze any? Reasons for answer.

7. (a) Two girls receive $2.10 for making button-holes. One makes 42, the other 28. How shall they divide the money?

(b) Mr. Brown paid one-third the cost of a building and Mr. Johnson one-half. Mr. Johnson's share of the rent is $500 per year more than Mr. Brown's. How much did each receive?

8. Indicate which of the following topics in a course in arithmetic should receive little emphasis, which moderate emphasis, and which great emphasis:

Cube root, complex fractions, accuracy in fundamentals, "cases" in percentage, taxes and public expenditures, greatest common divisor, speed in fundamentals, least common multiple, compound proportion, insurance, apothecaries' weight, savings and investments.

HISTORY AND CIVICS.

1. If history be regarded as concerned with the actions and achievements of the people,

(a) In founding and managing a stable government;

(b) In framing moral standards and acquiring practice in following them;

(c) in developing and regulating their industries; and

(d) in stimulating and conserving wholesome family and neighborhood customs and institutions;

What can the school do to help on right practice in these several ways?

2. If you could discuss but one of these two problems in our history:

(a) The struggle for and winning our independence as a nation (culminating in the Revolution and the war of 1812-15); or

(b) the achieving of national unity (through the rise and fall of slavery, and the multiplication of common interests between the north and south, between the east and west), which would you select and why?

3. What effect does or should elementary history studies have upon the ideals and practice of citizenship?

Discuss along with this the methods of teaching history to accomplish these results.

4. For pupils who do not reach high school which part of American history is more valuable—the 150 years of pre-revolutionary colonial life, or the 50 years since the Civil War? Why?

Your answer will depend upon what you conceive to be the purpose of history studies to such youth.

Answer either the first or second and either the third or fourth.

METHODS OF TEACHING.

1. Discuss the teacher's responsibility toward

(a) The alert, capable, willing pupil;

(b) The willing and studious, but slow pupil of only average ability;

(c) The capable, but indifferent or unwilling pupil; and

(d) The well-disposed, but born-short pupil.

How does the organization of the school help or hinder you in accomplishing these purposes?

2. In your teaching, what difference do you, or in your proposed teaching, would you make in your treatment of boys and girls just entering their teens, as to (a) instruction and (b) discipline?

3. Of the several studies in the most progressive elementary schools, which ones do you consider the most important for children who are destined to leave school before the high school? Why?

4. Give the educational argument for the introduction of hand and constructive exercises into the elementary schools. Into what grades should they go?

Give the argument from the industrial or economic situation, for including industrial and vocational work in the school course. In what grades does this belong?

Answer No. 4, and one of the other three questions.

GENERAL SCIENCE AND HYGIENE.

(Answer three out of four in each list.)

I. GENERAL SCIENCE.

1. Select one of the following, and give a brief account of its life history and its uses or dangers to man:
   (a) The common house-fly.
   (b) The common toad.
   (c) Some bird (to be selected).

2. (a) What are the functions of the root, leaf, and flower of a plant?
   (b) Explain how you would teach these functions to a class of fifth or sixth grade children.

3. What are the main purposes of nature study in grades below the high school?

4. Explain the composition of air, water and coal.

II. HYGIENE.

1. Discuss decay of the teeth under the following heads:
   (a) Prevalence among children of school age.
   (b) Causes.
   (c) Means of prevention.

2. In about 150 or 200 words set forth some of the most important requirements of school sanitation.

3. (a) How is the temperature of the body regulated?
   (b) What does heat regulation of the body have to do with health?

4. Explain the most important effects of exercise on the health.

QUESTIONS FOR 1916.

ARITHMETIC.

(Answer any ten)

1. Separate $15,456 into four parts proportional to 2, 3, 4, and 5.

2. A school district with an assessed valuation of $860,291 wishes to raise by special school tax the sum of $1460. What rate will it be necessary to levy?

3. A owns a 37½% interest in a store building which is worth $20,000. The building is insured for 87½% of its value. If the building is totally destroyed by fire, how much insurance indemnity should A receive?

4. What principal at 6% for 2 years 6 months will yield $187.50 interest?

5. Find the value of x in each of the following equations:

$2x-49=69$

$345-x=135$

$9x-c=a+b$

$\frac{3x-8=1}{4}$

$\frac{72-4x=56}{5}$

6. Define the following: poll tax, income tax, inheritance tax, internal revenue, tariff.

7.. The areas of two similar triangles are in the ratio of 3 to 1. The area of the larger is 1686 sq. feet and one of its sides is 97 feet. How long is the corresponding side of the other?

8. A insures his life for $5,000, the premium being $150 per year. He dies at the end of 10 years, after having paid 10 annual premiums. How much does his family gain by the transaction, money being worth 6%, simple interest?

9. "The arithmetic which is taught in the common schools should be the practical kind." Explain and illustrate the above statement.

10. Explain definitely what use you would make of drill in teaching number work.

11. What are the Courtis tests in Arithmetic?

METHODS AND MANAGEMENT.

(Answer any five.)

1. Describe a well-disciplined school as regards:
   (a) The degree of quiet;
   (b) The extent to which pupils are permitted to help one another in their lessons;
   (c) The number of rules;
   (d) The amount and kind of punishments inflicted.

2. Explain definitely what the teacher can do in the way of teaching children how to study.

3. What are some of the most important characteristics of the period of adolescence?

4. Explain in about one hundred words how you would teach composition in the intermediate grades.

5. Discuss the following statement: "All the great problems of the day must be regarded, in the last analysis, as educational problems".

6. Name two noted American educators (living or dead), and discuss briefly the work of each.

7. Tell what you can of the recently developed standard tests for measuring pupil proficiency in various subjects. Explain the value of such tests.

HISTORY AND CIVICS.

1. Cite important happenings—political, industrial, social and cultural, in American history between the close of the war of 1812-15, and the beginning of

the Civil War. What citizenship significance have any of these for school youth today?

2. If the amount of political history is to be reduced, in the upper elementary grades, what material would you substitute? Give somewhat detailed statement of such an outline.

3. What are the important features of American history since the Civil War to be emphasized for the seventh, eighth and ninth grades? Why?

4. What historical material can be used profitably, with children before the sixth school grade? Should it be confined to American history? Why? or why not? To Colonial history? Why? or why not?

Answer the first and second and either of the other two (according as you are interested in the primary, or grammar grades).

HYGIENE AND NATURE STUDY.

1. Indicate in a detailed outline a couse for the study of birds covering the four grades from the third to the sixth, inclusive—subject matter, method of treatment, amount of time given to it, etc.

2. What parts of physics have value for the household? Of chemistry? Give in detail an example of each.

3. Explain the habits and works of earthworms, bees.

4. Explain the processes involved in the various ways of cooking meats, and the dietetic advantages and disadvantages.

5. Describe standard means of ventilation, and their application to the school room: means of heating, and their relation to ventilation.

6. What are the food values of potatoes, sugar, vegetables?

Answer either the first or second; and two of the other four.

SCHOOL SAVINGS BANK SYSTEM.

It gives me pleasure to report that the School Savings Bank System continues in effective and successful operation. Inaugurated in August, 1911, under the plan submitted to the Board of Education by former Director Power, now Supervisor, the system has grown steadily with every passing year in popularity with the pupils of the Department and their parents, and also in business importance. Vice-President A. H. Giannini, of the Bank of Italy, who participated actively in the formulating of the original plan, and in whose institution the accumulated savings are deposited, reports the total of such deposits now on hand as $292,070.45, and the number of individual depositors as 17,026. These figures show a gratifying increase from the total of $68,187.37 of depositors, with 7,604 depositors, reported July 1, 1912, after the system had been in effect for one school year. During the past half-year, as is evidenced by comparing the present figures with those reported by Dr. Giannini in an address before the San Francisco Chapter of the American Institute of Banking last February, there has been an increase of $39,322.63 in the amount of deposits and 1,325 in the number of depositors, since on February 1st the amount on hand was $252,747.82, representing 15,701 individual accounts. During the first year that the system was in effect about one in every four pupils of the total in average daily attendance maintained accounts, while at present the proportion is one in two and three-quarters—certainly a gratifying proof of the growing popularity of the system.

DEFECTS IN SPEECH.

The Medical Department of the University of California (Affiliated Colleges) has conducted an exceptionally fine clinic in curing defects of speech. Classes have been held at the College and at one of our grammar schools. These have been well attended and have produced excellent results. We have many children suffering from various defects of speech which if uncorrected will seriously handicap them for life. Most of these defects yield readily to corrective measures if taken in childhood, but if neglected to adult life these defects are nearly or quite incurable. I believe that this work should be undertaken by the School Department.

STATE TEXT BOOK FUND COLLECTIONS.

Under date of July 31, 1916, there was forwarded from this office to State Superintendent Edward Hyatt at Sacramento, to be deposited in the State Text Book Fund, a certified check for six hundred and sixty-two dollars and fifty-eight cents ($662.58), which sum represents money received from pupils in the San Francisco public schools in payment for State text books carelessly lost or destroyed during the school years 1914-1915 and 1915-1916, as follows:

1914-1915	$413.23
1915-1916	249.35
Total	$662.58

The sending of the 1914-1915 remittance was deferred pending the rendering of an opinion by Attorney-General Webb, to whom Superintendent Hyatt had submitted the question, as to the proper disposition to be made of funds so collected. A previous remittance of eighty-four dollars and ninety-five cents ($84.95), representing collections for the school year 1913-1914, tentatively made, brings the total of such remittances to date up to $747.53.

SAN FRANCISCO PUPILS ESSAY CHAMPIONS.

It is with much satisfaction that I call attention herewith to the excellent showing made by pupils of our San Francisco public schools in the nation-wide "Thrift" contest. Out of the ten essays sent East by State Superintendent Edward Hyatt as the best examples of the work done by the school children of the entire State, four were written by San Francisco pupils. It is certainly something of which we well may be proud that our city, with a total average daily attendance of 46,562, as compared with 372,626 for the State as a whole, should furnish 40 per cent of the prize-winning essays, though possessing only a little over 12 per cent of the attendance. And to obtain four of the ten credits allotted to our entire State we sent but eight essays to Sacramento—there to compete with the scores submitted by all the other cities and counties of California. Probably nearly every school in the State, including, of course, those of all the most important cities north and south, was represented in the contest—a fact which cannot but add greatly to our satisfaction with its results. That satisfaction is further increased by the knowledge that the judge of the contest, State Superintendent Hyatt, is one whose official position as the representative of all the California Schools, as well as his high personal character, makes any question as to his absolute impartiality impossible.

California State Board of Education,
Office Commissioner of Vocational Education.

Sacramento, Jan. 3, 1916.

Supt. Alfred Roncovieri,
Superintendent of Schools,
San Francisco, California.

My Dear Supt. Roncovieri:

Relative to your communication of Dec. 31st. will say that some months ago I had the pleasure of visiting the Commercial High School in San Francisco and was tremendously impressed with the enthusiasm and interest in their work shown by the Principal and Teachers of that Institution.

The thing that appealed to me most strongly was the fact that the teachers of your Commercial High School make it a business to keep up with the demands of the commercial world. In every class that I visited I found the teachers using forms secured from business offices in San Francisco rather than from some text book, and these teachers seemed to know what the forms which they were teaching meant.

In my judgment San Francisco has a Commercial High School of which it can be justly proud.

I also visited the Humboldt Evening School during the latter part of last year and must say that I was astonished with what I observed there. I am sure that few people, even around the Bay region, appreciate the fact that San Francisco has for many years maintained such a thoroughly efficient evening vocational high school.

The thing that appealed to me in this Institution was the fact that the pupils in the school were being given the work which they desired rather than the work which some one else thought they desired. The teachers were men from the practical walks of life and they were instructing these young people largely in the technical subjects which supplemented their daily work.

I am free to say that I consider the Humboldt Evening High School one of the most effective Institutions in the State of California.

With best wishes for the New Year, I remain,

Yours very truly,
(Signed) EDWIN R. SNYDER,
Commissioner of Vocational Training.

ERS/DB

DEPARTMENT OF MUSIC, PUBLIC SCHOOLS.

Report of Miss Estelle Carpenter, Supervisor and Director of Music.

August 1, 1916.

Mr. Alfred Roncovieri,
Superintendent of Schools,
San Francisco, California.

My dear Sir:—

In reply to your request, I herewith submit the following report of the work done in the Music Department of the city schools ending June, 1916.

From the inspection of the work made during the past year, the results have shown a growth in many directions.

A deliberate process of education based upon scientific pedagogic and psychological principles has been pursued.

The process of interesting the child, through the singing of beautiful songs, has been the primary step in the musical education. By means of this interest the child has been lead through the various paths to a knowledge of technical facts, and the child has been led to study the subject with such a whole-souled interest that he gradually realizes in some measure the depth and beauty of music's meaning and influence.

Music is the language of the soul which is the source of spiritual life and worthy action. The emotions may be intensified and uplifted by the continuous use of the right kind of music. This will have the correct effect upon the impulses. There is no other subject that can so grip the whole child. It gives him poise, power, and a higher development, because it gives him a higher love. Through this subject, the best of the physical, mental and spiritual nature can be vivified and strengthened. Song-singing should be recognized as essential and as important as fresh invigorating air in the school-room. The power of song is a gift more precious than diamonds; it is a fountain of joy. It makes the words seem possible, "I am youth; eternal youth; I am the sun rising, the poet's singing; I am the new world; I am a little bird that has broken out of the egg. I am joy, joy, joy!" If rightly used music has the power to formulate the motives of life. It is the means by which all Art impulses may be stirred; it is the inherent right of each child to obtain an insight into this Art that will enrich life. A wish for the knowledge of this Art will be stimulated by the study of the subject in the classroom.

Much thought and labor has been given to the task of bringing Music to the comprehension of the immature mind.

The music study has been made to co-ordinate with the general school system. The course has been so prepared by the Director that there is a logical unfolding of the steps, and through these steps has come self-development and power. During the year outlines were planned and given out, covering all sections of the work. At the regular meetings, guidance as to methods was suggested to the grade teachers. One thousand teachers were addressed, and one hundred and fifty songs were sung. The regular teacher has given the regular instruction under the plans outlined by the Director, who gave aid by conferences, meeting, class lessons, and who supervised by visits and thus by various means directed and advised, encouraged and inspired. The teachers have been a very vital factor in carrying the work to the child. In the child development there must be great faith, great hope, great courage on the part of the teacher. I commend highly the faithful, skillful work of our teachers, and I appreciate the spirit of their earnest cooperation. Many teachers have a genuine musical interest which lends an artistic charm to the work; and there are many who are grounded in the elements of music. If a regular teacher is not capable in this subject an exchange of work is made. In some schools a special teacher of music is given charge of a number of classes. There are thirty-two such teachers in the Music Department besides a number who take the singing in their schools without extra compensation. These special teachers have been most helpful and I thank them for their work. I trust more of them will be appointed next year. In a large department some schools require more attention than others, so these schools have been visited more frequently.

The development of the child on all sides has been encouraged. Correct habits for voice production have been urged. In the lower grades some remarkable work has been done along the line of curing the so-called monotone. As the ancients expressed themselves through song and dance so to the child just beginning has been given steps for rhythm and the motion song for expression. The Eurythmics of Jacques Dalcroze have been simply used, and in upper grades various drills have been given for rhythmical forms. Ear training, oral and written dictation, tone production, song singing, phrasing, diction, interpretation, sight singing have all been developed. The sight singing was commenced at the beginning of the Associate Period when endurance, memory, drill and discipline come easily. In music appreciation the children listened to musical numbers and tried to recognize them. The Victrolas and grapaphones have been useful in this study. Interesting concerts have been given through their use and I hope that soon each school will own one of these instruments. A number of schools gave a musicale at the end of the term. All parents were invited, and great pleasure was derived by the children's participation. Work was carried on through the Adolescent Period. The stage of mutation was carefully watched and the voices helped. At this period the emotions predominate so the upper grades have been given the very best songs, such as "Handel's Largo"; selections from Mendelssohn's "Midsummer Night's Dream"; "Serenade" and "Who Is Sylvia" from Schubert; "Soldiers' Chorus" and "Praise Ye the Father" from Gounod; "Blue Danube" by Strauss; "Lift Thine Eyes", and selections from Wagner, Brahms, Dvorak, Lassen and Rubenstein. Modern composers have been represented by selections from Arthur Foote, Neidlinger, Farwell, Arthur Sullivan, Henry Hadley, Cadman and Paul Bliss. California composers have been represented by selections from Dr. H. J. Stewart, Oscar Weil, Metcalf, Pasmore, Savannah, Fickenscher and McCurrie.

Considering the very limited time allowed for music in each grade, and considering how many children enter school without acute tone perception and voice production the results in the music work have been remarkable.

There have been many visitors during the past year who have been favorably impressed with the work, and who have freely expressed their commendation.

A very great kindness was extended to the school children of San Francisco by Mrs. Giulio Minetti, Conductor, who gave an invitation to a series of concerts by the San Francisco People's Orchestra in the Civic Auditorium. There have been a number of small orchestra formed in various schools and all players are encouraged to join the High School Orchestra.

Mrs. May McGlade has been in charge of the high school music during the past year. Excellent courses have been given in theory, harmony, history of music, voice development, chorus and orchestra work. The choruses, glee clubs, and orchestras have been doing some notable work as shown in the regular rehearsals and the public performances in which they have taken part.

In the Cosmopolitan schools songs of the different countries have been taken in the native languages. In each intermediate school the work has been conducted by a special teacher and excellent results have been obtained.

The music work in the school has been a connecting link between the home and the community. The child often sings his school songs 'round the family hearthstone". The precious hours spent thus will strengthen the family life and the home ties.

Since the fire, 1906, there have been forty-four school dedications generally on Sunday. At all these functions the singing of the children was an important feature, and the Supervisor personally led the choruses at nineteen of these dedications. During last year the Sarah Cooper and Oriental schools were dedicated; and the term before, the Marshall and Washington Irving schools' dedication exercises took place. At the Mothers' Club meetings, the graduations, and patriotic exercises the children's singing has been an important feature. These school affairs develop pride and love of family, city and country, in both parent and pupil, and make for better citizenship. The singing of the children has entered into the life of the city. Amid the ruins of 1906, our children's voices through the choruses gave cheer and helpfulness to many a heart. From June 6, 1906, through the many dedications and great public choruses the singing of the children has occupied a unique place in the history of our city.

The Panama-Pacific International Exposition brought tremendous opportunities to all in a musical way, and many of the children and teachers gained much inspiration from this source. The concerts given by the bands and those given in Festival Hall will always be remembered. The graphaphone companies' lectures and concerts were most profitable. A free concert was given by Madame Schumann-Heink in Festival Hall, and by her invitation I directed the four thousand children in patriotic songs. I wish to express my deep appreciation for the wonderful kindness of Madame Schumann-Heink. Her marvelous singing will always be a much beloved memory. The children's singing contributed to the upbuilding of the Exposition, as a number of choruses sang at the ground breaking of Machinery Hall and Chinese site, and at the Liberty Bell performances. Also a chorus of three hundred children from various schools took part in the ground breaking exercises of the Civic Center.

In every way the study of music is encouraged and children are urged to attend concerts.

I wish to recommend the following:

(a) That two pianos be given to each large school.

(b) That in assigning teachers the musical ability be taken into consideration with the musical need of the school.

(c) That supplementary books be given to the teachers of the third grade, and to the children of the fourth and fifth grades to be selected by the Director.

(d) That music books destroyed by the fire by replaced to the schools.

(e) That supplementary octavo material be given to the Director for the use of the upper grade classes.

(f) That the Superintendent send to schools supplementary books "Stories of Great Musicians" by Hurne and Scobey.

(g) That a typewriting machine be sent to the office of the Director.

(h) That a Victor or phonograph be given to each school with sets of records.

I wish to thank the teachers for their good work and the principals for their support of the Music Department.

I am appreciative of the help given by the Assistant, and the cooperation of the special teachers.

I am deeply grateful to the Superintendent and the Deputy Superintendent, and the Honorable Board of Education for their assistance and kindness. I am,

Yours sincerely,

ESTELLE CARPENTER,
Director of Music.

REPORT OF DIRECTOR OF ART.

San Francisco, August 1, 1916.

Mr. Alfred Roncovieri,
Supt. of Schools,
San Francisco.

My dear Mr. Roncovieri:

In reply to your request for a report from my department for the past year, I desire to say, that I and my assistants have striven, to the best of our abilities, to follow the course of study, which you have prepared for us.

We have visited the schools regularly on an average of once a month, but this we feel to be insufficient for the supervision we deem necessary to accomplish the results we desire to obtain. And now that our schools have increased so extensively, our visits will of necessity be less frequent. I therefore desire to recommend that another assistant be added to my department. We feel gratified at our results in many classes of our schools, and at the commendation of our successes which have attracted the attention of distinguished educators who have visited our city.

With the increased demand of the industries of our nation for more and better design, we feel that this generation of the San Francisco children should be given every opportunity for training in the fundamentals which later will be useful in the pursuit of practical arts.

With a keen appreciation of the services of our teachers, and the support of our principals in carrying out our plans, and your unfailing courtesy, I remain,

Yours respectfully,

KATHERINE M. BALL,

Director of Art, San Francisco Public Schools.

REPORT OF SUPERVISOR OF HOME ECONOMICS, ELEMENTARY SCHOOLS.

June 9, 1916.

Mr. Alfred Roncovieri,
Superintendent of Schools,
San Francisco, Cal.

Dear Sir:

I beg to submit the following report of the Home Economics Department for the fiscal year 1915-1916.

Personnel—		
Supervisor	1	
Teachers in Intermediate schools	3	
Teachers in other grammar schools	11	
Teacher, part time	1	
	—	16
Plant—		
Domestic science laboratories		28
Practice dining-room		1
Enrollment and Cost—		
Average monthly enrollment, domestic science	4184.7	
Cost of cooking supplies and laundry	$1832.505	
Cost of cooking supplies and laundry, per pupil	0.44	
Visits to Domestic Science Laboratories—		
By school officials		59
By supervisor		274
By others		2000
Domestic Art—(This is exclusive of the work done in the Intermediate schools.)		
Schools in which sewing is taught		9
Classes taught by teachers of our home economics department		7
Classes taught by student-teachers from Lux School		23
Number of pupils taught, spring term		621

WHAT WE HAVE DONE DURING THE PAST YEAR.

Domestic Science.

I am happy to report that the character of the teaching is improving all the time, and that there is a growing feeling of co-operation with the teachers of academic subjects and with teachers of other "special" subjects.

At present our course in the selection and preparation of foods covers two years, and is given to the girls of the 7th and 8th grades. Pupils receive one lesson per week of 85, 90 or 120 minutes each. In the Intermediate schools a three years' course is given, and begins in the 8th grade.

During the spring term we had Visitors' Days at most of the laboratories, and parents and friends were invited to visit the room while a class was in session. At several laboratories special exhibits were prepared. At the Intermediate schools and at one other school the girls of the 8th grade presented an exhibit showing the relative food value of several common foods. This demonstration was modeled on some seen last year at the Exposition.

At two schools our pupils displayed and explained California food products, and we had a speaker from the Home Industry League. At another laboratory we gave a demonstration of child feeding, and several schools had exhibits of home cooking. The girls served refreshments prepared in class. We had several hundred guests who seemed pleased with both the class-work and the refreshments.

Domestic Art.

It is a matter of regret that a course in domestic art is not given in all our elementary schools. The work done in this line in the Intermediate schools is much appreciated by both the girls and their mothers, and there are many principals in other schools who would like to see similar sewing courses put in their schools.

A tentative plan for teaching sewing without extra teachers or equipment was tried by me last term. Four of my teachers had free periods which were devoted to domestic art, and seventeen student-teachers from the Lux school helped out in other schools.

The Lux School is an endowed school giving a two years' normal course in home economics. The State Board of Education requires that teachers in training do a certain amount of practice-teaching. The Lux students, to our mutual advantage, do their practice-teaching in our schools, teaching sewing to classes that could not otherwise be taught.

We began this arrangement during the spring term 1915, with two practice-teachers. Their work was so satisfactory that several principals asked for other practice-teachers to teach sewing, so that at present we have seventeen.

While the work is still too new and too incomplete to be judged as a domestic art course, it offers, I think, a good example of co-operation. The staff of the Lux School has been most helpful in planning work to meet our peculiar conditions; our principals have adjusted their school programs to meet the Lux time schedule, and several manual training teachers have helped us with sewing tables made in the shops as class work.

Desired Expansion.

I would like to see the home economics department expand in three directions.

1. A domestic art course, under a competent assistant supervisor.

2. Cafeterias or lunch-rooms established in schools were needed.

3. The work with foods now given, extended and improved.

The city budget does not provide funds for the first two items, but I hope that it will be possible to improve our present equipment for domestic science work. We need more cooking laboratories, and new mill-work at some of the old ones.

1. New laboratories. At present only twenty-eight of the fifty-one schools having girls in the 8th grades are provided with laboratories. Twenty-five per cent of our pupils have to leave their school to take cooking lessons. Twelve schools have an enrollment in the 7th and 8th grades to warrant the equipping of a domestic science room. In six schools the need seems to me to be urgent. The Fairmount School sends 165 girls to cooking every week, the Columbia School 145. The pupils of the McKinley, Grattan, Rochambeau and Yerba Buena schools are also numerous in our classes, and travel blocks from their schools to our laboratories.

2. I would like to have the mill-work at the Irving M. Scott, Horace Mann and Hearst schools scrapped, and up-to-date tables, etc., installed. These laboratories were equipped about twenty years ago, with makeshift furnishings.

3. I would like fresh paint and minor repairs at several laboratories and fly-screens at all windows not already provided with them.

4. I would like about half a dozen books of reference for each laboratory, and several sets of food charts, to be used in turn at different laboratories.

I would like to make some changes and improvements in the teaching of home economics in the grades. I think that we could make better use of several organizations that would be glad to help us train our girls for home life. In the schools I have always found principals and teachers willing to listen to any plans for correlation that I have suggested, and I have met with the most cordial co-operation when I have asked for information or help from a civic organization.

I expect many helpful suggestions from the report of Mrs. Henrietta W. Calvin, the home economics specialist of the staff of investigators who made the "School Survey" last spring. My teachers and I liked Mrs. Calvin, and hope that she liked our work and will show us how to improve it. We are looking for her report with interest.

Yours truly,

ELLEN M. BARTLETT,
Supervisor of Home Economics, Elementary Schools.

REPORT ON SPECIAL CLASSES FOR SUB-NORMAL CHILDREN.

Miss Louise M. Lombard in charge.

San Francisco, August 1, 1916.

Mr. A. Roncovieri,
Superintendent of Schools,
San Francisco, Cal.

My dear Sir:

I respectfully submit the following report of work in special classes for sub-normal children for past school year.

Three classes for sub-normal children are now organized—two at Ungraded Primary School and one in Buena Vista Primary School. During the past school year these classes have cared for fifty-three children. Of these number five have been sent on into regular grade work, one to Ethan Allen School and one motherless girl with immoral tendencies and decidedly sub-normal was admitted to Glen Ellen, State Home for Feeble Minded.

There are still in the grades with normal children, a hindrance to them and gaining little themselves, many of these children who require special care and training, showing urgent need for additional classes.

The need is also great for a new building to replace the one in which the classes at Ungraded Primary are conducted. The building is too small to accommodate the number of children cared for and entirely unsuited to the work. The grounds, which are large and well suited to gardening, cannot be used for this purpose as there is no protection and work done during the day is destroyed at night.

Respectfully,

LOUISE M. LOMBARD.

REPORT OF THE SCHOOL FOR THE DEAF.

Mr. Alfred Roncovieri,
Superintendent of Schools,
San Francisco, Cal.

Dear Sir:

In reply to your favor of June 13th asking for a report of the year's work in the Deaf Department for the last school year I would state that eight new pupils have been admitted to the school since last August. Two pupils were discharged—both semi-deaf. One who was in the Deaf Department two years was placed in a class for the hearing in the Golden Gate School. The other pupil, in attendance a year and a half, entered the Hamilton Intermediate School. Both these pupils came from regular hearing schools and had lost ground through partial deafness. Since discharging these pupils we have kept in touch with them and reports show they are working earnestly and doing well.

A new teacher, trained and experienced, was added to the corps this year, which has made it possible to grade the classes better. We now have thirty pupils enrolled.

All of the new pupils, seven of whom entered since February, had absolutely no language. They had never spoken and did not know that objects had names. Their sole means of communication were natural gestures.

Great effort has been made to improve the speech and speech-reading. Contests in speaking of all classes have been held every Friday in on of the class-rooms and aroused the ambition of children to master difficult sounds and otherwise improve in speech.

The Manual Training Class is a great pleasure and benefit. Seven boys have attended the John Swett School one period a week for instruction. Their very handicap is in a sense an advantage in the designing room as they are quiet and concentrate on their work.

For the first time since the Deaf Department was opened, drawing as taught in the hearing schools and under the supervision of the teachers of drawing, was introduced this year and has rendered a valuable service in creating a means for expression and power of observation.

The older girls received instruction in cooking at the Crocker School. There is, of course, some loss of time making the trip back and forth to these classes, the time coming out of the regular class work. This we regret.

The physical training introduced this year has helped very much in securing poise and posture. So far, we have used the exercises prescribed for the hearing children, adopting no special methods. The directions for these exercises are given orally, as far as possible, thereby training the children to an alertness in response to commands and directions, at the same time increasing their faculty in lip-reading.

The daily traveling to and from school has given these children self-reliance and has brought them in constant contact with hearing people. In a number of cases the older children take care of the little ones and there have been no accidents.

Instruction in sewing is carried on in the school-room. We want a sewing machine and have asked for it.

While the Exposition was in progress we were able to make a collection of raw materials from exhibits there, which furnish us the beginning of a school-room museum invaluable in the teaching of geography and nature study. As most of our teaching with this class of children must be objective we need an abundance of such material.

With an additional class we are in need of another school-room which is to be provided, I believe. We have also asked for a large closet to be built in in the southwest school-room.

There are frequent requests from adult deaf and hard of hearing for instruction in lip-reading. In many cases these people cannot afford private lessons. Their state is a very serious one and deserves relief. In a number of cities where the number justifies it provision is made for instruction in lip-reading to the adult deaf. These classes are usually conducted by experienced teachers of the deaf in night schools. I would suggest that this matter receive the consideration of the school authorities.

In a former letter to you I mentioned the need of better heating facilities in two of our school-rooms, the lack of which comes through some faulty construction of the school's heating plant. An effort was made last year to divert the heat from pipes leading to other rooms, to these cold rooms, but the result was far from satisfactory. As there seems no way to remedy this trouble with the present plant we would like stoves placed in these two rooms.

In conclusion I would say that there has been a gain along all lines of work.

We appreciate the co-operation of the Board of Superintendents and the Board of Education.

Very respectfully,

ALMA L. CHAPIN,

Teacher in charge of the San Francisco Day School for the Deaf.

DEPARTMENT OF PHYSICAL EDUCATION, ATHLETICS, SOCIAL AND LECTURE CENTERS.

July 31, 1916.

Mr. Alfred Roncovieri,
Superintendent of Schools,
San Francisco, Cal.

My dear Mr. Roncovieri:

In response to your request for a report concerning the work of the Department of Physical Education, Athletics, Social and Lecture Centers, may I ask you to accept my report of January 19th, 1916, in fulfillment of your request. To the report of January 19th, I wish to add the attached statement which shows the manner and the methods of expanding the work in physical education to include the high schools. The report of January 19th, together with the statement concerning the high school, brings the report of my Department up to date.

Yours sincerely,

E. B. DeGROOT.

BOARD OF EDUCATION—DEPARTMENT OF PHYSICAL EDUCATION, ATHLETICS, SOCIAL AND LECTURE CENTERS.

To Principals and Teachers of High Schools:

On June 20th the Board of Education created for the high schools the position of "Director of Physical Education and Athletics" and appointed the following persons to fill the positions thus created:

Polytechnic High School—Mr. Willis O. Hunter, Director of Physical Education and Athletics for Boys. Miss Gertrude Brown, Director of Physical Education and Athletics for Girls.

Lowell High School—Mr. Courteney Overin, Director of Physical Education and Athletics for Boys. Miss Clara Newhouse, Director of Physical Education and Athletics for Girls.

High School of Commerce—Mr. George G. Lorbeer. Director of Physical Education and Athletics for Boys. Miss Nita Sheffield, Director of Physical Education and Athletics for Girls.

Mission High School—Mr. Omar F. Bradway, Director of Physical Education and Athletics for Boys. Miss Nita Sheffield, Director of Physical Education and Athletics for Girls.

Girls High School—Mrs. Laura H. Tharp (reappointed), Director of Physical Education and Athletics.

The object of this action by the Board is to center the responsibility and leadership in all matters of physical education and athletics in one man for the boys, and one woman for the girls in each of the high schools.

The Directors of Physical Education and Athletics will become members of the faculty in their respective schools. They will be subordinate to the Principal and subject to all of his rules and regulations for the guidance of the faculty.

The Director of the Department of Physical Education. Athletics, Social and Lecture Centers will aid the Principal in establishing and carrying forward the work of physical education and athletics. He will be responsible for all technical procedure and the supervision of the methods, systems and practices of the Directors of Physical Education and Athletics.

The general plan of procedure will be extensive, rather than intensive, athletics; i. e., methods and practices which will center time and effort upon the mass of students, rather than upon the coaching of "first teams".

The Directors of Physical Education and Athletics will welcome the voluntary assistance of other members of the faculty in coaching and supervising teams for interschool contests. The work of volunteers, must, however, harmonize with the plans and the aims of the Director's of Physical Education and Athletics who, alone, will be held responsible to the Principal and the Department.

The Directors of Physical Education and Athletics will at once address themselves to carrying out the following aims. The extent to which some of the aims may be carried out will depend upon the physical facilities at hand and the measure of co-operation accorded the Directors of Physical Education and Athletics by the Principal and the members of the faculty.

AIMS OF THE DEPARTMENT OF PHYSICAL EDUCATION AND ATHLETICS IN HIGH SCHOOLS.

I. Physical Aims. The development of organic vigor through muscular exercise and the establishment of habits which lead to systematic physical exercise.

By means of:

Organized and directed play in the building or in the school yard.

Systematic classes in gymnastics in the building or in the school yard.

Folk, gymnastic, aesthetic and social dancing as part of a gymnastic course or as an unrelated exercise.

Class or group competition in games and athletic events wholly within the school.

Boxing, fencing and wrestling, arranged for groups on competitive or non-competitive basis.

Swimming, diving and life saving, arranged for groups on competitive or non-competitive basis.

Interschool competition in games, aquatics and athletic events arranged directly with other schools or through athletic leagues. (Interschool events for girls must be arranged only on the basis of an invitation to play or compete. The parts of "host" and "guest" must be strictly carried out.

Talks or lectures by the Director on physiology of exercise, hygiene and first aid.

Insistence upon the application of the laws of hygiene in exercise, bathing, dress and training.

Medical examination of heart, lungs and nervous system of all students who participate in events which call for a severe test of speed, strength or endurance.

Note.—As soon as feasible, these physical aims should be guaranteed to the student by certain required work for freshmen and sophomores, and by elective participation for juniors and seniors.

II.—Social and Ethical Aims. The awakening and development of social ideals and good conduct. Not to be attained by mere preachment, but through the experiences of the student, supplemented by interpretations of the Director, the Principal and members of the faculty who observe students in their play expressions.

By means of:

Participating in the "school spirit" engendered by athletic contests—loyalty.

Taking defeat gracefully and victory modestly—self-control.

Giving the "square deal" to team mates and adversaries alike—good sportsmanship.

Accepting the rulings of officials without "crabbing"—respect for authority.

Working together and subordinating self interests for common interests, as in team play—the essence of good citizenship.

Avoiding the use of profane and obscene language. Attention to proper dress upon the athletic field, in the gymnasium and about the school. Proper conduct and language in the presence of the opposite sex, especially at school dances and athletic functions. Guarding against slouchy, slovenly, tough expressions of any character—good manners.

Training; i. e., faithful, painstaking effort when upon the athletic field, and avoidance of tobacco, liquor, late nights and weak companions when off of the athletic field—moral stamina.

Respectfully,

E. B. DE GROOT,
Director of the Department.

RULES FOR THE ESTABLISHMENT AND OPERATION OF NEIGHBORHOOD CENTERS IN THE PUBLIC SCHOOL BUILDINGS OF SAN FRANCISCO.

The Board of Education will grant and promote, through its Department of Physical Education, Athletics, Social and Lecture Centers, the use of school buildings for evening neighborhood centers of the following character:

A—Social Centers. For the purpose of conducting neighborhood rallies, entertainments, clubs, etc., for any moral purpose except political or religious propaganda.

B—Lecture Centers. For the purpose of conducting lectures, discussions or debates upon any subject free from political or religious propaganda.

C—Music Centers. For the purpose of promoting neighborhood choruses or other musical interests of the people.

Note.—The term "Social Center" is here used to denote an inclusive neighborhood center. The social center may, therefore, include both lecture and music centers, as well as many other interests and activities.

By "political or religious propaganda" is not meant broad and liberal treatment of the civic and ethical questions of the day. The bar is against partisan or factional politics, and the promotion, criticism or giving offense to any religious faith or organization.

When neighborhood centers are established, the Board of Education will provide the following for each center:

One employe of the Board of Education to serve as leader, promoter and manager of the center.

Necessary janitorial service.

Light and heat.

A certain amount of equipment, repairs and supplies required for given activities.

Motion picture service in social centers once each month.

Stereopticon and operator in lecture centers.

Piano in music centers.

All other items of expense in the operation of a neighborhood center must be met by the patrons of the center. Club dues and admission fees may be collected and expended under the following rules:

1. Each club or unit group in the center must select a chairman or president and a secretary-treasurer, who will be responsible not only to the group they represent, but equally responsible to the manager of the center.

2. Dues or admission fees collected by any club or unit group of the center must be immediately deposited with the manager of the center. Deposit and receipt books must be used to insure accuracy and clear records involving all collections, deposits and disbursements of funds.

3. The sale of tickets for any entertainment must be conducted only at the entrance door at the time of the entertainment. Outside sale or huckstering of tickets will not be permitted.

4. All money derived from club dues or entertainments must be invested in the further equipment or operation of the center.

5. Admission fees to any form of entertainment must not be greater than 25c per person.

GENERAL RULES.

The regular closing time for evening centers shall not be later than 10 o'clock. The extended time for special functions shall not be later than 11 o'clock.

Children shall not be admitted to evening centers unless accompanied by adults.

The activities of the evening centers must be confined to those parts and facilities of the building that have been assigned for evening center use.

Smoking in or about the building will not be permitted. Spitting upon floors and other offensive acts will not be tolerated. Patrons of evening centers must be thoughtful of the rights and safeguards of children to whom must be guaranteed a sanitary, orderly and well kept school plant.

There must be strict adherence to all regulations imposed from time to time by the manager of the center. The manager will exercise advisory control and ultimate authority in all matters of operation.

REPORT OF ETHAN ALLEN SCHOOL (Parental School)—1915-1916.

Hon. A. Roncovieri, Superintendent of Schools.

Dear Sir: On July 26, 1915, we opened our school with 65 boys. On that day we paroled 16 boys. In addition to sending 16 boys to other schools, we allowed 19 boys to go to work. Of the paroled boys 2 were compelled to return, the rest keeping up with the class-work, in many cases having been promoted during the term, advancing a grade or two.

In December, 1915, we paroled 16 boys; 5 boys went to work; 8 boys graduated from 8-B grade from other schools. Many of our boys are now attending High School. The boys sent to work have proved satisfactory and all have been able to advance in the places we sent them.

Our school work is ungraded, consisting of grades from 1st to 8th. We follow the regular course of study, slightly modified, to meet the special conditions, so that a boy may fit in readily when paroled. This term we intend introducing type-writing and commercial arithmetic. The boys have a weekly paper and it is both interesting and a help to the school.

In addition to the curriculum, we have established and are carrying on successfully, rug-weaving, brush-making, basketry, cobbling, wood-work and gardening. We have now $110 in Bank of Italy from articles sold during the term.

This is the first term in the new Ethan Allen building—the ground surrounding this school, which was to have been used for the garden, was formerly a marble yard. The boys had to work very hard to transform these heaps of debris into a flourishing vegetable and flower garden. Our garden produces enough vegetables to supply the boys with a luncheon daily. We plant twice a year, thus giving us two crops. This year, in spite of the discouraging quality of the soil, our first crop was very successful, consisting of potatoes, beets, radishes, carrots, Swiss chard, beans, peas, onions, artichokes, cabbages and lettuce. We have a nice pumpkin patch and we are looking forward for "A nice crop of pumpkin pies" on Thanksgiving Day.

We also have a strawberry and blackberry patch and for the first year we had a fair crop.

Our varied activities have been helpful in strengthening the habits of concentration and industry and in many cases helping to assist the boy in determining his future work in life.

Our five showers and three bath tubs have helped much to secure habits of cleanliness—these are used daily.

The time of detention varies, because it takes a long time to undo years of bad habits. If we would receive these boys earlier, it would not be necessary to keep them so long. Our aim is to make this a corrective school, therefore if we could receive the boys after their first serious offense, the time for returning to their schools would be shortened.

Before corrective influences can be effective the physical condition must be improved, therefore a weekly dietary has been prepared with a view to supplying a right amount of each of the food elements necessary to improve the physical condition of the boy. I recommend that a physician be appointed to make weekly or semi-weekly visits to the school, examining the boys for physical defects as well as to general condition. This term we hope to establish a dental chair and have a dentist to examine the boys' teeth. We have also made arrangements to have a psychological test taken of every boy.

We have a Patrons' and Mothers' Club in connection with the school and we find that these are great factors in drawing closer bonds between home and school. Very often boys misunderstood at home are re-adjusted in their home relations through the closer relation established between the teacher and the child. A number of trained workers are going to be employed to visit homes and get a thorough understanding of home conditions in order to raise the standard.

During the vacation a trained worker was paid to visit the homes, every week, getting a full account of conduct. This is kept on record. By this means we keep in touch with all the boys during the vacation, which in my mind is far more important than regular school time. Very few if any of our boys get in trouble during the vacation.

We have a circulating library in connection with the school in order to cultivate a taste for good reading. During the term 150 books were donated.

I recommend the curfew law be strictly enforced, also the habit of peddling after dark, as the little money earned, together with the vast amount of liberty, gives them a desire to leave home and under these conditions they come under very evil influences.

Most respectfully,

RAE ALEXANDER, Principal.

UNIVERSITY OF CALIFORNIA—MUSEUM OF ANTHROPOLOGY.
LECTURES.

Affiliated Colleges, June 16, 1916.

Dr. Alfred Roncovieri,
Superintendent of Schools,
San Francisco.

Dear Dr. Roncovieri:

The following figures show the attendance of San Francisco grammar and high schools at the Museum of Anthropology for lectures during the preceding years:

1911-1912	1932
1912-1913	9273
1913-1914	9044
1914-1915	7532
1915-1916	6279

Note.—The lectures during the spring term, 1915, were cancelled on account of the illness of the lecturer. No grammar school classes were scheduled for the fall term, 1915, on account of the attendance of classes at the Exposition.

In December, 1915, the following circular was issued to teachers of 5th, 6th, 7th, and 8th grades:

"The University of California Museum of Anthropology at the Affiliated Colleges offers the following illustrated lectures to the children of the public schools of the City and County of San Francisco during the Spring Term, 1916. All of the lectures are supplementary to class-room work in history and geography.

"The lecture room of the Museum seats 180 pupils.

"Every afternoon and Monday, Wednesday and Friday forenoons are available for these lectures at the Museum. Attendance is purely optional on the part of the Principals and teachers; but in order to make definite arrangements, teachers desiring to attend with classes are requested to indicate their choice of lecture and time on the enclosed slip. The slip is to be returned without delay to the Superintendent's office. The schedule of lectures will then be prepared during the Christmas vacation.

"We have expectations that the United Railroads will furnish special cars to transport pupils direct from the school to the Museum, and then back to the school after the lecture. We shall furnish more exact information on this point later.

"The following are the lectures offered:

"Lecture No. 1. The Indians of California. The lecture is followed by a visit to the 'California Indian Hall', where the exhibit is explained to the pupils.

"Lecture No. 2. Spanish Explorers in the Southwest. The lecture is followed by a visit to the 'Southwestern Indian Hall', where the exhibit is explained to the pupils.

Lecture No. 3. Ancient Peru. The lecture is followed by a visit to the 'Peruvian Hall', where the exhibit is explained to the pupils.

"Lecture No. 4. Ancient Egypt. The lecture is followed by an explanation of the exhibit in the Museum's 'Egyptian Hall'.

"Lecture No. 8. Aboriginal Life in California. An illustrated lecture showing Ishi in his native wilds in Tehama county—an exposition of life in Californa three centuries ago. This lecture is followed by the examination of the collection of implements from Ishi's haunts.

"Lecture No. 19. The Races of the World. Particularly comprehensive and well illustrated. No exhibit.

"Lecture No. 11. The Indians of the Great Plains. The lecture is followed by a visit to the 'Plains Indian Room', where the exhibit is explained to the pupils.

"Lecture No. 12. The Races of Europe. This lecture is best suited for 7th and 8th grade pupils. It makes clear the racial and linguistic composition of the warring nations. Profusely illustrated. No exhibit.

"ALFRED RONCOVIERI, Supt. of Schools.

"Kindly fill out the following blank and return to this office.

"Name of teacher..
"Class ....
"School ....
"Lecture desired ....
"Approximate number of pupils who will attend..................................
"Day of week preferred...
"Forenoon (Monday, Wednesday and Friday only)............................
"Afternoon ...."

In May, 1916, the following circular was issued to teachers of 5th, 6th, 7th and 8th grades.

"The University of California Museum of Anthropology at the Affiliated Colleges is offering twelve illustrated lectures to the public schools of the City and County of San Francisco during the Fall Term, 1916. All of the lectures are supplementary to class-room work in history and geography.

"The lecture room of the Museum seats 180 pupils.

"Lectures will be given at 2:30 on every afternoon. Attendance is purely optional on the part of principals and teachers; but in order to make definite arrangements, teachers desiring to attend with classes are requested to indicate their choice of lecture and day on the enclosed slip. The slip is to be returned without delay to the Superintendent's office, as the schedule of lectures is to be prepared during the summer vacation.

"Classes from one school totaling seventy-five or more pupils (incluing teachers) and attending the same lecture at one time, may obtain a special car from the United Railroads at the ordinary street car rate or less. The United Railroads charged $7.50 for a special car regardless of the number of passengers. The special car calls for the pupils at or near their school and carries them direct to the Museum without change. After the lecture the car takes the pupils from the Museum back to the point of departure.

"The following are the illustrated lectures offered. With the exception of numbers 9 and 12, all are followed by a visit to the appropriate exhibit, which is explained by the lecturer.

"Lecture No. 1. The Indians of California.
"Lecture No. 2. Spanish Explorers in the Southwest.
"Lecture No. 3. Ancient Peru.
"Lecture No. 4. Ancient Egypt.
"Lecture No. 5. Greece and Rome.
"Lecture No. 6. The Totem Pole Indians.
"Lecture No. 7. The Eskimos.
"Lecture No. 8. The Filipinos.
"Lecture No. 9. The Races of the World.
"Lecture No. 10. The South Sea Islanders.
"Lecture No. 11. The Indians of the Great Plains.
"Lecture No. 12. The Races of Europe.

"The following report from Lecturer Gifford is interesting:

" 'It affords me pleasure to report to you the success of your scheme of optional attendance of grammar school classes at the lectures offered by the University of California Museum of Anthropology at the Affiliated Colleges. During the present term I have so far delivered forty-nine lectures to 3274 pupils. There are still ten more lectures to be given, so that the total for the spring term of 1916 will be close to 4000. You may be interested to know that I have also given during this spring term twenty-four lectures to 1109 San Francisco high school students.'

"Respectfully yours,

"ALFRED RONCOVIERI,
"Supt. of Schools."

May 10, 1916.

Your recent circular listing the twelve lectures offered by the Museum for the fall term of 1916, certainly has received a very general response. Applications for lectures for classes aggregating 15,577 pupils have been received. Unfortunately, we are not able to arrange afternoon lectures for all of these classes. I have, however, prepared a schedule which will allow of the afternoon attendance of 13,854 pupils at the Museum during the ensuing term. The large number of applications has necessitated the canceling of Lecture No. 7 on the Eskimos, for which classes aggregating 1723 pupils had applied. The lectures for the fall term will begin on Monday (August 7) of the second school week, and will end on Friday (December 15) of the next to the last school week.

I would be delighted if you would offer suggestions looking towards the improvement of our school lecture service.

With best wishes for a pleasant vacation, I remain,

Sincerely yours,

E. W. GIFFORD,
Associate Curator.

Encl. EWG/CR

TITLES OF TEXT-BOOKS IN USE IN SAN FRANCISCO HIGH SCHOOLS, SCHOOL YEAR 1915-1916.

Abbreviations of schools are: C, High School of Commerce; G., Girls High School; H., Humboldt Evening High School; L., Lowell High School; M., Mission High School; P., Polytechnic High School.

ENGLISH.

Title of Text and Publisher	Date of Adoption	Schools Using
Gayley & Young's Principles and Progress of English Poetry (MacMillan)	Oct. 1, 1909	All
Gayley's Classics Myths (Ginn)		G., C., P.
Gayley & Flaherty's Poetry of the People (Ginn)	Oct. 1, 1909	All
Brooks English Composition (American Book Co.) Books I and II	July 2, 1913	G. (Book II), C., H. L. (Book II), M., P.
Long's History of English Literature (Ginn)	July 23, 1910	G., P.
Bradley's Orations and Arguments (Allyn & Bacon)	Oct. 1, 1909	P.
Classics		

FRENCH.

Title of Text and Publisher	Date of Adoption	Schools Using
Chardenal's Complete French Course (Allyn & Bacon)	Aug. 24, 1912	G., L., M.
Francois' Introductory French Prose Composition (American Book Co.)	Aug. 30, 1911	G., C., L., M., P.
Francois' Alternative Exercises (American Book Co.)	Aug. 30, 1911	G.
Patton's Causerier en France (Heath)		G.
Walter & Ballard's Beginner's French (Scribners)	Jan. 5, 1915	C., P.
Fraser & Squair's Abridged French Grammar (revised) (Heath)	Jan. 6, 1914	C., P.
Ballard's Short Stories for Oral French (Scribners)	Jan. 5, 1915	P.
Classics		

GERMAN.

Title of Text and Publisher	Date of Adoption	Schools Using
Spanhoofd, Lehrbuch der Deutschen Sprache (Heath)	Oct. 1, 1909	G., H., L., M., P.
Muller & Wenckbach Gluck Auf (Ginn)	Oct. 1, 1909	G., M.
Walter & Krause's Beginner's German (Scribner)		
Walter & Krause's First German Reader (Scribner)	Jan. 6, 1914	C
Wesselholft German Composition (Heath)	Oct. 1, 1909	C
Bierwirth Elements of German Grammar (Holt)		C

Title of Text and Publisher	Date of Adoption	Schools Using
Pope German Composition (Holt)	Oct. 1, 1909	C
Bacon's German Grammar (Allyn & Bacon)	July 2, 1913	L.
Pope Writing and Speaking German (Holt)	Oct. 1, 1909	P.
Bacon's German Composition (Allyn & Bacon)	July 2, 1913	L.
Classics		
LATIN.		
Allen & Greenough's New Latin Grammar (Ginn)	Oct. 1, 1909	G., L., M.
Greenough, d'Ooge & Daniel's Second Year Latin (Ginn)	Oct. 1, 1909	G.
Allen & Greenough's Cicero's Orations and Letters (Ginn)	Oct. 1, 1909	G., H., L., M.
Greenough & Kittridge's Virgil (Ginn)	Oct. 1, 1909	G., M.
Rolfe & Dennison's Junior Latin Book (Allyn & Bacon)	July 2, 1913	L., M.
Fairclough & Brown's Virgil (Sanborn)	Oct. 1, 1909	L.
Peck's Ovid (Ginn)		L.
GREEK.		
Goodwin's Greek Grammar (revised) (Ginn)	Oct. 1, 1909	L.
Goodwin & White's Anabasis (Ginn)	Oct. 1, 1909	L.
Sterrett's Iliad (American Book Co.)	Oct. 1, 1909	L.
SPANISH.		
Worman's Spanish Book (I & II) (American Book Co.)	Oct. 1, 1909	C., P. (I)
Umphrey's Spanish Prose Composition (American Book Co.)	Oct. 1, 1909	C., P.
Harrison's Spanish Commercial Reader (Holt)		L.
Crawford's Spanish Composition (Ginn)		L.
Marion-Garennez-Introduction a la Lengua Castellana (Heath)		P.
MATHEMATICS.		
Hawkes, Luby, Touton First Course in Algebra (Ginn)	Jan. 6, 1914	G., C., H., L., M., P.
Betz & Webb, Plane Geometry (Ginn)	Jan. 6, 1914	G., C., H., L., M., P.
Taylor's Plane Trigonometry (Ginn)	Jan. 6, 1914	C., L.
Moore & Miner's Practical Business Arithmetic (Ginn)	Oct. 1, 1909	C.
Crockett's Elements of Plane and Spherical Trigonometry (American Book Co.)	Oct. 1, 1909	H., M.

Title of Text and Publisher	Date of Adoption	Schools Using
Hale's Practical Applied Mathematics (McGraw, Hill Book Co.)	Jan. 25, 1916	H.
Granville's Plane Trigonometry and Tables (Ginn)	Aug. 30, 1911	P.
Breckenridge. Mersereau & Moore's Shop Problems in Mathematics (Ginn)	Jan. 3, 1912	P.

HISTORY.

Title of Text and Publisher	Date of Adoption	Schools Using
West's Ancient World (revised) (Allyn & Bacon)	Jan. 6, 1914	G., C., M., L.
Harding's Essentials in Medieval and Modern History (Amer. Book Co.)	Jan. 6, 1914	G., C., L., M.
Cheyney's Short History of England (Ginn)	Oct. 1, 1909	G., M.
Muzzey's American History (Ginn)	Jan. 6, 1914	G., H., M.
Forman's Advanced Civics (revised) (Century Co.)	Jan. 6, 1914	G., C., M.
Bullock's Elements of Economics (Silver, Burdette Co.)	Aug. 30, 1911	G., C., L., M.
Reinach's Apollo (Scribner)	Aug. 30, 1911	G., L.
Andrew's Short History of England (Allyn & Bacon)	Aug. 6, 1914	C., L.
Sutton's Civil Government in California (American Book Co.)	Aug. 6, 1914	C., L.
Ely & Wicker's Elementary Principles of Economics (MacMillan)	Aug. 30, 1911	C.
Channing's Students History of the U. S. (MacMillan)	Oct. 1, 1909	C.
Myer's Medieval and Modern History (Ginn)	Oct. 1, 1909	H.
Ashley's American Government (MacMillan)	Aug. 30, 1911	H.
Davis' Readings in Ancient History (Allyn & Bacon)	Dec. 30, 1915	L.
Cheyney's Industrial and Social History of England (MacMillan)	Aug. 6, 1914	L.
Ogg's Social Progress of Contemporary Europe (MacMillan)	Dec. 30, 1915	L.
West's American History and Government (Allyn & Bacon)	Aug. 6, 1914	L., P.

SCIENCE.

Title of Text and Publisher	Date of Adoption	Schools Using
Snell's Elementary Household Chemistry (MacMillan)	Aug. 6, 1914	G., P.
Le Conte's Compendium of Geology (Appleton)	Aug. 30, 1911	G.
Young's Lessons in Astronomy (Ginn)	Oct. 1, 1909	G.

Title of Text and Publisher	Date of Adoption	Schools Using
Hunter's Elements of Biology (American Book Co.)	Jan. 5, 1915	G., M. first time Oct. 1909
Brownlee, Fuller, Hancock's First Principles of Chemistry (Allyn & Bacon)	Oct. 1, 1909	C., H., M., L., P.
Brownlee and Others Chemistry Manual (Allyn & Bacon)	Oct. 1, 1909	C., M., L., P.
Dryer's High School Physical Geography (American Book Co.)	Jan. 6, 1914	M.
Linville & Kelly's Text-book in General Zoology (Ginn)	July 23, 1910	L.
Andrew's Practical Course in Botany (American Book Co.)	Jan. 6, 1914	L.
Arey, Bryant, Clendenin & Morrey's Physiography (Heath)	July 2, 1913	L.
Snyder's First Year Science (Allyn & Bacon)	Aug. 5, 1915	P.

HOUSEHOLD ART.

Kinne & Cooley's Shelter and Clothing (MacMillan)		G.

COMMERCIAL.

Williams & Rogers Modern Illustrative Bookkeeping (American Book Co.)	Oct. 30, 1911	C., H., M.
Williams & Rogers Illustrated Banking (American Book Co.)	Oct. 30, 1911	C.
Belding's Correspondence (American Book Co.)	Oct. 30, 1911	C.
Gallagher-Marsh Shorthand Text-book (new edition)	Aug. 2, 1911	C., H., M.
Huffcut's Elements of Business Law (Ginn)	Oct. 1, 1909	C.
Nichols & Rogers Commercial Law		H.
Cutler & SoRelle Rational Typewriting		M.

TECHNICAL.

Bowditch American Practical Navigator (U. S. Hydrographic Office)		H.

APPENDIX TO "TEXT-BOOKS IN USE IN THE SAN FRANCISCO HIGH SCHOOLS".

The following list includes books adopted by the Board of Education since the close of the school year 1915-1916:

Title of Text and Publisher	Date of Adoption	Schools Using
Ashmun's Modern Prose & Poetry (Houghton, Mifflin Co.)	July 26, 1916	G.
Brewer's Oral English (Ginn & Co.)	"	C., L.
Hotchkiss & Drew's Business English (American Book Co.)		C.
Kutner's Commercial German (American Book Co.)		C.
Smith's Latin Lessons (Allyn & Bacon)		G., L., M.
Baker & Inglis High School Course in Latin Composition (Macmillan Co.)		G., L., M., P.
Espinosa & Allen's Elementary Spanish Grammar (American Book Co.)		C., L., M., P.
Roessler & Remy's First Spanish Reader (American Book Co.)		C., L., M., P.
Betz & Webb's Solid Geometry		C., L., M., P.
Gleason's A Greek Primer (American Book Co.)		L.
Moore's Industrial History of the United States (Macmillan Co.)		P.
Black & Davis' Practical Physics (Macmillan Co.)		All
Black's Laboratory Manual in Physics (Macmillan Co.)		All
Lallier's Elementary Manual of the Steam Engine (Van Nostrand)		P.
Bennett's Bookkeeping and Business Practice (American Book Co.)		C.
Robinson-Breasted's Outlines of European History Part I (Ginn & Co.)	Aug. 15, 1916	P.
Robinson-Beard's Outlines of European History, Part II (Ginn & Co.)		L., P.
Conn & Buddington's Advanced Physiology and Hygiene (Silver-Burdett Co.)		G., L.
Gowin & Wheatley's Occupations (Ginn & Co.)		P.

1916—	Number of Trials Paid for	Number of Defaults Paid for	Number of Appeals Paid for	Amount rec'd from Sundries	Number of Actions Paid for
July	222	188	13	$69.00	682
August	213	166	22	78.25	742
September	200	172	16	72.75	858
October	216	153	29	82.75	741
November	217	180	37	74.25	796½
December	201	158	29	56.75	719
1917—					
January	223	161	32	79.50	793
February	216	129	20	79.75	683
March	200	170	37	73.00	732
April	211	131	18	82.25	770
May	197	181	23	76.25	791
June	156	141	32	75.50	704
	2472	1930	308	$900.00	8966½

SPECIAL DEPOSIT FUND.

	Receipts	Disbursements
Cash balance July 1st, 1916, $888.02		
1916—July	$ 553.00	$ 817.62
August	937.40	729.75
September	386.00	563.35
October	593.40	473.40
November	2,918.45	889.25
December	496.97	2,651.92
1917—January	160.05	297.90
February	505.60	374.70
March	740.57	534.22
April	950.50	786.40
May	758.09	1,169.70
June	1,856.56	1,820.20
	$11,744.61	$11,108.41
Balance cash on hand July 1st, 1917		$ 636.20

Total number of Actions filed since April 18, 1906 97,081
Total number of Actions restored 1,400

Grand total of Actions filed since April 18, 1906 98,481

Respectfully submitted,

ROBERT W. DENNIS,
Justices' Clerk

Report of the Superintendent of Schools

San Francisco, July 1, 1917.

To the Honorable, the Board of Education,
in and for the City and County of San Francisco.

Ladies and Gentlemen:

I have the honor to submit herewith the annual report on the condition the public schools of this City and County, as required by the Charter, for the sixty-fifth fiscal year of the School Department, ending June 30, 1917.

ALFRED RONCOVIERI,
Superintendent of Common Schools, in and for the
City and County of San Francisco.

SCHOOL CALENDAR FOR 1916-1917.

Fall Term, 1916	In Session	Holidays
July 31—Aug. 25, 1916	20 days	
Aug. 28—Sept. 22, 1916	19 days	Labor Day—Sept. 4.
Sept. 25—Oct. 20, 1916	18 days	Columbus Day and day following—Oct. 12 and 13.
Oct. 23—Nov. 17, 1916	20 days	
Nov. 20—Dec. 15, 1916	17½ days	Thanksgiving Day and day following—Nov. 23 and 24. Half day Dec. 15.
Total	94½ days	

Spring Term, 1917	In Session	Holidays
Jan. 2—Jan. 26, 1917	19 days	
Jan. 29—Feb. 23, 1917	18½ days	Washington's and Lincoln's Birthdays—Feb. 22 and 12.
Feb. 26—Mar. 23, 1917	20 days	
Mar. 26—May 4, 1917	18½ days	May Day, 2 weeks vacation and half day for Red Cross meeting.
May 7—June 8, 1917	22½ days	Memorial Day—May 30.
Total	98½ days	

Spring Term	94½ days
Fall Term	98½ days
	193 days

Schools close June 8, 1917, and reopen July 30, 1917.

Note.—The financial data presented in this report were secured from various departments of the city and county government as herein specified in foot-notes, and are here presented without further verification by the Superintendent of Schools.

GENERAL STATISTICS.

Fiscal Year Ending June 30, 1917.

Population of the City and County (Estimated by multiplying the total average daily attendance of 46,862 by 11.2.)		524,854
Municipal Assessment—		
Real Estate	$477,963,094	
Personal Property	64,599,962	
Total	$542,563,056	
State Assessment, Operative	215,789,509	
Total Assessable		$758,352,565
Assessment just completed on which taxes will be collected for year 1917-1918—		
Municipal	$554,456,505	
State, Operative	237,146,831	
Total	$791,603,336	
Rate of County School Tax per $100 for the school year ending June 30, 1917 (Record of Board of Supervisors, September, 1917), apportioned to Common School Fund for Day and Evening Elementary Schools		$ .2140
Rate of County Tax per $100 valuation to produce $60 per average daily attendance pupil in the high schools, apportioned to Common School Fund for Day and Evening High Schools		.0560
Total Regular Rate levied for Common School Fund		$ .2700
Additional Rate, represented by receipts placed into funds other than the Common School Fund, but made available solely for school purposes		.1357
This .1357 is reported as follows:		
Kindergarten—Maintenance	.0028	
Elementary Schools—Building	.1020	
High Schools—Maintenance	.0246	
High Schools—Building	.0063	
Sub-Total		.4057
Additional Rate for Bond Redemption:		
1904 School Bond Redemption	.0129	
1908 School Bond Redemption	.0284	
1910 Polytechnic High School Bonds Redemption	.0046	
Sub-Total		.0459
Grand Total Rate per $100 levied for all School Purposes for 1916-17		.4516

(Exclusive of State apportionments, rents and other receipts not obtained by tax levy.)

ESTIMATED VALUE OF SCHOOL PROPERTY.

Kindergartens—

Valuation of Lots, School Houses and Furniture	$ 3,430.00
Valuation of Library Books	500.00
Valuation of School Apparatus	2,660.00
Total (Kindergartens)	$ 6,590.00

Elementary Schools—

Valuation of Lots, School Houses and Furniture	$10,897,662.00
Valuation of School Libraries	39,976.00
Valuation of School Apparatus	22,000.00
Total (Elementary Schools)	$10,959,638.00

High Schools—

Valuation of Lots, School Houses and Furniture	$ 3,109,114.00
Valuation of Laboratories	47,127.00
Valuation of Library Books and Apparatus	33,896.00
Total (High Schools)	$ 3,190,137.00
Grand Total	14,156,365.00

OUTSTANDING BONDED INDEBTEDNESS JUNE 30, 1917.

1904 Bonds at 3½%	$ 449,000.00
1908 Bonds at 5%	4,200,000.00
1910 Polytechnic High School Bonds at 4½%	500,000.00
Total	$ 5,149,000.00

RECEIPTS.

Receipts for the support of Kindergartens	$ 15,363.53
(Apportionment of City and County Funds.)	
Receipts for the support of day and evening Elementary Schools—	
Fiscal Year Ending June 30, 1917:	
(1) Balance on hand, July 1, 1916:	
(a) Common School Fund	72,328.72
(b) Bond Interest Funds (1904 and 1908)	126,110.47
(c) Public Building School Bond Fund (1908)	26,745.56
(2) Apportionment of State School Funds	670,107.92
(3) Apportionment of City and County Funds:	
(a) Common School Fund	1,066,066.42
(b) Bond Interest Funds (1904 and 1908)	239,145.74
(c) General Fund—by Board of Supervisors	385,042.84
(d) General Fund—by Board of Health (for employment of school Physicians and Nurses)	21,370.30
(e) General Fund—by Board of Police Commissioners (for employment of Truant Officer)	1,200.00
(4) From miscellaneous sources (rents, etc.)	99,498.27
Total (Elementary Schools)	$2,717,616.24

RECEIPTS—Continued.

Receipts for the support of day and evening High Schools—

(1) Balance on hand, July 1, 1916:	
(a) Common School Fund $	....
(b) Polytechnic High School, Bond Interest Fund (1910)..	12,706.78
(c) Polytechnic High School Bond Fund (1910)	13,977.97
(2) Apportionment of State School Funds	53,297.88
(3) Apportionment of City and County Funds:	
(a) Common School Fund	387,758.39
(b) Polytechnic High School Bond Interest Fund (1910)..	23,389.57
(c) General Fund—by Board of Supervisors	6,721.89
Total (High Schools)	$ 497,852.48
Grand Total Receipts	3,230,832.25

(Including Bond and Bond Interest Funds.)

EXPENDITURES.

Fiscal Year Ending June 30, 1917.

1. Salaries of all Teachers—	
Kindergarten	$ 11,702.77
Elementary	1,530,329.00
High School	339,372.90
Total	$1,881,404.67
2. Contingent Expenses (including salaries of administrative officials and employees, janitors, etc.), Supplies, Repairs, Rents, etc.—	
Kindergarten	$ 2,739.53
Elementary	348,412.57
High School....	64,008.98
Total	$ 415,161.08
3. Sites, Buildings and Furniture—	
Kindergarten	$ ....
Elementary	656,072.06
High School	45,435.66
Total	$ 701,507.72
4. Library Books—	
Kindergarten	$ ....
Elementary	4,600.00
*High School	....
Total	$ 4,600.00
5. Apparatus—	
Kindergarten	$ 921.23
Elementary	200.00
**High School	33,896.28
Total	$ 35,017.51
Grand Total Expenditures	3,034,690.98

*Item included under heading "Apparatus—High School."

**Includes library books.

RESUME

Receipts (including Bond and Bond Interest Funds)	$3,230,832.25
Expenditures	3,034,690.98
Balance	$ 196,141.27

Resume as applied to different types of schools.

Kindergartens:

Receipts	$ 15,363.53
Expenditures	15,363.53
Balance	0.00

Elementary Schools:

Receipts	$2,717,616.24
Expenditures	2,536,613.63
Balance	181,002.61

High Schools:

Receipts	$ 497,852.48
Expenditures	482,713.82
Balance	15,138.66

Balances:

Kindergarten	$ ....
Elementary Schools	181,002.61
High Schools	15,138.66
Total	$ 196,141.27

AVERAGE DAILY ATTENDANCE, AVERAGE NUMBER BELONGING AND ENROLLMENT FOR FIRST SCHOOL MONTH FROM JULY 3, TO AUGUST 25, 1916 (20 DAYS).

	Monthly Enrollment				Average	Average
				Aver. No.	Daily	No. Daily
Day Schools—	Boys	Girls	Total	Belonging	Attendance	Absent
Secondary Schools	1,978	2,764	4,742	4,519	4,404	115
Grammar Classes..	8,634	9,114	17,748	17,101	16,796	305
Primary Classes....	14,484	13,305	27,789	26,216	25,512	704
Totals	25,096	25,183	50,279	47,836	46,712	1,124
Evening Schools—						
Secondary Schools and Special........	1,758	949	2,707	1,920	1,772	148
Grammar Classes..	942	204	1,146	818	758	60
Primary Classes....	375	100	475	305	278	27
Totals	3,075	1,253	4,328	3,043	2,808	235

Totals of Day Schools Including High, Grammar and Primary:

Enrollment (Monthly) 50,27

Average Number Belonging 47,83
Average Daily Attendance 46,71

Average Number Daily Absent 1,12

Evening Schools Including High, Special, Grammar and Primary:

Enrollment (Monthly) 4,32

Average Number Belonging 3,04
Average Daily Attendance 2,80

Average Number Daily Absent........ 28

Grand Totals:

Enrollment (Monthly) 54,60

Average Number Belonging 50,87
Average Daily Attendance 49,52

Average Number Daily Absent........ 1,85

AVERAGE DAILY ATTENDANCE, AVERAGE NUMBER BELONGING AND ENROLLMENT FOR SECOND SCHOOL MONTH FROM AUGUST 28, TO SEPTEMBER 22, 1916 (19 DAYS).

	Monthly Enrollment			Aver. No.	Average Daily	Average No. Dail
Day Schools—	Boys	Girls	Total	Belonging	Attendance	Absent
Secondary Schools	1,949	2,716	4,665	4,525	4,357	168
Grammar Classes..	8,880	9,124	18,004	17,248	16,851	397
Primary Classes....	14,686	13,371	28,057	27,139	25,663	1,476
Totals	25,515	25,211	50,726	48,912	46,871	2,041
Evening Schools—						
Secondary Schools and Special........	1,651	891	2,542	1,831	1,656	175
Grammar Classes..	943	210	1,153	924	808	116
Primary Classes....	368	106	474	315	286	29
Totals	2,962	1,207	4,169	3,070	2,750	320

Totals of Day Schools Including High, Grammar and Primary:

Enrollment (Monthly) 50,72

Average Number Belonging ....
Average Daily Attendance ....

Average Number Daily Absent........ 2,04

Evening Schools Including High, Special, Grammar and Primary:

Enrollment (Monthly) 4,16

Average Number Belonging ....
Average Daily Attendance ....

Average Number Daily Absent........ 32

Grand Totals:

Enrollment (Monthly)	54,895
Average Number Belonging	51,982
Average Daily Attendance	48,912
Average Number Daily Absent	2,361

AVERAGE DAILY ATTENDANCE, AVERAGE NUMBER BELONGING AND ENROLLMENT FOR THIRD SCHOOL MONTH FROM SEPTEMBER 25, TO OCTOBER 20, 1916 (18 DAYS).

	Monthly Enrollment			Aver. No.	Average Daily	Average No. Daily
Day Schools—	Boys	Girls	Total	Belonging	Attendance	Absent
Secondary Schools	1,914	2,646	4,560	4,451	4,233	218
Grammar Classes	8,866	9,126	17,992	17,209	16,596	613
Primary Classes	14,651	13,355	28,006	26,538	25,327	1,211
Totals	25,431	25,127	50,558	48,198	46,156	2,042
Evening Schools—						
Secondary Schools and Special	1,296	869	2,165	1,695	1,522	173
Grammar Classes	1,118	216	1,334	876	784	92
Primary Classes	334	96	430	296	272	24
Totals	2,748	1,181	3,929	2,867	2,578	289

Totals of Day Schools Including High, Grammar and Primary:

Enrollment (Monthly)	50,558
Average Number Belonging	48,198
Average Daily Attendance	46,156
Average Number Daily Absent	2,042

Evening Schools Including High, Special, Grammar and Primary:

Enrollment (Monthly)	3,929
Average Number Belonging	2,867
Average Daily Attendance	2,578
Average Number Daily Absent	289

Grand Totals:

Enrollment (Monthly)	54,487
Average Number Belonging	51,065
Average Daily Attendance	48,734
Average Number Daily Absent	2,331

AVERAGE DAILY ATTENDANCE, AVERAGE NUMBER BELONGING AND ENROLLMENT FOR FOURTH SCHOOL MONTH FROM OCTOBER 23, TO NOVEMBER 17, 1916 (20 DAYS).

	Monthly Enrollment			Aver. No.	Average Daily	Average No. Daily
Day Schools—	Boys	Girls	Total	Belonging	Attendance	Absent
Secondary Schools	1,871	2,589	4,460	4,373	4,183	190
Grammar Classes..	8,778	9,071	17,849	17,283	16,692	591
Primary Classes....	14,610	13,374	27,984	26,469	25,488	981
Totals	25,259	25,034	50,293	48,125	46,363	1,762
Evening Schools—						
Secondary Schools and Special........	1,369	467	1,836	1,548	1,396	152
Grammar Classes..	889	509	1,398	875	772	103
Primary Classes....	334	90	424	295	270	25
Totals	2,592	1,066	3,658	2,718	2,438	280

Totals of Day Schools Including High, Grammar and Primary:

Enrollment (Monthly)	50,293
Average Number Belonging	48,125
Average Daily Attendance	46,363
Average Number Daily Absent	1,762

Evening Schools Including High, Special, Grammar and Primary:

Enrollment (Monthly)	3,658
Average Number Belonging	2,718
Average Daily Attendance	2,438
Average Number Daily Absent	280

Grand Totals:

Enrollment (Monthly)	53,951
Average Number Belonging	50,843
Average Daily Attendance	48,801
Average Number Daily Absent	2,042

AVERAGE DAILY ATTENDANCE, AVERAGE NUMBER BELONGING AND ENROLLMENT FOR FIFTH SCHOOL MONTH FROM NOVEMBER 20, TO DECEMBER 15, 1916 (17½ DAYS).

	Monthly Enrollment			Aver. No.	Average Daily	Average No. Daily
Day Schools—	Boys	Girls	Total	Belonging	Attendance	Absent
Secondary Schools	1,835	2,557	4,392	4,279	4,070	209
Grammar Classes..	8,661	8,965	17,626	17,264	16,663	601
Primary Classes....	14,349	13,112	27,461	26,424	25,412	1,012
Totals	24,845	24,634	49,479	47,967	46,145	1,822

Evening Schools—						
Secondary Schools and Special........	1,219	750	1,969	1,414	1,338	76
Grammar Classes..	813	200	1,013	822	778	44
Primary Classes....	351	77	428	398	282	116
Totals	2,383	1,027	3,410	2,634	2,398	236

Totals of Day Schools Including High, Grammar and Primary:

Enrollment (Monthly)	49,479
Average Number Belonging	47,967
Average Daily Attendance	46,145
Average Number Daily Absent	1,822

Evening Schools Including High, Special, Grammar and Primary:

Enrollment (Monthly)	3,410
Average Number Belonging	2,634
Average Daily Attendance	2,398
Average Number Daily Absent	236

Grand Totals:

Enrollment (Monthly)	52,889
Average Number Belonging	50,610
Average Daily Attendance	48,543
Average Number Daily Absent	2,058

AVERAGE DAILY ATTENDANCE, AVERAGE NUMBER BELONGING AND ENROLLMENT FOR SIXTH MONTH FROM JANUARY 2, TO JANUARY 26, 1917 (19 DAYS).

	Monthly Enrollment				Average	Average
Day Schools—	Boys	Girls	Total	Aver. No. Belonging	Daily Attendance	No. Daily Absent
Secondary Classes	2,115	2,916	5,031	4,864	4,711	153
Grammar Classes..	9,372	9,538	18,910	17,980	17,350	630
Primary Classes....	14,460	13,387	27,847	25,543	24,372	1,171
Total	25,947	25,841	51,788	48,387	46,433	1,954
Evening Schools—						
Secondary Schools and Special........	1,715	1,015	2,730	1,931	1,762	169
Grammar Classes..	945	209	1,154	931	866	65
Primary Classes....	384	61	445	288	262	26
Total	3,044	1,285	4,329	3,150	2,890	260

Totals of Day Schools Including High, Grammar and Primary:

Enrollment (Monthly) 51,788

Average Number Belonging 48,387
Average Daily Attendance 46,433

Average Number Daily Absent........ 1,954

Evening Schools Including High, Special, Grammar and Primary:

Enrollment (Monthly) 4,329

Average Number Belonging 3,150
Average Daily Attendance 2,890

Average Number Daily Absent........ 260

Grand Totals:

Enrollment (Monthly) 56,117

Average Number Belonging 51,537
Average Daily Attendance 49,323

Average Number Daily Absent........ 2,214

AVERAGE DAILY ATTENDANCE, AVERAGE NUMBER BELONGING AND ENROLLMENT FOR SEVENTH MONTH FROM JANUARY 29, TO FEBRUARY 23, 1917 (18½ DAYS).

	Monthly Enrollment			Aver. No.	Average Daily	Average No. Daily
Day Schools—	Boys	Girls	Total	Belonging	Attendance	Absent
Secondary Schools	2,106	2,866	4,972	4,808	4,573	235
Grammar Classes..	9,206	9,318	18,524	17,836	17,030	806
Primary Classes....	14,415	13,077	27,492	25,065	23,516	1,549
Total	25,727	25,261	50,988	47,709	45,119	2,590
Evening Schools—						
Secondary Schools and Special........	1,619	976	2,595	1,894	1,706	188
Grammar Classes..	911	209	1,120	878	800	78
Primary Classes....	385	67	452	284	262	22
Total	2,915	1,252	4,167	3,056	2,768	288

Totals of Day Schools Including High, Grammar and Primary:

Enrollment (Monthly) 50,988

Average Number Belonging 47,709
Average Daily Attendance 45,119

Average Number Daily Absent........ 2,590

Evening Schools Including High, Special, Grammar and Primary:

Enrollment (Monthly)	4,167
Average Number Belonging	3,056
Average Daily Attendance	2,768
Average Number Daily Absent	288

Grand Totals:

Enrollment (Monthly)	55,155
Average Number Belonging	50,765
Average Daily Attendance	47,887
Average Number Daily Absent	2,878

AVERAGE DAILY ATTENDANCE, AVERAGE NUMBER BELONGING AND ENROLLMENT FOR EIGHTH MONTH FROM FEBRUARY 26, MARCH 23, 1917 (20 DAYS).

	Monthly Enrollment			Aver. No.	Average Daily	Average No. Daily
Day Schools—	Boys	Girls	Total	Belonging	Attendance	Absent
Secondary Schools	2,050	2,799	4,849	4,698	4,492	206
Grammar Classes	9,101	9,371	18,472	17,605	16,965	640
Primary Classes	14,292	12,921	27,213	24,595	23,424	1,171
Total	25,443	25,091	50,534	46,898	44,881	2,017
Evening Schools—						
Secondary Schools and Special	1,550	917	2,467	1,741	1,602	139
Grammar Classes	876	208	1,084	841	768	73
Primary Classes	374	66	440	267	246	21
Total	2,800	1,191	3,991	2,849	2,616	233

Totals of Day Schools Including High, Grammar and Primary:

Enrollment (Monthly)	50,534
Average Number Belonging	46,898
Average Daily Attendance	44,881
Average Number Daily Absent	2,017

Evening Schools Including High, Special, Grammar and Primary:

Enrollment (Monthly)	3,991
Average Number Belonging	2,489
Average Daily Attendance	2,616
Average Number Daily Absent	233

Grand Totals:

Enrollment (Monthly)	54,525
Average Number Belonging	49,747
Average Daily Attendance	47,497
Average Number Daily Absent	2,250

AVERAGE DAILY ATTENDANCE, AVERAGE NUMBER BELONGING AND ENROLLMENT FOR NINTH MONTH FROM MARCH 26, TO MAY 4, 1917 (18½ DAYS).

	Monthly Enrollment			Aver. No.	Average Daily	Average No. Daily
Day Schools—	Boys	Girls	Total	Belonging	Attendance	Absent
Secondary Schools	1,951	2,699	4,650	4,539	4,294	245
Grammar Classes..	8,879	9,114	17,993	17,663	16,690	973
Primary Classes....	14,144	12,843	26,987	25,541	24,231	1,310
Total	24,974	24,656	49,630	47,743	45,215	2,528
Evening Schools—						
Secondary Schools and Special........	1,347	489	1,836	1,611	1,432	179
Grammar Classes..	813	589	1,402	819	746	73
Primary Classes....	311	63	374	309	290	19
Total	2,471	1,141	3,612	2,739	2,468	271

Totals of Day Schools Including High, Grammar and Primary:

Enrollment (Monthly)	49,630
Average Number Belonging	47,743
Average Daily Attendance	45,215
Average Number Daily Absent	2,528

Evening Schools Including High, Special, Grammar and Primary:

Enrollment (Monthly)	3,612
Average Number Belonging	2,739
Average Daily Attendance	2,468
Average Number Daily Absent	271

Grand Totals:

Enrollment (Monthly)	53,242
Average Number Belonging	50,482
Average Daily Attendance	47,683
Average Number Daily Absent	2,799

AVERAGE DAILY ATTENDANCE, AVERAGE NUMBER BELONGING AND ENROLLMENT FOR TENTH MONTH FROM MAY 7, TO JUNE 8, 1917 (22½ DAYS).

	Monthly Enrollment			Aver. No.	Average Daily	Average No. Daily
Day Schools—	Boys	Girls	Total	Belonging	Attendance	Absent
Secondary Schools	1,863	2,612	4,475	4,361	4,147	214
Grammar Classes	8,639	8,972	17,611	17,122	16,524	598
Primary Classes	13,858	12,584	26,442	24,983	24,008	975
Totals	24,360	24,168	48,528	46,466	44,679	1,787
Evening Schools—						
Secondary Schools and Special	1,191	798	1,989	1,424	1,284	140
Grammar Classes	742	186	928	762	702	60
Primary Classes	279	65	344	222	204	18
Totals	2,212	1,049	3,261	2,408	2,190	218

Totals of Day Schools Including High, Grammar and Primary:

Enrollment (Monthly)	48,528
Average Number Belonging	46,466
Average Daily Attendance	44,679
Average Number Daily Absent	1,787

Evening Schools Including High, Special, Grammar and Primary:

Enrollment (Monthly)	3,261
Average Number Belonging	2,408
Average Daily Attendance	2,190
Average Number Daily Absent	218

Grand Totals:

Enrollment (Monthly)	51,789
Average Number Belonging	48,874
Average Daily Attendance	46,869
Average Number Daily Absent	2,005

SOME SCHOOL STATISTICS FROM THE OPENING OF THE FIRST F

Year Ending Oct. 31.	No of Schools.	Teachers.	Pupils Enrolled.	Average Daily Attendance.	Populat
1850	1	2	150	....	
1851	1	4	325	....	
1852	7	15	700	445	
1853	....	16	2,870	1,182	
1854	....	19	4,199	1,727	
1855	....	29	4,694	1,638	
1856	9	61	3,347	2,516	
Year Ending June. 30.					
1857	....	60	2,821	2,155	
1858	....	67	5,273	2,521	
1859	11	75	6,201	2,829	56,8
1860	....	68	6,180	2,837	
1861	13	73	6,617	3,377	
1862	17	82	8,204	3,786	
1863	....	94	8,177	4,389	
1864	20	108	7,075	5,470	
1865	....	138	8,000	6,718	
1866	32	206	10,152	8,131	
1867	37	253	13,385	10,177	
1868	39	285	17,426	11,871	
1869	42	326	19,885	13,113	
1870	55	371	22,152	15,394	150,0
1871	56	416	26,406	16,978	
1872	56	480	27,664	18,272	
1873	58	506	27,722	18,550	
1874	64	510	29,449	19,434	
1875	64	552	31,128	21,014	
1876	66	574	34,029	22,761	
1877	66	632	37,268	24,899	
1878	65	672	38,672	26,292	
1879	64	696	38,129	27,075	
1880	59	686	38,320	28,150	234,14
1881	62	719	40,187	29,092	
1882	65	675	47,752	29,435	
1883	63	687	40,722	30,827	
1884	64	714	41,942	31,578	
1885	65	734	43,265	32,183	
1886	65	773	43,140	32,146	
1887	68	799	43,311	31,316	
1888	68	806	42,330	30,191	
1889	71	838	42,626	31,609	
1890	72	859	42,926	31,852	298,99
1891	73	879	43,626	31,809	
1892	75	897	46,172	32,431	
1893	76	929	45,775	32,799	
1894	73	866	44,349	32,939	
1895	75	904	44,822	32,974	
1896	76	927	45,435	33,508	
1897	77	974	46,564	33,581	
1898	92	1,070	50,101	35,116	
1899	90	1,074	48,972	36,830	
1900	86	1,061	48,058	35,004	342,78
1901	82	1,017	48,517	34,771	
1902	84	1,052	48,893	35,691	
1903	84	1,086	48,345	37,077	
1904	85	1,121	49,600	37,700	
1905	85	1,181	55,067	40,920	
1906	86	1,115	57,782	41,932	
1907	83	971	45,633	29,929	
1908	89	1,095	48,045	33,931	
1909	92	1,195	48,509	35,541	
1910	95	1,198	50,212	36,774	416,91
1911	100	1,227	51,462	37,736	
1912	105	1,308	53,160	40,448	
1913	105	1,423	53,757	42,820	
1914	104	1,478	57,852	44,388	
1915	104	1,485	61,941	46,562	

LIC SCHOOL BY J. C. PELTON, DECEMBER, 1849, TO JUNE 30, 1917.

enses for Purposes. c. Bonds)	Cost per Capita on Average Daily Attendance.	School Census Children 4 to 18 Years.	Value of School Property. (Estimated)	Assessment of City and County Property.
....	....	500	....	$ 21,621,214
....	....	1,510		14,016,903
$23,125	51.96	2,132		18,481,737
35,040	29.65	2,730		28,900,150
159,249	92.21	3,268		34,762,827
136,580	83.38	4,531		32,076,572
125,064	49.71	4,751		30,368,254
92,955	43.14	4,755		35,397,176
104,808	41.57	6,375		30,725,950
134,731	47.62	7,767		30,019,222
156,407	55.13	9,025		35,809,639
158,855	47.04	13,316		41,870,811
134,576	35.58	13,358		41,870,811
178,929	47.67	16,501		66,566,655
228,411	41.76	18,748		78,709,337
346,862	50.15	21,013		83,197,725
		5 to 15 Years.		
361,668	44.48	17,369	....	88,934,543
507,822	49.89	20,253	$1,057,000	96,740,159
416,654	35.09	23,306	1,368,000	109,360,825
397,842	30.34	24,817	1,531,000	106,414,128
526,625	33.56	27,055	1,729,800	114,759,510
705,116	41.53	28,971	1,786,400	106,391,876
668,262	36.02	31,936	1,810,000	105,025,534
611,818	35.45	34,676	....	288,533,256
		5 to 17 Years.		
689,022	35.40	38,084	2,227,620	212,407,505
707,445	33.71	41,029	2,367,000	264,000,000
867,755	38.12	46,238	2,505,500	269,105,141
732,324	29.41	53,210	2,585,000	260,576,978
989,259	37.62	55,899	2,711,000	254,702,960
876,489	32.37	62,105	3,047,303	244,477,360
809,133	28.74	58,492	3,073,000	217,487,074
827,324	28.44	55,115	3,137,000	253,545,476
735,435	24.98	55,880	3,137,000	222,336,400
791,175	25.66	58,061	3,137,000	201,992,152
797,452	25.25	63,029	3,137,000	201,763,762
840,367	25.80	69,000	3,137,000	223,509,560
815,778	25.37	74,079	3,189,000	230,386,325
843,297	26.93	78,246	3,184,575	230,151,009
926,662	30.69	59,517	3,230,598	251,746,111
916,644	28.99	60,642	4,772,180	273,389,616
983,014	31.35	61,144	4,757,724	306,041,440
,053,610	33.12	62,456	4,798,427	301,444,140
,098,839	33.88	63,933	4,932,754	311,566,079
,134,757	34.59	65,317	5,019,317	346,224,706
989,009	30.05	68,390	5,063,364	342,644,179
,043,067	26.09	70,006	5,140,258	325,108,898
,086,571	32.42	71,822	5,284,000	327,805,147
,222,941	36.52	74,840	5,354,859	330,401,154
,319,829	37.58	76,336	5,474,739	351,784,094
,507,163	40.92	75,292	5,514,200	405,111,615
,274,696	36.41	78,554	5,514,200	410,155,304
,152,631	30.27	82,173	5,207,600	413,417,241
,316,170	36.88	82,391	5,334,000	413,099,993
,822,585	35.67	91,386	5,649,651	419,968,644
,398,296	37.09	97,353	5,702,001	545,866,446
,403,349	34.29	98,127	5,800,000	502,892,359
498,275	35.73	101,836	6,984,000	524,230,946
825,433	44.28	77,367	6,207,010	375,932,477
934,355	57.01	87,696	6,379,000	429,632,592
701,236	47.86	88,058	7,206,573	454,334,160
307,948	89.98	74,729	8,733,285	492,867,037
137,825	83.18	abolished	10,161,492	545,057,591
744,073	92.54		12,536,929	605,488,153
829,054	77.70		11,983,657	604,793,249
504,838	78.95		12,600,202	623,847,729
224,429	69.25		16,929,218	647,207,514
817,831	60.13		14,020,943	749,000,000

PRINCIPALS AND SUPERVISORS AND TEACHERS EMPLOYED DURING THE YEAR ENDING JUNE 30, 1917.

	Principals			Teachers		
	Men	Women	Total	Men	Women	Total
Day High Schools	5	0	5	71	104	175
Evening High Schools	3	0	3	36	22	58
Day Elementary Schools	7	78	85	9	1,136	1,145
Evening Elementary Schools	4	2	6	11	30	41
	Supervisors					
Home Economics (Ev'ng Elementary)		1	1			8
Primary Grades (Day Elementary)		1				
Special Subjects (Day Elementary)						
Modern Languages				1	5	6
Drawing		1	1		7	7
Domestic Science		1	1		20	20
Manual Training	1	0	1	18		18
Physical Education	1			1	4	5
Music					1	1
Oral for Deaf					4	4
Defective Speech				1	1	2
Sub-normal		1	1		1	1
Kindergartens					14	14
Grand Total	21	86	107	148	1,352	1,500

Grand Total Principals and Supervisors 107
and Teachers 1,500

1,607

SCHOLASTIC PREPARATION OF TEACHERS.

Number of Teachers (including Principals.)

Who are graduates of University of California	198
Who are graduates of Leland Stanford Jr. University	85
Who are graduates of other Universities	56
Who are graduates of S. F. City Normal School	248
Who are graduates of Chico State Normal	24
Who are graduates of Los Angeles State Normal	4
Who are graduates of San Francisco State Normal	258*
Who are graduates of San Jose State Normal	182
Who are graduates of Santa Barbara State Normal	10
Who are graduates of Normal Schools of other States	87
Who are graduates of Lux School	9

CERTIFICATION OF TEACHERS.

No. holding regular certificates of High School Grade	243
No. holding special certificates of High School Grade	92
No. holding regular certificates of Grammar School Grade	1163
No. holding special certificates of Grammar School Grade	74
No. holding certificates of Primary School Grade	20
No. holding special Kindergarten Certificates	14

VOLUMES IN SCHOOL LIBRARIES AND STOREROOM (INCLUDING BOOKS FOR USE OF INDIGENTS).

	Volumes	Estimated Value
Day and Evening High Schools	7,585	$ 6,000
Day and Evening Elementary Schools and Kindergartens	104,110	40,476
In storeroom	2,500	1,250
Total	114,195	$47,726

NUMBER OF SCHOOLS.

Number of High Schools (Day)	5
Number of High Schools (Evening)	3
Number of Intermediate Schools (Specialized Grammar)	3
Number of Elementary Schools (Day)	82
Number of Elementary Schools (Evening)	5
Number of Kindergartens	14
Total	112

NUMBER AND TYPE OF CONSTRUCTION OF SCHOOL BUILDINGS.

	Elementary	High	Total
Number of Class "A" school buildings owned by the Department	5	2	7
Number of Class "B" school buildings	1	0	1
Number of Class "C" school buildings	11	3	14
Number of "Special Construction" school buildings (concrete and brick with wooden frame)	23	0	23
Number of wooden school buildings	47	0	47
	87	5	92

SCHOOL VISITATIONS.

Official visits of Superintendent and deputies	4,685
Official visits by members of the Board of Education	1,262
Visits by other persons	73,422

"STATE SCHOOL ENROLLMENT" AND ATTENDANCE STATISTICS FOR THE YEAR ENDING

	June 30, 1917	Increase (I) over or Decrease (D) from 1916	June 30, 1916
Day High Schools	6,002	I. 1,338	4,664
Evening High Schools	4,225	I. 343	3,882
Day Elementary Schools	49,746	D. 593	50,333
Evening Elementary Schools	3,973	D. 291	4,264
Kindergartens	1,155	I. 258	897
	65,101	I. 1,061	64,040

(Note: "State School Enrollment" admits no duplication. Pupils promoted during the year are enumerated only in the grades from which they were promoted.)

AVERAGE DAILY ATTENDANCE.

	June 30, 1917	Increase (I) over or Decrease (D) from 1916	June 30, 1916
Day High Schools	4,345	I. 493	3,852
*Evening High Schools	729	I. 65	* 664
Day Elementary	41,515	I. 214	41,301
*Evening Elementary Schools	556	D. 59	* 615
Kindergartens	524	I. 94	430
Total	47,669	I. 807	46,862

*The State law requires that the number of those actually present in elementary and secondary evening schools be divided by two for purposes of apportionment of State School Funds. There were, therefore, actually present in average daily attendance in elementary and secondary evening schools twice the numbers given above, or 1,285 and 1,279, respectively.

"STATE SCHOOL ENROLLMENT" BY GRADES AND SEX.

("State School Enrollment" admits no duplication. Pupils promoted during the year are enumerated only in the grades from which they were promoted.)

DAY SCHOOLS.

	Boys	Girls	Total
Kindergartens	577	578	1,155
Elementary Schools—			
First Grade	5,664	4,851	10,515
Second Grade	3,762	3,502	7,264
Third Grade	3,550	3,482	7,032
Fourth Grade	3,272	2,997	6,269
Fifth Grade	2,930	2,803	5,733
Sixth Grade	2,666	2,485	5,151
Seventh Grade	2,067	2,324	4,391
Eighth Grade	1,597	1,791	3,388
Total Elementary Schools	25,508	24,235	49,743
High Schools—			
First Year	1,290	1,747	3,037
Second Year	619	876	1,495
Third Year	364	491	855
Fourth Year	259	356	615
Total High Schools	2,532	3,470	6,002
Grand Total (Day Schools)	28,617	28,283	56,900

Note: The apparent disproportion of pupils in the first grades of the elementary and high schools in "State Enrollment" is further explained by the fact that the numbers 10,515 for elementary first grades and 3,037 for high school first grades is derived from three divisions of the first grade, whereas in all other grades the total numbers set opposite them are derived from two grades only.

EVENING SCHOOLS.

	Men	Women	Total
*Evening Elementary Schools—			
First Grade	462	76	538
Second Grade	182	47	229
Third Grade	285	53	338
Fourth Grade	408	94	502
Fifth Grade	305	42	347
Sixth Grade	363	82	445
Seventh Grade	381	94	475
Eighth Grade	385	79	464
Special Home-Economics	......	635	......
Totals	2,771	1,202	3,973
*Evening High Schools—			
First Year	2,209	792	3,001
Second Year	709	367	1,076
Third Year	119	15	134
Fourth Year	13	1	14
Totals	3,050	1,175	4,225
*Grand Totals (Evening Schools)	5,821	2,377	8,198
Grand Totals (Day Schools)	28,617	28,283	56,900
Grand Totals	34,438	30,660	65,098

*Evening schools enroll only pupils who are over 15 years of age, except a few who have been granted a permit to work, but who are over 14 years of age. Many adults are enrolled, both native born and foreigners.

GRADUATES.

Number of graduates from the elementary schools (day and evening).

	1916-17	1915-16
Boys	1,681	1,621
Girls	1,971	1,750
Totals	3,652	3,371

Number of graduates from the high schools (1916-1917).

	Day	Evening	
Boys	206	175	381
Girls	315	80	395
Totals	521	255	776

Number of graduates from high schools (1915-1916).

	Day	Evening	
Boys	179	223	402
Girls	254	82	336
Totals	433	305	738

REPORT OF THE BOARD OF EXAMINATION.

The Board of Examination is composed of: Superintendent Alfred Roncovieri, Chairman; Deputy Superintendent W. B. Howard, Secretary; Deputy Superintendent T. L. Heaton, Deputy Superintendent A. J. Cloud, Deputy Superintendent W. H. DeBell, Deputy Superintendent Mary Magner.

The Board of Examination has conducted one examination (December 1916), according to law, of persons desirous of securing certificates. It has met monthly and forwarded its recommendations to the Board of Education.

Herewith is a resume of its work:

Certificates granted on Credentials.

High School—	
Men	9
Women	29
	38
Grammar—	
Men	6
Women	188
	194
Specials—	
Men	11
Women	36
	47
Renewals—	
Men	4
Women	40
	44
On Examination. Grammar—	
Men	0
Women	3
	3
Rejected—	
Men	0
Women	3
	3
Number of Certificates issued	279
Number of Certificates renewed	44
Number of Applicants rejected	3
Amout fee collected of applicants, including renewals	$652

NECROLOGY.

Barthel, Mr. Franklin K........Supervisor Manual Training..........Died July 20, 1916
Church, Miss E. F..................Pacific Heights School.....................Died Aug. 24, 1916
McCormack, Miss J. V...........Lowell High School..........................Died Sept. 10, 1916
Marshall, Mrs. M. L...............Fairmount School...........................Died Nov. 4, 1916
Rowe, Mrs. Maude M............Laguna Honda School.....................Died Dec. 18, 1916
Shea, Miss M. T......................Crocker Intermediate School..........Died Jan. 8, 1917
Carson, Miss N.......................Washington Grammar School........Died Jan. 10, 1917
Johnson, Miss A. M...............Golden Gate School.........................Died March 1917
Backman, Mrs. F. L..............Lincoln Grammar School................Died June 24, 1917

STATISTICS OF RESIGNATIONS, DEATHS, AND APPOINTMENTS OF TEACHERS.

	Resigned	Died	Dropped From Roll	Total	Total Number of Teachers Appointed (all Schools)
1911-12	33	9	10	52	116
1912-13	38	9	4	51	86
1913-14	38	14	7	59	83
1914-15	38	4	4	46	107
1915-16	41	13	2	56	105
1916-17	44	9	11	64	153

REPORT OF SUPERVISOR OF DRAWING IN THE ELEMENTARY SCHOOLS

Mr. Alfred Roncovieri,
Supt. of Schools,
San Francisco.

My Dear Mr. Roncovieri:

In reply to your request for a report from my department for the past year, I desire to say that I am quite pleased with the results obtained in many of our schools.

While there has been no change in our Course of Study for the past three years, we are endeavoring to improve our methods of teaching it.

We have at present an exhibition of our work at the Palace of Fine Arts which has attracted considerable attention among San Francisco's art colony. Mr. J. Nelson Laurvik, the Director of the Palace has repeatedly written about it in the most flattering terms.

To advise you, regarding the esteem in which our results are held by well known authorities, I affix copies of two letters received by me at the close of last term.

Copy of a letter from Mr. Maxwell Armfield, the celebrated English artist, whose work is on exhibition at the Palace of Fine Arts.

San Francisco, Calif., June 5, 1917.

My dear Miss Ball,

I feel that I must send you a line to say how very much I enjoyed seeing the drawings of the children, yesterday.

I have not seen such promising work anywhere, in Europe or America.

Having taken classes myself in the most progressive London art school, The Central School of Arts and Crafts, I know a little of conditions there. My only regret in seeing your work is that you are not able to continue it into its logical unfoldment into craftsmanship.

However, even as it stands it is a bright spot in the dreary waste of art education as it is today.

Yours very truly,
MAXWELL ARMFIELD.

Copy of a letter from Professor Arthur B. Clark, head of Graphic Arts Department of Leland Stanford Junior University.

Stanford University, Calif., March 20, 1917.

My dear Miss Ball:

On returning from our trip of visiting art and drawing departments in San Francisco and Oakland on Saturday, I felt like writing you at once to express the thanks of the class for your kindness in explaining so clearly to us the ideas and principles underlying your teaching of art in the San Francisco schools; and even more to express my personal gratification that public school children anywhere have produced such splendid drawings as those which you showed to us.

The San Francisco children have had *real art* training, a thing which is extremely rare. I have seen a great many exhibitions of school drawings, from Boston to California, but I never saw a set of elementary or high school drawings in which the essentials of strong, emotional, creative art were so pronounced; and the teaching so successfully concentrated upon and directed toward the conditions which will produce natural, healthy, and powerful artistic emotion and expression. I consider this the highest aim of art training in the schools; not to train future artists but to give appreciation of art.

The reason I delayed writing was to let the excitement of the day wear off and to see if the whole twelve people of our company would continue as enthusiastic in their comments. The class meets only on Tuesdays and Thursdays, and I find them today just as enthusiastic an enraptured over the work as they were on Saturday, and when one considers that they include our most advanced students and four experienced teachers, one may feel that their approval is no small tribute.

Too often drawing teaching is dry and formal; in aiming to get uniform results, supervisors are prone to dodge the difficulties of their problem, and eliminate the conditions which permit mental activity and creative power on the part of the pupils. They aim at technical uniformity and get sterility. Loose, free handling in children's hands is the only condition which permits mental alertness, and joyful creative emotion. How I wish that art teachers everywhere could have heard your talk to us on Saturday morning and have seen your children's drawings, that this greatest of all principles could have inspired them!

Clive Bell in the book entitled "Art," page 287, says: "Art is not based on craft but on sensibility; it does not live by honest labor, but by inspiration." And on page 285: "Surely there can be no reason why almost every man and woman should not be a bit of an artist since almost every child is." And again; "Can we save the artist that is in almost every child?"

I feel very much encouraged to believe that we can in seeing your drawings.

I would like to see the spontaneous illustration as you formerly taught it, with all the natural mental characteristics of children's drawing so naively left alone (as Kerchensteiner of Munich, and Rouma of Belgium in their exhaustive studies of children's drawings have demonstrated to be typical). I would like to see this kind of drawing, and the object drawing and design, as you now teach them, carried on in every school of the United States, and I hope that some day they may be.

Again thanking you most heartily for the real help and inspiration which you have given us,

Most sincerely yours,

ARTHUR B. CLARK.

Trusting that such favorable comment may gratify you and you may appreciate the efforts of myself and my assistants in our efforts on behalf of the children of our city, I remain,

Yours very sincerely,

KATHERINE M. BALL.

REPORT OF DIRECTOR OF MUSIC IN THE ELEMENTARY SCHOOLS.

In reply to your request, I herewith submit the following report of the work done in the Music Department of the City Schools ending June, 1917.

The strong point of music that must account in a measure for the great social power it possesses, is its direct appeal to the instinctive and emotional life; for all men possess this life in common.

No sense appeals so directly and so forcibly to the emotions as sound. Sound surpasses all other senses in its universality and in the force of its effects. Music, with its variation, manifests this direct and quick power over the emotions to a high degree. The intimate association of the nerves of hearing and muscular sensation (all of which are affected by music), with those of the sympathetic nervous system, renders possible almost instantaneous changes in the central, especially the vital organs of the body. The changes in circulation are the most prominent of all these effects, and go far to account for the range and force of feelings which is possible for music to exert. Certain it is, in fact a matter of common experience, that while various classes and grades of music draw upon the emotional life with varying effects, the strong, the sympathetic, the vast in music seems to set us vibrating, by sympathy, in every nerve and fibre of the body as well as in the Spirit.

It is this universality, then, of the power of music to appeal to human emotions that gives it its breadth and depth of power. All music seems to contain something for everybody.

"The use of music in almost every clime under the sun bears witness to this same universality of music as a language of the emotions if not of the thoughts of men; of its power to hold, to arouse, to inspire, to incite to deeds; of its powers especially to draw men together in a community of feelings and hence through the exercise of their function as a human bond to further the development among men of those social emotions that make for unity and co-operation in community life. This art above almost any other, or at least next to speech (in fact, it was developed, so far as song is concerned, contemporaneously with speech and the dance), lends itself most readily to the different phases of human life, in society.

The Public School is a very important part of the social life of a community, and music in the Public School System is of fundamental importance. In education, mental and physical activities are being developed in a remarkable manner. The hopes for the future are in the rising generation. But in the hearts and minds of people there is too much the idea that happiness means "to have" instead of "to be." Modern life is fast becoming too material. Music in education is a counter-acting influence, and it is a medium by which the increased mental and physical activities are allied to the higher life qualities which make for character.

The heart and soul life may be promoted by music and song. Therefore in education music's place is one of the highest distinction.

The fundamental aim of public school music is a cultivation of the musical sense in the children; an appreciation of the best there is in music; an appeal through music so that the children will respond to the instinctive and emotional life of the music; a development of the inner natures of the children so that they will feel the quality of higher music. Through this awakening an interest will be so aroused that the technical and formal side of the subject will appeal to the intellectual in the children, and they will thus go forward anxious to learn more of a subject that means so much to their physical, mental and spiritual natures.

The organization and administration of the Music Department during the last year has been based upon the foregoing aims. Songs have been chosen carefully to meet all the moods of childhood, selections from the best composers have been rendered, and have been used as a basis for definite accomplished results. A love for good music and the inspiration coming from its right presentation and the correct rendition of it have certainly been developed. Added to this, power on the part of the children has made them able to express their feelings and imaginations in an artistic manner vocally and musically. Coupled with this power, has been shown a genuine interest in the varied sides of musical study, which has produced a strong endeavor to master the essentials of the subject. The various sides of music have been studied, such as, expression, rhythm, voice development, breathing, enunciation, ear-training, intervals, part-singing, oral and written dictation, sightsinging and theory. The ideals and aims of the most successful students of modern applied psychology and pedagogy have been embodied in the aims of this department. The changing voice of the boy has been watched carefully this year, and voices have been carefully segregated for the part singing. Musical appreciation has been greatly increased during the year by the recognition, on the part of the children, of well known patriotic Folk Songs and Classics. Talks have been given by the teachers on the great masters and their compositions. Musicales have been given at the various schools where the children have taken part collectively and individually. There have been many new phonographs incorporated into the equipment of the schools with an accompanying collection of very fine records. By these means the children have become acquainted with many of the treasures in the great store house of Music.

The work has been carefully planned by the Director of Music who has given during the year a series of lessons to the one thousand regular teachers. Outlines have been furnished covering all sides of the work. The meetings were given as grade meetings and attendance was compulsory. Two hundred songs were sung, and the work for the year was illustrated. A course of volunteer lessons has been given for all teachers. Subjects such as "Voice Development for Teachers," "The Child Voice," "Rhythm," "Art of Conducting," "Interpretation," "Sight-Singing," and "Children's Songs" have been lectured upon, and practical work has been given bearing upon these subjects. A course of eight lessons has been given to the teachers who have recently entered into the Department, and suggestions and directions have been given. Meetings are held with the Special Teachers of Music in the various schools four times a year and instruction is given for the work. The office of the Music Department has been open one day each week after school, and teachers wishing or requiring instruction have been aided.

The regular teacher is a very important factor in the instruction of music in the schools. I am pleased to report that many of our regular teachers are very musical. They have a love for the subject and they have studied much. Besides this, they are attending the best concerts and orchestras, and are extending their knowledge of the subject through lectures and reading. Added to this, they are excellent teachers and know how to impart their knowledge to the children. Whenever a teacher is capable of doing her own work, I have insisted on the work being done by herself; but if a teacher is not capable, she is required to exchange work with an able teacher in music. In some schools if there are a number of teachers who are not skilled in music, the work is given to one teacher who is certified and appointed by the Board of Education as a special teacher, and is given extra compensation. There are thirty such teachers in the Music Department. Some of these teachers are in Intermediate Schools where they take entire charge of the music. Besides these teachers, there are about twenty principals who are musical, and about one hundred and eighty-five teachers who are teaching a number of extra music classes without compensation. All these have been a wonderful help in the music work, and they have formed a power because of their interest and endeavor. I commend highly the faithful skillful work of our teachers, and I appreciate the spirit of their co-operation. During the past year no music was furnished me to give them on account of lack of funds. Still many of the teachers bought the music suggested, so that the children would have some new songs. Some schools have required more attention than others, so some schools have been visited more frequently. Where the principal has organized the work carefully, and the teachers have followed the directions given them by me, the work has been remarkable. I have heard and seen some exceptional work in the various schools. Aid has been given by me through conferences, meetings, class lessons, supervision by visits and in various other ways. I have directed, advised and encouraged the teachers. The various music teachers have helped those in their own buildings. Miss Edith Fleming, the Assistant, has carried out the work through her visits and lessons.

Many new pianos have been bought for the Department by the Board of

Education and they have proved a most welcome aid. A beautiful new organ has been given to the Girls' High Schools.

In the fall of the year, the Elementary Commissioner of Education, Dr. Margaret McNaught, asked me to meet with her and the Normal School Directors of Music to compile a Bulletin containing suggestions to teach music for the Rural Schools. I took a journey to Marysville and San Jose for this purpose, and after two meetings of intensive work, the Bulletin was compiled. It is of great interest and will be a great help to all teachers of the State.

The commencement exercises in most of the schools were entirely composed of choruses, which had been learned through the term as regular work. The character of these songs exemplified the high standard reached by the classes, as to selection and as to interpretation. Some of the part songs rendered were "Handel's Largo," "Lift Thine Eyes," "Serenade" by Gounod, Mendelssohn's "Spring Song," "Sextette," "Cradle Song" by Reis, "Eye Hath Not Seen" by Gaul, "On Wings of Music" by Mendelssohn, "Thou Art Like Unto a Flower" by Lizst, "Humoreske" by Dvorak, "List the Cherubic Hosts," "In Dreams I Hear the Seraps Fair" and many other songs from the well known operas and songs from the best composers. Selections from modern composers have been used, and also there has been a great interest in the use of songs written by our own California Composers: Oscar Weil, Dr. H. J. Stewart, John Metcalf, Henry Pasmore, Arthur Fickenscher, Samuel Savannah and Charles McCurrie.

During the moth of March, the dedication of the Redding School took place and the children of the grammar grades of the school sang a number of beautiful songs, in parts, under my direction. There were many compliments given to the singing. The great Madam Melba, who was present as a guest, was warm in her praises of the singing and conducting. Mr. Joseph Redding said that the children sang better than the choirs in the Cathedrals of Rome; and in the matter of attack the children's singing was equal to the chorus of the Bohemian Club. I drilled this chorus for three weeks with the assistance of Miss Hawkins, the special music teacher, Miss Geary and Miss Edson, the accompanist.

During the year of the Exposition, there were so many demands for children's choruses outside of the school premises, that the Board of Education deemed it advisable to deny such requests, and a rule was passed to that effect, and it has continued in operation.

Some three years ago I organized the society known as the San Francisco Public School Music Teachers' Association. It is composed of the teachers who are teaching music, and it meets for social and business purposes. During the past year a group of teachers have met under my direction to rehearse together The Folk Songs and the Patriotic Songs.

During the past year, the music work of the High Schools was extended. Two new teachers were added to the department, and recitations were arranged daily to be elected by the pupils. Mrs. Mary D. McGlade was appointed to take charge of the work in the Polytenchnic High School and also at the High School of Commerce. In the Polytechnic School Mrs. McGlade conducted a Girls' Glee Club and a Boys' Glee Club and classes in Harmony and History and Apprecia-tion of Music. There were about one hundred and seventy pupils enrolled in the music courses. An orchestra of about forty pieces was in charge of Mr. C. Lamp, the science instructor. During the year, in the plays given by the school, "Everyman" and "As You Like It," and at the graduations, the orchestra took part and Mrs. McGlade drilled and led the choruses. At the school rallies the Glee Clubs sang under her direction, as well as the whole school. At the High School of Commerce, she led about six hundred pupils in community songs, instructed a choral class, and organized and rehearsed the orchestra of the school. There were two musicales given in this school. During the year at the French play given at the school, the choruses and orchestra were under her direction.

At the close of the year Mrs. McGlade drilled and conducted the graduating exercises of the Humboldt Evening School. Through the past term at the Girls' High School, Mrs. McGlade rehearsed and directed a large orchestra of about thirty-five pieces made up of pupils from the combined High School Orchestras.

Mrs. Mary Carr Moore was given charge of the music work in the Girls' High School and the Mission High School. In the Girls' High School there were about two hundred pupils enrolled in the music courses. There were classes in Harmony, Musical History and Appreciation, and glee club and orchestra work. Mrs. Moore prepared the music with the pupils for an English play, a French play and a German play, and she also drilled and conducted the senior classes for two graduation exercises. In the Mission High School there were enrolled in the music course about one hundred and eighty pupils in the various classes in Harmony, Girls' Glee Club, Boys' Glee Club, Music History and Appreciation, and orchestra work. When the French play was produced Mrs. Moore drilled and conducted the choruses and orchestra. Two musicales were given during the year and the music for two graduations was drilled and conducted. In the original farce, by Mrs. Moore, called "Harmony," and which was produced by the pupils in the music courses of the Mission High School, four of the musical numbers were composed by the scholars. Mrs. Moore arranged and composed the musical numbers in this farce and drilled and conducted the orchestra and choruses.

Miss Constance Keehan was appointed to the Lowell High School and the High School of Commerce. In the Lowell High School there were about three hundred music students enrolled. There were classes in Harmony and Musical Appreciation and History, a Boys' Glee Club, a Girls' Glee Club, a mixed chorus and orchestra work. Musical numbers for two graduations were prepared and conducted by Miss Keohan in this school, also music for a French play, and a concert by the glee clubs and orchestra. In the High School of Commerce she had classes in Harmony and choral and at the end of the term she gave a cantata with the pupils, assisted by the orchestras of the Lowell High School and the High School of Commerce.

For a number of Years the work in music of the San Francisco State Normal School has been closely allied to the work in the Public Schools. Once a week after regular school hours, I have conducted courses of lectures on Public School Music, and these have been illustrated with songs and choruses.

During the year, I was made secretary of the Community Singing Committee, and there were established in three centre classes in public schools for adults. In the school work, the songs of the various countries have always been a part of my course of study, and the children have been required to learn certain songs by heart. In the great choruses which have been sung by the children under my direction, these songs always have formed a part of the program. In the various schools, there has been assembly singing and it has proved a great bond to further brotherhood and fellowship, as well as to further love of the Patriotic and Folk Songs. At the request of the Honorable Superintendent Roncovieri during the County Institute, I gave a few remarks on Community Music and led the eighteen hundred teachers in one Patriotic and Folk Songs. It was certainly a joy to conduct so attentive and responsive a body. At the institute on another day Mrs. McGlade spoke and led some songs.

After the Declaration of War, the first patriotic meeting was held in the Civic Auditorium. Mr. Charles Moore, the President of the Panama Exposition, formally presented to our city the great organ, and when the Honorable James Rolph, the Mayor of San Francisco, accepted the gift in behalf of the city, he also made a thrilling patriotic speech which stirred the audience to great enthusiasm. At the close of this meeting I directed the fifteen thousand present in the "Star Spangled Banner" and "America" to the accompaniment of the playing of Mr. Lemare. It was a never-to-be-forgotten occasion. The Honorable Board of

Education called a Red Cross Meeting for the teachers and there again we sang the Patriotic Songs under my direction. Since then there have been a number of unofficial gatherings where there have been requests for me to lead Patriotic Songs. This year I received an invitation to make an address at the National Education Association at the Music Section. Because of an urgent request, I will attend the Convention of the California Music Teachers' Association and deliver an address in July.

I am pleased to report that during the past year, there has been organized under my direction an Elementary School Orchestra with a membership of about forty, and there has been a genuine enthusiasm for the work. There is no fund to provide music for this organization. The children bought their own music. At the Crocker Intermediate School also there has been an orchestra organized. At the Horace Mann Intermediate School there is a well established orchestra, and in a number of grammar schools small orchestras have been formed. In each high school there is an orchestra, and there is another orchestra drawn from all the high schools.

San Francisco is fortunate in possessing so many musical opportunities. Concerts by the Golden Gate Band, and the Municipal Band. The San Francisco Symphony Orchestra, The Municipal Orchestra, The Philharmonic Orchestra, The Concerts on the great organ by Mr. Lemare, besides many other concerts have all been wonderful privileges.

In every way the study of music is encouraged, and children are urged to listen to good music, attend concerts and take lessons on the piano and other instruments.

Appreciation and enjoyment of music is a rich endowment. Social service is rendered by participation in choruses and by individual performances. Through this glorious Art the soul can be touched and can expand and thus "love, and lift, and live!"

"See deep enough and you see musically; the heart of Nature being everywhere Music, if you can only reach it."—Carlyle.

I wish to recommend the following:

a. That in transferring and assigning teachers, the musical ability be taken into consideration with the musical need of the school.

b. There is a great lack of equipment. It hampers Sight-singing. Supplemental books should be sent to the schools, one set (50 books) for each grade from the third grade through the eighth grade. I have recommended this before but ask again for these books, to be selected by the Supervisors.

c. That extra music needed in my office be supplied.

d. That orchestra music be allowed.

e. That books be allowed me for library.

f. That octave music be allowed for traveling library.

g. That a new piano be given to my office.

h. That a typewriter be allowed in my office. I am renting one now, as the clerical work and correspondence are exacting.

i. That I be allowed to select two assistants when funds allow.

j. That a phonograph with records be provided in my office.

I wish to mention again the good work of the teachers, the support given me by the Principals, the efficient work done by the assistant, Miss Edith Fleming, and all the Special Teachers of Music.

Thanking the Honorable Superintendent, the Deputy Superintendents, and the Honorable Board of Education for their co-operation and kindness, I am,

Sincerely yours,

(Signed) ESTELLE CARPENTER,
Director of Music.

REPORT OF THE DIRECTOR OF INDUSTRIAL EDUCATION AND VOCATIONAL TRAINING.

San Francisco, June 22, 1917.

Mr. Alfred Roncovieri,
Supt. of Schools.

Dear Sir: Pursuant to your request, I beg leave to submit the following report of the work done under my supervision during the past year:

The work of which I have charge, as the title of my office indicates, is composed of two parts; (1) industrial education and (2) vocational guidance. As the past year was my first in the department, and the work in industrial education was already established, while that of vocational guidance was quite new, most of my time was necessarily devoted to getting in touch with and keeping in shape the work in industrial education, though I must hasten to add that vocational guidance was by no means neglected, as will be shown later in this report.

The sudden death of the late Mr. Barthel left the then-called Manual Training Department without a head for over a month. During this time Deputy Superintendent Cloud gave as much time as he could to the task of keeping the department in running order. It pleases me to report that, in spite of the necessarily brief intervals that Mr. Cloud was able to devote to the needs of the Manual Training Department, he had the work so well organized by the time I had been elected and was started on my duties, that there were but a few things left to do to get the work of the Department under full swing.

Contrary to the custom of recent years the teachers of Manual Training were called together for professional instruction and discussion at least once a month during the past year. These monthly meetings, I am pleased to say, proved most interesting and profitable both to the teachers and to myself. The meetings brought the men together and got them to know each other as they had not done for some time past.

One point particularly worth while mentioning regarding the activities of the Department is the course of lessons in The Application of Art to Material which the men took. This course was given gratis by Mr. Pedro Lonos, the Director of the California Institute of Fine Arts. It was a course of twelve lessons and practice given on Monday evenings between the hours of seven and nine. I am proud to add that this art course was attended by every one of the teachers of Manual Training, most of them without a single absence.

As to the work in Vocational Guidance, I can only report, as I intimated before, that, owing to the arduous duties of becoming acquainted with an already well-established and extensive system of industrial education, I was able to give the guidance feature of my office but slight attention. I am pleased to believe, however, that we have made a start in a most propitious manner. During the first term I gave a course in Vocational Guidance (under the management of the Extension Division of the University of California) to a body of about twenty teachers. Some of these teachers are among those who were already giving guidance in the Polytechnic High School, some were from the Industrial Department, and others were teachers employed in the Intermediate Schools.

I want to take this opportunity to say a word in praise of the principals of our three Intermediate Schools. These three principals have co-operated in every possible way to bring about the success of such work in Vocational Guidance as we could undertake. Each one of these principals saw to it that several of his teachers became acquainted with the vocational guidance problem.

This co-operation of the principals explains how it is that we were able to give vocational guidance a fair start in each of the Intermediate Schools. Further progress of the vocational guidance work will largely depend upon our being able to put in the hands of the pupils books on the subject. It is for that reason that, at my suggestion, each of the Intermediate school principals has asked for a set of copies of Gowin and Wheatley's book entitled "Occupation," that being the best book yet on the market, for our purpose.

I trust that it will be possible for the Board of Education to supply during the coming year such stenographic and perhaps other help as will be necessary to put our plans concerning vocational guidance on the working basis which so important a phase of public school service justly deserves.

Respectfully,

CHAS. L. JACOBS,
Director of Industrial Education and Vocational Guidance.

REPORT OF ETHAN ALLEN SCHOOL.

On July 30, 1916, we opened our school with 55 boys. On that day we paroled 10 boys. On January 3, 1917, we paroled 16 boys. In addition to sending 10 boys to other schools, we allowed 14 to go to work. Of the paroled boys, 2 were compelled to return, the rest keeping up with the class work, in many cases being promoted during the term, advancing a grade or two. The boys sent to work have proven satisfactory and all have been able to advance in the places we sent them.

Our school work is ungraded, consisting of grades from the first to the eighth. We follow the regular course of study, slightly modified. In addition to the curriculum we have established rug weaving, brush making, cobbling, wicker furniture making, basketry, wood work, and gardening. Typing has been added to the school's work this term.

Enough vegetables are raised to supply over a hundred boys with a luncheon daily.

During the regular vacation it has been our custom to send many of the boys berry picking under the guidance of the Boys and Girls Aid. Their industry has enabled them to pay for the summer outing and given them a little money besides. The boys remaining in the city are looked after by a paid worker from the Juvenile Protective Association. She visits the homes at least four or five times during the vacation, getting a full account of conduct. This is kept on record. By this means we keep in touch with all the boys during the vacation, which, in my mind, is far more important than regular school time. Very few of our boys ever get in trouble during the vacation.

We have a circulating library in connection with the school in order to cultivate a taste for good reading. We also have a Balopticon and Stereopticon for lectures on history and geography. A set of stenographs and stereoscopes has been added to the school. This is used for teaching geography.

The five showers and three bath tubs have helped much to secure habits of cleanliness. These are used daily.

Respectfully,

(Signed) RAE ALEXANDER,
Principal.

SAN FRANCISCO DAY SCHOOL FOR THE DEAF.

July 14, 1917.

The close of the sixteenth year of the Day School for the Deaf finds us with an attendance of thirty children and a teaching staff of four.

The children have made good progress in their work during the year. Five left school within that time—two of them being large boys who have gone to work, one large girl to remain at home and two small children, both semi-deaf, to enter schools for the hearing.

Five new pupils have entered the school since last July, three of them partially deaf and coming from schools for the hearing in San Francisco, two others from the Berkeley School for the Deaf.

At the close of the school in June Miss Zaletta M. Wood resigned to return to her home in Providence, R. I., and Mrs. Anita Church to teach in the Los Angeles Day School for the Deaf. Miss Geraldine De Silva of the Ogden, Utah, school and Miss Claire Montgomery of the Los Angeles school were appointed to fill the vacancies.

Besides the regular school-work the older boys received instruction, once a week, in Manual Training at the Adams School, the older girls instruction in cooking at the Crocker School and in sewing under the supervision of their regular teacher. A sewing machine was added to our other school equipment this year.

At Christmas time members of the California Club very kindly subscribed five dollars toward providing a Christmas tree for this department.

A vacant school-room was placed at our disposal in January which gives us a sufficient number of rooms for the present number of children and teachers.

ALMA L. CHAPIN,
San Francisco Day School for the Deaf.

REPORT OF SPECIAL CLASSES FOR SUBNORMALS.

In July, 1916, there were three classes for the training of subnormal and retarded children. Two of these classes were in the Ungraded Primary School and one in the Buena Vista School. In September, 1916, the fourth class was opened in the Fairmount School and a trained teacher placed in charge.

During the year seventy-eight children have been enrolled in these classes. Of this number sixty-five were boys and thirteen were girls.

These children are given the academic work they are capable of receiving and are trained along manual and industrial lines. A large variety of hand work is given. The children assist in caring for the rooms and grounds and are given much practical assistance in personal cleanliness. In woodwork classes the boys make simple articles for home and school use and girls assist in making curtains and in the making and mending of their own clothing. Some of the boys also sew well.

The shacks at Ungraded Primary School are being torn down and a building espjecially designed for this line of work is being built. This will enable us to care for the children of this type in the district where there are many over-crowded schools and where the removal of the subnormal child is not only of great help to himself, but also a wonderful relief to the normal children and teachers.

LOUISE M. LOMBARD.

REPORT OF THE SPEECH CORRECTION DEPARTMENT SEPTEMBER, 1916—JUNE, 1917.

Total number pupils enrolled September, 1916—June, 1917.............................1115

Class 1.................... 538 Class 2.................... 577

Total number pupils left classes September, 1916—June, 1917......................... 413

Class 1.................... 175 Class 2.................... 238

Total number pupils entirely corrected and nearly corrected June 1917........ 287

Class 1.................... 154 Class 2.................... 133

Number pupils Peabody Center June, 1917..... 92

Class 1.................... 36 Class 2.................... 56

Pupils Excused........ 1

Class 1.................... 0 Class 2.................... 1

Number pupils Mission Grammar Center June, 1917.. 157

Class 1.................... 97 Class 2.................... 60

Pupils Excused........ 7

Class 1.................... 6 Class 2.................... 1

Number pupils Hancock Center June, 1917... 115

Class 1.................... 50 Class 2.................... 65

Pupils Excused........ 4

Class 1.................... 1 Class 2.................... 8

Number pupils John Swett Center June, 1917... 185

Class 1.................... 106 Class 2.................... 79

Pupils Excused........ 34

Class 1.................... 12 Class 2.................... 22

Number pupils Junipero Serra Center June, 1917... 118

Class 1.................... 55 Class 2.................... 63

Pupils Excused........ 10

Class 1.................... 4 Class 2.................... 6

Number pupils Lowell High Center June, 1917.. 10

Class 1.................... 10 Class 2.................... 0

Number pupils Mission High Center June, 1917.. 24

Class 1.................... 14 Class 2.................... 10

Number pupils John Swett High School Center June, 1917............................ 7

Class 1.................... 7 Class 2.................... 0

GENERAL REPORT OF ATTENDANCE AND PROGRESS.

	Pupils Corrected		Pupils not attending Center but receiving drill		Pupils attending Center		Pupils attending Center — Pupils greatly improved		Pupils improved		Pupils not improved	
	Class	Class	Cl.	Cl.	Cl.	Cl.	Cl.	Cl.	Cl.	Cl.	Cl.	Cl.
	1	2	1	2	1	2	1	2	1	2	1	2
	1	2	1	2	1	2	1	2	1	2	1	2
Peabody Center:												
Emerson		1		40	3		3					
Frank McCoppin			1	2	4	7	3	3	1	4		
Grant			1	5	2	1		1	2			
Lafayette						1		1				
Madison				30	2	2	2			2		
Pacific Heights				15	1	4	1	4				
Peabody					5	6	3	3	1	3	1	
Rochambeau				10	4	2	4			2		
Roosevelt				77	2		2					
Sutro				84	10	24	2	7	8	17		
Mission Grammar Center:												
Agassiz	1				6	2	No Final Report					
Balboa	Does not attend center											
Bryant					6	3	No Final Report					
Buena Vista					4		No Final Report					
Columbia					6		No Final Report					
Daniel Webster					1	14	No Final Report					
Edison			1	1	3	2	2		1	2		
Everett		1	1	4	6	1	1		5	1		
Douglass					4	2	No Final Report					
Hawthorne					1	8	1	2		6		
Irving M. Scott					1	4	No Final Report					
James Lick			9		10		2		6		2	
Le Conte				1		2		2				
Marshall	2		1	2	9	6	7	5	2	1		
Mission Grammar	3				8	3	5	1	3	1		
Noe Valley				3	7	8			7	8		
Patrick Henry			4		1		1					
Portola					6		No Final Report					
Starr King			5	15	4	2	1	2	3			
Sunnyside				2	3	2	1	2	2			
Visitacion Valley				2	2	4	2					
Hancock Center:												
Hancock					6	11	5	9	1	2		
Jean Parker	1		1	1	5	8	1	3	4	2		3
Sarah B. Cooper					5	15	5	8		7		
Garfield		1	5	1	5	2	5	2				
Oriental					1	4	No Final Report					
Sherman						2		2				
Spring Valley					5	6	No Final Report					
Washington Gr.					5	1	5	1				
Washington Irving		2			10	7	4	4	5	3	1	
Winfield Scott					1		No Final Report					
Yerba Buena					3	2	No Final Report					

GENERAL REPORT OF ATTENDANCE AND PROGRESS—Continued.

	Pupils Corrected		Pupils not attending Center but receiving drill		Pupils attending Center		—Pupils attending Center— Pupils greatly improved		Pupils improved		Pupils not improved	
	Class	Class	Cl.	Cl.	Cl.	Cl.	Cl.	Cl.	Cl.	Cl.	Cl.	Cl.
John Swett Center:												
Adams							5			2		
Crocker					8		No	Final	Report			
Denman					1	6	No	Final	Report			
F. Scott Key		6	1	11	1	4	1	1		2		1
Franklin	[illegible]				9	1	No	Final	Report			
Fremont					8	1	3		5			
Golden Gate	[illegible]	[illegible]			3	9	3	4		5		
Grattan				3	6	2	5		1	2		
Hamilton					4	2	No	Final	Report			
Hearst	5	1			6	5	3	3	3	2		
Henry Durant			1		2	1	2	1				
Jefferson						1	No	Final	Report			
John Swett	4	4		3	16	17	5	3	11			14
Lincoln					3	2	No	Final	Report			
McKinley	1			3	7	2	4		3	2		
Laguna Honda			6		2	1	2			1		
Redding		6			8	15	3	7	4	6	1	2
Ethan Allen					8		No	Final	Report			
Columbus					4	2	No	Final	Report			
Bay View									2			
Burnett				3		3		1		2		
Junipero Serra Center:												
Junipero Serra		1	3		10	13	10	5		8		
Bernal					7	2	3		4	1		
Cleveland	3	1			7	2	4	1	3			
Fairmount		1			7	9	7	4		5		
Farragut					2		No	Final	Report			
Haight			1	9	3	1	3	1				
Longfellow					4	5	No	Final	Report			
Monroe					2	3	No	Final	Report			
Sheridan					1	3		2	1	1		
Kate Kennedy					2	1	No	Final	Report			
Glenn Park	1	3		1	1	7		5	1	2		

The following schools have not been represented this term, January, 1917, to June, 1917.

Andrew Jackson
Balboa
Buena Vista (Children attend)
Harrison (Teacher attends)
Hunter's Point
Spring Valley
Jefferson (Child attends)

Winfield Scott (Child attends)
Dudley Stone
Moulder
Parkside
Commodore Sloat
Rincon
Michelangelo

REPORT OF TOTAL NUMBER CASES DEFECTIVE SPEECH 533

San Francisco School Department 1916-1917.

CLASSIFICATION.

Stammerers:	
Male	109
Female	36
Stutterers:	
Male	71
Female	16
Clutterers:	
Male	2
Female	1
Defective Articulation and Stammerers:	
Male	21
Female	4
Defective Articulation and Stutterers:	
Male	13
Female	2
Defective Articulation:	
Male	131
Female	54
Lispers:	
Male	22
Female	18
Stammerers, Stutterers and Clutterers:	
Male	4
Female	2
Stammerers and Stutterers:	
Male	10
Female	....
Stutterers and Lispers:	
Male	2
Female	....
Tongue-tied	3

CAUSES.

Heredity	66
Imitation	41
Injury	17
Shock	8
Tongue-tied	3
Malformation of mouth and throat..	2
Paralysis	3
Scarlet fever	11
Diphtheria	10
Illness (Whooping Cough, Measles, Mumps)	23
Mastoid operation	5
Rheumatism	1
Heart trouble	3
Spasms	1
Prenatal	2
Concussion of brain	1
Bronchial Asthma	1
Spinal Meningitis	5
Cerebral Spinal Meningitis	1
Deformed mouth due to operation	1
Confusion of Language	1

COMBINED CAUSES.

Heredity and Imitation	18
Heredity and Illness	14
Heredity and Injury	4
Heredity and Shock	2
Shock and Injury	10
Shock and Illness	5
Imitation and Illness	8
Diphtheria and Scarlet Fever	1
Scarlet Fever and Pneumonia	2
Scarlet Fever and Whooping Cough and Measles	3
Operation or Abscess in head	6
Operation for Adenoids and Tonsils	3
Operation in throat, Shock, Injury, Illness	1
No cause assigned	89

AGE DEFECT DEVELOPED.

2 years	15
3 years	14
4 years	23
5 years	20
6 years	16
7 years	21
8 years	13
9 years	7
10 years	9
11 years	6
12 years	7
13 years	4
On beginning to talk	199
On entering school	19
In school	3

GENERAL PHYSICAL CONDITION.

Fair	[illegible]7	Convulsions	1
Poor	[illegible]3	Asthma	1
Aenemic	15	Malformation of body	1
Nervous	25	Atrophied arm	1

MOUTH.

Negative	35	Jaw Undershot	1
Palate Small Arch	1	Jaw Overshot	2
Palate High Arch	11	Jaw Malformed	1
Palate Cleft	4	Jaw Sluggish	3
Palate Malformed	3	Jaw Narrow	2
Hare Lip	1	Jaw Broken	1
Tongue-tied	3	Oral Twitching	2

TEETH.

Fair	6	Irregular and Defective	12
Irregular	31	Malformation	1
Defective	143		

NOSE.

Negative	22	Fracture	1
Reflective Septum	9	Operated upon	2

THROAT.

Adenoids Moderate	9	Adenoids and Tonsils Removed	116
Adenoids Enlarged	1	Adenoids and Tonsils Hypertrophied	23
Tonsils Moderate	50	Tonsils Buried	2
Tonsils Enlarged	73	Tonsils Follicular	2
Adenoids Removed	5	Glands Swollen	18
Tonsils Removed	19	Glands Broken Down	1
Adenoids and Tonsils	12	Operation on Throat	2

UVULVA.

Missing	2	Biforated	1
Sluggish	1	Bifurcated	1

HEARING.

Defective	8	Mastoid Operation	5
Slightly Defective	29	Mastoiditis	1
Abscess back of Ear	2		

EYES.

Defective	20	Slight Conjunctivitis	5
Nystagmus	2	Crossed	1
Strabismus	8	Marginal Blepharitis	5

RACE.

English	121	English-Spanish	1
French	11	English-German	4
Italian	87	English-Portuguese	5
German	41	French-Irish	1
Russian	13	French-German	1
Belgian	1	French-American	2
Irish	36	French-Scotch	1
Scotch	1	French-Italian	1
Polish	3	German-American	3
Spanish	5	German-Spanish	1
Norwegian	3	German-Irish	2
Swedish	6	Italian-Irish	1
Danish	1	Irish-American	3
Hebrew	49	Irish-Spanish	1
Portuguese	9	Irish-Norwegian	1
Roumanian	2	Swedish-American	1
Greek	4	Russian-Roumanian	1
Mexican	4	Spanish-American	1
Japanese	1	Scotch-American	1
Chinese	4	Canadian-American	1
Negro	1		

LANGUAGE SPOKEN.

English	179	English-Norwegian	2
English-French	11	English-Roumanian	7
English-German	39	English-Japanese	1
English-Italian	84	English-Chinese	4
English-Yiddish	31	English-Greek	4
English-Spanish	11	English-Mexican-Italian	1
English-Russian	7	English-German-Spanish	1
English-Portuguese	5	English-French-Scotch	1
English-Polish	3		

MABEL F. GIFFORD,

Per GRACE E. McKENZIE,
Assistant.

DEPARTMENT OF PHYSICAL EDUCATION, ATHLETICS, SOCIAL AND LECTURE CENTERS.

Mr. Alfred Roncovieri,
Superintendent of Schools,
City and County of San Francisco.

Dear Sir: Pursuant to your instructions, I submit the following report concerning the operations of the Department of Physical Education, Athletics, Social and Lecture Centers for the school year ended June 30, 1917.

Physical Education in Elementary Schools: The time allotted to physical education in the elementary schools was twenty minutes per day, divided as follows: Five minutes each morning for corrective gymnastics (setting up drill), and seven minutes each afternoon for general gymnastics, followed by eight minutes of free play in the school yard. All gymnastic exercises were arranged in a progressive order with reference to time and the age and capability of pupils. The method employed in setting forth and applying gymnastic exercises was this:

(1) Lessons were prepared and printed on small cards for each grade. The lesson cards thus prepared were placed in the hands of classroom teachers who instructed the pupils.

(2) Classroom teachers were instructed and guided in the application of the lessons by a staff of four District Supervisors of Physical Education, each of whom served a district of the city containing twenty to twenty-five schools.

(3) Posture illustrations printed on cards twenty-two by twenty-eight inches were placed in each classroom. These illustrations set forth in striking manner the correct positions for pupils to take in standing and sitting. Thus, the "picture method" was employed to overcome faulty postures and to teach the correct carriage of the body at all times.

(4) A booklet of twenty-nine pages and twenty-one illustrations, entitled "Guide to the Plan of Physical Education in the Elementary Schools" was prepared and placed in the hands of principals and teachers. The purpose of the Guide was to furnish teachers with a convenient reference text concerning the nature, scope .and technique of physical education as applied to the conditions under which they were expected to work.

The plan of physical education in the elementary schools thus set forth was centered upon three objectives: (1) health education; (2) the development of organic vigor by means of selected exercises; (3) the maintenance of good posture as an aid to health, grace of movement and economy of effort.

Athletics in Elementary Schools: Interschool athletics were conducted on a large scale for boys in the upper grades in the grammar schools. The list of events and the number of participants set forth below will convey some idea of the extent and nature of this phase of our physical education work.

Annual Championship Swimming Meet, September 23, at Sutro Baths—400 boys participating.

Annual Championship Field Meet, October 7th, at Southside Playground—400 boys participating.

Annual Novice Field Meet, November 3rd, at Southside Playground—425 boys participating.

Annual Basketball Tournament, October 2nd to December 8th. Games conducted on various public playgrounds—75 teams participating.

Annual Soccor Football Tournament, January and February. Games conducted on various public playgrounds—26 teams participating.

Annual Baseball Tournament, March, April and May. Games conducted in public parks and playgrounds—67 teams participating.

Annual Championship Track Meet, April 28th, at Golden Gate Park Stadium—450 boys participating.

Annual Novice Track Meet, May 17th, at Golden Gate Stadium—430 boys participating.

The various schools involved in the above athletic schedule were supplied with basketballs, baseballs, bats, masks, gloves, footballs, and other necessary implements of games. Simple, inexpensive badges were awarded for individual excellence in the athletic contests. Team prizes in the form of silver cups, banners and placques were supplied by individuals and business firms who made their contributions through the Public Schools Athletic League, an organization of business and professional men who voluntarily co-operate with the Board of Education in promoting athletics among school boys. Since the inception of the Public School Athletic League work, the Board of Education has employed one man to supervise it. He arranges the programs, conducts the meets and tournaments, keeps the records and advises with principals and teachers. During the year under consideration, a teacher in each of forty schools volunteered to serve for slight extra pay ($5.00 per month for ten months) as "Teacher in Charge of Athletics." The duties of these teachers were outlined as follows:

"Each teacher or principal who volunteers to take the athletic league work will receive $5.00 per month, effective September to June, inclusive. Teachers who accept pay for conducting the P. S. A. L. work will be expected to

Post all P. S. A. L. notices that come to the school.

Select and enter boys in the various P. S. A. L. events.

See that entry blanks are properly handled in all detail.

Accompany teams to all games and events of the P. S. A. L.

Assume responsibility for the discipline of individuals and teams in all P. S. A. L.. events.

Be responsible for supplies and implements issued to the school for athletic work.

Carry out the instructions of the Supervisor of Athletics.."

This arrangement has not only been helpful to the Supervisor of Athletics, but it has resulted in a better quality of athletic achievement in all of the schools involved. The aims of our athletic league work have been—

(1) To supplement the formal physical exercises of the classroom with a type of physical education work designed to encourage self-expression and give soul satisfaction to the more active boys.

(2) To occupy the after school hours of boys with a constructive interest and occupation.

(3) To encourage good sportsmanship.

(4) To develop a robust body and a courageous spirit.

Physical Education and Athletics in High Schools: The year under consideration marks the first time that effort has been made to incorporate a scheme of physical education in the high schools. Heretofore, the Girls' High School only has had a special teacher of physical education who has endeavored to carry out a systematic plan of physical education. The other four high schools have merely had competitive athletics promoted by the students and supervised by regular teachers who gave extra time to this subject for slight extra pay. This year, the Board appointed special teachers of physical education and athletics in each of the high schools. These teachers were started in their work under the following instructions:

"BOARD OF EDUCATION, DEPARTMENT OF PHYSICAL EDUCATION, ATHLETICS, SOCIAL AND LECTURE CENTERS.

To Principals and Teachers of High Schools:

On June 20th, the Board of Education created for the high schools the position of 'Director of Physical Education and Athletics' and appointed the following persons to fill the positions thus created:

Polytechnic High School:

Mr. Willis O. Hunter,
Director of Physical Education and Athletics for Boys.
Miss Gertrude Brown,
Director of Physical Education and Athletics for Girls.

Lowell High School:

Mr. Courtenay Overin,
Director of Physical Education and Athletics for Boys.
Miss Clara Newhouse,
Director of Physical Education and Athletics for Girls.

High School of Commerce:

Mr. George C. Lorbeer,
Director of Physical Education and Athletics for Boys.

Miss Nita Sheffield,
Director of Physical Education and Athletics for Girls.

Mission High School:

Mr. Omar F. Bradway,
Director of Physical Education and Athletics for Boys.

Miss Nita Sheffield,
Director of Physical Education and Athletics for Girls.

Girls' High School:

Mr. Laura H. Tharp (Reappointed),
Director of Physical Education and Athletics.

The object of this action by the Board is to center the responsibility and leadership in all matters of physical education and athletics in each of the high schools in one man for the boys, and one woman for the girls.

The Directors of Physical Education and Athletics will become members of the faculty in their respective schools. They will be subordinate to the Principal and subject to all of his rules and regulations for the guidance of the faculty.

The Director of the Department of Physical Education, Athletics, Social and Lecture Centers, will aid the principal in establishing and carrying forward the work of physical education and athletics. He will be responsible for all technical procedure and the supervision of the methods, systems and practices of the Directors of Physical Education and Athletics.

The general plan of procedure will be extensive, rather than intensive, athletics; i. e., methods and practices which will center time and effort upon the mass of students, rather than upon the coaching of 'first teams.'

The Directors of Physical Education and Athletics will welcome voluntary assistance of other members of the faculty in coaching and supervising teams for interschool contests. The work of volunteers must, however, harmonize with the plans and the aims of the Directors of Physical Education and Athletics who, alone, will be held responsible to the Principal and the Department.

The Directors of Physical Education and Athletics will at once address themselves to carrying out the following aims. The extent to which some of the aims may be carried out will depend upon the physical facilities at hand and the measure of co-operation accorded the Directors of Physical Education and Athletics by the Principal and the members of the faculty..

AIMS OF THE DEPARTMENT OF PHYSICAL EDUCATION AND ATHLETIC IN HIGH SCHOOLS.

I—PHYSICAL AIMS:

The development of organic vigor through muscular exercises and the establishment of habits which lead to systematic physical exercise.

By means of

- Organized and directed play in the building or in the school yard.
- Systematic classes in gymnastics in the building or in the school yard.
- Folk, gymnastic, aesthetic and social dancing as a part of a gymnastic course or as an unrelated exercise.
- Class or group competition in games and athletic events wholly within the school.

Boxing, fencing and wrestling, arranged for groups on competitive or non-competitive basis.

Swimming, diving and life saving, arranged for groups on competitive or non-competitive basis.

Interschool competition in games, aquatics and athletic events arranged directly with other schools or through athletic leagues. (Interschool events for girls must be arranged only on the basis of an invitation to play or compete. The parts of 'hostess' and 'guest' must be strictly carried out.)

Talks or lectures by the Director on physiology of exercise, hygiene and first aid.

Insistence upon the application of the laws of hygiene in exercise, bathing, dress and training.

Medical examination of heart, lungs and nervous system of all students who participate in events which call for a severe test of speed, strength or edurance.

Note: As soon as feasible, these physical aims should be guaranteed to the student by certain required work for freshmen and sophomores, and by elective participation for juniors and seniors.

II—SOCIAL AND ETHICAL AIMS:

The awakening and development of social ideals and good conduct. Not to be attained by mere preachment, but through the experiences of the student, supplemented by the interpretations of the Director, the Principal and members of the faculty who observe students in their play exercises.

By means of:

Participating in the 'school spirit' engendered by athletic contests.—Loyalty.

Taking defeat gracefully and victory modestly.—Self-control.

Giving the 'square deal' to team mates and adversaries alike.—Good sportsmanship.

Accepting the ruling of officials without 'crabbing'—Respect for Authority.

Working together and subordinating self interests for common interests, as in team play.—The Essence of Good Citizenship.

Avoiding the use of profane and obscene language. Attention to proper dress upon the athletic field, in the gymnasium and about the school. Proper language and conduct in the presence of the opposite set, especially at school dances and athletic functions. Guarding against slouchy, slovenly, tough expressions of any character.—Good Manners.

Training; i. e., faithful, painstaking effort when upon the athletic field, and avoidance of tobacco, liquor, late nights and weak companions when off of the athletic field.—Moral Stamina.

Respectfully,

E. B. DE GROOT,
Director of the Department."

Very satisfactory progress has been made in the high schools in every phase of the physical education work. Competitive athletics among the boys were placed under a controlling influence that has resulted in better discipline and a higher degree of good sportsmanship. Athletics for girls were promoted and regulated in a manner to safeguard the health and social well being of all who participated. One unique feature of the work among girls has been the provision of a class in swimming once each week. Several hundred girls have been taught the most approved methods of swimming and life saving.

Social and Lecture Centers: The department has endeavored to meet the public demand for the establishment of neighborhood centers in public school buildings. The following announcement was issued for the guidance of all concerned.

"RULES FOR THE ESTABLISHMENT AND OPERATION OF NEIGHBORHOOD CENTERS IN THE PUBLIC SCHOOL BUILDINGS OF SAN FRANCISCO.

The Board of Education will grant and promote, through its Department of Physical Education, Athletics, Social and Lecture Centers, the use of school buildings for evening neighborhood centers of the following character:

A—Social Centers—for the purpose of conducting neighborhood rallies, entertainments, clubs, etc., for any moral purpose, except political or religious propaganda.

B—Lecture Centers—for the purpose of conducting lectures, discussions or debates upon any subject free from political or religious propaganda.

C—Music Centers—for the purpose of promoting neighborhood choruses or other musical interests of the people.

Note: The term 'Social Center' is here used to denote an inclusive neighborhood center. The social center may, therefore, include both lecture and music centers, as well as many other interests and activities.

By 'political or religious propaganda' is not meant broad and liberal treatment of the civic and ethical questions of the day. The bar is against partisan or factional politics and the promotion, criticism or giving offense to any religious faith or organization.

When neighborhood centers are established, the Board of Education will provide the following for each center:

One employe of the Board of Education to serve as leader, promoter and manager of the center.

Necessary janitorial service.

Light and heat.

A certain amount of equipment, repairs and supplies required for given activities.

Motion picture service in social centers once each month.

Stereopticon and operator in lecture centers.

Piano in music centers.

All other items of expense in the operation of a neighborhood center must be met by the patrons of the center.

Club dues and admission fees may be collected and expended under the following rules:

(1) Each club or unit group in the center must select a chairman or president and a secretary-treasurer, who will be responsible not only to the group they represent, but equally responsible to the manager of the center.

(2) Dues or admission fees collected by any club or unit group of the center must be immediately deposited with the manager of the center. Deposit and receipt books must be used to insure accuracy and clear records involving all collections, deposits and disbursements.

(3) The sale of tickets for any entertainment must be conducted only at the entrance door at the time of the entertainment. Outside sale or huckstering of tickets will not be permitted.

(4) All money derived from club dues or entertainments must be invested in the further equipment or operation of the center.

(5) Admission fees to any form of entertainment must not be greater than 25c per person.

GENERAL RULES.

The regular closing time for evening centers shall not be later than 10 o'clock. The extended time for special functions shall not be later than 11 o'clock.

Children shall not be admitted to evening centers unless accompanied by adults.

The activities of the evening centers must be confined to those parts and facilities of the building that have been assigned for evening center use.

Smoking in or about the building will not be permitted. Spitting upon floors and other offensive acts will not be tolerated. Patrons of evening centers must be thoughtful of the rights and safeguards of children to whom must be guaranteed a sanitary, orderly and well kept school plant.

There must be strict adherence to all regulations imposed from time to time by the manager of the center. The manager will exercise advisory control and ultimate authority in all matters of operation."

During the year under consideration, centers were maintained for short or long periods in the following schools:

Bryant School Social Center:

Monday each week—Dressmaking.
Tuesday each week—Millinery.
Wednesday each week—Millinery.
Last Friday each month—Neighborhood Rally.

Jean Parker Social Center:

One night each week—Community Singing.

Laguna Honda Social Center:

Thursday night each week—Community Singing.

Sutro Social Center:

One night each week—Community Singing.

Monroe Social Center:

Monday each week—Choral and Ukulele Club.
Friday each week—Spanish class.
Friday each week—Boys' Gymnasium Club.
Friday each week—Girls' Sewing Club.

Sunnyside Social Center:

First Friday each month—Motion Picture Entertainment.
Second Friday each month—Lecture.
Third Friday each month—Mothers' Club Entertainment.
Fourth Friday—Neighborhood Improvement Association Meeting.

John Swett Social Center:

Monday each week—Millinery and Dressmaking.
Monday each week—Cooking.
Monday each week—Spanish.

Monday each week—John Swett Junior Alumni Association.
First Wednesday each month—Neighborhood Rally.
Second Wednesday each month—Lecture.
Third Wednesday each month—Parent-Teachers Association.
Fourth Wednesday each month—John Swett Senior Alumni Association.
Wednesday each week—Class in English and American Laws and customs.

Visitacion Valley Social Center:

Monday each week—Community Singing.

Yerba Buena Social Center:

Monday each week—Girls' Dramatic Group.
Tuesday each week—Young Men's Dancing Group.
Wednesday each week—Millinery Group.
First Friday each month—Lecture.
Second Friday each month—Dance for "grown-ups."
Third Friday each month—Pay Show.
Fourth Friday each month—Neighborhood Rally.
Extra Friday—Extra.

The work of the Department of Physical Education, Athletics, Social and Lecture Centers has been maintained under a segregated budget amounting to a total of $25,400. This amount has covered all items of expense, including salaries, supplies, equipment, and even permanent improvements to school property incident to carrying out the various phases of the work of the department. The accomplishment in the light of the amount of money expended and the meager equipment at hand to facilitate the work has been very substantial. The success of the work of the department has, however, been due primarily to the hearty and sympathetic support of the Superintendent, the Deputy Superintendents, the members of the Board of Education, and to the generous co-operation of the principals and teachers throughout the School Department.

Very respectfully,

E. D. DE GROOT.

July 2, 1917.

Lightning Source UK Ltd.
Milton Keynes UK
UKHW021304180219
337443UK00006B/139/P